HANDBOOK OF RESEARCH ON ECONOMIC AND SOCIAL WELL-BEING

Handbook of Research on Economic and Social Well-being

Edited by

Conchita D'Ambrosio

Université du Luxembourg

Edward Elgar
PUBLISHING

Cheltenham, UK • Northampton, MA, USA

Published by
Edward Elgar Publishing Limited
The Lypiatts
15 Lansdown Road
Cheltenham
Glos GL50 2JA
UK

Edward Elgar Publishing, Inc.
William Pratt House
9 Dewey Court
Northampton
Massachusetts 01060
USA

A catalogue record for this book
is available from the British Library

Library of Congress Control Number: 2017953236

This book is available electronically in the **Elgar**online
Economics subject collection
DOI 10.4337/9781781953716

ISBN 978 1 78195 370 9 (cased)
ISBN 978 1 78195 371 6 (eBook)

Typeset by Servis Filmsetting Ltd, Stockport, Cheshire

Printed and bound in the United States.

Printed on ECF recycled paper containing 30% Post Consumer Waste.

Contents

Contributors

Carlotta Balestra, OECD Statistics Directorate, France

Luna Bellani, University of Konstanz, Germany; Institute of Labor Economics (IZA), Germany; and Dondena Centre for Research on Social Dynamics and Public Policy at Bocconi University, Italy

Romina Boarini, OECD, Office of Secretary-General (former Statistics Directorate), France

Cesar Calvo, Universidad de Piura, Peru

Bea Cantillon, Herman Deleeck Centre for Social Policy, University of Antwerp, Belgium

Olga Cantó, Universidad de Alcalá, Spain

Lidia Ceriani, Georgetown University, USA

Satya R. Chakravarty, Indian Statistical Institute, Kolkata, India

Nachiketa Chattopadhyay, Indian Statistical Institute, Kolkata, India

Mariateresa Ciommi, Università Politecnica delle Marche, Italy

Indranil Dutta, University of Manchester, UK

Lucio Esposito, University of East Anglia, UK

Alessio Fusco, Luxembourg Institute of Socio-Economic Research (LISER), Luxembourg

András Gábos, TARKI Social Research Institute, Hungary

Chiara Gigliarano, Università degli Studi dell'Insubria, Varese, Italy

Enrico Giovannini, Università degli Studi di Roma 'Tor Vergata', Italy

Tim Goedemé, Herman Deleeck Centre for Social Policy, University of Antwerp, Belgium

Carlos Gradín, Universidade de Vigo, Spain

Anne-Catherine Guio, Luxembourg Institute of Socio-Economic Research (LISER), Luxembourg

Michael Hoy, University of Guelph, Canada

Casilda Lasso de la Vega, Universidad del Pais Vasco / Euskal Herriko Unibertsitatea, Spain

Ricardo Mora, Universidad Carlos III de Madrid, Spain

Lars Osberg, Dalhousie University, Canada

Iñaki Permanyer, Centre d'Estudis Demogràfics, Universitat Autònoma de Barcelona, Spain

Coral del Río, Universidade de Vigo, Spain

Nicholas Rohde, Griffith University, Australia

Tommaso Rondinella, Italian National Institute of Statistics (Istat), Italy

Nicolas Ruiz, OECD Economics Department, France

Ernesto Savaglio, Università degli Studi 'G. d'Annunzio' Chieti-Pescara, Italy

Suman Seth, University of Leeds, UK; and Oxford Poverty and Human Development Initiative (OPHI), University of Oxford, UK

Jacques Silber, Bar Ilan University, Israel; and Luxembourg Institute of Socio-Economic Research (LISER), Luxembourg

Kam Ki Tang, University of Queensland, Australia

István György Tóth, TÁRKI Social Research Institute, Hungary

Stefano Vannucci, Università degli Studi di Siena, Italy

Paolo Verme, World Bank, USA

Antonio Villar, Universidad Pablo de Olavide, Spain; and Instituto Valenciano de Investigaciones Económicas (IVIE), Spain

Oscar Volij, Ben Gurion University of the Negev, Israel

Gaston Yalonetzky, University of Leeds, UK

Buhong Zheng, University of Colorado Denver, USA

Introduction
Conchita D'Ambrosio

The past decade has been characterized by a considerable flourishing of new concepts regarding individual and social well-being which have been investigated theoretically and empirically. The impetus for this new research came from increasing demand from both policy makers and society for measures of progress that went beyond the analysis of production and, at the same time, better datasets allowing individuals and households to be followed over their life courses. The aim of this *Handbook* is to provide extensive surveys of many of the recent themes that have been developed in this literature. It does so by offering a unique collection of less-traditional measures of well-being that are not otherwise easily accessible in a convenient and concise manner. Each topic is covered in two chapters: the first contains the theoretical approaches behind the indices; the second focuses more on empirical findings and issues related to the application of the measures.

When I accepted the invitation to edit the *Handbook* I thought that having two groups of experts write on the same subject was a good idea that, in addition to the choice of the topics, would have rendered the *Handbook* unique. I later regretted it: it was difficult to receive all the paired chapters from very busy experts who had non-stationary preferences. I hope the reader appreciates this time-consuming effort, which took four years to bear fruit.

This *Handbook* complements the other recent handbooks on similar topics: the 2009 *Oxford Handbook of Economic Inequality*, edited by W. Salverda, B. Nolan and T. Smeeding (Oxford University Press); the 2015 *Handbook of Income Distribution*, Volume 2, edited by A.B. Atkinson and F. Bourguignon (Elsevier); and the 2016 *Oxford Handbook of Well-being and Public Policy* edited by M.D. Adler and M. Fleurbaey (Oxford University Press).

At the same time, this *Handbook* builds on the handbooks published around 15 years ago: the 1999 *Handbook on Income Inequality Measurement*, edited by J. Silber (Kluwer), and the 2000 *Handbook of Income Distribution*, Volume 1, edited by A.B. Atkinson and F. Bourguignon (Elsevier).

A few lines follow to explain the choice and order of the topics. The *Handbook* starts by going beyond gross domestic product (GDP), in acknowledgement of the fact that production is not an appropriate indicator of individual and social well-being. Since its introduction, GDP has been extensively used to measure welfare, although it was never designed for this purpose. Criticism of its use as a measure of well-being, and attempts to overcome some of its most obvious limitations, first appeared in the 1970s, but it was not until the 1990s that viable alternatives to this approach began to emerge, stemming from pioneering work by leading welfare economists. A remarkable example of this new trend was the introduction of the Human Development Index (HDI) by the United Nations, which for the first time combined per capita income with non-income measures, such as life expectancy and education. With the Great Recession, a renewed emphasis has been put on the consequences of inequality and the distribution of resources; in this context, the high GDP growth experienced by many countries in the years preceding the crisis proved emblematic of the limitations of this indicator in reflecting economic and social conditions. The debate over the inadequacy of GDP has stimulated a great number of both national and international initiatives, giving rise to a new individual-centred set of measures and frameworks, some of which are reviewed in the first two chapters of this *Handbook*.

The measurement of human development and human poverty is addressed next: these were the first common efforts of most of the countries in the world to measure the well-being of their populations from multiple angles. The first *Human Development Report* was launched in 1990 and continues to be updated.

However, the issue of multidimensionality is particularly challenging, as it requires a formal review of the axiomatic approach characterizing its theoretical framework. Chapters 5 and 6 of the *Handbook* contain a discussion of the topic. This is accompanied by a review of the measurement of material deprivation, a concept which is closely linked to multidimensional poverty: while the latter accounts for both material and non-material dimensions of well-being, the indices of material deprivation refer to deprivations in the realm of material living conditions only.

The choice to move along to the topic of social exclusion was triggered by my personal view of the latter as persistence in the state of deprivation. The paternity of the term 'social exclusion' is usually attributed to René Lenoir (1974), a member of the French Government, who considered that France was threatened with internal disaggregation because of social exclusion. For Lenoir (1974), this term refers to individuals who are excluded from the welfare system because of their inadaptation to our society. At the European level, the concept of social exclusion became the reference paradigm for questions linked to poverty.

The analysis of persistence leads to the chapters on poverty over time. The introduction of a dynamic framework makes it possible to capture the heterogeneity of poverty in terms of individual intertemporal patterns, allowing researchers to discriminate between chronic poverty and transitory poverty, and to give more weightto consecutive poverty spells.

However, the measures of poverty over time illustrated in Chapters 9 and 10 are typically backward-looking. The two topics that follow, vulnerability to poverty and economic insecurity, are more concerned with the anticipation of future events. Although there is no consensus on the formal definition of these forward-looking concepts, empirical evidence reassuringly shows qualitatively similar results across different methods and definitions. Such findings suggest that, despite the future challenges, there already is some scope for public-policy recommendations.

Having tackled various forms of poverty, the *Handbook* then moves on to indicators of non-standard inequalities. While inequality is usually concerned with differences in the distribution of an attribute in the population, relative deprivation and satisfaction measures focus on one-sided differences only, either with respect to richer individuals or with respect to poorer ones. Moreover, differently from inequality, these two concepts do not necessarily refer to a set of individuals, but can also refer to single individuals. The desire to obtain measures of inequality at the individual level has thus contributed to the study of relative deprivation and relative satisfaction. The focus on these two concepts also calls for the introduction of relativist concerns in the theoretical models aimed at explaining a wide range of social phenomena. The dedicated chapter reviews the main theoretical models that have been developed that adopt a relativistic specification of utility, thus accounting for the presence of interpersonal comparisons. From a theoretical point of view, the acknowledgement of the role played by interpersonal comparisons requires the reformulation of some well-established concepts in microeconomics, such as those linked to the individual utility function. This process may consequently have important repercussions on the formulation of policy recommendations, for instance by bringing distributive considerations into the formulation of policies aimed at promoting economic growth.

The chapters dealing with social inequality follow. Social inequality is concerned with differences in variables other than income, including health, educational achievement, happiness, access to amenities, and so on, which are also often used to evaluate living standards in society. Although the measurement of inequality with respect to social variables is closely related to the measurement of income inequality, the types of variables under study have generated new measurement challenges. In particular, the chapter deals with ordinal variables and bounded cardinal variables.

Polarization is addressed next. As opposed to inequality, polarization focuses on clusters of individuals forming groups in different parts of a given distribution, particularly at its extremes, and the hollowing-out of the middle class. The interest in polarization can be partly attributed to the existing relationship between inequality and social instability and conflict. It has been widely argued that more polarized societies are more prone to social unrest and tension. While the adoption of inequality measures to empirically investigate this relationship has produced mixed and often inconclusive evidence, polarization indices have typically performed better in explaining episodes of social tension or conflict. From a theoretical point of view, many contributions to the polarization literature have tried to establish a clear distinction between the concept of inequality and that of polarization. As is the case with inequality, the concept of polarization can refer to both income and non-income variables, such as ethnicity or religion. Both income and social polarization are thus addressed in the two dedicated chapters.

Segregation, which is addressed next, is an even broader concept. The multifaceted nature of the concept has thus led to the development of numerous indices. The focus of the theoretical chapter is on axiomatic models. The rationale behind this choice is that the axiomatic approach, by emphasizing common and different properties of the various measures, can help to select the segregation indices that best suit the purposes of the researchers. The empirical chapter attempts to review the empirical literature covering various aspects of segregation: residential segregation by race or income; occupational segregation by gender, race or ethnic group; and school segregation.

The *Handbook* ends with the more general concepts of diversity and social fractionalization. Diversity can be applied in a variety of contexts. Its conceptualization and measurement have consequently been addressed by a number of disciplines, among which are ecology, biology, sociology and political science. Over the last decade, it has increasingly become an object of interest for economists and other social scientists. This growing interest has been motivated by a number of different concerns, from those for biodiversity and the development of conservation policies, to those for socioeconomic diversity. In particular, the latter is closely related to the concept of social fractionalization, which addresses the partitioning of a given population in different groups according to social attributes, such as language, religion or ethnicity. The empirical literature has focused on social fractionalization as a further predictor of social conflict, other than polarization. The two concepts capture different aspects of the distribution of a given population with respect to a set of characteristics, and exhibit two major differences. While fractionalization increases with the number of groups in the population, polarization decreases. Moreover, while most measures of polarization account for inter-group distances, indices of fractionalization are generally independent of this dimension. By capturing different aspects of inequality, these two concepts can thus help to explain different instances of social tension and conflict, as the empirical literature seems to suggest.

As briefly summarized above, this *Handbook* offers the reader a comprehensive overview of many measures of individual and social well-being and their applications. It is my hope that this collection will foster further discussion in the common effort to meet the growing demand for a more accurate measurement of these dimensions, which will be at the basis of future economic policies.

1. Going beyond GDP: theoretical approaches

Enrico Giovannini and Tommaso Rondinella

INTRODUCTION

In the aftermath of the Great Depression, the government of the United States needed a strong tool to assess the effectiveness of the policies undertaken to foster economic recovery. In this context, the initial framework of the System of National Accounts provided a powerful overview of the main dimensions of the economic system (production, consumption, savings, and so on) when most of the public attention was focused on the movements of the Dow-Jones index. The System, and its central indicator, the gross domestic product (GDP), was not only methodologically robust, but also supported by economic theory, the Keynesian one in particular, which guided Western societies after the crisis and the Second World War. GDP growth has thus become the main aim of societies and political action, as well as a synonym of development, well-being and progress. Yet, this has not always been the case. The ultimate purpose of human activities was happiness already for Aristotle in the *Nicomachean Ethics*, as well as, for example, during the enlightenment in Jeremy Bentham's work, and for the American Constitution.

Along with the development of the paradigm of economic growth, the second half of the twentieth century also saw an uninterrupted evolution of the criticisms of this solely economic approach. These were initially concentrated on the social aspects, stressing the fact that social conditions, standard of living and quality of life needed a broader set of indicators to be evaluated. From the 1970s, the environmental aspects emerged strongly: the fact that indefinite growth in production could not be possible, given the limited planetary boundaries; as well as increasing attention to the environmental externalities produced by the economic system. More recently, consciousness about the risks posed by climate change has strengthened the consensus around the irrationality of looking only at GDP growth.

This chapter aims at presenting the recent historical evolution of some of the theoretical concepts which underpinned the debate over the need to go 'beyond GDP'. We primarily focus on the approaches of multidimensionality and basic needs, utilitarianism and subjective well-being, and capabilities. We also present the methodological debate on aggregation, since the need to aggregate measures of the different domains of well-being is a constant issue which has never found a satisfactory answer on either the opportunity to aggregate or the best method to be used.

Two sections are then dedicated specifically to the measurement of inequalities and sustainability, fundamental elements of well-being and development posing measurement problems which are addressed in a number of ways. In particular, the issue of sustainability, which originally only considered the respect of ecological boundaries, raises formidable problems when extended to social aspects. Such problems are still in need of satisfactory solutions and therefore remain among the research issues lying ahead.

Further sections of the chapter are dedicated to more procedural and political issues, reflecting on the need to include citizens and stakeholders in the identification of the indicators to be used to go 'beyond GDP' if we aspire to measure what may have some democratic legitimacy. We then present the developments of the international debate in the last decade and the most relevant initiatives taken in the field of measuring national well-being. We conclude by highlighting the existing international convergence on the need of a broader set of national objectives represented by the debate over the Sustainable Development Goals.

1.1   ABOUT GDP

1.1.1   The GDP-Led Society

The 1929 crisis, which hit the United States and the rest of the world so hard, highlighted the fragility of the American economic system and of the tools policy makers would rely upon to prevent and better react to similar events. In 1931, the Department of Commerce was asked to provide estimates of national income: it was decided to rely on the expertise of the National Bureau of Economic Research (NBER), and especially on that of Simon Kuznets, who was already working on this issue. In 1934 Kuznets was able to present to the Congress a first full formulation of the national income as the 'part of the economy's end product that results from the efforts of the individuals who comprise a nation' (Kuznets, 1934, p. 1). After that, a series of Conferences on Research in Income and Wealth pulled together experts, academics, policy makers, institutions and key interest groups with the aim of continuously fine-tuning the System of National Accounts (SNA).

By the end of the 1930s, GDP and the SNA had taken a robust form, being based on a coherent theoretical framework. Moreover, with the publication of John Maynard Keynes's *General Theory* (Keynes, 1936), GDP was put at the centre of a broad macro-economic analysis model. Since Keynesian policies worked through monetary flows, a systematic measurement of aggregate economic activity (and employment) was strictly necessary. In the words of Robert Solow, Kuznets provided the 'anatomy' for Keynes's 'physiology' (European Parliament, 2007).

The SNA and GDP allowed for an effective management of national resources, playing a very relevant role during the recovery from the crisis and during the war, leading scholars to compare the use of GDP as a 'weapon' only the United States (US) could rely upon, to the consequence of the Manhattan Project. It allowed for the conversion of the civil economy into a war machine without hampering internal consumption, thus continuing to generate revenues for the war (Cobb et al., 1995; Fioramonti, 2013).

Yet, Kuznets himself (US Congress, Senate, 1934, pp. 5, 6) warned about the precautions to be taken when using GDP, the results of which are to be 'interpreted with a full realization of the definition of national income assumed, either explicitly or implicitly, by the measurement': the distinction between national and domestic measures ('the boundaries of a nation'); the lack of services provided by family members, housework in particular, and by owned durable goods; earning from odd jobs; relief and charity; changes in the value of assets; earnings from illegal pursuits. Besides what national income did or did not include, he also considered that it could not work as a measure of economic welfare 'unless the personal distribution of income is known'. Moreover, the use of a synthetic measure carries some risk, since 'the definiteness of the result suggests, often misleadingly, a precision and simplicity in the outlines of the object measured'. He was already taking into account the implications of bounded rationality, noticing how:

> the valuable capacity of the human mind to simplify a complex situation in a compact characterization becomes dangerous when not controlled in terms of definitely stated criteria. With quantitative measurements especially, the definiteness of the result suggests, often misleadingly, a precision and simplicity in the outlines of the object measured. Measurements of national income are subject to this type of illusion and resulting abuse, especially since they deal with matters that are the centre of conflict of opposing social groups where the effectiveness of an argument is often contingent upon oversimplification.

Despite Kuznets's own advice not to consider GDP as a measure of well-being, we know that this was exactly what was occurring then, and by the early 1950s GDP had become the undisputed key metric for economic performance and overall progress. After the Second World War, GDP grew along with most social outcome indicators; of course, economic growth has been the driver of a number of social improvements such as health conditions, education and opportunities for consumption, appearing as the perfect indicators for well-being and development, especially since, at that time, the negative impacts of economic growth on the environment, on social relationships and on time for leisure were not taken into account.

In his inaugural speech in 1949 on the international role to come for the United States, President Harry Truman stated, as the fourth and last point: 'we must embark on a bold new program for making the benefits of our scientific advances and industrial progress available for the improvement and growth of underdeveloped areas' (Truman, 1949, par. 44). According to many, the announcement of this fourth point of the Truman doctrine was the moment at which the idea of underdevelopment was established, as well as the equality between development and economic growth.

In 1960, Walt Rostow proposed an influential model of development stages based on the United States' industrialization and economic growth models. Rostow (1960) suggested a unique path towards development which passed from a traditional agricultural society to industrialization in a core sector, the so-called 'take-off', and to the following diffusion of an advanced market economy based on the US and Western model, to ultimately reach the stage of mass consumption. Three main conditions were required for take-off: the investment rate should rise from around 5 per cent to more than 10 per cent of national income; at least one manufacturing sector should start to grow rapidly; and the institutional framework must guarantee that domestic resources are mobilized for productive activities and not for consumption. After the high growth of a few industrial enterprises in key sectors (which may change from country to country), the increase in investment rates would lead the diffusion of industrial production into the 'maturity' stage leading to tertiary activities, urbanization of the population, decrease in fertility rates and a diminished attention to the perspectives of industrialization and material development. In particular, the social costs of further industrialization would appear as excessive, and new perspectives of social satisfaction would become attractive. The final stage of 'high mass consumption' would then be characterized by two major economic phenomena: an income which permits a level of consumption over the basic needs, and a tertiarization of the economy.[1]

According to Rostow, once the priorities of industrialization are met, societies can move towards three alternative scenarios (Solivetti, 1993): (1) the welfare scenario, a policy sustained by the state of social services, security, reduction of working hours for the whole population; (2) the mass-consumption scenario, based on private instead of public consumption; or (3) the scenario of national empowerment, based on military expenditures and international expansion. The mass-consumption society, together with a Keynesian approach, which looks at consumption as the major driver for GDP growth, would lead policy makers to see citizens only as consumers. This brought Kuznets himself to appeal for further caution in relation to the myth of GDP growth: 'Distinctions must be kept in mind between quantity and quality of growth, between its costs and return, and between the short and the long run. Goals for more growth should specify more growth of what and for what' (Kuznets, 1962, p. 29).

Such an 'economistic vision' of development was central to the political debate throughout the whole century. It was strongly supported by the 'neoliberal' ideas, which considered public intervention in the economy as useless or even harmful, since self-regulated free markets would have led to the optimal resource allocation. In particular, the idea of a 'trickle-down effect' in which, automatically and without the need for direct intervention, the benefits and the wealth produced by the industry would then slowly spread to all other sectors of society, made the existence of imbalances in the distribution of wealth within society in the short and medium term tolerable, if not required (Galenson and Leibenstein, 1955; Kuznets, 1955). During the second half of the century, the idea that economic development, and especially industrial growth, could automatically translate into a widespread prosperity for all citizens and for all the different sectors of society appeared well established.

1.1.2   GDP Limits as an Indicator of both Economic Performance and Well-Being

More recently, during the recent Great Recession, the fall and stagnation of GDP, especially in European countries, brought GDP growth to the centre of political debate once again. Yet, the 2008 crisis itself revealed some of the limits of the above-mentioned point of view, since looking only at GDP growth did not allow the approaching crisis to be seen: the economic system was clearly ill, but looking only at the increases in production (while ignoring poverty and private indebtedness) gave the impression that everything was going in the right direction.

The GDP-led society is based on the assumption that GDP growth is the goal when it comes to improving both economic performance and people's well-being. The criticisms over the use of GDP as a reference indicator address both aspects, and if the latter is easy to guess, the former is less straightforward.

The first part of the final report of the Stiglitz–Sen–Fitoussi Commission (Stiglitz et al., 2009) particularly addressed the limits of GDP in measuring economic performance. These refer, first of all, to the use of market prices in determining the utility of the different components of GDP. Market prices do not exist for certain goods and services which, nevertheless, deliver economic utility. That is the case of free public services, domestic work and voluntary work. And even when market prices exist, they may deviate from the social value: environmental externalities represent a typical example of such a deviation between the market and the social price. Moreover, quality changes in products can be very complex, and in some cases very rapid, setting a tremendous challenge to statisticians in the estimation of inflation. This has relevant implications in the evaluation of real income and real consumption, which deeply determine people's standard of living: overestimating inflation implies underestimating living conditions.

A second issue refers to depreciation in the fast-degrading current technological economy. Therefore, net measures should be preferred to gross values for a more accurate measure of overall performances. Other elements of weakness of GDP also relate to the differences which may arise between national and domestic measures in globalized economies. Focusing on income, more than on production, the national product may represent a better measure of economic performance.

Another possible distortion, mainly in cross-country comparisons, is due to the different valuation of public and private services; the former been valued for their cost (input), the latter for their market price (output). The same service will present a lower value in terms of GDP when provided by the public. Therefore, different institutional arrangements may lead to important differences when health and education services are prevalently public or private, since, due to the fact that productivity changes for government-provided services are systematically ignored, increases in public sector productivity may lead to underestimated GDP growth. Adjusted measures of income or output-based measures may reduce these discrepancies, guaranteeing the invariance principle.[2]

Finally, a well-known shortcoming in the use of GDP as an indicator of economic performance is in the valuation of defensive expenditures (those needed to mitigate the negative impacts of economic activities) as final goods or services. They should instead be considered as intermediate costs, and thus not accounted within GDP. Yet, the major difficulty here stands in the definition of which expenditures should be defined as defensive and which should not, the border being quite fuzzy.

The 'Stiglitz Report' identifies the net adjusted disposable income as a more appropriate general indicator for a country's economic performance. This indicator continues to refer to the System of National Accounts, but focuses much more on citizens' actual economic conditions by looking at disposable income, also taking into account taxation and social transfers, as well as the major public services which people can rely upon without having to pay for them.

If GDP is a flawed measure of economic performance, it is much clearer that it cannot fully represent well-being. Even if some of the determinants of well-being are somehow related to income, such as employment, education or health care, many very relevant aspects are totally independent: for example, social relationships, leisure, affects, quality of democracy, personal freedom, and so on. Moreover, as noted by Fleurbaey and Blanchet (2014), using GDP as a measure of well-being lacks analytical clarity in separating inputs, intermediate products, outputs and outcomes: from a well-being perspective, consumption is an outcome while public expenditure and investments are inputs, and their aggregation in a single measure would appear methodologically inexact.

1.2   BEYOND GDP

1.2.1   Social Trends and Standard of Living: The 1930s

The demand for an analytical framework to assess social and economic conditions of citizens and a theoretical approach to measure them has nevertheless been present throughout the whole twentieth century. Concepts such as well-being, welfare, standard of living, quality of life, progress and development have often been used to describe the final aim of political actions, and have been object of several theoretical and empirical studies.

The first efforts to synthetically measure the social conditions within a country were developed in the United States during the same years in which GDP was formalized by Simon Kuznets. Besides the need to better understand the economic system, it appeared necessary to evaluate the social impact of the crisis. In 1929, President Hoover established the Committee on Social Trends, chaired by Professor Wesley C. Mitchell, the founding director of the National Bureau of Economic Research (with whom Kuznets was a close collaborator) with the aim of helping 'to see where social stresses are occurring and where major efforts should be undertaken to deal with them constructively' (from President Hoover's Introduction, in Committee on Social Trends, 1933, p. v).

The Committee proposed to focus on social outcomes in order to provide a picture of American society and to highlight the relationships existing among emerging problems within a unifying framework: 'a basis for social action, rather than recommendations as to the form which action should take' (Committee on Social Trends, 1933, p. xciii). The proposal was based on three broader areas – physical heritage, biological heritage and social heritage[3] – and the final Report was accompanied by 12 monographs presenting a broad range of data, in some cases brand new data, dealing with: population; communication agencies; education; metropolitan communities; rural communities; races and ethnic groups; political, social and economic activities of women; recreation (Americans at play); the arts; health and environment; public administration; and growth of the federal Government.

At the same time, during the 1930s, a broad academic debate was taking place over the definition and the way of measuring the 'standard of living'. Scale of living, plane of living and level of living were all proposed as central concepts, though they never gained general acceptance (Bennett, 1937). Bennett defined the standard of living as 'per capita quantum of goods and services utilized annually by the inhabitants of a country' (Bennett, 1937, p. 317), a concept which, in his view, cannot be measured through statistics on national expenditure because of the difficulties in reducing data expressed in different currencies to a common monetary basis, and because of the scarcity and noncomparability of statistics on national income or expenditure. He thus built an index, using the scarce information available, to rank countries: the index included elements of economic well-being with important social outcomes such as mortality and fertility rates, deaths from preventable diseases, literacy, educational attainment, leather shoes sold, together with luxury items such as jewels and sugar. In practice, he built one of the first composite indexes on well-being which included data on food, clothing and adornments, shelter and its characteristics, transport and communication, as well as professional services (which included educational, medical, sanitary, religious, protective and recreational services).

In making explicit his difficulties in going beyond objective measures of goods and services availability, Bennett explained that the indicators he selected were:

> not designed to show whether or not the average person in the British Isles is happier or enjoys life more than the average person in Portugal, but merely to show whether and to what extent the one exceeded the other with reference to use of a limited though not a narrow aggregation of goods and services. (Bennett, 1937, p. 318)

1.2.2   The Social Indicators Movement

During the 1960s and 1970s the concept of development, which was central in the political debate, moved towards a much more complex dimension beyond GDP growth, leading to the idea that a multidimensional bulk of social indicators was needed to better understand reality and to guide policy decisions. In 1967, the *Populorum Progressio* encyclical written by Pope Paul VI evidenced the need to separate the concept of development from that of economic growth: 'The development We speak of here cannot be restricted to economic growth alone. To be authentic, it must be well rounded; it must foster the development of each man and of the whole man' (Paul VI, 1967, p. 3). Development of people means that man is the object of development, and that development can, and should, be evaluated according to the realization and fulfilment of people's needs and aspirations. This observation, which may appear trivial and obvious, is even revolutionary in the social sciences, since from the outset they have been characterized by what, following Ulrich Beck (1999), we might call 'methodological nationalism': the primary unit of analysis of research and study is society, and in particular the nation-state.

In 1969, Dudley Seers could affirm that 'we have all been aware that development consists in much else besides economic growth' (Seers, 1969, p. 1) and that among 'the challenges for the remainder of this century . . . the first is how to find measures of development to replace the national income, or more precisely to enable the national income to be given its true, somewhat limited, significance' (ibid., pp. 9–10). Development necessarily had to solve three major problems: poverty, unemployment and inequality: 'A "plan" which conveys no targets for reducing poverty, unemployment and inequality can hardly be considered a "development plan"' (ibid., p. 5).

This multidimensional approach based on outcomes is intended to overcome the drawbacks deriving from the use of a single monetary measure. In developed countries, particularly Sweden in the 1960s, the multidimensional approach led to the introduction of the concept of quality of life, defined in terms of control over resources such as money, property, knowledge, mental and physical energy, social relations and security. This approach, broadly known as the social indicators movement, focused on objective indicators of living conditions and on the ability of individuals to satisfy their interests and needs (Erikson, 1974, 1993; Beham et al., 2006).

The birth of the social indicators movement in the United States is often traced (Cobb and Rixford, 1998) to the publication in 1966 of *Social Indicators*, a project sponsored by the National Aeronautics and Space Administration (NASA) (Bauer, 1966), advocating for an increased collection of statistics for the publishing of an annual social report and for the development of a system of social accounts. Two years later, Robert Kennedy's famous speech at the University of Kansas evidenced the shortcomings of GDP as a measure of progress and as the objective of political action, and demonstrated a broader acceptance of a multidimensional approach towards development.

In 1969, upon the request of President Johnson, the Department of Health prepared a report 'to look at several important aspects of the quality of American life, and digest what is known about progress towards generally accepted social goals' (Department of Health, 1969). The report aimed not only at describing the social situation, but also at providing a tool for improving policy making, by:

> 1) providing more visibility to social problems and, 2) making possible better evaluation of public programs. The report deals with such areas as: health and illness; social mobility; the condition of the physical environment including pollution and housing; income and poverty; public order and safety; learning, science, and art; and participation and alienation. (Department of Health, 1969, p. 1)

The importance of social indicators was also recognized by the United Nations in the early 1970s. With the report *Contents and Measurement of Socioeconomic Development*, UNRISD (1970) enquired into the interrelations between the social and economic aspects of development through a comparative cross-national analysis and the building of indexes of socioeconomic development (Drewnowski and Scott, 1966; McGranahan et al., 1972). In 1973, the United Nations Statistical Commission started a process for the definition of a System of Social and Demographic Statistics (SSDS) with the purpose:

> to show what data are desirable on human beings, both individually and in groups, and on the institution with which they are connected and how these data should be organized in order to provide an information system which will be useful for description, analysis and policy making in the different fields of social life. (Stone, 1975, p. 3)

1.2.3   The Basic Needs Approach

At the same time, an important contribution to the debate around the measures of development came from the analysis of the economies and societies of least-developed countries (LDCs). The fact that development could not be measured by the growth of output had already been made clear during the 1950s by Sir Arthur Lewis (1955) in the very first pages of his influential *Theory of Economic Growth*. A further step forward in the conceptualization of development and well-being was represented by the diffusion of the theory of basic needs.

In the 1970s, the basic needs approach had become a mainstream idea in development, growing out of the work of the International Labour Office (ILO) World Employment Programme (WEP) bringing employment, people and human needs back to the centre of development strategy. Basic needs were said to include two elements:

> First, they include certain minimum requirements of a family for private consumption: adequate food, shelter and clothing, as well as certain household furniture and equipment. Second, they include essential services provided by and for the community at large, such as safe drinking water, sanitation, public transport and health, education and cultural facilities . . . The concept of basic needs should be placed within a context of a nation's overall economic and social development. In no circumstances should it be taken to mean merely the minimum necessary for subsistence; it should be placed within a context of national independence, the dignity of individuals and peoples and their freedom to chart their destiny without hindrance. (International Labour Office, 1976, pp. 24–25)

Even if, according to Bremner (1956), in the 1950s the concept of human need was periodically rediscovered, the theory on human needs can be considered to be primarily based on the work carried out by a psychologist, Abraham Maslow. In 1954 he published the book *Motivation and Personality* (Maslow, 1954) in which he proposed the theory that people have a hierarchy of psychological needs, which range from physiological needs to safety needs, love and belonging, esteem and self-actualization. The major criticisms to the so-called 'Maslow's pyramid' refer to its possible cultural bias, reflecting Western values and culture, for which it can hardly be considered a universal approach.

More recently, Sommers and Satel (2006) have referred to Maslow's lack of empirical findings to explain the progressive abandonment of his theories. Notwithstanding some conceptual weaknesses and operational difficulties, this intuitively appealing model has been very influential for decades. Lately, the needs approach has started evolving around the concept of development at human scale proposed by Manfred Max-Neef (Max-Neef et al., 1989), where needs are seen as a complex system: they cannot be seen as a hierarchy, and may be satisfied simultaneously but also may face significant trade-offs. Max-Neef developed a taxonomy of needs (subsistence, protection, affection, understanding, participation, leisure, creation, identity and freedom) defined through the existential categories of being, having, doing and interacting.

Doyal and Gough (1991) have moved further in this approach, differentiating between basic 'health needs' and the more cognitive 'autonomy'. Physical health needs are the fundamental requirements in order to stay alive. As with Maslow's hierarchy, health needs are the most important and will take precedence when they are threatened or impacted; autonomous needs are those necessary to make informed choices and to achieve conscious goals. They refer to mental health, cognitive skills and opportunities to engage in social participation:

> Objective basic needs consist, at the least, in those universal preconditions that enable sustained participation in one's form of life. At the most, they consist in those universal preconditions for critical participation in one's form of life – the capacity to situate it, to criticize it, and, if necessary, to act to change it. (Gough, 1994, p. 28)

Doyal and Gough identify 11 intermediate needs (or 'universal satisfier characteristics'), essential characteristics that contribute to improved physical health and autonomy. They are:

1. adequate nutritional food and water;
2. adequate protective housing;
3. a non-hazardous work environment;
4. a non-hazardous physical environment;
5. appropriate health care;
6. security in childhood;
7. significant primary relationships;
8. physical security;
9. economic security;
10. safe birth control and child-bearing;
11. appropriate basic and cross-cultural education.

For each of the eleven categories they identify two or more indicators in order to operationalize their theoretical framework. Having a list of indicators is also important from the theoretical point of view, to provide a formal boundary to the proposed concepts (which may otherwise lead to an infinite list of needs: the indicators chosen for empirical measurement deeply reflect the underlying conceptualization) and to strengthen the idea of describing 'objective needs' and gaining degrees of political relevance. Other than Maslow, the universal approach by Doyal and Gough has also been criticized for a cultural bias in the idea of universality.

1.2.4   The Millennium Development Goals

Within a similar approach it is possible to frame the set of indicators composing the Millennium Development Goals (MDGs) (UN, 2000), a set of time-bound targets foreseen in the so-called Millennium Declaration adopted by the UN General Assembly in 2000:

- Goal 1: eradicate poverty and hunger.
- Goal 2: achieve universal primary education.
- Goal 3: promote gender equality and empower women.
- Goal 4: reduce child mortality.
- Goal 5: improve maternal health.
- Goal 6: combat HIV/AIDS, malaria and other diseases.
- Goal 7: ensure environmental sustainability.
- Goal 8: develop a global partnership for development.

Their transparency and simplicity, along with their focus on multidimensional human needs, helped them gain overarching support going well beyond that gained by the economic growth objectives that had dominated previous development agendas. Nevertheless, their conceptual framework has been criticized for being incomplete and failing to take into account important elements of human development. Among these, one may mention demographic dynamics, inequalities, productive employment, decent work, social protection, social exclusion, biodiversity, persistent malnutrition, increase in non-communicable diseases, violence against women, reproductive health, peace and security, governance, the rule of law and human rights.

This simple framework has been also accused of not taking the enablers of development into adequate account, and in its monitoring system of not being able to consider the differences in initial conditions, thus undervaluing the results obtained, in particular, in sub-Saharan Africa (UN, 2012b). Some (e.g., Vandemoortele, 2007) have argued that the process which led to the definition of the goals and targets lacked a sufficiently broad participation, with the result that certain important topics were not considered. Yet, the centralized process allowed focus on a limited number of goals and targets, which is considered one of the strengths of the set.

Finally, the fact that the MDGs foresaw very clear targets for developing countries and much looser constraints for the advanced economies (through Goal 8 on a global partnership for development) may have suggested a sort of 'donor-centric agenda', where the idea of universality was somehow legitimized by the MDGs resulting from the approval of the United Nations General Assembly.

1.2.5 The Quality of Society

Since the 1980s and 1990s, increasing attention has been given to the concept of the quality of societies (Berger-Schmitt and Noll, 2000; Maggino, 2013) to broaden the view with respect to the notion of quality of life, stressing the difference between the individual and the societal dimensions. In this approach, the quality of societies is characterized in different ways (and most of the time is not made explicit, being part of the overall concept of well-being).

Veenhoven (1996) introduced the concept of 'liveability' of a nation to represent 'the degree to which its provisions and requirements fit with the needs and capacities of citizens'. Other concepts which have often characterized the analysis of the quality of societies are those of social cohesion, social exclusion and social capital. They all refer to the relationships existing among citizens. Social cohesion refers particularly to the existence of shared values, national or community identity, trust among members and low inequalities. Social exclusion is a concept which refers to a process and is linked to the analysis of disadvantageous social conditions such as poverty, deprivation, unemployment, familiar instability, migrations, lack of assistance leading to marginalization, and the breaking of relationships between the individual or household and the society. Finally, the concept of social capital refers to the collective or economic benefits derived from the preferential treatment and cooperation between individuals and groups. It thus looks at the strength of civic networks and organizations (clubs, parties, unions, non-governmental organizations, and so on), volunteering or cooperation among relatives, friends and neighbours.

In most multidimensional frameworks, the quality of society is represented by a domain of social relationships, a domain of safety and a domain of governance. The first usually refers to the quality of relationships with family, friends and neighbours, to the help given and received, and to the general trust in people. Safety typically refers to crime and violence, either registered or perceived, with sometimes quite different results. Governance is a broad and complex concept relative to the quality of the institutional system, sometimes referred to as 'quality of democracy', even though an authoritarian regime can be well governed, just as a democracy can be ill-administered, thus implying a separation of the two concepts which are often used to include the same phenomena.

Governance may refer to political stability, the trust in specific institutions and their transparency, the rule of law, the accessibility and effectiveness of public services, the participation in public life and debate (usually simplified as the voter turnout), the regulatory environment for business, the respect of civil rights (such as freedom of the press), the level of corruption, and so on. Fukuyama (2013, p. 3) proposed an operational definition of governance that takes as its starting point 'a government's ability to make and enforce rules, and to deliver services', separating it from the quality of democratic processes as well as the actual outcomes which may depend upon societal behaviours or budget constraints which fall outside the boundaries of institutional activity. According to Morlino, instead, good governance is one of the elements of democratic quality, where the ideal democracy is one that aims at the full implementation of freedom, equality and solidarity through a full-fledged guarantee of rights and adequate institutions. Elements for the analysis of the quality of democracies are the rule of law, electoral accountability, inter-institutional accountability, competition, participation, freedom, equality and responsiveness (Morlino et al., 2013).

The existing measures of governance have a number of limitations, often not being directly observable and thus being built through expert surveys, which are generally weak measures, especially when trying to create time-series data. Moreover, since the concept of 'good governance' is not exactly defined, different experts may intend different things when responding to the same survey question. Several measures dealing with governance or quality of democracy have been developed by public and private institutions (for a comprehensive list see www.democracybarometer.org). The World Bank's Worldwide Governance Indicators measure government effectiveness, regulatory quality, control of corruption, stability and absence of violence.

The Quality of Governance Institute has developed a set of measures of quality of governance for 136 countries worldwide, as well as a more detailed survey of 172 regions within the European Union. Its founder, Bo Rothstein (2011), starting from the idea that the basic characteristic of quality government is impartiality in the exercise of power, centres good governance on the ideas of corruption, social trust and inequality. Relevant examples are the Freedom House (2015) Index, the Polity measures by the Center for Systemic Peace, and the Varieties of Democracy project. The Bertelsmann Foundation elaborates both a set of Sustainable Governance Indicators (SGIs), dealing with policy performance, quality of democracy and governance, and a Transformation Index (BTI), which focuses on how effectively policymakers facilitate and steer development and transformation processes.

1.2.6   Utility and Subjective Well-Being

All the approaches analysed so far are based on objective measures and have to face the criticism of arbitrariness in the choice of the basic indicators and of their normative value. They can be contrasted to the American subjective well-being approach, according to which welfare and quality of life are to be considered as subjectively perceived and experienced by the individual. Accordingly, each individual is the best expert to evaluate their own quality of life (Noll, 2002): 'The quality of life must be in the eye of the beholder' (Campbell, 1972, p. 442).

During the twentieth century, the most influential approach towards the analysis of people's well-being can be framed within the 'welfare economics' approach. This can be initially attributed to the utilitarian theory, rooted in the works of Bentham and John Stuart Mill and first developed by Alfred Marshall and Cecil Pigou. Welfare economics sees welfare as the sum of individual preferences, therefore grounding the measure of well-being on subjective perceptions and expectations. Similarly, the 'American quality of life' (Noll, 2002) bases welfare measurement primarily on subjective indicators, and in the tradition of utilitarian philosophy and mental health research. Strongly influenced by social psychologists such as W.I. Thomas, known by his dictum that 'if men define situations as real, they are real in their consequences' (Thomas and Thomas, 1928, pp. 571–572), this approach ultimately defines welfare as subjective well-being.

Here, what is relevant to people and what produces utility cannot be simply measured in economic terms or willingness-to-pay. Equal amounts of money may have significantly different values among people, and psychological elements play a decisive role in the evaluation of quality of life. Perceptions of and impacts on personal well-being may vary significantly among individuals as a reaction to the same events or circumstances:

this depends on cultural backgrounds, systems of values, standards of living people are already used to, and personal expectations. What really matters is how people feel, whether they feel 'happy' or 'satisfied'. Yet, people adapt differently to the same situations, and raise their expectations very quickly once they have reached new standards, both material and immaterial. This phenomenon, known as the 'hedonic treadmill' (Brickman and Campbell, 1971), is at the basis of the support of measurement of well-being through subjective measures. Personality, personal goals, comparison with others and with the past, and culture all influence the way objective conditions and events affect subjective well-being (Diener, 2000; Beham et al., 2006).

Subjective well-being (often translated into the concepts of 'happiness' or 'life satisfaction') is therefore considered the ultimate goal of societies and the measures of overall life satisfaction are the most practicable indicators. According to Layard (2009, p. 1), 'the right single measure of progress must be the one that is self-evidently good. The only such measure is the Happiness of the population – and the equivalent absence of misery'.

Studies on subjective well-being naturally proposed the analysis of the relationship between happiness and income, leading to the 'Easterlin paradox'. Easterlin (1974) showed that within a developed country, even if richer people declare to be happier than poorer ones, the increase of income over time does not produce any increase in happiness. Moreover, in cross-country comparisons, no significant correlation emerges between income and happiness: richer countries are not happier than poorer ones. These are probably the results which more than any others contributed to the diffusion of the idea that well-being could not be measured through GDP.

There are, of course, many different ways to measure happiness and life satisfaction, and measures evolved over time (measures of happiness in the United States can be traced back to 1946; for a chronology, see Abdallah and Mahony's, 2012 work within the e-Frame project). The fundamental distinction in the different approaches towards subjective well-being is that between cognitive (or evaluative) and affective (or hedonic) measures: what people think of their life versus what people feel in their life.

The most common cognitive methods are based on a single direct question asking how happy or satisfied with life overall people are, on a proposed scale. In order to reduce measurement error, a few questions may be asked on different aspects of life satisfaction (for example, health, work, social and family life) to be combined into a single index using weights that reflect their average impact on answers to the single general question (Layard, 2010). A similar cognitive approach for the measurement of subjective well-being stands in the tradition of the so-called eudeimonia. Starting from the Aristotelian concept of a full realization of human potential, the eudeimonic approach measures well-being by asking people whether they consider what they do in their life as worthwhile. The adopted measurement scale itself adds a further subjective component, since the extremes of the scale (typically 0 and 10 in the so-called 'self-anchored' scale proposed by Cantril, 1965) are self-defined as the worst and the best possible conditions, according, therefore, to the interviewed perceptions, objectives and values.

The other major approach towards a unique measure of individual well-being is the 'hedonic approach', where well-being is defined as the balance between pleasure and pain. This kind of approach based on affects, is firstly found in the 'hedonic (or felicific) calculus' proposed by Jeremy Bentham (1789) for its 'greatest-happiness principle'. According to Bentham, the moral rightness or wrongness of any act depended on the amount of

Table 1.1   Components of subjective well-being

Pleasant affect	Unpleasant affect	Life satisfaction	Domain satisfaction
Joy	Guilt and shame	Desire to change life	Work
Elation	Sadness	Satisfaction with current life	Family
Contentment	Anxiety and worry	Satisfaction with past	Leisure
Pride	Anger	Satisfaction with future	Health
Affection	Stress	Significant other's views of	Finances
Happiness	Depression	one's life	One's group
Life	Self		
Ecstasy	Envy		

Source: Diener et al. (1999).

pleasure or pain that it produced. In principle, the felicific calculus could determine the moral status of any considered action by evaluating a number of 'circumstances', or variables to be taken into account: intensity, duration, certainty, propinquity, fecundity, purity, extent.

A more recent and very influential example in this field (Kahneman and Krueger, 2006) aims at distinguishing among different conceptions of utility rather than presuming to measure a single, unifying concept that motivates all human choices. It is the so-called 'U-index', which measures the percentage of time daily spent in unpleasant activities using a day reconstruction method (DRM) to evaluate features of individuals' perceptions of their experiences, beyond their utility as economists typically conceive of it.

These approaches can be considered as the fundamental elements of a multidimensional approach towards subjective well-being. The New Economics Foundation (Abdallah and Shah, 2012) proposes a synthesis of them into an index of 'overall well-being' considering life satisfaction, eudaimonia and affects. Yet, other taxonomies to subjective well-being have been proposed. One of the most influential is the multidimensional approach towards subjective well-being proposed in 1999 by Ed Diener, taking into account both affective and cognitive aspects, grouped into four major domains: pleasant affect, unpleasant affect, life satisfaction and domain satisfaction (see Table 1.1).[4]

Until recently, subjective measures had very little significance in the academic and political debate. Subsequently, happiness studies have contributed to granting increasing dignity to subjective measures by progressively understanding the strengths and weaknesses of those measures both in conceptual and in methodological terms.[5] More recently, and based on a very large world database with more than two million interviews, the Gallup-Healthways (2014) Global Well-Being Index (Gallup-Healthways, 2014) is built on a set of questions grouped into five areas of subjective well-being: purpose, social, financial, community and physical. In most countries, happiness appears flat over time. This flatness, at the root of the 'Easterlin paradox', can be explained on the one hand by the hedonic treadmill and the adaptation to modified standards of living, and on the other hand by the collective effort to improve relative social positions, which leads to economic growth but does not change relative positions much. As a matter of fact, one may think that 'the Easterlin paradox is not just a post-World War II phenomenon, but a more profound phenomenon of stability of subjective evaluation and feeling in our species' (Fleurbaey and Blanchet, 2014, p. 163). Fleurbaey and Blanchet also challenge the idea that happiness is self-evidently the ultimate goal: on the one hand, it is possible to look for happiness for external reasons, for example to carry out duties unencumbered by bad feeling or to be more pleasant to one's family and relatives or because of its positive effects on health. On the other hand, it has to be demonstrated that aspects other than happiness are not desirable in themselves, leaving happiness aside: 'the fact that many good things in life enhance happiness does not imply that people want them only for the pursuit of a greater happiness' (Fleurbaey and Blanchet, 2014, p. 170).

In the analysis made by Amartya Sen, the use of subjective well-being, and the utilitarian approach in general, finds its limits in its inability to take into account opportunities, freedoms and other relevant implications in terms of social justice. Utilitarianism ignores the existence of inequalities and violations of individual rights and freedoms, only evaluating total aggregate happiness. Happiness is then considered a restrictive vision of interpersonal comparison because of the adaptability to adversities. The utilitarian metric is unfair towards those suffering persistent privations, oppressed minorities, exploited workers or submissive housewives who no longer want a change but learned to bear their condition. Symmetrically, people with more expensive preferences may claim to be worst off. Happiness therefore becomes a flawed measure of societal well-being (Sen, 1985, 2013; Dworkin, 1981; Fleurbaey and Blanchet, 2014).

Fleurbaey and Blanchet also identify three major methodological problems arising in the submission of subjective questionnaires, which they call problems of scope, ranking and calibration. The 'scope problem' refers to common ambiguity about the exact target of the typical question, 'How are you satisfied with your life overall?', in which a number of elements are often unclear: the time frame (which could refer either to the current period or to the whole life), whether the condition of closest relatives is to be taken into account, or whether the community or country situation is to be considered. The scope problem is therefore very much dependent on the structure of the questionnaire and on the sequence of the questions which may bring the respondent to focus on different aspects of their life. The 'ranking problem' refers to the need for the respondent to quickly analyse all the relevant aspects affecting their satisfaction, and to rank them. Kahneman et al. (2006) observed that people tend to exaggerate the relevance of aspects under consideration at the moment, producing a 'focusing illusion', thus also this problem is strongly affected by the structure of the questionnaire. Finally, the 'calibration problem' refers to the difficulty in assigning a fixed score to open or fuzzy phenomena. To do this, one needs to define a standard or a term of comparison which can be identified in different ways, such as previous life experiences of the respondent, the kind of life they expected, or the lives of other people in the community or in the world. These problems produce a relevant heterogeneity among individuals, affecting the comparability of the results.

Despite these limitations and methodological caveats, subjective measures are broadening and increasingly affirming their usage. A policy application of happiness measures is offered by Richard Layard, who, in his renowned book *Happiness: Lessons from a New Science* (Layard, 2005), suggests that subjective well-being should influence the definition of the model of society we should attend to. In his view, referring to Bentham's principle of the 'greatest happiness', happiness must represent the unifying principle guiding laws and the rule of morality.[6] In this sense, any public or private decision 'should be judged by its impact on the happiness of all those affected by it, each person counting equally' (Layard, 2005, p. 112). More recently, Dolan, Layard and Metcalfe (Dolan et al., 2011) argue that different subjective well-being measures are to be used for different specific policy purposes. Evaluation measures should be used for specific life domains such as health, job and social relationships, or for public aspects such as the quality of services, aspects of the area or politics; while experience and eudeimonic measures should assess life in general or specific activities. On the basis of subjective well-being analysis, Layard (2005) identifies a number of policy options that can affect some of the determinants of happiness and life satisfaction, such as leisure and social relationships. Similarly, Abdallah and Shah (2012) call for improvements in ethnic inequalities, permanent employment contracts or reduced working hours in order to increase overall subjective well-being in the United Kingdom (UK).

1.2.7   Hybrid Approaches

In the context of the debate over the opportunity to use subjective indicators, scholars often agreed that welfare assessment should be based on a hybrid approach, taking into account both objective and subjective indicators (e.g., Allardt, 1993; Diener and Suh, 1997; Noll, 2002). In 1993 Erik Allardt proposed a broader and more inclusive approach which takes into account three major basic needs which everyone should fulfil: having, loving and being. 'Having' refers to necessary material conditions such as income, housing, employment, working conditions, health, education; 'loving' refers to affectivity and social relationships; 'being' refers to people's role in society and in the environment, involving political activities, leisure, work, opportunities to enjoy nature, and so on. The three broad issues need to be assessed through both objective and subjective indicators in order to provide a complete assessment of quality of life (Table 1.2).

Hybrid approaches are also the Happy Life-Expectancy, the Happy Income and the Happy Planet Index. Happy Life-Expectancy, proposed by Veenhoven (1996), multiplies life expectancy in years by average happiness on a 0–1 scale. The product 'can be interpreted as the number of years the average citizen in a country lives happily at a certain time' (Veenhoven, 1996, p. 1). The Happy Income Index, developed by Prinz and Bünger (2009) multiplies a measure of happiness for the median equalized household net income. The Happy Planet Index, proposed in 2006 by the New Economic Foundation

Table 1.2   Indicators to assess quality of life as proposed by Allardt (1993)

	Objective indicators	Subjective indicators
Having (material and impersonal needs)	1. Objective measures of the level of living and environmental conditions	4. Subjective feelings of dissatisfaction/ satisfaction with living conditions
Loving (social needs)	2. Objective measures of relationships to other people	5. Unhappiness/happiness – subjective feelings about social relations
Being (needs for personal growth)	3. Objective measures of people's relation to society and nature	6. Subjective feelings of alienation/ personal growth

Table 1.3   Harrison's hybrid framework of analysis

	Perception (attitude)	Reality (behavioural/outcomes)
Individual level	Happiness, life satisfaction, opinion about domains of life experience	Living conditions, educational attainment, job quality, income, access to resources etc. (micro-data)
Societal level	Perception of the quality of society or societal well-being	Features of society: crime rate, income distribution, quality of education and health, etc.

Source: Harrison (2014).

(NEF, 2006), was much more influential. It divides the happy life years by the ecological footprint, thus providing an indicator of the efficiency of a national system to satisfy the need to live a long and happy life using few natural resources. More recently, through the Midlife in the United States (MIDUS) surveys, Carol Ryff (Ryff et al., 2012) proposes an analysis of personal well-being which combines objective and subjective measures of physical and mental health, also taking into account a number of neurobiological mechanisms involving reactivity and recovery in the brain and physiological systems in the body.

Harrison (2014), instead, proposes a framework which distinguishes between objective and subjective measures as well as between individual and societal well-being (between quality of life and quality of society). This results in a tetracoric table with four different sectors of analysis for well-being: living conditions, happiness, features of society and perceptions of the quality of society (Table 1.3).

An attempt to bring together the objective and the subjective dimensions of well-being in a unique coherent framework was advanced by Giovannini (2015). When subjective and objective measures are considered together, because subjective well-being is influenced by a lot of conditions that could be captured by quantitative variables (employment, income, health, and so on), considering it as an additional dimension of well-being on top of the others could be seen as a duplication. Also, the other way round may imply causality: happier people may enjoy better health, have stronger social relationships and find a good job more easily. Leaving the subjective dimension completely out of the picture would mean missing an important element of well-being.

A possible solution to this dilemma is presented in Figure 1.1 (originally proposed by Giovannini and then slightly modified in the context of the New Development Paradigm, 2013). This approach is based on the idea that human beings have different capacities ('happiness skills' and/or 'resilience skills') of transforming into happiness what the economy and society produce in terms of outputs and outcomes. These happiness skills depend on both genetic characteristics and the way people are educated. The level of happiness has an impact on both the definition of human needs and the way the economy and society work. The scheme also considers that human 'needs' are not the only relevant ones, since ecosystem needs are also accounted for, as well as the existence of planetary boundaries.

While in the approach used for the development of several well-being frameworks the focus is on concrete outputs and outcomes, in this model there is an additional linkage between these results and subjective well-being, which in turn influences the way in which the needs are selected, as well as the functioning of societies and economies. In this way, a

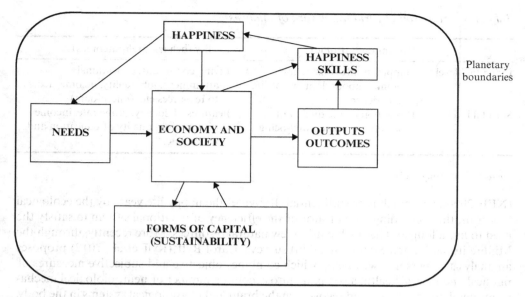

Figure 1.1   Key elements of a new development paradigm

'virtuous circle' is established and policy makers have an interest both in achieving better outputs and outcomes, and in maximizing the 'happiness or resilience skills' of people through proper education.[7] In this framework, policies should not be directly aimed at increasing happiness per se, but rather at improving the functioning of societies and economies, making them more sustainable and resilient; important characteristics for the medium- to long-term future of our world.

1.2.8   Capabilities Approach

The most influential approach beyond welfare economics and utilitarianism (Cobb, 2000), and for the funding of a multidimensional approach towards well-being, stands in the 'capabilities approach' developed by Nobel laureate Amartya Sen. Sen's contribution overcomes the most widespread approaches to the analysis and measurement of well-being: utility, opulence and basic needs.

We have already briefly presented some of Sen's criticisms towards the utilitarian approach (yet the analysis of the concept of utility pervades his works; see, for example, Sen, 1985, 1992). The 'opulence' approach is the one which identifies GDP and consumption, or in general the command over a mass of commodities, as measures of standard of living and well-being. Its limits are at the core of the whole theme treated in this chapter. In Sen's works, standard of living does not define a level of opulence, even if it is influenced by it. In his example, in comparing two poor people, the poorer may enjoy a higher standard of living if their metabolism needs less food, and therefore less money. Standard of living must refer to the life people are leading instead of the resources and means owned to live. The move towards increasing objectivity is considered correct, but opulence is not the target to be reached.

He also recalls the works of Karl Marx (1887 [1967]) and his idea of 'commodity fetishism' – the fact that social relations between people are perceived as economic relations among objects; and of Adam Smith (1776), who considered how 'the ability to appear in public without shame' would vary according to social customs and cultural conventions. In this way, Smith demonstrated the social nature of the relationship between commodities and living conditions: the 'capability' to appear in public without shame implies different requirements of the desired commodities and wealth, which vary according to the nature of the society one lives in (Sen, 1992).

The focus on the kind of life people live, on what people can or cannot do, on what people can or cannot be, becomes the centre of Sen's 'capability' approach (Sen, 1980). 'Capabilities' are the real opportunities people have in order to lead a valuable life; the ability to achieve actual results. The results obtained by the individuals are called 'functionings': 'Some functionings are very elementary, such as being adequately nourished, being in good health, etc., others may be more complex, but still widely valued, such as achieving self-respect or being socially integrated' (Sen, 1993, p. 31). Life is then seen as 'a combination of various "doings and beings", with quality of life to be assessed in terms of the capability to achieve valuable functionings' (ibid.). In this framework, material goods and economic resources are to be intended only as the means for achieving the functionings.

That is how the capability approach moves beyond the basic needs approach. The two are considered very important for their ability to shift attention towards the kind of life people are able to live. But their limit stands in the form in which basic needs must be considered. If they are considered in terms of commodities, the approach would still refer to the concept of opulence. While if one accepts that our interest is fundamentally in the kind of existence people lead, or may lead, then the basic needs should be formulated in line with functionings and capabilities. If what we value are functionings and capabilities, then the basic needs in terms of commodities are instrumentally, and not intrinsically, important (Sen, 1992).

The capabilities are strictly linked with the idea of freedom, another central aspect of Sen's approach. The value of a standard of living is given by the capability of leading different types of existence and, although it is necessary to give a particular importance to the life actually chosen, the availability of other choices has a certain value. Freedom is determinant in the move from the space of functioning to the space of capabilities (Sen, 1993, 2009; Fleurbaey and Blanchet, 2014). The presence of alternatives is an important element of advantage: people with the same functioning but with different capabilities present different levels of well-being. Here the typical example is the difference between fasting and starving. Freedom allows people to choose between different affiliations and cultures determining their preferred well-being. As explained by Nussbaum (2000, p. 87):

> if we were to take functioning itself as the goal of public policies, pushing citizens into functionings in a single determined manner, the liberal pluralist would rightly judge that we were precluding many choices that citizens may make in accordance with their own conceptions of the good, and perhaps violating their rights.

In Sen's example, well-being (and the goals of policy making) stands in the availability of access to health care services, not in the use of health care facilities by the whole population.

Sen never proposed a set of measures, refusing to subscribe to a definite list of capabilities, since he thought that this should be done through processes of public engagement and democratic discussion. Individuals' participation in the public sphere, besides being a fundamental pillar for individual functionings, is also the tool for the definition of the most appropriate measures according to the different contexts (see section 1.6 below). The main advantage of a definition of development based on the concept of choice is its apparent immunity from ethnocentric prejudices of character: the choice may in fact go in any direction, depending on the culture and values of reference (Riggs, 1984).

The other eminent scholar in the development of the capabilities approach, Martha Nussbaum, is far more specific than Sen. In order to provide the approach with political relevance (Holst, 2010) – that is, to have a greater political impact – she proposed a fundamental list of items that is intended to be both 'open-ended', 'subject to ongoing revision and rethinking, in the way that any society's account of its most fundamental entitlements is always subject to supplementation (or deletion)', and 'abstract and general': the items on the list are presented in a way that leaves 'room for the activities of specifying and deliberating by citizens and their legislatures and courts'. Elements of the list (Nussbaum, 2006, pp. 76–78) are:

1. Life;
2. Bodily health;
3. Bodily integrity;
4. Senses, imagination and thought;
5. Emotions;
6. Practical reason;
7. Affiliation;
8. Other species;
9. Play;
10. Control over one's environment.

Measurement is generally considered to be one of the weaknesses of the capabilities approach. Yet, Sen's approach has been translated into the concept of human development within the United Nations Development Programme (UNDP), as the conceptual basis for the extremely influential Human Development Index:

> The basic objective of human development is to enlarge the range of people's choices. These choices are not fixed forever. They change over time as circumstances and aspirations change. But at all levels of development, the three essential capabilities for human development are for people to lead long and healthy lives, to be knowledgeable and to have a decent standard of living. If these basic capabilities are not achieved many choices are simply not available and many opportunities remain inaccessible. (UNDP, Human Development Report 1/1990)

The *Human Development Report* (HDR) and its Human Development Index (HDI) are an important part of the measurement landscape, and the HDI (UNDP, 2010) is arguably the best-known alternative to GDP. (See also Seth and Villar, Chapters 3 and 4 in this *Handbook*.)

1.3 THE NEED TO AGGREGATE

The powerful influence of GDP largely stands in its ability to reduce complex information to a single number. Dashboards of indicators are able to show the multidimensionality, but suffer from a great difficulty in communicating the relevant messages, and the larger the set, the more difficult it is to communicate.

The increasing availability of data to the citizenship and the diffusion of information and communication technology have allowed almost anyone to produce and disseminate their own composite indicator. Therefore, over the years, a large number of synthetic measures of well-being have been developed by individual scholars, civil society organizations, companies and public institutions. In 2008, the OECD published a handbook for the building of composite indicators and the diffusion of some principles and steps which have to be followed to guarantee a minimum level of soundness in the applied methods, helping to improve the quality of the outputs (OECD and JRC, 2008). Of course, composite measures aggregating indicators of different natures are not limited to well-being measurement; examples are common in industrial competitiveness, environmental sciences, globalization and innovation (Bandura, 2008, collected 178 indexes on various economic, political, social and environmental measures), yet in a field characterized by multidimensional analysis such as the measurement of well-being, they have become relatively popular.

Aggregation represents one of the most controversial aspects of the 'beyond GDP' international debate because of its clashing strengths and weaknesses, independent of the actual method, which however represents a further complexity within the debate. In general, the choice to aggregate is the need to provide a measure of a complex 'latent construct' which is not directly observable. The relationship between the latent structure and the basic indicators is not straightforward and can be defined as either following a 'formative' or a 'reflective' approach (Maggino, 2009). In formative approaches, the construct is defined by (or composed of) a number of indicators. In this case, causality flows from the indicator to the construct. This is the case when measuring well-being: the definition of what is well-being, and thus its measure, stems from the indicators used. Alternatively, latent constructs are measured by indicators assumed to be reflective in nature: the indicators are seen as functions of the latent variable which is already known and defined, but is not directly observable. This is often the case in subjective measurement.

Having a single measure is preferable from various points of view (OECD and JRC, 2008): it is easy to interpret, it has a clear evolution over time, it allows immediate comparisons among countries or regions and with respect to other phenomena, it is immediately communicable, allows rankings which attract media attention, can summarize complex realities to support decision makers and can foster accountability. On the other hand, aggregation presents some drawbacks. First of all, the choice of the indicators to be used (what to aggregate) is often subjective or strongly limited by data availability. This may distort the meaning of the final output and may also be subject to political dispute. The choice of the basic elements should also foresee analytical clarity around the difference among inputs, intermediate factors, outputs or outcomes relative to the latent construct. Mixing elements of different kinds, which is quite common (especially when a large number of elements is considered), may lead to flawed aggregate measures.

Moreover, every aggregation foresees an implicit or explicit system of weighting. In the case of monetary indexes, such as the GDP, weighting relies on the use of market prices, providing the feeling that aggregation is not fully arbitrary (Fleurbaey and Blanchet, 2014). We have seen that the social preferences expressed by market prices may be strongly distorted, but still they provide a rationale which appears stronger than the simple arbitrary choice of weights (most of the time leading to an equal weighting, since any divergence from it appears very difficult to motivate). To grant legitimacy to the weighting system focus groups, Delphi methods or similar consultative processes are sometimes adopted.

Moreover, every weighting system implies some kind of 'substitutability' among the different factors in terms of well-being, and this is often considered to be critical. This theme is usually addressed in the environmental debate – namely in the difference between weak and strong sustainability (see section 1.5 below) – but is an ever-present obstacle: what increase in education is needed to offset a deterioration of health conditions? What increase in income may offset a 1 per cent lower proportion of workers satisfied in their job? And so on. Some non-linear correction may allow to build composite indicators with no perfect substitutability, favouring more balanced compositions of the basic indicators with respect to disequilibria. This is the case of the geometric mean adopted by the new version of the HDI, or the concave means proposed by Palazzi (2004), or the arithmetic mean adjusted by a 'penalty' coefficient related to the variability of each unit (method of the coefficient of variation penalty) developed by De Muro et al. (2011). Yet even these methods fail to completely solve the problem of the substitutability among basic indicators which affects any aggregation method, however sophisticated. Other shortcomings (OECD and JRC, 2008) of the use of composite indicators relate to the risk of them being poorly constructed, or to the fact that the construction process may not be transparent. Also, they are prone to lead to simplistic policy conclusions, or may be misused, for example to support a desired policy. Overall, we can affirm with Rosen (1991) that the justification for a composite indicator lies in its fitness for the intended purpose, and in peer acceptance.

In order to aggregate indicators with different units of measurement, typically through a weighted average, two major strategies may be considered: on the one hand, the reduction of all the values to 'pure numbers' through some kind of standardization of the values (ranks, normalization, rescaling, and so on); on the other hand, through a monetary aggregation in which every phenomenon is quantified in terms of its monetary value for society.

Indexes of the first kind are very common, given their effectiveness in communicating the desired message and their relative technical ease. The most relevant example in this field is certainly the Human Development Index (HDI) built by the UNDP in 1990 (UNDP, 1990). Yet, it was not the first one. The seminal experience in this field is the Index of Relative Standard of Living developed by Bennett in 1937, and over the century dozens of indexes of this kind have been built, each one selecting different indicators, thus proposing a different definition of development, well-being or progress. Among the most influential – all of them aggregating a large number of basic indicators – worth mentioning, in chronological order, are those developed by the United Nations Research Institute for Social Development (UNRISD): the Level of Living Index (Drewnowski and Scott, 1966), the Socioeconomic Development Index (SID) (UNRISD, 1970), the General Index of Development (McGranahan et al., 1972); also the Physical Quality of Life Index (PQLI) (Morris, 1979) and the Indexes of Quality of Life and the Environment by Prescott-Allen (2001). A hybrid procedure that combines composite and monetary frameworks is the Index of Economic Well-Being developed by Osberg and Sharpe (2002). More recently, the Canadian Index of Well-Being (2012), the OECD (2011b) Better Life Index and the Bhutanese Gross National Happiness (Ura et al., 2012) have proposed aggregate measure of well-being. In 2010, the UNDP, beside reviewing the aggregation methodology of the HDI, produced a Multidimensional Poverty Index based on the works by the Oxford Poverty and Human Development Initiative (OPHI) (UNDP, 2010).

On the other hand, some authors have proposed monetary measures of well-being with the aim of correcting GDP, and with the chance to actually compare GDP with the new measure. The seminal work in this field is the Measure of Economic Welfare (MEW) proposed by Nordhaus and Tobin (1972), that, starting from total household consumption (considered the real goal of economic activity), subtracts a number of components which are considered negative for economic welfare. These can be capital expenditures on replacements due to depreciation, or instrumental costs 'that are not directly sources of utility themselves but are regrettably necessary inputs to activities that may yield utility' (Nordhaus and Tobin, 1972, p. 7), for example the costs of commuting to work (within 'urban disamenities'), or some government expenditures such as police services, sanitation services, road maintenance and national defence. Nordhaus and Tobin then sum up imputations for capital services (health and education), leisure and non-market work. They do not adjust for environmental factors or depletion of natural resources, assuming the ability of manufactured capital to substitute any natural resources shortage. They continue to treat expenditures on pollution prevention as intermediate consumption.

Since then, a few other measures of the same kind have been developed, permanently including environmental aspects within the index. The most influential were the Economic Aspect of Welfare Index by Zolotas (1981) and the Index of Sustainable Economic Welfare (ISEW) by Cobb and Daly (1989), and the very similar Genuine Progress Indicator (GPI) proposed since 1995 by the non-profit organization Redefining Progress (Talberth et al., 2007), recently applied by Maryland government (http://green.maryland.gov/mdgpi/) and experimented on many countries (see Posner and Costanza, 2011; Kubiszewski et al., 2013). These experiences move forward with respect to the MEW (yet also face relevant criticisms; for example Neumayer, 1999) by fundamentally providing corrections for income inequalities (using either Gini or Atkinson indexes) and estimates of the costs due to natural resource depletion, usually through the actualization of the future costs needed for replacement or to generate renewable alternatives.

Most of the proposed measures show a common trend: the ISEW and GPI rise until the 1970s together with GDP, while they show a stable or even decreasing trend afterwards. Although different methods and countries show slightly different results, an overall message always emerges based on the fact that social and environmental costs outweigh the benefits of increased levels of consumption, leading to what Daly (1977) called 'uneconomic growth' (Daly, 1977, p. 100) and supporting the idea of the existence of a 'threshold hypothesis' proposed by Manfred Max-Neef, according to which 'for every society there seems to be a period in which economic growth (as conventionally measured) brings about an improvement in the quality of life, but only up to a point – the threshold point – beyond which, if there is more economic growth, quality of life may begin to deteriorate'

(Max-Neef, 1995, p. 117). Despite the large bulk of literature around aggregation and the many experiments done, agreement on the choice between aggregating or not has never been reached.

1.4 INEQUALITIES

The importance of inequalities in the analysis of well-being is derived from different elements (Rondinella, 2013). First of all is the need to qualify mean values which can hide very different phenomena and criticalities for selected social groups. Inequalities also have a relevant impact on perceived personal well-being, which can be strongly influenced by the individual's relative position within society or peer groups. Finally, a principle of social justice suggests that excessive inequalities are to the detriment of overall national well-being, even if it is not clear up to what threshold the reduction of inequalities – at least the income ones – is desirable. Therefore, all well-being dimensions need to be fairly distributed, and statistical systems must be able to identify excluded groups and lacking opportunities through measures of distribution among individuals, or the breakdown of indicators for different groups (for example, territories, gender, age, education, income, nationality).

The issue of inequalities traditionally refers to the economic ones, that is, income or wealth distribution. Besides the distributional measures which are usually used to assess inequalities, such as the interquintile or interdecile ratios, the Gini index or the Atkinson index, attention has been particularly directed towards poverty and low incomes, and only more recently, especially with the work by Atkinson et al. (2011), has there been increasing attention towards top incomes.

The analysis of income inequalities has been part of economic analysis since its origin. The Ricardian approach was centred on resource distribution; Marx considered the progressive concentration of wealth in the hands of a few capitalists to be unavoidable. During the twentieth century, Kuznets (1955) proposed a theory according to which, with the increase of income per capita, inequalities would initially rise and then start to decrease (Kuznets curve). With a new rise in economic inequalities since the last decades of the twentieth century, the issue is attracting renewed attention at the academic and political level. Influential publications are Piketty (2014), Stiglitz (2012), Wilkinson and Pickett (2008) and OECD (2008, 2011a, 2015), while it is worth remembering how recent social movements following the precipitation of the financial crisis had 'We are the 99 per cent' as their main slogan. Most of this analysis treats economic inequalities as a matter of social justice, including the implications for the working of the economic system, and the effects on other dimensions of well-being.

Less attention has been devoted to a more overarching, multidimensional approach to inequalities. Looking at equity issues when analysing the well-being of societies implies taking into account all well-being domains beyond traditional economic aspects. Actual applications of overarching analysis of well-being inequalities are reported in the OECD's *How's Life?* report (OECD, 2011b) for each of the 11 domains, as well as in the Italian Benessere Equo e Sostenibile (BES; Equitable and Sustainable Well-being) report (CNEL/Istat, 2013) in which, whenever applicable, indicators are analysed with respect to their distribution across different ages, genders, social groups and territories (Rondinella and Savioli, 2013).

Following the framework proposed by Saraceno and Schizzerotto (2009), the analysis of well-being inequalities can be carried out through three major approaches, that are not mutually exclusive. The most straightforward approach is based on outcomes, which considers the distribution of goods and services or the privileges and disadvantages that different people can rely upon. Secondly, it is possible to look at the relational inequalities, those emerging from different roles within the society. They refer to the broad concept of power, expressed by the ability to take and influence decisions, and the running of power systems and institutions. They also include the ability to determine one's own destiny, so-called 'agency'. In a democratic market society, where laws are supposed to guarantee equal rights to all, relational inequalities are those deriving from individual characteristics which can be acquired, such as knowledge background, educational attainment, working position in organizations and institutions. These characteristics refer to people's social status, and societies allowing for greater equality in this field are those where more social mobility occurs.

Lastly, one can consider the differences people face with regard to opportunities and their freedom to choose the best way to fulfil their expectations. The latter approach is derived from Sen's capabilities. A fair society guarantees equal capabilities to activate equal functioning through participation. This admits the existence of outcome inequalities, and its adoption may generate a conflict between equal opportunities and equal dignity.

1.5 SUSTAINABILITY

During the last decades of the twentieth century, concern over the environmental conditions of our planet and the impact of productive activities was constantly increasing. Since 1972, with the publication of the Club of Rome's report *Limits to Growth* (Meadows et al., 1972), the environmental issue and that of the sustainability of the productive system have played an increasingly relevant role in the debate over measures beyond GDP.

The idea of sustainability was initially linked to the ecological boundaries imposed by our planet on the economic system, and the concept of sustainable development was substantially composed by a 'beyond GDP' multidimensional vision of development, integrated by environmental indicators able to assess the sustainability of the process. The first attempts to build an operational measurement of sustainability were the monetary indexes, analysed above in section 1.3. In their work on the Measure of Economic Welfare (MEW), Nordhaus and Tobin also calculated a 'Sustainable MEW' by estimating total public and private wealth including reproducible capital, educational and health capital, and natural resources. In a comparison between the two measures they actually provided a first synthetic evaluation of welfare sustainability: 'When actual MEW is less than sustainable MEW, the economy is making even better provision for future consumers; when actual MEW exceeds sustainable MEW, current consumption in effect includes some of the fruits of future progress' (Nordhaus and Tobin, 1972, p. 7).

After that, similar monetary measures such as the Index of Sustainable Economic Well-being by Daly and Cobb, or the Genuine Progress Indicator, also focused the sustainability approach on environmental aspects and on the notion of planetary boundaries. They evaluated sustainability by discounting the actualized value of future costs of environmental damages from the monetary value of current well-being.

Planetary boundaries are at the core of another indicator that is still deeply influential in sustainability measurement: the Ecological Footprint proposed by Wackernagel and Rees (1996). The Ecological Footprint measures the demand of human activities on the Earth's ecosystems as compared with the planet's ecological capacity to regenerate. It represents the amount of biologically productive land and sea areas necessary to supply the resources a human population consumes, and to assimilate the associated waste. Footprint values are categorized for carbon, food, housing, and goods and services. It is expressed in global hectares per capita, and Wackernagel and Rees estimated that the available biological capacity for the six billion people on Earth was 1.8 global hectares per person, allowing them to estimate the 'total footprint number of Earths' needed to sustain the world's population the level of consumption at that time. It also allows for the estimation of the Ecological Debt Day (or Earth Overshoot Day): the day upon which humanity's resource consumption for the year exceeds the Earth's capacity to regenerate those resources in that year (Wakernagel et al., 2002). Using the sustainability boundaries of the Ecological Footprint, the Happy Planet Index (NEF, 2006), already presented above, proposes a measure of the efficiency of a national system to provide happy life years.

Yet sustainability has not always referred to ecological boundaries. The most relevant theoretical framework of analysis used to address sustainability is the one that became popular in 1987 as the central message of the so-called Brundtland Report, *Our Common Future*, of the World Commission on Environment and Development, where it was defined as 'development that meets the needs of the present without compromising the ability of future generations to meet their own needs' (World Commission on Environment and Development, 1987, p. 43).

In 1992 in Rio the United Nations Conference on Environment and Development (UNCED) proposed a global path towards sustainability within the Agenda 21 action plan, where special reference was made to the use of statistical indicators:

> Commonly used indicators such as the gross national product (GNP) and measurements of individual resource or pollution flows do not provide adequate indications of sustainability. Methods for assessing interactions between different sectoral environmental, demographic, social and developmental parameters are not sufficiently developed or applied. Indicators of sustainable development need to be developed to provide solid bases for decision-making at all levels and to contribute to a self-regulating sustainability of integrated environment and development systems. (UN, 1992, paragraph 40.4)

The adoption of Agenda 21 during this first Rio conference stimulated the construction of sustainable development indicator (SDI) sets. Moreover, Chapter 8 of Agenda 21 called on countries to adopt national sustainable development strategies (NSDS) (UN, 1992). These national strategies on sustainable development (SD) also led to the building of SD indicator sets in individual countries and by international organizations. The first was the SDI set recommended by the United Nations Commission on Sustainable Development (UNCSD) in the early 1990s. (See Hametner and Steurer, 2007 for a chronological review; while Smits et al., 2014 compared 55 national systems of sustainable indicator sets and composite indexes.)

In line with Agenda 21, in 1994 the OECD presented a set of environmental indicators in the so-called 'pressure–state–response' (PSR) framework. The indicators were classified into (1) indicators of environmental pressures ('pressure'); (2) indicators of environmental conditions ('state'); and (3) indicators of societal responses ('response') (OECD, 2003). The PSR framework, originating from environmental statistics, shows limitations when tied to sustainable development; nevertheless it was further adopted by various organisations. The UNCSD used a modified 'driving force–state–response' (DSR) framework, and the European Environmental Agency (EEA) adopted a 'driving force–pressure–state–impact–response' (DPSIR) version. In 1996, the UNCSD proposed a set of 134 SDIs in the 'driving force–state–response' framework, linked to the thematic chapters of Agenda 21. In connection to this SDI set, the UNCSD launched an international testing programme aimed at advancing the understanding, development and use of SDIs by governments; 22 countries covering all regions of the world participated in the testing programme. Authors have found two major weaknesses in the PSR framework: the uncertainties about the underlying causal linkages the framework implies; and an oversimplification of complex interlinkages between issues (Pintér et al., 2005; UNDESA, 2006).

Environmental sustainability has entered into most theoretical frameworks for the measurement of well-being, with the monitoring of climate change drivers, ecological footprint, material flows and the building of satellite environmental national accounts. Nevertheless, the same cannot be said for economic and social sustainability. The Brundtland Commission's definition of sustainability does not only refer to the environmental elements, but to the overall concept of development. The same can be said about the Rio Declaration.[8] Nowadays, the debate is very much concentrated on building an overarching model to evaluate the future sustainability of citizens' economic and social conditions within the ecological boundaries.

More recently, the International Social Science Council (ISSC) and United Nations Educational, Scientific and Cultural Organization (UNESCO) *World Social Science Report 2013* defines sustainability as:

> The capacity of a socio-ecological system to be maintained in conditions that allow for its continued functioning in perpetuity. In development and global environmental change contexts, it refers more specifically to the ability to maintain human well-being, social equity and environmental quality indefinitely, meeting current needs and desires while ensuring that future generations will still have coupled human environment systems available to them capable of providing goods and services for their needs and desires, without degrading these systems in the long term. (ISSC and UNESCO, 2013, p. 609)

The most common approach to overall sustainability is certainly the one based on the three traditional economic, social and environmental pillars. Yet, for example, due to the conceptual and methodological difficulties in measuring social sustainability, the Franco-German Report (CAE and GCEE, 2011) proposes a number of sustainability indicators only relative to the environmental and economic or financial terms, keeping them separate from the analysis of the quality of life.

Another approach is based on the concept of 'capital', as a way to evaluate the current and future stocks of capital and therefore sustainability. A different perspective is thus used for measuring economic performance shifting from flows to stocks, from income to wealth. The World Bank (2000, 2006) has carried out researches on this field proposing the so-called 'Genuine Saving' (or adjusted net saving) which includes in the measurement of human-made capital (gross national saving) the depreciation of fixed capital, discounts the damages caused by pollution, and adds education spending as a measure of human capital for future welfare. Genuine Saving shows how the use of non-renewable resources, without an investment in renewable ones, cannot continue indefinitely given the finite resource stocks (Daly and Posner, 2011).

A sustainability index of this kind is the Inclusive Wealth Index (IWI) presented at the Rio+20 Conference (UNU-IHDP and UNEP, 2012), following the United Nations' call for new ways of measuring progress in a green economy (UN, 2012a). The IWI proposes a stock of measures of productive capital assets, natural capital and human capital that moves forward with respect to previous measures, but recognizes the need for extra research in particular for the measurement of ecosystem services,[9] which the IWI starts to untangle.

According to the Joint UNECE/Eurostat/OECD Working Group on Statistics for Sustainable Development (UNECE, 2009), sustainable development is defined as 'an increase in well-being across the members of a society between two points in time', where well-being is 'a function of consumption in the broadest sense possible' that is far beyond the limits of marketable goods and services. Similarly, a broad definition of capital is considered in order to assess sustainability, referring to a non-declining per capita wealth over time, where wealth is defined as the sum of five stocks of capital: financial capital, produced capital, natural capital, human capital and social capital.

While the monetization of financial and produced capital is quite straightforward, monetizing natural and human capital is much more controversial, yet it has been done in a number of cases. Also, social capital appears very difficult to express in monetary terms. From an operational point of view, a selection of mixed monetary and non-monetary indicators does not permit the quantification of an overall 'stock of well-being'; leaving aside the very controversial issue of substitutability among different forms of capital, an issue that returns every time researchers produce aggregate measures from heterogonous phenomena.

Beside stock indicators, the United Nations Economic Commission for Europe (UNECE) approach identifies flow elements needed to assess changes over time and monitor the determinants of such changes. The central problem in the capital approach to sustainable development, therefore, is in the definition of 'shadow prices' (see World Bank, 2006; Arrow et al., 2010; Hamilton, 2012) which, when they can be identified, may lead to important differences in the final results, even when starting from the same set of indicators. Moreover, the use of shadow prices implies a substitutability among components, following an approach of so-called 'weak sustainability' aiming at maintaining total capital without regard to the partitioning among the different components, as opposed to the 'strong sustainability' that does not make allowances for the substitution of human and human-made capital for natural capital.

More recently, the Joint UNECE/OECD/Eurostat Task Force (2012) abandons the capital approach, proposing different sets of available indicators in order to address three dimensions of human well-being following what was proposed by the Brundtland Commission: human well-being of the present generation in one particular country ('here and now'), the well-being of future generations ('later') and the well-being of people living in other countries ('elsewhere'). Sustainable development is therefore measured through sets of indicators which alternatively refer to one of the three dimensions or to one of 20 domains (or themes): subjective well-being, consumption and income, nutrition, health, housing, education, leisure, physical safety, trust, institutions, energy resources, non-energy resources, land and ecosystems, water, air quality, climate, labour, physical capital, knowledge capital and financial capital.

Sustainability is sometimes addressed through different concepts, in particular those of resilience and/or vulnerability. We can refer to vulnerability as the exposure to material, physical or psychological harm from one or more risks; and resilience as the ability to minimize well-being losses after a crisis (Morrone, 2012). An OECD project explored the usefulness of the 'asset-based' approach to provide a common framework for the statistical measurement of vulnerable populations focusing on the resources (assets) people can draw on to manage diverse risks. In the OECD definition, 'a person (or household) is vulnerable to future loss of well-being below some socially-accepted norms if he or she lacks (or is strongly disadvantaged in the distribution of) assets which are crucial for resilience to risks' (OECD, 2010).

The 2014 *Human Development Report* (UNDP, 2014) is dedicated to this approach, yet it focuses on the concept of 'human vulnerability' to describe 'the prospects of eroding people's capabilities and choices' (UNDP, 2014, p. 1). In this approach, the 'sustained enhancement of individuals' and societies' capabilities is necessary to reduce these persistent vulnerabilities'. Similarly, human resilience ensures that 'people's choices are robust, now and in the future, and enabling people to cope and adjust to adverse events' (UNDP, 2014, p. 1). All these experiences represent important efforts in moving in the right direction towards extending the measurement of sustainability beyond the environmental sphere.

1.5.1 Green Economy and Green Growth

A model for economic activity that is mindful of planetary boundaries has recently been developed around the ideas of the 'green economy' and 'green growth'. The concept of the 'green economy' was implicitly drawn from economic theories of the 1970s that began to consider resources such as the environment and energy as productive factors. Following the Stern Review (Stern, 2006) on the effects of climate change and the subsequent economic policy initiatives, the theme of the green economy began to spread and international bodies started to define it. In 2008, with the burst of the economic crisis, the United Nations Environment Programme (UNEP) asked national governments to sign a Global Green Deal to support a progressive change of unsustainable production and consumption patterns towards a greener economy. UNEP believed that transformation was inevitable to prevent further economic crises that could bring the global economy towards irreversible recession.

The green economy has been defined as a set of activities aimed at 'improving the human well-being and social equity, while significantly reducing environmental risks and ecological shortages' (UNEP, 2011). The green economy is a low-carbon, resource-efficient and socially inclusive model of development. Growth in income and employment are driven by investments and technologies that reduce carbon emissions and pollution, improve energy efficiency and resources, and prevent the loss of biodiversity and ecosystem services. The development path should maintain, enhance and, if necessary, rebuild natural capital as a critical economic resource and as a source of public benefits.

The OECD (2009) emphasizes economic growth, defining as 'green growth' all actions to promote growth and economic development and, at the same time, to ensure that the natural heritage continues to provide resources and environmental services that underpin our well-being. To do this, investments and innovation need to be accelerated to make sustained growth possible and create new economic opportunities. The pursuit of green growth must involve an increase in productivity; a reduction of waste and energy consumption; new ways of creating value and the management of environmental issues; the development of new markets for technology, green products and services; and the pursuit of economic stability, with less volatile resource prices.

The European Commission, through the European Environment Agency (EEA) has defined the green economy as 'one in which environmental, economic and social policies and innovations enable society to use resources efficiently, thereby enhancing human well-being in an inclusive manner, while maintaining the natural systems that sustain us' (EEA, 2012, p. 10). It highlights the inability to continue to support 'brown growth' and stresses the natural limits in terms of quantity and quality of resources that the Earth can provide, and the quantity and quality of pressures it can absorb.

The green economy is therefore not only a preferable approach to economic development, but in the long term it is the only way to support economic growth. Still, in measuring green growth, or green employment, the biggest limitation emerges from data availability. A taxonomy of which economic activities need to be included is still missing, leading to different operational approaches with decreasing feasibility. A first approach includes in the green economy those businesses operating in sectors that can be more directly related to the topic of the environment: the treatment of water resources, waste management, energy production, the protection of natural resources, and interventions to protect the land and reclaim soils. A second approach looks at those companies that have introduced in the productive process actions aimed at reducing resource use and the resulting environmental pressures, or that have introduced innovations for the production of sustainable goods and services. All firms producing in an environmentally friendly manner, certified or not, can be traced in this sense, but they are difficult to detect on the basis of the available administrative information. Within the industrial sector special attention therefore needs to be given to eco-industries, because of their high growth expectation, low pollution and ability to provide green technologies. Eco-industries are therefore a wide aggregate of activities that industrial policies should constantly refer to (on green industrial policies, see Rondinella, 2012). According to the OECD and Eurostat (1999, p. 9) definition, eco-industries are: 'activities which produce goods and services to measure, prevent, limit, minimize or correct environmental damage to water, air and soil, as well as problems related to waste, noise and eco-systems. This includes technologies, products and services that reduce environmental risk and minimize pollution and resources'. A measure of this kind is currently not available, yet estimates of the dimension of the green sector, and of the number of green jobs, have been proposed by Ecorys (2009), Schepelman et al. (2009) and Oko-Institute (2011).

An even more enlarged measure can be considered, starting from the relationships between institutional actors – public administration, citizens, businesses – where consumer demand for goods and services geared towards environmental sustainability induces firms to find a market space to operate in the green economy, guaranteed by public administrations' intervention with awareness-raising tools, regulation, certification and warranty. A further enlargement of the concept, closer to that of strong sustainability, involves rethinking the relationship between economic development and nature, directing production towards the use of natural capital in an amount not exceeding the capacity of nature to reproduce it; an attitude that requires the interaction of economy, society and institutions in the long term, and which also includes the idea of development that a company intends to pursue.

1.5.2 On the Inclusion of Environmental and Energy Variables in Macroeconomic Modelling[10]

Since the work of the Club of Rome, the literature on economic modelling considering energy and environment has been extended considerably. Models tackle a large number of different phenomena related to the inclusion of energy and environmental elements into the economic system. Issues taken into account vary broadly according to the different aims of the research. Some are macroeconomic models that consider the whole economic system and aim at including green variables, which is usually done through the use of KLE or KLEM (capital, labour, energy, materials) production functions; others are energy models exclusively focused on the energy and environmental systems, such as energy production, energy use and emissions (NEP, 2010). The composition of these two approaches has generated a large number of models at national, regional and global levels. Yet, most of the current econometric models include only energy aspects, with few considering broader environmental issues.

At one end of the spectrum one finds aggregated computable general equilibrium (CGE) models. They try to include the entire macroeconomy in which the energy system is a part, and each sector is represented by a production function designed to simulate the potential substitutions between the main factors of production. Among the most recent ones, ENV-Linkages has 22 sectors and 12 regions (Burniaux and Chateau, 2008); GEMINI-E3 has 18 sectors of which five are energy sectors (Bernard and Vielle, 2008); IMACLIM-R has 12 sectors and 12 regions (Sassi et al., 2010). ENV-Growth (OECD, 2012b) has just one sector, but proposes a global model that considers 175 countries.

But CGE models present the limit of relying on very restrictive assumptions relative to the functioning of the economy, especially in the short and medium run. CGE models are supply models where the hypothesis of perfect price flexibility often ensures the full and optimal use of production factors and thus rules out permanent or transitory less-than-optimum equilibrium such as the presence of involuntary unemployment. This is overcome by neo-Keynesian macroeconomic models that try to give a more realistic representation of the actual functioning of the economy, explicitly taking into account slow adjustments of prices and quantities. Therefore, CGE models are best suited for long-term analysis where the economy may be approximated as being in general equilibrium, while macroeconomic models may be the preferred choice for short to medium time horizons. The ThreeME (Reynès et al., 2011) model of the Observatoire français des conjonctures économiques (OFCE) is disaggregated in 24 sectors with an explicit distinction between four types of energy and five types of transports, and allows for the neo-Keynesian short-term macroeconomic modeling approach to catch up with the most advanced computable general equilibrium model (CGEM) in terms of sectorial analysis.

A third approach is represented by hybrid models incorporating the features of both macroeconometric models (CGE or macroeconomic models) and technology-rich engineering economic models. Since CGE and macroeconomic models, at least tradition-ally, include only a rather rough description of the technological components included in the energy system, and since engineering-economic models, on the other hand, exclude the non-energy parts of the macroeconomy, linking these two approaches has been a way of extending the modelling. The most relevant of these is Cambridge Econometrics (2012) E3ME which combines the features of an annual short- and medium-term sectorial model estimated by formal econometric methods with the detail and some of the methods of the CGE models, providing analysis of the movement of the long-term outcomes for key E3 indicators in response to policy changes.

The other big challenge, still scarcely developed in the macroeconomic modelling lit-erature, is the inclusion of environmental variables other than greenhouse gas emissions, which are usually taken into account, or the material flows included in KLEM function. Some models, such as the OECD's (2012a, 2012b), are endowed with sector-specific production input factors such as land in agriculture or deforestation. The outputs of the whole system may then be transmitted to the environment, producing externalities such as local air pollution, material use and waste. The implications over the possible trans-formation of the transport network may be considered as further outcomes. The markets typically transmit these effects through the level of activity creating demand for inputs of materials, fuels and labour; through wages and prices affecting incomes; and through incomes leading in turn to further demand for goods and services.

1.6   LEGITIMACY AND PARTICIPATIVE PROCESSES

The selection of a theoretical framework, and of the related indicators, implies the over-coming of a purely political problem of the priorities implicitly or explicitly set when choosing what to measure. This is well summarized by the 'motto' within the Stiglitz–Sen–Fitoussi report – 'what we measure affects what we do' (Stiglitz et al., 2009, p. 7) – linking the technical and the political sides of these exercises. A participative approach in the selection of the actual indicators to be used to measure well-being has also been always recommended by Sen who, as we saw before, never suggested an actual measurement for his capability approach since he considered that a phase of public deliberation was strictly necessary for the operationalization of the theory.

Public deliberation can be defined as the process of exchange of information and opin-ions by a group which is facing a common decision and is represented by the unavoidable discursive dimension through which collective preferences are formed and expressed. It is thus necessary to take into account every context and communicative channel, whether institutional or not, which publicly expresses interests and problems affecting a democratic community (Bohman and Rehg, 1997; Elster, 1998). Public deliberation may generate legitimate and bounding norms if it derives from a free agreement, in the absence of external constraints, among peers who can freely introduce themes, needs and claims. Essential conditions are the equality of participants, the inclusion of all actors involved, the ability of each to introduce their interest, the pursuit of a discursive agreement and a stance towards the common good (Habermas, 1985; Sunstein, 2008; Rondinella et al., 2011). In the definition of a set of progress indicators, public deliberation therefore becomes an essential step to grant the process the necessary legitimacy.

While public deliberation may be a necessary condition for political legitimacy, it may not be a sufficient one. The latter position can be found in Rawls (1971), for whom a conception of justice is acceptable if it can be justified as reasonable in public deliberations. Hence, for Rawls, what matters is procedure. This approach is criticized by Martha Nussbaum, who considers procedure as secondary: a particular procedure is valid if and only if it generates a valid outcome – 'Justice is in the outcome, and the procedure is a good one to the extent that it promotes this outcome' (Nussbaum, 2006, p. 82, quoted in Holst, 2010).

The production and circulation of statistical information is central to the creation of knowledge and in the expansion of the set of information used to decide (Giovannini, 2009), steering political decisions and helping citizens form their own opinions on the measured social phenomena. If end-users are involved in the selection or even the elaboration of indicators, chances increase that the information – based on shared values and knowledge – becomes relevant in the subsequent choices. This is the reason why, in the selection of indicators, attention is often given to the different stakeholders that will be affected by the proposed tool. With regard to this, Scrivens and Iasiello (2010) identify three fundamental characteristics of a set of progress indicators to impact on political decision-making: the set must be legitimized; fit for purpose – which implies choosing the most feasible way to disseminate them: composite index, headline indicators or extended set of indicators; and coupled with incentives motivating stakeholders to act on the basis of the information delivered. In this sense the legitimacy of the set of indicators derives from the shared conviction that the indicators adequately represent all the relevant issues. Within democratic systems, public decision making through civil society actors' involvement may supply a precious source of political legitimation.

Thus, broad participation (Hardi and Zdan, 1997) becomes essential for the purpose of selecting indicators, allowing citizens to play an active role within the community and to grant legitimacy to their choices. Moreover, according to Hall and Rickard (2013, pp. 43–44), the activation to participatory processes:

> strengthens the machinery of democracy . . . helps societies to better understand their own identities and circumstances . . . renders goals and values explicit . . . creates [a] stronger sense of shared ownership for new policies and renders societies more capable of addressing its problems and more resilient to large scale shocks.

Operatively, the academic literature presents three major approaches towards selection strategies: top-down, bottom-up and the so-called 'bidirectional method' (Michalos et al., 2011). Top-down methods are those in which the set of indicators is directly selected by the expert proposing the tool. The bottom-up method relies on the participation of a number of stakeholders, members of a specific territorial area, who set the priorities (see Atkisson, 1997; Valentin and Spangerberg, 2000). The 'bidirectional method' is a mixed approach in which stakeholder consultation is accompanied by the work of a group of experts. While the top-down approach, in which the expert decides dimensions and indicators, cannot boast any political legitimacy (Innes, 1990), a pure bottom-up approach, however legitimated on a political basis, may be valid only at a local level (therefore not taking into account the global implications of consumption behaviours) and may not consider all the implications arising from the use of specific indicators. The bidirectional method is a pragmatic method that guarantees legitimacy, methodological quality and coherence with general objectives of sustainable well-being beyond the local community. Rondinella et al. (2017) recently adapted Archon Fung's analytical framework on the varieties of participation processes (Fung, 2006) to a number of experiences of shared definition of sets of well-being indicators. They use Fung's dimensions of who participates, how they communicate and make decisions, and how discussion is linked with public action. This creates an analytical space that is useful to classify participative processes and to provide a general impression of the overall architecture: the broader the participation, the more densely populated is the space. They also distinguish between consultation and deliberation within participative processes: consultation is basically made of surveys of opinions, which may or may not be considered by a central decision maker; deliberation consists in the definition of venues for discussion among stakeholders in order to let them converge through dialogue and argumentative exchange towards a common decision.

The deliberative approach is mainstreaming among national experiences. In Italy (CNEL/Istat, 2013) the selection of indicators has been carried out through the dialogue between a scientific commission of experts, a national steering committee with entrepreneurs, unions, and civil society at large, supported by public meetings, a national survey, a blog and an online questionnaire. Most parts of the Italian society had the chance to influence the decisional process in some way. Similarly, in the United Kingdom, the Office for National Statistics (ONS, 2012) set up a national consultation made of an advisory forum, a technical group and a broad national consultation of 175 events with 2750 people, and 34 000 consulted online or via other channels. The building of the Canadian Index of Well-Being was also based on a very long process of discussion between experts and social actors throughout the whole country (Canadian Index of Well-Being, 2012). The Australian Measures of Australia's Progress (MAP) (ABS, 2002) aims at improving the system of indicators though a Web 2.0 consultation on three main areas of interest:

- Aspirations: broad goals that reflect what Australians care about.
- Outcomes: more specific goals that demonstrate progress towards these aspirations.
- Measures: how we check to see whether Australia is moving towards these outcomes.

These experiences led to similar but still different results (which are shown in the following section) and confirmed Sen's view of the necessity of participatory processes for the definition of the actual measures of national well-being, in order to reflect people's cultural background, overall conditions and future priorities.

1.7   POLITICAL DEVELOPMENTS OF THE 2000s

Throughout the decade of the 2000s, the debate around moving 'beyond GDP' as a measure of well-being and progress has gained momentum (Giovannini and Rondinella, 2012; Giovannini, 2015). Since 2001, when Giovannini became Chief Statistician of the OECD, the OECD has promoted several initiatives to raise awareness of the importance of measuring and fostering the progress of societies, of the need to develop new measures and to improve the use of existing ones. In 2004, with the first World Forum on Statistics, Policy and Knowledge held in Palermo, the 'beyond GDP' debate speeded up. Three years later, the Istanbul Declaration[11] (OECD, 2007, p. 1) highlighted an international consensus on the need to 'undertake the measurement of societal progress in every country, going beyond conventional economic measures such as GDP per capita' and launched the Global Project on Measuring the Progress of Societies as a worldwide benchmark for those who wish to measure and assess the progress of their societies.

In this context, the most relevant and authoritative work in the field was developed. The Commission on the Measurement of Economic Performance and Social Progress (the 'Stiglitz–Sen–Fitoussi Commission'), set up by French President Nicolas Sarkozy and hosting, among others, five Nobel Prize laureates, produced a final report in September 2009 calling for a 'shift [of] emphasis from measuring economic production to measuring people's well-being' (Stiglitz et al., 2009, p. 12). The Commission's aims have been to identify the limits of GDP as an indicator of economic performance and societal progress; to consider what additional information might be required for the production of more relevant indicators of social progress; to assess the feasibility of alternative measurement tools; and to discuss how to present statistical information in an appropriate way. The structure of the report – composed of economic performance, quality of life and sustainability – has itself become a widespread framework of analysis, which has been adopted by, among others, the Franco-German Ministerial Council (CAE and GCEE, 2011) and Statistics Austria (2014). The recommendations from the Report are presented in Box 1.1.

In 2009, Group of 20 (G20) leaders asked for work on measurement methods that 'better take into account the social and environmental dimensions of economic development', as an inherent part of the implementation of the new Framework for a Strong, Sustainable and Balanced Growth (G20, 2009). Another important development occurred with the European Commission's Communication, *GDP and Beyond: Measuring Progress in a Changing World* (European Commission, 2009), which fulfils the commitment made at the Beyond GDP Conference, where the President of the Commission clearly stated that 'It's time to go beyond GDP' (Barroso, 2007). The Communication defined a roadmap for action committing itself to work in several areas to improve existing measures.[12]

It is against this background that within the European Statistical System (ESS) the Sponsorship Group[13] on Measuring Progress, Well-Being and Sustainable Development was established with the mandate of coordinating activities on the issue of the recommendations from the Stiglitz Commission Report and the European Commission's Communication (European Statistical System, 2011).[14] The key challenge within the ESS is to implement the recommendations arising from these converging initiatives, in order to deliver richer statistical information and further enhance harmonisation at the international level, in particular in Europe.

A further step forward is represented by the 'Sofia Memorandum' produced in 2010 by the 96th conference of Directors General of the National Statistical Institutes (DGINS). It recognizes the validity of the Stiglitz Commission's recommendations and lists a number of improvements that national statistical institutes should adopt, such as: to reconcile National Accounts aggregates with household survey data, to give more attention to the household perspective, to capture distributional aspects, to harmonize environmental measures and to improve timeliness of quality-of-life statistics (DGINS ESSC, 2010).

In February 2010, the Franco-German Ministerial Council decided to ask the French Conseil d'Analyse Économique (CAE) and the German Council of Economic Experts (GCEE) to follow up on Stiglitz's outcomes. The CAE and GCEE published a report on 'Monitoring economic performance, quality of life and sustainability' (CAE and GCEE,

---

BOX 1.1   RECOMMENDATIONS FROM THE STIGLITZ COMMISSION

'Recommendation 1: When evaluating material well-being, look at income and consumption rather than production'

'Recommendation 2: Emphasise the household perspective'

'Recommendation 3: Consider income and consumption jointly with wealth'

'Recommendation 4: Give more prominence to the distribution of income, consumption and wealth'

'Recommendation 5: Broaden income measures to non-market activities'

'Recommendation 6: Quality of life depends on people's objective conditions and capabilities. Steps should be taken to improve measures of people's health, education, personal activities and environmental conditions. In particular, substantial effort should be devoted to developing and implementing robust, reliable measures of social connections, political voice, and insecurity that can be shown to predict life satisfaction'

'Recommendation 7: Quality-of-life indicators in all the dimensions covered should assess inequalities in a comprehensive way'

'Recommendation 8: Surveys should be designed to assess the links between various quality-of-life domains for each person, and this information should be used when designing policies in various fields'

'Recommendation 9: Statistical offices should provide the information needed to aggregate across quality-of-life dimensions, allowing the construction of different indexes'

'Recommendation 10: Measures of both objective and subjective well-being provide key information about people's quality of life. Statistical offices should incorporate questions to capture people's life evaluations, hedonic experiences and priorities in their own survey'

'Recommendation 11: Sustainability assessment requires a well-identified dashboard of indicators. The distinctive feature of the components of this dashboard should be that they are interpretable as variations of some underlying "stocks". A monetary index of sustainability has its place in such a dashboard but, under the current state of the art, it should remain essentially focused on economic aspects of sustainability'

'Recommendation 12: The environmental aspects of sustainability deserve a separate follow-up based on a well-chosen set of physical indicators. In particular, there is a need for a clear indicator of our proximity to dangerous levels of environmental damage (such as associated with climate change or the depletion of fishing stocks)'

2011) which, starting from the domains and indicators of the Stiglitz Commission, discusses how comprehensiveness and accuracy of an indicator set might be traded off optimally with parsimony and cost to provide a reliable basis for regular, timely and digestible reporting on economic performance, quality of life and sustainability.

In the same year, with the expiration of the Lisbon Strategy for growth and jobs, the governments of the European Union launched the Europe 2020 strategy, a set of guidelines of action establishing mid-term political economy targets which extend economic growth to a few aspects which should characterize the European model (following a 'GDP and beyond' approach, rather than a 'beyond GDP' one). These guidelines aim at increasing European competitiveness, maintaining a social market economy and improving resource efficiency. Europe 2020 sets European and national targets for eight indicators which countries have to achieve by 2020. Europe 2020 is certainly the most advanced institutionalization of a set of progress indicators. The indicators emerged as the outcome of a political debate within the European Council; targets have been fixed for each country and indicator, and the monitoring system is envisaged within the European Semester of economic policy coordination. This implies that governments must not only monitor the dynamic of the indicators but also define the measures to achieve the goals (see Rondinella, 2014, on policy use of well-being indicators).

In 2010 the UNDP also moved closer to a multidimensional approach. In particular, the 2010 *Human Development Report* introduces the Inequality-Adjusted Human Development Index (IHDI), which is a measure of the level of human development of people in a society that accounts for inequality; the Gender Inequality Index to better expose differences in the distribution of achievements between women and men; and the Multidimensional Poverty Index (MPI), which complements money-based measures by considering multiple deprivations and their overlapping deprivations in three dimensions: education, health and living conditions.

Within the OECD, another theoretical framework that reduces the emphasis on economic indicators in favour of a multidimensional approach, which considers social and environmental well-being just as important as economic well-being, was developed in 2009 (Hall et al., 2009). The authors define the 'well-being of a society' (or societal well-being) as the sum of the human well-being and the ecosystem condition; and 'progress of a society' (or societal progress) as the improvement in human well-being and the ecosystem condition. Moreover, in their definition, progress:

- Is a multidimensional concept, encompassing both material and immaterial aspects of well-being;
- Is a dynamic concept, which requires both looking back at the past and considering future paths (and particular emphasis is placed on the future when one considers the sustainability of the current level of well-being);
- Refers to the experiences of people, and what they value as important for their lives and societies. Taking the individual as a point of departure for analysis does not imply neglecting communities, but it requires evaluating them by virtue of what they bring to the people living in them. (Hall et al., 2009, p. 10)

The framework advanced by the OECD for 'equitable and sustainable well-being' (Figure 1.2) is built around the concept of 'human well-being' which, with its individual and social components, represents the final aim of societal progress. Human well-being is supported by three domains which are considered as means: culture, economy and governance. All this refers to the human system that is strongly linked to the ecosystem through the impact of human activities on nature (resource management) and on the 'environmental services' we can enjoy and provide to the ecosystem.

Nowadays it is quite common for policy-oriented reports on current and future challenges to recognize the need to go 'beyond GDP'. For example, the UN Rio+20 Conference declaration, *The Future We Want* (UNCSD, 2012, par. 38), clearly states that:

We recognise the need for broader measures of progress to complement GDP in order to better inform policy decisions, and in this regard, we request the UN Statistical Commission in consultation with relevant UN System entities and other relevant organisations to launch a programme of work in this area building on existing initiatives.

Similarly, in *Now for the Long Term*, the report of the Oxford Martin Commission for Future Generations (2013, p. 26), states that:

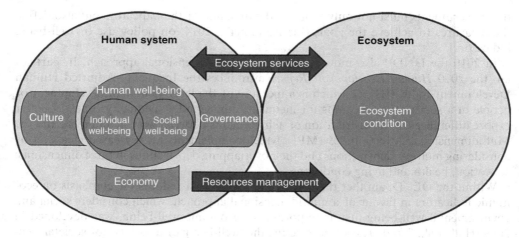

Source: Hall et al. (2009).

Figure 1.2   Equitable and sustainable well-being

To enable a deeper understanding of global inequality, it is time to shift the focus away from GDP and increase attention on measures of household income and distribution. Job targets should be reconsidered in light of the changing nature of employment, including by considering the adoption of new metrics, which take into account informal and voluntary working arrangements.

The most recent, and possibly most significant, recognition of this paradigm shift is represented by the Synthesis Report on the Post-2015 Agenda (UN, 2014a, p. 22) of the United Nations Secretary-General Ban Ki-moon:

Economic growth should lead to shared prosperity. As such, the strength of an economy must be measured by the degree to which it meets the needs of people, and on how sustainably and equitably it does so. We need inclusive growth, built on decent jobs, livelihoods and rising real incomes for all and measured in ways that go beyond GDP and account for human well-being, sustainability and equity. Ensuring that all people, including women, persons with disabilities, youth, aged, and migrants have decent employment, social protection, and access to financial services, will be a hallmark of our economic success . . .
   Member States have recognized the importance of building on existing initiatives to develop measurements of progress on sustainable development that go beyond gross domestic product. Thus, work on developing alternative measures or progress, beyond GDP, must receive the dedicated attention of the United Nations, international financial institutions, the scientific community, and public institutions. These metrics must be squarely focused on measuring social progress, human well-being, justice, security, equality, and sustainability. Poverty measures should reflect the multi-dimensional nature of poverty. New measures of subjective well-being are potentially important new tools for policy-making.

In September 2015, the UN General Assembly adopted a resolution (UN, 2015) defining a framework for the Post-2015 Agenda comprising 17 Sustainable Development Goals (SDGs) and 169 Targets moving forward with respect to the MDGs. While the latter were substantially aimed at reducing extreme poverty in developing countries, the SDGs also involve commitments for rich countries; they aim at reducing inequalities within and between countries; call for sustainable consumption and production patterns; and monitor fair governance and justice. The whole list of Goals comprises:

- Goal 1. End poverty in all its forms everywhere;
- Goal 2. End hunger, achieve food security and improved nutrition and promote sustainable agriculture;
- Goal 3. Ensure healthy lives and promote well-being for all at all ages;
- Goal 4. Ensure inclusive and equitable quality education and promote lifelong learning opportunities for all;
- Goal 5. Achieve gender equality and empower all women and girls;
- Goal 6. Ensure availability and sustainable management of water and sanitation for all;
- Goal 7. Ensure access to affordable, reliable, sustainable and modern energy for all;
- Goal 8. Promote sustained, inclusive and sustainable economic growth, full and productive employment and decent work for all;
- Goal 9. Build resilient infrastructure, promote inclusive and sustainable industrialization and foster innovation;
- Goal 10. Reduce inequality within and among countries;
- Goal 11. Make cities and human settlements inclusive, safe, resilient and sustainable;
- Goal 12. Ensure sustainable consumption and production patterns;
- Goal 13. Take urgent action to combat climate change and its impacts;
- Goal 14. Conserve and sustainably use the oceans, seas and marine resources for sustainable development;
- Goal 15. Protect, restore and promote sustainable use of terrestrial ecosystems, sustainably manage forests, combat desertification, and halt and reverse land degradation and halt bio-diversity loss;
- Goal 16. Promote peaceful and inclusive societies for sustainable development, provide access to justice for all and build effective, accountable and inclusive institutions at all levels;
- Goal 17. Strengthen the means of implementation and revitalize the global partnership for sustainable development.

(UN, 2015)

The paradigmatic change is confirmed by the last Target of the last Goal (17.19) which calls for the development of 'measurements of progress on sustainable development that complement gross domestic product' (UN, 2015).

In March 2016 the UN Statistical Commission agreed on the global indicator frame-work for the Post-2015 Agenda, a set of 230 indicators[15] (UN, 2016). The framework is expected to be monitored by the United Nations at global level due to the different rel-evance that indicators have at country level. The framework and the monitoring process at national level is instead thought to be:

> voluntary and country-led, will take into account different national realities, capacities and levels of development and will respect policy space and priorities. As national ownership is key to achieving sustainable development, the outcome from national-level processes will be the foun-dation for reviews at the regional and global levels, given that the global review will be primarily based on national official data sources. (UN, 2015)

1.7.1 Theoretical Frameworks Developed at National Level

It is not possible to provide a complete review of the many tools for the measurement of well-being which have been developed across the globe. Broad and diversified collections are carried out by the European Parliament (Goossens, 2007; and the Beyond GDP initiative, http://www.beyond-gdp.eu), which examine different indicators through a strengths, weaknesses, opportunities, threats (SWOT) analysis, by Gadrey and Jany-Catrice (2005) and by Afsa et al. (2008). The broadness of the subject is also demonstrated by the entries on the OECD website Wikiprogress.org. Here we can only focus on a few recent initiatives carried out at national and international level that incorporate much of the debate described so far. These recent trends propose a dashboard of indicators sometimes aggregated into a single measure, and at other times built around the centrality of subjective well-being measures.

A framework of the latter kind is proposed by the Office for National Statistics (ONS) in the United Kingdom for the Measures of National Well-being (MNW) initiative. In this case the central element is represented by individual well-being intended as people's overall subjective assessment which, in practice, is represented by the three indicators quoted above: life satisfaction; positive and negative emotions; and feeling that life is worthwhile (eudemonia). Individual well-being is considered to be directly affected by a number of factors grouped into six areas: our relationships; health; what we do; where we live; personal finance; and education and skills. Finally, three more contextual domains are considered: governance, the economy and the natural environment. For all the measures considered in the ten domains, equality, fairness and sustainability are to be taken into account (Figure 1.3).

Another approach explicitly taking into account equity and sustainability is proposed

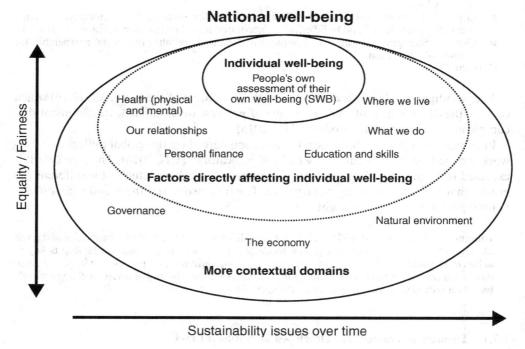

Source: Beumont (2011).

Figure 1.3   MNW framework

in Italy by the CNEL/Istat (2013) BES initiative, promoted by Giovannini when he was President of Istat. The BES initiative proposes a set of 134 indicators grouped into 12 domains. Whenever applicable, indicators are analysed with respect to their distribution throughout territories and social groups; that is, providing their disaggregation for regions, sex, age, education, nationality or economic condition. Indicators are also presented in their time evolution in order to show recent trends and suggest future conditions. Since 2015, a set of composite indicators for some of the 12 domains are also computed. In Buthan, the will to measure gross national happiness instead of GDP goes back to the 1970s. The framework used has developed over time and currently includes nine domains and the building a composite index.[16]

In 2002 the Australian Bureau of Statistics (ABS) set up a dashboard of indicators (Measures of Australia's Progress, MAP[17]) around the traditional domains of society, economy and environment (with 15 subdomains). An evolution of the initiative was proposed by ABS in 2010 and named MAP2.0, asking Australians to share, via e-mail, letter or via a website, what progress means to them and what dimensions are to be considered. A step further is then represented by the Australia National Development Index (www.andi.org.au) for which a further broadening of a national debate is foreseen, bringing together actors from academia and the third sectors.

In 2004 the Atkinson Charitable Foundation initiated a consultation process in Canada which led in 2009 to the launch of the Canadian Index of Well-Being, a composite index based on eight domains of eight indicators each. The Canadian experience is of great relevance for citizens' consultations since, over a number of years, many communities and stakeholders throughout the different states have contributed to the debate over the national priorities.

Following a consolidated experience on the issue, OECD's Better Life Initiative proposed a framework of analysis based on 11 domains which are analysed separately in the *How's Life?* report (OECD, 2011b) so as to offer a comprehensive picture of multidimensional well-being at international level. The report dedicates special attention to inequalities as a central element in well-being assessment, providing a valuable presentation of multidimensional inequalities related to every dimension. Moreover, online software allows users to freely assign weights to the different domains so as to provide rankings of OECD countries according to individual priorities. Tools of this kind help to communicate a fundamental issue which is present in most national initiatives: the relevance of a discussion over the priorities that every set of indicators implicitly or explicitly suggests, a discussion which, as we saw before, can be overcome only through a deliberative process able to grant legitimacy to the chosen approach. (See also Balestra et al., Chapter 2 in this *Handbook*.)

Table 1.4 presents these frameworks all together, showing how they are similar while displaying minor differences. Most of the domains overlap in all frameworks (even if labelled or aggregated differently, which actually implies slightly different meanings), giving way to the emergence of a fundamental picture made of health, education, living standards, work, social relationships, safety, governance and environment. Subjective well-being is not always included, as well as macroeconomic aspects considered in the UK and Australia. The broadest framework is the Italian one, which, unlike the others, includes research and innovation, and landscape and cultural heritage, following the dictate of the national Constitution.

Table 1.4 Well-being domains in selected frameworks

SSF	MNW	BES	Buthan	MAP	CIW	Better Life Index
Material living standards	Personal finance	Economic well-being	Living standards	Economy (household economic well-being)	Living standards	Income
	Economy			Economy - (housing)		Housing
				Economy (national income; national wealth; productivity)		
Health	Health	Health	Health	Society health	Healthy populations	Health
Education	Education and skills	Education and culture Research and innovation	Education; culture	Society education and training	Education; leisure and culture	Education
Personal activities	What we do	Work and life balance	Time use	Society work	Time use	Jobs; work–life balance
Political voice and governance	Governance	Policy and institutions; quality of services	Good governance	Society democracy, governance and citizenship	Democratic engagement	Civic engagement
Social connections and relationships	Our relationships	Social relationships	Community vitality	Society family, community and social cohesion	Community vitality	Community
Environment	Natural environment	Environment	Ecological diversity and resilience		Environment	Environment
		Landscape and cultural heritage				
Insecurity	Where we live	Safety		Society crime		Safety
	Individual well-being	Subjective well-being	Psychological well-being			Life satisfaction

Note: SSF = Stiglitz–Sen–Fitoussi Report; MNW = Measures of National Well-being; CIW = Canadian Index of Well-being.

1.8   CONCLUSION: GLOBAL CONVERGENCE AND FUTURE CHALLENGES

Nowadays, we witness a progressive convergence at the international level towards multidimensional measures of well-being that are able to take into account both equity and sustainability. Measures of well-being, development and sustainability are increasingly following similar patterns, and the set of Sustainable Development Goals (SDGs) for the 2030 Agenda agreed upon by United Nations in September 2015 represents a significant achievement. In parallel, the measurement of the overall impact of business activities using similar concepts is under development.

Demographic growth, population ageing and financial markets' 'short-termism' may generate worries over social and economic sustainability, starting from the sustainability of welfare systems. Powerful measures of sustainability still represent the most difficult challenge ahead: shadow prices may solve a number of problems, but they still present difficulties, in particular when it comes to assessing elements of human and social capital. On the other hand, approaches based on vulnerability and resilience can contribute to better framing some domains, such as health, even if they cannot fit into approaches based on monetary stocks and thus into a single measure.

The global landscape is now very different from the one we used to know in the twentieth century. We can no longer talk about a world divided between industrialized countries and the Global South. Emerging countries are now economic powers; production, trade and financial systems are deeply globalized. Every country, even if with different objectives, is fighting against poverty, deprivation and social exclusion, and for universal access to basic services. Moreover, natural resource distribution and future availability are affecting all countries: efforts to achieve sustainable development need to be global and coordinated.

The multidimensional approach aimed at achieving equitable and sustainable well-being is becoming universal, although individual countries need to develop it according to their specificities, capabilities and priorities. Such an overarching approach appears to be applicable in both OECD and non-OECD countries (Giovannini, 2013) and is now embedded in the Sustainable Development Goals.

In this chapter we have only marginally dealt with the linkages between well-being measures and policy making. We believe that better measures can lead to better policies. For example, policy impact assessment is currently focused on economic measures, fundamentally referring to the cost–benefit analysis. We still lack integrated models of monitoring and assessment of policies that use well-being indicators in a holistic way. The development of econometric models that can take into account the impact of different policies over societal progress is another challenge lying ahead.

Finally, we should not forget that statistical capacity is very diverse in developed and developing countries. New technologies may help in reducing costs for the production of statistics, and improving the timeliness of data, in the context of the so-called 'data revolution'.[18] From this point of view, the improvement of theoretical foundations and the enhancement of statistical capacities are both equally important to achieve a better knowledge of the state of well-being of people and of the planet.

NOTES

1. 'Real income per head rose to a point where a large number of persons gained a command over consumption which transcended basic food, shelter, and clothing; and the structure of the working force changed in ways which increased not only the proportion of urban to total population, but also the proportion of the population working in offices or in skilled factory jobs – aware of and anxious to acquire the consumption fruits of a mature economy.

   In addition to these economic changes, the society ceased to accept the further extension of modern technology as an overriding objective. It is in this post-maturity stage, for example, that, through the political process, Western societies have chosen to allocate increased resources to social welfare and security. The emergence of the welfare state is one manifestation of a society's moving beyond technical maturity; but it is also at this stage that resources tend increasingly to be directed to the production of consumers' durables and to the diffusion of services on a mass basis, if consumers' sovereignty reigns' (Rostow, 1960, p. 6).

2. According to the invariance principle, 'a movement of an activity from the public to the private sector or vice-versa, should not change our measure of performance, except to the extent that there is an effect on quality or access' (Stiglitz et al., 2009, p. 33).

3. http://socialarchive.iath.virginia.edu/xtf/view?docId=united-states-presidents-research-committee-on-social-trends-cr.xml.

4. For a comprehensive presentation of subjective well-being measures, see the OECD Guidelines (OECD, 2013), Ryan and Deci (2001), Diener et al. (2010), Dolan and Metcalfe (2011) and Abdallah and Mahony (2012).

5. The debate over the relevance and the robustness of subjective measures is very well presented by Fleurbaey and Blanchet (2014).

6. Bentham (1789) wrote: 'It has been shown that the happiness of the individuals, of whom a community is composed, that is their pleasures and their security, is the end and the sole end which the legislator ought to have in view: the sole standard, in conformity to which each individual ought, as far as depends upon the legislator, to be made to fashion his behavior'.

7. See, for example, http://www.positivepsychology.org.

8. 'Principle 1: Human beings are at the center of concerns for sustainable development. They are entitled to a healthy and productive life in harmony with nature' (UNCED, 1992).

9. They are provisioning services (production of foods, fuels, fibres, water and genetic resources); cultural services (recreation, spiritual and aesthetic satisfaction, and scientific information); regulating services (controlling variability in production, pests and pathogens, environmental hazards, and many key environmental processes); and supporting services (the main ecosystem processes) (UN, 2012a).

10. This review is the fruit of a collaboration with Elena Grimaccia at Istat.

11. Adopted by the European Commission, the OECD, the Organization of the Islamic Conference, the United Nations, the United Nation Development Programme and the World Bank.

12. Key actions are: complementing GDP with environmental and social indicators; near real-time information for decision-making; more accurate reporting on distribution and inequalities; developing a European Sustainable Development Scoreboard; extending National Accounts to environmental and social issues.

13. Sponsorship Group co-chaired by the Eurostat and the National Statistical Institute of France (FR-INSEE) Directors General, with the participation of 16 member states (Presidents and Directors General of National Statistical Institutes: Austria, Bulgaria, Czech Republic, Germany, Denmark, Estonia, France, Italy, Luxembourg, Netherlands, Norway, Poland, Sweden, Slovenia, Slovakia, United Kingdom) as well as the OECD and UNECE.

14. The activities on the 'GDP and beyond' Communication and the Stiglitz report in the European Commission and in the European Statistical System (ESS) are also coordinated by the Inter-departmental Co-ordination Group co-chaired by Eurostat and DG Environment Directors General, with the participation of 11 Commission DGs and three agencies.

15. Indicators are classified into three tiers: a first tier for which an established methodology exists and data are already widely available; a second tier for which a methodology has been established but for which data are not regularly available; and a third tier for which an internationally agreed methodology has not yet been developed (UN, 2016).

16. http://www.grossnationalhappiness.com/.

17. http://www.abs.gov.au/.

18. See the report of the Independent Experts Advisory Group, established by the UN Secretary General (UN, 2014b).

REFERENCES

Abdallah, S. and S. Mahony (2012) Stocktaking report on subjective well-being, Deliverable 2.1, e-Frame project, www.eframeproject.eu.

Abdallah, S. and S. Shah (2012) 'Well-being patterns uncovered: an analysis of UK data', New Economics Foundation, London.

Afsa, C., D. Blanchet, V. Marcus, P.-A. Pionnier, L. Rioux, M.M. d'Ercole, G. Ranuzzi and P. Schreyer (2008) 'Survey of existing approaches to measuring socio-economic progress', Joint Insee–OECD document prepared for the first plenary meeting of Commission on the Measurement of Economic Performance and Social Progress, http://www.stiglitz-sen-fitoussi.fr/en/documents.htm.

Allardt, E. (1993) 'Having, loving, being: an alternative to the Swedish model of welfare research', in M.C. Nussbaum and A. Sen (eds), *The Quality of Life*, Clarendon Press, Oxford.

Arrow, K.J., P. Dasgupta, L.H. Goulder, K.J. Mumford and K. Oleson (2010) 'Sustainability and the measurement of wealth', NBER Working Paper no. 16599, December.

Atkinson, T., T. Piketty and E. Saez (2011) 'Top incomes in the long run of history', *Journal of Economic Literature*, 49(1), pp. 3–71.

Atkisson, A. (ed.) (1997) *The Community Handbook: Measuring Progress Toward Healthy and Sustainable Communities*, Redefining Progress, San Francisco, CA.

Australian Bureau of Statistics (ABS) (2002) *Measuring Australia's Progress*, ABS, Canberra.

Bandura, R. (2008) *A Survey of Composite Indices Measuring Country Performance: 2008 Update*, United Nations Development Programme – Office of Development Studies.

Barroso, J.M. (2007) 'Beyond GDP international initiative, 2007. Opening speech', http://www.beyond-gdp.eu/proceedings/bgdp_proceedings_intro_ses1.pdf.

Bauer, R.A. (ed.) (1966) *Social Indicators*, MIT Press, Cambridge, MA.

Beck, U. (1999) *Che cos'è la globalizzazione. Rischi e prospettive della società planetaria*, Roma, Carocci.

Beham, B., S. Drobnič and R. Verwiebe (2006) *Literature Review, Theoretical Concepts and Methodological Approaches of Quality of Life and Work*, Deliverable of EU project Quality, Utrecht University, Utrecht.

Bennett, M.K. (1937) 'On measurement of relative national standards of living', *Quarterly Journal of Economics*, 51(2), pp. 317–336.

Bentham, J. (1789) *An Introduction to the Principles of Morals and Legislation*, London, http://www.econlib.org/library/Bentham/bnthPML4.html.

Berger-Schmitt, R. and H.H. Noll (2000) 'Conceptual framework and structure of a European system of social indicators', EU Reporting Working Paper no. 9, TSER Project, Towards a European System of Social Reporting and Welfare Measurement, Subproject, European System of Social Indicators.

Bernard, A. and M. Vielle (2008) 'GEMINI-E3, a general equilibrium model of international–national interactions between economy, energy and the environment', *Computational Management Science*, 5(3), pp. 173–206.

Beumont, J. (2011) 'Measuring national well-being: discussion paper on domains and measures', Office for National Statistics, London.

Brickman, P. and D. Campbell (1971) 'Hedonic relativism and planning the good society', in M.H. Apley (ed.), *Adaptation-Level Theory: A Symposium*, Academic Press, New York, NY.

Bohman, J. and W. Rehg (eds) (1997) *Deliberative Democracy: Essays on Reason and Politics*, MIT Press, Cambridge, MA.

Bremner, R.H. (1956) *From the Depths: The Discovery of Poverty in the United States*, New York University Press, New York, NY.

Burniaux, J. and J. Chateau (2008) 'An overview of the OECD ENV-Linkages Model', OECD Economics Department Working Paper no. 653, OECD Publishing, http://dx.doi.org/10.1787/230123880460.

CAE and GCEE (2011) 'Monitoring economic performance, quality of life and sustainability', Joint Report as requested by the Franco-German Ministerial Council, Conseil des Ministres Franco-Allemand, Fribourg-en Brisgau, 10 December 2010.

Cambridge Econometrics (2012) *E3ME: An Economy–Energy–Environment Model of Europe, Technical Manual, Version 5.5*, Cambridge Econometrics.

Campbell, A. (1972) 'Aspiration, satisfaction, and fulfilment', in A. Campbell and P.E. Converse (eds), *The Human Meaning of Social Change*, Russel Sage Foundation, New York, NY.

Canadian Index of Wellbeing (2012) *How are Canadians Really Doing? The 2012 CIW Report*, Canadian Index of Wellbeing and University of Waterloo, Waterloo, ON.

Cantril, H. (1965) *The Pattern of Human Concerns*, Rutgers University Press, New Brunswick, NJ.

CNEL/Istat (2013) *Rapporto BES 2013. Il benessere equo e sostenibile in Italia*, Istat, Rome.

Cobb, C.W. (2000) *Measurement Tools and the Quality of Life*, Redefining Progress, San Francisco, CA.

Cobb C., T. Halstead and J. Rowe (1995) 'If the GDP is up, why is America down?', *Atlantic*, https://www.theatlantic.com/past/docs/politics/ecbig/gdp.htm.

Cobb, C.W. and C. Rixford (1998) *Lessons Learned from the History of Social Indicators*, Redefining Progress, San Francisco, CA.

Cobb, J. and H. Daly (1989), *For the Common Good*, Beacon Press, Boston, MA.

Committee on Social Trends (1933) *Recent Social Trends in the United States*, McGraw Hill Book Company, New York, NY.

Daly, H. (1977) *Steady-State Economics*, W.H. Freeman, San Francisco, CA.

Daly, L. and S. Posner (2011) *Beyond GDP: New Measures for a New Economy*, Demos, New York, NY.

De Muro, P., M. Mazziotta and A. Pareto (2011) 'Composite indices of development and poverty: an application to MDGs', *Social Indicators Research*, 104(1), pp. 1–18.

Department of Health, Education, and Welfare (1969) 'Towards a social report', Department of Health, Education, and Welfare, Washington, DC.

DGINS ESSC (2010) *Sofia Memorandum. Measuring Progress, Well-Being and Sustainable Development*, http://www.dgins-sofia2010.eu/.

Diener, E. (2000) 'Subjective well-being: the science of happiness and a proposal for a national index', *American Psychologist*, 55, pp. 34–43.

Diener E., J. Helliwell and D. Kahneman (2010), *International Differences in Well-Being*, Oxford University Press, Oxford.

Diener E. and E. Suh (1997) 'Measuring quality of life: economic, social and subjective indicators', *Social Indicators Research*, 40, pp. 189–216.

Diener, E., E.M. Suh, R.E. Lucas and H.L. Smith (1999) 'Subjective well-being: three decades of progress', *Psychological Bulletin*, 25, pp. 276–302.

Dolan, P., R. Layard and R. Metcalfe (2011) 'Measuring subjective wellbeing for public policy: recommendations on measures', Special Paper No. 23, Centre for Economic Performance, School of Economics and Political Science, London, http://cep.lse.ac.uk/pubs/download/special/cepsp23.pdf.

Dolan, P. and R. Metcalfe (2011) 'Comparing measures of subjective well-being and views about the role they should play in policy', ONS, London.

Doyal, L. and I. Gough (1991) *A Theory of Human Need*, Macmillan, New York, NY.

Drewnowski, J. and W. Scott (1966) 'The Level of Living Index', United Nations Research Institute for Social Development, Report No. 4. UNRISD, Geneva.

Dworkin, R. (1981) 'What is equality? Part 1: Equality of welfare', *Philosophy and Public Affairs*, 10(3), pp. 185–246.

Easterlin, R.A. (1974) 'Does economic growth improve the human lot? Some empirical evidence', in P.A. David and M.W. Reder (eds), *Nations and Households in Economic Growth; Essays in Honor of Moses Abramovitz*, Academic Press, New York, NY.

Ecorys (2009) 'Study on the competitiveness of the EU eco-industry', within the Framework Contract of Sectorial Competitiveness Studies – ENTR/06/054, Final report.

EEA (2012) 'Environmental indicator report 2012 – Ecosystem resilience and resource efficiency in a green economy in Europe. Part I. Introduction', European Environment Agency, Copenhagen.

Elster, J. (ed.) (1998) *Deliberative Democracy*, Cambridge University Press, Cambridge.

Erikson, R. (1974) 'Welfare as a planning goal', *Acta sociologica*, 17(3), pp. 273–288.

Erikson, R. (1993) 'Descriptions of inequality: the Swedish approach to welfare research', in M. Nussbaum and A. Sen (eds), *The Quality of Life*, Clarendon Press, Oxford.

European Commission (2009) Communication from the Commission to the Council and the European Parliament 'GDP and Beyond: Measuring Progress in a Changing World', (COM/2009/0433 final).

European Parliament (2007) 'Alternative progress indicators to gross domestic product (GDP) as a means towards sustainable development', Policy Department Economic and Scientific Policy Study.

European Statistical System (2011) Sponsorship Group on Measuring Progress, Well-being and Sustainable Development, 'Final Report' adopted by the European Statistical System Committee.

Fioramonti, L. (2013) *Gross Domestic Problem: The Politics Behind the World's Most Powerful Number*, Zed Books, London.

Fleubaey, M. and D. Blanchet (2014) *Beyond GDP: Measuring Welfare and Assessing Sustainability*, Oxford University Press, Oxford.

Freedom House (2015) 'Freedom in the world 2015. Discarding democracies/Return to the iron fist', Freedom House.

Fukuyama, F. (2013) 'What is governance?', Working Paper no. 314, Centre for Global Development.

Fung, A. (2006) 'Varieties of participation in complex governance', *Public Administration Review*, 66(1), pp. 66–75.

G20 (2009) 'Leaders' statement', Pittsburgh Summit, 24–25 September, http://www.pittsburghsummit.gov/mediacenter/129639.htm.

Gadrey, J. and F. Jany-Catrice (2005) *Les noveaux indicateurs de richesse*, La Découverte, Paris.

Galenson, W. and H. Leibenstein (1955) 'Investment criteria, productivity and economic development', *Quarterly Journal of Economics*, 69(3), pp. 343–370.

Gallup-Healthways (2014) 'State of Global Well-being Index. Results of the Gallup–Healthways Global Well-Being Index', Gallup-Healthways, http://www.well-beingindex.com.

Giovannini, E. (2009) 'Bringing statistics to citizens: a "must" to build democracy in the XXI century', in M. Segone (ed.), *Country-Led Monitoring and Evaluation Systems. Better Evidence, Better Policies, Better Development Results*, UNICEF, Geneva.

Giovannini, E. (2013) 'Using "equitable and sustainable well-being" to build the post-MDGs framework', *IDS Bulletin*, 44(5/6), pp. 89–96.

Giovannini, E. (2015) '"Beyond GDP" ten years after Palermo: where do we stand?', *Rivista internazionale di studi sociali*, 128(1), pp. 3–15.

Giovannini, E. and T. Rondinella (2012) 'Measuring equitable and sustainable well-being in Italy', in F. Maggino (ed.), *Quality of Life in Italy: Research and Reflections*, Springer, New York, NY and London.

Goossens, Y. (2007) 'Alternative progress indicators to gross domestic product (GDP) as a means towards sustainable development', European Parliament, Study IP/A/ENVI/ST/2007-10.

Gough, I. (1994) 'Economic institutions and the satisfaction of human needs', *Journal of Economic Issues*, 28(1), pp. 25–66.

Habermas, J. (1985) *Etica del discorso*, Laterza, Roma-Bari.

Hall, J., E. Giovannini, A. Morrone and G. Ranuzzi (2009) 'A framework to measure the progress of societies', Working Paper no. 34, OECD Statistics Directorate, OECD Publishing, Paris.

Hall, J. and L. Rickard (2013) *People, Progress and Participation – How Initiatives Measuring Social Progress Yield Benefits Beyond Better Metrics*, Bertelsmann Stiftung, Gütersloh.

Hametner, M. and R. Steurer (2007) 'Objectives and indicators of sustainable development in Europe: a comparative analysis of European coherence', *ESDN Quarterly Report*, December, European Sustainable Development Network, http://www.sd-network.eu/.

Hamilton, K. (2012) 'Comments on Arrow et al. "Sustainability and the measurement of wealth"', *Environment and Development Economics* 17(3), 356–361, Cambridge University Press, Cambridge.

Hardi, P. and T. Zdan (1997) *Principles in Practice*. International Institute for Sustainable Development, Winnipeg.

Harrison, E. (2014) 'More than the sum of the parts? Individual well-being and quality of society as research paradigms in Europe', presentation at conference, Social Monitoring and Reporting in Europe: The Quality of Society and Individual Quality of Life – How do they relate?, Villa Vigoni, 23–25 June.

Holst, C. (2010) 'Martha Nussbaum's outcome-oriented theory of justice: philosophical comments', ARENA Working Paper no. 16, December, Arena Centre for European Studies, University of Oslo.

Innes, J. (1990) *Knowledge and Public Policy: The Search for Meaningful Indicators*, 2nd edn, Transaction Publishers, New Brunswick, NJ and London.

International Labour Office (ILO) (1976) *Employment, Growth and Basic Needs: A One World Problem*, Praeger, New York, NY.

ISSC and UNESCO (2013) *World Social Science Report 2013, Changing Global Environments*, OECD Publishing and UNESCO Publishing, Paris.

Joint UNECE/Eurostat/OECD Task Force (2012) *Draft Report of the Joint UNECE/Eurostat/OECD Task Force on Measuring Sustainable Development*, United Nations Economic Commission for Europe, Geneva.

Kahneman, D. and A.B. Krueger (2006) 'Developments in the measurement of subjective well-being', *Journal of Economic Perspectives*, 20(1), pp. 3–24.

Kahneman, D., A.B. Krueger, D. Schkade, N. Schwarz and A.A. Stone (2006) 'Would you be happier if you were richer? A focusing illusion', CEPS Working Paper no. 125, May.

Keynes, J.M. (1936) *The General Theory of Employment, Interest and Money*, Palgrave Macmillan, London.

Kubiszewski, I., R. Costanza, C. Franco, P. Lawn, J. Talberth, T. Jackson and C. Aylmer (2013) 'Beyond GDP: measuring and achieving global genuine progress', *Ecological Economics*, 93, pp. 57–68.

Kuznets, S. (1934) 'National income, 1929–32', NBER bulletin 49, New York, NY.

Kuznets, S. (1955) 'Economic growth and income inequality', *American Economic Review*, 45, pp. 1–28.

Kuznets, S. (1962) 'How to judge quality', *New Republic*, 147, pp. 29–31.

Layard, R. (2005) *Happiness: Lessons from a New Science*, Penguin Books, London.

Layard, R. (2009) 'Why subjective well-being should be the measure of progress', OECD World Forum on Statistics, Knowledge and Policy – Charting Progress, Building Visions, Improving Life, Busan, Korea, 27–30 October.

Layard, R. (2010) 'Measuring subjective well-being', *Science*, 327(5965), pp. 534–535.

Lewis, A. (1955) *The Theory of Economic Growth*, Routledge, London.

Maggino, F. (2009) 'The state of the art in indicators construction in the perspective of a comprehensive approach in measuring well-being of societies', Working Paper, Università degli Studi di Firenze.

Maggino, F. (2013) 'Defining and measuring well-being and the role of happiness', in E. Zamfir and F. Maggino (eds), *The European Culture for Human Rights: The Right to Happiness*, Cambridge Scholars Publishing, Cambridge.

Marx, K. (1887 [1967]) *Capital: A Critique of Political Economy*, Vol. 1, International Publishers, New York, NY.

Maslow, A. (1954) *Motivation and Personality*, Addison Wesley Longman, New York, NY.

Max-Neef, M. (1995) 'Economic growth and quality of life: a threshold hypothesis', *Ecological Economics*, 15(2), 115–118.

Max-Neef, M.A., A. Elizalde and M. Hopenhayn (1989) *Human Scale Development: Conception, Application and Further Reflections*, Apex, New York, NY.

McGranahan, D.V., C. Richard-Proust, N.V. Sovani and M. Subramanian (1972) *Contents and Measurement of Socioeconomic Development. A Staff Study of the United Nations Research Institute for Social Development*, UNRISD, New York, NY.

Meadows, D.H., G. Meadows, J. Randers and W.W. Behrens III (1972) *The Limits to Growth*, Universe Books, New York, NY.

Michalos, A.C., B. Smale, R. Labonté, N. Muhajarine, K. Scott, M. Guhn, A.M. Gadermann, B.D. Zumbo, A. Morgan, K. Moore, L. Swystun, B. Holden, H. Bernardin, B. Dunning, P. Graham, A.-S. Brooker and I. Hyman (2011) 'The Canadian Index of Well-being. Technical Report 1.0', Canadian Index of Well-being and University of Waterloo, Waterloo.

Morlino, L., D. Piana and F. Raniolo (eds) (2013) *La qualità della democrazia in Italia*, Il Mulino, Bologna.

Morris, M.D. (1979) *Measuring the Conditions of the World's Poor: The Physical Quality of Life Index*, Pergamon, New York, NY.

Morrone, A. (2012) 'Vulnerability measures in the BES framework', Paper presented at SIS 2013 Statistical Conference, Advances in Latent Variables – Methods, Models and Applications, Brescia – Department of Economics and Management, 19–21 June.

NEF (2006) *Happy Planet Index. An Index of Human Well-Being and Environmental Impact*, New Economics Foundation, London.

NEP (2010) 'Coordinated use of energy system models in energy and climate policy analysis – lessons learned from the Nordic Energy Perspective project'.

Neumayer, E. (1999) 'The ISEW – not an Index of Sustainable Economic Welfare', *Social Indicators Research*, 48, pp. 877–101.

New Development Paradigm (2013) 'Happiness: towards a new development paradigm', Report of the Kingdom of Buthan, http://www.newdevelopmentparadigm.bt.

Noll, H.H. (2002) 'Social indicators and quality of life research: background, achievements and current trends', in N. Genov (ed.), *Advances in Sociological Knowledge over Half a Century*, International Social Science Council, Paris.

Nordhaus, W. and J. Tobin (1972) 'Is growth obsolete?', in W. Nordhaus and J. Tobin, *Economic Research: Retrospect and Prospect, Volume 5, Economic Growth*, NBER, Cambridge, MA.

Nussbaum, M. (2000) *Women and Human Development: The Capabilities Approach*, Cambridge University Press, Cambridge.

Nussbaum, M. (2006) *Frontiers of Justice: Disability, Nationality and Species Membership*, Harvard University Press, Cambridge, MA.

OECD (2003) *OECD Environment Indicators. Development, Measurement and Use*, OECD Publishing, Paris.

OECD (2007) *Istanbul Declaration*, Final declaration of the OECD 2nd World Forum on Measuring and Fostering the Progress of Societies, Istanbul, 30 June, http://www.oecd.org/dataoecd/14/46/38883774.pdf.

OECD (2008) *Growing Unequal? Income Distribution and Poverty in OECD Countries*, OECD Publishing, Paris.

OECD (2009) *Green Growth: Overcoming the Crisis and Beyond*, OECD Publishing, Paris.

OECD (2010) *Green Growth Strategy Interim Report: Implementing our Commitment for a Sustainable Future*, C/MIN(2010)5.

OECD (2011a) *Divided We Stand: Why Inequality Keeps Rising*, OECD Publishing, Paris.

OECD (2011b) *How's Life? Measuring Well-Being*, OECD Publishing, Paris.

OECD (2012a) *OECD Environmental Outlook to 2050: The Consequences of Inaction*, OECD Publishing, Paris.

OECD (2012b) Long-term economic growth and environmental pressure: reference scenarios for future global projections, Working Party on Climate, Investment and Development, ENV/EPOC/WPCID(2012)6.

OECD (2013) *Guidelines on Measuring Subjective Well-Being*, OECD Publishing, Paris.

OECD (2015) *In It Together: Why Less Inequality Benefits All*, OECD Publishing, Paris.

OECD and Eurostat (1999) *The Environmental Goods and Services Industry – Manual for Data Collection and Analysis*, OECD Publishing, Paris.

OECD and JRC (2008) *Handbook on Constructing Composite Indicators: Methodology and User Guide*, OECD Publishing, Paris.

Oko-Institut (2011) 'The vision scenario for the European Union. 2011 update for the EU-27', www.oeko.de, Berlin.

ONS (2012) *Measuring National Well-being, First Annual Report on Measuring National Well-being*, Office for National Statistics, www.ons.gov.uk.

Osberg, L. and A. Sharpe (2002) 'An index of economic well-being for selected OECD countries', *Review of Income and Wealth*, 48(3), pp. 91–316.

Oxford Martin Commission for Future Generations (2013) 'Now for the long term', Oxford Martin School, Oxford.

Palazzi, P. (2004) Lo sviluppo come fenomeno multidimensionale. Confronto tra ISU e un indice di sviluppo sostenibile, *Moneta e Credito*, 227(2), pp. 279–309.

Paul VI (1967) *Populorum Progressio*, Encyclical of Pope Paul VI on the Development of Peoples, 26 March.

Piketty, T. (2014) *Capital in the Twenty-First Century*, Belknap Press, Cambridge, MA.

Pintér, L., P. Hardi and P. Bartelmus (2005) *Sustainable Development Indicators: Proposals for a Way Forward*, International Institute for Sustainable Development, Winnipeg.

Posner, S. and R. Costanza (2011) 'A summary of ISEW and GPI studies at multiple scales and new estimates for Baltimore City, Baltimore County, and the State of Maryland', *Ecological Economics*, 70(11), pp. 1972–1980.

Prescott-Allen, R. (2001) *The Well-being of Nations: A Country-by-Country Index of Quality of Life and the Environment*, Island Press, Washington, DC.

Prinz, A. and B. Bünger (2009) 'Living in a material world: happy income and happy life years', CAWM – Discussion Paper No 15.

Rawls, J. (1971) *A Theory of Justice*, Belknap / Harvard University Press, Cambridge, MA.

Redefining Progress (2004) *The Genuine Progress Indicator 1950–2002 (2004 update)*, www.RedefiningProgress.org.

Reynès, F., Y. Yeddir-Tamsamani and G. Callonnec (2011) 'Presentation of the three-me model: multi-sector macroeconomic model for the evaluation of environmental and energy policy', Document de travail de l'OFCE, No. 2011-10, OFCE.

Riggs F.W. (1984) 'Development', in G. Sartori (ed.), *Social Science Concepts: A Systematic Analysis*, SAGE, London.

Rondinella, T. (2012) 'Green industrial policies: economic recovery and emission reduction in Europe', in B. Galgoczi (ed.), *Green Industries and Creating Jobs*, ETUI, Bruxelles.

Rondinella, T. (2013) 'How to look at an unequal well-being', paper presented at SIS 2013 Statistical Conference, Advances in Latent Variables – Methods, Models and Applications, Brescia – Department of Economics and Management, 19–21 June.

Rondinella, T. (2014) 'Policy use of progress indicators', in T. Rondinella, M. Signore, D. Fazio, et al. (eds), *Map on Policy Use of Progress Indicators*, e-Frame – European Framework for Measuring Progress, EU FP7 Project, Deliverable 11.1, www.eframeproject.eu.

Rondinella, T. and M. Savioli (2013) 'Una lettura del Benessere Equo e Sostenibile in Italia in chiave territoriale', Autonomie Locali e Servizi Sociali, n.2, Il Mulino, Bologna.

Rondinella, T., E. Segre and D. Zola (2011) 'L'indicatore di Qualità regionale dello sviluppo italiano (Quars) e altri casi studio internazionali', Rivista delle Politiche Sociali n.1, Ediesse, Roma.

Rondinella, T., E. Segre and D. Zola (2017) 'Participative processes for measuring progress: deliberation, consultation and the role of civil society', *Social Indicators Research*, 130(3), pp. 959–982.

Rosen, R. (1991) *Life Itself: A Comprehensive Inquiry into Nature, Origin, and Fabrication of Life*, Columbia University Press, New York, NY.

Rostow, W.W. (1960) *The Stages of Economic Growth: A Non-communist Manifesto*, Cambridge University Press, New York, NY.

Rothstein, B. (2011) *The Quality of Government: Corruption, Social Trust, and Inequality in International Perspective*, University of Chicago Press, Chicago, IL.

Ryan, R.R.M. and E.L. Deci (2001) 'On happiness and human potentials: a review of research on hedonic and eudaimonic well-being', *Annual Review of Psychology*, 52, pp. 141–166.

Ryff, C., E. Friedman, T. Fuller-Rowell, G. Love, Y. Miyamoto, J. Morozink, B. Radler and V. Tsenkova (2012) 'Varieties of resilience in MIDUS', *Social and Personality Psychology Compass*, 6(11), pp. 792–806.

Saraceno, C. and A. Schizzerotto (2009) 'Introduzione', in A. Brandolini, C. Saraceno and A. Schizzerotto (eds), *Dimensioni della disuguaglianza in Italia: povertà, salute, abitazione*, Collana della Fondazione Ermanno Gorrieri per gli studi sociali, Il Mulino, Bologna.

Sassi, O., R. Crassous, J.-C. Hourcade, V. Gitz, H. Waisman and C. Guivarch (2010) 'IMACLIM-R: a modelling framework to simulate sustainable development pathways', *International Journal of Global Environmental Issues*, 10(1/2), pp. 5–24.

Schepelmann, P., M. Stock, T. Koska, R. Schüle and O. Reutter (2009) 'A green new deal for Europe, A report by the Wuppertal Institute for Climate, Environment and Energy', Green European Foundation, Wuppertal.

Scrivens, K. and B. Iasiello (2010) 'Indicators of "societal progress": lessons from international experiences', OECD Statistics Working Papers, 2010/4, OECD Publishing, Paris.

Seers, D. (1969) 'The meaning of development', *International Development Review*, 44, https://www.ids.ac.uk/files/dmfile/themeaningofdevelopment.pdf.

Sen, A. (1980) 'Equality of what?', in S. McMurrin (ed.) *Tanner Lectures on Human Values*, Cambridge University Press, Cambridge.

Sen, A. (1985) *Commodities and Capabilities*, North-Holland, Amsterdam.

Sen, A. (1992) *The Standard of Living: Lecture 1, Concepts and Critiques and Lecture 2, Lives and Capabilities*, University of Utah Press, Salt Lake City, UT.

Sen, A. (1993) 'Capability and well-being', in M.C. Nussbaum and A. Sen (eds), *The Quality of Life*, Clarendon Press, Oxford.

Sen, A. (2009) *The Idea of Justice*, Allen Lane, London.

Sen, A. (2013) 'Infelicità delle istituzioni europee', Lecture at the Festival delle Scienze of Rome, Il Sole 24 Ore, 27 January.

Smith, A. (1776) *An Inquiry into the Nature and Causes of the Wealth of Nations*, http://en.wikisource.org/wiki/The_Wealth_of_Nations.

Smits, J.P., R. Hoekstra and N. Schoenaker (2014) 'The e-Frame Convergence Report: Taking Stock of the Measurement Systems for Sustainable Development and the Opportunities for Harmonisation', e-Frame Project, Deliverable D2.5, www.eframeproject.eu.

Solivetti, L.M. (1993) *Società tradizionali e mutamento socio-economico*, NIS, Rome.

Sommers, C. and S. Satel (2006) *One Nation Under Therapy: How the Helping Culture Is Eroding Self-Reliance*, St Martin's Press, London.

Statistics Austria (2014), 'How's Austria?', http://www.statistik.at/web_en/statistics/------/hows_austria/index.html.

Stern, N. (2006) *Stern Review on the Economics of Climate Change (pre-publication edition). Executive Summary*, HM Treasury, London.

Stiglitz, J. (2012) *The Price of Inequality: How Today's Divided Society Endangers Our Future*, W.W. Norton & Company, New York, NY.

Stiglitz, J., A. Sen and J.-P. Fitoussi (2009) 'Report by the Commission on the Measurement of Economic Performance and Social Progress', www.stiglitz-sen-fitoussi.fr.

Stone, R. (1975) *Towards a System of Social and Demographic Statistics*, United Nations, New York, NY.

Sunstein, C. (2008) *Infotopia: How Many Minds Produce Knowledge*, Oxford University Press, Oxford.

Talberth, J., C. Cobb and N. Slattery (2007) *The Genuine Progress Indicator 2006: A Tool for Sustainable Development*, Redefining Progress, Oakland, CA.

Thomas, W.I. and D. Thomas (1928) *The Child in America*, Alfred Knopf, New York, NY.

Truman, H.S. (1949) 'Truman's inaugural address', 20 January, http://www.bartleby.com/124/pres53.html.

UN (1992) 'Agenda 21 – Global Programme of Action on Sustainable Development', http://sustainabledevelopment.un.org/agenda21/.

UN (2000) *General Assembly Resolution 55/2 of 8 September 2000*.

UN (2012a) 'United Nations Secretary-General's High Level Panel Report on Global Sustainability – resilient people, resilient planet: a future worth choosing'.

UN (2012b) 'Realizing the future we want for all: report to the Secretary-General', United Nations, New York, NY.

UN (2014a) 'The road to dignity by 2030: ending poverty, transforming all lives and protecting the planet', Synthesis Report of the Secretary-General on the post-2015 Sustainable Development Agenda, United Nations General Assembly, A/69/700.

UN (2014b) 'A world that counts: mobilising the data revolution for sustainable development', Report to the UN Secretary-General of the Independent Advisory Experts Group on Data Revolution, www.undatarevolution.org.

UN (2015) 'Transforming our world: the 2030 Agenda for Sustainable Development', A/RES/70/1.

UN (2016) 'Report of the Inter-agency and Expert Group on Sustainable Development Indicators to the Statistical Commission', E/CN.3/2016/2/Rev.1.

UNCED (1992) 'Report of the United Nations Conference on Environment and Development', Rio de Janeiro, June 1992, http://www.un.org/documents/ga/conf151/aconf15126-1annex1.htm.

UNCSD (2012) 'The future we want', Outcome document adopted at Rio+20, Rio de Janeiro, June, http://www.un.org/en/sustainablefuture/.

UNDESA (2006) 'Global trends and status of indicators of sustainable development', UN Department of Economic and Social Affairs, New York, NY.

UNDP (1990) *Human Development Report*, Oxford University Press, New York, NY.

UNDP (2010) *Human Development Report 2010. The Real Wealth of Nations: Pathways to Human Development*, United Nations Development Programme, New York, NY.

UNDP (2014) *Human Development Report. Sustaining Human Progress: Reducing Vulnerabilities and Building Resilience*, United Nations Development Programme, New York, NY.

UNECE (2009) *Measuring Sustainable Development*, United Nations Economic Commission for Europe, Geneva.

UNEP (2011) 'Towards a green economy: pathways to sustainable development and poverty eradication – a synthesis for policy makers', United Nations Environment Programme, www.unep.org/greeneconomy.

UNRISD (1970) *Contents and Measurement of Socioeconomic Development*, Praeger, New York, NY.

UNU-IHDP and UNEP (2012) *Inclusive Wealth Report 2012. Measuring Progress Toward Sustainability*. Cambridge University Press, Cambridge.

Ura, K., S. Alkire, T. Zangmo and K. Wangdi (2012) *A Short Guide to Gross National Happiness Index*, Centre for Bhutan Studies, Thimphu.

US Congress, Senate (1934) 'National income, 1929–32', S. Doc. 124, 73rd Cong., 2d sess.

Valentin, A. and J. Spangerberg (2000) 'A guide to community sustainability indicators', *Environmental Impact Assessment Review*, 20, 381–392.

Vandemoortele, J. (2007) 'The MDGs: "M" for misunderstood?', WIDER Angle, No. 1, https://www.wider.unu.edu/publication/mdgs-%E2%80%98m%E2%80%99-misunderstood.

Veenhoven, R. (1996) 'Happy life expectancy: a comprehensive measure of the quality-of-life in nations', *Social Indicators Research*, 39, pp. 1–58.

Wackernagel, M. and W. Rees (1996) *Our Ecological Footprint*, New Society Publishers, Philadelphia, PA.

Wackernagel, M., N.B. Schulz, D. Deumling, A. Callejas Linares, M. Jenkins, V. Kapos, C. Monfreda, J. Loh, N. Myers, R. Norgaard and J. Randers (2002) 'Tracking the ecological overshoot of the human economy', *Proceedings of the National Academy of Sciences* 99(14), pp. 9266–9271.

Wilkinson, R. and K. Pickett (2008) *The Spirit Level: Why Equality is Better for Everyone*, Penguin Books, London.

World Bank (2000) *Genuine Saving as a Sustainability Indicator*, World Bank, Washington, DC.

World Bank (2006) *Where is the Wealth of Nations?*, World Bank, Washington, DC.

World Commission on Environment and Development (1987) 'Report of the World Commission on Environment and Development: Our Common Future', transmitted to the General Assembly as an Annex to document A/42/427, 'Development and international co-operation: environment', http://www.un-documents.net/wced-ocf.htm.

Zolotas, X. (1981) *Economic Growth and Declining Social Welfare*, New York University Press, New York, NY.

2.   Going beyond GDP: empirical findings
Carlotta Balestra, Romina Boarini and Nicolas Ruiz

2.1   INTRODUCTION

Nations need indicators that measure progress towards achieving their goals: economic, social and environmental. Standard economic indicators such as gross domestic product (GDP) are useful for measuring the macroeconomic performance of countries and informing policy makers about the position of the economy in the business cycle. Although GDP was never designed to measure social or economic welfare, for decades it has enjoyed supreme status as the predominant benchmark of economic and social progress (Kuznets, 1934; Marcuss and Kane, 2007; McCulla and Smith, 2007).

GDP's current role poses a number of problems (Bleys, 2012; Nordhaus and Tobin, 1973; Sen, 1985b, 1998; Fleurbaey, 2009; Stiglitz et al., 2009). At the level of society as a whole, GDP interprets every expense as positive and does not distinguish welfare-enhancing activities from welfare-reducing ones (Cobb et al., 1995; Talberth et al., 2007). For example, an oil spill increases GDP because of the associated cost of clean-up and remediation, but it obviously detracts from overall well-being (Costanza et al., 2004). GDP also leaves out many components that enhance welfare but do not involve monetary transactions and therefore fall outside the market. For example, the act of picking vegetables from a garden and cooking them for family or friends is not included in GDP, while buying a similar pre-prepared meal in a grocery store involves an exchange of money and a subsequent GDP increase (Kubiszewki et al., 2013).[1] Moreover, at the level of the person, there are many aspects beyond monetary metrics that are important for their well-being, such as the need to feel valued and respected by others, the extent to which aspirations are fulfilled, and the care and affection that are provided by close family and friends (Boarini et al., 2006; Costanza et al., 2009; OECD, 2011a).

These criticisms were first raised during the mid-1970s with worries about ecological limits to growth and an increasing concern over the relative weights to be given to economic and social aspects of human progress, for developed as well as for developing countries. Some early initiatives took place at that time, in particular the attempt by Nordhaus and Tobin (1973) to develop a measure of economic welfare, based on GDP, but correcting GDP for its most evident limitations (Christian, 1974; OECD, 1982, 1986). Following these early moves, interest in alternative approaches to GDP temporarily fell, with other pressing but more traditional problems taking centre stage, such as stagflation or rapid increase in unemployment rates and the GDP-targeted policies needed to address them.

Interest in alternatives or complements to GDP resumed progressively during the 1990s. Emblematic of this new trend was the creation of the United Nations Human Development Index (HDI) that combines GDP with measures of health and educational achievement (see Seth and Villar, Chapter 3 in this *Handbook*). More recently, the Great Recession seems to have given further impetus, strengthening the perception that the strong pace of GDP growth during the period of the Great Moderation reflected, at least in some countries, the accumulation of unsustainable levels of private and public debt, the inadequate pricing of risk, and the consequences of wider inequalities (Stiglitz, 2010; Atkinson and Morelli, 2011). In addition, that experience has greatly reinforced people's sentiment that economic growth in the years of the Great Moderation was not lifting all boats, and that the costs of the crisis are today falling disproportionately upon those who have least benefited from the economic expansion of the 2000s. This sentiment may be at the root of the social unrest that characterised much of the world in 2011, from the Arab Spring to Occupy Wall Street in the United States, from the *indignados* taking the streets in Madrid, Athens and Jerusalem to movements for a more open and accountable democratic system in Moscow; these being only some examples of a much more widespread expression of people's discontent with the functioning of political systems and of their call for an economy with a more human face.

The discussion and research on well-being measures has evolved in parallel to these world events, finding expression in some major initiatives. The report by the Commission on the Measurement of Economic Performance and Social Progress (the Stiglitz–Sen–Fitoussi report) published in 2009 (Stiglitz et al., 2009) concluded that 'the time was right to shift emphasis from measuring economic production to measuring people's well-being'. Other international initiatives such as the European Commission's GDP and Beyond project (Eurostat, 2009a) and the Organisation for Economic Co-operation and Development (OECD) Global Project on Measuring the Progress of Societies (OECD, 2011a) added to the impetus to look for – and to use – new approaches to the measurement of quality of life and progress. The OECD, for example, sees this as 'better statistics for better policies for better lives'. These international initiatives have gone hand in hand with a large number of national initiatives, in the form of public national consultations (in Australia and the United Kingdom), parliamentary commissions (in Germany and Norway), national roundtables (in Italy, Spain and Slovenia) and in a variety of other forms (for example, in Japan, China and Korea). All in all, the initiatives on 'going beyond GDP' are increasingly numerous, reflecting the widespread recognition that well-being statistics are critical for informing policy making on a range of aspects that matter to the life of ordinary people.[2] The interested reader is referred to Appendix 2.1 for a summary of several initiatives measuring well-being developed by a number of OECD countries' National Statistical Offices.

The creativity called forth by the failings of GDP gave birth to a plethora of indicators and frameworks. While different in scope and proposal, most of these metrics share a number of distinctive features: (1) they focus on the individuals, rather than on the economy; (2) they consider the distribution of well-being in the population alongside average achievements of each country; (3) they are multidimensional; (4) they balance objective measures and subjective judgements; and (5) they assess both current and future well-being, considering the latter in terms of a number of key resources (observable today) that have the potential to generate well-being over time.

Over recent years the literature on 'going beyond GDP' has been growing exponentially. In the process of writing this chapter so many new publications became available that the review is outdated even before it is completed. Hence, our aim here is not to provide an exhaustive overview of the available works on the subject, but rather to stress some of the most challenging issues in the operationalisation of the frameworks that try to convey a broader picture of societal progress, and to sketch some of the techniques that have been used to get around those issues. On the surface, some of these problems appear to be methodological in nature, but a closer look reveals that measurement is always involved. Well-being, prosperity, happiness, quality of life and other definitions that generally figure in the literature are in some sense useless unless they are properly defined, operationalised and measured in a way that is relevant and helpful for policy discussions (Smith et al., 2013).

Some of the issues that are addressed in this chapter relate to what should be taken into account, and to who decides what is valuable. The choice of components inevitably reflects a set of values and/or beliefs, but which actor should decide what matters to life, and on which grounds? In addition to the questions of 'what counts' and 'who decides' is the question of 'how to count'. This arises at different levels: the choice of subjective or objective indicators; the way of introducing inequality; the decision of whether or not to aggregate and which set of weights to use.

The rest of this chapter is organised as follows. Section 2.2 deals with one-dimensional alternatives to GDP, mainly focused on individuals and households. Section 2.3 introduces a multidimensional framework for assessing people's well-being and gives an overview of the issues related to the capability approach and of a number of its empirical applications. Both Section 2.2 and Section 2.3 account for the distribution of well-being outcomes across the population. Section 2.4 discusses the aggregation of heading components and single indicators, a distinctive issue related to any multidimensional framework, and reviews some of the most famous composite indices of well-being. Section 2.5 offers an alternative approach to well-being, based on subjective measures and people's perceptions. Section 2.6 zooms out, by considering the sustainability of well-being over time. Section 2.7 concludes.

2.2   ONE-DIMENSIONAL ALTERNATIVES TO GDP

Stiglitz et al. (2009) argues that assessing an individual's economic situation is more relevant than focusing on indicators for the entire economy. For instance, the median household income – an income measure that better reflects the actual material living standards of a 'typical' household – has evolved quite differently from GDP per capita in a number of countries. Against this background, this section assesses material living standards by focusing more directly on the household perspective, moving progressively from the macro to the micro perspective and then to distributional issues.

2.2.1   From GDP to Non-Market Activities

GDP does focus on measuring economic activities that occur within a country's domestic market. However, economic activity covers more than market production. It also includes non-market activities; namely services provided by the government, by households for themselves and by the 'third sector'. Government services do actually appear in the national accounts, although adjustments are made so that they fit within the accounting framework, as they are non-market by definition. On the contrary, only a few countries regularly generate systematic empirical data on any substantial portion of the third sector.[3] Those doing so tend to use national legal definitions, thus making any comparative study difficult. Application of consistent rules for deciding on which organisations are part of the non-profit sector is a key motivation for the United Nations *Handbook on Non-Profit Institutions in the System of National Accounts*, which offers countries a standard set of guidelines for gathering data on the non-profit sector so that it can be seen and analysed as a distinct sector in national economic accounts. The resulting 'satellite accounts on non-profit institutions' pull together a much more comprehensive and reliable picture of the civil society sector than previously available, making it possible to gauge its contribution and track its evolution over time.[4] As part of this process, statistical agencies are also called on to estimate the scale and value of the volunteer work these organisations mobilise, and to include this in estimates of economic activity (UN, 2003).

Stiglitz et al. (2009) suggest that a more complete picture of overall production could be drawn by constructing comprehensive and periodic accounts of household activity that complete national accounts. In spite of the inherent measurement difficulties (namely, the choice of estimates for labour costs), recent improvements in the statistical infrastructure of many countries (for example, more detailed data on wages, improved data on non-market activities, and time-use surveys) have led many countries to produce household production satellite accounts (for example, Australia, Canada, Finland, Germany, Hungary, Mexico, Switzerland and the United Kingdom) that complement the traditional estimates of economic activity, and that are able to provide a more comprehensive assessment of the material well-being of households (Ahmad and Koh, 2011; Holloway et al., 2002).

A relevant illustration of the size of the household unpaid work is provided by time-use surveys (Figure 2.1). On average, across the OECD area, individuals devote 26.5 hours per week to housework (for example, childcare, care for the elderly, cooking), only two hours less than the weekly time spent on paid work. Substantial variation exists among countries: in Japan, on average, people spend on unpaid work only one-quarter of the time spent on paid activities. At the other end of the scale, in Mexico and Turkey, people spend more than 36 hours per week on chores and unpaid care activities.

The development of satellite accounts to account for the household and the non-profit sector implies the conversion of the measured output of the specific sector in monetary terms to allow a practical comparison with the national accounts, and more specifically with GDP. Some scholars (see Cassiers and Thiry, 2009) caution against the attempt to assess in monetary terms some activities that precisely have as a main characteristic their intrinsic value and not being valuable in monetary terms. As an example, is child care of the same value if it is provided by a babysitter rather than by parents? How far could the satellite accounts expand? For these authors, if conversion of time into monetary terms is emphasised, then the focus tends to be on materialistic outcomes. It therefore overshadows the direct contribution to well-being that results from a specific non-market activity.

While it is beyond the scope of this chapter to elaborate in greater detail the technical questions concerning the valuation of unpaid work, or to give an extensive overview of the results of different measurement methods,[5] it is worth mentioning that the Human Development Report 1995, using a uniform approach with extra gross wages of a domestic worker as the relevant market price, found that unpaid work accounts for 72 per cent of gross national product (GNP) in Australia, 53 per cent in Germany and 45 per cent in Finland. The report concludes that, whatever the method used, the value of unpaid work in industrial countries is considerable: 'It is at least half of gross domestic product and it accounts for more than half of private consumption'. On a global level:

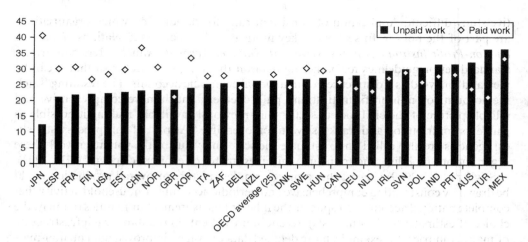

Notes: For all figures, the following ISO codes for countries are used: AUS: Australia; AUT: Austria; BEL: Belgium; CAN: Canada; CHE: Switzerland; CHL: Chile; CHN: China; CZE: Czech Republic; DEU: Germany; DNK: Denmark; ESP: Spain; EST: Estonia; FIN: Finland; FRA: France; GBR: United Kingdom; GRC: Greece; HUN: Hungary; IND: India; IRL: Ireland; ISL: Iceland; ISR: Israel; ITA: Italy; JPN: Japan; KOR: Korea; LUX: Luxembourg; MEX: Mexico; NLD: Netherlands; NOR: Norway; NZL: New Zealand; POL: Poland; PRT: Portugal; SVK: Slovak Republic; SVN: Slovenia; SWE: Sweden; TUR: Turkey; USA: United States; ZAF: South Africa.
Countries are ranked in ascending order of the gender gap in unpaid work.
Data refer to 2011 for Japan and the United States; 2010 for Canada and Norway; and 2009–10 for Estonia, Finland, France, New Zealand and Spain. Data refer to 2009 for Korea and Mexico; 2008–09 for Austria and Italy; and 2008 for Turkey. Data refer to 2006 for Australia, China, the Netherlands and Turkey; 2005 for Belgium, Ireland and the United Kingdom; 2003–04 for Poland; and 2001–02 for Germany. Data refer to 2001 for Denmark; 2000-01 for Slovenia and Sweden; 2000 for South Africa; 1999–2000 for Hungary; and 1999 for India and Portugal.
For details on the definitions of unpaid work and total work see Miranda (2011).

Source: Authors' calculations based on time-use surveys.

Figure 2.1   Housework and paid work: worked hours per person per week, various years

> if these unpaid activities were treated as market transactions at the prevailing wages, they would yield huge monetary valuations – a staggering \$16 trillion, or about 70 per cent more than the officially estimated \$23 trillion of global output . . . Of this \$16 trillion, \$11 trillion is the non-monetized, 'invisible' contribution of women. (UNDP, 1995, p.97)

2.2.2   From GDP to Household Adjusted Disposable Income

Beyond aggregate economic conditions, a narrower focus on households can be operated within the National Accounts sphere. A natural staring point is the concept of household adjusted disposable income per capita. Available in a wide range of countries, it is considered as the measure that best reflects people's economic resources at the aggregate level, combining information on a large number of market and non-market resources.

Household adjusted disposable income is obtained by adding to the flows that make up people's gross income (earnings, self-employment and capital income, as well as current monetary transfers received from other sectors) the social transfers in-kind that households receive from governments (such as education and health care services), and then subtracting the taxes on income and wealth and the social security contributions paid by households. This measure can be expressed in both gross and net terms, with the difference being households' consumption of fixed capital.[6]

While recent work referred to the net measure (see, e.g., OECD, 2011a), the evidence presented below will rely on the gross measure, mainly because of better data availability.[7] It is worth emphasising some of the major limitations generally associated with household income measures, including the one being used here; in particular: (1) indirect taxes are not included in the measure of taxes paid by households, implying that their impact is captured only to the extent they are reflected in prices; and (2) the deflation procedure cannot rely on different price indices by income groups (see below).

Not surprisingly, cross-country differences in household adjusted disposable income per capita are large (Figure 2.2). For the countries analysed, household adjusted disposable income is highest in the United States, about six times as high as in South Africa, where it is the lowest. Household adjusted disposable income per capita is closely related to GDP per capita, with a pairwise correlation of 0.94 over the countries and years for which data are available. Indeed, cross-country comparisons in material living standards are weakly affected by the use of household adjusted disposable income instead of GDP. There are nonetheless some exceptions, such as Luxembourg and Ireland, faring much better in terms of GDP than in terms of household income, reflecting the strong impact of net transfers from abroad, as highlighted in previous studies (see OECD, 2011a).

However, when looking at the differences between growth of GDP and that of household income in recent years, GDP appeared to have grown considerably more than households' economic resources in many countries. The gap was particularly large in Korea, Central European countries (namely, the Czech Republic, Hungary, Poland and Slovenia) and Estonia (Figure 2.3). In fact, only a few countries with large commodity-producing sectors experienced stronger gains in household incomes relative to GDP (for example, Norway and Russia and, to a lesser extent, Australia).

Many factors underlie this growing gap, including: a faster rise in corporate savings and reinvested profits than in employee compensation – resulting in a lower share of primary income accruing to households; a stronger tendency towards outward transfers of firms' profits; and changes in redistribution policies through taxes and social benefits. Discrepancies between GDP and household adjusted disposable income may also be reflective of resources that will in principle increase household material living standards in the future (for example, reinvested profits) or may diminish it (for example, higher consumption today financed through external debt). Properly disentangling the various factors underlying these differences is a research area in its early stages (see Karabarbounis and Neiman, 2013, for a recent development in this field).

2.2.3   From Macro to Micro Sources

National Accounts provide aggregate amounts of households' resources that are then expressed on a per capita basis to adjust for differences in population size, therefore measuring material living standards of the average household in the country. However, one needs to turn to micro sources of information to look at more representative population groups or at specific parts of the income distribution. Yet a number of issues arise when moving from macro to micro sources, generating discrepancies between the associated

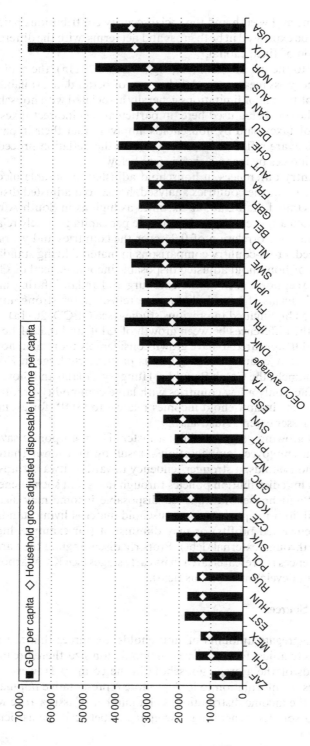

Notes: Household gross adjusted disposable income per capita and GDP per capita are expressed in USD, constant prices, constant purchasing power parities (PPPs), OECD base year 2005. For household gross adjusted disposable income per capita, PPPs are those for actual individual consumption of households; while in the case of GDP per capita, PPPs for the GDP deflator are used.

Data refer to 2010 for Australia, Canada, Chile, Japan, Mexico, Poland, Switzerland, the United States, the Russian Federation and South Africa; 2009 for Luxembourg; and 2006 for New Zealand.

Source: OECD calculations based on National Accounts Database.

Figure 2.2 Cross-country patterns in GDP and household disposable income, 2011

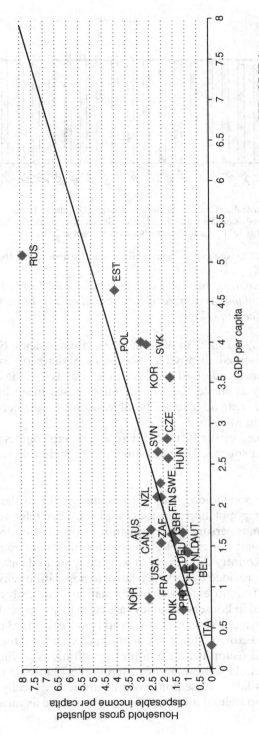

Notes: Household gross adjusted disposable income per capita and GDP per capita are expressed in USD, constant prices, constant PPPs, OECD base year 2005. For household gross adjusted disposable income per capita PPPs are those for actual individual consumption of households; while in the case of GDP per capita, PPPs for the GDP deflator are used.

For New Zealand the last available observation is 2006, for Luxembourg 2009; and for Australia, Canada, Chile, Japan, Mexico, Poland, the Russian Federation, South Africa, Switzerland and the United States it is 2010.

Source: OECD calculations based on National Accounts Database.

Figure 2.3   Real annual growth rates of GDP and household disposable income: cross-country patterns, average annual growth rates in percentages, 1997–2011

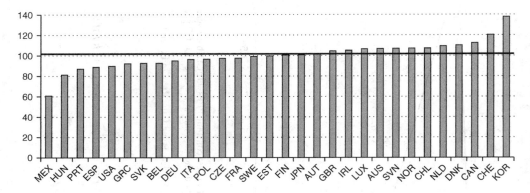

Note: Data refer to 2009 except for Australia, Canada, Denmark, France, Germany, Israel, Mexico, the Netherlands, Norway, Sweden, the United Kingdom and the United States, for which the last available observation is 2010; for Korea for which it is 2011; and for Switzerland for which it is 2008.

Source: OECD calculations based on OECD National Accounts and Income Distribution Databases.

Figure 2.4   *From macro to micro sources: survey-based mean household disposable income per consumption unit as a share of SNA-based mean adjusted disposable income per capita (%)*

respective estimates of households' incomes. To illustrate these discrepancies, Figure 2.4 presents survey-based mean household disposable income as a share of System of National Accounts (SNA)-based mean adjusted disposable income. Across the countries for which information is currently available, the ratio of micro-based mean household disposable income to macro-based mean adjusted disposable income ranges between 138 per cent in Korea and 61 per cent in Mexico.

These differences can be explained by the fact that micro and macro sources have distinct objectives, coverage and data sources. Here are some of the main differences and their implications:

- The scope of the reference population. National Accounts refer to the resident population as derived from population censuses, while surveys refer to private households (that is, they exclude persons living in institutions) and often do not take all of the territory into account (for example, overseas territories are excluded for France). In addition, cross-country differences in weighting methods may impact on the population estimates provided by surveys relative to population censuses. On average, across the 19 OECD countries for which information is currently available, the population estimates used in household surveys are close to 98 per cent of their National Account counterpart, but lower in Austria and New Zealand (93 per cent).
- The scope of the household sector. National Accounts data available at the international level for the household sector include non-profit institutions serving households (NPISH), while household surveys do not. Across the 13 OECD countries for which information is available,[8] these non-profit institutions typically account for around 0.2 per cent of household adjusted disposable income as measured in the National Accounts.

- The definition of income components. In National Accounts, household income includes several non-cash components – such as income imputed for in-kind public services (for example, health and education), for owner-occupied housing and for some types of financial assets – that surveys generally exclude. Conversely, benefits from some retirement schemes are not included in household income in the National Accounts, while they are in surveys. Also, measures of self-employment income may differ between the two sources. This is because of the impact of depreciation allowances and of inventory accounting in the 'tax' definition of self-employment income used in household surveys. This issue may be especially important for countries where unincorporated enterprises are widespread.
- Survey non-response. Household surveys are affected by non-response, which is not random along the income distribution as it increases with the level of income (Deaton, 2005). This means that household surveys generally fail to measure and track top incomes, while they can also have some difficulty reaching the poorest. Moreover, non-response rates vary across countries. For example, in the 2008 wave of the European Union Statistics on Income and Living Conditions (EU-SILC), the non-response rate exceeded 30 per cent in Belgium, Denmark, Luxembourg and Norway; while it stood below 10 per cent in Portugal and the Slovak Republic (see Atkinson and Marlier, 2010).
- Equivalisation. While macro-based estimates of household incomes are usually measured on a per capita basis, micro-based estimates refer to the concept of 'equivalised' (or 'per consumption unit') household disposable income. The notion of equivalisation implies that the income attributed to each person in a household reflects income sharing within the household and adjusts for household needs. It is assumed that these needs increase with household size, but less than proportionally. A number of 'scales' exist for such adjustment, but all tend to inflate the aggregate amounts measured by surveys.

To have a better understanding of such differences and how to solve them, there have been some ongoing international efforts to produce statistical methods and disaggregated global data to take into account individual household situations in the National Accounts. Two international projects were launched in 2011 in this vein: the OECD/Eurostat EG DNA (Expert Group on Disparities in a National Account Framework) project covering 16 countries (Australia, France, Germany, Italy, Israel, Japan, Korea, Mexico, the Netherlands, New Zealand, Portugal, Slovenia, Sweden, Switzerland, Turkey and the United States), and a similar effort at the EU level, covering 27 EU countries (see Fesseau and Mattonetti, 2013).

2.2.4 From Mean to Median Household Income

In general, survey-based median as opposed to mean income comes closer to being representative of typical household economic resources (see Stiglitz et al., 2009; the move to median income is one of the key recommendations of the report). In practice, an observed shortfall of median relative to mean household incomes also provides a preliminary assessment of inequality.

Cross-country differences in median household disposable income are larger than in mean household disposable income. Median household disposable income is highest in Luxembourg, about eight times as high as in Mexico, while mean household disposable income is less than seven times higher (Figure 2.4, Panel A). Despite these differences, using median instead of mean equivalised household disposable income does not affect cross-country comparisons in material living standards: indeed, across countries and years for which the data are available, the correlation between the level of mean and median equivalised incomes is equal to 0.99 and the associated country ranking almost identical (Figure 2.5, Panels B and C).[9] This general pattern hides some notable exceptions: Chile and the United States feature higher material living standards in terms of mean than median incomes; while the opposite occurs in the case of Belgium and the Nordic countries, due to relatively low income inequality.

Since the mid-1990s mean and median incomes have moved in tandem. Hence, as was the case for mean income, median income lagged GDP growth in a large number of countries (Figure 2.6). As a result, mean income growth outpaced median income growth in approximately half of OECD countries, implying that incomes in the middle of the distribution lost ground relative to those in the upper tail of the distribution. The largest gaps in mean versus median income growth rates occurred in Austria, Australia, France, Denmark, Canada and the United States. At the same time, the OECD countries characterised by higher levels of inequality – for example, Chile, Mexico and Turkey, as well as Spain – experienced a substantive narrowing of the gap between mean and median incomes amid different GDP growth rates.

2.2.5   Escaping the 'Tyranny of Averages' by Assessing Income Inequality

Average income is a meaningful statistic, but it does not tell the whole story about living standards across different groups of the population when GDP growth does not tend to 'raise all boats' equally, and the main impact of economic expansion is felt by the better-off with little if any benefits trickling down to the poorer income groups. Widening economic disparities observed in the last three decades have therefore emphasised the need for supplementing average values of economic resources with some measures of dispersion. As we have seen, median income provides a better measure of what is happening to the 'typical' individual or household than average income, and as such is already a first stage toward a proper account of inequality. But for policy purposes, it is also important to know what is happening at the bottom of the income distribution, or at the top.

The overall shape of the distribution of household disposable income differs significantly across OECD countries. Such differences may be highlighted through summary indexes of the underlying distribution. Figure 2.7 shows levels of the best-known of these indexes (the Gini coefficient) in the mid-1990s and late 2000s. Some OECD countries such as Chile and Mexico, but also Turkey, the United States and Israel, have a much more unequal income distribution than others. By contrast, the Nordic and Eastern European countries are characterised by lower income inequalities. Over time, income inequality increased in most OECD countries, especially in Sweden, Netherlands and Denmark; while it fell in a few, such as Turkey, Ireland, Belgium, Greece and Chile.

The Gini coefficient is only one among many summary indexes of the underlying distribution. In fact, different summary indexes are especially sensitive to different parts of the distribution, and an acute monitoring of inequality requires several indicators, as country ranking may partly depend on the specific inequality measure used. Table 2.1 shows how four other summary measures of income inequality compare to the Gini

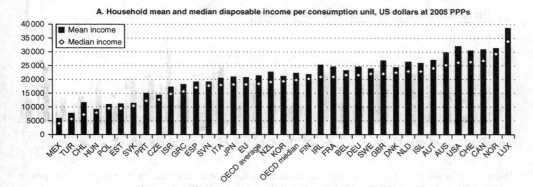

A. Household mean and median disposable income per consumption unit, US dollars at 2005 PPPs

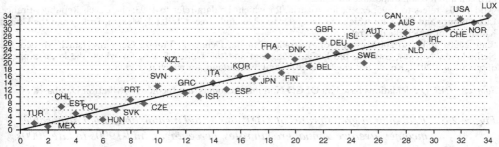

B. GDP per capita ranking (x-axis) and mean disposable income per consumption unit ranking (y-axis)

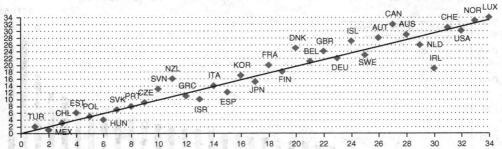

C. GDP per capita ranking (x-axis) and median disposable income per consumption unit ranking (y-axis)

Notes: All disposable income indicators used in this and the following sections refer to the concept of 'equivalised' (or 'per consumption unit') household disposable income. The notion of equivalisation implies that the income attributed to each person in a household reflects income sharing within the household and adjusts for household needs. It is assumed that these needs increase with household size, but less than proportionally (total household income is divided by the square root of household size).

In the case of mean and median equivalised household disposable incomes, PPPs are those for private consumption of households. For GDP per capita, PPPs for the GDP deflator were used.

Latest available year is 2010 for Australia, Canada, Denmark, France, Germany, Israel, Mexico, the Netherlands, Norway, Sweden, the United Kingdom and the United States; 2011 for Korea; and 2008 for Switzerland.

Source: OECD calculations based on OECD National Accounts and Income Distribution Databases.

Figure 2.5 GDP, mean and median household disposable incomes, years around 2009

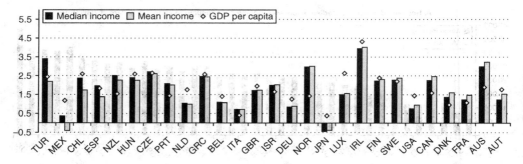

Notes: For median and mean equivalised household disposable incomes, PPPs are those for private consumption of households. For GDP per capita, PPPs are those for the GDP deflator.
Countries are sorted in ascending order according to the difference between the annual average growth rates of mean and median disposable incomes.
'Mid-1990s' refers to 1995; except for Austria, for which the data refer to 1993; the Czech Republic, France, Luxembourg and Chile, for which the data refer to 1996; and Greece, Ireland, Mexico, Turkey and the United Kingdom, for which the data refer to 1994.
'Late 2000s' refers to 2009; except for Australia, Canada, Denmark, France, Germany, Israel, Mexico, the Netherlands, Norway, Sweden, the United Kingdom and the United States, for which the latest available observation is 2010; Korea, for which it is 2011; and Switzerland, for which it is 2008.

Source: OECD calculations based on OECD National Accounts and Income Distribution Databases.

Figure 2.6   *Real annual growth rates of GDP, mean and median household disposable incomes, average annual growth rates, percentages, mid-1990s to late 2000s*

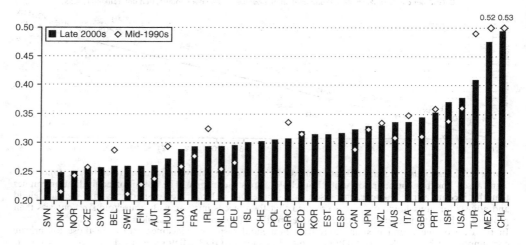

Notes: Data refer to the mid-2000s instead of the late 2000s for Greece and Switzerland.
For Austria, Belgium, the Czech Republic, Estonia, Finland, Iceland, Luxembourg, Poland, Portugal, the Slovak Republic, Slovenia, Spain and Switzerland, the values are provisional.

Source: OECD Income Distribution Database.

Figure 2.7   *Gini index of income inequalities, late 2000s*

Table 2.1 Levels of income inequality

	Gini Coefficient		Mean Log Deviation		Standard Coefficient of Variation		Interdecile Ratio P90/P10		Interdecile Ratio P50/P10	
	Level	Rank	Level	Rank	Level	Rank	Level	Rank	Level	Rank
Australia	0.30	16	0.17	15	039	9	3.95	15	2.09	18
Austria	0.27	4	0.13	8	0.33	3	3.27	10	1.82	7
Belgium	0.27	9	0.13	6	0.30	1	3.43	14	1.97	14
Canada	0.32	18	0.18	17	0.59	17	4.12	17	2.14	20
Czech Republic	0.27	5	0.12	4	0.38	8	3.20	5	1.74	2
Denmark	0.23	1	0.10	2	0.60	18	2.72	1	1.75	3
Finland	0.27	7	0.13	7	0.81	24	3.21	6	1.86	11
France	0.28	13	0.14	9	0.37	7	3.39	13	1.82	8
Germany	0.30	15	0.16	14	0.45	13	3.98	16	2.08	17
Greece	0.32	21	0.18	16	0.43	12	4.39	21	2.18	21
Hungary	0.29	14	0.14	10	0.48	15	3.36	12	1.78	6
Iceland	0.28	12	0.16	13	0.54	16	3.10	4	1.76	4
Ireland	0.33	22	0.19	18	0.79	22	4.41	22	2.29	22
Italy	0.35	25	0.24	23	1.10	25	4.31	20	2.11	19
Japan	0.32	20	0.20	20	0.41	11	4.77	25	2.43	26
Korea	0.31	17	0.20	22	0.35	5	4.73	24	2.50	27
Luxembourg	0.26	3	0.12	3	0.30	2	3.25	8	1.86	10
Mexico	0.47	30	0.41	28	2.70	28	8.53	30	2.86	30
Netherlands	0.27	8	3.23	7	1.86	12				
New Zealand	0.34	23	4.27	19	2.06	16				
Norway	0.28	11	0.16	12	0.46	14	2.83	3	1.77	5
Poland	0.37	26	0.26	24	0.71	20	5.63	26	2.42	25
Portugal	0.42	28	0.31	26	1.13	26	6.05	28	2.35	24
Slovak Republic	0.27	5	0.13	5	0.37	6	3.26	9	1.86	13
Spain	0.32	19	0.20	21	0.41	10	4.59	23	2.32	23
Sweden	0.23	2	0.10	1	0.65	19	2.79	2	1.72	1
Switzerland	0.28	10	0.15	11	0.34	4	3.29	11	1.83	9
Turkey	0.43	29	0.32	27	1.45	27	6.49	29	2.67	28
United Kingdom	0.34	23	0.20	19	0.71	21	4.21	18	1.99	15
United States	0.38	27	0.29	25	0.81	23	5.91	27	2.69	29
Average OECD	0.31	–	0.19	–	0.66	–	4.16		2.09	–
Corr. with Gini coeff.	–	–	0.99	–	0.80	–	0.96		0.88	–

Note: The mean log deviation is the average value of the natural logarithm of the ratio of mean income to the income of each decile. The squared coefficient of variation is the variance of average income of each decile, divided by the square of the average income of the entire population. The P90/P10 inter-decile ratio is the ratio of the upper bound value of the ninth decile to that of the first. The P50/P10 inter-decile ratio is the ratio of median income to the upper bound value of the first decile. All these summary indicators have different upper and lower bounds: the mean log deviation and inter-decile ratios have a lower value of 1 and no upper bound, while the squared coefficient of variation has a lower bound of 0 and upper bound of infinity.

Source: OECD Income Distribution Database.

coefficient. Overall, these different measures tell a consistent story: cross-country correlations between different inequality measures and the Gini coefficient are above 0.95 for the mean log deviation and the P90/P10 inter-decile ratio, and around 0.80 for the square coefficient of variation and the P50/P10 inter-decile ratio.[10]

2.2.6   Top Incomes

Income inequality has been growing over the last two decades or so. But in fact, most of the rise took place at the top of the distribution (see Piketty and Saez, 2013): rich households have been doing much better than both low- and middle-income households. The magnitudes involved in such a rise have substantial implications on how households fare with GDP growth, and why moving beyond GDP for the monitoring of economic performance appears to be essential. In particular, the rise in inequality at the top can explain why the majority of households cannot reconcile the aggregate income growth figures with the performance of their incomes.

Taking a dynamic view from 1975 up to the 2007 financial crisis, the top percentile managed to capture a very large fraction of the growth in pre-tax incomes, especially in English-speaking countries: around 47 per cent of total growth went to the top 1 per cent in the United States, 37 per cent in Canada, and above 20 per cent in Australia and the United Kingdom. By contrast, in Nordic countries, but also in France, Italy, Portugal and Spain, it was the bottom 99 per cent of the population that benefited from more growth, receiving about 90 per cent of the increase in total pre-tax income between 1975 and 2007 (Figure 2.8).

The bottom 99 per cent obviously form a very large and heterogeneous group; therefore,

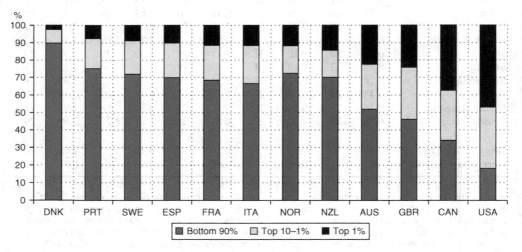

Note: Incomes refer to pre-tax incomes, excluding capital gains.

Source: World Top Income Database.

Figure 2.8   *Share of income growth going to income groups, 1975–2007; one fifth or more of total income growth is captured by the top 1 per cent*

a closer look needs to be taken at the evolution of incomes in different subgroups. For example, Figure 2.8 splits this group into the upper-middle class (top 10–1 per cent) and the bottom 90 per cent. About 80 per cent of total income growth has been captured by the top 10 per cent in the United States, and around two-thirds in Canada. In Australia and the United Kingdom, the top 10 per cent benefited from about half of the income growth. Income growth was shared more equally in other OECD countries for which data are available, but in all cases the top of the distribution benefited from growth proportionally more than the rest of the population.

The disproportionate surge in top incomes helps to explain why so many people have not felt their incomes rising in line with national GDP growth. From the mid-1970s to the late 2000s, the United States' average income grew at an annual rate of 1 per cent. However, the vast majority of the population did not see their incomes rising by anything close to this rate. In fact, if one strips out the growth that went to the top 1 per cent, the annual growth rate of the remaining 99 per cent was only 0.6 per cent. Excluding the top income percentile may also change the country ranking considerably in terms of annual income growth. For instance, average real income growth is lower in France than in the United States over the period, but France performed better than the United States when considering income growth of the bottom 99 per cent.

2.3 A MULTIDIMENSIONAL FRAMEWORK FOR MEASURING WELL-BEING

The opportunity to move from an income-based perspective to account for the constitutive plurality of human life has been widely advocated by the sociological literature on social welfare and poverty that traditionally considers a plurality of indicators to describe the quality of life of individuals and households (Townsend, 1985; Aberg, 1987; Allardt, 1993). In recent years, the economists' debate on well-being has also been strongly renewed by the essential contribution of Sen (1987, 1992, 1993, 1994, 1997). Health, longevity, knowledge and education, social relations and subjective feelings, since then, are considered as constitutive elements of human life that should not be ignored if we are interested in assessing people's welfare.

The basic assumption of any multidimensional approach to well-being analysis is that there are relevant dimensions of well-being which economic resources alone are not able to capture. Income and consumption are only rough measures of the quality of life because they are not able to fully describe what people can really achieve, and because higher income does not necessarily result in higher quality of life. A first case in point is health. Figure 2.9 shows that the relationship between GDP per capita and average life expectancy at birth among OECD countries is positive but not linear, flattening out once reaching a GDP per capita of around US$40 000. A similar non-linear relationship holds between GDP per capita and air pollution (measured in terms of PM10 concentration; Figure 2.10).

These two patterns suggest that, in higher-income countries, the level of GDP per capita is not linearly related to good health status and low air pollution – the more so, the higher the GDP per capita of the country concerned. While such patterns are described here with reference to OECD countries, the same log-linear pattern holds when observed across a broader

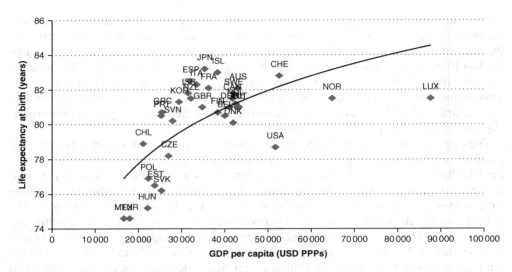

Notes: Data on life expectancy at birth refer to 2013 for Mexico; and 2011 for Canada and the United States.
GDP per capita is expressed in dollars, at current prices and current PPPs.

Source: OECD Health Data, OECD National Accounts.

Figure 2.9   GDP per capita and life expectancy at birth, 2012

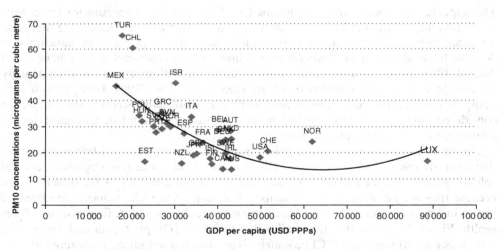

Notes: Air pollution is measured through the concentrations of fine suspended particulates less than 10 microns in diameter (micrograms per cubic metre).
Data are urban population weighted PM10 levels in residential areas of cities with more than 100 000 residents.
GDP per capita is expressed in dollars, at current prices and current PPPs.

Sources: World Bank; OECD 2008; OECD National accounts.

Figure 2.10   GDP per capita and air pollution, 2011

range of countries in the world. These simple correlation results are corroborated by a range of studies using multivariate analysis that control for other factors at the country level (Di Tella and MacCullough, 2004; Di Tella et al., 2010; Helliwell, 2003; Fleche et al., 2011; Boarini et al., 2012) as well as by analysis based on individual-level data highlighting the presence of decreasing marginal returns from income to health status (Furnée et al., 2010).

2.3.1 The Capability Approach

Sen's 'capability approach', which rests on 'a person's capability to have various functioning vectors and to enjoy the corresponding well-being achievements' (Sen, 1985a), is widely recognised as one of the more complete and comprehensive approaches to welfare analysis, in which a plurality of well-being dimensions are considered, the relationships among them are investigated, and through which deprivation and inequality assume a new and clear meaning. In recent years the number of empirical studies based on the capability approach (CA) has been increasing considerably. This section represents an attempt to give an overview of the topics and issues that have been discussed in CA applications, mainly in OECD countries. Due to the notably large number of CA studies, we applied selection criteria to keep this overview limited to certain topics. We review papers that provide empirical applications of the CA framework,[11] focusing on well-being outcomes (rather than inequality or human development or single dimensions of well-being) and referring to the whole population (rather than specific demographic or socioeconomic groups).[12] First, we briefly summarise theoretical issues of the CA framework; then we concentrate on the use of capabilities versus functionings and on the selection of relevant dimensions; and we briefly address measurement and weighting techniques.

Sen's approach offers a broad theoretical framework to assess individual welfare based on the two notions of 'capabilities' and 'functionings'. Functionings describe individuals' aspects of life, what persons are and do. To assess well-being, these functionings usually incorporate several intrinsic values irreducible to each other, such as 'being nourished', 'being in good health', 'being well-sheltered', 'being educated' or 'moving about freely' (Sen, 1992; Kuklys, 2005). While the notion of the capability set is a derived notion, it is central to the whole approach.[13] Capability refers to 'the various combinations of functionings (beings and doings) that the person can achieve. Capability is, thus, a set of vectors of functionings, reflecting the person's freedom to lead one type of life or another . . . to choose from possible livings' (Sen, 1992, p. 40). Capability thus captures not only achievements but also unchosen alternatives; it scans the horizon to notice roads not taken. It tells 'whether one person did have the opportunity of achieving the functioning vector that another actually achieved' (Sen, 1985b). Naturally, there is a link between functionings and capabilities: the opportunities to live a 'good life' are affected by certain attributes of the individual – a starving or uneducated person would have fewer choices than a healthy, educated person. Yet the capabilities approach goes far beyond individual attributes to analyse the role of social environment on human choice and agency: an individual in an open, free society would enjoy a larger set of potential functionings than one in a closed, oppressive society (Robeyns, 2005).

Hence, what mainly characterises the CA with respect to other multidimensional approaches of well-being is that it is not simply a way to enlarge the evaluative well-being to variables other than income, but it is a radically different way to conceive the meaning of well-being, taking into account freedom of choice (Sen, 1985a; Alkire and Sarwar, 2009; Anand et al., 2009; Anand et al., 2011). Quality of life arguably depends not on the mere existence of resources but on what they enable people to do and be, and people's ability to convert resources into a valuable functioning varies in important ways: 'The value of the living standard lies in the living, and not in the possessing of commodities, which has derivative and varying relevance' (Sen, 1987, p. 25). Undoubtedly, the richness of such theoretical argumentation is not easy to translate into practical terms.

2.3.2   Using Functionings and Capabilities to Assess Well-Being: Challenges and Applications

The capability approach is certainly more demanding at a methodological level if compared with more standard or income-centred approaches to well-being; it is also hard to constrain and to manage in the traditional framework of welfare and poverty analysis, if we want to fully preserve its informative and interpretative contents. The challenging character of the capability approach has called its operationalisation into question (Robeyns, 2000; Comim, 2008). An empirical application of the capability approach indeed requires: (1) the choice of the evaluative space (functionings versus capabilities space); (2) a list of relevant functionings and capabilities; (3) a set of indicators related to the selected dimensions of well-being and adequate criteria to measure and represent them; (4) to decide how (and if) aggregate the elementary indicators to obtain an overall evaluation for each single dimension of well-being; and (5) to decide how (and whether) to add up all the dimensions and to reach an overall evaluation of well-being.

While Sen himself has outlined some real advantages in being able to relate the analysis of well-being on the wider information base of a capability set rather than on the space of the functioning achieved, the information requirement increases and the set of available options is not easily or directly observable, since one would have to measure not only the outcome but all the options potentially open to an individual vis-à-vis hypothetical states of the world (Anand et al., 2005, 2009; Anand and van Hees, 2006). This is empirically very challenging and explains why so far most of the existing literature has focused on measuring the functionings space than the capabilities space (see Anand et al., 2005, 2009; and Anand and van Hees, 2006 for notable exceptions). In some cases, however, assessing functionings may be sufficient or even more adequate (Volkert and Schneider, 2011). Fleurbaey (2006) points out that there could be good reasons for a quality-of-life measure to include some achieved functionings, and he provides several reasons for this. The first is related to equality or inclusion: if groups differ systematically in the level of achieved functionings, then one may conclude that the members of those groups did not have access to the same capabilities, unless there are plausible reasons why they would systematically choose differently (Robeyns and van der Veen, 2007; Robeyns, 2003). The second is that for some groups such as the severely disabled, or small children, or people in intensive care, functionings may be the best indicator that we can have. In such cases functionings data alone are feasible.

With reference to the possibility of achieving a consensus about a list of functionings and capabilities to involve in an empirical analysis of well-being, some authors have promoted full-fledged lists of functionings or at least argued for providing a methodology to select such a list (Robeyns, 2005). Nussbaum's (2011, 2006, 2000) list of 'central human capabilities' contains 'life, bodily health, bodily integrity, senses, imagination, and thought, emotions, practical reason, affiliation, (being able to live with concern for) other species, play, control over one's political and material environment'. Nussbaum sees here 'timeless' central human capabilities as general goals that can be specified by different societies in various ways. She considers her list as evolutionary, including various ways of revision depending on how different societies want to specify their central human capabilities. Nussbaum (2009) argues that the existence of a list of domains or central capabilities is important for the critical force of the CA. Although Sen (2004) is not entirely against the use of lists, he has emphasised that a given list may not be helpful, as different purposes may necessitate different lists.

Other authors argue that the list of things people value should reflect people's values and priorities and therefore it should be effectively drawn from deliberative and participative processes (Crocker, 2008). Bottom-up participative procedures have been implemented to empirically derive a list of capabilities (Biggeri et al., 2006; Burchardt and Vizard, 2011).

Leaving aside Nussbaum's top-down high-level list, most scholars have approached the question by focusing on different, often ad hoc selections of functionings, mostly based on data availability (Qizilbash, 2013). Some empirical works focus on a small selection of dimensions, such as the three dimensions in the illustration carried out by Sen (1985a). Alternatively, other empirical applications include a large list of dimensions (Anand et al., 2005; Chiappero-Martinetti, 2000; Klasen, 2000; Robeyns, 2006). Dimensions can be captured by a single indicator or, most frequently, by a range of indicators. A good illustration is Drèze and Sen (2002), which focuses on three dimensions but includes a list of more than 30 indicators.

Alkire (2002) gives an extensive overview of some 40 lists produced by philosophers, psychologists and other social scientists, and reaches a quite surprising conclusion. Despite the large variety of approaches the specific proposals are strikingly similar. This is the case, for instance, for the lists of dimensions that have been proposed for international comparisons by the OECD (2011a) or the European Statistical System (Eurostat, 2011a). All proposals include material consumption and housing quality, health, job market status and leisure, the quality of social interactions and of the natural environment. The consensus is more widespread about the first layer of encompassing dimensions, while it tends to dissipate when one turns to a second layer of more specific dimensions or indicators (Decancq et al., 2015).

The issue of how to choose a set of appropriate indicators for the representation of the manifold dimensions of well-being is obviously related to the availability of statistical data, or to the decision to conduct ad hoc interviews to collect an adequate information set, as well as to the kind of assessment one wants to pursue. The rich informational requirement involved in the capability approach is one of the reasons often advocated to justify the choice of more traditional approaches to poverty and well-being analysis. Most data reflect achieved functionings rather than capabilities, although in some cases information on capabilities may be available directly from household surveys, for example in questions such as: 'Do you have/do x – if you do not is that because you do not want x, or because you are not able to obtain/do x?' (Alkire, 2005). Questions on material deprivation framed in this fashion are, for instance, available in the EU-SILC.

Most studies are based on micro-data collected for reasons different from those for which the research is conducted (that is, secondary data). In most cases the analysis is carried out using household surveys (Anand et al., 2005; Chiappero-Martinetti, 2000; Di Tommaso, 2007; Klasen, 2000) or census data (Roche, 2008). Some other empirical applications are carried out with data tailored on the specific research question that the researcher wants to address (that is, primary data) (Anand and van Hees, 2006; Biggeri et al., 2006; Qizilbash and Clark, 2005).

Moreover, in a multidimensional framework, the question of how and whether to aggregate available statistical information into an aggregate index becomes complex, as it can be conducted on different and/or subsequent levels (see also Chakravarty and Chattopadhyay, Chapter 5 in this *Handbook*; Guio, Chapter 6 in this *Handbook*). First, we could be interested in moving from the space of elementary indicators to the overall evaluation of a given functioning for each unit of analysis; alternatively, the aggregation could involve the whole set of functionings for obtaining an overall picture of the individual or household standard of living; finally, we could be interested in merging the individual well-being assessments into a synthetic index of social multidimensional well-being (Decancq and Lugo, 2013). In the case of aggregation, an additional complication arises, regarding how to trade-off the different dimensions of well-being, that is, how to weigh different functionings and capabilities vis-à-vis each other (Slesnick, 1998). While partial orderings might suffice in some cases, one can safely assume that the more relevant and useful comparisons will involve trade-offs between different dimensions. An aggregation of the functionings/capabilities vector into some summary measure that would allow such trade-offs, or a scheme of weights for that matter, has so far been rather ignored in the literature (Binder, 2014).

Finally, applications in the capability approach make use of a variety of statistical techniques, also depending on the purpose of the analysis. The most common aggregation techniques include: scaling techniques (for example, the HDI), fuzzy set theory (Chiappero-Martinetti, 2000; Qizilbash, 2002; Addabbo et al., 2004; Roche, 2008), multivariate data reduction techniques (Schokkaert and Van Ootegem, 1990; Krishnakumar and Nagar, 2008; Roche, 2008) and the regression approach (Kuklys, 2005; Anand and van Hees, 2006). Additionally, empirical applications generally use partial scaling or stochastic dominance when they opt for a non-aggregation solution (e.g., Brandolini and D'Alessio, 1998; Robeyns, 2006).[14]

2.3.3   Taking into Account Multidimensional Inequalities

Besides uneven distribution of income, there is increasing evidence that inequalities characterise all areas of life, such as social connections, civic engagement, personal security and exposure to environmental pollution (OECD, 2011a). A straightforward approach to take the multidimensionality of well-being into account in an inequality exercise is to consider each dimension separately, that is, to study the evolution of inequality dimension by dimension (examples of this approach are by Atkinson et al., 2002; World Bank, 2005). This method clearly goes beyond a sole focus on incomes and may provide additional insights.

For instance, inequalities due to socioeconomic background are very large when considering people's self-reported health status, regardless of the structures of the health systems of the countries considered (Figure 2.11); a socioeconomic gradient in health status is also evident when looking at objective measures of health status, such as life

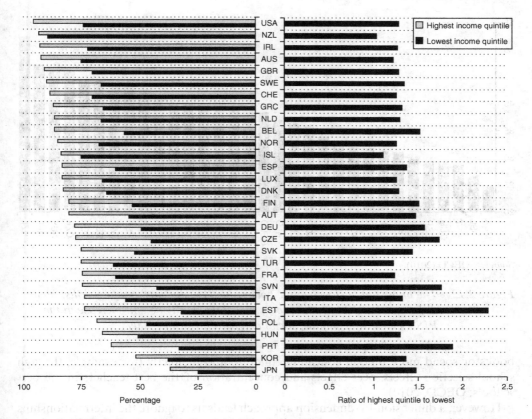

Notes: Values shown in the right-hand panel refer to the ratio between the share of adults in the top income quintile reporting good or very good health, and the corresponding share of adults in the bottom income quintile.
Data refer to 2008 for Turkey; and 2007 for Australia, Japan and New Zealand.
Adults are generally defined as individuals over 15 years old.

Source: OECD Health Data; European Union Statistics on Income and Living Conditions (EU-SILC).

Figure 2.11   *Inequalities in health: adults reporting good or very good health, by income quintile; percentage and ratio of highest to lowest quintile, years around 2009*

expectancy, across people with different education, income or occupation. The reasons for these gradients are many.

As socioeconomic disadvantage grows, people live and work in more difficult circumstances, with harmful effects on their health. In addition, behaviours that are detrimental to health status, such as smoking, excess drinking and poor nutrition, tend to increase with greater socioeconomic disadvantage. Finally, disadvantaged people have greater problems in accessing appropriate health care. Similarly, education is another area where differences in family socioeconomic conditions play a huge role in shaping individuals' educational outcomes (for example, Figure 2.12). The influence of family background on students' competences plays out directly (for example, higher-income parents have more

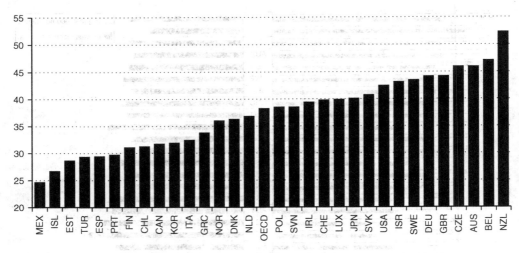

Source: OECD (2010).

Figure 2.12   The impact of socioeconomic background on students' reading skills; point difference in PISA reading score associated with one unit increase in the PISA index of economic, social and cultural status, 2009

books or spend more time in educating children) and indirectly (for example, through school selection effects, peer effects and concentration of the best teachers in the best schools; OECD, 2010).

However, a dimension-by-dimension approach leads us to ignore the interrelationships and possible correlations between the dimensions of well-being. In a multidimensional context two different forms of inequality must be taken into account. The first form is related to the concept of the single-dimensional inequality concerning the spread of the distribution (Kolm, 1977), and is called 'distribution-sensitive inequality'. The second form of inequality, in contrast, is typically multidimensional in nature since it is based on the existing correlation among different components of human development (Atkinson and Bourguignon, 1982), and is called 'association-sensitive inequality'. This latter form of multidimensional inequality is important for two reasons. First, evidence suggests that the various components of well-being are synergistically related to one another (OECD, 2011a; Boarini et al., 2012). When all dimensions are strongly correlated, then higher achievement in one dimension strongly enforces higher achievements in other dimensions, and any one dimension is sufficient for measuring well-being. Conversely, less correlation among dimensions makes multidimensional analysis more informative. Therefore, the degree of association among dimensions clearly has relevance for multidimensional evaluations of societal progress (Seth, 2009). However, proper knowledge about the relationship among dimensions is required, since dimensions could be either substitutes for or complements to each other (Bourguignon and Chakravarty, 2003). Second, the association-sensitive inequality is important from the point of view of policy recommendations. A society where one individual is top-ranked in all dimensions, another second-ranked in all dimensions, and so on, is arguably more unequal than a society with the same distributional profiles in each dimension but where some individuals are top-ranked in some dimensions, and other individuals in other dimensions. To neglect these interrelationships would be to iron out one of the primary motivations for a multidimensional approach to inequality (Decancq and Lugo, 2009).

Both forms of inequality have already been incorporated in the construction of various multidimensional poverty indices (Tsui, 2002; Bourguignon and Chakravarty, 2003) and inequality indices (Tsui, 1995, 1999; Bourguignon, 1999). Gajdos and Weymark (2005) obtain a multidimensional generalised Gini social evaluation function that turns out to be a weighted average of the one-dimensional Gini index of the different dimensions. Seth (2009) proposed a class of HDIs, based on generalised means and equal degree of substitution between any two dimensions, which is sensitive to both forms of multidimensional inequality. The class of indices is applied to the Mexican census data for the year 2000 and it is shown how the ranking of states is altered by association-increasing transfers. Decancq and Lugo (2009) propose two indices for measuring inequality of multidimensional well-being, derived from two underlying social evaluation functions, thought of as multivariate generalisations of the Gini coefficient, in which both the levels and the position of individuals in the overall distribution matter for the social evaluation. These functions aggregate both across the dimensions of well-being and across individuals. The two social evaluation functions differ only with respect to the sequencing of aggregations. The authors illustrate both indices using Russian household data between 1995 and 2005 for four dimensions of well-being (that is, expenditure, health, schooling and housing quality) and show that the sequencing of both aggregations turns out to be essential in terms of levels of inequality.

2.4 TO AGGREGATE OR NOT?

Faced with a 'large and eclectic dashboard' (Stiglitz et al., 2009, p. 62), there is an understandable desire to reduce the dimensionality to form a single composite index. Indeed, one of the reasons why GDP per capita has held the throne for so long despite its limitations as a welfare metric is the fact that it allows for monitoring nations' economic well-being through one single headline number. Parsimony matters, because a single headline indicator is easier to interpret than dashboards of indicators expressed in different units. This is why headline numbers are so attractive. Composite indices are an appealing tool for summarising complex information, but they can also be too simplistic and reductive.

By summarising into one number a multiplicity of components, composite indices make it possible to assess overall well-being at a point in time as well as its progress over time. However, they rely on several assumptions and their validity and robustness is hence conditional upon the soundness of these assumptions. Assumptions underlying the construction of composite indices include: the underlying theoretical framework and the structure of the index (nesting, number of dimensions, number of subdimensions, and so on); the imputation methods used for missing data; the normalisation technique applied to each indicator; and the choice of weights and aggregation techniques (OECD, 2008; Ravallion, 2011).

An early contribution was the Physical Quality of Life Index (Morris, 1979), which is a weighted average of literacy, infant mortality and life expectancy. Along similar lines, the most famous example is now the Human Development Index (HDI) proposed by the United Nation Development Programme (UNDP) in 1990. To balance comparisons between countries based on GDP per capita at purchasing power parity (PPP), the UNDP extended the analysis to health and educational achievement, regarded as two major aspects of development and progress. Health outcomes are measured in terms of life expectancy at birth, in years. Educational achievement is measured through mean of years of schooling for adults aged 25 years, and expected years of schooling for children of school-entering age. The two sub-indices are combined into an education index using the arithmetic mean. These three dimensions – economic prosperity (GDP), health (life expectancy) and education – are attributed equal importance in the composite index.

Once dimensions have been selected, the question is how to aggregate different metrics. The HDI method is based on rescaling each dimension relative to its most likely range of variation. Maximum and minimum values for life expectancy are set at 85 and 20 years. The educational index is scaled along the full range available for a percentage, namely [0; 100]. Finally, GDP per capita at PPP (in log) is scaled relatively to a minimum of $100 and a maximum of $75 000. For countries whose GDP per capita exceeds $75 000, their GDP index is set to 1.[15]

The HDI index leads to a country ranking that differs (sometimes significantly) from that based on GDP. For instance, in 2013, the United States of America (USA) had the second-highest GDP per capita among OECD countries, but stood in fifth position in terms of HDI. Conversely, Austria jumped from twentieth to seventh place. While differences in HDI between developed countries are usually small, the HDI provides substantial changes in international ranking for middle- and low-income countries: countries such as Madagascar, Ecuador and Georgia improve their rank by more than 20 in the HDI comparison.[16]

In a similar spirit to the HDI, the Multidimensional Poverty Index (MPI) was developed by Alkire and Santos (2010). The authors chose three dimensions and ten components for the MPI: two for health (malnutrition and child mortality), two for education (years of schooling and school enrolment), and six aiming to capture 'living standards' (including both access to services and proxies for household wealth). Keeping with the HDI, the three headings of the MDI (health, education and living standards) are weighted equally to form the composite index. According to the MDI, a household is identified as being poor if it is deprived across at least 30 per cent of the weighted indicators. While the HDI uses aggregate country-level data, the MPI uses household-level data, which are then aggregated to the country level.[17]

The OECD's Better Life Index (www.oecdbetterlifeindex.org), developed by the organisation on the occasion of its 50th anniversary, is an interactive composite index. The Better Life Index extends the scope of previous multidimensional indexes of well-being, by including 11 dimensions (housing, income, jobs, community, education, civic engagement, environment, health, work–life balance, safety and life satisfaction) measured through 24 indicators. Both objective measures (for example, life expectancy) and subjective measures (for example, life satisfaction) are considered. The tool has been designed to involve people in the discussion on well-being and, through this process, to learn what matters the most to them. This interactive web-based tool enables citizens to compare well-being across countries by giving their own weight to each of the 11 dimensions explored in the OECD well-being framework. The web application allows users to see how countries' average achievements compare, based on the user's own personal priorities in life, and enables users to share their index and choices of weights with other people in their networks, as well as with the OECD. The Better Life Index is regularly updated and enhanced. Since its creation, the tool has been enriched with additional indicators and key measures on inequalities and gender differences.

Since its launch in May 2011, the Better Life Index has attracted more than six million visitors from just about every country on the planet and has received more than 13 million page views. More than 90 000 users have shared their indexes with the OECD, generating information on the importance that users attach to various life dimensions and on how these preferences differ across countries and the demographic characteristics of users. The feedback gathered from these users shows that, on average, life satisfaction, health status and education are the dimensions deemed most important, although all dimensions are found to resonate with people's sense of well-being.

Although intrinsic to the concept of composite indicators, the issue of weighting (both headings or dimensions, and indicators) has for a long time been underestimated in the construction of such aggregate measures (Decancq and Lugo, 2013; Hagerty and Land, 2007). There are typically two levels at which weights can be defined in composite indices. First there are the (typically equal) weights on the headline components (for example, education, health and income in the HDI), which are normally explicit. These headline components are, however, functions of one or more primary variables (for example, mean of years of schooling for adults aged 25 years, and expected years of schooling for children of school-entering age in the education component of the HDI). This is the second level at which weights can be defined, and it is here that weights are generally unknown and the trade-offs that they embed are difficult to determine (Ravallion, 2011).[18]

Little is told about the uncertainties that exist about the weights and the robustness tests performed, even though country ranking is likely to change under different weights and functional aggregation forms. The most common method of testing robustness is to calculate the correlation coefficients between alternative versions of the composite index, such as obtained by changing the weights. Alkire et al. (2010) provide correlation coefficients between various MPIs obtained by varying the weights, with 50 per cent weight on one of the deprivations, and 25 per cent on each of the other two (instead of one-third on each). The correlation coefficients are all above 0.95, and the authors conclude that the index is 'quite robust to the particular selection of weights' (Alkire et al., 2010, p. 4). However, usually little information is given to the users to assess properly the sensitivity of these indices to changes in weights. One notable exception to composite indices that set weights ad hoc is the interactive website of the OECD Better Life Index (BLI), which allows users to vary the weights of the index and immediately gives the corresponding country rankings.[19]

2.5   SUBJECTIVE APPROACHES TO WELL-BEING

Besides gathering together various objective indicators of living conditions, an alternative method that attempts to capture different meaningful well-being dimensions consists of directly measuring the quality of life as experienced by agents. After all, if well-being has to do with the kind of life that one aspires to live, then overall satisfaction with life as a whole should be relevant (Schokkaert, 2007).

The interest of economists, since the classics, embraced questions on life satisfaction and its drivers. The value of the investigation of the wealth–happiness nexus was also recognised, among others, by Malthus (1798), Marshall (1890 [1947]), Veblen (1899) and, more recently, Dusenberry (1949) and Hirsch (1976). However, until more recent times, in the absence of ample and multi-country empirical data, the debate remained confined within the realms of philosophy and the history of economic thought.[20] The recent availability of cross-sectional and longitudinal survey data on life satisfaction in a large number of countries gave researchers the opportunity to verify empirically (and not just to assume) what matters for individuals and what policy makers should take into account when trying to promote personal and societal well-being.

While measures of subjective well-being (SWB) may not be appropriate as a single sufficient measure of quality of life (Fleurbaey and Blanchet, 2014), they could have many roles in quality-of-life measures: 'Happiness is not all that matters, but first of all, it does matter (and that is important), and second, it can often provide useful evidence on whether or not we are achieving our objectives in general' (Sen, 2008).[21] First, evaluative data on subjective well-being might be conceived of as one dimension of quality of life, to be explored alongside other important dimensions such as being healthy, being well nourished, and working. If two people shared the same resources, but only one was joyful and fulfilled, while the other was miserable, this could be important to notice. Second, it has been argued that human perception is fundamental to understanding an individual's well-being, as the only person who knows whether someone is feeling well is that person themselves (Layard, 2005): in other words, 'the best way to measure whether someone feels happy or satisfied is to ask them' (NEF, 2011). Another argument for measuring subjective well-being is that paternalism can be avoided, as individuals are asked about their views about their own well-being which allows them to make their own assessment of it. This is in contrast to the checklist compiled by researchers and policy makers (Waldron, 2010). Aware of the importance of supplementing objective metrics with subjective measures, the Stiglitz–Sen–Fitoussi Commission put subjective well-being into the limelight as a possible supplement to traditional measures of development such as GDP ('Measures of subjective well-being provide key information about people's quality of life'; Stiglitz et al., 2009).

Empirical studies on subjective well-being pose a series of methodological problems that cannot be easily solved. First of all, how should 'happiness' be measured? Usually, subjective well-being is measured on the basis of people's self-assessment. Yet there are different aspects considered in the indicators of SWB:[22] (1) life satisfaction, defined as the overall judgement people make regarding their life at a particular point in time; and (2) hedonic experience of positive or negative affects, conceived of as the flow of positive or negative emotions.

The first aspect, life satisfaction, is usually measured by asking people to self-assess their satisfaction with life in general, or relative to some specific area (job, health, and so on), ordering the answers on the basis of a 0–10 Likert scale. The second aspect, hedonic experience, is measured on the basis of a person's report of an event, at the time or shortly afterwards. These two points of view measure different aspects of SWB and hence are likely to produce different empirical evidence. For instance, respondents' income level seems to matter more to their answers to life satisfaction questions than it does to their answers to questions designed to gauge the innate character component of happiness (affect), as gauged by questions such as 'How many times did you smile yesterday?' (Deaton and Kahneman, 2010). In contrast, psychosocial wealth is more strongly correlated with emotional well-being than life satisfaction. Specifically, supportive social relationships are strongly tied to positive feelings, and greater autonomy is associated with less negative feelings; these patterns hold across international samples (Diener al., 2010; Tay and Diener, 2011). Compared with everyday emotional experiences, cognitive evaluations that invite people to think about whether they are living the 'best possible' life may be influenced more by material consumption (Oishi and Schimmack, 2010). Thus, there may not be one single ingredient to happiness.

Second, SWB questions are vulnerable to order bias: that is, where they are placed in a survey. People will respond differently to an open-ended happiness question that is at the beginning of a survey than to one that is framed or biased by the questions posed beforehand, such as those about whether income is sufficient or the quality of their job. Bias in answers to happiness surveys can also result from unobserved personality traits and related errors that affect how the same individuals answer a range of questions. This latter source of bias is particularly troublesome in cross-country studies, where inference could be biased by cultural traits (for example, it may be considered polite and correct in a given culture to declare oneself always satisfied; while in another, people may tend to overcomplain) and language differences (OECD, 2012).[23]

2.5.1 What Message Does Life Satisfaction Convey when Compared to Income?

Despite potential methodological pitfalls, cross-sections of large samples across countries find remarkably consistent patterns in SWB measures. In particular, the relation between life satisfaction and income has been extensively studied. A few clear facts are as follows.

There are large differences in life satisfaction across countries of the world (Deaton, 2008, 2011; Stevenson and Wolfers, 2008; Sacks et al., 2010; Inglehart et al., 2008; Hagerty and Veenhoven, 2003).[24] Part of these differences stem from differences in material standards and aspects of quality of life such as social connectedness, access to employment, health, environmental quality and political freedom (see OECD, 2011a, for a review). Average national income, measured by GDP per capita, is positively associated to life satisfaction, but this relationship is non-linear (Figure 2.13). This suggests that an increase in GDP per capita in a poor country is likely to bring a greater (absolute) improvement in the average life satisfaction than the same increase in GDP per capita in a richer country.[25]

There is substantial variation in subjective well-being within countries too. While some countries have relatively equal distribution of life satisfaction (for example, in much of Western Europe, Israel, Japan and New Zealand) other countries display much greater variance (OECD, 2011a). The difference in inequality between the most equal country (the Netherlands) and the least equal ones (Chile, the Slovak Republic and Portugal) is equal in size to the gap in average life satisfaction between the highest and lowest country in the OECD (Figure 2.14). Part of the within-country variance in life satisfaction is due to socioeconomic differences (Blanchflower and Oswald, 2004; Clark and Oswald, 1996; Diener, 1984; Diener et al., 1993; Diener and Biswas-Diener, 2002; Diener and Oishi, 2000; Dolan et al., 2008; Duncan, 1975; Easterlin, 1974; Easterlin and Angelescu, 2009;

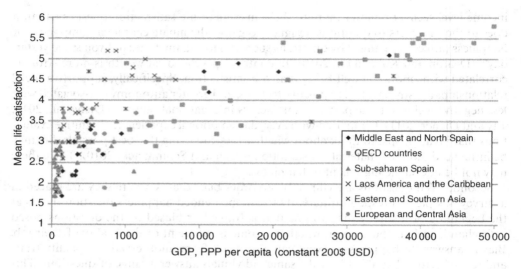

Note: The Cantril ladder is measured on a scale from 0 to 10.

Source: OECD calculations based on Gallup World Poll and World Bank (2011).

Figure 2.13   Link between life satisfaction and GDP per capita, by regions, 2011 (Cantril ladder, mean value)

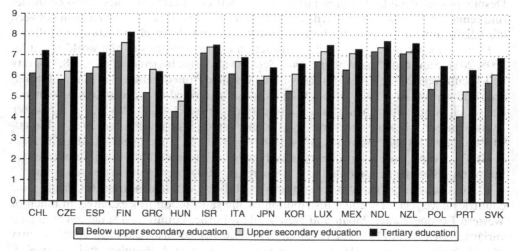

Source: Gallup World Poll.

Figure 2.14   Life satisfaction across people with different education, 2010

Frey and Stutzer, 2002b; Gardner and Oswald, 2001, 2007; Hagerty, 2000; Schyns, 2002). Among the countries shown here, Portugal, Spain, Slovenia and Hungary have particularly large gaps in life satisfaction between people with and without tertiary education. This is also true in many of the non-OECD countries observed, and in particular in South Africa and Indonesia.

The obvious omission from the set of stylised facts discussed above is how the relationship between GDP and national subjective well-being changes over time. The lack of a strong time-series correlation between changes in average income and changes in measures of subjective well-being in wealthy countries, combined with the existence of a strong correlation between the same two measures at the individual level, was noted by Richard Easterlin (1974), and is generally referred to as the 'Easterlin paradox'. The Easterlin paradox argues that a higher rise in personal income leads to higher subjective well-being for that person, but that a rise in average incomes for a country does not give rise to a corresponding increase in the country's average subjective well-being. Figure 2.15 shows that in a number of OECD countries life satisfaction has not increased substantially in the past 40 years, providing support to the Easterlin paradox.

Many explanations have been put forward to explain the Easterlin paradox. The first is that income is an important determinant of well-being until basic needs are met, then other factors become more significant, such as social capital and good relations (Veenhoven, 1991; Lane, 2000). This implies that, at low per capita income levels, small improvements make a big difference in terms of average country life satisfaction; while at high income levels, the same changes have a negligible impact. This 'subsistence level' or satiation point could be as low as US$10 000 per annum (as reported in McMahon, 2006) or as high as US$30 000 per annum (as reported by Proto and Rustichini, 2013). The proposition of the satiation point is also supported by Clark et al. (2008) and Frey and Stutzer (2002a) and seems in line with the results of the literature on happiness as reported in Boarini et al. (2006), Bruni and Porta (2005), Layard (2005), Schokkaert (2007) and others.

The second explanation is that people's aspirations adjust to the rise in income, offsetting the increase in material well-being. That means that people tend to adapt to changes in their environment (Easterlin, 2002; Frey and Stutzer, 2002b). This explanation reconciles evidence on the concave instantaneous utility functions and the insignificance of the income effect of happiness in the long run. From an empirical point of view hedonic adaptation is calculated by testing whether the sum of current and lagged (personal or household) income coefficients in a life satisfaction regression are significantly different from zero. When the null hypothesis is not rejected we have evidence of full adaptation; that is, current (generally positive) and lagged (generally negative) income effects compensate each other. From a theoretical point of view this implies that the concave utility function assumption does hold in a given instant of time, but not across time. Frey and Stutzer (2000) illustrate this concept by showing that, with a given increase in income, we move along the shape of the utility function in the current period (a positive and significant non-linear effect), but later on, the monetary achievement triggers a rise in expectations which causes a downshift of the instantaneous utility curve. If this dynamic is repeated in time and the different observed combinations of income and utility are matched at given time intervals, we may end up having a flatter or flat relationship, which is consistent with the Easterlin paradox.

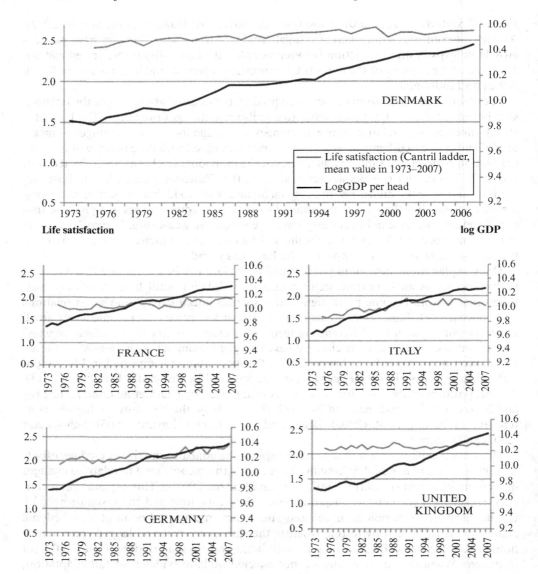

Notes: Life satisfaction refers to the mean value on the Cantril ladder on a scale from 0 to 10. GDP per capita is measured in US dollars, constant prices, constant PPPs.

Source: OECD calculations based on the Eurobarometer and the OECD National Accounts.

Figure 2.15   *Life satisfaction and log of GDP per head trends in selected OECD countries, 1973–2007*

The third explanation is that individuals do not look just at their own income, but also compare it with the average income of their reference group.[26] Competition with others may create 'treadmill effects' up to the extreme case of fully relative preferences where only relative and not absolute income matters. In such a context, an increase in personal income, paralleled by an equal increase in income of the entire reference group, would not affect individual life satisfaction. This is equivalent to saying that, with competition on income considered as a zero sum game, the dominance of the relative income effect may paradoxically eliminate any significant impact of a positive change in personal income (Frank, 2005; Layard, 2005).[27] Writings on comparisons include Hagerty (2000), Luttmer (2005), Fliessbach et al. (2007), Clark and Senik (2010), Daly et al. (2010) and Layard (2010).

The debate on the Easterlin paradox, however, is still open. For instance, Castriota (2006) observes that the paradox does not apply to Italy when using Eurobarometer data for the last decade. More recently, the paradox has been questioned by Stevenson and Wolfers (2008), who analyse multiple rich datasets including the USA, the EU and developing countries, spanning in some cases to several decades. They claim that data do not show any evidence of the existence of a point of satiation, and find a positive link between growing wealth and life satisfaction, in both rich and poor countries. Similarly, Sacks et al. (2010) find that life satisfaction increases in line with increase in the log of per capita GDP. At the current state of empirical data, it is difficult to reject any hypothesis on statistical grounds with respect to whether no relationship or a positive relationship between income and subjective well-being over time is proposed. Another position that can be taken is to accept that there is no clear-cut trend, positive or negative, in self-reported subjective well-being over periods of 20 to 30 years in rich countries. Instead, the results indicate that there is more to subjective well-being than just income.

2.5.2   Non-Financial Correlates of Life Satisfaction

Research combining the use of individual and societal variables stresses the importance of some key non-financial correlates of life satisfaction. Particular attention has been paid to the relationship between life satisfaction and unemployment. Unemployment first of all reduces the individual well-being of those personally affected.[28] In their seminal work on the United Kingdom, Clark and Oswald (1994, p. 655) summarise their results as follows: 'Joblessness depresses well-being more than any other single characteristic including important negative ones such as divorce and separation'. For Germany, based on individual panel data, Winkelmann and Winkelmann (1998) find a negative effect of personal unemployment on life satisfaction that would require a sevenfold increase in income to compensate. Importantly, in these two analyses, indirect effects (such as income losses) that may – but need not – accompany personal unemployment are kept constant. Being unemployed therefore has costs over and above the potential decrease in the material living standard (Stutzer and Frey, 2010).

Other non-financial correlates of life satisfaction include family relationships (Diener, 2000); health and education (Frey and Stutzer, 2002b; Ross and Van Willigen, 1997; Van Praag et al., 2003); social ties and institutional quality (Helliwell, 2003); and income inequality (Alesina et al., 2001; Alois, 2014). These research findings also suggest that the improvement in individuals' well-being due to these factors generally exceeds that associated to the financial gain that they may bring to individuals. In a number of cases, however, the non-financial correlates of subjective well-being identified by these studies are themselves significantly correlated to GDP per capita.

Some correlates seem to be universally associated to life satisfaction, while other variables are more strongly associated with life satisfaction in some cultures than in others (Tov and Diener, 2013). As might be expected, fulfilling basic needs for food, shelter and safety, and having socially supportive relationships, are associated with greater life satisfaction across various demographic groups (Diener et al., 2010) and regions of the world (Tay and Diener, 2011). In addition, psychological needs – such as competence (mastery of important skills), and autonomy or personal freedom – are also associated with greater life satisfaction in cross-cultural samples (Diener et al., 2010; Sheldon et al., 2011; Tay and Diener, 2011). On the contrary, self-esteem and sense of personal freedom correlate more strongly with life satisfaction in European and North American countries (Diener and Diener, 1995; Oishi et al., 1999) than in Asian or Latin American countries. In contrast, having harmonious relationships and spending time with loved ones are more strongly associated with life satisfaction and positive emotions for Asians and Latin Americans compared with Europeans and North Americans (Kwan et al., 1997; Oishi et al., 1999).

2.6   GDP AND BEYOND: THE SUSTAINABILITY ANGLE[29]

2.6.1   The Sustainable Development Paradigm and the Link with Moving Beyond GDP

One important research stream within the 'GDP and beyond' agenda has focused on the question of sustainability. By 'sustainability' people usually refer to the idea that the well-being levels currently enjoyed by the current generations can be sustained over time thanks to the preservation of various forms of capital that yield well-being today (OECD, 2013b). This definition is grounded in the seminal UN-sponsored Brundtland Report (World Commission on Environment and Development, 1987) at the origin of the sustainable development paradigm. More specifically, sustainable development was defined as: 'development that meets the needs of the present without compromising the ability of future generations to meet their own needs'. Needs were described as being 'socially and culturally determined', and development referred to progress towards a wide range of economic and social goals. The report identified three pillars of sustainable development: the environmental, the economic and the social.

Since the publication of the Brundtland Report, many different approaches to measuring sustainable development have been developed (see, e.g., Stiglitz et al., 2009; United Nations, 2009, 2014, for reviews). These approaches have in common the idea that sustainability requires managing resources or capital stocks; however, they can differ greatly when it comes to the practical measures of these resources and what this implies for their management. These approaches include:

- Adjusted or 'green' GDP measures. These measures take GDP as a starting point and include various 'corrections' such as subtractions for aspects of consumption that do not contribute positively to welfare (for example, congestion) or that cause damage to the environment (for example, greenhouse gas emissions) or, more rarely, additions to reflect the value of non-market activities (for example, leisure). Nordhaus and Tobin's (1973) Measure of Economic Welfare provided one of the early examples of this approach, focused on people's welfare; and Daly and Cobb's (1989) Index of Sustainable Economic Welfare, which includes natural assets, and deductions for environmental damage, is another application of the same approach.

- Total wealth and savings measures. Like the former measures, total wealth and saving measures start from GDP but consider whether the capital stocks that underpin current economic consumption are being adequately maintained over time. Thus, the sustainability of economic outcomes over time is the main focus. Examples in this category include Nordhaus and Tobin's Sustainable Measure of Economic Welfare (SMEW), and the more recent UN University International Human Dimensions Programme (UNU-IHDP) and UN Environment Programme (UNEP) *Inclusive Wealth Report 2012*. The World Bank's (2006, 2011) concept of Adjusted Net Savings (ANS) also belongs to this category; this approach explores the annual flows relevant to the maintenance of the 'total wealth of a country', focusing on the level of investment (or savings) necessary to keep pace with the current consumption of resources. ANS equal the sum of SNA monetary measures of investment in produced capital (such as machinery and equipment), human capital (expenditures on education) and knowledge capital (research and development expenditures); monetary estimates of the depreciation or degradation of natural capital are then subtracted from these to produce an estimate of 'net' (or genuine) national savings.

- Footprint measures. Footprints focus on consumption of the natural resource component of total wealth, and whether this consumption is occurring at a sustainable rate, relative to the total stocks of resources that are available. The best-known indicators in this group are the Global Footprint Network's National Footprint Accounts (e.g., Global Footprint Network, 2010; Borucke et al., 2013). One feature of the footprint approach is that it captures the 'elsewhere' dimension of sustainability, by directly examining the extent to which countries' demands for biocapacity exceed what is available to them nationally. Countries with greater biocapacity than footprints are considered to be in a state of 'surplus', whilst countries with footprints larger than their available biocapacity are in a state of 'ecological overshoot'.

- Other composite indices. These often combine physical (rather than monetary) indicators about current well-being and levels of consumption. For example, the New Economics Foundation's Happy Planet Index (NEF, 2012) combines information about life expectancy, life satisfaction and ecological footprint, to estimate the 'ecological efficiency' with which current well-being is generated. Similarly, Van der Kerk and Manuel's (2012) Sustainable Society Index (SSI) combines measures of human well-being, environmental well-being and economic well-being. The SSI has a total of 21 indicators grouped under eight different categories, to explore the evolution of three different types of well-being between 2006 and 2012 in 151 countries; an aggregate overall SSI score is also available.

- Dashboards or sets of indicators. At the national level, many countries have adopted sustainable development indicator sets that cover a wide range of topics, using a 'dashboard' approach; that is, without aggregation either within or across domains. For example, the Swiss Federal Statistical Office's (2013) MONET framework includes 17 key indicators, covering current well-being and its distribution, the efficiency of resource and energy use, and the human, financial and natural resources left to future generations. Statistics New Zealand (2008) adopted a similar approach, with four broad indicator groups, 15 topics and 85 indicators overall. The United Kingdom Government's Department for Environment, Food and Rural Affairs (DEFRA, 2010) developed a National Indicator Suite with 68 indicators, ranging from greenhouse gas emissions, natural resources and waste, through to social measures such as crime and community participation, employment and poverty, and education. The monitoring framework developed for the EU Sustainable Development Strategy (Eurostat, 2009b, 2011b) similarly includes ten headline indicators ranging from socioeconomic development (GDP growth) to official development assistance, sustainable transport, good governance, and climate change and energy.

These approaches provide a very different picture of sustainability among different countries, suggesting that the actual method used to measure sustainability matters a great deal. In particular the largest source of differences can be found between the approaches that emphasise environmental resource consumption (for instance, the Ecological Footprint and the Happy Planet Index, where the richest countries perform the most poorly), and those measures that emphasise investment in economic sustainability (for instance, the Adjusted Net Savings and the Inclusive Wealth estimates where the richest countries perform relatively well; see Neumayer, 2012). A pitfall of the majority of these approaches is that they do not offer any direct assessments of social aspects of sustainability, mainly because of lack of adequate indicators.

Existing approaches to sustainable development also differ widely in the extent to which they make a conceptual distinction between needs 'here and now', 'later' and 'elsewhere', as emphasised by the UNECE–Eurostat–OECD Task Force (United Nations, 2014). 'Here and now' refers to the needs of present generations; 'later' to the needs of future generations; and 'elsewhere' to the needs of people in other countries – thus addressing the issue of transboundary impacts (both now and in the future). Sustainable development dashboards often blend measures of current consumption and needs with measures of resource management that are more future-oriented. Many sustainable development approaches are restricted to measuring sustainability at the national level (for example, Inclusive Wealth, Adjusted Net Savings and many dashboard approaches) which makes it more difficult to incorporate transboundary and global issues. Footprint measures, on the other hand, can be used to assess whether a country's consumption outpaces its national supply of resources, thus indicating the pressure that the country exerts on resources outside its national boundaries.

2.6.2   Conceptual Foundations of Measures of Sustainability: The Capital Approach

Since the Brundtland Report and its many practical interpretations, many scholars have reframed the sustainability question by highlighting the need to make clear at the outset the issue of 'what to sustain' (see, e.g., Neumayer, 2012; Fitoussi and Stiglitz, 2013; Fleurbaey and Blanchet, 2014). Against this background, it is important to distinguish between the specification of the goals that are to be achieved (the 'what') and the specification of what is required to achieve those goals in a sustainable or lasting way (the 'how'). While some of the approaches discussed above conflate the two (for example, the Happy Planet Index), scholars' approaches (usually those who recommend a dashboard of indicators, for example, the joint UNECE–OECD–Eurostat Task Force for Measuring Sustainable Development) set instead a clear measurement boundary between the levels of well-being that should be maintained over time and the means needed to achieve this.

Even when this distinction is clearly made, the measurement of the 'what to sustain' and the 'how to sustain' is very challenging. The 'what', for instance, is bound to a normative judgement that inherently depends on what future generations may wish to achieve, which can of course be different from what matters to current generations (in terms of both levels and composition). A further complication arises from the fact that there is lot of uncertainty about the future state of the world, and even if we have perfect information and understanding of the 'production function' of each well-being outcome today, which is far from being the case, there will be unpredictable shocks. This uncertainty introduces a new type of normative judgement which was not present in the case of well-being evaluation today: that is, judgements on whether to focus on low-probability events that could lead to large changes in the well-being achievements in the future, or high-probability cases associated to smaller changes in well-being outcomes. All this implies that, as future well-being outcomes cannot be predicted with confidence, the assessment of the sustainability of current well-being will need to be based on observations of the relevant drivers. This notion of relevant drivers lies at the core of the capital approach that underpins most of the approaches to measuring sustainability of well-being, reviewed in the previous section.

Well-being drivers are of many types, and they vary depending on the specific well-being dimension considered. The determinants of the well-being achievement of an individual at a distant future point (for example, future health) include other types of the individual's well-being achievements that cumulate over time (for example, future skills), as well as other factors such as individual characteristics, contextual factors and factors 'actionable' by humans. Therefore capital stocks are one of the important drivers of well-being over time, although they are not the only relevant determinants of it.

Different types of capital have in common the fact of building up over time (through investment and depreciation) and of being subject to possible rapid and irreversible changes. These capital variables are the link between the present and the future; through them, the choice made by one generation may be expected to influence the opportunities available to the next generation. The so-called 'capital approach' usually includes capitals that are conventionally labelled as economic, natural, human and social capitals (see OECD, 2013b for a discussion of these four types of capital as well as possible indicators measuring them). By highlighting how human activities and behaviours impact on the resources that will be available to future generations, the capital approach can 'be used by nations to guide their investment strategies for sustainability' (UNU-IDHP and UNEP, 2012).

2.6.3   Practical Measurement Issues Raised by the Capital Approach

A limited understanding of how stocks of resources generate well-being over time and how these stocks interact with non-capital drivers of well-being

While attractive in theory, the practical implementation of the capital approach raises a number of issues. One is that although research into the drivers of different well-being outcomes is reasonably well advanced in some domains (for example, economic well-being or physical health), in other aspects (for example, mental health, personal security) detailed examination of drivers remains underdeveloped. In particular, there is not always a clear distinction between drivers of well-being that can be seen as a form of capital, and drivers of well-being that do not belong to this category (for instance, trust is sometimes considered as a well-being outcome in itself, but also as a component of social capital). Similarly, not very much is known about how drivers interact with one another to produce multiple well-being outcomes; partly because in many cases outcomes are examined in isolation rather than jointly. Therefore, in practice, even if there is agreement on what has to be sustained over time (namely, what are the well-being outcomes that would be worthwhile ensuring to future generations), we do not have the full set of knowledge that tells us why well-being evolves in such and such direction. Developing such knowledge is therefore a critical future research agenda.

Assumptions on substitutability of stocks are controversial

The other difficulty is related to the concrete use of the capital approach to develop an explicit test for judging the sustainability of a nation's economic development. For instance, some institutions have used this approach and considered a country's development path as not sustainable when it has involved declining per capita levels of total wealth over time (e.g., World Bank, 2006, 2011; UNU-IHDP and UNEP, 2012). To do that, however, all capital stocks must be valued according to a common unit (for example, money) and then aggregated into a measure of total wealth, which requires making the assumption that these stocks are substitutable to some degree (so-called 'weak sustainability'). While this process of valuation and aggregation makes the trade-offs inherent in managing resources explicit, and thus possibly subject to a democratic debate, it has also the shortcoming of sometimes making heroic assumptions on the future well-being value (that is, the future well-being returns that should compound all well-being costs and benefits) of the different capital stocks. These assumptions do not only include normative judgements about views of a good life, but also also include less subjective factors such as productivity improvements and shocks to the system.

If, as many believe (see below), substitutability is less than perfect, assessing sustainability through total aggregated wealth could hide unsustainable imbalances across the different stocks of resources for well-being. For example, Rockström et al. (2009) identified nine 'planetary boundaries' which, if crossed, could lead to important natural subsystems shifting into a new state, with 'deleterious or potentially even disastrous consequences for humans'. Rockström et al. further estimate that three of these boundaries – those relating to biodiversity loss, climate change and human interference with the nitrogen cycle – have already been transgressed.

In practice, most approaches to sustainability assessment assume limited rather than perfect substitutability (UNU-IHDP and UNEP, 2012; OECD, 2011b; Heal, 2011). This in turn suggests that some, although not necessarily all, capital stocks may need to be maintained at some critical level for a system to remain 'sustainable'. Limits to substitutability are most frequently raised with respect to biodiversity and ecosystems (Heal, 2011) but they potentially apply to other resources such as human and social capital (United Nations, 2009) as well. Imperfect substitutability is not necessarily in contradiction with monetisation of stocks, which can prove relevant for comparing the value of different capital stocks. Imperfect substitutability however implies that the sometimes standard definition of sustainability adopted by some approaches – for example, maintaining a country's per capita total capital base – is not sufficient. Rather, a more complex assessment is required: one that examines both total asset value (where valuations based on a common unit are feasible), and the values of individual resources.

In these conditions the sustainability of well-being can only be assessed through a comprehensive dashboard of indicators, measured in different – and not necessarily comparable – units. This is indeed the first recommendation of the Stiglitz–Sen–Fitoussi's commission on sustainability.[30] A dashboard of indicators is meant to act as a signalling device, pointing to specific problematic areas where policy makers should focus. Declining per capita stocks of capital in any single area sends a warning, irrespective of the trend of total resources. Further empirical research should focus on identifying where the limits to substitutability lie, right across the range of capital inputs for well-being. These limits are currently most studied and understood for the environment, where thresholds and non-linear effects are the most apparent and considered by some as potentially catastrophic (Rockström et al., 2009). However, from a larger well-being perspective, human, economic and social capital cannot be fully substituted for one another, and it would be important to gather sufficient empirical evidence that quantifies the magnitude of these trade-offs and the actions needed to conform them.

Measuring sustainability beyond capital stocks

Finally, changing future circumstances could alter both how stocks are used to produce well-being and the efficiency with which well-being outcomes are generated. Preserving the current stock of resources for future generations may be insufficient to sustain well-being if demand on resources grows, or if efficiency of resource use declines. Physical measures of stock levels therefore need to be complemented with indicators that can reflect pressure[31] on resources, and the efficiency[32] with which resources can be converted to well-being.

There are a variety of ways in which resource productivity or efficiency can be measured. Typically, measures involve comparing different capital flows; so, for example, in economic productivity terms, the flow of GDP might be compared to the flow of carbon emissions. However, human and social capitals are not 'consumed' to produce well-being in quite the same manner that natural and economic resources are typically consumed. Although both human and social capital can deteriorate over time (for example, through neglect), in some cases using knowledge and skills may strengthen them. Efficiency or productivity as applied to human and social capital may therefore be best conceived in terms of returns on investment (or well-being impact), rather than returns to 'consumption' per se (for example, how higher educational attainment leads to higher economic and social outcomes).

The Ecological Footprint provides an example of efficiency measure. This is used in the Human Development Report (2013), and in the Happy Planet Index (2012), albeit in relation to only a limited set of well-being outcomes. To generate an efficiency measure such as the Happy Planet Index, well-being outcomes are compared to the Ecological Footprint required to achieve them. Such measures show how efficiently environmental 'consumption' delivers returns to well-being. Monitoring these measures over time could indicate whether technological advancement, coupled with changing lifestyles and living standards, is leading to greater or worse efficiency of resource use.

Although the sustainability literature includes many examples that implicitly link capital flows and different types of well-being outcomes, there are no commonly accepted international measures of efficiency. Productivity or efficiency measures would be inadequate as sustainability measures in isolation, because they give little indication of whether overall resource stocks are being maintained. Nonetheless, efficiency measures can complement stocks by providing more immediate policy signals about how effectively resources are being put to use.

Sustainability as a global issue

The global nature of some forms of capital, and the transboundary impacts that one country can have on the resources of others, means that sustainability cannot be monitored only at the national level. However, most of the existing approaches measuring sustainability ignore its global dimension (OECD, 2013b; World Bank, 2006, 2011; and the Inclusive Wealth Report, UNU-IHDP and UNEP, 2012). Global factors that should be included in sustainability assessment pertain to two distinct categories of resources:

- Shared capital: that is, capital assets without clearly demarked national boundaries. Natural capital in particular consists of several shared resources, such as climate, weather systems, oceans, biodiversity and natural habitats. Other forms of capital can also be shared: for example, cross-border trade agreements and peace agreements might be examples of social (or institutional) capital that is both shared and global. Conversely, cross-border conflicts can be thought of as shared liabilities that threaten global stocks of social capital.
- Transboundary impacts: even where assets are physically located within national boundaries, their management here and now can have an impact on future well-being elsewhere. For example, although rainforests are found only in certain climate zones, the well-being benefits that they generate in terms of both biodiversity and carbon sinks are enjoyed globally.

The sustainability of well-being cannot, therefore, be considered only within the boundaries of a nation. This remains a critical aspect to develop in the future.

2.7   WAYS FORWARD AND CONCLUSIONS

The last 30 years have seen great progress in the development of alternative measures of well-being, as testified by the large range of national initiatives and research articles on the theme. Despite these significant efforts, the well-being agenda still has a long way to go, especially concerning its statistical aspects (see OECD, 2011a, 2013b). Well-being and progress are complex concepts, and many of their dimensions are, by construction, hard to measure (for example, psychological aspects of well-being; and in general, subjective dimensions of well-being). Some of the greatest statistical challenges are:

- The necessity to strengthen the measurement of well-being in specific domains of life where existing sources are either underdeveloped or simply do not exist (for example, quality of employment, quality of housing, mental health and disability, non-cognitive skills, measures of time crunches and time stress, quality of social relations and social network support, civic engagement, and so on).
- The need to improve cross-country comparability of existing instruments and indicators, for example by developing international standards for those dimensions where none currently exist (for example, subjective well-being, household wealth distribution) or where existing standards and guidance are not consistently applied across countries (time use, victimisation surveys).
- The need to increase the frequency and timeliness of existing surveys, and to increase their sample size so as to develop well-being indicators for specific groups of the population (for example, ethnic minorities, native populations) or geographical areas of the country considered (for example, regions).
- The necessity to carry out comprehensive surveys that collect data on multiple dimensions of life at the same time, in order to inform on the joint distribution of achievements (see Ruiz, 2011). Measuring the joint distribution of outcomes is also key to understanding which dimensions of well-being play a causal role on others (for example, how education influences health) and what are the most important well-being drivers.
- The necessity to better understand what are the key drivers for each dimension of concern, so as to identify the set of policies best apt at improving achievements in each of them, as well as the trade-off and synergies between different policy instruments.

The research agenda on well-being is also vast. Some of the most challenging avenues forward include understanding the complex relationship between the various dimensions of well-being, both at individual and society level (Stiglitz et al., 2009), and assessing the policy drivers of well-being to understand how government intervention can effectively enhance people's lives.

NOTES

1. Although estimations of domestic production are still fragile and national accountants do not always have sufficiently accurate data to include this production in their aggregates, domestic production has been recently estimated at 35 per cent of GDP for France, 30 per cent for the United States, and 40 per cent for Finland (Stiglitz et al., 2009).
2. The growing interest in the 'going beyond GDP' ideas has resulted in an explosion of alternative measures over the last 15 years. In an extensive review of composite indicators measuring country performance, Bandura (2005) reported a growing trend in both the quantity of indices available and the variety of issuing institutions (either public or private). Bandura found that approximately 80 per cent of the indices in the study had been elaborated in the 1991–2005 period, and that almost half of all indices available in 2005 were developed after 2000. The author also noted that the issues covered by the indices have broadened and

moved away from traditional topics such as economic issues to also include gender aspects, environmental performance, corruption, globalisation and competitiveness. In a 2008 update, 43 indices were added to the inventory of alternative measures (Bandura, 2008; Bleys, 2012).

3. The concept of the 'third sector' encapsulates the 'sphere of economic activities that occupied the space between the point where the private sector ends and the point where the state sector begins'. Such social institutions are variously referred to as non-profit, voluntary, civil society or non-governmental organisations, and collectively as the third, voluntary, non-profit or independent sector (UN, 2003).

4. Satellite accounts are a framework that enables attention to be focused on a certain field or aspect of economic and social life. They are produced in the context of national accounts, but are more flexible as they allow concepts, definitions, accounting rules and classifications to be changed, where it improves analysis.

5. Landefeld et al. (2009) show in a study for the United States (US) that extending the production boundary to include household production of non-market services, not already included in GDP, would increase US GDP by 19 per cent using the replacement cost approach (using housekeeper's hourly wages), and 62 per cent using the opportunity cost approach (using average hourly wages). Interestingly, however, average annual real growth over the period, 1985–2004, differed by only 0.1 per cent between the two approaches.

6. Consumption of fixed capital is defined as the reduction in the value of the fixed assets used in production. At the household level, the most important fixed asset is usually housing. Under the National Accounts framework, consumption of fixed capital is estimated by applying a depreciation rate to the current value of each capital asset, that is, its current market price. The depreciation rate varies across countries and depends on the assumption about assets' service lives (that is, how long the asset is assumed to be used; for example, in the United States it is assumed that the service life of a dwelling is 80 years). Depreciation functions may be geometric (US assumption for dwellings) or linear. On average across OECD countries for which data are available, consumption of fixed capital represents -5 per cent of net adjusted household disposable income.

7. There are well-known measurement issues in the estimation of households' consumption of fixed capital, suggesting that gross adjusted disposable income may be more appropriate for cross-country comparative purposes. The difference between the two series (net and gross) is modest, and the correlation between them close to 1 (0.99).

8. The breakdown into households and non-profit institutions serving households – that is, categories S14 and S15, respectively, in SNA – is not available for the following countries: Australia, Austria, Canada, Chile, Denmark, Germany, Israel, Korea, Luxembourg, Switzerland, the United Kingdom and South Africa. The figures presented in this chapter use a measure that includes both sectors.

9. The correlation between National Accounts-based household adjusted disposable income per capita and micro-based median household disposable income per consumption unit is equal to 0.93.

10. Depending on the measure used, some countries improve their ranking based on some summary measures, while others worsen their ranking based on some others, but overall the different measures tell a consistent story.

11. Some studies deal with a specific aspect related to the capability approach operationalisation, such as subjective perception of capability (e.g., Anand et al., 2005; Anand and van Hees, 2006), adaptive preferences (Burchardt, 2005) or differences in functioning conversion factors (Kuklys, 2005; Binder and Broekel, 2012).

12. Studies that concentrate on specific subgroups of population, such as children or women, include Addabbo and Di Tommasio (2008), Di Tommaso (2007), Biggeri et al. (2006) and Robeyns (2006).

13. Fleurbaey (2006) highlights that functionings are 'selected achievements' that matter from a normative point of view; for instance, achievements that go beyond subjective well-being and encompass objective achievements. Functionings matter beyond resources, as people may have different attributes and needs, and can achieve different levels of well-being with the same amount of resources. Capabilities need to be considered alongside achievements, to take into account the importance of freedom for human life (that is, the possibility of choosing one's own functionings).

14. For an extensive review of the statistical techniques used in the applications of the capability approach, see Chiappero-Martinetti and Roche (2009).

15. An alternative way to aggregate different metrics consists in calculating an aggregate monetary equivalent of well-being, which puts together various components of well-being expressed through the same monetary metric. For a discussion on this method, see Fleurbaey and Gaullier (2009) and Jones and Klenow (2010).

16. There have been a number of spin-offs from the HDI, including the Gender Empowerment Measure, which is a composite of various measures of gender inequalities in political participation, economic participation and decision-making, and power over economic resources.

17. Alkire and Foster constructed an inequality-adjusted version of the MDI that combines information on both 'average' achievements and on inequalities in the MDI achievements within each country (Alkire and Foster, 2010).

18. Subjective questions in surveys can also offer useful clues as to the appropriate weights, although this type of data raises its own problems, such as those stemming from psychological differences between respondents, including latent heterogeneity in the interpretation of the scales used in survey questions (Ravallion, 2011; Ravallion and Lokshin, 2002).

19. www.oecdbetterlifeindex.org.

20. Although the terms 'happiness' and 'life satisfaction' will be used interchangeably hereinafter, it should be borne in mind that they are not synonyms. Questions about life satisfaction ask respondents to make an overall evaluation of their lives. The results are often interpreted as measures of happiness, but happiness can also be thought of as relating to affect, and can be measured from experiential questions, for example about smiling a lot or feeling happy, or the absence of depression, often during the day before the interview. See OECD (2013a) for a detailed discussion of evaluative and affective measures of subjective well-being.

21. Subjective indicators of well-being are obviously not limited to measures of global satisfaction. They can also be used to measure the satisfaction provided by work or state of health, for example. They can thus help to select and rank the objective variables of quality of life, or even help to weight them better if it is decided to aggregate them into composite indicators, as one can consider that individuals are the best judges of their quality of life.

22. Subjective measures of life satisfaction have only rarely been used to build summary indicators of well-being. An exception is the Inequality-Adjusted Happiness (IAH) produced by Veenhoven and Kalmijn (2005). This indicator is based on the mean and the variance of the distribution of questions on satisfaction with life as whole. The index gives equal weight to the utilitarian and egalitarian viewpoints.

23. The word 'happiness' has nuances which vary according to different languages. In Anglo-Saxon languages it is more akin to a concept in which happiness is the fruit of chance: the English word 'happiness' has its root in the verb 'to happen', and *gluck* ('happiness' in German) is close in meaning to 'luck'. The meaning is different again in French (*bonheur*) and Italian (*felicità*), where it is more akin to a concept of personal responsibility and cultivation of virtues.

24. Criticisms have been raised of the use of subjective well-being for developing countries, as differences in cultural attitudes and limited access to information and resources may affect individuals' self-assessment, especially for poor people (Sen, 2008). However, it is also important not to overstate this effect. Subjective measures are valuable additional resources, which – if interpreted with caution and contrasted with more objective indicators – can contribute to a better understanding of individuals' well-being.

25. Approximately 70 per cent of the historical data on happiness and life satisfaction are based on European and North American respondents (Tov and Au, 2013), thus representing only 16 per cent of the world population. However, over the past two decades, cross-national studies such as the World Values Survey and the Gallup World Poll have now surveyed samples representing 80−95 per cent of the world population (Tov and Diener, 2013).

26. A difficulty here consists in defining the reference group: do we compare to work colleagues, friends or neighbours? Mostly, we do not know, although some relatively unusual data on the self-reported direction of comparisons appears in the European Social Survey (see Clark and Senik, 2010).

27. Interestingly, research has found that in emerging and transition countries, for lower levels of income and high social mobility, a negative difference between one's own income and the income of peers may paradoxically translate into a positive effect on life satisfaction. The standard rationale which may explain this anomaly is the so-called 'tunnel effect hypothesis' (Hirschman and Rothschild, 1973): if an individual is stuck in a traffic jam and observes after a while that a car in the contiguous lane starts moving, they may be happy for it, since this is a signal that they too will soon also be starting to move.

28. For references and a discussion of psychological and social factors determining the drop in life satisfaction of people who become unemployed, see Frey and Stutzer (2002a). The specific effect of social work norms on unemployed people's subjective well-being is studied empirically in Clark (2003) and Lalive and Stutzer (2010).

29. This section largely draws from OECD (2013b), Chapter 6.

30. The recommendation reads: 'Sustainability requires a well-identified dashboard of indicators. The distinctive feature of the components of this dashboard is that they are interpretable as variations of some underlying "stocks"'.

31. For instance, rising populations imply that greater investment will be needed to maintain per capita stocks levels. In the case of finite non-renewable resources (such as fossil fuels or ecosystem services), this implies that the production of well-being will either need to shift away from these resources (to be less dependent on consuming them), and/or that efficiency gains in their use will need to be achieved in the interim.

32. Future environmental, economic, social or technological shifts may also affect capital stocks and their productivity (or the efficiency with which they can be converted to well-being outcomes). One example is climate change, which may have wide-reaching effects on capital stocks and the well-being that can be derived from them, ranging from the productivity of agricultural land to impacts on human capital through health risks (see OECD, 2012, Box 3), and labour supply (Zivin and Neidell, 2010). Other crises

created by economic or social instability, such as recessions or wars, could also affect the value of total resources that are available to support well-being in individual nations. Technological advancements, on the other hand, may improve the efficiency of resource use, enabling countries to achieve more well-being with fewer resources in the future.

REFERENCES

Aberg, R. (1987), 'Working conditions', in R. Erikson and R. Aberg (eds), *Welfare in Transition: A Survey of Living Conditions in Sweden 1968–1981*, Oxford: Clarendon Press, pp. 102–116.

Addabbo, T. and M.L. Di Tommasio (2008), 'Children's capabilities and family characteristics in Italy', ReCent Working Papers Series No. 22.

Addabbo, T., M.L. Di Tommaso and G. Facchinetti (2004), 'To what extent fuzzy set theory and structural equation modelling can measure functionings? An application to child well-being', CHILD Working Paper No. 30.

Ahmad, N. and S.H. Koh (2011), 'Incorporating household production into international comparisons of material well-being', OECD Statistics Directorate Working Paper No. 7.

Alesina, A., R. Di Tella and R. MacCulloch (2001), 'Inequality and happiness: are Europeans and Americans different?', National Bureau of Economic Research Working Paper No. 8198, Cambridge, MA: NBER.

Alkire, S. (2002), 'Dimensions of human development', *World Development*, 30, pp. 181–205.

Alkire, S. (2005), 'Subjective quantitative studies of human agency', *Social Indicators Research*, 74, pp. 217–260.

Alkire, S. and J.E. Foster (2010), 'Designing the Inequality-Adjusted Human Development Index', Oxford Poverty and Human Development Initiative (OPHI), Working Paper No. 37, University of Oxford.

Alkire, S. and M.E. Santos (2010), 'Acute multidimensional poverty: a new index for developing countries', Oxford Poverty and Human Development Initiative (OPHI), Working Paper No. 8, University of Oxford.

Alkire, S. and M.B. Sarwar (2009), 'Multidimensional measures of poverty and well-being', Oxford Poverty and Human Development Initiative, Oxford Department of International Development, University of Oxford, https://ora.ox.ac.uk/objects/uuid:ec55c162-bbb3-464c-b811-10298503ff90.

Alkire, S., M.E. Santos, S. Seth and G. Yalonetzky (2010), 'Is the multidimensional poverty index robust to different weights?', Oxford Poverty and Human Development Initiative, University of Oxford.

Allardt, E. (1993), 'Having, loving, being: an alternative to the Swedish model of welfare research', in M. Nussbaum and A.K. Sen (eds), *The Quality of Life*, Oxford: Clarendon Press, pp. 88–95.

Alois, P. (2014), 'Income inequality and happiness: is there a relationship?', LIS Working Papers Series, No. 614.

Anand, P. and M. van Hees (2006), 'Capabilities and achievements: an empirical study', *Journal of Socio-Economics: Special Section – The Socio-Economics of Happiness*, 35(2), pp. 268–284.

Anand, P., G. Hunter, I. Carter, K. Dowding, F. Guala and M. Van Hees (2009), 'The development of capability indicators', *Journal of Human Development Capabilities*, 10, pp. 125–152.

Anand, P., G. Hunter and R. Smith (2005), 'Capabilities and well-being: evidence based on the Sen–Nussbaum approach to welfare', *Social Indicators Research*, 74(1), pp. 9–55.

Anand, P., J. Krishnakumar and N.B. Tran (2011), 'Measuring welfare: latent variable models for happiness and capabilities in the presence of unobservable heterogeneity', *Journal of Public Economics*, 95, pp. 205–215.

Atkinson, A.B. and F. Bourguignon (1982), 'The comparison of multi-dimensioned distributions of economic status', *Review of Economic Studies*, 49, pp. 183–201.

Atkinson, A.B. and E. Marlier (2010), *Income and Living Conditions in Europe*, Luxembourg: Publications Office of the European Union.

Atkinson, A.B. and S. Morelli (2011), 'Inequalities and banking crises, a first look', unpublished.

Atkinson, A.B., B. Cantillon, E. Marlier and B. Nolan (2002), *Social Indicators: The EU and Social Exclusion*, Oxford: Oxford University Press.

Bandura, R. (2005), 'Measuring country performance and state behavior: a survey of composite indices, UNDP/ODS Background Paper, New York: United Nations Development Programme, Office of Development Studies.

Bandura, R. (2008), 'A survey of composite indices measuring country performance: 2008 update', UNDP/ODS Working Paper, New York: United Nations Development Programme, Office of Development Studies.

Biggeri, M., R. Libanora, S. Mariani and L. Menchini (2006), 'Children conceptualizing capabilities: results of a survey conducted during the first Children's World Congress on Child Labour', *Journal of Human Development*, 7(1), pp. 59–84.

Binder, M. (2014), 'Subjective well-being capabilities: bridging the gap between the capability approach and subjective well-being research', *Journal of Happiness Studies*, 15(5), pp. 1197–1217.

Binder, M. and T. Broekel (2012), 'The neglected dimension of well-being: analyzing the development of "conversion efficiency" in Great Britain', *Journal of Socio-Economics*, 41(1), pp. 37–47.

Blanchflower, D.G. and A.J. Oswald (2004), 'Well-being over time in Britain and the USA', *Journal of Public Economics*, 88(7/8), pp. 1359–1386.

Bleys, B. (2012), 'Beyond GDP: classifying alternative measures for progress', *Social Indicators Research*, 109, pp. 355–376.

Boarini, R., M. Comola, C. Smith, R. Manchin and F. De Keulenaer (2012), 'What makes it for a better life. The determinants of subjective well-being in OECD countries: evidence from the Gallup World Poll', OECD Statistics Department Working Paper No. 47, Paris.

Boarini, R., A. Johansson and M. Mira d'Ercole (2006), 'Alternative measures of well-being', OECD Economics Department Working Paper, Paris.

Borucke, M., D. Moore, G. Cranston, K. Gracey, K. Iha, J. Larson, E. Lazarus, J.C. Morales, M. Wackernagel and A. Galli (2013), 'Accounting for demand and supply of the biosphere's regenerative capacity: the National Footprint Accounts' underlying methodology and framework', *Ecological Indicators*, 24, pp. 518–533.

Bourguignon, F. (1999), 'Comment to "Multidimensioned approaches to welfare analysis" by E. Maasoumi', in J. Silber (ed.), *Handbook of Income Inequality Measurement*, Boston, MA, USA; Dordrecht, Netherlands; London, UK: Kluwer Academic, pp. 477–484.

Bourguignon, F. and S.R. Chakravarty (2003), 'The measurement of multidimensional poverty', *Journal of Economic Inequality*, 1, pp. 25–49.

Brandolini, A. and G. D'Alessio (1998), 'Measuring well-being in the functioning space', plenary paper, 13th International Economics Association Congress, Buenos Aires.

Bruni, L. and P.L. Porta (eds) (2005), *Economics and Happiness. Framing the Analysis*, Oxford: Oxford University Press.

Burchardt, T. (2005), 'Are one man's rags another man's riches? Identifying adaptive expectations using panel data', *Social Indicators Research*, 74(1), pp. 57–102.

Burchardt, T. and P. Vizard (2011), '"Operationalizing" the capability approach as a basis for equality and human rights monitoring in twenty-first-century Britain', *Journal of Human Development and Capabilities*, 12(1), pp. 91–119.

Cassiers, I. and G. Thiry (2009), 'Au-delà du PIB: reconcilier ce qui compte et ce que l'on compte', Discussion Papers No. 75, Université catholique de Louvain, Institut de Recherches Economiques et Sociales (IRES).

Castriota, S. (2006), 'Education and happiness: a further explanation to the Easterlin Paradox', CEIS Departmental Working Paper.

Chiappero-Martinetti, E. (2000), 'A multidimensional assessment of well-being based on Sen's functioning approach', *Rivista Internazionale di Scienze Sociali*, 108(2), pp. 207–239.

Chiappero-Martinetti, E. and J.M. Roche (2009), 'Operationalization of the capability approach', in E. Chiappero-Martinetti (ed.), *Debating Global Society: Reach and Limits of the Capability Approach*, Milan: Fondazione Giangiacomo Feltrinelli, pp. 157–203.

Christian, D.E. (1974), 'International social indicators: the OECD experience', *Social Indicators Research*, 1(2), pp. 169–186.

Clark, A.E. (2003), 'Unemployment as a social norm: psychological evidence from panel data', *Journal of Labor Economics*, 21(2), pp. 323–351.

Clark, A.E., P. Frijters and M. Shields (2008), 'Relative income, happiness and utility: an explanation for the Easterlin paradox and other puzzles', *Journal of Economic Literature*, 46(1), pp. 95–144.

Clark, A.E. and A.J. Oswald (1994), 'Unhappiness and unemployment', *Economic Journal*, 104(424), pp. 648–659.

Clark, A.E. and A.J. Oswald (1996), 'Satisfaction and comparison income', *Journal of Public Economics*, 61(3), pp. 359–381.

Clark, A.E. and C. Senik (2010), 'Who compares to whom? The anatomy of income comparisons in Europe', *Economic Journal*, 120(544), pp. 573–594.

Cobb, C., T. Halstead and J. Rowe (1995), 'If the GDP is up, why is America down?', *Atlantic Monthly*, 276, pp. 59–78.

Comim, F. (2008), 'Measuring capabilities', in F. Comim, M. Qizilbash and S. Alkire (eds), *The Capability Approach: Concepts, Measures and Application*, Cambridge: Cambridge University Press, pp. 157–200.

Costanza, R., J. Erickson, K. Fligger, A. Adams, C. Adams, B. Altschuler, S. Balter, B. Fisher, J. Hike, J. Kelly, T. Kerr, M. McCauley, K. Montone, M. Rauch, K. Schmiededkamp, D. Saxton, L. Sparacino, W. Tusinski and L. Williams (2004), 'Estimates of the Genuine Progress Indicator (GPI) for Vermont, Chittenden County and Burlington, from 1950 to 2000', *Ecological Economics*, 51(1/2), pp. 139–155.

Costanza, R., M. Hart, S. Posner and J. Talberth (2009), 'Beyond GDP: the need for new measures of progress', Pardee Paper No. 4, Boston, MA: Pardee Center for the Study of the Longer-Range Future.

Crocker, D.A. (2008), *Ethics of Global Development: Agency, Capability and Deliberative Democracy*, Cambridge: Cambridge University Press.

Daly, H. and J. Cobb (1989), *For the Common Good*, Boston, MA: Beacon Press.

Daly, M., A.J. Oswald, D. Wilson and S. Wu (2010), 'Dark contrasts: the paradox of high rates of suicide in happy places', *Journal of Economic Behavior and Organization*, 80(3), pp. 435–442.

Deaton, A. (2005), 'Measuring poverty in a growing world (or measuring growth in a poor world)', *Review of Economics and Statistics*, 87, pp. 1–19.

Deaton, A. (2008), 'Income, health, and well-being around the world: evidence from the Gallup World Poll', *Journal of Economic Perspectives*, 22(2), pp. 53–72.

Deaton, A. (2011), 'The financial crisis and the well-being of Americans', NBER Working Paper No. W17128, Cambridge, MA: National Bureau of Economic Research.

Deaton, A. and D. Kahneman (2010), 'High income improves evaluation of life but not emotional well-being', *Proceedings of the National Academy of Science of the United States of America*, 107(38), pp. 16489–16493.

Decancq, K., M. Fleurbaey and E. Schokkaert (2015), 'Inequality, income, and well-being', in A.B. Atkinson and F. Bourguignon (eds), *Handbook of Income Distribution Vol. II*, Amsterdam: North-Holland, pp. 67–140.

Decancq, K. and M.A. Lugo (2009), 'Measuring inequality of well-being with a correlation-sensitive multidimensional Gini index', Economics Series Working Papers, No. 459, University of Oxford, Department of Economics.

Decancq, K. and M.A. Lugo (2013), 'Weights in multidimensional indices of wellbeing: an overview', *Econometric Reviews*, 32(1), pp. 7–34.

Department for Environment, Food and Rural Affairs (DEFRA) (2010), 'Measuring progress: sustainable development indicators 2010', London: Department for Environment, Food and Rural Affairs, http://sd.defra.gov.uk/documents/SDI2010_001.pdf.

Di Tella, R. and R. MacCulloch (2004), 'Happiness adaption to income beyond "basic needs"', in E. Diener, J. Helliwell and D. Kahneman (eds), *International Differences in Well-Being*, New York: Oxford University Press, pp. 217–247.

Di Tella, R., J. Haisken-De New and R. MacCulloch (2010), 'Happiness adaptation to income and to status in an individual panel', *Journal of Economic Behavior and Organization*, 76, pp. 834–852.

Di Tommaso, M.L. (2007), 'Children capabilities: a structural equation model for India', *Journal of Socio-Economics*, 36, pp. 436–450.

Diener, E. (1984), 'Subjective well-being', *Psychological Bulletin*, 95(3), pp. 542–575.

Diener, E. (2000), 'Subjective well-being: the science of happiness and a proposal for a national index', *American Psychologist*, 55(1), pp. 34–43.

Diener, E. and M. Diener (1995), 'Cross-cultural correlates of life satisfaction and self-esteem', *Journal of Personality and Social Psychology*, 68, pp. 653–663.

Diener, E. and R. Biswas-Diener (2002), 'Will money increase subjective well-being?', *Social Indicators Research*, 57(2), pp. 119–169.

Diener, E. and S. Oishi (2000), 'Money and happiness: income and subjective wellbeing across nations', in E. Diener and E.M. Suh (eds), *Subjective Well-being across Cultures*, Cambridge, MA: MIT Press, pp. 185–218.

Diener, E., E. Sandvik, L. Seidlitz and M. Diener (1993), 'The relationship between income and subjective well-being: relative or absolute?', *Social Indicators Research*, 28, pp. 195–223.

Diener, E., W. Ng, J. Harter and R. Arora (2010), 'Wealth and happiness across the world: material prosperity predicts life evaluation, whereas psychosocial prosperity predicts positive feeling', *Journal of Personality and Social Psychology*, 99, pp. 52–61.

Dolan, P., T. Peasgood and M.P. White (2008), 'Do we really know what makes us happy? A review of the economic literature on the factors associated with subjective well-being', *Journal of Economic Psychology*, 29, pp. 94–122.

Drèze, J. and A.K. Sen (2002), *India: Development and Participation*, 2nd edn, Oxford: Oxford University Press.

Duncan, O.D. (1975), 'Does money buy satisfaction?', *Social Indicators Research*, 2(3), pp. 267–274.

Dusenberry, J. (1949), *Income, Saving and Theory of Consumer Behavior*, Cambridge, MA: Harvard University Press.

Easterlin, R.A. (1974), 'Does economic growth improve the human lot? Some empirical evidence', in P.A. David and M.W. Reder (eds), *Nations and Households in Economic Growth: Essays in Honour of Moses Abramovitz*, New York, USA and London, UK: Academic Press, pp. 89–125.

Easterlin, R.A. (ed.) (2002), *Happiness in Economics*, Cheltenham, UK and Northampton, MA, USA: Edward Elgar Publishing.

Easterlin R. and L. Angelescu (2009), 'Happiness and growth the world over: time series evidence on the happiness–income paradox', IZA Discussion Paper No. 4060, Bonn.

Eurostat (2009a), 'GDP and Beyond'. http://epp.eurostat.ec.europa.eu/portal/page/portal/gdp_and_beyond/introduction.

Eurostat (2009b), *Sustainable Development in the European Union: 2009 Monitoring Report of the EU Sustainable Development Strategy*, Eurostat Statistical Books, European Union, http://epp.eurostat.ec.europa.eu/cache/ITY_OFFPUB/KS-78-09-865/EN/KS-78-09-865-EN.PDF.

Eurostat (2011a), 'Report on the Sponsorship Group on Measuring Progress', http://epp.eurostat.ec.europa.eu/portal/page/portal/pgp_ess/0_DOCS/estat/SpG_progress_wellbeing_report_after_ESSC_adoption_22Nov1.pdf.

Eurostat (2011b), *Sustainable Development in the European Union: 2011 Monitoring Report of the EU Sustainable Development Strategy*, Eurostat Statistical Books, European Union, http://epp.eurostat.ec.europa.eu/cache/ITY_OFFPUB/KS-31-11-224/EN/KS-31-11-224-EN.PDF.

Fesseau, M. and M. Mattonetti (2013), 'Distributional measures across household groups in a national accounts framework: results from an experimental cross-country exercise on household income, consumption and saving', OECD Statistics Working Papers No. 53, Paris: OECD Publishing.

Fitoussi, J.-P. and J.E. Stiglitz (2013), 'On the measurement of social progress and wellbeing: some further thoughts', *Global Policy*, 4(3), pp. 290–293.

Fleche, S., C. Smith and P. Sorsa (2011), 'Exploring determinants of subjective well-being in OECD countries: evidence from the World Value Survey', OECD Economics Department Working Paper No. 921, Paris: OECD Publishing.

Fleurbaey, M. (2006), 'Capabilities, functionings and refined functionings', *Journal of Human Development*, 7(3), pp. 299–310.

Fleurbaey, M. (2009), 'Beyond GDP – the quest for a measure of social welfare', *Journal of Economic Literature*, 47(4), pp. 1029–1075.

Fleurbaey, M. and D. Blanchet (2014), *Beyond GDP: Measuring Welfare and Assessing Sustainability*, Oxford: Oxford University Press

Fleurbaey, M. and G. Gaullier (2009), 'International comparisons of living standards by income equivalent', *Scandinavian Journal of Economics*, 111(3), pp. 597–623.

Fliessbach, K., B. Weber, P. Trautner, T. Dohmen, U. Sunde, C.E. Elger and A. Falk (2007), 'Social comparison affects reward-related brain activity in the human ventral striatum', *Science*, 318, pp. 1305–1308.

Frank, R. (2005), 'Does absolute income matter?', in L. Bruni and P.L. Porta (eds), *Economics and Happiness: Framing the Analysis*, Oxford: Oxford University Press, pp. 65–90.

Frey, B.S. and A. Stutzer (2000), 'Happiness, economy and institutions', *Economic Journal*, 110, pp. 918–938.

Frey, B.S. and A. Stutzer (2002a), 'What can economists learn from happiness research?', *Journal of Economic Literature*, 40(2), pp. 402–35.

Frey, B.S. and A. Stutzer (2002b), *Happiness and Economics: How the Economy and Institutions Affect Well-Being*, Princeton, NJ, USA and Oxford, UK: Princeton University Press.

Furnée C.A., W. Groot and G.A. Pfann (2010), 'Health and income: a meta-analysis to explore cross-country, gender and age differences', *European Journal of Public Health*, 21(6), pp. 775–780.

Gajdos, T. and J.A. Weymark (2005), 'Multidimensional generalized Gini indices', *Economic Theory*, 26(3), 471–496.

Gardner, J. and A.J. Oswald (2001), 'Does money buy happiness? A longitudinal study using data on windfalls', Mimeo, Warwick University.

Gardner, J. and A.J. Oswald (2007), 'Money and mental well-being: a longitudinal study of medium-sized lottery wins', *Journal of Health Economics*, 26(1), pp. 49–60.

Global Footprint Network (2010), 'National Footprint Accounts, 2010 edition', www.footprintnetwork.org.

Hagerty, M.R. (2000), 'Social comparisons of income in one's community: evidence from national surveys of income and happiness', *Journal of Personality and Social Psychology*, 78(4), pp. 764–771.

Hagerty M.R. and K.C. Land (2007), 'Constructing summary indices of quality of life: a model for the effect of heterogeneous importance weights', *Sociological Methods and Research*, 35(May), pp. 455–496.

Hagerty, M.R. and R. Veenhoven (2003), 'Wealth and happiness revisited – growing national income does go with greater happiness', *Social Indicators Research*, 64(1), pp. 1–27.

Heal, G. (2011), 'Sustainability and its measurement', NBER Working Paper Series No. 17008, Cambridge, MA: National Bureau of Economic Research, http://www.nber.org/papers/w17008.

Helliwell, J. (2003), 'How's life? Combining individual and national variables to explain subjective well-being', *Economic Modelling*, 20(2), pp. 331–360.

Hirsch, F. (1976), *Social Limits to Growth*, Cambridge, MA: Harvard University Press.

Hirshman, A. and M. Rothschild (1973), 'The changing tolerance for income inequality in the course of economic development', *Quarterly Journal of Economics*, 87, pp. 544–566.

Holloway, S., S. Short and S. Tamplin (2002), 'Household satellite account (experimental) methodology', Newport: UK Office for National Statistics.

Inglehart, R., R. Foa, C. Peterson and C. Welzel (2008), 'Development, freedom, and rising happiness: a global perspective (1981–2007)', *Perspectives on Psychological Science*, 3(4), pp. 264–285.

Jones, C.I. and P.J. Klenow (2010), 'Beyond GDP? Welfare across countries and time', NBER Working Paper, No. 16352, Cambridge, MA: National Bureau of Economic Research.

Karabarbounis, L. and B. Neiman (2013), 'The global decline of the labour share', NBER Working Paper Series No. 191136, Cambridge, MA: National Bureau of Economic Research.

Klasen, S. (2000), 'Measuring poverty and deprivation in South Africa', *Review of Income and Wealth*, 46, pp. 33–58.

Kolm, S.-C. (1977), 'Multidimensional equalitarianisms', *Quarterly Journal of Economics*, 91, pp. 1–13.

Krishnakumar, J. and A. Nagar (2008), 'On exact statistical properties of multidimensional indices based on principal components, factor analysis, MIMIC and structural equation models', *Social Indicators Research*, 86, pp. 481–496.

Kubiszewki, I., R. Costanza, C. Franco, P. Lawn, J. Talberth, T. Jackson and C. Aylmer (2013), 'Beyond GDP: measuring and achieving global genuine progress', *Ecological Economics*, 93, pp. 57–68.

Kuklys, W. (2005), *Amartya Sen's Capability Approach: Theoretical Insights and Empirical Applications*, Berlin: Springer.

Kuznets, S. (1934), *National Income 1929–32*, New York: National Bureau of Economic Research.

Kwan, V.S.Y., M.H. Bond and T.M. Singelis (1997), 'Pancultural explanations for life satisfaction: adding relationship harmony to self-esteem', *Journal of Personality and Social Psychology*, 73, pp. 1038–1051.

Lalive, R. and A. Stutzer (2010), 'Approval of equal rights and gender differences in well-being', *Journal of Population Economics*, 23(3), pp. 933–962.

Landefeld, J.S., B.M. Fraumeni and C.M. Vojtech (2009), 'Accounting for household production: a prototype satellite account using the American Time Use Survey', *Review of Income and Wealth*, 55(2), pp. 205–225.

Lane, R. (2000), *The Decline of Happiness in Market Democracies*, New Haven, CT: Yale University Press.

Layard, R. (2005), *Happiness: Lessons from a New Science*, London: Penguin.

Layard, R. (2010), 'Measuring subjective well-being', *Science*, 327, pp. 534–535.

Luttmer, E. (2005), 'Neighbors as negatives: relative earnings and well-being', *Quarterly Journal of Economics*, 120, pp. 963–1002.

Malthus, T. (1798), *An Essay on the Principles of Population*, London: Published for J. Johnson.

Marcuss, D. and R.E. Kane (2007), 'US national income and product statistics born of the Great Depression and World War II', *Bureau of Economic Analysis: Survey of Current Business*, 87(2), pp. 32–46.

Marshall, A. (1890 [1947]), *Principles of Economics*, London: Macmillan.

McCulla, S.H. and S. Smith (2007), 'Measuring the economy: a primer on GDP and the national income and product accounts', Bureau of Economic Analysis, US Department of Commerce.

McMahon, D. (2006), *Happiness: A History*, New York: Atlantic Monthly Press.

Miranda, V. (2011), 'Cooking, caring and volunteering: unpaid work around the world', OECD Social, Employment and Migration Working Papers, No. 116, Paris: OECD Publishing.

Morris, D. (1979), *Measuring the Condition of the World's Poor: The Physical Quality of Life Index*, New York: Pergamon.

Neumayer, E. (2012), 'Human development and sustainability', *Journal of Human Development and Capabilities*, 13(4), pp. 561–579.

New Economics Foundation (NEF) (2011), *Measuring Our Progress*, London: New Economics Foundation, http://www.neweconomics.org/publications/measuring-our-progress.

Nordhaus, W.D. and J. Tobin (1973), 'Is growth obsolete?', in M. Moss (ed.), *The Measurement of Economic and Social Performance*, Studies in Income and Wealth, 38, Cambridge, MA: National Bureau of Economic Research, pp. 1–80.

Nussbaum, M. (2000), *Women and Human Development: The Capabilities Approach*, Cambridge: Cambridge University Press.

Nussbaum, M. (2006), *Frontiers of Justice: Disability, Nationality, Species Membership*, Cambridge, MA: Harvard University Press.

Nussbaum, M. (2009). 'Capabilities as fundamental entitlements: Sen and social justice', in K. Schneider and H.-U. Otto (eds), *From Employability Towards Capability*, Luxembourg: Inter-Actions, pp. 15–43.

Nussbaum, M. (2011), *Creating Capabilities: The Human Development Approach*, New York: Harvard University Press.

OECD (1982), *The OECD List of Social Indicators*, Paris: OECD Publishing.

OECD (1986), *Living Conditions in OECD Countries: Compendium of Social Indicators*, Paris: OECD Publishing.

OECD (2008), *Growing Unequal?: Income Distribution and Poverty in OECD Countries*, Paris: OECD Publishing.

OECD (2010), *PISA 2009 Results: Overcoming Social Background. Equity in Learning Opportunities and Outcomes. Volume II*, Paris: OECD Publishing.

OECD (2011a), *How's Life? Measuring Well-Being*, Paris: OECD Publishing.

OECD (2011b), *Divided We Stand: Why Inequality Keeps Rising*, Paris: OECD Publishing.

OECD (2012), *OECD Environmental Outlook to 2050*, Paris: OECD Publishing.

OECD (2013a), *Guidelines on Measuring Subjective Well-being*, Paris: OECD Publishing.

OECD (2013b), *How's Life? 2013 – Measuring Well-Being*, Paris: OECD Publishing.

Office for National Statistics (ONS) (2012), *Measuring National Well-being – Life in the UK 2012*, Newport: UK Office for National Statistics, http://webarchive.nationalarchives.gov.uk/20160105183326/http://www.

ons.gov.uk/ons/rel/wellbeing/measuring-national-well-being/first-annual-report-on-measuring-national-well-being/art-measuring-national-well-being-annual-report.html.

Office for National Statistics (ONS) (2014), *Measuring National Well-being – Life in the UK 2014*, Newport: UK Office for National Statistics, http://webarchive.nationalarchives.gov.uk/20160106200454/http://www.ons.gov.uk/ons/dcp171766_352740.pdf.

Oishi, S. and U. Schimmack (2010), 'Culture and well-being: a new inquiry into the psychological wealth of nations', *Perspectives on Psychological Science*, 5, pp. 463–471.

Oishi, S., E.F. Diener, R.E. Lucas and E.M. Suh (1999), 'Cross-cultural variations in predictors of life satisfaction: perspectives from needs and values', *Personality and Social Psychology Bulletin*, 25, pp. 980–990.

Piketty, T. and E. Saez (2013), 'Top incomes and the Great Recession: recent evolutions and policy implications', *IMF Economic Review*, 61, pp. 456–478.

Proto, E. and A. Rustichini (2013), 'A reassessment of the relationship between GDP and life satisfaction', *PLoS ONE*, 8(11), http://dx.doi.org/10.1371/journal.pone.0079358.

Qizilbash, M. (2002), 'Development, common foes and shared values', *Review of Political Economy*, 14(4), pp. 463–480.

Qizilbash, M.A.K. (2013), 'On capability and the good life: theoretical debates and their practical implications', *Philosophy and Public Policy Quarterly*, 31(2), pp. 35–42.

Qizilbash, M.A.K. and D. Clark (2005), 'The capability approach and fuzzy poverty measures: an application to the South African context', *Journal of Social Indicators Research*, 74, pp. 103–129.

Ravallion, M. (2011), 'Mashup indices of development', *World Bank Research Observer*, 27(1), pp. 1–32.

Ravallion, M. and M. Lokshin (2002), 'Self-rated economic welfare in Russia', *European Economic Review*, 46, pp. 1453–1473.

Robeyns, I. (2000), 'An unworkable idea or a promising alternative? Sen's capability approach re-examined', CES Discussion Paper 00.30, University of Leuven.

Robeyns, I. (2003), 'Sen's capability approach and gender inequality: selecting relevant capabilities', *Feminist Economics*, 9(2/3), pp. 61–92.

Robeyns, I. (2005), 'The capability approach: a theoretical survey', *Journal of Human Development*, 6(1), pp. 93–114.

Robeyns, I. (2006), 'Measuring gender inequality in functionings and capabilities: findings from the British Household Panel Survey', in P. Bharati and M. Pal (eds), *Gender Disparity: Manifestations, Causes and Implications*, New Dehli: Anmol Publishers, pp. 236–277.

Robeyns, I. and R.J. van der Veen (2007), 'Sustainable quality of life: conceptual, analysis for a policy-relevant empirical specification', MNP Report 550031006, Bilthoven and Amsterdam: Environmental Assessment Agency and University of Amsterdam, http://www.mnp.nl/en/publications/2007/Sustainablequalityoflife.ht.

Roche, J.M. (2008), 'Monitoring inequality between social groups: a methodology combining fuzzy set theory and principal component analysis', *Journal of Human Development: Special Issue: Selected Papers from the 2007 International Conference of the Human Development and Capability Association*, 9(3), pp. 427–452.

Rockström, J., W. Steffen, K. Noone, A. Persson, F.S. Chapin III, E.F. Lambin, T.M. Lenton, M. Scheffer, C. Folke, H.J. Schellnhuber, B. Nykvist, C.A. de Wit, T. Hughes, S. van der Leeuw, H. Rodhe, S. Sörlin, P.K. Snyder, R. Costanza, U. Svedin, M. Falkenmark, L. Karlberg, R.W. Corell, V.J. Fabry, J. Hansen. B. Walker, D. Liverman, K. Richardson, P. Crutzen and J.A. Foley (2009), 'A safe operating space for humanity', *Nature*, 461, pp. 472–475.

Ross, C. and M. Van Willigen (1997), 'Education and the subjective quality of life', *Journal of Health and Social Behaviour*, 38, pp. 275–297.

Ruiz, N. (2011), 'Measuring the joint distribution of household's income, consumption and wealth using nested Atkinson measures', OECD Statistics Directorate Working Paper No. 5, Paris: OECD Publishing.

Sacks, D.W., B. Stevenson and J. Wolfers (2010), 'Subjective well-being, income, economic development and growth', NBER Working Paper No. 16441, Cambridge, MA: National Bureau of Economic Research.

Schokkaert, E. (2007), 'Capabilities and satisfaction with life', *Journal of Human Development*, 8(3), pp. 415–430.

Schokkaert, E. and L. Van Ootegem (1990), 'Sen's concept of the living standard applied to the Belgian unemployment', *Recherches Economiques de Louvain*, 56, pp. 429–450.

Schyns, P. (2002), 'Wealth of nations, individual income and life satisfaction in 42 countries: a multilevel approach', *Social Indicators Research*, 60(1/2/3), pp. 5–40.

Sen, A.K. (1985a), *Commodities and Capabilities*, Amsterdam: North-Holland.

Sen, A.K. (1985b), 'Well-being, agency and freedom: the Dewey Lectures 1984', *Journal of Philosophy*, 82, pp. 169–221.

Sen, A.K. (1987), *The Standard of Living*, Cambridge: Cambridge University Press.

Sen, A.K. (1992), *Inequality Reexamined*, New York, USA and Oxford, UK: Oxford University Press.

Sen, A.K. (1993), 'Capability and well-being', in M. Nussbaum and A.K. Sen (eds), *The Quality of Life*, Oxford: Clarendon Press, pp. 30–53.

Sen, A.K. (1994), 'Well-being, capability and public policy', *Giornale degli economisti e annali di economia*, 7/8/9, pp. 333–348.

Sen, A.K. (1997), *On Economic Inequality: Expanded Edition with a Substantial Annexe by James Foster and Amartya Sen*, Oxford: Clarendon Press.

Sen, A.K. (1998), *Development as Freedom*, Oxford: Oxford University Press.

Sen, A.K. (2004), 'Capabilities, lists, and public reason: continuing the conversation', *Feminist Economics*, 10(3), pp. 77–80.

Sen, A.K. (2008), 'The economics of happiness and capability', in L. Bruni, F. Comim and M. Pugno (eds), *Capability and Happiness*, New York: Oxford University Press, pp. 16–27.

Seth, S. (2009), 'Inequality, interactions, and human development', *Journal of Human Development and Capabilities*, 10(3), 375–396.

Sheldon, K.M., C. Cheng and J. Hilpert (2011), 'Understanding well-being and optimal functioning: applying the Multilevel Personality in Context (MPIC) model', *Psychological Inquiry*, 22, pp. 1–16.

Slesnik, D.T. (1998), 'Empirical approaches to the measurement of welfare', *Journal of Economic Literature*, 36, pp. 2108–2165.

Smith, L.M., J.L. Case, H.M. Smith, L.C. Harwell and J.K. Summers (2013), 'Relating ecosystem services to domains of human well-being: foundation for a US index', *Ecological Indicators*, 28, pp. 79–90.

Statistics New Zealand (2008), 'Measuring New Zealand's progress using a sustainable development approach 2008', www.stats.govt.nz/browse_for_stats/environment/sustainable_development/sustainable-development. aspx.

Stevenson, B. and J. Wolfers (2008), 'Economic growth and subjective well-being: reassessing the Easterlin paradox', *Brookings Papers on Economic Activity*, 1, pp. 1–87.

Stiglitz, J. (2010), *Freefall: America, Free Markets, and the Sinking of the World Economy*, New York: W.W. Norton.

Stiglitz, J.E., A.K. Sen and J-P. Fitoussi (2009), *Mismeasuring Our Lives: Why GDP Doesn't Add Up*, New York: New Press.

Stutzer, A. and B.S. Frey (2010), 'Recent advances in the economics of individual subjective well-being', Discussion Paper Series / Forschungsinstitut zur Zukunft der Arbeit, No. 4850.

Swiss Federal Statistical Office (2013), 'Sustainable development – a brief guide 2013: 17 key indicators to measure progress', www.bfs.admin.ch/bfs/portal/en/index/themen/21/01/new.html?gnpID=2013-267.

Talberth, J., C. Cobb and N. Slattery (2007), *The Genuine Progress Indicator 2006: A Tool for Sustainable Development*, Oakland, CA: Redefining Progress, http://rprogress.org/publications/2007/GPI%202006.pdf.

Tay, L. and E. Diener (2011), 'Needs and subjective well-being around the world', *Journal of Personality and Social Psychology*, 101, pp. 354–365.

Tov, W. and E.W.M. Au (2013), 'Comparing well-being across nations: conceptual and empirical issues', in I. Boniwell and S. David (eds), *Oxford Handbook of Happiness*, Oxford: Oxford University Press, pp. 449–464.

Tov, W. and E. Diener (2013), 'Subjective well-being', in K.D. Keith (ed.), *Encyclopedia of Cross-Cultural Psychology*, Malden, MA: Wiley-Blackwell, pp. 1239–1245.

Townsend, P. (1985), *Poverty in the United Kingdom*, London: Penguin.

Tsui, K.-Y. (1995), 'Multidimensional generalizations of the relative and absolute inequality indices: the Atkinson–Kolm–Sen approach', *Journal of Economic Theory*, 67, pp. 251–265.

Tsui, K.-Y. (1999), 'Multidimensional inequality and multidimensional generalized entropy measures: an axiomatic derivation', *Social Choice and Welfare*, 16, pp. 145–157.

Tsui, K.-Y. (2002), 'Multidimensional poverty indices', *Social Choice and Welfare*, 19, pp. 69–93.

United Nations (UN) (2003), *Handbook on Non-Profit Institutions in the System of National Accounts*, New York: United Nations.

United Nations (UN) (2009), *Measuring Sustainable Development*, New York, USA and Geneva, Switzerland: United Nations, prepared in cooperation with the OECD and the Statistical Office for European Communities (Eurostat).

United Nations (UN) (2014), *Conference of European Statisticians Recommendations on Measuring Sustainable Development*, New York, USA and Geneva, Switzerland: United Nations, prepared in cooperation with the OECD and the Statistical Office for European Communities (Eurostat).

United Nations Development Programme (UNDP) (1995), *Human Development Report 1995*, New York: Oxford University Press.

United Nations Development Programme (UNDP) (2013), *Human Development Report 2013 – The Rise of the South: Human Progress in a Diverse World*, New York, http://hdr.undp.org/en/media/HDR_2013_EN_com plete.pdf.

UNU-IHDP and UNEP (2012), *Inclusive Wealth Report 2012. Measuring Progress towards Sustainability*, Cambridge: Cambridge University Press.

Van de Kerk, G. and A. Manuel (2012), *Sustainable Society Index 2012*, The Hague: Sustainable Society Foundation.

Van Praag, B.M.S., P. Frijters and A. Ferrer-i-Carbonell (2003), 'The anatomy of subjective well-being', *Journal of Economic Behavior and Organization*, 51, pp. 29–49.
Veblen, T. (1899), *The Theory of the Leisure Class*, New York: Dover Publications.
Veenhoven, R. (1991), 'Is happiness relative?', *Social Indicators Research*, 24, pp. 1–34.
Veenhoven, R. and W.M. Kalmijn (2005), 'Inequality-adjusted happiness in nations: egalitarianism and utilitarianism married in a new index of societal performance', *Journal of Happiness Studies*, 6, pp. 421–455.
Volkert, J. and F. Schneider (2011), 'The application of the capability approach to high-income OECD countries: a preliminary survey', CESifo Working Paper No. 3364.
Waldron, S. (2010), 'Measuring subjective well-being in the UK', http://www.statistics.gov.uk/articles/nojournal/workingpaper-measuringsubjective well-beingintheuk.pdf.
Winkelmann, R. and L. Winkelmann (1998), 'Why are the unemployed so unhappy? Evidence from panel data', *Economica*, 65(257), pp. 1–15.
World Bank (2005), *World Development Report 2006: Equity and Development*, Washington DC: World Bank Publications.
World Bank (2006), *Where is the Wealth of Nations? Measuring Capital for the 21st Century*, Washington, DC: World Bank.
World Bank (2011), *The Changing Wealth of Nations: Measuring Sustainable Development in the New Millennium*, Washington, DC: World Bank.
World Commission on Environment and Development (WCED) (1987), *Our Common Future* (the Brundtland Report), Oxford: Oxford University Press.
Zivin, J.G. and M.J. Neidell (2010), 'Temperature and the allocation of time: implications for climate change', NBER Working Paper No. 15717, Cambridge, MA: National Bureau of Economic Research.

APPENDIX 2.1: SELECTED EXAMPLES OF INITIATIVES TO MEASURE WELL-BEING BY OECD COUNTRIES' NATIONAL STATISTICAL OFFICES

In recent years, many OECD countries' National Statistical Offices have carried out measures of well-being and progress beyond the boundaries of gross domestic product. Below are selected examples of such initiatives.

Australia

The Australian Bureau of Statistics (ABS) published its first report, *Measures of Australia's Progress* (MAP) in 2002, with updates in 2010 and 2012. In 2011, the ABS carried out an extensive community consultation (MAP 2.0) to improve its framework, involving a wide range of individuals, community leaders and experts to provide guidance on the goals and aspirations of Australians. The feedback collected through a series of conferences, web consultations and panels exposed some of the gaps in the picture provided by the indicators included in the MAP report, leading to the identification of governance as a new domain of progress. The outcomes of this consultation were used by the ABS to improve the statistical framework used to measure progress, and were reflected in the MAP report released in November 2013. See www.abs.gov.au/AUSSTATS/abs@.nsf/mf/1370.0.55.001?opendocument#from-banner=LN.

Austria

In 2012, Statistik Austria launched a new dataset, *How's Austria?*, comprising 30 headline indicators in the areas of material wealth, quality of life, and environmental sustainability. In the same year, the Ministry of Economy together with the Austrian Institute of

Economic Research (Österreichisches Institut für Wirtschaftsforschung, WIFO) published a study (*Mehr als Wachstum*; that is, 'More than growth'), which complemented the set of comparative indicators used by the OECD for its *How's Life?* report with additional indicators on those domains that were identified as especially relevant by Austrian people. Through a dedicated survey, Austrian people were asked to rate the importance of different indicators and dimensions for their own well-being. Based on this information, the WIFO report aggregated these various indicators to derive a composite index of Austrian well-being. See http://www.statistik.at/, http://www.statistik.at/web_en/statis tics/hows_austria/index.html.

France

The French government played a pivotal role in promoting the 'beyond GDP' agenda. Following the establishment of the Commission on the Measurement of Economic Performance and Social Progress (the so-called Stiglitz–Sen–Fitoussi Commission) in 2007, the French National Statistical Office (INSEE) launched a series of measurement initiatives. See http://www.insee.fr/fr/themes/document.asp?ref_id=ip1428.

Germany

In 2011, the Parliament established a Commission on Growth, Well-Being, Quality of Life – Ways to Sustainable Economics and Societal Progress in the Social Market Economy. Over the following months, the Commission discussed the importance of economic growth for the economy and society, the possibility of developing new indicators of well-being and progress, and the issue of sustainability (in particular, the need to decouple economic growth from resource use). The Commission's final report, issued in March 2013, proposed a set of indicators for measuring progress in three domains: the economy ('GDP, income distribution, and government debt'), the ecology ('greenhouse gases, nitrous oxide, and biodiversity'), and social wealth ('employment, education, health, and freedom').

Italy

In 2011, the Italian Statistical Office (ISTAT) and the National Council on the Economy and Labour (CNEL) established a joint Steering Group on the Measurement of Progress in Italian Society, which included representatives from businesses, trade unions and civil society. The Group developed a multidimensional framework for measuring 'equitable and sustainable well-being' (BES: *benessere equo e sostenibile*), building on an open consultation with experts, the civil society and citizens. As part of this initiative, ISTAT conducted surveys to identify the dimensions of well-being that are most relevant for Italian people. The Group published its report in 2013, and indicators will be systematically updated by ISTAT. See http://en.istat.it/salastampa/comunicati/non_calendario/20101227_00/ Cnel_EN.pdf.

Mexico

The national statistical office (INEGI) has developed better well-being statistics in three ways: first, by promoting discussions on the subject through seminars and conferences organised with many regional partners; second, by including new questions on subjective well-being in a range of existing surveys (household income and expenditure survey, time use survey, consumer confidence and public perception survey); and third, by promoting the use of the new set of well-being indicators in policy making. Several municipalities and state governments have launched initiatives on using evidence from new well-being metrics in their policy process. See http://www.inegi.org.mx/.

United Kingdom

In 2010, the UK Prime Minister invited the National Statistician to run a 'national debate', asking citizens 'What matters?' to them. This initiative was run by the Office of National Statistics (ONS) Measuring National Well-Being programme, which included the establishment of online and offline platforms to interact with people and organisations. More than 34 000 contributions were made through these platforms, with initial findings from the national debate and consultation published in June 2011. In July 2012, the ONS released its first annual subjective well-being estimates and a revised set of domains and measures. In November 2012, the first report on *Life in the UK – 2012* (and the national well-being 'wheel', which included the well-being indicators) was published (ONS, 2012). In March 2014, the ONS released the second edition of *Life in the UK* (ONS, 2014). The ONS measures of national well-being are now being combined with the Department for Environment, Food and Rural Affairs (DEFRA) Sustainable Development Indicators. See www.ons.gov.uk/ons/guide-method/user-guidance/well-being/publications/measuring-what-matters--national-statistician-s-reflections-on-the-national-debate-on-measuring-national-well-being.pdf.

Portugal

Statistics Portugal has also started to publish a set of well-being indicators on its website. See http://www.ine.pt/xportal/xmain?xpid=INE&xpgid=ine_main).

3. Human development and poverty: theoretical approaches
Suman Seth and Antonio Villar

> Developing better measures is not an end in itself but a means to enhance policies that improve people's lives. (Ángel Gurría, OECD Secretary-General)

3.1 INTRODUCTION

Gross domestic product (GDP) has become the yardstick to evaluate the overall economic performance or even the social well-being of a country or a region. The underlying assumption is that the well-being of an individual depends on their expenditure capacity, so that disposable income can be interpreted as a summary measure of their consumption opportunities. As the GDP is the market value of all new goods and services produced and provided in a given region during a year – or, equivalently, the total income of all individuals in the region in that year – it can be regarded as the macro counterpart of individual incomes or a measure of social well-being.

There are many problems associated with the use of GDP as a measure of social well-being, and the use of consumption expenditure as a measure of individual well-being. The problems associated with the use of GDP are clear: only market transactions are considered; quality is not computed; distributive aspects are ignored; and stocks or durable goods and infrastructures are practically out of the picture. GDP also leaves out activities of the informal sector, which can be significantly large in developing countries; and public sector activities are valued at cost due to the lack of markets and prices (Spence, 2009). The use of consumption expenditure as a measure of individual well-being is also far from unproblematic because it may leave out many factors – such as the quality of health or the value of knowledge – that are crucial for human flourishing but cannot be measured due to the lack of market prices. For a more detailed discussion of the flawed assumptions behind using per capita GDP as a measure of development, see Alkire and Deneulin (2009). Yet GDP and related indicators are used primarily because we have not yet found a better alternative that is so generally accepted.

GDP certainly captures a relevant part of the economic performance of a society, but it is far from being a complete measure of economic development and certainly further from being a sufficient measure of human development and social well-being. In fact, it is improbable that any single indicator can capture human development or social well-being, which is multifaceted by nature. This, rather, requires a multidimensional approach, which was recognized soon after GDP became a standard and has been discussed ever since.[1] Like human development, human deprivation or poverty is also usually understood in terms of deprivation in income or consumption expenditure. However, as Ruggeri Laderchi et al. (2003) showed in the case of India, non-deprivation in income did not necessarily mean non-deprivation in health and education. In fact, human deprivation or poverty, like human development, is also multifaceted and requires a multidimensional approach. A number of indices based on multiple dimensions have been developed in many areas of research, especially regarding inequality, poverty, subjective well-being, education and health, to name a few. Some of these indices are composite indices and others are more sophisticated multidimensional indices. The relevance of this approach led the Organisation for Economic Co-operation and Development (OECD) to issue a manual on the construction of composite indices (Nardo et al., 2008).

Note that moving from one to several dimensions, when approaching the development of a society, creates a number of difficult issues that call for agreement and compromise. The key points are: (1) Which are the most relevant dimensions to be considered? (2) How can we approximate those dimensions by means of specific variables whose data are available? (3) How should those variables be aggregated into a single index in order to get a systematic evaluation criterion? The difficulty of tackling all those issues explains a good deal about the persistence of GDP as the main index for economic growth and development. In spite of the different proposals put forward, no general agreement was reached on the adoption of a new standard, at least until the launching of the Human Development Index in 1990.

Since its inception, the Human Development Index (HDI) has become the most successful index to use multiple dimensions that address economic development and social well-being. Besides the HDI, the United Nations Development Programme (UNDP) in subsequent Human Development Reports has introduced several other indices, of which the more well-known ones are the Human Poverty Index (HPI) for measuring poverty, the Gender-Related Development Index (GDI) for capturing inequality in human development across gender, and the Gender Empowerment Index (GEM) for measuring women's empowerment. Each of these measures has evolved over time in terms of the selection of indicators and methodology. In this chapter, we restrict our analysis to the measures of human development and human deprivation or poverty, leaving aside the discussion of indices developed for other purposes.

The first Human Development Report (HDR) was launched in 1990 and since then global HDRs have been produced yearly. Indices in the HDR proposed by the United Nations have mostly been applications of Amartya Sen's idea of functionings and capabilities (Sen, 1985). These indices have been used frequently to measure the development and poverty of nations. Many countries have also produced national Human Development Reports, whose indices contain subnational level information. The indices in these reports have gone through several changes over time. We divide this timeline into two segments: pre-2010 and post-2010, because in the 2010 Human Development Report titled *The Real Wealth of Nations: Pathways to Human Development*, all indices have gone through significant amendments.

3.2 INDICES IN THE HUMAN DEVELOPMENT REPORTS, 1990–2009

The global HDRs have introduced various indices of human development, poverty, gender inequality, gender empowerment, and a few others. In this chapter, we focus on the indices of human development and poverty.

3.2.1   The Index for Measuring Human Development

The HDI was introduced in the first HDR in 1990. The HDI soon became popular, and each new edition had a large impact in the mass media because of its intuitive character and the large number of countries in the evaluation. This approach to measuring human development identified health, knowledge and material well-being as the key dimensions for social and economic development. Achievement in health was measured by the indicator life expectancy at birth (H), which is the number of years that a newborn is expected to live, according to the actual pattern of mortality rates within each country. Knowledge, understood as educational achievements, was approximated by a composite indicator: a mixture of literacy rate (E_1) and gross enrolment rate (E_2) (with weights of 2/3 and 1/3, respectively). Finally, material well-being was associated with the logarithm of the per capita GDP (Y).

Each of these four indicators was normalized with respect to a maximum and a minimum possible performance. This was essential in order to make the performance across indicators comparable. The maximum possible performances for these four indicators were denoted by H^{max}, E_1^{max}, E_2^{max} and Y^{max}, and the minimum possible performances were denoted by H^{min}, E_1^{min}, E_2^{min} and Y^{min}, respectively. Each of the four indicators was normalized as $i_N = (i - i^{min})/(i^{max} - i^{min})$ for $i = H$, E_1, and E_2 and $Y_N = (\ln Y^{max} - \ln Y)/(\ln Y^{max} - \ln Y^{min})$ for material well-being. The Human Development Index was defined as the arithmetic mean of the normalized values of those three dimensions and is expressed as:

$$HDI = \frac{1}{3}\left(H_N + \frac{2}{3}E_{1N} + \frac{1}{3}E_{2N} + Y_N\right) = \frac{1}{3}(H_N + E_N + Y_N).$$

Although the life expectancy indicator has been used consistently to assess the health dimension, different indicators have been used to measure the knowledge dimension, and different transformations of the same indicator have been used to gauge the material well-being dimension over time. In the first HDR, the knowledge dimension was assessed only by the adult literacy rate. From the second HDR onwards, the knowledge dimension was assessed by both the adult literacy rate and mean years of schooling. In the 1995 HDR, the mean years of schooling indicator was replaced by the combined enrolment ratio indicator. This pair of indicators was used until 2009. The well-being indicator, on the other hand, has been assessed throughout by per capita GDP, but with different transformations. In the first HDR, the logarithmic transformation was used, but in consecutive reports an equally distributed equivalent transformation (based on Atkinson, 1970) was used; until the 1999 HDR, when the transformation was switched back to the logarithmic scale following the suggestions of Anand and Sen (2000).

An index of human development, however, measures the progress of an entire society. The index ensures that any overall progress in human development is supported by an increase in its value, and any decline is evaluated by a decrease. An index of human development nevertheless ignores the underlying causes of progress or decline. Progress may occur with continual improvements in the lives of those already enjoying high levels of human development, while neglecting the lives of those actually needing improvement. In other words, progress may take place despite a large section of the population remaining deprived of basic needs, capabilities and public services. The pursuit of progress in human development remains incomplete until existing deprivations in the population are successfully eradicated.

3.2.2 Indices for Measuring Human Deprivations

Although the first attempt to assess deprivations using a poverty index was made in the 1996 Human Development Report, the first four HDRs presented the HDI as a complement of the country's deprivation. A country's deprivation in three dimensions was understood as a shortfall in that country's performance from the best possible performance in that dimension. A deprivation score was assigned to each of the four indicators as $D_i = (i^{max} - i)/(i^{max} - i^{min})$ for $i = H$, E_1, and E_2, and $D_Y = (\ln Y^{max} - \ln Y)/(\ln Y^{max} - \ln Y^{min})$. Then the overall deprivation score was obtained as $D = (D_H + D_E + D_Y)/3$. The HDI was the complement of the overall deprivation score, such that $HDI = (1 - D)$. It is straightforward to verify that this formulation is equivalent to the traditional HDI formulation: the simple average of performances in three dimensions. Thus, in the early Human Development Reports, an effort was made to link the HDI to the concept of deprivation, albeit at the country level.

However, deprivation at the country level may not necessarily be sensitive to deprivations at the individual level within countries. The HDI, even when presented as the complement of country-level deprivation, may not be sensitive to individual deprivations. Anand and Sen (1997) refer to measuring human development as a 'conglomerate approach', and measuring poverty as a 'deprivation approach'. A poverty index, unlike an index of development, is solely focused on those who fail to meet the deprivation cut-off. Every poverty index is supposed to satisfy the 'focus axiom', which requires that the poverty index should not be sensitive to the performance of those who are non-deprived or non-poor.[2]

Like human development, human deprivation is also multidimensional. Reducing deprivation in one dimension – such as income – may not necessarily translate to the reduction of deprivations in other dimensions. The earliest attempt to introduce a poverty index – referred to as the Capability Poverty Measure (CPM) – was made in the 1996 Human Development Report. The CPM was a composite index or a simple average of the basic capability shortfalls in three dimensions: living a healthy and well-nourished life, having the capability of safe and healthy reproduction, and being literate and knowledgeable. The corresponding indicators were the percentage of children under five years who were underweight, the percentage of births not attended by trained health personnel, and the percentage of women aged 15 years and above who were illiterate. Note that the three chosen indicators did not capture the deprivations of the entire population, but only deprivations among women and children.

In the 1997 HDR, two different poverty indices were introduced: one for the developing countries, referred to as HPI-1; and another for the industrialized countries, referred to as HPI-2. The HPI-1 consisted of three dimensions (like the HDI): (1) a long and healthy life; (2) knowledge; and (3) a decent standard of living. Deprivation in the long and healthy life dimension was measured by the percentage of people not expected to survive to the age of 40 (P_1). Deprivation in the knowledge dimension was assessed by the percentage of adults who were illiterate (P_2). Finally, deprivation in the standard-of-living dimension was an average of deprivations in three indicators: the percentage of people without access to safe water (P_{31}), the percentage of people without access to health services (P_{32}), and the percentage of moderately and severely underweight children under the age of five years (P_{33}). Thus, the third dimension – a decent standard of living – was measured as $P_3 = (P_{31} + P_{32} + P_{33})/3$. However, given the lack of frequent data on access to health services, from the 2001 HDR onwards, this third dimension has been measured by the average of the first and the third indictors only, such that $P_3 = (P_{31} + P_{33})/2$. The HPI-1 was a composite index of the three dimensions using the well-known formulation of the general mean of order three, and can be expressed as HPI-1 $= [(P_1^3 + P_2^3 + P_3^3)/3]^{1/3}$.

The choice of indicators for the HPI-1, however, was not suitable for the much richer industrialized countries because there would not be any deprivation in any of these indicators. An alternative index consisting of four dimensions, referred to as HPI-2, was developed for the industrialized countries. The first dimension related to the survival of citizens to a relatively early age, as measured by the percentage of people not expected to survive to the age of 60 years (P_1). The second dimension was knowledge, which was assessed by the percentage of people who were functionally illiterate as defined by the OECD (P_2). The third related to a decent standard of living, measured by the percentage of people living below the income poverty line, which was 50 percent of the median disposable household income (P_3). The fourth dimension related to non-participation or exclusion as gauged by the rate of long-term (12 months or more) unemployment of the labour force (P_4). The HPI-2 also used the generalized mean to formulate the HPI-2 such that HPI-2 $= [(P_1^3 + P_2^3 + P_3^3 + P_4^3)/4]^{1/3}$.

3.2.3   A Critical Evaluation of the pre-2010 Indices

Certainly, these additional indicators were novel and represented progress towards a more comprehensive measure of development and poverty. Yet, these indices of human development and poverty have also received much criticism.[3] Let us first discuss the criticisms attributed to the HDI. The main ones refer to:

1. *The nature of the selected dimensions.* Some relevant aspects of human development were missing, such as social integration and sustainability.
2. *The choice of indicators.* Even though the choice of indicators was significantly affected by the availability of data, it was not clear that the indicators used for approximating health, education and material well-being were the most sensible ones. Moreover, the nature of the three variables involved made the interpretation of the HDI as a summary statistic of a representative agent difficult.
3. *The absence of time-consistent data.* Due to frequent data revisions of indicators between subsequent years, inter-temporal comparisons using HDI became difficult.
4. *The lack of concern for distributive issues.* It is only natural to think that the measurement of human development should compute not only 'the size of the cake', but also the way in which it is distributed.
5. *The additive structure of the index.* Aggregating different components by the arithmetic mean had strong implications for their substitutability (linear indifference curves) and makes the index dependent on the normalization methods applied to different indicators.

6. *The lack of theoretical justification of the formula.* This makes it difficult to analyse the suitability of this index vis-à-vis other alternatives. Moreover, it induces the use of the HDI as an ordinal measure (a criterion to produce a ranking), and not as a cardinal measure that would help in evaluating the size of the differences between countries.

Like the HDI, the pre-2010 poverty indices could also be subject to criticism. Let us start with the Capability Poverty Measure or CPM, which faced two major criticisms. The first is related to the selection of indicators. The three chosen indicators did not capture the deprivations of the entire population; but only deprivations among women and children. Indeed, women and children should receive particular attention in any poverty eradication policy, but a poverty index for a country should not be restricted to a particular section of the population. The second criticism was due to the particular functional form used to aggregate and to obtain the composite poverty index. Like the HDI, the CPM used the arithmetic mean, ensuring that any increase in the deprivation in one dimension could be compensated by an equal-sized reduction in another dimension.

The HPIs, however, had one methodological improvement over the CPM in that the HPIs used a different order of general mean for aggregation rather than the arithmetic mean. The general mean of order $\alpha \geq 1$ of any n positive real values $x_1, \ldots, x_n$ is defined as $([x_1^\alpha + \cdots + x_n^\alpha]/n)^{1/\alpha}$. The arithmetic mean is also a general mean with order $\alpha = 1$ and is equal to $(x_1 + \cdots + x_n)/n$. As the value of parameter α increases, more emphasis is given to the larger values. In the HPI formulation, the use of a higher order of α places more emphasis on the larger deprivations. This ensures that an increase in deprivation in one indicator that has a relatively larger deprivation should be compensated by a much larger improvement in another indicator with a relatively lower deprivation. Also, a more equal distribution of deprivations across indicators is rewarded.

Another improvement appears to be in the selection of indicators. Unlike in the CPM, the indicators in the HPIs were not biased towards a particular section of the population, such as women and children; they captured deprivations across a wider range of population. Different indicators, however, were still based on different sets of the population. Consider the HPI-1 for example. The indicator for a long and healthy life was based on the living population, but was also affected by the number of people who died. The indicator for knowledge captured deprivations among the adult population only. Finally, one indicator for standard of living captured deprivations among the entire population, while the other captured deprivations only among children. Because the population sets were different across indicators, it was not possible to capture the multiplicity or the extent of deprivations for a particular group of people. In other words, the HPIs were not useful for understanding who within a country was more or less poor. This criticism could also be partially attributed to the use of composite indices for measuring poverty in general.

A composite index is built by first obtaining a comprehensive deprivation score for each indicator across the population and then aggregating these comprehensive deprivation scores to obtain the index. We can clearly see that, like the HDI, for the CPM and for the HPIs, the data for different indictors were collected from different sources and for different population subgroups. For any multidimensional index of poverty, however, information on all indicators ought to be collected from the same dataset so that the information on each indicator is available for each person or at least for each household. Thus, the construction of a multidimensional poverty index involves two stages: *identification* of those who are poor and *aggregation* of the deprivation information of the poor to obtain the overall index. For composite indices of poverty, there is no difference between the terms 'deprived' and 'poor' because people are separately identified as poor in each indicator in order to obtain the comprehensive deprivation score for that indicator. In multidimensional poverty analysis, however, the terms 'deprived' and 'poor' have a clear distinction. A person is considered deprived in an indicator if the person fails to meet the threshold in that indicator. By being deprived a person may not necessarily be considered poor, though. It is the identification function based on the joint deprivations that identifies a person as poor or non-poor (see the example in section 3.3.3).[4]

One clear distinction between composite indices of poverty and multidimensional indices of poverty is, thus, the consideration of joint deprivations at the identification stage. The second major difference is that a multidimensional index requires the information on all indicators to be available from the same dataset; whereas, a composite index may be constructed by collating information from different sources. This second difference may make a composite index appear more flexible and the multidimensional index appear more demanding. However, if it is feasible to capture joint deprivations, then the ability to capture them may outweigh the flexibility of composite indices. Certainly, the construction of the CPM and HPIs was innovative at a time when the measurement of poverty was dominated by the income approach – such as $1 a day and $2 a day – but they were merely composite indices and fell short of being truly multidimensional indexes of poverty.

3.3   INDICES IN THE HUMAN DEVELOPMENT REPORT 2010 AND ONWARDS

The twentieth anniversary of the HDR was taken as the right occasion to refurbish these indices, after launching an open discussion among specialists concerning possible improvements.[5] As a result, some substantial changes were introduced in the design of the HDI, a complementary index known as the Inequality-adjusted HDI (IHDI) was introduced, and the HPI-1 was replaced by a completely new index of poverty: the Multidimensional Poverty Index (MPI). Let us first discuss the modifications in the HDI, and then outline the MPI.

3.3.1   The Human Development Index

The 2010 Human Development Index is a more solid construct than its predecessor, even though it keeps most of the essential traits of the traditional HDI. In particular, it: (1) maintains the three-dimensional nature of the index; (2) continues to consider health, education and material well-being to be the only key dimensions to evaluate human development; (3) holds the equal-weight assumption for those variables; (4) keeps the normalization convention already adopted and the evaluation of material well-being in terms of logs; and (5) recurs to a mean in order to aggregate the normalized variables into a single number. There are, however, three major modifications in the 2010 Human Development Index that improve its analytical power. First, the indicators for measuring the achievements in material well-being and education were replaced. Table 3.1 presents

Table 3.1   The dimensions and indicators of the old and new HDI

Dimensions	Indicators	
	Pre-2010 HDI	2010 HDI
Health (*H*)	Life expectancy at birth	Life expectancy at birth
Knowledge (*E*)	Adult literacy rate	Mean years of schooling
	Gross enrolment ratio	Expected years of schooling
Material well-being (*Y*)	GDP per capita (PPP USD)	GNI per capita (PPP USD)

Note: GNI = gross national income; PPP = purchasing power parity.

the pre-2010 and 2010 HDI indicators for the three dimensions. Second, a time-consistent series for each indicator, using 1980 as a starting point, was developed, allowing system-atic inter-temporal comparisons to be made. Third, instead of using the arithmetic mean, achievements in the three dimensions are aggregated using the geometric mean, thus adopting the following formula:

$$HDI_{2010} = \left(\frac{H - H^{min}}{H^{max} - H^{min}} \times \frac{E - E^{min}}{E^{max} - E^{min}} \times \frac{\ln Y - \ln Y^{min}}{\ln Y^{max} - \ln Y^{min}} \right)^{1/3}$$

where *H*, *E*, and *Y* are the indicators measuring achievements in health, knowledge and material well-being dimensions, respectively, and the minimum and maximum goalposts are used in order to normalize each variable within the [0, 1] interval. Let us now devote some time to conducting a more in-depth analysis of the improvements to the 2010 HDI over the pre-2010 HDI.

The first significant modification in the 2010 HDI is the amendment of the indica-tors. Indeed, the choice of the indicators that approximate the achievements in the three selected dimensions is a key element of the construction of the index. Life expectancy at birth was kept as the indicator for assessing the health dimension, so there is no novelty regarding this dimension. The normalization of this indicator, according to the 2016 HDR, is obtained by taking $H^{max} = 85$ and $H^{min} = 20$. The 2010 version of the HDI, however, measures material well-being in terms of the logarithmic transformation of per capita gross national income rather than that of the per capita GDP. This entails taking into account the incomes of nationals living abroad and the proceeds of firms operating in other countries. This is a minor improvement in the design of the index. The nor-malization of this indicator, according to the 2016 HDR, is obtained by taking $Y^{max} = \$75\,000$ and $Y^{min} = \$100$.

The change in the variable that measures educational achievements was a major one, and was really needed. The excessive weight given to the literacy rate in the traditional HDI made it unsuitable for capturing differences in human capital, particularly in devel-oped countries. Among the several alternatives for measuring educational achievements, the 2010 HDI selected yet another composite variable: the geometric mean of 'mean years of education' (adults) and 'expected years of schooling' (children), suitably normalized. Getting the normalized variable for education requires first normalizing each partial index and then taking an arithmetic mean of the two normalized values. According to the 2016 HDR, to normalize mean years of education the maximum value is set equal to 15 years, and to normalize the expected years of schooling the maximum value is set equal to 18 years; whereas, the minimum goalpost is set equal to zero in both cases.

The second major improvement in the 2010 HDI is the reconstruction of time-consistent values for the HDI according to the new method. This allows for comparing the evolution of this index and yields interesting results on the dynamics of the different countries.

The third major improvement is the use of geometric mean as an aggregator rather than the arithmetic mean. Using the arithmetic mean to aggregate achievements in the three dimensions into a real-valued indicator has a number of drawbacks, despite the appeal of its intuitive character. The arithmetic mean is an additive aggregation procedure that implies assuming perfect substitutability between components (linear indifference curves). It amounts to admitting that we can substitute, for instance, expected life and years for education at a constant rate, no matter the average level of health. A constant rate of substitution independent of the level of the variable is hard to justify in many contexts, and particularly in this one. Moreover, an additive index of this sort generates a ranking that is sensitive to the normalization of the different indictors. Namely, a change in the arbitrary normalization of the raw variables induces changes in the ranking that the index produces (because changing the normalization amounts to modifying the weights with which those variables enter the index).

The need for a change in the aggregation process was widely recognized in the literature. Many authors agreed on the need to replace the arithmetic mean with a more general nonlinear type of mean, most particularly the geometric mean (see Chakravarty, 2003; Foster et al., 2005; Herrero et al., 2010a; Seth, 2009, 2013, among others, for a discussion). The geometric mean is a well-known aggregator in economics. It corresponds to the familiar symmetric Cobb–Douglas formula for production and utility functions and exhibits much better properties regarding substitutability among the variables. Also note that the geometric mean penalizes the dispersion of variables that are aggregated; whereas, the arithmetic mean is insensitive to the distribution of the variables being averaged.[6]

How does our vision of human development change with the new index? The 2010 Human Development Report says in this respect (p. 217):

> The methodological improvements in the HDI, using new indicators and the new functional form, result in substantial changes ... Adopting the geometric mean produces lower index values, with the largest changes occurring in countries with uneven development across dimensions. The geometric mean has only a moderate impact on HDI ranks.

Indeed, the new HDI discriminates more than the old one (the coefficient of variation is 40 per cent higher) and yields a good deal of shifts in the ranking, mostly due to the change in the variable that measures education. See Klugman et al. (2011) for a detailed discussion.

3.3.2   Adjusting Inequality in Human Development

There is a general consensus on the need to take into account distributive considerations when evaluating economic growth or human development. This can now be accomplished easily because there are statistics on income inequality for many countries, and we have a well-established theory that permits linking the evaluation of the size and the distribution of income. It is therefore striking that the Human Development Report waited for

20 years to include distributive considerations into the HDI, in spite of several proposals being put forward (e.g., Anand and Sen, 1994; Hicks, 1997; Foster et al., 2005; Herrero et al., 2010a, 2010b; Seth, 2009, 2013).

The 2010 Human Development Report includes a new index that addresses the distribution of the different variables: the Inequality-adjusted Human Development Index (IHDI). This index has the same structure as the 2010 HDI, but each constituent variable has previously been adjusted by a discount rate that measures the inequality of its distribution within each country. That is, the IHDI is the geometric mean of the inequality-adjusted values of the variables for health, education and material well-being:

$$I(H) = f_H(H)(1 - A_H), I(E) = f_E(E)(1 - A_E), I(Y) = f_Y(Y)(1 - A_Y)$$

where A_C, for $C = H, E, Y$, is the inequality measure of the corresponding variable, and $f_C(C)$ describes the transformation of the original values into normalized values (with logs in the case of the per capita GNI). According to this formulation, inequality reduces the achievements in each variable. The term $f_C(C)A_C$ is a measure of the loss due to inequality.

The report adopts Atkinson's (1970) inequality index for the value of the inequality aversion parameter $\varepsilon = 1$, which yields an inequality-adjusted measure for each indicator corresponding to the geometric mean of individual achievements (see Foster et al., 2005; Alkire and Foster, 2010 for details). The IHDI is given by the formula:

$$IHDI = \sqrt[3]{I(H) \times I(E) \times I(Y)}.$$

However, the variables used for computing the inequality measures are not necessarily computed from the same variables used for computing the partial indices for the HDI. Thus, $f_H(H)$, $f_E(E)$, and $f_Y(Y)$ are the partial indices for the HDI such that $f_H(H)$ is the life expectancy at birth, $f_E(E)$ is the geometric mean of expected years of schooling and mean years of schooling, and $f_Y(Y)$ is the corresponding partial index based on GNI per capita. In contrast, the inequality measure for the knowledge dimension has been computed using years of schooling among adults only as it is not possible to capture inequality across the expected years of schooling variable. Similarly, the inequality measure for the material well-being dimension has been computed from various variables such as per capita disposable income, per capita consumption expenditure or income imputed from asset indices.[7] The inequality measure for the health dimension, however, is computed using the same indicator used for constructing the corresponding partial indicator, yet the computation of the inequality measure is not straightforward: the measure is not computed by capturing inequality across the health status of the entire population; rather, inequality is computed across the mortality rates for different age groups (for a detailed discussion, see Kovacevic, 2010a).

3.3.3　A New Index for Measuring Human Deprivations

In the 2010 Human Development Report, UNDP introduced a new index of multidimensional poverty referred to as the Multidimensional Poverty Index (MPI) for developing countries, which was proposed by Alkire and Santos (2010). This shows the UNDP's

Table 3.2   Dimensions, indicators, deprivation cut-offs, and weights of the MPI[8]

Dimension	Indicator	A person in a household is deprived if:
Health	Nutrition	Any woman or child in the household with nutritional information is undernourished
	Mortality	Any child has died in the household
Education	Schooling	No household member has completed five years of schooling
	Attendance	Any school-aged child in the household is not attending school up to class 8
Standard of living	Electricity	The household has no electricity
	Sanitation	The household's sanitation facility is not improved, or it is shared with other households
	Water	The household does not have access to safe drinking water, or safe water is more than a 30-minute walk (round trip)
	Flooring material	The household has a dirt, sand or dung floor
	Cooking fuel	The household cooks with dung, wood or charcoal
	Assets	The household does not own more than one of these items: radio, telephone, TV, bike, motorbike or refrigerator; and does not own a car or truck

Source: Alkire et al. (2011).

willingness to mark a clear departure from the use of composite indices to multidimensional indices that are able to capture joint distributions across the population. Like the HDI and the HPI-1, the MPI also has three dimensions – education, health and standard of living – but it consists of ten indicators. The indicators and their deprivation cut-offs are reported in Table 3.2. The health dimension and the education dimension consist of two indicators each, and the standard of living dimension consists of six indicators. Thus, two indicators in the MPI, child mortality and access to safe drinking water, are the same as those in the HPI-1.

The method of the MPI is an adaptation of the Adjusted Headcount Ratio proposed by Alkire and Foster (2007, 2011). Unlike the HPI-1, the MPI is computed directly from the survey dataset rather than the indicators being computed from different sources. Let us provide a brief outline of the method with an exemplar country with n individuals and d indicators. In case of the MPI, $d = 10$. Let us refer to the performance of a person in an indicator by achievement. The achievements of all n persons in d dimensions is represented by the $n \times d$-dimensional matrix X. The achievement of any person i in indicator j is denoted by x_{ij}. The weight attached to indicator j is denoted by $w_j > 0$ such that $\sum_j w_j = 1$. Each indicator has its own deprivation cut-off. A person failing to meet the cut-off is identified as deprived in that dimension. The deprivation cut-off of indicator j is denoted by z_j. Subject to the deprivation cut-off, person j is assigned a deprivation status score in indicator j, which is denoted by g_{ij} such that $g_{ij} = 1$ if person i is deprived in indicator j and $g_{ij} = 0$, otherwise. In the next step, a deprivation score is obtained for each person i such that $c_i = \sum_j w_j g_{ij}$. The deprivation score of each person is the weighted average of deprivation status scores. Note that at the two extremes, $c_i = 0$ if person i is not deprived in any indicator and $c_i = 1$ if person i is deprived in all indicators, and so $c_i \in [0,1]$.

Not all those who are deprived in any indicator are identified as poor, however. The identification step involves a poverty cut-off k. A person is identified as poor whenever $c_i \geq k$, and non-poor whenever $c_i < k$. If the value of k is positive but lower than the minimum weight assigned to any indicator such that $0 < k < \min\{w_1,\ldots,w_d\}$, then the identification approach is referred to as the union approach. By the union approach, a person is identified as poor even when they are deprived in a single indicator. On the other extreme, an intersection approach identifies a person as poor only if the person is deprived in all indicators, or when $k = 1$. Both of these approaches may be too stringent, and in that case an alternative middle ground may be found by using an intermediate approach, such that $\min\{w_1,\ldots,w_d\} < k < 1$. Once individuals are identified as poor and non-poor, then a censored distribution of deprivation scores is obtained, such that $c_i(k) = c_i$ if $c_i \geq k$ and $c_i(k) = 0$ for all $c_i < k$. The adjusted headcount ratio, denoted by M_0, is computed from the censored distribution scores as $M_0 = [\sum_i c_i(k)]/n$.

The MPI uses a particular set of indicators and deprivation cut-offs, a particular set of weights, and a certain value of poverty cut-off. The three dimensions, ten indicators, and the corresponding deprivation cut-offs are already outlined in Table 3.2. Like the HDI and the HPI-1, the MPI weighs each dimension equally, and furthermore the weight within each dimension is equally distributed across indicators. For example, the mortality indicator in the health dimension is assigned a weight equal to 1/6; whereas the assets indicator in the standard of living dimension is assigned a weight equal to 1/18. The poverty cut-off for the MPI is equal to one-third of the weighted indicators, or $k = 1/3$. Thus, a person within a household is identified as poor if the household's deprivation score is equal to or larger than 1/3. Note that the identification takes place at the household level but not at the individual level because it is difficult to obtain data at the individual level. Because the identification takes place at the household level, it is not possible to capture the difference in achievements that may exist within a household. Despite this shortcoming, the construction of the MPI is a big leap forward in the measurement of poverty.

The MPI also has certain useful properties. First, it can be expressed as a product of two terms. One is the multidimensional headcount ratio (H), which is the proportion of the population living in households that are deprived in at least one-third of weighted indicators or with deprivation scores equal to or larger than one-third. If we denote the number of poor by q, then $H = q/n$. The other term is the average deprivation score among the poor (A). By definition, H lies between 0 and 1: it is equal to 1 when everyone is identified as poor, and is equal to 0 when there are no poor at all. The range of A, however, is not as straightforward. Whenever there is at least one poor person, A lies between k and 1, but if there is no poor person in the society, then A cannot be defined. The second useful feature is that the MPI can be expressed as a weighted average of the censored headcount ratios of the ten indicators. The censored headcount ratio of an indicator is the proportion of the population that is identified as multidimensionally poor and is simultaneously deprived in that indicator. The third useful property is that the MPI is decomposable across any population subgroup, which means that the overall MPI can be expressed as the weighted average of subgroup MPIs where the weight attached to each subgroup is equal to its relative population share.

3.4   A CRITICAL EVALUATION OF THE 2010 INDICES

Although the indices introduced in the 2010 HDR overcame many limitations of the indices introduced in the previous HDRs, there is still room for improvement. In this section, we devote some time to critically assess these 2010 indices.

3.4.1   The Human Development Index

The new HDI is regarded as containing major improvements with respect to measuring educational achievements, the construction of time-consistent data series, the new aggregation formula, and the introduction of distributive considerations. Yet it has also opened an important discussion about some methodological issues, which refer to the nature of the index and its internal structure. From a purely theoretical viewpoint, there are some flaws in the design of the new HDI that should be addressed (see Herrero et al., 2012). From an empirical perspective, the 2010 HDI received a number of criticisms related to the apparent performance of African countries and the questionable trade-offs between variables, according to the new method (see Ravallion, 2012).

Most of the criticisms are related to the change in the aggregation procedure. Some argue that the change in the aggregation formula does not significantly alter the ranking of the countries (most of the changes are actually due to the new education variable); whereas, the geometric mean is a less intuitive concept than the arithmetic mean. Moreover, there are empirical outcomes regarding the resulting rates of substitution between dimensions that have shed some doubts about the advantage of the new formulation (see the discussions in the blog 'Let's Talk Human Development', Ravallion, 2012; Zambrano, 2011, 2016; Klugman et al., 2011). Finally, there are also criticisms on some modelling choices, particularly regarding the use of logs for the income variable and the normalization strategy (see Herrero et al., 2010b, 2012). Let us critically evaluate the new HDI in more detail.

Choice of weights
The 2010 HDI preserves the number and the nature of the selected dimensions and the equal-weight principle of the traditional HDI. There is no novelty in those respects, and the criticisms that applied to the pre-2010 HDI also apply here. The choice of equal weights for the different dimensions was made essentially on the basis that there was no rationale to give more weight to any of those essential aspects of human development (see UNDP, 1995, p. 48). The 2010 edition of the HDR keeps this weighting system. Yet, as Anand and Sen (1997) have pointed out, one may well consider that 'the weights in the HDI should be traced either to individual preferences, some collective social choice process, or to a strong normative argument'. In an empirical paper regarding 1975–2005, using principal components techniques, Nguefack-Tsague et al. (2011) provide a statistical justification for the HDI weighting scheme.[9]

Any precise weighting scheme, however, is difficult to agree upon universally, and therefore, instead of just debating the selection of a particular weighting scheme, it is important to understand how robust the comparisons are with respect to the choice of the initial weighting scheme, to possible alternatives. Different tools for sensitivity and robustness analyses have been developed in order to test the robustness of rankings generated by the composite indices. For example, Foster et al. (2009, 2013) propose a tool for testing the robustness of pair-wise comparisons with respect to the initial weighting scheme. Applying the tool to the HDI ranking for various years, they find that nearly 70 per cent of all the HDI pair-wise comparisons to be fully robust. 'Fully robust' means that 70 per cent of the pair-wise comparisons did not alter, no matter which alternative weighting schemes were selected when the weights were strictly positive and summed up to 1.[10]

Choice of variables

Do the three dimensions of HDI sufficiently cover all facets of development? Certainly, the answer is no. In particular, the question of sustainability is essential and should be incorporated into the index – the sooner the better.[11] Also, including some aspects of social exclusion may improve the measurement of the differential impact of economic fluctuations. However, caution is necessary when increasing the number of dimensions, because: (1) the larger number of dimensions makes the aggregation procedure more difficult; and (2) the larger number of variables makes choosing a precise weighting scheme more complex.

The precise dimensions that should be added are a matter of great debate, which is beyond the scope of this chapter. However, we provide a critical evaluation of the variables that have been used to measure the three dimensions of the new HDI.

The health variable   Life expectancy at birth is an estimate of the average number of years for a newborn in a given society at a given point in time. It is obtained from the mortality tables of the existing population as follows. First, one determines the probability of death at age γ, p_γ, and then computes the corresponding survival probability at that age, given by $\bar{p}_\gamma = 1 - p_\gamma$. The number of survivors at age γ in a given year, S_γ, is simply $S_\gamma = S_{\gamma-1}\bar{p}_\gamma$, under the convention of starting from a fictitious population $S_0 = 100\,000$. Life expectancy at age γ (assuming that agents live during half of the year in which they die) is calculated as:

$$e_\gamma = \frac{1}{2} + \frac{1}{S_\gamma} \sum_{i=\gamma+1}^{\infty} S_i = \frac{1}{2} + \sum_{i=\gamma+1}^{\infty} \left(\prod_{j=\gamma+1}^{i} \bar{p}_j \right).$$

Life expectancy at birth is simply e_0, that is, the average number of years that a person born in the year of reference will live.

It is clear from the formulation on the right in the above equation that life expectancy at any reference age y is independent of the demographic structure of a country, which allows consistent comparison of health in countries with different population pyramids.[12] Life expectancy at birth is a variable that provides a sensible approximation of the measurement of a long and healthy life. Although the data are available for most countries, this variable is rather elementary in construct. The data show that developed countries exhibit very high values of life expectancy at birth, with a small variance; while they exhibit more relevant differences in the demographic structure. Therefore, life expectancy at birth tends to overestimate the development capacities of those countries with a relatively older population, and to underestimate the development capacities of those countries with a younger population (typically, developing countries). In future revisions of the health variable, quality of life (for example, in terms of quality-adjusted life years [QALYs] or self-perceived health states) and the population structure (for example, the relative size of the working-age population) should be considered in addition to the quantity of life. Finally, there is also a more essential consideration as to whether this is the type of indicator that fits best to evaluate human development.

The education variable   The change in the variable measuring educational achievements was probably the most needed one. The HDI 2010 substituted the old combination of literacy rate and gross enrolment rates with another composite variable that consists of the geometric mean of 'mean years of education' (among adults) and 'expected years of schooling' (among children), suitably normalized. These two new partial indicators are certainly more informative, and capture the essential differences in the level of human capital among countries.

Yet the way in which the composite education variable has been constructed has two disadvantages worth considering. The use of the geometric mean in order to create the composite variable of education makes the indicators' impact on the HDI less transparent. Moreover, the geometric mean of the two partial indicators of education amounts to unjustifiably penalising improvements in the educational expectations of the young, as the geometric mean fosters the equalization of the component variables. Consequently, improvements in children's schooling are only partially reflected in the index of education, which makes incentives to invest in education less apparent. From a different perspective, it is worth taking into account that the empirical evidence suggests that, after some minimal threshold, it is the quality of education and not the years of schooling indicator that better explains differences in development. The Programme for International Student Assessment (PISA) studies provide a rich database that may be considered for the future incorporation of the quality of education (for example, by computing quality-adjusted years of schooling).

The income variable   As in the traditional HDI, the new version measures material well-being in terms of logs of an income variable (per capita GDP before 2010, and per capita GNI afterwards). The use of logs implies that the effect of one additional unit of a given variable decreases with the level at which this happens. This is the conventional way of describing how the consumption of a given good relates to personal welfare and is an expression of the 'decreasing marginal utility' principle. The Human Development Report provides this type of explanation to justify the use of logarithms when measuring material well-being: an additional euro has a different impact depending on the level of well-being at which it is gained. The obvious question is: Why is this principle applied to the income variable and not to the other ones in the HDI? Why is it that an additional year of life or education has the same value no matter the level at which it occurs?

A reasonable explanation of this asymmetry goes along the lines of the axiomatics provided in Zambrano (2014) (see also Klugman et al., 2011 for a wider discussion). When raw variables are interpreted as estimates of capabilities, direct indicators should be distinguished from indirect indicators of capabilities and thus variables should receive differential treatment. Even though this is a consistent approach that might justify the use of logs for the income variable, it involves some drawbacks. First, it does not fit very well with some of the novelties of the HDI 2010 (especially with respect to the inequality-adjusted measures discussed in the next subsection). Second, it imposes restrictions on the normalization formula, as one cannot take minimum values below 1 for the logged variable, no matter the units in which we measure income. Third, it has a relevant impact on the substitutability of the underlying primary variables reported in Table 3.1, as the meaning of substitutability is not very clear (or, alternatively, prevents making sensible calculations of marginal rates of substitution).

Rights   We shall be extremely brief on this point as this is a well-known problem: the HDI does not take into account human rights. People in charge of the Human Development Reports are well aware of this. As an example, the heading of Figure 4.1 in the 2010 HDR reads as follows: 'A high Human Development Index does not mean democracy, equality or sustainability.' Equality has already been addressed, for example by the introduction of the IHDI, and dealing with sustainability is on the agenda. What about democracy? For example, the compliance with some basic rights, as identified in the Universal Declaration of Human Rights of 1948.

The objective of involving as many countries as possible has led to the neglect of this basic question in the existing HDI and forced those interested to look elsewhere when seeking a measure of the basic rights of citizens. This is an arguable strategy, because it seems to send the message that those aspects are not as important.

Modelling flaws

The preceding discussion regarding the choice of variables is partly a matter of judgement. We now discuss an aspect that can be regarded as a conceptual flaw in the way the HDI is modelled.

As the variables for assessing the three human development dimensions are measured in different units, some normalization is required. Following the procedure already used in the traditional HDI, the normalization formula chosen by the 2010 HDI preserves the maximum and minimum goalposts. However, the interpretation of maximum and minimum goalposts is somewhat different, as follows. Maximum goalposts are mostly regarded as a technical device to keep the range of variables within a compact interval. Minimum goalposts, on the contrary, are given an ethical content and are interpreted as minimum admissible values (a kind of subsistence level).

We have already seen that a given raw variable, X, is transformed into a normalized variable, x, according to the formula:

$$x = \frac{X - X^{min}}{X^{max} - X^{min}},$$

where X^{max} and X^{min} are the corresponding goalposts. That is, we transform the original values into relative gains so that all the transformed variables move into the [0, 1] interval. Note that the normalized variables are all unit-free, and that the above formula can be regarded as a linear transformation of the original variable, $x = aX'$, where $a = \frac{1}{X^{max} - X^{min}}$ defines the units in which the variable is measured and $X' = X - X^{min}$ is the net value of the variable.

This way of normalizing the variables, however, has three negative implications:

1. It makes the whole construction of the HDI dependent on the arbitrary choices of the normalization parameters. In particular, changing the minimum goalpost can revert (and indeed it does) the ranking and modify the relative valuations.[13] This is

unfortunate because the dependence of the ranking on the arbitrary choice of normalization values was one of the main criticisms of the arithmetic mean. Note that the multiplicative formula of the 2010 HDI implies that changing the maximum goalposts only affects the units of measurement and therefore it alters neither the ranking nor the relative values of any two countries.[14]

2.   Deducting any positive value from the original variables (that is, using minimum goalposts) worsens the picture we get of lower-performing countries, while having practically no impact on those countries with higher values. As a consequence, the gap between top and bottom countries increases artificially. A simple example using the health variable illustrates this: a minimum goalpost of 20 years implies computing one-half of Afghanistan's life expectancy and three-quarters of Japan's corresponding value.

3.   The use of a minimum goalpost in the normalization may have a very large effect on the marginal rates of substitution due to the behaviour of the slope of a Cobb–Douglas function when a given component approaches 0. Therefore, subtracting whatever amount to an already very close-to-zero magnitude will increase substantially (and again artificially) the associated marginal rates of substitution. This is the main reason behind the polemic substitution rates found in Ravallion (2012); see Herrero et al. (2012) for a discussion and a calculation of marginal rates of substitution without using minimum goalposts.

3.4.2   The Inequality-Adjusted Human Development Index

The 2010 edition of the HDI (at last) took distributive issues into account. It introduced inequality measures not only regarding income but also with respect to the two other dimensions. Distributive considerations are introduced by calculating the egalitarian equivalent worth of a given value. That is, if $f_C(C)$ is the mean value of a reference variable C and A_C is an inequality measure, then the egalitarian equivalent value is given by $f_C(C)[1 - A_C]$. This is a well-founded conceptual construction, provided that two requirements are fulfilled: (1) both the inequality measure and the mean value should refer to the very same variable; and (2) more equality leads to better possible world. Unfortunately, all variables that are used for the construction of the IHDI do not seem to satisfy those requirements.

Take the income variable first. The egalitarian-equivalent income fits neither with the use of logs nor with the normalization choice. If we measure inequality over the income distribution vector, as is done in the 2010 report, we cannot consistently use the log of income as the reference variable. Moreover, the normalization used (with or without logs) is also inconsistent, as the chosen inequality measure is sensitive to the choice of minimum goalposts in the normalization.[15] If we want to keep the interpretation of the capability approach proposed in Zambrano (2011), one should measure inequality over the vector of log income values. Be that as it may, the inconsistency with the normalization choice remains, unless one measures inequality over the distribution of the normalized individual logged variables. But the meaning of that exercise is far from clear. Measuring income in logs for the HDI and measuring inequality without logs or normalization, as is done in various HDRs, violates requirement (1) stated above.

In order to understand why the second requirement is not fulfilled, let us consider the health dimension, where it is not clear whether more equality leads to a more desirable state. Recall that inequality in the health dimension is not based on the inequality in health conditions of the population in a given time period, but it is based on the inequality in life spans across different age groups in a given time period (Kovacevic, 2010b). Consider two distributions of life expectancies across age groups with the same average life expectancies at birth. Suppose, one distribution is obtained from the other distribution by improving the life span of the youngest group and at the same time by reducing the life span of the eldest group due to some epidemic disease. Although the average life expectancy remains unchanged, it is not clear why the latter distribution should reflect a more desirable state due to the unfortunate demise of some of its oldest members. Even acknowledging this limitation though it is quite tough to find a proper indicator to reflect health conditions of the citizens of a country, the present way of computing health inequality is hard to justify and requires further research for improvement.

Another area of concern for the IHDI is the ignorance of the joint distribution of well-being in various dimensions. In terms of measuring poverty, the UNDP has moved in the right direction by introducing a poverty measure that captures the joint distribution of deprivations rather than computing a composite index of poverty. The same, however, has not been true for the HDI or the IHDI. The chosen indicators have not been obtained from a single survey, and thus not from the same set of individuals or households within a country. In this sense, the IHDI (and certainly the HDI) still remains a composite of dashboard indices and is being prevented from graduating to a multidimensional index capturing joint deprivations. Is it possible to capture the joint distribution of achievements? The answer is yes, but this requires the data on all indicators to be available from a single survey and across all individuals or households, as in case of the MPI. An extension of the class of indices developed by Foster et al. (2005) has been proposed by Seth (2009, 2013), which captures the joint distribution of achievements and has been used to compute the UNDP's Gender Inequality Index in 2010. This index is in the same class of indices to which the IHDI belongs and may be used when the data are available.

3.4.3   The Multidimensional Poverty Index

The UNDP's efforts towards upgrading the measurement of poverty from using a composite index (HPI) to a multidimensional index (MPI) capturing joint distribution is indeed novel. However, there is still room for improvement in certain aspects. One is the consideration of inequality across the poor; and the second is the different types of robustness of the ranking or pair-wise comparisons with respect to different parameters, such as alternative choices of deprivation cut-offs, poverty cut-offs and weighting schemes.

Consideration of inequality while measuring poverty has been customary following Sen (1976). By construction, the MPI is an average of weighted deprivations that the poor experience, and is not sensitive to inequality across the poor. There are various alternative poverty measures that use binary indicators as the MPI does, but are sensitive to inequality across the poor (see Bossert et al., 2009; Jayaraj and Subramanian, 2009; Rippin, 2011). However, there is a crucial trade-off that should be taken into consideration. The inequality-sensitive poverty indices do not allow the overall indices to comprehend the contribution of each indicator or dimension to overall poverty, which is crucial for policy analysis (Alkire and Foster, 2016). Given that both properties are important, whether it is possible to find a framework to incorporate both is a subject for further research. For a potential solution, see Seth and Alkire (2017).

A second improvement should come from developing a tool that may be used to test the robustness of rankings and country comparisons with respect to the choice of parameters in the MPI's construction. Although Alkire and Santos (2010, 2014) tested the robustness of country rankings with respect to a few alternative weighting schemes, a range of poverty cut-offs, and a few different alternative sets of deprivation cut-offs, a sounder and more concrete approach is required.

3.5   CONCLUDING REMARKS

In this chapter, we present a critical evaluation of the indices for measuring human development and poverty in various Human Development Reports. We show how these indices have evolved over time to capture various aspects of well-being and deprivations. The introduction of simplified indices in the early reports was required to catch the attention of the mass media and policy makers to put the concept of human development on the agenda. However, a simplified index is not sufficient for capturing the complexity of human lives and their development and deprivations. These make the construction of the indices more complex. More complex indices, however, make their interpretation difficult. Hence, further research is required to amend the indices in a direction that maintains the intuitive interpretations of the indices and, at the same time, captures the complex realities of human development and deprivations.

Another important issue with these indices is the requirement of data. We have reiterated that the consideration of joint distribution is imperative in order to graduate an index of well-being or poverty from its composite index status to a truly multidimensional index status. The UNDP has moved in this direction by introducing a multidimensional measure of poverty. However, a move in the same direction has not been possible for the measurement of human development, primarily due to the lack of appropriate data. Our proposals for theoretical improvements cannot be materialized without solving the data constraints first.

ACKNOWLEDGEMENTS

We are grateful to Sabina Alkire, Milorad Kovacevic, and Eduardo Zambrano for valuable comments. This work was done while the second author was visiting the Department of Mathematics for Decisions at the University of Florence, Italy. Thanks are due for the hospitality and facilities provided there. The research is covered by the projects ECO2010-21706 and SEJ-6882/ECON with financial support from the Spanish Ministry of Science and Technology, the Junta de Andalucía and the FEDER (Fonds Européen de Développement Économique et Régional / European Fund for Economic and Regional Development).

NOTES

1. For example, the United Nations 1954 report on the standards of living, the 'basic needs approach' fostered by the International Labour Organization in 1974, the Physical Quality of Life Index (PQLI) put forth by Morris (1979) and reformulated by Ram (1982), or the proposals of the Daj Hammarskjöld Foundation (Max-Neef, 1984). For more recent critiques, see Boarini et al. (2006), Stiglitz et al. (2009) or Fleurbaey (2009).
2. We discuss in section 3.2.3 that the terms 'deprived' and 'poor' are not synonymous when multiple dimensions are involved in the construction of a poverty index.
3. We here follow Herrero et al. (2010b). See also the contributions in Anand and Sen (1994), Hicks (1997), Sagar and Najam (1999), Osberg and Sharpe (2002), Philipson and Soares (2001), Pinilla and Goerlich (2005), Foster et al. (2005), Becker et al. (2005), Stiglitz et al. (2009), Seth (2009) and Herrero et al. (2010c).
4. See, however, the discussion in Villar (2013).
5. See the research papers 2010 series of the United Nations Development Programme and, particularly, the contributions by Alkire and Foster (2011, 2010), Herrero et al. (2010b), Kovacevic (2010a) and Alkire and Santos (2010).
6. Given the small values of the normalized variables, changes in rankings induced by substituting the arithmetic mean by the geometric mean will be small. The changes in the relative values, though, are more relevant and reflect the dispersion of the partial indices.
7. Income inequality is calculated with respect to the original distribution without logarithmic transformations.
8. For the 2014 HDR, certain notable revisions to the MPI indicators were made, such as (i) 'stunting of under five children' was used instead of 'overweight' as a health indicator, (ii) a few asset indicators were added to better reflect rural poverty, (iii) the definition of deprivation in school attainment was changed to 'at least 6 years of education' instead of 'at least 5 years' etc. For further details, see Kovacevic and Calderon (2016).
9. For a discussion on different techniques for setting weights for multidimensional indices, see Decancq and Lugo (2013).
10. For further discussions on robustness and sensitivity analyses of the composite indices, see Nardo et al. (2008), Cherchye et al. (2008), Permanyer (2011) and Seth and McGillivray (2016).
11. The 2011 edition of the Human Development Report pays particular attention to this issue. The United Nations team responsible for the report is actively working on this topic, trying to find ways of incorporating the sustainability dimension in the HDI. **See also** Costantini and Monni (2005), Neumayer (2011) and Llavador et al. (2011).
12. The independence of life expectancy from the demographic structure is a way of avoiding the 'composition effect' that appears when using the average mortality rates. Indeed, it might be the case that country A has a lower average mortality rate than country B, while country A exhibits higher mortality rates at all age intervals. The reason is that specific mortality rates vary a lot across cohorts, and the relative size of the different cohorts may induce this counter-intuitive outcome. That is why life expectancy is preferred.
13. When calculating the HDI 2010 by normalizing the raw variables as shares of the same maximum values used in the report (that is, letting minimum goalposts equal to 0), some 30 per cent of the countries change their ranking by five or more positions.
14. A change in the minimum goalpost modifies both the units in which the variables are measured and the net value. The first only affects the scale and does alter the ranking in a multiplicative formula (as happens with changes in the maximum goalposts). The second impact is indistinguishable from a change in the level of the raw variable and that is why the ranking is altered.
15. We consider here the family of relative inequality measures, which is taken as reference in the 2010 report.

REFERENCES

Alkire, S. and Deneulin, S. (2009) 'The Human Development and Capability Approach', in Deneulin, S. and Shahani, L. (eds), *An Introduction to Human Development and Capability Approach*, Earthscan: London.

Alkire, S. and Foster, J.E. (2007) 'Counting and Multidimensional Poverty Measures', OPHI Working Paper 7, Oxford Poverty and Human Development Initiative, University of Oxford.

Alkire, S. and Foster, J.E. (2010) 'Designing the Inequality-Adjusted Human Development Index (IHDI)', OPHI Working Paper 37, Oxford Poverty and Human Development Initiative, University of Oxford.

Alkire, S. and Foster, J.E. (2011) 'Counting and Multidimensional Poverty Measurement', *Journal of Public Economics*, 95 (7): 476–487.

Alkire, S. and Foster, J. (2016) 'Dimensional and Distributional Contributions to Multidimensional Poverty', Working Paper 100, Oxford Poverty and Human Development Initiative, University of Oxford.

Alkire, S., Roche, J.M., Santos, M.E. and Seth, S. (2011) 'Multidimensional Poverty Index 2011: Brief Methodological Note', Oxford Poverty and Human Development Initiative, Oxford University. Available at http://www.ophi.org.uk/wp-content/uploads/MPI_2011_Methodology_Note_4-11-2011_1500.pdf.

Alkire, S. and Santos, M.E. (2010) 'Acute Multidimensional Poverty: A New Index for Developing Countries', Working Paper 38, Oxford Poverty and Human Development Initiative, Oxford University.

Alkire, S. and Santos, M.E. (2014) 'Measuring Acute Poverty in the Developing World: Robustness and Scope of the Multidimensional Poverty Index', *World Development*, 59: 251–274.

Anand, S. and Sen, A. (1994) 'Human Development Index: Methodology and Measurement', Human Development Report Office Occasional Paper 12, New York: United Nations Development Programme.

Anand, S. and Sen, A.K. (1997) 'Concepts of Human Development and Poverty: A Multidimensional Perspective', United Nations Development Programme (UNDP) Human Development Report 1997 Papers: Poverty and Human Development, New York.

Anand, S. and Sen, A. (2000) 'The Income Component of the Human Development Index', *Journal of Human Development*, 1 (1): 83–106.

Atkinson, A.B. (1970) 'On the Measurement of Inequality', *Journal of Economic Theory*, 2 (3): 244–263.

Becker, G.S.T., Philipson, T.J. and Soares, R.R. (2005) 'The Quantity and Quality of Life and the Evolution of World Inequality', *American Economic Review*, 95: 277–291.

Boarini, R., Johansson, A. and Mira d'Ercole, M. (2006) 'Alternative Measures of Well-being', OECD Social, Employment and Migration Working Papers No. 33, Paris: OECD.

Bossert, W., Chakravarty, S.R. and D'Ambrosio, C. (2009) 'Multidimensional Poverty and Material Deprivation with Discrete Data', *Review of Income and Wealth*, 59 (1), 29–43.

Chakravarty, S.R. (2003) 'A Generalized Human Development Index', *Review of Development Economics*, 7: 99–114.

Cherchye, L., Ooghe, E. and Puyenbroeck, T.V. (2008) 'Robust Human Development Rankings', *Journal of Economic Inequality*, 6: 287–321.

Constantini, V. and Monni, S. (2005) 'Sustainable Human Development for European Countries', *Journal of Human Development*, 6 (3): 329–351.

Decancq, K. and Lugo, M.A. (2013) 'Weights in Multidimensional Indices of Well-Being: An Overview', *Econometric Reviews*, 32: 7–34.

Fleurbaey, M. (2009) 'Beyond GDP: The Quest for a Measure of Social Welfare', *Journal of Economic Literature*, 47 (4): 1029–1047.

Foster, J.E., López-Calva, L.F. and Székely, M. (2005) 'Measuring the Distribution of Human Development: Methodology and an Application to Mexico', *Journal of Human Development*, 6: 5–29.

Foster J.E., McGillivray, M. and Seth, S. (2009) 'Rank Robustness of Composite Indices', OPHI Working Paper 26, Oxford Poverty and Human Development Initiative, University of Oxford.

Foster J.E., McGillivray, M. and Seth, S. (2013) 'Composite Indices: Rank Robustness, Statistical Association and Redundancy', *Econometric Reviews*, 32: 35–56.

Herrero, C., Martínez, R. and Villar, A. (2010a) 'Multidimensional Social Evaluation: An Application to the Measurement of Human Development', *Review of Income and Wealth*, 56: 483–497.

Herrero, C., Martínez, R. and Villar, A. (2010b) 'Improving the Measurement of Human Development', Human Development Reports Research Papers 2010–12.

Herrero, C., Martínez, R. and Villar, A. (2012) 'A Newer Human Development Index', *Journal of Human Development and Capabilities*, 13: 247–268.

Herrero, C., Soler, A. and Villar, A. (2010c) 'Desarrollo Humano en España (1980–2007)', Fundación Bancaja.

Hicks, D.A. (1997) 'The Inequality Adjusted Human Development Index: A Constructive Proposal', *World Development*, 25 (8): 1283–1298.

Jayaraj, D. and Subramanian, S. (2009) 'A Chakravarty–D'Ambrosio View of Multidimensional Deprivation: Some Estimates for India', *Economic and Political Weekly*, 45 (6): 53–65.

Klugman, J., Rodriguez, F. and Choi, H.-J. (2011) 'The HDI 2010: New Controversies, Old Critiques', Human Development Research Paper 2011/1.

Kovacevic, M. (2010a) 'Review of HDI Critiques and Potential Improvements', Human Development Research Paper 2010/33.

Kovacevic, M. (2010b) 'Measurement of Inequality in Human Development – A Review,' Human Development Research Paper 2010/35, UNDP Human Development Report Office.

Kovacevic, M. and Calderon, C. (2016) 'UNDP's Multidimensional Poverty Index: 2014 Specifications,' Occasional Paper, UNDP Human Development Report Office.

Llavador, H., Roemer, J.E. and Silvestre, J. (2011) 'Sustainability in the Presence of Global Warming: Theory and Empirics', Human Development Research Paper 2011/05.

Max-Neef, M. (1984), 'Desarrollo a escala humana. Conceptos, aplicaciones y algunas reflexiones', Barcelona: Icaria/Nordan.

Morris, M.D. (1979) 'Measuring the Condition of the World's Poor: The Physical Quality of Life Index', Washington, DC: Overseas Development Council.

Nardo, M., Saisana, M., Saltelli, A., Tarantola, S., Hoffman, A. and Giovannini, E. (2008) 'Handbook on Constructing Composite Indicators: Methodology and User's Guide', Paris: Joint Research Centre (JRC) of the European Commission and OECD.

Neumayer, E. (2011) 'Sustainability and Inequality in Human Development', Human Development Research Paper 2011/04.

Nguefack-Tsague, G., Klasen, S. and Zucchini, W. (2011) 'On Weighting the Components of the Human Development Index: A Statistical Justification', *Journal of Human Development and Capabilities*, 12 (2): 183–202.

Osberg, L. and Sharpe, A. (2002) 'An Index of Economic Wellbeing for Selected OECD Countries', *Review of Income and Wealth*, 48: 291–316.

Permanyer, I. (2011) 'Assessing the Robustness of Composite Indices Rankings', *Review of Income and Wealth*, 57: 306–326.

Philipson, T. and Soares, R. (2001) 'Human Capital, Longevity, and Economic Growth', mimeo, University of Chicago.

Pinilla, F. and Goerlich, F.J. (2005) 'Renta per capita y potencial de calidad de vida (QLP) en España (1981–1999)', *Investigaciones Regionales*, 4: 53–74.

Ram, R. (1982) 'Composite Indices of Physical Quality of Life, Basic Needs Fulfillment, and Income: A "Principal Component" Representation', *Journal of Development Economics*, 11: 227–247.

Ravallion, M. (2012) 'Troubling Tradeoffs in the Human Development Index', *Journal of Development Economics*, 99 (2): 201–209.

Rippin, N. (2011) 'A Response to the Weaknesses of the Multidimensional Poverty Index (MPI): The Correlation Sensitive Poverty Index (CSPI)', German Development Institute.

Ruggeri Laderchi, C., Saithand, R. and Stewart, F. (2003) 'Does it Matter that We Do not Agree on the Definition of Poverty? A Comparison of Four Approaches', *Oxford Development Studies*, 31 (3): 243–274.

Sagar, A.D. and Najam, A. (1999) 'The Human Development Index: A Critical Review', *Ecological Economics*, 25: 249–264.

Sen, A.K. (1976) 'Poverty: An Ordinal Approach to Measurement', *Econometrica*, 44: 219–231.

Sen, A.K. (1985) *Commodities and Capabilities*, Oxford: Oxford University Press.

Seth, S. (2009) 'Inequality, Interactions, and Human Development', *Journal of Human Development and Capabilities*, 10: 375–396.

Seth, S. (2013) 'A Class of Distribution and Association Sensitive Multidimensional Welfare Indices', *Journal of Economic Inequality*, 11 (2): 133–162.

Seth S. and Alkire, S. (2017) 'Did Poverty Reduction Reach the Poorest of the Poor? Complementary Measures of Poverty and Inequality in the Counting Approach', *Research of Economic Inequality*, 25: 63–102.

Seth, S. and McGillivray, M. (2016) 'Composite Indices, Alternative Weights, and Comparison Robustness'. OPHI Working Paper 106, University of Oxford.

Spence, R. (2009) 'Economic Growth', in Deneulin, S. and Shahani, L. (eds) *An Introduction to Human Development and Capability Approach*, London: Earthscan.

Stiglitz, J.E., Sen, A. and Fitoussi, J-P. (2009) 'Report by the Commission on the Measurement of Economic Performance and Social Progress', Paris: Centre de recherche en économie de Sciences Po.

United Nations Development Programme (UNDP) (various years), *Human Development Report*, New York: Oxford University Press.

Villar, A. (2013) 'Welfare Poverty Measurement', mimeo, Pablo de Olavide University.

Zambrano, E. (2011) 'Functionings, Capabilities and the 2010 Human Development Index', Human Development Report Office.

Zambrano, E. (2014) 'An Axiomatization of the Human Development Index', *Social Choice and Welfare*, 42 (4): 853–872.

Zambrano, E. (2016) 'The "Troubling Tradeoffs" Paradox and a Resolution', *Review of Income and Wealth*, 63 (3): 520–541.

4. Human development and poverty: empirical findings
Suman Seth and Antonio Villar

4.1 INTRODUCTION

The concept of human development, which is a process of enlarging people's choices, is a broad concept and inherently multidimensional. It is already well established that we cannot obtain a comprehensive picture of human development by merely looking at the performance of any single dimension such as income. This is so because not all variables that affect human development evolve similarly. Table 4.1 presents illustrations of certain countries from the 1990 Human Development Report (HDR) that show mismatches between performances in monetary and non-monetary dimensions. The first set of three countries – Sri Lanka, Jamaica and Costa Rica – had high life expectancy and adult literacy rates and low infant mortality rates despite low levels of per capita gross national product (GNP). In contrast, the second set of three countries – Brazil, Oman and Saudi Arabia – had much lower life expectancy and adult literacy rates and higher infant mortality rates despite much higher levels of per capita GNP.

The lack of perfect synergies between monetary and non-monetary dimensions has shifted the focus from a merely economic growth-led development process to a more holistic process of development that focuses on monetary as well as non-monetary dimensions. This more holistic process of development calls for a multidimensional approach to measurement. It should be borne in mind that the objective of measurement exercises is to capture and reflect various aspects of human development that assist in guiding better policies towards improving human lives. It is thus crucial that these measurement

Table 4.1   The gross national product versus other social indicators

Country	GNP per capita (USD)	Life expectancy (years)	Adult literacy rate (%)	Infant mortality (per 1000 live births)
Modest GNP per capita with high human development				
Sri Lanka	400	71	87	32
Jamaica	940	74	82	18
Costa Rica	1610	75	93	18
High GNP per capita with modest human development				
Brazil	2020	65	78	62
Oman	5810	57	30	40
Saudi Arabia	6200	64	55	70

Source: Human Development Report 1990, Table 1.1.

exercises are technically sound yet are amenable to practical issues and policy guidance at the same time.

There may be two distinct ways to assess progress when multiple dimensions are involved. One is to look at progress in different dimensions separately and the other is to aggregate performance into a single index to assess overall progress. One can find good arguments in favour of each of those mechanisms.

There are two key arguments for looking at performance in different dimensions separately. One is that it avoids the loss of information that occurs when we aggregate performance in different dimensions into a single index. The other is that it does not require making difficult decisions regarding the relative importance of the different dimensions and the suitability of various aggregation procedures. We also find good reasons to favour a synthetic measure. First, a single index summarizing overall performance may send a more powerful message than a dashboard of large number of isolated indices (Stiglitz et al., 2009). This is the reason why the GNP or gross domestic product (GDP) and the Human Development Index (HDI) have become more popular and have played a more effective role in policy design than the dashboard of Millennium Development Goals indicators (see section 4.4). Second, a single real-valued index satisfies completeness and transitivity. Completeness permits full comparability whereas transitivity ensures consistent evaluations. Third, looking at different dimensions separately implies ignoring the joint distribution of achievements across the population. We discuss this issue in detail later on.

The HDI is one of the social indices, introduced in various Human Development Reports in the past two decades, with the objective of creating a family of rich and highly informative indices to assess the degree of development in a large number of countries. Those indicators are aimed at answering a basic question: How have countries progressed in terms of human development over the past decades? The data using the new HDI, introduced in the 2010 HDR, show a relevant worldwide improvement in the level of human development for the period 1980–2013 in all dimensions, even though the rate of improvement varies in different periods. Table 4.2 provides a summary of the evolution in global human development by groups of countries, according to their level of human development. Countries experiencing larger increases in the HDI are the medium or low human development countries.

The average yearly HDI growth rate for the period 1980–2013 in the world is 0.77 per

Table 4.2   The growth of HDI in the world, 1980–2013, by groups of countries

	Average annual HDI growth				
	1980–2013	1980–1990	1990–2000	2000–2013	2008–2013
Very high human development	0.53	0.52	0.62	0.37	0.20
High human development	1.14	1.04	0.81	1.04	0.60
Medium human development	1.41	1.22	1.09	1.17	0.79
Low human development	1.31	0.64	0.95	1.56	0.77
World	0.77	0.66	0.67	0.73	0.41

Source: Human Development Report 2014.

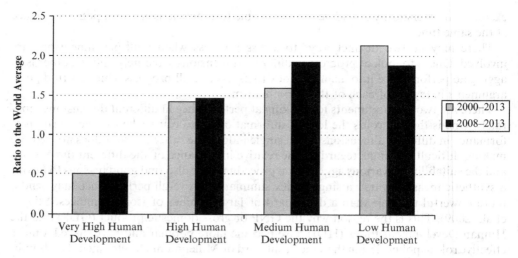

Figure 4.1   The ratio of regional growth to overall growth in HDI

cent, with values of 0.53 per cent for the most developed countries and 1.31 per cent for the less developed ones. Notice that the period 2000–2013 shows larger differences in favour of those countries with low human development, which conveys a rather positive message. The 2008 crisis clearly affected the evolution of human development by reducing the annual rates of growth, as shown in the last column of Table 4.2. Yet it might be worth noting that the slowdown is mostly a scale effect, as the shares in average growth have remained quite stable, as Figure 4.1 shows. The vertical axis measures the ratio of the average annual HDI growth in different HDI categories to the overall average annual HDI growth, which is directly computed using the numbers in Table 4.2. For example, the ratio of the average annual HDI growth of very high human development countries to the world average for the period 2000–2013 is computed as 0.37/0.73 = 0.5, which is the height of the corresponding grey bar in Figure 4.1.

The rest of this chapter is structured as follows. In section 4.2, we discuss certain practical concerns about the HDI and how they have been empirically addressed. In section 4.3, we discuss various inequality-adjusted human development indices and explore the relationship between the level of human development and the level of inequality. In section 4.4, we discuss the empirical studies relating to the poverty indices reported in Human Development Reports. Section 4.5 concludes.

4.2   PRACTICAL CONCERNS ABOUT THE HDI

The country rankings generated by the HDI have received a large amount of global attention. A number of practical issues, however, have raised concerns over the application of the index. The first issue that has received a great deal of attention is the choice of equal weights for each of the three dimensions (Kelley, 1991; Desai, 1991). It has been argued that the equal weight structure entails a very strong value judgement. Rankings or comparisons may alter if an alternative weighting structure entailing a different value judgement is selected. This concern has been acknowledged in the literature and various data-driven techniques, such as principal component analysis (UNDP, 1993; Noorbakhsh, 1998; Nguefack-Tsague et al., 2011) and data envelopment analysis (Mahlberg and Obersteiner, 2001; Despotis, 2005), have been used to devise alternative weighting structures. Some of these applications have agreed with the equal weight structure and some have disagreed. An interesting study was pursued by Chowdhury and Squire (2006), who conducted an opinion survey among experts from different countries. Their study found that experts somewhat agreed with the equal weight structure of the HDI.

Whichever way the weighting structure is determined, there is always some degree of arbitrariness in the choice, and so another branch of literature has taken an alternative route. Instead of developing a new technique for weighting dimensions, these studies have proposed conducting sensitivity analysis (Saisana et al., 2005) and robustness tests (Cherchye et al., 2008; Foster et al., 2009; Permanyer, 2011; Seth and McGillivray, 2016) with respect to the choice of initial weights. These robustness and sensitivity analyses test whether or not a given pair-wise comparison is fully robust to alternative weighting structures, and if the comparison is not fully robust then to what extent the comparison is robust. Foster et al. (2009) found that nearly 70 per cent of all pair-wise HDI comparisons for various years were fully robust. This implies that no matter how the initial equal weighting structure is altered, 70 per cent of all pair-wise comparisons would not change.[1] When the initial equal weights were allowed to vary by 25 per cent in any direction, then nearly 92 per cent of pair-wise HDI comparisons were robust. Thus, although there has been a strong animosity towards the choice of equal weights, empirical findings tend to agree with this choice (even when there may be particular cases where the directions of pair-wise comparisons alter).

The issue of robustness with respect to the choice of weights is linked to a second issue related to the correlation or statistical association between the component dimensions. If the statistical associations between component dimensions are high, then any debate over the choice of weights loses most of its significance. Cahill (2005) used six alternative weighting structures to compute the HDI ranking using the three highly correlated dimensions of HDI, and found HDI rankings across countries to be very highly correlated to each other. In fact, in a hypothetical world, if all three dimensions of the HDI were perfectly positively associated, then any two alternative weighting structures would agree over every pair-wise comparison (Foster et al., 2013). If an overall index provides similar rankings to any of its component indices, then what additional information does the aggregate index provide? This was precisely the point made by McGillivray (1991). The Spearman's rank correlation coefficients between the three dimensions as well as the rank correlation between the HDI and its component dimensions appeared to be very high (ranging between 0.74 and 0.97 using the data from 1990 Human Development Report). McGillivray and White (1993) also found a very high correlation between HDI rankings and the rankings based on per capita GNP that the HDI was trying to replace. This type of high association between HDI rankings and rankings according to its component dimensions, as well as the high association between HDI rankings and per capita GNP rankings, may mean that the HDI is a redundant index (McGillivray, 1991).

This way of understanding redundancy of an index, however, can be debated. First, note that even though the rank correlation coefficients were high when they were computed across all countries, they were not necessarily high across subgroups of countries. For example, the rank correlation coefficients ranged between -0.14 and 0.4 when McGillivray (1991) considered only the low human development countries. Put differently, a high rank correlation between two long lists of country outcomes is perfectly compatible with very large differences between individual realizations. Second, the high statistical associations existed at the aggregate level across countries. This may not necessarily imply that such high associations exist between dimensions at more disaggregated levels: across states or provinces, across municipalities or across households. Therefore, a deeper analysis and understanding of the redundancy aspect of an index is required.

A third issue that is often raised relates to the particular functional form used for aggregating the dimensional performances. Note that the traditional HDI until 2009 is obtained by linearly aggregating the performance in three dimensions, which also assumed a strong value judgement. Besides, linear aggregation has a number of draw-backs. It implies assuming perfect substitutability between the components values; that is, it amounts to admitting that we can substitute, for instance, expected life years by education at a constant rate, no matter the average level of health (see Ravallion, 2012 for a discussion on trade-offs between dimensions). In addition, an additive index gener-ates a ranking that is sensitive to the normalization of the different dimensions, where a change in the arbitrary normalization of the underlying variable induces changes in rankings. To counter these limitations of the linear HDI, the 2010 HDR introduced a new aggregation formulation based on the geometric mean as discussed in Chapter 3 of this *Handbook*. The country rankings produced by the new HDI were not found to be strikingly different from the rankings produced by the linear HDI using the 2010 country data (UNDP, 2010, p. 227).

The geometric mean is a well-known aggregator in economics, corresponding to the familiar symmetric Cobb–Douglas formula for production and utility functions, and exhibits much better properties regarding substitutability among the dimensions. However, the benefit of using the geometric mean formulation may not be fully enjoyed unless appropriate normalizations of the original underlying variables are undertaken. The country rankings are still sensitive to the selection of the minimum values for nor-malization. For the construction of the HDI, the normalized value of each dimension is obtained by subtracting the minimum value from the original variable in each dimension, and then dividing by the difference of the maximum and the minimum values. Any change in the minimum values still alters country rankings. One way of addressing this problem is to set the minimum values equal to zero and then to normalize each dimension by divid-ing the related variable by the corresponding maximum value only (Herrero et al., 2010; Alkire and Foster, 2010).

All the relevant practical issues involving the measurement of human development are very important but ignore one key practical issue, which is the consideration of dis-tributional aspects. The discussion until now assumes that dimensional indices are first somehow obtained and then meaningfully aggregated to obtain the index. By doing this, dimensional indices and thus the HDI ignore the existing inequality in human develop-ment. In the next section, we discuss how distributional concerns have been incorporated into the measurement of human development.

4.3 DISTRIBUTIONAL CONCERNS WHILE MEASURING HUMAN DEVELOPMENT

The first attempt to incorporate the distributional aspects into the measurement of human development was made by Anand and Sen (1995) who captured inequality across gender in the same three dimensions of the HDI. The index, well known as the Gender-related Development Index (GDI), is based on equally distributed equivalent achievements (Atkinson, 1970), which is equivalent to the generalized means with a particular restriction on the relevant parameter. The generalized mean of order α of a vector $y = (y_1, \ldots, y_n)$ with n positive achievements is defined as:

$$\mu_\alpha(y) = \begin{cases} \left[\dfrac{1}{n}\sum_{i=1}^{n} y_i^\alpha\right]^{1/\alpha} & \text{for } \alpha \neq 0 \\ \left[\displaystyle\prod_{i=1}^{n} y_i\right]^{1/n} & \text{for } \alpha = 0 \end{cases}.$$

The parameter α is an inequality aversion parameter. When $\alpha = 1$, then $\mu_1(y)$ is the average of all achievements in y without any consideration of inequality between the n elements. However, when $\alpha < 1$, then $\mu_\alpha(y)$ is the equally distributed equivalent achievement of y, which implies that $\mu_\alpha(y)$ would yield the same level of overall achievement if each of the n achievements were equal to $\mu_\alpha(y)$. The higher the aversion to inequality (smaller the value of α) is, the lower the value of $\mu_\alpha(y)$ is.

The GDI is computed in two steps. First, an equally distributed equivalent achievement for each of the three dimensions is calculated using the male and female achievements. Then, in the second step, the GDI of a country is computed as a simple average of the three equally distributed equivalent achievements. The GDI can be seen as a gender-inequality-adjusted Human Development Index. The loss in human development due to gender inequality can be computed as (HDI – GDI)/HDI. Figure 4.2 presents a scatter-plot showing the relation between HDI levels (horizontal axis) and percentage losses in human development due to inequality between gender (vertical axis) across 130 countries for year 1992. There does not appear to be any relationship between the HDI levels and losses in human development due to gender inequality. Thus, it cannot be claimed that countries with lower human development have larger gender disparities. In fact, certain high-medium HDI countries, such as Saudi Arabia and Algeria, appear to have had high levels of gender inequality; whereas certain low human development countries, such as Angola and Tanzania, appear to have had very low levels of gender inequality.

Gender inequality captures inequality between two genders but ignores inequality within groups. Even when human development levels are less unequal across genders, large inequalities may exist across the population. An attempt to incorporate distributional aspects using a much wider perspective was made by Hicks (1997). In order to capture inequality, Hicks computed a Gini coefficient for income distribution, educational distribution and longevity distribution, as follows. The Gini coefficient for income distribution is computed using the data on income shares by quintile. In other words, the Gini coefficient is computed from certain discrete points from the Lorenz curves. The Gini coefficient of the education distribution is also computed from certain discrete data

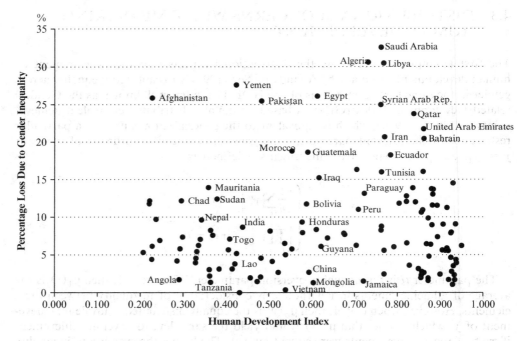

Source: Computation used data from Human Development Report 1995, Tables 1.1, 1.2 and 3.1.

Figure 4.2   HDI and loss due to gender inequality across 130 countries in 1992

points by classifying the education data into six categories: no education, some primary education, completed primary education, some secondary education, completed secondary education and some higher education. Finally, the Gini coefficient of the longevity distribution is obtained from mortality statistics (death rates) that were available across age, gender and rural/urban residence for nine consecutive years.

The inequality-adjusted index for each dimension is then computed by multiplying the dimensional achievement by a factor that is inversely related to the corresponding Gini coefficient. Let us denote the original dimensional achievements of the three dimensions of the HDI by x_1, x_2 and x_3 and the corresponding dimensional Gini coefficients by G_1, G_2 and G_3. The inequality-adjusted index of dimension i is computed as $x_i \times (1 - G_i)$. The Inequality-Adjusted HDI, referred to by Hicks as the IAHDI, is a simple average of the three dimensional inequality-adjusted indices such that:

$$\text{IAHDI} = \frac{1}{3}\sum_{i=1}^{3} x_i \times (1 - G_i).$$

Note that in an ideal situation where there is no inequality across the categories, each inequality-adjusted dimensional index is equal to the corresponding dimensional achievement and the IAHDI is equal to the HDI. On the other hand, if inequality in each dimension increases but the average achievement remains the same, the IAHDI falls, discounting for the higher inequality.

Hicks applied the index to 20 developing countries using HDI data for year 1995 and showed how the country rankings changed when the HDI was adjusted for existing inequality (see Hicks, 1997, Table 4). For example, Costa Rica and the Republic of Korea had the same level of HDI – of 0.883 and 0.882, respectively – in 1995. However, the levels of inequality in all three dimensions were higher in Costa Rica than in the Republic of Korea. As a result, the IAHDI of Costa Rica was much lower (0.561) than that of the Republic of Korea (0.621). Using HDI and IAHDI values, Hicks computed the percentage loss in the level of well-being due to existing inequality in the three dimensions by (HDI – IAHDI)/HDI. The percentage loss ranged from 29.6 per cent for the Republic of Korea to 56.6 per cent for Guatemala and Bangladesh.

Another attempt to incorporate distributional concerns into the measurement of the HDI was made by Foster et al. (2005). Instead of the Gini coefficient to capture inequality across each distribution, they propose a framework based on generalized means. A simple average or arithmetic mean of all elements in y can be obtained by setting $\alpha = 1$, which we denote as μ. The Atkinson measure of inequality of order α can be defined as $I_\alpha = (\mu - \mu_\alpha)/\mu$ for $\alpha < 1$. This relationship can be expressed as $\mu_\alpha = \mu(1 - I_\alpha)$. Foster et al. first propose computing the general mean of order α for each distribution – income, education and health – where inequality within each distribution is captured through the Atkinson measure of inequality. In the second stage, the three dimensional general means are again aggregated using a general mean of order α to obtain the inequality-adjusted HDI. Note that the generalized means capture inequality within the distributions during the first stage, and the second stage generalized mean ensures that the overall index is discounted or reduced if the performance in three dimensions is not uniform.

The authors apply the family of inequality-adjusted HDI to a data sample from the 2000 Mexican Population Census. The sample contains 10 099 182 individual records from 2.2 million households, each with information on income and education. However, the Population Census did not include any information on health, and so individual-level health information was imputed from municipality-level data, which ensured that inequalities in health across households living in different areas were still captured.

In order to make this human development index as comparable as possible with the traditional HDI, certain adjustments are made to the variables. As income is only one component of gross domestic product, adjustments are made to household income. Two variables are used to capture the education status of the sample households, as in the traditional HDI. One is the literacy variable, which is computed as the proportion of literate individuals over 14 years of age compared to the total number of individuals older than 14. The other is the attendance variable, which is the proportion of 6–24-year-old individuals attending school. As in the traditional HDI, the education index for each individual is constructed by giving a two-thirds weight to the literacy variable and a one-third weight to the attendance variable. However, the health indicator is slightly different, using infant mortality or infant survival rates as proxies for the health conditions. Note that this variable is available only at the municipality level and not at the household level, and so inequality across health is captured only at the municipality level.

They compute the HDIs ($\alpha = 1$) and inequality-adjusted HDIs ($\alpha = -2$) nationally and for all 32 states of Mexico (see Foster et al., 2005, Table 1). The loss of well-being due to inequality is computed as (HDI – IAHDI)/HDI. At the national level, the loss in well-being due to inequality appears to be 26 per cent. However, the loss in well-being varies

Table 4.3   Inequality and human development

	HDI	Inequality-adjusted HDI (IHDI)	Overall loss (%)
Very high human development	0.890	0.780	12.3
High human development	0.735	0.590	19.7
Medium human development	0.614	0.457	25.6
Low human development	0.493	0.332	32.6

Source: Human Development Report 2014.

widely from state to state: from nearly 14 per cent in Distrito Federal and Baja California, to 38 per cent in the state of Oaxaca. The losses in well-being in the states of Chiapas, Guerrero and Zacatecas are more than 30 per cent. The use of an inequality-adjusted HDI causes the ranks of the states to change markedly.

A particular measure from the Foster et al. (2005) family of measures has been used by Alkire and Foster (2010), who propose using the measure for $\alpha = 0$ (geometric mean), which satisfies certain interesting and policy-relevant properties. Note that meaningful comparison of the HDI that is based on the geometric mean (that is, the new HDI formulation introduced in the 2010 HDR that replaced the traditional linear formulation of the HDI) and the inequality-adjusted HDI proposed by Alkire and Foster (2010) requires that no logarithmic transformation is applied to the income variable. If a logarithmic transformation is applied, then there would be an excess emphasis on income inequality because a logarithmic transformation is already a concave transformation.

The data referring to the inequality-adjusted HDI (Table 4.3) reveal two key messages. First, inequality-adjusted values may change the ranking of individual countries considerably, no matter the level of development (see the Appendix Table 4A.1). Second, the overall loss due to inequality is, on average, inversely proportional to the degree of development (we shall come back to this point later on).

A somewhat different approach to reflect inequality in the level of human development has been followed by Grimm et al. (2008), who computed HDIs for different income groups. Grimm et al. apply their approach to 13 developing countries, where each country has a household income survey and a Demographic Health Survey (DHS). The household income survey is used to compute the indices for education and income, and the DHS is used to compute the life expectancy indices.

In order to compute the quintile-based indices, it is important to match the quintiles across two surveys for each country. Grimm et al. propose two alternative approaches for this purpose. One is a regression-based method where one first needs to identify a common set of variables in both surveys that correlate with the income variable in the income survey. The set of variables should include some characteristics of household heads, some characteristics of households, and some information on housing conditions. Income is then regressed on the set of common variables from the income survey, and the regression coefficients are used to predict household incomes in the DHS, which are used to construct the cumulative distribution of income and thus the income quintiles. The other approach is to use principal component analysis to construct the cumulative distribution of the asset index and then the asset quintiles. In this alternative approach, it is assumed that the asset quintiles yield a classification that is consistent with what is obtained by observed income in the respective income surveys.

Once the quintiles are classified, the dimensional indices of income and education indices are constructed from the income surveys and the health indices are constructed from the health surveys. The HDIs from the dimensional indices are constructed using a weighted average, where the weight structure is the same as that of the traditional HDI.

In order to reflect inequality in the HDIs, the authors compute the ratio of HDI between the richest and the poorest quintile. Their results reveal stark differences across countries. They analyse the data for 13 developing countries and two industrialized countries (see Grimm et al., 2008, Table 1). The 13 developing countries are Bolivia, Burkina Faso, Cameroon, Columbia, Cote d'Ivoire, Guinea, Indonesia, Madagascar, Mozambique, Nicaragua, South Africa, Vietnam and Zambia. Of these 13 countries, the high inequality countries are Guinea, Burkina Faso, Zambia and Madagascar, where the HDI for the richest income quintile is 1.7 times or higher than the poorest quintile. For the second group of countries – Bolivia, Cameroon, Nicaragua, Cote d'Ivoire, Mozambique and South Africa – the ratios of the richest to the poorest range between 1.5 and 1.7. For the third group of countries, consisting of Colombia, Vietnam and Indonesia, the ratio of the HDI for the richest to the poorest quintile is smaller but still ranges between 1.3 and 1.5.

One consistent aspect of all these studies is that the level of human development is inversely related to the level of inequality in human development, both across countries and within countries. In Figure 4.3, we present four diagrams in four panels. In each diagram, the level of human development is presented on the horizontal axis and the level of inequality on the vertical axis. Panel I presents the relationship across 20 developing countries as computed by Hicks (1997). Panel II presents the relationship across 32 Mexican states as computed by Foster et al. (2005). Panel III presents the relationship across 13 developing countries as computed by Grimm et al. (2008). Finally, Panel IV presents the relationship between HDI and the percentage loss in human development due to inequality using the inequality-adjusted HDI across 132 countries reported in the 2013 Human Development Report. It is evident that the data from each of these four sources demonstrate a strong negative relationship between the level of HDI and inequality in human development.

4.3.1 Sensitivity to Joint Distribution

Unlike in the single dimensional context, analysis in the multidimensional context entails two distinct forms of inequality. The first pertains to the spread of the distribution across persons, analogous to unidimensional inequality. The second, in contrast, deals with the joint distribution among dimensions. This second form of inequality is important because a change in the joint distribution may alter individual-level evaluations as well as overall inequality. Let us look at the following example of two achievement matrices, where rows denote persons and columns denote dimensions:

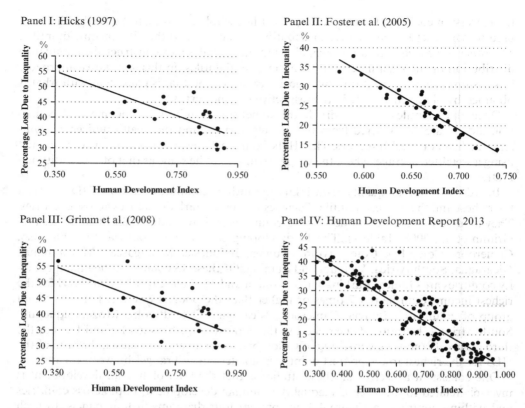

Figure 4.3   Comparison of the HDI level and inequality in human development

$$\text{Achievement Matrix I} \quad \begin{bmatrix} 0.90 & 0.90 & 0.90 \\ 0.30 & 0.80 & 0.80 \\ 0.30 & 0.40 & 0.40 \end{bmatrix} \qquad \text{Achievement Matrix II} \quad \begin{bmatrix} 0.90 & 0.90 & 0.90 \\ 0.30 & 0.40 & 0.80 \\ 0.30 & 0.80 & 0.40 \end{bmatrix}$$

It is evident from Achievement Matrix I that person 1 has higher levels of achievement in all three dimensions. Person 2 has higher achievements in the second and third dimensions than that of Person 3, but enjoys the same level of achievement in the first dimension. If we look at the distribution of achievements in each of the three dimensions in Achievement Matrix II, it is clear that each dimensional distribution is identical to the corresponding dimensional distribution in Achievement Matrix I. In other words, the distribution of achievement for the first dimension is (0.30, 0.30, 0.90), that for the second dimension is (0.40, 0.80, 0.90), and that for the third dimension is (0.40, 0.80, 0.90). Therefore, any distributional analysis of human development using the methods presented earlier in this section would result in identical conclusions for both achievement matrices. This is because none of these methods reflect the joint distribution of achievements.

Should, then, any distributional analysis yield the same conclusion? Clearly, in Achievement Matrix I, the third person is the worst-off in all dimensions; unlike in

Achievement Matrix II, where the third person enjoys higher achievement in the second dimension than the second person. Although the dimensional distributions are identical across two distributions, the joint distributions are clearly different. In this sense, one may argue that inequality across the population is higher in Achievement Matrix I than in Achievement Matrix II. In fact, the association between dimensions in Achievement Matrix I is higher, as if the matrix were obtained from Achievement Matrix II by increasing the association between dimensions. In the literature on multidimensional inequality, poverty and welfare measurement, this type of transformation of achievement matrices is known under different names: basic rearrangement (Boland and Proschan, 1988), basic rearrangement-increasing transfer (Tsui, 2002), correlation increasing switch (Bourguignon and Chakravarty, 2003), correlation increasing arrangement (Deutsch and Silber, 2005), association increasing transfer (Seth, 2009, 2013), correlation increasing transfer (Tsui, 1999) and unfair rearrangement principle (Decancq and Lugo, 2012).[2] There is thus a clear need for methods that may capture this second form of inequality.

One such family of indices that incorporates this second as well as the first form of inequality has been proposed by Seth (2009, 2013). These indices, like the family of measures proposed by Foster et al. (2005), are based on generalized means. However, the order of aggregation is different. First, each person's achievements across all dimensions are aggregated using a generalized mean of order β to obtain an overall well-being score for each person, and then these overall well-being scores are aggregated using a generalized mean of order α to obtain the inequality-adjusted human development index. Thus, the family of indices has two parameters: α and β. When $\alpha = \beta \leq 1$, then the sub-family of indices coincide with the Foster et al. (2005) family of indices. When $\alpha < \beta \leq 1$, then if two joint distributions have identical dimensional distributions but different associations between dimensions, then the level of human development is lower when the association between dimensions is higher.

Seth (2009) applied the index to the same Mexican dataset used by Foster et al. (2005), but because of certain differences in normalizations the final values differ from those of Foster et al. The ranking of 32 states is indeed different when an index sensitive to both forms of inequality is used. However, the point of using such an index can be clarified by using an example shown in Table 4.4, following Seth (2009). The state of Tabasco was chosen at random and the achievements transformed in such a way that each dimensional distribution remains unchanged but the association between dimensions increases. Table 4.4 summarizes the post-transfer human development scores of Tabasco for different approaches. Note that the development scores of Tabasco that are based on the traditional HDI ($\alpha = \beta = 0$) and the Foster et al. index ($\alpha = \beta = -2$) are the same in the pre- and post-transformation situation. However, Tabasco's level of human development falls when an index sensitive to both forms of inequality is used. Before transformation,

Table 4.4   Level of human development before and after transformation

State	HDI	Foster et al. (2005)	Seth (2009)
	($\alpha = 1, \beta = 1$)	($\alpha = -2, \beta = -2$)	($\alpha = -3, \beta = -1$)
Pre-transformation	0.719	0.296	0.254
Post-transformation	0.719	0.296	0.244

Tabasco scored 0.254, whereas after transformation the score drops to 0.244. Therefore, a higher association between dimensions adversely affects Tabasco's level of human development.

Seth (2013) also applied an index from this family to study the change in well-being between 1997 and 2000 in Indonesia, using the Indonesian Family Life Surveys. The normalizations of the indicators are slightly different from the normalizations used by Foster et al. (2005) and Seth (2009). Instead of normalizing all variables between 0 and 1, Seth (2013) pursues an approach analogous to poverty analysis by identifying a threshold for each dimension below which a person is identified as deprived, and is otherwise not deprived. Then the achievements of each person in each dimension are divided by the corresponding threshold and these normalized values are assumed to be comparable across dimensions. For example, a person receives a value of 1 whenever the person is deprived in any dimension. This type of normalization implicitly assumes that the level of well-being is not bounded from above. Another major difference in the empirical study of Seth (2013) from Foster et al. (2005) and Seth (2009) is the choice of indicators. Although the same three dimensions – standard of living, education and health – are used, standard of living is assessed by per capita expenditure, education is assessed by years of education completed, and health is assessed by the body mass index. The study focuses only on those who are 15 years old or older.

The study produced an interesting finding. When an index with $\alpha = \beta = 1$ (traditional HDI formulation) is used, then no statistically significant change in well-being is observed, either at the national level or across rural and urban areas. However, when an index with $\alpha = -1$ and $\beta = 0.1$ is used, then the level of well-being increases statistically significantly both at the national level and across rural and urban areas. Why did the level of well-being improve when adjusted for inequality? It turns out that although average per capita expenditure fell between 1997 and 2000, inequality also went down. Even though the pair-wise association between dimensions was higher in 2000 than in 1997, which adversely affects the level of well-being, the reduction in inequality within dimensions dominated the increase in association.

Note that not considering the information regarding joint distribution during multidimensional evaluation is indeed an important omission. On the other hand, an analysis including it requires that information on all dimensions and indicators should be available for each unit of analysis from the same source. If this requirement appears too stringent, then the distributional analysis may be conducted using the methods outlined earlier in this section. However, given that more and more data have become available in recent years, further research is required to develop methods that reflect both forms of inequality in the multidimensional context.

4.4   POVERTY ANALYSIS AND APPLICATIONS

Both the measurement of human development and its distributional issues are concerned with overall progress without paying particular attention to those who are impoverished. With the objective of dealing with the issue of human impoverishment, Anand and Sen (1997) created the Human Poverty Index (HPI). As they explain, the relationship between the HDI and the HPI should be seen as the relationship between the per capita gross

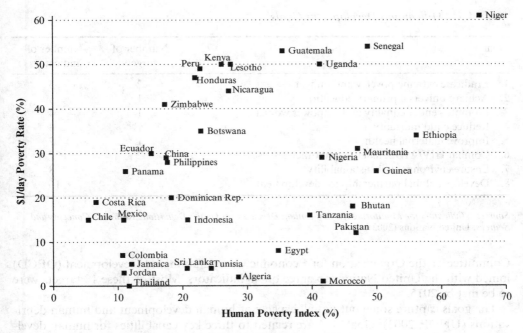

Source: Based on Human Development Report 1997, Table 1.1.

Figure 4.4 The relationship between the HPI and $1/day across developing countries

national product, which measures overall progress in terms of incomes, and an income-based index of poverty. In the 1997 edition of the Human Development Report, two separate HPIs were computed for developing countries and for industrialized countries. The HPIs were generalized means of dimensional deprivations that are outlined in the theoretical chapter on the measurement on human development and human poverty, Chapter 3 of this *Handbook*. The HPIs of developing countries were not found to be highly correlated with the $1/day poverty rates as presented in the 1997 Human Development Report, as shown in Figure 4.4.

Even though, like the traditional HDI, the HPI was a composite index, it did not earn similar popularity for two main reasons. First, it is not intuitively as appealing as the HDI. The formulation is not as straightforward as the HDI, and thus it is difficult to provide an intuitive interpretation of the HPI that could be used for meaningful purposes. The second reason is that, unlike the $1/day poverty measure of the World Bank, the HPI could not provide an answer to this question: How many poor are there in a country? For meaningful policy analysis, it is probably more useful to look at deprivation in each indicator separately, or at a dashboard of indicators such as those in the Millennium Development Goals (Table 4.5).

In the United Nations Millennium Declaration of 2000, eight Millennium Development Goals (outlined in Table 4.5), consisting of 18 time-bound targets, were adopted by 189 countries. In order to accomplish these goals and targets, international organizations such as the World Bank, the International Monetary Fund and the Development Assistance

Table 4.5   Millennium Development Goals

Goal	Number of targets	Number of indicators
1. Eradicate extreme poverty and hunger	2	5
2. Achieve universal primary education	1	3
3. Promote gender equality and empower women	1	4
4. Reduce child mortality	1	3
5. Improve maternal health	1	2
6. Combat HIV/AIDS, malaria and other diseases	2	7
7. Ensure environmental sustainability	3	8
8. Develop a global partnership for development	7	16

Source: Indicators for Monitoring the Millennium Development Goals: Definitions Rationale Concepts and Sources, United Nations (2003).

Committee of the Organisation for Economic Co-operation and Development (OECD) joined with the United Nations to agree on 48 indicators. Most of these 18 targets were to be met by 2015.

The goals capture some but not all aspects of human development and human deprivations (UNDP, 2003). Goals 1–6 are related to three key capabilities for human development. Goal 1 on reducing poverty and hunger is related to the capability of having a decent standard of living. Goals 2 and 3 on achieving universal primary education and promoting gender equality (especially in education) and empowering women are related to the key capability of being educated. And goals 4, 5 and 6 on reducing child mortality, improving maternal health and combating major diseases are related to the key capability of living a long and healthy life. Goals 7 (ensuring environmental sustainability) and 8 (develop a global partnership for development) are not directly related to a key capability, but are related to essential conditions for human development.

Progress since 2000, however, has not been uniform across all indicators. As the data in Table 4.6 reflect, 70 or more developing countries either met the targets or made sufficient progress in indicators such as extreme poverty, improved water, and education gender parity; however, another 70 or more countries either made insufficient progress or were moderately to seriously off-target with respect to indicators such as under-5 mortality, undernourishment, improved sanitation, maternal mortality and infant mortality. In fact, only 26 developing countries met the target or made sufficient progress in improving maternal mortality, and only 14 countries met the target or made sufficient progress in improving infant mortality.

Indeed, a dashboard of indicators conveys more information in terms of progress in different dimensions. It conveys better than a composite index where progress has been made and where progress has not. However, a dashboard of indicators has certain limitations. First, it lacks of a single outline figure such as GDP. If one looks at the MDGs to learn whether a country has made progress or not, a conclusion can only be reached if the country has improved in all indicators, or has deteriorated in all indicators. Apart from these two cases, it is hard to make any conclusion on progress. It is very difficult to go through all 48 indicators every time to draw any conclusion. Second, although a

Table 4.6 *Number of developing countries with progress status in selected MDG*
  indicators

Goal	Target/indicator	MDG target met	Sufficient progress	Insufficient progress	Moderately off target	Seriously off target
1	Extreme poverty ($1.25/day)	66	12	7	4	24
7	Improved water	64	6	4	11	40
3	Education gender parity	61	12	8	8	32
2	Primary completion	44	9	10	9	44
4	Under-5 mortality	35	14	20	34	39
1	Undernourishment	34	7	9	7	70
7	Improved sanitation	32	10	8	8	60
5	Maternal mortality	8	18	7	26	74
4	Infant mortality	6	9	18	32	77

Source: World Bank, http://data.worldbank.org/mdgs/progress-status-across-groups-number-of-countries
(accessed 30 April 2014).

dashboard of indicators shows how many people are deprived in various indicators, it
does not reflect how many people are poor at a certain point in time (Alkire et al., 2011).
Third, a dashboard of indicators, like any composite index (such as the HPI), does not
consider the joint distribution of deprivations. For further discussions of these issues, see
Chapter 3 of Alkire et al. (2015a).

Let us consider the following example, drawing on Alkire and Foster (2011). It is similar
in spirit to the example presented in the previous section:

Deprivation Matrix I

Deprivation Matrix II

$$
\begin{array}{ccc}
\text{Income} & \text{Health} & \text{Sanitation} \\
\begin{bmatrix}
1 & 0 & 0 \\
0 & 1 & 0 \\
0 & 0 & 1
\end{bmatrix}
\end{array}
\qquad
\begin{array}{ccc}
\text{Income} & \text{Health} & \text{Sanitation} \\
\begin{bmatrix}
0 & 0 & 0 \\
0 & 0 & 0 \\
1 & 1 & 1
\end{bmatrix}
\end{array}
$$

Suppose there are two hypothetical societies with three persons. The deprivation
profile of the two societies in three MDG indicators are summarized in Deprivation
Matrices I and II, where rows denote persons. In the matrix, an element equal to 1 implies
that the person is deprived in the indicator; whereas, if the element is equal to 0, it implies
that the person is not deprived. It is clear that in Deprivation Matrix I, each person has
one deprivation. On the other hand, in Deprivation Matrix II, only one person faces all
three deprivations. Both a composite index (such as the HPI) and a dashboard of indicators (for example, consisting of the three indicators) would find an identical level of
poverty in these two societies. In other words, neither composite indices nor dashboards
of indicators can identify such differences. Why is understanding such differences crucial
in practice? Note that, in order to alleviate these deprivations in the second society, it
is more efficient if the three different ministries responsible for these three indicators
coordinate with each other to assist the person facing all deprivations. The second reason

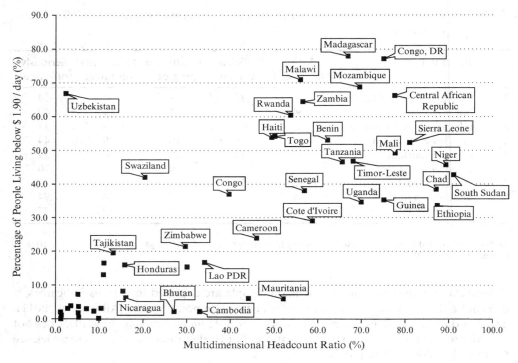

Source: Data from Alkire et al. (2016).

Figure 4.5   Disparity between $1.90/day poverty rates and MPI poverty rates across developing countries

is that it may be possible in the second society, unlike in the first society, that the third person actually represents a minority group living in abject poverty within an affluent society.

Any poverty measurement exercise, following Sen (1976), involves two important steps: identification and aggregation. The identification step amounts to singling out who the poor are. This crucial step was ignored by both the HPI and the dashboard of MDG indicators. In the innovative 2010 Human Development Report, the new Multidimensional Poverty Index (developed by Alkire and Santos, 2010) respected these two steps. The construction of the MPI and its properties are outlined in detail in Chapter 3 of this *Handbook*. The MPI identifies a person as poor if the person is deprived in one-third or more of the ten weighted indicators. The MPI does not necessarily identify the same group of people identified as living below $1.90/day, the income poverty threshold used by the World Bank to assess global income poverty (Ferreira et al., 2016). In Figure 4.5, we compare the percentage of population identified as living below $1.90/day and the percentage of the population identified as the MPI poor. Although there appears to be a positive correlation, there are several exceptions. For example, let us look at countries where 40–50 per cent of the population live below $1.90/day: Swaziland, Tanzania, Timor-Leste, Mali, South Sudan and Niger. Multidimensional headcount ratios for these

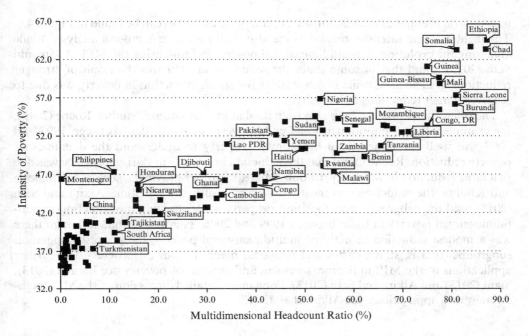

Source: Data from Alkire et al. (2016).

Figure 4.6   Incidence versus intensity of poverty

countries, however, vary from 20 per cent to 91 per cent. Several other similar examples may be found in Figure 4.5. Inter-temporal analyses have also shown that reductions in monetary poverty and MPI poverty do not go hand in hand. For a cross-country example, see Alkire et al. (2015b); and for an application in India, see Alkire and Seth (2015).

The MPI has three interesting features that make it amenable to empirical applications: (1) the MPI is presented as a product of the percentage of the population that is poor (known as the 'multidimensional headcount ratio', or the incidence of poverty) and the average number of weighted deprivations that the poor people experience (the intensity of poverty); (2) the MPI is additively decomposable so that the national MPI can be expressed as a population-weighted average of subgroup MPIs; and (3) the MPI can be expressed as a weighted average of post-identification dimensional deprivations.

The usefulness of the first property can be seen in the example in Figure 4.6, where we plot the relationship between the incidence and intensity of poverty across developing countries. The MPI is a product of incidence and intensity, and thus it may be possible that the same level of MPI can be obtained by different combinations of incidence and intensity. If the same level of MPI is obtained from a lower level of incidence but a higher level of intensity, then this means that a smaller fraction of poor people are deprived in a larger number of indicators on average. Let us compare Sierra Leone and Nigeria. Nearly 81 per cent of the population are MPI poor in Liberia compared to only around 53 per cent of the population in Nigeria. However, the poor experience similar levels of poverty intensity, on average, in both countries. Several other examples can be found in Figure 4.6. The incidence and intensity breakdown is also useful for inter-temporal analysis. While analysing the evolution of multidimensional poverty in India using the MPI, Alkire and Seth (2015) found that in some states the reduction in MPI was the result of stronger reductions in incidence; while in other states the strong reduction in poverty was due to relatively larger reductions in intensity.

The other two properties have also been used in various country studies. Roche (2013), for example, studied multidimensional child poverty in Bangladesh between 1997 and 2007 and used the dimensional breakdown property to understand the dynamics of poverty reduction. Roche found that the reduction in poverty in Barisal province was due to a large reduction in water deprivation, whereas in other provinces, such as Chittagong and Khulna, the reduction was mostly driven by health and nutrition. Alkire and Seth (2015) used the subgroup decomposition property while studying the reduction in multidimensional poverty in India between 1999 and 2006. They found that, although there was a modest reduction in national multidimensional poverty, the poorest population subgroups (that is, states, castes and religions) made the slowest progress. For further applications of the MPI in the measurement and analysis of poverty, see Batana (2013), Siani (2013) and Alkire and Seth (2013). For a more detailed discussion of the MPI methodology and applications, see Alkire et al. (2015a).

4.5   CONCLUDING REMARKS

This chapter provides a brief outline of the practical issues surrounding the measurement of human development and poverty. The key aspects are multidimensionality, inequality and poverty; three elements for which there is a large list of contributing factors and a variety of modelling choices.

Discussing multidimensionality implies analysing how to select the relevant dimensions of a given problem, deciding how to weigh their relative importance, and choosing how to aggregate (or not) those dimensions into a single indicator. A dashboard of indicators is sometimes regarded as a better practical choice because it saves the analyst from making those difficult modelling choices. Yet, single-valued indicators provide a summary measure of a complex phenomenon, making it easier to grasp the evolution of human development and poverty. Be that as it may, there are two considerations worth introducing here. First, that both approaches can be regarded as complementary rather than as alternatives. So a single-valued indicator coupled with additional information on particular aspects of human development may be very useful. Second, in both scenarios one has to deal with the problem of interdependent variables in order to gain a sound assessment of the situation.

In the case of multidimensional measures, we find the choice of three equally weighted dimensions to be the most common. This choice seems to be an acceptable approach regarding the equal weights of those three dimensions even though, sooner rather than later, the sustainability dimension should be introduced. Substituting the arithmetic mean with the geometric mean, as a way of aggregating those dimensions, seems a substantial improvement, even though there are still some pending issues, particularly regarding the normalization strategy and the use of logs for the income dimension (see Chapter 3 of this

Handbook for a discussion). As a consequence, the resulting rates of substitution for those countries with lower levels of human development may become rather odd.

Taking distributive aspects into account is a major step forward in the measurement of human development. In spite of the different proposals made at different points in time, it took 20 years to introduce this aspect into the assessment of human development. The method for incorporating inequality into the measurement of human development has so far been intuitive and solid. Yet there are still some inconsistencies: income is measured in logs, whereas income distribution is measured without. There are also some difficulties in interpreting what inequality means with respect to education and health, as it is not clear that a uniform distribution dominates another in which the younger generation exhibits higher values.

The measurement of poverty has been substantially revised since 2010. It now consists of a multidimensional index that applies to less-developed countries, and is much richer and sounder than former proposals. Yet it is somehow unfortunate to lose the poverty index for highly developed countries at a time when the economic crisis has hit some sectors of those countries very hard.

ACKNOWLEDGEMENTS

This work was done while the second author was visiting the Department of Mathematics for Decisions at the University of Florence, Italy. Thanks are due for the hospitality and facilities provided there. The research is covered by the projects ECO2010-21706 and SEJ-6882/ECON with financial support from the Spanish Ministry of Science and Technology, the Junta de Andalucía and the FEDER (Fonds Européen de Développement Économique et Régional / European Fund for Economic and Regional Development).

NOTES

1. How many pair-wise comparisons are there? If there are 100 countries, then the number of total possible pair-wise comparisons is $100 \times 99/2 = 4950$.
2. If Achievement Matrix II is obtained from Achievement Matrix I, the transformation is referred to as 'weak rearrangement' by Alkire and Foster.

REFERENCES

Alkire, S. and Foster, J. (2010). Designing the Inequality-Adjusted Human Development Index (IHDI). Working Paper 37, Oxford Poverty and Human Development Initiative, University of Oxford.
Alkire, S. and Foster, J. (2011). Counting and multidimensional poverty measurement. *Journal of Public Economics*, 95(7), 476–487.
Alkire, S., Foster, J. and Santos, M.E. (2011). Where did identification go?. *Journal of Economic Inequality*, 9(3), 501–505.
Alkire, S., Foster, J.E., Seth, S., Santos, M.E., Roche, J.M. and Ballon, P. (2015a). *Multidimensional Poverty Measurement and Analysis*, Oxford: Oxford University Press.
Alkire, S., Jindra, C., Robles, G. and Vaz, A. (2016). Multidimensional Poverty Index – Summer 2016: brief methodological note and results. OPHI Briefing 42, Oxford Poverty and Human Development Initiative, University of Oxford, http://www.ophi.org.uk/multidimensional-poverty-index/mpi-2015/mpi-data/.

Alkire, S., Roche, J.M. and Vaz, A. (2015b). Changes over time in multidimensional poverty: methodology and results for 34 countries. OPHI Working Paper 76, University of Oxford.

Alkire, S. and Santos, M.E. (2010). Acute multidimensional poverty: a new index for developing countries. OPHI Working Paper 38, University of Oxford; also published as Human Development Research Paper 2010/11.

Alkire, S. and Seth, S. (2013). Selecting a targeting method to identify BPL households in India. *Social Indicators Research*, 112(2), 417–446.

Alkire, S. and Seth, S. (2015). Multidimensional poverty reduction in India between 1999 and 2006: where and how?. *World Development*, 72, 93–108.

Anand, S. and Sen, A. (1995). Gender inequality in human development: theories and measurement. Occasional Paper 19, United Nations Development Programme, New York, August.

Anand, S. and Sen, A. (1997). Concepts of human development and poverty: a multidimensional perspective. United Nations Development Programme, Human Development Papers, 1–20.

Atkinson, A.B. (1970). On the measurement of inequality. *Journal of Economic Theory*, 2(3), 244–263.

Batana, Y.M. (2013). Multidimensional measurement of poverty among women in sub-Saharan Africa. *Social Indicators Research*, 112(2), 337–362.

Boland, P.J. and Proschan, F. (1988). Multivariate arrangement increasing functions with applications in probability and statistics. *Journal of Multivariate Analysis*, 25(2), 286–298.

Bourguignon, F. and Chakravarty, S.R. (2003). The measurement of multidimensional poverty. *Journal of Economic Inequality*, 1(1), 25–49.

Cahill, M.B. (2005). Is the Human Development Index redundant?. *Eastern Economic Journal*, 31, 1–5.

Cherchye, L., Ooghe, E. and Van Puyenbroeck, T. (2008). Robust human development rankings. *Journal of Economic Inequality*, 6(4), 287–321.

Chowdhury, S. and Squire, L. (2006). Setting weights for aggregate indices: an application to the commitment to development index and human development index. *Journal of Development Studies*, 42(5), 761–771.

Decancq, K. and Lugo, M.A. (2012). Inequality of wellbeing: a multidimensional approach. *Economica*, 79(316), 721–746.

Desai, M. (1991). Human development: concepts and measurement. *European Economic Review*, 35(2), 350–357.

Despotis, D.K. (2005). A reassessment of the Human Development Index via data envelopment analysis. *Journal of the Operational Research Society*, 56(8), 969–980.

Deutsch, J. and Silber, J. (2005). Measuring multidimensional poverty: an empirical comparison of various approaches. *Review of Income and Wealth*, 51(1), 145–174.

Ferreira, F.H., Chen, S., Dabalen, A., Dikhanov, Y., Hamadeh, N., Jolliffe, D., Narayan, A., Prydz, E.B., Revenga, A., Sangraula, P., Serajuddin, U. and Yoshida, N. (2016). A global count of the extreme poor in 2012: data issues, methodology and initial results. *Journal of Economic Inequality*, 14(2), 141–172.

Foster, J.E., Lopez-Calva, L.F. and Szekely, M. (2005). Measuring the distribution of human development: methodology and an application to Mexico. *Journal of Human Development*, 6(1), 5–25.

Foster, J., McGillivray, M. and Seth, S. (2009). Rank robustness of composite indices. Working Paper 26, Oxford Poverty and Human Development Initiative, University of Oxford.

Foster, J.E., McGillivray, M. and Seth, S. (2013). Composite indices: rank robustness, statistical association, and redundancy. *Econometric Reviews*, 32(1), 35–56.

Grimm, M., Harttgen, K., Klasen, S. and Misselhorn, M. (2008). A human development index by income groups. *World Development*, 36(12), 2527–2546.

Herrero, C., Martínez, R. and Villar, A. (2010). Improving the measurement of human development. United Nations Development Programme.

Hicks, D.A. (1997). The inequality-adjusted human development index: a constructive proposal. *World Development*, 25(8), 1283–1298.

Kelley, A.C. (1991). The Human Development Index: 'handle with care'. *Population and Development Review*, 17, 315–324.

Mahlberg, B. and Obersteiner, M. (2001). Remeasuring the HDI by data envelopment analysis. International Institute for Applied Systems Analysis Interim Report, 1, 069.

McGillivray, M. (1991). The Human Development Index: yet another redundant composite development indicator?. *World Development*, 19(10), 1461–1468.

McGillivray, M. and White, H. (1993). Measuring development? The UNDP's Human Development Index. *Journal of International Development*, 5(2), 183–192.

Nguefack-Tsague, G., Klasen, S. and Zucchini, W. (2011). On weighting the components of the human development index: a statistical justification. *Journal of Human Development and Capabilities*, 12(2), 183–202.

Noorbakhsh, F. (1998). The Human Development Index: some technical issues and alternative indices. *Journal of International Development*, 10(5), 589–605.

Permanyer, I. (2011). Assessing the robustness of composite indices rankings. *Review of Income and Wealth*, 57, 306–326.

Ravallion, M. (2012). Troubling tradeoffs in the human development index. *Journal of Development Economics*, 99(2), 201–209.

Roche, J.M. (2013). Monitoring progress in child poverty reduction: methodological insights and illustration to the case study of Bangladesh. *Social Indicators Research*, 112(2), 363–390.

Saisana, M., Saltelli, A. and Tarantola, S. (2005). Uncertainty and sensitivity analysis techniques as tools for the quality assessment of composite indicators. *Journal of the Royal Statistical Society: Series A (Statistics in Society)*, 168(2), 307–323.

Sen, A. (1976). Poverty: an ordinal approach to measurement. *Econometrica: Journal of the Econometric Society*, 44(2), 219–231.

Seth, S. (2009). Inequality, interactions, and human development. *Journal of Human Development and Capabilities*, 10(3), 375–396.

Seth, S. (2013). A class of distribution and association sensitive multidimensional welfare indices. *Journal of Economic Inequality*, 11(2), 133–162.

Seth, S. and McGillivray, M. (2016). Composite indices, alternative weights, and comparison robustness. OPHI Working Paper 106, University of Oxford.

Siani, J. (2013). Has poverty decreased in Cameroon between 2001 and 2007? An analysis based on multidimensional poverty measures. *Economics Bulletin*, 33(4), 3059–3069.

Stiglitz, J., Sen, A. and Fitoussi, J.P. (2009). The measurement of economic performance and social progress revisited: reflections and overview. Commission on the Measurement of Economic Performance and Social Progress, Paris.

Tsui, K.Y. (1999). Multidimensional inequality and multidimensional generalized entropy measures: an axiomatic derivation. *Social Choice and Welfare*, 16(1), 145–157.

Tsui, K.Y. (2002). Multidimensional poverty indices. *Social Choice and Welfare*, 19(1), 69–93.

United Nations (2003), Indicators for monitoring the Millennium Development Goals, definitions, rationale, concepts, and sources. New York.

United Nations Development Programme (UNDP) (various years). *Human Development Report*, New York: Oxford University Press.

APPENDIX

Table 4A.1   Human Development Index (HDI), inequality–adjusted Human Development Index (IHDI) and Multidimensional Poverty Index 2013

HDI rank	Country	HDI	IHDI	Loss due to inequality (%)	Rank difference of HDI and IHDI	MPI
Very high human development						
1	Norway	0.944	0.891	5.6	0	–
2	Australia	0.933	0.860	7.8	0	–
3	Switzerland	0.917	0.847	7.7	−1	–
4	Netherlands	0.915	0.854	6.7	1	–
5	United States	0.914	0.755	17.4	−23	–
6	Germany	0.911	0.846	7.1	1	–
7	New Zealand	0.910	–	–	–	–
8	Canada	0.902	0.833	7.6	−2	–
9	Singapore	0.901	–	–	–	–
10	Denmark	0.900	0.838	6.9	0	–
11	Ireland	0.899	0.832	7.5	−1	–
12	Sweden	0.898	0.840	6.5	3	–
13	Iceland	0.895	0.843	5.7	5	–
14	United Kingdom	0.892	0.812	8.9	−4	–
15	Hong Kong, China (SAR)	0.891	–	–	–	–
15	Korea (Republic of)	0.891	0.736	17.4	−20	–
17	Japan	0.890	0.779	12.4	−6	–
18	Liechtenstein	0.889	–	–	–	–
19	Israel	0.888	0.793	10.7	−4	–
20	France	0.884	0.804	9.0	−2	–
21	Austria	0.881	0.818	7.2	4	–
21	Belgium	0.881	0.806	8.5	0	–
21	Luxembourg	0.881	0.814	7.6	3	–
24	Finland	0.879	0.830	5.5	9	–
25	Slovenia	0.874	0.824	5.8	9	0.000
26	Italy	0.872	0.768	11.9	−1	–
27	Spain	0.869	0.775	10.9	1	–
28	Czech Republic	0.861	0.813	5.6	9	0.010
29	Greece	0.853	0.762	10.6	0	–
30	Brunei Darussalam	0.852	–	–	–	–
31	Qatar	0.851	–	–	–	–
32	Cyprus	0.845	0.752	11.0	−3	–
33	Estonia	0.840	0.767	8.7	3	0.026
34	Saudi Arabia	0.836	–	–	–	–
35	Lithuania	0.834	0.746	10.6	−3	–
35	Poland	0.834	0.751	9.9	−2	–
37	Andorra	0.830	–	–	–	–
37	Slovakia	0.830	0.778	6.3	9	0.000

Table 4A.1 (continued)

HDI rank	Country	HDI	IHDI	Loss due to inequality (%)	Rank difference of HDI and IHDI	MPI
Very high human development						
39	Malta	0.829	0.760	8.3	5	–
40	United Arab Emirates	0.827	–	–	–	0.002
41	Chile	0.822	0.661	19.6	−16	–
41	Portugal	0.822	0.739	10.1	0	–
43	Hungary	0.818	0.757	7.4	7	0.016
44	Bahrain	0.815	–	–	–	–
44	Cuba	0.815	–	–	–	–
46	Kuwait	0.814	–	–	–	–
47	Croatia	0.812	0.721	11.2	−2	0.016
48	Latvia	0.810	0.725	10.6	0	0.006
49	Argentina	0.808	0.680	15.8	−4	0.011
High human development						
50	Uruguay	0.790	0.662	16.1	−8	0.006
51	Bahamas	0.789	0.676	14.3	−3	–
51	Montenegro	0.789	0.733	7.2	5	0.006
53	Belarus	0.786	0.726	7.6	6	0.000
54	Romania	0.785	0.702	10.5	4	–
55	Libya	0.784	–	–	–	–
56	Oman	0.783	–	–	–	–
57	Russian Federation	0.778	0.685	12.0	3	0.005
58	Bulgaria	0.777	0.692	11.0	5	–
59	Barbados	0.776	–	–	–	–
60	Palau	0.775	–	–	–	–
61	Antigua and Barbuda	0.774	–	–	–	–
62	Malaysia	0.773	–	–	–	–
63	Mauritius	0.771	0.662	14.2	−2	–
64	Trinidad and Tobago	0.766	0.649	15.2	−6	0.020
65	Lebanon	0.765	0.606	20.8	−17	–
65	Panama	0.765	0.596	22.1	−18	–
67	Venezuela (Bolivarian Republic of)	0.764	0.613	19.7	−10	–
68	Costa Rica	0.763	0.611	19.9	−11	–
69	Turkey	0.759	0.639	15.8	−3	0.028
70	Kazakhstan	0.757	0.667	11.9	9	0.001
71	Mexico	0.756	0.583	22.9	−13	0.011
71	Seychelles	0.756	–	–	–	–
73	Saint Kitts and Nevis	0.750	–	–	–	–
73	Sri Lanka	0.750	0.643	14.3	1	0.021
75	Iran (Islamic Republic of)	0.749	0.498	33.6	−34	–
76	Azerbaijan	0.747	0.659	11.8	7	0.021
77	Jordan	0.745	0.607	18.6	−5	0.008

Table 4A.1   (continued)

HDI rank	Country	HDI	IHDI	Loss due to inequality (%)	Rank difference of HDI and IHDI	MPI
High human development						
77	Serbia	0.745	0.663	10.9	12	0.000
79	Brazil	0.744	0.542	27.0	−16	0.011
79	Georgia	0.744	0.636	14.5	4	0.003
79	Grenada	0.744	–	–	–	–
82	Peru	0.737	0.562	23.7	−9	0.043
83	Ukraine	0.734	0.667	9.2	18	0.008
84	Belize	0.732	–	–	–	0.018
84	Macedonia (Former Yugoslav Republic of)	0.732	0.633	13.6	7	0.002
86	Bosnia and Herzegovina	0.731	0.653	10.6	13	0.002
87	Armenia	0.730	0.655	10.4	15	0.001
88	Fiji	0.724	0.613	15.3	6	–
89	Thailand	0.722	0.573	20.7	−2	0.006
90	Tunisia	0.721	–	–	–	0.004
91	China	0.719	–	–	–	0.056
91	Saint Vincent and the Grenadines	0.719	–	–	–	–
93	Algeria	0.717	–	–	–	–
93	Dominica	0.717	–	–	–	0.018
95	Albania	0.716	0.620	13.4	11	0.005
96	Jamaica	0.715	0.579	19.0	1	–
97	Saint Lucia	0.714	–	–	–	–
98	Colombia	0.711	0.521	26.7	−10	0.022
98	Ecuador	0.711	0.549	22.7	−3	0.024
100	Suriname	0.705	0.534	24.2	−6	0.024
100	Tonga	0.705	–	–	–	–
102	Dominican Republic	0.700	0.535	23.6	−4	0.009
Medium human development						
103	Maldives	0.698	0.521	25.4	−7	0.018
103	Mongolia	0.698	0.618	11.5	16	0.065
103	Turkmenistan	0.698	–	–	–	–
106	Samoa	0.694	–	–	–	–
107	Palestine, State of	0.686	0.606	11.7	13	0.005
108	Indonesia	0.684	0.553	19.2	5	0.066
109	Botswana	0.683	0.422	38.2	−21	–
110	Egypt	0.682	0.518	24.0	−5	–
111	Paraguay	0.676	0.513	24.1	−5	0.064
112	Gabon	0.674	0.512	24.0	−5	0.070
113	Bolivia (Plurinational State of)	0.667	0.470	29.6	−10	0.089
114	Moldova (Republic of)	0.663	0.582	12.2	16	0.007
115	El Salvador	0.662	0.485	26.7	−7	–

Table 4A.1 (continued)

HDI rank	Country	HDI	IHDI	Loss due to inequality (%)	Rank difference of HDI and IHDI	MPI
Medium human development						
116	Uzbekistan	0.661	0.556	15.8	14	0.008
117	Philippines	0.660	0.540	18.1	10	0.064
118	South Africa	0.658	–	–	–	0.044
118	Syrian Arab Republic	0.658	0.518	21.2	4	0.021
120	Iraq	0.642	0.505	21.4	0	0.045
121	Guyana	0.638	0.522	18.2	10	0.030
121	Viet Nam	0.638	0.543	14.9	15	0.017
123	Cape Verde	0.636	0.511	19.7	4	–
124	Micronesia (Federated States of)	0.630	–	–	–	–
125	Guatemala	0.628	0.422	32.8	−8	0.127
125	Kyrgyzstan	0.628	0.519	17.2	10	0.019
127	Namibia	0.624	0.352	43.6	−22	0.187
128	Timor–Leste	0.620	0.430	30.7	−3	0.360
129	Honduras	0.617	0.418	32.2	−6	0.072
129	Morocco	0.617	0.433	29.7	0	0.048
131	Vanuatu	0.616	–	–	–	0.129
132	Nicaragua	0.614	0.452	26.4	4	0.072
133	Kiribati	0.607	0.416	31.5	−4	–
133	Tajikistan	0.607	0.491	19.2	9	0.054
135	India	0.586	0.418	28.6	0	0.283
136	Bhutan	0.584	0.465	20.4	9	0.119
136	Cambodia	0.584	0.440	24.7	7	0.212
138	Ghana	0.573	0.394	31.3	−1	0.139
139	Lao People's Democratic Republic	0.569	0.430	24.5	8	0.174
140	Congo	0.564	0.391	30.7	0	0.181
141	Zambia	0.561	0.365	35.0	−4	0.328
142	Bangladesh	0.558	0.396	29.1	4	0.253
142	Sao Tome and Principe	0.558	0.384	31.2	0	0.154
144	Equatorial Guinea	0.556	–	–	–	–
Low human development						
145	Nepal	0.540	0.384	28.8	3	0.217
146	Pakistan	0.537	0.375	30.1	2	0.230
147	Kenya	0.535	0.360	32.8	0	0.229
148	Swaziland	0.530	0.354	33.3	−2	0.086
149	Angola	0.526	0.295	44.0	−17	–
150	Myanmar	0.524	–	–	–	–
151	Rwanda	0.506	0.338	33.2	−4	0.350
152	Cameroon	0.504	0.339	32.8	−2	0.248
152	Nigeria	0.504	0.300	40.3	−14	0.240

Table 4A.1   (continued)

HDI rank	Country	HDI	IHDI	Loss due to inequality (%)	Rank difference of HDI and IHDI	MPI
Low human development						
154	Yemen	0.500	0.336	32.8	−2	0.283
155	Madagascar	0.498	0.346	30.5	2	0.357
156	Zimbabwe	0.492	0.358	27.2	7	0.172
157	Papua New Guinea	0.491	–	–	–	–
157	Solomon Islands	0.491	0.374	23.8	11	–
159	Comoros	0.488	–	–	–	–
159	Tanzania (United Republic of)	0.488	0.356	27.1	8	0.332
161	Mauritania	0.487	0.315	35.3	−2	0.352
162	Lesotho	0.486	0.313	35.6	−2	0.156
163	Senegal	0.485	0.326	32.9	3	0.439
164	Uganda	0.484	0.335	30.8	5	0.367
165	Benin	0.476	0.311	34.6	0	0.412
166	Sudan	0.473	–	–	–	–
166	Togo	0.473	0.317	32.9	4	0.250
168	Haiti	0.471	0.285	39.5	−3	0.248
169	Afghanistan	0.468	0.321	31.4	7	0.353
170	Djibouti	0.467	0.306	34.6	2	0.139
171	Côte d'Ivoire	0.452	0.279	38.3	−2	0.310
172	Gambia	0.441	–	–	–	0.324
173	Ethiopia	0.435	0.307	29.4	5	0.564
174	Malawi	0.414	0.282	31.9	1	0.334
175	Liberia	0.412	0.273	33.8	−1	0.485
176	Mali	0.407	–	–	–	0.558
177	Guinea−Bissau	0.396	0.239	39.6	−4	0.462
178	Mozambique	0.393	0.277	29.5	2	0.389
179	Guinea	0.392	0.243	38.0	−1	0.506
180	Burundi	0.389	0.257	33.9	2	0.454
181	Burkina Faso	0.388	0.252	35.0	2	0.535
182	Eritrea	0.381	–	–	–	–
183	Sierra Leone	0.374	0.208	44.3	−3	0.388
184	Chad	0.372	0.232	37.8	1	0.344
185	Central African Republic	0.341	0.203	40.4	−2	0.430
186	Congo (Democratic Republic of the)	0.338	0.211	37.6	1	0.392
187	Niger	0.337	0.228	32.4	3	0.605

Source: Human Development Report 2014.

5. Multidimensional poverty and material deprivation: theoretical approaches
Satya R. Chakravarty and Nachiketa Chattopadhyay

5.1 INTRODUCTION

Even in the early twenty-first century many people of the world face difficulty in making ends meet. This manifestation of poverty, which arises because of insufficiency of income to cover expenses, is a denial of human rights. However, well-being of a population depends also on many attributes and dimensions other than income (Kolm, 1977; Townsend, 1979; Streeten, 1981; Sen, 1985, 1987; Ravallion, 1996; Thorbecke, 2008; Stiglitz et al., 2009). Examples of such dimensions are housing, literacy, environmental conditions, life expectancy at birth, provision of public goods, and so on. In other words, the well-being of a population, hence its poverty, is a multidimensional phenomenon. A person with sufficiently high income may not always be well off with respect to some non-monetary dimension of life. An example may be insufficient quantity of a public good. Many rich people in several developing and underdeveloped countries suffer or even die from malaria or dengue in the rainy season because of badly organized malaria prevention programs, a local public good. Likewise, it is unlikely that an old homeless person is sufficiently well off with respect to income. Trade-off between income and a non-income dimension may not be possible to improve the level of living of a person.

Therefore targeting of poverty alleviation is still one of the major economic policies in many countries of the world. To formulate anti-poverty policies it is necessary to know the level of poverty. This in turn necessitates the quantification of the extent of poverty. Hence, the construction of a multidimensional index, a quantifier of the level of multidimensional poverty, is a worthwhile exercise. The June and September 2011 issues of the *Journal of Economic Inequality* published a series of forum articles on multidimensional indices of achievement and poverty. These contributions nicely elucidate conceptual problems on the concerned matters.[1]

According to Sen (1976), income poverty measurement problem involves two exercises: (1) the identification of the poor; and (2) aggregation of the characteristics of the poor into an overall indicator of poverty. The first problem is generally solved by specifying a poverty line that represents the income required for a subsistence level of living. A person is regarded as income poor if his income falls below the poverty line. Loosely speaking, the second problem requires aggregation of income shortfalls of the poor from the poverty line. Sen also suggested a sophisticated index of income poverty which is senative to the redistribution of income among the poor, and income shortfall from the poverty line.[2]

Following Sen (1976) several authors, including Tsui (2002), Bourguignon and Chakravarty (2003), Chakravarty and Silber (2008) and Alkire and Foster (2011a), suggested postulates for a multidimensional poverty index. Essential to the formulation of these axioms is that each person possesses a vector of basic needs or dimensions, which represent different dimensions of well-being, and a direct method of identification of the poor verifies whether the person has 'minimally acceptable levels' (Sen, 1992, p. 139) of these dimensions. These 'minimally acceptable levels' represent the cut-off points for different dimensions for a person to be non-poor in the dimensions. A person is regarded as deprived in a dimension if the observed level falls below the cut-off. We then say that the person is characterized by a functioning failure. One then looks at poverty directly in terms of shortfalls of dimensional quantities, that is, the extents of deprivations, from respective cut-off points or directly in terms of number of functioning failures. An aggregation of these shortfalls and number of functioning failures, defined in an unambiguous way, gives us an indicator of multidimensional poverty. It may be important to note that the cut-off points are determined independently of the attribute distributions.

The objective of this chapter is to present a brief discussion on the axiomatic approach to the measurement of multidimensional poverty and material deprivation. The distinction between multidimensional poverty and material deprivation we follow is the one that has been endorsed by the European Union. As stated above, a multidimensional poverty index takes into account all dimensions of well-being, including non-material dimensions such as communing with friends; whereas a material deprivation index is concerned with functioning failures and deprivations related to material living conditions (see Guio, 2005; Whelan and Maître, 2009; Guio et al., 2009). In their report prepared for the Commission of Economic Performance and Social Progress, constituted by the French Government, Stiglitz et al. (2009) stated that dimensions related to material living standards should be included for the evaluation of multivariate well-being.

The next section presents the postulates for a multidimensional poverty index. Section 5.3 discusses some functional forms for such an index. In section 5.4 we make a discussion on some material deprivation indices. Finally, section 5.5 concludes.

5.2   AXIOMS FOR AN INDEX OF MULTIDIMENSIONAL POVERTY

The objective of this section is to analyze the properties for a multidimensional poverty index. In a society of n-persons, person i possesses an m-vector $x_i = (x_{i1}, x_{i2}, \ldots, x_{im})$ of attributes, where $x_{ij} \geq 0$ for all i and j. We refer to x_{ij} as the achievement of individual i in attribute or dimension j. The vector x_i is the ith row of an $n \times m$ distribution matrix $X \in M^n$, where M^n is the set of all $n \times m$ matrices whose entries are non-negative real numbers. The distribution of attribute j ($j = 1, 2, \ldots, m$) among the n persons is represented by the column x_j of the matrix $X \in M^n$. Let $M = \cup_{n \in N} M^n$, where N is the set of all positive integers. That is, M is the set of all distribution matrices with m columns. For any $n \in N, X \in M^n$, we write $n(X)$ (or n) for the corresponding population size. Initially we exclude the possibility that a variable can be of qualitative type, for instance, whether a person is physically handicapped or not.

In this multidimensional set up, a cut-off point is defined for each dimension. These cut-off points give the minimal quantities of the m attributes necessary for maintaining a subsistence standard of living. Let $z = (z_1, \ldots, z_m)$ be the vector of cut-off points, where $z_i > 0$ for all i. The vector z is assumed to be an element of the set $Z \subset \mathcal{R}^m_{++}$, strictly positive part of the m-dimensional Euclidean space. Person i is said to be deprived or non-deprived in dimension j according as $x_{ij} < z_j$ or $x_{ij} \geq z_j$ and he is called non-deprived if $x_{ij} \geq z_j$ for all j. We say that a person has functioning failure in dimension j if he is deprived in the dimension. Equivalently, dimension j is a meager dimension for the person. The number of meager dimensions of a person is his functioning failure score. For any pair (i, j), let $\hat{x}_{ij} = \min(x_{ij}, z_j)$ be the attribute quantity censored at z_j. For $n \in N$, $X \in M^n$, we write $\hat{X}$ for the censored distribution matrix corresponding to X. A person is called non-deprived in a distribution matrix if he is not deprived in any attribute.

For specifying the number of poor here, Bourguignon and Chakravarty (2003) defined the poverty indicator variable:

$$\rho(x_i;z) = 1 \text{ if } \exists \text{ a dimension } j \text{ such that } x_{ij} < z_j, = 0, \text{ otherwise.} \tag{5.1}$$

Then the number of poor persons in the multidimensional structure is given by:

$$n_p(X) = \sum_{i=1}^{n} \rho(x_i;z). \tag{5.2}$$

This method of identifying the set of multidimensional poor persons is referred to as the union method of identification. One minor problem with this method is that a person who is non-deprived in all dimensions except one in which the shortfall from the cut-off point is quite low will be identified as poor. Such a person may not regard himself as poor. However, the union method has established itself as a prominent identification criterion because of its easy implementation and long usage. (Chakravarty, 2018, discusses several advantages of this notion of identification.) An alternative identification approach is the intersection method, which says that a person is poor if he is deprived in all dimensions, and this leads us to identify the number of poor as the total number of persons who are deprived in all dimensions. In this method a person with a high functioning failure score $l < m$ will not be identified as poor (see Tsui, 2002; Atkinson, 2003; Bourguignon and Chakravarty, 2003).

Alkire and Foster (2011) defined person i as multidimensionally poor if $x_{ij} < z_j$ holds for k many values of j, where k is some integer between 1 and m. Clearly, this intermediate identification method coincides with the union or the intersection method according as $k = 1$ or m (see also Gordon et al., 2003). In all these identification methods, we assign equal importance to each dimension. A more general case is to assume that different dimensions are assigned different positive weights and let c_i be the sum of weights assigned to the dimensions in which person i is deprived. In this general case person i is identified as poor if and only if $c_i \geq k$, where $m \geq k > 0$. If we denote the weight assigned to dimension j by w_j and if $\min_j w_j \geq k$, then we get the union method, whereas the intersection method drops out as a special case of this general criterion if $m = k$. An example of the weights can be $w_1 = \frac{m}{2}$ and $w_j = \frac{m}{2(m-1)}, 2 \leq j \leq m$ (see Alkire and Foster, 2011a). We can refer to k as identification threshold in this intermediate set-up. The choice of dimensional weights is definitely an issue of value judgment. As Ravallion (2011a) argued, the weights should have consistency with 'well-informed choices by poor people'.[3]

In the following discussion we assign equal importance to each dimension and follow the union criterion of identification. (See Atkinson, 2003, for arguments in favor of equal importance.) A person will be called non-poor or rich if he is not poor under the specific identification method. Clearly, a non-deprived person is non-poor. For any $n \in N$, $X \in M^n$, $z \in Z$, we denote the set of all poor persons in X by $\Pi(X;z)$. For any given

$z \in Z$ we write the number of poor persons in $X \in M^n$ by $|\Pi(X;z)|$. Clearly, $|\Pi(X;z)|$ $= n_p(X)$.The head count ratio, the proportion of persons in poverty, is $\frac{|\Pi(X;z)|}{n}$.

A multidimensional poverty index P is a non-constant real valued function defined on $M \times Z$, that is, $P : M \times Z \rightarrow \mathcal{R}$, where $\mathcal{R}$ is the real line. For any $X \in M$ and $z \in Z$, $P(X;z)$ gives the extent of poverty corresponding to X and the threshold vector z.

The properties suggested below for an arbitrary P are generalizations of different postulates proposed for an income poverty index. In stating these axioms we assume the union method of identifying the poor in this multidimensional framework. Our discussion applies equally well to any other method of identification.

Weak Focus (WFC): For any $(X; z) \in M \times Z$ and for any non-poor person i and dimension j, an increase in x_{ij}, given that all other achievement levels in X remain fixed, does not change the poverty value $P(X;z)$.

Strong Focus (SFC): For any $(X;z) \in M \times Z$ and for any person i and dimension j, an increase in $x_{ij} \geq z_j$, given that all other achievement levels in X remain fixed, does not change the poverty value $P(X;z)$.

Normalization (NOM): For any $(X;z) \in M \times Z$ if $x_{ij} \geq z_j$ for all i and j, then $P(X;z) = 0$.

Symmetry (SYM): Given for any $(X;z) \in M \times Z$, $P(X;z) = P(\pi X;z)$, where π is any $n \times n$ permutation matrix.[4]

Monotonicity (MON): For any $(X;z) \in M \times Z$, person i and attribute j such that $x_{ij} < z_j$, a reduction in x_{ij}, given that other achievement levels in X remain fixed, increases the poverty value $P(X;z)$.

Principle of Population (POP): For any $(X;z) \in M \times Z$, $P(X;z) = P(X^{(l)};z)$, where $X^{(l)} =$

$$\begin{pmatrix} X^1 \\ X^2 \\ \cdots \\ X^l \end{pmatrix}, \text{ where each } X^i = X \text{ and } l \geq 2 \text{ is any integer.}$$

Continuity (CON): Given $z \in Z$, $P(X;z)$ varies continuously with respect to changes in attribute quantities such that the poverty status of any person does not change.

Subgroup Decomposability (SUD): For any $X^1, X^2, \ldots, X^l \in M$ and $z \in Z$, $P(X;z) = \sum_{i=1}^{l} \frac{n_i}{n} P(X^i; z)$, where

$$X = \begin{pmatrix} X^1 \\ X^2 \\ \cdots \\ X^l \end{pmatrix} \in M, n_i \text{ is the population size associated with } X^i \text{ and } \sum_{i=1}^{l} n_i = n.$$

Increasingness in Subsistence Levels of Attributes (INS): For any $X \in M$, $P(X;z)$ is increasing in z_j, where j is a deprived dimension.

Non-Poverty Growth (NPG): For any $(X;z) \in M \times Z$, if Y is obtained from X by adding a rich person to the society, then $P(Y;z) < P(X;z)$.

Ratio Scale Invariance (SCI): For all $(X^1;z^1) \in M \times Z$, $P(X^1;z^1) = P(X^2;z^2)$, where $X^2 = X^1 \Omega$, $z^2 = z^1 \Omega$ and $\Omega = \text{diag}(\omega_1,\omega_2,\ldots\omega_m)$, $\omega_i > 0$ for all i, is an m-rowed diagonal matrix.

According to WFC, if a rich person, who is non-deprived in all dimensions, gets more in a dimension, then poverty does not change.[5] SFC means that giving a person more in a dimension in which he is non-deprived, does not change the extent of poverty, even if he is deprived in one or more of the other dimensions. Thus, trade-off between two dimensions of a person who is deprived in one but non-deprived in the other is not possible. This definitely does not exclude the possibility of a trade-off if the person is deprived in both dimensions. The two focus axioms do not rule out the possibility of dependence of the poverty index on the non-poor population size. NOM attaches the value 0 to a poverty index in the situation when everybody is non-poor. In view of SYM, any characteristic other than the attribute levels, for instance the marital status of the individuals, is immaterial for poverty measurement. MON demands that the value of the poverty index increases if the condition of a poor person in a dimension in which he is deprived worsens. POP enables us to view poverty in average terms. It becomes helpful for cross-population (for example, for inter-temporal and interregional) poverty comparisons. CON means that small changes in attribute quantities that do not change the poverty position of a person will not generate an abrupt jump in the value of the poverty index.

SUD demands that when a population is partitioned into several subgroups, say l, with respect to some homogeneous characteristic such as age, sex or region, then total poverty is given by the population share weighted average of poverty levels of different subgroups. The percentage contribution of subgroup i to global poverty is $(n_i P(X^i;z))/nP(X;z)100$, where X^i is the sub-matrix of X corresponding to subgroup i with population size n_i. Such contributions enable us to isolate subgroups of the population that are more afflicted by poverty (see Anand, 1983; Chakravarty, 1983, 2009; Foster et al., 1984; Foster and Shorrocks, 1991). Repeated applications of SUD shows that we can write the poverty index as:

$$P(X;z) = \frac{1}{n}\sum_{i=1}^{n} P(x_i;z). \tag{5.3}$$

Since $P(x_i;z)$ depends only on person $i's$ attributes, we refer to it as 'individual poverty function'. Evidently, P in (5.3) satisfies SYM and POP.

An increase in the threshold limit of a deprived dimension will increase the deprivation of a poor person and hence poverty increases in such a case. NPG demands that poverty will decrease if a rich person migrates to the society. Given SFC, this holds if the non-poor population size is inversely related to the poverty index. SCI says that the poverty index remains unaltered under scale transformations of dimensional quantities and threshold limits. This enables us to look at the extent of deprivation in any dimension j in terms of proportionate shortfall or deprivation $(1 - \frac{x_{ij}}{z_j})$ of the attribute quantity from the cutoff.

The next axiom deals with the redistribution of attributes among the poor. For $X, Y \in M$, with $X \neq Y$, X is said to uniformly majorize Y if $X = BY$ for some $n \times n$ non-permutation bistochastic matrix. This means that we transform the distribution matrix Y into the matrix X by some equalizing transfers (see Kolm, 1977; Tsui, 2002; Savaglio, 2006; Weymark, 2006; Chakravarty, 2009; Bosmans et al., 2015). Given that the meager attribute quantities of the poor in X are obtained from those in Y by a sequence of equalizing operations, a poverty index which is sensitive to the redistribution of attributes among the poor should regard X as less poverty stricken than Y.

Transfers Principle (TRF): For any $z \in Z$, $X, Y \in M$ if X uniformly majorizes Y then $P(X;z) < P(Y;z)$, given that the transfers are among the meager dimensions of the poor.

It may be worthwhile to note that this transfer axiom is not the only way of generalizing the single-dimensional principle of transfers to the multidimensional set-up. As Fleurbaey and Trannoy (2003) noted, TRF requires that one distribution matrix is obtained from another by transferring achievements in all the dimensions in the same proportion. This is a very strong requirement. Next, transfer across some of the dimensions may not be possible. Examples are ordinal dimensions; say, self-reported health status and educational attainments. As an alternative, they suggested Pigou–Dalton bundle transfer across transferable dimensions between two persons where the donor is richer than the recipient in all the dimensions and the transfer does not allow the recipient to be richer than the donor in any dimensions. (See Fleurbaey and Maniquet, 2011; Lasso de la Vega et al., 2010; Chakravarty and Lugo, 2016; Chakravarty, 2018, for further discussion.)

To understand the next property, which clearly indicates the distinguishing features between single and multidimensional poverty, we consider the two-person two-dimension case, where each person is deprived in both the dimensions. Assume that $x_{11} > x_{21}$ and $x_{12} < x_{22}$. Let there be a switch of quantities in dimension 2 between the two persons. This switch increases the correlation between the dimensions since person 1 who had more in dimension 1 has now more in dimension 2 also. If the two dimensions are substitutes, then one will compensate the lack of another in the definition of individual poverty. Consequently, the correlation-increasing switch will increase poverty. Clearly, the mean of each attribute remains unaltered under the switch. A similar argument will establish that poverty should decrease under a correlation increasing switch if the two dimensions are complements (see Atkinson and Bourguignon, 1982). In the general case with m dimensions, the rearrangement of dimensions are made in a way such that one of the persons receives at least as much of every dimension as the other, and more of at least one dimension (see Weymark, 2006; Chakravarty, 2009, 2018; Decancq, 2014).

Following Bourguignon and Chakravarty (2003), the postulate can be stated formally for substitutes as:

Increasing Poverty under Correlation Increasing Switch (IPC): Assume that $z \in Z$ is given. Under SUD, for any $X \in M$, if $Y \in M$ is obtained from X by a correlation-increasing switch between two poor persons, then $P(X;z) < P(Y;z)$, given that the two attributes are substitutes.

The corresponding property, which requires poverty to decrease under such a switch when the dimensions are complements, is denoted by DPC. If a poverty index remains unchanged under a correlation-increasing switch, then the dimensions are regarded as 'independents'.

The next postulate, suggested by Alkire and Foster (2011a), says that if a poor person who is non-deprived in a dimension becomes deprived in the dimension, then poverty increases.

Dimensional Monotonicity (DIM): Suppose the distribution matrices $Y \in M$ and $X \in M$ are related as follows: for some attribute j' and a person i' who is poor in X, $x_{ij} \geq z_j$, $y_{ij} = x_{ij} - \delta < z_j, \delta > 0$ for $(i, j) = (i', j')$ and $y_{ij} = x_{ij}$ for all $(i, j) \neq (i', j')$. Then $P(X;z) < P(Y;z)$.

5.3   SOME FUNCTIONAL FORMS FOR INDICES OF MULTIDIMENSIONAL POVERTY

In this section we discuss some functional forms for multidimensional poverty indices. The first example we consider is the Bourguignon and Chakravarty (2003) index $P_{\alpha,\theta}(X;z)$, one of the most widely used indices in the literature, which is defined as:

$$P_{\alpha,\theta}(X;z) = \frac{1}{n} \sum_{i \in \Pi(X;z)} \left[\sum_{j=1}^{m} a_j \left(1 - \frac{\hat{x}_{ij}}{z_j} \right)^\theta \right]^{\alpha/\theta}, \tag{5.4}$$

where $\alpha > 0$, $\theta > 0$ are parameters, and $a_j > 0$ for all $j = 1, 2, \cdots, m$ with $\sum_{j=1}^{m} a_j = 1$.

Under these parametric restrictions, the subgroup decomposable (hence symmetric and population replication invariant) index $P_{\alpha,\theta}$ satisfies MON, CON, SCI, INS, NPG and DIM. By construction the third bracketed term on the right hand side of (5.4) is the individual poverty function. This index can be interpreted as follows. A power transformation with power θ is first applied to the poverty shortfalls in the individual dimensions. These transformed shortfalls across dimensions are aggregated into an overall gap using the positive weights $a_j's$. Multidimensional poverty is then defined as the average of such gaps raised to the power α over the whole population. The weight a_j reflects the importance that a policy maker assigns to dimension j. It may also be interpreted as the priority that the government assigns for removing poverty from the jth dimension of well-being. $P_{\alpha,\theta}$ can be regarded as a simple parametric multidimensional generalization of the Foster–Greer–Thorbecke (1984) single-dimensional index.

The index $P_{\alpha,\theta}$ takes on its maximum value 1 if all the persons are fully deprived in all dimensions, that is, $x_{ij} = 0$ for all pairs (i, j) where $i = 1,2,\cdots, n; j = 1,2,\cdots, m$. On the other hand, as specified in NOM, the index achieves its lower bound 0 if there is no poor person in the society. For $\alpha=1$, $\theta=1$, the index becomes the average of a weighted sum of individual poverty shortfalls in different dimensions. TRF is satisfied when θ is greater than 1. The index will satisfy IPC or DPC according as α is greater or less than θ. The parameter θ represents the curvature of the isopoverty contour. For any finite $\theta > 1$, the isopoverty contours are strictly convex to the origin and as the value of θ increases, under ceteris paribus assumptions, the contours become more convex. The elasticity of substitution between proportionate shortfalls corresponding to two dimensions is $\frac{1}{\theta - 1}$. Thus, for $\theta = 1$, there is perfectly elastic tradeoff between the proportionate deprivations and as $\theta \rightarrow \infty$ we get the rectangular isopoverty contour. For a given θ, as the value of α increases, higher weight is assigned to attribute-wise transfers lower down the scale.

Given $\alpha = 1$, as $\theta \rightarrow \infty$, the corresponding limiting form of $P_{\alpha,\theta}$ is given by:

$$P_{\alpha,\theta}(X;z) = \frac{1}{n} \sum_{i \in \Pi(X;z)} \left(\max_{j} \left\{ 1 - \frac{\hat{x}_{ij}}{z_j} \right\} \right). \qquad (5.5)$$

Since the two-dimensional individual isopoverty curves corresponding to the formula (5.5) are of rectangular shape, there is no scope for substitutability between the two relative shortfalls in this case. The informational requirement of this index is minimal; we only need information on the relative shortfalls $(1 - \hat{x}_{ij}/z_j)$ to perform the aggregation. (See Bourguignon and Chakravarty, 1999, for further discussion.)

For $\alpha = \theta$, $P_{\alpha,\theta}$ coincides with the indices suggested by Chakravarty et al. (1998). In this case we can rewrite the index as $\sum_{j=1}^{m} a_j [\frac{1}{n} \sum_{i \in \Pi(X;z)} (1 - \frac{\hat{x}_{ij}}{z_j})^{\theta}]$. Thus, the overall poverty is a weighted average of poverty levels for individual dimensions. This property is known as the factor decomposability axiom. Under the union identification rule, the contribution of dimension j to overall poverty is given by the amount $a_j P(x_{.j};z_j)$, where $P(x_{.j};z_j) = \sum_{i \in \Pi(X;z)} \frac{1}{n} (1 - \frac{\hat{x}_{ij}}{z_j})^{\theta}$. The set of indices $P(x_{.j};z_j)$, where $j = 1, 2,\dots, m$, constitutes a portfolio of dimensional indices. Such a dashboard of individual dimensional indicators enables us to summarize the dimension-wise poverty levels (see Atkinson et al., 2002; Stiglitz et al., 2009). A dashboard-based aggregate index of poverty ignores interdimensional association.

Complete elimination of poverty from dimension j will reduce total poverty exactly by this quantity. The percentage contribution of dimension j to overall poverty becomes $100(a_j P(x_{.j};z_j))/P(X;z)$ (see Chakravarty et al., 1998; Chakravarty and Silber, 2008; Chakravarty, 2009). Here, under the union method of identification, the two decomposition postulates can be employed simultaneously. This type of two-way splitting of poverty becomes especially helpful when the limited resources of the society may not be sufficient for removal of poverty from one entire subgroup or for one dimension of the entire population.

Lasso de la Vega and Urrutia (2011) and Lasso de la Vega et al. (2009) developed an axiomatic characterization of $P_{\alpha,\theta}$ as a multidimensional deprivation index using several intuitively reasonable axioms defined on the set of individual deprivations in different dimensions. Among these axioms, monotonicity demands increasingness of the deprivation index with respect to dimensional individual deprivations. According to the weak dimension separability axiom, if deprivation for a subset of the set of dimensions reduces while the deprivations in the other subset remain unchanged for all individuals, then overall deprivation should decrease. Homotheticity requires that a common proportional change in all individual dimensional deprivation levels in two societies will not change the ranking of the societies with respect to their overall deprivations. A highly innovative feature of their characterization is that the framework is quite general in the sense that any notion of deprivation, including multidimensional poverty, fits with the framework.

Often investigation of the relationship between poverty, economic growth and inequality is motivated by policy-related issues such as 'trickledown' effects of economic growth and the impact of structural adjustment programs to stabilize the economy (see, e.g.,

Ravallion and Huppi, 1991; Datt and Ravallion, 1992; Kakwani, 1993; Lipton and Ravallion, 1995). The Watts (1968) multidimensional poverty index suggested by Tsui (2002), Chakravarty et al. (2008) and Chakravarty and Silber (2008) can be employed to show that a change in poverty can be disaggregated into a multidimensional growth component and a multidimensional redistribution component. The growth component shows the effect of economic growth on poverty change assuming that inequality does not change; the redistribution component isolates the effect of change in inequality, given that the means of the dimensions remain unchanged.

The Watts index is defined as:

$$P_W(X;z) = \frac{1}{n} \sum_{i \in \Pi(X;z)} \sum_{j=1}^{m} \delta_j \ln\left(\frac{z_j}{\hat{x}_{ij}}\right), \tag{5.6}$$

where $x_{ij} > 0$ for all i, j and at least one of the non-negative weights δ_j is positive. It is easy to verify that subgroup decomposable index P_W fulfills NOM, MON, CON, TRF and DIM. Since P_W does not change under a correlation increasing switch, it treats the attributes as 'independents'. The parameter δ_j is a scale parameter in the sense that given $(X;z)$, an increase in δ_j for any j will increase the value of P_W. The index P_W is a normalized version of a Maasoumi–Lugo (2008) multidimensional poverty index based on the 'aggregate poverty line approach'.

To identify the growth and redistribution components explicitly, suppose X^1 and X^2 denote the attribute matrices of a society in periods 1 and 2 and the corresponding population sizes are n_1 and n_2 respectively. Then assuming that the cut-off points are fixed, the poverty change between the two periods is given by:

$$\Delta P = P_W(X^2;z) - P_W(X^1;z)$$

$$= \left[\frac{|\Pi(X^2;z)|}{n_2}\left(\frac{1}{|\Pi(X^2;z)|}\sum_{j=1}^{m}\sum_{i \in \Pi(X^2;z)}\delta_j\log\frac{\eta_j^2}{x_{ij}^2}\right) - \frac{|\Pi(X^1;z)|}{n_1}\left(\frac{1}{|\Pi(X^1;z)|}\sum_{j=1}^{m}\sum_{i \in \Pi(X^1;z)}\delta_j\log\frac{\eta_j^1}{x_{ij}^1}\right)\right]$$

$$+ \left[\frac{|\Pi(X^2;z)|}{n_2}\sum_{j=1}^{m}\delta_j\log\frac{z_j}{\eta_j^2} - \frac{|\Pi(X^1;z)|}{n_1}\sum_{j=1}^{m}\delta_j\log\frac{z_j}{\eta_j^1}\right], \tag{5.7}$$

where η_j^t denotes the mean of the quantities of attribute j owned by the poor in period t ($t = 1, 2$). The first of the two third-bracketed terms on the right-hand side of (5.7) gives the redistribution component showing the change in poverty resulting from a change in inequality of the poor, keeping the means of their attribute quantities constant. The inequality index that appears here is the multidimensional extension of Theil's mean logarithmic deviation (see also Tsui, 1999). The second term of the expression, which we interpret as the growth component, gives the change in the poverty index resulting from changes in means of attribute quantities of the poor while holding their inequality constant (see Chakravarty, 2009).

Alkire and Foster (2011) suggested an index using a 'dual cut-off method' of identification.[6] For any distribution matrix X, they defined the deprivation index of person i in dimension j as $d_{ij}^\alpha = (1 - x_{ij}/z_j)^\alpha$ if $x_{ij} < z_j$ while $d_{ij}^\alpha = 0$ if $x_{ij} \geq z_j$, where $\alpha > 0$. This function is then used to identify the poor persons in their framework as follows: define $d_{ij}^{\alpha}(k) = d_{ij}^{\alpha}$ if the functioning failure score of person i is at least k, while $d_{ij}^{\alpha}(k) = 0$ if the functioning failure score is less than k. That is, we consider the transformed normalized shortfalls $(1 - x_{ij}/z_j)^{\alpha}$ of person i in different dimensions and check whether he has positive shortfalls in at least k dimensions, in which case he is regarded as multidimensionally poor. Equivalently, we say that person i is poor in the Alkire–Foster sense if his functioning failure score is at least k. The Alkire–Foster multidimensional poverty index is then defined as:

$$P_{AFM}(k;X,z) = \frac{1}{nm} \sum_{i \in \Pi(X;z)} \sum_{j=1}^{m} d_{ij}^{\alpha}(k). \tag{5.8}$$

where for $\alpha \geq 0$. This subgroup decomposable ratio scale invariant index satisfies NOM, MON, CON and DIM. It meets TRF for $\alpha > 1$. It is insensitive to a correlation increasing switch for all $\alpha \geq 0$. Note that in (5.8) if we replace $1/m$ by $b_j > 0$, where $\sum_{j=1}^{m} b_j = 1$ and α by $\alpha_j > 0$ for all $1 \leq j \leq m$, then we get an alternative form of the index suggested by Chakravarty et al. (1998).[7]

P_{AFM} is the sum of α powers of the normalized deprivations of the poor divided by the maximum possible value that the sum can take. Duclos and Tiberti (2016) argued that a minor change in an achievement can lead to a discontinuous jump in P_{AFM} because of the underlying identification criterion. However, it satisfies the restricted continuity axiom we have assumed here.

As we have mentioned in the introduction, some of the dimensions of well-being may be represented by ordinal variables. Therefore, each variable representing such a dimension can be transformed using an increasing function which may or may not be the same across dimensions. Thus, for each j, x_{ij} will be transformed into $f_j(x_{ij})$, where f_j be an arbitrary increasing function. Also for each j, the threshold limit becomes $f_j(z_j)$. Now, given that the dimensions are ordinally measurable, information invariance will demand that irrespective of the method of aggregation the multidimensional poverty based on x_{ij} and z_j values should be same as that calculated using $f_j(x_{ij})$ and $f_j(z_j)$ values, where $1 \leq i \leq n$ and $1 \leq j \leq m$. Since $(1 - f_j(x_{ij})/f_j(z_j))$ may not be equal to $(1 - x_{ij}/z_j)$, $1 \leq i \leq n$ and $1 \leq j \leq m$, the indices based on deprivations $(1 - x_{ij}/z_j)$ do not fulfill the necessary information invariance assumption. However, the headcount ratio verifies the required information invariance restriction. Consequently, if some of the dimensions are measurable on ordinal scale and the remaining dimensions satisfy ratio scale measurability, then the headcount ratio is an appropriate index of multidimensional poverty. Another index that survives this information invariance requirement is the Alkire–Foster (2011a) dimension adjusted headcount ratio defined as the total number of functioning failure scores of the poor in the Alkire–Foster sense divided by nm, the maximum functioning failure score that could be experienced by all people. This index drops out as the limiting case of P_{AFM} as $\alpha \to 0$. It satisfies the Alkire–Foster DIM axiom. However, the headcount ratio fails to verify this axiom.[8]

In all the indices considered above the additive aggregation has been used both across dimensions and across individuals. Tsui (2002) axiomatically characterized the following family of subgroup decomposable scale invariant indices which involves a multiplicative aggregation across dimensions:

$$P_{TR}(X;z) = \frac{1}{n} \sum_{i \in \Pi(X;z)} \left[\prod_{j=1}^{m} \left(\frac{z_j}{\hat{x}_{ij}} \right)^{r_j} - 1 \right], \tag{5.9}$$

where $x_{ij} > 0$ for all i,j and the parameters $r_j > 0$ have to be chosen such that different axioms are satisfied. This family is a generalization of the single-dimensional Chakravarty (1983) index to the multivariate set up. In the general case the restrictions on the parameters r_j for TRF to be satisfied are quite complicated. For $m = 2$, the restrictions $r_1(r_1 + 1) > 0$ and $r_1 r_2(r_1 r_2 + 1) > 0$ are required for satisfaction of TRF. These two inequalities are ensured by positivity of r_1 and r_2. Positivity of $r_1 r_2$ guarantees that P_{TR} increases under a correlation increasing switch.

The ratio scale invariance axiom reflects a particular notion of value judgment. An alternative notion of value judgment is translation invariance which requires that adding a constant to the dimension level of each person in any dimension and the corresponding threshold does not change poverty. Thus, while ratio scale invariance treats poverty in terms of normalized deprivations, translation invariance views poverty with respect to absolute deprivations $(z_j - x_{ij})$. A multidimensional poverty index $P:M \times Z \rightarrow \Re$ is called absolute or translation invariant if for any $(X;z) \in M \times Z$, $P(X;z) = P(X + \Gamma; z + q)$, where $(X + \Gamma; z + q) \in M \times Z$ and the matrix Γ having the same dimension as that of X possesses identical rows $q = (q_1,q_2, \cdots ,q_m)$. Tsui (2002) derived the following unique class of multidimensional absolute poverty indices:

$$P_{TA}(X;z) = \begin{cases} \frac{1}{n} \sum_{i \in \Pi(X;z)} \left[\prod_{j=1}^{m} \exp c_j(z_j - \hat{x}_{ij}) - 1 \right] \\ \frac{1}{n} \sum_{i \in \Pi(X;z)} \sum_{j=1}^{m} h_j(z_j - \hat{x}_{ij}) \end{cases} \tag{5.10}$$

where $c_j, h_j > 0$ for all j. Furthermore, the parameters c_j are restricted in such a way so that $\prod_{j=1}^{m} \exp c_j(z_j - \hat{x}_{ij})$ is strictly convex. The first expression in (5.10) is a generalization of the Zheng (2000) single-dimensional index. On the other hand, the second expression is the multidimensional extension of the absolute poverty gap.

Often it may be necessary to make a comparison between two distribution matrices on the basis of their poverty levels. The ranking should naturally remain the same even if the dimension quantities and threshold levels in the two matrices are expressed in differing measuring units. An axiom that guarantees this requirement is known as unit consistency (Zheng, 2007a, 2007b). To understand the issue more explicitly, let us consider the problem of ranking two countries with respect to their multidimensional poverty levels, where the dimensions involved are life expectancy and income. Assume that income is measured in the currency of country I, say dollars, and life expectancy is measured in years. It is observed that country II has higher poverty than country I. Now, if we decide to measure income in the currency of country II, say euros, and life expectancy in months, unit consistency will demand that the poverty ranking of the two countries should not change as a consequence these changes in the units of measurement of the dimensions. Formally, the unit consistency axiom can be stated as:

Unit Consistency (UCO): For any $X^1, X^2 \in M$ and two given threshold vectors $z^1, z^2 \in Z$, if $P(X^1; z^1) < P(X^2; z^2)$, then $P(X^1 \Omega; z^1 \Omega) < P(X^2 \Omega; z^2 \Omega)$ for all $\Omega = \text{diag}(\omega_1, \omega_2, \ldots \omega_m), \omega_i > 0$ for all i.

It should be clear that all ratio scale invariant multidimensional poverty indices are unit consistent, but there may exist unit consistent indices which may not satisfy ratio scale invariance.

Diez et al. (2008) and Chakravarty and D'Ambrosio (2013) independently characterized the following family of subgroup decomposable, continuous, unit consistent multidimensional poverty indices:

$$P_U(X;z) = \frac{\rho}{n \prod\limits_{j=1}^{m} z_j^{\lambda_j - \varepsilon}} \sum_{i \in \Pi(X;z)} \left[\prod_{j=1}^{m} z_j^{\lambda_j} - \prod_{j=1}^{m} \hat{x}_{ij}^{\lambda_j} \right], \qquad (5.11)$$

where ε is a real number and the parameters ρ and λ_j have to be chosen such that $\rho \lambda_j > 0$ for all $1 \leq j \leq m$. Furthermore, IPC(DPC), holds if and only if $\rho \lambda_i \lambda_j > 0 (\rho \lambda_i \lambda_j < 0)$, where $i \neq j = 1, 2, \ldots, m$.

Given λ_j, P_U becomes a relative index if and only if $\varepsilon = 0$. However, for any real ε unit consistency is satisfied. Therefore, (5.11) gives us a large class of unit consistent multidimensional poverty indices. However, this family does not satisfy translation invariance for any suitable choice of ε and $\lambda_j, 1 \leq j \leq m$.

In the two-attribute case, for TRF to hold it is necessary and sufficient that $\rho \lambda_1 (\lambda_1 - 1) < 0$ and $\lambda_1 \lambda_2 (1 - \lambda_1 - \lambda_2) < 0$. If the two attributes are complements, for simplicity of analysis we may assume that $\rho = 1$. Then for any $\lambda_1, \lambda_2 \in (.5, 1)$ all the conditions stated above are satisfied. Given other things, as the value of λ_j increases in the interval $(.5, 1)$ the reduction in the poverty index will be larger the higher is the value of λ_j. On the other hand, if the two attributes are substitutes, we can choose $\rho = -1$. Then for any $\lambda_1, \lambda_2 \in (-1, -.5)$, all the conditions are verified. To see this explicitly, note that if $\rho = -1$, IPC will be satisfied whenever $\lambda_1 \lambda_2 > 0$. The two TRF conditions then become $\lambda_1 (\lambda_1 - 1) > 0$ (since $\rho = -1$) and $\lambda_1 \lambda_2 (1 - \lambda_1 - \lambda_2) < 0$. These three inequalities are fulfilled simultaneously for any $\lambda_1, \lambda_2 \in (-1, -.5)$.

For $m = 1$, P_U in (11) coincides with the first member of the Dalton class of unit consistent income poverty indices characterized by Zheng (2007b). Therefore, P_U can be regarded as a generalization of the Zheng single-dimensional unit consistent poverty index to the multidimensional framework. It may be noted that the Zheng index itself is a two-parameter generalization of the Chakravarty (1983) and the Clark et al. (1981) indices.

In a different approach, Decancq et al. (2015) proposed to use preferences of the individuals to aggregate dimensions. Let R_i stand for the ith individual's preference relation defined on the bundles of m-dimensional private consumption goods. Thus, for any two bundles u_i and u_i', $u_i R_i u_i'$ means that individual i is at least as well off at u_i as at u_i'. We write u to denote an allocation, a list of bundles across individuals. $R_{(n)}$ is the vector of preferences of the persons. In this model an economic situation is described by $(u, R_{(n)})$. The indifference component corresponding to R_i is denoted by I_i. Their axiomatic characterization reveals that only one preference relation, namely the Leontief preference can be chosen and the resulting index turns out to be:

$$P(u;R_{(n)}) = G\left[\frac{1}{n}\sum_{i=1}^{n}\phi(1 - \min\{1,\mu(u_i,R_i)\})\right], \tag{5.12}$$

where $G \to [0,1] \to \mathcal{R}$ is continuous and increasing, $\phi \to [0,1] \to \mathcal{R}$ continuous, decreasing and convex and $\mu(u_i,R_i) = \mu$ if and only if $u_i R_i z$. The poverty line vector z is identified such that a person is poor if and only if he consumes a bundle to which he prefers z. The individual poverty function μ can be any decreasing convex function computed from the fraction of z to which a person is indifferent. The formulation allows high degree of flexibility regarding the choice of z in the sense that it becomes dependent on the degree of freedom of the policy analyst.

5.4 MATERIAL DEPRIVATION

Material deprivation is a state of economic strain which arises out of enforced inability of a person to reach minimal levels of consumption in dimensions related to material living conditions. It is not a consequence of the choice 'not to do'. Qualitative dimensions such as social cohesion are not within the purview of the measurement of material deprivation. In line with Europe 2020, examples of deprivations of dimensions that may be used in the measurement of material deprivation are: inability to pay unexpected expenses; lacking the capacity to afford a meal with meat, chicken, fish (or vegetarian protein equivalent) every second day; and inability to afford a durable good such as a washing machine, color television, telephone or car.

Bossert et al. (2013b) characterized a multidimensional index, a weighted sum of functioning failures, and used it to evaluate material deprivation in the European Union. Variables relevant for measuring deprivation were assumed to be discrete in nature. More precisely, a functioning failure has been assigned a value of 1, whereas the absence of a functioning failure has been identified with a value of 0. This rules out the possibility of using continuous variables, so that an axiom like SCI becomes inappropriate. They have employed the union method of identification. Thus, a person becomes materially deprived if his functioning failure score is at least 1.

The characterization involves three axioms, namely, zero normalization, additive decomposability in attributes and subgroup decomposability. According to zero normalization, if in a one-person society the person is not deprived in any dimension, then the index value is 0. However, the index value is positive if the functioning failure score is at least 1. Additive decomposability requires that for all $n \in N$, $X,Y \in M^n$, $D(X + Y) = D(X) + D(Y)$, where D is the material deprivation index. To understand this axiom, suppose that a person's income can be broken down into two components, salary income and non-salary income, which are reported in matrices X and Y, respectively. If this kind of breakdown is not possible for a dimension, then the corresponding entry in one of the matrices can be the actual level of achievement, and in the other matrix the entry can be 0. Additive decomposability then says that the sum of deprivations based on the individual matrices is the same as that based on the added matrix. This axiom has been used extensively in the literature on social index numbers (see Chakravarty, 2003). Additivity is definitely a strong condition. However, sometimes an additive index can avoid problems that arise with a non-additive index. For instance, consider the new Human Development Index: the geometric mean of the normalized country-level dimensional achievements over corresponding minimum values. In this index if achievement in one of the dimensions approaches its minimum value, then the index value approaches 0 irrespective of the achievement levels in other dimensions, and this leads to many undesirable conclusions (see Chakravarty, 2011a, 2011b). 'The less appealing properties of the new index could have been avoided to a large extent, while allowing imperfect substitutability, by using the alternative index proposed here, exploiting the aggregation function proposed by Chakravarty (2003) – in fact a straightforward generalization of the functional form used by the old HDI' (Ravallion, 2012, p. 208).

The Bossert et al. (2013b) material deprivation index is defined as:

$$B(X) = \frac{1}{n} \sum_{i \in S(X)} \sum_{j=1}^{m} \psi_j,$$ (5.13)

where $n \in N$, $X \in M^n$ are arbitrary, $S(X)$ is the set of all persons who are materially deprived in X and $\psi_j > 0$ is the weight assigned to the jth dimension.[9] The interpretation of ψ_j is same as that we have provided for a_j in (5.4). Recall that in the Alkire and Foster (2011a) intermediate identification method, the counting formula using unequal weights for dimensions is used without any characterization. Lasso de la Vega (2010) used the counting approach based on this identification method to examine dominance conditions for poverty orderings. Aaberge and Peluso (2011) employed rank dependent social evaluation criteria to compare deprivation counts of distributions. Jayaraj and Subramanian (2010) applied the index B to measure deprivation in India.

5.5 CONCLUSIONS

We have argued that poverty should be measured in terms of shortfalls of dimensions of well-being from respective minimally acceptable levels for different individuals in a society. We then presented certain properties for an index of poverty in such a structure, followed by a discussion on some poverty indices. An analysis of material deprivation has also been presented.

However, it may not always be possible to get detailed information on achievement levels of different dimensions, and hence the deprivation status of a person in a dimension may not be clear. There can be a wide range of threshold limits for different dimensions which co-exist in reasonable harmony. This indicates that the deprivation status of a person in a dimension may be fuzzy. Alternative approaches to the multidimensional poverty measurement based on fuzzy set theory have been suggested, among others, by Cerioli and Zani (1990) Chiappero-Martinetti (1994, 2000), Cheli and Lemmi (1995), Chakravarty (2006) and Lemmi and Betti (2006).

Given that there are now many poverty indices it may be worthwhile to check whether for given threshold limits one distribution matrix becomes more (or less) poverty-stricken than another by a certain class of poverty indices. The determination of threshold limits for different dimensions has been an issue of debate for a long time. Quite often a significant degree of arbitrariness is involved in the construction of the threshold values (see Sen,

1981; Ravallion, 1994; Foster and Sen, 1997; Foster, 2000; Bourguignon and Chakravarty, 2003). In view of this, it may be interesting to look at multidimensional poverty orderings by a given index for a range of threshold limits. Attempts along this line have been made by Duclos et al. (2006a, 2006b) and Bourguignon and Chakravarty (2009).

NOTES

1. See Alkire and Foster (2011b), Alkire et al. (2011), Birdsall (2011), Chakravarty (2011a), Ferreira (2011), Klugman et al. (2011a, 2011b), Lustig (2011a, 2011b), Ravallion (2011a, 2011b), Roodman (2011), Silber (2011), Thorbecke (2011), Aaberge and Brandolini (2015), Alkire et al. (2015), Chakravarty and Lugo (2016) and Duclos and Tiberti (2016).
2. Extensive discussions on income poverty indices and their properties can be found in Blackorby and Donaldson (1980), Kakwani (1980), Foster (1984, 2000), Donaldson and Weymark (1986), Cowell (1988, 2016), Chakravarty (1990, 2009), Foster and Sen (1997), Zheng (1997) and Lambert (2001).
3. Discussion on techniques for setting weights can be found in Sen (1992), Atkinson et al. (2002), Brandolini and D'Alessio (2009), Decanq and Lugo (2013), Foster et al. (2013) and Aaberge and Brandolini (2015).
4. An $n \times n$ matrix with non-negative entries is called a bistochastic matrix if each of its rows and columns sums to 1. A bistochastic matrix is called a permutation matrix if it has exactly one positive entry in each row and column.
5. WFC was introduced and analysed in details by Bourguignon and Chakravarty (2003).
6. Alkire and Foster (2011b) and Alkire et al. (2015) provide further discussion on this identification method.
7. Discussion on union based versions of some members of the Alkire–Foster family can also be found in Bourguignon and Chakravarty (2003), Deutsch and Silber (2005) and Chakravarty and Silber (2008).
8. Dimensional monotonicity is one of the basic postulates of the Nicholas–Ray (2011) counting-based intertemporal multidimensional deprivation measure. A related measure of social exclusion suggested by Chakravarty and D'Ambrosio (2006) also satisfies this postulate.
9. Bossert et al. (2013a) extended this index to an inter-temporal framework.

REFERENCES

Aaberge, R. and A. Brandolini (2015), 'Multidimensional poverty and inequality', in A.B. Atkinson and F. Bourguignon (eds), *Handbook of Income Distribution*, Vol. 2A, Amsterdam: North-Holland.
Aaberge, R. and E. Peluso (2011), 'A counting approach for measuring multidimensional deprivation', Universita di Verona, Dipartimento di Economia, WP No.7.
Alkire, S. and J.E. Foster (2011a), 'Counting and multidimensional poverty measurement', *Journal of Public Economics*, 95, 476–487.
Alkire, S. and J.E. Foster (2011b), 'Understandings and misunderstandings of multidimensional poverty measurement', *Journal of Economic Inequality*, 9, 289–314.
Alkire, S., J.E. Foster and M. Santos (2011), 'Where did identification go?', *Journal of Economic Inequality*, 9, 501–505.
Alkire, S., J.E. Foster, S. Seth, M.E. Santos, J.M. Roche and P. Ballon (2015), *Multidimensional Poverty Measurement and Analysis*, Oxford: Oxford University Press.
Anand, S. (1983), *Inequality and Poverty in Malaysia: Measurement and Decomposition*, New York: Oxford University Press.
Atkinson, A.B. (2003), 'Multidimensional deprivation: contrasting social welfare and counting approaches', *Journal of Economic Inequality*, 1, 51–65.
Atkinson, A.B. and F. Bourguignon (1982), 'The comparison of multidimensional distributions of economic status', *Review of Economic Studies*, 49, 183–201.
Atkinson, A.B., B. Cantillion, E. Marlier and B. Nolan (2002), *Social Indicators: The EU and Social Inclusion*, Oxford: Oxford University Press.
Birdsall, N. (2011), 'Comment on multidimensional indices', *Journal of Economic Inequality*, 9, 489–491.
Blackorby, C. and D. Donaldson (1980), 'Ethical indices for the measurement of poverty', *Econometrica*, 58, 1053–1060.

Bosmans, K., K. Decancq and E. Ooghe (2015), 'What do normative indices of multidimensional inequality really measure?. *Journal of Public Economics*, 130, 94–104.

Bossert, W., L. Ceriani, S.R. Chakravarty and C. D'Ambrosio (2013a), 'Intertemporal material deprivation', in G. Betti and A. Lemmi (eds), *Poverty and Social Exclusion: New Methods of Analysis*, London: Routledge.

Bossert, W., S.R. Chakravarty and C. D'Ambrosio (2013b), 'Multidimensional poverty and material deprivation', *Review of Income and Wealth*, 59, 29–43.

Bourguignon, F. and S.R. Chakravarty (1999), 'A family of multidimensional poverty measures', in D.J. Slottje (ed.), *Advances in Econometrics, Income Distribution and Scientific Methodology: Essays in Honor of C. Dagum*, Heidelberg: Physica-Verlag.

Bourguignon, F. and S.R. Chakravarty (2003), 'The measurement of multidimensional poverty', *Journal of Economic Inequality*, 1, 25–49.

Bourguignon F. and S.R. Chakravarty (2009), 'Multidimensional poverty orderings: theory and applications', in K. Basu and R. Kanbur (eds), *Arguments for a Better World: Essays in Honor of Amartya Sen. Volume 1: Ethics, Welfare and Measurement*, Oxford: Oxford University Press.

Brandolini, A. and G. D'Alessio (2009), 'Measuring well-being in the functioning space', in E. Chiappero Martinetti (ed.), *Debating Global Society: Reach and Limits of the Capability Approach*, Milan: Feltrinelli Editore.

Cerioli, A. and S. Zani (1990), 'A fuzzy approach to the measurement of poverty', in C. Dagum and M. Zenga (eds), *Income and Wealth Distribution, Inequality and Poverty*, New York: Springer-Verlag.

Chakravarty, S.R. (1983), 'A new index of poverty', *Mathematical Social Sciences*, 6, 307–313.

Chakravarty, S.R. (1990), *Ethical Social Index Numbers*, New York: Springer.

Chakravarty, S.R. (2003), 'A generalized human development index', *Review of Development Economics*, 7, 99–114.

Chakravarty, S.R. (2006), 'An axiomatic approach to multidimensional poverty measurement via fuzzy sets', in A. Lemmi and G. Betti (eds), *Fuzzy Set Approach to Multidimensional Poverty Measurement*, New York: Springer.

Chakravarty, S.R. (2009), *Inequality, Polarization and Poverty: Advances in Distributional Analysis*, New York: Springer.

Chakravarty, S.R. (2011a), 'A reconsideration of the tradeoffs in the new human development index', *Journal of Economic Inequality*, 9, 471–474.

Chakravarty, S.R. (2011b), 'On tradeoffs in the human development indices', *Indian Journal of Human Development*, 5, 517–525.

Chakravarty, S.R. (2018), *Analyzing Multidimensional Well-Being: A Quantitative Approach*, New Jersey: Wiley.

Chakravarty, S.R. and C. D'Ambrosio (2006), 'The measurement of social exclusion', *Review of Income and Wealth*, 52, 377–398.

Chakravarty, S.R. and C. D'Ambrosio (2013), 'A family of unit consistent multidimensional poverty indices', in V. Berenger and F. Bresson (eds), *Monetary Poverty and Social Exclusion around the Mediterranean Sea*, New York: Springer.

Chakravarty, S.R., J. Deutsch and J. Silber (2008), 'On the Watts multidimensional poverty index and its decomposition', *World Development*, 36, 1067–1077.

Chakravarty, S.R. and M.A. Lugo (2016), 'Multidimensional indicators of inequality and poverty', in M. Adler and M. Fleurbaey (eds), *Handbook of Well-Being and Public Policy*, Oxford: Oxford University Press.

Chakravarty, S.R., D. Mukherjee and R. Ranade (1998), 'On the family of subgroup and factor decomposable measures of multidimensional poverty', *Research on Economic Inequality*, 8, 175–194.

Chakravarty, S.R. and J. Silber (2008), 'Measuring multidimensional poverty: the axiomatic approach', in N. Kakwani and J. Silber (eds), *Quantitative Approaches to Multidimensional Poverty Measurement*, New York: Palgrave Macmillan.

Cheli, B. and Lemmi A (1995), 'A "totally" fuzzy and relative approach to the multidimensional analysis of poverty', *Economic Notes*, 24, 115–134.

Chiappero-Martinetti, E. (1994), 'A new approach to evaluation of well-being and poverty by fuzzy set theory', *Giornale Degli Economisti e Annali di Economia*.

Chiappero-Martinetti, E. (2000), 'A multidimensional assessment of well-being based on Sen's functioning approach', *Rivista Internazionale di Scienze Sociali*, 108, 207–239.

Clark, S., R. Hemming and D. Ulph (1981), 'On indices for the measurement of poverty', *Economic Journal*, 91, 515–526.

Cowell, F.A. (1988), 'Poverty measures, inequality and decomposability', in D. Bos, M. Rose and C. Seidl (eds), *Welfare and Efficiency in Public Economics*, New York: Springer.

Cowell, F.A. (2016), 'Inequality and poverty measures', in M. Adler and M. Fleurbaey (eds), *Handbook of Well-Being and Public Policy*, Oxford: Oxford University Press.

Datt, G. and M. Ravallion (1992), 'Growth and redistribution components of change in poverty measures: a decomposition with applications to Brazil and India in the 1980s', *Journal of Development Economics*, 38, 275–295.

Decancq, K. (2014), 'Copula-based measurement of dependence between dimensions of well-being', *Oxford Economic Papers*, 66, 681–701

Decancq, K., M. Fleurbaey and F. Maniquet (2015), 'Multidimensional poverty measurement: shouldn't we take preferences into account?', mimeo, Brussels: CORE.

Decancq, K. and M.A. Lugo (2013), 'Weights in multidimensional indices of well-being: an overview', *Econometric Reviews*, 32, 7–34.

Deutsch, J. and J. Silber (2005), 'Measuring multidimensional poverty: an empirical comparison of various approaches', *Review of Income and Wealth*, 51, 145–174.

Diez, H. M.C. Lasso de la Vega and A.M. Urrutia (2008), 'Multidimensional unit and subgroup consistent inequality and poverty measures: some characterization results', *Research on Economic Inequality*, 16, 189–211.

Donaldson, D. and J.A. Weymark (1986), 'Properties of fixed-population poverty indices', *International Economic Review*, 27, 667–688.

Duclos, J.-Y., D.E. Sahn and S.D. Younger (2006a), 'Robust multidimensional poverty comparisons', *Economic Journal*, 116, 943–968.

Duclos, J.-Y., D.E. Sahn and S.D. Younger (2006b), 'Robust multidimensional poverty comparisons with discrete indicators of well-being', in S.P. Jenkins and J. Micklewright (eds), *Poverty Inequality Re-examined*, Oxford: Oxford University Press.

Duclos, J-Y. and L. Tiberti (2016), 'Multidimensional poverty indices: a critical assessment', in M. Adler and M. Fleurbaey (eds), *Handbook of Well-Being and Public Policy*, Oxford: Oxford University Press.

Ferreira, F. (2011), 'Poverty is multidimensional. But what are we going to do about it?', *Journal of Economic Inequality*, 9, 493–495.

Fleurbaey, F. and F. Maniquet (2011), *A Theory of Fairness and Social Welfare*. New York: Cambridge University Press.

Fleurbaey M. and A. Trannoy (2003), 'The impossibility of a Paretian egalitarian', *Social Choice Welfare*, 21, 319–329.

Foster, J.E. (1984), 'On economic poverty measures: a survey of aggregate measures', in R.L. Basmann and G.F. Rhodes (eds), *Advances in Econometrics, Vol. 3*, Greenwich, CT: JAI Press.

Foster, J.E. (2000), 'Poverty indices', in A. de Janvry and R. Kanbur (eds), *Poverty, Inequality and Development: Essays in Honor of Erik Thorbecke*, New York: Springer.

Foster, J.E., J. Greer and E. Thorbecke (1984), 'A class of decomposable poverty measures', *Econometrica*, 42, 761–766.

Foster, J.E., M. McGillivray, M. and S. Seth (2013), 'Composite indices: rank robustness, statistical association and redundancy', *Econometric Reviews*, 22, 35–56.

Foster, J.E. and A.K. Sen (1997), *On Economic Inequality, with a Substantial Annexe by J.E. Foster and A.K. Sen*, Oxford: Oxford University Press.

Foster, J.E. and A.F. Shorrocks (1991), 'Subgroup consistent poverty indices', *Econometrica*, 59, 687–709.

Gordon, D., S. Nandy, C. Pantazis, S. Pemberton and P. Townsend (2003), 'The distribution of child poverty in the developing world', Bristol: Centre for International Poverty Research.

Guio, A.-C. (2005), 'Material deprivation in the EU', *Statistics in Focus*, Population and Social Conditions, Living Conditions and Welfare, 21/2005, Luxembourg: Eurostat.

Guio, A.-C., A. Fusco and E. Marlier (2009), 'An EU approach to material deprivation using EU-SILC and Eurobarometer data', IRISS Working Paper 2009-19.

Jayaraj, D. and S. Subramanian (2010), 'A Chakravarty–D'Ambrosio view of multidimensional deprivation: some estimates for India', *Economic and Political Weekly*, 45, 53–65.

Kakwani, N.C. (1980), 'On a class of poverty measures', *Econometrica*, 48, 437–446.

Kakwani, N.C. (1993), 'Poverty and economic growth with application to Côte D'Ivoire', *Review of Income and Wealth*, 39, 121–139.

Klugman, J., F. Rodriguez and H.-J. Choi (2011a), 'The HDI 2010: new controversies, old critiques', *Journal of Economic Inequality*, 9, 249–288.

Klugman, J., F. Rodriguez and H.-J. Choi (2011b), 'Response to Martin Ravallion', *Journal of Economic Inequality*, 9, 497–499.

Kolm, S.C. (1977), 'Multidimensional egalitarianism', *Quarterly Journal of Economics*, 91, 1–13.

Lambert, P.J. (2001), *The Distribution and Redistribution of Income*, Manchester: Manchester University Press.

Lasso de la Vega, M.C. (2010), 'Counting poverty orderings and deprivation curves', *Research on Economic Inequality*, 18, 153–172.

Lasso de la Vega, M.C. and A.M. Urrutia (2011), 'Characterizing how to aggregate the individuals' deprivations in a multidimensional framework', *Journal of Economic Inequality*, 9, 183–194.

Lasso de la Vega, M.C., A.M. Urrutia and A. Sarachu (2009), 'The Bourguignon and Chakravarty multidimensional poverty family: a characterization', ECINEQ WP 2009-109.

Lasso de la Vega, M.C., AM. Urrutia and A. Sarachu (2010), 'Characterizations of multidimensional inequality measures which fulfill the Pigou–Dalton bundle principle', *Social Choice and Welfare*, 35, 319–329.

Lemmi, A. and G. Betti (eds) (2006), *Fuzzy Set Approach to Multidimensional Poverty Measurement*, New York: Springer.

Lipton, M. and M. Ravallion (1995), 'Poverty and policy', in J. Behrman and T.N. Srinivasan (eds), *Handbook of Development Economics*, Vol. 1, Amsterdam: North-Holland.

Lustig, N. (2011a), 'Multidimensional indices of achievements and poverty: what do we gain and what do we lose? An introduction in JOEI Forum on multidimensional poverty', *Journal of Economic Inequality*, 9, 227–234.

Lustig, N. (2011b), 'Multidimensional indices of achievements and poverty: comments', *Journal of Economic Inequality*, 9, 469–469.

Maasoumi, E. and M.A. Lugo (2008), 'The information basis of multivariate poverty assessments', in N. Kakwani and J. Silber (eds), *Quantitative Approaches to Multidimensional Poverty Measurement*, New York: Palgrave Macmillan.

Nicholas, A. and R. Ray (2011), 'Duration and persistence in multidimensional deprivation: methodology and Australian application', *Economic Record*, 88, 106–126.

Ravallion, M. (1994), 'Measuring social welfare with and without poverty lines', *American Economic Review*, 84, 359–364.

Ravallion, M. (1996), 'Issues in measuring and modeling poverty', *Economic Journal*, 106, 1328–1343.

Ravallion, M. (2011a), 'On multidimensional indices of poverty', *Journal of Economic Inequality*, 9, 235–248.

Ravallion, M. (2011b), 'The Human Development Index: a response to Klugman, Rodriguez and Choi', *Journal of Economic Inequality*, 9, 475–478.

Ravallion, M. (2012), 'Troubling tradeoffs in the Human Development Index', *Journal of Development Economics*, 99, 201–209.

Ravallion, M. and M. Huppi (1991), 'Measuring changes in poverty: a methodological case study of Indonesia during an adjustment period', *World Bank Economic Review*, 5, 57–82.

Roodman, D. (2011), 'Composite indices', *Journal of Economic Inequality*, 9, 483–484.

Savaglio, E. (2006), 'Three approaches to the analysis of multidimensional inequality', in F. Farina and E. Savaglio (eds), *Inequality and Economic Integration*, London: Routledge.

Sen, A.K. (1976), 'Poverty: an ordinal approach to measurement', *Econometrica*, 44, 219–231.

Sen, A.K. (1981), *Poverty and Famines*, Oxford: Clarendon Press.

Sen, A.K. (1985), *Commodities and Capabilities*, Amsterdam: North-Holland.

Sen, A.K. (1987), *Standard of Living*, Cambridge: Cambridge University Press.

Sen, A.K. (1992), *Inequality Re-examined*, Cambridge, MA: Harvard University Press.

Silber, J. (2011), 'A comment on the MPI index', *Journal of Economic Inequality*, 9, 479–481.

Stiglitz, J.E., A. Sen and J.-P. Fitoussi (2009), *Report by the Commission on the Measurement of Economic Performance and Social Progress*, CMEPSP.

Streeten, P. (1981), *First Things First: Meeting Basic Human Needs in Developing Countries*, Oxford: Oxford University Press.

Thorbecke, E. (2008), 'Multidimensional poverty: conceptual and measurement issues', in N. Kakwani and J. Silber (eds), *The Many Dimensions of Poverty*, New York: Palgrave Macmillan.

Thorbecke, E. (2011), 'A comment on multidimensional poverty indices', *Journal of Economic Inequality*, 9, 485–487.

Townsend, P. (1979), *Poverty in the United Kingdom*, Harmondsworth: Penguin.

Tsui, K.-Y. (1999), 'Multidimensional inequality and multidimensional generalized entropy measures: an axiomatic derivation', *Social Choice and Welfare*, 16, 145–157.

Tsui, K.-Y. (2002), 'Multidimensional poverty indices', *Social Choice and Welfare*, 19, 69–93.

Watts, H. (1968), 'An economic definition of poverty', in D.P. Moynihan (ed.), *On Understanding Poverty*, New York: Basic Books.

Weymark, J.A. (2006), 'The normative approach to the measurement of multidimensional inequality', in F. Farina and E. Savaglio (eds), *Inequality and Economic Integration*, London: Routledge.

Whelan, C.T. and B. Maître (2009), 'Europeanization of inequality and European reference groups', *Journal of European Social Policy*, 19, 117–130.

Zheng, B. (1997), 'Aggregate poverty measures', *Journal of Economic Surveys*, 11, 123–162.

Zheng, B. (2000), 'Minimum distribution-sensitivity, poverty aversion and poverty orderings', *Journal of Economic Theory*, 95, 116–137.

Zheng, B. (2007a), 'Unit-consistent decomposable inequality measures', *Economica*, 74, 97–111.

Zheng, B. (2007b), 'Unit-consistent poverty indices', *Economic Theory*, 31, 113–142.

6. Multidimensional poverty and material deprivation: empirical findings
Anne-Catherine Guio

6.1 INTRODUCTION

It is now widely acknowledged that poverty is more than a lack of sufficient income and that it needs to be measured as a multidimensional concept (see, e.g., Alkire and Foster, 2011a; Atkinson, 2003, 2011; Bossert et al., 2013; Bourguignon and Chakravarty, 2003; Chakravarty et al., 2008; Duclos et al., 2006; Ferreira, 2011; Maasoumi and Lugo, 2008; Ravallion, 2011; Tsui, 2002; Stiglitz et al., 2009; Alkire et al., 2015). As explained by Kakwani and Silber (2008, p. 15): 'The most important development of poverty research in recent years is certainly the shift of emphasis from a uni- to a multidimensional approach to poverty'. However, despite this wide recognition of the intrinsic multidimensional nature of poverty, there are many divergences in the academic literature on how to measure this multidimensional aspect (see, for example, Chakravarty and Chattopadhyay, Chapter 5 in this *Handbook*, and the June 2011 issue of the *Journal of Economic Inequality* devoted to this topic). As explained in this chapter, the disagreements are notably about the choice of indicators and dimensions (see section 6.3), the way to aggregate these indicators and dimensions (see the discussion in section 6.2), and the aggregation options (section 6.4).

Discussion on multidimensional poverty is not confined to academic literature but has largely penetrated the institutional and policy levels. There are many examples of multidimensional approaches of poverty measurement, compiled and disseminated by international institutions to allow systematic cross-country comparisons. A selection of a few emblematic examples is provided below, in order to illustrate the methodological choices behind different approaches.

6.2 EXAMPLES OF MULTIDIMENSIONAL APPROACHES TO POVERTY USED BY INTERNATIONAL INSTITUTIONS

6.2.1 Example of a Composite Multidimensional Indicator: The Human Development Index

I start this review with the United Nations Development Programme's Human Development Index (HDI), one of the most emblematic multidimensional indexes (for detailed description and analysis, see Seth and Villar, Chapter 3 in this *Handbook*). The HDI combines three dimensions: long and healthy life, access to knowledge and decent standard of living (see Table 6.1).

There are a number of criticisms which have been raised against the HDI, mainly

Table 6.1   Human Development Index (HDI) and components, by region and HDI groups, 2014

Region and HDI group	HDI	Life expectancy at birth (years)	Expected years of schooling (years)	Mean years of schooling (years)	Gross national income per capita (PPP $)
Region					
Arab States	0.666	70.6	12.0	6.4	15 722
East Asia and the Pacific	0.710	74.0	12.7	7.5	11 449
Europe and Central Asia	0.748	72.3	13.6	10.0	12 791
Latin America and the Caribbean	0.748	75.0	14.0	8.2	14 242
South Asia	0.607	68.4	11.2	5.5	5 605
Sub-Saharan Africa	0.518	58.5	9.6	5.2	3 363
HDI group					
Very high human development	0.896	80.5	16.4	11.8	41 584
High human development	0.744	75.1	13.6	8.2	13 961
Medium human development	0.630	68.6	11.8	6.2	6 353
Low human development	0.505	60.6	9.0	4.5	3 085
Developing countries	0.660	69.8	11.7	6.8	9 071

Notes: Indicators are population-weighted and calculated based on HDI values for 187 countries. PPP is purchasing power parity (PPP). Very high human development countries regroup countries whose HDI is higher than 0.800; High human development countries regroup countries whose HDI ranges from 0.700 to 0.799; Medium human development countries regroup countries whose HDI ranges from 0.550 to 0.699 and low human development countries regroup countries whose HDI is lower than 0.550.

Source: Human Development Report 2015, Table 1.

linked to the choice of dimensions and constitutive variables within each dimension, their weighting and the functional form of the composite index (see, e.g., Ravallion, 2011; Lustig, 2011). There is, however, a general recognition that the existence of such indexes 'has succeeded in de-emphasizing a growth-centric view of development' (Lustig, 2011, p. 2). Complementing money-based measures with non-income dimensions such as the HDI offers a different view of poverty, which is illustrated by the difference in national ranking, when one uses either per capita income only or the HDI.

Combining different dimensions into a single index raises questions, however, as this implies a substitution rate (trade-off) between dimensions (see, e.g., Ravallion, 2011). Furthermore, the dimensions aggregated in the HDI are measured via distinct sources and do not take into account the combination of problems at the individual level. There are two types of aggregation. The first type, as for the HDI, summarizes information across individuals at the dimension level (for example, employment, health, housing, low income) and then aggregates it across dimensions. The second approach aggregates the information across dimensions at the individual level (for example, persons or households), which are then summed up over individuals to form an aggregated indicator. This latter approach requires access to data collected at the individual (or household) level on different dimensions via a common source. To avoid possible confusion between the two forms of aggregation, the former is referred to below as 'composite' indicators and the latter as 'aggregated' indicators (see Marlier et al., 2007, for a detailed discussion of the policy implications of the two approaches). Some authors refer to 'marginal indices' to designate composite indices, as they capture only the marginal distributions of dimensions; and to 'multidimensional measure reflecting joint distribution' to indicate that aggregated indices take into account the joint distribution of deprivations at individual level (see Alkire, 2011, p. 6).

6.2.2 Example of Aggregated Multidimensional Indicator: The Multidimensional Poverty Index

The Multidimensional Poverty Index (MPI) developed by Alkire and Santos (2010) for the 2010 Human Development Report (UNDP, 2010) offers a worldwide illustration of an aggregated indicator based on individual accumulation of deprivations. The MPI has three dimensions – health, education and living standard – and ten indicators (see Figure 6.1). It measures the magnitude of overlapping deprivations at the household level. It follows a method developed by Alkire and Foster (2011a, 2011b) to generate multidimensional indexes of poverty which fulfil desirable axioms, are decomposable and can be used with a large variety of data (including discrete and continuous data). The method

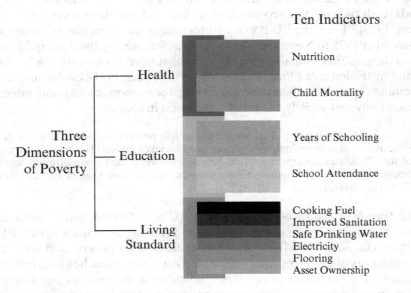

Source: Oxford Poverty and Human Development Initiative (OPHI), Ten Indicators, http://www.ophi.org.uk/multidimensional-poverty-index/.

Figure 6.1   Composition of the MPI

is a 'dual cut-off method': for each dimension, a threshold is defined to identify those deprived, and for all dimensions taken together a 'poverty cut-off' is chosen (in terms of the minimum number of deprivation dimensions to be considered as poor).

The MPI is the product of two components: the poverty incidence (that is, the percentage of people who are poor) and the poverty intensity (that is, the average share of dimensions in which poor people are deprived). The 2016 figures show that 30 per cent of the people living in the 102 countries analysed were living in multidimensional poverty. In terms of intensity, poor people were deprived on average in half the sum of the weighted constitutive ten indicators (see Figure 6.1).[1] This illustrates the importance of taking into account the way people cumulate deprivations in aggregation process. Figure 6.2 presents the worldwide incidence of the MPI.

The MPI is presented by its authors as an index which can be used as an analytical tool to identify multidimensionally poor people, show aspects in which they are deprived, and help to reveal the interconnections among deprivations (Alkire et al., 2015). Since its launch, the MPI has stirred controversy (e.g., Rippin, 2010), which has raised interesting questions which I will come back to later in this chapter.

6.2.3   Example of a Multidimensional Dashboard: The EU Portfolio of Commonly Agreed Social Indicators

Almost 40 years ago, the European Union (EU) emphasized the multidimensional nature of poverty. Indeed, back in 1975 the EU Council of Ministers defined the poor as 'individuals or families whose resources are so small as to exclude them from the minimum acceptable way of life of the Member State in which they live', with 'resources' being defined as 'goods, cash income plus services from public and private sources' (EU Council of Ministers, 1975).[2] Then, the EU Poverty 1 Programme was launched, covering the period from December 1975 to November 1981. This was followed by the Poverty 2 Programme, providing for specific Community action to combat poverty (January 1985 to December 1988), and by the Poverty 3 Programme (July 1989 to June 1994), establishing a medium-term Community action programme concerning the economic and social integration of the economically and socially less privileged groups in society.

> These Poverty Programmes 1–3 allowed considerable progress to be made in the description, quantification and understanding of poverty and social exclusion. However, it is only from the end of the 1990s, and even more so from March 2000 when the Lisbon Strategy was launched, that social protection and inclusion have become *specific policy areas* for EU cooperation. (Marlier et al., 2007, p. 18)[3]

Since the launch of the Lisbon Strategy, the EU Social Protection Committee and its Indicators Sub-Group have been developing and refining commonly agreed EU indicators in the social field. They first focused on indicators for poverty and social exclusion (that is, indicators of low income, heath, employment, education, housing, and so on) and then extended their activities to also cover indicators in the areas of pensions as well as healthcare and long-term care.[4] To do so, the Indicators Sub-Group has agreed on a broad common methodological framework for the development of the indicators portfolio. Some principles concern the portfolio as a whole, whereas others concern each individual indicator (see Social Protection Committee Indicators Sub-Group, 2015):

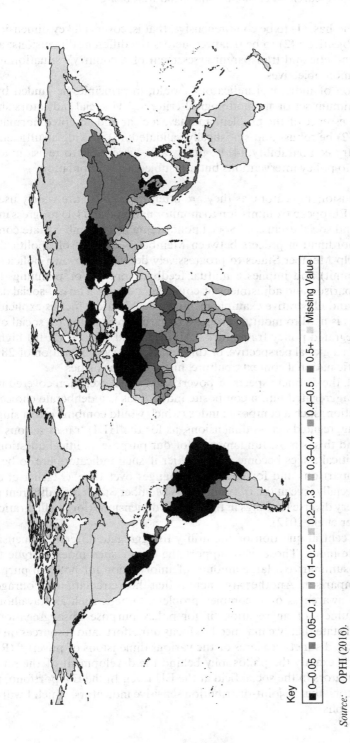

Key

■ 0–0.05　■ 0.05–0.1　■ 0.1–0.2　■ 0.2–0.3　■ 0.3–0.4　■ 0.4–0.5　■ 0.5+　■ Missing Value

Source: OPHI (2016).

Figure 6.2 MPI level in the 102 countries for which it is computed, 2016

- The portfolio has: (1) to be comprehensive, that is, covers all key dimensions of the common objectives; (2) to be balanced across the different dimensions; and (3) to enable a synthetic and transparent assessment of a country's situation in relation to the common objectives.
- The selection of individual indicators should, in principle, be guided by the following minimum set of methodological criteria. EU social indicators should: (1) capture the essence of the problem and have a clear and accepted normative interpretation; (2) be robust and statistically validated; (3) provide a sufficient level of cross-country comparability; (4) be timely and susceptible to revision; and (5) be responsive to policy interventions but not subject to manipulation.

EU 'social inclusion' indicators, as they are often referred to, are widely used by EU countries and the European Commission to monitor national and EU progress in the fight against poverty and social exclusion. Social policy remains a Member State competence, but the policy coordination process between Member States (a 'soft' political process) is 'designed to help Member States to progressively develop their own policies' (March 2000 Lisbon Summit) and implies a mutual feedback process of planning, targeting, monitoring, comparison and adjustment of countries' policies. The EU social dashboard is a very specific and illustrative example of how a dashboard which is explicitly agreed by Member States is used to monitor progress toward agreed common social objectives, as part of an integrated policy framework.[5] Atkinson and Marlier (2010) highlight the possible lessons, in a global perspective, of this multi-country cooperation of 28 Member States, with specific national contexts, culture, history and priorities.

At the EU level, the distinct aspects of poverty and social exclusion covered in the EU portfolio are not aggregated into a composite index. This is a deliberate choice. Indeed, to guide policy action, such a composite index (which would combine into a single figure the information aggregated across dimensions, as for the HDI) 'raises serious technical issues but also, and this is most fundamental for our purpose, political questions. Those technical and political issues become even trickier if such indicators are to be used for international comparisons and for measuring changes over time' (Marlier et al., 2007, p. 185) This is especially true in the EU context, as Member States have different performances and show very diverse rankings in the various dimensions (for an illustration of this variety, see Marlier et al., 2012).

This raises the central question of the utility to aggregate different dimensions into a single composite index. Those who support the use of such indexes argue that they are important to summarize a large amount of information for political purposes and cross-country comparison. Another argument is that their circulation encourages public use and increases awareness on a complex problem. Others, such as Ravallion (2011), question the usefulness of aggregation 'if for policy purposes disaggregation will be indispensable' and state that 'we may need to focus our efforts and resources on developing the best possible distinct measures of the various dimensions of poverty' (Ravallion, 2011, p. 17). This is exactly the philosophy behind the development of the set of commonly agreed indicators in the social field at the EU level. In the EU portfolio, there are aggregated indicators, that is, joint-distribution sensitive indicators, which I will focus on in the next paragraphs.

6.2.4   Example of Aggregated One-Dimensional Index: The EU Indicator of Material Deprivation

Since 2009, the EU set of social inclusion indicators described above includes material deprivation (MD) indicators with a view to complementing the income poverty measures and better reflecting huge differences in living standards across the EU (especially since the last two EU enlargements, in 2004 and 2007). The EU MD indicators are aggregated indicators which combine nine material and social items that are customary in all Member States. These nine items are: coping with unexpected expenses; one week's annual holiday away from home; avoiding arrears; a meal with meat, chicken, fish or vegetarian protein equivalent every second day; keeping the home adequately warm; a washing machine; a colour TV; a telephone; a personal car. The indicator focuses on enforced lacks – that is, lacks due to insufficient resources and thus problems of affordability – rather than lacks resulting from choices or lifestyle preferences (Mack and Lansley, 1985). I will come back to this and show that the construction of such MD indicators shares many of the questions raised by the multidimensional poverty literature, despite the fact that such MD indicators do not aim at covering all aspects of poverty and social exclusion (for example, health, employment, education, income), in contrast to many multidimensional poverty indexes. Indeed, the EU MD indicator can be considered as unidimensional; that is, its constituents aim at reflecting a common underlying latent concept of 'deprivation' (see section 6.4).

Figure 6.3 illustrates the interest of complementing the income poverty measure with material deprivation indicators at the EU level to better reflect differences in standard of living. The EU income poverty indicator is a relative measure, defined as the proportion of people living in a household whose total equivalized income is below 60 per cent of the median national equivalized household income. The range of national material deprivation rates across Member States in 2015 is wide: from less than 5 per cent in Sweden and Luxembourg, up to 40 per cent in Romania and Greece and 49 per cent in Bulgaria; the EU-28 weighted average is 17 per cent. This range is much broader than income poverty rates, which vary between 10 per cent in the Czech Republic, and 20–25 per cent in Croatia, Greece, Estonia, Bulgaria, Spain, Lithuania, Latvia and Romania (EU-28 average: 17 per cent). These results reflect the fact that 'the differences in average living standards across countries as well as the distribution within them now come into play' (Marlier et al., 2012, p. 313). This is particularly clear in Hungary and Cyprus (which have an extremely high level of deprivation but a below-EU-average income poverty rate) as well as, though to a lesser extent, the Czech Republic (lowest poverty risk in the EU, together with the Netherlands, but intermediate performance on deprivation). By contrast, Spain and Estonia have a very high poverty risk but a below-average proportion of deprivation. There are two reasons for these differences. First, the change in concept (income versus deprivation); second, the move from a country-based measure to an EU-wide criterion (see also Fusco et al., 2010).

6.2.5   The EU Social Inclusion Target

In June 2010, the Lisbon Strategy was replaced by the Europe 2020 Strategy on smart, sustainable and inclusive growth, with five headline targets to be achieved by 2020. One of

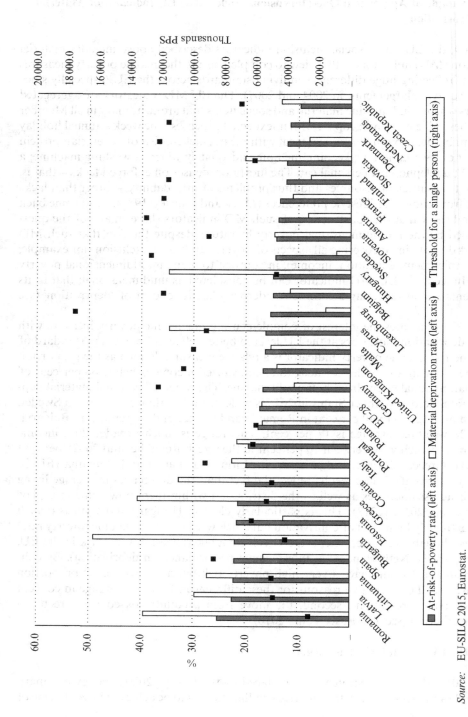

Source: EU-SILC 2015, Eurostat.

Figure 6.3   At-risk-of-poverty rate and threshold and deprivation rate, EU Member States, 2015

these targets is a social inclusion target (the first ever EU target in the social field), which consists of the following: 'promoting social inclusion, in particular through the reduction of poverty, by aiming to lift at least 20 million people out of the risk of poverty and social exclusion in the EU' (European Council, 2010).[6] To monitor progress towards this target, the EU Council of Ministers agreed on a new type of aggregated indicator. With a view to reflecting the multidimensional nature of poverty and social exclusion, this indicator of 'at risk of poverty or social exclusion' is defined as a combination of three subindicators measured at individual level:

- The standard EU 'at-risk-of-poverty' indicator (see above).
- An indicator of 'severe material deprivation' (that is, the EU MD indicator presented above, with the threshold raised from three to four out of the nine items).
- An indicator of (quasi-)joblessness (that is, people living in households where, on average, members aged 18–59 have worked less than 20 per cent of their total work potential during the income reference period).[7]

As illustrated in Figure 6.4, the aim of the Venn diagrams is to present the joint distribution of the three components and to go a step further in the analysis than simply presenting the total number of people suffering from at least one problem. Contrasting such Venn diagrams by country shows that the degree of overlap and the relative share of the three components vary within the EU. In Bulgaria (BG), the circle 'severe material deprivation' is much larger than is observed for the other countries; that is, there is a much higher proportion of people suffering from severe material deprivation (whether or not combined with one or both of the other two problems). In other countries such as Luxembourg (LU), the targeted population is mainly composed of people at risk of poverty (that is, the two other circles are small and overlap a lot with the poverty risk). And in countries such as Ireland (IE), it is the problem of (quasi-)joblessness that is prevalent. In the Netherlands (NL), the three problems are of limited amplitude. Besides looking at the social inclusion target, it is therefore useful for policy purposes to analyse the three individual indicators separately, and their degree of overlap.

These examples of multidimensional indicators or dashboards monitored by international institutions (HDI, MPI, commonly agreed EU social indicators, EU material deprivation indicator, EU social inclusion target) illustrate the political interest for considering the multidimensional nature of poverty. They also highlight the complexity of the methodological choices behind the construction of such approaches. In the rest of the chapter, I review some of these choices and illustrate the divergence of views found in the literature. Two main questions are developed below: (1) the selection of the dimensions; and (2) the aggregation process.

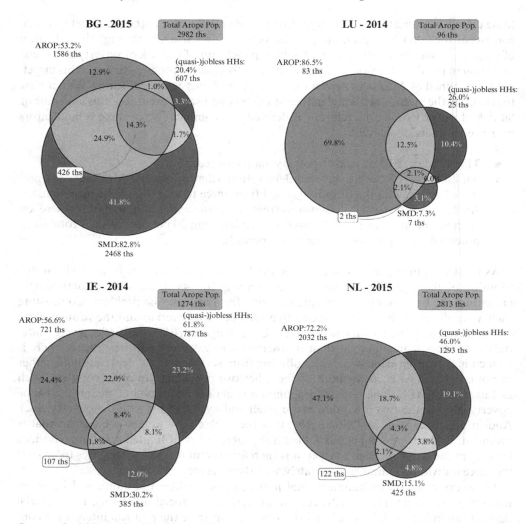

Source: Social Protection Committee (2016).

Figure 6.4   *Composition of the population at-risk-of-poverty or social exclusion*
(AROPE): population at-risk-of-poverty (AROP), living in (quasi-)
jobless households (HH) and/or severely materially deprived (SMD), % and
thousands of people (ths)

6.3   THE DIFFICULT CHOICE OF DIMENSIONS AND CONSTITUTIVE ITEMS

The starting point of many papers on multidimensional poverty is the Sen's capabilities
and functionings theory (Sen, 1976, 1979, 1985, 1993). As explained by Alkire (2008,
p. 90):

The capability approach proposes that social arrangements should be primarily evaluated according to the extent of freedom people have to promote or achieve plural functionings they value. It follows that the capability approach views poverty as a deprivation of the valuable freedoms and evaluates multidimensional poverty in the space of capabilities.

According to the capability approach, poverty is therefore measured in the space of 'the freedom to live the life one values' (Ruggeri Laderchi et al., 2003, p. 244). The 'key issue is how to define the configuration of relevant attributes, including their minimal thresholds, that constitute an acceptable level of functioning' (Thorbecke, 2008, p. 5). This choice is very context-specific. Although Martha Nussbaum proposed a list of capabilities to be applied in many contexts (Nussbaum, 1988), Amartya Sen argued against 'a "canonical" list of capabilities, that is expected to apply to all times and places' (Alkire, 2008, p. 96).

The importance of the context and society where people live on the choice and composition of dimensions was also highlighted by Peter Townsend in the 1960s. According to Townsend (1979, p. 31):

Poverty can be defined objectively and applied consistently only in terms of the concept of relative deprivation . . . Individuals, families and groups in the population can be said to be in poverty when they lack the resources to obtain the type of diet, participate in the activities and have the living conditions and amenities which are customary, or at least widely encouraged or approved, in the societies to which they belong. Their resources are so seriously below those commanded by the average individual or family that they are, in effect, excluded from ordinary living patterns, customs or activities.

Townsend's approach and work were instrumental not only in the United Kingdom, where research on material deprivation was initiated (see Gordon and Pantazis, 1997), but also in the whole of Europe (Guio, 2009; Guio et al., 2012), Australia (Bray, 2001) and New Zealand (Perry, 2002; Jensen et al., 2002); for a review, see for example Boarini and Mira d'Ercole (2006) and Nolan and Whelan (2011). Most of the MD analyses encompass items related to the satisfaction of basic needs, affordability of durables, affordability of leisure and social activities, availability of housing amenities, measures of financial stress, housing conditions and local environment characteristics.

Although there are divergences between the material deprivation and multidimensional poverty research, the central question remains broadly the same: how to select the dimensions that people 'value' (Sen) or 'which are customary, or at least widely encouraged or approved, in the societies to which people belong' (Townsend). There is a difficult trade-off between contextualizing the choice of dimensions (in order to take into account the specific values of one type of society) and the need for a certain degree of universality (which encompasses different ways of living relevant for different persons and cultures). This question of the degree of universality of the definition of poverty is obviously central in international comparisons.

To escape from experts' arbitrariness (paternalism, ethnocentrism, and so on), the choice of dimensions and variables requires normative assumptions or information on public consensus about what constitutes a 'right' baskets of dimensions to be included in the analysis. To do this, some studies rely on a human rights-based approach. Relying on the Universal Declaration of Human Rights, 'Human rights indicators: a guide to measurement and implementation' was published by the Office of the High Commissioner for Human Rights (OHCHR, 2012). This guide aims to assist in developing indicators (quantitative and qualitative) to measure progress in the implementation of international human rights norms and principles. The guide identifies specific indicators for a selected set of rights, but also emphasizes the importance of making the monitoring process 'country-owned and sufficiently decentralized, as well as inclusive for the different stakeholders to reflect their concerns', via the formation of civil society working groups to 'map . . . human rights standards for selected issues and identify . . . relevant indicators/benchmarks' (OHCHR, 2012).

Other studies use a framework of human needs to guide the selection of dimensions and their constituents; see, for example, Maslow's hierarchy of needs (Maslow, 1943) or the human scale defined by Max-Neef (1992). Ramos and Silber (2005), for example, implement a framework developed by Allardt (1993) who stresses three different dimensions: 'having' (this aspect encompasses economic resources, housing, employment, working conditions, health, education), 'loving' (degree of satisfaction with social life) and 'being' (ability to make decisions, political activities, leisure, opportunities to enjoy nature, meaningful work, and so on).

The selection of dimensions can also be determined by 'public consensus' (political goals such as the Sustainable Development Goals) or via empirical evidences in people's value (Silber, 2007). Many surveys on value judgement are available and can provide guidance for these approaches (see, for example, the World Values Survey). An example of such use in the selection process is provided at the EU level by the 2007 Eurobarometer survey which was launched by the European Commission to collect evidence in the 27 EU countries on what is needed for people to live a decent life in the country where they live (see TNS, 2007 for a description of the survey). This was largely inspired by the methodology developed by Mack and Lansley (1985) in Great Britain, taking the consensual judgement of individuals into account to identify 'social needs' in order to exclude as much as possible experts' value judgements as to what constitutes an acceptable standard of living. According to Mack and Lansley, an item supported by at least 50 per cent of interviewees constitutes a 'socially perceived necessity', so that their approach can be seen as a consensual definition of deprivation. Such data can also be used to weight the different dimensions into an aggregated indicator (see Guio, 2009; Guio et al., 2009). Figure 6.5 shows a heat map of the percentage of respondents identifying each deprivation item as a necessity in the EU Member States and for the EU as a whole. The heat map shows that there is considerable variation across EU countries with significantly higher proportions of the population in Greece (EL) and Cyprus (CY) considering items to be necessities than the people of Denmark (DK) and the Netherlands (NL). However, while the proportions considering each item to be a necessity varies, there is little variation between countries in the rank order of deprivation items; that is, in general the items which are ranked highly in one country will also be ranked highly in all other countries, and vice versa (low-ranked items in one country are low-ranked in all other countries).

Information on values and choices can also be obtained by a deliberative process which 'aims to draw out people's actual values and priorities using group discussions and participatory analyses' (Alkire, 2008, p. 103). This is the approach followed, for example, to construct the Canadian Index of Wellbeing (see Michalos and Sharp, 2010; Moore et al., 2010), and the process of concerted indicators proposed by the Council of Europe to define social cohesion and well-being (see Council of Europe, 2005, 2011).

In practice, the selection of dimensions and constituent variables is also greatly constrained by the data availability and quality. This is a particular tricky issue when one

	EU27	EU15	NMS12	EL	CY	RO	BG	HU	PT	HR	LV	SK	EE	SI	LU	MT	IE	AT	PL	D-E	FI	UK	DE	FR	D-W	SE	ES	CZ	BE	IT	LT	DK	NL
Medical Care when needed	77%	77%	78%	92%	92%	77%	82%	85%	81%	82%	75%	77%	81%	85%	80%	81%	63%	84%	75%	87%	80%	78%	83%	72%	82%	87%	73%	79%	76%	68%	60%	85%	78%
An indoor flushing toilet for sole use of the household	69%	70%	66%	87%	90%	65%	58%	75%	74%	75%	62%	69%	66%	82%	78%	73%	69%	77%	65%	69%	59%	75%	69%	71%	69%	60%	64%	70%	67%	69%	42%	48%	69%
No leakingroof, damp walls, floors, foundation	68%	68%	67%	81%	74%	76%	74%	54%	69%	71%	71%	70%	78%	75%	68%	68%	68%	75%	65%	80%	75%	72%	74%	69%	73%	78%	56%	64%	69%	62%	55%	61%	62%
Buying medicine when needed	74%	74%	76%	91%	91%	79%	81%	83%	82%	77%	73%	69%	75%	87%	82%	78%	64%	80%	72%	83%	77%	71%	80%	70%	79%	82%	72%	76%	75%	70%	58%	78%	68%
A place to live with hot, running water	67%	67%	65%	86%	82%	74%	51%	73%	74%	72%	55%	68%	52%	81%	71%	62%	62%	80%	62%	63%	60%	71%	66%	74%	67%	65%	59%	64%	62%	64%	41%	49%	59%
A place to live with its own bath or shower	63%	63%	63%	87%	90%	66%	58%	72%	71%	71%	59%	66%	58%	80%	72%	66%	65%	75%	61%	59%	50%	69%	59%	63%	59%	53%	62%	65%	57%	66%	42%	35%	49%
Bed + bedding for everyone	68%	67%	70%	86%	85%	71%	80%	80%	79%	72%	70%	73%	74%	71%	81%	83%	62%	68%	65%	82%	69%	66%	75%	69%	73%	78%	53%	72%	65%	64%	56%	64%	58%
To be able to keep one's home adequately warm	62%	62%	61%	83%	70%	58%	64%	78%	59%	68%	68%	59%	64%	75%	70%	39%	62%	81%	61%	73%	69%	64%	68%	64%	67%	55%	53%	50%	61%	58%	45%	55%	54%
Buying medical equipment when needed	66%	66%	66%	83%	81%	70%	73%	72%	74%	70%	67%	65%	69%	79%	77%	72%	60%	77%	62%	75%	67%	63%	70%	66%	68%	79%	68%	66%	64%	57%	49%	73%	59%
Regular medical and dental checkups	62%	62%	65%	81%	79%	69%	70%	68%	73%	68%	64%	65%	63%	78%	68%	66%	58%	72%	63%	72%	56%	62%	67%	59%	66%	61%	61%	63%	55%	57%	46%	68%	43%
A warm winter coat	65%	63%	71%	88%	67%	80%	84%	77%	71%	70%	61%	76%	73%	63%	79%	32%	64%	71%	68%	69%	73%	58%	68%	66%	67%	71%	60%	63%	61%	56%	46%	64%	45%
A place to live where one doesn't risk being forced to leave	57%	55%	64%	71%	68%	79%	66%	73%	61%	67%	60%	54%	75%	61%	63%	55%	62%	63%	59%	50%	63%	58%	47%	59%	47%	42%	61%	50%	55%	57%	44%	38%	39%
No crime violence or vandalism in the area	49%	48%	51%	75%	70%	60%	52%	68%	61%	51%	60%	57%	61%	42%	41%	66%	62%	51%	44%	48%	50%	56%	44%	47%	42%	41%	44%	32%	52%	45%	47%	37%	43%
Fresh fruit and vegetables once a day	49%	48%	52%	74%	61%	66%	58%	54%	78%	57%	50%	57%	40%	59%	51%	49%	58%	47%	49%	52%	38%	50%	44%	41%	42%	41%	61%	27%	43%	44%	34%	35%	41%
Not too much pollution or other environmental problems	42%	41%	47%	70%	68%	54%	50%	61%	54%	52%	50%	52%	59%	42%	35%	57%	53%	46%	40%	38%	44%	46%	39%	36%	39%	37%	33%	34%	47%	40%	39%	38%	39%
2 pairs of shoes suitable to the climate	58%	55%	68%	88%	79%	77%	79%	71%	67%	68%	67%	73%	64%	63%	74%	43%	61%	67%	65%	66%	58%	44%	63%	58%	62%	70%	55%	59%	49%	49%	46%	60%	35%
Refrigerator	58%	56%	66%	87%	89%	71%	75%	69%	78%	70%	60%	72%	60%	77%	75%	84%	54%	72%	62%	65%	61%	43%	64%	55%	63%	70%	58%	62%	50%	48%	50%	54%	35%
Well-maintained and kept in a decent state of repair	42%	41%	48%	69%	51%	58%	50%	59%	47%	60%	49%	49%	46%	41%	40%	48%	52%	52%	42%	40%	34%	43%	35%	42%	34%	27%	49%	34%	38%	41%	35%	30%	22%
Cooker big enough for HH	42%	39%	53%	82%	64%	69%	75%	57%	75%	58%	45%	52%	45%	71%	71%	75%	53%	58%	39%	58%	34%	41%	54%	37%	53%	66%	18%	48%	36%	17%	52%	43%	29%
A place to live with well maintained public amenities	34%	32%	42%	58%	47%	54%	45%	54%	48%	42%	48%	40%	43%	30%	28%	39%	48%	36%	37%	21%	26%	41%	23%	28%	23%	20%	31%	28%	28%	35%	35%	18%	26%
Access to local public transport	38%	36%	43%	62%	44%	52%	53%	50%	59%	45%	44%	41%	48%	35%	49%	36%	42%	33%	39%	41%	36%	40%	35%	37%	33%	30%	40%	29%	37%	30%	28%	21%	25%
Meat, chicken or fish at least once every two days	43%	42%	46%	53%	29%	62%	54%	39%	76%	50%	52%	38%	43%	30%	35%	39%	56%	36%	47%	34%	46%	36%	29%	41%	28%	39%	58%	22%	47%	44%	32%	37%	35%
A place to live that is not too dark, with enough natural light	39%	36%	48%	77%	57%	55%	55%	61%	61%	53%	45%	51%	47%	46%	38%	48%	52%	55%	43%	38%	30%	36%	35%	29%	35%	28%	31%	34%	32%	39%	33%	21%	27%
Repairing or replacing major electrical goods	40%	39%	42%	65%	49%	39%	59%	60%	54%	51%	45%	43%	37%	50%	63%	56%	46%	44%	35%	43%	39%	35%	35%	48%	33%	31%	43%	42%	40%	34%	34%	30%	27%
Washing machine	48%	45%	59%	74%	85%	56%	67%	66%	65%	61%	48%	68%	52%	77%	71%	74%	45%	60%	56%	61%	46%	34%	55%	41%	53%	37%	51%	59%	38%	39%	39%	21%	33%
A place to live without too much noise	28%	26%	36%	59%	51%	46%	41%	41%	49%	37%	40%	37%	39%	25%	23%	39%	46%	36%	33%	18%	22%	34%	19%	23%	19%	15%	25%	20%	21%	27%	30%	15%	18%
Being able to get basic banking services	29%	29%	28%	34%	38%	37%	35%	21%	36%	38%	32%	33%	37%	39%	41%	30%	36%	31%	23%	44%	41%	33%	32%	36%	29%	26%	25%	21%	36%	16%	24%	24%	25%
A place to live with enough space and privacy for everybody	31%	28%	42%	55%	44%	48%	46%	46%	42%	41%	46%	36%	51%	40%	31%	36%	45%	34%	42%	26%	26%	32%	24%	32%	24%	16%	25%	26%	25%	24%	32%	18%	18%
A place to live with enough space to invite friends and family	25%	23%	33%	40%	39%	41%	36%	40%	37%	35%	35%	29%	31%	29%	24%	20%	41%	27%	31%	18%	20%	26%	21%	21%	22%	14%	22%	17%	20%	22%	28%	15%	15%
Smart clothes	24%	19%	39%	43%	44%	53%	38%	37%	22%	26%	50%	56%	34%	18%	16%	33%	43%	41%	34%	21%	33%	23%	13%	14%	12%	20%	30%	26%	16%	12%	20%	9%	15%
Some new, not 2nd hand clothes	30%	26%	44%	75%	67%	62%	49%	44%	39%	39%	45%	52%	31%	33%	36%	37%	45%	36%	40%	24%	23%	21%	21%	25%	21%	26%	38%	21%	14%	21%	27%	14%	11%
Replacing worn out or broken furniture	21%	20%	27%	57%	40%	34%	44%	30%	40%	33%	37%	26%	19%	24%	28%	15%	33%	19%	23%	19%	12%	19%	16%	18%	15%	13%	28%	17%	15%	16%	23%	10%	10%
Buying presents for family or friends at least once a year	17%	14%	29%	26%	24%	34%	28%	41%	14%	16%	41%	32%	33%	13%	16%	7%	17%	13%	23%	23%	18%	18%	16%	14%	14%	20%	7%	31%	16%	10%	21%	17%	12%
Fixed telephone	18%	18%	22%	53%	35%	35%	41%	18%	12%	37%	13%	16%	13%	24%	28%	53%	19%	12%	18%	26%	8%	16%	25%	18%	25%	22%	12%	4%	12%	13%	9%	12%	12%
Spending a small amount of money each week on oneself	14%	13%	22%	23%	20%	28%	27%	19%	15%	19%	28%	18%	24%	10%	15%	11%	21%	14%	23%	16%	16%	14%	16%	9%	15%	6%	11%	9%	10%	10%	17%	8%	9%
Colour TV	19%	14%	39%	45%	55%	53%	61%	47%	35%	35%	36%	34%	28%	24%	19%	35%	16%	14%	31%	25%	15%	13%	17%	9%	15%	14%	9%	23%	10%	11%	34%	11%	5%
Being able to decorate one's home	13%	10%	23%	16%	9%	22%	20%	21%	16%	31%	16%	24%	30%	12%	10%	5%	17%	11%	29%	13%	9%	13%	11%	8%	10%	5%	7%	11%	10%	9%	12%	6%	7%
Paying for one week annual holiday away from home	15%	13%	25%	44%	27%	35%	33%	29%	17%	19%	22%	20%	23%	22%	13%	4%	16%	13%	23%	12%	11%	12%	9%	16%	8%	17%	8%	10%	12%	12%	14%	8%	10%
Participating in a regular leisure or sports activity	13%	12%	16%	17%	15%	19%	19%	22%	17%	19%	17%	16%	23%	32%	23%	15%	18%	11%	13%	11%	13%	11%	10%	11%	10%	13%	15%	13%	15%	9%	11%	13%	13%
Inviting friends or family for dinner at home once a month	12%	10%	20%	22%	17%	23%	26%	24%	13%	19%	22%	16%	17%	8%	10%	5%	14%	10%	20%	7%	9%	10%	8%	9%	9%	9%	9%	8%	8%	10%	13%	8%	9%
Going out once a month (restaurant, cinema, disco or concert, etc.)	11%	9%	18%	29%	21%	27%	26%	20%	13%	18%	27%	20%	19%	10%	14%	10%	14%	11%	14%	7%	10%	10%	7%	8%	7%	6%	8%	10%	9%	9%	13%	4%	5%
Car	17%	17%	20%	50%	84%	26%	32%	13%	29%	34%	20%	23%	21%	31%	32%	42%	23%	10%	14%	15%	13%	9%	10%	30%	9%	19%	16%	13%	14%	18%	19%	7%	4%
Buying newspapers, magazines and books	13%	10%	22%	19%	14%	29%	30%	27%	14%	14%	29%	27%	23%	13%	16%	12%	18%	12%	19%	16%	14%	8%	15%	7%	15%	13%	8%	13%	9%	10%	17%	7%	10%
Mobile phone	12%	9%	24%	26%	41%	35%	34%	21%	22%	15%	38%	25%	33%	14%	20%	32%	17%	12%	16%	8%	21%	7%	5%	6%	4%	9%	10%	20%	8%	9%	22%	10%	4%
Going to the hairdresser regularly	11%	9%	20%	12%	4%	33%	27%	21%	13%	14%	28%	21%	25%	9%	12%	15%	19%	10%	15%	15%	10%	7%	10%	5%	10%	9%	12%	8%	8%	8%	22%	5%	9%
Computer	9%	6%	17%	10%	18%	26%	22%	12%	13%	18%	20%	17%	19%	11%	11%	20%	9%	6%	14%	7%	8%	6%	6%	5%	5%	8%	5%	9%	6%	8%	13%	10%	6%
Internet connection	7%	5%	14%	8%	12%	20%	19%	10%	11%	15%	19%	13%	19%	8%	11%	18%	8%	6%	12%	5%	8%	5%	4%	4%	4%	9%	4%	7%	6%	6%	11%	9%	5%

Notes: Deprivations coloured in red have high proportions of the population agreeing that they are necessities, deprivations coloured in green have low percentages of the population agreeing that they are necessities. Although there is some variation between countries (that is, left to right across the heat map) the ordering of necessities within countries (that is, top to bottom in the heat map) is very similar.
Country abbreviations: BE: Belgium, BG: Bulgaria, CZ: Czech Republic, DK: Denmark, DE: Germany, D-E: East Germany, D-W: West Germany; EE: Estonia, IE: Ireland, EL: Greece, ES: Spain, FR: France, HR: Croatia, IT: Italy, CY: Cyprus, LV: Latvia, LT: Lithuania, LU: Luxembourg, HU: Hungary, MT: Malta, NL: The Netherlands, AT: Austria, PL: Poland, PT: Portugal, RO: Romania, SI: Slovenia, SK: Slovakia, FI: Finland, SE: Sweden, UK: United Kingdom.

Source: Eurobarometer special no. 279, Wave 67.1 (computations: http://www.poverty.ac.uk/).

Figure 6.5 Heat map of the 2007 Eurobarometer perception of necessities results, by EU Member States

wants to look at the joint distribution of the attributes (which requires a common source for all of them). In many cases, dimensions and variable selection are data-driven.

Empirical criteria can also help in identifying relevant constitutive indicators (see, e.g., Dickes, 1989; Eurostat, 2002; Guio, 2009; Perry, 2002; Whelan, 1993; Gordon et al., 2000; Pantazis et al., 2006; Guio et al., 2012). So, for instance, in their in-depth analysis of the thematic module on MD included in the EU Statistics on Income and Living Conditions (EU-SILC) survey, Guio et al. (2012, 2017) propose an analytical framework for developing robust aggregate indicators for social monitoring purposes at national and EU levels. In this framework, they start by analysing the dimensional structure of the full set of eligible items, in order to explore the underlying structure to the data. Then, they assess the robustness of the items; both the robustness of each individual item (validity and suitability tests) and the robustness of the set of items taken together (reliability and additivity):

1. Suitability of the items: this test aims at checking that citizens in the different countries (as well as the different population subgroups within each country) consider them necessary for people to have an 'acceptable' standard of living in the country where they live. This can be checked by using consensus survey or, if available, by using information on the proportion of people wanting an item; that is, either people who have the item, or who would like to have it but cannot afford it (or are prevented from having it due to other reasons than affordability).
2. Validity of individual items: to ensure that each item exhibits statistically significant relative risk ratios with independent variables known to be correlated with the latent dimension (for example, material deprivation).
3. Reliability of the scale: to assess the internal consistency of the scale as a whole; that is, how closely related the set of items are as a group.
4. Additivity of items: to test that, say, someone with an MD indicator score of 2 is in reality suffering from more severe MD than someone with a score of 1; that is, that the indicator's components add up.

The last two criteria (additivity and reliability of the scale) are relevant only because items are summed up in an aggregated indicator.

Although this is the most common option, aggregation is not the only possibility to deal with multidimensionality, as explained above. We can look at the separate aspects in a dashboard and study the joint distribution between attributes without aggregating them. As we are reminded by Duclos et al.:

> It is possible for a set of univariate analyses done independently for each dimension of well-being to conclude that poverty in A is lower than poverty in B while a multivariate analysis concludes the opposite, and vice-versa. The key to these possibilities is the interaction of the various dimensions of well-being in the poverty measure and their correlation in the sampled populations. (Duclos et al., 2006, p. 945)

Ferreira and Lugo (2012) propose different intermediate approaches in-between the use of a dashboard and the computation of an aggregated index; they suggest focusing on the joint distribution of attributes. One of these approaches is the Venn diagram used at the EU level to present the components of the social inclusion target (see section 6.2). Another option is to use Copula function (Decancq, 2009; Quinn, 2007) or multivariate stochastic dominance techniques (see, e.g., Duclos et al., 2006). The latter can be used to compare a few (two or three) multidimensional distributions in order to determine whether one distribution dominates another for a range of cut-off lines (that is, the poverty frontier in multiple dimensions). However, this approach can yield only to partial ordering and is difficult to implement in the case of numerous dimensions. These may be considered as strong arguments for aggregation by some authors. There remain, however, many disagreements on the way to aggregate the different dimensions (e.g., Alkire and Foster, 2011b; Ravallion, 2011; Lustig, 2011; Thorbecke, 2008), as discussed in the next subsection.

6.4   ISSUES RELATED TO AGGREGATION

Among the issues related to aggregation, the question of how to combine dimensions (and how to combine variables into dimensions) is central. There are many proposals of multidimensional indexes with desirable axiomatic properties (see the companion Chapter 5 by Chakravarty and Chattopaddhyay in this *Handbook*; Chakravarty et al., 2008; Bourguignon and Chakravarty, 2003; Lasso de la Vega and Urrutia, 2011). The Bourguignon and Chakravarty (2003) index is one of the most famous examples and can be seen as a generalization of the Forster–Greer–Thorbecke unidimensional index. Many other authors have developed multidimensional indexes, with a common concern to ground their index in a social welfare function.

There are, however, difficulties in positioning poverty measures in a social welfare framework, as recognized by Alkire and Foster:

> Much of the exercise of selecting a welfare function is by definition normative and has many degrees of freedom. There will likely be a multiplicity of acceptable functions, and even if a unique welfare function could be agreed upon there is no unique transformation from welfare function to poverty measure. (Alkire and Foster, 2011b, quoted in Lustig, 2011, p. 5)

The specification of such a welfare function raises the question of the degree of the substitutability or complementarity of dimensions. If dimensions are substitutes, this implies possible trade-offs between them. If they are complements, an improvement in one dimension increases the utility of another. In practice, many indicators have a simple counting method (see Atkinson, 2003), that is, a simple sum (eventually weighted) of the dimensional components. An arithmetical sum implies that dimensions are supposed to be perfect substitutes (the rate at which one dimension can compensate another is constant). When revised in 2010, the HDI shifted from an arithmetical to a geometrical average for this reason.

The method of identification of the poor is also a complex question in the case of multiple dimensions. There are two main (extreme) positions:

- the intersection approach: if a person falls short in all attributes, then they will be considered as poor, as for example in the Irish official 'consistent poverty measure' which focuses only on people who suffer from both material deprivation and income poverty; and
- the union approach: a shortfall in one dimension is a sufficient condition to be poor, as for example in the EU social inclusion target presented above.

An intermediate position (see Alkire and Foster, 2011a, 2011b) is to define a minimal number of dimensions where the person has to be deprived to be considered poor (union and intersection being extreme cases of this more general case). Similarly, in the MD literature, those cumulating a minimal number of deprivations are considered as deprived, the threshold ranging in theory between one and the total number of items or dimensions.

The aggregation process raises the question of how to weigh the different dimensions (and the variables within each dimension), which is central to the critics opposed to aggregation. Choosing the variables or dimensions in the list is the first kind of crude weighting (giving 1 to each item retained, and 0 to those not in the list). Once dimensions and variables are chosen, the question of weighting deserves explicit justification, except 'if either the union or the intersection identification approaches are used' (Alkire, 2011, p. 15). In all other situations, this step is crucial, as this has an impact on the 'trade-off' between the dimensions (Decancq and Lugo, 2013).

Decancq and Lugo (2013) present a very rich typology of approaches to set weights in a multidimensional context. Some are data-driven, others are normative. Their paper shows that giving equal weighting is not trivial, even if many papers choose this option for clarity and communication reasons. Other authors prefer to use data-driven weighting. A first example is provided by the frequency-based approach in which each item or dimension is weighted by a function of the proportion of persons who are not deprived (prevalence weighting).[8] The idea behind this choice is that the higher the proportion of people who have the item, the more likely a person lacking it will feel deprived. One important question is related to the choice of the reference population to determine the prevalence; that is, in evaluating their situation, are respondents influenced mostly by their perceptions of how they are doing compared to others in their own country, or beyond national border lines? Or, on the contrary, do they compare themselves to people belonging to a closer group that they belong to (socially or geographically)? Halleröd (1995) proposed to define weights for small homogeneous subgroups (in terms of age and other socio-economic characteristics) and used different sets of weights to take into account differences in preferences for different subgroups within the country. At the other extreme, Guio (2009) tested the impact of using nationally defined weights and EU-defined weights in the EU MD indicator. As highlighted by Decancq and Lugo (2013, p. 12), the frequency-based approach:

> hinges on the (implicit) assumption that the relative importance of the different dimensions, and hence the opinion on the 'good life', depends crucially and only on the relative deprivation levels across the different dimensions. In general, this seems a strong and rather restrictive assumption about the nature of the evaluation process about the 'good life'.

Another example of data-driven weighting is provided by the use of 'consensus' weights, that may be computed on the basis of surveys gathering social views on what is more desirable; that is, goods or dimensions considered as necessary by a larger proportion of the population should receive greater weights, in comparison to the other items or dimensions. Data presented in Figure 6.5 were, for example, used to define national 'consensus weighting' at the EU level in the construction of weighted MD indicators (see Guio, 2009; Guio et al., 2009; Bossert et al., 2009).

Multivariate statistical tools may also be used to determine data-driven weights. Aggregation can be derived from multivariate analysis, mainly latent variables approaches.

'The main idea behind the latent variable approach is that the different dimensions of development (deprivation) cannot be directly measured, but can be represented by latent variables manifesting themselves through a set of achievements' (Krishnakumar, 2008, p. 125). Examples of such techniques are provided below (see Silber, 2007; Krishnakumar, 2008; Kakwani and Silber, 2008, for a review):

- Principal component analysis (see, e.g., Klasen, 2000; Krishnakumar, 2008).
- Multiple correspondence analysis (MCA) (Assellin and Tuan Anh, 2008, who link MCA with axiomatic view; Deutsch et al., 2013).
- Factor analysis (Nolan and Whelan, 1996; Guio, 2009; Luzzi et al., 2008; Dekkers, 2008; Dewilde, 2004; Guio et al., 2012).
- Cluster analysis (Guio et al., 2012; Hirschberg et al., 1991; Luzzi et al., 2008).
- Rash models and item response theory (e.g., Dickes et al., 1984; Cappellari and Jenkins, 2007; Fusco and Dickes, 2008; Martini and Vanin, 2013; Raileanu Szeles and Fusco, 2013; Guio et al., 2012).
- Multiple indicators and multiple causes (MIMIC) (see Krishnakumar, 2008; Montgomery and Hewett, 2004).
- Structural equation modelling (Krishnakumar, 2008), or linear structural relations (LISREL) modelling (see Tomlinson et al., 2008).

The goal of such tools is the reduction of information, via the derivation of one (or a few) latent dimension(s) which regroup observed variables.

The main criticism of data-driven weighting comes from the fact that the resulting weights are difficult to justify from a normative point of view, are not independent of the dataset used (coverage, time) and are not easily given an intuitive interpretation. Alternatively, weighting may be derived from participatory process, which present the advantage of taking into account the value judgement of people, but may present other drawbacks (subjectivity, representativeness, costs). Some interactive tools propose the users of the indicators to set their own weights. This is, for example, the case of the OECD Better Life Index portal (http://www.oecdbetterlifeindex.org/), where users are invited to aggregate 11 key dimensions (education, housing, environment, job, health, community, environment, and so on) and to rate these dimensions depending on the importance they attach to them.

6.5   CONCLUSIONS

Despite the fact that it is now widely acknowledged that poverty is more than a lack of sufficient income, and needs to be measured as a multidimensional concept, there is great disagreement on the way to measure this multidimensionality. Recent decades saw an explosion of proposals, at both the academic and the international institutions level, which benefited from the increasing awareness of the importance of monitoring the different aspects of poverty, and from the impressive number of datasets made available for research which cover different dimensions of poverty.

A brief overview of these various attempts shows that there remains a huge space of freedoms on how to treat this multidimensional information. These decisions are neither trivial, nor neutral on the results and the way to report and use them at the political level. Sensitivity analysis is essential to quantify the impact of alternative methodological choices.

The literature review presented in this chapter shows for example the advantages and disadvantages of using dashboards, of aggregating information via multidimensional indexes, or of looking at the joint distribution of attributes without aggregating them. In many situations, however, a mix of these different tools is needed to fully apprehend the multidimensional nature of poverty.[9]

Data quality and availability is crucial in this process, as the possibility to study the different dimensions for the same individuals, within a unique source, is crucial for joint distribution analysis and indexes. Techniques such as data matching offer alternatives when some dimensions are lacking in a survey, as they allow for coupling dimensional information from different datasets for similar individuals.

NOTES

1. See Alkire et al. (2016).
2. Interestingly, the Council amended this definition in 1985 and enlarged the concept of 'resources' in order to take into account material, cultural and social aspects: 'the persons whose resources (material, cultural and social) are so limited as to exclude them from the minimum acceptable way of life in the Member State to which they belong' (EU Council of Ministers, 1985).
3. In order to understand better the policy dynamic that has progressively led to this cooperation, Marlier et al. (2007) suggest that it is worth looking at six 'EU texts' that have played a particularly important role in this shift (see pages 18–21 and Appendix 2a).
4. For the current list of EU social protection and social inclusion indicators, see Social Protection Committee Indicators Sub-Group (2015).
5. Although via a 'softer' process, other international organizations monitor the progress of countries via dashboards or composite or aggregated indicators (see, for example, the indicators supporting the Sustainable Development Goals, or the OECD 'Society at a Glance' publications).
6. See Frazer et al. (2014) for a discussion of the target.
7. See the Eurostat website for exact definitions and national figures for each indicator and the target as a whole. The three dimensions are measured at the individual level on the basis of a common source: the EU Statistics on Income and Living Conditions (EU-SILC) survey.
8. See, for example, Brandolini (2008), Desai and Shah (1988), Deutsch and Silber (2005), Förster (2005), Muffels and Fouarge (2004), Tsakloglou and Papadapoulos (2002) and Willits (2006).
9. Measuring global poverty by complementing income-based measures by a multidimensional dashboard of outcome indicators, which include a multidimensional index, was proposed by A.B. Atkinson who chaired the Commission on Global Poverty of the World Bank (World Bank, 2017). Another example of such combination is given by the United Nations Children's Fund (UNICEF) application Multiple Overlapping Deprivation Analysis (MODA) for Children, which focuses on child deprivations and provides many unidimensional results, multidimensional overlap analyses, as well as aggregated indexes for a range of possible cut-off points (using the Alkire and Foster method). All these tools are provided with possible decomposition analysis and profiling methods, to allow a large range of analyses and crossing the results.

REFERENCES

Alkire, S. (2008), 'Choosing dimensions: the capability approach and multidimensional poverty', in Kakwani, N. and Silber, J. (eds), *The Many Dimensions of Poverty*, New York: Palgrave Macmillan, pp. 89–119.
Alkire, S. (2011), 'Multidimensional poverty and its discontents', OPHI Working Paper No. 46.
Alkire, S. and Foster, J. (2011a), 'Counting and multidimensional poverty measurement', *Journal of Public Economics*, 95(7): 476–487.

Alkire, S. and Foster, J. (2011b), 'Understandings and misunderstandings of multidimensional poverty measurement', *Journal of Economic Inequality*, 9(2): 289–314.

Alkire, S., Foster, J., Seth, S., Santos, M.E., Roche, J.M. and Ballon, P. (2015), *Multidimensional Poverty Measurement and Analysis*, Oxford: Oxford University Press.

Alkire, S., Jindra, C., Robles, G. and Vaz, A. (2016), 'Multidimensional Poverty Index 2016: brief methodological note and results', OPHI Briefing 42, University of Oxford.

Alkire, S. and Santos, M.E. (2010), 'Acute multidimensional poverty: a new index for developing countries', OPHI Working Paper Series No. 38, Oxford University.

Allardt, E. (1993), 'Having, loving, being: an alternative to the Swedish model of welfare research', in Nussbaum, M. and Sen, A. (eds), *The Quality of Life*, Oxford: Clarendon Press, pp. 88–94.

Assellin, L.-M. and Tuan Anh, V. (2008), 'Multidimensional poverty and multiple correspondence analysis', in Kakwani, N. and Silber, J. (eds), *Quantitative Approaches to Multidimensional Poverty Measurement*, Basingstoke: Palgrave Macmillan, pp. 80–103.

Atkinson, A.B. (2003), 'Multidimensional deprivation: contrasting social welfare and counting approaches', *Journal of Economic Inequality*, 1: 51–65.

Atkinson, A.B. (2011), 'On lateral thinking', *Journal of Economic Inequality*, 9(3): 319–328.

Atkinson, A.B. and Marlier, E. (2010), 'Analysing and measuring social inclusion in a global context', New York: United Nations.

Boarini, R. and Mira d'Ercole, M. (2006), 'Measures of material deprivation in OECD countries', Document de travail de l'OCDE sur les affaires sociales, l'emploi et les migrations, no. 37, Paris: OCDE.

Bourguignon, F. and Chakravarty, S. (2003), 'The measurement of multidimensional poverty', *Journal of Economic Inequality*, 1(1): 25–49.

Bossert, W., Chakravarty, S. and D'Ambrosio, C. (2009), 'Multidimensional poverty and material deprivation', ECINEQ Working Paper, 2009-129.

Bossert, W., Chakravarty, S.R. and D'Ambrosio, C. (2013), 'Multidimensional poverty and material deprivation with discrete data', *Review of Income and Wealth*, 59: 29–43.

Brandolini, A. (2008), 'On applying synthetic indices of multidimensional well-being: health and income inequalities in selected EU countries', Banca d'Italia, Temi di discussion 668.

Bray, J.R. (2001), 'Hardship in Australia', Department of Family and Community Services, Occasional paper no. 4.

Cappellari, L. and Jenkins, S.P. (2007), 'Summarizing multiple deprivation indicators', in Jenkins, S.P. and Micklewright, J. (eds), *Inequality and Poverty: Re-examined*, Oxford: Oxford University Press, pp. 166–184.

Chakravarty, S., Deutsch, J. and Silber, J. (2008), 'On the Watts multidimensional poverty index and its decomposition', *World Development*, 36(6): 1067–1077.

Council of Europe (2005), 'Methodological guide to the concerted development of social cohesion indicators – methodological guide'.

Council of Europe (2011), 'Involving citizens and communities in securing societal progress for the well-being of all – methodological guide'.

Decancq, K. (2009), 'Copula-based measurement of dependence between dimensions of well-being', HEDG Working Paper 09/32, University of York.

Decancq, K. and Lugo, M.A. (2013), 'Weights in multidimensional indices of well-being: an overview', *Econometric Reviews*, 32(1): 7–34.

Dekkers, G. (2008), 'Are you unhappy? Then you are poor! Multi-dimensional poverty in Belgium', *International Journal of Sociology and Social Policy*, 28(11/12): 502–515.

Desai, M. and Shah, A. (1988), 'An econometric approach to the measurement of poverty', *Oxford Economic Papers*, 40: 505–522.

Deutsch, J. and Silber, J. (2005), 'Measuring multidimensional poverty: an empirical comparison of various approaches', *Review of Income and Wealth*, 51(1): 145–174.

Deutsch, J., Silber, J. and Verme, P. (2013), 'On measuring social exclusion: a new approach with an application to FYR Macedonia', in Ruggeri Laderchi, C. and Savastano, S. (eds), *Poverty and Exclusion in the Western Balkans: New Directions in Measurement and Policy*, New York: Springer Verlag, pp. 99–116.

Dewilde, C. (2004), 'The multidimensional measurement of poverty in Belgium and Britain: a categorical approach', *Social Indicator Research*, 68, 331–369.

Dickes, P. (1989), 'Pauvreté et conditions d'existence. Théories, modèles et mesures', Document PSELL, No. 8, Walferdange: CEPS/INSTEAD.

Dickes, P., Gailly, B., Hausman, P. and Schaber, G. (1984), 'Les désavantages de la pauvreté: définitions, mesures et réalités en Europe', *Mondes en développement*, 12(45): 131–190.

Duclos, J.-Y., Sahn, D. and Younger, S. (2006), 'Robust multidimensional poverty comparisons', *Economic Journal*, 116(514): 943–968.

EU Council of Ministers (1975), 'Council Decision of 22 July 1975 Concerning a Programme of Pilot Schemes and Studies to Combat Poverty', 75/458/EEC, OJEC, L 199, Brussels.

EU Council of Ministers (1985), 'Council Decision of 19 December 1984 on Specific Community Action to Combat Poverty', 85/8/EEC, OJEC, L 2, Brussels.

European Council (2010), 'European Council 17 June 2010: Conclusions', Brussels: European Council.

Eurostat (2002), 'Income, poverty and social exclusion: second report', Luxembourg: OPOCE.

Ferreira, F. (2011), 'Poverty is multidimensional. But what are we going to do about it?', *Journal of Economic Inequality*, 9(3): 493–495.

Ferreira, F. and Lugo, M.A. (2012), 'Multidimensional poverty analysis: looking for a middle ground', Policy Research Working Paper No. 5964.

Förster (2005), 'The European social space revisited: comparing poverty in the enlarged European Union', *Journal of Comparative Policy Analysis*, 7(1): 29–48.

Frazer, H., Guio, A.-C., Marlier, E., Vanhercke, B. and Ward, T. (2014), 'Putting the fight against poverty and social exclusion at the heart of the EU agenda: a contribution to the mid-term review of the Europe 2020 strategy', OSE Paper Series, Research Paper 15, Brussels: OSE.

Fusco, A. and Dickes, P. (2008), 'The Rasch model and multidimensional poverty measurement', in Kakwani, N. and Silber, J. (eds), *Quantitative Approaches to Multidimensional Poverty Measurement*, Houndmills: Palgrave Macmillan, pp. 49–62.

Fusco, A., Guio, A.-C. and Marlier, E. (2010), 'Characterising the income poor and the materially deprived in European countries', in Atkinson, A.B. and Marlier, E. (eds), *Income and Living Conditions in Europe*, Luxembourg: OPOCE, pp. 133–153.

Gordon, D., Adelman, L., Ashworth, K., Bradshaw, J., Levitas, R., Middleton, S., Pantazis, C., Patsios, D., Payne, S., Townsend, P. and Williams, J. (2000), *Poverty and Social Exclusion in Britain*, York: Joseph Rowntree Foundation.

Gordon, D. and Pantazis, C. (1997), *Breadline Britain in the 1990s*, Ashgate: Aldershot.

Guio, A.-C. (2009), 'What can be learned from deprivation indicators in Europe?', Eurostat Methodologies and working papers, Luxembourg: Office for Official Publications of the European Communities (OPOCE).

Guio, A.-C., Fusco, A. and Marlier, E. (2009), 'A European Union approach to material deprivation using EU-SILC and Euro-barometer data', IRISS WP 2009-19, December.

Guio, A.-C., Gordon, D. and Marlier, E. (2012), 'Measuring material deprivation in the EU: indicators for the whole population and child-specific indicators', Eurostat Methodologies and working papers, Luxembourg: Office for Official Publications of the European Communities (OPOCE).

Guio, A.-C., Gordon, D., Najera, H. and Pomati, M. (2017), 'Revising the EU material deprivation variables', Eurostat Methodologies and working papers, Luxembourg: Office for Official Publications of the European Communities (OPOCE).

Halleröd, B. (1995), 'The truly poor: direct and indirect measurement of consensual poverty in Sweden', *Journal of European Social Policy*, 5(2): 111–129.

Hirschberg, J.G., Maasoumi, E. and Slottje, D.J. (1991), 'Cluster analysis for measuring welfare and quality of life across countries', *Journal of Econometrics*, 50: 131–150.

Jensen, J., Spittal, M., Crichton, S., Sathiyandra, S. and Krishnan, V. (2002), 'Direct measurement of living standards: the New Zealand ELSI scale', Wellington: Ministry of Social Development.

Kakwani, N. and Silber, J. (2008), *The Many Dimensions of Poverty*, New York: Palgrave Macmillan.

Klasen, S. (2000), 'Measuring poverty and deprivation in South Africa', *Review of Income and Wealth*, 46: 33–58.

Krishnakumar, J. (2008), 'On exact statistical properties of multidimensional indices based on principal components, factor analysis, MIMIC and structural equation models', *Social Indicator Research*, 86: 481–496.

Lasso de la Vega, C. and Urrutia, A. (2011), 'Characterizing how to aggregate the individuals' deprivations in a multidimensional framework', *Journal of Economic Inequality*, 9(2): 183–194.

Lustig, N. (2011), 'Multidimensional indices of achievements and poverty: what do we gain and what do we lose? An introduction to the JOEI Forum on multidimensional poverty', *Journal of Economic Inequality*, 9(2): 227–234.

Luzzi, G.F., Flückiger, Y. and Weber, S. (2008), 'A cluster analysis of multidimensional poverty in Switzerland', in Kakwani, N. and Silber, J. (eds), *Quantitative Approaches to Multidimensional Poverty Measurement*, London: Palgrave Macmillan, pp. 63–79.

Maasoumi, E. and Lugo, M.-A. (2008), 'The information basis of multivariate poverty assessments', in Kakwani, N. and Silber, J. (eds), *Quantitative Approaches to Multidimensional Poverty Measurement*, London: Palgrave Macmillan, pp. 1–29.

Mack, J. and Lansley, S. (1985), *Poor Britain*, London: George Allen & Unwin.

Marlier, E., Atkinson, A.B., Cantillon, B. and Nolan, B. (2007), *The EU and Social Inclusion: Facing the Challenges*, Bristol: Policy Press.

Marlier, E., Cantillon, B., Nolan, B., Van den Bosch, K. and Van Rie, Ti. (2012), 'Developing and learning from EU measures of social inclusion', in Besharov, D.J. and Couch, K.A. (eds), *Counting the Poor: New Thinking about European Poverty Measures and Lessons for the United States*, International Policy Exchange Series, New York: Oxford University Press, pp. 299–341.

Martini, M.-C. and Vanin, C. (2013), 'A measure of poverty based on the Rasch model', in Torelli, N., Pesarin, F. and Bar-Hen, A. (eds), *Advances in Theoretical and Applied Statistics*, Berlin and Heidelberg: Springer-Verlag, pp. 327–337.

Maslow, A.H. (1943), 'A theory of human motivation', *Psychological Review*, 50(4): 370–396.

Max-Neef, M.A. (1992), *Human Scale Development*, New York, USA and London, UK: Apex Press.

Michalos, A. and Sharp, A. (2010), 'An approach to the Canadian Index of Wellbeing (CIW), methodology report', Canadian Index of Wellbeing, Toronto.

Montgomery, M.R. and Hewett, P.C. (2004), 'Urban poverty and health in developing countries: household and neighborhood effects', Policy Research Division Working Paper No. 184, New York: Population Council.

Moore K., Swystun, L., Holden B., Bernardin, H., Dunning, B. and Graham, P. (2010), 'Democratic engagement domain report', Canadian Index of Wellbeing, Toronto.

Muffels, R. and Fouarge, D. (2004), 'The role of European welfare states in explaining resources deprivation', *Social Indicators Research*, 68(3): 299–330.

Nolan, B. and Whelan, C.T. (1996), 'The relationship between income and deprivation: a dynamic perspective', *Revue économique*, 3: 709–717.

Nolan, B. and Whelan, C.T. (2011), *Poverty and Deprivation in Europe*, Oxford: Oxford University Press.

Nussbaum, M. (1988), 'Nature, function, and capability: Aristotle on political distribution', *Oxford Studies in Ancient Philosophy*, Supplement: 145–184.

OHCHR (2012), 'Human rights indicators: a guide to measurement and implementation', United Nations, Unit of the Rights Commissioner, Geneva.

OPHI (2016), *Global Multidimensional Poverty Index Databank*, Oxford Poverty & Human Development Initiative (OPHI), University of Oxford.

Pantazis, C., Townsend, P. and Gordon, D. (2006), 'The necessities of life', in Pantazis, C., Gordon, D. and Levitas, R. (eds), *Poverty and Social Exclusion in Britain: The Millennium Survey*, Bristol: Policy Press, pp. 89–122.

Perry, B. (2002), 'The mismatch between income measures and direct outcome measures of poverty', Centre for Social Research and Evaluation, Ministry of Social Development, New Zealand.

Quinn, C. (2007), 'Using copulas to measure association between ordinal measures of health and income', HEDG Working Paper 07/24, University of York.

Raileanu Szeles, M. and Fusco, A. (2013), 'Item response theory and the measurement of deprivation: evidence from Luxembourg data', *Quality and Quantity*, 47: 1545. https://doi.org/10.1007/s11135-011-9607-x.

Ramos, X. and Silber, J. (2005), 'On the application of efficiency analysis to the study of the dimensions of human development', *Review of Income and Wealth*, 51(2): 285–309.

Ravallion, M. (2011), 'On multidimensional indices of poverty', *Journal of Economic Inequality*, 9(2): 235–248.

Rippin, N. (2010), 'Poverty severity in a multidimensional framework: the issue of inequality between dimensions', Courant Research Center, Discussion Paper No. 47, University of Göttingen.

Ruggeri Laderchi, C., Saith, R. and Stewart, F. (2003), 'Does it matter that we don't agree on the definition of poverty? A comparison of four approaches', QEH Working Paper Series 107, University of Oxford.

Sen, A.K. (1976), 'Poverty: an ordinal approach to measurement', *Econometrica*, 44(2): 219–231.

Sen, A.K. (1979), 'Issues in the measurement of poverty', *Scandinavian Journal of Economics*, 81(2): 285–307.

Sen, A.K. (1985), *Commodities and Capabilities*, Oxford: India Paperbacks.

Sen, A.K. (1993), 'Capability and wellbeing', in Nussbaum, M. and Sen, A. (eds), *The Quality of Life*, Oxford: Oxford University Press, pp. 30–66.

Silber, J. (2007), 'Measuring poverty: taking a multidimensional perspective', *Hacienda Publica Espanola*, 182(3): 29–73.

Social Protection Committee (2016), 'Social Protection Committee Annual Report 2016: review of the social protection performance monitor and developments in social protection policies', European Union.

Social Protection Committee Indicators Sub-Group (2015), 'Portfolio of EU Social Indicators for the Monitoring of progress towards the EU Objectives for social protection and social inclusion (2015 Update)', Brussels: European Commission.

Stiglitz, J.E., Sen, A. and Fitoussi, J.-P. (2009), 'Report by the Commission on the Measurement of Economic Performance and Social Progress'.

Thorbecke, E. (2008), 'Multidimensional poverty: conceptual and measurement issues', in Kakwani, N. and Silber, J. (eds), *The Many Dimensions of Poverty*, New York: Palgrave Macmillan, pp. 3–19.

TNS (2007), 'Poverty and social exclusion. Report on the Special Eurobarometer 279/ Wave 67.1', Brussels.

Tomlinson, M., Walker, R. and Williams, G. (2008), 'Measuring poverty in Britain as a multi-dimensional concept', *Journal of Social Policy*, 42(2): 215–233.

Townsend, P. (1979), *Poverty in the United Kingdom*, Hardmonsworth: Penguin Books.

Tsakloglou, P. and Papadopoulos, F. (2002), 'Aggregate level and determining factors of social exclusion in twelve European countries', *Journal of European Social Policy*, 12(3): 211–225.

Tsui, K.-Y. (2002), 'Multidimensional poverty indices', *Social Choice and Welfare*, 19(1): 69–93.

UNDP (2010), *Human Development Report 2010: The Real Wealth of Nations: Pathways to Human Development*, New York: Palgrave Macmillan.

Whelan, B. (1993), 'Non-monetary indicators of poverty', in Berghman, J. and Cantillon, B. (eds), *The European Face of Social Security: Essays in Honour of Herman Deleeck*, Aldershot: Avebury, pp. 24–42.

Willits, M. (2006), 'Measuring child poverty using material deprivation: possible approaches', Working Paper No. 28, Department of Work and Pensions.

World Bank (2017), 'Monitoring global poverty. Report of the Commission on Global Poverty', Washington, DC: World Bank Group.

7. Social exclusion: theoretical approaches
Luna Bellani and Alessio Fusco

7.1 INTRODUCTION

The sociological and socioeconomic literature has provided important contributions to the analysis of economic and social well-being. In this framework, a research strand aiming at measuring well-being not only on the basis of individuals' income, but directly through the observation of their living conditions and the strength of their link with the society, has emerged progressively since the 1970s. This includes the work of Townsend (1979) on multiple deprivation (see Chapter 5 by Chakravarty and Chattopadhyay, and Chapter 6 by Guio, in this *Handbook*), followed by, among others, the work of Paul Dickes (1989) on poverty of living conditions (see also Dickes et al., 1984), the important contribution of the Irish researchers from the Economic and Social Research Institute (ESRI) on the concept of consistent poverty (see Nolan and Whelan, 1996, 2011) or recent work within European task forces and networks on material deprivation (e.g., Guio, 2009; Fusco et al., 2010).[1] In parallel with these contributions, the concept of social exclusion, which is the topic of this chapter, slowly emerged. The exclusion of individuals from the minimum living standards of the society they belong to, and from participation in the life of the society, are key elements of these approaches. Social exclusion highlights the difficulties encountered by rich societies in sharing the fruits of their prosperity with all their members (Ringen, 1987).

The concept of social exclusion is quite broad. Despite being at the heart of many national and international debates, the borders of this concept are difficult to draw (Paugam, 1996a). For some researchers, this non-rigorous concept does not bring anything new and constitutes a 'catch-all' concept allowing analysis of a wide variety of phenomena such as poverty or deprivation (Levitas, 1996). For others, it is precisely the ambiguity of the topic to which social exclusion refers that makes its conceptualization difficult (Vleminckx and Berghman, 2001). The impact of the concept of social exclusion on the conceptualization of poverty within the European institutions has been important (Room, 1995).[2]

The aim of this chapter is to review the theoretical approaches of social exclusion. After explaining the context in which this concept emerged in the European Union institutional framework (section 7.2), the characteristics of social exclusion drawn from the sociological literature are presented (section 7.3) followed by the formalization of these characteristics with the economic axiomatic approach (section 7.4). Finally, section 7.5 concludes.

7.2   THE EMERGENCE OF THE SOCIAL EXCLUSION CONCEPT WITHIN THE EUROPEAN UNION

The sociological analysis of poverty comes back to the work of Simmel (1908) and highlights the link between individuals and the society. The concept of social exclusion was built around the French view of poverty which does not directly study the issue of poverty but analyses the link between a category of individuals (who can be labelled the poor) and the society.[3] The paternity of the term 'social exclusion' is usually attributed to René Lenoir (1974), a member of the French Government, who considered that France was threatened by internal disaggregation because of social exclusion. For Lenoir (1974), this term refers to individuals excluded from the welfare system because of various forms of maladjustment to society. At the European level, the concept of social exclusion became the reference paradigm for questions linked to poverty, but only after a long process. Indeed, in the early years of the European Communities, the social question was outranked by questions related to economic cooperation. As mentioned by Ferrera et al. (2002), the initial Treaties reflected the idea that economic growth would benefit all individuals through a trickle-down effect. The questioning of this principle led to a progressive transition from a purely economic and commercial cooperation to an entity also dealing with social issues. Indeed, the social dimension took on more importance in the European Union only in the 1970s, with the adoption by the European Commission in January 1974 of a Social Action Programme recognizing that the European Communities have an independent role to play in the building of social policies and proposing, in cooperation with the Member States, the implementation of specific measures to fight poverty (Atkinson et al., 2002; Marlier et al., 2007; Frazer et al., 2010).

Poverty is at the heart of the interest in social questions, which led to the devising of a set of specific programmes, known as the poverty programmes, the aim of which was to improve the knowledge and quantitative description of poverty. Despite modest funding, the three poverty programmes allowed poverty and policies aiming at its reduction to be placed on the European agenda (Alcock, 2006). The programme of Social Action Poverty 1 (1975–1981) was based on a small number of studies and pilot projects. At the end of this programme the European Commission estimated that there were 38 million poor people in Europe, on the basis of the official definition of poverty which stated that the poor are 'the individuals or families whose resources are so small that they are excluded from the minimum way of life in the country where they live' (Council, 1975). Starting with this programme, the social dimension received more attention on the European Union agenda. The second poverty programme (1985–1988) marked a major evolution in terms of concepts and definitions, with a slow move from the concept of poverty to the concept of social exclusion (O'Higgins and Jenkins, 1990; Hagenaars et al., 1994). At the beginning of this programme the 1975 definition was slightly modified, and according to Council (1985) the poor are the individuals whose resources (material, cultural and social) are so small that they are excluded from the minimum way of life in the country where they live. Compared to the 1975 definition, the 1985 definition shows an enlargement of the definition of poverty and clearly points to a multidimensional concept of poverty. Later on, researchers associated with the research programme Poverty 3 would consider that this enlarged definition of poverty points to the concept of social exclusion (Vleminckx and Berghman, 2001).

This first step toward the elaboration of the concept of social exclusion continued at the end of the 1980s with the adoption in the official language of the European Community of the term 'social exclusion' to replace the term 'poverty' in an official document. In reality, the adoption of this term has a political connotation and was done with the aim of replacing the term 'poverty' which was found by governments to be too accusatory for referring to the existing problems (Berghman, 1995; Room, 1995). From this moment on, the use of the term 'social exclusion' became more and more widespread in the official terminology of the European Union.

Following Poverty 2, the Poverty 3 programme (1989–1994) was launched with the aim to promote the economic and social integration of the least economically and socially privileged groups. The need to integrate the social dimension into the European construction was emphasized. A set of reasons were also advanced for the replacement of the term 'poverty' by 'social exclusion' in the conclusions to Poverty 3, where it is mentioned that the nature of poverty has changed since the mid-1970s. Social exclusion reflects the structural crisis of the society (Paugam, 1996b), and new phenomena such as urban crisis, homelessness, racial tensions, long-term unemployment and households' indebtedness are more visible. Poverty can no longer be seen as a residual or a simple lack of resources that can be solved automatically through economic growth. Its structural character and mechanisms must be acknowledged, as well as the multidimensional nature of the mechanisms that leads to exclusion of social exchanges, practices and rights that are intrinsic to the economic and social integration. Henceforth, transfer policies are not necessarily efficient and social policies must be rethought to renew the link between the individual and the society. As mentioned by Nolan and Whelan (1996, p. 189):

> talking of social exclusion rather than poverty highlights the gap between those who are active members of society and those who are forced to the fringes, the increasing risks of social disintegration, and the fact that, for the persons concerned and for society, this is a process of change and not a set of fixed and static situations.

The different poverty programmes allowed improvement of our understanding and ability to quantify poverty within the European Union beyond the income poverty paradigm. After that, the Treaty of Amsterdam in 1997 was the first communitarian treaty mentioning the fight against social exclusion (Ferrera et al., 2002; Atkinson et al., 2002), and the so-called Lisbon strategy gave further impetus to the European cooperation in the social domain. The Lisbon strategy was based on the strategic aim to become, within ten years (2000–2010), 'the most competitive and dynamic knowledge-based economy . . . with more and better jobs and greater social cohesion'. This goal made it necessary to have a global strategy aiming to promote economic and employment growth, and to combat social exclusion. It also introduced a specific approach in the treatment of the social dimension (the open method of coordination or OMC).[4] This incorporation of social inclusion among the explicit goals of the European Union constituted a major step in the importance given to the social dimension within the Union. This step was followed by the agreement at the Nice European Council in December 2000 on the community goals in terms of fighting poverty and social exclusion. In the original spirit of the Lisbon strategy, economic policies, employment policies and social policies were supposed to have the same importance. However, following a mid-term evaluation of the Lisbon process, the Lisbon strategy was refocused on growth and employment, while the social process was maintained but received less importance than the others. It should be noted that, within the OMC, high importance was given to the regular reporting on a set of social indicators, in order for each Member State to better compare their situation and exchange good practice in terms of devising and implementing social policy. The first list of indicators was defined in Laeken and regularly updated afterwards.

Since the end of the Lisbon strategy in 2010, the concept of social exclusion has also been fully integrated in the recently defined Europe 2020 strategy, the aim of which is for the European Union to become a smart, sustainable and inclusive economy (Frazer et al., 2010; Atkinson et al., 2017). This strategy includes a social inclusion target, which represents an important step forward in the EU political commitment to combat poverty and social exclusion. This target aims at reducing by 20 million the number of individuals at risk of poverty and social exclusion (AROPE). The AROPE target is based on a combination of three indicators: the number of people considered at risk of poverty, the number of materially deprived persons, and the number of people aged 0–59 living in 'jobless' households.

The evolution of the way social issues were handled in the European Union illustrates their increasing importance. Initially, they were neglected in favour of prioritizing economic considerations. They then took on increasing importance through the Poverty programmes until the Lisbon process and the Europe 2020 strategy where they are among the explicit goals of the European cooperation, together with economic growth and employment. The progressive enlargement of the definition of poverty through the different Poverty programmes pointed, in the early 1990s, to the need for the introduction of a new concept, the concept of social exclusion, the characteristics of which are explained in more details in the next section.

7.3   THEORETICAL APPROACH: THE SOCIOLOGICAL VIEW

Despite the importance of the concept of social exclusion and the numerous publications referring to it, the borders of this concept are difficult to trace (Silver, 1995; Paugam, 1996b; Atkinson, 1998a). In this section, we review the sociological and socioeconomic literature to identify the main characteristics of this concept which evolved over time. For Lenoir (1974), social exclusion refers to the social maladjustment of different groups of the population, and to those who do not benefit from the economic growth. Following the oil crisis of the 1970s, this reference to maladjustment was eclipsed by the appearance of the phenomenon of new poverty and precariousness. Many contributions, mainly in France, associated social exclusion with problems linked to unemployment, highlighting the importance of the situation on the labour market to explain situations of exclusion (Castel, 1995; Paugam, 1996c; Maurin, 2002). This narrower view on social exclusion was criticized (Atkinson, 1998a) and replaced, on the basis of European work at the beginning of the 1980s. Perhaps one of the most complete definitions of social exclusion is the one suggested by Vleminckx and Berghman (2001, p. 37): 'social exclusion could be defined as a concoction (or blend) of multidimensional and mutually reinforcing processes of deprivation, associated with a progressive dissociation from social milieu, resulting in the isolation of individuals and groups from the mainstream of opportunities society has to offer'. This definition highlights the notion of a *social link*, and suggests that social exclusion possesses a double nature: it refers to a *state of multidimensional disadvantage* but also to the *process* through which an individual progressively become marginalized.

The notion of a *social link* between the individual and the society is central to the concept of social exclusion and highlights the fundamentally relational aspect of this concept (Room, 1995; Sen, 2000).[5] The analysis of social exclusion is based on the notion of a group. A group is a set whose cohesion is directed by several rights and duties. Social exclusion is the process through which individuals are progressively being untied from this set. This process is sometimes referred to as the rupture of the social link, social disintegration or disaffiliation (Castel, 1995), social disqualification (Paugam, 1996c) or marginalization. At the national level, the question of the social link highlights the concept of national unity and citizenship, according to which exclusion or inclusion is to be defined (Silver, 1994, 1995). The question of poverty is then linked to the violation of the social rights linked to citizenship and to the lack of social integration (Shaffer, 2007).[6] Different views or paradigms on the organization of the society, of national identity or of political ideology, will result in different conception of social exclusion. For Silver (1995, p. 65), there are at least three such paradigms: 'solidarity', 'specialization' and 'monopoly':

> Each of the three paradigms attributes exclusion to a different cause, and is grounded in a different political philosophy: republicanism, liberalism or social democracy. Each provides an explanation of multiple forms of social disadvantage – economic, social, political, and cultural – and thus encompasses theories of citizenship and racial-ethnic inequality as well as poverty and long-term unemployment.

Without going into the details, it can be noted that the French conception of social exclusion highlights the notion of solidarity, while the Anglo-Saxon conception is more individualized (specialized) and materialistic:

> Anglo-Saxon sociological literature on 'social exclusion' often refers to the discourse of citizenship, participation, and partnership and is often characterised by a multidimensional approach; the French sociological discourse on 'social exclusion' is often associated with issues of identity, class, marginalisation, rupture and vulnerability. (Vleminckx and Berghman, 2001, p. 31)[7]

The emphasis on the link between society and the individual allows two conclusions to be reached. First, contrary to the ambiguity that might exist regarding the relative or absolute aspect of the poverty concept, social exclusion is inherently a relative concept (Paugam, 1996a; Atkinson, 1998a) and cannot accommodate an absolute version. To determine whether someone is excluded or not, reference should be made to a group or a community in a given place and time.[8] Second, while the poverty concept is centred around the individual and the resources that are at their disposal, the concept of social exclusion also takes into consideration the resources of the community an individual lives in: 'deprivation is caused not only by lack of personal resources but also by insufficient or unsatisfactory community facilities, such as dilapidated schools, remotely-sited shops, poor public transport networks and so on; indeed, such an environment tends to reinforce and perpetuate household poverty' (Room, 1995, p. 238). From a political point of view, this analysis highlights the importance of investing in community resources and not only targeting action on the households.

Social exclusion goes beyond the lack of financial resources and refers to a *state of disadvantage in different domains*, which bears some similarities with the concept of deprivation. As mentioned by de Haan (1999), 'the concept focuses on the multidimensionality of deprivation, on the fact that people are often deprived of different things at the same time. It refers to exclusion (deprivation) in the economic, social and political sphere' (see also Atkinson and Davoudi, 2000). Individuals can be excluded from different domains or dimensions of the society to which they belong, such as the labour market, the welfare state, access to education and health care, and so on. Vleminckx and Berghman (2001) mention that in the Poverty 3 programme, it was suggested that social exclusion had to be defined in terms of a failure of one or several of the following four systems: (1) the democratic and legal system, which promotes civic integration; (2), the labour market, which promotes economic integration; (3) the welfare state, which promotes social integration; and (4) family and communitarian systems, which promote interpersonal integration. The link with the society depends on these four complementary systems and determines different types of populations and difficulties according to their accumulation or not. The dimensions of social exclusion are interrelated. The exclusion in one dimension can lead to the exclusion in another one. Individuals can cumulate disadvantages. Low-skilled individuals are more likely to be unemployed or in precarious jobs which in turn may negatively affect their political power, social network and the quality of their interpersonal integration. Therefore, tackling social exclusion implies taking into account the complex interrelations among the various dimensions of this phenomenon.

The idea of *dynamic process* is the main feature of social exclusion. As mentioned by Room (1995, p. 237): 'it is not enough to count the numbers and describe the characteristics of the socially excluded; it is also necessary to understand and monitor the *process* of social exclusion and to identify the factors that can trigger entry or exit from situations of exclusion'. Indeed, the trajectories generated from the different social and economic forces leading to disaffiliation can be numerous and varied; the ability to explain the circumstances that will lead to poverty constitute a research priority in the field of social exclusion. Hence, as underlined by Giddens (1998, p. 104), 'exclusion is not about graduations of inequality, but about mechanisms that act to detach groups of people from the social mainstream'.

The multiplicity of processes, as well as the potential triggering factors and trajectories of the break of the social link, is not simple to measure. Different paths, coming from the interaction between individual personal characteristics and their environment, can lead to social exclusion. Hence, it is difficult to find a common structure, a pattern of social exclusion. Indeed, in the case of an erosion of resources, progressive or abrupt, triggered by a factor, individuals can be taken into 'spirals of precariousness' from which they cannot escape, and that lead them into situations of exclusion (Paugam, 1995, 1996c). At the end, individuals are trapped in their situation, unable to escape it by themselves and without any positive prospects (Vleminckx and Berghman, 2001). This last point corresponds to what Atkinson (1998a, p. 14) considers as primary in the situation of exclusion: 'people are excluded not just because they are currently without a job or income but because they have little prospects for the future'. This lack of positive prospects concerns not only individuals, but also their children, which highlights the possibility of intergenerational transmission of social exclusion.

The dynamic aspect of exclusion allows the study of the process of inter-temporal investment or disinvestment. The forms of capital at the disposal of individuals are investments of the past, and their analysis over time allows an understanding how situations of vulnerability arise and how the processes of erosion of these resources happen (Shaffer, 2007). For Walker (1995), there is a similarity between long-term income poverty and social exclusion: individuals experiencing long-term income poverty also have a low chance of escaping it, and then their link with society is weak. However, Atkinson (1998a) suggests that exclusion is not only long-term income poverty, which is one of the factors that leads to it. He considers that, in addition to being at the margin of the society, it is in the negation of the positive prospects of individuals that exclusion lies. Then, the role and aim of social policies change and are no longer limited to transfer policies, but include policies of activation, to promote access to public services, of social integration and against discrimination.

Another important question lies in the voluntary or involuntary nature of social exclusion. Indeed, social exclusion can be voluntary when individuals exclude themselves deliberately; or involuntary when it is not intentional (Giddens, 1998). In the first case, we can exclude ourselves from the labour market if we choose to live on social assistance; in the second case we can be excluded from the labour market or from access to credit as a result of the decisions of other individuals.[9] Atkinson (1998a, p. 14) highlights the importance of agency in the framework of social exclusion: 'In terms of failure to achieve the status of inclusion, we may be concerned not just with a person's situation, but also the extent to which he or she is responsible. Unemployed people are excluded because they are powerless to change their own lives'. In a similar way, Sen (2000) highlights the distinction between active and passive exclusion. When migrants are deprived of rights linked to the citizenship of their host country, exclusion is active, as it is the result of the decisions of another agent; when exclusion is not due to a deliberated act, for example in the case of unemployment in an economic recession, exclusion is passive.[10]

7.4 MEASUREMENT: THE ECONOMICS APPROACH

As far as the measurement of social exclusion is concerned, to the best of our knowledge two branches of contributions have emerged in the economic literature.[11] The first branch focuses on the empirical measurement of social exclusion. In this branch, Tsakloglou and Papadopoulos (2002), following the idea that social exclusion is a dynamic process generated by a state of multidimensional deprivation, first construct static indicators of deprivation in particular fields (income, living conditions, necessity of life and social relations). Then, they aggregate this information in order to obtain a static indicator of cumulative disadvantage. Finally, individuals at high risk of cumulative disadvantage in at least two out of three years are classified as being at high risk of social exclusion.

The second branch of the literature develops instead an axiomatic approach to the measurement of social exclusion. In this branch we have two theoretical contributions: Chakravarty and D'Ambrosio (2006) and Bossert et al. (2007). The first contribution by Chakravarty and D'Ambrosio (2006) proposes an index of social exclusion built on the definition of exclusion as lack of participation in social institutions, where this lack of participation is then operationalized as capability failures. An individual's capability failure is defined as the number of functionings from which the person is excluded over a certain period of time, and a weighted sum of these functionings failures describes what they call the individual deprivation score.

The social exclusion measure proposed is thus a function of the deprivation scores of different individuals in the society. More formally, they characterize the family of exclusion measures whose members satisfy normalization, monotonicity, subgroup decomposability, and have non-decreasing marginals. In practice, these measures are equal to 0 if nobody is socially excluded (normalization), increase if the deprivation score of a person increases (monotonicity), and according to subgroup decomposability, for any partitioning of the population with respect to some socioeconomic or demographic characteristic, they are equal to the sum, weighted by the population share, of the exclusion levels of each group. Finally, non-decreasingness of marginal social exclusion ensures that in aggregating individual deprivation scores into an overall indicator of exclusion, a higher deprivation score does not get a lower weight than a lower score.

The measure proposed considers the multidimensionality of the concept in constructing the individuals' capability failures, while the relativity of the concept is captured by the non-decreasing marginals' axioms. The dynamic aspect of social exclusion is embedded directly in the definition of the functioning failures. In the empirical application these are in fact constructed by using as the threshold being deprived for at least four years out of six.

The second contribution in this field is Bossert et al. (2007). Although sharing the same approach with the previous one, the commonalities between the two contributions are rather minor. Both assume functioning-failure profiles to constitute the primary inputs for the analysis, but Bossert et al. (2007), focusing on the dynamic aspects of social exclusion, define it as chronic relative deprivation in terms of functionings.[12] The individual index of social exclusion that they propose is given by the sum of individual deprivation measures weighed by the number of consecutive periods spent in deprivation. This weighting system is used in order to take into account the persistence of deprivation over time, so that a higher weight is given to consecutive periods in a state of deprivation than to isolated ones.

An aggregate measure of social exclusion is then characterized as the average of the individual levels of social exclusion. Again, more formally, Bossert et al. characterize an aggregate measure of social exclusion, which satisfies anonymous individual invariance, conditional exclusion additivity, exclusion identity and two-person one-period normalization with individual measures of social exclusion that satisfy single-period equivalence, temporal independence, conditional additive decomposability and conditional average decomposability.

The axioms imposed on the individual social exclusion measure are used to derive a particular way of taking into account persistence over time, which is peculiar to this contribution. In more detail: 'single-period equivalence' states that, if there is only one time period, the individual's social exclusion coincides with the individual's measure of deprivation. 'Temporal independence' requires the index to be insensitive with respect to the number of consecutive periods in which the set of those with fewer functioning failures is empty.[13] 'Conditional additive decomposability' requires that the measure of the individual's social exclusion is additively decomposable in any two-subset partition of the periods if the two components of the partition are separated by a period in which the individual has minimal functioning failure; while 'conditional average decomposability' ensures that the temporal pattern of the individual functioning failures is properly taken into consideration.

Thus, the aggregate measure of social exclusion proposed in this contribution depends on the individual levels of social exclusion only; and, moreover, the identities of the individuals are irrelevant ('anonymous individual invariance'), and if everyone in society experiences the same degree of social exclusion, then the aggregate level of social exclusion is equal to that value as well ('exclusion identity').

As mentioned above, these contributions, although based on the same type of approach (axiomatic), differ in many aspects. First of all they use a different definition of social exclusion: Bossert et al. start with the characterization of an index of deprivation, and they consider social exclusion as persistence in the state of deprivation; while Chakravarty and D'Ambrosio focus directly on social exclusion as lack of participation in social institutions. This also leads to a different definition of minimal deprivation in the society: while for Chakravarty and D'Ambrosio that minimal level is achieved when nobody is excluded from any functioning, in the Bossert et al. framework a minimal value of individuals' social exclusion is reached if everybody has the same number of capability failures, however small or large it may be. Furthermore, the way each contribution treats the central notion of persistence is an important distinguishing feature. The dynamic aspect of social exclusion in Chakravarty and D'Ambrosio is captured directly in the construction of the functioning failures; while Bossert et al. argue that social exclusion can be interpreted as persistence in the state of deprivation. As a consequence, the axiom systems and the characterizations of exclusion measures are very different, both conceptually and formally.

7.5 CONCLUSION

There is the traditional concept of poverty, which by now is restricted to denote a lack of disposable income, and there is the comprehensive concept of social exclusion, that refers to a breakdown of malfunctioning of the major societal systems that should guarantee full citizenship. Poverty, then, is part of – a specific form of – social exclusion. The latter is broader and should not necessarily encompass an element of poverty. In between poverty and social exclusion there is the concept of relative deprivation. In theory, relative deprivation is in line with the social exclusion concept; in practice, however, its operationalisation has generally rendered it a broader version of the poverty concept. (Berghman, 1995, p. 20)

The link between social exclusion and poverty is a widely debated topic. Indeed, if poverty and social exclusion, are not identical, they also bear similarities, and it is common to see them side by side in the expression 'poverty and social exclusion', even in the recently adopted Europe 2020 AROPE target. The use of this expression suggests that these 'almost twin' concepts are highly interrelated, but not synonymous (Abrahamson, 2002). As mentioned by Atkinson (1998a), some authors use them interchangeably, while others consider that they are clearly different (Berghman, 1995; Abrahamson, 2002). The origin of this situation lies in the parallel evolution of the traditions that tried to analyse these concepts, until the confrontation of these two fields of research at the European level allowed the elaboration of a wider framework of analysis (Room, 1995).

The concept of social exclusion is a multidimensional approach of persistent poverty which is essentially relative and based on the link between the individual and the society. Poverty and social exclusion are close but different concepts. While poverty focuses on distributional issues, social exclusion emphasizes relational aspects. Poverty character-izes individuals and households; while social exclusion characterizes their belonging to a group, justifying the integration of public resources in the analysis. Poverty is seen as a residual from market competition, while social exclusion is structural. Hence, in theory, social exclusion is a wider concept than poverty, and the analysis of poverty through the social exclusion concept allows us to take into account a wider range of resources to determine individual well-being.[14]

As underlined by Sen (2000), the added value brought about by the concept of social exclusion is not its novelty, but the cogency with which the relational aspect, trajectories and processes that can lead individuals into poverty is emphasized. Social exclusion also emphasizes the structural nature of the problem linked to social organization and to dis-crimination which some groups are exposed to. This emphasis on the notion of the group suggests a complementarity with the poverty approach.

ACKNOWLEDGEMENTS

This research has been supported by core funding for the Luxembourg Institute of Socio-Economic Research (LISER) from the Ministry of Higher Education and Research of Luxembourg and by funding from the Luxembourg Fonds National de la Recherche through an AFR postdoctoral grant for Luna Bellani and through the Luxembourg Fonds National de la Recherche CORE funding scheme project PersiPov (Contract C10/LM/783502) for Alessio Fusco.

NOTES

1.   See Fusco (2007) for an overview of material deprivation approaches, and other chapters in this *Handbook*.
2.   The concept of social exclusion mainly pertains to developed countries even if some contributions have tried to transpose it to developing countries (see, e.g., Rodgers et al., 1995; Saith, 2007).
3.   This line of research led to a large number of studies, especially in France, with the work of Bourdieu (1986, 1993), Paugam (1995, 1996a) on disqualification and Castel (1995) on disaffiliation (see Paugam, 2005, for an overview).
4.   The OMC is a mutual feedback process of planning, monitoring, examination, comparison and adjust-ment of national (and subnational) social policies, all of this on the basis of common objectives agreed for the European Union (EU) as a whole. The aim of this peer review exercise, which involves the European Commission and all 27 Member States, is to share experiences and practices with a view to reaching a greater convergence on key EU social protection and social inclusion objectives. Central to this frame-work is the definition of a list of commonly agreed indicators which follow a principle-based approach (Atkinson et al., 2002).
5.   Sen (2000) underlines that relational exclusions have both a constitutive importance and an instrumental importance. The constitutive importance highlights the importance of the situation of exclusion itself; it refers to the state of being excluded. The instrumental dimension highlights the contribution of the state of exclusion in the perpetuation of the situation of exclusion; it refers to the process. Exclusion from the labour market has a constitutive relevance and also contributes to the appearance of other forms of exclu-sion (instrumental importance).
6.   The notion of social rights goes back to the work of Marshall (1950) on citizenship and social class. At the national level, social exclusion can be understood as a violation of the rights of a citizen. As underlined by Vleminckx and Berghman (2001, p. 31), on the basis of Marshall's work, the 'progressive extension of civil,

then political and finally social rights, results in equal status, making citizenship the basis of social integration in capitalist societies'. Civil rights (individual liberty and freedom of expression, property rights, and so on), political rights (voting) and social rights are the three elements of citizenship. For Marshall, social rights refer to 'the right to a modicum of economic welfare and security, to fully share in the social heritage and to live the life of a civilized being according to the standards prevailing in society' (quoted by Vleminckx and Berghman, 2001: 32). This corresponds to the way Atkinson (1998b) justifies a study of poverty in terms of minimum rights.

7. The monopoly paradigm refers to the work of Weber and highlights the existence of hierarchical power relations in the constitution of social order. Hence, in this view that became widespread in Scandinavian countries and in the United Kingdom, monopoly is responsible for exclusion (de Haan, 1999).

8. In a horizontal vision of the stratification of society, the excluded are the outsiders who are located at the periphery, by contrast with the insiders who are located at the centre (Abrahamson, 2002).

9. With regard to the voluntary aspect of social exclusion, Burchardt et al. (1999, p. 229) suggest an operational definition of social exclusion: 'an individual is socially excluded if (a) he or she is geographically resident in a society but (b) for reasons beyond his or her control he or she cannot participate in the normal activities of citizens in that society and (c) he or she would like to so participate'.

10. Sen (2000) argues that denying immigrants the political right to vote through long and difficult procedures to acquire the citizenship of the host country is a form of active exclusion and makes their social integration harder.

11. A contribution somehow in-between these two approaches is Poggi (2007). In her paper, she derives a general class of social exclusion measures, identifying the socially excluded individuals using Sen's capability approach.

12. Refer to Chapter 15 in this *Handbook* on relative deprivation for a description of this deprivation index.

13. This is due to the way the deprivation measure is defined as product of two factors. One factor reflects the incapacity to identify with other members of society: the lack of identification. The second factor captures the aggregate alienation with respect to those who are better off.

14. In practice, it is not unusual to find papers that go beyond a definition of poverty as static, descriptive, unidimensional and narrowly based on financial resources. For example, Nolan and Whelan (1996) note that, if the research on poverty may have been 'guilty' of limiting the measurement of poverty to its static and income aspect, it does not mean that dynamic and multidimensional aspects were omitted in the conceptualization of this phenomenon. Conversely, Saunders (2003) saw it as ironic that the empirical literature looking at the measurement of social exclusion, with the exception of some works by Paugam (1995, 1996c), concentrated on the characteristics and conditions of individuals excluded in certain domains of life, rather than on the processes themselves.

REFERENCES

Abrahamson, P. (2002). 'Indicators for social inclusion: making a distinction between poverty and social exclusion', *Politica Economica*, 17(1), pp. 49–54.

Alcock, P. (2006). *Understanding Poverty*, 3rd edition, Palgrave Macmillan, London.

Atkinson, A.B. (1998a). 'Social exclusion, poverty and unemployment', in Atkinson, T., Hills, J. (eds), *Exclusion Employment and Opportunity*, CASE Paper no. 4, Center for Analysis of Social Exclusion, London, pp. 1–20.

Atkinson, A.B. (1998b). *Poverty in Europe*, Blackwell Publishers, Oxford.

Atkinson, A.B., Cantillon, B., Marlier, E., Nolan, B. (2002). *Social Indicators: The EU and Social Inclusion*, Oxford University Press, Oxford.

Atkinson, A.B., Guio, A.-C., Marlier, E. (2017). *Monitoring Social Inclusion in Europe*, Publication Office of the European Union, Statistical Books, Luxembourg.

Atkinson, R., Davoudi, S. (2000). 'The concept of social exclusion in the European Union: context, development and possibilities', *Journal of Common Market Studies*, 38(3), pp. 427–448.

Berghman, J. (1995). 'Social exclusion in Europe: policy context and analytical framework', in Room, G. (ed.), *Beyond the Threshold: The Measurement and Analysis of Social Exclusion*, Policy Press, Bristol, pp. 10–28.

Bossert, W., D'Ambrosio, C., Peragine, V. (2007). 'Deprivation and social exclusion', *Economica*, 74(296), pp. 777–803.

Bourdieu, P. (1986). 'Forms of capital', in Richardson, J. (ed.), *Handbook of Theory and Research for the Sociology of Education*, Greenwood Press, New York, pp. 241–258.

Bourdieu, P. (ed.) (1993). *La misère du monde*, Seuil, Paris.

Burchardt, T., Le Grand, J., Piachaud, D. (1999). 'Social exclusion in Britain 1991–1995', *Social Policy and Administration*, 33, pp. 227–244.

Castel, R. (1995). *Les Métamorphoses de la question sociale. Une chronique du salariat*, Paris: Fayard.
Chakravarty, S.R., D'Ambrosio, C. (2006). 'The measurement of social exclusion', *Review of Income and Wealth*, 52(3), pp. 377–398.
Council (1975). 'Council decision of 22 July 1975 concerning a programme of pilot schemes and studies to combat poverty', 75/458/EEC, OJEC, L199, Brussels.
Council (1985). 'Council decision of 19 December 1984 on specific community action to combat poverty', 85/8/EEC, OJEC, L2, Brussels.
de Haan, A. (1999). 'Social exclusion: towards a holistic understanding of deprivation', Villa Borsig Workshop, Series Inclusion Justice and Poverty Reduction.
Dickes, P. (1989). 'Pauvreté et conditions d'existence. Théories, modèles et measures', Document PSELL n°8, Walferdange, CEPS/INSTEAD.
Dickes, P., Gailly, B., Hausman, P., Schaber, G. (1984). 'Les desavantages de la pauvrete: définitions, mesure et réalités en Europe', *Mondes En Développement*, 12(45), pp. 131–190.
Ferrera, M., Matsaganis, M., Sacchi, S. (2002). 'Open coordination against poverty: the new EU social inclusion process', *Journal of European Social Policy*, 12(3), pp. 227–239.
Frazer, H., Marlier, E., Nicaise, I. (2010). *A Social Inclusion Roadmap for Europe 2020*, Antwerp: Garant.
Fusco, A. (2007). *La Pauvreté, un Concept Multidimensionnel*, Editions l'Armattan, Collection L'Esprit Economique, Paris.
Fusco, A., Guio, A.-C., Marlier, E. (2010). 'Characterizing the income poor and the materially deprived in European countries', in Atkinson, A.B, Marlier, E. (eds), *Income and Living Conditions in Europe*, OPOCE, Luxembourg, pp. 133–153.
Giddens, A. (1998). *The Third Way*, Cambridge Polity Press, Cambridge.
Guio, A.-C. (2009). 'What can be learned from deprivation indicators in Europe?', Eurostat methodologies and working papers, Eurostat, Luxembourg.
Hagenaars, A.J.M., de Vos, K., Zaidi, A. (1994). *Poverty Statistics in the Late 1980s: Research Based on Micro-Data*, Eurostat, Luxembourg.
Lenoir, R. (1974). *Les exclus. Un Français sur Dix*, Le Seuil, Paris.
Levitas, R. (1996). 'The concept of social exclusion and the new Durkheimian hegemony', *Critical Social Policy*, 46(14), pp. 5–20.
Marlier, E., Atkinson, A.B., Cantillon, B., Nolan, B. (2007). *The EU and Social Inclusion: Facing the Challenges*, Policy Press, Bristol.
Marshall, T.H. (1950). *Citizenship and Social Class and Other Essays*, Cambridge University Press, Cambridge.
Maurin, E. (2002). *L'égalité des Possibles. La Nouvelle Société Française*, La République des Idées, Seuil, Paris.
Nolan, B., Whelan, C.T. (1996). *Resources, Deprivation and Poverty*, Clarendon Press, Oxford.
Nolan, B., Whelan, C.T. (2011). *Poverty and Deprivation in Europe*, Oxford University Press, Oxford.
O'Higgins, M., Jenkins S. (1990). 'Poverty in the EC: 1975, 1980, 1985', in Teekens, R., van Praag, B. (eds), *Analysing Poverty in the European Community*, Eurostat News Special Edition 1-1990, Eurostat, Luxembourg, pp. 187–211.
Paugam, S. (1995). 'The spiral of precariousness: a multidimensional approach to the process of social disqualification in France', in Room, G. (ed.), *Beyond the Threshold: The Measurement and Analysis of Social Exclusion*, Policy Press, Bristol, pp. 49–79.
Paugam, S. (ed.) (1996a). *L'Exclusion. L'Etat des Savoirs*, Editions la Découverte, Paris.
Paugam, S. (1996b). 'Introduction. La constitution d'un paradigme', in Paugam, S. (ed.), *L'Exclusion. L'Etat des Savoirs*, Collection Textes à l'Appui, La Découverte, Paris, pp. 7–19.
Paugam, S. (1996c). 'Poverty and social disqualification: a comparative analysis of cumulative social disadvantage in Europe', *Journal of European Social Policy*, 6(4), pp. 287–303.
Paugam, S. (2005). *Les formes élémentaires de la pauvreté*, Collection le lien social, PUF, Paris.
Poggi, A. (2007). 'Does persistence of social exclusion exist in Spain?', *Journal of Economic Inequality*, 5(1), pp. 53–72.
Ringen, S. (1987). *The Possibility of Politics*, Clarendon Press, Oxford.
Rodgers, G., Gore, C., Figueiredo, J. (eds) (1995). *Social Exclusion: Rhetoric, Reality, Responses*, UNDP, International Institute for Labor Studies, Genève.
Room, G. (ed.) (1995). *Beyond the Threshold. The Measurement and Analysis of Social Exclusion*, Policy Press, Bristol.
Saith, R. (2007). 'Social exclusion: the concept and application to developing countries', in Stewart, F., Saith, R., Harriss-White, B. (eds), *Defining Poverty in the Developing World*, Palgrave Macmillan, Houndmills, pp. 75–90.
Saunders, P. (2003). 'Can social exclusion provide a new framework for measuring poverty', SPRC Discussion Paper No. 127.
Sen, A.K. (2000). 'Social exclusion: concept, application, and scrutiny', Social Development Paper No. 1, Asian Development Bank.

Shaffer, P. (2007). 'New thinking on poverty: implications for globalisation and poverty reduction strategies', DESA Working Paper series, United Nations Department for Economic and Social Affairs.

Silver, H. (1994). 'Social exclusion and social solidarity: three paradigms', *International Labour Review*, 133(5/6), pp. 531–578.

Silver, H. (1995). 'Reconceptualizing social disadvantage, three paradigms of social exclusion', in Rodgers, G., Gore, C., Figuereido, J. (eds), *Social Exclusion: Rhetoric, Reality, Responses*, UNDP, International Institute for Labor Studies, Genève.

Simmel, G. (1908). 'Der Arme', in Simmel, G., *Soziologie. Untersuchungen über die Formen der Vergesellschaftung*, Georg-Simmel-Gesamtausgabe Band 11, Frankfurt a.M., S. 512–555.

Townsend, P. (1979). *Poverty in the United Kingdom*, Penguin Books, Harmondsworth.

Tsakloglou, P., Papadopoulos, F. (2002). 'Identifying population groups at high risk of social exclusion: evidence from the ECHP', in Muffels, R.J.A., Tsakloglou, P., Mayes, D.G. (eds), *Social Exclusion in European Welfare States*, Edward Elgar Publishing, Cheltenham, UK and Northampton, MA, USA, pp. 135–169.

Vleminckx, K., Berghman, J. (2001). 'Social exclusion and the welfare state: an overview of conceptual issues and policy implications', in Mayes, D.G., Berghman, J., Salais, R. (eds), *Social Exclusion and European Policy*, Edward Elgar Publishing, Cheltenham, UK and Northampton, MA, USA, pp. 27–46.

Walker, R. (1995). 'The dynamics of poverty and social exclusion', in Room, G. (ed.), *Beyond the Threshold. The Measurement and Analysis of Social Exclusion*, Policy Press, Bristol, pp. 102–128.

8. Social exclusion: empirical findings
Bea Cantillon, András Gábos, Tim Goedemé and István György Tóth

8.1 INTRODUCTION

In recent decades, we have seen strong investment – both in Europe and elsewhere in the world – in the collection of data on the material and immaterial living conditions of individuals and the households to which they belong (see, among others, Stiglitz et al., 2009). Back in the 1980s, the Luxembourg Income Study (LIS) was the first project to allow cross-country comparison of such data from national sources. Thanks to the European Community Household Panel Survey or ECHP (which has since been superseded by the European Union Statistics on Income and Living Conditions or EU-SILC), there are now European data series based on largely harmonized survey methods.

The improved availability of data, the growing insights into the drivers of poverty and social exclusion, and increasing attention in society towards these issues as important dimensions of social progress have, in recent decades, paved the way for the development of sets of effective social indicators. The use of such indicators is now widely diffused. At the global level, institutions such as the World Bank and the United Nations Development Programme (UNDP) have developed indicators with a view to putting poverty on political agendas (such as the number of people living on less than US$1 a day, and the Sustainable Development Goals); in the EU, the Lisbon Agenda (2000–2010) linked the goals of enhancing social inclusion and combating poverty with those of achieving economic and employment growth, and in support of this process a set of social indicators was developed; more recently, the Organisation for Economic Co-operation and Development (OECD), the European Commission, the European Parliament, the Club of Rome and the World Wide Fund for Nature (WWF) have launched the 'Beyond GDP' initiative, which aims at 'developing indicators that are as clear and appealing as GDP [gross domestic product], but more inclusive of environmental and social aspects of progress. Economic indicators such as GDP were never designed to be comprehensive measures of prosperity and well-being' (see the Beyond GDP website[1]). Nationally, too, many governments are making efforts to develop indicators of, among other things, social exclusion (for example, Canada, the United Kingdom and Ireland). Increasingly, then, the notion is gaining ground that economic growth (especially as measured by GDP) should not be the only policy goal, and that situations where some population groups are excluded from the benefits of growth should be remedied through adequate policy making. In this context, statistical measures of social exclusion are of the greatest importance: it is crucial for countries to be able 'to assess their current performance according to an explicit set of criteria, to determine whether or not they are making progress in fighting poverty and social exclusion, and to compare the impact of different policy measures undertaken to promote social inclusion' (Atkinson and Marlier, 2010a).

We take the position of Vleminckx and Berghman (2001) referred to in Bellani's and Fusco's Chapter 7 in this *Handbook*, that social exclusion is an inherently ambiguous concept that cannot be operationalized unequivocally, as it is essentially a relative, graduated and multidimensional notion. Social exclusion is a relative notion, because it is defined in relation to the general level of the economic and social well-being in (a group of) countries or population groups at a given point in time. As such, social exclusion is a relative concept in two senses. First, what is regarded as an acceptable way of life depends largely on the reference group taken: is it the population within a given country, the EU as a whole, regional or local communities? The second sense in which social exclusion may be relative concerns the uprating of the standards over time. Income poverty thresholds may for instance be determined relative to current living standards, but in examining changes over time we may wish to scale by the overall increase in living standards, or to maintain it constant in purchasing power. Social exclusion is a graduated notion because it concerns many different circumstances, ranging from insecurity over exclusion from a minimal acceptable way of life, to situations of being entirely excluded from society, such as the homeless. Finally, social exclusion is multidimensional because it encompasses cumulative deprivation in relation to income, housing, education and health care.

In this chapter, we review empirical trends in social exclusion in Europe. We pay particular attention to the EU social indicators that are meant to measure social exclusion. We do so because these are the indicators that are most often used for evaluating policies directed at tackling social exclusion. More in particular, we focus on the at-risk-of-poverty indicator, which is a relative income poverty measure, the share of jobless households and material deprivation. The chapter begins with a brief introduction to the EU social indicators and how they relate to the concept of social exclusion. In section 8.3 we take a closer look at the levels and trends of these indicators: what do they tell us about the evolution of social inclusion within the Union? In addition, we look at how the indicators overlap and interact, both from a cross-sectional and a longitudinal perspective. Subsequently, we turn to the link with employment and redistribution, given that these are the two factors that policy makers promote most often for tackling social exclusion in Europe. Section 8.4 concludes.

8.2 THE EUROPE 2020 SOCIAL INCLUSION INDICATORS AND THE MEASUREMENT OF SOCIAL EXCLUSION

Even though social indicators were in use in several European social reports and the so-called 'poverty programmes' since the mid-1970s, there were no official indicators endorsed by the European Council. This changed in December 2001, when the European Council adopted 18 social indicators of poverty and social exclusion. In subsequent years, the portfolio of indicators was extended. One major change was the addition of an indicator of material deprivation in 2009 (European Commission, 2010). In June 2010 another important step was taken when the European Council defined a specific target in its Europe 2020 strategy: '20 million less [sic] people should be at risk of poverty and exclusion according to three indicators (at-risk-of-poverty; material deprivation; jobless household), leaving Member States free to set their national targets on the basis of the most appropriate indicators, taking into account their national circumstances and priorities' (European Council, 2010). Post-crisis, the eurozone has reinforced the methods of enforcing compliance with budgetary standards; chief amongst these changes are the Macroeconomic Imbalance Procedure (MIP). Additionally, the new overall governance framework for the EU, the European Semester, has added to the strength of supranational macroeconomic surveillance. More recently, the MIP was supplemented with some auxiliary social indicators, and the European Semester was complemented with social headline indicators (for example, unemployment levels and changes, and working-age poverty rates).

The definition of the Europe 2020 target is based on the union of three indicators of poverty and social exclusion: the low-income proportion (the at-risk-of-poverty indicator), an indicator of severe material deprivation and an indicator of the work intensity of the household. The target is defined as the absolute number of the population which is poor or socially excluded according to at least one of these three indicators.

Being at risk of poverty means living in a household with an equivalized net disposable household income below 60 per cent of the median equivalized net disposable household income of the country in which one lives. Disposable household income is equivalized using the modified OECD equivalence scale which attaches a weight of 1 to the first adult, a weight of 0.5 to all other household members aged 14 and over, and a weight of 0.3 to household members aged less than 14. The equivalized household income is obtained by dividing total disposable household income by the sum of the individual equivalence weights. All household members 'receive' the same equivalized household income. In other words, it is assumed that the living standard of all household members is the same (e.g., Atkinson et al., 2002; Marlier et al., 2007). In general, disposable income includes all income from all household members (wages, profits, property income, social benefits) minus social contributions and direct taxes. Property, imputed rent, production for own consumption, as well as most other income in kind is excluded from the income concept.[2]

Severe material deprivation is measured by an index of nine items related to financial stress and the enforced lack of some durables. All persons living in a household which at the moment of the interview lacks at least four out of nine items[3] are considered to be severely materially deprived. The list of items as well as the threshold is the same across all EU Member States (see Guio, 2009; Wolff, 2010). In May 2012, the Working Group on Living Conditions agreed to revise the list of deprivation items (Guio et al., 2012),[4] resulting in the change of the related parts of the EU-SILC questionnaire since 2015, and the switch to an alternative material deprivation indicator.

The third indicator relates to the work intensity of the household. It is calculated by adding up the total number of months all household members of working age have worked during the income reference period, expressed in full-time equivalents. This is divided by the total number of months they could have worked and for which information is available. If the ratio is below 0.20, the household is considered to have a very low work intensity. Persons aged 60 and over are not counted in this measure.

Obviously, the three indicators separately do not encompass the concept of social exclusion, as discussed in the accompanying theoretical Chapter 7 in this *Handbook*. The at-risk-of-poverty and low-work intensity indicators are one-dimensional measures, while material deprivation is focused on a very limited number of items that aim to capture one aspect of social exclusion, namely material well-being. Low work intensity adds one important dimension: work is important not only as a source of income, but also as a means to social participation and inclusion. In what follows, we not only focus on the three dimensions separately, but we also pay attention to the degree to which these various indicators overlap and people can be considered deprived in more than one dimension. As all three indicators relate to a specific status at one moment in time we also briefly review some recent evidence on the processes related to entering or exiting poverty, household joblessness and material deprivation.

The principal data source for calculating the EU social indicators is the EU Statistics on Income and Living Conditions (EU-SILC), a representative sample of persons living in private households in the EU Member States and several other countries. The data provide detailed information on income and living conditions and are collected from both survey data and register data, depending on the country. Variables are partially *ex ante*, partially *ex post* harmonized. Clearly, comparability could be improved in a non-negligible way if efforts for harmonization were increased (e.g., Glaser et al., 2015). In most countries, data are collected in accordance with a four-year rotational panel design, meaning that respondents stay in the sample for four years, while each year one-quarter of the sample is replaced by a fresh panel. This also allows data users to track changes within households over time, even though a four-year time window is rather limited. The European Commission has proposed to extend the panel duration to six years in its proposal for a regulation on a common framework for European statistics relating to persons and households (Atkinson et al., 2017). For more information on the EU-SILC, see Marlier et al. (2007), Atkinson and Marlier (2010b) and Decancq et al. (2014).

8.3   SOCIAL EXCLUSION IN EUROPE

8.3.1   Basic Trends

Innumerable studies have relied on these data in trying to chart and understand the phenomenon of social exclusion in a cross-national perspective: trends have been revealed; the size and composition of the groups of socially excluded have been compared; policy impacts have been examined; and the relationship between social exclusion on the one hand and social, demographic and economic changes on the other has been scrutinized. One of the facts to have been learnt from such studies is that the structure of poverty and social exclusion is quite similar in different countries: lone-parent households, low-skilled persons, migrants and social benefit claimants are invariably at greater risk of social exclusion. Between countries, there are substantial differences in levels of social exclusion, depending on the overall level of development, the scope and efficiency of social redistribution, the functioning of the labour market, and the socio-demographic composition of the population. In the new EU Member States, the proportion of the population with relatively low incomes decreased quite significantly in the years prior to the current financial crisis, as did the proportion of households with very low work intensity. However, the available data would appear to suggest that this progress has been wiped out by the major downturn that hit around the end of the first decade of the twenty-first century. The Scandinavian countries traditionally report the lowest poverty rates, but since the end of the 1990s they have experienced a persistent increase. The other European welfare

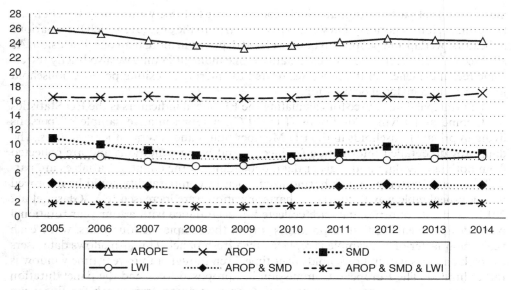

Source: Eurostat online database (accessed July 2016).

Figure 8.1   *Trends in the percentage at risk of poverty or social exclusion (AROPE), at risk of poverty (AROP), severe material deprivation (SMD) and low work intensity (LWI), as well as their intersections, EU-SILC 2005–2014, EU-27 weighted average*

states have exhibited a remarkable degree of stability: after the somewhat divergent movements of the 1980s, no further progress has been made in reducing poverty and social exclusion. Strikingly, many countries have seen a steady decline in poverty among elderly persons, but an increase in child poverty. While the chosen policy pathways may diverge, the driving factors behind poverty and social exclusion are invariably linked with evolutions in employment and how it is distributed between work-poor and work-rich families, as well as with the prevalence of in-work poverty and the effectiveness of social redistribution.

Figure 8.1 sheds some more light on recent trends in the Europe 2020 poverty reduction indicators, aggregated at the level of all EU Member States, except for Croatia (for which the time series is more limited). About 24 per cent of the EU population was at risk of poverty or social exclusion in 2014,[5] a reduction of about 1.5 percentage points since 2005, and an increase since 2009 of 1 percentage point. This is a sizeable share of the EU population. However, social exclusion is more about people combining different types of hardship. The percentage of the EU population experiencing both income poverty and material deprivation is much lower, around 4.5 per cent.[6] A little less than half of this group also experiences a very low household work intensity (remember that elderly persons are not included in this measure). Changes in the intersection of these measures have been much less pronounced compared to changes in the union. If we turn to the separate components, it is clear that the percentage at-risk-of-poverty remained stable

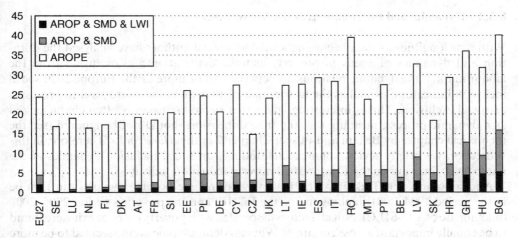

Notes: Bars are cumulative.
AT = Austria; BE = Belgium; BG = Bulgaria; CY = Cyprus; CZ = Czech Republic; DE = Germany; DK = Denmark; EE = Estonia; ES = Spain; FI = Finland; FR = France; GR = Greece; HR = Croatia; HU = Hungary; IE = Ireland; IT = Italy; LT = Lithuania; LU = Luxemburg; LV = Latvia; MT = Malta; NL = the Netherlands; PL = Poland; PT = Portugal; RO = Romania; SE = Sweden; SI = Slovenia; SK = Slovakia; UK = United Kingdom.

Source: Eurostat online database (accessed July 2016).

Figure 8.2 *At risk of poverty or social exclusion (AROPE), intersection of at risk of poverty (AROP) and severe material deprivation (SMD) and the intersection including very low work intensity (LWI), EU-SILC 2014*

until the crisis, and started to increase more recently. In contrast, severe material deprivation and low work intensity were substantially on the decline until 2008–2009, after which they increased again. In other words, Europe still has a long way to go to reach the Europe 2020 social inclusion target.

Obviously, levels of poverty and social exclusion differ markedly across countries. Figure 8.2 provides some more detail. Even though in purely monetary terms Romanian inhabitants are poorer (e.g., Decancq et al., 2014), the percentage of the population confronted with all three adverse situations captured by the Europe 2020 poverty reduction indicator is highest in Bulgaria, reaching 5 per cent of the population. It is lowest in Sweden, where an estimated 0.1 per cent of the population is confronted at the same time with income poverty, severe material deprivation and a very low work intensity. Notably, when focusing on the intersection of the three indicators, the geographical distribution is much less clear-cut than one would expect. This is somewhat less the case if we instead focus on just severe material deprivation and income poverty. Measured in that way, social exclusion is highest in Bulgaria, Romania and Greece, in which severe material deprivation has nearly doubled between 2008 and 2014. In contrast, it is lowest in the Scandinavian countries, Luxembourg and the Netherlands. The combination of severe material deprivation and AROP is also relatively prevalent in the other Southern European as well as Eastern European countries, except for Slovenia, the Czech Republic and Estonia (for further analysis, see Eurostat, 2014).

8.3.2   Dynamics and Interrelations at the Micro Level

With new longitudinal data becoming available, several authors have analysed the duration and dynamics of spells in poverty; material deprivation and exclusion from the labour market; the dynamic relationship between two or more of the Europe 2020 social inclusion indicators; as well as the factors that contribute at the micro level to processes of social exclusion. This is interesting, given that social exclusion is often characterized as a dynamic process, meaning that the time dimension should not be ignored (see the theoretical chapter by Bellani and Fusco, Chapter 7 in this *Handbook*). Therefore, in this subsection we briefly review some recent findings on social inclusion dynamics at the micro level, focusing on the Europe 2020 poverty reduction indicators.

Andriopoulou and Tsakloglou (2015) analysed income poverty dynamics in Europe in the period 1994–2001 (making use of the ECHP) and the pre-crisis period 2005–2008 (making use of EU-SILC). Not all factors associated with poverty entry or exit were found to be equally important across countries. Whereas demographic events seemed to be more strongly associated with poverty transitions in Northern European countries, income events – and in particular, changes in the household head's labour earnings – were found to be particularly important in the Mediterranean countries. Some factors associated with poverty transitions were found to be important in both periods, such as events associated with second earners (for example, finding a job or increasing earnings). Other factors played a more important role in one period than in another. For instance, demographic events were found to have a stronger effect for poverty entries in the pre-crisis period than in the 1990s, whereas for poverty exits demographic events seemed to be more important in the 1990s. Also quite notably, employment events were found to be more important for ending a poverty spell than unemployment events for starting a poverty spell. Finally, it should be stressed that apart from these general patterns, the authors found much heterogeneity in the relative importance of the factors that shape poverty transitions across European countries.

In another study, Ward and Ozdemir (2013) analysed the longitudinal EU-SILC data, spanning the 2007–2010 survey years, to assess the persistence of low work intensity. In particular, they defined persistent low work intensity as living in a household where the work intensity is below 20 per cent in the 2010 survey year and at least two out of three previous years. On average, about 8 per cent of the population was found to be living in a household confronted with persistent low work intensity. This is on average 65 per cent of the population confronted with a low work intensity in 2010. However, strong differences exist between countries, correlated to overall levels of low work intensity: the highest percentages were found in Belgium and the United Kingdom (about 12 per cent of the population below age 65), and the lowest in Luxembourg, Spain, Estonia and Latvia (all below 5 per cent). The authors also found that in all countries, those living in households with a persistent low work intensity have a substantially higher persistent risk of poverty than others of working age, emphasizing the importance of employment for avoiding persistently low income.

Papadopoulos and Tsakloglou (2015) also looked at persistent forms of social exclusion. In particular, they examined to what degree chronic forms of relative material deprivation overlap with long-term poverty at the micro level. They covered 22 European countries and tracked household situations between 2005 and 2008, also making use of the EU-SILC. Not very surprisingly, their analysis revealed very substantial cross-country differences in the population shares of those classified as being at high risk of chronic cumulative disadvantage. The highest levels of aggregate risk of chronic relative material deprivation were recorded in some countries of Southern and Central-Eastern Europe, and the Baltic countries, and the lowest in a number of Northern and continental European countries, broadly in line with what we find with the EU indicator of severe material deprivation. Concomitantly, the overlap between chronic material deprivation and income poverty varies strongly across countries. Even though the overlap between both indicators is considerable everywhere, it is not complete. This indicates that both forms of adverse conditions refer to distinct phenomena. The authors also identify the risk factors of chronic relative material deprivation and chronic income poverty: in almost all countries that they included in the analysis, a lack of full employment at the individual level, having low educational qualifications, being a member of a lone-parent household or living in a household headed by a woman, led to higher risks of chronic relative material deprivation and longitudinal poverty.

Finally, on the basis of longitudinal EU-SILC data for eight EU Member States related to the period between 2004 and 2010, Ayllón and Gábos (2017) studied to what extent being at risk of poverty, being severely materially deprived or living in a household with low work intensity in one year is related to being in the same status one year later ('state dependence'), and whether being in a given status predicts the occurrence of one of the others in subsequent periods ('feedback effects'). Of the three forms of hardship, material deprivation is the phenomenon least affected by state dependence, and low work intensity is most affected. In terms of feedback effects between poverty and material deprivation, the authors find clear evidence of a feedback loop only in the Central-Eastern European countries, where both phenomena reinforce each other. However, they do not observe these effects in other countries. Feedback effects between other pairs of indicators were also found in some countries, but the pattern is much more diverse. Having a low work intensity status today was much more strongly associated with income poverty or material deprivation at the moment of observation rather than having consequences later. Employment policies that reduce low work intensity clearly fight poverty in the first instance, but also severe material deprivation, via current effects.

8.3.3 Employment, Social Protection and Poverty Before, During and After the Crisis[7]

Much of the European discourse on social inclusion and the reduction of poverty has emphasized the link between employment and social exclusion. Therefore, in this section we briefly elaborate on the link between the two factors, and how this is mediated by social transfers. Indeed, the level of household income and consequently the risk of poverty is most directly determined by the labour market attachment and the earning capacity of household members on the one hand, and by the welfare state-provided social transfers on the other hand. The mechanisms of how changes in individual employment and in the social benefit system translate into changes in poverty outcomes are complex (Cantillon and Vandenbroucke, 2014). First, while employment is an individual-level concept, decisions related to labour market participation are often made at household level, jointly with or conditioned on the similar decisions of other household members, and often together with decisions on demographic outcomes, such as leaving the parental home, cohabitation, marriage, childbearing, and care for dependent household members (e.g. Becker, 1981; Del Boca, 2002). Further, poverty and social exclusion are household-level concepts and the link with employment should be made at household level as well. Depending on how the newly evolving jobs are distributed across households according to their work intensity and what the underlying dynamics of this process are, changes in the overall risk of income poverty may differ strongly; also, the design of and the changes in the welfare benefit system contribute to variances between member states (Marx et al., 2013).[8] In the following, we deal with both factors – employment and social transfers – but not all channels through which they exert their effect on poverty will be discussed here.

One of the key issues concerning the Europe 2020 targets relates to the relationship between employment and poverty. Employment growth became one of the priorities of the Lisbon agenda in 2000. The strategy envisaged that employment and economic policies should raise the employment rate[9] to as close to 70 per cent as possible by 2010 and, as part of that goal, they should increase the employment rate for women to more than 60 per cent by the same year. In early 2010, the European Commission launched the Europe 2020 strategy, to support recovery from the crisis and to set out where the EU wants to be by 2020. In order to monitor the progress, the Commission proposed a set of headline targets for the EU, including a new employment target: namely that 75 per cent of the population aged 20–64 should be in employment by 2020.

While many countries failed to meet the employment target, the pre-crisis Lisbon era was generally marked by an increase in employment rates. According to the Eurostat data, the employment rate of the EU-27 working-age population (15–64 years) in 2010 was 64.1 per cent, 1.9 percentage points higher than in 2000, but still close to 6 percentage points short of the Lisbon target of 70 per cent. This gap was partly due the unfavourable economic situation observed in almost all countries during 2009 and 2010. If the employment peak of 65.8 per cent from 2008 were used as a benchmark, the gap would be smaller, but would still exist. However, the relative success in employment (especially before the economic crisis) did not bring about corresponding massive drops in poverty rates: in the EU-27 countries the at-risk-of-poverty rate stayed practically unchanged between 2005 and 2010 (16.5 per cent), with a slight increase (from 15.7 per cent to 16.4 per cent) in the EU-15, according to the Eurostat data based on the EU-SILC.[10] This fact provoked studies expressing disappointment regarding the poverty reduction capacity of employment growth and of social expenditure (Cantillon et al., 2014; Marx et al., 2013; Corluy and Vandenbroucke, 2014; Hills et al., 2014).

Cantillon et al. (2014) describe that the disappointing trends of the poverty standstill (no decline or even increase in times of employment growth) can be largely attributed to the deteriorating efficiency of the social protection systems of the European welfare states. Their analysis (based on combined ECHP and EU-SILC data for the period 1995–2008) points out that in the Nordic welfare states (mostly as a result of loosening social safety nets) the decline of pre-transfer poverty – that followed employment growth – was cancelled out by a decline in the poverty-reducing effect of cash transfers. This was also found in most of the Continental countries. Job polarization and an increase in the number of persons living in jobless households resulted in an increase of pre-transfer poverty in the Southern European countries. This could not be fully compensated by a small improvement in poverty reduction efficiency of social transfers. In the new Member States, the decreasing poverty trends could by and large be associated with the fact that additional employment (where it existed) strongly benefited the work-poor households.

8.3.4   Trends in National Employment and Poverty, 2005–2012/13

Data on individual employment trends (annual average of employment rate for age 20–64, percentage, men and women together), on poverty trends (AROP(a)[11] for age group 20–59) and on pre-transfer AROP(a) rates (preAROP(a)[12]) are also shown in Figures 8.3–8.7. The countries in the figures are grouped by the similarities of the employment trajectories they present. We differentiate between five distinct country groups, according to the time trends in individual employment patterns.

Group A (see Figure 8.3) includes Greece, Spain, Cyprus, Bulgaria, Ireland, Slovenia and Portugal. These member states are characterized by increasing employment among the active age population in the first half of the period in analysis. After reaching its peak in 2008 (2007 in Spain), a large drop in employment started and continued, with no signs of recovery until 2013 (2012 in Ireland). Poverty rates in countries belonging to Group A have shown no change until the breakout of the crisis, but being on the rise right after.[13] Employment and poverty trends seem to co-move very strongly in this group. The country by country presentations in Figure 8.3 show mirrored trends for these two indicators.[14]

In Group B (see Figure 8.4), showing trends for Slovakia, Denmark, Italy, the Netherlands, Sweden, Hungary and Finland, the employment drop around 2008 was also measurable; however, it did not seem to be followed by a long-term declining trend. The paths these countries followed after 2008 are not uniform, though. Some (Sweden and Hungary, for example) show recovery by 2012; others seemed to stagnate (Slovakia and Finland after 2010), and some (such as Italy) were on a slight decline afterwards. Trends of poverty rates in Group B vary to a great extent, although an increasing trend can be observed in all of them but the Netherlands during the crisis period. They were on the rise in Finland, Sweden and Denmark; showed a U-shape in Slovakia, Hungary and (in some periods) in Italy; and they seemed to stagnate in the Netherlands. The mirrored trends of employment and poverty seem to be prevalent here as well, with the exception of the Finnish data between 2005 and 2008, when both employment and poverty were on the rise.[15]

Group C (Figure 8.5) contains the three Baltic countries: Estonia, Latvia and Lithuania. Within this group there is a continued employment growth between 2006 and 2008, followed by a large drop in the two years afterwards. Between 2011 and 2013 a quick recovery of labour markets can be seen, reaching the start levels (2005) by 2013. Poverty rates are relatively high and fairly volatile in Group C. The volatility in Lithuania is unusually high. In some periods (most notably in 2010 and 2011 in Estonia and Latvia), poverty was on the rise in periods of employment expansion. The most important finding in this group is that the period between 2008 and 2012 witnessed a special non-linearity: employment first declined and then increased within the same period. This warrants care in analysing time trends in two subsequent periods. We suggest for this group the separation of periods the 2008–2010 and 2010–2012 when further analysis is carried out.

In Group D (Figure 8.6), showing data for Malta, Poland, Germany and Austria, employment never really declined throughout the period (except a slight drop in Poland between 2009 and 2010). There are, however, differences between these four countries.

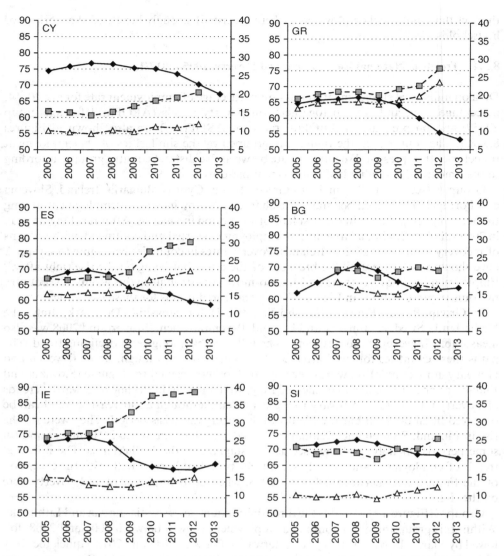

Notes: Cross-sectional waves for years 2005 until 2012 were used. Data for 2012 are subject to revisions in subsequent releases; data for Bulgaria and Romania are available from 2007 onwards; data for Malta are available from 2009 onwards.
In the EU-SILC, the income reference year is the calendar year preceding the survey year (excepting Ireland and the UK, where the 12-month period prior to the interview consists the reference period).
Years displayed in our graphs are survey years, similarly to the Eurostat protocol.

Source: Employment rate: Eurostat Statistical Database, AROP(a), preAROP(a): own calculations based on EU-SILC.

Figure 8.3   *Country-specific presentations of employment (left axis) and AROP(a) (right axis) trends in countries with large continued drop after 2008 (Group A) (squares: preAROP(a), triangles: AROP(a), diamonds: employment), (%)*

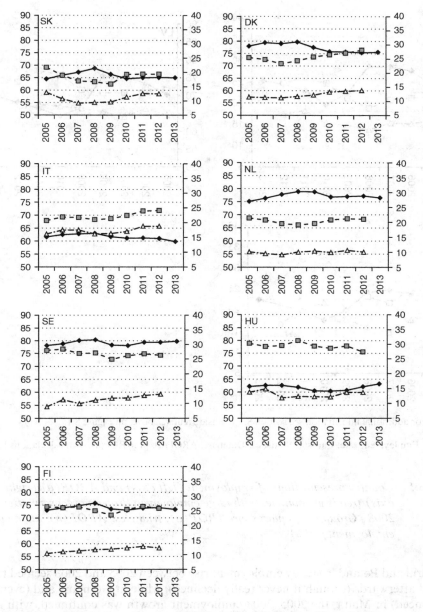

Note: For additional information see section 8.3.1 'Basic Trends', above, on Figure 8.1.

Source: Employment rate: Eurostat Statistical Database, AROP(a), preAROP(a): own calculations based on EU-SILC.

Figure 8.4   *Country presentations of employment (left axis) and AROP(a) (right axis) trends in countries with slight employment drop (with or without recovery) after 2008 (Group B) (squares: preAROP(a), triangles: AROP(a), diamonds: employment), (%)*

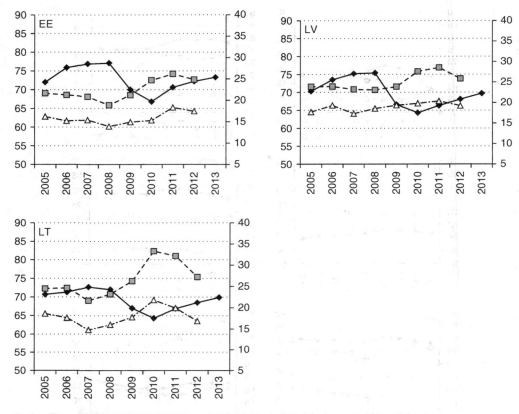

Note: For additional information see section 8.3.1 'Basic Trends', above, on Figure 8.1.

Source: Employment rate: Eurostat Statistical Database, AROP(a), preAROP(a): own calculations based on EU-SILC.

Figure 8.5   Country presentations of employment (left axis) and AROP(a) (right axis) trends in countries with large employment drop and recovery after 2008 (Group C) (squares: preAROP(a), triangles: AROP(a), diamonds: employment), (%)

In Austria and Poland, a steady employment rise between 2005 and 2008 seemed to have stopped afterwards (though it never really declined); while in Germany and (even more pronounced) in Malta, the 2005–2008 employment growth was continued, with a relatively strong further employment growth after 2010. Poverty trends mirror employment trends in Poland, follow employment trends in Germany, and do not seem to change between 2005 and 2011 in Austria (though in the most recent year a large increase was measured by the first release of the EU-SILC 2012), when countries in Group D are analysed. The Malta series is shorter than the others, making it difficult to observe trends.

Finally, in Group E (Figure 8.7), comprising Belgium, the Czech Republic, France,

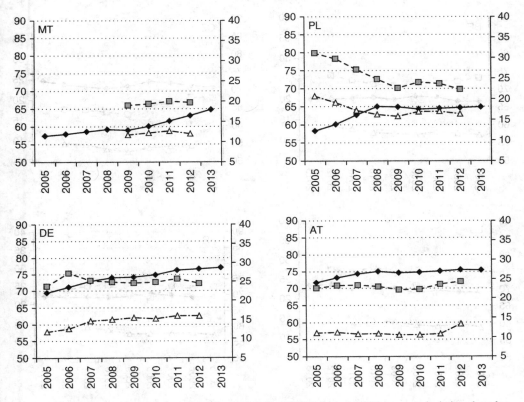

Source: Employment rate: Eurostat Statistical Database, AROP(a), preAROP(a): own calculations based on EU-SILC.

Figure 8.6 *Country presentations of employment (left axis) and AROP(a) (right axis) trends in countries with longer employment increase periods with no drops (Group D) (squares: preAROP(a), triangles: AROP(a), diamonds: employment), (%)*

Luxembourg, Romania and the United Kingdom, only slight changes (as compared to the first four country groupings) are observed in employment trends. For poverty, we see diverse trends in Group E. In Romania and in the Czech Republic, longer decline spells (2007–2010 and 2005–2009, respectively) of poverty were followed by a sharp increase afterwards (in 2011–2012 and 2010–2012, respectively). In Belgium, Luxembourg and the United Kingdom, similarly small changes in employment figures were accompanied by only relatively small changes in poverty over time. In France, a stable employment rate was paralleled by a rising trend of poverty.

To summarize the above trends differently: we have seen that relatively larger changes in employment seem to have been accompanied by reverse trends in poverty rates: when employment increases, poverty declines in most of the cases. However, trends of poverty under no change in employment regimes turn out to be very heterogeneous, perhaps

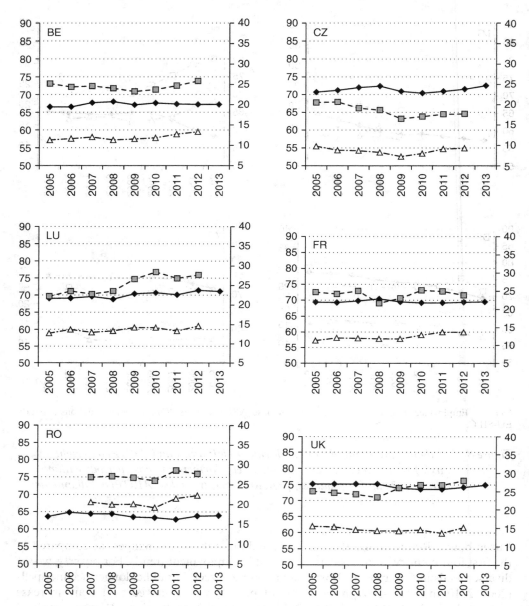

Source: Employment rate: Eurostat Statistical Database, AROP(a), preAROP(a): own calculations based on EU-SILC.

Figure 8.7   Country presentations of employment (left axis) and AROP(a) (right axis) trends in countries where there was no substantial change in employment rate throughout the period (Group E) (squares: preAROP(a), triangles: AROP(a), diamonds: employment), (%)

due to different policies in labour markets and in social transfers. Also, the elasticity of poverty change to employment seems to vary in different countries.

The magnitude of the correlation between employment and poverty is estimated by Gábos et al. (2015). According to their panel regression estimates, pre-transfer poverty to employment elasticity has been 60 per cent, whereas post-transfer poverty to employment elasticity has been around 25 percent on average, in the EU in the period between 2004 and 2012. The elasticity of the employment–poverty ratio, while it looks sizeable for the whole sample on average, seems to have some variations across countries and periods. The authors' estimates show that the relationship between employment and post-transfer poverty does not differ significantly across the pre-crisis and the crisis periods.

8.3.5   A Counterfactual Analysis of the Poverty Reduction Effect of National Social Expenditures

To consider now the relationship and joint development of AROP(a) rates and preAROP(a) rates, we turn back for a moment to Figures 8.3–8.7. As seen there, in some of the countries (see Greece and Bulgaria), the differences between AROP(a) rates and preAROP(a) rates are relatively small; while in other countries (Ireland and Slovenia, for example) they are much larger. This can be taken as a measure of the extent of the social redistribution in the given countries. Also, the distance between AROP(a) and preAROP(a) is not necessarily constant over time. In some countries (such as Greece, Bulgaria and Slovenia), the two lines seem to go in parallel; while in others (such as Ireland, Cyprus and Spain) they seem to start diverging after the breakout of the crisis.

To measure the distance in the at-risk-of-poverty rate before and after social transfers (excluding pensions),[16] the standard measure of withdrawal rates, defined as the difference between AROP(a) and preAROP(a), expressed in percentage of the preAROP(a) rates, can be applied here. The following formula is used,

$$PRI = (preAROP(a)\text{-}AROP(a))/preAROP(a)*100,$$

where PRI stands for Poverty Reduction Index. This is, of course, a counterfactual, symbolizing (but, due to arising endogeneities and behavioural reactions, not 'measuring') the effectiveness of social expenditures in reducing poverty. The time trend of PRI for the Member States (organized into the structure of our country grouping introduced in section 3.3.1) is shown in Table 8.1.

At the beginning of the crisis (2008), PRI was the highest (above 50 per cent) in the Nordic countries (Denmark, Sweden and Finland), in Belgium, Ireland, Austria, the Czech Republic, Hungary and Slovenia; but also high in France and the Netherlands (between 45 per cent and 50 per cent in 2008, but higher than 50 per cent before that). Half of these countries belong to group B (slight employment drop after 2008), but they also represent groups A (large continued drop in employment after 2008) and E (no substantial change in employment), as well as D (longer employment increase periods with no drop), but the latter only by Austria. If we look at the trends for the entire period (2005–2012), the majority of these countries experienced a significant decrease in PRI, with the important exception of Ireland. In some countries, the poverty reduction effect of the social transfers fell between 2005 and 2012 by more than 10 per cent (Belgium, Austria,

Table 8.1 Poverty Reduction Index of social expenditures in the EU Member States, 2005–2012 (%)

		2005	2006	2007	2008	2009	2010	2011	2012	2008/2005	2012/2008
	BG	–	–	15.3	24.3	22.0	28.8	21.3	22.2	–	0.92
	CY	34.1	35.8	34.9	33.0	41.4	38.7	42.9	41.8	0.97	1.27
	ES	22.2	21.6	21.2	22.4	24.0	29.3	29.5	27.4	1.01	1.22
A	GR	14.1	12.5	13.6	13.6	12.8	14.0	13.1	13.9	0.96	1.02
	IE	42.4	46.2	52.8	58.3	62.9	63.6	63.2	61.5	1.38	1.05
	PT	29.1	31.4	31.6	30.7	30.8	36.9	33.9	33.3	1.06	1.08
	SI	56.4	55.1	56.18	52.0	54.5	53.2	49.8	52.0	0.92	1.00
	DK	54.9	54.4	51.9	51.9	52.6	49.8	49.8	50.8	0.95	0.98
	FI	60.3	57.7	57.0	53.1	49.3	51.5	51.6	52.3	0.88	0.99
	HU	54.6	49.3	60.0	60.7	58.4	57.7	53.5	50.0	1.11	0.82
B	IT	21.9	20.0	19.4	23.0	23.6	24.1	21.5	22.1	1.05	0.96
	NL	52.8	54.1	53.3	47.5	46.9	52.4	49.9	52.3	0.90	1.10
	SE	68.2	60.5	63.2	59.1	52.8	54.8	52.7	50.1	0.87	0.85
	SK	40.5	43.5	45.8	43.7	39.6	41.5	35.3	35.5	1.08	0.81
	EE	25.2	28.5	26.2	26.3	29.8	38.0	30.0	29.8	1.04	1.13
C	LT	24.1	28.5	31.7	31.0	32.3	34.5	38.1	38.0	1.29	1.23
	LV	25.9	19.3	25.5	19.7	19.0	28.2	28.6	25.5	0.76	1.29

	AT	50.8	51.8	53.7	52.5	52.3	52.4	53.9	44.8	1.03	0.85
D	DE	50.3	53.7	41.7	39.3	36.6	38.3	37.7	34.6	0.78	0.88
	MT	-	-	-	-	38.4	37.0	36.5	39.1	-	-
	PL	33.5	35.8	36.5	34.6	30.3	29.66	28.40	26.8	1.03	0.77
	BE	55.2	52.4	51.2	53.0	50.4	50.3	48.5	48.6	0.96	0.92
	CZ	52.4	57.4	54.6	55.7	56.1	53.1	48.3	47.5	1.06	0.85
	FR	54.0	50.1	52.1	45.4	48.6	48.8	45.0	42.6	0.84	0.94
E	LU	42.5	41.7	42.9	43.2	46.5	50.1	50.2	47.2	1.02	1.09
	RO	-	-	23.2	26.3	24.8	26.2	24.5	19.4	-	0.74
	UK	38.3	37.9	40.2	39.2	45.3	45.9	49.1	46.0	1.02	1.17

Note: AT = Austria; BE = Belgium; BG = Bulgaria; CY = Cyprus; CZ = Czech Republic; DE = Germany; DK = Denmark; EE = Estonia; ES = Spain; FI = Finland; FR = France; GR = Greece; HU = Hungary; IE = Ireland; IT = Italy; LT = Lithuania; LU = Luxemburg; LV = Latvia; MT = Malta; NL = the Netherlands; PL = Poland; PT = Portugal; RO = Romania; SE = Sweden; SI = Slovenia; SK = Slovakia; UK = United Kingdom.

Source: Own calculations based on EU-SILC. Data for Malta are missing for 2005–2008 and observations for Romania and Bulgaria are missing for 2005 and 2006.

Finland), or even by 20 per cent or more (as in France and Sweden). In general, this drop in effectiveness was an almost continuous trend (especially in Belgium, Denmark and Sweden), but the crisis made a real difference between dynamics before and after 2008.[17] In some countries, such as the Czech Republic, Hungary[18] and Austria, a distinctive U-shape is visible: the pre-crisis period was characterized by a pick-up in PRI values with a significant fall afterwards (otherwise, similar to Slovakia or Poland). To the contrary, in France, Slovenia and Finland (as well as in Germany), the loss in the poverty reduction effectiveness took place in the pre-crisis period, while no significant change occurred in the crisis period. We notice here that in Ireland, having one of the highest PRIs in 2008, the distance between AROP(a) and preAROP(a) increased significantly (by 45 per cent) throughout the whole period, mainly due to strong improvement between 2005 and 2008 (38 per cent), followed by a much smaller increase afterwards (5 per cent).

The lowest PRIs in 2008 were observed in the Mediterranean countries (Greece, Spain, Italy, Cyprus and Portugal), in the Baltic States, as well as in some other new Member States (Bulgaria, Poland and Romania); the poverty reduction effect of social transfers in all these countries being near one-third or below. According to the individual employment trends, these countries belong mainly to groups A and C (large employment drop and recovery after 2008). Also, one may observe that in many of these member states, the effectiveness of the social transfers improved between 2005 and 2012. This is especially the case of Lithuania (by 58 per cent), Cyprus (24 per cent), Spain (23 per cent), the United Kingdom (21 per cent) and Portugal (14 per cent), while in the other member states no significant change between the 2005 and 2012 levels was observed. The Greek case is a specific one, where the poverty reduction index levelled during the whole period was analysed at a very low rate: 13–14 per cent.

Looking at PRI trends in the pre-crisis and the crisis period from another point of view, the picture is very mixed. In countries belonging to the groups with clearly negative employment outcomes (A and B), PRIs improved or did not change significantly before the crisis. This holds for all the countries in groups A and B, except the Nordic member states, where PRI decreased in both of the periods. Also, a large drop in PRI was observed in the Netherlands before the crisis, and in Slovakia after the crisis. In countries from groups D and E (good or relatively good employment outcomes between 2005 and 2012), with the exception of Luxembourg and the United Kingdom, the PRI decreased or did not change significantly in either of the periods. We need to mention that there were two countries – the Netherlands and, more interestingly, Latvia – where the poverty-reducing capacity of social expenditures seemed to deteriorate during the crisis shocks, but then it improved and reached the pre-crisis levels.

Summarizing our findings related to PRI (see Table 8.2), one may observe that in countries with high poverty reduction effects of social transfers by 2008, the poverty alleviation capacity of cash benefits either diminished or levelled between 2008 and 2012. Half of the countries with medium PRI, however, did seemingly make greater efforts to compensate the negative effects of the crisis via income redistribution. In these countries, poverty trends were mixed: in the Netherlands the poverty rate stayed unchanged; in Cyprus and the UK it increased significantly, but not greatly. In Estonia and Lithuania, the volatility of the poverty rates was very high in this period, as were individual employment rates. In some other countries with a medium level of PRI, no sizeable change in the poverty reduction effect of transfers could be observed. Countries with a low PRI level show dif-

Table 8.2   EU Member States' classification according to the poverty reduction effects of social transfers

PRI in 2008	Increase between 2008 and 2012	No sizeable change between 2008 and 2012	Decrease between 2008 and 2012
High PRI	–	Ireland, Denmark, Finland, Slovenia, Belgium	Hungary, Sweden, Austria, the Czech Republic
Medium PRI	Cyprus, Estonia, Lithuania, the Netherlands, the UK	Portugal, (Malta), France, Luxembourg	Slovakia, Germany,
Low PRI	Latvia, Spain	Greece, Bulgaria, Italy	Romania, Poland

Note: High PRI: PRI in 2008: >50%, Low PRI in 2008: <25%. Increase between 2008 and 2012: increase in PRI value by at least 10%. Decrease between 2008 and 2012: decrease by at least 10%.

Source: Own classification based on figures in Table 8.1.

ferent patterns in the crisis period: Latvia and Spain increased the effectiveness of poverty reduction, while in Romania and Poland PRI diminished by one-quarter compared to the 2008 levels.

All in all, it can be concluded that public social expenditures remained an important factor in the fight against poverty. However, the effectiveness of social systems declined in the crisis years in many countries, mostly in those where the poverty reduction index was high before the crisis (such as in Austria, the Czech Republic, Hungary and Sweden) but not only there (see, for example, Poland and Romania, where the pre-crisis poverty alleviation performance was low and even decreased between 2008 and 2012).

8.4   CONCLUSIONS

Although social policy making has been informed by social indicators for a considerable time – at both the European and other levels – and despite the regular publication of and political debate over league tables and targets, combined with growing insight into the relationship between policy making and policy outcomes, we have witnessed little progress in the promotion of social inclusion over the past ten years. Notwithstanding some areas of success, the overall conclusion must be that, even before the crisis, levels and trends in social exclusion in Europe were disappointing, especially if we focus on those at risk of poverty. The lack of substantial progress in the fight against social exclusion stands in stark contrast to the ambitious policy goals formulated by the EU. Moreover, since the crisis, severe material deprivation and low work intensity have increased again. Whereas the situation has worsened since the crisis, in many countries, the most important drivers of increasing poverty among the working-age population are the increase in the share of jobless households and a marked increase in their poverty risk. Yet, it would not be warranted to conclude that these trends are just transitory, merely related to the crisis. They were indeed already observable before the crisis: at that time in many countries' work-poor households benefited less from job growth while the poverty-reducing capacity of social protection decreased to the detriment of especially these households. This indicates severe and increasing structural difficulties to reduce poverty and social exclusion. Undoubtedly, external inegalitarian forces such as globalization, technological progress and individualization are to a large extent accountable for downward pressures on low-paid work and consequential social protection (see, e.g., Cantillon et al., 2015; OECD, 2011).

Today, the large heterogeneity within the EU is growing and endangers its social model. The current 'soft' governance of 'social Europe' has not brought us closer to the EU-level poverty reduction targets or social convergence. Without denying the importance of the current social *acquis*, we need new ways to think about 'social Europe'. So far, efforts by the EU to eradicate poverty and social exclusion have failed, both on a substantive level and on a governance level. The substantive shift towards activation and more inclusive labour markets has not resulted in lower poverty rates (Cantillon, 2011). The current *social acquis*, which is open and flexible, lacks the necessary bite to truly address growing incapacities of national welfare states. A more forceful and effective application of social indicators requires a clarification of the underlying normative assumptions, as well as a better understanding of the relationship between policy design and outcomes, in conjunction with a more substantial investment in indispensable statistical capacity. These would be important steps to define indicators and targets that could be more helpful for successfully monitoring and tackling social exclusion in Europe.

NOTES

1. http://ec.europa.eu/environment/beyond_gdp/background_en.html (accessed 16 October 2017).
2. The impact of imputed rent on poverty and inequality estimates has been studied by, among others, Frick and Grabka (2003), and Sauli and Törmälehto (2010). The measurement and impact of including production for own consumption is discussed in Paats and Tiit (2010). Brandolini et al. (2010) employ an even wider income concept: they focus on the total net worth, which takes account of as many assets and debts as possible. For an exercise including services as income in kind, see Verbist (2011) and Verbist and Matsaganis (2014).
3. The household: (a) has been in arrears on mortgage, rent payments, utility bills, hire purchase instalments or other loan payments over the last 12 months; (b) does not have the capacity to afford paying for one week's annual holiday away from home; (c) does not have the capacity to afford a meal with meat, chicken, fish or vegetarian protein equivalent every second day; (d) does not have the capacity to face unexpected financial expenses equal to the at-risk-of-poverty threshold (monthly average) estimated on the basis of the EU-SILC of two years ago; (e) cannot afford to keep the home adequately warm; (f) does not have a telephone because it cannot afford it; (g) does not have a colour TV because it cannot afford it; (h) does not have a washing machine because it cannot afford it; and (i) does not have a car because it cannot afford it.
4. The items on durables (excepting the car) were dropped from the list and seven new items were added (Guio et al., 2012, pp. 13, 68). Among these new items, two are measured at household level: the household: (a) does not have a computer and internet because it cannot afford it; and (b) does not have the capacity to replace worn-out furniture. The five additional items are measured at individual level. The household is considered as deprived if at least half of the adults (persons aged 16 or over); (c) do not have the capacity to replace worn-out clothes by some new (not second-hand) ones; (d) do not have two pairs of properly fitting shoes (including a pair of all-weather shoes) because they cannot afford it; (e) cannot afford to spend a small amount of money each week on themselves; (f) cannot regularly participate in a leisure activity such as sport, cinema, concert because they cannot afford it; (7) cannot get together with friends and family (relatives) for a drink or meal at least once a month because they cannot afford it. For register countries there is only one respondent for the questions asked at the individual level. In these cases, the value of the respondent's answer is applied to all household members.
5. Note that the data mix information on 2013 (especially income and work intensity) and 2014 (in particular demographic information and material deprivation). In the text, we refer to the survey year.

6. For a more detailed analysis of the intersection between material deprivation and income poverty (also called 'consistent poverty') see, for instance, Whelan and Maître (2010) and Kis and Gábos (2015).
7. The empirics of this section is derived from Gábos et al. (2015). For more conclusions based on the same working paper see also Gábos et al. (forthcoming).
8. Corluy and Vandenbroucke (2014) provide an insight into the effects of unequal distribution of employment over households in the EU Member States between 1995 and 2008. They find that in most of the countries, the actual household joblessness rate was higher in both 1995 and 2008 than would be expected on the basis of a random distribution.
9. Employment rate is defined as the number of persons in employment as a percentage of the population of working age (20–64 years). The indicator is based on the EU Labour Force Survey (EU-LFS), a large individual sample, in which all definitions apply to persons aged 15 years and over living in private households. Persons carrying out obligatory military or community service are not included in the target group of the survey, as is also the case for persons in institutions or collective households such as boarding houses, halls of residence and hospitals. The employed population consists of those persons who did any work for pay or profit for at least one hour during the reference week, or were not working but had jobs from which they were temporarily absent.
10. There are no consistent figures for the at-risk-of-poverty rate for the Lisbon era (2000–2010). The reason for this is the shift in the data source from the European Community Household Panel (ECHP) survey to the EU-SILC in the case of the EU-15 Member States during the first half of the 2000s. The EU-10 new Member States are part of the EU-SILC from its start. Overall, 2005 is the first survey year for which figures are available of all the EU-25 countries (Bulgaria and Romania joining the EU-SILC in 2007).
11. AROP(a) refers to at-risk-of-poverty rate of the active-age population. Headcount of individuals (aged 20–59) whose income falls below the at-risk-of-poverty threshold is established as 60 per cent of median equivalent income of total population. It should be noted that throughout this chapter we use the notation AROP(a) instead of AROP, to inform the reader that the population in analysis are those aged 20–59.
12. preAROP(a) is the pre-transfer poverty rate and represents the at-risk-of-poverty rate calculated by removing all active-age cash benefits (except pensions) from household incomes.
13. The question emerges of why the decline in poverty rates in Greece, Slovenia and Bulgaria continued after 2008. Perhaps it is due to the fact that in the EU-SILC we have survey years, meaning that the survey year 2008 refers to incomes received by the households in 2007. Alternatively, the explanation can lie in the fact that the effects of the crisis may have reached these countries somewhat later than the other countries.
14. Exceptions being poverty rates in Bulgaria in 2011 and in Slovenia in 2009. Given the fact that these two data points seem to be bumps in trends, one might rather suspect some accidental phenomena or some data problems.
15. Data problems are to be suspected in 2006 for both Sweden and Hungary.
16. All active-age cash benefits accruing to individuals aged 20 to 59; that is, unemployment benefits, sickness/invalidity pay, social assistance, family-related allowances and/or housing allowances (pensions excluded). Social transfers refer to the per capita amount of the benefits, originally measured on a household level.
17. Indicated by the two last columns of Table 8.1.
18. A suspicious jump in the 2006 Hungarian poverty figures is most likely due to data error.

REFERENCES

Andriopoulou, E. and Tsakloglou, P. (2015). Mobility into and out of poverty in Europe in the 1990s and the pre-crisis period: the role of income, demographic and labour market events. Antwerp: Herman Deleeck Centre for Social Policy, University of Antwerp.

Atkinson, A.B., Cantillon, B., Marlier, E. and Nolan, B. (2002). *Social Indicators: The EU and Social Inclusion*. Oxford: Oxford University Press.

Atkinson, A.B., Guio, A.-C. and Marlier, E. (eds) (2017). *Monitoring Social Inclusion in Europe*. Luxembourg: Publications Office of the European Union.

Atkinson, A.B. and Marlier, E. (2010a). *Analysing and Measuring Social Inclusion in a Global Context*. New York: United Nations.

Atkinson, A.B. and Marlier, E. (eds) (2010b). *Income and Living Conditions in Europe*. Luxembourg: Publications Office of the European Union.

Ayllón, S. and Gábos, A. (2017). The interrelationships between the Europe 2020 poverty and social exclusion indicators. *Social Indicators Research*, 130(3), 1025–1049.

Becker, G.S. (1981). *A Treatise on Family*. Cambridge, MA: Harvard University Press.

Brandolini, A., Magri, S. and Smeeding, T.M. (2010). Asset-based measurement of poverty. *Journal of Policy Analysis and Management*, 29(2), 267–284.

Cantillon, B. (2011). The paradox of the social investment state: growth, employment and poverty in the Lisbon era. *Journal of European Social Policy*, 21(5), 432–449.

Cantillon, B., Collado, D. and Van Mechelen, N. (2015). The end of decent social protection for the poor? The dynamics of low wages, minimum income packages and median household incomes. Antwerp: Herman Deleeck Centre for Social Policy – University of Antwerp.

Cantillon, B., Van Mechelen, N., Pintelon, O. and Van den Heede, A. (2014). Social redistribution, poverty and the adequacy of social protection. In B. Cantillon and F. Vandenbroucke (eds), *Reconciling Work and Poverty Reduction: How Successful are European Welfare States?* (pp. 157–184). Oxford: Oxford University Press.

Cantillon, B. and Vandenbroucke, F. (2014). *Reconciling Work and Poverty Reduction: How Successful are European Welfare States?*. Oxford: Oxford University Press.

Corluy, V. and Vandenbroucke, F. (2014). Individual employment, household employment, and risk of poverty in the European Union: a decomposition analysis. In B. Cantillon and F. Vandenbroucke (eds), *Reconciling Work and Poverty Reduction: How Successful are European Welfare States?* (pp. 94–130). Oxford: Oxford University Press.

Decancq, K., Goedemé, T., Van den Bosch, K. and Vanhille, J. (2014). The evolution of poverty in the European Union: concepts, measurement and data. In B. Cantillon and F. Vandenbroucke (eds), *Reconciling Work and Poverty Reduction in Europe: How Successful are European Welfare States?* (pp. 60–93). Oxford: Oxford University Press.

Del Boca, D. (2002). The effect of child care and part time opportunities on participation and fertility decisions in Italy. *Journal of Population Economics*, 15(3), 549–573.

European Commission (2010). *ISG Activity Report 2009*. Brussels: European Commission.

European Council (2010). European Council 17 June 2010 Conclusions. Brussels: European Council.

Eurostat (2014). Luxembourg: Publication Office of the European Union.

Frick, J.R. and Grabka, M.M. (2003). Imputed rent and income inequality: a decomposition analysis for Great Britain, West Germany and the US. *Review of Income and Wealth*, 49(4), 513–537.

Gábos, A., Branyiczki, R., Lange, B. and Tóth, I.G. (2015). Employment and poverty dynamics in the EU countries before, during and after the crisis. ImPRovE Working Paper 15/06, Antwerp: Herman Deleeck Centre for Social Policy – University of Antwerp. http://improve-research.eu/?wpdmact=process&did=Nz QuaG90bGluaw==.

Gábos, A., Branyiczki, R., Lange, B. and Tóth, I. (forthcoming), Employment and poverty dynamics in the EU countries before, during and after the crisis. In B. Cantillon, T. Goedemé and J. Hills (eds), *Decent Incomes for the Poor: Improving Policies in Europe*. Oxford: Oxford University Press.

Glaser, T., Kafka, E., Lamei, N., Lyberg, L. and Till, M. (2015). European comparability and national best practices of EU-SILC: a review of data collection and coherence of the longitudinal component. Vienna: Statistics Austria.

Guio, A.-C. (2009). What can be learned from deprivation indicators in Europe? Eurostat Methodologies and Working Papers. Luxembourg: Office for Official Publications of the European Communities.

Guio, A.-C., Gordon, D. and Marlier, E. (2012). Measuring material deprivation in the EU. Indicators for the whole population and child-specific indicators. Eurostat Methodological and Working Papers. Luxembourg: Publications Office of the European Union.

Hills, J., Paulus, A., Sutherland, H. and Tasseva, I. (2014). *A Lost Decade? Decomposing the Effect of 2001–11 Tax-Benefit Policy Changes on the Income Distribution in EU Countries*. Antwerp: Herman Deleeck Centre for Social Policy, University of Antwerp.

Kis, A.B. and Gábos, A. (2015). Consistent poverty across the EU. Antwerp: Herman Deleeck Centre for Social Policy – University of Antwerp.

Marlier, E., Atkinson, A.B., Cantillon, B. and Nolan, B. (2007). *The EU and Social Inclusion: Facing the Challenges*. Bristol: Policy Press.

Marx, I., Horemans, J., Marchal, S., Van Rie, T. and Corluy, V. (2013). Towards a better marriage between job growth and poverty reduction. Amsterdam: AIAS.

OECD (2011). *Divided We Stand: Why Inequality Keeps Rising*. Paris: OECD Publishing.

Paats, M. and Tiit, E.-M. (2010). Income from own-consumption. In A.B. Atkinson and E. Marlier (eds), *Income and Living Conditions in Europe* (pp. 179–194). Luxembourg: Publications Office of the European Union.

Papadopoulos, F. and Tsakloglou, P. (2015). Chronic material deprivation and long-term poverty in Europe in the pre-crisis period. Antwerp: Herman Deleeck Centre for Social Policy – University of Antwerp.

Sauli, H. and Törmälehto, V.-M. (2010). The distributional impact of imputed rent. In A.B. Atkinson and E. Marlier (eds), *Income and Living Conditions in Europe* (pp. 155–178). Luxembourg: Publications Office of the European Union.

Stiglitz, J.E., Sen, A. and Fitoussi, J.-P. (2009). Report by the Commission on the measurement of economic performance and social progress. Paris: INSEE.

Verbist, G. (2011). The 'forgotten' income component? The inequality effect of including the value of public services in the income concept. *Reflets et perspectives de la vie économique*, 50(4), 169–178.

Verbist, G. and Matsaganis, M. (2014). The redistributive capacity of services in the EU. In B. Cantillon and F. Vandenbroucke (eds), *Reconciling Work and Poverty Reduction in Europe: How Successful are European Welfare States?* (pp. 185–211). Oxford: Oxford University Press.

Vleminckx, K. and Berghman, J. (2001). Social exclusion and the welfare state: an overview of conceptual issues and policy implications. In D.G. Mayes, J. Berghman and R. Salais (eds) *Social Exclusion and European Policy* (pp. 27–46). Cheltenham, UK and Northampton, MA, USA: Edward Elgar Publishing.

Ward, T. and Ozdemir, E. (2013). Measuring low work intensity – an analysis of the indicator. Antwerp: Herman Deleeck Centre for Social Policy – University of Antwerp.

Whelan, C.T. and Maître, B. (2010). Comparing poverty indicators in an enlarged European Union. *European Sociological Review*, 26(6), 713–730.

Wolff, P. (2010). 17% of EU Citizens were at-risk-of-poverty in 2008 (No. 9/2010). Luxembourg: Eurostat.

9. Poverty over time: theoretical approaches
Michael Hoy and Buhong Zheng

9.1 INTRODUCTION

The importance of time in poverty measurement has recently received its due attention from researchers. In his ground-breaking work on poverty measurement, Sen (1976) pointed out the deficiency of official poverty measures and laid out the fundamentals for a more comprehensive analysis of poverty. In the early stages of the poverty measurement literature, the objective (understandably) was to understand the notion of poverty and to delineate the ideal properties that a poverty measure should possess. To that end, researchers limited their attention to static poverty measurement; that is, measuring poverty over a single time period and restricted to a single dimension of well-being (usually income or consumption). All individuals were also assumed to be homogenous except for the chosen dimension. After three decades of research, we now have a comprehensive understanding of the issues in static poverty measurement. This large literature has identified a set of key axioms for poverty measurement and developed classes of sophisticated poverty measures in the context of a static or single period environment.[1]

Although the inadequacy of omitting other dimensions of well-being and the dynamic aspect of poverty over time were well recognized as important problems, only in the last decade or so have these issues become major topics of research in poverty measurement. When multidimensionality and the time factor are incorporated into poverty measurement, as expected, the picture once again becomes quite complicated. Now even the answer to the basic issue of 'who is poor?' is no longer straightforward. In the case of unidimensional (income/consumption) poverty measurement for a single time period, a person is classified poor if his income or consumption falls below a pre-established poverty line (although exactly to determine the line may not be that simple). This is the so-called focus axiom. If a person's poverty status depends on multiple dimensions such as income and health or multiple periods of time, then it is no longer a simple dichotomous choice of a person being above or below the poverty line. It is questionable whether the focus axiom, which is central to Sen's pioneering approach, should be applied separately to each element being measured or to some aggregate value of the entire range of measurement. In these more complex environments, we must decide how to aggregate deprivation across several dimensions or many time periods as well as across individuals in coming to a measure of poverty for a society as a whole. In the case of static, unidimensional poverty measurement, (absent any income transfers) a non-poor individual does not affect the poverty deprivation of any other (unrelated) poor individual. In other words, there are no poverty interactions (mitigation or aggravation) from people above the poverty line when aggregating poverty for a population; poverty measurement is about those who are poor. In contrast, for a given individual who may live some periods in poverty and some periods out of poverty, it is not convincing that we ought to adopt the same types of aggregation arguments from an intrapersonal perspective. The assessment of an individual's poverty over his lifetime depends on his experience in periods of poverty *and* depends to some degree on his experience in periods spent out of poverty. The specific pattern of those experiences matters as well.

This is to say that an individual's lifetime poverty experience resulting from time spent in poverty may be mitigated by episodes of being well-off. This is not to say that he transfers his income or consumption from well-off periods to the poverty periods, but rather his suffering of deprivation in periods of poverty can be soothed somewhat by his contentment of good days spent out of poverty. A person who has spent a great deal of his previous years in poverty may be more vulnerable to a current year in poverty and suffer more than someone who experiences poverty only for that year. Besides the frequency of poverty spells within an individual's lifetime, the pattern may also matter. Consider two individuals who have spent the same number of years in poverty over their lifetimes. If one individual's pattern of poverty spells were consecutive or bunched closely together, we may consider this person to have had a worse poverty experience than if the same number of poverty experiences were spread out more evenly over his lifetime. The concern with chronic poverty is long-standing (e.g., Godley, 1847, p. 2). However, only recently have axiomatic treatments of lifetime or dynamic poverty measures been explored.

Our goal in this chapter is to review the ongoing debate about what should matter in defining, conceptualizing and measuring intertemporal or lifetime poverty and how to best capture those characteristics that do impact on lifetime poverty experiences.[2] For example, there are strong differences of opinion on whether the extent to which a person's income exceeds the poverty line when a person experiences periods of relative affluence should compensate for periods when a person does experience poverty. Also, although it is widely accepted that chronic poverty is a serious concern when judging the impact of poverty spells experienced by individuals, there have been several alternative specifications on how to incorporate this aspect into a lifetime poverty measure. This literature on developing formal or axiom-based measures of inter-temporal or lifetime poverty is mostly recent but growing quite rapidly. We hope that this review will enhance further developments in this important area of poverty measurement research.

Our focus is to review the literature that proposes how to conceptualize or develop specific measures of inter-temporal or lifetime poverty. We address alternative perspectives about how one should take into account the frequency and pattern of episodes of poverty (and non-poverty) over a person's lifetime when measuring the impact on that person's lifetime well-being from a perspective of social deprivation. In doing so, we recognize that it is too early in this literature to come to a consensus on choosing from among the various proposed measures. However, we hope that our review helps to direct questions in moving forward.

We acknowledge that measurement issues that arise in empirical applications are very important when choosing a specific measure or even a general approach to measuring lifetime poverty. Panel data, for example, typically involve a relatively small fraction of consecutive years of people's lives. We leave such concerns about data availability aside for the most part as we believe it is important first to sort out what is most relevant to take into account when developing measures of intertemporal or lifetime poverty before adopting such measures for empirical application.

In section 9.2 we present a set of axioms which capture the various approaches to intertemporal or lifetime poverty measurement in this budding literature. We then, in section

9.3, review a subset of the papers that have proposed specific combinations and variants of these axioms. Our selection is not exhaustive but rather we choose those papers that we believe best illustrate the various approaches that have been taken to measure lifetime poverty. In section 9.4 we provide some remarks about the approaches taken thus far and make suggestions for future development of this literature.

9.2   AXIOMS

Suppose an individual lives through T periods of time and, judged by his consumption, he is poor for some periods and is not poor for the other periods.[3] How should one assess his poverty level over his lifetime? Putting this more abstractly, given a lifetime consumption profile $\mathbf{x} = (x_1, x_2, \ldots, x_T)$, what is the the poverty level associated with $\mathbf{x}$? In measuring poverty, an income level must be identified as the poverty line which decides whether the individual has, in any given period, experienced poverty or nonpoverty. It is reasonable to imagine that the poverty line may not be identical in every period of time. For simplicity, however, we assume that the poverty line remains constant at a consumption level z over the T periods. Consequently, we may denote the lifetime poverty of $\mathbf{x}$ as $P(\mathbf{x}; z)$. We assume that all issues surrounding the measurement of poverty in each time period are settled. Poverty in each period t is measured by $p_t \equiv p(x_t; z)$, $t = 1, \ldots, T$, and the individual deprivation function $p(\cdot;\cdot)$ satisfies the usual conditions of *continuity*, *focus*, *monotonicity* and *transfer* established in the static poverty measurement literature (e.g., Zheng, 1997).

Throughout the chapter we present simple numerical examples to illustrate axioms. In some instances it is useful to use income profiles while in other cases we adopt the commonly used normalized poverty gaps,[4] which we will call a (lifetime) poverty profile, $\mathbf{p}$. For example, if the poverty line is $z = 10$, the income profile $\mathbf{x} = (5, 12, 1, 15, 20)$ generates the poverty profile $\mathbf{p} = (\frac{1}{2}, 0, \frac{9}{10}, 0, 0)$. Using $\mathbf{p}$ rather than $\mathbf{x}$ to capture lifetime poverty is appropriate only if one restricts the measure of lifetime poverty to be independent of income levels in non-poverty periods. Doing so rules out any possible mitigation effects. In such cases we can write $P(\mathbf{x}; z) = P(\mathbf{p})$. However, if one wishes to allow for mitigation effects, the vector $\mathbf{p}$ will typically ignore important information.

In the context of lifetime poverty measurement, it is useful to define poverty spells and non-poverty spells. A poverty spell consists of consecutive poverty periods or a block of poverty in which the individual lives below the poverty line for the entire duration of time. A non-poverty spell consists of consecutive non-poverty periods. The goal of measuring $P(\cdot;\cdot)$ is to incorporate the levels of poverty and possibly non-poverty of these different spells into a single poverty value for the entire T periods. In what follows we critically review some of the major axioms that have been proposed on $P(\cdot;\cdot)$. We also take into account any single (isolated) period of poverty or non-poverty as a trivial spell.

The first axiom on $P(\cdot;\cdot)$ is a common regularity condition in almost all poverty and inequality measurement approaches. The axiom is a continuity requirement: $P(\cdot;\cdot)$ is a continuous function of all arguments involved. It is certainly desirable that a small perturbation in any consumption of the poverty line should not dramatically alter the picture of poverty assessment. Following the literature of static poverty measurement, depending on whether the individual's poverty status in any period is changed or not as a result of an increase or a decrease in consumption, two levels of continuity axioms can be distinguished.

The Weak Continuity Axiom: $P(\cdot;\cdot)$ is continuous in each period's individual consumption provided that the individual's poverty status remains unchanged in all periods.

The Strong Continuity Axiom: $P(\cdot;\cdot)$ is continuous in each period's individual consumption even if the individual's poverty status changes in some periods.

The next axiom we discuss is generalized from the focus axiom in the static poverty measurement literature. There, in the context of a single period, the focus axiom makes poverty measurement exclusively a concern for people living below the poverty line; only changes made below the poverty line will affect the poverty level of an individual or a society. If an individual's consumption is greater than the poverty line then the poverty value of the individual is zero.

While the focus axiom distinguishes poverty measurement from inequality measurement and other welfare measurement, the generalization of it to the intertemporal context is less straightforward than for the continuity axiom. It seems reasonable to assert that a person who has never experienced a spell of poverty – even a single period – within his lifetime should be classified as non-poor while anyone who has experienced at least one spell of poverty should classified as poor. Determining how to extend the focus axiom to an individual's lifetime stream of consumption or income is not such a clear matter. Several authors have adopted a strict generalization of the focus axiom that requires that, in any non-poor period, the extent to which consumption exceeds the poverty line is irrelevant for lifetime/inter-temporal poverty measurement. In this case, one can use the censored income profile rather than the actual income profile as basic data.

The Strict Focus Axiom: $P(\mathbf{x}; z) = P(\mathbf{y}; z)$ if $\mathbf{y}$ is obtained from $\mathbf{x}$ by changing only the consumption levels that are above the poverty line without any income crossing the poverty line.

The acceptance of the strict focus axiom is conditioned on the presumptions that: (1) each time period is distinct and the boundary between the periods is a natural one with no uncertainty about what this level should be; (2) if one uses income as data, there is no consumption/income smoothing between different time periods; and (3) a non-poverty period cannot mitigate or influence the suffering of any poverty period. These are strong assumptions as it should be easily persuaded that the level of consumption in a non-poverty period may indeed affect the overall assessment of poverty over the T periods. For example, comparing two individuals who have identical periods of poverty and, in those periods, have identical consumption levels below the poverty line (say both had poor childhoods), if one individual enjoys a high standard of living in all non-poverty periods (say a successful investment banker) while the other person makes a living barely above the poverty line (say, a poor economist?), it is difficult to argue that the lifetime poverty of the first individual is the same as the second individual when all T periods are considered.

It is well recognized that the use of an accounting period such as a year is more or less an arbitrary choice. It follows that whether a consumption level above the poverty line affects the level of overall (lifetime) poverty depends upon the accounting period used. In the extreme case, if poverty of the entire lifetime is measured as a single period, then every single (annual, monthly, or other period of measurement) consumption (above or below) matters.

Even if one accepts the legitimacy of any specific accounting period, it is still difficult to argue that the well-being of a non-poverty period has no influence on the poverty level over a lifetime. As many authors have recognized, a well-to-do period may enable a person to better cope with poverty deprivation in the following periods (such as by receiving better health care and intake of better nutrition).[5] This effect may be rather like someone with a better immune system being able to better fight off an infection. If this is the case, then higher consumption in a non-poverty period may be helpful in reducing lifetime poverty. On the other hand, when the individual (say the aforementioned investment banker) assesses his lifetime poverty at the end of period T, he may lament his memories of poverty sufferings early in his life, but may also savor his time of comfortable living in the good times. All things considered, he may conclude that 'Although I had some tough moments in my life, I also had many moments of luxury and so life as a whole has been not too bad at all.' This is in stark contrast to the focus axiom used in aggregating poverty across different people in a given period. There, it is indeed reasonable to argue that one person's wealthy living does not alleviate another (unrelated) person's suffering from poverty. Here we are measuring the same individual's poverty across different time periods (an issue also echoed in multidimensional poverty measurement where an individual's different dimensions of living could be intrinsically connected).

We believe that the strict focus axiom is too restrictive; it eliminates any possibility that lifetime poverty assessment may be mitigated by periods of good living above the poverty line. We propose to keep a more relaxed version of the focus axiom which imposes the requirement of the focus axiom to each time period but not to the lifetime as a whole. For ease of reference, we refer to this focus requirement as a weak focus axiom.

The Weak Focus Axiom: the measurement of poverty in each time period satisfies the focus axiom as it is usually defined in the static poverty measurement literature.

As in the static poverty measurement literature, a consumption increase in any time period should not increase lifetime poverty, all other things staying the same. If the increase happens in a poverty period, then overall poverty should decrease. This axiom mirrors the monotonicity axiom and is similarly labelled as follows:

The Monotonicity Axiom: $P(\mathbf{x}; z) \leq P(\mathbf{y}; z)$ if $\mathbf{x}$ is obtained from $\mathbf{y}$ by increasing the individual's consumption in any single time period; $P(\mathbf{x}; z) < P(\mathbf{y}; z)$ if in that time period of $\mathbf{y}$ the individual's consumption happens to be below the poverty line.

Although we could also distinguish the monotonicity axiom into a weak version (no period's poverty status is altered as a result of consumption increase) and a strong version (poverty status may change in some periods) as in static poverty measurement, such an exercise is less pronounced for lifetime/inter-temporal poverty measurement since the situations calling for this distinction do not seem to arise in the current context.

While all above axioms are derived from static poverty measurement, the following axiom introduces something new and specific to lifetime/inter-temporal poverty measurement: it concerns the pattern or distribution of poverty spells over the lifetime. It stipulates that chronic poverty, a situation in which people live in poverty for an extended duration of time, intensifies poverty deprivation and increases the level of lifetime poverty in a manner over and above the contribution of each of the individual time period's poverty experience. In this new literature, a number of authors have argued for having this requirement for a measure of lifetime/inter-temporal poverty. Technically, this axiom can be stated as follows:

The Chronic Poverty Axiom: Suppose there are only two distinct and non-adjacent poverty periods $s < t$ in the lifetime consumption profile $\mathbf{x}$. If $\mathbf{y}$ is obtained from $\mathbf{x}$ by moving the two periods of poverty further apart, that is the two poverty periods become $s' = s - n < t + n = t'$ for some $n > 0$, then $P(\mathbf{y}; z) \leq P(\mathbf{x}; z)$.[6]

Is this a reasonable requirement for lifetime/inter-temporal poverty measurement? Clearly not everyone is convinced that it is. For example, Foster (2007, p. 17) explicitly expressed his doubt, and Calvo and Dercon (2009) seem to embrace the idea but fall short of making it an axiom. To many of us, this is a pertinent property for chronic poverty measurement: it captures precisely why clustering poverty periods together will make life more miserable. As an analogy, consider a form of poverty, say hunger, and suppose one has to go to bed hungry three days in a given week. Now suppose one could also choose meal distribution to decide which three days that hunger will strike, what will be the most-hungry distribution of meals and what will be the least-hungry distribution? It is easy to be convinced that the most devastating distribution would be to have hunger three days in a row without a full meal in between, while the most tolerable distribution would be to have the hungry days evenly distributed with full meals served between hungers (say, hungry on Monday, Wednesday and Friday and full meals on Sunday, Tuesday, Thursday and Saturday). Another analogy of the importance of chronic episodes is that of suffering of unbearable summer heat. In a place without air-conditioning (as in Moscow in the middle of July 2010 when the 10th Social Choice and Welfare Meeting was held there), consecutive sizzling days are much worse than having some cool breeze in between so that one can rest well to better cope physically and psychologically with scorching heat on the following days.

Although one may accept the notion that chronic poverty is more harmful to an individual's well-being than is sporadic episodes of poverty, there are many different possible formulations and interpretations of chronicity of poverty and how it affects lifetime poverty from which to choose. To Bossert et al. (2012), Dutta et al. (2013) and to some degree Calvo and Dercon (2009), contiguous periods of poverty will generate greater impact than that caused by the same amount of poverty experiences but which are interspersed by periods of non-poverty. To Hoy and Zheng (2008, 2011), Hoy, et al. (2012), Zheng (2012), Mendola et al. (2009), and Mendola and Busetta (2012), the impact of these poverty periods upon lifetime poverty intensifies as they move closer in time to each other even in the absence of contiguity, with the effect reaching its maximum when they cling together without any non-poverty hiatus. For ease of reference, we enlist this consecutive-poverty-period interpretation of chronic poverty as a strict axiom of chronic poverty.

The Strict Chronic Poverty Axiom: Suppose there are two distinct and nonadjacent poverty periods $s < t$ in the lifetime consumption profile $\mathbf{x}$. Now if $\mathbf{y}$ is obtained from $\mathbf{x}$ by changing the temporal locations of these two poverty experiences to periods s' and t', with $s' < t'$, then $P(\mathbf{x}; z) < P(\mathbf{y}; z)$ if and only if $s' = t' - 1$.

Several papers have entertained a decomposability condition that requires the lifetime/inter-temporal poverty to be some weighted average of poverty over different time periods. Calvo and Dercon (2009) present a version that is a direct copy of the decomposability condition in poverty aggregation over individuals.

The Strong Decomposition Axiom: For any $1 < k < T$,

$$P(x_1,\ldots,x_k,x_{k+1},\ldots,x_T;z) = \frac{k}{T}P(x_1,\ldots,x_k;z) + \frac{T-k}{T}P(x_{k+1},\ldots,x_T;z).$$

Clearly, this strong axiom simply views lifetime poverty as a weighted sum of all periods' poverty, that is, $P(\mathbf{x};z) = \frac{1}{T}\sum_{t=1}^{T}p_t$, and as such the chronic poverty axiom in either strict or general form cannot be satisfied.

Bossert et al. (2012) employ a decomposition property but do not apply the strong decomposition rule to the entire consumption profile; rather, they apply it to poverty spells (consecutive periods of poverty). That is, the aggregate poverty level of consecutive poverty periods is a normalized sum of each period's poverty. For the entire consumption profile with spells of non-poverty and spells of poverty, they propose a different decomposition rule (they call it between-spell decomposition).

The Weak Decomposition Axiom: If $x_k \geq z$ or $x_{k+1} \geq z$, then:

$$P(x_1,\ldots,x_k,x_{k+1},\ldots,x_T;z) = \frac{k}{T}P(x_1,\ldots,x_k;z) + \frac{T-k}{T}P(x_{k+1},\ldots,x_T;z).$$

Notice that weak decomposition rules out the importance of how close in time poverty spells occur, except when periods of poverty are consecutive. For example, consider the following two poverty profiles $\mathbf{p} = (\frac{1}{2},0,\frac{1}{2},\frac{1}{4},0,0)$ and $\mathbf{p}' = (\frac{1}{2},0,\frac{1}{2},0,\frac{1}{4},0)$ arising from income profiles $\mathbf{x}$ and $\mathbf{x}'$. Choosing $k = 3$, we have from strong decomposability that poverty must be equal for $\mathbf{p}$ (that is, $\mathbf{x}$) and $\mathbf{p}'$ (that is, $\mathbf{x}'$) since, writing the lifetime poverty values in terms of poverty profiles, we have that $P(\mathbf{p}) = \frac{1}{2}P(\frac{1}{2},0,\frac{1}{2}) + \frac{1}{2}P(\frac{1}{4},0,0)$ and $P(\mathbf{p}') = \frac{1}{2}P(\frac{1}{2},0,\frac{1}{2}) + \frac{1}{2}P(0,\frac{1}{4},0)$ must deliver the same value. For weak decomposability, it is true that $P(\mathbf{p}') = \frac{1}{2}P(\frac{1}{2},0,\frac{1}{2}) + \frac{1}{2}P(0,\frac{1}{4},0)$, but it is not required that $P(\mathbf{p}) = \frac{1}{2}P(\frac{1}{2},0,\frac{1}{2}) + \frac{1}{2}P(\frac{1}{4},0,0)$ and so it is not necessary that $P(\mathbf{p}) = P(\mathbf{p}')$ since there are consecutive poverty experiences in periods 3 and 4. Thus, weak decomposability allows closeness of periods of poverty experiences to matter as long as these periods are consecutive. One might feel this does not go far enough. For example, weak decomposability would not distinguish between poverty profile $\mathbf{p} = (\frac{1}{2},0,\frac{1}{4},0,0,0)$ and $\mathbf{p}' = (\frac{1}{2},0,0,0,\frac{1}{4},0)$ even though the two poverty experiences occur closer in time in the former case.

Finally, if one rejects the strong version of the focus axiom and accepts only the weak version, then it is natural to entertain the possibility that a non-poverty (affluent) period may mitigate the deprivation experienced in a poverty period. This mitigation amounts to extending the monotonicity axiom in some way above the poverty line. Dutta et al.

(2013) consider the mitigation of a non-poverty (affluent) period on an immediately subsequent period of poverty. They assumed that the affluent period has a 'fixed effect': the magnitude of mitigation does not vary continuously with the level of the 'affluence'. Hoy and Zheng (2011) and Zheng (2012) stipulate that the mitigation effect may depend on the level of well-being in non-poverty periods in a continuous way. For simplicity, here we consider these two versions of a mitigation axiom.

The Weak Mitigation Axiom: $P(\mathbf{x}; z) < P(\mathbf{y}; z)$ if $\mathbf{x}$ is obtained from $\mathbf{y}$ by increasing the individual's consumption in non-poverty period t such that $x_t > \delta > y_t > z$ for some δ; but $P(\mathbf{w}; z) = P(\mathbf{x}; z)$ if $\mathbf{w}$ is obtained from $\mathbf{y}$ such that $w_t > \delta > y_t > z$ even though $w_t > x_t$.

This means that there is some cut-off value, δ, which exceeds the poverty line, such that income in a non-poor period will mitigate the effect of poverty experiences in other periods but only up to some specified cut-off level δ. For example, if $z = 10$ and $\delta = 15$, then $\mathbf{x} = (20, 5, 5)$ will generate less lifetime poverty than $\mathbf{y} = (12, 5, 5)$ even though the only income that differs between these two profiles is in a non-poor period. However, the mitigation effect only comes into play up to the limit $\delta = 15$, and so $\mathbf{w} = (25, 5, 5)$ generates the same lifetime poverty as does $\mathbf{x}$ even though $w_1 > x_1$. This result occurs since it is only the extent to which x_1 and w_1 may exceed y_1 up to the limit δ that matters. Increases beyond δ have no further mitigating effect. When the mitigation process is allowed to be continuous and the effect to be increasing with consumption, we obtain the following strong form of the axiom which Hoy and Zheng (2011), Hoy et al. (2012) and Zheng (2012) adopt.

The Strong Mitigation Axiom: $P(\mathbf{x}; z) \leq P(\mathbf{y}; z)$ if $\mathbf{x}$ is obtained from $\mathbf{y}$ by increasing the individual's consumption in non-poverty period t such that $x_t > y_t > z$.

For the above example, the strong mitigation axiom allows for the possibility that $\mathbf{x} = (25, 5, 5)$ displays less poverty than $\mathbf{y} = (20, 5, 5)$. There is no limit imposed on the extent to which increasing income in a non-poor period can mitigate lifetime poverty caused by poverty experienced in other periods of life.

Besides these axioms, authors have also proposed other more specific requirements to characterize their chronic poverty measures. Due to space limitations and the lack of generality of some of the additional axioms, we will not list them all here. But when describing the various specific measures in the next section, we briefly discuss some of the interesting properties these measures may possess.

9.3   POVERTY MEASURES

In this section, with the help of the above axioms, we review and evaluate the different approaches to conceptualizing inter-temporal/lifetime poverty and the corresponding poverty measures generated. Rather than try to review every approach currently on offer, we focus on a subset of papers. We believe we have chosen papers that represent most of the various important distinctions existing in the literature at this time.

9.3.1   The Rodgers–Rodgers Measure of Chronic Poverty

Rodgers and Rodgers (1993) were probably among the first authors to measure poverty over time in a manner that takes into account not only poverty incidence but also poverty intensity. Most studies of poverty over time prior to their work can be labeled as 'poverty dynamics' – the activities of people moving into and out of poverty – which considers persistence of poverty as the topic of concern. In comparison to this earlier literature on persistent poverty, Rodgers and Rodgers (1993) do not limit assessment of poverty in any given period to an indicator variable that uses only information about whether a person is poor or not poor. The previous literature essentially used the headcount ratio as the only measure of poverty. They were also concerned about the possibility of individuals being able to transfer income across periods (for example, from non-poor periods into poor periods) which, although an important issue, can be treated separately from our main consideration of how consumption over time should be aggregated in a way that is sensitive to chronic poverty concerns and other properties (such as early poverty concerns) that depend on the pattern of poverty experiences over a lifetime.

Rodgers and Rodgers were led by their concerns to consider an individual's permanent income as the relevant statistic for measuring chronic poverty. If a person's permanent or average lifetime income were below the poverty line, then that would imply that income smoothing could not eliminate lifetime poverty. In Rodgers–Rodgers' approach, the total poverty of an individual is simply the sum of all years' poverty values:

$$\sum_{t=1}^{T} p_t.$$

They measure chronic poverty as the poverty of the permanent income x^* gauged against the poverty line z:

$$p(x^*; z)$$

and transitory poverty is measured as the residual term:

$$\sum_{t=1}^{T} p_t - p(x^*; z).$$

Rodgers and Rodgers' 'permanent income' is essentially the average income over the T periods.[7] As such, their measure of 'chronic poverty' completely ignores the focus axiom; the strict or the weak version. Income shortfall in a period can be completely compensated by high incomes of any other periods. The distribution of poverty incidence has virtually no effect on the degree of chronic poverty: whether poverty is concentrated in a few periods or evenly distributed across all T years make no difference. Also, whether the poverty periods are contiguous or spaced more or less evenly by non-poverty spells in between does not matter either. It follows that their measure of chronic poverty does not satisfy either version of the chronic poverty axiom. Clearly, the measure also is not decomposable in either sense of decomposability stated above.[8] The measure, however, satisfies both the continuity axiom (both versions) and the monotonicity axiom.

To illustrate these properties, consider an example of a population with three individuals who live over three years, with income profiles $\mathbf{x} = (5, 14, 5)$, $\mathbf{y} = (5, 5, 14)$, and

$\mathbf{w} = (5, 5, 20)$. Using the relative poverty gap measure $p_t = p_t(x_t; z) = (1 - x_t/z)$ with $z = 10$, we obtain individual's lifetime poverty to be $P(\mathbf{x}; z) = 1$, $P(\mathbf{y}; z) = 1$, $P(\mathbf{w}; z) = 0$. The presumption underlying the Rodgers–Rodgers approach is that, if the interest rate is zero and so individuals can costlessly spread their income between periods, then $\mathbf{w}$ displays no permanent poverty, since $\mathbf{w}_P = (10, 10, 10)$ is the vector of permanent income and $\mathbf{x}$ and $\mathbf{y}$ display equal amounts of permanent poverty (per year) of amount 0.2 each; that is, since $\mathbf{x}_P = \mathbf{y}_P = (8, 8, 8)$. Rodgers–Rodgers's approach equates poverty measured using permanent income with chronic poverty. This is reasonable if perfect smoothing is possible, but not otherwise.[9] If we consider the opposite extreme that no smoothing occurs across time periods, and so consumption in period t is simply income in that period, then the pattern of income/consumption should matter with $\mathbf{y}$ displaying greater chronic poverty than $\mathbf{x}$. Where $\mathbf{w}$ would compare to $\mathbf{y}$ in terms of chronic poverty depends on how one feels about the importance of mitigation. Rodgers–Rodgers's measure involves what one might consider 'perfect mitigation' since one high income in any period, including the last period of life, can completely mitigate any poverty experienced earlier in life.

It is also worth noting that while the Rodgers–Rodgers measure of chronic poverty does not reflect the focus axiom even in the weak sense, their measure of total poverty demands the strict focus axiom. In this sense, their measure of chronic poverty tends to be underestimated and the transitory portion tends to be overestimated. These conclusions are evident from the above numerical examples.[10] However, their objects of measurement are income and perfect smoothing is possible. Taken together, this means that assessing how their measures relate to the type of axioms used in the current literature is not a straightforward exercise.

The Rodgers–Rodgers approach belongs to what is referred to as the 'components' approach of lifetime poverty measurement. One goal of this approach is to separate total poverty into permanent (or chronic) poverty and transient poverty. This is a different sort of decomposability than we have addressed in this chapter. More recent noteworthy contributions in this vein include Jalan and Ravallion (2000) and Duclos et al. (2010).

9.3.2   The Calvo–Dercon Approach

Calvo and Dercon (2009) provide a comprehensive exposure of the various issues in poverty measurement over time. They employed a set of four figures of different temporal arrangements of poverty and non-poverty spells to illustrate three key questions in poverty measurement over time: the issue of 'compensation of poverty spells by non-poverty spells'; the issue of discounting poverty in the past or the future; and the issue of whether a 'prolonged episode of poverty' causes 'greater harm' than isolated poverty spells. Their goal, however, is not to draw any definitive conclusion on any of these issues but rather to investigate the ways these concerns can be incorporated into the measurement of lifetime poverty.

In constructing a lifetime poverty measure $P(\cdot; \cdot)$ over the T periods, Calvo and Dercon view the process as composed of three distinct operations: focus, transformation and aggregation. The focus step is to truncate income or any calculated variable above the poverty line; the transformation step is to transform income in order to preserve the Pigou–Dalton principle of transfers; the aggregation step is to aggregate over the T periods to come up with a single summary index of poverty. They consider the implications of taking these three steps in all possible orders. For example one could first aggregate all incomes over the T periods to obtain a 'permanent income', then apply a poverty measure to the 'permanent income', which amounts to a combined step of focus and transformation. The resulting poverty measure from this aggregation–focus–transformation order is in fact equivalent to the chronic poverty measure that Rodgers and Rodgers defined. By examining all six possible sequences that these steps can display, Calvo and Dercon constructed four sets of poverty measures, but concluded that only two sets of them can be regarded as lifetime measures of poverty: one is the Rodgers–Rodgers measure and the other is a member of the family proposed by Foster (2007) – noted below – which corresponds to the sequence of focus–transformation–aggregation. In fact, if one applies focus as the first step, then there is no possibility of any mitigation effect since the income levels in out-of-poverty will have been truncated and so no information relating to potential mitigation survives that step. They point out that this may be considered a merit or a flaw, depending on one's perspective.

Calvo and Dercon point out that the transformation step, which stipulates that a transfer of income from a more poor spell to a less poor spell should increase aggregate poverty, is not non-controversial in a lifetime poverty measure. If the reduction in consumption occurs in a more poor spell which is isolated (that is, is not preceded or followed by a spell of poverty) while the increase in consumption occurs in a less poor spell which occurs within an uninterrupted sequence of poor spells, then one might argue that it is at least possible that lifetime income would fall. For example, with $z = 10$, one might argue that the income profile (14, 3, 10, 5, 4, 2), displays less lifetime or chronic poverty than (14, $3 - \delta$, 10, 5, $4 + \delta$, 2) for $0 < \delta < 1$ and sufficiently small even though such a conclusion violates the transformation axiom. The rationale for such a conclusion would be that although the person is made worse off in a spell of deeper poverty, the person is made better off in a period that occurs amongst a sequence of poverty spells.

Their measures, however, cannot successfully address all three issues of 'compensation', 'discounting' and 'prolonged poverty' that Calvo and Dercon raised. To partially address the prolonged poverty concern – or the chronic poverty axiom in this chapter – they proposed to multiply each period's poverty with that of the previous period.

9.3.3   The Foster Measure of Chronic Poverty

The chronic poverty measure proposed by Foster (2009) relies on a poverty duration (frequency) cut-off in addition to the use of a poverty line. A person must live in poverty a sufficient fraction of periods of his life in order to be deemed chronically poor. This approach requires a consensus on this cut-off value. Clearly, such a consensus is unlikely to be achieved and in practice different studies invoke different definitions. For example, the US Census Bureau defines 'chronic poverty' as 'people in poverty every month for the duration of a longitudinal survey panel (typically 3 to 4 years)', while Hulme and Shepherd (2003) consider that 'an individual experiences significant capability deprivations for a period of five years or more'. Implicitly, their requirement demands five successive years (or more) of poverty experience. Note that in both cases it seems that chronic poverty requires an unbroken poverty spell. In Foster's approach, however, chronic poverty does not require contiguous periods of poverty and all that matters is the fraction of time the individual lives in poverty over the T periods.

Suppose it is settled that an individual experiences chronic poverty if he spends fraction τ (or more) of his T periods in poverty. If the individual in question has experienced q periods in poverty, then Foster's measure of chronic poverty with a general poverty deprivation function p_t is:

$$P(\mathbf{x};z) = \begin{cases} \frac{1}{T}\sum p_t & \text{if } q/T \geq \tau \\ 0 & \text{if } q/T < \tau \end{cases}$$

Foster's measure can be straightforwardly calculated and easily interpreted. It also clearly spells out who are counted as 'chronically poor'. This simplicity, however, comes at a cost: the measure does not satisfy the strong continuity axiom although it does satisfy the weak continuity axiom. Consider, for example, two profiles of poverty values $\mathbf{p} = (\frac{1}{2},0,0,\frac{1}{2},\frac{1}{2},0,\frac{1}{2})$ and $\mathbf{p}' = (\frac{1}{2},0,\varepsilon,\frac{1}{2},\frac{1}{2},0,\frac{1}{2})$ and assume the threshold for chronic poverty is five periods.[11] According to Foster's approach, there is no chronic poverty in $\mathbf{p}$ but chronic poverty is present in $\mathbf{p}'$ and its (chronic) poverty level is $\frac{2+\varepsilon}{7}$ which is strictly positive. Thus the Foster measure is not continuous at $\varepsilon = 0$. That is, suppose in the third period the relative poverty gap of ε approaches 0 (that is, income approaches the poverty line z). Once income crosses the poverty line, the Foster measure experiences a sudden drop from a value greater than 2/7 to zero. By way of construction, the Foster measure also does not satisfy a strict version of the monotonicity axiom; an increase in the income of a non-chronically poor individual in any poverty period will not reduce the level of the overall poverty.

Since Foster's definition of a chronic poverty measure is not sensitive to the contiguity or closeness of poverty periods, the measure automatically fails to satisfy any version of the chronic poverty axiom. The measure does satisfy both versions of the decomposability axiom. It satisfies the strict version of the focus axiom and allows no mitigation of poverty by non-poverty spells. It also satisfies decomposability by population subgroup and also allows for decomposability in the sense of the components approach; that is, what fraction of total poverty in the population is due to chronic or permanent poverty and what is due to transient poverty.

9.3.4 The Bossert–Chakravarty–D'Ambrosio Measure

In contrast to all three approaches above, Bossert et al. (2012) states unequivocally that a lifetime/inter-temporal measure of poverty should reflect the persistence of poverty that an individual may experience. They believe that 'the negative effects of being in poverty are cumulative, hence a two-period poverty spell is much harder to handle than two one-period spells that are interrupted by one (or more) periods out of poverty'. But to them, the poverty experience of an individual intensifies only when the poverty periods are uninterrupted (contiguous). Consequently any poverty measure flowing out of that notion will satisfy the strict chronic poverty axiom (which they characterized) but not the general chronic poverty axiom that Hoy and Zheng (2011) advanced. Relying upon the weak decomposability axiom and several other axioms, they characterize a new measure of intertemporal poverty:

$$P(\mathbf{x};z) = \frac{1}{T}\sum_{t=1}^{T}m(p_t)p_t$$

where $p_t \geq 0$ is period t's level of poverty and $m(p_t)$ is the number of consecutive poverty periods that encompass period t as a member.

The Bossert et al. measure shares with the Foster measure a simplicity of form: both reflect an average of per-period poverty and both subscribe to the strong focus axiom and so no mitigation effect is accepted. The different weights used in these two measures (the Foster measure is a simple average while the Bossert et al. measure is a weighted average), however, make them behave very differently: while the Foster measure is insensitive to the temporal pattern of poverty episodes, the Bossert et al. measure registers an increase in poverty whenever two or more poverty periods move next to each other. This increase, however, is not a continuous process: when two isolated poverty periods move toward each other, nothing happens until the two periods are connected (that is, contiguous). In other words, the Bossert et al. measure may not satisfy the strong continuity axiom although it does satisfy the weak one. Consider, for example, two distributions of snapshot poverty over seven time periods, $\mathbf{p} = (\frac{1}{2},0,0,\frac{3}{7},\frac{3}{7},0,\frac{1}{2})$ and $\mathbf{q} = (\frac{1}{2},0,0,\frac{1}{2},\frac{1}{2},0,\frac{1}{2})$. The Bossert et al. indices for $\mathbf{p}$ and $\mathbf{q}$ are $\frac{19}{49}$ and $\frac{21}{49}$. Thus, $\mathbf{p}$ has *less* poverty than $\mathbf{q}$. Now consider $\mathbf{p}' = (\frac{1}{2},0,\varepsilon,\frac{3}{7},\frac{3}{7},0,\frac{1}{2})$ whose poverty index is $\frac{21\varepsilon + 25}{49}$. Since for an arbitrarily small value $\varepsilon > 0$, $\frac{21\varepsilon + 25}{49} > \frac{21}{49}$, $\mathbf{p}'$ now has more poverty than $\mathbf{q}$. Thus, the Bossert et al. measure is not continuous at $p_t = 0$.

Bossert et al.'s requirement that only contiguous periods of poverty will intensity poverty experience may also lead to what can be called a 'time-unit inconsistency' problem. As is well accepted and as we noted above, the use of any specific time unit for poverty measurement, such as a year or a month, is somewhat arbitrary. For example, as mentioned before, in defining chronic poverty, the US Census Bureau adopts 'month' as the time unit while the Chronic Poverty Research Centre used 'year' as the basic unit for one period. It is clear that a sufficient number of 'consecutive months in poverty' implies 'consecutive years in poverty' but the reverse is not true. It follows that an individual who experiences consecutive years in poverty may not experience any consecutive months in poverty. Consequently, Bossert et al.'s measurement of poverty using a year as a unit can be very different from using a month. Ideally, one would expect some consistency – at least of a qualitative nature – in poverty measurement when the time unit varies; otherwise the conclusion can be easily manipulated. It is easy to construct a numerical example to demonstrate this issue for the Bossert et al. measure.

The Bossert et al. measure satisfies weak, but not strong, decomposability. One cannot break up a profile into two subsequences and satisfy decomposability unless the point at which the break occurs does not involve consecutive periods of poverty experiences. Therefore, as noted in the section on axioms, unlike for measures that satisfy strong decomposability, the two poverty profiles $\mathbf{p} = (\frac{1}{2},0,\frac{1}{2},\frac{1}{4},0,0)$ and $\mathbf{p}' = (\frac{1}{2},0,\frac{1}{2},0,\frac{1}{4},0)$ are not required in their setup to have the same amount of lifetime poverty but would under strong decomposability.

Dutta et al. (2013) start from the framework of Bossert et al.'s approach but note that they do not allow the distribution of non-poverty spells to play a role in determining overall lifetime poverty. This is a consequence of Bossert et al.'s use of the strict focus axiom. It follows that whether non-poverty periods are grouped together or separately is irrelevant; it is also the case that there is no effect on overall poverty if some non-poverty period's income should increase. Dutta et al. argue that both should matter. Furthermore, they believe the order of non-poverty periods (or 'affluence periods' in their terminology) should matter as well: a non-poverty period can mitigate a poverty period that follows but not a prior poverty period. In this sense, affluence can prepare one better for poverty but cannot *ex post* mitigate a previous spell of poverty. To satisfy this additional consideration, Dutta et al. proposed and characterized the following poverty measure:

$$P(\mathbf{x};z) = \frac{1}{T}\sum_{t=1}^{T} \frac{[1 + m(p_t)]^\alpha}{[1 + n(p_t)]^\beta}\, p_t^\gamma$$

where $m(p_t)$ is now the number of consecutive poverty periods prior to the tth period, $n(p_t)$ is the number of non-poor periods immediately prior to the tth period, and parameters α, β and γ are all positive. It is easy to see that Dutta et al.'s measure increases as poverty periods cluster ($m(p_t)$ increases) and decreases as non-poverty periods cluster in advance of a poor period ($n(p_t)$ increase). Note that the mitigation of poverty from preceding non-poverty experiences dissipates immediately after one period of poverty is experienced.

Like Bossert et al.'s measure, Dutta et al.'s (base) measure satisfies only the weak continuity axiom. Although it is sensitive to how non-poverty periods are grouped together, it still satisfies the strict focus axiom since it is insensitive to any income increases above the poverty line. To make the poverty measure at least partially responsive to the level of income in a non-poverty period, Dutta et al. modified their measure by replacing $n(p_t)$ with $\tilde{n}(p_t) = \Sigma\lambda_t$ and $\lambda_t = \tilde{\lambda} > 1$ if the consumption is above a certain threshold δ and 1 if otherwise. The resulting measure then satisfies the weak mitigation axiom albeit not the strong one.

9.3.5 The Mendola–Busetta Measure

Mendola and Busetta (2012) – and Mendola et al. (2011) – explicitly take the time eclipsed between a pair of poverty periods into account in modelling the persistence of poverty over time. Their 'cumulative hardship hypothesis' is consistent with the chronic poverty axiom and different from the strict axiom adopted by Bossert et al. (2012) and Dutta et al. (2013) in that two periods of poverty generate a greater effect on lifetime poverty as they move closer to each other even if they do not become contiguous. Their individual aggregate poverty measure over the T periods is defined as:[12]

$$P(\mathbf{x};z) = A(T) \sum_{\substack{p_t>0;p_s>0 \\ s>t}} \frac{(p_t + p_s)/2}{s - t}\, \omega$$

where $A(T)$ is a positive normalization factor and ω is a 'decay factor' that discounts the individual's poverty experience if it occurs early in life.

The Mendola–Busetta measure satisfies the strong focus axiom, the weak continuity axiom and the general chronic poverty axiom. Like the Foster measure, it does not satisfy the strong continuity axiom since it implicitly assumes that an individual is counted as chronically poor only if he experiences at least two periods of poverty. Whenever a threshold is established for being identified as 'chronically poor', the strong continuity axiom will be violated. The measure also does not satisfy either of the decomposability axioms and does not allow for poverty mitigation.

9.3.6   The Hoy–Zheng Measure

Hoy and Zheng (2008, 2011) proposed the chronic poverty axiom as a key requirement for a lifetime poverty measure to capture the persistence aspect of poverty over time. They argued that each period of poverty leaves a mark on the lifetime experience of poverty, but it is also reasonable to consider an individual's lifetime as a whole in the poverty evaluation process. With a few other axioms, Hoy and Zheng axiomatically characterize the following measure of lifetime poverty:

$$P(\mathbf{x};z) = \beta(T)\left\{\sum_{t=1}^{T}\alpha(t,T)p_t\right\} + (1 - \beta(T))\bar{p}$$

where $\bar{p} = p(\bar{x},z)$ and $\bar{x}$ is the average of $\mathbf{x} = (x_1, x_2, \ldots, x_T)$; $\alpha(t, T) \geq 0$ and $0 \leq \beta(T) \leq 1$.

For this poverty measure, the part $\sum_{t=1}^{T}\alpha(t,T)p_t$ is a weighted average of all periods' poverty and $\bar{p} = p(\bar{x},z)$ is the poverty level if the entire lifetime is viewed as a single period. The parameter $\beta(T)$ plays the role of a 'memory' factor in the sense that if $\beta(T) = 1$ (that is, the case of 'perfect memory'), then what matters for lifetime poverty measurement is each period's poverty experience; and if $\beta(T) = 0$ (that is, the case of 'no memory'), then what matters for lifetime poverty measurement is the lifetime considered as a whole and individual periods of poverty experience do not matter. For $0 < \beta(T) < 1$, both individual poverty incidence and lifetime assessment play a role in shaping overall poverty. In this last case, the strong poverty mitigation axiom is satisfied.

In order for the poverty measure to satisfy the chronic poverty axiom, the function $\alpha(t, T)$ must be concave; that is, $\partial\alpha^2(t, T)/\partial t^2 < 0$. Clearly, a measure with this property will imply that lifetime poverty intensifies as poverty periods cluster, and its impact reaches its maximum when all poverty periods are contiguous. This intensifying process is continuous, unlike for both the Bossert et al. and the Dutta et al. measures. For example, the following three poverty profiles represent an increasing degree of chronic poverty, respectively: $(\frac{1}{2},0,0,0,0,\frac{1}{2})$, $(0,\frac{1}{2},0,0,\frac{1}{2},0)$, and $(0,0,\frac{1}{2},\frac{1}{2},0,0)$.

Another axiom that Hoy and Zheng (2011) introduced is the early poverty axiom: they argue that poverty experiences occurring in early stages of life are more damaging. Poverty in childhood affects physical and mental health later in life. This early poverty axiom amounts to requiring $\partial\alpha(t, T)/\partial t < 0$. Considering all possible values of $\alpha(t, T)$ that satisfy these conditions, Hoy and Zheng (2011) derived a set of dominance conditions that can determine when one poverty profile will possess unambiguously more lifetime poverty than another.[13]

The linear structure of the Hoy–Zheng measure allows no interaction between different periods of poverty. As pointed out in Hoy et al. (2012), there is also a potential restriction or conflict between the chronic poverty axiom and the early poverty axiom. To allow for a more flexible interaction between poverty periods and more direct poverty mitigation, Zheng (2012) axiomatically characterizes a class of gravitational measures of lifetime poverty:

$$P(\mathbf{x};z) = \sum_{s \le t} F_{st}(p_s, p_t, \upsilon_{st})$$

where F_{st} is continuous in each argument and is increasing in p_s and p_t and decreasing in υ_{st} $= t - s + 1$ and $F(0, 0, \upsilon) = 0$. This class is referred to as 'gravitational measures' because it is modelled after Newton's Universal Law of Gravitation: 'the force is proportional to the product of the two masses and inversely proportional to the square of the distance between the point masses'. Examples of this class include:

$$P(\mathbf{x};z) = \sum_{s \le t} \frac{p_s^\alpha p_t^\beta}{\upsilon_{st}^\gamma}$$

and:

$$P(\mathbf{x};z) = \sum_{s \le t} p_s^\alpha p_t^\beta \left(1 - \frac{\upsilon_{st}}{T}\right)^\gamma$$

where α, β and γ are positive parameters.

As can be easily seen from the above two examples, the Zheng measure implies that the closer are any two poverty spells (smaller is υ_{st}), the greater is the lifetime poverty (that is, the greater is the contribution of each pair of poverty experiences p_s, p_t). Also, an increase in (snapshot) poverty intensity in a given period t will have a greater impact on lifetime poverty the closer is any preceding period in which poverty is experienced. Thus, poverty profile $\mathbf{p} = (0, \frac{1}{2}, 0, \frac{1}{2})$ generates higher lifetime poverty than does $\mathbf{p}' = (\frac{1}{2}, 0, 0, \frac{1}{2})$ and the effect of greater poverty in period four would be more pronounced in the case of $\mathbf{p}$ than in $\mathbf{p}'$ (that is, the difference in lifetime poverty between $\widetilde{\mathbf{p}} = (0, \frac{1}{2}, 0, \frac{1}{2} + \varepsilon)$ and $\mathbf{p} = (0, \frac{1}{2}, 0, \frac{1}{2})$ is greater than the difference between $\widetilde{\mathbf{p}}' = (\frac{1}{2}, 0, 0, \frac{1}{2} + \varepsilon)$ and $\mathbf{p}' = (\frac{1}{2}, 0, 0, \frac{1}{2})$, for $0 < \varepsilon \le \frac{1}{2}$). This latter property seems desirable as the poverty experience in the fourth period in the former case occurs for someone in a more vulnerable state since the most recent poverty experience happened more recently.

The new measure satisfies strong focus, strong continuity, monotonicity, chronic poverty but not decomposability and poverty mitigation. To enable it to satisfy the poverty mitigation axiom, Zheng (2012) redefines p_t to allow it to take negative values to reflect the level of well-being in a non-poverty period. Modelling the new interaction among poverty and non-poverty periods, Zheng (2012) further characterizes a generalization of the gravitational measures as follows:

$$P(\mathbf{x};z) = \sum_{p_t > 0; s \le t} F_{st}(p_s, p_t, \upsilon_{st})$$

where F_{st} is continuous and increasing in p_s and p_t and decreasing in $\upsilon_{st} = t - s + 1$, and $F_{st}(p_s, p_t, \upsilon_{st}) > 0$ if $p_s > 0$ and $p_t > 0$; $F_{st}(p_s, p_t, \upsilon_{st}) < 0$ if $p_s < 0$ and $p_t > 0$; and $F(0, 0, \upsilon) = 0$. An example of this class is:

$$P(\mathbf{x};z) = \sum_{s \le t; p_t > 0} \text{sign}(p_s) |p_s|^\alpha p_t^\beta \left(1 - \frac{\upsilon_{st}}{T}\right)^\gamma.$$

In addition to what we have reviewed, there is other recent work on measuring poverty over time. For example, both Günther and Maier (2008) and Hojman and Kast (2009) invoked the notion of 'loss aversion' in measuring multi-period poverty and characterize classes of poverty measures that rank increasing income streams as having less poverty than decreasing income streams. This amounts to assigning higher weights to later periods' poverty than early ones. Given the arguments that favour more emphasis on poverty early in life (that is, see the empirical support mentioned as justification for Hoy and Zheng's early poverty axiom), it is debatable whether 'loss aversion' is an appropriate requirement for a lifetime poverty measure. Gradin et al. (2012) also question the standard approach of poverty aggregation across people – a topic that is not reviewed in this chapter – and proposed a procedure that is sensitive to the inequality of well-being across the population. For the sake of keeping the chapter short, we do not go into details of these additional papers.

9.4   CONCLUSIONS

The recent literature on how one should conceptualize and measure an individual's poverty status over their lifetime has drawn attention to this important perspective of social deprivation. It has also shed light on many important considerations involving properties such as poverty persistence, chronic poverty, the relative importance of poverty at different stages of one's life, and so on. The literature is, however, in its beginning stages and we expect that, over the next decade or two, much more research will be done along these lines for finding the most suitable approach for measuring lifetime poverty.

The papers we have chosen to review intensively in this chapter raise some very interesting debates. To begin, even the simple focus axiom, which is widely accepted in the well-developed literature on static unidimensional poverty measurement, is not easy to extend in a straightforward and non-controversial manner. Should the focus axiom apply to each period of life or should it apply more broadly to average or lifetime permanent income? Or is a less simple version of the focus axiom appropriate? One specific view that has been expressed by a number of authors has been the notion that the level of income or consumption in non-poor periods of life may compensate or mitigate the effects of living in poverty in other periods. We have referred to this idea as the property of mitigation and authors have suggested alternative ways in which mitigation may matter. Some of the issues raised include: (1) whether only a preceding period of affluent living should mitigate a period of poverty or whether subsequent periods of affluence should also matter; (2) how should the magnitude of income in an affluent period matter; and (3) how should the closeness in time between experiences of affluence and poverty matter. If one wants to allow for mitigation effects that depend on the level of income in non-poor periods of life, then one cannot simply start with a vector (temporal profile) of incomes that have been censored at the 'per period' poverty line to use as data in measuring a person's lifetime poverty and so the focus axiom from static poverty measurement must be modified.

Another important advance related to this literature has been the attention that the phenomenon of chronic poverty has received. The concept of chronic poverty is a long-standing one and has (directly or indirectly) received substantial attention in the empirical literature on duration and persistence of poverty as well as the notion of dynamics into and out of poverty, including research involving the phenomenon of poverty traps; characterized as 'any self-reinforcing mechanism which causes poverty to persist' (Azariadis and Stachurski, 2005). The 'spells approach' to measuring lifetime poverty has brought interesting nuances to the discussion. Should we categorize a person as being chronically poor based on the fraction of years of his life that he lives in poverty? Should it matter whether periods spent in poverty are clustered close together in time or are interspersed more or less evenly within periods of affluent living? If one answers 'yes' to this second question, must periods of poverty be uninterrupted (contiguous) or just close in time to each other in order to be viewed as contributing more to chronic poverty?

Answers to these sorts of questions, including the issue of mitigation, may best be answered by empirically measuring people's well-being, using either subjective or objective measures, after they have experienced different patterns of poverty up to a given point in their lifetimes. If the pattern matters to their ultimate health and sense of well-being, including their feelings of social deprivation, then determining how the pattern matters may be helpful in deciding which conceptualizations and which of the many measures of lifetime poverty are most appropriate. Deciding (eventually) on a fairly limited set of measures may be viewed as important to debates on what measures are best for alleviating poverty at the societal level. Different policies will lead to different effects on the duration and pattern of poverty experienced by various individuals in society. It is therefore important that the measures used to reflect these implications provide the 'right' trade-offs when measuring the impact on individuals' lifetime poverty profiles. There are additional future challenges for this literature, which include integrating theory with empirical applications as well as formulating lifetime poverty experience within a multidimensional framework. The literature has also, for the most part, presumed (at least implicitly) that individuals live the same number of periods. As noted by Kanbur and Mukherjee (2007), this is especially a concern when more people die young in one population compared to another, since removing those individuals from the calculation may reduce the size of population that is poor and hence the measure of societal poverty.

NOTES

1. For a survey of static poverty measurement, see, for example, Foster and Sen (1997), Zheng (1997) and Chakravarty (2009).
2. Empirical applications of chronic poverty measures are reviewed by del Rio et al., Chapter 10 in this *Handbook*.
3. In this chapter we do not distinguish between poverty based on income or consumption levels. However, it is clear that if one were to include income smoothing possibilities, these would be two very different problems.
4. Income x generates normalized poverty gap $(z - x)/z$ for $x \leq z$ and 0 for $x > z$.
5. Calvo and Dercon (2009, p. 31) remark that 'some may argue that hardship at some point in life may be acceptable if it is followed by much better outcomes in other periods'.
6. For some measures, this axiom is satisfied with the strong inequality applying; that is, $P(y; z) < P(x; z)$. However, other measures require that chronic poverty be experienced only when poverty occurs in adjacent periods.
7. It is then adjusted up by discounted savings (when a period's income is above the mean), and down by discounted borrowing (when income is below the mean income).
8. Rodgers and Rodgers (1993) represents the so-called component approach of measuring poverty over time: the total poverty observed over a certain period of time is decomposed into a component of 'chronic poverty' and a component of 'transitory poverty'. This is an altogether different perspective on decomposability.

9. Of course, for a person to be able to implement equal consumption in each period (that is, smooth income perfectly), would depend not just on having a zero interest rate but also requires knowing with certainty what his future income would be when deciding how much to borrow or save.
10. Note also, for example, that if income in a non-poor period were to increase by one unit while income in a poor period which occurs within a sequence of poor periods were to decrease by one unit, overall poverty would rise, chronic poverty would remain unchanged, and so transitory poverty would also rise.
11. The values in **p** and **p′** are not incomes but values of poverty that are computed from the respective income distributions.
12. Mendola et al. (2011) proposed a somewhat different yet more complicated measure along the same lines. To preserve space, we do not review the other measure here.
13. Hoy and Zheng (2008) demonstrate empirically, using Panel Study of Income Dynamics (PSID) data, that adding additional axiomatic requirements, such as their early and chronic poverty axioms, leads to substantial increases in the power of the partial orderings that one can infer when making pairwise (individual) lifetime poverty comparisons.

REFERENCES

Azariadis, C. and J. Stachurski (2005), Poverty traps. In P. Aghion and S. Durlauf (eds), *Handbook of Economic Growth*, Vol. 1, Part A, pp. 295–384. Amsterdam: Elsevier, North-Holland.
Bossert, W., S.R. Chakravarty and C. D'Ambrosio (2012), Poverty and time. *Journal of Economic Inequality*, 10, 145–162.
Calvo, C. and S. Dercon (2009), Chronic poverty and all that: the measurement of poverty over time. In T. Addison, D. Hulme and R. Kanbur (eds), *Poverty Dynamics: Interdisciplinary Perspectives*, pp. 29–58. Oxford: Oxford University Press.
Chakravarty, S. (2009), *Inequality, Polarization and Poverty, Advances in Distributional Analysis*, New York: Springer.
Duclos, J.Y., A. Araar and J. Giles (2010), Chronic and transient poverty: measurement and estimation, with evidence from China. *Journal of Development Economics*, 91, 266–277.
Dutta, I., L. Roope and H. Zank (2013), On intertemporal poverty measures: the role of affluence and want. *Social Choice and Welfare*, 11, 741–762.
Foster, J. (2007), A class of chronic poverty measures. Department of Economics Vanderbilt University working paper no. 07-W01.
Foster, J. (2009), A class of chronic poverty measures. In T. Addison, D. Hulme and R. Kanbur (eds), *Poverty Dynamics: Interdisciplinary Perspectives*, pp. 59–76. Oxford: Oxford University Press.
Foster, J. and A. Sen (1997), On economic inequality: after a quarter century. Annex to the enlarged edition of Amartya Sen, *On Economic Inequality*, Oxford: Clarendon Press.
Godley, J.R. (1847), Observations on an Irish Poor Law, addressed to the Committee of Landed Proprietors, assembled in Dublin, January, Grant & Bolton, Dublin, Ireland.
Gradin, C., C. del Rio and O. Canto (2012), Measuring poverty accounting for time. *Review of Income and Wealth*, 58, 330–354.
Günther, I. and J. Maier (2008), Poverty, vulnerability and loss aversion. unpublished mimeo.
Hojman, D. and F. Kast (2009), On the measurement of poverty dynamics. HKS Faculty Research Working Paper Series RWP09-035, John F. Kennedy School of Government, Harvard University.
Hoy, M. and B. Zheng (2008), Measuring lifetime poverty. Department of Economics, University of Guelph Discussion Paper No. 2008-14.
Hoy, M. and B. Zheng (2011), Measuring lifetime poverty. *Journal of Economic Theory*, 146, 2544–2562.
Hoy, M., B.S. Thompson and B. Zheng (2012), Empirical issues in lifetime poverty measurement. *Journal of Economic Inequality*, 10, 163–189.
Hulme, D. and A. Shepherd (2003), Conceptualizing chronic poverty. *World Development*, 31, 303–423.
Jalan, J. and M. Ravallion (2000), Is transient poverty different? Evidence for rural China. *Journal Development Studies*, 36, 82–99.
Kanbur, R. and D. Mukherjee (2007), Premature mortality and poverty measurement. *Bulletin of Economic Research*, 59, 339–359.
Mendola, D. and A. Busetta (2012), The importance of consecutive spells of poverty: a path-dependent index of longitudinal poverty. *Review of Income and Wealth*, 58, 355–374.
Mendola, D., A. Busetta and A.M. Milito (2009), The importance of consecutive spells of poverty: a longitudinal poverty index. IRISS Working Paper Series, Series A, 21.

Mendola, D., A. Busetta and A.M. Milito (2011), Combining the intensity and sequencing of the poverty experience: a class of longitudinal poverty indices. *Journal of the Royal Statistical Society*, 174, 953–973.

Rodgers, J. and J. Rodgers (1993), Chronic poverty in the United States. *Journal of Human Resources*, 28, 25–54.

Sen, A. (1976), Poverty: an ordinal approach to measurement. *Econometrica*, 44, 219–231.

Zheng, B. (1997), Aggregate poverty measures. *Journal of Economic Surveys*, 11, 123–162.

Zheng, B. (2012), Measuring chronic poverty: a gravitational approach. Working Paper, Department of Economics, University of Colorado Denver.

10. Poverty over time: empirical findings
Carlos Gradín, Olga Cantó and Coral del Río

10.1 INTRODUCTION

The modern analysis of poverty began more than a century ago by quantifying the extent of this phenomenon in a cross-section of individuals in a particular territory. Since the pioneering works at the turn of the nineteenth century by Charles Booth (1889) and Seebohm Rowntree (1901), referring to London and York, respectively, many studies have extended the analysis of poverty all over the world. This literature boomed during the last decades mostly because there was an increasing concern about poverty, and its combat was included in the political agenda. Lyndon Johnson's War on Poverty in the United States (US), the Lisbon strategy and Europe 2020 agenda in the European Union (EU), and the United Nations (UN) Millennium and Sustainable Development Goals are outstanding examples of this. In any case, the rapidly growing literature on the analysis of poverty was possible thanks to the availability of more data, mostly cross-sectional, and the development of a more rigorous conceptual and methodological framework on poverty measurement.

Poverty was identified from the very beginning as a dynamic phenomenon, and therefore its analysis over time became a priority. The ways of introducing time into the measurement of poverty have been diverse; the most obvious and common method is to build a series of poverty indices that allow for the analysis of poverty trends in time based on two or more cross-sections of individuals. This simple approach allows tracking the relevance of poverty over time, but at the same time it conceals relevant issues regarding the dynamic nature of poverty as a time-varying state for each affected individual. Indeed, many people may fall into poverty at any time due to a variety of factors affecting their household, such as a change in their labor market outcomes (for example, losing a job), in their composition (for example, a divorce, a new born-child) or in their benefit eligibility (for example, losing unemployment compensation). The likelihood of being in poverty varies across individuals, and also through the life cycle, something that was already suggested by Rowntree (1901). Consequently, a cross-sectional poverty rate does not provide us with any information about the flows of individuals in and out of poverty. In fact, the change in the poverty rate between two given periods is just the net result of entries and exits of poverty. Thus, a stable poverty rate in time is compatible with a high and a low rotation of individuals in and out of poverty.

Given the dynamic nature of poverty, a relevant part of the literature has focused on developing an inter-temporal analysis of the phenomenon in a variety of different ways. In fact, in recent times there has clearly been increasing research interest in this particular field, given the recent publication of various books, reports and monographs in journals, and the organization of some specialized conferences. The main research concern in this field is to discover the main causes of poverty and thereby to identify which policies may be more effective in reducing it. There is a wide consensus in the literature on the heterogeneity of the poverty phenomenon in terms of the individual inter-temporal pattern, leading to a fundamental distinction in the causes of poverty and, consequently, in the best alleviating policies. The main way the literature has dealt with this heterogeneity has been to try to distinguish between poverty that represents a temporary state (called transitory, temporary or transient poverty) from poverty representing a long-term or deep lack of well-being (persistent, permanent or chronic poverty). There are various reasons why making such a distinction is adequate. Both types of poverty are of a clearly different nature, with different implications in terms of the well-being of the poor. While increasing human and physical assets (as well as the returns to those assets) would be a more effective policy in reducing chronic poverty, insurance and income-stabilization schemes would be more appropriate in order to deal with transitory poverty (e.g., Jalan and Ravallion, 1998).

The literature on poverty over time has been in constant development since the end of the 1970s, trying to find adequate answers to three main questions. The first of these is to provide an adequate measure of total inter-temporal poverty observed along a given time span, and to give some dimension of the relevance of chronic and transitory poverty within it. In fact, in recent years the issue of how to actually measure total inter-temporal poverty has become most prominent in the research agenda and still remains an open question, with an incipient and growing empirical literature. The second issue is to identify the main characteristics associated with each inter-temporal poverty type, and its major determinants and consequences on individual welfare. Finally, the key issue is to identify which are the most effective policies in combatting the poverty phenomenon, by adequately focusing each alleviating policy on the individuals with a particular time poverty profile.

The analysis of poverty in a cross-section of individuals basically requires two stages (Sen, 1976). The first stage is identification, when the researcher needs to choose in which dimensions individual well-being will be assessed, based on the available data. This stage usually requires fixing a poverty line that allows separation of the poor from the non-poor population. The second stage is aggregation, when the researcher must summarize the information collected at the individual level into an index of poverty for the whole society. In measuring poverty over time, the literature also needs to deal with these two stages, but in a more complex way than when only one single period is involved, due to the necessity of considering different possible inter-temporal well-being patterns. Indeed, there are at least three fundamental methodological issues involved in the analysis of dynamic poverty.

First, regarding the identification of the poor, in the same way as when approaching the measurement of static poverty, the most common choice is to use the information on needs-adjusted household income or consumption over a specific accounting period (a month, a year) and to identify the poor using the poverty line (either relative or absolute) that is most common in each geographical context, even if there is an observable increasing interest in exploring poverty in a multidimensional perspective. Note, however, that the implications of this choice in a dynamic framework are significantly greater than in a static one given that, in this inter-temporal context, the intrinsic variability of each variable in time and the existence of measurement error will imply changes in the value of the reference variable which do not really reflect any changes in well-being, thus leading to the risk of overestimating transitory poverty. In this vein, Clark and Hulme (2010), for example, claim that well-being measures based on a more holistic concept – such as literacy, nutritional status or housing quality – would produce a significantly different picture than when using income or consumption. Additionally, the identification process here may involve a twofold strategy, because of the variability in well-being over time: apart from identifying the poor in each period, the researcher often wants to separate the chronic from the transitory poor, or even to compute an individual inter-temporal poverty index as the basis for a subsequent aggregation across society as a whole. Given the large number of possible different inter-temporal poverty trajectories, it is not straightforward to determine which particular profiles are to be considered as being part of chronic poverty, and that usually depends strongly on the approach followed and on the available data.

Second, the aggregation stage of poverty is also more complex in the dynamic framework than in the static framework, because one needs to summarize in a single index all poverty profiles over time. This implies dealing with fundamental questions such as the extent to which people are able to smooth their consumption along a time span, whether consecutive years in poverty should be treated differently to non-consecutive ones, or whether any discount factor should be used when aggregating poverty from different years. Most of the literature has overcome this lack of an appropriate conceptual framework by focusing on the incidence of poverty and poverty flows, or by averaging across individuals. Surprisingly, it was not until recently that the measurement of inter-temporal poverty became a central issue in the discussion.

Finally, the need for inter-temporal individual information in a dynamic analysis is clearly more demanding of data than in any conventional cross-sectional analysis. Hence, this strongly restricts the set of databases available for undertaking this type of study. Most researchers use panel data with a variety of time spans, sample sizes and designs. The main problem here is the limited availability of this kind of data, due to high collection costs. In some cases, in order to reduce these high costs the length in time covered by the panel is short or the number of observations sampled is relatively small. Additionally, panels can be problematic due to sample bias arising from high attrition rates, an inherent difficulty of tracking households over time, or linked to migration flows during the observation period. Not surprisingly, the empirical expansion of this field has taken place in parallel with the increasing availability of appropriate data.

A few outstanding panels in some mostly developed countries have been tracking a significant number of households for long time spans and, therefore, have become the main source of empirical analysis of poverty dynamics in the world. The first of these is the Panel Study of Income Dynamics (PSID) for the US collected by the University of Michigan since 1968.[1] In 1984, the Deutsche Institut für Wirtshaftsforschung (DIW) started collecting data for the German Socio-Economic Panel (SOEP), and somewhat later, in 1991, a similar panel was initiated for the United Kingdom (UK) by the Institute for Social and Economic Research (ISER): the British Household Panel Survey (BHPS).[2] Further, in the early 1990s the European Statistical Office, Eurostat, decided to launch the European Community Household Panel (ECHP), an eight-year multi-country panel survey including information on 15 European Union countries which provided extremely valuable information in order to analyze income dynamics in the European Union at that time. Unfortunately, Eurostat did not continue to collect this dataset (it covers only the 1994–2001 period) and in 2004 the ECHP was replaced by the European Union Survey on Income and Living Conditions (EU-SILC), a panel survey of a much more limited scope that consists of four-year rotating data. Yet, this survey is larger than the ECHP, given that it expanded its sample including information from the new EU and associated countries.

With the exception of the ECHP and the EU-SILC, panel surveys all over the world have been mostly used in poverty dynamics research for single-country studies, so there is a considerable lack of cross-national research in the field. Some projects that have tried to mitigate this problem by collecting comparable information from several heterogeneous panels are the Panel Comparability Project (PACO) at former CEPS/INSTEAD (Centre d'Etudes de Populations, de Pauvreté et de Politiques Socio Economiques / International Network for Studies in Technology, Environment, Alternatives, Development) now the Luxembourg Institute of Socio-Economic Research (LISER) that was run for only a few years, and the Cross National Equivalent Files (CNEF) prepared since 1970 by Cornell University, first, and later by the Ohio State University.[3] Despite these difficulties, a few studies have been able to provide some cross-country comparative analyses.[4] In the following sections of this chapter we summarize the answers to the most relevant questions previously posed that have been provided by the literature on poverty over time, based on a large variety of empirical findings.

10.2   THE RELEVANCE OF CHRONIC AND TRANSITORY POVERTY

Some theories popularized during the 1960s had promulgated the idea of poverty as a permanent state in both developing and industrialized countries, and the poor as an isolated population living in their own subculture.[5] Contrary to these ideas, a large empirical literature since the late 1970s has confirmed, in a variety of ways and for different geographical areas, the existence of significant flows into and out of poverty. Notwithstanding this continuous rotation within the poor, the literature has also identified that a significant subpopulation suffers poverty persistently or recurrently. Thus the fact is that the poverty phenomenon can only be adequately understood by analyzing its dynamics, and it is crucial to be able to quantify these phenomena in order to identify different poverty profile determinants and consequences and, therefore, to establish which policies are more likely to be most effective in each case. Let us highlight first the main findings regarding the quantification of these flows, and then go into more detail regarding the causes and consequences of different poverty profiles in the next section.

10.2.1   Empirical Evidence on Poverty Dynamics

Poverty flows into and out of poverty
The most striking results regarding poverty flows came from the analysis of the time spent in poverty, applying survival analysis. In their classic paper, Bane and Ellwood (1986) showed that most poverty spells in the US are in fact quite short.[6] Using data from the PSID for the 1970s and the US official definition of poverty they estimated that almost 45 percent of new poverty spells are expected to end after one single year. Further, about 70 percent will end after just three years, and no more than 12 percent of these new poverty spells are expected to last more than nine years. Several studies have extended this kind of

analysis to other countries.[7] For example, Jenkins and Rigg (2001) estimated that, using 60 percent of the median income as a poverty line and the BHPS during the 1990s, 54 percent of new entrants to poverty manage to leave after one year in the UK. This percentage of leavers grows to almost 80 percent after three years, while only about 8 percent of these new entrants remained poor after a seven-year period. Therefore, these authors' results draw a very similar pattern of poverty persistence in the UK compared to that previously obtained for the US: 'one of relatively short spells for the majority, but relatively long spells for a significant minority' (Jenkins and Rigg, 2001, p. 78).

A few studies have shown the actual variety in individual inter-temporal poverty patterns across countries; but unfortunately, due to data limitations, their results are generally based on short panels.[8] For example, according to Fouarge and Layte (2005), the proportion of new spells expected to be finished by the first year in western EU countries during 1995–1998 (using 60 percent of the national median as a poverty line) was found to vary between 45 percent in Portugal and the UK, and 55–56 percent in Belgium, Spain and Denmark. After three years, the proportion of spells that are expected to have ended ranges between 72 percent in France, and 79 percent in Denmark.

In general, high values of poverty entry and exit rates every year show that there is a large rotation within the poor in a particular country. For example, Valletta (2006), analyzing the CNEF for the 1990s based on equivalent disposable income, reported during six years and a poverty line fixed at a conservative 50 percent of the median, shows that in Canada and the US, on average, 4.5 percent and 5.5 percent of the non-poor population, respectively, falls into poverty from one year to the next. These percentages are slightly smaller in the UK and Germany (3.8 percent and 3.1 percent, respectively). Similarly, a relatively large percentage of the poor are able to leave poverty the following year, even if there are large differences between countries: 55 percent in the UK, 42 percent in Germany, 37 percent in the US, and 32 percent in Canada. Mean spell duration over the whole period analyzed (a biased estimate of the true expected spell duration) is lowest in the UK (1.6 years) and largest in Canada (2.6 years), with intermediate values in Germany and the US: 1.9 and 2.1 years, respectively. Interestingly, poverty flows appear to be particularly sensitive to the business cycle, but also show long-term trends. For example, Stevens (1994) showed this to be true for the US, finding that after conditioning on the business cycle, there was a declining trend in poverty exit rates for the period 1970–1987. In the same vein, Jenkins (2011) finds that the decline in poverty rates in the UK between 1991 and the mid-2000s was driven by the rise in the poverty exit rate (which went from 30 percent in 1995 to 40 percent in 2003), although with fluctuations during the period, while the entry rate was largely stabilized around 8–9 percent.

There are, thus, some country-specific profiles in terms of poverty dynamics. As Valletta (2006, p. 269) underlines: 'In particular, individuals in Great Britain face relatively high entry and exit rates to and from poverty and a relatively low mean duration, while Canada has relatively low exit rates and high mean duration'. Consequently, it is possible to assess the extent to which poverty is more or less persistent in each country. It turns out that poverty is more persistent in the US and Canada, where the percentage of individuals who are poor all six observed years is 3.9 percent of the total population in the US and 3.5 percent in Canada, which is in contrast with 1.4 percent in Germany and only 0.4 percent in the UK. However, it is important to note, as Bane and Ellwood (1986) did, that the long-term poor make up a large part of the group of the poor in any given year.[9] This is the consequence of those in longer spells being more likely to be sampled as being in poverty in any given year. These authors estimated that more than a half of the cross-sectional poor in the US are in fact in a spell expected to last more than nine years (and that about 26 percent of the poor had already been poor for more than nine years). As a consequence of this intense rotation within the poor each year, the proportion of population affected by poverty over a few years is much larger than the usual cross-sectional poverty rates indicate. For example, Valletta (2006) obtains that the proportion of ever-poor (as opposed to persistently poor) individuals is approximately twice the average annual poverty rate in all four analyzed countries. This proportion of ever-poor individuals ranges from 18 percent in Germany and 21 percent in the UK, to 25 percent in Canada and 30 percent in the US. In the words of Rodgers and Rodgers (1993, p. 28) these findings using the Bane and Ellwood (1986) spells approach:

> reconciled the conflicting views of the 1960s (that poverty is mostly long term) and 1970s (that poverty is mostly short term) by demonstrating that a large percentage of those who are poor at a particular point in time are in long-term poverty, but only a small percentage of the ever-poor population experience a long poverty spell.

This same type of cross-country exercise is undertaken in OECD (2008) for a larger group of countries – 17 Organisation for Economic Co-operation and Development (OECD) countries – although for a shorter time span (three years around the 2000s), based on income before taxes and after public transfers and using heterogeneous sources.[10] Placing the poverty threshold at 50 percent of the median, this report found that the poverty exit rate was on average 40 percent (above 50 percent in only two countries: the Netherlands and Denmark; and below 30 percent in only three countries: Canada, the US and Ireland). The entry rate was on average about 5 percent (with the largest value in Australia and Spain: above 6 percent; and the lowest in Luxembourg, Germany and Austria: below 3 percent). The percentage of ever-poor population ranged from 10 percent in Luxembourg to 25 percent in Australia, and the proportion of persistent poor (poor in all three years) was above 7 percent in Australia, Greece, Ireland, Portugal and the US; but lower than 2 percent in Denmark and the Netherlands.

Intense rotation within the poor has also been found in completely different economic contexts, and also when absolute poverty lines are used. For example, Gustafsson and Sai (2009) estimated that in a sample of rural households in China during the early 2000s from the China Household Income Project (CHIP) data and according to the National Bureau of Statistics usual low income threshold, the poverty entry rate between two consecutive years is about 4 percent and the poverty exit rate is about 45–50 percent. Further, less than 4 percent of the rural Chinese sample was poor over three consecutive years, compared with a 16 percent of the sample that was ever poor. These numbers are similar to what has been obtained for developed countries using relative poverty thresholds. In contrast, Gaiha and Deolalikar (1993), using a panel survey of rural South India (from the International Crops Research Institute Semi-Arids Tropics, ICRISAT) obtained that 88 percent of the individuals in the sample were poor at least once during the nine-year period between 1975/76–1983/84, with a high proportion (one in four of them, or 22 percent of the sample) being always below the poverty threshold. Indeed, in their literature review on poverty dynamics in the developing world based on 13 studies from ten countries, using heterogeneous data sources, periods and welfare measures, Baulch and

Hoddinott (2000) show that the proportion of those ever poor for all the consecutive years considered is generally lower than the proportion of those who are sometimes poor, but they note that there is a high variability in this difference depending on the country considered.

The existence of intense flows out of poverty must not be misunderstood, in the sense that it should not be perceived that poverty is no longer a problem. In fact, in most countries the quality of many poverty exits is very low and poverty recurrence is high. In the particular case of the US, Stevens (1999) noticed that many exits out of poverty are only temporary, with people recurrently falling back into poverty after a short while: half of those leaving poverty return to it within the following four years. Jenkins and Rigg (2001) find a similar pattern in the UK and conclude that 30 percent of those leaving poverty fall back into poverty again within the following year, although they also notice that those who manage to stay out of poverty longer face a much lower risk of returning back to poverty (a re-entry rate of 7 percent after five years). Thus, these results underline the importance of considering a multiple-spell approach to the analysis of poverty dynamics, although it might be necessary to make some adjustments in order to deal with measurement error to prevent spurious interruptions of spells both in and out of poverty. Indeed, some studies have investigated in more detail how the length of spells in and out of poverty influences future poverty risk (e.g., Cantó, 2002; Fouarge and Layte, 2005; Biewen, 2006; Andriopoulou and Tsaglokou, 2011; Arranz and Cantó, 2012).

Permanent income approach

In order to prevent considering as transitory poverty some small changes in income or consumption that are not economically relevant, some studies use an alternative way of measuring chronic poverty. Rodgers and Rodgers (1993, p. 26, agreeing with Rainwater, 1981), claim that 'longer income periods are better suited to understanding the nature of chronic poverty than shorter income periods' because permanent income (or the lack of it) is the principal influence on people's standard of living and style of life. Rodgers and Rodgers (1993, p. 31) define permanent income for T years as 'the maximum sustainable annual consumption level that the agent could achieve with his or her actual income stream over the same T years, if the agent could save and borrow at prevailing interest rates'. Thus inter-year income transfers are assumed to be feasible in order to smooth consumption (although there is evidence suggesting the existence of liquidity constrains among the poor, for example, Jappelli, 1990). In practice in these papers, the interest rate is generally assumed to be constant and equal for borrowing and saving, and very often is fixed at a zero rate. In this setting, permanent income is commonly calculated as the mean income or consumption in the relevant period and then compared with average needs over that same period.[11]

The proportion of chronic poor based on permanent income, by construction, must be larger than when considering only those who are always poor, given that we are now also including as chronic poor those individuals whose income or consumption when out of poverty does not compensate the poverty gap when in poverty.[12] According to Valletta (2006), using this new criterion the proportion of chronic poor in the US and Canada increases from 3.9 percent and 3.5 percent (always poor) to 10.6 percent and 9.1 percent, respectively; while in the case of Germany and the UK it increases from 1.4 percent and

0.4 percent (always poor) to 4.4 percent and 2.9 percent, respectively. Interestingly, the differences between countries using this other measure become even wider.

The idea of permanent income in order to approach the measurement of individual well-being has inspired a whole branch of the poverty dynamics literature (the so-called components approach), especially fruitful in country-specific studies for developing countries, as another way to measure the relevance of chronic and transitory poverty.[13] In this approach the main focus is to decompose total poverty in its permanent and transitory components. Thus, transient poverty is what results from the variability of well-being in time, while chronic poverty is what remains when this variability is eliminated. Chronic poverty is, then, the level of poverty one obtains when substituting, for each individual, the value of yearly income or consumption by that of the permanent income. The poverty index most commonly used in order to obtain total poverty is the mean for all years and all individuals of $(1 - y_{it})^2$, where y_{it} is the income/consumption for individual i at moment t, normalized for differences in demographics and prices, and relative to the poverty gap, thus y_{it} takes the value 1 for someone at the poverty line. This index is based on the squared poverty gap index, the Foster–Greer–Thorbecke index with parameter equal to 2, $FGT(2)$, that apart from considering incidence also incorporates intensity and inequality to the measurement of total poverty. In a similar way, chronic poverty is then measured by substituting y_{it} by the mean income or consumption for the whole time span and then transitory poverty is obtained as the difference between total and chronic poverty (Jalan and Ravallion, 1998).[14] Using this method, Jalan and Ravallion (1998) obtain for the 1985–1990 period that half of total poverty in rural China is chronic while the other half is transitory. Further, out of the total cross-sectional poor every year the percentage of chronically poor is over 50 percent and was continuously increasing over the period.[15]

The method of this study has been largely replicated for a long list of mostly developing countries. For example, Mills and Mykerezi (2009), using the Russian Longitudinal Monitoring Survey (RLMS) for the period 1994–2003, find a significantly lower percentage of chronic poverty: 14 percent (37 percent when focusing only on 2000–2003). However, Nega et al. (2010) and Haddad and Ahmed (2003), although based on very small samples, find chronic poverty to account for about two-thirds of total poverty in four rural communities in northern Ethiopia (2004–2006) and Egypt (1997–1999).

10.2.2 Measuring Aggregate Inter-Temporal Poverty

All previous empirical studies on poverty dynamics reveal that there has been an increasing interest in the literature in summarizing the information provided by a panel of individuals and consequently in constructing consistent aggregate poverty measures that take into account individual income/consumption profiles across time. The main advantage of these measures is that they will allow for ranking different distributions in terms of poverty accounting for many relevant dynamic features at the same time. Despite this being a promising line of research (Jäntti and Jenkins, 2015), no consensus has been yet reached regarding which characteristics this inter-temporal poverty measure should have, and thus the empirical evidence is still scarce and is mostly devoted to testing different methodological points, while the results are quite sensitive to the underlying assumptions made by researchers.

Following a components approach provides a family of measures that allow for the possibility of fully compensating low and high income periods, thus underlying the relevance of permanent income in poverty analyses. Moreover, the use of a permanent income concept summarizing individual inter-temporal profiles makes it particularly easy to construct a chronic poverty measure with similar properties as those usually required in cross-sectional poverty analysis, such as incidence, intensity and inequality among the poor. In this case, however, the corresponding chronic poverty measure is insensitive to the number of periods that individuals spend below the poverty line, and thus prevents researchers from identifying the role of poverty duration.

In contrast, most of the literature discussed in the previous section, that is usually referred to as the spells approach (Yaqub, 2000), emphasizes the duration of poverty in time, thus defining chronic poverty as that part of the phenomenon that lasts for all (or most) of the observation time span. The transitory poor are then all other shorter poverty experiences, including those who suffer poverty only occasionally and those who experience it recurrently. However, within this approach most poverty analysis only accounts for either the incidence of poverty with different time patterns or the mean poverty spell duration. Thus, it does not consider either per-period poverty intensity or inter-temporal variability (inequality of per-period individual poverty gaps along time) in a composite measure of persistent poverty. This gap has recently been filled by a number of contributions aimed at integrating other dimensions of poverty such as intensity and inequality and even the possibility of income compensation within this duration-based approach. Nevertheless, this has revealed itself as a quite difficult task, since the introduction of the time dimension in poverty analysis necessarily involves various value judgements which remain controversial: Is persistent poverty more severe than recurrent poverty? How should persistence in poverty be defined? When in a lifetime is a poverty spell more harmful for well-being? To what extent may incomes from non-poverty periods mitigate the effects of poverty gaps? Is there a social preference for equality among individuals or among per-period individual poverty gaps?

Using an extension of the *FGT* index that allows incorporating per-period poverty gap intensity and inequality, Foster (2007, 2009) shows that chronic poverty in Argentina in the early 2000s was about 91 percent of total poverty, a percentage that is higher than the usual results obtained by earlier approaches. The chronic poor account for 64 percent of the ever poor, while the percentage of poverty periods that belong to the chronically poor account for 79 percent of the total. All of this suggests that income deficits are larger for the chronically poor. This group is identified by using a double cut-off; that is, those who spend a minimum number of periods below the poverty line (for example, three out of four). Total poverty is defined to be the average of per-period normalized poverty gaps across all the poor, while chronic poverty is this average only across those identified as chronically poor. Taking advantage of the decomposability properties of these measures, the contribution of six Argentinian regions to overall chronic poverty is quantified. For example, the north-east of the country registers a high chronic poverty incidence, given that even though only 15 percent of the population live there, it accounts for 26–28 percent of total chronic poverty.

Individual poverty trajectories

Foster's approach incorporates a duration cut-off and a preference for equality in an aggregate measure of chronic poverty in an easy and intuitive manner. However, poverty periods are treated equally regardless of whether they are in a longer or shorter spell, given that once individuals are identified as chronically poor, all their per-period observations are assumed to be independent from each other. However, as mentioned above, the literature on poverty duration suggests that the longer a person has been poor, the lower is their likelihood of escaping poverty and the greater the lack of well-being. Not surprisingly, several papers have recently incorporated, in a variety of ways, the sensitivity of inter-temporal poverty to poverty persistence and have showed its empirical relevance.

Bossert et al. (2012) use a similar extended *FGT* index to analyze inter-temporal poverty in the EU (ECHP 1994–2001). Their approach introduces the sensitivity to spells duration in the aggregate measure by weighting each per-period poverty gap by the length of the spell to which that period belongs. Portugal and Greece turn out to be the countries with more inter-temporal poverty regardless of whether longer spells are penalized or not, while Denmark and Finland are among those with the lowest poverty. However, Austria and particularly Spain, with a high level of temporary poverty, show less severe poverty once persistency is taken into account, precisely the opposite of what happens in Germany.

Gradín et al. (2012) extend this approach, considering different degrees of sensitivity to duration, as well as incorporating a social preference for equality among individual poverty profiles rather than among per-period individual poverty gaps, used in the two previous approaches. This last feature is introduced in order to reconcile the way in which poverty is measured in a static and a dynamic framework, following Sen's ideas on the dimensions of poverty. The empirical results show that Portugal presents not only a higher proportion of population ever poor, and a higher average duration and persistency, but also a higher inequality of poverty experiences among individuals, accumulating in one country all features that negatively impact on inter-temporal poverty. Denmark is the opposite case to Portugal because it accumulates all poverty-reducing features. However, again, it is not necessarily true that countries with high (low) levels of inter-temporal poverty will always increase (decrease) their index when inequality among individuals is considered: inter-temporal poverty is relatively less severe in Spain (due to a high rotation in poverty), while it remains roughly invariant at low levels in Germany.[16] Aaron and Ray (2012) have extended this approach to analyze inter-temporal multidimensional deprivation in Australia.

Hoy and Zheng (2011) analyze lifetime poverty instead of inter-temporal poverty of a population over a number of years. In this context, poverty is assumed to be aggravated with poverty spells experienced at earlier stages of life based on evidence showing that it 'not only affects consumption in later periods but also leaves an inherently deeper mark on lifetime deprivation' (Hoy and Zheng, 2011, p. 2545). Duration is also considered as the accumulation of (not necessarily consecutive) poverty periods in time.[17] In an empirical analysis using these and some of the previous approaches, Hoy et al. (2012) analyze lifetime poverty in the US using the PSID from 1967 to 1992, showing the extent to which non-whites robustly suffer more chronic poverty than whites.

Finally, the role of spell duration on inter-temporal poverty measurement has been considered in a variety of other ways. Mendola and Busetta (2012), unlike Hoy and Zheng's view, consider that more recent spells are the most relevant, and non-poverty spells have a particularly relevant role, so they measure longitudinal poverty taking into account the distance between poverty periods. Calvo and Dercon (2009) instead introduced sequence sensitivity by weighting each year's poverty gap by the gap in the previous year, and used discounting factors to handle poverty gaps in different periods.

Income compensation over time

As noted in the previous section, duration-sensitive longitudinal poverty approaches generally assume that households cannot compensate (not even partially) the income deficit during poverty spells with income from other periods spent out of poverty. This is precisely the opposite idea to that of the components approach which does not consider duration, assuming that full compensation is actually possible. Different studies have proposed a variety of methodologies in order to introduce more flexibility in income compensation, and have assessed the empirical relevance that different views about the role of compensation have on ranking inter-temporal poverty across households. This point is relevant from an empirical point of view, as Calvo and Dercon (2009) show, using data from rural Ethiopia, that there are high correlations among inter-temporal measures but with considerable differences in ranking households by poverty depending on the different views on the role of compensation.

Hoy and Zheng's previously discussed approach is a clear case of how duration and (partial) compensation can be integrated in the same setting. Their lifetime poverty measure is a weighted average of two terms, one reflecting sensitivity to duration, and the other being a measure of permanent poverty (when the mean consumption is below the poverty line). Foster and Santos (2012) analyze urban chronic poverty in Argentina between 2001 and 2003, using a measure that penalizes inequality in income distribution over time while allowing for several degrees of income substitutability across periods. As expected, they show that chronic poverty increases as lower income substitutability across periods is allowed for. This is because the higher costs of transferring income between periods aggravate the difficulties of some of the people initially considered as being in transitory poverty. However, under all considered assumptions the percentage of chronically poor is always high (53–58 percent), and chronic poverty represents most of total poverty (89–98 percent). Furthermore, they are able to provide a measure of the different contribution of different periods to total inter-temporal poverty. For example, the crisis period from December 2001 onwards (75 percent of the sample) accounts for 85–87 percent chronic poverty in Argentina.

Finally, another relevant feature of inter-temporal income compensation that has attracted the attention of researchers in recent times is the fact that compensation may be more difficult in periods of extreme poverty, given the long-term consequences of extreme deficits (for example, severe malnutrition), and because 'fluctuations in well-being have a greater negative impact, the poorer the individual' (Porter and Quinn, 2008, p. 27).

10.3   DETERMINANTS OF POVERTY DYNAMICS

The empirical work on poverty dynamics has mostly identified two distinct types of poverty: chronic and transitory (which may be recurrent). We have already seen that the available empirical research has quantified the relevance of these two types of poverty as well as the magnitude of flows into and out of poverty. In this section we show that many research papers have also identified the main demographic and socioeconomic characteristics associated to chronic and transitory poverty, as well as the mechanisms through which poverty transitions occur, and the long-term consequences of persistent poverty, especially during childhood. These issues are especially important for policy design.

10.3.1   Characterization of Poverty by Type

A first main result of the empirical literature is to highlight the fact that the chronic or persistently poor are actually different from the transitory poor. This is a consistent conclusion regardless of the particular approach used.

For instance, the approaches based on the duration of poverty, such the pioneering work undertaken by Duncan (1984) for the US, show that the characteristics of the persistently poor differ markedly from those of individuals who have experienced just one year in poverty.[18] In fact, the characteristics of the temporarily poor are not very different from those of the rest of the population, while two-thirds of the chronic poor in the US are either elderly or black females with low chances to escape poverty through work or marriage. Other studies using a similar method, such as Oxley et al. (2000), OECD (2001, 2008) and Valletta (2006), have also obtained that female headship is consistently associated with persistent poverty in most of the countries analyzed. In fact, this seems to be the case in all of the 18 countries studied by the OECD (2008), and most strongly in Austria, Belgium, Denmark and Finland. In general, this result reflects the situation of two different demographic groups: single elderly women without children, and young women with children. Indeed, in most of the countries studied, chronic poverty risk is higher for single-adult households with children, who face a risk of persistent poverty that is twice as high as that of the whole population, particularly in Japan, the Netherlands and Denmark. Additionally, a high persistent poverty risk is also associated with either low educational attainment of the household head (except in Germany) or head aged 65 or over, particularly in Australia, Italy and Japan. Finally, individuals belonging to workless households have a chronic poverty risk that is almost five times higher than that of the whole population, especially in Canada, Denmark and the Netherlands. In a quite different context – rural China – Gustafsson and Sai (2009) show that a large household size or the low education of the household head is a stronger determinant of persistent poverty than of temporary poverty. Interestingly, they also stress that some particular characteristics of the village are more associated with persistent poverty, such as being situated up in the mountains or having a low average household income.

Similar households' characteristics are shown to be associated with the chronic component of poverty in various developing countries. As Jalan and Ravallion (1998) note, referring to China, household size, presence of children and education are more important to determine chronic poverty than they are to determine transient poverty. Temporary poverty is more the consequence of the exposure of households to uninsured income risk (lack of physical assets). Indeed, as Yaqub (2000) asserts, it appears as if both in developing and affluent countries the poor manage their few assets against welfare fluctuations; however, the transitory poor are able to dominate such smoothing transactions, while the chronic poor cannot. Muller (2003) highlights the greatest association of main inputs (land and labor) with the chronic component of poverty in Rwanda. In a more general way, the report by the Chronic Poverty Research Centre (Shepherd, 2011) concludes that the main determinants of chronic poverty are insecurity, limited citizenship, spatial disadvantage, social discrimination and poor-quality work opportunities.

10.3.2   Characterizing Flows Into or Out of Poverty

A second main set of results of the empirical literature on poverty dynamics identifies the characteristics and events that are most associated with poverty transitions (entries and exits). For this purpose, many studies have estimated individual transition probabilities into and out of poverty as functions of individual or household demographic and socio-economic characteristics (for example, age, gender, household structure, education, labor status) and demographic or labor market events (for example, beginning a job, having a wage rise). If a certain factor promotes (or deters) a poverty exit, people with that characteristic will experience shorter (longer) poverty spells, and thus the factor should be associated with transitory (chronic) poverty. The models used in these studies, pioneered in the US by Levy (1977) and Hill (1981), are referred to in the literature as 'first-order Markov chains' and assume that the probability of a transition is independent of the individual's situation in previous periods of time different from the current one.

Comparing a variety of developed countries, Duncan et al. (1993) show that the income starting position (that is, the distance to the poverty line or poverty gap) is an important determinant of the probability of a transition out of poverty. Their results show that transition rates among families with incomes close to the poverty line are very similar among a group of European countries and the US and Canada. However, given that poor individuals in Germany, Ireland, Luxembourg, the Netherlands and Sweden have a level of income that is closer to the median in comparison with the US or Canada, there are large differences between these two groups of countries regarding the relevance of persistent poverty. Regarding other determinant characteristics, in an EU cross-country comparison using the ECHP between 1994 and 2000, Fouarge and Layte (2005) conclude that single parents are more likely to be persistently poor and have a lower probability of leaving poverty. Also, joblessness and a low educational level (even when employment status is controlled for) are associated with a high risk of persistent poverty.

There is also evidence for developing countries. For example, Gaiha (1988) finds that the access to cultivable land combined with modern agricultural inputs play a decisive role in poverty transitions in rural India. Similarly, Stampini and Davis (2006) conclude for rural households in Nicaragua that agricultural activities serve as a poverty exit strategy as long as they are associated with a certain accumulation of assets. In a more comparative approach, Krishna (2007) highlights that ill-health and the costs of health care are one of the most important reasons pushing households into poverty in Asia, sub-Saharan Africa and Latin America. Also, this author underlines that poverty escapes are associated with income diversification, access to employment and social networks, even if through informal employment.

10.3.3   Trigger Events

Bane and Ellwood (1986) underlined the need not only to describe the characteristics of those who transit into and out of poverty but also to identify which events are most associated with these transitions. As noted by Jenkins (2000), a change in equivalized income that triggers a transition is reflecting a change in income (income events) or/and in household composition (demographic events). Therefore, trigger events can be related to changes in either one or both of these variables. The comparative analyses undertaken by Duncan et al. (1993), Oxley et al. (2000), Layte and Whelan (2003) and OECD (2008) suggest that finding a job, getting married or starting to receive a social insurance or assistance benefit increases the probability of moving out of poverty; while becoming unemployed, getting divorced or losing a social benefit increases the likelihood of falling into poverty.[19] However, in general, most poverty transitions are concomitant with income events related to changes in employment and earnings (for example, finding or losing a job, more or less hours of work, changes in head's earnings) while fewer of them are associated to demographic events (for example, childbirth, marriage, divorce, children leaving home).[20] Indeed, Duncan et al. (1993) conclude that in all six countries that they study, employment events are the most frequent cause of both poverty entries and exits. In contrast, marriage accounts only for one-tenth of all poverty exits in three out of the six countries. Finally, social insurance events appear to play a significant role only in some particular countries.

As a consequence, Layte and Whelan (2003) underline the importance of country institutions and welfare regimes, given that they find that social welfare and market incomes play different roles in poverty transitions across countries, and that Southern European welfare regimes focus poverty risks on the experience of the household's primary earner to a far greater extent than Northern European welfare states. Not surprisingly, the OECD (2001) report concludes that a more extensive welfare state and a higher share of social spending to low-income households clearly contribute to decrease poverty persistence; and, in contrast, a higher share of low-paid employment contributes to increase it.

10.3.4 True State Dependence

The wide evidence about poverty persistence shows that experiencing poverty during a specific time period increases the probability of undergoing poverty in subsequent periods. Thus, one of the possible causes of poverty persistence that has attracted more attention in the literature is poverty itself. In the words of Cappellari and Jenkins (2004, p. 598), this happens because 'the experience of poverty itself might induce a loss of motivation, lowering the chances that individuals with given attributes escape poverty in the future'. This effect is identified in the literature as 'true or genuine state dependence' (GSD).[21] The adjectives 'true' or 'genuine' refer to the fact that this effect should not be confounded with other adverse attributes (such as low human capital, poor assets, and so on) that characterize the poor population and make them less likely to escape from poverty. If GSD is an important determinant of poverty persistency, it calls for policies aiming to break the vicious circle of poverty given that past poverty experiences may alter the individual's chances of experiencing it again through changes in the individual's preferences or set of opportunities.

Pioneering work on the matter was undertaken by Hill (1981) for the US, but the introduction of modern panel data econometrics allows for a better identification of GSD. As Cappellari and Jenkins (2004) explain, the estimation of GSD in the first-order Markovian models of transition probabilities can be biased in different ways. A first important bias is related to the fact that individuals are not randomly distributed within the initially poor (initial conditions bias). For example, low-educated individuals are more likely to be in poverty when sampled, so the estimated coefficient on education in the transition probability will be biased because its effect will include its role in determining initial poverty, and not just its influence on a poverty transition. A second bias is generated by the fact that between the initial and final period attrition occurs, and some individuals are not effectively observed at a second moment in time. If attrition is not random in terms of individual characteristics, obtained results will be biased. Furthermore, in these models it is necessary to take into account not only observed characteristics (for example, education or labor status) but also other individual-specific unobserved attributes (for example, motivation or ability). Cappellari and Jenkins (2004) estimate a substantial value of GSD for the UK: if the probability of being poor one year is 53 percentage points higher for those who were poor in the previous year, the gap remains at 31 percentage points after controlling for individual heterogeneity (both observed and unobserved). GSD is shown to be also relevant in other countries such as Germany (Biewen, 2009), Australia (Buddlemeyer and Verick, 2008) and Spain (Ayllón, 2013).

10.3.5   Long-Term Consequences of Chronic Poverty

The importance of analyzing and designing sound policies to fight chronic or persistent poverty is reinforced by new evidence that highlights the long-term consequences of experiencing severe and persistent poverty, especially during childhood. Several studies, such as Hoelscher (2004) and Magnuson and Votruba-Drzal (2009), have surveyed abundant evidence confirming that children who experience persistent poverty are at risk of suffering poor outcomes across important domains later in life, even if, in some cases, the causality is complex to determine. However, a large body of literature underlines that the consequences of poverty spells in childhood are likely to persist (Machin, 1998; Engle and Black, 2008), so that experiencing childhood poverty affects one's life chances by increasing family stress and reducing parental investments. More specifically, empirical evidence shows that deep and early poverty, holding other characteristics constant, is related to lower levels of children's achievement and educational attainment, and to child and young adult antisocial and problematic behavior. Indeed, Hirsch (2006) identifies a variety of long-term consequences of not ending child poverty in the UK: greater chance of material hardship in adulthood, linked to continuing economic disadvantage; knock-on effects on health, psychological well-being and ability to achieve life goals; and future consequences for the child's own children in the far future.

Similarly, Gregg et al. (1999) and Ermisch et al. (2001) conclude that young adults who as children suffered from financial hardship have higher chances of earning low wages, being unemployed, spending time in prison (in the case of men) and becoming a lone parent (in the case of women). In general, these authors find that education is an important 'transmission mechanism'; and poverty was found to be, by far, the most important force linking childhood development with subsequent social and economic outcomes. Indeed, the study demonstrated an intergenerational link in the cycle of family disadvantage: looking at the tested cognitive ability, at an early age, of the children whose parents had themselves grown up in socially disadvantaged situations, the average cognitive ability among them was lower. This suggests a potentially important cross-generational link that may well spill over to affect the subsequent economic fortunes of the children of disadvantaged individuals. Results for developing countries, in a report by Suryadarma et al. (2009), also conclude that, for instance, in Indonesia chronically poor children have worse health and education outcomes than other children, reducing their future opportunities. As a consequence, several papers have investigated poverty dynamics focusing on households with children, such as Jenkins and Schluter (2003) in the UK and Germany, and Gradín and Cantó (2012) in Spain.

Some other studies have focused on the distinctive long-term effects of poverty depending on its inter-temporal type. In the context of developing countries, Bhatta and Sharma (2006) indicate that poverty in Nepal has a negative impact on individual asset accumulation, so that there is a significant difference in the level of human capital accumulation between transient and chronically poor individuals. Indeed, even if household wealth and human capital are related to both poverty profiles, the relationship is more strongly related to chronic poverty. The chronically poor have a lower level of human capital, and the gap with the transient poor can be largely explained by the differences in the characteristics of the two groups. Another study, on Pakistan by Arif and Bilquees (2007), concludes that the chronically poor are more likely to depend on debt than the non-poor, while this is not the case of the transient poor. In this same line of argument, Baulch and Hoddinott (2000) conclude from the information of a variety of studies that being in poverty reflects the interlinked factors of low endowments, low returns to those endowments and vulnerability to shocks. These authors note that in one direction this means that households with larger endowments and greater returns to them are less vulnerable to shocks; but also, in the other direction, it means that vulnerability to shocks may have grave consequences on endowments and consequently will also increase the likelihood of experiencing persistent poverty.

10.4 FINAL REMARKS

Since the late 1970s the literature on poverty dynamics has helped to shape our understanding of poverty. Some features have contributed in this process. There is an increasing availability of panel data in a variety of countries, although the lack of long-period panel data in most countries and comparability issues are still probably the main obstacles that the literature faces. This explains why most research focuses on short-term dynamics instead of on a more comprehensive lifetime perspective. The literature has also taken advantage of the availability of increasingly sophisticated statistical and econometric tools designed for panel data analysis, in parallel to what happened with another dynamic phenomenon such as unemployment in labor economics. These techniques, compared with more descriptive approaches, have allowed several potential biases to be tackled, and avoiding spurious effects. A third crucial element is the progressive construction of a conceptual framework. This work is still unfinished, and different views prevail. Examples of this are the spells versus components approaches to the measurement of chronic poverty, and the difficulties to include in a single measure the level of inter-temporal poverty in a panel of individuals. However, there are also significant efforts made in order to reconcile these different views, and to provide a common framework for the measurement of both static and longitudinal poverty. Similarly, the literature on poverty dynamics could take advantage of further coordination with that of income mobility; but so far, as Jenkins

(2011) has noted, they have evolved with little overlap, with the latter much more focused on measurement issues and the former being more policy-oriented.

A few lessons can be taken from this empirical literature. We now know that there are significant inflows and outflows in poverty even in a short time interval, and at the same time we also know that there is a high inertia to stay in poverty or to fall back again after a short time out of it. Therefore, despite the large poverty rotation observed, chronic poverty remains a significant portion of the poverty phenomenon and therefore its very negative long-term consequences should be a matter for political concern. We now also have some idea about the distinctive characteristics of the persistent and transient poor, and about the main mechanisms that push people in and out of poverty, and therefore effective poverty-alleviating policies are more clearly determined. We also know that there is a great variety of inter-temporal poverty across countries, strongly dependent on the prevailing welfare regime, even if the actual country ranking may depend on what we consider important in the analysis of the poverty phenomenon.

ACKNOWLEDGEMENT

We acknowledge financial support from Ministerio de Economía, Industria y Competitividad (ECO2013-46516-C4-2-R), Xunta de Galicia (GRC2015/014), and Comunidad de Madrid (S2015/HUM-3416-DEPOPOR-CM).

NOTES

1. Other panel data that have also been used in the US are the National Longitudinal Surveys (NLS), since 1979, and the Survey of Income and Program Participation (SIPP), since 1983, with varying panel durations.
2. Since 2009 this panel has been incorporated in the new and large Understanding Society panel survey for the UK undertaken by the same institution.
3. This project includes equivalently defined variables for the mentioned PSID, SOEP and BHPS, plus the Household Income and Labour Dynamics survey in Australia (HILDA), the Canadian Survey of Labour and Income Dynamics (SLID), the Swiss Household Panel (SHP), the Korean Labor and Income Panel Study (KLIPS) and the Russian Longitudinal Monitoring Survey (RLMS-HSE).
4. Alternatives to the use of panel data, which will not be discussed in this survey, are the use of retrospective information available in cross-sections, the construction of pseudo-panels that follow several cohorts of individuals over time, and the use of static proxies of chronic poverty (severe poverty, multiple deprivations in relative stable dimensions, and so on).
5. Outstanding examples are Oscar Lewis's (1959) *Five Families: Mexican Case Studies in the Culture of Poverty*, and Michael Harrington's (1962) *The Other America: Poverty in the United States*.
6. A poverty spell is defined as 'beginning in the first year that income was below the poverty line after having been above it, and as ending when income was above the poverty line after having been below' (Bane and Ellwood, 1986, p. 7). In order to overcome potential measurement error, these authors eliminated from their analysis one-year spells either into or out of poverty if they either began or ended with an income change that was less than one-half the needs standard.
7. Examples of other country-specific studies are Stevens (1994, 1999) for the US (see Cellini et al., 2008, for a survey on research for this country); Devicenti (2001) and Jenkins (2000) for the UK (see Smith and Middleton, 2007; Jenkins, 2011 for reviews of research on this country); Addabbo (2000) for Italy; Eberharter (2001) and Biewen (2006) for Germany; Finnie and Sweetman (2003) for Canada; and Cantó (2002) and Bárcena and Cowell (2006) for Spain.
8. Outstanding examples of cross-country comparative studies are the pioneering works by Duncan et al. (1993, 1995). More recently, other similar studies have been undertaken by Oxley et al. (2000), OECD (2001, 2008), Whelan et al. (2002, 2003), Fouarge and Leyte (2005) and Valletta (2006), among others.

9. In fact their approach was a criticism of earlier studies – such as Duncan (1984), Coe et al. (1982), Coe (1978), Rainwater (1981) – that tabulate how many people were found to be poor for specific periods over a fixed time frame (for example, two out of ten years). Despite this limitation, this descriptive approach has also complemented the analysis of spell duration in more recent research.

10. Previously, another two OECD studies analyzed a more restricted set of countries: OECD (2001) analyzes 12 EU countries (using the ECHP), the US (PSID) and Canada (SLID) over three years (1993–1995); while Oxley et al. (2000) analyze six countries (Canada, Germany, the Netherlands, Sweden, the UK and the US) over a six-year period, using various surveys and tax files.

11. Although permanent income is usually measured using the mean of the individual stream of income or consumption – such as in Duncan and Rodgers (1991), Rodgers and Rodgers (1993) and Jalan and Ravallion (1998) – the literature provides other similar approaches. For example, Duclos et al. (2010) follow a normative approach using the equally distributed equivalent (EDE) poverty gap. Others such as Duncan and Rodgers (1991) interpret permanent income as the individual-specific effect estimated using a fixed-effect regression of income-to-needs ratio on households' characteristics, while the error term captures the transitory component. Other studies have followed similar model-based approaches to estimating permanent income, such as Gaiha and Deolalikar (1993), Stampini and Davis (2006) and Hasegawa and Ueda (2007).

12. OECD (2001) denominates this chronic poverty as 'permanent-income poverty'. Alternatively, other studies extend chronic poverty based on duration, relaxing the measure and also classifying as chronic poor those individuals who spend most, but not all, of the observation time below the poverty line. An outstanding example of this is the persistent-at-risk-of-poverty rate that Eurostat usually calculates, and which is defined as the share of persons with an equivalized disposable income below the national risk-of-poverty threshold (60 percent of the contemporary median) in the current year and in at least two of the preceding three years.

13. In a much earlier, different approach, Lillard and Willis (1978) estimated components-of-variance models to describe the evolution of earnings and income over time. Stevens (1999) and Devicienti (2001) conclude that, in comparison with other approaches, these components-of-variance models perform worse in fitting observed patterns of poverty in the US and the UK, respectively.

14. Rodgers and Rodgers (1993), however, compute the transitory component for each year and then average over all the periods.

15. Duclos et al. (2010), however, obtain somewhat lower estimates for the transitory poverty component in rural China (around 23 percent); their calculations are based on the use of EDE poverty gaps and after correcting for the bias coming from using short panels.

16. Note that the last two inter-temporal poverty measures may be considered as generalizations of Foster's chronic poverty index; despite the fact that they do not explicitly use a time threshold to define who is chronically poor, they can be easily adapted accordingly. Furthermore, spells duration-based approaches may be affected by spurious income fluctuations around the poverty line due to measurement error. In the context of aggregate measurement of inter-temporal poverty, Porter and Yalonetzky (2012) show with data from rural Ethiopia that the use of fuzzy poverty lines makes Foster's (2009) and Gradín et al.'s (2012) measures more robust.

17. This measure, in a similar way to others, involves a weighted average of per-period poverty levels. Here, weights depend on lifetime poverty profiles and are increasing with 'closeness' of poverty spells in time.

18. Individual and household characteristics are generally defined at the beginning of the period.

19. Some of these comparative analyses take into account that small changes in income for individuals near the poverty threshold may lead to transitions that have no significance in terms of individual welfare.

20. Similar results are obtained in single-country studies (e.g., Muffels et al., 1999; Jenkins, 2000; Jenkins and Rigg, 2001; Cantó, 2003).

21. More specifically, GSD reflects the 'scarring' effect promoting persistence that may affect the ability of poor household members to keep or take up an adequate job. Biewen (2009) mentions five of such mechanisms: (a) adverse incentives associated with the poverty trap; (b) a process of demoralization, loss of motivation or depreciation of human capital; (c) health problems such as abuse of alcohol or other drugs; (d) a reduction of one's social network due to a change in the living milieu and an increase in 'bad' contacts; and (e) strain on marriages or cohabitative relationships, and possibly an increase in the probability of a household split.

REFERENCES

Aaron, N. and R. Ray (2012), 'Duration and Persistence in Multidimensional Deprivation: Methodology and Australian Application', *Economic Record*, 88 (280), 106–126.

Addabbo, T. (2000), 'Poverty Dynamics: Analysis of Household Income in Italy', *Labor*, 14 (1), 119–144.

Andriopoulou, E. and P. Tsaglokou (2011), 'The Determinants of Poverty Transitions in Europe and the Role of Duration Dependence', IZA Discussion Paper 5692, Bonn: Institute for the Study of Labor.

Arif, G.M. and F. Bilquees (2007), 'Chronic and Transitory Poverty in Pakistan: Evidence from a Longitudinal Household Survey', *Pakistan Development Review*, 46 (2), 111–127.

Arranz, J.M. and O. Cantó (2012), 'Measuring the Effect of Spell Recurrence on Poverty Dynamics – Evidence from Spain', *Journal of Economic Inequality*, 10 (2), 191–217.

Ayllón, S. (2013), 'Understanding Poverty Persistence in Spain', *Series – Journal of The Spanish Economic Association*, 4, 201–233.

Bane, M.J. and D.T. Ellwood (1986), 'Slipping Into and Out of Poverty', *Journal of Human Resources*, 21 (1), 1–23.

Bárcena, E. and F.A. Cowell (2006), 'Static and Dynamic Poverty in Spain, 1993–2000', *Hacienda Pública Española*, 179 (4), 51–77.

Baulch, B. and J. Hoddinott (2000), 'Economic Mobility and Poverty Dynamics in Developing Countries: Introduction to Special Issue', *Journal of Development Studies*, 36 (6), 1–24.

Bhatta, S.D. and S.K. Sharma (2006), 'The Determinants and Consequences of Chronic and Transient Poverty in Nepal', CPRC Working Paper 66, Manchester: Chronic Poverty Research Centre.

Biewen, M. (2006), 'Who are the Chronic Poor? An Econometric Analysis of Chronic Poverty in Germany', *Research on Economic Inequality*, 13, 31–62.

Biewen, M. (2009), 'Measuring State Dependence in Individual Poverty Histories when there is Feedback to Employment Status and Household Composition', *Journal of Applied Econometrics*, 24 (7), 1095–1116.

Booth, C. (1889), *Life and Labour of the People*, London, UK: Macmillan.

Bossert, W., S.R. Chackravarty and C. D'Ambrosio (2012), 'Poverty and Time', *Journal of Economic Inequality*, 10 (2), 145–162.

Buddelmeyer, H. and S. Verick (2008), 'Understanding the Drivers of Poverty Dynamics in Australian Households', *Economic Record*, 84 (266), 310–321.

Calvo, C. and S. Dercon (2009), 'Chronic Poverty and All That: The Measurement of Poverty Over Time', in T. Addison, D. Hulme and R. Kanbur (eds), *Poverty Dynamics: Interdisciplinary Perspectives*, Oxford: Oxford University Press, pp. 29–58.

Cantó, O. (2002), 'Climbing Out of Poverty, Falling Back In: Low Incomes' Stability in Spain', *Applied Economics*, 34 (15), 1903–1916.

Cantó, O. (2003), 'Finding out the Routes to Escape Poverty: The Relevance of Demographic vs. Labour Market Events in Spain', *Review of Income and Wealth*, 49 (4), 569–589.

Cappellari, L. and S.P. Jenkins (2004), 'Modelling Low Income Transitions', *Journal of Applied Econometrics*, 19 (4), 593–610.

Cellini, S., S. McKernan and C. Ratcliffe (2008), 'The Dynamics of Poverty in the United States: A Review of Data, Methods, and Findings', *Journal of Policy Analysis and Management*, 27 (3), 577–605.

Clark, D. and D. Hulme (2010), 'Poverty, Time and Vagueness: Integrating the Core Poverty and Chronic Poverty Frameworks', *Cambridge Journal of Economics*, 34 (2), 347–366.

Coe, R.D. (1978), 'Dependency and Poverty in the Short and Long Run', in G.J. Duncan and J.N. Morgan (eds), *5000 American Families: Patterns of Economic Progress*, Vol. 6, Ann Arbor, MI: Institute for Social Research, University of Michigan, pp. 273–296.

Coe, R.D., G.J. Duncan and M.S. Hill (1982), 'Dynamic Aspects of Poverty and Welfare Use in the United States', Paper presented at Conference on Problems of Poverty, Clark University, August.

Devicienti, F. (2001), 'Poverty Persistence in Britain: A Multivariate Analysis using the BHPS, 1991–1997', *Journal of Economics*, 9 (1), 1–34.

Duclos, J., A. Araar and J. Giles (2010), 'Chronic and Transient Poverty: Measurement and Estimation, with Evidence from China', *Journal of Development Economics*, 91 (2), 266–277.

Duncan, G.J. (ed.) (1984), *Years of Poverty, Years of Plenty*, Ann Arbor, MI: Survey Research Center, Institute for Social Research, University of Michigan.

Duncan, G.J., B. Gustafsson, R. Hauser, G. Schmauss, S. Jenkins, H. Messinger, R. Muffels, B. Nolan, J.-C. Ray and W. Voges (1995), 'Poverty and Social-Assistance Dynamics in the United States, Canada and Western Europe', in K. McFate, R. Lawson and W.J. Wilson (eds), *Poverty, Inequality and the Future of Social Policy: Western States in the New World Order*, New York: Russell Sage Foundation, pp. 67–108.

Duncan, G.J., B. Gustafsson, R. Hauser, G. Schmauss, H. Messinger, R. Muffels, B. Nolan and J.-C. Ray (1993), 'Poverty Dynamics in Eight Countries', *Journal of Population Economics*, 6 (3), 215–234.

Duncan, G.J. and W. Rodgers (1991), 'Has Children's Poverty Become More Persistent?', *American Sociological Review*, 56 (4), 538–550.

Eberharter, V.V. (2001), 'Poverty Inequality and Poverty Mobility in Germany in the 1990s', *Journal of Income Distribution*, 10 (1–2), 13–25.

Engle, P.L. and M.M. Black (2008), 'The Effect of Child Poverty on Child Development and Educational Outcomes', *Annals of the New York Academy of Sciences*, 1136, 243–256.

Ermisch, J., M. Francesconi and D.J. Pevalin (2001), 'Outcomes for Children of Poverty', Research Report 158, London: Department for Work and Pensions.

Finnie, R. and A. Sweetman (2003), 'Poverty Dynamics: Empirical Evidence for Canada', *Canadian Journal of Economics*, 36 (2), 291–325.

Foster, J.E. (2007), 'A Class of Chronic Poverty Measures', Working Paper 07-W01, Department of Economics, Vanderbilt University.

Foster, J.E. (2009), 'A Class of Chronic Poverty Measures', in T. Addison, D. Hulme and R. Kanbur (eds), *Poverty Dynamics: Interdisciplinary Perspectives*, Oxford: Oxford University Press, pp. 59–76.

Foster, J.E. and M.E. Santos (2012), 'Measuring Chronic Poverty', OPHI Working Paper 52, Oxford Poverty and Human Development Initiative, University of Oxford.

Fouarge, D. and R. Layte (2005), 'Welfare Regimes and Poverty Dynamics: The Duration and Recurrence of Poverty Spells in Europe', *Journal of Social Policy*, 34 (3), 407–426.

Gaiha, R. (1988), 'Income Mobility in Rural India', *Economic Development and Cultural Change*, 36 (29), 279–302.

Gaiha, R. and A.B. Deolalikar (1993), 'Persistent, Expected and Innate Poverty: Estimates for Semi-Arid Rural South India, 1975–1984', *Cambridge Journal of Economics*, 17 (4), 409–421.

Gradín, C. and O. Cantó (2012), 'Why are Child Poverty Rates so Persistently High in Spain?', *Manchester School*, 80 (1), 117–143.

Gradín, C., C. del Río and O. Cantó (2012), 'Measuring Poverty Accounting for Time', *Review of Income and Wealth*, 58 (2), 330–354.

Gregg, P., S. Harkness and S. Machin (1999), *Child Poverty and Its Consequences*, Ref. 389, York: Joseph Rowntree Foundation.

Gustafsson, B. and D. Sai (2009), 'Temporary and Persistent Poverty among Ethnic Minorities and the Majority in Rural China', *Review of Income and Wealth*, 55 (1), 588–606.

Haddad, L. and A. Ahmed (2003), 'Chronic and Transitory Poverty: Evidence from Egypt, 1997–99', *World Development*, 31 (1), 71–85.

Harrington, M. (1962), *The Other America: Poverty in the United States*, New York: Macmillan Publishers.

Hasegawa, H. and K. Ueda (2007), 'Measuring Chronic and Transient Components of Poverty: A Bayesian Approach', *Empirical Economics*, 33 (3), 469–490.

Hill, M.S. (1981), 'Some Dynamic Aspects of Poverty', in M.S. Hill, D.H. Hill and J.N. Morgan, *5000 American Families: Patterns of Economic Progress. Analyses of the First Twelve Years of the Panel Study of Income Dynamics*, Vol. 9, Ann Arbor, MI: Institute for Social Research, pp. 93–120.

Hirsch, D. (2006), *The Cost of Not Ending Child Poverty: How We Can Think About It, How It Might Be Measured and Some Evidence*, York: Joseph Rowntree Foundation.

Hoelscher, P. (2004), *A Thematic Study Using Transnational Comparisons to Analyse and Identify What Combination of Policy Responses are Most Successful in Preventing and Reducing High Levels of Child Poverty*, Final Report, European Commission, DG Employment and Social Affairs.

Hoy, M. and B. Zheng (2011), 'Measuring Lifetime Poverty', *Journal of Economic Theory*, 146 (6), 2544–2562.

Hoy, M., B.S. Thompson and B. Zheng (2012), 'Empirical Issues in Lifetime Poverty Measurement', *Journal of Economic Inequality*, 10 (2), 163–189.

Jalan, J. and M. Ravallion (1998), 'Transient Poverty in Postreform Rural China', *Journal of Comparative Economics*, 26, 338–357.

Jäntti, M. and S.P. Jenkins (2015), 'Income Mobility', in A.B. Atkinson and F. Bourguignon (eds), *Handbook of Income Distribution*, Volume 2A, Oxford: North-Holland, pp. 807–935.

Jappelli, T. (1990), 'Who is Credit Constrained in the US Economy?', *Quarterly Journal of Economics*, 105 (1), 219–234.

Jenkins, S.P. (2000), 'Modelling Household Income Dynamics', *Journal of Population Economics*, 13 (4), 529–567.

Jenkins, S.P. (2011), *Changing Fortunes: Income Mobility and Poverty Dynamics in Britain*, Oxford: Oxford University Press.

Jenkins, S.P. and J. Rigg (2001), 'The Dynamics of Poverty in Britain', Department of Work and Pensions, Research Report No. 157, Corporate Document Services, Leeds.

Jenkins, S.P. and C. Schluter (2003), 'Why are Child Poverty Rates Higher in Britain than in Germany? A Longitudinal Perspective', *Journal of Human Resources*, 38 (2), 441–465.

Krishna, A. (2007), *One Illness Away: Why People Become Poor and How They Escape Poverty*, Oxford: Oxford University Press.

Layte, R. and C.T. Whelan (2003), 'Moving In and Out of Poverty: The Impact of Welfare Regimes on Poverty Dynamics in the EU', *European Societies*, 5 (2), 167–191.

Levy, F. (1977), 'How Big is the American Underclass?', Working Paper 0090-1, Washington, DC: Urban Institute.

Lewis, O. (1959), *Five Families: Mexican Case Studies in the Culture of Poverty*, New York: Basic Books.

Lillard, L. and R. Willis (1978), 'Dynamic Aspects of Earning Mobility', *Econometrica*, 46 (5), 985–1012.

Machin, S. (1998), 'Childhood Disadvantage and Intergenerational Transmissions of Economic Status', in A.B. Atkinson and J. Hills (eds), *Exclusion, Employment and Opportunity*, LSE Research Paper No. CASEpaper CASE/4, London: LSE STICERD, pp. 55–64.

Magnuson, K. and E. Votruba-Drzal (2009), 'Enduring Influences of Childhood Poverty', in S. Danziger and M. Cancian (eds), *Changing Poverty, Changing Policies*, New York: Russell Sage, pp. 153–179.

Mendola, D. and A. Busetta (2012), 'The Importance of Consecutive Spells of Poverty: A Path Dependence Index of Longitudinal Poverty', *Review of Income and Wealth*, 58 (2), 355–374.

Mills, B. and E. Mykerezi (2009), 'Transient and Chronic Poverty in the Russian Federation', *Post Communist Economies*, 21 (3), 283–306.

Muller, C. (2003), 'Censored Quantile Regressions of Chronic and Transient Seasonal Poverty in Rwanda', *Journal of African Economies*, 11 (4), 503–541.

Muffels, R., D. Fouarge and R. Dekker (1999), 'Longitudinal Poverty and Income Inequality: A Comparative Panel Study for the Netherlands, Germany and the UK', European Panel Analysis Group, EPAG, Working Paper 1.

Nega, F., E. Mathijs, J. Deckers, M. Haile, J. Nyssen and E. Tollens (2010), 'Rural Poverty Dynamics and Impact of Intervention Programs upon Chronic and Transitory Poverty in Northern Ethiopia', *African Development Review*, 22 (1), 92–114.

OECD (2001), 'When Money is Tight: Poverty Dynamics in OECD Countries', *Employment Outlook*, Paris: OECD, pp. 37–87.

OECD (2008), *Growing Unequal? Income Distribution and Poverty in OECD Countries*, Paris: OECD, pp. 155–175.

Oxley, H., T. Dang and P. Antolín (2000), 'Poverty Dynamics in Six OECD Countries', *OECD Economic Studies*, 30, 7–52.

Porter, C. and N.N. Quinn (2008), 'Intertemporal Poverty Measurement: Tradeoffs and Policy Options', CSAE Working Paper 2008–21.

Porter, C. and G. Yalonetzky (2012), 'Fuzzy Chronic Poverty: A Proposed Response to Measurement Error for Intertemporal Poverty Measurement', Paper prepared for the 32nd General Conference of the International Association for Research in Income and Wealth, Boston, MA.

Rainwater, L. (1981), 'Persistent and Transitory Poverty: A New Look', Working Paper no. 70, Joint Center for Urban Studies of MIT and Harvard University.

Rodgers, J.R. and J.L. Rodgers (1993), 'Chronic Poverty in the United States', *Journal of Human Resources*, 28 (1), 25–54.

Rowntree, B.S. (1901), *Poverty: A Study of Town Life*, London: Macmillan.

Sen, A. (1976), 'Poverty: An Ordinal Approach to Measurement', *Econometrica*, 44 (2), 219–231.

Shepherd, A. (2011), *Tackling Chronic Poverty: The Policy Implications of Research on Chronic Poverty and Poverty Dynamics*, Manchester: Chronic Poverty Research Centre.

Smith, N. and S. Middleton (2007), 'A review of poverty dynamics research in the UK', Joseph Rowntree Foundation.

Stampini, M. and B. Davis (2006), 'Discerning Transient from Chronic Poverty in Nicaragua: Measurement with a Two-Period Panel Data Set', *European Journal of Development Research*, 18 (1), 105–130.

Stevens, A.H. (1994), 'The Dynamics of Poverty Spells: Updating Bane and Ellwood', *AEA Papers and Proceedings*, 84, 34–37.

Stevens, A.H. (1999), 'Climbing Out of Poverty, Falling Back in: Measuring the Persistency of Poverty Over Multiple Spells', *Journal of Human Resources*, 34 (3), 557–588.

Suryadarma, D., Y.M. Pakpahan and A. Suryahadi (2009), 'The Effects of Parental Death and Chronic Poverty on Children's Education and Health: Evidence from Indonesia', CPRC Working Paper 133, Chronic Poverty Research Centre.

Valletta, R.G. (2006), 'The Ins and Outs of Poverty in Advanced Economies: Government Policy and Poverty Dynamics in Canada, Germany, GB and the United States', *Review of Income Wealth*, 52 (1), 261–284.

Whelan, C.T., R. Layte and B. Maître (2002), 'Persistent Deprivation in the European Union', *Schmollers Jahrbuch: Journal of Applied Social Science Studies*, 122 (1), 31–54.

Whelan, C.T., R. Layte and B. Maître (2003), 'Persistent Income Poverty and Deprivation in the European Union: An Analysis of the First Three Waves of the European Community Household Panel', *Journal of Social Policy*, 32 (1), 1–18.

Yaqub, S. (2000), 'Poverty Dynamics in Developing Countries', Institute of Development Studies, Development Bibliography, University of Sussex.

11. Vulnerability to poverty: theoretical approaches
Cesar Calvo

11.1 INTRODUCTION

The future can inspire hope, but also fear. The economic literature on poverty has gradually come to realise that hardship today is often compounded with sombre expectations for tomorrow. Some of the non-poor may likewise feel the threat of a downturn looming. Since households are vulnerable to future shocks that may force them down into poverty, both theoretical and empirical work need to assess the *ex ante* implications of this threat. Even before shocks materialise, this vulnerability affects households: it clouds their present, it reduces their subjective well-being and it shapes their behaviours.

The concept of 'vulnerability to poverty' captures these concerns. As in the case of the usual, *ex post* poverty concept, it is founded on the conviction that failure to reach some critical 'poverty line' causes hardship of an entirely different nature from, say, the 'mild discomforts' which a household above that threshold might experience. Life below the poverty line is grim, and both the affected households and societies at large must work towards the reduction of poverty. In the case of vulnerability to poverty, the possibility of such hardship is assessed *ex ante*, before it strikes the household.

This chapter discusses the existing theoretical proposals about how best to define vulnerability to poverty, which immediately bear implications as to how we should measure it, and indeed as to why we should care about it in the first place. The structure follows an underlying divide between proposals placing the threshold in the space of well-being and proposals placing it in the space of outcomes (say, consumption levels). The former are concerned with the risk of the household failing to reach some well-being standard, while the latter focus on the threat of a shortfall with respect to some minimal outcome level.

The literature also includes a third group of proposals, which see vulnerability as inability to cope with shocks, as failure to protect outcome levels in the face of the inevitable ups and down of life. In this chapter, the fact that a household cannot insure itself against shocks and thus experiences random outcomes certainly lies at the root of the concept of vulnerability, but does not capture it entirely. Following the two main strands within the literature, vulnerability here pays attention both to this inability to cope and, crucially, also to its consequences; in particular, to shortfalls from some critical threshold, in terms of either well-being or outcome levels.

Section 11.2 lays down the notation and defines key concepts which jointly compose either of these two possible views of vulnerability. Section 11.3 addresses the first of them and considers vulnerability as a shortfall in expected utility. Following this lead, section 11.4 goes over the theoretical literature where vulnerability prompts households to mitigate their exposure to future poverty, paradoxically at the cost of sacrificing their chances to improve their overall expectations for the future. Whether this future will come shortly or lies rather far ahead is not without consequences for vulnerability assessments, and section 11.5 explores these implications. Section 11.6 addresses the second main view of vulnerability and defines it as the expectation of critically low outcomes, that is as the threat of a poverty episode. Section 11.7 dwells on issues regarding aggregation over several households. Section 11.8 concludes.

11.2 BASIC PROPERTIES

Let x_t stand for some relevant outcome level at time t, and let it determine utility at that point in time u_t, that is, $u_t = U(x_t)$, where a capital letter is used, here and hereafter, to signal a function. Let z stand for a poverty line defined in the space of outcomes, so a household is poor if $x_t < z$. Even though other outcomes may be as important as consumption, we refer to x_t as consumption for the sake of concreteness.

At time t, the household is uncertain about $t + 1$, due to random shocks that may hit at $t + 1$ and impinge on x_{t+1}. This exposure to uninsured shocks is crucial to the concept of vulnerability, to the point that 'vulnerability' is often tantamount to inability to stabilise and secure future consumption levels, as seminally in Morduch (1994) and later in, for example, Glewwe and Hall (1998), Amin et al. (2003) and Gerry and Li (2010). As mentioned above, vulnerability in this chapter will encompass this inability and, furthermore, the threat that some downfalls may go beyond what is socially acceptable, as captured by the poverty line z.

Let E_t be the expected-value operator based on information at time t, so, for example, $E_t[x_{t+1}]$ is the expectation at t for consumption in the next period. Assuming for simplicity a finite number m of possible states of the world at $t + 1$, let vectors $\mathbf{x}_{t+1}$, $\mathbf{u}_{t+1}$ and $\mathbf{p}$ contain values for consumption, utility and probabilities for those m states. In this case, $E_t[x_{t+1}] = \mathbf{p}'\mathbf{x}_{t+1}$, $E_t[u_{t+1}] = \mathbf{p}'\mathbf{u}_{t+1}$ and we can define vulnerability at time t as follows:

$$\upsilon_t = V(z, x_t, \mathbf{p}, \mathbf{x}_{t+1}) \tag{11.1}$$

For ease of exposition, we assume function V is differentiable. State-specific utility values in $\mathbf{u}_{t+1}$ may determine vulnerability through $u_{t+1} = U(x_{t+1})$, but this is not imposed since some views of vulnerability will give no role to utility. All views will however agree in paying attention to states of the world where consumption is low. Intuitively, vulnerability cannot decrease if consumption $x_{t+1,s}$ decreases in any s-th state. Function V should thus be monotonic:

$$[Monotonicity] \quad \frac{\partial V(z, x_t, \mathbf{p}, \mathbf{x}_{t+1})}{\partial x_{t+1,s}} \leq 0 \tag{11.2}$$

Beyond this monotonicity property, there is no strong consensus on other attributes of function V. Any further desideratum will be present in only part of the literature. For the purpose of this chapter, we focus on three decisive properties. First, consider *reference dependence*, which claims that current consumption x_t should matter, since low future consumption will be arguably harder to bear if the household has got used to a high living standard. Formally:

$$[Reference\ dependence] \quad \frac{\partial V(z, x_t, \mathbf{p}, \mathbf{x}_{t+1})}{\partial x_t} > 0 \tag{11.3}$$

Second, function V could be required to exhibit *risk sensitivity*, since the very uncertainty over their future dents the well-being of the vulnerable:

$$[Risk\ sensitivity]\ V(z, x_t, \mathbf{p}, \mathbf{x}_{t+1}) > V(z, x_t, \mathbf{p}, E_t[x_{t+1}]\mathbf{1}) \tag{11.4}$$

where $\mathbf{1}$ is a vector whose elements are all 1. Vulnerability would be lower if the expected consumption level were attained with certainty.

Third, the states looming as a threat are arguably those where poverty strikes. In this vein, a *focus* property should ensure that states with $x_{t+1,s} > z$ receive no attention besides the fact that poverty has been prevented:

$$[Focus]\ \frac{\partial V(z, x_t, \mathbf{p}, \mathbf{x}_{t+1})}{\partial x_{t+1,s}} = 0\ \text{if}\ x_{t+1,s} > z \tag{11.5}$$

The appeal of this property depends on the answer to the following question. Suppose a farmer faces two scenarios. A drought may occur and hence they may face poverty. Otherwise, if it rains, they will be rich. 'Does she becomes less vulnerable if the harvest in the rainy scenario improves, with no change in the harvest if the drought occurs?' (Calvo and Dercon, 2013). Opting for a negative answer, which is reasonable but not compelling, clearly invokes the *focus* property. The literature includes this stance and also the opposite, allowing the non-poor state to compensate for the poor state.

The convenience of other sensible properties might be raised, such as *scale invariance* in $\mathbf{x}_{t+1}$ and z. However, *reference dependence*, *risk sensitivity* and *focus* will suffice as a useful structure to discuss the main views of vulnerability in the literature. We now turn to this discussion.

11.3   VULNERABILITY AS LOW EXPECTED UTILITY

As early as in Chambers (1989), vulnerability 'refers to exposure to contingencies and stress . . . which is defencelessness, meaning lack of means to cope' (p. 1). Exposure to uninsured risks causes stress and undermines well-being. Economics has long been aware of this intuition, and has formalised it as risk aversion, which is secured by concavity in $U(x)$. A stream of the literature has drawn on this concept and relates vulnerability closely to the deleterious effect of risk exposure on the expected utility of a risk-averse household.

Consider the following two proposals:

$$V^L = U(z) - E_t[U(x_{t+1})],\ \text{with}\ U' > 0\ \text{and}\ U'' < 0 \tag{11.6}$$
$$[\text{Ligon and Schechter (2003)}]$$

$$V^G = \text{Max}\{U(z|x_t) - E_t[U(x_{t+1}|x_t)],\ 0\} \tag{11.7}$$
$$[\text{Günther and Maier (2014)}]$$

where the notation drops the arguments in $V(z, x_t, \mathbf{p}, \mathbf{x}_{t+1})$. Ligon and Schechter (2003) provided the seminal view of vulnerability to poverty as a shortfall in the *ex ante* expected utility of a risk-averse individual, as compared to their utility when the poverty line x is secured with no risk. Since x_{t+1} only enters their definition through the concave utility function, *risk sensitivity* is secured by construction.

Since they place their critical threshold in the space of utility, Ligon and Schechter (2003) omit the *focus* property and thus allow the possibility of rich states ($x_{t+1,s} \geq z$) to compensate for states threatening with poverty. Likewise, they pay no attention to *reference dependence*, which is a major concern for Günther and Maier (2014). In (11.7), V^G brings into consideration that households take their current consumption x_t as reference and dread the possibility of falling down to a lower living standard (even if the fall is not deep enough to plunge them into poverty). This is indeed a recurring notion in the literature (e.g., Povel, 2015). Formally, they draw on prospect theory results, and in particular on loss aversion, which also secures a weak form of *risk sensitivity*, even if $U'' = 0$ for most consumption values.[1]

Günther and Maier (2014) do consider a *focus* on the threat of falling below the poverty line, but only to a limited extent: vulnerability is said to be zero if expected utility is higher than utility at $x_{t+1} = z$ with certainty. However, as in V^L, this expected utility could be high due to some very rich states of the world, even if the threat of extreme poverty looms in others. The strong, outcome-based *focus* property in (11.5) will only come into full effect in section 11.6, under a different view of vulnerability.

11.4 VULNERABILITY AND HOUSEHOLD CHOICES

With or without *reference dependence*, if vulnerability mirrors expected utility, then a forward-looking utility-maximiser household will also minimise vulnerability, and hence vulnerability can be thought of as driving household choices. This view is explicit in (11.6) and can be said to underlie a larger literature where vulnerability is invoked as an explanation for reduced, perhaps inefficiently low, risk-taking among the poor. In (11.7), this is only partially true due to its *focus*, which disregards efforts to raise expected utility beyond $U(z)$.

If choices promising higher returns also imply higher risks (of greater poverty), then the poor may be led into a poverty trap by their own efforts to reduce their vulnerability. Morduch (1994) brought to light this link between vulnerability and poverty, which can however be traced back to the seminal model in Sandmo (1971), where greater wealth implies greater willingness to take entrepreneurial risks, provided risk aversion decreases in wealth. The same early intuition is present in Stiglitz (1974), where sharecropping is an optimal, stable contract between the landlord and his poor tenants, since it implicitly provides the latter with insurance.

A number of models later followed this vein, with Banerjee (2000) providing the most explicit formalisation of the fact that 'the poor are vulnerable: they are afraid of any losses because losses cause them too much pain' (p. 135). The poor have 'too much to lose' if things go wrong, and paradoxically this will scare them away from opportunities to escape poverty whenever they entail some risk. These opportunities can take several forms, but two instances will suffice to illustrate.

In Fafchamps and Pender (1997), a profitable investment is also irreversible, and risk-averse preferences exhibit precautionary-savings motives. Households will hence need to pile up savings beyond the cost of the (indivisible) investment asset, since this asset cannot be turned into cash in the case of a negative shock, and these cautious households will never sacrifice entirely their access to readily available resources. Vulnerability thus implies a higher savings threshold and a greater difficulty to escape poverty. Likewise, in Eswaran and Kotwal (1989), risk-averse poor households look for credit as a safety net in the case of a negative shock; if their poverty restricts their access to credit, they will again reduce their exposure and forfeit investments even if their expected returns are high.

All these arguments highlight that efforts to minimise vulnerability (that is, to maximise expected utility) include choices aiming to smooth income (or assets) over states of the world, even at the cost of reducing expected earnings. The literature consistently provides instances of empirical support for this idea, for example as in Dercon (1998) and Dercon and Christiaensen (2011). However, this is only true if households fail to insure their consumption from the uncertainty surrounding their income sources. Even though they may resort to formal and, with greater likelihood among the poor, informal insurance contracts, households typically find no access to complete insurance (Dercon, 2002). Both to ensure clarity and for later use, we now formalise these ideas.

Let w_{t+1} denote income, and allow for a random shock ε_{t+1} on this income (with $E_t[\varepsilon_{t+1}] = 0$ and $Var_t[\varepsilon_{t+1}] = \sigma_{t+1}^2$):

$$w_{t+1,s} = \mu_{t+1} + \varepsilon_{t+1,s} \tag{11.8}$$

where subscript s denotes the s-th state of the world and μ_{t+1} is a non-random value. Next, consider the household effort to insure their consumption from income shocks. To this end, let $b_{t+1,s}$ be an insurance payment due to the household if the s-th state occurs:

$$b_{t+1,s} = -\lambda\varepsilon_{t+1,s}, \text{ with } 0 \leq \lambda \leq 1 \tag{11.9}$$

where λ measures the completeness of the insurance contract. Note (11.9) imposes fair insurance (that is, $E_t[b_{t+1}] = 0$). From (11.8) and (11.9), available income in the s-th state depends on the expected income μ_{t+1}, the realised income shock $\varepsilon_{t+1,s}$, and the degree of insurance λ:

$$w_{t+1,s} + b_{t+1,s} = \mu_{t+1} + (1 - \lambda)\varepsilon_{t+1,s}, \text{ with } 0 \leq \lambda \leq 1 \tag{11.10}$$

If $\lambda = 1$, insurance is complete and the household secures $w_{t+1,s} = \mu_{t+1}$ regardless of the state actually occurring.

Given (11.10), the household consumption function may be written as follows:

$$x_{t+1,s} = X(\mu_{t+1} + (1 - \lambda)\varepsilon_{t+1,s}) \tag{11.11}$$

Vulnerability assessments feed on this state-specific consumption function. To highlight this link with greater clarity, ignore intertemporal transfers momentarily and assume all available income is consumed:

$$x_{t+1,s} = \mu_{t+1} + (1 - \lambda)\varepsilon_{t+1,s} \tag{11.12}$$

Lastly, taking V^L for concreteness and then feeding (11.12) into a second-order Taylor approximation of (11.6):

$$v_t^L \approx U(z) - U(\mu_{t+1}) - \frac{U''(\mu_{t+1})}{2}(1 - \lambda)^2\sigma_{t+1}^2 \qquad (11.13)$$

In (11.13), as their vulnerability worries households at t, they will forgo opportunities to raise their expected income μ_{t+1} whenever they come at the cost of a significantly higher exposure to uninsured risk, as measured by $(1 - \lambda)^2\sigma_{t+1}^2$. As discussed above, in this view vulnerable households fear any risk to lose the little they have, and this fear may lock them into persistent poverty.

Lastly, we use this setup to note that (11.12) clarifies the rationale for the outcome-based *focus* property in (11.5), which prevents high-consumption states from compensating for poverty-striken states. So to speak, consumption in the rainy scenario already discounts the insurance payment to protect consumption if a drought occurs. Vulnerability is assessed on state-specific consumption $x_{t+1,s}$, *after* all such insurance efforts have been made.

11.5   THE TIME FRAME OF VULNERABILITY

Echoing the bulk of the literature, the discussion has referred to the threat of a poverty episode in one particular period in the future. In the notation above, $t + 1$ could lie one month, one year, or one whole decade ahead. The choice should make no dramatic difference if consumption levels in all future periods exhibited a strong positive correlation *ex ante*. However, arguments to the contrary exist.

For instance, in the presence of poverty traps, households may be willing to suffer severe consumption shortfalls in the near future so as to avoid the risk of persistent poverty in the longer run (Carter and Lybbert, 2012). They realise that long-run consumption will stabilise at a dismally low level if they dissave their assets for the sake of short-run consumption; say, if they sacrifice their ox, they will never be able to buy another one to plough their land and their productivity will be permanently low.

Formally, taking $t + 2$ as the long-run:

$$x_{t+2,s} = \begin{cases} \underline{x} & \text{if } a_{t+1,s} < \hat{a} \\ \overline{x} & \text{if } a_{t+1,s} \geq \hat{a} \end{cases} \qquad (11.14)$$

where $a_{t+1,s}$ denotes savings at the end of $t + 1$ when the s-th state occurs and $\hat{a}$ is a critical threshold condemning those below to low future consumption $\underline{x} < \overline{x}$. Assuming households maximise $U(x_{t+1}, x_{t+2}) = \ln(x_{t+1}) + \beta\ln(x_{t+2})$ with $0 < \beta < 1$, the consumption function in (11.11) takes an explicit form:

$$x_{t+1,s} = \begin{cases} \mu_{t+1} + (1 - \lambda)\varepsilon_{t+1,s} & \text{if } \varepsilon_{t+1,s} < \hat{\varepsilon} \\ \mu_{t+1} + (1 - \lambda)\varepsilon_{t+1,s} - \hat{a} & \text{if } \varepsilon_{t+1,s} \geq \hat{\varepsilon} \end{cases} \qquad (11.15)$$

and:

$$x_{t+2,s} = \begin{cases} \underline{x} & \text{if } \varepsilon_{t+1,s} < \bar{\varepsilon} \\ \bar{x} & \text{if } \varepsilon_{t+1,s} \geq \bar{\varepsilon} \end{cases} \tag{11.16}$$

where $\bar{\varepsilon} = \frac{1}{1-\lambda}(\frac{\bar{a}x^{\beta}}{x^{\beta}} - \mu_{t+1})$ is a threshold dividing long-run poverty from high long-run consumption. Provided $\varepsilon_{t+1,s} \geq \bar{\varepsilon}$, bad shocks are not bad enough to obscure the long-run future, and vulnerability to long-run poverty $V_t(x_{t+2})$ remains unaffected. Households sacrifice the short run for the sake of the future, and thus they are vulnerable to immediate hardship in the face of such bad shocks. Worse shocks however, such that $\varepsilon_{t+1,s} < \bar{\varepsilon}$, force households to give up their future, since protecting it would require extreme short-run deprivations. Their vulnerability to poverty in the near future $V_t(x_{t+1})$ thus lessens, to the cost of a dramatic rise in vulnerability $V_t(x_{t+2})$ for the longer horizon. Clearly, the time frame of the vulnerability assessment matters. Note this is not due to the additional uncertainties of a longer time span, since ε_{t+1} has remained the only source of risk.

11.6   VULNERABILITY AS EXPECTED POVERTY

An increasingly dominant view among policy-makers follows a different path. They find the concept of vulnerability to poverty relevant because it helps them predict who will be poor in the future, and thus provides them with a tool to craft a forward-looking policy. Vulnerability relates to how much poverty the policy-maker should expect, and vulnerability indices are judged according to their success in predicting future poverty (Celidoni, 2013).

On the flip side, concerns about expected utility are allowed to fade, not least due to pragmatic reasons: both utility functions and their parameters are unknown, as well as subjective probabilities. Hence, the expected-utility view is deemed to provide little guidance to fine-tune policy in practice, and furthermore this advice will be clouded by doubts about the true reasons behind the choice of parameters. From this standpoint, expected poverty offers a gain in both empirical guidance and transparency, as it builds explicitly on the set of parameters and probabilities shaping the stance of the policy-maker (Christiaensen and Subbarao, 2005). The rationale for the switch from the utility space to that of outcomes is thus pragmatic.

Let $P(z, x_t)$ denote a household poverty function and define $e_t = z - x_t$ as the gap between the poverty line and consumption. In many instances, for example in the well-known FGT index (Foster et al., 1984), poverty is determined by this gap: $P(z, x_t) = \tilde{P}(e_t)$. With this notation, we may summarise the existing proposals as follows:

$$V^R = E_t[\tilde{P}(e_{t+1})] \tag{11.17}$$
[Ravallion (1988)]

$$V^D = E_t[\tilde{P}(D(z, x_t) - x_{t+1})] \tag{11.18}$$
[Dutta et al. (2011)]

$$V^C = V^L \text{ in (6), with } U(x_t) = \frac{1}{\theta}\left(\frac{\text{Min}\{x_t, z\}}{z}\right)^{\theta} \text{ and } \theta < 1 \tag{11.19}$$

[Calvo and Dercon (2013)]

By exploring the consequences of uncertainties in consumption on expected (aggregate) poverty, Ravallion (1988) paved the way for this whole stream of the literature, even though his piece did not use the term vulnerability. He allowed $\tilde{P}(e_{t+1})$ to take any specification within the Atkinson class of poverty measures, and showed that greater risk will raise expected poverty if the consumption function in (11.11) is concave. The concavity of consumption in available resources thus secures *risk sensitivity*.

In the case of the headcount, that is, $\mathrm{FGT}_{t+1}(\alpha = 0)$, Ravallion (1988) finds a more demanding condition: the consumption function must be quasi-concave and the consumption mode must be above the poverty line. That *risk sensitivity* hinges on a rather strong condition is significant because most of the subsequent empirical literature estimates vulnerability as the probability of facing poverty in the future, that is, $E_t[\mathrm{FGT}_{t+1}(\alpha = 0)]$, which is the household-level equivalent to the aggregate headcount.

In particular, the specification in (11.17) also captures a more recent strand of proposals aiming to find a 'vulnerability line' z_v, such that a current outcome below this line ($x_t < z_v$) can be interpreted as a high probability of falling into poverty in the future. This approach arises from the practitioners' need to easily identify the vulnerable, and policy papers have provided it with insightful foundations. For instance, in Cafiero and Vakis (2006), z_v includes insurance as part of the basket of basic needs, while López-Calva and Ortiz-Juarez (2014) and Dang and Lanjouw (2014) resort to empirical household-specific estimates of the probability of future poverty and set z_v at the consumption level of those whose probability rises above a given threshold. Gallardo (2013) defines z_v as the sum of z and the standard downside mean-semideviation of consumption (as a measure of the risk of poverty), but otherwise differs from (11.17), since his proposal does not build on expected poverty, but on poverty at the expected consumption level, that is, $\tilde{P}(E_t[e_{t+1}])$.

As for *focus*, it is clearly built into (11.17) by construction, since $\tilde{P}(e_{t+1,s})$ is evaluated in each s-th state of the world.[2] On the other hand, *reference dependence* is entirely ignored.

The view of Dutta et al. (2011) differs both because *reference dependence* is acknowledged and because *focus* is compromised. As in, for example, López-Calva and Ortiz-Juarez (2014), they also modify the standard poverty line, but with a different aim. Dutta et al. (2011) propose a hybrid line combining the usual minimal consumption level z with the desire to preserve initial living standards x_t – for instance, $D(z,x_t) = z^\alpha x_t^{1-\alpha}$. They allow both for a higher line when current consumption rises ($0 < \alpha < 1$), in line with the loss aversion conjecture, and also for a lower line ($\alpha > 1$), because arguably a higher x_t implies that the household will have better means to cope in the future if misfortune strikes. While this second case ($\frac{\partial D(z,x_t)}{\partial x_t} < 0$) is appealing, a proper discussion goes beyond the scope of this chapter, since it touches on manifold issues related to the analysis of poverty over time, for example as in Calvo and Dercon (2009) and in Hoy and Zheng in Chapter 9 of this volume. In either case, their proposal drops the *focus* property, since $D(z, x_t) - x_{t+1} < 0$ does not discard $z - x_{t+1} > 0$ (nor $x_t - x_{t+1} > 0$).

Lastly, Calvo and Dercon (2013) propose $V^C = E_t[\frac{1}{\theta}(1 - [\frac{\mathrm{Min}\,\{x_{t+1},z\}}{z}]^\theta)]$, which is both the expected value of the poverty measure in Chakravarty (1983) and, as expressed in (19), the particular case of the expected-utility V^L definition for $U(x_t) = \frac{1}{\theta}(\frac{\mathrm{Min}\,\{x_t,z\}}{z})^\theta$. This proposal may thus be seen a bridge between the expected-poverty and the expected-utility views, largely due to the poverty specification in Chakravarty (1983), which does not depend on the poverty gap and does not impose the form $\tilde{P}(e_{t+1})$. Seen as an expected-utility case, V^C relies on the usual CES utility function, which is however turned unusual by the censoring of x_t at the poverty line, as imposed by $Min\{x_t, z\}$. While not appealing at first glance, this censoring is the cost to secure *focus*. The well-known CES function provides however the benefit of ensuring that *risk sensitivity* is both active and also well-behaved (unlike the cases under V^R and V^D), with risk aversion decreasing in income as typically found in empirical work since Binswanger (1981).[3] On the downside, *reference dependence* is entirely absent.

While each of these proposals will exhibit some drawback, they all can certainly contribute to policy-making. Poverty alleviation programmes should benefit from the foresight of future poverty episodes. Planning efforts should gain efficiency from antici-pating where, when and whom poverty will strike next. Yet the toolkit provided by the vulnerability literature remains far from widespread use in actual targeting decisions. To some extent, this is due to the challenges posed by the empirical estimation of vulnerabil-ity, which Ceriani discusses in Chapter 12 of this *Handbook*. However, arguably part of the reason is rooted elsewhere, in the lack of theoretical foundations for forward-looking targeting decisions. Suppose empirical estimation challenges are overcome and policy-makers know which households will be poor next year and how poor they will be; should available resources be relocated from the currently poor to help those households reduce their vulnerability? The answer is far from obvious and will probably build on several smaller, theory-loaded questions.

For instance, if a currently poor household is also among those in poverty next year, is this more worrisome than seeing two different households in poverty in either year? Can vulnerability-reducing insurance policies trigger moral hazard and other undesired side-effects? If current poverty and future expected poverty are correlated across households, what are the implications for targeting purposes? These questions remain open, and their answers will enable policy-makers to reap the fruits of the progress made to date on the theory of vulnerability as the threat of future poverty.

11.7 AGGREGATION

Lastly, since the view of vulnerability as expected poverty is largely inspired by the concern of policy-makers, it needs to pay attention to aggregation issues. Knowing that a number of households are individually exposed to the threat of poverty provides only partial information about the extent of poverty looming on society at large. Under any of the usual definitions of aggregate poverty, for example, $FGT_{t+1}(\alpha)$, the policy-maker is interested *inter alia* in how many households may suffer poverty simultaneously. Individual vulnerability is blind to outcomes for other households and hence to such simultaneity.

In the literature, aggregation has however typically taken the form of simple averages of individual vulnerability indices, as for example in Imai et al. (2011). Thus, no attention is paid to correlations among household consumption levels over all possible states of the world. Drawing on the properties of multidimensional poverty measures (which do care about correlations among households, albeit over the set of relevant well-being dimen-sions), Calvo and Dercon (2013) provide the following proposal:

$$\overline{V}^C = \frac{1}{\theta}\left(1 - \mathrm{E}_t\left[\left\{\prod_{i=1}^{n}\left(\frac{\mathrm{Min}[z,x_{t+1,i}]}{x_{t+1,i}}\right)^{\frac{1}{n}}\right\}^{\theta}\right]\right), \text{ with } \theta < 1 \qquad (11.20)$$

where the bar in $\overline{V}$ denotes this is an aggregate measure for a population with n households. Making loose use of the properties in section 11.2, which were defined for the individual case, visual inspection shows that *reference dependence* is absent, whereas *monotonicity* and *focus* are in place. The upper limit on θ can be equally proved to secure the aggregate equivalent to *risk sensitivity*, but the role of this parameter goes beyond this property.

Since Keeney (1979), the literature on multivariate risk is aware of the dilemma between *catastrophe avoidance* and *risk equity*. In (11.20), $\theta > 0$ would prioritise *risk equity*, that is, if household consumption levels in each state of the world were reshuffled among household so that the *same* households suffer poverty in all states, then the policy-maker would say society has become more vulnerable to poverty. Such concern for *risk equity* comes at the cost of *catastrophe avoidance*, which requires $\theta < 0$ and implies that the policy-maker first and foremost dreads states of the world where poverty is widespread (regardless of how these poor households fare in other states).

Aggregation thus raises the question on how to judge any correlation among households in their consumption levels over all states of the world. A stronger positive correlation may lead to higher ($\theta < 0$) or lower ($\theta > 0$) aggregate vulnerability, depending on the view of the policy-maker. In turn, this view will shape policies aiming to reduce vulnerability. If the threat of widespread poverty (*catastrophe avoidance*) dominates other concerns, then the policy-maker will pay greater attention to the reduction of covariant risks (for example, macroeconomic downturns or plagues). If she cares more strongly about *risk equity*, then policies to mitigate idiosyncratic risks (for example, crime or job-related accidents) will be called upon.

11.8 CONCLUSION

This chapter reviews the theoretical literature on vulnerability and finds two competing views, with different policy implications. First, vulnerability as low expected utility stresses the danger of self-perpetuating poverty. The poor may shy away from decisions paving their way out of poverty whenever these decisions entail some degree of additional uncertainty. They feel vulnerable and thus they protect the little they have. From this point of view, insurance and safety nets may be instrumental to reduce their sense of defencelessness and unleash their energy to fight for their own success. This should also hold true for households narrowly above the poverty trap, which will be especially wary of shocks forcing them to dissave and thus condemning them to long-run poverty.

Second, vulnerability as expected poverty requires the policy-maker to think through and be explicit about her priorities. For instance, the ability to foretell (however imprecisely) who will be poor will only prompt stark policy implications when the policy-maker is ready to relocate available resources to protect these households, sometimes unavoidably to the detriment of programmes targeting the currently poor. Likewise, strategies to reduce aggregate vulnerability will determine the relative importance of idiosyncratic and covariant sources of risk depending on the relative strength of her concern for risk equity and for the threat of widespread poverty. These are no simple questions and go beyond the scope of economics. Their answers will necessarily draw on interdisciplinary work.

NOTES

1. For instance, in Günther and Maier (2014), $U(x_{t+1}|x_t) = x_{t+1} + \beta(x_{t+1} - x_t)$, with $\beta = \begin{cases} 1 & \text{if } x_{t+1} \geq x_t \\ 2 & \text{if } x_{t+1} < x_t \end{cases}$

2. For any function $\tilde{P}(e_t)$, $\tilde{P}(e_t) = \tilde{P}(\text{Max}\{e_t, 0\})$.

3. As first pointed out by Ligon and Schechter (2002), common poverty measures such as FGT($\alpha = 2$) entail increasing risk aversion when fed into (11.17).

REFERENCES

Amin, Sajeda, Ashok S. Rai and Giorgio Topa (2003), 'Does microcredit reach the poor and vulnerable? Evidence from northern Bangladesh', *Journal of Development Economics* **70**(1), 59–82. http://www.sciencedirect.com/science/article/pii/S0304387802000871.

Banerjee, Abhijit (2000), 'The two poverties', *Nordic Journal of Political Economy* **26**, 129–141.

Binswanger, Hans P. (1981), 'Attitudes toward risk: Theoretical implications of an experiment in rural India', *Economic Journal* **91**(364), 867–890. http://www.jstor.org/stable/2232497.

Cafiero, Carlo and Renos Vakis (2006), 'Risk and vulnerability considerations in poverty analysis: Recent advances and future directions', Social Protection Discussion Paper 610, World Bank.

Calvo, Cesar and Stefan Dercon (2009), 'Chronic poverty and all that: The measurement of poverty over time', *in* T. Addison, D. Hulme and R. Kanbur, (eds), *Poverty Dynamics: Interdisciplinary Perspectives*, New York: Oxford University Press, pp. 29–58.

Calvo, Cesar and Stefan Dercon (2013), 'Vulnerability to individual and aggregate poverty', *Social Choice and Welfare* **41**(4), 721–740. http://dx.doi.org/10.1007/s00355-012-0706-y.

Carter, Michael R. and Travis J. Lybbert (2012), 'Consumption versus asset smoothing: Testing implications of poverty trap theory in Burkina Faso', *Journal of Development Economics* **99**(2), 255–264.

Celidoni, Martina (2013), 'Vulnerability to poverty: An empirical comparison of alternative measures', *Applied Economics* **45**(12), 1493–1506. http://dx.doi.org/10.1080/00036846.2011.624271.

Chakravarty, Satya R. (1983), 'A new index of poverty', *Mathematical Social Sciences* **6**(3), 307–313. http://www.sciencedirect.com/science/article/pii/0165489683900641.

Chambers, Robert (1989), 'Editorial introduction: Vulnerability, coping and policy', *IDS Bulletin* **20**(2), 1–7. http://dx.doi.org/10.1111/j.1759-5436.1989.mp20002001.x.

Christiaensen, Luc J. and Kalanidhi Subbarao (2005), 'Towards an understanding of household vulnerability in rural Kenya', *Journal of African Economies* **14**(4), 520–558. http://jae.oxfordjournals.org/content/14/4/520.abstract.

Dang, Hai-Anh and Peter Lanjouw (2014), 'Welfare dynamics measurement: Two definitions of a vulnerability line and their empirical application', Policy Research Working Paper 6944, World Bank.

Dercon, Stefan (1998), 'Wealth, risk and activity choice: Cattle in western Tanzania', *Journal of Development Economics* **55**(1), 1–42.

Dercon, Stefan (2002), 'Income risk, coping strategies, and safety nets', *World Bank Research Observer* **17**(2), 141–166. http://wbro.oxfordjournals.org/content/17/2/141.abstract.

Dercon, Stefan and Luc Christiaensen (2011), 'Consumption risk, technology adoption and poverty traps: Evidence from Ethiopia', *Journal of Development Economics* **96**(2), 159–173.

Dutta, Indranil, James Foster and Ajit Mishra (2011), 'On measuring vulnerability to poverty', *Social Choice and Welfare* **37**(4), 743–761. http://dx.doi.org/10.1007/s00355-011-0570-1.

Eswaran, Mukesh and Ashok Kotwal (1989), 'Credit as insurance in agrarian economies', *Journal of Development Economics* **31**(1), 37–53. http://www.sciencedirect.com/science/article/pii/0304387889900308.

Fafchamps, Marcel and John Pender (1997), 'Precautionary savings, credit constraints, and irreversible investment: Theory and evidence from semi-arid India', *Journal of Business and Economics Statistics* **15**(2), 180–194.

Foster, James, Joel Greer and Eric Thorbecke (1984), 'A class of decomposable poverty measures', *Econometrica* **52**(3), 761–776.

Gallardo, Mauricio (2013), 'Using the downside mean-semideviation for measuring vulnerability to poverty', *Economics Letters* **120**(3), 416–418. http://www.sciencedirect.com/science/article/pii/S0165176513002607.

Gerry, Christopher J. and Carmen A. Li (2010), 'Consumption smoothing and vulnerability in Russia', *Applied Economics* **42**(16), 1995–2007. http://dx.doi.org/10.1080/00036840701765403.

Glewwe, Paul and Gillette Hall (1998), 'Are some groups more vulnerable to macroeconomic shocks than others? Hypothesis tests based on panel data from Peru', *Journal of Development Economics* **56**(1), 181–206. http://www.sciencedirect.com/science/article/pii/S0304387898000583.

Günther, Isabel and Johannes K. Maier (2014), 'Poverty, vulnerability, and reference-dependent utility', *Review of Income and Wealth* **60**(1), 155–181. http://dx.doi.org/10.1111/roiw.12081.

Imai, Katsushi S., Raghav Gaiha and Woojin Kang (2011), 'Vulnerability and poverty dynamics in Vietnam', *Applied Economics* **43**(25), 3603–3618. http://dx.doi.org/10.1080/00036841003670754.

Keeney, Ralph (1979), 'Equity and public risk', *Operations Research* **28**(3), 527–534.

Ligon, Ethan and Laura Schechter (2002), 'Measuring vulnerability: The director's cut', Discussion Paper 86, WIDER-UNU.

Ligon, Ethan and Laura Schechter (2003), 'Measuring vulnerability', *Economic Journal* **113**(486), C95–C102.

López-Calva, Luis F. and Eduardo Ortiz-Juarez (2014), 'A vulnerability approach to the definition of the middle class', *Journal of Economic Inequality* **12**(1), 23–47. http://dx.doi.org/10.1007/s10888-012-9240-5.

Morduch, Jonathan (1994), 'Poverty and vulnerability', *American Economic Review* **84**(2), 221–225. http://www.jstor.org/stable/2117833.

Povel, Felix (2015), 'Measuring exposure to downside risk with an application to Thailand and Vietnam', *World Development* **71**, 4–24. http://www.sciencedirect.com/science/article/pii/S0305750X13002489.

Ravallion, Martin (1988), 'Expected poverty under risk-induced welfare variability', *Economic Journal* **86**(393), 1171–1182.

Sandmo, Angmar (1971), 'On the theory of the competitive firm under price uncertainty', *American Economic Review* **61**(1), 65–73.

Stiglitz, Joseph (1974), 'Incentives and risk sharing in sharecropping', *Review of Economic Studies* **41**(2), 219–255.

12. Vulnerability to poverty: empirical findings
Lidia Ceriani

12.1 INTRODUCTION

Poverty has been always studied in a world of certainty. However, if the aim of studying poverty is not only improving the well-being of whom is deprived today, but also preventing people from becoming poor in the future, a new, forward-looking perspective must be adopted. Since future distributions of outcomes are unknown, analyzing poverty in a world of uncertainty becomes essential. The literature has recently started studying uncertainty as a determinant part of poverty itself, referring to this issue as 'Vulnerability to poverty'. World Development Report 2000/2001, for instance, underlines that: 'poverty is more than inadequate income or human development, it is also vulnerability and a lack of voice, power, and representation Reducing vulnerability – to economic shocks, natural disasters, ill health, disability, and personal violence – is an intrinsic part of enhancing well-being' (World Bank, 2001, p. 12).

Vulnerability is a relatively young stream of the welfare economics literature. Although the idea of linking the economics of poverty with the economics of uncertainty dates back to the seminal work of Morduch (1994), almost all contributions were developed in the last decade, and only a few have been published to date in peer-reviewed journals.

12.2 DEFINITIONS

The increasing prominence of interventions designed to address vulnerability shows large interest and a wide agreement among economists about the importance of enriching welfare (and poverty) analysis by adding this new concept, but there is still no consensus about its definition. This is not surprising, when we think that the debate about the definition of poverty is not ended yet. The concept of vulnerability is perhaps more complicated to grasp, since it inflates the poverty analysis semantic sphere, introducing another complex and not easily understandable notion: uncertainty.

The different approaches found in the literature can be grouped into three main classes of definitions: (1) vulnerability as disability to cope with risk; (2) vulnerability as risk of poverty; and (3) vulnerability as low expected utility. The empirical findings described in this chapter mainly belong to the second definition, with a few exceptions (see, e.g., Morduch, 1994; Jalan and Ravallion, 1999; Devereux et al., 2006).

12.2.1 Vulnerability as Disability to Cope with Risk

A seminal idea of vulnerability in Morduch (1994) has been followed up by many other economists who have investigated vulnerability (Glewwe and Hall, 1998; Banerjee, 2000;

Christianensen and Boisvert, 2000; Skoufias and Quisumbing, 2003; Kurosaki, 2006). They all understand vulnerability as lack of insurance against shocks.

Individuals, notably in low-income countries, do not have access to effective insurance mechanisms,[1] and are therefore exposed to income fluctuations due to erratic weather, price variability, crop failures or human illness. If insurance mechanisms were effective, individuals could smooth consumption over time, by pooling risks or by borrowing against adverse shocks, independently of income fluctuations.[2] In this framework, an individual is defined vulnerable if their current consumption falls below the poverty line although their permanent income stays above it.

Although Morduch (1994) is the first to link vulnerability to the lack of access to consumption-smoothing mechanisms, his approach still lies in a static framework: vulnerability is just one dimension of a multidimensional concept of poverty (Morduch, 1994, p. 224). Similarly, according to Banerjee (2000), vulnerability is intended as one of two distinct aspects of poverty, the first one being desperation. Vulnerability, according to Banerjee (2000), means being afraid of any losses, because 'losses cause poor people too much pain' (Banerjee, 2000, p. 135). As a consequence, poor people underinvest, perpetuating their poverty status. We can find, implicitly, the same conceptualization in Christianensen and Boisvert (2000). They point out that:

> people who anticipate not being able to smooth consumption through borrowing, asset liquidation or insurance, engage in less risky activities, resulting in a lower variance of income. However, strategies focused at reducing the variance of income typically also lead to a reduction in average income, shifting the probability distribution of consumption to the left, and thereby increasing the probability of consumption shortfall (Christianensen and Boisvert, 2000, p. 6).

Vulnerability as lack of consumption-smoothing mechanisms not only affects individuals' well-being, but it is also detrimental to the overall economy. Elbers et al. (2007), for example, show that, because of the behavioral response of vulnerable individuals, uninsured exposure to risk in developing countries substantially reduces growth.

12.2.2 Vulnerability as Risk of Poverty

A second stream of the literature defines vulnerability as the *ex ante* risk that an individual will be poor in the future. In contrast with poverty, which is an *ex post* measure of a household well-being, vulnerability is therefore a forward-looking measure of a household's well-being. Therefore, as suggested by Chaudhuri et al. (2002), whereas the status of 'poor' is observable, the status of 'vulnerable' can only be estimated or inferred.

Within this framework, we can then recognize two different approaches. Some scholars concentrate on vulnerability as the likelihood of suffering poverty in the future (Pritchett et al., 2000; Chaudhuri et al., 2002; Suryahadi and Sumarto, 2003; Kuhl, 2003; Dang and Lanjouw, 2016). Others consider both the likelihood of being poor and the extent of future poverty (Christiaensen and Subbarao, 2005; Christianensen and Boisvert, 2000; Calvo and Dercon, 2013).

12.2.3   Vulnerability as Low Expected Utility

Ligon and Schechter (2003) adopt a utilitarian approach to measuring vulnerability. The authors define vulnerability as the difference between a household's utility derived from certainty equivalent consumption and its expected utility derived from actual consumption. In this framework, vulnerability depends not only on the mean of households' consumption, but also on its variation. Consumption variation can be further decomposed in aggregate and idiosyncratic risk. Günther (2014) expands this concept by introducing reference-dependent utility.

12.3   MEASUREMENT AND DATA

Once vulnerability has been defined, scholars must assess the following steps: (1) choosing a vulnerability indicator; (2) developing a method for forecasting future outcomes and variability of the vulnerability indicator; and (3) determining a vulnerability threshold. Choices made at each step are mainly driven by data availability and by the type of society targeted by the study; for instance, whether there are panel data or cross-country data, or whether the society is rural, developed or not developed.

12.3.1   Vulnerability Indicator

In order to quantify vulnerability and specify its determinants, we should first choose the indicator of well-being that we intend to use in the analysis. Consumption is the widely used indicator for assessing vulnerability to poverty, for different reasons. First, if we believe in the permanent income hypothesis, consumption has the advantage of incorporating information about household ability to smooth income shocks. Second, in developing countries and among rural communities (the main target of vulnerability studies), self-consumption is a relevant part of overall consumption, which will not be captured by expenditures, earnings or income. Finally, in societies where the informal sector is large, income data are less reliable. Other reasons might be contingent upon the country and the period of analysis. For instance, Glewwe and Hall (1998) underline that due to very high inflation in Peru in 1990, consumption data were easier to deflate since they were based on the same reference period for all households (in contrast to income data).

Nevertheless, other indicators have been used in the literature: expenditures (Pritchett et al., 2000; Skoufias and Quisumbing, 2003; Ligon and Schechter, 2003), earnings (Bourguignon et al., 2004), income (Pritchett et al., 2000; Zhang and Wan, 2008; Bérgolo et al., 2010; Jadotte, 2011; Chiwaula et al., 2011; Landau et al., 2012; Bronfman, 2014), non-monetary indicators, such as the Food Consumption Score computed by the World Food Programme and the Crowding Index computed by the United Nations High Commissioner for Refugees (UNHCR) (Verme et al., 2016). And, in multidimensional frameworks, leisure time (Calvo, 2008), health and nutrition (Devereux et al., 2006).

12.3.2   Forecasting Future Outcomes

The major challenge in determining a person's vulnerability status involves the estimate of the future distribution of the chosen indicator for each individual (or household). The main restriction on the possible approaches to estimate the fluctuation of the chosen outcome comes from data availability. As pointed out by Chaudhuri et al. (2002), the analysis of household vulnerability to poverty (as probability to be poor in the future), requires estimation of both expected consumption and the variance of consumption for each household. The best-case scenario (see, e.g., Skoufias and Quisumbing, 2003; Landau et al., 2012) would be to have a panel dataset of at least three observations, and information both on income and consumption.

Nevertheless, vulnerability studies mainly focus on developing countries, where this form of data is difficult to find. Hence, scholars developed methods for using cross-section data (Novignon et al., 2012; Chiwaula et al., 2011; Jadotte, 2011; Günther and Harttgen, 2009; Bourguignon et al., 2004; Glewwe and Hall, 1998). As explained in Bourguignon et al. (2004), these methods rely on recovering individual earning dynamics from pseudo-panel data. The baseline hypothesis is that all individuals within a cohort are subject to a similar stochastic earning process. Therefore, observing the evolution of the mean and the variance of earnings within a cohort in repeated cross-sections is sufficient to estimate the common characteristics of individual earning processes. This approach has been criticized (see, e.g., Calvo and Dercon, 2013) because it is based on the hypothesis that cross-section data contain information on all possible states of the world; if we want to include in the analysis covariate risks, this may not be the case.

Some of the studies are able to compare results using both cross-section and panel data (Chaudhuri et al., 2002; Bourguignon et al., 2004; Bérgolo et al., 2010; Bérgolo et al., 2012; Landau et al., 2012; Bronfman, 2014; Dang and Lanjouw, 2016), and therefore to perform cross-validation testing to check the accuracy of the estimates based on cross-section information. In general, we can conclude that cross-sectional and panel vulnerability measures are very close to each other, except when strong economic shocks hit the economy. In particular, Chaudhuri et al. (2002) find that the cross-sectional vulnerability estimates well identify those among the non-poor who are likely to remain non-poor, and those among the poor who are more likely to remain poor. Bérgolo et al. (2010) and Bérgolo et al. (2012) find that cross-sectional vulnerability estimates capture the probability of future poverty especially for those households at the bottom of the income distribution (even if with some exclusion errors). Dang and Lanjouw (2016) find that although synthetic panels do not accurately predict those who remain poor over time, differences between the estimates and true rates drawn from panel estimates are very small, falling within 2–4 percentage points. Similarly, Bronfman (2014) estimates that at most only 3.6 percent of individuals falling into poverty in a given year were not predicted to be vulnerable in the cross-section model. Performing a validation exercise on Argentina, Bérgolo et al. (2012) reveal a possible issue in using a cross-section setting to address vulnerability: given the 2001–2002 crisis, vulnerability computed on 2001 data underestimated the 2002 poverty rate by more than 10 percentage points. Analyzing vulnerability using cross-sections may therefore lead to under- (over-) estimating poverty in case of a strong negative (positive) shock.

The following presents the different empirical models used to estimate vulnerability according to the dataset used in the analysis, namely: (1) single cross-section; (2) repeated cross-section and pseudo-panels; and (3) panels.

Single cross-section

Chaudhuri et al. (2002)[3] develop a method for estimating expected outcome (in this case consumption) and its volatility by using a single cross-section dataset. The underlying assumption is that most of the observed cross-sectional variation in consumption levels across households is due to differences in observable characteristics. For each household h, Chaudhuri et al. (2002) estimate the following model (12.1)–(12.2):

$$\ln y_h = X_h\beta + e_h \tag{12.1}$$

$$\sigma^2_{e,h} = X_h\theta \tag{12.2}$$

where y_h is household h consumption level, which is assumed to be log-normally distributed; X_h is the set of household observable characteristics, such as household size, location, educational attainment, employment status and demographic characteristics of household head; and community characteristics (that is, the presence of transport facilities, industries, credit institutions, cooperatives or the access to clean water); β is a vector of parameters; and e_h represents the idiosyncratic shock to consumption, which is assumed to be identically and independently distributed over time for each household.

Equations (12.1)–(12.2) are estimated using three-step feasible generalized least squares procedures. The first step involves an ordinary least squares (OLS) estimation of equation (12.1). This yields consistent estimates of the parameter affecting consumption $\hat{\beta}$, and of the residuals. As underlined in Chiwaula et al. (2011), the disturbance term e_h is assumed to account for the unexplained variance, capturing idiosyncratic shocks that contribute to different levels in the vulnerability outcome for households that are otherwise observationally equivalent. In the second step, the log of the squared residuals is regressed on the same variables as in the first step. This yields consistent estimates of the effect of household characteristics on the variance of the outcome ($\hat{\theta}$). The last step corrects for inefficiency of the OLS model by weighting it with the square root of the predicted values of the second step.

Given the estimates $\hat{\beta}$ and $\hat{\theta}$, expected value and variance of log consumption become, respectively, $\hat{E}[\ln y_h|X_h] = X_h\hat{\beta}$, and $\hat{V}[\ln y_h|X_h] = X_h\hat{\theta}$. Household estimated vulnerability – the probability that, given the set of characteristics X_h, consumption c_h will fall below the poverty line z – is then defined by:

$$\hat{v}_h = \hat{P}_h(\ln y_h < \ln z) = \Phi\left(\frac{\ln z - X_h\hat{\beta}}{\sqrt{X_h\hat{\theta}}}\right) \tag{12.3}$$

where $\Phi(\cdot)$ is the cumulative density of the standard normal.

Note that this model relies on two basic assumptions. First, heteroscedasticity, which allows each household outcome's variance to depend on the respective household's characteristics, as in equation (12.2). Second, log normality in the distribution of the chosen vulnerability outcome, which allows to examine how household characteristics affect the mean and the variance of the vulnerability outcome, as in equation (12.3).

Günther and Harttgen (2009) expand the method proposed by Chaudhuri et al. (2002) with multilevel analysis. Taking into account the hierarchical data structure – lower levels (households) are nested in higher levels (communities) allows the author to differentiate between the impact of idiosyncratic household-specific shocks and covariate community-specific shocks.

The main critique to this approach (see, e.g., Ligon and Schechter, 2003; Calvo and Dercon, 2013) derives from the fact that all unobservable sources of persistence in household consumption level are ruled out by assuming that β does not change over time. Moreover, the structure of the economy is assumed to be relatively stable, ruling out any possible aggregate shock. The only uncertainty about the future stream of consumption comes from the uncertainty about idiosyncratic shocks, e_h, household h will experience in the future.

Repeated cross-sections and pseudo panels

Bourguignon et al. (2004) develop a model to obtain estimates of future earnings using repeated cross-sections under the hypothesis that earnings follow a first-order autoregressive process and that individuals enter and exit randomly from the labor force between two successive periods (see also Cuesta et al., 2011 for the same approach applied to income mobility). The logarithm of earnings for individual i, belonging to age cohort j at period t, is described by:

$$\ln y_{it}^{j} = X_{it}^{j}\beta_{i}^{j} + \eta_{it}^{j} \tag{12.4}$$

where X_{it}^{j} is the set of individual characteristics and η_{it}^{j} stands for the unobserved determinant as well as the transitory component of outcomes. By assumption, residuals η_{it}^{j} follow a first-order autoregressive process:

$$\eta_{it}^{j} = \rho^{j}\eta_{it-1}^{j} + \varepsilon_{it}^{j} \tag{12.5}$$

where ε_{it}^{j} is the shock in the earnings variable and it is assumed to have variance $\sigma_{\varepsilon_{jt}}^{2}$. If individuals enter and exit randomly from the labor force between two successive periods (second hypothesis), the variance of the earnings shocks follows the following pattern:

$$\sigma_{\eta_{jt}}^{2} = \rho^{j2}\sigma_{\eta_{jt-1}}^{2} + \sigma_{\varepsilon_{jt}}^{2} \tag{12.6}$$

We can first estimate equation (12.4) for each cohort j for each period t and get estimates of the variance of residuals $\sigma_{\varepsilon_{jt}}^{2}$. Then, provided that at least three subsequent cross-sections are available, estimate of ρ^{j} are found from equation (12.6). Finally, the residuals provides the estimates for the variance $\sigma_{\varepsilon_{jt}}^{2}$.

Panels

When panel data are available, the simplest approach (see Christiaensen and Subbarao, 2005; Bourguignon et al., 2004; Suryahadi and Sumarto, 2003) is assuming that the outcome y is determined by the following stochastic process:

$$\ln y_{it} = \beta X_i + e_i \tag{12.7}$$

where $\ln y_{it}$ is the logarithm of the outcome, X_i is a vector of individual (household) characteristics (sex, age, location,. . .), β is a vector of parameters to be estimated and e_i is a disturbance term with mean zero. The variance of the disturbance term ($\sigma^2_{e_i}$) is determined by:

$$\sigma^2_{e_i} = X_i \tau \tag{12.8}$$

where τ is also a vector of parameters. Three-step feasible generalized least squares are used to estimate values of $\hat{\beta}$ and $\hat{\tau}$. These parameters, together with X_i can be used to calculate expected log outcome:

$$E\left[\ln y_{it}|X_i\right] = X_i \hat{\beta} \tag{12.9}$$

and the outcome variance:

$$Var[\ln y_{it}|X_i] = \hat{\sigma}^2_{e_i} = X_i \hat{\tau} \tag{12.10}$$

Let y be log normally distributed (Chaudhuri et al., 2002; Christianensen and Boisvert, 2000). Let z be the poverty line and establish a threshold probability value above which an individual (a household) is considered vulnerable (see section 12.3.3). The probability that an individual with characteristics X_i will be poor becomes:

$$\upsilon_{it} = Pr(\ln y_{it} < \ln z|X_i) = \Phi\left(\frac{\ln z - X\hat{\beta}}{\sqrt{X_i \hat{\tau}}}\right).$$

According to Kuhl (2003), for instance, individual characteristics may be grouped as follows:

$$X_i = (A_i', I_i', G_i', D_i', K_i')$$

where A_i' is a vector of aggregate shocks such as rainfall or drought hitting the whole members of the society. I_i' is a vector of negative idiosyncratic shocks affecting a single household. G_i' collects the positive idiosyncratic shocks experienced by a single household. D_i' are variables to control for seasonal variation in consumption due to a household choice as a response to changes in their external environment. K_i is a vector of controls for household composition. Hoddinott and Quisumbing (2003) propose a slight variation of the model, adding a set of binary variables identifying each subgroups of the population separately.

Some authors concentrate only on idiosyncratic risks (Amin et al., 2003):

$$E(y^i|\overline{X}, X^i) = \alpha^i + \eta_t + X_t^i \beta^i$$

where $\overline{X}$ is the vector of aggregate variables and X^i is the vector of idiosyncratic variables of the $i - th$ individual.

On the other hand, Glewwe and Hall (1998) focus on household level consumption response to aggregate shocks:

$$E(y^i|\overline{X}, X^i) = \alpha^i + \eta_t + X^i\beta_t$$

Note that here we have the idiosyncratic vector of time-invariant household characteristics X^i, but with time-varying coefficients β_t.

Even if we assume that the true distribution of possible outcomes in the next period (y_{it+1}) could be known, however, the joint distribution of the states of the world s and y_{it+1} is not known. Kamanou and Morduch (2005) generate a distribution of possible future outcomes for households using bootstrap technique, based on their observed characteristics and consumption fluctuations of similar households. Starting with the base year of a panel, they draw a large number (1000) of independent bootstrap samples. With each bootstrap sample, they construct a regression equation to predict the change in consumption based on its correlation with a set of household covariates. Then, they predict per capita expenditure of the future period for each household in each of the bootstrap samples by augmenting the linear part of the predicted value with a shock drawn at random from the empirical distribution of the regression residuals (these are Monte Carlo estimates of future period consumption). Using these samples, the authors compute the next period level of poverty for each household in each of the 1000 samples and then the expected value of poverty as the mean of the bootstrap sample.

12.3.3 Vulnerability Threshold

In the framework of vulnerability as risk of falling into poverty in the future, a vulnerability threshold must be defined; those whose probability of falling into poverty is above the vulnerability threshold will be then defined as vulnerable. Most studies (Pritchett et al., 2000; Christianensen and Boisvert, 2000; Suryahadi and Sumarto, 2003; Christiaensen and Subbarao, 2005; Chiwaula et al., 2011) set this threshold arbitrarily at 0.5: if the probability of falling into poverty is more than 50 percent, an individual is defined as vulnerable. Formally:

$$v_{h,t+k} = 1 - [P(\ln y_h > \ln z)]^k \geq 0.5,$$

which is equivalent to a 29 percent or higher probability to fall below the poverty line in any given year when $k = 2$. As noted by Pritchett et al. (2000), setting the vulnerability threshold to 0.5 has two attractive features. First, it makes intuitive sense to say an individual is vulnerable if they face a 50 percent or higher probability of falling into poverty in the future. Second, it coincides with the one-period-ahead risk of poverty of an individual who is just at the poverty line and faces a mean zero shock. This implies that, in the limit, as the time horizon goes to zero, being poor and being vulnerable coincide. In a recent contribution, Dang and Lanjouw (2016) propose two vulnerability lines defined on the basis of, respectively, an insecurity and a vulnerability index. The first vulnerability threshold is such that a specified proportion of the population with a consumption level above that line will fall below the poverty line in the future. The second vulnerability threshold is such that individuals who are above the poverty line and below the vulnerability line will be poor in the future.

12.4   RESULTS

This section reviews the main results in terms of sources of risk and vulnerability profiles drawn from the empirical vulnerability literature. Vulnerability has been investigated in a large variety of countries, mainly developing countries. Table 12.1 summarizes the country coverage of the existing empirical literature.

12.4.1   Sources of Risk

Households are exposed to a large variety of shocks, both covariates and idiosyncratic. Households should be able to insure consumption against idiosyncratic shocks better than against covariate shocks: since covariate shocks hit the whole community at the same time, risk pooling mechanisms within the community fail to reduce variability of outcomes. On the other hand, insurance across communities might be difficult because of information asymmetries and enforcement failures (see also Günther and Harttgen, 2009 and references therein). Borrowing the classification found in Kozel et al. (2009), the different shocks can be classified as follows. Covariates stocks include macro-shocks, such as terms-of-trade shocks, price shocks or financial crises; climate shocks such as droughts or flooding; agriculture production shocks due to pests, insects or frosts; cattle diseases and insect infestations; natural disasters such as storms, earthquakes, tsunami; and finally, social and political instability such as war, civil conflict and violence. Idiosyncratic shocks include health shocks (both illnesses and deaths); labor market shocks, such as job losses and wage cuts; and other shocks such as corruption, violence, theft, fire, loss of property and local and family disputes. Since household surveys were not designed to provide a full coverage of the impact of shocks on household welfare (as noted by Günther and Harttgen, 2009), only a subset of these shocks are analyzed in the empirical literature. Usually, covariate shocks are found to have a larger impact on households' consumption than idiosyncratic shock (Günther and Harttgen, 2009; Ligon and Schechter, 2003; Dercon and Krishnan, 2000; Christiaensen and Subbarao, 2005). On the other hand, Heltberg and Lund (2009) find that in Pakistan, health shocks, and in particular the illness or death of household members are more frequent, costly and severe shocks than covariate shocks.

Climate shocks
Calvo and Dercon (2013) find that both scarce rainfall, below 60 percent of the usual rainfall distribution, and too much rain, are the main source of risk for households in Ethiopia. Also for Ethiopia, Dercon and Krishnan (2000) find a significant and positive effect of rainfall on log consumption. De la Fuente (2010) finds that in rural Mexico low rainfall levels increase the magnitude of the household threat of future poverty, but positive fluctuations above the average reduce the vulnerability of households. Datt and Hoogeveen (2003) find that the largest share of poverty increase in the Philippines in the period 1997–1998 is imputable to the drought beginning September 1997, caused by El

Table 12.1   Country coverage of empirical vulnerability studies

Region	Country	References
Asia	Bangladesh	Skoufias and Quisumbing (2003)
	China	Chaudhuri (2003)
		Jalan and Ravallion (1999)
		Zhang and Wan (2008)
	Indonesia	Chaudhuri et al. (2002)
		Pritchett et al. (2000)
	India	Dang and Lanjouw (2016)
	Pakistan	Heltberg and Lund (2009)
	Republic of Korea	Bourguignon et al. (2004)
	The Philipphines	Datt and Hoogeveen (2003)
	Vietnam	Dang and Lanjouw (2016)
	Syrian Refugees*	Verme et al. (2016)
Africa	Ethiopia	Calvo and Dercon (2013)
		Dercon and Krishnan (2000)
		Skoufias and Quisumbing (2003)
	Cameroon	Chiwaula et al. (2011)
	Kenya	Christiaensen and Subbarao (2005)
	Nigeria	Chiwaula et al. (2011)
	Madagascar	Günther and Harttgen (2009)
	Malawi	Devereux et al. (2006)
	Mali	Skoufias and Quisumbing (2003)
Latin America	Argentina	Bérgolo et al. (2010)
		Bérgolo et al. (2012)
	Bolivia	Bérgolo et al. (2010)
	Brazil	Bérgolo et al. (2010)
	Chile	Bérgolo et al. (2010)
		Bérgolo et al. (2012)
		Bronfman (2014)
	Colombia	
	Costa Rica	
	Dominican Republic	
	Ecuador	Bérgolo et al. (2010)
	El Salvador	
	Guatemala	
	Haiti	Jadotte (2011)
	Honduras	Bérgolo et al. (2010)
	Mexico	Bérgolo et al. (2010)
		Skoufias and Quisumbing (2003)
		de la Fuente (2010)
	Nicaragua	
	Panama	Bérgolo et al. (2010)
	Paraguay	
	Peru	Calvo (2008)
		Bérgolo et al. (2010)
		Glewwe and Hall (1998)
	Uruguay	Bérgolo et al. (2010)
	Venezuela	Bérgolo et al. (2010)

Table 12.1   (continued)

Region	Country	References
Europe and Central Asia	Bulgaria	Ligon and Schechter (2003)
	Germany	Landau et al. (2012)
	Great Britain	Worts et al. (2010)
	Republic of Serbia	Ersado (2006)
	Russia	Skoufias and Quisumbing (2003)
North America	United States	Worts et al. (2010)
		Dang and Lanjouw (2016)

Note: * The study analyzes the welfare of Syrian refugees living in Jordan and Lebanon.

Niño. In particular, the adverse weather effect increases significantly with ownership of land. Ersado (2006) finds that rainfall variability and its deviations from the long-run normal are associated with increased vulnerability in Serbia. Dercon and Krishnan (2000) report that the most frequently quoted cause of hardship among rural communities in Ethiopia in 1994–1995 was harvest failure due to drought, frost and waterlogging.

Health shocks

Novignon et al.'s (2012) findings suggest that the current health status of a household plays a crucial role in determining the household's vulnerability to poverty: as the general household health declines, future consumption is expected to reduce, making the household vulnerable to poverty in future. In their study on Pakistan, Heltberg and Lund (2009) found that idiosyncratic health shocks have the greatest impact on a household's vulnerability, and Calvo and Dercon (2013) find that serious illnesses are a significant covariate in determining vulnerability. On the other hand, days of illness per adult has no statistically significant effect in determining vulnerability, according to the estimates of Dercon and Krishnan (2000), as well as the incidence of poor health in the household, according to Ersado (2006).

Labour market shocks

Datt and Hoogeveen (2003) analyze the impact of two different labor market shocks in the Philippines crisis in 1998: reduced wages and job losses (both within the country and abroad). They find that the labor market shocks had a 12 percent negative impact on per capita consumption of affected households, and that the shock was greater the more educated the household head and the more commercially developed the communities.

12.4.2   Vulnerability Profiles

This section concentrates on the main covariates used in the literature for assessing future poverty status, underlying the different findings. Since vulnerability definitions, indicators and methods of estimate, country of analysis and type of datasets, vary between the different contributions, this section is intended as a descriptive overview. Nevertheless, although general normative statements cannot be drawn, some similarities are found.

Gender

Gender of the household head has usually no significant effect on vulnerability (see, e.g., Chaudhuri et al., 2002; Dercon and Krishnan, 2000; Ersado, 2006). Ligon and Schechter (2003) find that even if the gender of the household head does not affect vulnerability, female-headed households bear greater aggregate risk than male-headed ones. Bérgolo et al. (2010) find that, among 18 countries in Latin America, gender disparities are significant only in Costa Rica and Venezuela: families where the household head is a woman were more likely to be vulnerable in Costa Rica in years 1992, 1997, 2002 and 2007, and in Venezuela in years 1992, 1998, 2002 and 2006. On the other hand, Glewwe and Hall (1998) find that female-headed households were less vulnerable than male-headed households in Peru in the late 1980s (the result is significant only at the 10 percent level). On the same lines, male-headed households are more vulnerable than female-headed households in the study conducted in Ghana by Novignon et al. (2012).

Education

All studies find that education is always significantly correlated with vulnerability: households with better-educated heads are less vulnerable. Bourguignon et al. (2004), in their study of Korea, find that households where education attainment of the head is above 12 years are non-vulnerable, while workers with less education experience greater vulnerability to falling into poverty. Similar results are found in Chaudhuri et al. (2002) for Indonesia in 1996–1999: 63 percent of the population living in households headed by individuals with at most a primary school education are vulnerable to poverty. On the other hand, within the population in the two highest educational attainment categories, the fraction of vulnerable individuals is less than 1 percent. Bérgolo et al. (2010) find that the educational gaps are highest in most Central American countries, Bolivia, Ecuador and Peru, with almost the entirety of low–educated households being classified as vulnerable to poverty.

Occupation

Effects of occupation status on vulnerability are mainly driven by country and period of analysis. As expected, vulnerability decreases with the share of employed individuals in the household (see, e.g., Ersado, 2006; Ligon and Schechter, 2003). Households headed by self-employed individuals shows higher rates of vulnerability, while salaried workers show more stability (see Chaudhuri et al., 2002; Bérgolo et al., 2010). Studying the Republic of Haiti in 2001, Jadotte (2011) finds that unemployed individuals, domestic workers and self-employed individuals are the most vulnerable, and that unemployment and self-employment show similar vulnerability patterns. Ligon and Schechter (2003) also find that vulnerability decreases with the number of pensioners in the household.

Sector of activity

Chaudhuri et al. (2002) report that the incidence of vulnerability is lower for salaried workers in the public and private sectors than it is for those in other employment categories. Landau et al. (2012) show that in Germany, during the period 1992–2008, the incidence of vulnerability was lowest among households in which the head was employed in services, banking and insurance, or energy sectors. In their study of Indonesia, Pritchett et al. (2000) find that the three sectors accounting for the highest percentage of vulnerable individuals were trade, followed by services and then industry. In Haiti, working in the non-farm sector is associated with lower vulnerability (see Jadotte, 2011); as opposed to Bulgaria, where agricultural households bear no more risk than other households (see Ligon and Schechter, 2003). On the other hand, Glewwe and Hall (1998) find for Peru that households headed by blue-collar workers, white-collar workers and government workers are neither more nor less vulnerable than other households. On the same lines, Bourguignon et al. (2004) report that in Korea there is no difference in vulnerability among sectors (tradable and non-tradable manufactory). In rural Ethiopia, households involved in permanent cropping farms are less vulnerable than households involved in other types of farming (Calvo and Dercon, 2013).

Type of settlement
In Ghana, according to Novignon et al. (2012) estimates, the incidence of vulnerability in 2005–2006 was more than double among urban households than among rural households. Also according to Ligon and Schechter (2003), Bulgarian households living in villages (as opposed to cities) are less vulnerable. On the other hand, Chaudhuri et al. (2002) report that vulnerability in Indonesia in the late 1990s, was mainly a rural phenomenon (20 percent of the urban population is vulnerable, 60 percent of the rural population). The result is consistent with Calvo's (2008) findings for Peru: rural households are more vulnerable to consumption poverty (although they are less vulnerable to leisure poverty). Distance to town is a strong predictor of vulnerability in rural Ethiopia (Calvo and Dercon, 2013). Günther and Harttgen (2009) find that rural households are mainly vulnerable because of low expected mean consumption, while urban vulnerability is mainly driven by high consumption vulnerability. In general, rural households seem to be vulnerable to both idiosyncratic and covariate shocks, while urban households are more exposed to idiosyncratic than covariate shocks.

Possession of land or livestock
In studies of rural communities, possession of assets such as land or livestock is usually taken into account, and it is found to lessen exposure to vulnerability. Calvo and Dercon (2013) report that the larger the livestock, the lower the vulnerability in rural Ethiopia. Ersado (2006) finds for rural Serbia that livestock holding alleviates the effect of idiosyncratic shock but it has no impact on aggregate risk. Livestock possession, particularly large livestock, has a positive impact on households' income also according to Jadotte's (2011) analysis of Haiti. However, large livestock do not insure households against income drop in the presence of a bad-weather shock as small livestock do. Chiwaula et al. (2011) find that livestock are used as a buffer against income fluctuations in Cameroon, while the value of agricultural assets mitigate the negative effect of shocks in Nigeria: as a consequence, the majority of vulnerable households are vulnerable because their asset base is too low.

12.5   CONCLUDING REMARK

This chapter has reviewed the principal empirical contributions to the vulnerability literature. It provided an overview of the different definitions, surveyed the main measurement strategies and commented on the different results. It was found that although there is no consensus about the definition, the interpretation of vulnerability as risk of poverty prevails. Measurement choices are mainly driven by data availability and by the type of society targeted in the study: current literature mainly concentrate on developing countries and uses cross-section datasets. In terms of vulnerability profiles, the different covariates usually have the expected signs; in particular, not being endowed with assets (personal assets, such as education; or physical assets, such as land or livestock) is highly correlated with being vulnerable. Covariate risks are usually accountable for the larger part of vulnerability.

The analysis of vulnerability to poverty is still a young research field, and further research should concentrate, first of all, on a strong definitional effort to clarify the object of analysis. From a methodological point of view, there is space and scope to develop multi-period vulnerability indices: when studying the effects of a policy on individuals' well-being we should not concentrate only on immediate effects, but rather try to look further ahead at paths and patterns of poverty and risk. Moreover, as happened with poverty analysis, research should elaborate on the few multidimensional approaches to vulnerability developed so far. Empirical analysis should develop further by following two different and complementary approaches. On the one hand, identify policies which affect vulnerability. On the other, trace its effects on the economic system: for example, measuring the impact of perceived vulnerability on consumption habits and financial markets. Finally, there could be advantages in cross-imputing covariate shocks that affected one country or some communities within a country to other countries or communities, to simulate possible risk scenarios and develop more effective safety nets and insurance mechanisms.

NOTES

1. See Townsend (1994) for an evaluation of risk-bearing mechanisms in villages in South India.
2. If individuals face aggregate shocks affecting the entire population, or covariate shocks (for instance, natural disasters, or monetary crisis), any insurance mechanism might fail, see Günther and Harttgen (2009) for a discussion.
3. The same approach is then adopted by Christiaensen and Subbarao (2005), Chiwaula et al. (2011), Günther and Harttgen (2009) and Verme et al. (2016).

REFERENCES

Amin, Sajeda, Ashok S. Rai and Giorgio Topa (2003), Does microcredit reach the poor and vulnerable? evidence from northern Bangladesh. *Journal of Development Economics*, 70, 59–82.
Banerjee, Abhijit (2000), The two poverties. *Nordic Journal of Political Economy*, 26, 129–141.
Bérgolo, Marcelo, Guillermo Cruces, Leonardo Gasparini and Andrés Ham (2010), Vulnerability to poverty in Latin America empirical evidence from cross-sectional data and robustness analysis with panel data. Working Paper 170, Chronic Poverty.
Bérgolo, Marcelo, Guillermo Cruces and Andrés Ham (2012), Assessing the predictive power of vulnerability measures: evidence from panel data for Argentina and Chile. *Journal of Income Distribution*, 21, 28–64.
Bourguignon, François, Chor ching Goh, and Dae Il Kim (2004), Estimating individual vulnerability to poverty with pseudo-panel data. Policy research working paper, World Bank.
Bronfman, Javier (2014), Measuring vulnerability to poverty in Chile using the National Socio Economic

Characterization Panel Survey for 1996, 2001, 2006. MPRA Paper 62689, University Library of Munich, Germany.

Calvo, Cesar (2008), Vulnerability to multidimensional poverty: Peru, 1998–2002. *World Development*, 36, 1011–1020.

Calvo, Cesar and Stefan Dercon (2013), Vulnerability to individual and aggregate poverty. *Social Choice and Welfare*, 41, 721–740.

Chaudhuri, Shubham (2003), Assessing vulnerability to poverty: concepts, empirical methods and illustrative examples. Technical report, Columbia University.

Chaudhuri, Shubham, Jyotsna Jalan and Asep Suryahadi (2002), Assessing household vulnerability to poverty from cross-sectional data: A methodology and estimates from indonesia. Discussion Paper Series 0102-52, Columbia University, Department of Economics.

Chiwaula, Levinson S. Rudolf Witt and Hermann Waibel (2011), An asset-based approach to vulnerability: The case of small-scale fishing areas in Cameroon and Nigeria. *Journal of Development Studies*, 47, 338–353.

Christiaensen, Luc and Kalanidhi Subbarao (2005), Toward an understanding of household vulnerability in rural Kenya. *Journal of African Economies*, 14, 520–558.

Christianensen, L. and R.N. Boisvert (2000), On measuring household food vulnerability: Case evidence from northern Mali. Working paper, World Bank.

Cuesta, J., H. Nopo and G. Pizzolitto (2011), Using pseudo-panels to measure income mobility in Latin America. *Review of Income and Wealth*, 57, 224–246.

Dang, Hai-Anh H. and Peter F. Lanjouw (2016), Welfare dynamics measurement: Two definitions of a vulnerability line and their empirical application. *Review of Income and Wealth*.

Datt, Gaurav and Hans Hoogeveen (2003), El Niño or El Peso? Crisis, poverty and income distribution in the Philippines. *World Development*, 31, 1103–1124.

de la Fuente, Alejandro (2010), Remittances and vulnerability to poverty in rural Mexico. *World Development*, 38, 828–839.

Dercon, S. and P. Krishnan (2000), Vulnerability, seasonality and poverty in Ethiopia. *Journal of Development Studies*, 36, 25–53.

Devereux, Stephen, Bob Baulch, Alexander Phiri and Rachel Sabates-Wheeler (2006), Vulnerability to chronic poverty and malnutrition in Malawi. Report, DFID Malawi.

Elbers, Chris, Jan Willem Gunning and Bill Kinsey (2007), Growth and risk: Methodology and micro evidence. *World Bank Economic Review*, 21, 1–20.

Ersado, Lire (2006), Rural vulnerability in Serbia. Policy Research Working Paper Series 4010, World Bank.

Glewwe, P. and G. Hall (1998), Are some groups more vulnerable to macroeconomic shocks than others? Hypothesis tests based on panel data from Peru. *Journal of Development Economics*, 56, 181–206.

Günther, Isabel (2014), Poverty, vulnerability, and reference-dependent utility. *Review of Income and Wealth*, 60.

Günther, Isabel and Kenneth Harttgen (2009), Estimating households vulnerability to idiosyncratic and covariate shocks: A novel method applied in Madagascar. *World Development*, 37, 1222–1234.

Heltberg, Rasmus and Niels Lund (2009), Shocks, coping, and outcomes for Pakistan's poor: Health risks predominate. *Journal of Development Studies*, 45, 889–910.

Hoddinott, John and Agnes Reynes Quisumbing (2003), Methods for microeconometric risk and vulnerability assessments. Social Protection Discussion Papers 29138, World Bank.

Jadotte, Evans (2011), Vulnerability to poverty: A microeconometric approach and application to the Republic of Haiti. In *Inequality of Opportunity: Theory and Measurement* (Juan Gabriel Rodríguez, ed.), vol. 19 of Research on Economic Inequality, Emerald Group, Bingley, pp. 179–216.

Jalan, Jyotsna and Martin Ravallion (1999), Are the poor less well insured? Evidence on vulnerability to income risk in rural China. *Journal of Development Economics*, 58, 61–81.

Kamanou, Gisele and Jonathan Morduch (2005), Measuring vulnerability to poverty. In *Insurance Against Poverty* (Stephan Dercon, ed.), WIDER Studies in Development Economics, Oxford University Press, Oxford, UK and New York, USA.

Kozel, Valerie, Pierre Fallavier and Reena Badani (2009), *Risk and Vulnerability Analysis in World Bank Analytic Work, 2000–07*. In *Social Protection and Labor at the World Bank, 2000–2008*, (Robert Holzmann, ed.) World Bank, Washington, DC.

Kuhl, Jesper J (2003), Disaggregating household vulnerability – analyzing fluctuations in consumption using a simulation approach. Paper for the Northeast Universities Development Consortium Conference Yale University.

Kurosaki, Takashi (2006), Consumption vulnerability to risk in rural Pakistan. *Journal of Development Studies*, 42, 70–89.

Landau, Katja, Stephan Klasen and Walter Zucchini (2012), Poverty, equity and growth in developing and transition countries: statistical methods and empirical analysis. Discussion Papers 118, Georg-August-Universität Göttingen.

Ligon, Ethan and Laura Schechter (2003), Measuring vulnerability. *The Economic Journal*, 113, C95–C102.

Morduch, Jonathan (1994), Poverty and vulnerability. *American Economic Review*, 84, 221–225.

Novignon, Jacob, Justice Nonvignon, Richard Mussa and Levison Chiwaula (2012), Health and vulnerability to poverty in Ghana: Evidence from the Ghana living standards survey round. *Health Economics Review*, 2, https://doi.org/10.1186/2191-1991-2-11.

Pritchett, Lant, Asep Suryahadi and Sudarno Sumarto (2000), Quantifying vulnerability to poverty: A proposed measure, applied to Indonesia. Working Paper 2437, World Bank.

Skoufias, Emmanuel and Agnes R. Quisumbing (2003), Consumption insurance and vulnerability to poverty: A synthesis of the evidence from Bangladesh, Ethiopia, Mali, Mexico and Russia. FCND Discussion Paper 155, IFPRI.

Suryahadi, Asep and Sudarno Sumarto (2003), Poverty and vulnerability in Indonesia before and after the economic crisis. *Asian Economic Journal*, 17, 45–64.

Townsend, Robert M. (1994), Risk and insurance in village India. *Econometrica*, 62, 539–591.

Verme, Paolo, Chiara Gigliarano, Christina Wieser, Kerren Hedlund, Marc Petzoldt and Marco Santacroce (2016), *The Welfare of Syrian Refugees: Evidence from Jordan and Lebanon*. World Bank, Washington, DC.

World Bank (2001), *World Development Report 2000/2001: Attacking Poverty*. Oxford University Press, New York.

Worts, Diana, Amanda Sacker and Peggy McDonough (2010), Falling short of the promise: Poverty vulnerability in the United States and Britain, 1993–2003. *American Journal of Sociology*, 116, 232–271.

Zhang, Yuan and Guanghua Wan (2008), Can we predict vulnerability to poverty?. Research Paper 2008/82, UNU-Wider.

13. Economic insecurity: theoretical approaches
Nicholas Rohde and Kam Ki Tang

13.1 INTRODUCTION

To the average householder the concept of economic insecurity needs no introduction. Most people will be familiar (or at least be able to empathize) with the sense of stress or anxiety that is associated with an uncertain financial future. Fear of events such as unemployment, losses in asset values, unexpected expenses and property crime detract from our current sense of well-being,[1] and hence the anxiety stemming from these sources is deserving of scientific examination. Up until recently, however, research into insecurity has been largely neglected by academic economists. There are probably a couple of reasons for this being the case. Firstly, insecurity is by its very nature a phenomenon that deals with unobservable, forward-looking expectations rather than what has happened in past. Secondly, it is highly subjective and idiosyncratic; two seemingly similar individuals may have wildly different perceptions about the future and hence one may feel much more insecure than the other. These underlying issues make objective and comprehensive measurement difficult, a fact which seems to have discouraged serious quantitative research.

However, there is an increasing acceptance that economic insecurity is an important welfare concept. The clearest recognition of this comes from the United Nations Development Programme's (UNDP) 1994 Human Development Report (HDR) which introduces and defines the broader notion of human security. This is defined over seven areas: economic, food, health, environment, personal, community and political security. The document states that economic security 'requires an assured basic income for individuals, usually from productive and remunerative work or, as a last resort, from a publicly financed safety net' (HDR, p. 25). Osberg and Sharpe (2012) point out that these statements have the virtue of coming from human rights declarations which have a legitimate claim to reflect the preferences of the people they represent. Given the wide-ranging authority of the United Nations, this constitutes strong evidence of the degree to which individuals and their governments value a sense of economic safety.

Aside from this formal recognition, the importance of economic insecurity can also be seen in the literature on subjective well-being. For example, research based on survey data from Dominitz and Manksi (1997) and Scheve and Slaughter (2004) highlighted the links between employment security and job satisfaction, and found that more secure workers were significantly happier in their jobs than those whose positions were more vulnerable. And if secure individuals are happier in their jobs, it is also likely that this sense of satisfaction is correlated with higher scores on other indicators of well-being. Indeed, this is the case, as work by Offer et al. (2012), Barnes and Smith (2011), Andersen (2002) and Smith et al. (2009) demonstrates. Insecure individuals exhibited elevated obesity levels, greater tobacco use and had a tendency to abuse alcohol. These results are not altogether surprising, as economic insecurity is by definition a state of mental unease and is therefore likely to induce behavioural reactions that lead to other health problems.[2]

While the individual costs of insecurity are fairly clear, the associated problems are not confined to those who suffer it directly. For example, Haurin (1991) observed that income volatility (commonly taken as a source of economic insecurity) has a significant impact upon investment in housing; and other authors such as Kimball and Weil (2009) have modelled links between risk aversion, precautionary savings and consumption. The implication is that a widespread sense of economic insecurity has the potential for broad macroeconomic consequences such as elevated unemployment and declining output growth. This in turn can create a vicious circle which reinforces the original sense of insecurity and further exacerbates the worsening macroeconomic conditions.

Although economic insecurity has serious implications for well-being, a commonly accepted framework for analysis has yet to be established. As a consequence, empirical studies on the topic have tended to be vaguely ad hoc, where each work produces its own definition of 'economic insecurity' and then proposes its own techniques to quantify it. As such, there is some ambiguity about the precise meaning of the term, and a much larger level of uncertainty about how it should be measured. Despite this lack of clarity, there are many common themes that can be found across the existing literature, and the purpose of this chapter is to unite some of these shared themes. We do not seek to develop a coherent theoretical framework for economic insecurity, but rather limit our focus to discussing some of the generally agreed-upon issues involved in defining and measuring the phenomenon.

The remainder of the chapter is organized as follows. Section 13.2 provides an intuitive guide to economic insecurity and contrasts this concept with other forms of welfare analysis. Section 13.3 reviews three different approaches to measurement, namely: the use of survey instruments, the methods developed by Osberg and Sharpe and the International Labour Organization based upon aggregate data, and estimation techniques that employ unit record data. Finally, section 13.4 provides a brief summary and gives some concluding comments.

13.2   WHAT IS ECONOMIC INSECURITY?

Economic insecurity is a notion of welfare (or the lack of it). Given that there is a diverse range of welfare concepts such as vulnerability, poverty and happiness, there is a need to place economic insecurity in the context of these other phenomena. We are especially interested in the value-added of developing such a concept and how it could relate to the formation of economic policy. We start by considering the following example as a way to introduce the idea and to explain how it differs from the other aforementioned notions of well-being.

Example 1: Eddie and Josh both work in the manufacturing industry in the United States (US) and both earn the same income y. While Eddie's job is perfectly secure, there is a $0 < p < 1$ probability that Josh's company will shut down the local production facility and move to China, leaving him unemployed. Josh is well aware of this and is anxiously awaiting his employer's final decision.

It should seem intuitive that Josh will feel less secure about his financial future than Eddie; however, existing measures of welfare may not reflect Josh's disadvantaged position. As both parties are currently equally well off, it is only the expectation concerning his future income that Josh will be worried about. If we observe the state of the world where his job is not outsourced (and hence his future income is the same as Eddie's), their realized incomes will show no evidence of a well-being gap existing between the two, despite the fact that Josh was knowingly exposed to an anxiety-producing risk. Accordingly, we can say that attempts to measure insecurity based purely upon observed factors will not capture the negative psychological effects of risks that did not eventuate, and hence neglect an important component of economic insecurity.

Even in the state of the world where Josh does lose his job, it is still unlikely that the full effect of this event will be captured by existing welfare measures. Unless his income falls below a given level (which is unlikely, given the social protection afforded in developed economies like the US), Josh will not be classed as poor[3] and may not qualify as vulnerable.[4] While his income certainly has the potential to be mobile,[5] mobility is generally defined over an entire distribution rather than at the individual level. And while Josh's income may change only marginally (perhaps due to unemployment benefit), his sense of identity derived through his employment will be compromised through redundancy and affect his well-being accordingly.[6] For these reasons it is important to look beyond traditional economic measures based directly upon incomes when thinking about insecurity.

Given that material factors alone are insufficient for our purpose, we may look for guidance to the broader welfare concept of happiness. This constitutes a subjective state of well-being that takes into account all factors – past, current or future – that matter to the individual concerned. Subject to the availability of information it incorporates expectations about different states of the world, not just the one that eventuated. To the extent that Josh is aware of his uncertain future, *ceteris paribus*, he should be less happy than Eddie. However, the comprehensiveness of happiness as a notion of well-being can be problematic in that, unless we can control for all extraneous factors, happiness measures will be too general to pinpoint economic insecurity.

Example 1 illustrates that the essential element that distinguishes economic insecurity from other well-being concepts is that economic insecurity involves risk. In fact, economic insecurity is defined by many as 'the anxiety associated with the exposure to economic risks', as seen in the pioneering works of Osberg (1998), Hacker (2006), Stiglitz et al. (2009) and Bossert and D'Ambrosio (2013). At this level, the definition is probably in line with many people's own experience and is therefore fairly intuitive. Nevertheless, as anxiety is not easily quantified, in practice researchers have to settle with the assumption that there is an 'anxiety function' of which 'economic risk' is a key input. This is akin to the standard economic presumption of the existence of a utility function, of which consumption is a major input. As such, the operational definition of economic insecurity is essentially reduced to 'the exposure to economic risks'. Nonetheless, insecurity is not the same as risk and, thus, is a distinct concept of its own, as illustrated with the following example.

Example 2: Kath has just made a large financial investment. Her investment horizon is over ten years and she chooses to put a substantial proportion of her portfolio in high-return and high-risk equities. In this instance Kath has an exposure to risk. However, as long as her exposure is in line with her preference, it should not cause her undue anxiety. This demonstrates that a voluntary assumption of risk does not have to imply a sense of economic insecurity. Thus a second essential element that characterizes economic insecurity is that the exposure to risk has to be involuntary.

The terms 'risk' and 'uncertainty' are often used interchangeably; however, they are not synonymous. The *MacMillan Dictionary of Modern Economics* (1992) defines risk as 'a context in which an event occurs with some probability or where the size of an event has a probability distribution'. That is, risk is defined in terms of a platonic knowledge of a complete set of outcomes and associated probabilities, such as the flipping of a fair coin. Conversely the *Penguin Dictionary of Economics* (2004) defines uncertainty as a situation where 'there is a plurality of outcomes to which objective probabilities cannot be assigned'. As far as insecurity is concerned, uncertainty is the more relevant concept, as households are unlikely to know either the full range of possible economic futures or their respective probabilities. Furthermore, unlike the exposure to risk which can be voluntary or involuntary, the exposure to uncertainty by nature is almost always involuntary. Once we define economic insecurity as exposure to uncertainty instead of risk, then there is no need to redundantly state that it is involuntary exposure. However, it is possible that a person simultaneously has voluntary exposure to risk and involuntary exposure to uncertainty. In example 2, while Kath may be voluntarily exposed to financial risk, she may still be insecure due to a sense of financial uncertainty. So far, our discussion has focused on exposure to uncertainty in income or wealth. But that is not the only source of economic insecurity, as illustrated by the next example.

Example 3: Emily's son has recently been diagnosed with a serious illness requiring costly treatment. While her family has some health insurance, she is unsure as to whether this will cover the considerable expenses in part, or even at all. In this case, the source of economic insecurity comes not from exposure to uncertainty in income or wealth, but from exposure to uncertainty in expenditure, or more precisely, in the ability to fund the needed expenditure. This illustrates that economic insecurity is about financial need as much as financial capacity, or simply about financial shortfall.[7]

To summarize we can conclude that the notion of economic insecurity is concerned with the adverse well-being effect of (involuntary) exposure to uncertainty in enduring an uninsured financial shortfall. As such, it is distinct from other existing welfare concepts including poverty, vulnerability and mobility, risk and uncertainty, yet it overlaps with them to varying degrees. In the rest of the chapter we will use this definition as a theoretical benchmark to assess various indices that have been used to measure economic insecurity.

13.3 MEASUREMENT CONCEPTS

Given the welfare costs of economic insecurity, there is some interest in how it may be measured such that it is as consistent as possible with the definition provided above. In practice, however, a number of simplifying assumptions tend to be made which, while imperfect, allow this otherwise difficult problem to be analytically tractable. There are a number of approaches that have been employed in the literature so far and we review the major quantitative techniques below. Initially we consider measuring insecurity at the national level using broad descriptive statistics such as unemployment and poverty rates. Following this we focus on techniques for measurement at the individual level. This is done by examining different aspects of economic insecurity such as job security, income and wealth insecurity, and the alternative methods that have been applied in each case.

13.3.1 Aggregate Measures of Insecurity

If we are interested in assessing trends in insecurity at the national level or in making broad cross-country comparisons, it is practical to use measures based upon aggregate national indices. The methods used for making such comparisons have been developed in a number of works by both academic researchers and the International Labour Organization, and work by combining a variety of indicators of economic risk to form a general summary index.

Osberg and Sharpe (2012) base their Index of Economic Security (IES) (as part of their broader Index of Economic Wellbeing) on a number of measures of risk stemming from ill-health, unemployment, divorce and widowhood, and old age. Their general approach is to take a broad range of indicators that capture most of the accepted drivers of economic risk and combine them to form a single representative index. One drawback of the IES, however, is that it measures historically realized hazards rather than perceptions of the future. While this is at odds with our characterization above, they can be reconciled in practice if we accept the assumption made by the authors that the degree of insecurity felt is proportional to realized objective risks. This reduces insecurity to its operational definition and allows the authors to produce meaningful measurements that are consistent with our working definition. Osberg and Sharpe construct the IES for both richer and poorer countries, and employ slightly different methods in each case. We now consider both instances below.

Aggregate measures of economic insecurity in richer countries
To build the IES for developed countries, Osberg and Sharpe measure their four sources of economic risk as follows:

- For insecurity in the event of sickness, a proxy index is used based on the percentage of disposable household income spent on health care services.
- Insecurity associated with unemployment comes from both the current unemployment rate and the average proportion of earnings replaced by unemployment benefits.
- Insecurity associated with widowhood is measured by combining the probability of divorce, the poverty rate among single female parent families, and the average poverty gap ratio among single female parent families. This requires a definition of poverty, which is assumed to be below half of the median equivalent income.
- Insecurity due to old age is measured by the poverty rate and average poverty gap ratio (multiplicatively) experienced by households headed by a person of over 65.

In order to aggregate the four components into the overall IES, a linear scaling technique is used where each component is given a numerical weight proportional to the relative size of the population affected by that risk. It is assumed that unemployment affects the population of working age (15–64), illness affects everyone, widowhood affects all married women and their children who are under 18, and old-age poverty affects the population of 65 or above. A difficulty, however, with such a weighting system is that the demographic structure can differ both from country to country and over time, and hence changes in aggregate insecurity may be driven by factors such as shifting age profiles.

However, there is a simple solution if the index is a simple linear weighted function, for example:

$$I_1 = S_1 D_1 \qquad (13.1)$$

where I_1, S_1, and D_1 are, respectively, the insecurity index, socioeconomic measures, and demographic measures at period 1. In this case, change in insecurity over two periods, say, 0 and 1, can be decomposed into the change in socioeconomic conditions that give rise to insecurity for a given demographic structure, plus the change in demographic structure for given socioeconomic conditions:

$$I_1 - I_0 = 0.5(S_1 - S_0)(D_1 + D_0) + 0.5(S_1 + S_0)(D_1 - D_0) \qquad (13.2)$$

Cross-country comparison can be conducted in a similar way with the assistance of some socioeconomic and demographic benchmarks.

Aggregate measures of economic insecurity in poorer countries
Although much of the concern over economic insecurity has focussed on developed countries, the phenomenon is arguably even more important in poorer nations. The nature of economic risk is markedly different in poor countries, and this requires some changes in the way that insecurity should be measured. Two notable differences are:

- Social safety nets such as unemployment insurance are limited (often to the point of non-existence) in poor nations and hence the lack of this security feature must be factored into the analysis.
- While relative poverty is the main concern in rich countries, in poor countries absolute poverty is the primary concern.

Consistent with their approach for richer countries, Osberg and Sharpe consider economic risks related to health, employment, widowhood and old age. However, the effect of sickness on insecurity is now measured by the percentage of household discretionary income (disposable income net of food expenditures) spent on health care services. While in rich countries the food cost share of disposable income is small and can be neglected, in poor countries the food cost share is larger and food is of higher priority than health care.

Unemployment risk is measured by an agglomeration of agricultural and non-agricultural labour statistics. This aspect is of crucial importance, as most people are either employed by petty trading or farm their own land, and there is often no social welfare or unemployment insurance system to provide support. For risks related to widowhood, male mortality rates and the national poverty rates and depths are used.[8] Insecurity stemming from old age is then measured by national poverty rate and depth, due to missing micro-data on elderly poverty. In poor countries without public pension systems, many elderly still have to work, hence there is not much difference between poverty among the elderly and poverty among the young.

Once these modified indicators are derived, they are again aggregated to build a summary statistic that can be used to make cross-sectional and longitudinal comparisons. Although there are some differences in the approaches for richer and poorer countries,

Osberg and Sharpe (2012) argue that as the central features of the index are the same, the insecurity index can still be compared across these strongly heterogeneous countries.

Aggregate measures from the International Labour Organization
The International Labour Organization's (ILO) index of economic security represents an alternative to the Osberg and Sharpe method. The ILO index uses aggregate data to measure seven different aspects of economic safety at the national level, where larger values indicate a more secure population. The index uses information on incomes, representation (that is, bargaining rights), three types of work-related security (labour market, employment, job security and working conditions) and skill development. Indicators on these phenomena are normalized and aggregated, with income security and representation security given twice the weight of the other variables, such that a unit change in the normalized indicators of these variables will have double the influence of the other five. The ILO measure is extremely broad, with the set of 90 countries covering 86 per cent of the world population.

13.3.2   Individual-Level Measures of Insecurity

Measuring insecurity at the individual or household level presents a different set of challenges to measurement at the aggregate level. When using aggregate data it is fair to assume that an increase in a factor such as the unemployment rate will drive an increase in the average level of economic insecurity. This is essentially a 'law of large numbers' argument that subjective factors will become unimportant at the aggregate level. However, when it comes to individuals, subjective perceptions and other personal characteristics cannot be assumed to average out, as we are examining each statistical unit in isolation. This form of analysis therefore requires a different set of techniques and a stronger set of assumptions than measurement based upon aggregate data. The following section presents some methods for examining insecurity at the micro level and we focus on labour market insecurity, income insecurity and wealth security.

13.3.3   Survey-Based Methods

Perhaps the most effective way of obtaining information on perceived risks is to use surveys of subjective expectations. These instruments have been almost exclusively used to measure job insecurity (Sverke et al., 2006),[9] and hence this is the area where we will focus, although there is no particular reason why the approach cannot be used more broadly.

The strongest appeal of surveys is that they have the ability both to be forward-looking and to capture the idiosyncratic characteristics of individuals. This capacity to draw subtle and nuanced information from subjects has stimulated a great deal of interest in determining the most meaningful features. Greenhalgh and Rosenblatt (1984) were among the first to investigate the issue, defining job insecurity as the 'perceived powerlessness to maintain desired continuity in a threatened job situation' (ibid., p. 438). These authors outline three elements implicit within their definition: the probability of a threat, the severity of that threat, and the feeling of powerlessness to overcome the threat. Each of these elements captures a different aspect of job insecurity, all of which are accessible if the appropriate survey instrument is used.[10] Questions can also be targeted to elicit deliberately objective or subjective interpretations of job security. For example, some researchers have asked respondents about their likelihood of having the same job in the foreseeable future (De Witte, 1999; Mohr, 2000; Roskies et al., 1993), a question that has a relatively objective overtone. Other questionnaires take a subjective approach, using phrases such as 'I worry about', 'I fear I will' and 'I feel uneasy about' (Armstrong-Stassen, 1994; Barling and Kelloway, 1996; Burke, 1991; Mauno et al., 2001),[11] and therefore get more closely to the crux of feelings of insecurity in their subjects.

As there are multiple dimensions to feelings of job insecurity, there is value in combining the results of a number of different survey questions in a single index. For example, an individual may feel threatened by the prospect of demotion or a pay cut, but not by the prospect of job loss. Or a second individual may face a high probability of losing their position, but is confident in their ability to get a replacement job quickly and easily. To account for this, Sverke et al. (2006) and several other authors have developed multiple-item scales (Sverke et al., 2002; Gorsuch, 1997; Spector, 1992). In one case, Ashford et al. (1989) analysed job insecurity by considering five related, though distinct, components: perceptions of (1) threats to job features; (2) the importance of each feature; (3) the threat of the occurrence of adverse events that would affect the total job (for example, temporary lay-off); (4) the importance of each event; and (5) feelings of powerlessness to handle such threats. Job insecurity is then measured as a function of all five inputs.[12]

13.3.4 Estimation Methods

An alternative to the use of survey instruments is to produce measures based upon high-quality unit record data, such as those available from the US Panel Study of Income Dynamics. This represents a cheaper alternative to conducting surveys and allows researchers to examine the relationships between the insecurity experienced by an individual and a number of other variables of interest such as their age, race and health. While it is possible to measure household economic risk with some degree of validity, there are a few assumptions that need to be made before the results can be interpreted as indicators of insecurity. To begin with, an anonymity assumption is required such that we can treat equivalent data points symmetrically. Thus, we assume away personal factors such as the temperaments of the individuals involved, which in theory would be relevant to the analysis.[13] We also rely upon the same assumptions used by Osberg and Sharpe, of realized risk being a proxy for future risk, and insecurity being proportional to objective risk. These assumptions are strong at the individual level and may not always be reasonable; however, they are required to allow us to construct measures from microdata sets when explicit questions on insecurity are unavailable.

Provided that the above assumptions are deemed acceptable, a straightforward approach is to restrict ourselves to job security and to take an estimate of the latent probability of an individual becoming unemployed.

Let $U = \begin{Bmatrix} 0 \\ 1 \end{Bmatrix}$ denote a dummy variable that indicates unemployment while $\mathbf{x}$ is a $n \times k$ data matrix, where there are n individuals and k covariates. We may then use the model:

$$\hat{p}(U = 1|\mathbf{x}) = \Phi(\mathbf{x}'\hat{\boldsymbol{\beta}}) \tag{13.3}$$

for the probability of job loss, where $\Phi(.)$ is a normal (or logistic) CDF, β is a $k \times 1$ coefficient matrix, and $\hat{p} \in (0,1)$ is an intuitive insecurity measure in that a high probability of job loss will highlight insecure individuals or households. Clearly the choice of independent variables will have some impact upon the fitted values, and it would be important to include labour market variables such as job type and industry alongside demographic variables. Other variations on this theme involve extending the analysis to panel data, or using Bayesian methods to establish posterior unemployment probabilities that are updated through time (Smith et al., 2009).

Of course the main reason that job loss will drive insecurity is that it will impact negatively upon income, which leads us to the broader concept of income insecurity. There are a few methods used to measure insecurity in income, and one such measure comes from Smith et al. (2009) who regress annual income y on a time trend t for each household and then take the distribution of the predicted values. For income stream $y = y_1, y_3, \ldots y_T$ where T is the most recent time period, we assume that $E(y|T + 1) = \beta_0 + \beta_1(T + 1)$ where the estimated variance of the forecast $\widehat{\mathrm{var}}\,(f)$ is used to generate the measure.

The forecast then follows a Student t distribution with $T - k$ degrees of freedom. If we consider a poverty line y^* then the probability of falling below it thus becomes:

$$\int_{-\infty}^{y^*} t_{t-k}\left(\beta_0 + \beta_1(T + 1), \hat{\sigma}^2\left[1 + \frac{1}{T} + \frac{(T + 1 - \bar{t})^2}{\sum(t_i - \bar{t})^2}\right]\right) \tag{13.4}$$

which forms an intuitive measure of insecurity. A natural extension of this method is to try using other covariates besides the time trend in generating the income function. This would capture a number of other determinants of income and hence produce more precise estimates. Nevertheless this extension would have its own set of problems in that the econometric estimates of forecasted income distribution may not reflect those anticipated by the household. For example, a household with unique characteristics and therefore an unusual set of explanatory variables is likely to have a high variance in the income forecast simply due to limited local data.

A solution to this problem is to eschew the forecast variance and produce estimates based upon other details from the model. If we take the above time-series regression it seems fair to assume that insecurity: (1) decreases with time-trend β_1; (2) decreases with the average income μ_y; and (3) increases with error variance σ^2 (Nichols and Rehm, 2014). That is, a positive trend is more secure, a high average income is more secure, and noise around an income trend drives insecurity. An appropriate combination of these three factors will then be useful for measuring income insecurity. One such method would be to standardize each indicator to the unit interval using $s_v = (v - v_{min})/(v_{max} - v_{min})$ where v is the variable of interest and then employ a linear scaling $I(y) = \chi s_{\beta_1} + \psi s_{\bar{y}} + \omega s_{\hat{\sigma}^3}$ where χ, ψ and ω are the respective dimension weights. Noting that $I_{\hat{\sigma}^2}(y) > 0$, $I_{\hat{\beta}_1}(y) < 0$ and $I_{\bar{y}}(y) < 0$, we can infer that the correct signs for the weights are $\chi, \psi < 0$, $\omega > 0$. As the 'correct' values of these parameters are probably not knowable, the sensitivity of $I(y)$ with respect to the chosen values should be investigated.

An alternative approach based upon the income stream comes from Cruces (2005, 2006), Makdissi and Woden (2003) and Rohde et al. (2014), who examine the volatility in y using tools from the income inequality literature. The idea is that if incomes are volatile through time, this can be a sign of insecurity. To account for this, it is possible to consider the utility associated with income y_t. A simple concave transformation of y_t is $u_t(\alpha) = y_t^{1-\alpha}/(1 - \alpha)$ where α captures aversion to risk.

Applying this to each time period gives the average utility $\bar{u} = \frac{1}{T}\Sigma_{t=1}^{T} u_t$, while a fixed income stream that gives the same utility is $y^{CE} = [\bar{u}(1 - \alpha)]^{\frac{1}{1-\alpha}}$. Here y^{CE} refers to a constant 'certainty equivalent' income level devoid of volatility risk. An asymmetrical index of insecurity can be given by $I(y) = 1 - y^{CE}/\bar{y}$ which is a longitudinal analogue to Atkinson's (1970) inequality measure.[14] This measure satisfies a number of appealing properties as an insecurity measure, such as scale invariance (that is, that volatility is independent of scale) and an appropriate sensitivity to intertemporal transfers, such that smoother, more reliable income streams are measured as less insecure. Like the probability of job loss, $I(y) \in (0,1)$ and has the further attractive interpretation as the proportion of income that is wasted due to intertemporal instability. By averaging these values across a sample it is possible to obtain an estimate of the welfare costs of income volatility conditional on risk aversion parameter α. A difficulty with this approach, however, is that there is no clear way to establish which sources of volatility will drive insecurity and which will not. For example, a process of steady advancement will yield an increasing income that will appear insecure, despite being symptomatic of a process independent of the uncertainty that drives insecurity. To make sure that measures are appropriate at the household level, Rohde et al. (2014) censor the index such that households with positive income time trends are classified as perfectly secure. That is, the household-specific score is:

$$I^*(y) = \begin{cases} I(y) \text{ if } \hat{\beta}_1 < 0 \\ 0 \text{ if } \hat{\beta}_1 \geq 0 \end{cases} \tag{13.5}$$

where $\hat{\beta}_1$ remains the estimated slope on the time trend regression.

Another approach used by Hacker et al. (2012) and Smith et al. (2009) is to consider insecurity as downside risk, measuring the tendency for incomes to fall from their previous levels. Most incomes will grow over time due to inflation, output growth and advancement, cases where $y_t < y_{t-1}$ will be rather unusual and indicative of underlying stress. One such measure based upon this mechanism is:

$$I(y) = \frac{1}{T-1}\sum_{t=1}^{T-1} b_t \text{ where } b_t = \begin{cases} 1 \text{ if } y_t < y_{t-1} \\ 0 \text{ if } y_t > y_{t-1} \end{cases} \tag{13.6}$$

The index used by Hacker et al. (2012) builds upon this, classifying a household as insecure if it experiences a sharp drop in income or a sharp increase in out-of-pocket medical expense, and lacks a sufficient financial safety net. Let us define m_t as these medical expenses and a_t as a dichotomous indicator of sufficient liquid assets,[15] then Hacker's measure[16] at time t is:

$$I(y,m,a) = \begin{cases} 1 \text{ if } (y_t^* - y_{t-1}^*) + (m_{t-1} - m_t) < -0.25 \times y_t^* \text{ and } a_t = 0 \\ 0 \text{ otherwise} \end{cases} \tag{13.7}$$

where y_t^* is defined as available income. The measure is thus dichotomous, classing households as having experienced a significant adverse event or being safe from that event.

An index with a similar theme is employed by Bucks (2011), who aggregates multiple dichotomous indicators at the household level. If there are f such indicators (such as being uninsured, poor or denied credit) a household may be insecure if it meets g criteria where $f \geq g$. Using the Alkire and Foster (2011) method these indicators can be condensed into a single index. In the example below (five households over three criteria) we have the 5×3 indicator matrix Q. If a household is required to be insecure over $f = 2$ dimensions then only the second household meets the criteria. Censoring the secure values in Q gives Q^* below:

$$Q = \begin{bmatrix} 0 & 0 & 1 \\ 1 & 0 & 1 \\ 0 & 0 & 0 \\ 0 & 1 & 0 \\ 1 & 0 & 0 \end{bmatrix} \quad Q^* = \begin{bmatrix} 0 & 0 & 0 \\ 1 & 0 & 1 \\ 0 & 0 & 0 \\ 0 & 0 & 0 \\ 0 & 0 & 0 \end{bmatrix} \tag{13.8}$$

We then observe that the sample is insecure over two out of 15 possible household dimensions, and this value is used as the insecurity score. A stricter criterion wherall three indicators must be present would yield a value of 0, while a broader rule of classifying a household as insecure if it is at risk over one category would give a total score of 5/15. Given that there is no clear-cut rule for determining the appropriate cut-off, some sensitivity analysis should also be used as to the appropriate value of g when employing this method.

The above indices capture one or more facets of insecurity and aggregate these into a single indicator. However, an alternative approach comes from Bossert and D'Ambrosio (2013) who observe that eventually all economic risks are fundamentally threats to security, employing the idea that wealth represents the claim over all entitlements that can be relied upon in the case of a negative shock. These authors thus produce an axiomatically justified index based upon fluctuations of a household's wealth stream. Denoting this $w = w_1, w_2, \ldots w_T$ where w is wealth and T is the current period, the index may be written as:

$$V_t = -w_T + \sum_{\substack{t \in T \\ w_t < w_{t-1}}} \alpha_t (w_t - w_{t-1}) + \sum_{\substack{t \in T \\ w_t > w_{t-1}}} \beta_t (w_t - w_{t-1}) \tag{13.9}$$

where α_t and β_t are weighting series applied to gains and losses that can be chosen at the analyst's discretion subject to a few restrictions. The Bossert–D'Ambrosio work is unique in the sense that it provides a full characterization of individual insecurity based upon axioms designed to ensure that the index is forward looking. The axioms the authors employ are labelled: (1) single period monotonicity (SPM); (2) a proximity property (PP); (3) homogeneity (H); (4) temporal aggregation (TA); and (5) weak loss priority (WLP), and their measure is built bottom-up from these fundamentals.

The central idea is that insecurity in the current period is a monotonically decreasing function of current wealth (the SPM axiom), such that greater wealth implies a larger buffer of resources against adverse events. This is combined with the TA axiom which imposes that insecurity is a sum of the current wealth level and past fluctuations. The role of the changes in wealth from one period to the next (and consequently the α_t and β_t series) is to capture the experiences of the household over time. For example, declining wealth will drive more insecurity once the level w_T is accounted for, while a household that recovers from a financial setback will gain confidence from their success, which shows up as decreased insecurity. In addition the authors note that more recent fluctuations will be psychologically more powerful than those that occurred in the distant past, and use the PP axiom to discount changes in the distant past more heavily, which implies that $\alpha_t > \alpha_{(t-1)} > 0$ and $\beta_t > \beta_{(t-1)} > 0 \; \forall t \in T$. Further, as there is a noted psychological asymmetry in preferences against losses relative to gains (Tversky and Kahneman, 1991), the WLP axiom places more emphasis on losses than gains, implying $\alpha_t > \beta_t$. Lastly, as the authors are reluctant to scale their index, the homogeneity axiom H leaves the index unstandardized such that positive, zero and negative scores of any magnitude are possible, where negative scores indicate less insecurity.

Given the series $\{w_t\}$, the value of V crucially depends on the chosen values of sequences $\{\alpha_t\}$ and $\{\beta_t\}$. An example of sequences that satisfy PP and WLP is $\alpha_t = \frac{\phi}{2t-1}$ and $\beta_t = \frac{\alpha_t}{2}$ and these are the functional forms recommended by the authors. A noticeable robustness issue with the index is that rescaling the above sequences of α_t (and thus β_t) by choosing any real positive number for ϕ will still satisfy PP and WLP. However, different values will change the relative importance of the current wealth w_T and past wealth fluctuations in determining the level of economic insecurity. Again, as there is no clear rationale for choosing any particular value, some sensitivity analysis should accompany this approach.

An attractive property of the Bossert–D'Ambrosio measure is that with a slight modification it becomes directly decomposable into separate elements from different wealth factors. Let us suppose that $w_t = w_{1t} + w_{2t} + \ldots w_{kt}$ such that each wealth observation is the sum of k components such as housing equity, savings and financial assets. If the WLP axiom is jettisoned the index may be written as:

$$V_T = -w_T + \sum_{t \in T} \theta_t (w_t - w_{t-1}) \tag{13.10}$$

where θ_t has the same properties as the α_t series. Substituting the summation for w_t gives:

$$V_T = -\sum_{j=1}^{k} w_{jT} + \sum_{t \in T} \theta_t \left(\sum_{j=1}^{k} w_{jt} - \sum_{j=1}^{k} w_{jt-1} \right). \tag{13.11}$$

Noting that this is also a linear sum over j we can write:

$$V_T = \sum_{j=1}^{k} \left[-w_{jT} + \sum_{t \in T} \theta_t (w_{jt} - w_{jt-1}) \right] \tag{13.12}$$

which in turn yields:

$$V_T = \sum_{j=1}^{k} V_{jT} \tag{13.13}$$

allowing the insecurity index to be decomposed into the insecurity associated with each input. This decomposition allows for the contribution of each factor to be observable and hence may be used to diagnose the sources of fluctuations in the index.

13.4   CONCLUSION

This chapter has provided an introduction to the emerging literature on economic insecurity and discussed some of the current approaches used for quantitative analysis. We have focused in particular on three different approaches to measurement: measures constructed from aggregate data, directly administered questionnaires, and econometric measures based on household-level surveys. The chapter has argued that survey-based methods are desirable in their ability to measure subjective and idiosyncratic character- istics of insecurity; however, their expense makes them impractical for many researchers. Alternatively, we have shown that indices constructed from aggregate data are relatively simple to calculate and are useful for making cross-national comparisons and examining income trends, but are unable to shed light on determinants of insecurity at the micro level. Lastly, we have claimed that indices constructed from household-level data are practical for studying the effects and distributional characteristics of insecurity, but these techniques require some heavy-handed assumptions which may not always be accept- able. It is our view that progress in this last area represents an important field for future research on economic insecurity.

Finally, it is noted that while progress in research in economic insecurity has been rapid, measurement techniques are still best thought of as exploratory rather than definitive. This is unsurprising, given both the subjectivity of the phenomenon and the only recent attention that it has received. Indeed, given that insecurity was virtually unstudied by economists before the pioneering works of Dominaintz and Manski, Osberg and Sharpe, and Hacker, the progress that has been made since then has been rapid. Nevertheless there is still a long way to go before research into insecurity reaches a stage of maturity comparable to other fields of well-being analysis.

ACKNOWLEDGEMENTS

The authors would like to thank Prasada Rao and Lars Osberg for their invaluable com- ments, and Thi Cao and Sonja Kobinger for their excellent research assistance. This research was supported under the Australian Research Council's Discovery Projects funding scheme (DP120100204).

NOTES

1. See Osberg and Sharpe (2012) for more on this argument.
2. Further psychological evidence of the impact of economic insecurity upon people's perceptions comes from Tversky and Kahneman (1991), whose development of prospect theory emphasizes the asymmetrical psychological costs associated with losses relative to gains.
3. An individual is considered poor if they fall below a poverty line in terms of income or consumption.
4. Vulnerability captures *ex ante* the downside risk in economic well-being (Dutta et al., 2011; Dercon, 2005; see also Chapter 12 by Ceriani and Chapter 11 by Calvo in this *Handbook*). Also see Osberg (2010) for discussion of the similarity and difference between vulnerability and insecurity.
5. See Fields (2005) for a survey on mobility.
6. Akerlof and Kranton's (2000) work on economics and identity suggests that individuals who are unable to meet norms with respect to employment and consumption will face certain social costs. For example,

somebody who loses their job may also lose an important aspect of their identity, such as being the house-hold breadwinner.

7. It should be noted that we are assuming that avoidance options of financial hazards such as insurance are not adequately available. Otherwise, there should be no shortfall once the avoidance options are exercised. For instance, although insurance can help mitigate the costs of financial hazards, it is available only for a limited range of adverse events such as car theft or house fire.

8. Due to missing microdata on poverty rate and depth among single women, the national poverty rates and depths are used instead.

9. In addition to survey work on job security, there exists some research on subjective assessments of other types of insecurity such as health problems (related to a lack of insurance) and victimization by burglary (Dominitz and Manski, 1997). These authors use the US Survey of Economic Expectations, which directly asks for self-assessment on the subject's state of security with respect to the given threats. Survey work by Brunton-Smith and Sturgis (2011) also identifies subjective insecurity associated with crime, while Simard et al. (2010) measure subjective fear of illness due to cancer.

10. Following Greenhalgh and Rosenblatt (1984), a number of related characterizations have been proposed, each designed to shed light on a slightly different aspect of the phenomenon. These include job insecurity as 'one's expectations about continuity in a job situation' (Davy et al., 1997), 'an employee's perception of a potential threat to continuity in his or her current job' (Heaney et al., 1994), 'a discrepancy between the level of security a person experiences and the level she or he might prefer' (Hartley et al., 1991), and 'the subjectively experienced anticipation of a fundamental and involuntary event' (Sverke et al., 2002).

11. The sense of job security has also been measured by questions such as 'How certain are you about your future employment in this organization?' (Davy et al., 1997; Lim, 1997).

12. Related work comes from Roskies et al. (1993), who consider a different set of aspects: the likelihood of termination, early retirement, demotion, impaired working conditions and long-term job insecurity.

13. There is also the possibility that observable features of the data (such as unemployment or income volatility) which would seemingly indicate insecurity may be voluntarily undertaken. This complicates the analysis as the propensity for an individual to willingly expose themself to risk is probably positively correlated with their sense of economic security.

14. It may be necessary to mean-equalize the waves of a sample such that volatility as a result of output growth is removed.

15. This variable is set equal to 1 when the household has enough liquid wealth to compensate for lost income until expected recovery, or to cover lost income for six years.

16. Hacker et al. (2012) also add debt service, an equivalence scale and the qualification that individuals are not transitioning into retirement. The authors also express a preference for interpreting the measure as an average over population subgroups rather than at the individual level.

REFERENCES

Akerlof, G. and Kranton, R. (2000). 'Economics and identity', *Quarterly Journal of Economics*, 115(3), 715–753.

Alkire, S. and Foster, J. (2011). 'Counting and multidimensional poverty measurement', *Journal of Public Economics*, 95(7/8), 476–487.

Andersen, J. (2002). 'Coping with long-term unemployment: economic security, labour market integration and wellbeing: results from a Danish panel study, 1994–1999', *International Journal of Social Welfare*, 11(3), 178–190.

Armstrong-Stassen, M. (1994). 'Coping with transition: a study of layoff survivors', *Journal of Organizational Behaviour*, 15(7), 597–621.

Ashford, S., Lee, C. and Bobko, P. (1989). 'Content, cause, and consequences of job insecurity: A theory-based measure and substantive test', *Academy of Management Journal*, 32, 803–829.

Atkinson, A. (1970). 'On the measurement of inequality', *Journal of Economic Theory*, 2, 244–263.

Barling, J. and Kelloway, K. (1996). 'Job insecurity and health: the moderating role of workplace control', *Stress Medicine*, 12, 253–259.

Barnes, M. and Smith, T. (2011). 'Tobacco use as response to economic insecurity: evidence from the National Longitudinal Survey of Youth', *B.E. Journal of Economic Analysis and Policy*, 9(1), 1–27.

Bossert, W. and D'Ambrosio, C. (2013). 'Measuring economic insecurity', *International Economic Review*, 54(3), 1017–1030.

Brunton-Smith, I. and Sturgis, P. (2011). 'Do neighbourhoods generate fear of crime? An empirical test using the British Crime Survey', *Criminology*, 49(2), 331–369.

Bucks, B. (2011). 'Economic vulnerability in the United States: measurement and trends', Paper prepared for the IARIW–OECD Conference on Economic Insecurity, Paris.

Burke, R. (1991). 'Job insecurity in stockbrokers', *Journal of Managerial Psychology*, 6(5), 10–16.

Cruces, G. (2005). 'Evaluating the impact of income fluctuations on poverty: theory and an application to Argentina', Economic Commission for Latin America and the Caribbean.

Cruces, G. (2006). 'Accounting for income fluctuations in distributional analysis: theory and evidence for Argentina', ECLAC STICERD-LSE.

Davy, J., Kinicki, A. and Scheck, C. (1997). 'A test of job security's direct and mediated effects on withdrawal cognitions', *Journal of Organizational Behavior*, 18(4), 323–349.

Dercon, S. (2005). 'Vulnerability: a micro perspective', Paper presented at the ABCDE for Europe World Bank Conference, Amsterdam.

De Witte, H. (1999). 'Job insecurity and psychological wellbeing: review of the literature and exploration of some unresolved issues', *European Journal of Work and Organizational Psychology*, 8, 155–177.

Dominitz, J. and Manski, C. (1997). 'Perceptions of economic insecurity', *Public Opinion Quarterly*, 61(2), 261–287.

Dutta, I., Foster, J. and Mishra, A. (2011). 'On measuring vulnerability to poverty', *Social Choice and Welfare*, 37(4), 743–761.

Fields, G. (2005). 'The many facets of income mobility', Ithaca, NY: ILR School Cornell University.

Gorsuch, R. (1997). 'Exploratory factor analysis: its role in item analysis', *Journal of Personality Assessment*, 68(3), 532–560.

Greenhalgh, L. and Rosenblatt, Z. (1984). 'Job insecurity: toward conceptual clarity', *Academy of Management Review*, 9(3), 438–448.

Hacker, J. (2006). *The Great Risk Shift: The Assault on American Jobs, Families, Health Care, and Retirement and How You Can Fight Back*, New York: Oxford University Press.

Hacker, J., Huber, G., Rehm, P., Schlesinger, M., Valletta, R. and Craig, S. (2012). 'The Economic Security Index: a new measure for research and policy analysis', Federal Reserve Bank of San Francisco Working Paper Series, 21.

Hartley, J., Jacobson, D., Klandermans, B. and van Vuuren, T. (1991). *Job Insecurity: Coping with Jobs at Risk*, London: SAGE.

Haurin, D. (1991). 'Income variability, homeownership, and housing demand', *Journal of Housing Economics*, 1(1), 60–74.

Heaney, C., Israel, B. and House, J. (1994). 'Chronic job insecurity among automobile workers: effects on job satisfaction and health', *Social Science and Medicine*, 38(10), 1431–1437.

Kimball, M. and Weil, P. (2009). 'Precautionary saving and consumption smoothing across time and possibilities', *Journal of Money, Credit and Banking*, 41(2/3), 245–284.

Lim, V. (1997). 'Moderating effects of work-based support on the relationship between job insecurity and its consequences', *Work and Stress*, 11(3), 251–266.

Makdissi, P. and Woden, Q. (2003). 'Risk-adjusted measures of wage inequality and safety nets', *Economics Bulletin*, 9(1), 1–10.

Mauno, S., Leskinen, E. and Kinnunen, U. (2001). 'Multi-wave, multi-variable models of job insecurity: applying different scales in studying the stability of job insecurity', *Journal of Organizational Behavior*, 22(8), 919–937.

Mohr, G. (2000). 'The changing significance of different stressors after the announcement of bankruptcy: a longitudinal investigation with special emphasis on job insecurity', *Journal of Organizational Behavior*, 21(3), 337–359.

Nichols, A. and Rehm, P. (2014). 'Income risk in 30 countries', *Review of Income and Wealth*, 60, S98–116.

Offer, A., Pechey, R. and Ulijasazek, S. (2012). 'Obesity under affluence varies by welfare regimes: The effect of fast food, insecurity, and inequality', *Economics and Human Biology*, 8(3), 297–308.

Osberg, L. (1998). 'Economic insecurity', Discussion Papers 0088, University of New South Wales, Social Policy Research Centre.

Osberg, L. (2010). 'Measuring economic insecurity and vulnerability as part of economic wellbeing: concepts and context', Department of Economics at Dalhousie University working papers archive, Dalhousie, Department of Economics.

Osberg, L. and Sharpe, A. (2012). 'Measuring economic insecurity in rich and poor nations', CSLS Research Reports 2012-03, Centre for the Study of Living Standards.

Rohde, N., Tang, K. and Rao, D.S. (2014). 'Distributional characteristics of income insecurity in the US, Germany and Britain', *Review of Income and Wealth*, 60, S159–176.

Roskies, E., Louis-Guerin, C. and Fournier, C. (1993). 'Coping with job insecurity: How does personality make a difference?', *Journal of Organizational Behavior*, 14(7), 617–630.

Scheve, K. and Slaughter, M. (2004). 'Economic insecurity and the globalization of production', *American Journal of Political Science*, 48(4), 662–674.

Simard, S., Savard, J. and Ivers, H. (2010). 'Fear of cancer recurrence: specific profiles and nature of intrusive thoughts', *Journal of Cancer Survivorship*, 4(4), 361–371.

Smith, T., Stoddard, C. and Barnes, M. (2009). 'Why the poor get fat: weight gain and economic insecurity', *Forum for Health Economics and Policy*, 12, 5.

Spector, P. (1992). 'A consideration of the validity and meaning of self-report measures of job conditions', in C.L. Cooper and I.T. Robertson (eds), *International Review of Industrial and Organizational Psychology*, Vol. 7, New York: Wiley, pp. 123–151.

Stiglitz, J., Sen, A. and Fitoussi, J.P. (2009). 'Report by the Commission on the Measurement of Economic Performance and Social Progress', Technical Report.

Sverke, M., Hellgren, J. and Näswall, K. (2002). 'No security: a meta-analysis and review of job insecurity and its consequences', *Journal of Occupational Health Psychology*, 7(3), 242–264.

Sverke, M., Hellgren, J. and Näswall, K. (2006). 'Job insecurity: a literature review', SALTSA Report No. 1, Stockholm: National Institute for Working Life.

Tversky, A. and Kahneman, D. (1991). 'Loss aversion in riskless choice: a reference-dependent model', *Quarterly Journal of Economics*, 106(4), 1039–1061.

United Nations Development Programme (UNDP) (1994). *Human Development Report 1994*, New York: Oxford University Press.

14. Economic insecurity: empirical findings
Lars Osberg

INTRODUCTION

Economic well-being is partly determined by the affluence or deprivations which individuals experience in the immediate present, and it is also partly determined by the worries or pleasures created by their expectations of future experiences. From the poorest to the richest, people both live in the present, and anticipate the future. Economic insecurity is, as a consequence, an important determinant of economic well-being[1] and Chapter 13 by Rohde and Tang in this *Handbook* has therefore discussed some of the theoretical issues raised by the term 'economic insecurity'.

However, theoretical concepts will have little influence on actual economic policy unless a practical empirical measurement strategy can be found. The focus of this chapter therefore is to examine how economic insecurity has been measured in the literature and to discuss some of the implications of different measurement strategies. Although the prevalence and implications of economic insecurity are quite often discussed in the popular press, the term is relatively rare in academic economics discourse.[2] Osberg (1998, p. 17) defined it as 'the anxiety produced by a lack of economic safety – that is, by an inability to obtain protection against subjectively significant potential economic losses'. However, anxiety about the future fits poorly into a '*Homo economicus*' vision of rational utility-maximizing economic agents dispassionately calculating their probabilities of positive or negative outcomes and choosing which risks[3] to take and how much insurance to obtain. In addition, academic economists have often preferred to assume away some of the key issues which produce economic insecurity, such as incomplete insurance markets or involuntary unemployment. Hence, the economics literature on insecurity is thin, and the authors who do use the term have often adopted different empirical measurement strategies. This survey therefore begins by trying to clarify the common conceptual elements in available definitions of economic insecurity.

Partly because economic insecurity is a relatively new research agenda within economics, statistical agencies have not collected data for this specific purpose, and there has been no standardization of international data collection methods. Yet measurement without context is meaningless: a statement like 'economic insecurity in Canada was 75 in the year 2013' would, by itself, mean nothing. Because comparability, either over time or across societies, is essential to the meaning of measurement, and because 'purpose-built' data are not available, empirical researchers have had to use data that were collected for other purposes. As this survey will demonstrate, data constraints have therefore fundamentally influenced the existing literature. The existing empirical measures of economic insecurity are thus best seen as provisional approximations; if and when better fundamental data sources become available, one may expect that they will be used, instead of the older data which were not designed for this specific purpose and are not necessarily optimal. However, the conundrum is that statistical agencies cannot be expected to develop better data on economic insecurity until they have some evidence that such measurement might matter, for some socially important issues.

Section 14.1 of this chapter begins by discussing existing definitions and measurement problems. It then summarizes four measurement strategies developed in the current emerging empirical literature on economic insecurity, while section 14.2 presents some recent empirical findings. Section 14.3 is a conclusion while Appendix 14.1 discusses some linked literatures.

14.1 EMPIRICAL MEASURES OF ECONOMIC INSECURITY (EXPLICITLY SELF-LABELLED AS SUCH)

14.1.1 Definitions

The term 'economic insecurity' is sometimes used as if its meaning were so obvious that no explicit verbal definition is necessary, notwithstanding the author's emphasis on the importance of the concept.[4] However, when the search term is 'economic insecurity', the explicit definitions found in the top five most 'Google-popular' web articles[5] are:

1. 'Economic insecurity describes the risk of economic loss faced by workers and households as they encounter the unpredictable events of social life' (Western et al., 2012).
2. 'economic insecurity arises from the exposure of individuals, communities and countries to adverse events, and from their inability to cope with and recover from the costly consequences of those events' (United Nations, 2008).
3. 'economic insecurity is the anxiety produced by a lack of economic safety, that is, by an inability to obtain protection against subjectively significant potential economic losses' (Osberg, 1998).
4. 'Economic insecurity is perhaps best understood as the intersection between "perceived" and "actual" downside risk' (Jacobs, 2007).
5. 'An individual's perception of the risk of economic misfortune' (Scheve and Slaughter, 2004).

A common element in these definitions is that individuals will feel economically insecure when they perceive an uninsurable, significant downside economic risk; that is, a hazard or danger looms in their economic future, with a non-trivial likelihood but not with certainty, and they are unable to insure or avoid or ignore this danger. Each of these definitions also frames economic insecurity in fairly general terms (not just the specific hazards, such as job security or food security, discussed in Appendix 14.1). Each looks forward at future hazards, that is, downside risks; which implies that concepts of volatility or uncertainty or risk aversion are quite different ideas from economic insecurity, because they also include the probability of upside events.[6] In looking forward, each of these definitions also concerns expectations of future states; current experiences and past events plausibly influence the estimation of future hazards, but they are not in themselves the issue.[7]

However, these conceptual definitions do not directly guide empirical measurements in specifying what periods of time are most relevant for the measurement of economic insecurity. Because time is continuous, but analysts have to choose whether to think of events as occurring within daily, weekly, monthly, annual or longer periods of time, any index of economic security must specify the accounting period within which flows are cumulated and any net negative shocks to individuals are calculated.

Implicitly, specifying a particular time period presumes that the timing of whatever happens within the specified period can be ignored; for example, if a calendar year accounting framework is used in calculating an individual's annual income, it is presumed not to matter if cash actually arrived on 3 January or 30 December. For income and consumption purposes, this can be called the 'perfect capital market, within periods' assumption, and it has long been known to have important measurement consequences. For example, Ruggles (1991, p. 167) used the Survey of Income and Program Participation in the United States (US) (which recorded monthly income flows) to show that the incidence of monthly income poverty in a year was about three times greater than the incidence of annual income poverty.

Although within-year poverty dynamics disappear from statistical measurement when analysts use annual income data, in reality a weekly or monthly loss (especially if combined with lack of credit access) may be highly relevant for individuals' subjective insecurity.[8] In practice, the accounting period used in most academic analyses of 'economic security' has been annual. This implies consistency with the annual income period used for most analyses of poverty, or of the distribution of income or national output trends, which is an advantage. However, it also implies an understatement of the incidence of transitions which occur with shorter durations.[9]

If economic insecurity is an issue of forward-looking expectations, and if expectations are rationally formed by individuals, one would expect that the population weighted sum of expected hazards (for example, unemployment), summed across all people, will equal the total hazard experienced (for example, the observed unemployment rate). Nevertheless, this is quite different from saying that it is unemployed people who are insecure about joblessness. The expected probability of unemployment in period t, conditional on personal characteristics and employment history in prior periods, will in general differ across persons. However, everyone at risk of unemployment has reason to be somewhat insecure, because the luck of the draw determines whether or not a particular individual actually becomes unemployed. A forward-looking perspective argues that researchers should predict each individual's level of economic insecurity by estimating the expected probability of a hazard at each point in time (for example, the probability of unemployment in period t) as a function of previous periods' data.

Hence, an econometric implication of an 'expectation of downside risk' perspective is that only prior periods' data should be used to predict insecurity in period t. One should not use current experience of a hazard (for example, unemployment or income loss) in period t to measure an individual's economic insecurity in the same period, because expectations of future events cannot be driven by simultaneous realizations of those events.[10] Implicitly, each period is seen as an instant of time.

However, the problem with this purism is that the data available to researchers are longer-term, often annual. With coarsely grained data, it is plausible that within-period expectations can be partly driven by prior within-period events. For example, with annual data, 'economic insecurity' about unemployment for the year as a whole might plausibly be an issue heavily influenced by being unemployed in January, even if the person had employment in most of the rest of the year. The econometric implication is that current-period data on personal experience of hazards (for example, a person's experience of unemployment) can be used as an 'experiential' measure. Using subjective and objective data from Chile and Mexico, Espinosa et al. (2014) conclude that the most significant variable in determining subjective economic insecurity is current exposure to adverse events, which produces great anxiety and concern about, and the inability to recover from, these bad events.

14.1.2 Three Summary Micro-measures of Economic (In)Security

Economic insecurity has been measured both at the national level and at the individual level; within the 'micro-based' measurement approach, economic insecurity has been conceived of as a large income loss experience, an inadequate wealth buffer stock against shocks, and a downward deviation from trend income. Each of these approaches has its particular strengths and weaknesses; this section complements Chapter 13 by Rohde and Tang in this *Handbook*, which also discusses the conceptual basis of measurement of economic insecurity.

The large income loss approach
The Economic Security Index (ESI) of Jacob Hacker (2008; Hacker et al. 2010, 2012; henceforth H) is a 'micro-based' index of aggregate economic security in the US. The underlying conceptual definition of economic security is: 'the degree to which individuals are protected against hardship-causing economic losses' (Hacker et al., 2012, p. 5).[11] More specifically, the ESI calculates:

> an annual index that represents the share of individuals who experience at least a 25 percent decline in their inflation-adjusted 'available household income' from one year to the next (except when entering retirement) and who lack an adequate financial safety net to replace this lost income until it returns to its original level. (Hacker et al., 2012, p. 8)

Hence, the key idea is really the frequency of large net income declines: the empirical calculations do not so much measure the 'protection' of individuals as they calculate the frequency of large (25 per cent or more) declines in income.[12] There is no attempt to measure the social protection mechanisms of the welfare state, such as eligibility for unemployment insurance benefits or the replacement rate in unemployment insurance benefits for lost earnings.

Available micro-data measure the outcomes which individuals actually experience, but rarely have a convincing way of measuring the unobserved, unchosen options which could have been picked. At the individual level, therefore, there can always be reasonable debates about which outcomes were determined by individual choice and which outcomes were the result of constraints imposed on the individual. Hacker et al. cannot distinguish, at the individual level, between large involuntary losses in income (for example, due to lay-off) and large voluntary declines in income (for example, because of voluntary labour force withdrawal). On average, one would expect interpersonal variation in tastes to be offsetting, or at the most to produce a consistent bias in level estimates, so estimates of macro trends in economic insecurity should be reliable: if preferences have a distribution that does not change fortuitously over time, trends in average outcomes should reflect changes in the constraints facing individuals. However, micro-econometric analysis of causes and micro estimation of implications can be seriously affected.

Hacker et al. explicitly reject the use of public opinion data regarding perceptions of experiences and instead use Panel Study of Income Dynamics (PSID) micro-data to ask how many individual Americans experience substantial (25 per cent or more) declines in total available household annual income from all sources. Hence, subjective 'anxiety' is not the focus of measurement. The 25 per cent criterion which distinguishes losses large enough to cause insecurity from 'small' declines that can be ignored is recognized to be somewhat arbitrary, in much the same way as any specific poverty line criterion of deprivation can be seen as somewhat arbitrary. However, the important issue in both cases is robustness: whether alternative plausible specifications give approximately the same results. Hacker et al. assure readers that the 25 per cent criterion is consistent with polling data on self-perceptions of hardship, and that trends in the ESI are qualitatively similar with alternative thresholds.[13]

Conceptually, the ESI has three major components: losses in equivalent income,[14] medical spending dynamics, and wealth holdings. Because their focus is on net declines in generalized purchasing power – rather than on access to specific commodities (such as food or housing) – Hacker et al. consider it desirable not to distinguish between variations in earnings or transfer payments or other different types of income, and they consequently aggregate earnings, transfers and all other sources of income. Both the time frame and the accounting period are a single calendar year; measurement of economic insecurity is seen as being about how many people, in a particular past year, experienced an income decline that was large enough to be hard to cope with, given their current wealth stock.

Since their emphasis is on insecurity trends in the US, where uninsured medical expenses are a leading cause of household bankruptcies, Hacker et al. explicitly deduct the amount of medical out-of-pocket spending from after tax income in order to get 'available disposable income'.[15] And because wealth which can be accessed to replace lost income provides a sense of security which buffers the impact of income shocks, Hacker et al. exclude from the 'insecure' population anyone with sufficient liquid financial wealth to cope with a large income shock.[16] Household holdings of private wealth therefore play an important role in this framework as a buffer stock protection against deprivation. By contrast, the protective role of the state through social assistance or social insurance (for example, unemployment insurance or worker's compensation or public pensions) is not specifically identified. Fluctuations in total income from all sources are the measured variable, so variations in transfer income cannot be distinguished from market risk in earned income.

The buffering role of private wealth

In a quite different way, 'wealth' is the central component of the indices constructed by Bossert and D'Ambrosio (2009, 2013; henceforth BD). Their starting point is the definition of economic insecurity as 'the anxiety produced by the potential exposure to adverse events and by the anticipation of the difficulty in recovering from them'. Because of their focus on the psychological state of anxiety in the anticipation of adverse future events, they ask the question: what is it that can make a person feel less anxious?

BD suggest that wealth represents a buffer stock that can be turned to in the case of any adverse future event, so each individual's present economic insecurity depends on the current wealth level that person possesses and its past changes. Current assets are important since the wealthier an individual is, the bigger the buffer stock which can be relied on in case of an adverse future event. Because an individual's past experiences play a role in shaping self-confidence on how well the individual can do in case of an adverse event, past wealth losses will increase insecurity, while past wealth gains will decrease it. They argue that in assessing whether a person feels insecure, it is not enough just to look at the wealth that an individual has at a particular point in time. For BD the accounting period is annual, but subjective economic insecurity is driven by events over a number of past years. Past declines in wealth are thought of as representing adverse shocks, not as voluntary anticipated dissaving (for example, the spending of savings in retirement). Hence, the hypothesis is that the more losses individuals have experienced, the more they will feel insecure about their future, even conditional on having the same amount of wealth at that moment. D'Ambrosio and Rohde (2014, henceforth DR) offer an empirical application of BD. Their proposed measure of insecurity therefore is a weighted sum of current wealth and past losses and gains in wealth, where past declines are more heavily weighted than past increases (loss aversion is the rationale) and where events farther in the past get less weight than more recent events.

The concept of 'wealth' has found many alternative definitions in empirical economic research: Wolff (1991), for example, provided an early discussion of whether and how to count the discounted present value of employer pensions or social security benefits as part of household wealth.[17] Conceptually, Bossert and D'Ambrosio (2013, p. 3) argue that 'wealth' should be:

> defined in a comprehensive manner – wealth is assumed to encompass everything that may help an individual in coping with adverse events. The wealth of an individual includes, for instance, claims on governments, family, friends etc. Sen (1976) refers to these claims as entitlements – consumption bundles available to an agent given her rights and opportunities.[18]

However, there are huge practical problems in comprehensive measurement of 'entitlements' or 'everything that may help an individual in coping with adverse events'. Because entitlements to benefits under the social insurance or social assistance programmes of the welfare state are typically codified in legislation, they can be summarized (in a 'macro' sense) and they are included in the Osberg and Sharpe 'macro' measure of economic insecurity.[19] Informal social entitlements are much more hypothetical as protections: the strength (or weakness) of such potential claims can only really be observed when adverse events play out. Micro-data on perceptions of such protections are limited.[20] Hence, in practice, DR do not use a broad measure of entitlements. Instead, the net marketable private assets of households – that is, the sum of financial assets (including homeowner's equity) less total liabilities – is their measure of wealth.

Both the H and the DR perspectives include only private stocks of marketable individual wealth in their empirical measurements of economic insecurity. Both research groups exclude the present value of public and private pension entitlements. Neither perspective fits very well with the life cycle consumption/savings model, which predicts asset accumulation during working years and dissaving during retirement.

Moreover, an indicator of the complexities of measuring economic insecurity is their disagreement about the treatment of housing wealth (which is the main marketable asset held by most households, for example, in the US and Italy). Because H see insecurity as arising from an inability to maintain current consumption in the event of a large income shock, they rule out home equity as a plausible source of security. The illiquid nature of housing equity is key: 'hard to sell when you need cash right now' might be a way of summarizing their perspective. Because the market value of net home equity is not considered, renters and owners are implicitly treated as equivalently exposed to income shocks.

For DR, who do include the value of home equity, the main consideration is that wealth is a buffer against possible anxieties about the future, but past experiences of negative wealth shocks reduce the value of that buffer. Housing wealth is seen as providing a sense of security equivalent to other wealth – that is, in proportion to net home equity – so rising house prices produce increased security, while falling real estate prices cause insecurity.

Neither the H nor DR think of housing as a primary good. The value of security in the sense of home owners dependably receiving a stream of housing services – 'always having a roof over your head' – is not part of either discussion. Historically, some countries have had a judicially enforceable 'right to housing' and the UN Universal Declaration of Human Rights explicitly identifies such a right.[21] Furthermore, the literature on homelessness emphasizes the social exclusion and profound psychological effects which a lack of housing produces. Arguably, having a place to stay is a variable which is dichotomous,[22] not continuous, and the percentage of persons exposed to such a risk might be considered part of economic insecurity.[23]

In practice, owner-occupied housing can be quite volatile in market values; a notable recent example is the increase in US house prices from 2000 to 2007, and the subsequent collapse. Since middle-class American households had had easy access to mortgage financing, many were highly leveraged; Wolff (2012, p.9) estimates that as a result 'between 2007 and 2010, median wealth plunged by a staggering 47 percent'. Both the volatility of housing prices and the special characteristics of housing as a commodity can thus affect the measurement of economic insecurity. If housing equity is excluded from measurement of economic insecurity (as H would advocate), neither the increase in US middle-class net worth prior to 2008 nor the collapse in net worth after 2008 enters the calculation of economic insecurity. From the perspective of DR, however, an estimate of the level of economic insecurity in the US in the 2000–2007 period should reflect the rising house values of that period, and estimates of economic insecurity for each year from 2008 to 2011 should reflect, with greater weight, the net home equity losses of the latter period. The 'right to housing' perspective, on the other hand, would argue that the important time trend to capture is the changing fraction of households at risk of homelessness (that is, foreclosure) or the percentage who are mortgage-free and effectively insulated from market uncertainties.

In a political economy sense, both H and DR emphasize privately held assets, which rather pushes social insurance and the role of the welfare state out of the centre of the 'economic insecurity' stage. However, because they differ in how they conceive of housing wealth, cyclical volatility in housing prices does not influence trends in economic insecurity in Hacker's calculations, but does drive middle-class insecurity in DR's world-view.

Downside income volatility relative to trend

Rohde et al. (2014, henceforth RTR, p. S159) start from the definition: 'the concept (economic security) broadly refers to a state of stress or anxiety felt by individuals when contemplating their financial futures'. They emphasize that this concept is therefore inherently 'forward-looking' but share with BD the perspective that building a micro-based index leaves no option but to use 'backward-looking' data on individuals' past experiences; like BD, they emphasize that this is done in order to estimate individuals' perceptions of the future. However, they emphasize the importance of past volatility of income and not of wealth.[24]

As they note, a number of countries have panel data on household incomes which measure the income stream of household i as $y_i = (y_{i1}, y_{i2}, \ldots, y_{iT})$ over T time periods, usually annual. The question they address is how to construct from such data an insecurity index I_i for each household, and then aggregate such an index over households. RTR are quite conscious that indices of dispersion in past incomes such as the coefficient of variation, or the Theil or Gini indices, pay no attention to sequence. An income stream in which incomes jump around (such as 10, 25, 15, 30, 20) has the same coefficient of variation, and produces the same Gini or Theil index, as a sequence (such as 10, 15, 20, 25, 30) in which those same incomes arrived in a steadily increasing pattern – which might be a predictable career progression. If we want to measure 'economic insecurity', it would seem essential to distinguish between volatile and predictable variations over time. RTR therefore use their panel data to estimate a time series regression of the form $y_{it} = a + \beta t + e_{it}$ for each household and only consider volatility for incomes that have lost ground relative to the household's overall trend. This implies that a downward deviation from a descending trend is assumed equivalent to a downward deviation of the same size from an ascending trend, which could well be questioned. Like H and BD, they do not distinguish between market and transfer income.

There are numerous studies of short-term volatility of incomes, sometimes referred to as 'transitory' variation. These studies typically start by drawing a distinction between observed current income (y) and 'permanent' income ($E(y)$, where E denotes the expectation operator). The two differ because in each period there is some realization y_T of a mean zero random shock (hence observed income in any period is $y = E(y) + y_T$).[25] The income volatility/instability literature emphasizes trends in the variance of y_T. Rohde et al. are quite clear in distinguishing themselves from this literature: they are not interested in positive income shocks. If, for example, the variance of transitory income were to increase because a new lottery scheme introduced some chance of very large short-term income gains, this would not affect economic insecurity.[26]

14.1.3   A Compound 'Macro' Index

Although their verbal definition of the underlying concept of economic insecurity is very general, subjective and forward-looking (see Osberg, 1998), the Osberg and Sharpe (2002, 2005, 2009, 2014) measurement strategy in practice is quite focused. Only four specific hazards are identified and it is assumed that changes in the subjective level of anxiety about a lack of economic safety are proportionate to changes in objective risk. Objective changes in risk are evaluated using aggregate macro-data for the year and country in question.[27] The four economic risks identified (that is, unemployment, sickness, widowhood and old age) are specified because these are specifically named in Article 25 of the United Nations Universal Declaration of Human Rights.

Because their index of economic security is one component of the Index of Economic Well-Being (IEWB) Osberg and Sharpe refer to it as the 'IEWB Index of Economic Security'. And since security is thought of as just the opposite of insecurity, security from each hazard is calculated as equal to the negative of each insecurity. Like the IEWB itself, it is a compound index with four components.

Insecurity in the event of unemployment is conceptually driven by the probability of unemployment and the magnitude of financial loss that unemployment can produce, as indicated by the unemployment rate and the average proportion of earnings that are replaced by unemployment benefits. Insecurity in the event of sickness is seen as driven by the financial risk imposed by illness, which in international comparisons is dominated by the coverage of public health care and is estimated by the percentage of disposable household income spent by households on health care services that is not reimbursed by public or private health insurance. Insecurity in the event of 'widowhood' is modelled as the hazard of women and children becoming poor because they lose access to male earnings due to family break-up; that is, the hazard is equal to (the probability of divorce) multiplied by (the poverty rate among single female parent families) multiplied by (the average poverty gap ratio among single female parent families). The final component of the IEWB economic security domain is the risk of poverty in old age, which is proxied by the poverty intensity (calculated as the poverty rate multiplied by the average poverty gap ratio) experienced by households headed by a person 65 and over.

These component indices are all clearly 'macro' in nature. The employment security component, for example, attempts to measure the aggregate chance of unemployment and the coverage which unemployment insurance offers, on average, to offset the risk of that hazard; it does not add up micro-data on the unemployment experience of individuals. For this component, as for the financial cost of illness, the role which private wealth could play as an individual's buffer has been ignored.

While unemployment directly causes a loss of earnings, and illness directly causes health care costs, the UN Universal Declaration also identifies widowhood and old age, because these states of life are economic hazards in the probabilistic sense that they increase the likelihood of future deprivation; a likelihood that is influenced by a wide range of public policies. Hence, the calculation of these components of the IEWB index emphasizes the probability, and depth, of poverty associated with these states.

In addition to arguing that economic insecurity should be modelled in the aggregate – as a macro characteristic of a given population – the IEWB Index of Economic Security is closely tied to the specific hazards identified in Article 25 of the Universal Declaration of Human Rights.[28] The IEWB perspective is that public policy cannot mitigate or offset all possible economic hazards (and should not attempt to try), and that informing public policy debates is the purpose of social index construction. In the IEWB perspective, the set of all anxieties about all future possible economic hazards includes some which are not legitimate objectives of public policy.[29] The IEWB index only considers specific contingencies ('security in the event of unemployment, sickness, widowhood and old age') identified in Article 25 of the 1948 Universal Declaration of Human Rights (and reiterated in numerous other human rights covenants since then). Because these human rights documents have been ratified by legislatures and constitutional conventions which can claim democratic legitimacy, they can credibly claim to reflect societal preferences about the legitimate objectives of public policy. Whatever their personal level of wisdom or intelligence, no individual researcher or author can plausibly claim that they speak for society as a whole.

14.1.4   Discussion

The fact that there are several candidate empirical measurements of the same general underlying concept of economic (in)security should not be thought unusual. In economics, broad general concepts often have a number of possible alternative measurements, and the issue at hand determines which is used; income is an example.

In income distribution analysis, equivalent disposable individual income is the most common object of analysis. Using an equivalence scale,[30] disposable household money income (the sum of labour earnings, interest, dividends and money transfer payments, minus direct taxes) is divided by the number of equivalent adults in each household and attributed equally to each household member. However, in public finance the taxable income of tax units is the key income concept; economies of household scale are not part of that calculation, but distinctions between individuals within the same household can be quite important. In macroeconomics, gross domestic product (GDP)[31] per capita is often used as the national income measure and the 'household sector' is defined to include much more – for example, charitable foundations – than just 'households' in the income distribution literature (that is, co-residing persons who share consumption).

Each measure of income is calculated quite differently, from different databases and including different components; for example, imputed income from home ownership is part of GDP calculations, but typically omitted from measurements of the income tax base and the distribution of income; while the value of identifiable government services received is discussed in public finance, but only sometimes included in measures of the distribution of household income. Although realized capital gains are sometimes part of taxable income obtained from tax data, they are rarely included in household income measurement and omitted entirely in GDP measurement. Unrealized capital gains are an addition to command over resources and potential consumption, and arguably should be measured for both income distribution and tax purposes, but almost never are. In short, the analytical concept of income espoused by Hicks (1946) and Simons (1938 [1969]) is in practice far from realized, and the differing measures of income used for different purposes align only approximately. It has taken a long period of harmonization (through the Canberra Group at the household level, and the System of National Accounts revisions at the macro level) to get some semblance of consistency within each sub-specialty, but harmonization between the distributional, public finance and national income accounting literatures remains a work in progress.

Nevertheless, the diversity of measurement choices made for 'income' has not stopped economists from using this concept in useful ways. In practice, the diversity of measurement choices has been driven by the different questions asked in different specialty areas in economics. 'Economic (in)security' is an equally broad general concept which is at a much earlier stage in the measurement development process; empirical variation is to be expected.

14.2   EMPIRICAL FINDINGS

In estimating the Economic Security Index, H were interested in measuring long-term time trends within a single country (the US). Fortunately, for this purpose, the US is one of the very few countries with the panel micro-datasets necessary to examine year-to-year income declines for individuals over a long period (1985–2010).[32] Their core conclusion (Hacker et al., 2014, p. S19) was that: 'economic insecurity has risen substantially over the last quarter of a century; levels of insecurity – though elevated across the board – are much higher among those with limited education, as well as among racial minorities and younger workers; and the recent downturn is producing particularly deep losses'. Their decomposition of trends in the ESI and the impact of medical out-of-pocket (MOOP) expenditures and debt finance charges shows that both MOOP and debt costs have little variation over time; the key driver of both long-term trends and cyclical fluctuations in the ESI is the percentage of households reporting a large year-to-year income decline.

By contrast with H's focus on long-term trends in a single country, DR are interested in cross-national comparisons and a much more short-term issue: the impacts of the Great Recession of 2008. In estimating the distribution of economic insecurity in Italy and the USA, using data from 1994 to 2010, their choice of countries was mainly dictated by data availability: the Survey of Household Income and Wealth (SHIW) and the Panel Study of Income Dynamics (PSID) are among the few longitudinal datasets that regularly sample household wealth. The major finding they emphasize is that in both countries, although to a greater extent in the US, the Great Recession produced a dramatic change in insecurity levels. They note that there was a notable distributional shift from higher values to lower (on average), and a substantial increase in the dispersion of the index. Both countries developed a heavy tail indicating an increased proportion of very insecure households; however, there was little evidence of change in the proportion in the upper tail of the distribution. In assessing the impact of past shocks to wealth on current feelings of insecurity, it is clear that long-ago shocks should have less influence than more recent shocks, but DR have to assume some specific decay rate to operationalize their measure.

A striking feature of their results is the difference between the US and Italy in the distribution of security: in Italy, far more of the mass of the distribution of security is in positive territory. In both countries, the Great Recession produced a significant shift downward in the distribution of security, but the Italian distribution is still far less peaked than the American.

Both H and DR are interested in how economic insecurity has varied over time, but RTR focus on how the cost of economic insecurity varies within societies, and how much it has been mitigated by government at each point in the income distribution. They use the Cross National Equivalence File (CNEF) panel data on household incomes for the US, the United Kingdom (UK) and Germany for 1991–2007 (thereby excluding the impacts of the Great Recession, which started in 2008). Because their concern is the extent to which downward deviations from trend income are on average mitigated by government transfers, at different points in the income distribution, they estimate an earnings trend for each person for the period as a whole, look at downward deviations in income, and ask how much of a decline in certainty equivalent income would have generated a similar decline in utility. Hence, their measure of insecurity is calculated for the period as

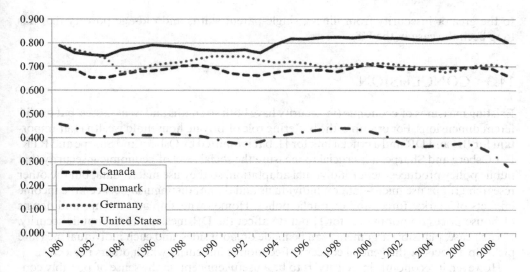

Figure 14.1   Estimates of the IEWB Index of Economic Security

a whole, for each person in each country, for market income and for income after taxes and transfers.

If economic insecurity were distributed equally by income class, then each 10 per cent of income recipients would end up getting 10 per cent of total insecurity, and a plot of the cumulative distribution of insecurity and the cumulative distribution of population (ordered by income) would be a straight line with a 45-degree slope. If low-income people bear more insecurity than average, the plot line lies above 45 degrees at low incomes. This is very much the case for the US market incomes, and is only somewhat reduced by taxes and transfers at the bottom; while at the top of the income distribution there is, after taxes and transfers, less than proportionate insecurity. The concentration of insecurity among the less well-off is even more pronounced in the UK, and the offsetting impact of government is even less, throughout almost all of the income distribution. In Germany, by contrast, there is less inequality in market income insecurity to begin with, and the impact of taxes and transfers roughly equalizes the impact of income insecurity throughout the income distribution.

Compared to all these 'micro'-oriented studies, the 'macro' approach of Osberg and Sharpe (2014) has the great disadvantage that the distribution of economic insecurity within a country cannot be examined. However, secondary macro-data are often available, and have been for some time; hence the advantage of this approach is that cross-nationally comparable estimates of trends, such as in Figure 14.1, can be constructed for many affluent nations (and cross-sectional estimates for both rich and poor nations are possible).

With long spans of data, for a number of countries, there is a stronger empirical basis for concluding, for example, that the United States has been an outlier among developed nations in its relatively high level of economic insecurity. When unemployment was low in the US – that is, prior to the Great Recession – the lower levels of unemployment insurance protection characteristic of the US were somewhat offset by more rapid access to re-employment. More recently, long-term unemployment has risen in the US, which adds to the greater insecurity from illness, single-parent status and old-age poverty that has long been the case in the US.

14.3   CONCLUSION

Existing measures of economic (in)security have both strengths and weaknesses, but on different dimensions. For example, the buffering role of private household wealth is all-important for BD and DR and a crucial link for H, but is omitted by Osberg and Sharpe and RTR. For Osberg and Sharpe, it is crucial to measure the social level of economic insecurity that public policy produces, net of individual adaptation, so they use macro-data; but the other research groups use micro-data on individuals and do not distinguish between the income impacts of market forces and of public policy. Home ownership and the ups and downs of house prices do not matter for H but do affect the DR measure of economic security. In each case, plausible arguments can be made on both sides, and each individual measure picks up aspects of the general concept of economic insecurity which others neglect.

However, if 'economic insecurity' is to be a useful concept, in the sense of possibly contributing to better economic and social decision making, there should be some conceivable link to public policy. At any point in time, in any given society, public policy[33] establishes the rules of the economic game for individuals, and thereby produces an average level of exposure to downside risk. For example, to some degree the state shares with individuals the financial risk of hazards such as unemployment or illness, through programmes such as unemployment insurance or public health insurance. Although individuals may have varying levels of personal anxieties and risk preference, and can decide to avoid or mitigate their personal economic hazards as much as possible (or, alternatively, can decide to increase their personal risk exposure), public policy sets the context for such decisions. Knowing the benefit or wage replacement rate determined by the provisions of the unemployment insurance or the degree of public 'co-pay' embedded in public health insurance systems, individuals can decide how much to save privately as an additional private buffer stock against the costs of illness or unemployment. The argument for macro-based indices is partly that the purpose of social index construction is to inform debates on public policy, so the average level of downside risk should be measured in an aggregate macro sense.[34,35]

With micro-based indices, issues of endogeneity at the individual level can often impede analysis of the role that economic insecurity plays in causing individual outcomes. When an index of the economic insecurity of each individual in a population is constructed using data on their individual characteristics and outcomes, by construction each individual has a different level of economic insecurity. The temptation then is to use each individual's measured economic insecurity in micro-econometric estimations of individual-level outcomes. However, although individuals' measured economic insecurity can be correlated with other characteristics of the same individuals, assessment of causality is often more problematic,[36] but causality is crucial to the implications of economic insecurity. Because group estimates answer the social policy question of the risks to which a population is exposed, and the protections for which that population is eligible,[37] they can be useful in circumventing issues of endogeneity and reverse causality at the individual level.

In the end, the empirical findings from the four different methods surveyed in this chapter are different, but quite consistent. Each study has been very much constrained by the data available, and the questions asked of the data have been different in each case. Nevertheless, although the US is compared to different nations in different ways in each study, all the studies agree in concluding that economic insecurity is highest in the US in the years under analysis; and an accumulating body of results concur that this adversely affects health and well-being outcomes. For example, Offer et al. (2010) have used the Osberg and Sharpe IEWB estimates of economic insecurity to explain cross-country differences in the prevalence of obesity, while Smith et al. (2013) use the ESI index for the same purpose (with the same finding of a strong impact).[38] RTR use Australian microdata and a battery of alternative possible empirical measures to estimate the impact of economic insecurity on mental health, and similarly find robust results.

We do not yet know which measurement method produces the best explanatory measure of economic insecurity; indeed, although it is possible that one, and only one, measurement method is the very best in all possible cases, it is probable that some aspects of economic insecurity are more important for some problems and that other measures may dominate for other issues. At this stage of the literature, it is reassuring to find robustness: that empirical findings about the implications of economic insecurity are qualitatively similar under different operational definitions. As the empirical research on economic insecurity accumulates, it will become clearer which measurement strategy is most fruitful for which particular problem. For now, there is strong evidence that economic insecurity matters, but there is not yet a single clearly dominant empirical measurement method.

NOTES

1. Narayan et al. (2000), for example, report the life self-descriptions of poor people in a sample of poor countries, who repeatedly stress both their immediate deprivations and their anxieties about the future. See also ILO (2004).
2. Osberg (1998, p. 17) defined economic insecurity as 'the anxiety produced by a lack of economic safety – that is, by an inability to obtain protection against subjectively significant potential economic losses'. The EconLit database (https://www.ebsco.com/products/research-databases/econlit, accessed 3 May 2013) had 154 hits for the term 'economic insecurity'; by contrast, 'risk' had 91 353 hits.
3. Some writers (e.g., Akay et al., 2009) distinguish between 'risk' (referring to known probabilities of future hazard) and 'ambiguity' or 'uncertainty' (referring to unknown probabilities of hazards). This chapter avoids that distinction and uses the term 'risk' for both. This chapter also uses the terms 'security' and 'insecurity' as simply the opposites of each other.
4. As Appendix 14.2 notes, the Minsky and Whalen (1996) and Leggett (1964) articles remain web-popular and discuss large topics: respectively, the importance of economic insecurity for the structural survival of capitalism, and the formation of class consciousness. Neither article provides an explicit definition of economic insecurity, although the context indicates that unemployment is probably what they mean. See also Gustman et al. (2010) and Poterba et al. (2011).
5. See Appendix 14.2 for a summary. In some cases, for example Catalano (1991), the 'definition' provided is in the form of example issues (such as job loss) rather than by the articulation of conceptual equivalents.
6. Greater risk is not, per se, the issue: giving somebody a lottery ticket would increase the variance of the distribution of their possible future outcomes, but would not make them more insecure.
7. Individuals may well mourn past losses and/or regret past decisions, but unless that changes their estimation of future events or their anxiety about the future, insecurity is unaffected.
8. The administrators of social assistance programmes have long known that families can get very cold and very hungry in much less than a week, if they have no cash and no access to credit to tide them over a short period without income.
9. The Hacker measure of insecurity (ESI; see below and the theoretical Chapter 13 in this *Handbook*) is

based on the criterion of a 25 per cent income loss, but an annual accounting period understates the impact of spells of loss stretching over the year end. To illustrate this, imagine two individuals (Bob and Jim – otherwise the same), who have the same constant monthly rate of pay and both experience the loss of five months of income during the calendar years 2011 to 2013. If Bob loses his income from 1 July 2012 until 30 November 2012, his 2012 income is 5/12 lower than his 2011 income, and his 2013 income is back to the 2011 level. The ESI counts Bob as experiencing a significant (greater than 25 per cent) income loss during 2012. By contrast, if Jim loses his income from 15 October 2012 until 15 March 2013, his 2012 income is only 21 per cent (= 2.5/12) below his 2011 income and his 2013 income is the same as his 2012 income. Jim does not get counted as taking a year-to-year income loss of more than 25 per cent, but his only difference from Bob is the delay in timing. The same issue arises for medical out-of-pocket spending associated with an ailment spreading over the year end. The problem of annual accounting period end points is unlikely to affect aggregate trends qualitatively, but it would affect estimates of levels and does reinforce the prevalence of insecurity.

10. In panel data analyses, using only *t-1* and earlier period data in estimation of period *t*, insecurity can substantially limit sample size and explained variance.
11. Their view is thus consistent with the definition of economic security as: 'A situation of having a stable source of financial income that allows for the on-going maintenance of one's standard of living currently and in the near future', http://www.businessdictionary.com/definition/economic-security. html#ixzz2rnDT8cDS.
12. If an individual experiencing unemployment had prior year earnings of Y_l and in the year when unemployment occurred had earnings of Y_u and received unemployment benefits of B, Hacker et al. measure the decline (D) in net income (that is, $D = Y_l - (Y_u + B)$) and consider a person insecure if $D/Y_l > 0.25$. The approach of Osberg and Sharpe (see section 14.1.3 below) is based on the idea that the hazard of unemployment produces a market income loss of ($Y - Y_u$) and the degree of protection of individuals depends on the replacement rate (R); that is, the percentage of market income loss replaced by unemployment benefits $R = B/(Y_l - Y_u)$.
13. Similarly, they state that exclusion of families experiencing losses in equivalent income stemming from changes in family size does not affect the level or trend of the ESI.
14. If household size increases (due to birth or marriage or other demographic change) but money income is constant, the equivalent income of all household members will fall, and conversely for household size declines. The ESI uses the Citro and Michael (1995, p.178) preferred equivalence scale. For a family with A adults and K children, the number of equivalent adults is $(A + PK)^\alpha$ where $P = 0.7$ and $\alpha = 0.65$ or $\alpha = 0.75$, implying that one additional child or adult household member, with no income of their own, would decrease equivalent income by less than 25 per cent.
15. Also, debt servicing costs for households with negative net worth are deducted. If health care reform in the US is successful, presumably the health care cost element in the calculation of the ESI will diminish in importance over time.
16. 'Liquid financial wealth' is defined as all wealth holdings besides the primary home, personal vehicles and earmarked retirement savings. 'Sufficient' is defined as equal to or greater than the cumulative loss for the median individual with their socio-demographic characteristics who also experienced such a loss.
17. Because any calculation of net present value is sensitive to the assumed interest rate, a decline in interest rates (as experienced since 2007 in many countries) will increase the current wealth equivalent of defined benefit plan pension entitlements, but it is problematic to think that this increases economic security.
18. The conditionality of protective 'entitlements' is not addressed. Financial assets can be spent for any purpose; access to those resources is not contingent on events or past behaviour. However, the entitlements provided by the welfare state or kinship networks may be contingent on the process that generated deprivation (for example, in Canada, unemployment benefits are not available to those unemployed individuals who have quit their jobs, just those who are laid off; and in any country, a homeless person will probably find that their brother-in-law is much more likely to accommodate them if their house burned down, and much less likely to take them in if they cheated on their spouse and have been locked out as a result).
19. For example, Osberg and Sharpe (2011) use Organisation for Economic Co-operation and Development (OECD) calculations of the average percentage of lost earnings replaced by unemployment benefits (that is, the 'gross replacement rate') for two earnings levels and three family situations. Source: OECD, Tax-Benefit Models, http://www.oecd.org/document/3/0,3343,en_2649_34637_39617987_1_1_1_1,00.html.
20. International comparisons of the percentage of people who believe that they know someone they could rely on in time of need are available at http://www.oecdbetterlifeindex.org/topics/community/. However, the extent to which personal contacts could be depended on is not known.
21. Article 25 of the United Nations Universal Declaration of Human Rights declared: 'Everyone has the right to a standard of living adequate for the health and well-being of himself and of his family, including food, clothing, housing and medical care and necessary social services the right to security in the event of unemployment, sickness, disability, widowhood, old age or other lack of livelihood in circumstances beyond his

control.' See also Article 11(1) of the International Covenant on Economic, Social and Cultural Rights (United Nations: High Commission for Human Rights), http://www.ohchr.org/EN/ProfessionalInterest/Pages/CESCR.aspx.

22. If, for example, an attempt was made to include security of housing in the measurement of 'economic security', the percentage of the population owning their house mortgage-free, or the percentage exposed to the hazard of foreclosure (that is, with little, no or negative home equity) might be part of the index.

23. Mortgage-free home ownership protects against the hazard of eviction. Also, home equity can reduce the hazard of poverty in old age when the imputed value of in-kind housing services received by home owners is not counted in calculations of eligibility for, or payments of, income assistance (as, for example, in Canada).

24. They are careful to note: 'Reflecting this limited scope . . . we refer to our results as measurements of "income volatility" or "income insecurity" rather than "economic insecurity"' (ibid., p. S160).

25. Footnote 2 of Sologon and O'Donoghue (2014, p. S206) gives an idea of the scope of the literature: 'Relevant studies exploring the trends in volatility are: McCurdy (1982), Abowd & Card (1989), Moffitt & Gottschalk (1995, 1998, 2002, 2008), Baker (1997), Baker & Solon (2003), Dickens (2000b), Ramos (2003), Kalwij & Alessie (2003), Cappellari (2004), Gustavsson (2004), Nichols (2008), Nichols & Zimmerman (2008), Sologon & O'Donoghue (2010), Sologon (2010), Shin & Solon (2011).'

26. Appendix 1 discusses the connection between income volatility, economic mobility and economic (in)security.

27. Green et al. (2000, p. 1) report that 'subjective employment insecurity tracks the unemployment rate', while Dominitz and Manski (1996, p. 4) report that 'Expectations and realizations of health insurance coverage and of job loss tend to match up closely' for the United States.

28. Not all the hazards named in Article 25 of the UN Universal Declaration of Human Rights are modelled: lack of data has prevented attention to the hazard of disability. The deprivation of primary commodities ('food, clothing, housing and medical care and necessary social services') has also not been addressed.

29. For example, speculators may worry about the possibility of a collapsing stock market or a decline in commodity prices. In the BD approach, the reasons for past changes in wealth are irrelevant, so those changes in wealth would show up.

30. In rich countries, a number of candidate scales (for example, the Luxembourg Income Study or OECD scales) use household size and composition to account for economies of scale in consumption; while poor countries more often use age and gender 'calorie-equivalencies' to calculate the necessary food expenditures per household.

31. Net national income (NNI) is the national income accounting concept which accounts for depreciation and net foreign ownership; whether it better measures income flows depends heavily on the issue under examination.

32. Micro-data from three panel surveys of the US population were used: the Survey of Income and Program Participation (SIPP) for 1985–2010, and the Current Population Survey (CPS) for 1986–2010, plus the Panel Study of Income Dynamics (PSID) from 1969 (see Hacker et al., 2014).

33. Public policy includes both macroeconomic and microeconomic policy choices. Monetary policy, for example, influences the level of aggregate demand and thereby helps to establish the risk of unemployment for all citizens, while social policy on income supports and unemployment benefits help to determine the costs of job loss for those who actually become unemployed.

34. One analogy is the hazard of death or injury in a traffic accident. No society can escape making a set of policy choices which affect the vehicle accident rate (for example, the standards established for road construction, the speed limits on highways and the laws surrounding drunk driving). In any given context, individuals will then choose how fast and how carefully to drive. Even knowing that public behaviour is somewhat endogenous (for example, people may drive faster on better roads), the inescapable social decision is, 'What base level of hazard do we want?'

35. To assess the implications of economic insecurity, macro-based estimates of economic insecurity can also be used in cross-country macro time series and cross-sectional regressions.

36. At any given level of social protection, those most anxious about the future can save more and build a larger buffer of private savings, while the relatively less anxious can effectively increase their exposure to shocks by choosing to acquire debt. These individual decisions are conditional on the general level of social protection, but a cross-sectional comparison of individuals within a given society at a point in time will show the more anxious to have more observed private wealth; that is, greater subjective insecurity can cause greater assets.

37. Since micro-econometric estimation of the impacts of economic insecurity on individuals' outcomes requires regressors which are plausibly exogenous to individuals' micro decisions, a macro-based estimate can be thought of as an 'intention to treat' instrumental variable to use in micro-econometric estimation of the impacts of economic insecurity. For example, Rohde et al. (2014) use Australia's Household Income and Labour Dynamics (HILDA) panel data and local average unemployment risk exposure in their analysis of the implications of economic insecurity for mental health.

38. Watson (2013) and Watson et al. (2016) estimate the impact of greater individual economic insecurity on the probability that individuals will gain weight, using differences-in-differences techniques with panel micro-data from Canada's National Population Health Survey, before and after the 'natural experiment' of Canada's 1996 changes to unemployment insurance. See also Smith (2009, 2012) and Wisman and Capehart (2010).

REFERENCES

Akay, A., P. Martinsson, H. Medhin and S. Trautmann (2009), 'Attitudes toward uncertainty among the poor: evidence from rural Ethiopia', IZA Discussion Paper 4225.
Bossert, W. and C. D'Ambrosio (2009), 'Measuring economic insecurity', Working Paper.
Bossert, W. and C. D'Ambrosio (2013), 'Measuring economic insecurity', *International Economic Review*, 54 (3), 1017–1030.
Bryceson, D. (1990), *Food Insecurity and the Social Division of Labour*, Basingstoke: Macmillan Press.
Catalano, R. (1991), 'The health effects of economic insecurity', *American Journal of Public Health*, 81, 1148–1152.
Citro, C.F. and R.T. Michael (eds) (1995), *Measuring Poverty: A New Approach*, National Research Council, Washington, DC: National Academy Press.
D'Ambrosio, C. and N. Rohde (2014), 'The distribution of economic insecurity: Italy and the USA over the Great Recession', *Review of Income and Wealth*, 60, S33–S52.
Dominitz, J. and C.F. Manski (1996), 'Perceptions of economic insecurity: evidence from the survey of economic expectations', NBER WP 5690.
Espinosa, J., J.R. Friedman and C. Yevenes (2014), 'Adverse shocks and economic insecurity: evidence from Chile and Mexico', *Review of Income and Wealth*, 60, S141–S158.
Green, F., A. Felstead and B. Burchell (2000), 'Job insecurity and the difficulty of regaining employment', *Oxford Bulletin of Economics and Statistics*, 62, 855–883.
Greenhalgh, L. and Z. Rosenblatt (1984), 'Job insecurity: toward conceptual clarity', *Academy of Management Review*, 9 (3), 438–448.
Guha-Khasnobis, B., S.S. Acharya and B. Davis (eds) (2007), *Food Insecurity, Vulnerability and Human Rights Failure: Studies in Development Economics and Policy*, London: Palgrave Macmillan.
Gustman, A.L., T.L. Steinmeier and N. Tabatabai (2010), 'What the stock market decline means for the financial security and retirement choices of the near-retirement population', *Journal of Economic Perspectives*, 24 (1), 161–182.
Hacker, J. (2008), *The Great Risk Shift: The New Economic Insecurity and the Decline of the American Dream*, rev. and exp. edn, New York: Oxford University Press.
Hacker, J.S., G. Huber, A. Nichols, P. Rehm, M. Schlesinger, R.G. Valletta and S. Craig (2012), 'The economic security index: a new measure for research and policy analysis', Federal Reserve Bank of San Francisco WP 2012-21, available at http://www.frbsf.org/publications/economics/papers/2012/wp12-21bk.pdf.
Hacker, J.S., G.A. Huber, A. Nichols, P. Rehm, M. Schlesinger, R.G. Valletta and S. Craig (2014), 'The economic security index: a new measure for research and policy analysis', *Review of Income and Wealth*, 60, S5–S32.
Hacker, J.S., G.A. Huber, P. Rehm, M. Schlesinger and R. Valetta (2010), *Economic Security at Risk*, New York: Rockefeller Foundation.
Hicks, J.R. (1946), *Value and Capital*, 2nd edn, Oxford: Clarendon Press.
International Labour Organization (ILO) (2004), *Economic Security for a Better World*, Geneva: ILO.
Jacobs, E. (2007), 'The politics of economic insecurity', *Brookings Institution: Issues in Governance Studies*, 12, 1–13.
László, K.D., H. Pikhart, M.S. Kopp, M. Bobak, A. Pajak, S. Malyutina, G. Salavecz and M. Marmot (2010), 'Job insecurity and health: a study of 16 European countries', *Social Science and Medicine*, 70 (6), 867–874.
Leggett, J. (1964), 'Economic insecurity and working class consciousness', *American Sociological Review*, 29, 226–234.
Macdonald, B.-J. and L. Osberg (2014), 'Canadian retirement incomes: how much do financial market returns matter?', *Canadian Public Policy*, 40 (4), 315–335.
Maxwell, S. (2001), 'The evolution of thinking about food security', in S. Devereux and S. Maxwell (eds), *Food Security in Sub-Saharan Africa*, Durban: University of Natal Press, Institute of Development Studies, pp. 13–31.
Minsky, H.P. and C.J. Whalen (1996), 'Economic insecurity and the institutional prerequisites for successful capitalism', *Journal of Post Keynesian Economics*, 19 (2), 155–170.

Narayan, D., R. Chambers, M.K. Shah and P. Petesch (2000), *Crying Out for Change: Voices of the Poor*, Vol. 3, New York: Oxford University Press for the World Bank.

Offer, A., R. Pechey and S. Ulijaszek (2010), 'Obesity under affluence varies by welfare regimes: the effect of fast food, insecurity, and inequality', *Economics and Human Biology*, 8, 297–308.

Osberg, L. (1998), 'Economic insecurity', SPRC Discussion Paper 88, Social Policy Research Centre, University of New South Wales, Sydney.

Osberg, L. and A. Sharpe (2002), 'An index of economic well-being for selected OECD countries', *Review of Income and Wealth*, 48 (3), 291–316.

Osberg, L. and A. Sharpe (2005), 'How should we measure the "economic" aspects of well-being?', *Review of Income and Wealth*, 51 (2), 311–336.

Osberg, L. and A. Sharpe (2009), 'New perspectives on the economic security component of the index of economic well-being', Toronto, Canada: Canadian Economics Association 43rd Annual Conference.

Osberg, L. and A. Sharpe (2011), 'Moving from a GDP-based to a well-being-based metric of economic performance and social progress. Results from the index of economic well-being for OECD countries, 1980–2009', CSLS Research Report 2011-12.

Osberg, L. and A. Sharpe (2014), 'Measuring economic insecurity in rich and poor nations', *Review of Income and Wealth*, 60, S53–S76.

Poterba, J.M., S.F. Venti and D.A. Wise (2011), 'The composition and drawdown of wealth in retirement', *Journal of Economic Perspectives*, 25 (4), 95–117.

Rohde, N., K.K. Tang and D.S. Prasada Rao (2014), 'Distributional characteristics of income insecurity in the US, Germany and Britain', *Review of Income and Wealth*, 60 (1), S159–S176.

Ruggles, P. (1991), 'Short- and long-term poverty in the United States: Measuring the American underclass', in L. Osberg (ed.), *Economic Inequality and Poverty: International Perspectives*, Armonk, NY: M.E. Sharpe, pp. 157–192.

Scheve, K. and M.J. Slaughter (2004), 'Economic insecurity and the globalization of production', *American Journal of Political Science*, 48 (4), 662–674.

Sen, A. (1976), 'Famines as failures of exchange entitlements', *Economic and Political Weekly*, 11, 1273–1280.

Simons, H.C. (1938 [1969]), 'The definition of income', reprinted in R.H. Parker and G.C. Harcourt (eds) (1969), *Readings in the Concept and Measurement of Income,* Cambridge: Cambridge University Press, pp. 63–73.

Smith, T.G. (2009), 'Reconciling psychology with economics: obesity, behavioral biology, and rational overeating', *Journal of Bioeconomics*, 11, 249–282.

Smith, T.G. (2012), 'Behavioural biology and obesity', in A. Offer, R. Pechey and S. Ulijaszek (eds), *Insecurity, Inequality, and Obesity in Affluent Societies*, Oxford: Oxford University Press, pp. 69–81.

Smith, T.G., S. Stillman and S. Craig (2013), 'The US obesity epidemic: new evidence from the Economic Security Index', paper presented at the Agricultural and Applied Economics Association's 2013 AAEA Annual Meeting, Washington, DC, 4–6 August.

Smith, T.G., C. Stoddard and M.G. Barnes (2009), 'Why the poor get fat: weight gain and economic insecurity', *Forum for Health Economics and Policy*, 12 (5), 1–29.

Sologon, D.M. and C. O'Donoghue (2014), 'Shaping earnings insecurity: labour market policy and institutional factors', *Review of Income and Wealth*, 60 (S1), S205–S232.

Sverke, M., J. Hellgren and K. Näswall (2002), 'No security: A meta-analysis and review of job insecurity and its consequences', *Journal of Occupational Health Psychology*, 7 (3), 242–264.

United Nations (2008), 'World Economic and Social Survey 2008. Overcoming economic insecurity', Department of Economic and Social Affairs, available at http://www.un.org/en/development/desa/publications/ (accessed 17 January 2017).

Watson, B. (2013), 'Three essays on the health implications of economic insecurity', PhD dissertation, Dalhousie University, Halifax, Canada.

Watson, B., L. Osberg and S. Phipps (2016), 'Economic insecurity and the weight gain of Canadian adults: a natural experiment approach', *Canadian Public Policy*, June, 115–131.

Western, B., D. Bloome, B. Sosnaud and L. Tach (2012), 'Economic insecurity and social stratification', *Annual Review of Sociology*, 38, 341–359.

Winship, S. (2012), 'Bogeyman economics: has economic insecurity been overstated?', National Affairs Article, Winter, http://www.brookings.edu/research/articles/2012/01/bogeyman-economics-winship.

Wisman, J.D. and K.W. Capehart (2010), 'Creative destruction, economic insecurity, stress, and epidemic obesity', *American Journal of Economics and Sociology*, 69 (3), 936–982.

Wolff, E.N. (1991), 'The distribution of household wealth: methodological issues, time trends and cross-sectional comparisons', in L. Osberg (ed.), *Economic Inequality and Poverty: International Perspectives*, Armonk, NY: M.E. Sharpe, pp. 60–92.

Wolff, E.N. (2012), 'The asset price meltdown and the wealth of the middle class', NBER Working Paper No. 18559.

APPENDIX 14.1: LESSONS FROM RELATED CONCEPTS AND LITERATURES

Most people would probably consider having a job, buying food or making financial decisions to be economic activities, so job security, food security and financial security presumably concern aspects of economic security. However, although there are large literatures associated with each concept, these bodies of work have been quite distinct, and each topic has been analysed in isolation. Nevertheless, the difficulties of measurement of these types of insecurity point to some of the complexities of measuring a broader concept.

For example, the large literature on job insecurity has often addressed its impacts on individual health or on job performance. Precisely because the hazard being considered is very specific – whether a person's current worker–firm job match will be terminated by the employer – it has been possible to use very direct questions for measurement purposes. In László et al. (2009), for example, respondents in 16 European countries were asked to what extent they agreed with the statement, 'My job security is poor'. Those responding 'strongly agree' and 'agree' were regarded as having job insecurity. Health status was similarly self-evaluated, and the conclusion drawn was that: 'an important proportion of middle-aged individuals in Europe are affected by job insecurity and . . . having an insecure job is associated with an increased risk of poor health in most of the countries'. The question used by Burgard et al. (2009) was even more specific: 'How likely is it that during the next couple of years you will involuntarily lose your main job – not at all likely, not too likely, somewhat likely, or very likely?' Using two large US panel data sets spanning 1986 to 2005, they conclude: 'even after adjusting for socio-demographic and job characteristics, health prior to baseline, neuroticism, hypertension and smoking status, and objective employment insecurity before baseline or over follow-up, perceived job insecurity remains a significant predictor of subsequent health' (Burgard et al., 2009, p. 787). The meta-analysis of Sverke et al. (2002) concluded: 'job insecurity has detrimental consequences[1] for employees' job attitudes, organizational attitudes, health, and, to some extent, their behavioral relationship with the organization'.

This literature has been facilitated by the fact that the respondent's current main job provides a clear, unique referent, and voluntary quits are not the issue: the research focus is on the probability that the employer will terminate a person's current job. Context is not addressed, and no attempt is made to measure any offsetting complicating consequences of job loss. Whether or not unemployment insurance benefits partially offset the financial cost of job loss, or whether increased earnings from other family members can be expected to help maintain household consumption, or whether replacement jobs are easily available, greatly affect the consequences of job loss, but the answers to questions on these issues are typically not included as part of a measure of job security. This clear focus on 'job security' and inattention to context and mitigating circumstances keeps the measurement problem relatively simple.

Although 'job security' refers to the hazard of losing a specific job, 'employment security' refers to the more general hazard of wanting, but not being able to get, any paid job. Although arguably more relevant for well-being, as the generality of the hazard and the focus of research widens in scope, measurement difficulties also increase. For example, in project-driven industries such as construction or live music or film, workers typically get a series of firm–employee matches; no particular job lasts very long, but when demand is strong, individuals may get a degree of employment security. Likewise, in a macro-economy with low unemployment, even casual workers may get steady work, albeit from a sequence of employers. Both these examples illustrate the importance of macroeconomic context for the micro-measurement of insecurity. Although job security and employment security share the core issue of the availability of continuing employment, job security focuses solely on the current worker–firm match, but the availability of other jobs is crucial to employment security.

Defining and measuring 'food security' also has both a macro and a micro meaning, which do not necessarily imply each other. In the macro sense, regions or localities may be 'food-secure' if a given area at a point in time has aggregate stocks of food sufficient to nourish the entire resident population. However, whether or not individuals actually go hungry depends on the micro distribution of entitlements to consumption within and among households (see Sen, 1981). Although food security has been the subject of high-profile international summit conferences (most recently, in 1996 and 2009) and the focus of agricultural and trade policy within nations,[2] its definition is far from unam-biguous. Maxwell (2001, p. 15), for example, has noted that 'food security' has at least 32 distinct definitions in the published literature. He argues that over time the focus of the food security literature has shifted from a concern with aggregate food production to an emphasis on the household poverty that often determines individual access to available food. Even when food quantity is sufficient, in a total calories-per-day sense, the vitamin and micronutrient intake necessary for health may be lacking. Webb and Thorne-Lyman (2007) therefore emphasize the multidimensionality of food security and argue that it is not enough to focus just on preventing low household income.[3]

Both food security and job security have thus been linked to wider issues, but the meas-urement problem for each is vastly reduced by their relatively narrow focus. Both achieve vividness of communication and clarity of purpose in public policy discussions by focus-ing on one specific dimension of deprivation. Financial security is, in principle, a concept that could be much broader than either; that is, if it were interpreted to mean 'having enough financial resources to feel secure'.[4] If so, it arguably would be broad enough to approximate economic security.

However, the term 'financial security' is most commonly used in the context of retire-ment and/or old age. Regrettably, although the term is often used in the economics litera-ture on retirement, sometimes this is done without any accompanying explicit definition (see, e.g., Gustman et al., 2010; Poterba et al., 2011). When the meaning of a concept is left implicit, and no explicit definition or measure is proposed, it becomes difficult to know what issues are, or are not, relevant. However, because the context of most usage of the term 'financial security' indicates that only the elderly and near-elderly are under consideration, 'financial security' has in practice become a concept focused on a specific phase of the life cycle. Nevertheless, the question remains of how to frame the hazard in question. Should one think of: (1) the risk of poverty in old age; or (2) the risk of being unable to maintain, during retirement years, approximately the same living standards as during the individual's working life?[5]

This list of security issues is incomplete, but it already illustrates some of the complicat-ing dimensions potentially important to measurement of economic (in)security. The job/employment security distinction illustrates the fact that specificity and clarity of survey evidence sometimes comes with a cost in relevance, and that accurate measurement of a micro hazard can depend on macro context. The food security literature reminds us that we can think of security as a macro characteristic of society or as a micro issue facing individuals, which do not necessarily imply each other; and that the hazards producing insecurity can be thought of as multidimensional or as insufficient aggregate total resources. The financial security literature indicates that social concern about insecurity may be limited to a particular stage of life and that one can think of insufficient resources as relative to own prior norms of consumption, or in terms of the probability and depth of poverty. Each issue is important in its own right, each concerns a specific dimension of economic insecurity, and each illustrates some problematic aspects of measurement.

Osberg (2010) has also discussed how, despite their tendencies to mutual ignorance and non-citation of each other, the literatures on economic vulnerability, social security, social insurance and social protection address many of the same issues as the economic insecurity literature. Underlying all these discussions is the core problem that important uninsurable hazards threaten the future of economic agents, even in countries with well-developed welfare states and sophisticated private insurance markets, and especially in poor countries that lack both.

Notes

1. Note that correlations are measured, but causality is inferred (Greenhalgh and Rosenblatt, 1984; László et al., 2010).
2. Food security has been, and remains, a particularly important issue for agricultural policy, and government legitimacy, in very poor countries; see, for example, Bryceson's (1990) analysis of Tanzania. See also Maxwell (2001).
3. Guha-Khasnobis et al. (2007) have also linked food security to vulnerability and human rights.
4. Indeed, a Google web search on the term 'economic insecurity' will produce, as top item, the Wikipedia definition, which sees the two terms as synonymous; see Appendix A. Broader still is the Human Resources and Skills Development Canada (HRSDC) description, which argues: 'Financial security is about achieving material well-being. It's about having an adequate income to meet basic needs such as housing, food, and clothing. It's also about being able to take advantage of opportunities and lead a rewarding life.' See http://www4.hrsdc.gc.ca/d.4m.1.3n@-eng.jsp?did=4. Since there is no mention in the HRSDC discussion of adverse risks or uncertainties (specific or general), and despite the generality, the phrasing implies that this is not an exhaustive 'definition', it is not pursued further.
5. Although a retirement income target equal to 70 per cent of pre-retirement earnings has often been advocated by financial planners, it has quite limited information content regarding post-retirement living standards (see MacDonald and Osberg, 2014).

APPENDIX 14.2

Table 14A.1   Most 'Google popular' usages of 'economic insecurity'

Definition	Source (accessed 7 May 2013)
'Economic security or financial security is the condition of having stable income or other resources to support a standard of living now and in the foreseeable future. It includes: • probable continued solvency • predictability of the future cash flow of a person or other economic entity, such as a country • employment security or job security. Financial security more often refers to individual and family money management and savings. Economic security tends to include the broader effect of a society's production levels and monetary support for non-working citizens.'	Wikipedia, http://en.wikipedia.org/wiki/Economic_security
'Economic insecurity describes the risk of economic loss faced by workers and households as they encounter the unpredictable events of social life.'	Western et al. (2012), http://www.annualreviews.org/doi/abs/10.1146/annurev-soc-071811-145434
'The Economic Security Index . . . tracks the proportion of Americans who see their "available household income" – their household income after paying for medical care and servicing their financial debts – decline by 25 percent or more from one year to the next and who lack sufficient financial wealth (such as savings) to replace this lost income.'	http://www.economicsecurityindex.org/
'Economic Insecurity has been measured with community-level indicators such as the unemployment rate [and] as the undesirable job or financial experiences of individuals. Losing a job or income, or being unable to pay one's bills are examples'	Catalano (1991), http://www.ncbi.nlm.nih.gov/pmc/articles/PMC1405640/
'economic insecurity arises from the exposure of individuals, communities and countries to adverse events, and from their inability to cope with and recover from the costly consequences of those events'	UNDP (2008), http://www.un.org/en/development/desa/policy/wess/wess_archive/2008wess.pdf
'the anxiety produced by a lack of economic safety, i.e. by an inability to obtain protection against subjectively significant potential economic losses'	Osberg (1998), http://www.sprc.unsw.edu.au/media/File/dp088.pdf
'Economic insecurity is perhaps best understood as the intersection between "perceived" and "actual" downside risk, which carry nearly equal importance in politics.'	Jacobs (2007), http://www.brookings.edu/research/papers/2007/09/politics-jacobs

Table 14A.1   (continued)

Definition	Source (accessed 7 May 2013)
'the broadest measure of economic insecurity is the risk of losing a job or experiencing a significant drop in income'	Winship (2012), http://www.brookings.edu/research/articles/2012/01/bogeyman-economics-winship
Google Scholar (additional listings)	
'An individual's perception of the risk of economic misfortune'	Scheve and Slaughter (2004), http://onlinelibrary.wiley.com/doi/10.1111/j.0092-5853.2004.00094.x/full
'We measure respondents' perceptions of near-term economic insecurity through their responses to questions eliciting subjective probabilities of three events: What do you think is: ... the percent chance that you will have health insurance coverage 12 months from now? ... the percent chance that someone will break into (or somehow illegally enter) your home and steal something, during the next 12 months? ... the percent chance that you will lose your job during the next 12 months?'	Dominitz and Manski (1996), http://www.nber.org/papers/w5690
No explicit definition of economic insecurity – implicitly used as equivalent to unemployment	Minsky and Whalen (1996), http://www.jstor.org/stable/4538526
No explicit definition of economic insecurity – implicitly used as equivalent to unemployment	Leggett (1964), http://www.jstor.org/stable/2092125

15. Relative deprivation and satisfaction: theoretical approaches
Lucio Esposito

15.1 INTRODUCTION

The interest in the concepts of relative deprivation and relative satisfaction is motivated by the fact that the divide between 'haves' and 'have-nots' not only raises ethical concerns, but also has important consequences for our everyday life. It has been argued that economic inequality triggers violence, crime and social unrest; an unequal distribution of resources has been indicated as a cause of suicide, mental distress and various illnesses; and as having an influence on migration, educational achievements, marriage decisions and voting patterns; see Williams (1984), Stark and Taylor (1991), Wagner and Zick (1995), Alesina and Perotti (1996), Barber (2001), Hillemeier et al. (2003), Eibner and Evans (2005), Veenstra (2005), Subramanian and Kakawi (2006), Fesnic and Viman-Miller (2009), Gravelle and Sutton (2009) and Watson and McLanahan (2011). Not surprisingly, economic inequality has been studied at great length under a number of disciplines including economics, sociology, psychology, anthropology and political science.

But why do we need the concepts of relative deprivation and relative satisfaction when we could simply talk about inequality? Answering this question leads to clarifying the conceptual relationship between inequality and relative deprivation or relative satisfaction. When thinking of relative deprivation and relative satisfaction, the word 'relative' is a clear indication that the achievements of a certain individual *i* are to be evaluated against the achievements of other people in society, which are taken as a sort of benchmark. Relative deprivation and relative satisfaction exist (that is, they are different from zero) when these other benchmark achievements are different from those of individual *i*. This line of reasoning leads to a banal but important consideration, namely that inequality in the distribution of the relevant benefit is the condition *sine qua non* for the existence of relative deprivation and relative satisfaction. Therefore, one could say, the two phenomena thus analysed are closely related to inequality. However, there is an important difference between the concept of inequality and those of relative deprivation and relative satisfaction. While the former necessarily refers to a set of individuals as a whole, the latter can also refer to single individuals. In other words, one can safely think of the level of inequality or of relative deprivation in society. However, while it makes sense to talk about the relative deprivation or relative satisfaction of a certain individual, the same cannot be said about inequality. This difference, and the desirability to obtain indicators at the individual level, motivate the study of relative deprivation and relative satisfaction.

This chapter is organized as follows. Section 15.2 presents a review of the interest in relative deprivation and relative satisfaction in the literature, showing evidence that academic interest in the topic has a fairly long history. Next, the section reviews the main theoretical models produced on the basis of a relativistic specification of utility. Section

15.3 deals with measurement and is divided into three subsections. The first one deals with different approaches to measurement, the second introduces the main indices proposed by the literature, and the third presents extensions in a dynamic and multidimensional setting. It may be worth mentioning that in this chapter the dynamic element is considered only with respect to reference incomes; the idea of individual i's relative deprivation or satisfaction with respect to a benchmark represented by their own achievements in a previous period are beyond the scope of this chapter. Section 15.4 deals with the concept of the reference group, and section 15.5 concludes.

15.2   A REVIEW OF THE LITERATURE ON RELATIVIST CONCERNS

The concepts of relative deprivation and relative satisfaction have long been explored by economists as well as by scholars from a number of other disciplines, in particular sociology (Merton, 1938; Stouffer et al., 1949; Festinger, 1954; Runciman, 1966; Townsend, 1979), psychology (Bradburn, 1969; Crawford and Naditch, 1970; Morrison, 1971; Easterlin, 1974) and anthropology (Foster, 1965, 1972; Acheson, 1972; Thompson and Roper, 1976). In economics, the interest in these concepts can be traced back to the often-quoted 'linen shirt argument' put forward by Adam Smith (1776). In eighteenth-century England, possession of goods such as a linen shirt or leather shoes was important not for their intrinsic value but because they granted inclusion in the social life of the village. Marx (1849) wrote extensively on the germane role that interpersonal comparisons and status have on social dynamics. A similar stance can be found in Veblen's (1899) notions of conspicuous leisure and consumption. A significant statement can be found in the words of one of the fathers of modern welfare economics, who asserts that a 'proportion of the satisfaction yielded by the incomes of rich people comes from their relative, rather than from their absolute, amount' (Pigou, 1932, p. 90). Perhaps even more explicitly, John Stuart Mill states that 'Men do not desire merely to be *rich*, but to be *richer* than other men . . . The avaricious or covetous man would feel little or no satisfaction in the possession of any amount of wealth if he were the *poorest* amongst all his neighbours or fellow-countrymen' (Mill, 1941, p. 49, posthumously published contribution).

It was only with Duesenberry (1949), however, that these ideas received a more precise formalization. The question, 'What kind of reaction is produced by looking at a friend's new car or looking at houses or apartments better than one's own?' (ibid., p. 27) motivated his proposal of a utility function going beyond the absolute income approach. According to his relative income hypothesis, utility was not only positively dependent on own income, but also negatively affected by other people's income levels. What he named the 'demonstration effect' would drive people to demand more or better goods when other people are seen to possess them. In other words, the fact that other people are observed to enjoy certain goods would be the element triggering some latent preference for these goods. This implies a formal acknowledgement of consumption externalities, which take place when consumption by some people generates costs or benefits for others. A similar idea can be found in Leibenstein's (1950) 'bandwagon effect', which is defined as 'the case where an individual will demand more (less) of a commodity at a given price because some or all other individuals in the market also demand more (less) of the commodity' (ibid., p. 190).

Interdependent preferences are also studied by Pollack (1976), who uses utility functions that depend not only on the absolute value of consumption, but also on the average level of consumption in society.

The implications of interpersonal comparisons and status for consumer behaviour were studied at length by Hirsch (1976) and Frank (1985). Hirsch gives the example of competition for status through status symbols such as watches. Acquiring luxurious watches rather than ordinary ones does not provide concrete improvements on one's situation other than signalling membership to elitist groups in society. Frank proposes an illustrative prisoner's dilemma-like thought experiment, where he shows how working in a 'distasteful' but better-remunerated dusty mine could become the dominant strategy merely for the concern of losing ground in the income hierarchy. Since these contributions, goods which are demanded for the status they confer are called 'positional goods'. The conceptual interest for positional goods has also gone beyond consumer behaviour and the economic discipline, and has been extended to the philosophical analysis of inequality (e.g., Brighouse and Swift, 2006). An interesting comparison can be made between Hirsch's example of the appetite for a luxurious watch and Adam Smith's linen shirt argument. In both cases the willingness to possess the relevant good is motivated by interpersonal comparisons and by the achievement of a social type of functioning. However, while in the linen shirt argument the focus is on not being at the bottom of society and therefore excluded, inherent in Hirsch's example of luxurious watches is the desire to feature at the top of the social hierarchy. Consumption behaviour in presence of relativist concerns is also analysed in the more recent papers by Bagwell and Bernheim (1996), Corneo and Jeanne (1997) and Hopkins and Kornienko (2004), to cite a few. Bagwell and Bernheim (1996) investigate the conditions under which the desire to signal wealth gives rise to 'Veblen effects' (defined as the willingness to pay larger prices for equivalent goods), and show that this does not happen when the marginal cost of consuming the positional good is larger for poorer individuals. Corneo and Jeanne (1997) develop a model where consumers demand a positional good in order to signal membership of an elitist group. They consider cases where consumers are snobbish and conformist, and show that in the latter case the market demand curve can have a positive slope. Hopkins and Kornienko (2004) emphasize the strategic nature of the choice of individual-level consumption. They model the concern for status as a simultaneous move game and analyse it in the framework of symmetric Nash equilibrium. By using techniques from auction theory, they derive a number of results including that relativist concerns increase as society becomes richer.

Theoretical models adopting a relativistic specification of utility and accounting for the externality implied by the 'keeping up with the Joneses' motivation have been developed to study not only consumption behaviour, but a number of other social outcomes and economic issues. The social nature of consumption behaviour is used by Leibenstein (1975) to explain fertility decline; for him, 'social status considerations' are 'critical to the explanation of the utility cost of children' (ibid., p. 2). The choice to restrain family size would stem from the consideration that having many children may decrease consumption possibilities and hence cause downward social mobility. In an earlier paper, Leibensein (1962) noted how the externalities arising from interpersonal comparisons represent a challenge to the Pareto principle, and analysed the implications this may bring about for social choice rules derivable from democratic ideals. Akerlof and Yellen (1990) devote a whole section to relative deprivation theory in their model of unemployment, although relative deprivation is conceptualized mainly in terms of fairness perception about the remuneration obtained according to the effort made in the workplace.

A number of contributions have focused on the implications of relativist concerns for taxation and public finance. Boskin and Sheshinski (1978) show that accounting for relative deprivation provides an additional reason for redistribution, and can remove the possibility that increasing tax rates may end up in a reduction of tax revenues via disincentive effects. Ng (1987) analyses the problem of the optimal level of public expenditure in the presence of relative income effects, taking into account the externalities arising from private expenditure. In a model where investment in education is carried out to maximize lifetime utility, and people care about status, Lommerud (1989) shows that it can be optimal for the government to tax away income differences and employ educational subsidies to increase people's willingness to invest in education. Ireland (1998, 2001) studies a number of issues affecting the design of taxation schemes in the presence of positional goods and competition for status. Ljungqvist and Uhlig (2000) argue that the policy objective of neutralizing the effect of consumption externalities can be achieved by taxing consumption at a flat marginal rate. Papers by Aronsson and Johansson-Stenman (2008, 2010) show how the optimal provision of public goods and the optimal taxation of labour and capital income in the presence of relativist considerations are still an area of active research. Bilancini and Boncinelli (2012) study the impact of redistributive policies in the presence of relativist concerns by focusing on how social status is computed and evaluated. They derive different results according to whether status depends in an ordinal or a cardinal way on individuals' relative position in the economic hierarchy.

Abel (1990) and Galí (1994) introduce a relativist specification of the utility function to analyse the implications on asset pricing models and financial decisions taken by economic agents. Portfolio choices and optimal exposure to risk are shown to be affected by the introduction of these externalities and by the way these are modelled. Risky choices are also explored by Robson (1992). He investigates the implications of relativist concerns for risk-taking using a Neumann–Morgenstern type of utility function which includes not only absolute wealth but also a status variable given by ordinal rank in the wealth distribution. Robson shows that in this way it is possible to account for apparently contradictory behaviour such as simultaneously purchasing insurance and participating in lotteries, and derives additional results on the equilibrium wealth distribution in terms of Pareto inefficiency and existence of a middle class.

Another important area in which the implications of status effects and a relativist specification of utility have been studied is that of savings and economic growth. Cole et al. (1992) develop a model where differences in growth rates across countries are explained through the existence of a non-market sector which generates concerns for relative position in the income distribution and generates multiple equilibria. In a two-class growth model where individuals care about both absolute consumption and the social perception of their wealth rank, Corneo and Jeanne (1999) find that both too much equality and too much inequality are detrimental to economic growth. Moreover, differently from the model without status, the steady growth rate of the economy is affected by the initial level of wealth inequality. Corneo and Jeanne (2001) carry out a similar analysis in the realm of an endogenous growth model and show that the steady growth rate of the economy increases with both the strength of the status-seeking motive and the initial level of equality in the distribution of wealth. Cooper et al. (2001) explain the flat trend of happiness through a growth model in which 'normal goods' confer utility directly, while 'status goods' do at the expense of other individuals. As the economy grows, resources for innovation are progressively transferred to status goods, and the share of resources spent on these goods increases. This process is shown to have negative long-term effects on utility. Along similar lines, Eaton and Eswaran (2009) explain the Easterlin (1974) paradox of constant self-reported happiness despite rising real income, using a general equilibrium model which incorporates a positional good (which they call a 'Veblen good'). They show that as productivity increases, the 'Veblen good' tends to absorb all the additional productivity, and that this mechanism is detrimental for social capital. In a two-period model, Direr (2001) analyses the effect of relative consumption on aggregate saving and shows that a rise in consumption inequalities has a negative impact on saving compared to the case where agents do not care about relative income.

15.3   MEASUREMENT

15.3.1   Approaches

The following quote from Runciman (1966) is generally considered the conceptual starting point for the measurement of relative deprivation and relative satisfaction:

> We can roughly say that [a person] is relatively deprived of X when (i) he does not have X; (ii) he sees some other person or persons, which may include himself at some previous or expected time, as having X; (iii) he wants X; (iv) he sees it as feasible that he should have X. (ibid., p. 10)

These words motivated the first formal approach to measurement in economics, proposed by Yitzhaki (1979). The Yitzhaki approach does not directly rely on individual comparisons, nor does it extend the analysis directly into the utility space; see also Yitzhaki (1980). Each income level is explicitly said to represent a different bundle of commodities that a certain individual is able to consume, and the value of each bundle is a function of its scarcity. Relative deprivation of individual *i* is given by the sum of the values of the existing bundles that they are not able to consume, while relative satisfaction is given by the sum of those they can consume. Yitzhaki (2010) stresses that since his approach does not rely on the existence of interpersonal comparisons and consumption externalities, no contrast is created with standard neoclassical economic theory.

Building upon an additional remark by Runciman (1966, p. 10) – 'The magnitude of a relative deprivation is the extent of the difference between the desired situation and that of the person desiring it' – Hey and Lambert (1980) provide an alternative motivation to Yitzhaki's (1979) framework. They consider interpersonal comparisons explicitly and extend Yitzhaki's approach directly into the utility space. As remarked by Yitzhaki (1980), Hey and Lambert start from a more micro perspective, emphasizing one-to-one comparisons, to the point that in the realm of the comparison between two individuals the overall income distribution is irrelevant. In other words, in conceptualizing and measuring the relative deprivation or satisfaction generated by the comparison between individuals *i* and *j*, only the characteristics of these two individuals matter. It follows that it is indifferent whether *i* and *j* are the richest or the poorest persons in society or whether there are many or a few individuals richer or poorer than them.

This way of looking at relative deprivation and relative satisfaction is reflected in what has become the common approach to the quantification of these phenomena, which consists in a summation at two stages; see also Chakravarty and Chakraborty (1984), Paul (1991), Chakravarty and Chattopadhyay (1994), Podder (1996), Chakravarty (1997), Esposito (2010) and Bossert and D'Ambrosio (2014). An individual deprivation (satisfaction) function provides the deprivation (satisfaction) felt by individual *i* when comparing their situation to that of individual *j*. The sum of these values represents *i*'s total relative deprivation or satisfaction; all individual magnitudes are then added together to obtain the aggregate figure. The main source of disagreement among scholars is the shape of the individual deprivation or satisfaction function, which has the achievements of individuals *i* and *j* as arguments. This function can be considered the cornerstone of such an approach. Indeed, the validity of an additive approach at two stages strongly relies on the possibility to interpret the image of individual *i*'s deprivation or satisfaction function 'at *j*' as the magnitude of individual *i*'s sense of deprivation or satisfaction arising when they compare themself to individual *j*.

It should be noted that although in Yitzhaki (1979) and Hey and Lambert (1980) the quantification of relative deprivation and relative satisfaction receives roughly equal attention, most of the theoretical literature on measurement has focused on the development of deprivation indices rather than satisfaction indices. While it is not easy to fully illustrate the reasons for such stark asymmetry, an important reason can be certainly presented as follows. In his rejoinder to Hey and Lambert, Yitzhaki (1980) stresses the fact that his understanding of 'satisfaction' has to be understood in the light of the economics tradition of focusing on what an individual possesses or achieves; the deprivation aspect would simply be the other side of the coin, which is typically of interest to sociologists. As has been argued, the approach by Hey and Lambert (1980) is more directly based on the idea of interpersonal comparisons. In this framework, the notion of 'relative deprivation' is to be understood as the feeling of frustration arising as a consequence of a more restricted access to functionings compared to others in society. If we were to build the idea of 'relative satisfaction' as a sort of mirror image of this feeling, then we would have to construct it as a feeling of 'elation' (Chakravarty, 1997) experienced by individual *i* as a reaction to seeing that individual *j* is poorer. But when we do this we encounter two considerable difficulties. Firstly, many of us would encounter an ethical resistance to admitting that seeing people poorer than us gives us some sort of satisfaction. We have no hesitation, and feel no embarrassment, in acknowledging that we do not want to lag behind others. However, while not wanting to have less than others can be comfortably seen as a human weakness, desiring more than others (or, more precisely, gaining pleasure out of having more than others) is promptly associated with an array of negative sentiments such as greediness, along with a Hobbesian view of human nature. It is interesting to notice that Hey and Lambert (1980, p. 572) wonder whether in their framework '"gloating" rather than "satisfaction" may be a more appropriate term'. In the psychological literature it has been noted that this idea may indeed generate a sense of guilt (Brickman and Bulman, 1977). Secondly, the empirical evidence on the existence of a feeling of 'relative satisfaction' is much weaker compared to the case of relative deprivation. While there is a body of literature attesting the distress caused by 'looking upward' and seeing people richer than us, the same cannot be said about an enjoyment deriving from 'looking down-ward' and seeing people poorer than us. Scholars are actually in profound disagreement in this respect. Stutzer (2004) argues for the inexistence of looking downward effects, while some evidence in favour of the looking downward thesis is found by Ferrer-i-Carbonell (2005) (although only for the Eastern Germans subset of their sample), by Vendrik and Woltjer (2007) adopting the framework of Kahneman and Tversky's (1979) prospect theory, and by Corazzini et al. (2012) on the basis of a cross-country questionnaire study. Blanchflower and Oswald (2004) find inconclusive evidence and conclude that indeed 'much remains to be understood' (ibid., p. 1378).

It can be illustrative to look at the (generalized and simplified) framework of 'self-cen-tred inequality' used by Fehr and Schmidt (1999). It can be seen that the door is left open to the possibility of both 'looking upward' and 'looking downward' comparisons effects. Call u_i and y_i the utility and the income level of individual i, respectively. For the sake of simplicity imagine that society is made of three individuals h, i and k whose incomes are described by the income vector $\tilde{y} = (y_h, y_i, y_k)$ assumed to be arranged in increasing order. According to Fehr and Schmidt (1999, p. 822, equation 1), the utility of individual i is given by the following equation:

$$u_i(y) = \underbrace{\varphi_{abs}(y_i)}_{\substack{\text{absolute income} \\ \text{component}}} + \underbrace{\alpha_{rd}\varphi_{rd}(y_i, y_k)}_{\substack{\text{relative deprivation} \\ \text{component}}} + \underbrace{\alpha_{rs}\varphi_{rs}(y_i, y_h)}_{\substack{\text{relative satisfaction} \\ \text{component}}}, \tag{15.1}$$

where α_{rd} and α_{rs} can be interpreted as weights attached to relative deprivation and relative satisfaction component, respectively. As it would be natural to expect, Fehr and Schmidt assume $\alpha_{rd} < 0$, meaning that relative deprivation has a negative impact on individual utility. However, they are far less definite about the sign of α_{rs}. They note that although they acknowledge that for some people α_{rs} can be positive (in line with the looking downward argument that relative satisfaction has a positive impact on individual utility), a focus on fairness considerations may actually justify a negative sign. (See Clark and D'Ambrosio, 2015 for additional discussion on these and other points.)

15.3.2 Tools

In order to introduce more formally the measurement tools proposed by the literature, some basic notation is in order. Let $\mathcal{N}$, $\mathfrak{R}_+$ and $\mathfrak{R}_{++}$ be the sets of positive integers, non-negative and positive real numbers, respectively. For $N \in \mathcal{N}$, $\mathfrak{R}_{++}^n$ denotes the positive orthant of the Euclidean n-space $\mathfrak{R}^n$. In a fixed set of n individuals, let $y = (y_1, y_2, \ldots, y_n)$ $\in \mathfrak{R}_{++}^n$ be the vector of incomes arranged in strictly increasing order, where similarly to our previous formulation y_i denotes the income of individual i. Relative deprivation and relative satisfaction of the individual i in the comparison with individual j are given by the individual deprivation function which has the general form $f(y_i, y_j)$: $\mathfrak{R}_{++} \times \mathfrak{R}_{++} \to \mathfrak{R}_+$. The function f, which we described as the cornerstone of the double summation approach, should be able to adequately represent the feelings of deprivation or satisfaction felt by individual i when they compare with individual j. We can readily be more precise about the functional form of f considering that relative deprivation is felt only towards richer individuals, whilst relative satisfaction is felt only towards poorer individuals. It follows that the individual deprivation and satisfaction functions, respectively, will take the forms:

$$d_i = \begin{cases} d(y_i, y_j) & \text{if } y_i < y_j \\ 0 & \text{if } y_i \geq y_j \end{cases} \tag{15.2}$$

$$s_i = \begin{cases} s(y_i, y_j) & \text{if } y_i > y_j \\ 0 & \text{if } y_i \leq y_j \end{cases} \tag{15.3}$$

The first stage of the double summation approach aggregates the magnitudes deriving from one-to-one comparisons in an index of total relative deprivation or satisfaction of individual i. These indices take the general form $g(y_i, y): \Re_{++} \times \Re_{++}^n \rightarrow \Re_{+}$. Total relative deprivation and relative satisfaction of individual i can be written as follows, respectively:

$$RD_i = \frac{1}{n}\sum_{j=1}^{n} d_i \tag{15.4}$$

$$RS_i = \frac{1}{n}\sum_{j=1}^{n} s_i \tag{15.5}$$

The second stage of the double summation approach provides the aggregate (average) level of relative deprivation and relative satisfaction in society. This is done by summing up all individual levels RD_i and RS_i and normalizing by the population size. Relative deprivation and relative satisfaction in society, respectively, are given by the indices:

$$RD = \frac{1}{n}\sum_{i=1}^{n} RD_i \tag{15.6}$$

$$RS = \frac{1}{n}\sum_{i=1}^{n} RS_i \tag{15.7}$$

The first index proposed in the literature was the one by Yizthaki (1979), for which, as we have seen in the previous section, Hey and Lambert (1980) provided an alternative motivation. This index is based upon a linear type of individual deprivation or satisfaction function, where the extent of the feeling felt by individual i is equal to the income gap between individual j's income and i's. The individual relative deprivation and satisfaction functions, respectively, are the following:

$$d^{Y-HL}(y_i, y_j) = y_j - y_i \tag{15.8}$$
$$s^{Y-HL}(y_i, y_j) = y_i - y_j \tag{15.9}$$

The index proposed by Yizthaki (1979) and Hey and Lambert (1980) has received two alternative axiomatic characterizations: see Ebert and Moyes (2000) and Bossert and D'Ambrosio (2006). The aggregate index RD^{Y-HL} is known to be equivalent to the absolute Gini coefficient, that is, the product between the Gini coefficient $G(x)$ and mean income $\mu(x)$. Given that $RD^{Y-HL} = G(x)\mu(x)$ we have that aggregate relative satisfaction according to Yizthaki (1979) and Hey and Lambert (1980) can be written as $RS^{Y-HL} = \mu(x)[1 - G(x)]$.[1] A graphical relationship between the Gini coefficient and indices of relative deprivation *à la* Yitzhaki (1979) and Hey and Lambert (1980) has been shown by Kakwani (1984); the Gini coefficient is the area below a relative deprivation curve representing the gaps between an individual's income and the incomes of individuals richer than them (here the income gap is normalized by mean income, as is the case for the individual deprivation proposed by Chakravarty, 1997). Duclos (2000) has shown that the S-Ginis of Donaldson and Weymark (1980) and Yitzhaki (1983) – which are weighted gaps between the line of perfect income equality and the Lorenz curve for a distribution of income – can be interpreted as indices of relative deprivation based on linear individual functions. Later, a transformation of the S-Ginis was characterized by Tsui and Wang (2000) using the concept of 'net marginal deprivation', which is based on the idea of monotonicity of relative deprivation (that is, an increase in the income of individual *i* generates an increase in the deprivation felt by individuals poorer than *i* and a decrease in her own feeling of deprivation). Building upon transformations of the RD_i^{Y-HL} index, Chakravarty and Chakraborty (1984) obtain generalized relative deprivation indices which correspond to different welfare functions; the Yitzhaki index is obtained as a special case of the indices they propose. Berrebi and Silber (1985) propose an alternative interpretation of the Gini coefficient in terms of relative deprivation, and illustrate how various indices of inequality can be seen as indices of relative deprivation responding to alternative definitions of phenomenon of relative deprivation. An additional generalization of the Gini index leading to two different classes of indices of relative deprivation is offered by Verme (2011).

Paul (1991) offered the first contribution challenging the linearity of individual relative deprivation functions $d(y_i, y_j)$ in reference income. The rejection of linearity was motivated by the idea that that 'A person feels less envious with respect to an increase in the income of a rich person than with respect to a corresponding increase in the income of a person who is richer than him but poorer than the rich man' (ibid., p. 337). He proposes a concave individual deprivation function which is based on an envy parameter $\beta \in \Re_{++}$ larger than 1 and can be written as follows:

$$d^{PA} = (y_j / y_i)^{1/\beta} - 1 \tag{15.10}$$

Podder (1996) justifies concavity in a similar way, recurring to the well-established concept in sociologic theory that our feeling of deprivation is more sensitive to advancements achieved by people who are closer to our situation; see, among others, Festinger (1954). Podder proposes an individual relative deprivation function based on the following logarithmic functional form:

$$d^{PO} = \ln y_j - \ln y_i \tag{15.11}$$

Esposito (2010) proposes an index of relative deprivation that is not only concave but, differently from previous indices, it is also upper-bounded.[2] This is motivated by Runciman's (1966, p. 10) idea that even if it can be accepted that 'a man may say with perfect truth that he wants to be as rich as the Aga Khan', these 'fantasy wishes' should be considered as irrelevant in evaluating deprivation. Moreover, upper-boundedness also introduces a limit to the increase in the deprivation felt by individual i as a consequence of the addition of one particular rich individual; this property can be found valuable in a reading of relative deprivation in terms of social exclusion.[3] The functional form is as follows:

$$d^E = 1 - (y_i/y_j)^\beta \tag{15.12}$$

with $\beta \in \Re_{++}$. As β increases, differences in the sense of deprivation felt towards richer individuals gradually diminish (the relative deprivation felt towards a richer individual tends to 1 regardless of how rich they are) and the relative deprivation of individual i tends to the headcount of people richer than them. In this way, higher values of β increase the importance of unfulfilled 'closer' aspirations and lower the imaginary threshold of what Runciman (1966) refers to as fantasy wishes.

Bossert and D'Ambrosio (2014) propose and characterize an index of deprivation more sensitive to closer individuals without eliminating the original structure of Hey and Lambert. The generalized income shortfall deprivation measure is based on an increasing and strictly concave function of (15.8).

15.3.3   D-Squared: Relative Deprivation Domains and Dynamics

The basic approach described in the previous section postulates that the relative deprivation felt by individual i when they compare with individual j is a function of their income levels at the present time; or, more generally, that comparisons take place within one single domain and are based only on current achievements. This framework can be extended along two lines to take into account the different domains in which interpersonal comparisons take place, and different dynamics concerning individual i's and individual j's achievements. For example, it may be the case that individual i compares not only their income but also their level of education with that of individual j. Similarly, we know that individual i feels relatively deprived if individual j is richer than them; however, the intensity of this feeling may vary according to whether this hierarchy was also in place yesterday, or whether individual j has just 'overtaken' individual i in the income scale.

The desirability to take into account a dynamic element in the evaluation of relative deprivation was first pointed out by Hirschman and Rothschild (1973) when they described a phenomenon labelled the 'tunnel effect'. According to this idea, increasing relative deprivation may be leading in the short run to a positive externality for the individual with a lower level of achievement, by generating optimism and fostering the view of a better future for them. However, if these positive expectations are not met, then in the medium and long run this feeling would gradually reverse and turn into a negative externality, as normally expected in classic relative deprivation theory; studies of this topic include Ravallion and Lokshin (2000) and Senik (2004). Bossert and D'Ambrosio (2007) develop a system of measurement covering multiple time periods which not only takes into account individual income gaps but also incorporates dynamic considerations. In the measure they suggest the income gap between individual i and richer individual j receives a premium, or a larger weight, if in the previous period individual j was not richer than individual i.

D'Ambrosio and Frick (2012) generalize the utility function (15.1) to account for a dynamic component of both relative deprivation and relative satisfaction (see ibid., p. 289, equation 7). Their empirical analysis using panel data from Germany over the period 1992–2007 suggests that 'an individual's wellbeing is negatively affected by the comparison with permanently richer individuals . . . and is positively affected by the comparison with permanently poorer individuals' (ibid., p. 298). In addition, they find evidence that while the idea of the 'tunnel effect' was developed with reference to developing and more volatile societies, it can also play a major role for people living in more economically advanced and stable societies such as today's Germany.

The issue of considering multiple domains in the evaluation of relative deprivation is motivated by the notion that interpersonal comparisons take place in a wide range of domains rather than only in the income space. For example, the work by Quinn (2006) points to the importance of relative concerns in the domain of housing quality and durables. Further insights are provided by the contributions of Solnick and Hemenway (1998, 2005) and Carlsson et al. (2007), who point to heterogeneity in relativist concerns across dimensions. According to these findings, people would feel relative deprivation more intensely in certain domains than in others. Incorporating this heterogeneity in relative concerns across domains into measurement implies using a system of different weights and/or functional forms to account for relative deprivation in different domains. Such a framework would imply engaging with the challenge of further aggregation across domains; for theoretical work on this issue in the case of absolute deprivation, see Tsui (2002) and Bourguignon and Chakravarty (2003). However, as is the case for the measurement of absolute deprivation in a multidimensional setting, an obstacle to that is the nature of most multidimensional data: many variables are categorical or at most ordinal, but very unlikely continuous. This implies serious restrictions in the possibility to use more nuanced functional forms. For a more detailed discussion of these issues, see the chapters on social exclusion, and on multidimensional poverty and material deprivation, contained in this *Handbook*.

15.4   REFERENCE GROUP

So far this chapter has neglected the question of to whom we actually compare ourselves and our achievements. Interpersonal comparisons typically take place within the so-called reference group: the subset of society composed by the persons an individual compares themself to. Hyman (1942) defines the reference group as the set of people exerting relevant influence on those individuals who take them as a reference point for evaluating their own situation. Deutsch and Gerard (1955) pointed out two routes through which reference groups affect the individual, namely normative and informational. Normative social influence is the desire to conform to the expectations of the reference group, while informational social influence affects the acceptance of the information obtained from the reference group as evidence about reality. Both these types of influences can be seen as being in place in the case of relative deprivation and relative satisfaction. The levels of achievements attained by the reference group become accepted evidence of social expectations which are met (in the case of relative satisfaction) or not met (in the case of relative deprivation). Park and Lessig (1977) pointed out how the reference group could be concrete or imaginary, and remarked how both matter in terms of individuals' aspirations formation and social behaviour.

The criteria adopted for the demarcation of reference groups are demographic lines and similarities such as race, gender and education (Eibner and Evans, 2004), or age, class, religion and political values, and geographical proximity (Bylsma and Major, 1994). The decision to consider a whole country as a reference group is often made for the sake of simplicity, although in most cases this choice lacks a sound justification. The underlying assumption grounding this choice is that people compare themselves to others by virtue of belonging to the same country. This assumption is likely to be inaccurate, in particular for countries which are very large and heterogeneous in their social and demographic background. The heterogeneity of reference groups within a society is indeed attested by a number of papers such as Osler et al. (2003), Clark and Senik (2010) and Mangyo and Parker (2011). Acknowledging heterogeneity in group formations may also lead to relaxing the 'close' reference group assumptions made by Yitzhaki (1982), according to which if individual j belongs to individual i's reference group, then individual i also belongs to individual j's reference group. While it is true that reference groups are often shaped by the communality of socio-demographic criteria such as those mentioned above, it is not necessarily true that these characteristics restrain reference group formation and bind it to happen across closed boxes. Reference groups may also be multiple, and vary according to the domain in which interpersonal comparisons take place.

Van Praag (2011) encourages researchers to increase their effort towards a sounder specification of reference groups. As also advocated by Gravelle and Sutton (2009), a more in-depth understanding of the mechanisms with which reference groups are chosen is paramount in order to identify and measure interpersonal comparisons effects. The literature in fact still lacks a formal framework able to fully account for the nuances in the creation of reference groups. Motivated by this gap in the literature, Van Praag (2011) introduces the concepts of reference distribution and social filter to account for different intensities with which comparisons are made; see also Van Praag and Ferrer-i-Carbonell (2004, Chapter 8). The idea is to provide a formulation of the reference group which goes beyond the classic dichotomy: either an individual belongs to individual i's reference group or they do not. Membership to the reference group would become a polytomous (and possibly continuous) variable, enabling individual relative deprivation or relative satisfaction to be modelled in a more nuanced way.

15.5   CONCLUSION

From this chapter it is clear that relative deprivation and relative satisfaction are long-standing research topics for the academic community. Economists are no exception to that. It is also clear that economists have engaged seriously in the task of introducing relativist concerns in models aiming at explaining a wide range of social phenomena. It would be erroneous, however, to think that these contributions represent a large proportion of academic work in economics. The large majority of economists' academic production still overlooks externalities arising from interpersonal comparisons. An article by Frank (2005) appearing in the *New York Times* is forcefully entitled 'The mysterious disappearance of James Duesenberry'; in the piece it is argued how Duesenberry's theory, 'which clearly outperforms the alternative theories that displaced it in the 1950s . . . is no longer even mentioned in leading textbooks'. The very same point is made in Frank (2008). How is that possible?

A formal and conclusive agreement on the necessity to acknowledge the effects of interpersonal comparisons would certainly have serious repercussions. At a theoretical level, economics would have to abandon or somehow reformulate theoretical pillars such as the notion of Pareto improvement. It would then become more difficult to promote economic growth without seriously bringing the distributive element into the picture. Anti-egalitarian arguments based on incentive effects or a larger propensity to save among the rich may not suffice to defend an exclusive focus on the increase in absolute income. The consequent demand for redistribution and the implications of a more socio-political nature can be readily imagined. If researchers in this field keep on providing compelling evidence, whether of a theoretical or an empirical nature, economists from all fields will be bound to rethink much of their work and to look at economic issues through different and less deprived lenses. And the availability of authoritative and highly accessible accounts of the costs of inequality, such as Wilkinson and Pickett (2009) and Stiglitz (2012), is bound to increase the awareness of policy makers at a national and international level.

NOTES

1. For generalization of the relationship between deprivation and satisfaction functions, see Chakravarty and Mukherjee (1999).
2. Note that the individual deprivation function in Chakravarty (1997) is 'indirectly' upper bounded, since the interpersonal income gaps are normalized by the mean income in society. However, such normalization implies that the relative deprivation between individual i and individual j is affected, via the change in the mean income, by the variation in the income of a third person.
3. For a conceptual link between relative deprivation and the multidimensional phenomenon of social exclusion see also Bourguignon (1999), Sen (2000), Atkinson and Bourguignon (2001) and Bossert et al. (2007).

REFERENCES

Abel, A.B. (1990), 'Asset Prices under Habit Formation and Catching Up with the Joneses', *American Economic Review*, 80 (2), 38–42.
Acheson, J. (1972), 'Limited Good or Limited Goods? Response to Economic Opportunity in a Tarascan Pueblo', *American Anthropologist*, 72 (5), 1152–1169.
Akerlof, G.A. and J.L. Yellen (1990), 'The Fair Wage–Effort Hypothesis and Unemployment', *Quarterly Journal of Economics*, 105 (2), 255–284.
Alesina, A. and R. Perotti (1996), 'Income Distribution, Political Instability, and Investment', *European Economic Review*, 40 (6), 1203–1228.
Aronsson, T. and O. Johansson-Stenman (2008), 'When the Jones's Consumption Hurts: Optimal Public Good Provision and Nonlinear Income Taxation', *Journal of Public Economics*, 92 (5/6), 986–997.
Aronsson, T. and O. Johansson-Stenman (2010), 'Positional Concerns in an OLG Model: Optimal Labor and Capital Income Taxation', *International Economic Review*, 51 (4), 1071–1095.
Atkinson, Anthony Barnes and François Bourguignon (2001), 'Poverty and Inclusion from a World

Perspective', in Joseph E. Stiglitz and Pierre A. Muet (eds), *Governance, Equity and Global Markets*, Oxford: Oxford University Press, pp. 151–164.

Bagwell, L.S. and B.D. Bernheim (1996), 'Veblen Effects in a Theory of Conspicuous Consumption', *American Economic Review*, 86 (3), 349–373.

Barber, J.G. (2001), 'Relative Misery and Youth Suicide', *Australian Journal of Psychiatry*, 35 (1), 49–57.

Berrebi, Z.M. and J. Silber (1985), 'Income Inequality Indices and Deprivation: A Generalization', *Quarterly Journal of Economics*, 100 (3), 807–810.

Bilancini, E. and L. Boncinelli (2012), 'Redistribution and the Notion of Social Status', *Journal of Public Economics*, 96 (9), 651–657.

Blanchflower, D.G. and A.J. Oswald (2004), 'Well-Being Over Time in Britain and the USA', *Journal of Public Economics*, 88 (7), 1359–1386.

Boskin, M.J. and E. Sheshinski (1978), 'Optimal Redistributive Taxation when Individual Welfare Depends upon Relative Income', *Quarterly Journal of Economics*, 92 (4), 589–601.

Bossert, W. and C. D'Ambrosio (2006), 'Reference Groups and Individual Deprivation', *Economics Letters*, 90 (3), 421–426.

Bossert, W. and C. D'Ambrosio (2007), 'Dynamic Measures of Individual Deprivation', *Social Choice and Welfare*, 28 (1), 77–88.

Bossert, W. and C. D'Ambrosio (2014), 'Proximity-Sensitive Individual Deprivation Measures', *Economics Letters*, 122 (2), 125–128.

Bossert, W., C. D'Ambrosio and V. Peragine (2007), 'Deprivation and Social Exclusion', *Economica*, 74 (296), 777–803.

Bourguignon, François (1999), 'Absolute Poverty, Relative Deprivation, and Social Exclusion', in Gudrun Kochendörfer-Lucius and Boris Pleskovic (eds), *Inclusion, Justice and Poverty Reduction*, Berlin: Villa Borsig Workshop Series, pp. 1–4.

Bourguignon, F. and S.R. Chakravarty (2003), 'The Measurement of Multidimensional Poverty', *Journal of Economic Inequality*, 1 (1), 25–49.

Bradburn, Norman (1969), *The Structure of Psychological Well Being*, Chicago, IL: Aldine Publishing Company.

Brickman, Philip and Ronnie Bulman (1977), 'Pleasure and Pain in Social Comparison', in Jerry Suls (ed.), *Social Comparison Processes: Theoretical and Empirical Perspectives*, Washington, DC: Hemisphere, pp. 149–186.

Brighouse, H. and A. Swift (2006), 'Equality, Priority, and Positional Goods', *Ethics*, 116 (3), 471–497.

Bylsma, W.H. and B. Major (1994), 'Social Comparisons and Contentment: Exploring the Psychological Costs of the Gender Wage Gap', *Psychology of Women Quarterly*, 18 (2), 241–249.

Carlsson, F., O. Johansson-Stenman and P. Martinsson (2007), 'Do You Enjoy Having More Than Others? Survey Evidence of Positional Goods', *Economica*, 74 (296), 586–598.

Chakravarty, S.R. (1997), 'Relative Deprivation and Satisfaction Orderings', *Keio Economic Studies*, 34 (2), 17–31.

Chakravarty, S.R. and A.B. Chakraborty (1984), 'On Indices of Relative Deprivation', *Economics Letters*, 14 (2/3), 283–287.

Chakravarty, S.R. and N. Chattopadhyay (1994), 'An Ethical Index of Relative Deprivation', *Research on Economic Inequality*, 5, 231–240.

Chakravarty, S.R. and D. Mukherjee (1999), 'Measures of Deprivation and Their Meaning in Terms of Satisfaction', *Theory and Decision*, 47 (1), 89–100.

Clark, Andrew E. and Conchita D'Ambrosio (2015), 'Attitudes to Income Inequality: Experimental and Survey Evidence', in Anthony B. Atkinson and François Bourguignon (eds), *Handbook of Income Distribution*, Vol. 2A, Amsterdam: North-Holland, pp. 1147–1208.

Clark, A.E. and C. Senik (2010), 'Who Compares to Whom? The Anatomy of Income Comparisons in Europe', *Economic Journal*, 120 (544), 573–594.

Cole, H.L., G.J. Mailath and A. Postlewaite (1992), 'Social Norms, Savings Behavior, and Growth', *Journal of Political Economy*, 100 (6), 1092–1125.

Cooper, B., C. Garcia-Penalosa and P. Funk (2001), 'Status effects and negative utility growth', *Economic Journal*, 111 (473), 642–665.

Corazzini L., L. Esposito and F. Majorano (2012), 'Reign in Hell or Serve in Heav'n? A Cross-country Journey into the Absolutist vs Relativist Perception of Wellbeing', *Journal of Economic Behaviour and Organization*, 81 (3), 715–730.

Corneo, G. and O. Jeanne (1997), 'Conspicuous Consumption, Snobbism and Conformism', *Journal of Public Economics*, 66 (1), 55–71.

Corneo, G. and O. Jeanne (1999), 'Social Organization in an Endogenous Growth Model', *International Economic Review*, 40 (3), 711–726.

Corneo, G. and O. Jeanne (2001), 'On Relative-Wealth Effects and Long-Run Growth', *Research in Economics*, 55 (4), 349–358.

Crawford, S. and M. Naditch (1970), 'Relative Deprivation, Powerlessness, and Militancy: The Psychology of Social Protest', *Psychiatry*, 33 (2), 208–233.

D'Ambrosio, C. and J.R. Frick (2012), 'Individual Wellbeing in a Dynamic Perspective', *Economica*, 79 (314), 284–302.

Deutsch, M. and H.B. Gerard (1955), 'A Study of Normative and Informational Influence Upon Individual Judgement', *Journal of Abnormal and Social Psychology*, 51 (3), 629–636.

Direr, A. (2001), 'Interdependent Preferences and Aggregate Saving', *Annales d'Economie et de Statistique*, ENSAE, 63/64, 297–308.

Donaldson, D. and J.A. Weymark (1980), 'A Single Parameter Generalization of the Gini Indices of Inequality', *Journal of Economic Theory*, 22 (1), 67–86.

Duclos, J.-Y. (2000), 'Gini Indices and the Redistribution of Income, International Tax and Public Finance', *International Tax and Public Finance Journal*, 7 (2), 141–162.

Duesenberry, J.S. (1949), *Income, Saving and the Theory of Consumer Behaviour*, Cambridge, MA: Harvard University Press.

Easterlin, Richard A. (1974), 'Does Economic Growth Improve the Human Lot? Some Empirical Evidence', in Paul A. David and Melvin W. Reder (eds), *Nations and Households in Economic Growth: Essays in Honor of Moses Abramovitz*, New York: Academic Press, pp. 89–125.

Eaton, C.B. and M. Eswaran (2009), 'Well-being and Affluence in the Presence of a Veblen Good', *Economic Journal*, 119 (539), 1088–1104.

Ebert, U. and P. Moyes (2000), 'An Axiomatic Characterization of Yitzhaki's Index of Individual Deprivation', *Economics Letters*, 68 (3), 263–270.

Eibner, Christine and William Evans (2004), 'The Income–Health Relationship and the Role of Relative Deprivation', in Kathryn Neckerman (ed.), *Social Inequality*, New York: Russell Sage Foundation, pp. 545–568.

Eibner, C.E. and W. Evans (2005), 'Relative Deprivation, Poor Health Habits and Mortality', *Journal of Human Resources*, 40 (3), 591–620.

Esposito, L. (2010), 'Upper Boundedness for the Measurement of Relative Deprivation', *Review of Income and Wealth*, 56 (3), 632–639.

Fehr, E. and K.M. Schmidt (1999), 'A Theory of Fairness, Competition, and Cooperation', *Quarterly Journal of Economics*, 114 (3), 817–868.

Ferrer-i-Carbonell, A. (2005), 'Income and Well-Being: An Empirical Analysis of the Comparison Income Effect', *Journal of Public Economics*, 89 (5), 997–1019.

Fesnic, F.N. and R. Viman-Miller (2009), 'What Drives the Vote for the Extreme Right? Absolute Vs. Relative Deprivation', APSA 2009 Toronto Meeting Paper.

Festinger, L. (1954), 'A Theory of Social Comparison Processes', *Human Relations*, 7 (2), 117–140.

Foster, G.M. (1965), 'Peasant Society and the Image of Limited Good', *American Anthropologist*, 67 (2), 293–315.

Foster, G.M. (1972), 'The Anatomy of Envy: A Study in Symbolic Behavior', *Current Anthropology*, 13 (2), 165–202.

Frank, R.H. (1985), 'The Demand for Unobservable and Other Nonpositional Goods', *American Economic Review*, 75 (1), 101–116.

Frank, R.H. (2005), 'The Mysterious Disappearance of James Duesenberry', *New York Times*, 9 June, http://www.nytimes.com/2005/06/09/business/09scene.html?_r=0 (accessed 20 January 2013).

Frank, R.H. (2008), 'Should Public Policy Respond to Positional Externalities?', *Journal of Public Economics*, 92 (8–9), 1777–1786.

Gali, J. (1994), 'Keeping Up with the Joneses: Consumption Externalities, Portfolio Choice, and Asset Prices', *Journal of Money, Credit, and Banking*, 26 (1), 1–8.

Gravelle, H. and M. Sutton (2009), 'Income, Relative Income, and Self-Reported Health in Britain 1979–2000', *Health Economics*, 18 (2), 125–145.

Hey, J.D. and P.J. Lambert (1980), 'Relative Deprivation and the Gini Coefficient: Comment', *Quarterly Journal of Economics*, 95 (3), 567–573.

Hillemeier, M.M., J. Lynch, S. Harper, T. Raghunathan and G.A. Kaplan (2003), 'Relative or Absolute Standards for Child Poverty: A State-Level Analysis of Infant and Child Mortality', *American Journal of Public Health*, 93 (4), 652–657.

Hirsch, Fred (1976), *Social Limits to Growth*, Cambridge, MA: Harvard University Press.

Hirschman, A.O. and M. Rothschild (1973), 'The Changing Tolerance for Income Inequality in the Course of Economic Development, with a Mathematical Appendix', *Quarterly Journal of Economics*, 87 (4), 544–566.

Hopkins, E. and T. Kornienko (2004), 'Running to Keep in the Same Place: Consumer Choices as a Game of Status', *American Economic Review*, 94 (4), 1085–1107.

Hyman, H.H. (1942), 'The Psychology of Status', *Archives of Psychology*, 269, 94–102.

Ireland, N.J. (1998), 'Status-Seeking, Income Taxation and Efficiency', *Journal of Public Economics*, 70 (1), 99–113.

Ireland, N.J. (2001), 'Optimal Income Tax in the Presence of Status Effects', *Journal of Public Economics*, 81 (2), 193–212.

Kahneman, D. and A. Tversky (1979), 'Prospect Theory: An Analysis of Decision under Risk', *Econometrica*, 47 (2), 263–291.

Kakwani, N. (1984), 'The Relative Deprivation Curve and its Applications', *Journal of Business and Economic Statistics*, 2 (4), 384–394.

Leibenstein, H. (1950), 'Bandwagon, Snob and Veblen Effects in the Theory of Consumers' Demand', *Quarterly Journal of Economics*, 65 (2), 183–207.

Leibenstein, H. (1962), 'Notes on Welfare Economics and the Theory of Democracy', *Economic Journal*, 286 (72), 299–319.

Leibenstein, H. (1975), 'The Economic Theory of Fertility Decline', *Quarterly Journal of Economics*, 89 (1), 1–31.

Ljungqvist, L. and H. Uhlig (2000), 'Tax Policy and Aggregate Demand Management under Catching up with the Joneses', *American Economic Review*, 90 (3), 356–366.

Lommerud, K.E. (1989), 'Educational Subsidies when Relative Income Matters', *Oxford Economic Papers*, 41 (1), 640–652.

Mangyo, E. and A. Parker (2011), 'Relative Deprivation and Health: Which Reference Groups Matter?', *Journal of Human Resources*, 46 (3), 459–481.

Marx, K. (1849), 'Wage Labour and Capital', in K. Marx and F. Engels, *Selected Works, Vol. 1*, Moscow: Progress Publishers, pp. 142–174.

Merton, K.R. (1938), 'Social Structure and Anomie', *American Sociological Review*, 3 (5), 672–682.

Mill, John S. (1941), *On Social Freedom*, New York, Columbia University Press.

Morrison, D.E. (1971), 'Some Notes Toward a Theory of Relative Deprivation, Social Movements, and Social Change', *American Behavioral Scientist*, 14 (5), 675–690.

Ng, Y.K. (1987), 'Relative Income Effects and the Appropriate Level of Public Expenditure', *Oxford Economic Papers*, 39 (2), 293–300.

Osler, M., U. Christensen, P. Due, R. Lund, I. Andersen, F. Diderichsen and E. Prescott (2003), 'Income Inequality and Ischaemic Heart Disease in Danish Men and Women', *International Journal of Epidemiology*, 32 (3), 375–380.

Park, C.W. and V.P. Lessig (1977), 'Students and Housewives: Differences in Susceptibility to Reference Group Influence', *Journal of Consumer Research*, 4 (2), 102–110.

Paul, S. (1991), 'An Index of Relative Deprivation', *Economics Letters*, 36 (3), 337–341.

Pigou, Arthur C. (1932), *The Economics of Welfare*, London, Macmillan.

Podder, N. (1996), 'Relative Deprivation, Envy and Economic Inequality', *Kyklos*, 49 (3), 353–376.

Pollak, R. (1976), 'Interdependent Preferences', *American Economic Review*, 66 (3), 309–320.

Quinn, M.A. (2006), 'Relative Deprivation, Wage Differentials and Mexican Migration', *Review of Development Economics*, 10 (1), 135–153.

Ravallion, M. and M. Lokshin (2000), 'Who Wants to Redistribute? The Tunnel Effect in 1990s Russia', *Journal of Public Economic*, 76 (1), 87–104.

Robson, A. (1992), 'Status, the Distribution of Wealth, Private and Social Attitudes to Risk', *Econometrica*, 60 (4), 837–857.

Runciman, Walter G. (1966), *Relative Deprivation and Social Justice*, London: Routledge.

Sen, A.K. (2000), 'Social Exclusion: Concept, Application and Scrutiny', Social Development Papers No. 1, Manila: Office of Environment and Social Development, Asian Development Bank.

Senik, C. (2004), 'When Information Dominates Comparison: Learning from Russian Subjective Panel Data', *Journal of Public Economics*, 88 (9/10), 2099–2133.

Smith, Adam (1776), *An Inquiry into the Nature and Causes of the Wealth of Nations*, Oxford: Clarendon Press.

Solnick, S.J. and D. Hemenway (1998), 'Is More Always Better? A Survey about Positional Goods', *Journal of Economic Behavior and Organization*, 37 (3), 373–383.

Solnick, S.J. and D. Hemenway (2005), 'Are Positional Concerns Stronger in Some Domains than in Others?', *American Economic Review*, 95 (2), 147–151.

Stark, O. and E. Taylor (1991), 'Migration Incentives, Migration Type: The Role of Relative Deprivation', *Economic Journal*, 101 (408), 1163–1178.

Stiglitz, Joseph E. (2012), *The Price of Inequality: How Today's Divided Society Endangers Our Future*, New York: W.W. Norton & Company.

Stouffer, Samuel A., Edward A. Suchman, Leland C. De Vinney, Shirley A. Star and Robin M. Williams Jr. (1949), *The American Soldier: Adjustments during Army Life 1*, Princeton, NJ: Princeton University Press.

Stutzer, A. (2004), 'The Role of Income Aspirations in Individual Happiness', *Journal of Economic Behavior and Organization*, 54 (1), 89–109.

Subramanian, S.V. and I. Kawaki (2006), 'Being Well and Doing Well: On the Importance of Income for Health', *International Journal of Social Welfare*, 15 (Suppl. 1), S13–S22.

Thompson, R.W. and R.E. Roper (1976), 'Relative Deprivation in Buganda: The Relation of Wealth, Security, and Opportunity to the Perception of Economic Satisfaction', *Ethos*, 4 (2), 155–187.

Townsend, Peter (1979), *Poverty in the United Kingdom*, London: Allen Lane and Penguin Books.

Tsui, K.Y. (2002), 'Multidimensional Poverty Indices', *Social Choice and Welfare*, 19 (1), 69–93.

Tsui, K.Y. and Y.Q. Wang (2000), 'A New Class of Deprivation-Based Generalized Gini Indices', *Economic Theory*, 16 (2), 363–377.

Van Praag, B. (2011), 'Well-Being Inequality and Reference Groups: An Agenda for New Research', *Journal of Economic Inequality*, 9 (1), 111–127.

Van Praag, Bernard M. and Ada Ferrer-i-Carbonell (2004), *Happiness Quantified: A Satisfaction Calculus Approach*, Oxford: Oxford University Press.

Veblen, Thorstein (1899), *The Theory of the Leisure Class*, New York: Macmillan.

Veenstra, G. (2005), 'Social Status and Health: Absolute Deprivation or Relative Comparison, or Both?', *Health Sociologic Review*, 14 (2), 121–134.

Vendrik, M.C. and G.B. Woltjer (2007), 'Happiness and Loss Aversion: Is Utility Concave or Convex in Relative Income?', *Journal of Public Economics*, 91 (7), 1423–1448.

Verme, P. (2011), 'Two Classes of Generalized Deprivation Indexes', *Economics Bulletin*, 31 (3), 2021–2029.

Wagner, U. and A. Zick (1995), 'The Relation of Formal Education to Ethnic Prejudice: Its Reliability, Validity and Explanation', *European Journal of Social Psychology*, 25 (1), 41–56.

Watson, T. and S. McLanahan (2011), 'Marriage Meets the Joneses: Relative Income, Identity, and Marital Status', *Journal of Human Resources*, 46 (3), 482–517.

Wilkinson, Richard G. and Kate Pickett (2009), *The Spirit Level: Why More Equal Societies Almost Always Do Better*, London: Allen Lane.

Williams, K.R. (1984), 'Economic Sources of Homicide: Reestimating the Effects of Poverty and Inequality', *American Sociologic Review*, 49 (2), 283–289.

Yitzhaki, S. (1979), 'Relative Deprivation and the Gini Coefficient', *Quarterly Journal of Economics*, 93 (2), 321–324.

Yitzhaki, S. (1980), 'Relative Deprivation and the Gini Coefficient: Reply', *Quarterly Journal of Economics*, 95 (3), 575–576.

Yitzhaki, S. (1982), 'Relative Deprivation and Economic Welfare', *European Economic Review*, 17 (1), 99–113.

Yitzhaki, S. (1983), 'On an Extension of the Gini Index', *International Economic Review*, 24 (3), 617–628.

Yitzhaki, S. (2010), 'Is there Room for Polarization?', *Review of Income and Wealth*, 56 (1), 7–22.

16. Relative deprivation and satisfaction: empirical findings
Paolo Verme

16.1 INTRODUCTION

This chapter provides a review of the empirical literature that attempted to test the relative income and relative deprivation hypotheses in economics. The relative income and relative deprivation hypotheses are treated as one and the same hypothesis. As discussed in more detail in the next section, in economics the relative income hypothesis as put forward by Duesenberry (1949) in the context of savings, and the relative deprivation hypothesis formalized by Runciman (1966) in the context of social status, converged empirically into testing the same hypothesis, simply stated as follows:

The evaluation of individual utility depends – among other factors – on relative income, one's own income relative to the income of others.

The empirical literature on the relative income and relative deprivation hypotheses is vast and cuts across the social sciences. To set the boundaries of the review, the chapter covers only published papers in economics journals as found in JSTOR and Econpapers by using the search terms 'relative income' and 'relative deprivation' in titles and keywords. This initial search provided more than 200 hits. From this initial set of papers I kept only papers that used relative income as one of the explanatory factors in the specification of the empirical models, therefore removing titles in specific areas of economics that tested for non-income dimensions of deprivation. A second screening was undertaken using the references in these papers. This left a final core of approximately 50 papers.

The relative income hypothesis as stated by Duesenberry (1949) emerged as one of the core issues in economics for a short period of time after its publication before being replaced by the life-cycle hypothesis put forward by Modigliani and others. The relative deprivation hypothesis stated by Runciman (1966) has been very popular across the social sciences since its publication and started to become popular in economics from the 1980s following an article by Yitzhaki (1979) that attempted to operationalize the relative deprivation hypothesis into a measure of relative deprivation. This literature focused on relative income as a measure of relative deprivation and mainly concerned itself with the measurement of relative deprivation rather than with the test of the relative income hypothesis. It is only during the last decade, and thanks to the popularity of the literature on happiness, that the relative deprivation/relative income hypothesis has become more mainstream in economics. As a result, tests of the relative income hypothesis have started to appear in high-ranking journals including the *Journal of Economic Literature*, the *Economic Journal* and the *Journal of Public Economics*, bringing to new life the original relative income hypothesis proposed by Duesenberry (1949).

The chapter is structured as follows. In the next section, I review the main intellectual contributions that led to the formulation and testing of the relative income hypothesis. It is shown how this hypothesis has been a catalyst for some of the important theories that emerged in economics during the second half of the twentieth century. Section 16.3 states the relative income hypothesis in its simplest form. Section 16.4 reviews the construction of the empirical models used to test the relative income hypothesis. Section 16.5 discusses the econometric problems that typically affect the literature that used these models. Section 16.6 summarizes the empirical results related to absolute income and relative income in papers that attempted to test the relative income hypothesis.

16.2 ECONOMICS AND THE RELATIVE INCOME HYPOTHESIS

The root of the relative income hypothesis is to be sought at the very roots of economics. It is therefore useful to start our search with one of the very first definitions of utility as given by Bentham:

> By utility is meant that property in any object, whereby it tends to produce benefit, advantage, pleasure, good, or happiness, (all this in the present case comes to the same thing) or (what comes again to the same thing) to prevent the happening of mischief, pain, evil, or unhappiness to the party whose interest is considered. (Bentham, 1789 [1907], p. 2)

In its original conception, utility was the property that objects have in providing pleasure or preventing displeasure. Maximizing utility was therefore understood as the maximization of collective pleasure or the minimization of collective displeasure, the main societal objective advocated by both Bentham and Mill.

The theory of revealed preferences provided economics with a means to measure utility, so that income or consumption could be used to measure utility and the utility maximization problem could be mathematically stated and empirically tested. These developments also helped to clarify one of the most complex and controversial issues in economics, namely the shape of the individual utility function and its aggregation in society. Pigou (1920) advocated utilitarianism as a way to maximize social welfare in a world with identical utilities functions across individuals and decreasing marginal utilities. This implied that, given a societal total income, societal utility could be maximized through the reallocation of income from the richer to the poorer until perfect income equality would be achieved. The paradox of this view was evidently that the maximization of utility could be achieved only with perfect income equality. Others, such as Dalton (1920) and Tinbergen (1970), argued instead that, in a real world of differing individual utilities, equal incomes do not necessarily amount to equal utilities, so that the optimal level of inequality may in fact be different from zero. This debate highlighted how different hypotheses about individual utilities could lead to very different optimal solutions for societies. It also introduced the notion of relativity, intended as utility functions relative to individual tastes for commodities.

The economics profession had also long accepted the notion of interdependent utilities: the idea that individual utilities also depend on the utility of others. Both Adam Smith and Karl Marx in different passages noted the importance of relative wealth as opposed to absolute wealth. In *The Wealth of Nations* Adam Smith (1776 [1976], pp. 869–870) wrote that: 'By necessaries I understand not only the commodities which are indispensably necessary for the support of life, but whatever the custom of the country renders it indecent for creditable people, even of the lowest order, to be without'. Marx (1847 [1933], p. 33) himself wrote that: 'A house may be large or small; as long as the neighboring houses are likewise small, it satisfies all social requirement for a residence. But let there arise next to the little house a palace, and the little house shrinks to a hut'. Veblen (1898) later noticed that people's consumption is also functional in expressing status and position in society, a concept later developed by Frank (1985) in his theory of positional goods. Here the relativity concept acquires a new dimension. Not only are people different in their own evaluation of commodities, but the value function also depends on the commodities of others. This greatly complicates the maximization problem of societal utility, as utility becomes a function of both absolute income and relative income or rank.

The formalization of interdependent utilities did not gain much traction in economics until Duesenberry (1949) proposed a relative income hypothesis to explain savings behavior in the United States (US). Looking at data between 1869 and 1929, Kuznets (1942) had noticed that aggregate savings did not increase as a proportion of income over time, while evidence from cross-sectional budget surveys during the period 1935–1942 showed that the household savings rate increased with income. In an effort to explain the mismatch between income and savings behavior in longitudinal studies, Duesenberry (1949) proposed the so-called 'relative income hypothesis'. His basic intuition was that households are concerned about community consumption standards, and that this concern leads to savings rates being an increasing function of a household's position in the income distribution: 'for any given relative income distribution, the percentage of income saved by a family will tend to be unique, invariant, and increasing function of its percentile position in the income distribution' (ibid., p. 3). Duesenberry also noticed that social comparisons are not symmetric. People tend to discount or ignore downward comparisons, while they consider or even overvalue upward comparisons. This further complicates the assessment of societal utility as the shape of the individual utility function becomes more complex and difficult to detect in empirical studies.

The relative income hypothesis is in contrast with the better-known permanent income hypothesis (Modigliani and Brumberg, 1954; Friedman, 1957), which superseded the relative income hypothesis and eventually became the core teaching in economics. The permanent income hypothesis can explain the cross-section positive relation between income and savings share with transitory deviations from permanent income that in the long run tend to cancel each other out, which provides an explanation for the lack of correlation between saving rates and incomes in longitudinal studies. The popularity of the permanent income hypothesis eventually marginalized the relative income hypothesis for decades; witness the fact that the Duesenberry hypothesis has seldom been tested empirically.

At the same time that Duesenberry was putting forward his relative income theory, Stouffer et al. (1949) published a very extensive study on the US Army during World War II that pinpointed a number of striking facts about soldiers' reported well-being. They noted, for example, that African American soldiers stationed in the Southern United States were happier than African American soldiers stationed in the Northern states.

More generally, the happiness of the American soldier largely depended on the specific context and the reference group, the group of people that soldiers compared themselves with. This idea would be re-elaborated two decades later by Runciman (1966) in a theory of social justice. Runciman defines the situation of relative deprivation as one where an individual is deprived of a status or commodity, sees other persons as having these assets, and wishes to have these assets. In addition to turning the initial findings of Stouffer et al. into a full theory of social justice, Runciman's contribution is essential in understanding the role of the reference group, the group of people individuals compare themselves with. This group can be different across people and can be defined across different characteristics, complicating further the question of societal aggregation of utilities.

Although very appealing, this definition was rather complex to operationalize in empirical research and found little support in economics until a decade later. The concept of relative deprivation used in empirical research in economics was first put forward by Yitzhaki (1979) and is confined to the income sphere. Yitzhaki proposed to measure any individual relative deprivation as the sums of incomes of the people richer than the observed individual. The sum of these measures across a population would then represent the relative deprivation measure for a society. This is evidently a gross simplification of Runciman's relative deprivation theory, but one that provided appealing empirical applications. Not only could relative deprivation be measured by simply summing up income distances, but also, as shown by Yitzhaki, the relative deprivation measure at the societal level was equivalent to the absolute Gini index (the Gini multiplied by the mean).

This last property of the Yitzhaki relative deprivation measure is particularly important for our review as it allows us to relate the debate on the aggregation of individual utilities with the debate on relative income and relative deprivation. By adopting income as a unit measure, the Yitzhaki measure is de facto a relative income measure, while the fact that this measure at the societal level is equal to the absolute Gini index implies that this measure can be used to measure the degree of equality of a society. In a nutshell, the more unequal a society is, the more relatively deprived this society will be. Moreover, while the Gini index per se is a cross-section measure of inequality, the absolute Gini also considers mean income. This implies that, the Gini index being equal, with increasing mean incomes over time, relative deprivation increases. In longitudinal studies that try to explain individual and societal behavior with changing levels of incomes, this property could potentially help to explain the inconsistency between longitudinal and cross-section studies on happiness and incomes.

A few years before Yitzhaki's constribution, Easterlin (1974 [1995]) noticed another inconsistency between longitudinal and cross-section data, a paradox that would eventually lead research on happiness for years to come and revive the relative income hypothesis. Easterlin noticed that the US and other Western countries had been growing in income per capita for several decades without any corresponding rise in reported happiness levels. For example, while income per capita in the US almost doubled between 1973 and 2004, happiness – as measured by the General Social Survey – showed no trend. This paradox quickly acquired popularity across the social sciences, confirming the initial intuition and providing some possible explanations in disciplines as diverse as political science (Inglehart, 1990) and psychology (Diener et al., 1995). The search for a solution to the Easterlin paradox has also largely hovered around the idea that, beyond a minimum absolute income necessary for living, relative income becomes more important than absolute income for explaining happiness. As noted in Verme, 2009: 'the inconsistent relation between happiness and income in longitudinal studies is generally explained with theories of relative deprivation or rising expectations' (p.150). This would explain why in richer societies average happiness and average absolute income do not covariate as expected, while richer people tend to be happier than poorer people.

Economics was a latecomer in this debate, despite the obvious relation between happiness and utility when one looks at the original definition of utility as stated by Bentham, where happiness and utility are one and the same concept. Early contributions included several contributions from the Dutch Leiden School (see, for example, Kapteyn et al., 1978; Van Herwaarden and Kapteyn, 1979; Layard, 1980; Frank, 1985) but mainstream economics long resisted the idea of considering self-reported happiness as a direct measure of utility. The initial skepticism was related to the measurement of happiness, thought as unreliable, but these concerns were progressively removed by advances in psychology that showed the robustness of answers to happiness questions. In fact, it is the recognition by the economics profession of the role of psychological factors in decision making that eventually provided credibility to the relative income hypothesis in economics.

The seminal work of Kahneman and Tversky (1979) is key to understanding this step forward in economics, and also to better understand the relative income hypothesis and its possible tests. Kahneman and Tversky (1979) showed that what matters for individuals when they make choices is not the status quo but changes from a reference point. This can be interpreted in two ways for the study of the relative income hypothesis. The reference point can be interpreted as the reference group, which can be defined as self-selected groups of peers in society or, alternatively, as one's own status in the past or in the future. In their work, Kahneman and Tversky have mainly focused on the latter, showing how the value function is concave in gains and convex in losses, and also how the value function is steeper for losses than for gains (Tversky and Kahneman, 1991). As will be seen below, findings related to the relative income hypothesis are very much in line with prospect theory in that they provide significant evidence on this behavioral asymmetry. Also important of this body of work is the concept of *ex ante* decisions utility versus *ex post* experienced utility. While Kahneman and Tvesrky worked extensively on the former, they also recognized that the latter had been little studied. But models where the dependent variable refers to past or current experiences rather than future projections – such as models that use happiness or life satisfaction as the dependent variable – focus on *ex post* utility and offer a significant bulk of evidence on how *ex post* utility is shaped.

This brief review of the literature that dealt directly or indirectly with the relative income hypothesis provides the essential guidelines for empirical modeling. Utility is equated to happiness, or considered a latent variable measured with happiness. Income is a measure of revealed preferences, but contributes to utility in its relative form in addition to the absolute form. Individual utilities are therefore interdependent and shaped by the reference group. The reference group (or point) may relate to the same individual in the past or the future, or to groups of individuals in the same society. These comparisons may lead to convex or concave individual utility functions. After stating the relative income hypothesis more formally, the chapter will review how all these aspects are captured by models that attempt to test the relative income hypothesis.

16.3 THE RELATIVE INCOME HYPOTHESIS

In essence, the test of the relative income hypothesis revolved around the test of how measures of relative income enter the happiness/utility equation, with what sign, what shape and what level of significance. More formally, the empirical literature on the relative income hypothesis essentially tests one main hypothesis and two sub-hypotheses, as follows:

H1: Satisfaction is negative in positive values of relative income.

H1a: Satisfaction is concave in positive values of relative income. With increasing values of relative income, satisfaction increases with decreasing marginal returns.

H1b: Satisfaction is convex in negative values of relative income. With decreasing values of relative income, satisfaction decreases with increasing marginal returns.

In testing these hypotheses, it is necessary to keep in mind that different authors have opted for different types of data (cross-section, cross-country, panel), different types of welfare measures (income, consumption, expenditure, wages), different types of observational unit (individual, household, population groups, countries), different types of dependent variables (happiness, life satisfaction, job satisfaction), different numbers of steps for the multi-steps indicators, different types of key variables transformations (log, squared, cubic), different types of estimators (ordered logit or probit, ordinary least squares), different types of estimations (with/without fixed effects, with/without clustering) and different sets of control variables (household, individual and community characteristics). This makes comparisons across empirical results an arduous task, and the truth of the matter is that I could not find two studies the results of which could be entirely compared. However, one obvious test of the relative income hypothesis is the consistency of the sign and significance of the relative income variable across different types of models, countries and times.

16.4 EMPIRICAL SPECIFICATIONS

To simplify the exposition, I consider utility and happiness as one concept and relative income and relative deprivation as one measure. Therefore, in what follows, I will refer to utility and relative income only. Let U be utility, x a vector of incomes, r a measure of relative incomes and Z a vector of controls, whether demographics or fixed effects. The subscripts i refer to individuals, c to countries or cohorts, and t to time.

The relation between utility and income can be modeled in several ways depending on what we think individuals consider when deriving utility from income. The simplest possible specification and also the most common in economics is that utility derives from absolute income in any point in time so that:

$$U_i = f(x_{it}).$$

Critics of this approach argued that individuals are in fact concerned about relative income rather than absolute income so that:

$$U_i = f(r_i),$$

where r is relative income, which can be defined with different specifications. For example, Easterlin (1974[1995]) proposed a utility function defined in relative terms only with $U_i = U_i \frac{C_i}{\sum_{j \in s} a_{ij} C_j}$, where C is consumption rather than income and a is a weight attached to individual consumption (see below for more details).

However, the most common specifications in empirical analyses that attempt to test the relative income hypothesis make utility a function of both absolute and relative income so that

$$U_i = f(x_{it}, r_t).$$

This type of specification is the focus of this chapter. Econometric specifications of the utility function that include both absolute and relative incomes mostly rely on measures of life satisfaction or happiness as proxies for utilities. This evidently implies that self-reported happiness is a reliable variable that conveys true information on individual utility, a question which has been debated in the literature in the past, but that now finds broad consensus in economics (see Easterlin, 1974[1995]; Diener, 1984; Clark et al., 2008).

These types of specifications have two main sources of variety. The first and perhaps the greatest source of variety relates to the different specifications of r. In some studies r is a share of income over mean income $x/\bar{x}$ (Duesenberry, 1949; Layard, 1980; Persson, 1995), while for others r is a distance of income from mean income $(x - \bar{x})$, (Akerlof, 1997; Corneo and Jeanne, 1997). Johansson-Stenman et al. (2002) compared the two types of formulations and found that the 'ratio' approach performed better than the 'distance' approach. However, in my review I could not find other similar tests, and both approaches continue to be widely used in empirical research. Some studies also use income rank as a measure of relative income (Frank, 1985; Van de Stadt et al., 1985). Frank (1985), for example, suggests a maximization problem in which the utility index is expanded to allow for the effect of rank.

The income variable is usually a continuous variable, but some authors have also used income measured in steps (see, for example, McBride, 2001). The relative income hypothesis has also been tested with household as opposed to individual income, and with different measures of welfare such as income, consumption or expenditure. Ferrer-i-Carbonell (2005) used family income as a form of relative income, while Oshio et al. (2011) used household income in place of income. Many datasets, especially in poorer countries, do not contain information on incomes, or contain information on incomes that is not reliable because of under-reporting. In these cases, scholars prefer to use consumption or expenditure as a proxy of income. While these choices are routinely made to test the relative income hypothesis, it is also evident that income and consumption are two conceptually different measures in economics (differentiated by savings) that cannot be simply equated or compared.

The second greatest source of differences in these types of models relates to the choice of the reference group when defining relative income r. Assume that mean income (or median incomes in some papers) is the variable that defines relative income. The question is over what group this mean should be estimated. This reference group can be the whole society, subsamples of the population, samples of other populations, the same unit of observation *i* in other points in time such as the past or the future, or reference points used by individuals in the past such as the income levels of parents.

Clark et al. (2008) define as internal reference points self-comparisons with past and future incomes, as opposed to external reference points where the reference group is represented by other members of society or other societies. McBride (2001) refers to the external or sociological norm when people compare themselves with others, and to the internal or psychological norm when people compare themselves with their own status in the past. Similarly, Luttmer (2005) and Ferrer-i-Carbonell (2005) refer to parallel and longitudinal comparisons. Parallel comparisons are comparisons with peers, while longitudinal comparisons are comparisons with richer (upwards comparisons) or poorer (downwards comparisons) people. More generally, Verme (2010) refers to 'alter' comparisons when people compare themselves with other people in society in the same point in time (cross-section comparisons), and 'ego' comparisons when people compare themselves with their own past status or their own expected status in the future (self-comparisons). In essence, we can think of at least five types of reference groups: richer and poorer individuals in the present (upward and downward comparisons), past and future own status (past and future self-comparisons), and comparisons with peers (parallel comparisons), as depicted in Figure 16.1.

Both McBride (2001) and Verme (2010) propose utilities functions that combine the alter/external and the ego/internal dimensions so that:

$$U_{it} = f\{(x_{it}/g(e_{it}, a_{ijt}))\},$$

where g (.) is a function of both the ego (e) and alter (a) value systems. In McBride, the econometric specification of such model results in:

$$H_{ict} = \beta_1 \log(x_{it}) + \beta_2 \log(e_{it}) + \beta_3 \log(a_{ict}) + \alpha_{it} + \alpha_t + \varepsilon_{ict},$$

where H is a measure of happiness, A is a time-varying individual specific effect and α_{it} and α_t are the time variant and time-invariant individual effects respectively.

The mechanism for the selection of the reference group is also central to the understanding of the relative income hypothesis. The empirical literature has explored different possibilities. Some studies focused on testing systematically the relative income hypothesis using reference groups defined across different characteristics (Van de Stadt et al., 1985; Ferrer-i-Carbonell, 2005; Akay and Martinsson, 2011). These different characteristics may be based on personal characteristics such as age and education, or location characteristics such as region or town. For example, Van de Stadt et al. (1985) used education, age and employment; Persky and Tam (1990) used other people in the same region; and McBride (2001) used people in the same country as the reference group.

A slightly more complex approach to the identification of the reference group is to model utilities in two stages. In the first stage, income or wages are modeled based on a number of personal characteristics that people use to select the reference group. In a second stage, predicted income is used in a utility function either in conjunction or as

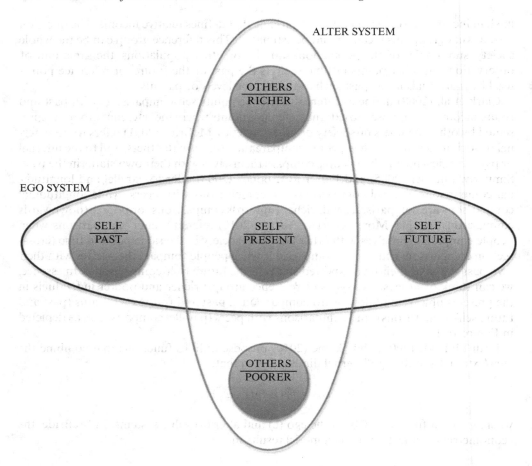

ALTER SYSTEM

OTHERS
RICHER

EGO SYSTEM

SELF
PAST

SELF
PRESENT

SELF
FUTURE

OTHERS
POORER

Source: Verme (2010).

Figure 16.1   Individual evaluation system of happiness/satisfaction

a replacement of relative income (see, for example, Clark and Oswald, 1996; Izem and Verme, 2008; Silber and Verme, 2010; Verme, 2011a; Verme, 2011b). This approach arises from the concern that people self-select their own reference groups based on their peers, where peers are defined on the basis of similar personal characteristics, and also on the idea that what may define relative income is the distance between one's own status and one's own expected status, an information conveyed by the predicted values of income.

Irrespective of the choice of reference income and reference group, estimations of the happiness/utility equation almost always rely either on ordered probit (or logit) for categorical ordered dependent variables or on ordinary least squares (OLS) estimators for continuous dependent variables. Ferrer-i-Carbonell and Frijters (2004) showed that an ordered logit or probit specifications lead to very similar results, although this review will show that most authors opted for an ordered probit estimation.

Variables transformations are also an important source of diversity across empirical studies. The equations would normally be in log form as the standard approach with continuous independent variables. But some studies opted to focus on testing the linearity of the income–happiness relation using quadratic or cubic transformations of the income variable.

Most applications would also add a set of control variables Z defining personal, household or communities characteristics, and also a set of fixed effects, usually based on spatial criteria such as regions or urban and rural areas. If relative income is modeled in terms of predicted income, and predicted income is estimated using a set of personal and/or household characteristics, these characteristics should normally not be used also in the utility model, although this is not always the case in empirical papers.

In essence, the standard econometric model to test the relative income hypothesis can be described as:

$$U_i = \beta_1 \ln(x_i) + \beta_2 \ln(r_i) + \gamma Z_i,$$

where β_1 and β_2 are the parameters of interest.

The distinction between cross-section and longitudinal models also leads us to three types of studies: those that rely on one cross-section survey focusing therefore on individuals or households within a single country, cross-country studies and longitudinal studies. The empirical specification of relative income models is essentially the same, with the only difference being the change in subscripts, but the interpretation of the coefficients is evidently different. For example, the great debate on the Easterlin paradox revolved around the paradox of countries showing little increase in happiness as they grew richer, but this is very different from considering individual happiness and income within these same countries. The measurement of collective utility over time and the measurement of individual utility over a given society in a given point in time are two very different lines of investigation, even if the concept of relative income is central in both types of studies.

Provided that cross-section and longitudinal data are available, one can of course try to reconcile the two types of relative income hypotheses. Di Tella et al. (2003) offer, for example, one of the most comprehensive models by considering individuals, countries and time, trying to test the relative income hypothesis using countries and time as reference:

$$U_{ict} = \beta_1 \ln(x_{ict}) + \beta_2 \ln(x_{ict}/\bar{x}_{jt}) + \beta_3 \ln(\bar{x}_{ct}/\bar{x}_c) + \gamma Z_{ict}$$

These complex relations are nicely depicted in Figure 16.2 from Clark et al. (2008) where the cross-section within countries' relation between happiness and income is superimposed over the longitudinal cross-country relation. The figure shows how difficult is to capture these relations in one equation, especially if the empirical model is linear. It also shows that we can think of two forms of relative income hypotheses. One is relative income across individuals within countries, while the second is relative income across time.

The longitudinal approaches to the study of relative income also extend to the question of adaptation. The basic idea is that people become accustomed to current income and, if income does not change in real terms, the utility that derives from income diminishes over time simply because of habituation. The question of habituation is well known in psychology with prominent experiments on lottery winners showing how people quickly adapt to the new welfare status and rapidly return to the level of happiness enjoyed before

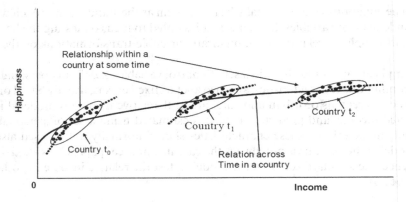

Source: Clark et al. (2008).

Figure 16.2   Happiness and income

winning the lottery. This is important for the relative income hypothesis because it would imply that income has diminishing returns over time so that when people compare their income with their own income in the past the present income is discounted by the habituation factor.

16.5   ECONOMETRIC AND MEASUREMENT ISSUES

The test of the relative income hypothesis – as it implies the specification and estimation of econometric models – is a microcosm of econometric issues that plague any empirical model. This section briefly reviews the main econometric issues that have been specifically found to complicate the test of the relative income hypothesis.

16.5.1   The Choice of the Welfare Measure

Income is often the measure of choice for well-being in rich countries, but microeconomists working on developing countries tend to use consumption or expenditure ('consumption' for short) as a proxy of income. That is because reported income is often underestimated and more volatile than consumption or expenditure. However, the difference between income and consumption is savings, and savings change significantly across the distribution of incomes, with the poor having zero or low savings and the rich having large savings. In addition, consumption may or may not include consumption of public goods that consumers have already paid for via taxation, and the difference between income and consumption also depends on whether we consider pre-tax or post-tax incomes. Regressions that attempt to explain deprivation or satisfaction with consumption tend to underestimate the impact of income, either because consumption is likely to have less variance than consumption (less significance) or because income is larger than consumption (lower coefficient). Headey and Wooden (2004) find some evidence of this phenomenon, concluding that the impact of income on satisfaction is typically underestimated.

There is also a difference in using household as opposed to individual incomes. The choice depends on how we believe individuals make value assessments of their own status when comparing their status with the status of others. For example, a young individual may have a low salary but live in a very wealthy family. This person may assess her/his own status on the basis of her/his family wealth rather than individual income. Hence, modeling household or individual relative income requires different behavioral assumptions, the interpretation of the coefficients estimated is different and, ultimately, models that use income or consumption are not strictly comparable.

16.5.2   Identification of the Reference Groups

Relative income is 'relative' in that it refers to the income of a reference group. Reference groups can be group- or individual-specific and researchers need to pinpoint the relevant reference group to assess the importance of relative income for satisfaction or deprivation. The problem is that very few studies actually ask respondents what their reference group is, and most of the time researchers either use the whole population as the reference group, or a subset of the population which is defined based on normative criteria chosen by the researchers themselves. This is what McBride (2001) refers to as problem 2: the lack of direct data on norms.

There are a few approaches to address this problem. A popular method is to estimate predicted incomes based on a number of personal characteristics that are generally thought to be used by people to compare themselves with others, such as age and education. However, including or excluding important variables can result in very different estimates and this approach is often criticized for being too 'normative'. The use of average incomes of peer groups such as co-workers or neighbors, which is also a popular approach to the selection of reference groups, may not be a better option. Knight and Song (2006) find, for example, that 68 percent of survey respondents in China reported that their main comparison group consisted of individuals in their own village. While this may be regarded as a high share, it does not exhaust the whole population and leaves over a third of the population who look for reference points outside their own village. In addition, this kind of localized knowledge is very rare in empirical studies. Also, depending on psychological factors, individuals may have a different approach to choosing the reference group, and these different approaches result in heterogeneity that cannot easily be captured in empirical studies. As noted by Clark et al. (2008, p. 24), 'the empirical happiness literature is still in its infancy on this issue'.

16.5.3   Discreteness of the Dependent Variable

In happiness/satisfaction/utility models, utility is a latent variable Z which is a proxy of the true level of utility S. The latent variable is represented by the scores R of the dependent variable. With ordered logit or probit models, what is captured is the ordinal information that the dependent variable provides, but not the cardinal information. Since S is a continuously differentiable monotonously function of R (Vendrik and Woltjer, 2006), ordinal properties of S are the same as those of Z but the cardinal properties such as concavity and convexity may differ (Vendrik and Woltjer, 2007). As discussed in previous sections, testing the concavity or convexity of the utility function is important to test hypotheses H1a and H1b, and this requires a different setting from the standard latent dependent variable model.

16.5.4   Timing

As in any causal or correlation study, researchers must be knowledgeable about the time distance between cause and effect or between two correlated phenomena. Feelings of satisfaction such as life satisfaction may be the result of past recollection of income, the last income received or future income expectations. Feelings of satisfaction or deprivation may also derive from life events that occurred in the past and altered the perception of income. Many of these factors are not observed in empirical studies. In fact, we will see that very few studies use lagged income variables.

16.5.5   Multicollinearity

In happiness models it is common to use variables constructed on income, such as relative income or income inequality in conjunction with absolute income itself. This may lead to multicollinearity that can affect both the significance and the size of the coefficients. As noted by Kosicki (1987, p. 426), the basic problem in determining whether rank matters is collinearity between income rank and the level of income. The way to resolve the dilemma, as he suggests, is to include both the level of income and income rank in the equation, and at the same time, generate as much variation in rank independent of variation in the level of income as possible, for example by comparing people across different communities.

   It is also possible that the introduction of fixed effects generates collinearity with core explanatory variables such as relative income. The use of fixed effects is very common in happiness studies that use relative income as explanatory variable. As fixed effects tend to be variables representing communities or areas, they may be at similar levels of aggregation as the reference group used to measure relative income. This increases the likelihood of correlation between relative income and fixed effects. In a review of studies on the relation between income inequality and happiness, Verme (2011a) has shown how in empirical models multicollinearity between fixed effects and core explanatory variables may explain the empirical heterogeneity of results. Addressing this problem is not simple and often boils down to a trade-off between losing on the explanatory power of the model and depicting more accurately the sign and significance of the inequality–happiness relation.

16.5.6   Omitted Variables

It is widely recognized that happiness models can explain only a limited part of the variation in happiness; witness the fact that the R squared and pseudo-R squared obtained from these models are typically low. It is possible therefore that the real explanations behind variations in happiness lie behind some of the omitted variables. Di Tella and MacCulloch (2008) examined a series of potential omitted variables which could explain why increasing income has not led to more happiness, using Eurobarometer and US General Social Survey (GSS) data. Variables used included life expectancy, pollution, unemployment, inflation, hours worked, divorce rate, crime and income inequality. Their results show that most of these variables are correlated with life satisfaction as expected. However, their inclusion as right-hand-side variables does not explain why rising income has not produced rising well-being. That is because these additional variables have mostly also improved over time without increasing happiness. In their own words: 'introducing omitted variables worsens the income-without-happiness paradox'. While these tests are not conclusive, the fact that the explanatory power of the happiness models is very low indicates that the results on relative income should be taken with caution. Significance of the relative income variable simply indicates that this is a variable that contributes, with income and among many other unobserved variables, to well-being.

16.5.7 Non-linearity, Concavity and Convexity of the Utility Function

It is also very little understood whether the relation between income and satisfaction is non-linear, and what function would best describe this relation. One of the explanations of the Easterlin paradox is that, as a country becomes richer, income becomes less relevant for happiness. This would imply decreasing marginal returns from income (as predicted by orthodox economic theory) and a concave utility function. Many papers test this hypothesis using different sets of data (cross-section, longitudinal or panel data) but a few use variables transformations of income and relative income that would allow looking at the shape of the utility function.

16.5.8 Behavioral Asymmetries

Perhaps one of the most complex behaviors to model is the question of upward/downward or past/future comparisons. This chapter has discussed how the literature has hypothesized different value functions for both types of comparisons in the works of, for example, Duesenberry (1949) for upward/downward comparisons (alter comparisons), and in the work of Kahneman and Tversky for past/future comparisons (ego comparisons). The central problem is the question of asymmetry of comparisons across these two dimensions and how to model such asymmetry. Vendrik and Woltjer (2007) is one of the few papers that provides formal tests of these hypotheses, but the empirical literature is otherwise silent on these questions.

16.5.9 Observational Equivalence

It is possible that the observation of a constant level of satisfaction over time at the aggregate level (such as for a country) can be explained by different factors. For example, this constancy could be explained by a reference group constituted by internal reference points (comparison with one's own income in the past) or by a reference group constituted by both internal and external reference points (where 'external' is the comparison with other people). It is also possible that positive and negative developments over time cancel each other out across individuals, resulting in no change at the aggregate level. Studies that have attempted to address these issues are very few.

16.5.10   Inconsistent Estimates

The use of ordered categorical models such as ordered probits and logits can lead to inconsistent estimates (Maddala, 1983). Ferrer-i-Carbonell and Frijters (2004) test whether results on the relative income hypothesis are sensitive to the use of OLS or categorical ordered models and find no significant differences between the use of the two models. However, controlling for fixed effects reduces the size of the positive coefficient on income. To address this problem one would need panel data, good instruments for personality traits or variables that observe personality traits directly – a rare feature of economics studies.

16.6   EMPIRICAL RESULTS

As already mentioned, the sources of differences across the specification of empirical models for testing the relative income hypothesis are many, from the choice of the welfare variable, to the choice of country and time, to the choice of the estimation method. We have noted that this diversity does not allow comparing results across studies. We have also noted that comparing the signs and significance of the relative income variable across different empirical models is per se a robustness test of the relative income hypothesis. This is what is done in this section by cataloguing a selected sample of empirical works across types of studies and according to results.

Absolute income is almost invariably used in conjunction with relative income to test the relative income hypothesis. We start therefore with results on absolute income before reviewing results on relative income. A first observation is that empirical models that try to explain happiness with absolute and relative income can explain only a small part of the variation in happiness. Ferrer-i-Carbonnell (2005) noticed that the pseudo-R2's for all regressions tested in the paper were between 0.07 and 0.08. This is in accordance with the general finding in the literature that only about 8–20 percent of individual subjective well-being depends on observed variables that are typically used in these types of models (Kahneman et al., 1999). Therefore, testing the relative income hypothesis does not amount to testing whether this variable is the most relevant factor in explaining happiness, but boils down to testing whether this variable is consistently significant in happiness equations.

Almost all studies find a positive association between absolute income and satisfaction. This evidence is consistent with studies that use cross-section surveys, panel data and cross-country studies. Cross-section studies on single countries have consistently found a positive and significant relation between income and life satisfaction or happiness with or without demographic controls. This is true for developed countries (Blanchflower and Oswald, 2004; Shields and Wheatley Price, 2005) as well as for developing countries (Graham and Pettinato, 2002; Lelkes, 2006). The main difference between developed and developing countries seems to be the slope of the relation: steeper for poorer economies as compared to richer economies. Panel data have been used to control for unobserved heterogeneity, such as personality traits. This section of the literature also concludes that changes in absolute incomes are correlated with changes in happiness (Winkelmann and Winkelmann, 1998; Ravallion and Lokshin, 2002; Ferrer-i-Carbonell and Frijters, 2004; Senik, 2004; Ferrer-i-Carbonell, 2005; Clark et al., 2005).

Some of the work with panel data has also gone further in an effort to establish a causality link between income and satisfaction by instrumenting income with exogenous shocks. Frijters et al. (2004b) used the average increase in incomes in East Germany after reunification, and the average decrease in incomes in Russia after the collapse of the Soviet Union, as exogenous shocks and find a greater effect of income on happiness than in much of the previous literature. Gardner and Oswald (2007) use information on lottery winnings in the British Household Panel Survey (BHPS) as reflecting exogenous income movements. In both the level and panel equations, lottery winnings are found to significantly reduce mental stress scores. These studies are consistent in finding a positive and significant relation between income and happiness, and concord in finding different slopes of the income–satisfaction relation across countries and across groups of people (Clark et al., 2005; Frijters et al., 2004a; Lelkes, 2006). A few cross-country longitudinal studies also used gross domestic product (GDP) per capita instead of income, controlling for country fixed-effects, and found a positive relation, in contrast with the Easterlin paradox (Di Tella et al., 2003; Helliwell, 2003; Alesina et al., 2004).

Despite the fact that the overwhelming majority of studies find a positive relation between income and happiness, there are a few studies that find a negative relation. This has been labeled the case of the 'frustrated achievers' (Graham and Pettinato, 2002; Becchetti and Rossetti, 2009; Brockmann et al., 2009), to underscore the fact that even an increase in income can result in decreased satisfaction. For example, using the German Socio-Economic Panel Survey (SOEP), Becchetti and Rossetti (2009) found that half of the achievers – defined in terms of people who improved on their income during the last period – are frustrated, meaning that they declared a reduction in life satisfaction. This is one of the few studies that actually split happy and unhappy achievers into two groups, avoiding in this way the averaging of negative and positive income-satisfaction relations.

Several studies also find that income exhibits decreasing marginal returns on satisfaction for individuals within countries and across countries, and that this is true especially over time (Diener and Lucas, 1999; Layard, 2005). This would be partly explained by the role of positional goods and the reference group, two factors that change along with income (Duesenberry, 1949; Frank, 1985). In essence, expectations, needs and the reference group are continuously adjusted to higher incomes, so that the effect of an increase in marginal income is short-lived. This literature provides a possible explanation for the Easterlin paradox. In low-income countries, an increase in average incomes increases average happiness; but in high-income countries this elasticity is no longer at work, and factors other than income such as religion, social networks and freedom become more important for explaining changes in happiness.

The sign and significance of the relation between happiness and relative income in empirical studies is less consistent than the observed relation between happiness and absolute income. The majority of studies find a negative and significant relation, as postulated by the relative income hypothesis (when controlling for absolute income). Studies that use averages of incomes across predefined reference groups as relative income are perhaps the most common, and results are quite consistent in finding a negative relation between relative income and life satisfaction (Ferrer-i-Carbonell, 2005; Blanchflower and Oswald, 2004; Graham and Felton, 2006; Kapteyn and van Herwaarden, 1980; Kapteyn et al., 1997; McBride, 2001). Alpizar et al. (2005) use a group of students from Costa Rica and a specifically designed questionnaire to test the relative income hypothesis using the ratio approach and the differential approach with both income and consumption measures. They find a negative and significant sign for relative income in all equations.

Two studies that use the German SOEP data (D'Ambrosio and Frick, 2007, 2012) find that the role of relative deprivation (measured with the Yitzhaki, 1979 income measure) in explaining subjective well-being carries a negative sign and is more important than the role of absolute income. Interestingly, these studies also find that both absolute and relative income in the past contribute to shape the perception of well-being in the present, what is referred to as the 'ego' comparisons.

For China, there is overwhelming evidence that relative income and deprivation is very important in both urban and rural areas. Knight and Song (2006), using a sample of Chinese households, find that people who perceived their own income to be above average were much happier than those who perceived their own income to be below average, after controlling for absolute income. Appleton and Song (2008) and Knight and Gunatilaka (2008) find that relative income is very important in rural China to explain happiness, and Wang and Vander Weele (2011) find that relative deprivation is very relevant in explaining happiness for urban residents.

Despite the evidence reported for countries like China and Costa Rica, several studies that have focused on poorer countries found that relative income is positively correlated with happiness or satisfaction. For example, Ravallion and Lokshin (2010) find a positive sign for a relative income measure using a survey from Malawi, and the same sign is found by Senik (2004) for Russia, and by Kingdon and Knight (2007) for South Africa.

There is also evidence that relative income predicted with an income equation is a significant factor that explains satisfaction. In these types of models, predicted income is interpreted as the income that people expect, given their own characteristics and relatively to the characteristics of the reference group, where the reference group can be the whole population or selected subsets of the population. Hamermesh (1977) uses the residual from a wage equation as reference income and finds this residual to have a positive and significant effect on job satisfaction. Clark and Oswald (1996), using a similar approach with a sample of British employees, find both income and reference income to be significant and with opposite signs in a job satisfaction regression. Sloane and Williams (2000) also find a negative and significant relation between job satisfaction and the reference income predicted with a wage equation. Verme (2010) and Silber and Verme (2012) using the Consortium of Household Panels for European Socio-Economic Research (CHER) find that deprivation indices constructed with predicted income values are consistently and negatively correlated with income satisfaction.

Measures of relative deprivation have been found by several authors to be negatively associated with happiness or life satisfaction. Oshio et al. (2011) find the Yitzhaki measure of relative deprivation to be negatively associated with happiness for China and Korea. Silber and Verme (2012) find various measures of relative deprivation constructed with predicted income to be negatively associated with satisfaction.

The choice of the reference group is an important determinant of the outcome of the relative income–happiness relation. Most researchers use 'alter' comparisons, comparisons with other groups in society based on predefined characteristics. In Ferrer-i-Carbonell (2005) the reference group contains all the individuals with a similar education level, in the same age bracket, and living in the same region. Akay and Martinsson (2011) used several types of reference groups to test the relative income hypothesis in northern

Ethiopia but found no significance of relative income, as opposed to absolute income which is always found to be significant. Persky and Tam (1990) assume that all individuals living in the same region are part of the same reference group. McBride (2001) includes in the reference group of each individual all people in the USA who are in the age range of five years younger and five years older than the individual concerned. Van de Stadt et al. (1985) define the reference group according to education level, age and employment status. It was not possible to detect in the review particular reference groups as being better than others in finding a significant relation between happiness and relative income. All that can be said is that most scholars use individual characteristics, either directly in the happiness equation or indirectly with the estimation of predicted income.

A number of studies find evidence that both the internal (ego) comparisons and external (alter) comparisons matter. Knight et al. (2009) find this result for rural China, where relative income seems to be more important than absolute income in explaining happiness, while both past and expected incomes are also found to be relevant for present happiness. Verme (2010), using a set of European panel surveys, concludes that absolute income is more important than relative income in explaining happiness, but also that relative income consistently carries a negative and significant sign in equations where the dependent variable is satisfaction with income.

Some studies indicate upward and downward asymmetries in social comparisons. These asymmetries were originally suggested by Duesenberry (1949) when he noticed how people tend to make upwards comparisons rather than downwards comparisons. Frank (1985) also explored this aspect in relation to the role of positional goods and found similar results. For Taiwan, Tao and Chiu (2009) find a weak role of absolute income in explaining happiness, a non-significant role of downward comparisons, and a positive and significant role for upward and parallel comparisons (the latter measured in terms of predicted income). According to these authors, relative income is a better predictor of happiness than absolute income.

Corazzini et al. (2011) designed a questionnaire to explore the relativist versus absolutist perception of well-being and administered this questionnaire to respondents in eight countries: four low-income and four high-income countries. Results indicate that well-being is perceived mainly in relative terms, with the strength of relativism being higher for respondents in high-income countries. They also find that interpersonal comparisons take place by looking both 'upward' and 'downward' along the income scale, and that both rank and the magnitude of reference incomes are important in assessing well-being.

Relative income has also been found to be a key element in the understanding of a number of factors related to happiness, such as the case of the frustrated achievers, and adaptation. Becchetti and Rossetti (2009) find that relative income contributes to explain the case of the frustrated achievers; those individuals who report higher income but lower satisfaction as compared to the past. The adaptation hypothesis – whereby individuals tend to adapt quickly to an improved welfare status and, in consequence, derive less utility from the same level of welfare – has also found substantial support in various studies across countries such as the United Kingdom (Clark, 1999) and Germany (Grund and Sliwka, 2003; Di Tella et al., 2005), and also in cross-country studies (Van Praag and Frijters, 1999). Clark et al. (2016) find no adaptation to income poverty.

REFERENCES

Akay, A. and Martinsson, P. (2011) Does relative income matter for the very poor? Evidence from rural Ethiopia. *Economics Letters*, 110(3), 213–215.

Akerlof, G.A. (1997) Social distance and social decisions. *Econometrica*, 65, 1005–1027.

Alesina, A., Di Tella, R. and MacCulloch, R. (2004) Inequality and happiness: are Europeans and Americans different?. *Journal of Public Economics*, 88(9/10), 2009–2042.

Alpizar, F., Carlsson, F. and Johansson-Stenman, O. (2005) How much do we care about absolute versus relative income and consumption?. *Journal of Economic Behavior and Organization*, 56, 405–421.

Appleton, S. and Song, L. (2008) Life satisfaction in urban China: components and determinants. *World Development*, 36, 2325–2340.

Becchetti, L. and Rossetti, F. (2009) When money does not buy happiness: the case of 'frustrated achievers'. *Journal of Socio-Economics*, 38, 159–167.

Bentham, J. (1789 [1907]) *An Introduction to the Principles of Morals and Legislation*, Clarendon Press, Oxford.

Blanchflower, D.G. and Oswald, A.J. (2004) Well-being over time in Britain and the USA. *Journal of Public Economics*, 88, 1359–1386.

Brockmann, H., Delhey, J., Christian, W. and Yuan, H. (2009) The China puzzle: falling happiness in a rising economy. *Journal of Happiness Studies*, 10(4), 387–405.

Clark, A.E. (1999) Are wages habit-forming? Evidence from micro-data. *Journal of Economic Behavior and Organization*, 39, 179–200.

Clark, A.E., D'Ambrosio, C. and Ghislandi, S. (2016) Adaptation to poverty in long-run panel data. *Review of Economics and Statistics*, 98, 591–600.

Clark, A.E., Etile, F., Postel-Vinay, F., Senik, C. and Van der Straeten, K. (2005) Heterogeneity in reported well-being: evidence from twelve European countries. *Economic Journal*, 115, C118–C132.

Clark, A.E., Frijters, P. and Shields, M. (2008) Relative income, happiness and utility: an explanation for the Easterlin paradox and other puzzles. *Journal of Economic Literature*, 46(1), 95–144.

Clark, A.E. and Oswald, A.J. (1996) Satisfaction and comparison income. *Journal of Public Economics*, 61, 359–381.

Corazzini, L., Esposito, L. and Majorano, F. (2011) Exploring the absolutist vs relativist perception of poverty using a cross-country questionnaire survey. *Journal of Economic Psychology*, 32(2), 273–283.

Corneo, G. and Jeanne, O. (1997) Conspicuous consumption, snobbism and conformism. *Journal of Public Economics*, 66, 55–71.

Dalton, H. (1920) The measurement of the inequality of incomes. *Economic Journal*, 30(119), 348–361.

D'Ambrosio, C. and Frick, R.J. (2007) Income satisfaction and relative deprivation: an empirical link. *Social Indicators Research*, 81(3), 497–519.

D'Ambrosio, C. and Frick, J.R. (2012) Individual wellbeing in a dynamic perspective. *Economica*, 79(314), 284–302.

Diener, E. (1984) Subjective wellbeing. *Psychological Bulletin* 95(3), 542–575.

Diener, E., Diener, M. and Diener, C. (1995) Factors predicting the subjective well-being of nations. *Journal of Personality and Social Psychology*, 69, 851–864.

Diener, E. and Lucas, R.E. (1999) Personality and subjective well-being. In Kahneman, D., Diener, E. and Schwarz, N. (eds), *Foundations of Hedonic Psychology: Scientific Perspectives on Enjoyment and Suffering*, Russell Sage Foundation, New York, pp. 213–229.

Di Tella, R. and MacCulloch, R. (2008) Gross national happiness as an answer to the Easterlin Paradox?. *Journal of Development Economics*, 86(1), 22–42.

Di Tella, R., MacCulloch, R. and Haisken-deNew, J.P. (2005) Happiness adaptation to income and to status in an individual panel. Harvard Business School Working Paper.

Di Tella, R., MacCulloch, R. and Oswald, A.J. (2003) The macroeconomics of happiness. *Review of Economics and Statistics*, 85, 809–827.

Duesenberry, J.S. (1949) *Income, Saving and the Theory of Consumer Behavior*, Harvard University Press, Cambridge, MA.

Easterlin, R.A. (1995) Will raising the incomes of all increase the happiness of all?. *Journal of Economic Behavior and Organization*, 27(1), 35–47.

Ferrer-i-Carbonell, A. (2005) Income and well-being: an empirical analysis of the comparison income effect. *Journal of Public Economics*, 89, 997–1019.

Ferrer-i-Carbonell, A. and Frijters, P. (2004) The effect of methodology on the determinants of happiness. *Economic Journal*, 114, 641–659.

Frank, R.H. (1985) The demand for unobservable and other non-positional goods. *American Economic Review*, 75, 101–116.

Friedman, M. (1957) *A Theory of the Consumption Functions*, Oxford University Press, London.

Frijters, P., Shields, M.A. and Haisken-DeNew, J.P. (2004a) Money does matter! Evidence from increasing real incomes in East Germany following reunification. *American Economic Review*, 94, 730–741.
Frijters, P., Shields, M.A. and Haisken-DeNew, J.P. (2004b) Changes in the pattern and determinants of life satisfaction in Germany following reunification. *Journal of Human Resources*, 39, 649–674.
Gardner, J. and Oswald, A.J. (2007) Do divorcing couples become happier by breaking up?. *Journal of the Royal Statistical Society: Series A (Statistics in Society)*, 169(2), 319–336.
Graham, C. and Felton, A. (2006) Inequality and happiness: insights from Latin America. *Journal of Economic Inequality*, 4(1), 107–122.
Graham, C. and Pettinato, S. (2002) *Happiness and Hardship: Opportunity and Insecurity in New Market Economies*, Washington, DC: Brookings Institution Press.
Grund, C. and Sliwka, D. (2003) The further we stretch the higher the sky: on the impact of wage increases on job satisfaction. University of Bonn, Bonn Econ Discussion Paper 2003-1.
Hamermesh, D.S. (1977) Economic aspects of job satisfaction. In Ashenfelter, O. and Oates, W. (eds), *Essays in Labor Market Analysis*, Wiley, New York, 53–72.
Headey, B. and Wooden, M. (2004) The effects of wealth and income on subjective well-being and ill-being. *Economic Record*, 80, 24–33.
Helliwell, J.F. (2003) How's life? Combining individual and national variables to explain subjective well-being. *Economic Modelling*, 20(2), 331–360.
Inglehart, R. (1990) *Cultural Shift in Advanced Industrial Society*, Princeton University Press, Princeton, NJ.
Izem, R. and Verme, P. (2008) Relative deprivation with imperfect information. *Economics Bulletin*, 4(7), 1–9.
Johansson-Stenman, O., Carlsson, F., and Daruvala, D. (2002) Measuring future grandparents' preferences for equality and relative standing. *Economic Journal*, 112, 362–383.
Kahneman, D., Diener, E. and Schwarz, N. (1999) *Well Being: The Foundations of Hedonic Psychology*, Russell Sage, New York.
Kahneman, D. and Tversky, A. (1979) Prospect theory: an analysis of decision under risk. *Econometrica*, 47(2), 263–291.
Kapteyn, A., van de Geer, S., van de Stadt, H. and Wansbeek, T. (1997) Interdependent preferences: an econometric analysis. *Journal of Applied Econometrics*, 12, 665–686.
Kapteyn, A. and van Herwaarden, F.G. (1980) Independent welfare functions and optimal income distribution. *Journal of Public Economics*, 14, 375–397.
Kapteyn, A., Van Praag, B.M.S. and Van Herwaarden, F.G. (1978) Individual welfare functions and social reference spaces. *Economics Letters*, 1(2), 173–177.
Kingdon, G. and Knight, J. (2007) Community, comparisons and subjective well-being in a divided society. *Journal of Economic Behavior and Organization*, 64, 69–90.
Knight, J. and Gunatilaka, R. (2008) Income, aspirations and the hedonic treadmill in a poor society. University of Oxford, Department of Economics.
Knight, J. and Song, L. (2006) Subjective well-being and its determinants in rural China. Mimeo.
Knight, J., Song, L. and Gunatilaka, R. (2009) Subjective well-being and its determinants in Rural China. *China Economic Review*, 20, 635–639.
Kosicki, G. (1987) A test of the relative income hypothesis. *Southern Economic Journal*, 54(2), 422–434.
Kuznets, S. (1942) National income and taxable capacity. *American Economic Review*, 32(1), Part 2, Supplement, Papers and Proceedings of the 54th Annual Meeting of the American Economic Association, March, pp. 37–75.
Layard, R. (1980) Human satisfaction and public policy. *Economic Journal*, 90, 737–750.
Layard, R. (2005) *Happiness: Lessons from a New Science*, Allen Lane, London.
Lelkes, O. (2006) Tasting freedom: happiness, religion and economic transition. *Journal of Economic Behavior and Organization*, 59(2), 173–194.
Luttmer, E.F. (2005) Neighbors as negatives: relative earnings and well-being. *Quarterly Journal of Economics*, 120(3), 963–1002.
Maddala, G.S. (1983) *Limited Dependent and Qualitative Variables in Econometrics*, Cambridge University Press, Cambridge.
Marx, K. (1847 [1933]) Relation of wage-labour to capital. In Marz, K., *Wage Labour and Capital*, transl. 1891 by Frederick Engels, 1933 reprint, available at http://www.marxists.org/archive/marx/works/1847/wage-labour/ch06.htm.
McBride, M. (2001) Relative-income effects on subjective well-being in the cross-section. *Journal of Economic Behavior and Organization*, 45, 251–278.
Modigliani, F. and Brumberg, R.H. (1954) Utility analysis and the consumption function: an interpretation of cross-section data. In Kenneth K. Kurihara (ed.), *Post-Keynesian Economics*, Rutgers University Press, New Brunswick, NJ, pp. 388–436.
Oshio, T., Nozaki, K. and Kobayashi, M. (2011) Relative income and happiness in Asia: evidence from nationwide surveys in China, Japan and Korea. *Social Indicators Research*, 104, 351–367.

Persky, J. and Tam, M.Y. (1990) Local status and national social welfare. *Journal of Regional Science*, 30(2), 229–238.

Persson, M. (1995) Why are taxes so high in egalitarian societies?. *Scandinavian Journal of Economics*, 97, 469–476.

Pigou, A.C. (1920) *The Economics of Welfare*, Macmillan & Co., London.

Ravallion, M. and Lokshin, M. (2002) Self-rated economic welfare in Russia. *European Economic Review*, 46(8), 1453–1473.

Ravallion, M. and Lokshin, M. (2010) Who cares about relative deprivation?. *Journal of Economic Behavior and Organization*, 73(2), 171–185.

Runciman, W.G. (1966) *Relative Deprivation and Social Justice*, Routledge & Kegan Paul, London.

Senik, C. (2004) When information dominates comparison: a panel data analysis using Russian subjective data. *Journal of Public Economics*, 88, 2099–2123.

Shields, M.A. and Wheatley Price, S. (2005) Exploring the economic and social determinants of psychological well-being and perceived social support in England. *Journal of the Royal Statistical Society: Series A (Statistics in Society)*, 168(3), 513–537.

Silber, J. and Verme, P. (2010) Distributional change, reference groups and the measurement of relative deprivation. *Research on Economic Inequality*, 18, 197–217.

Silber, J. and Verme, P. (2012) Relative Deprivation, reference groups and the assessment of the standard of living. *Economic Systems*, 36(1), 31–45.

Sloane, P.J. and Williams, H. (2000) Job satisfaction, comparison earnings, and gender. *Labour*, 14(3), 473–501.

Smith, A. (1776 [1976]) *An Inquiry into the Nature and Causes of the Wealth of Nations*, Glasgow Edition 1976, R.H. Campbell & A.S. Skinner, Glasgow.

Stouffer, S.A., Suchman, E.A., DeVinney, L.C., Star, S.A. and Williams, R.M. Jr. (1949) *The American Soldier (1). Adjustment During Army Life*. Princeton University Press, Princeton, NJ.

Tao, H. and Chiu, S. (2009) The effects of relative income and absolute income on happiness. *Review of Development Economics*, 13(1), 164–174.

Tinbergen, J. (1970) A positive and normative theory of income distribution. *Review of Income and Wealth*, 16(3), 221–234.

Tversky, A. and Kahneman, D. (1991) Loss aversion in riskless choice: a reference-dependent model. *Quarterly Journal of Economics*, 106(4), 1039–1061.

Van de Stadt, H., Kapteyn, A. and van de Geer, S. (1985) The relativity of utility: evidence from panel data. *Review of Economics and Statistics*, 67(2), 179–187.

Van Herwaarden, F.G. and Kapteyn, A. (1979) Empirical comparison of the shape of welfare functions. *Economics Letters*, 3(1), 71–76.

Van Praag, B.M.S. and Frijters, P. (1999) The measurement of welfare and well-being: the Leiden approach. In Kahneman, D., Diener, E. and Schwarz, N. (eds), *Foundations of Hedonic Psychology: Scientific Perspectives on Enjoyment and Suffering*, Russell Sage Foundation, New York, pp. 413–433.

Veblen, T. (1898) *The Theory of the Leisure Class*, Macmillan, New York.

Vendrik, M.C.M. and Woltjer, G.B. (2006) Happiness and loss aversion: when social participation dominates comparison. METEOR Research Memorandum RM/06/027, Faculty of Economics and Business Administration, Maastricht University.

Vendrik, M.C.M. and Woltjer, G.B. (2007) Happiness and loss aversion: is utility concave or convex in relative income?. *Journal of Public Economics* 91, 1423–1448.

Verme, P. (2009) Happiness, freedom and control. *Journal of Economic Behavior and Organization*, 71(2), 146–161.

Verme, P. (2010) Happiness, deprivation and the alter ego. In Deutsch, J. and Silber, J. (eds), *The Measurement of Individual Well-being and Group Inequalities: Essays in Memory of Z.M. Berrebi*, Routledge, New York.

Verme, P. (2011a) Life satisfaction and income inequality. *Review of Income and Wealth*, 57(1), 111–127.

Verme, P. (2011b) Two classes of generalized relative deprivation indices. *Economics Bulletin*, 31(3), 2021–2029.

Wang, P. and Vander Weele, T.J. (2011) Empirical research on factors related to the subjective well-being of Chinese urban residents. *Social Indicators Research*, 101, 447–459.

Winkelmann, L. and Winkelmann, R. (1998) Why are the unemployed so unhappy? Evidence from panel data. *Economica*, 65, 1–15.

Yitzhaki, S. (1979) Relative deprivation and the Gini coefficient. *Quarterly Journal of Economics*, 93, 321–324.

17. Social inequality: theoretical approaches
Casilda Lasso de la Vega

17.1 INTRODUCTION

The analysis of the inequality in the distribution of income has attracted the attention of many economists for quite some time now and a great number of different problems have been addressed and deeply analysed. There are two key concepts that underlie the measurement of income inequality. The first is that there is no inequality when everybody enjoys the mean income, or to put it differently, the mean income is taken as the equality reference point. The second basic concept is the Pigou–Dalton principle, which establishes that a transfer of income from a poorer person to a richer one increases inequality. Based on these two concepts researchers have developed a huge number of tools for ranking distributions according to their inequality.

There are variables other than income, including health, educational achievement, happiness, access to amenities, and so on, that are also often used to evaluate living standards in society. In this chapter, all these non-income variables are simply called social variables. In recent years, there has been a growing interest in measuring inequality among these social variables, and as a consequence, a large body of research has been generated. This research has two major strands. The first strand focuses on the assessment of the 'pure inequality' of the distribution of the social variable of interest, without considering the economic status of the individuals. In other words, this analysis is not interested in detecting whether the people in the various categories are rich or poor. However, the concern about to what extent inequality in health, education, and so on is related to unequal economic status has led researchers to develop a second research strand that has been termed 'socioeconomic inequality'.

Although the measurement of pure inequality of social variables is closely related to the measurement of income inequality, new problems have arisen, most of which have to do with the type of variables that represent the distributions. In fact the social variables can be both cardinal and ordinal. For instance, self-reported data about health status, happiness or educational attainments are collected from responses in ordered categories ranging, for example, from 'very good' or 'excellent' to 'poor' or 'very poor', without cardinal interpretation. The standard tools for measuring income inequality cannot be used without first assigning a cardinal number to each social category. Although sophisticated mechanisms have been proposed for this purpose,[1] the inequality indices are very sensitive to cardinal scales and different inequality rankings may ensue depending on the scale. Thus, if there is no way to overcome the arbitrariness of the cardinalization, inequality comparisons of ordinal distributions using the traditional procedures may not be robust.[2]

An alternative approach to the measurement of inequality in the distribution of ordinal variables has been suggested by Allison and Foster (2004). They propose taking the median as the equality reference point and introduce a partial ordering (the counterpart of the Lorenz order) that allows the comparison of ordinal distributions with equal medians. Families of inequality indices that are consistent with this partial ordering have been proposed and characterized by Blair and Lacy (2000), Abul Naga and Yalcin (2008), Kobus and Milos (2012) and Lazar and Silber (2013).

Nevertheless, Cowell and Flachaire (2017) have recently questioned the use of the median status as the equality reference point for ordinal distributions. As an alternative to each individual's status, they suggest just aggregating a function of the number of individuals that are better- or worse-off than the given individual. By using this approach and some basic axioms they characterize a family of inequality indices that incorporates various degrees of inequality aversion.

Sometimes the social data are represented by cardinal variables, for example, nutritional intake, life expectancy, mortality rate or literacy. Nevertheless, even in these cases, the application of the conventional inequality procedures is not straightforward since in most cases the individuals' characteristics are represented by bounded variables. Consequently, these characteristics may be represented both by attainments towards the perfect state, and by shortfalls from the maximal value. But the choice of representation may well affect comparisons of inequality across populations and, indeed, their inequality rankings will usually be reversed. Clarke et al. (2002) were the first to tackle this problem.

If the inequality rankings of social states remain unchanged when focusing either on the attainment side or on the shortfall side, it is said that there is consistency between the two notions of inequality. Lambert and Zheng (2011) analyse deeply the partial inequality orderings within Zoli's (1999) setting. They remark that relative inequality and all currently documented intermediate inequality concepts fail to meet consistency. Consistent indices have been derived by Erreygers (2009b), Lambert and Zheng (2011) and Chakravarty et al. (2016). Finally, Bosmans (2016) introduces a more general setting that proposes separate measures for attainments and shortfalls. All these papers take into account the distributions of attainments and shortfalls separately, and search for consistency in the respective inequality levels. By contrast, Lasso de la Vega and Aristondo (2012), Aristondo and Lasso de la Vega (2013) and Kjellsson and Gerdtham (2013) propose considering a unified framework where the attainment and shortfall distributions can be jointly analysed, and introduce inequality indices and invariant conditions for this setting.

All the results mentioned so far focus on the measurement of pure inequality of distributions of social variables. Regarding the literature on socioeconomic inequality, the second strand in the research on inequality with social variables, the first empirical papers on this topic were based on the concentration curve methodology. See, for instance, Wagstaff and van Doorslaer (2000) and van Doorslaer and van Ourti (2011) for a survey of the papers devoted to the concentration curve and the concentration index, and the practical guide published by O'Donnell et al. (2008). However, new approaches (including the equality of opportunity approach) have recently been developed for measuring socioeconomic inequalities (see Fleurbaey and Schokkaert, 2012). All these mentioned surveys cover the main methodological developments and questions, and provide extensive treatments of the measurement of socioeconomic inequality. The reader interested in these topics is referred to them.

This chapter concentrates solely on the measurement of pure inequality in distributions with social variables. It is organized into two main sections. Section 17.2 is devoted to reviewing results in the measurement of inequality when the social variables are ordinal, whereas section 17.3 focuses on bounded cardinal variables. Thus subsection 17.2.1 introduces the notation regarding categorical distributions, and subsection 17.2.2 discusses the use of the standard income inequality procedures for measuring inequality of ordinal distributions. Subsection 17.2.3 introduces the approach proposed by Allison and Foster (2004), and the social inequality indices derived within this approach are reviewed in subsection 17.2.4. Finally, Cowell and Flachaire's (2017) approach is introduced in subsection 17.2.5. As regards the measurement of inequality of bounded distributions in section 17.3, subsection 17.3.1 begins with the notation and basic definitions, and in subsection 17.3.2 the results derived by Lambert and Zheng (2011) are summarized. Subsection 17.3.3 examines indices that rank distributions of attainments and shortfalls consistently, and subsection 17.3.4 introduces the alternative approach mentioned above that jointly analyses the distributions of attainments and shortfalls. Section 17.4 concludes.

17.2 MEASURING SOCIAL INEQUALITY WITH ORDINAL DATA

17.2.1 Notation

Consider a social variable such as health level, educational attainment, happiness or access to amenities, having n categories with $2 \leq n < \infty$. The number of categories is given and fixed. Assume categorical statuses are listed in increasing order. A population categorical distribution is represented by a vector $x = (x_1, \ldots, x_n)$, where x_i is the number of observations in category i. A distribution is degenerated if $x_i = 0$ for some i. The normalized distribution will be denoted by $p = (p_1, \ldots, p_n)$, where p_i is the proportion of people in category i, with $\sum_{i=1}^{n} p_i = 1$. The cumulative population proportion is $P_i = \sum_{j=1}^{i} p_j$, and $P = (P_1, \ldots, P_n)$ is the cumulative distribution. A category m is the median of x if half of the population has a categorical status below or equal to it and the other half is above or equal to it. The distribution P may be split into two vectors $P^L = (P_1, \ldots, P_{m-1})$ and $P^H = (P_m, \ldots, P_n)$. We will write $P = (P^L, P^H)$ as needed.

Let Ω denote the set of categorical distributions defined over n categories, and $\Omega_m \subset \Omega$ those distributions with median m. We also let Λ denote the set of cumulative distributions defined over n categories. Two particular distributions belonging to Ω will be used in the following. On the one hand the normalized distribution that corresponds to a society where everybody belongs to the median category will be represented by $\hat{\pi} = (0, \ldots, 0, 1, 0, \ldots, 0)$. The corresponding cumulative distribution will be denoted by $\hat{\Pi} = (\hat{\Pi}^L, \hat{\Pi}^H)$, with $\hat{\Pi}^L = (0, \ldots, 0)$ and $\hat{\Pi}^H = (1, \ldots, 1)$. On the other hand, the normalized distribution $\tilde{\pi} = (0.5, 0, \ldots, 0, 0.5)$, where half the population is in the lowest state and the other half enjoys the highest category level. This distribution has not specific median. Indeed any $m \in \{1, 2, \ldots, n\}$ can be considered as median state. Denote by $\tilde{\Pi} = (0.5, 0.5, \ldots, 0.5, 1)$ the cumulative distribution of $\tilde{\pi}$. Accordingly, $\tilde{\Pi} = (\tilde{\Pi}^L, \tilde{\Pi}^H)$ with $\tilde{\Pi}^L = (0.5, \ldots, 0.5)$ and $\tilde{\Pi}^H = (0.5, \ldots, 0.5, 1)$.

17.2.2   Standard Procedures for Measuring Social Inequality with Ordinal Data

We are interested in ranking two categorical distributions according to their inequality. If we want to use the standard inequality methods we may either compute any inequality index or apply an inequality dominance criterion. In both cases we must select a scale that assigns a numerical value to each categorical status. Formally, a scale is a positive vector $c = (c_1, c_2, \ldots, c_n)$, that assigns the cardinal value c_i to category i, with $c_1 \leq c_2 \leq \ldots \leq c_n$, that is, higher categorical status have higher values. The average level of distribution x given the scale c is $c(x) = \sum_{i=1}^{n} p_i c_i$. C represents the set of all feasible scales.

Given any categorical distribution, a variety of procedures have been proposed for selecting a scale (e.g., Wagstaff and van Doorslaer, 1994; van Doorslaer and Jones, 2003). However it is clear that the choice is arbitrary and it is easy to prove that the mean is highly sensitive to the scale. So the traditional inequality indices, which are all mean-based, are likely to fail to rank categorical distributions since different inequality rankings may ensue depending on the scale.[3]

With respect to the dominance criteria[4] that guarantee unanimous orderings at a variety of inequality indices, only the first-order dominance criteria, based on the quantiles of the distribution, avoid the need for using a scale. The question that arises is whether it is possible to establish conditions that guarantee unanimous inequality rankings regardless of the scale used to assign numerical values to the categories. Allison and Foster (2004) and Zheng (2008) explore these kinds of conditions. For establishing these results we need some previous definitions.

Definition 1. Given any two categorical distributions, x and y, we say that distribution x first order dominates distribution y if $P_j \leq Q_j$ for all $j = 1, \ldots, n$, where P_j and Q_j are the cumulative population shares in the bottom j categories of x and y respectively.

First order dominance incorporates neither the mean nor the transfer principle. Then no scale is needed to check this criterion. However the following proposition (Allison and Foster, 2004) shows the implications when any scale is chosen:

Proposition 1. Distribution x first order dominates distribution y if and only if the mean of x is as large as the mean of y for all scales c.

The implementation of the second-order dominance criteria is based on the Lorenz curves.

Definition 2. Given a categorical distribution x and a scale c, for each cumulative population share, P_l:

1. the generalized Lorenz ordinate is the (normalized) cumulated total categorical level, that is, $GL(x; c; P_l) = \sum_{i=1}^{l} p_i c_i$. The generalized Lorenz curve is the linear segment of the n Lorenz coordinates and the origin $(0,0)$.
2. The relative Lorenz ordinate is $RL(x; c; P_l) = \sum_{i=1}^{l} p_i c_i / c(x)$. The relative Lorenz curve is the linear segment of the n relative Lorenz coordinates and the origin $(0, 0)$.

3. The absolute Lorenz ordinate is $AL(x;c;P_l) = \sum_{i=1}^{l} p_i(c_i - c(x))$. The absolute Lorenz curve is the linear segment of the n absolute Lorenz coordinates and the origin $(0, 0)$.

Definition 3. We say that categorical distribution x generalized (respectively relative or absolute) Lorenz dominates distribution y for the scale c if the generalized (respectively the relative or the absolute) Lorenz curve of x lies nowhere below and somewhere strictly above that of y.

Whereas first order dominance does not depend on the scale adopted, Lorenz dominance depends on the cardinal values assigned to each category. The following proposition (Zheng, 2008) shows that generalized Lorenz dominance, when required for all possible scales, collapses to first order conditions. In other words, in measuring welfare with categorical variables nothing but first-order dominance is useful:

Proposition 2. Distribution x generalized Lorenz dominates distribution y for all scales c if and only if distribution x first order dominates distribution y.

Since welfare comparisons are established using the generalized Lorenz dominance we get the following result (Zheng, 2008):

Corollary 1. Distribution x welfare dominates distribution y in any degree of stochastic dominance for all scales c if and only if distribution x first order dominates distribution y.

The impossibility result established in Proposition 3 below (Zheng, 2008) shows that the relative (absolute) Lorenz curves are not appropriate tools to rank any non-degenerate distributions when different scales are considered:

Proposition 3. For any two non-degenerate categorical distributions x and y, the relative (absolute) Lorenz curve of x lies nowhere below that of y for all scales c if and only if $x = y$.

In conclusion, neither standard inequality measures nor Lorenz dominance can be applied in ranking inequality of categorical distributions. Moreover, Lorenz dominance has restricted relevance in ranking social welfare.

17.2.3   The Allison–Foster Approach for Measuring Social Inequality

Allison and Foster (2004) introduce an alternative procedure for measuring inequality that deals well with ordinal data. They propose to replace the mean by the median as equality reference point and introduce a median-based approach where the notion of inequality as 'spread out' is formalized as follows:

Definition 4. Given any two categorical distributions x and y, x has greater spread than y, written $x \geqslant_{AF} y$, if:

1.   *x* and *y* has the same median category *m*,
2.   for all categories *j* < *m* we have $P_j \geq Q_j$, and
3.   for all categories *j* ≥ *m* we have $P_j \leq Q_j$

where P_j and Q_j are the cumulative population shares in the bottom *j* categories of *x* and *y* respectively.

The ranking $\geq_{AF}$ is a partial ordering.[5] Note that if distribution *x* has greater spread than distribution *y*, then *y* first order dominates *x* below the median and *x* first order dominates *y* above and for the median. It is clear that this ranking suits ordinal data since results do not depend on the numerical value assigned to the categories.

The partial ordering $\geq_{AF}$ can be represented by a curve that Allison and Foster (2004) call the *S*-curve, constructed as follows. Given a scale *c*, we represent the linear cumulative distribution of the categorical distribution. The resulting curve is rotated 90° and then, the portion of the curve below the median category is flipped up, as shown in Figures 17.1 and 17.2. The base of the curve represents the percentage of population that belongs to the median category.

Note also that the *S*-curves are based in the percentages of populations belonging to each category and hence they are invariant under replications of the population.

In the same way as the Lorenz curve represents the Lorenz ordering for income distributions, the ordering $\geq_{AF}$ may be represented by the *S*-curve. First of all, two limiting curves correspond to the two extreme situations. If everybody belongs to the median category, the curve coincides with the horizontal axis. This distribution can be considered to have the least spread. The opposite situation occurs when half of the population has the least categorical level and the other half enjoys the highest category. Then the *S*-curve becomes two segments of equal length, parallel to the horizontal axis through the maximum respective levels. This society can be considered to have the highest spread. In other words, given any distribution $x \in \Omega_m$, we always get $\bar{\pi} \geq_{AF} x$ and $x \geq_{AF} \hat{\pi}$.

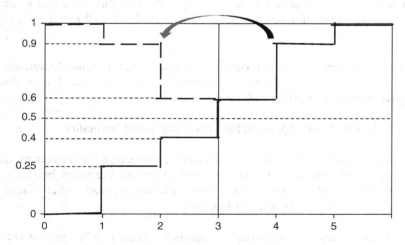

Figure 17.1   The CDF for categorical distribution x = (5, 3, 4, 6, 2)

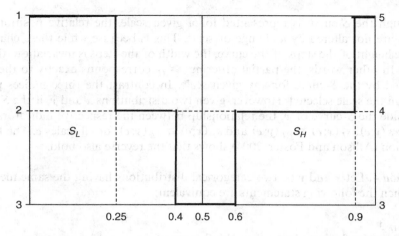

Figure 17.2   The S-curve for the categorical distribution **x** = (5, 3,4,6, 2)

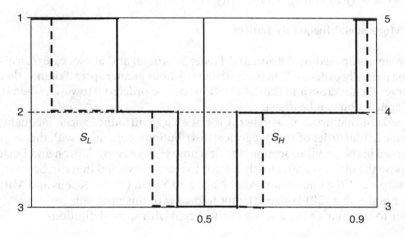

Figure 17.3   The S-curve for categorical distribution **x** = (5, 3, 4, 6, 2), *in solid line, lies*
inside that of **y** = (2, 4, 7, 6, 1), *in dotted line*

In addition, given two distributions **x** and **y**, if the S-curve of **x** lies inside the S-curve of **y**, as displayed in Figure 17.3 for instance, then **x** has greater spread than **y**, that is, **x** $\geqslant_{AF}$ **y**. In contrast, when the S-curves cross the distributions cannot be ranked according to the partial ordering $\geqslant_{AF}$, and nothing can be concluded about which distribution has more spread.

Moreover, as the Gini index is computed from the area determined by the Lorenz curve, some indices may be obtained from the area below the S-curve. Specifically, Allison and Foster (2004) propose three indicators. For a given scale **c**, $s(\mathbf{x}; c)$ is twice the area below the $s_L(\mathbf{x}; c)$ twice the area to the left of 0.5, and $s_H(\mathbf{x}; c)$ computed as twice the area to the right of 0.5. It is clear that $s(\mathbf{x}; c) = s_L(\mathbf{x}; c) + s_H(\mathbf{x}; c)$

Although the *S*-curve is represented for a given scale, the relative positions of the *S*-curves are not altered by a change of scale. This is because while these changes will affect the height of the steps of the curve, the width of the steps is invariant to the choice of scale. In other words, the partial ordering $\succcurlyeq_{AF}$ corresponds exactly to the ranking established by the *S*-curve for any given scale. In contrast the three indices proposed depend on the scale selected. However, given two distributions *x* and *y*, if the *S*-curve of *x* lies inside the *S*-curve of *y*, the relationship between the respective indicators is clear: $s(x;c) \geq s(y;c)$, $s_L(x;c) \geq s_L(y;c)$ and $s_H(x;c) \geq s_H(y;c)$ for all scales *c*. The following proposition (Allison and Foster, 2004) shows that the reverse also holds:

Proposition 4. Let *x* and *y* be two categorical distributions having the same median category. Then the following statements are equivalent:

1. $x \succcurlyeq_{AF} y$
2. the *S*-curve of *x* is no lower than the *S*-curve of *y*;
3. $s(x;c) \geq s(y;c)$ for all scales *c*;
4. $s_L(x;c) \geq s_L(y;c)$ and $s_H(x;c) \geq s_H(y;c)$ for all scales *c*.

17.2.4　More Social Inequality Indices

The approach proposed by Allison and Foster is ordinal and allows categorical distributions to be partially ordered. When a distribution *x* has greater spread than *y*, their respective S-curves do not cross and the distributions can be ordered. However, when the curves cross no conclusion can be drawn.

The question that arises is whether it is possible to introduce social inequality indices that provide a total order of the categorical distributions, consistent with the $\succcurlyeq_{AF}$ / ordering. As noted in the previous section, the first answer is given by Allison and Foster (2004) who propose the index $s(x;c)$, closely related to the *S*-curve and that can be interpreted as the counterpart of the Gini index. Abul Naga and Yalcin (2008), Kobus and Milos (2012) and Lazar and Silber (2013) also attempt to deal with this problem.

In order to summarize these results let us begin with some definitions:

Definition 5. A social inequality index is a non-constant function $I: \Omega \times C \rightarrow \mathbb{R}$ whose typical image, denoted by $I(x,c)$, represents the level of inequality in a categorical distribution *x* with *n* categories, given a scale *c*.

The following four properties are the counterparts for a social inequality measure of the basic properties assumed in the income inequality field.

Continuity (CON). *I* is a continuous function in $\Omega \times C$.

Continuity is quite basic and requires that small changes either in the categorical distribution or in the scale produce small changes in the inequality level. Consequently, the inequality level does not abruptly change as the population in each category and/or the scale is slightly altered. The next requirement guarantees that the index be consistent with the $\succcurlyeq_{AF}$ ordering:

Aversion to Median Preserving Spreads (EQUAL). For all $x, y \in \Omega_m$, if $x \succcurlyeq_{AF} y$ then $I(x,c) \geq I(y,c)$ for all scales c.

The $\succcurlyeq_{AF}$ ordering is defined on the cumulative proportion of the population in each category. Then if an index satisfies EQUAL it is invariant under replications of the population. EQUAL also guarantees that individuals are treated symmetrically in the sense that no other attribute but the category to which individuals belong matters in measuring social inequality.

If inequality is regarded as cardinal and not only as an ordinal concept, some normalization properties are useful. The following two axioms impose the cardinalization of the measure in the two extreme situations:

Lower-Normalization (LNOR). $I(\hat{x}, c) = 0$ for all scales c, where $\hat{x}$ is a categorical distribution in which all the population has the median category level.

Higher-Normalization (HNOR). $I(\bar{x}, c) = 1$ for all scales c, where $\bar{x}$ is a categorical distribution where half of the population belongs to the category with the lowest status and the other half enjoys the highest level.

It has already been argued that $\hat{x}$ corresponds to the situation with least spread. We assume that in this case inequality is equal to 0. By contrast $\bar{x}$ enjoys the highest spread, and HNOR demands the level of inequality to be equal to 1. Similarly to what happens in the traditional income inequality framework, LNOR and EQUAL imply that I takes non-negative values.

Finally, the next two properties require some kind of invariance under changes in the scale:

Scale Invariance (SCALINV). For all $x, y \in \Omega$, I is scale invariant if $I(x,c) \leq I(y,c)$ for some scale c implies $I(x,c') \leq I(y,c')$ for all scales c'.

Scale Independence (SCALINDEP). For all $x \in \Omega$, $I(x,c) = I(x,c')$ for all scales c and c'.

SCALINV demands that the inequality rankings of categorical distributions should not be sensitive to the choice of numerical scale. In turn SCALINDEP requires that the inequality levels are not affected by the cardinal values assigned to each category. Clearly SCALINDEP is stronger than SCALINV.

The following proposition, proved by Abul Naga and Yalcin (2008), characterizes the continuous social inequality indices consistent with the $\succcurlyeq_{AF}$ ordering which are invariant to the choice of scale.

Proposition 5. $I: \Omega \times C \rightarrow \mathbb{R}$ is an inequality index that satisfies CON, EQUAL, LNORM and SCALINV if and only if:

$$I(x,c) = \Delta\{\chi[\Phi(P),c] - \chi[\Phi(\hat{\Pi}),c]\}$$

for all $x \in \Omega$ and for all scales c, where P is the cumulative distribution of x and:

- $\Delta: \mathbb{R} \to \mathbb{R}_+$ is an increasing continuous function with $\Delta(0) = 0$;
- $\Phi: \Lambda \to \mathbb{R}$ is a continuous function which preserves the ordering $\geqslant_{AF}$; and
- $\chi: rang(\Phi) \times C \to \mathbb{R}$ is a continuous increasing function in its first argument.

The family characterized in Proposition 5 is quite broad. Interesting examples can be obtained with specific formulations. Choosing $\chi(t,c) = t$ and Δ the constant function $1/(\Phi(\overline{\overline{\Pi}}) - \Phi(\hat{\Pi}))$, which preserves normalization, yields the following family of indices:

$$I(\mathbf{x},c) = \frac{\Phi(P) - \Phi(\hat{\Pi})}{\Phi(\overline{\overline{\Pi}}) - \Phi(\hat{\Pi})}$$

with P the cumulative distribution of $\mathbf{x}$.

All these indices are clearly SCALINV since they do not depend on c explicitly.

Examples of particular interest arise when $\Phi(P) = \sum_{i=1}^{n-1} f(P_i)$ with a $f:[0, 1] \to [0, 1]$ continuous function, increasing in $[0,0.5]$ and decreasing in $[0.5,1]$ such that $f(0) = f(1) = 0$ and $f(0.5) = 1$. Some possible specifications for f and the corresponding indices are presented in Box 17.1 (see Blair and Lacy, 2000; Abul Naga and Yalcin, 2008; Lazar and Silber, 2013; Reardon, 2009). In particular the family $I_{\alpha,\beta}$, proposed by Lazar and Silber (2013), is a continuous modification of the family of indices introduced by Abul Naga and Yalcin (2008). The two parameters α and β allow researchers to accommodate different sensitivity judgments. For a given β, as α increases the inequality index becomes more sensitive to the dispersion below the median. By contrast, as α decreases the opposite is true, that is, the family becomes more sensitive to the cumulative probability mass at the bottom of the distribution. It is easy to show that the limiting case gives:

$$I_{1,1}(\mathbf{x}) = I_A(\mathbf{x}) = 1 - \frac{2\sum_{i=1}^{n}|P_i - 0.5| - 1}{n - 1},$$

referred to as the 'absolute value measure' (Abul Naga and Yalcin, 2008).

In many applied analyses, the population is split into groups according to social characteristics including region, race, gender, and so on. In these cases it is quite useful to invoke properties which allow the inequality in each group to be related to overall inequality. Imagine that we are interested in comparing the social inequality between men and women in a society. Imagine that M and W are the total population of men and women respectively. Let us denote by $\alpha = \frac{M}{W}$. Let x_1 and x_2 be the respective categorical distributions. It is clear that $\mathbf{x} = \alpha x_1 + (1 - \alpha)x_2$ corresponds to the categorical distribution of the whole population. Similarly, if P_1 and P_2 are the respective cumulative distributions then $P = \alpha P_1 + (1 - \alpha)P_2$ is the global cumulative distribution. The aggregativity axiom proposed by Shorrocks (1984) requires that the overall inequality can be represented as an increasing transformation of the subgroup inequalities. The counterpart of the aggregativity axiom for social inequality indices is introduced by Kobus and Milos (2012) as follows:

BOX 17.1   EXAMPLES OF SOCIAL INEQUALITY INDICES

$$I_{BL}(x) = 1 - \frac{4}{n-1}\sum_{i=1}^{n-1}(P_i - 0.5)^2$$

$$f_{BL}(t) = 1 - 4(t - 0.5)^2$$

$$I_1(x) = -\frac{1}{n-1}\sum_{i=1}^{n-1}[P_i\log_2 P_i + (1 - P_i)\log_2(1 - P_i)]$$

$$f_1(t) = -[t\log_2 t + (1 - t)\log_2(1 - t)]$$

$$I_2(x) = \frac{4}{n-1}\sum_{i=1}^{n-1} P_i(1 - P_i)$$

$$f_2(t) = 4t(1 - t)$$

$$I_3(x) = \frac{2}{n-1}\sqrt{P_i(1 - P_i)}$$

$$f_3(t) = 2\sqrt{t(1 - t)}$$

$$I_4(x) = 1 - \frac{1}{n-1}\sum_{i=1}^{n-1}|2P_i - 1|$$

$$f_4(t) = 1 - |2t - 1|$$

$$I_{\alpha,\beta}(x) = \frac{\sum_{i=1}^{m-1}(2P)^{\alpha} + \sum_{i-m}^{n}2(1 - P)^{\beta}}{n - 1},\ \alpha,\beta > 0$$

$$f_5(t) = \begin{cases} (2t)^{\alpha} & 0 \le t \le \dfrac{1}{2} \\ (2(1 - t))^{\beta} & \dfrac{1}{2} \le t \le 1 \end{cases} \quad \alpha,\beta > 0$$

Aggregativity (AGGR). A social inequality index $I: \Omega \times C \to \mathbb{R}$ is aggregative if there exists a function Q such that for any $\alpha \in (0,1)$ and for any $x, x_1, x_2 \in \Omega$ with $x = \alpha x_1 + (1 - \alpha)x_2$

$$I(x,c) = Q(I(x_1,c), I(x_2,c), \alpha, c)$$

where Q is continuous and strictly increasing in its first two arguments.

This axiom is interesting in applied analysis since it allows policy makers to target the groups in which inequality is particularly high in order to achieve a maximum reduction in inequality levels. Proposition 6 (Kobus and Milos, 2012) characterizes the aggregative social inequality indices:

Proposition 6. $I: \Omega \times C \to \mathbb{R}$ is an inequality index that satisfies CON, EQUAL, LNORM, HNORM, SCALINDEP and AGGR if and only if:

$$I(x,c) = \Delta\left(\sum_{i=1}^{n}a_i P_i\right)$$

for all $x \in \Omega$ and for all scales c, with $\Delta \mathbb{R} \rightarrow [0,1]$ a continuous function with $\Delta(\sum_{i=1}^{n} a_i \hat{P}_i) = 0$ and $\Delta(\sum_{i=1}^{n} a_i \bar{P}_i) = 1$. Moreover, either:

Δ is a strictly increasing function and $a_i \geq a_{i+1}$ when $i < m$ and $a_i \leq a_{i+1}$ when $i \geq m$
or:
Δ is a strictly decreasing function and $a_i \leq a_{i+1}$ when $i < m$ and $a_i \geq a_{i+1}$ when $i \geq m$

Among the indices listed in Box 17.1 only the absolute value measure I_{11} is aggregative.

17.2.5 An Alternative Approach for Measuring Inequality with Ordinal Data

The contributions reviewed so far suggest taking the median as equality reference point in the measurement of inequality of distributions in ordinal variables. In addition all the proposed measures are based on quantiles. Cowell and Flachaire (2017) have recently questioned this approach and propose instead three alternative ingredients in the measurement. First of all they introduce, for each individual i, that belongs to category $n(i)$, the status, which can be given by either the downward-looking version:

$$s_i = \sum_{l=1}^{n(i)} p_l$$

or by the upward-looking version:

$$s_i' = \frac{1}{n} \sum_{l=n(i)}^{n} p_l$$

In the two versions, individual i's status lies between 0 and 1. If everybody belongs to the same category – that is, in the case of perfect equality – then the two versions take the value 1. Thus, the second ingredient in their framework is proposing, as a equality reference point, not the median but the maximum possible value of status.

Finally, on the basis of some basic axioms they characterize the following family of inequality indices:

$$I_\alpha(s) = \begin{cases} \dfrac{1}{\alpha(\alpha-1)}\left[\dfrac{1}{n}\sum_{1 \leq i \leq n}(s_i^\alpha - 1)\right] & \text{if } \alpha \neq 0, \alpha < 1 \\ -\dfrac{1}{n}\sum_{1 \leq i \leq n} \log s_i & \text{if } \alpha = 0 \end{cases}$$

The α parameter captures the sensitivity of the index to the different parts of the distribution: the lower the value of the parameter, the more sensitive to part of the distribution close to 0.

This family, similar to the well-known 'generalized entropy' family in the income inequality setting, allows for inequality comparisons of distributions in ordinal variables.

17.3 MEASURING SOCIAL INEQUALITY WITH CARDINAL DATA

The previous section reviewed the measurement of social inequality with ordinal variables. When the data are cardinal, a different kind of problem appears. Distributions of health, education, and so on are usually represented by bounded variables. For any bounded variable that represents say the attainments, it is natural to define the corresponding shortfall variable as the difference between the bound and the attainment. Inequality comparisons across populations may not coincide for attainments and shortfalls. In fact, the inequality rankings will usually be reversed. As long as we compare populations with the same means, the standard dominance criteria guarantee that inequality dominance in the distribution of attainments coincides with that in the distribution of shortfalls (see Lambert and Zheng, 2011). But when the means differ, even in the simplest case with only two individuals, the results may not be robust. Consider the following two-person distributions: $\mathbf{x} = (35,15)$ and $\mathbf{y} = (65,35)$ displayed in Figure 17.4. The respective means are $\mu(\mathbf{x}) = 25$ and $\mu(\mathbf{y}) = 50$. In order to compare the inequality levels of these distributions some invariance condition needs to be invoked. Assume a relative point of view. Then distribution $\mathbf{x}$ is relative-equivalent to distribution $\mathbf{x}^* = (70,30)$. In a non-ambiguous way $\mathbf{x}^*$ is more unequal than $\mathbf{y}$. Thus the relative inequality level is higher in the first population than in the second. Now imagine that the bound is $\alpha = 100$ and focus

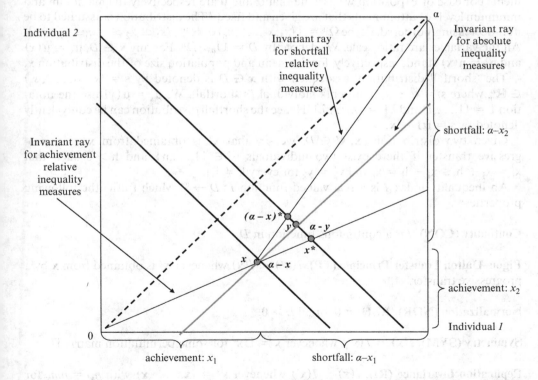

Figure 17.4   Relative and absolute invariance conditions for attainments and for shortfalls

on the shortfall side. The corresponding shortfall distributions are $\alpha - x = (65,85)$ and $\alpha - y = (35,65)$. Again, from a relative point of view the first situation is equivalent to $(\alpha - x)* = (43.3,56.6)$ which displays unambiguously less inequality than $\alpha - y$. Now the conclusion is that the inequality level is lower in the first population than in the second. Focusing either on attainments or on shortfalls leads to contradictory conclusions.

Note that in this case assuming an absolute point of view will lead to the same inequality rankings of attainments or of shortfalls. Indeed, from an absolute point of view, $x = (35,15)$ is equivalent to $x** = (60,40)$, more unequal than $y = (65,35)$. The respective shortfall distributions are $\alpha - x = (65,85)$, absolute equivalent to $(\alpha - x) = (40,60)$, still more unequal than $\alpha - y = (35,65)$.

As can be seen in Figure 17.4 the other intermediate invariant rays between relative and absolute yield contradictory results. Consequently, since the choice between the attainments and the shortfalls is arbitrary, it seems desirable that the evaluation of the inequality should be consistent whether working with attainments or with shortfalls. This section reviews the contributions to this matter.[6]

17.3.1   Notation

We consider a population consisting of $n \geq 2$ individuals. An 'attainment distribution' is represented by a vector $x = (x_1, x_2, \ldots, x_n)$, $\in \mathbb{R}^n_{++}$ where x_i represents individual i's attainment. For ease of exposition we assume that α and 0 are respectively the maximum and minimum levels of attainments that are given and fixed.[7] The distribution is assumed to be non-decreasingly ordered. Let be $\Omega^n = \{(x_1, x_2, \ldots, x_n) \in \mathbb{R}^n_{++} / x_1 \leq x_2 \leq \ldots \leq x_n < \alpha\}$. All the variables are ratio-scale. We denote by $D = \cup_{n \geq 2} \Omega^n$. For any $x \in D$, $\mu_x = \mu(x)$ and $n_x = n(x)$ stand, respectively, for the mean and population size of the distribution x.

The 'shortfall distribution' associated with $x \in D$ is denoted by $s = (s_1, s_2, \ldots, s_n) \in \mathbb{R}^n_+$, where $s_i = \alpha - x_i$ represents individual i's shortfall. We $\mu_x = \mu(x)$ use the notation $1 = (1, \ldots, 1)$ and $\lambda 1 = (\lambda, \ldots, \lambda)$. Hence the shortfall distribution can be equivalently denoted by $s = \alpha 1 - x$.

Given two distributions $x, x' \in D$, we say that x' is obtained from x by a progressive transfer if there exist two individuals $i, j \in \{1, \ldots, n\}$ and $h > 0$ such that $x'_i = x_i + h \leq x_j - h = x'_j$ and $y'_k = y_k$ for every $k \neq i, j$.

An inequality index I is a real valued function $I : D \to \mathbb{R}$ which fulfils the following properties:

Continuity (CON). I is a continuous function in D.

Pigou–Dalton Transfer Principle (TP). $I(x') < I(x)$ whenever x' is obtained from x by a progressive transfer.

Normalization (NOR). $I(\lambda 1) = 0$ for all $\lambda > 0$.

Symmetry (SYM). $I(x) = I(x')$ whenever $x = \Pi x'$ for some permutation matrix Π.

Replication Invariance (RI). $I(x) = I(x')$ whenever $x' = (x, x, \ldots, x)$ with $n_{x'} = mn_x$ for some positive integer m.

The crucial axiom in inequality measurement is the Pigou–Dalton transfer principle which requires that a transfer from a richer person to a poorer one decreases inequality. In addition, the indices are usually assumed to be normalized with the inequality level equal to 0 when everybody has exactly the same distribution value. Symmetry establishes that the inequality index should be insensitive to a reordering of the individuals. Finally, replication invariance allows populations of different sizes to be compared. These four properties are considered to be inherent to the concept of inequality and have come to be accepted as basic properties for an inequality index.

In empirical applications, the population is often classified into groups. In order to relate the overall inequality to the inequality in each group, Shorrocks (1980) introduces the decomposability property that requires the overall inequality may be decomposed as the sum of the between- and the within-group components.[8] The between-group component is defined as the inequality level of a hypothetical distribution in which each person's value is replaced by the mean of their subgroup. The within-group component is a weighted sum of the subgroup inequality levels.

To formalize this property, assume that a population of n individuals is split into $K \geq 2$ mutually exclusive subgroups with distribution $\mathbf{x}^j = (\mathbf{x}^j_1, \ldots, \mathbf{x}^j_{n_j})$, where $\mu_j = \mu(\mathbf{x}^j)$ denotes the mean of the jth subgroup and $n_j = n(\mathbf{x}^j)$ represents its size for all $j = 1, \ldots, K$. Let inequality in group j be written $I_j = I(\mathbf{x}^j)$. Let us denote by $\mathbf{x}^B = (\mu_1 \mathbf{1}_{n_1}, \ldots, \mu_K \mathbf{1}_{n_K})$ the distribution in which each person's value is replaced by the respective subgroup mean.

Decomposability (DECOMP). An index I is decomposable if the following relationship holds:

$$I(\mathbf{x}^1, \ldots, \mathbf{x}^K) = I(\mathbf{x}^W) + I(\mathbf{x}^B)$$
$$= \sum_{j=1}^{K} w^j(\mu_1, \ldots, \mu_K; n_1, \ldots, n_K) I(\mathbf{x}^j) + I(\mu_1 \mathbf{1}_{n_1}, \ldots, \mu_K \mathbf{1}_{n_K})$$

where $w^j(\mu_1, \ldots, \mu_K; n_1, \ldots, n_K) \geq 0$ is the weight on subgroup j's inequality level $I_j = I(\mathbf{x}^j)$ in the within-group term $j = 1, \ldots, K$.

Some popular indices, as the Gini coefficient, are not decomposable. Ebert (2010) suggests a weak decomposable axiom as follows:

Weak Decomposability (WDECOMP). An inequality index $I: D \to \mathbb{R}$ is weak-decomposable if for every $n = (n_1, n_2)$, where $n_1 > 1$ are $n_2 > 1$ are integers, there exist positive weight functions $w^1(n_1, n_2)$, $w^2(n_1, n_2)$ and $u(n_1, n_2)$ such that:

$$I(\mathbf{x}^1, \mathbf{x}^2) = w^1(n_1, n_2) I(\mathbf{x}^1) + w^2(n_1, n_2) I(\mathbf{x}^2) + u(n_1, n_2) + \sum_{1 \leq i \leq n_1} \sum_{1 \leq j \leq n_2} I(x^1_i, x^2_j)$$

where $\mathbf{x}^l$ is any arbitrary distribution over the population with size n_l with $l = 1, 2$.

Ebert (2010) characterizes the weak decomposable inequality indices that satisfy normalization and replication invariance.

Table 17.1   (λη) inequality orderings

	η=0	0<η<1	η=1
λ=0	Absolute	Absolute	Absolute
0<λ<1	Absolute	Zoli	Krtscha
λ=1	Absolute	Besley and Preston/ Pfingsten	Relative

17.3.2   Standard Inequality Procedures for Measuring Social Inequality with Bounded Cardinal Data

In order to compare distributions with different means, we need to assume some invariance criteria. Zoli (1999) proposes an inequality partial ordering in terms of two parameters $\lambda \in [0,1]$ and $\eta \in [0,1]$ that includes the relative, the absolute and the intermediate inequality orderings proposed by Pfingsten (1986), Bossert and Pfingsten (1990), Besley and Preston (1988) and Krtscha (1994). According to Zoli (1999) we get the following definition:

Definition 6. Given $\mathbf{z}, \mathbf{w} \in \Omega^n$, $\mathbf{z}$ is unambiguously less *(λη)* unequal than $\mathbf{w}$ if and only if $(\mathbf{z} - \mu(\mathbf{z})\mathbf{1})/(\eta\mu(\mathbf{z}) + (1 - \eta))^\lambda$ generalized Lorenz dominates $(\mathbf{w} - \mu(\mathbf{w})\mathbf{1})/(\eta\mu(\mathbf{w}) + (1 - \eta))^\lambda$. Vectors $\mathbf{z}$ and $\mathbf{w}$ are said to be *(λη)* inequality-equivalent if each weakly dominates the other in the sense of the specific partial ordering.

Table 17.1 displays the different invariance criteria according to the values of the parameters λ and η. Specifically, each of the cases $\lambda = 0$ and $\eta = 0$ corresponds to the absolute inequality criterion. When $\eta = 1$ the relative criterion is obtained for $\lambda = 1$, whereas for $0 < \lambda < 1$ we get the Krtscha (1994) intermediate point of view.

Proposition 7 below, proved by Lambert and Zheng (2011), establishes that apart from the absolute criterion, that is, when $\lambda\eta = 0$, no consistency is obtained. In other words, absolute dominance in terms of attainments guarantees absolute dominance in terms of shortfalls (Proposition 8), whereas for the rest, it is always possible to choose distributions that reverse the rankings (Proposition 9):

Proposition 7. If $\mathbf{x}$ and $\mathbf{y}$ are (λη) inequality equivalent for the Zoli partial inequality ordering with parameters $\lambda \in [0,1]$ and $\eta \in [0,1]$ then:

1. if $\lambda\eta = 0, \mathbf{s}_x = \alpha\mathbf{1} - \mathbf{x}$ and $\mathbf{s}_y = \alpha\mathbf{1} - \mathbf{y}$ are (λη) inequality equivalent;
2. if $\lambda\eta \neq 0$, $\mathbf{s}_x = \alpha\mathbf{1} - \mathbf{x}$ has unambiguously less (λη) inequality than $\mathbf{s}_y = \alpha\mathbf{1} - \mathbf{y}$ if $\mu(\mathbf{x}) < \mu(\mathbf{y})$ and $\mathbf{s}_x = \alpha\mathbf{1} - \mathbf{x}$ has unambiguously more (λη) inequality than $\mathbf{s}_y = \alpha\mathbf{1} - \mathbf{y}$ if $\mu(\mathbf{x}) > \mu(\mathbf{y})$.

Proposition 8. For the absolute inequality concept, $\mathbf{x}$ is unambiguously less unequal than $\mathbf{y}$ if and only if $\mathbf{s}_x = \alpha\mathbf{1} - \mathbf{x}$ is unambiguously less unequal than $\mathbf{s}_y = \alpha\mathbf{1} - \mathbf{y}$.

Proposition 9. Let I be an inequality index which respects the Zoli partial inequality ordering with parameters $\lambda \in [0,1]$ and $\eta \in [0,1]$ with $\lambda\eta \neq 0$. Distributions of attainments $\mathbf{x}$ and $\mathbf{y}$ can be found for which $I(\mathbf{x}) \leq I(\mathbf{y})$ and $I(\alpha\mathbf{1} - \mathbf{x}) > I(\alpha\mathbf{1} - \mathbf{y})$.

17.3.3 Inequality Indices for Measuring Social Inequality with Bounded Cardinal Data

With respect to the inequality indices, Lambert and Zheng (2011) introduce the next consistency criterion:

Definition 7. An inequality index I measures attainment inequality and shortfall inequality consistently if $I(\mathbf{x}) < I(\mathbf{y}) \Leftrightarrow I(\alpha\mathbf{1} - \mathbf{x}) < I(\alpha\mathbf{1} - \mathbf{y})$ for all $\mathbf{x}, \mathbf{y} \in D$.

A stronger requirement is introduced by Erreygers (2009b), demanding that the inequality of attainments and the inequality of shortfalls should coincide:

Definition 8. An inequality index I is complementary if $I(\mathbf{x}) = I(\alpha\mathbf{1} - \mathbf{x})$ for all $\mathbf{x} \in D$.

Lambert and Zheng (2011) aim at characterizing consistent inequality indices. They carry out the characterization among two specific families of inequality indices defined as follows:

Definition 9.

1. A rank-independent index of absolute inequality I_{RI} takes the form:

$$I_{RI}(\mathbf{x}) = \frac{1}{n}\sum_{1 \leq i \leq n} u(x_i - \mu(\mathbf{x}))$$

for $\mathbf{x} \in \Omega^n$, where $u: \widetilde{\mathbb{R}} \to \widetilde{\mathbb{R}}$ is strictly convex and twice differentiable and $u(0) = 0$.
2. A rank-dependent index of absolute inequality I_{RD} takes the form:

$$I_{RD}(\mathbf{x}) = \frac{1}{n}\sum_{1 \leq i \leq n} w(p_i)(x_i - \mu(\mathbf{x}))$$

for $\mathbf{x} \in \Omega^{*n}$, where $p_i = (2i - 1)/2n$ is the rank of x_i and $w: [0,1] \to \mathbb{R}$ is strictly increasing.

Proposition 10. $I_{RI}(\mathbf{x})$ measures attainment inequality and shortfall inequality consistently if and only if $u(t) = u(-t)$ for all $t \neq 0$. Then $I_{RI}(\mathbf{x}) = I_{RI}(\alpha\mathbf{1} - \mathbf{x})$.

$I_{RD}(\mathbf{x})$ measures attainment inequality and shortfall inequality consistently if and only if $w(1 - p) = -w(p)$ for all $p \in [0,1]$. Then $I_{RD}(\mathbf{x}) = I_{RD}(\alpha\mathbf{1} - \mathbf{x})$.

Proposition 10 shows that, despite assuming only consistency, all the indices turn out to be complementary. All the functions $u(t) = t^{2k}$, where k is a positive integer, satisfy the criterion in part 1 of Definition 9. In these cases $I_{RI}(\mathbf{x})$ is the $(2k)$th central moment of $\mathbf{x}$. When $k = 1$ we get the variance. In turn, if $w(p) = 2p - 1$, the criterion in part (b) is satisfied. In this case $I_{RD}(\mathbf{x})$ is the absolute Gini coefficient of $\mathbf{x}$.[9] Note that the only decomposable consistent index obtained is the variance.

As mentioned, Ebert (2010) characterizes the inequality indices that are weakly decomposable. In a recent work Chakravarty et al. (2016) show the implication of imposing an absolute point of view. They establish the following result:

Proposition 11. Let I: $D \rightarrow \mathbb{R}$ be an inequality index that satisfies NOR for any two-person society. Then I is an absolute index that satisfies CON, SYM, RI and WDECOMP if and only if:

$$I_\psi(\mathbf{x}) = \frac{2}{n^2} \sum_{1 \le i \le n} \sum_{1 \le j \le n} \psi(|x_i - x_j|)$$

where ψ: $D \rightarrow \mathbb{R}$ a continuous function with $\psi(0) = 0$. In addition, I_ψ satisfies TP if and only if the function ψ is non-decreasing.

All the indices of the family are complementary. Note that when $\psi(t) = t$ we get four times the absolute Gini coefficient, whereas for $\psi(t) = t^2$ the variance is found.

17.3.4 A Unified Framework for Measuring Social Inequality with Bounded Cardinal Data

The previous section has reviewed how the standard inequality procedures behave when the distributions are bounded. It is concluded that only the absolute invariant criterion may rank the distributions of attainments and of shortfalls consistently.

Lasso de la Vega and Aristondo (2012), Aristondo and Lasso de la Vega (2013) and Kjellsson and Gerdtham (2013) propose an alternative framework in which attainment and shortfall distributions can be jointly analysed. Whereas the first two introduce indicators for doing so, Kjellsson and Gerdtham (2013) focus on the criteria of invariance that should be satisfied.

Aristondo and Lasso de la Vega (2013) consider the distributions of attainments and shortfalls jointly and evaluate the inequality as the divergence between the joint distribution and the hypothetical situation in which all the individuals enjoy the mean. In other words, they propose evaluating the divergence between the distributions $(\mathbf{x}, \alpha 1 - \mathbf{x})$ and $(\mu(\mathbf{x})1, (\alpha - \mu(\mathbf{x}))1)$. Assessing these divergences imposes a value judgement since it is crucial to determine what distributional changes guarantee that the divergences do not vary and, consequently, the inequality level remains unaltered.

Joint distributions of attainments and shortfalls are defined from points of view consistent with concerns for relative, absolute or intermediate inequality within Zoli's (1999) framework.[10] The $(\lambda\eta)$ joint distribution is defined as follows:

$$\mathbf{x}_{\lambda\eta} = \left(\frac{\mathbf{x} - \mu(\mathbf{x})1}{(\eta\mu(\mathbf{x}) + (1 - \eta))^\lambda} + 1, \frac{(\alpha 1 - \mathbf{x}) - (\alpha - \mu(\mathbf{x}))1}{(\eta(\alpha - \mu(\mathbf{x})) + (1 - \eta))^\lambda} + 1 \right)$$

All these distributions have a mean equal to 1.

Once the divergence between the joint and the reference mean distributions is introduced, the standard inequality measures will evaluate this divergence. Consider an inequality measure $I_{\lambda\eta}$ invariant according to the $(\lambda\eta)$ invariance condition, and, for any given $\mathbf{x} \in D$, the joint distribution $\mathbf{x}_{\lambda\eta}$. If we are interested in analysing simultaneously the attainment and the shortfall inequality from a $(\lambda\eta)$ invariant point of view, we may think of applying inequality measure $I_{\lambda\eta}$ to joint distribution $\mathbf{x}_{\lambda\eta}$.

Specifically, Aristondo and Lasso de la Vega (2013) propose considering the joint indicator associated with $I_{\lambda\eta}$, denoted by $I_{\lambda\eta}^J$, as the indicator that, for each distribution $\mathbf{x} \in D$, takes the following value:

$$I_{\lambda\eta}^J(\mathbf{x}) = I_{\lambda\eta}(\mathbf{x}_{\lambda\eta})$$

Proposition 12 below states that some properties fulfilled by $I_{\lambda\eta}$ are inherited by the joint indicators:

Proposition 12. If $I_{\lambda\eta}$ is a $(\lambda\eta)$ invariant inequality measure satisfying CON, TP, SYM, RI and NOR the joint indicator associated, $I_{\lambda\eta}^J$, also satisfies CON, TP, SYM, RI and NOR. In addition $I_{\lambda\eta}^J(\mathbf{x}) = I_{\lambda\eta}^J(\alpha\mathbf{1} - \mathbf{x})$ for any distribution $\mathbf{x} \in D$.

The joint indicator $I_{\lambda\eta}^J$ satisfies all the properties usually assumed for an inequality measure and so it captures the joint distribution inequality.

Since $I_{\lambda\eta}^J(\mathbf{x}) = I_{\lambda\eta}^J(\alpha\mathbf{1} - \mathbf{x})$, Proposition 1 allows the derivation of complementary indices according to Erreygers' designation, both rank-dependent and rank-independent.

Lasso de la Vega and Aristondo (2012) also propose complementary indicators taking the generalized mean of the inequality of attainments and inequality of shortfalls. In particular, the arithmetic mean indicator associated with an inequality index has the following form:

$$I^1(\mathbf{x}) = \frac{I(\mathbf{x}) + I(\alpha\mathbf{1} - \mathbf{x})}{2}$$

Proposition 13 below shows that the joint indicator $I_{\lambda\eta}^J$ associated with a decomposable index $I_{\lambda\eta}$ is exactly the arithmetic mean indicator associated with $I_{\lambda\eta}$:

Proposition 13. If $I_{\lambda\eta}$ is a $\lambda\eta$ invariant decomposable inequality measure then:

$$I_{\lambda\eta}^J(\mathbf{x}) = I_{\lambda\eta}^1(\mathbf{x}) = \frac{I_{\lambda\eta}(\mathbf{x}) + I_{\lambda\eta}(\alpha\mathbf{1} - \mathbf{x})}{2}$$

for any distribution $\mathbf{x} \in D$.

Since the decomposable relative, absolute and Bossert–Pfingsten type of intermediate inequality measures are characterized,[11] Proposition 13 provides quite an easy way to compute the joint indicators associated to the members of these families.

Now we focus on these specific joint indicators associated with decomposable measures. Following Kjellsson and Gerdtham (2013), their behaviour under equi-proportionate changes in attainments and in shortfalls is analysed.[12] Consider an equi-proportional increase in attainments. For any $\theta > 0$ such that $\mathbf{x} + \theta\mathbf{x} \in D$ we find:

$$I^J_{\lambda\eta}(x + \theta x) = \frac{I_{\lambda\eta}(x + \theta x) + I_{\lambda\eta}(\alpha 1 - (x + \theta x))}{2}$$

Equi-proportional decreases in shortfalls lead to:

$$I^J_{\lambda\eta}(x + \theta(\alpha 1 - x)) = \frac{I_{\lambda\eta}(x + \theta(\alpha 1 - x)) + I_{\lambda\eta}((\alpha 1 - x) - \theta(\alpha 1 - x))}{2}$$

for all $\theta > 0$ such that $x + \theta(\alpha 1 - x) \in D$.

We get the following proposition (Aristondo and Lasso de la Vega, 2013):

Proposition 14. If $I_{\lambda\eta}$ is a $\lambda\eta$ invariant decomposable inequality measure then for any distribution $x \in D$

1. $I^J_{\lambda\eta}(x) \leq I^J_{\lambda\eta}(x + \theta x)$ for all $\theta > 0$ with $x + \theta x \in D$, and
2. $I^J_{\lambda\eta}(x) \geq I^J_{\lambda\eta}(x + \theta(\alpha 1 - x))$ for all $\theta > 0$ with $x + \theta(\alpha 1 - x) \in D$.

In words, the joint indicators associated with $\lambda\eta$ invariant decomposable measures do not decrease under equi-proportional increases in attainments, and do not increase under equi-proportional decreases in shortfalls. They are *hs*-relative indicators according to Kjellsson–Gerdtham's designation. As stressed by Kjellsson and Gerdtham (2013, p. 8), the *hs*-relative invariant condition represents 'a new compromise concept for a bounded variable by explicitly considering the two relative invariance equivalent criteria, defined with respect to attainments and shortfalls, to represent the polar cases of defensible positions'.

As mentioned before, measuring inequality with a decomposable index allows policy makers to target the subgroups in which inequality is higher. The following proposition shows that for any point of view assumed, it is always possible to find joint indicators that are decomposable:

Proposition 15. The joint indicators associated with the second Theil measure, GE_0, variance and the members of the BP family $BP_{\beta,0}$ are decomposable measures.

In all cases the weights on subgroup j's inequality level for which the respective decomposable decompositions hold are $w^j = n_j/n$.

As proved in the proposition, the weights in the within-group component depend only on the subgroup population shares. Then the decomposition satisfies the path independence property (Foster and Shneyerov, 2000). This means that the variations in between-group inequality as measured by these indices do not affect the within-group term, contrary to what happens with most of the decompositions.

17.4 CONCLUDING COMMENTS

The first attempts to measure inequality of distributions of social variables, including health status, educational attainments, life expectancy, mortality rate, and so on, used the tools developed for the measurement of income inequality. However, in contrast with the income, these social variables are usually measured either on ordinal scales or on bounded variables. Yet ordinal scales have no cardinal meaning and the role played by the mean as the equality reference point is no longer appropriate. Besides, the Pigou–Dalton principle simply cannot be applied. In turn, bounded variables can be represented in terms of attainment towards the perfect state or shortfalls from that value, but the inequality rankings may change when focusing either on the attainment side or on the shortfall side. These peculiar characteristics of social variables have led researchers to question the adequacy of the standard inequality tools and to propose more appropriate ones. This chapter has consisted of two main sections. Section 17.2 has reviewed the alternative approaches suggested hitherto for capturing dispersion in the distributions with ordinal variables. In turn, section 17.3 has summarized the problems that appear and the procedures focused on identifying inequality measures that are not sensitive to whether the outcomes are represented by attainments or by shortfalls.

ACKNOWLEDGEMENTS

The author acknowledges the support of the Spanish Ministerio de Educación y Ciencia under project ECO2015-67519-P and the Gobierno Vasco, under the project IT568-13. The author is indebted to Oscar Volij for his help and support.

NOTES

1. For instance, van Doorslaer and Jones (2003) and Wagstaff and van Doorslaer (1994) survey most of these methods.
2. See, for example, Kakwani (1980), van Doorslaer and Jones (2003), Allison and Foster (2004), Erreygers (2009a) and Zheng (2008). This difficulty also appears with the dominance criteria as shown by Zheng (2008).
3. See, for example, Kakwani (1980), van Doorslaer and Jones (2003), Allison and Foster (2004), Erreygers (2009a) and Zheng (2008).
4. A thorough introduction to the literature on income distributions and to the various Lorenz dominances can be found in Lambert (2001).
5. As usual $>AF$ and $\sim AF$ will represent the asymmetric and symmetric parts of $\geqslant_{AF}$.
6. This section focuses on the results obtained when the same inequality index is used to measure distributions of achievements and shortfalls corresponding to the same attribute. Bosmans (2016) introduces an interesting alternative framework in which different measures for each of these two distributions are allowed.
7. Lasso de la Vega and Aristondo (2012) derive conditions that guarantee robustness when the bounds change.
8. It is clear that the decomposability property is stronger than the aggregativity axiom introduced by Shorrocks (1984) and mentioned in subsection 17.2.4.
9. Erreygers (2009b) also characterizes two complementary indices that are minor variations of the variance and the absolute Gini coefficient.
10. Although this definition is a bit more general than the one introduced in Aristondo and Lasso de la Vega (2013), it is straightforward to show that all their results hold in this setting.
11. Shorrocks (1980) showed that the only family of relative decomposable inequality measures is the generalized

entropy (GE) family. Specifically, the second Theil measure is defined by $GE_0(\mathbf{x}) = \sum_{i=1}^{n} \ln(\mu(\mathbf{x})/x_i)/n$. Chakravarty and Tyagarupananda (1998) in a differentiable framework, and Bosmans and Cowell (2010) in a continuous one, characterize the family of absolute decomposable inequality measures. The variance, given by $\mathbf{V}(\mathbf{x}) = \sum_{i=1}^{n}(x_i - \mu(\mathbf{x}))^2/n$, belongs to this family. Finally, Chakravarty and Tyagarupananda (2009) prove that the unique decomposable Bossert-Pfingsten type of intermediate inequality measures is a two-parameter transformation of the GE family. The eminent member that will play a role will be $BP_{\beta,0}(\mathbf{x}) = \frac{1}{n}\sum_{i=1}^{n} \ln(\frac{\mu(\mathbf{x}) + c}{x_i + c})$ where $c = (1-\beta)/\beta$ and $0 < \beta < 1$.

12. Specifically, they formalize a new criterion of invariance considering the two equi-proportional distribution changes, with regard to attainments and to shortfalls, respectively, as the extreme cases.

REFERENCES

Abul Naga, R.H. and T. Yalcin (2008), Inequality measurement for ordered response health data. *Journal of Health Economics*, 27, 1614–1625.

Allison, R.A. and J.E. Foster (2004), Measuring health inequality using qualitative data. *Journal of Health Economics*, 23, 505–552.

Aristondo, O. and C. Lasso de la Vega (2013), Measuring the inequality of bounded distributions: a joint analysis of attainments and shortfalls. *Research on Economic Inequality*, 21, 33–52.

Besley, T.J. and I.P. Preston (1988), Invariance and the axiomatics of income tax progression: a comment. *Bulletin of Economic Research*, 40, 159–163.

Blair, J. and M.G. Lacy (2000), Statistics of ordinal variation. *Sociological Methods and Research*, 28, 251–280.

Bosmans, K. (2016), Consistent comparisons of attainment and shortfall inequality: a critical examination. *Health Economics*, 25, 1425–1432.

Bosmans, K. and F. Cowell (2010), The class of absolute decomposable inequality measures. *Economics Letters*, 109, 154–156.

Bossert, W. and A. Pfingsten (1990), Intermediate inequality: concepts, indices and welfare implications. *Mathematical Social Sciences*, 19, 117–134.

Chakravarty, S. and S. Tyagarupananda (1998), The subgroup decomposable absolute indices of inequality. In S.R. Chakravarty, D. Coondoo and R. Mukherjee (eds), *Quantitative Economics: Theory and Practice, Essays in Honor of Professor N. Bhattacharya*, Allied Publishers, New Delhi, pp. 247–257.

Chakravarty, S. and S. Tyagarupananda (2009), The subgroup decomposable intermediate indices of inequality. *Spanish Economic Review*, 11, 83–97.

Chakravarty, S.R., N. Chattopadhyay and C. D'Ambroiso (2016), On a family of achievement and shortfall inequality indices. *Health Economics*, 25, 1503–1513.

Clarke, P.M., U.G. Gerdtham, M. Johannesson, K. Bingefors and L. Smith (2002), On the measurement of relative and absolute income-related health inequality. *Social Science and Medicine*, 55, 1923–1928.

Cowell, F.A. and E. Flachaire (2017), Inequality with ordinal data. *Economica*, 84, 290–321.

Ebert, U. (2010), The decomposition of inequality reconsidered: weakly decomposable measures. *Mathematical Social Sciences*, 60, 94–103.

Erreygers, G. (2009a), Correcting the concentration index. *Journal of Health Economics*, 28, 504–515.

Erreygers, G. (2009b), Can a single indicator measure both attainment and shortfall inequality?. *Journal of Health Economics*, 28, 885–893.

Fleurbaey, M. and E. Schokkaert (2012), Equity in health and health care. In Mark V. Pauly, Thomas G. Mcguire and Pedro P. Barros (eds), *Handbook of Health Economics*, Vol. 2, Elsevier B.V., pp. 1003–1092. https://www.elsevier.com/books/handbook-of-health-economics/pauly/978-0-444-53592-4.

Foster, J. and A. Shneyerov (2000), Path independent inequality measures. *Journal of Economic Theory*, 91, 199–222.

Kakwani, N.C. (1980), *Income Inequality and Poverty: Methods of Estimation and Policy Applications*, Oxford University Press, Oxford.

Kjellsson, G. and U.G. Gerdtham (2013), Lost in translation – rethinking the inequality equivalence for bounded health variables. *Research on Economic Inequality*, 21, 3–32.

Kobus, M. and P. Milos (2012), Inequality decomposition by population subgroups for ordinal data. *Journal of Health Economics*, 31, 15–21.

Krtscha, M. (1994), A new compromise measure of inequality. In W. Eichhorn (ed.), *Models and Measurement of Welfare and Inequality*, Springer, Heidelberg, pp. 111–119.

Lambert, P. (2001), *The Distribution and Redistribution of Income*, 3rd edn, Manchester University Press, Manchester.

Lambert, P. and B. Zheng (2011), On the consistent measurement of attainment and shortfall inequality. *Journal of Health Economics*, 30, 214–219.

Lasso de la Vega, C. and O. Aristondo (2012), Proposing indicators to measure achievement and shortfall inequality consistently. *Journal of Health Economics*, 31, 578–583.

Lazar, A. and J. Silber (2013), On the cardinal measurement of health inequality when only ordinal information is available on individual health status. *Health Economics*, 22, 106–113.

O'Donnell, O., E. van Doorslaer, A. Wagstaff and M. Lindelow (2008), Analyzing health equity using household survey data. World Bank, Washington, DC.

Pfingsten, A. (1986), Distributionally-neutral tax changes for different inequality concepts. *Journal of Public Economics*, 30, 385–393.

Reardon, S.F. (2009), Measures of ordinal segregation. In J. Bishop (ed.) *Occupational and Residential Segregation*, Research on Economic Inequality series, Vol. 17, Emerald, Bingley, pp.129–155.

Shorrocks, A.F. (1980), The class of additively decomposable inequality measures. *Econometrica*, 48, 613–625.

Shorrocks, A.F. (1984), Inequality decomposition by population subgroups. *Econometrica*, 52, 1369–1385.

van Doorslaer, E. and A.M. Jones (2003), Inequalities in self-reported health: validation of a new approach to measurement. *Journal of Health Economics*, 22, 61–87.

van Doorslaer, E. and T. van Ourti (2011), Measuring inequality and inequity in health and health care. In P. Smith and S. Glied (eds), *The Oxford Handbook of Health Economics*, Oxford University Press, Oxford, pp.837–869.

Wagstaff, A. and E. van Doorslaer (1994), Measuring inequalities in health in the presence of multiple category morbidity indicators. *Health Economics*, 3, 281–291.

Wagstaff, A. and E. van Doorslaer (2000), Equity in health care finance and delivery. In A.J. Culyer and J.P. Newhouse (eds), *Handbook of Health Economics*, Vol. 1B, Elsevier/North-Holland, Amsterdam, pp.1803–1862.

Zheng, B. (2008), Measuring inequality with ordinal data: a note. *Research on Economic Inequality*, 16, 177–188.

Zoli, C. (1999), A generalized version of the inequality equivalence criterion: a surplus sharing characterization, complete and partial orderings. In H. de Swart (ed.), *Logic, Game Theory and Social Choice*, University Press, Tilburg, pp.427–441.

18. Social inequality: empirical findings
Indranil Dutta and Gaston Yalonetzky

18.1 INTRODUCTION

In recent years, especially since the 2008 Global Financial Crisis, socioeconomic inequality has soared to the front pages of the public discourse.[1] Furious debates have taken place in our public forums and sometimes violent skirmishes have erupted in the streets from heated sentiments around inequality.

In addition to income and wealth inequalities, academics, policy-makers and lay people have long expressed concerns over other forms of inequality, generally referred to as 'social inequality'. However, there is a broad range of interpretations about what social inequality stands for, which can be both complementary and legitimate notions of the concept. For example, in chapter 17 in this *Handbook*, Lasso de la Vega interprets social inequality as notions and measurements of inequality over non-monetary dimensions of life, for example health, education, subjective well-being, and so on. By contrast, other people define social inequality as the uneven distribution of a valuable well-being attribute (for example, income, health) across social groups.[2] More recently the interest in between-group inequality has arisen both through the literature on so-called horizontal inequality and its relationship to social conflict (see Esteban and Ray, 2008; Stewart, 2009; Dutta et al., 2014), and also the literature on inequality of opportunity, where the groups are typically defined by circumstances beyond the individuals' control.

The aim of this chapter is to review some of the main recent contributions in the empirical literature on social inequality. We start with the interpretation of Lasso de la Vega (Chapter 17 in this *Handbook*) and review empirical papers which have applied recent measurement techniques for: (1) ordinal data; and (2) bounded cardinal data. Then we follow the more traditional interpretation and review some of the recent work on between-group inequality. We divide the latter area by the type of data, as the methods required for cardinal and ordinal variables are different. We also illustrate some of the measurement methods with our own empirical cases. However, we do not review the rich literature on inequality of opportunity, since it has been covered very competently by Roemer and Trannoy (2015).

In a broad sense the traditional interpretation of social inequality reflects the gap between groups which might be indicative of a systematic bias. Intrinsically thus the focus on group inequality becomes more imperative vis-à-vis interpersonal inequality. According to Stewart et al. (2005) there are also strong instrumental reasons encompassing both efficiency and distributional concerns to focus on group inequality. The efficiency aspect of social inequality arises from the fact that talented individuals belonging to a particular disadvantaged group might be constrained and hence unable to contribute their maximum potential. Affirmative actions to counter group inequalities, such as those in the US, have been efficiency-enhancing (Badgett and Hartmann, 1995; Holzer and Neumark, 2000). When it comes to distributional issues, there are theoretical reasons and empirical evidence to the effect that distributional concerns can engender social conflict. Persistence of group inequality in the future also brings about conflict. In fact Acemoglu and Robinson (2012) argue that it is the threat of unrest arising from social inequality that leads to the evolution of the more egalitarian institutions. Thus it is no surprise that Majumdar and Subramanian (2011, p. 105) claim that social inequality 'is politically more salient and consequential than are interpersonal disparities'.

Since social inequality measures the difference between the groups, it is inevitably dependent on how the groups are defined. It is therefore possible that for the same outcome variable, social inequality can be high according to one definition of groups, while low if we change the definition. These various possibilities reflect that individuals do not necessarily belong to one group but identify themselves with multiple groups. In this chapter, however, we take the group formations as given. For our empirical exercise we shall explore inequality using different definitions of groups.

While the popular discourse has focused mainly on income inequality, the notion of social inequality can encompass inequality over a broader range of outcomes such as health, education and happiness (Lasso de la Vega, Chapter 17 in this *Handbook*). For example, Dorling (2011) highlights the importance of education as an important reason for the persistence of social inequality. Many of these variables, such as health and happiness, are ordinal in nature. While we can apply standard inequality measures and group decomposition techniques to measure social inequality for cardinal variables, it is significantly more challenging to measure inequality for ordinal variables. One goal of the chapter is to illustrate how practitioners have implemented some of the methods in detail.

A prominent theme in social inequality is the presence of the so-called gradients: for example, the well-documented health gradient across income groups (Marmot, 2005). The measurement of this phenomenon has been formalised through concentration curves (Kakwani et al., 1997). However, concentration curves may not be an appropriate technique when the variable of interest is ordinal. We describe some new results in this area.

The rest of the chapter proceeds as follows. After a brief section where the notation is introduced, section 18.3 reviews applications of methods for the measurement of inequality with ordinal data. This section, firstly, mentions cardinalisation methods briefly, in order to then move on to the ordinal frameworks of: (1) Allison and Foster (2004); (2) Abul Naga and Yalcin (2008), Lazar and Silber (2013); and (3) Cowell and Flachaire (2012). A subsection also discusses recent methods to measure between-group, or socio-economic, inequality with ordinal data by Zheng (2011) and Apouey and Silber (2013). Then section 18.4 provides brief methodological discussions and empirical illustrations of between-group inequality methods for cardinal data. We first discuss methods for socio-economic inequality when groups are defined by unordered variables. Then we move on to methods for between-group inequality when the socioeconomic group is defined by a continuous variable. A final subsection discusses empirical papers on between-group inequality with bounded cardinal variables. The chapter concludes with some final remarks.

18.2 NOTATION

Consider a society with n individuals with achievements $(x_1, x_2, \ldots, x_n)$ along some dimension such as income or health or happiness. Let there be G socioeconomic groups with population $(n_1, n_2, \ldots, n_G)$ and population share is $(s_1, s_2, \ldots, s_G)$, where $s_l = n_l/n$ and $n = \sum_{l=1}^{G} n_l$. These socioeconomic groups could also be ranked in an increasing order if we consider the groups in terms of income, or a similar variable with higher and lower values. On the other hand, if we consider the groups in terms of say ethnicity, geographical regions, or any other variable with unordered categories, such rankings of the groups are not possible. For achievements such as income, which can be measured in terms of cardinal numbers, let the average achievement of the groups in that dimension be given as $(\bar{x}_1, \bar{x}_2, \ldots, \bar{x}_G)$. The average achievement across the whole population is: $\bar{x} \equiv \sum_{i=1}^{G} s_i \bar{x}_i$.

When it comes to ordinal variables, consider the distribution to be spread over m (fixed) categories. A scale over the m categories is represented as $c = (c_1, c_2, \ldots, c_m)$ where $c_j > c_i$ for $j > i$. For any ordinal distribution X, let $\tilde{n}_X = [\tilde{n}_X^1, \ldots, \tilde{n}_X^j, \ldots, \tilde{n}_X^m]$ where $\tilde{n}_X^j$ is the number of people in category j. The categories are ranked in ascending order such that category j is ranked higher than category i, with category m being the highest category. Let $f(j)$ and $F(j)$, respectively, be the proportion of population in the jth category and the cumulative proportion of population in the jth category of distribution X (or in a lower category). When it comes to group-wise distribution across the different categories we denote $f_X^l(j)$ and $F_X^l(j)$, respectively, as the proportion of lth subgroup in the jth category and the cumulative proportion of the lth subgroup in the jth category of distribution X (or in a lower category).

Finally, we say that distribution Y first-order stochastic dominates (F-dominates) X if $F_Y(j) \leq F_X(j)$, $\forall j = 1, \ldots, m$, with strict inequality holding at least for one value of j.

18.3   SOCIAL INEQUALITY WITH ORDINAL DATA

18.3.1   Cardinalising the Ordinal Variables

When measuring inequality with variables based on ordered categories, one approach is to attribute a number to each category and then apply the standard measures of inequality for cardinal data. The two broad methods for converting ordinal rankings are scaling and regressions. The first method applies standard scales to the ordinal rankings in order to convert them into cardinal numbers. The second method assumes that the ordinal variables come from an underlying cardinal distribution and uses regressions to reveal the cardinal numbers. We discuss these methods below.

Linear scales

For many variables of interest, such as health, life satisfaction or happiness, the information is mainly self-assessed and of ordinal nature. A common approach to deal with such variables is to cardinalise them and apply appropriate inequality measurement methods for cardinal variables.[3] One such instance is the study on happiness inequality by Veenhoven (1990). In a series of research papers Veenhoven investigates life satisfaction with the question: '*Taken everything together, how satisfied or dissatisfied are you with your life these days?*' The respondents are asked to choose from a ten-point scale, with 1 being 'extremely dissatisfied' and 10 being 'extremely satisfied'. Note that although the answers are over a ten-point scale, it is effectively an ordinal variable. The variable is cardinalised by taking a linear scale of the response. Using standard inequality measures such as the standard deviation, Veenhoven (1990) finds that inequality of life satisfaction is lower in more developed countries.

As has been demonstrated *inter alia* by Allison and Foster (2004) and Dutta and Foster (2013), when it comes to ordinal or categorical data, standard measures of inequality such as the standard deviation, coefficient of variation and Gini coefficient may yield inconsistent results under different scales. This is because, in order to derive the level of inequality using these measures, the categorical data need to be scaled. For instance, in the General Social Survey (GSS), the household head is asked: '*Taken all together, how would you say things are these days – would you say that you are very happy, pretty happy or not too happy?*' Suppose '*very happy*' is ranked higher than '*pretty happy*', which in turn is ranked higher than '*not too happy*'. To measure inequality of happiness we need to know how far apart these categories are from each other. We may use a scale, say $c = (1, 2, 3)$, where '*very happy*' is at 3, '*pretty happy*' is at 2 and '*not too happy*' is at 1. Once the scale is established, the standard measures can be applied to derive the level of inequality. There is, however, no reason that we should be restricted to a particular scale. We can take another scale, for example, of $c' = (1, 3, 9)$. The levels of inequality calculated using the standard measures will clearly change, but, more worryingly, the order of distributions in terms of their level of inequality may also be altered. Thus, for instance in the United States (US) case, it may happen that under one scale 1994 has lower happiness inequality compared with say 2000, yet another scale may show the opposite result. In such circumstances it becomes difficult to understand whether inequality is increasing or decreasing over time. Furthermore, it becomes difficult to undertake any consistent comparative analysis, whether it is across regions or between groups.

Regression-based approaches

A more sophisticated way of cardinalising the ordinal variables is to use either ordered probit regressions or interval regressions. Regression-based approaches have been used by van Doorslaer and Jones (2003) and Madden (2010), among others, in the context of health. First let us take up the ordered probit regression. Suppose we have a self-assessed health variable, which reports the different categories, such as poor, fair, good and excellent, used by individuals in order to assess their health. The method relies on the assumption that the actual value of the health status is latent but comes from a normal distribution and these ordinal categories just represent cut-off points in that distribution. This can be represented as:

$$x_i = k, \text{ if } \delta_k \leq \tilde{x}_i \leq \delta_{k+1} \text{ where } k = 1, \ldots, m$$

where $\tilde{x}_i$ is the latent variable derived from socioeconomic factors h_i:

$$\tilde{x}_i = h_i \beta + \varepsilon_i,$$

where $\varepsilon_i \sim N(0, \sigma^2)$. A likelihood function is used to estimate the value of β from which $\tilde{x}_i$ is calculated. From there one can calculate the inequality measure.

On the other hand, one can use an established distribution of health to calculate the cut-off points for the different ordinal categories and then undertake an interval regression. Van Doorslaer and Jones (2003) use the the Health Utility Index (HUI) as the reference distribution and derive the cut-off points from it. In doing so they assume that there is a stable mapping from the HUI to self-assessed health. For example, the HUI (Health Utility Mark 3) was developed with the 2001 Canadian Community Household Survey (CCHS). For each individual, the method transforms eight domains of health status into a 'utility score' relying on health weights, in turn based on community preferences. The index is finally normalized between 0 and 1, with 0 meaning death and 1 denoting perfect health (van Kippersluis et al., 2009).

Madden (2010) uses both the ordered probit and interval regression methods to study health inequality in Ireland from 2003 to 2006, using the European Union Survey of Living Conditions. The ordinal data are converted to cardinal scale, using regressions based on a broad set of socioeconomic factors, which include education and marital status. Once the level of health has been estimated from the regressions, Madden calibrates the inequality using generalised entropy measures and the ordinal inequality measures (Abul Naga and Yalcin, 2008). The analysis shows that while there is very little difference in which regression method is used for converting the ordinal data into cardinal data, there is considerable difference between using standard measures and using measures for ordinal inequality. It is to these latter measures that we next turn.

18.3.2   Pre-orderings for Ordinal Variables

In the approaches discussed above there are strong underlying assumptions, whether in terms of different scales or in terms of the distribution of the variables. In their seminal paper, Allison and Foster (2004) provide a novel approach based on distributional dispersion around the median of an ordinal variable. They note that one of the measures of central tendency that is order-preserving under scale transformations is the median. The median, therefore, becomes a natural choice from which to evaluate the dispersion in the distribution of an ordinal variable.

As explained by Lasso de la Vega (Chapter 17 in this *Handbook*), under the Allison–Foster framework, inequality in an ordinal setting is considered as the 'spread away from the median category' and is captured through the notion of *S-dominance*, which is defined as the following:

Definition 1 *S-dominance*: *Consider two ordinal distributions with the same number of categories, X and Y, and with common median category, k. Distribution Y S-dominates X if and only if $\forall j = 1, \ldots, k - 1$, $F_Y(j) \leq F_X(j)$, and $\forall j = k, \ldots, n$, $F_Y(j) \geq F_X(j)$.*

Compared to Y, distribution X has a greater population share in the categories below the median, and a greater population share in the categories above the median. Hence X has a greater spread away from the median compared to Y. More people are concentrated in the middle for distribution Y than distribution X, or in other words, the 'spread' of Y's distribution is lower. Thus Y *S-dominates* X will be associated with X having higher inequality than Y, for any inequality index measuring inequality interpreted as the spread away from the median.

Dutta and Foster (2013) and Balestra and Ruiz (2015) have shown that in the case of a variable with only three categories, if X and Y are two different distributions, then it must be the case that either there is an F-dominance relationship between them or an

S-dominance relationship between them. The intuition behind this result is that two distributions with three categories either cross once or do not cross at all.

S-dominance was the first pre-order capturing a sensible notion of ordinal inequality. However it is significantly limited by its unsuitability for comparing distributions with different medians. Aiming at filling this gap Abul Naga and Yalcin (2010) proposed a measurement framework for median-independent ordinal inequality, including both a pre-order and indices. The approach takes off from the realisation that distributions with different medians are not directly comparable in terms of ordinal inequality based on spreads away from a common median. However, a transformation of these distribution is comparable. Let $\Pi_X(j) \equiv |F_X(j) - 0.5|$. Then we can measure inequality as spreads away distribution-specific medians. For example, when the whole population is in the same category i, the transformed distribution is: $\Pi_X(j) = 0.5, \forall j$. That defines the benchmark of equality, as in the case of the Allison–Foster ordering. On the other extreme, the case of maximum inequality, which takes the form of extreme bipolarisation, occurs when half of the population is in the bottom category and the other half is in the top category. In that case we have: $\Pi_X(j) = 0 \ \forall j < m$.

The dominance condition proposed by Abul Naga and Yalcin (2010) for comparing distributions with different medians can be expressed in alternative equivalent ways. We here reproduce the formulation by Abul Naga et al. (2016) which is based on an interpretation of Abul Naga and Yalcin (2010, p. 12, proposition 5.4.) and requires sorting Π_X in ascending order. We define the ordered vector of transformed distributions as Π_X^*. So, for instance, $\Pi_X^*(1) \equiv \min[\Pi_X(1), \Pi_X(2), \ldots, \Pi_X(m-1)]$ and $\Pi_X^*(m-1) \equiv \max[\Pi_X(1), \Pi_X(2), \ldots, \Pi_X(m-1)]$, and so on. The formulation by Abul Naga et al. (2016) is then:

Definition 2 *MI-dominance: Consider two ordinal distributions with the same number of categories, X and Y. Distribution Y MI-dominates X if and only if* $\forall j = 1, \ldots, m - 1 : \Pi_X^*(j) \leq \Pi_Y^*(j) \text{ and } \exists i | \Pi_X^*(i) < \Pi_Y^*(i).$

The condition of MI-dominance in Definition 2 tells us that distribution X is closer to the benchmark of maximum bipolarization than Y (and further away from the benchmark of equality). Any ordinal inequality index which is coherent with MI-dominance yields a higher value when evaluated for X than for Y. Finally, as Abul Naga and Yalcin (2010) note, S-dominance implies MI-dominance, but the reverse is not true.

Empirical illustration

We compare the inequality among African-Americans in the US from 1994 to 2012. We construct a square matrix with ten rows and ten columns, with each row and column representing a year from our sample (Table 18.1). Each cell of the matrix describes whether the distributions of the concerned two years are based on *F-dominance* or *S-dominance*.

In order to understand Table 18.1, let us consider the year 1996. The first cell in the row labelled 1996, compares the happiness distribution in 1996 with 1994 and the *F* in that cell shows that 1996 *F-dominates* 1994. If we compare the two distributions, the share of the population in the worst category (*not too happy*) was, $f_{1996}(1) = 0.175 < f_{1994}(1) = 0.215$. The share of the population in the best category (very happy) was $f_{1996}(3) = 0.242 > f_{1994}(3) = 0.176$. This implies that 1996 *F-dominates* 1994. If we continue on the same row and

Table 18.1   Dominance comparisons for happiness in the US

	1994	1996	1998	2000	2002	2004	2006	2008	2010	2012	F	S
1994								S			0	1
1996	F		F		S			F	S	F	4	2
1998	F				S			F	S	S	2	3
2000	F	F	F		S			F	F	F	6	1
2002	F							F			2	0
2004	F	F	F	F	F		F	F	F	F	9	0
2006	F	F	F	F	S			F	F	F	7	1
2008											0	0
2010	F				S			F			2	1
2012	F				S			F	S		2	2
F	8	3	4	2	1	0	1	8	3	4	34	
S	0	0	0	0	6	0	0	1	2	1		11

Note: F and S stands for F-Dominance and S-Dominance. The last two columns shows the number F-Dominant and S-Dominant relations for each row. Similarly the last two rows show the number of F-Dominant and S-Dominant relations for each column.

Source: Authors' calculations using GSS data.

Table 18.2   Dominance comparisons for happiness across racial groups in the US 2006

2006	Whites	Blacks	Others
Whites		F	F
Blacks			
Others		S	

Note: F and S stand for F-Dominance and S-Dominance.

compare the distribution of happiness of 1994 with 2002, we find that the share of the population in the worst category is $f_{1996}(1) = 0.175 < f_{2002}(1) = 0.215$ and the share of the population in the best category is $f_{1996}(3) = 0.242 < f_{2002}(3) = 0.295$. Thus in this comparison, 1996 *S-dominates* 2002. Although in this case there are more *F-dominating* relations than *S-dominating* ones, the majority of cases are non-comparable, which is reflected in the blank spaces in the table.

The comparisons can certainly be done across time, but also across groups for a given period. For instance if we compare the distributions of happiness across the three groups in 2006, we get Table 18.2, which shows that the happiness distribution of White Americans *F-dominates* African-Americans and Others in 2006.

As earlier, this can be inferred from the distributions of the worst and the best categories. For the worst category, $f_w(1) = 0.102 < f_B(1) = 0.165$ and the share of the population in the best category (very happy) was $f_w(3) = 0.347 > f_B(3) = 0.274$. Similarly, when we compare White Americans and Others we find $f_w(1) = 0.102 < f_O(1) = 0.150$ and $f_w(3) = 0.347 > f_O(3) = 0.253$. On the other hand if we compare the distribution of African-

Americans and Others, we note that the former have a higher proportion in the best and worst category while Others have a higher proportion in the median category. Thus Others *S-dominate* African-Americans.

Examples from the literature
Madden (2011) provides an interesting application of F- and S-dominance comparisons in an assessment of levels and distribution of subjective well-being indicators in Ireland between 1994 and 2001. Relying on the eight annual waves of the panel dataset Living in Ireland Survey (LII), Madden (2011) concentrates on several life satisfaction variables involving work, finance, housing, leisure, health and GHQ-12 (a mental health measure based on a General Health Questionnaire). In order to assess changes in the average levels of life satisfaction, Madden (2011) performs F-dominance comparisons, since whenever first-order dominance with ordinal variables holds, one can safely conclude that one distribution will exhibit higher social welfare than another one for any choice of (arbitrary) scales for the variable's ordered categories. Then, in order to assess changes in inequality over these ordinal variables, the author performs S-dominance comparisons.

For the case of work satisfaction, Madden (2011) finds only two instances of F-dominance (out of 28 possible pairwise year comparisons). However, several S-dominance relationships emerge. In particular, 1994 and 1996 are dominated by all their respective subsequent years (for example, 1994 dominated by 1995, 1996, and so on, up to 2001), highlighting reductions in work satisfaction inequality in latter years. By contrast, very few S-dominance relationship are apparent in the case of finance satisfaction, but plenty of F-dominance relationships appear, which tend to favour latter years over former years, to the point that 1999, 2000 and 2001 F-dominate every year preceding them, respectively. This means that the most recent years in the studied period are unambiguously better than their predecessors in terms of finance satisfaction.

The cases of housing and leisure satisfaction are similar to that of work satisfaction: few F-dominance relationships, but several S-dominance relationships usually pointing to inequality reductions in more recent years. In both cases 1994 is S-dominated by all the subsequent years. Finally, the two health satisfaction variables exhibit less clear patterns, although 2000 and 2001 tend to S-dominate most preceding years, again pointing toward inequality reduction over these well-being dimensions.

Balestra and Ruiz (2015) conduct F-dominance and S-dominance analysis for education and subjective well-being using the 2010 wave of the Gallup World Poll, which covers all Organisation for Economic Co-operation and Development (OECD) countries, plus Brazil, Indonesia, Russia and South Africa. Their education variable has three categories (primary, secondary and tertiary education). Their life satisfaction variable is measured originally with a Cantril ladder ranging from 0 to 10. However, the authors transform it into a three-category variable (Category 1: 0–4, Category 2: 5–8, Category 3: 9–10). That way, for both variables, the authors can apply the aforementioned proposition whereby in any comparison involving three-category variables there is bound to be either F-dominance or S-dominance (but not both, obviously). The authors find that 82 percent of all dominance relationships are of the F-type in the case of life satisfaction, whereas for education 80 percent of relationships are likewise first-order dominance.

18.3.3   Ordinal Inequality Measures

Notation
Let Ω be the set of all distributions. Consider a distribution $X \in \Omega$, with k as the median category and $F_X(0) = 0$. The mean happiness of distribution X below the median can be expressed as:

$$\mu_X^L(c) = 2\left(\sum_{j=1}^{k-1} c_i(F_X(j) - F_X(j-1)) + c_k(0.5 - F_X(k-1)) \right), \quad (18.1)$$

and the mean happiness of distribution X above the median can be written as:

$$\mu_X^U(c) = 2\left(\sum_{j=k+1}^{m} c_i(F_X(j) - F_X(j-1)) + c_k(F_X(k) - 0.5) \right). \quad (18.2)$$

An ordinal inequality measure is a function $I : \Omega \to \mathbb{R}_+$. The Allison and Foster (2004) inequality measure is given by:

$$I_X^{AF}(c) = \mu_X^U(c) - \mu_X^L(c). \quad (18.3)$$

We note that a limitation of $I_X^{AF}(c)$ in (18.3) is that it depends on the arbitrary scale given to the ordered categories of the variable. Other ordinal inequality indices, like those mentioned below, do not suffer from this problem, as they map only from scale-invariant cumulative distribution functions. At least if Y S-dominates X then it will be the case that $I_X^{AF}(c) > I_Y^{AF}(c)$ for every possible scale c. That is, $I_X^{AF}(c)$ is a measure of inequality as spread away from the common median.

Empirical illustration
Based on the above notion of dominance, several ordinal measures have been developed. For empirical illustrations, we employ the measures developed by Allison and Foster (2004) (mentioned above in equation 18.3) and Abul Naga and Yalcin (2008) (mentioned below in equation 18.4). Unlike the dominance-based methods, these measures provide complete rankings, although they are scale-dependent in the case of the indices proposed by Allison and Foster (2004). As explained by Lasso de la Vega (Chapter 17 in this *Handbook*) the measures proposed by Abul Naga and Yalcin (2008) are not scale-dependent, since they map from the vector of cumulative probabilities. However, they do depend on the number of categories in the ordinal variable. The measure we consider for our own empirical illustration in this section of the chapter is based on Allison and Foster (2004) (henceforth, the AF measure).

In this section, we shall extensively use the US General Social Survey (GSS), which collects data on individual levels of happiness along with a rich set of personal information. Although the GSS dataset is collected for a long period, for our empirical illustrations we focus on the period 1994 to 2012, where data have been collected every two years. In each of these years, a nationally representative sample was chosen. It is one of the longest and most consistent surveys available for the US and has been extensively used in the literature (see Alesina et al., 2004; Di Tella et al., 2006; Stevenson and Wolfers, 2008). The questions on attitudes and self-assessment of happiness and health are asked to the household head. The yearly average ages of the respondents range between 44 to 48 years.

Table 18.3   *Ordinal inequality measure of happiness across racial groups in the US*

	Whites			Blacks			Others			Total		
	AF1	AF2	AF3	AF1	AF2	AF3	AF1	AF2	AF3	AF1	AF2	AF3
1994	1.700	2.164	1.236	1.562	1.484	1.640	1.451	1.661	1.242	1.671	2.056	1.287
1996	1.675	2.136	1.214	1.668	1.802	1.533	2.181	2.862	1.500	1.706	2.138	1.273
1998	1.772	2.292	1.252	1.648	1.726	1.569	1.918	2.252	1.584	1.766	2.213	1.319
2000	1.761	2.323	1.200	1.708	1.895	1.522	1.602	1.840	1.365	1.743	2.228	1.257
2002	1.767	2.271	1.264	2.037	2.198	1.877	1.237	1.322	1.152	1.766	2.198	1.334
2004	1.812	2.299	1.324	2.014	2.365	1.663	1.575	1.702	1.448	1.811	2.249	1.373
2006	1.795	2.287	1.304	1.759	1.976	1.541	1.615	1.821	1.410	1.763	2.177	1.349
2008	1.789	2.228	1.350	2.034	1.911	2.158	1.823	2.139	1.507	1.824	2.179	1.470
2010	1.720	2.092	1.348	1.786	1.876	1.697	1.614	1.588	1.641	1.720	2.012	1.427
2012	1.880	2.358	1.403	1.681	1.768	1.594	1.731	2.041	1.421	1.833	2.234	1.433

Note: AF1, AF2 and AF3, stands for the Allison and Foster inequality measure under the scales $(-2, 0, 2)$, $(-2, -1, 2)$ and $(-2, 1, 2)$.

Source: Authors' calculations based on GSS data.

Using the US GSS data from 1994 to 2012 we estimate the AF inequality measure for each of the different racial groups separately. For robustness purposes we use three different scales: $(-2, 0, 2)$; $(-2, -1, 2)$ and $(-2, 1, 2)$, to represent the weights given to the three categories, starting with the worst category of '*not too happy*'. The scales reflect, respectively, a linear scale, a convex scale and a concave scale. In the linear scale the increase in the scale is at a constant rate; for the convex scale the increase happens at an increasing rate; and finally, for the concave scale the increase happens at a decreasing rate. Table 18.3 shows the results. Although we calibrate the results for the the AF inequality measure, for a three-category case under a linear scale the AF measure is a monotonic transformation of the Abul Naga–Yalcin measure (Dutta and Foster, 2013).

The first three columns of Table 18.3 show the AF inequality index for White Americans under a linear scale (AF1), a convex scale (AF2), and a concave scale (AF3). The next six columns do the same calibrations for African-Americans and Others. The final three columns focus on the overall inequality. The broad trends in terms of total inequality vary slightly depending on the scale used. According to the linear scale, total happiness inequality initially increased in the mid- to late 1990s but declined over the next decade. On the other hand, both the AF2 and AF3 show that inequality broadly increased. Although there was a slight dip in 2010, all the measures show that inequality had increased in 2012. The happiness inequality of White Americans follows broadly similar trends. Overall inequality seems to be increasing for all the different scales, except for 2010 when there clearly had been a reduction of inequality. When it comes to African-Americans inequality trends seems to be quite different. For them, happiness inequality has been choppy. It increased dramatically around the early 2000s. In recent years inequality has decreased and, unlike Others, the trend continues even for 2012. For the Others, there was a sharp increase in inequality in the mid-1990s after which it declined, reaching the lowest values in the early 2000s. Thereafter, the trend points towards higher inequality, though it is below the mid-1990's level. In terms of the level of happiness on an average over the ten years covered, whether African-Americans have a higher level of inequality compared to White Americans depends on the scale used. For the linear scale and concave scales, African-Americans do have a higher average inequality. However, when we take a convex scale, the White Americans do have higher average happiness inequality. Thus it is not unambiguous as the case for income inequality between the two racial groups, where White Americans typically have lower inequality.

Examples from the literature

Jones et al. (2011) studied inequality in responsiveness indicators of health systems across 25 countries. Relying on the World Health Survey, they focused on 'health responsiveness' for in-patient services and chose the domains of 'clarity of communication', 'dignity', 'confidentiality' and 'prompt attention'. For each variable there were five response categories ranging from 'very bad' to 'very good'; and for each variable the authors compute three indices from two now popular families of overall inequality for ordinal variables. Firstly, they choose two indices from the two-parameter Abul Naga–Yalcin family (Abul Naga and Yalcin, 2008):

$$ANY_{\alpha,\beta} = \frac{\sum_{j=1}^{k-1} [F(j)]^{\alpha} - \sum_{j=k}^{m} [F(j)]^{\beta} + (m + 1 - k)}{D_{\alpha,\beta} + (m + 1 - k)}, \ \alpha, \beta \geq 1 \quad (18.4)$$

where $D_{\alpha,\beta} = (k - 1)(0.5)^{\alpha} - (1 + (m - k)(0.5)^{\beta})$. Their first choice is the so-called symmetric case of $(\alpha, \beta) = (1, 1)$. Then, in order to emphasize inequalities below the median responsiveness value, their second choice becomes $(\alpha, \beta) = (1, 4)$. Their third index is a one-parameter family proposed by Apouey (2007):

$$AP_{\tau} = 1 - \frac{2^{\tau}}{m - 1} \sum_{j=1}^{m-1} |F(j) - 0.5|^{\tau}, \ 0 \leq \tau \leq 1 \quad (18.5)$$

where $\tau = 0.73$.[4] For the four variables, the inequality country ranking is fairly robust across the three inequality indices. In the case of 'dignity', Croatia, France and Ireland consistently appear as (relatively) high-inequality countries; whereas Portugal, the Netherlands and Spain turn up among the countries with the lowest inequality (relative to the other countries on the list). Regarding 'prompt attention', Sweden, Ireland and Hungary are among the most unequal; whereas Bosnia, Germany and Spain show up among the least unequal. As for 'confidentiality', Croatia, Hungary and Ireland often appear in the top inequality slots; while Slovenia, Portugal and Spain appear more frequently at the bottom. Finally, in the 'clarity of communication' ranking, Croatia and Ireland top the list as the two most unequal countries across all indices; whereas Portugal, Spain and Slovenia again tend to show relatively low inequality levels vis-à-vis other countries (Jones et al., 2011, p. 621, Table 2). The authors conclude that 'The indices vary across countries, with, in general, countries of Northern Europe exhibiting greatest inequality and Southern European countries least inequality' (Jones et al., 2011, p. 625).

In a previously mentioned study, Madden (2011) also computes members of (18.4) and (18.5) for six indicators of life satisfaction in Ireland (1994–2001): work, finance, housing, leisure, health and GHQ (mental health). In particular, the author computes $ANY_{1.1}$, $ANY_{1.5}$ and $ANY_{0.6}$. For most variables the author finds significant inequality reduction (except an occasional bump) robustly across the three indices. However in the case of health, the inequality trend is basically flat throughout the period.

Wang and Yu (2015) also computed different members of (18.5) in their study of self-assessed health inequality in China between 1997 and 2009, using the Chinese Health and Nutrition Survey (CHNS). Specifically they computed $AP_{0.1}$, $AP_{0.5}$, $AP_{0.9}$, AP_1 and $AP_{0.415}$.[5] All their computations consistently report increases in self-assessed health inequality in China during the studied period. The national results seem to be mainly influenced by the inequality increases in urban areas, whereas in rural areas the upward trend was temporarily interrupted between 2004 and 2006. Meanwhile, in every year, health inequality in urban areas is consistently higher than in rural areas. All the results are remarkably robust to the five choices of τ.

Costa Font and Cowell (2013) is the first application of the inequality measurement method proposed by Cowell and Flachaire (2012) (explained by Lasso de la Vega Chapter 17 of this *Handbook*). The family of inequality indices developed by Cowell and Flachaire (2012) is given by:

$$
CF_\alpha = \begin{cases} \frac{1}{\alpha(\alpha - 1)}\left[\frac{1}{n}\sum_{i=1}^{n} \widetilde{s}_i^{\alpha} - 1 \right] & \text{if } \alpha \neq 0, \\ -\frac{1}{n}\sum_{i=1}^{n} \ln \widetilde{s}_i & \text{if } \alpha = 0, \end{cases} \tag{18.6}
$$

where $\widetilde{s}_i$ is the 'status' of individual i, which can be measured in two potential ways: (1) as the proportion of people in the same category as i or below; or (2) as the proportion of people in the same category as i or above. Effectively, the first method, called 'downward-looking status', implies that $\widetilde{s}_i$ is a cumulative distribution function; whereas the second method, called 'upward-looking status', states that $\widetilde{s}_i$ is a survival function. Costa Font and Cowell (2013) seek to gauge the sensitivity and robustness of cross-country rankings of health inequality to two key choices pertaining to the Cowell–Flachaire family: (1) the choice of α; and (2) the choice of how to measure $\widetilde{s}_i$. They use the World Health Survey from 2002 and a measure of self-assessed health with five categories.

The authors find ample evidence of re-rankings across different choices of α (which they make range from -2 to 0.99), pointing to the empirical relevance of that methodological choice. For example, in the case of downward-looking status and OECD countries, health inequality in France moves from the highest position at low levels of α to the lowest inequality value (compared against Australia, Austria, Estonia, Finland, Belgium, Denmark and Germany) when α approaches 0.99. Finland also starts with the second-highest inequality level when $\alpha = -2$, but then becomes the least unequal country when α is around -0.3, and finally sees its inequality value increase to become the third-highest unequal country when $\alpha = 0.99$. For other countries, such as Denmark and Belgium, the level of inequality remains relatively constant across the range of α. The narrower case of comparing Sweden, Norway and Finland is likewise stark: all possible rankings between these three countries exist, depending on the choice of α.

Similar patterns of massive re-rankings, but also with countries exhibiting steady inequality levels, occur in different regions of the world studied by the authors. Moreover, the choice of upward- versus downward-looking status can also produce rerankings. One nice summary of the authors' findings is in Costa Font and Cowell (2013, p. 15, Table 1), where they report the rank correlation between downward-looking and upward-looking status for different values of α. Interestingly, they find that the highest degree of positive rank concordance between the two status measurement options takes place when α gets closer to 0.99. When α is negative, the authors find that the rank correlations are negative as well.

In addition to their dominance analysis (mentioned above), Balestra and Ruiz (2015) also compute inequality indices for education and subjective well-being using the 2010 wave of the Gallup World Poll. As mentioned, both their education and life satisfaction variables bear three categories. Following the ideas of Abul Naga and Yalcin (2008), the authors propose an inequality index which is very similar in spirit to a member of the family proposed by Apouey (2007), and also similar to one of the functional forms proposed by Reardon (2009). The index is the following:

$$BR = 1 - \left[\frac{2\sum_{j=1}^{m} |F(j) - 0.5| - 1}{m - 1} \right] \tag{18.7}$$

We note that the sum on the right-hand side of (18.7) is done over the whole m categories of the variable. That is why the -1 element is necessary on the numerator of the ratio on the right-hand side. So that whenever there is maximum inequality (with $F(j) = 0.5$, $\forall j = m - 1$), $BR = 1$. By contrast, had the sum been performed between $j = 1$ and $j = m - 1$ then we would simply have AP_1 from (18.5).

Applying (18.7), the authors find that the US, Estonia, South Africa and Hungary are the most unequal countries in terms of life satisfaction. At the other extreme, Belgium, the Netherlands, Italy and Luxembourg emerge as the least unequal. Meanwhile, for education, India, Brazil, Portugal and Iceland are the most unequal; whereas Slovenia, the Czech Republic, Germany and Denmark are the least unequal countries.

Lv et al. (2015) axiomatically characterise a measure which essentially adds up functions of all the pairwise differences between individuals in terms of categories across all possible individual pairs (akin to a Gini-style summation). The measure is given as:

$$LWX = \sum_{i=1}^{m} \sum_{j \neq i}^{m} g(|i - j|) f(i) f(j) \tag{18.8}$$

where $g:[1, 2,\ldots, m - 1] \to (0, \infty)$ and $0 < g(1) < g(2) < \ldots < g(m - 1)$. This measure satisfies a 'median-preserving spread' where an increase in the spread of the distribution, keeping the median category the same, leads to increased inequality. Different choices of g are admissible. For example, $g(i) = \frac{2i}{m-1}$ applied in (18.8) yields the absolute Gini coefficient for ordinal variables; which, as the authors note, is also one of the functional forms used by Reardon (2009) (mentioned below). The authors apply this class of indices to measure health inequality in the different provinces of China, covering both rural and urban areas, using the China Household Income Project Survey, which uses subjective well-being questions to measure individuals' health status.

18.3.4 Between-Group Inequality for Ordinal Variables when the Socioeconomic Variable is Unordered

Fusco and Silber (2014) provide a comprehensive empirical illustration of the most recent methods to measure between-group inequality when the variable of interest is ordinal (for example, self-assessed health) and the groups are defined by a variable with unordered categories (for example, gender, ethnicity, and so on). The main idea behind this methods is that each socioeconomic group has its own distribution of the ordinal variable of interest. The benchmark of complete socioeconomic equality is achieved in this framework when all group-specific distributions are identical. Hence socioeconomic inequality in this context means distributional dissimilarity across groups. There are several recent methodological contributions to the measurement of this form of distributional dissimilarity, including Reardon (2009), Silber and Yalonetzky (2011), D'Ambrosio and Permanyer (2015) and Permanyer (Chapter 19 in this *Handbook*).[6]

The authors use the European Union Statistics on Income and Living Conditions (EU-SILC) 2009 dataset in order to perform a comparison of socioeconomic inequality in self-assessed health with five categories across 13 European countries: Austria, Belgium, Switzerland, Cyprus, Estonia, Spain, France, Greece, Ireland, Italy, Luxembourg, Latvia and the UK. Their socioeconomic categories are nationals and foreigners. They choose the following two indices from the Reardon family:

$$R1 = 1 - \frac{\sum_{i=1}^{G} s_i \sum_{j=1}^{m-1} 4F_i(j)[1 - F_i(j)]}{\sum_{j=1}^{m-1} 4F(j)[1 - F(j)]}, \tag{18.9}$$

$$R2 = 1 - \frac{\sum_{i=1}^{G} s_i \sum_{j=1}^{m-1} 2\sqrt{F_i(j)[1 - F_i(j)]}}{\sum_{j=1}^{m-1} 2\sqrt{F(j)[1 - F(j)]}}, \tag{18.10}$$

where $F(j)$ is the cumulative distribution function (evaluated at j) for the whole population, whereas $F_i(j)$ is the respective statistic just for group i. The rationale of indices from the Reardon family like (18.9) and (18.10), is that the denominators on the right-hand side measure total inequality in the ordinal inequality over the whole population (note that the values are 0 if and only if everybody in the population is concentrated in the same category, whereas these denominators are maximal when half the population is in the bottom category and the other half is in the top category). Meanwhile the numerators in the right-hand side ratios measure the sum of within-group ordinal inequality across all groups. Following an argument based on Jensen's inequality, it is easy to show that: (1) the numerator can never be higher than the denominator; and (2) the numerator equals the denominator if and only if all the group distributions are identical. Hence the members of the Reardon family measure between-group inequality indirectly, as the proportion of total inequality not 'explained' by the sum of within-group inequalities (Silber and Yalonetzky, 2011).[7]

Fusco and Silber (2014) also choose the index with $\alpha = 2$ (square of absolute distances) from the following family proposed by Silber and Yalonetzky (2011):

$$SY1 = \frac{2^\alpha}{m-1} \sum_{i=1}^{G} s_i \sum_{j=1}^{m-1} |F_i(j) - F(j)|^\alpha, \alpha > 0. \tag{18.11}$$

The authors also choose a Gini-style index proposed by Silber and Yalonetzky (2011):

$$SY2 = \sum_{i=1}^{G} \sum_{l>i}^{G} s_i s_l \sum_{j=1}^{m-1} |F_i(j) - F_l(j)|. \tag{18.12}$$

Both the indices in (18.11) and (18.12) (the latter only when $G = 2$) fulfil a set of desirable properties, and measure between-group inequality across group distributions directly, as a form of distributional dissimilarity. Finally, Fusco and Silber (2014) compute a member from the family proposed by D'Ambrosio and Permanyer (2015), which is based on the old notion of distributional overlap (Weitzman, 1970), combined with elements from the more recent polarisation literature (Esteban and Ray, 1994):

$$DP = \sum_{i=1}^{G} \sum_{l=1}^{G} s_i^{1+\alpha} s_l \left[1 - \sum_{j=1}^{m} \min f_i(j), f_l(j) \right] \tag{18.13}$$

Fusco and Silber (2014) choose $\alpha = 0.71$. The indices in (18.13) are equal to 0 if and only if all group distributions are equal.

Fusco and Silber (2014) find a very high degree of rank correlation across the four indices used. In fact the lowest correlation is 0.941 (between (18.10) and (18.13) with $\alpha = 0.71$). When it comes to health inequality between nationals and foreigners, the authors find that, among the 13 European countries, Austria, Belgium, Luxembourg and Switzerland tend to be the least unequal, whereas Estonia and Latvia top the list.

18.3.5   Between-Group Inequality for Ordinal Variables when the Socioeconomic Variable is Ordered

In this section we discuss comparing the distributions of an ordinal variable of interest in terms of a socioeconomic gradient. When it comes to cardinal variables, the concentration curve (and the indices associated with it) is used to measure inequality between groups defined by another cardinal variable. Otherwise, even with a cardinal variable of interest, we can measure inequality between groups defined by unordered categories (for example, ethnic group) using traditional inequality indices (for example, see section 18.4 below). However, in many cases, such as self-reported health or life satisfaction, the variable of interest is ordinal. In this context, Zheng (2011) pioneered the methods to compare the distributions of ordinal variables in terms of their socioeconomic gradients. We briefly discuss these methods before we apply them in an empirical illustration.

We can represent an ordinal distribution X over m different categories and G different socioeconomic groups, through the following matrix:

$$X = \begin{bmatrix} f_1(1) & \cdots & f_1(m) \\ \cdot & \cdots & \cdot \\ \cdot & \cdots & \cdot \\ \cdot & \cdots & \cdot \\ f_G(1) & \cdots & f_G(m) \end{bmatrix}$$

If we consider the socioeconomic classes to be ranked in an ascending order, then we ask matrix X to satisfy a 'monotone' condition whereby if being in socioeconomic groups u is preferable to group t, that is, $t < u$, then $\sum_{j=1}^{k} f_t(j) > \sum_{j=1}^{k} f_u(j)$ for all $k = 1, \ldots, m$. The intuition is that groups ranked higher on the socioeconomic variable defining them (for example, income quintiles) will have a greater proportion of the population in the better categories of the variable of interest (for example, self-assessed health) than lower socioeconomic groups. On the other hand, for variables which are undesirable such as ill health, then the intuition would be reversed. We would want higher-ranked socioeconomic groups to have higher proportions of people in the lower categories.

When it comes to comparing the matrices of distributions, Zheng (2011) proposes several comparison rules based on both welfare and inequality criteria, such as rank dominance, and generalised Lorenz dominance. Our focus in this chapter is on inequality criteria, for which Zheng (2011) proposes several dominance rules such as absolute Lorenz dominance and relative Lorenz dominance. Here we highlight the rule based on absolute Lorenz dominance (AL-dominance).

Consider any distribution X. Let θ: $(\theta_1, \ldots, \theta_G)$ be the distribution of people over the socio-economic categories. We denote $\tilde{\theta}_l = \sum_{i=1}^{l} \theta_i$, $l = 1, 2, \ldots, G$ and $\alpha_X^{kl} = \sum_{i=1}^{l} \sum_{j=k}^{m} \theta_i f_i(j)$.

Definition 3 *Consider two ordinal distributions of achievements X and Y each divided into G groups. Then X Absolute Lorenz dominates Y if and only if:*

$$\tilde{\theta}_l \alpha_X^{Gk} - \alpha_X^{lk} \leq \tilde{\theta}_l \alpha_Y^{Gk} - \alpha_Y^{lk}$$

for all $j = 1, 2, \ldots, m$ and all $l = 1, 2, \ldots, G - 1$ with the inequality holding strictly for at least some pairs (j, l).

Therefore, one distribution would dominate the other if it has lower cumulative proportion of the population in the lower categories.

More recently, two additional approaches to the measurement of socioeconomic inequality when the two variables are ordinal have been proposed by Apouey and Silber (2013). The first approach relies on the construction of a particular type of concentration curve.[8] Let $f(h, y)$ be the joint probability of having a health status of h ($h = 1, 2, \ldots, H$) and a group status of y ($y = 1, 2, \ldots, Y$). Let $F(h, y)$ be the respective cumulative distribution function. If the two variables (that of interest and that defining the groups) are independent from each other, then it should be the case that: $f(h, y) = f(h)f(y)$, where $f(h)f(y)$ is, naturally, the expected probability of finding people with a joint value of h and y if the two variables were independent. Hence we can measure socioeconomic inequality with two ordinal variables as departures from the situation of contingency-table independence. Apouey and Silber (2013) show how a categorical concentration curve can be constructed by plotting the accumulation of observed probabilities ($f(h, y)$) on the vertical axis, against the cumulation of the expected probabilities ($f(h)f(y)$) on the horizontal axis; but crucially performing the accumulation not from the lowest values of $f(h)f(y)$ (that is, ranking the observations in terms of expected probabilities). Rather, the population needs to be ranked in ascending order in terms of the ratio of observed to expected probabilities $\frac{f(h,y)}{f(h)f(y)}$, and then the accumulation on both axes is performed. If the two variables are independent then the concentration curve will overlap with the 45-degree line. Otherwise, the concentration curve is a convex curve akin to the Lorenz curve. The further the distance from the 45-degree line, the higher the degree of association between the two variables. Then a concentration index can be computed by measuring the area between the concentration curve and the 45-degree line.

Additionally, the authors show that several meaningful socioeconomic inequality indices can be computed, as long as they are sensitive to the difference between observed and expected probabilities for each and every (h, y) duplet. One of the examples provided by the authors is the following Theil-like index:

$$TAS = \sum_{y=1}^{Y} \sum_{h=1}^{H} f(h)f(y) \ln\left[\frac{f(h,y)}{f(h)f(y)}\right] \tag{18.14}$$

The second approach proposed by Apouey and Silber (2013) is basically a bivariate extension of the ordinal inequality indices, especially those of Apouey (2007) and Reardon (2009). More than measures of socioeconomic gradient, this approach proposes a way of measuring bivariate bipolarization (see Permayer, Chapter 19 in this *Handbook*). The maximum degree of bivariate bipolarization is achieved, in this framework, whenever $F(h, y) = 0.5 \ \forall(h, y)$. Meanwhile, the minimum degree of bipolarization occurs when $\exists(i, j)$ | $F(i, j,) = 1 \ \forall h \geq i \wedge y \geq j \wedge F(i, j,) = 0 \ \forall h < i \wedge y < j$. The two bivariate indices proposed by the authors are:

$$B1 = 1 - \frac{2\sum_{y=1}^{Y} \sum_{h=1}^{H} |F(h,y) - 0.5|}{HY} \tag{18.15}$$

$$B2 = \frac{4}{HY} \sum_{y=1}^{Y} \sum_{h=1}^{H} F(h,y)[1 - F(h,y)] \tag{18.16}$$

Empirical illustration

For an empirical application we follow closely the paper by Chen and Zheng (2014), which explores the socioeconomic inequalities associated with happiness. The data for this paper come from the General Social Survey in the US. As described before, the happiness response is over three categories: 'not too happy', 'pretty happy' and 'very happy'. When it comes to the socioeconomic status, Chen and Zheng (2014) choose income as the indicator, with income quintiles as the different categories. In GSS data there are several income variables, all of which are not necessarily informative in terms of breaking down into quintiles. Chen and Zheng (2014) choose Income06, which is grouped data on family income before tax. Using Current Population Survey cut-offs, they generate the quintile information for each household. Thus, $\theta = (0.2, 0.2, 0.2, 0.2, 0.2)$. Note that while happiness is based on the household head's response, the socioeconomic status is for the whole family.

We compare below the happiness distribution for 2008 and 2010 from Chen and Zheng (2014, p. 226, Table 1). For example in 2008, the distribution across the three happiness categories of 'not too happy', 'pretty happy' and 'very happy', for the poorest quintile are, 0.2677, 0.5249 and 0.2074, respectively. The distribution across the same categories for the second-poorest quintile is 0.1854, 0.5851 and 0.2295, respectively. Similarly, the distributions for the third and the fourth quintile across the three happiness categories are: 0.1403, 0.5166, 0.3431 and 0.561, 0.5727, 0.3712, respectively. The distribution of the top quintile in 2008 is given by 0.312, 0.5489 and 0.42. In implementing the Lorenz dominance conditions, one first needs to check whether the 'monotone assumption' that is, there is a income gradient in happiness, is satisfied. In this example, if we compare the bottom two quintiles we see, $0.1854 < 0.2677$, and $0.1854 + 0.5851 < 0.2677 + 0.5249$. We can check for each of the other quintiles and show that there is a income gradient in happiness in 2008. We can similarly show a income gradient of happiness in 2010. Implementing the condition for absolute Lorenz dominance comparisons leads to the following matrices for 2008 and 2010, respectively:

$$\frac{1}{5}\begin{bmatrix} 0.13 & 0.11 \\ 0.18 & 0.16 \\ 0.19 & 0.19 \\ 0.11 & 0.11 \end{bmatrix} \text{ and } \frac{1}{5}\begin{bmatrix} 0.11 & 0.08 \\ 0.13 & 0.15 \\ 0.12 & 0.15 \\ 0.08 & 0.08 \end{bmatrix}.$$

To calculate the first cell of the 2008 matrix, with $l = 1$ and $G = 1$, first add up all the values under 'pretty happy' and 'very happy' categories for all the quintiles, multiplied by the weight of the quintiles which is 0.2, yielding 0.86388. Note that since $l = 1$, we will multiply 0.2 to 0.86388. Next, subtract the total proportion of people in the top two categories for the lowest quintile, which is $(0.2677 + 0.5249)$ multiplied by 0.2. This should result in (0.13 times 0.2) after rounding off. Cell-wise comparison of the above two matrices shows that the distribution of 2010 has a lower value that that of 2008. Thus 2010 absolute Lorenz dominates 2008. However, as is evident from the Chen and Zheng (2014) paper, unlike the welfare dominance relations, the number of inequality dominance relations are limited as the conditions are more difficult to satisfy.

Examples from the literature
The above-mentioned study of Wang and Yu (2015) also applies the method of Zheng (2011) to income-related health inequality in China between 1997 and 2009 (with data

points in 1997, 2000, 2004, 2006 and 2009). They partition income levels into thirds, while the self-assessed health variable has four categories. When performing Lorenz dominance comparisons of income–health matrices between years, they find that while 2006 and 2009 are incomparable, both years separately dominate all previous years, that is, 1997, 2000 and 2004, in the sense that 2006 and 2009 feature more socioeconomic health inequality (that is, related to income) unambiguously. They also find that 2000 features more socioeconomic inequality than 1997. For each year, the authors also compare the income–health matrices of urban and rural areas. Every year, urban areas show higher socioeconomic inequality than rural areas.

Apouey and Silber (2013) apply their two measurement approaches to the measurement of an income–health gradient with ordinal data, using EU-SILC datasets for 24 European countries. They use two data points: for all countries they have data in 2011, but then for some countries they also have initial data in 2004, or 2005 or 2006. Hence they refer to 2004–2006 as the 'first year of data'. Their health variable is self-assessed with five categories, and their income variable is provided in quintiles. For their first approach, they compute a Gini index which measures the area between the 45-degree line and the concentration curve described above (the one constructed by ranking observations according to the ratios of observed to expected probabilities).[9] In the first year of data, Austria, Iceland and Italy exhibit the lowest Gini values; whereas Estonia, Lithuania and Portugal show up with the highest level of socioeconomic inequality. Meanwhile, in 2011, Iceland, Italy and France top the list of the least unequal countries; whereas Belgium, Portugal and Bulgaria show the highest inequality. Interestingly, only ten out of the 24 countries experience socioeconomic inequality reductions between the initial year and 2011.

Apouey and Silber (2013) also compute B1 (18.15) and B2 (18.16) for the same dataset. The rankings in each year differ slightly between the two bipolarisation indices. Likewise, in most cases the two indices move in the same direction between the initial year and 2011. Interestingly, even though the two indices are normalised between 0 and 1, the range of B2 tends to be higher than B1's. Further details appear in Apouey and Silber (2013, pp. 21–22, 24–25, tables 1 and 2).

18.4   BETWEEN-GROUP SOCIAL INEQUALITY WITH CARDINAL DATA

18.4.1   Data

When it comes to measuring social inequality, where we are interested in the differences between groups, any data with group-based information would suffice (for example, income means by ethnic group). In that sense, quantifying social inequality would be less demanding than total inequality in terms of data requirements. However, for most purposes we have to rely on household surveys to measure social inequality. The lack of proper household surveys is a big impediment to more widespread measurements of social inequality.

18.4.2 Measures of Between-Group Inequality when the Socioeconomic Variable is Unordered

When the groups are defined by unordered variables (for example, ethnicity) and the variable of interest is cardinal (for example, income), the literature measures between-group inequality by comparing the degree of dispersion across distributional standards for each group.[10] For example, one could take the mean of each group's distribution and compute an inequality index over the means. More frequently, practitioners remove all inequality within each group by replacing each group member's income with the respective group mean. Then, finally, they compute an inequality index over the whole population and its smoothed distribution. They interpret this latter value as the between-group component of total inequality. Meanwhile the within-group component can be obtained by subtracting the between-group component from the total inequality value, for a chosen index.

As explained by Lasso de la Vega (Chapter 17 in this *Handbook*), the first class of inequality indices fully decomposable into a between-group and a within-group component was identified and axiomatically characterized by Shorrocks (1980). It turns out that this is the class of generalized-entropy indices:

$$
GE(\alpha) = \begin{cases} \frac{1}{n\alpha(\alpha - 1)} \sum_{i=1}^{n} [(\frac{x_i}{\bar{x}})^{\alpha} - 1] & \text{if } \alpha \neq 0,1, \\ \frac{1}{n} \sum_{i=1}^{n} \frac{x_i}{\bar{x}} ln(\frac{x_i}{\bar{x}}) & \text{if } \alpha = 1 \\ -\frac{1}{n} \sum_{i=1}^{n} ln(\frac{x_i}{\bar{x}}) & \text{if } \alpha = 0, \end{cases}
\tag{18.17}
$$

Several famous inequality indices are members of the generalized entropy family. For example, $\alpha = 2$ yields half the squared coefficient of variation, $\alpha = 1$ yields the Theil index, and $\alpha = 0$ yields the mean log deviation. Now the respective between-group components of $GE(\alpha)$ are the following:

$$
BGE(\alpha) = \begin{cases} \frac{1}{G\alpha(\alpha - 1)} \sum_{i=1}^{G} s_i [(\frac{\bar{x}_i}{\bar{x}})^{\alpha} - 1] & \text{if } \alpha \neq 0,1, \\ \frac{1}{G} \sum_{i=1}^{G} s_i \frac{\bar{x}_i}{\bar{x}} ln(\frac{\bar{x}_i}{\bar{x}}) & \text{if } \alpha = 1 \\ -\frac{1}{G} \sum_{i=1}^{G} ln(\frac{\bar{x}_i}{\bar{x}}) & \text{if } \alpha = 0, \end{cases}
\tag{18.18}
$$

Foster and Shneyerov (2000) identified a second family of inequality indices that are decomposable into between- and within-group components. They call it the family of 'path-independent' families. Their idea is that, in principle, one could generate between-group inequality components by smoothing the distribution through replacing each individual's income with any generalized mean (for example, the Euclidean mean, the harmonic mean, the geometric mean) in addition to the arithmetic mean. For each type of mean used, the authors found the only inequality indices for which the within-group component is the weighted sum of each within-group inequality, where the weights are the group population shares. These are the path-independent inequality indices. Crucially, they found that in the case of smoothing with the arithmetic mean, the only Shorrocks-decomposable, path-independent inequality index is the mean log deviation, that is, $GE(0)$. Unfortunately, $GE(0)$ requires $x_i > 0$ $\forall i = 1, 2, \ldots, n$, although this should not be a problem for between-group inequality analysis in practice, since usually: $\bar{x}_i > 0$ $\forall i = 1, 2, \ldots, G$.[11]

Empirical illustration

There is considerable evidence in many countries of income inequality between regions, ethnic groups and gender. In the US, for instance, compared to White Americans, Hispanics and African-Americans earn 24 and 25 percent less, respectively (Fryer Jr, 2011). These inter-group comparisons give a good overview of the social inequality in society.

We use the between-group Theil index, that is, $BGE(1)$, to calculate the contributions of the different racial groups on overall inequality in the US in the last decade based on the US GSS data from 1994 to 2010. The analysis below is based on the respondents' income. The income information for the respondents show the income intervals that they belong to. We have assumed the average of the interval as the income of respondent. The population in the GSS is divided in to three racial categories: White Americans, African-Americans and Others. Table 18.4 presents the group contributions of the groups to the overall inequality.

It is interesting to note from Table 18.4 that White Americans have a positive value which indicates that they have a higher income share compared to their population share; on the other hand, the negative values of African-Americans indicate the opposite situation. What it shows is that White Americans contribute positively to the inequality and Blacks contribute negatively. The overall inequality, which is a summation of the group contributions, does not show any strong patterns. It increased in the early 2000s, followed by a decrease, and then an increase again. On the other hand, if we look into the within-

Table 18.4   Decomposition of the Theil income inequality index by racial group in the US

	Between-group inequality			Within-group inequality		
	Whites	Blacks	Others	Whites	Blacks	Others
1994	0.02	−0.02	0.01	0.30	0.25	0.32
1996	0.03	−0.02	−0.01	0.28	0.29	0.36
1998	0.05	−0.03	−0.01	0.33	0.29	0.32
2000	0.04	−0.03	0.00	0.33	0.40	0.22
2002	0.07	−0.03	−0.02	0.47	0.36	0.39
2004	0.04	−0.03	−0.01	0.36	0.32	0.35
2006	0.06	−0.02	−0.03	0.35	0.36	0.35
2008	0.04	−0.04	0.01	0.56	0.27	0.98
2010	0.06	−0.03	−0.01	0.36	0.33	0.45
2012	0.06	−0.03	−0.02	0.58	0.44	0.40

Source: Authors' calculation based on GSS data.

group inequality, the Whites have the lowest inequality compared to the other two groups. For both African-American and White Americans, compared to the Others the inequality within the group is lower in 2010 compared to 1994.

Examples from the literature

Applying the same decomposition of the Theil index, Galbraith and Hale (2009) looked into spatial inequality in the US in terms of income. Using the Bureau of Economic Analysis (BEA) data, they calculate both within-state and between-state inequality inequality for the period 1969 to 2006. The within-state component reflects the between-county inequality. The BEA definition of income is quite comprehensive, including rents, dividends and government payments apart from wages and salaries. Their main results are in Figure 18.1.[12]

During this period, while there has been a slight decrease in between-state inequality, the much larger within-state inequality has seen a significant increase. Further investigation reveals that the increase in inequality is higher in states where the dominant sectors are information technology (IT), finance and insurance. To some extent this seems to be picking up the worsening income distribution in the US during the dot-com bubble, but

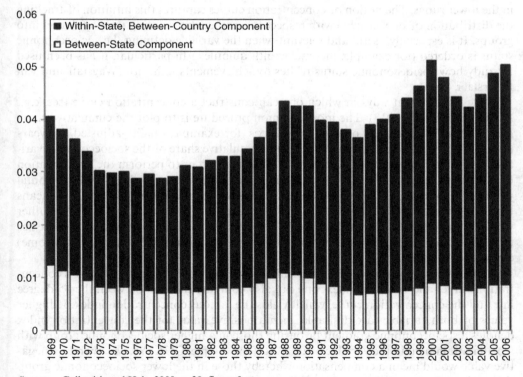

Source: Galbraith and Hale, 2009, p. 20, figure 9.

Figure 18.1   Income inequality in the US

also the huge increase in the finance sector remuneration during the early years of the last decade.

Other members of the generalized entropy family have also been used in applied work on between-group inequality, especially in the inequality-of-opportunity literature. For example, Roemer (2014) uses the coefficient of variation, while Ferreira and Gignoux (2011) use the mean-log deviation due to its path-independence decomposability property. In both cases the groups are defined by circumstances beyond the individuals' control. Hence this component can be interpreted as a lower bound of the illegitimate portion of total inequality.

18.4.3   Measures of Between-Group Inequality when the Socioeconomic Variable and the Variable of Interest are Continuous: Concentration Curves

Often we are interested in understanding the joint distribution of two variables of simultaneous interest. For instance, it is relevant, particularly from a policy perspective, to explore how health and socioeconomic status are distributed. The widely cited Whitehall study (Marmot et al., 1991) finds a strong health gradient with respect to socioeconomic levels. The study shows that those at higher positions in Whitehall, the United Kingdom (UK) government's administrative hub, fare better in terms of health compared to those in the lower rungs. The notion of concentration curves captures this intuition of tracking the distribution of one variable with respect to another one defining the population into groups. It is especially useful and relevant when the variable defining the socioeconomic status is ordered (for example, income, wealth quintiles.) In particular, it has been used to study how socioeconomic status relates to achievements in health (Wagstaff and van Doorslaer, 2000).

There are different ways in which one can construct a concentration curve (see, e.g., Apouey and Silber, 2013). The most common procedure is to plot the cumulative share of the variable of interest on the vertical axis, for example, quality-adjusted life years (QUALY) or years of education, against the cumulative share of the socioeconomic variable (for example, income) on the horizontal axis. In order to perform the accumulation of both variables, people need to be ranked in ascending order according to the horizontal variable. If the ensuing concentration curve runs along the 45-degree line, then it means that there are no differences in, say, QUALY, across different income levels. In other words, there is no income gradient for QUALY. By contrast, if the concentration curve lies to the bottom of the 45-degree line, then it means that richer people (in terms of income) enjoy more QUALY.[13]

In a manner analogous to the relationship between the Lorenz curve (which is a concentration curve) and the Gini index, one can also compute the area between the 45-degree line and the concentration curve, which yields the famous concentration index. If higher values of both variables are desirable, then a positive value for the concentration index denotes a socioeconomic gradient favouring those in a higher socioeconomic group with a better attainment in the variable of interest (for example, QUALY). Meanwhile, a negative value would mean a compensation whereby those in the lower socioeconomic group enjoy a better value of the variable on the vertical axis.

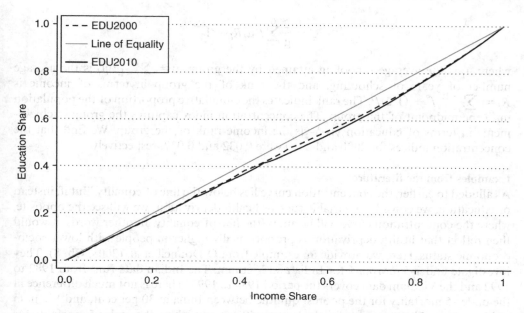

Notes: EDU2000 and EDU2010 stands for the educational achievement of the respondents in the year 2000 and 2010 respectively.

Source: Authors' own calculation using GSS data.

Figure 18.2   Education concentration curves for the US: 2000 and 2010

Empirical illustration

Let us consider the GSS data from the US again. Suppose we are interested in understanding how the level of education varies with respect to income. The appropriate technique would be to use the concentration curve. Education in the GSS data is given as the number of years in schooling of the respondent. We have taken the respondents' income in the survey, which is given as grouped information, as an indicator of the respondents' socioeconomic status. We plot the concentration curves for 2000 and 2010 in Figure 18.2.

On the horizontal axis we have the cumulative percentage of the population, starting from the lowest income to the highest. On the vertical axis, we have the cumulative share of education achieved by each of these income percentiles. Since education is a 'good', the concentration curve lies below the line of inequality. In both 2000 and 2010, we observe that the lower-income groups have disproportionately less education. One can interpret this as resulting in greater concentration of education in the richer groups. To some extent this is not surprising, as it is quite well established that there is a strong positive gradient between income and education. What is interesting to note is that the year-2000 concentration curve is nested within the year-2010 curve, thus indicating that the concentration of education in the richer income groups has indeed increased during the first decade of the twenty-first century in the US. In order to quantify the level of such concentration, we need an index. One of the popular concentration indices was proposed by Kakwani et al. (1997). For grouped data it is calculated as follows:

$$C = \frac{2}{\mu} \sum_{l=1}^{G} f^{l} \mu_{l} R_{l} - 1$$

where μ_{l} is the average schooling attained by the group, $\mu = \sum_{l=1}^{G} f^{l} \mu_{l}$ is the average number of years of schooling, and the rank of the group in terms of income is $R_{l} = \sum_{t=1}^{l-1} f^{t} + (1/2)f^{l}$. The rank indicates the cumulative proportion of the population until the midpoint of the group. The concentration index captures the group's achievements in terms of education vis-à-vis the income rank of the group. We find that the concentration indices for 2000 and 2010 were 0.032 and 0.037, respectively.

Examples from the literature
As alluded to earlier, the concentration curve lies below the line of equality. But if, instead of education, we consider a variable such as health deprivation, we will see the opposite, where the concentration curve will lie above the line of equality. In other words, it would then reflect that health deprivation is proportionally higher in people with lower socioeconomic status. Here we provide an example from O'Donnell et al. (2008, Ch. 8). They investigate under-5 mortality for India and Vietnam. The Indian data runs from 1982 to 1992 and the Vietnam data covers the period 1989 to 1998. There is not much difference in the under-5 mortality for the poorest quintile between India at 30 per cent, and Vietnam at 31 per cent. The gap arises for the bottom 40 per cent where the under-5 mortality for India rises to 59 per cent and in Vietnam it increases to 48 per cent. For the bottom 60 per cent, the increase is similar, with India at 79 per cent and Vietnam at 69 per cent. Finally, for the bottom 80 per cent, the gap narrows to 93 per cent under-5 mortality in India and 85 per cent in Vietnam. We plot the concentration curves for these data.

As is clear from Figure 18.3, the concentration curve lies above the line of equality, thus reflecting the fact that under-5 mortality is a 'bad'. Further, the concentration curve for Vietnam lies inside the concentration curve for India, thus indicating that the burden of

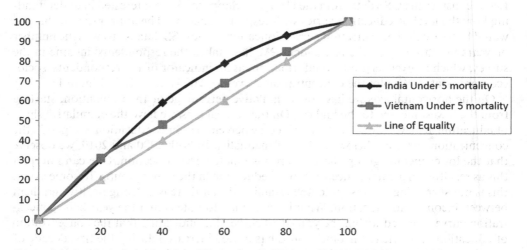

Source: Authors' calculation based on O'Donnell et al. (2008, pp. 99–100, Tables 8.1 and 8.2).

Figure 18.3   Concentration curves of under-5 mortality in India and Vietnam

the under-5 mortality falls more disproportionately on the poor in India than in Vietnam. In fact the concentration index for Vietnam is 0.64 compared to India's 0.44.

Frick and Ziebarth (2013) test the sensitivity of the income–health concentration index in Germany to different choices of income and wealth, as well as of health indicators. Relying on the German Socio-Economic Panel Study (SOEP), they try out four income variables, two wealth variables, four subjective health variables and four 'quasi-objective' health variables. For each combination of income (or wealth) and health indicator they compute the concentration index in two steps. Firstly, they implement one of its most common formulas:

$$CI = \frac{2}{\mu_h} cov(h_i, r_i^w),$$ (18.19)

where h_i is the health value of individual i, r_i^w is the rank of individual i in wealth (or income) variable w, and μ_h is the mean value of the health indicator. In practice, the authors used several health measures, some of which they treat as directly continuous. For other health variables which are clearly ordinal, for example self-assessed health variables with a limited number of response categories, the authors partition the domain of responses and transform these variables into binary-response indicators (hence the computation of μ_h ceases to be dependent on an arbitrary scale, even though there may be more than one justifiable way of dichotomizing the domain of the raw variable). In the second stage they normalize CI using the Wagstaff correction method, so that the concentration indices of health variables with different bounds and means become comparable:

$$WCI = \frac{\mu_h(b_h - a_h)}{(b_h - \mu_h)(\mu_h - a_h)} CI,$$ (18.20)

The authors compute 80 concentration indices, interacting the eight health variables with ten income–wealth variables (the six described above, plus four cases in which only positive values are considered). Among their main findings, they conclude that the change of socioeconomic variable affects the value of the concentration index the most whenever they use binary measures of self-assessed health. At the other extreme, the impact of a change in the socioeconomic variable is significantly milder when the health variables are 'quasi-objective' (for example, grip strength measured by hand dynamometer).

18.4.4 Between-Group Social Inequality with Bounded Cardinal Data

Only recently, a theoretical literature has explored and clarified the potential inconsistencies arising from the choice between attainment and shortfall variables when measuring inequality with bounded cardinal data (Erreygers, 2009a; Lambert and Zheng, 2011; Aristondo and Lasso de la Vega, 2013; Kjellsson and Gerdtham, 2013; Chakravarty et al., 2015. As is clear from Lasso de la Vega (Chapter 17 in this *Handbook*), the seminal theoretical papers were published between 2009 and 2013. Hence we should not expect many empirical applications applying the lessons of these theoretical papers as of the timing of this writing. But in the future, most research on bounded variables will surely adopt the indices that guarantee consistent inequality assessments between choices of attainment and shortfall variables. In the meantime, we found four recent illustrative papers on bounded cardinal variables, all of them related to health issues.[14]

Baeten et al. (2013) study the trends in socioeconomic health inequality in China between 1991 and 2006, that is, during part of the prolonged period of high economic development. They follow a cohort over six waves of the China Health and Nutrition Survey (CHNS). Their health measure is self-reported and bounded from above and below. Moreover, they are interested in so-called Income-Related Health Inequality (IRHI), that is, a measure of health inequality between income groups. Effectively they need a concentration index that is consistent to choices between attainment and shortfall variables (given the variable's double-bounded nature). For that purpose they compute the adjusted concentration index proposed by Erreygers (2009b), which is translation invariant:

$$CE = \frac{8}{n^2 (h^{max} - h^{min})} \sum_{i=1}^{n} z_i h_i, \tag{18.21}$$

where h_i is the health level of individual i, which can take maximum and minimum values of h^{max} and h^{min}, respectively.[15] $z_i = \frac{n+1}{2} - r_i$, that is, z_i is the deviation of individual i's income rank (r_i) from the median income rank (that is, $\frac{n+1}{2}$), where $r_i = 1$ for the richest individual and $r_i = n$ for the poorest individual. Therefore, clearly z_i is positive for people in the top half of the income distribution, and negative for those at the bottom half. As Baeten et al. (2013) explain, this effectively means that $CE > 0$ if the rich have overall better health than the poor. Conversely, $CE < 0$ implies that, overall, the health distribution is rather pro-poor. If only grouped data are available, then CE should be expressed in terms of the G groups as opposed to the n individuals.

Baeten et al. (2013) also perform interesting time decompositions to explain changes in IRHI in China. Here we will just report two basic findings. First, a steady increase in CE from 0.013 in 1991 to 0.0175 in 1993 to 0.0315 in 1997, followed by a plateau through 2000 (0.0332) and 2004 (0.0329), ending with a resumption of increased inequality toward 2006 (0.0408). In summary, a threefold increase in socioeconomic health inequality in China between 1991 and 2006. Second, a regional breakdown shows different patterns (Ibid., p. 1224, figure 5). The inland-rural trend is remarkably similar to the national trajectory. The coastal-rural trend is also similar to the national and inland-rural trend, but showing less inequality than the two latter, especially at the end of the period. By contrast the inland-urban regions show a steady increase from the beginning (no plateau) and the highest inequality levels during most years (1997 being the exception). Finally, the coastal-urban region exhibits the lowest levels of IRHI all through the period. More interestingly, after a plateau between 1991 and 1993, followed by a steep increase between 1993 and 1997, the trend continues with a mild but steady decline until the end of the studied period.

An early application of consistent inequality indices is provided by van Kippersluis et al. (2009), who studied the distribution of health and income-related health in 11 European Union countries between 1994 and 2001. Their main interest was to disentangle age and cohort effects for the mean levels of self-assessed health (constructed using the HUI mentioned above) and its levels of total and socioeconomic inequality, that is, both the degree of dispersion across the whole population and the degree of inequality in self-assessed health across ordered groups (income in their case). Since the authors are concerned by the bounds of their health variable, they use the adjusted concentration index of Erreygers (2009b) for measuring socioeconomic inequality, that is *CE*. For total inequality, they use the adjusted Gini index, also proposed by Erreygers (2009b), which is essentially *CE*, where now z_i in (18.21) depends not on the ranking of a socioeconomic variable like income, but instead on the ranking of h_i itself. The authors corroborate deteriorations in mean self-assessed health across the life cycle health for men and women in Belgium, Denmark, France, Germany, the Netherlands, the United Kingdom, Greece, Ireland, Italy, Portugal and Spain. More interestingly, they find that overall health inequality (as measured by the adjusted Gini) increases with age in all countries, whereas socioeconomic inequality (as measured by *CE*) remains remarkably constant throughout most of the life span, often decreasing at the very end, during the last years of life.

Kjellsson et al. (2015) relay the main lessons learned from the theoretical work from epidemiology and health economics on the attainment-shortfall inconsistency problem. They explain that in the case of bounded variables there are three choices of inequality measurement: (1) absolute; (2) relative-attainment; and (3) relative-shortfall. They further illustrate how (2) and (3) are inconsistent. Then they provide an example of socioeconomic inequality in child mortality among four Eastern European countries (Russia, Poland, the Czech Republic and Lithuania). The idea is that infant mortality rate is a bounded variable, and actually the shortfall counterpart to the infant survival rate. As an absolute index of socioeconomic inequality they use the 'slope index of inequality' (SII), a measure which is popular in the public health literature. The SII is constructed as follows: society is divided into *G* socioeconomic groups with a continuous or ordered variable, for example income deciles, or deciles for an index of material deprivation. Then for each socioeconomic group a distributional standard is computed, for example the mean survival rate for each decile. Then the distributional standard is regressed against the socioeconomic variable and a constant, for example the mean survival rates against the socioeconomic variable. The slope coefficient accompanying the regressor is the SII (see Murage et al., 2012).

Kjellsson et al. (2015) then construct an attainment-relative (ARII) and shortfall-relative (SRII) index by performing simple transformations on the SII. According to the SII, Russia has the highest socioeconomic inequality in mortality (19.4) followed by the Czech Republic (14.3), Lithuania (13.7) and Poland (11.7). Interestingly the ranking (which is consistent in the absolute case between the two choices of variable) is preserved in the computation of the ARII (with respective values of 1.02, 1.015, 1.014, 1.012). However, the SRII yields a different ranking. Shockingly, now Russia (2.4) emerges as the least unequal country, followed by Poland (2.6), Lithuania (3.3), and the Czech Republic (3.9).

Silber (2015) assesses trends in socioeconomic health inequality across Southern and South-Eastern Asia (Bangladesh, Cambodia, India, Indonesia, the Maldives, Nepal, Pakistan, the Philippines, Timor Leste and Vietnam) over the last 25 years. The author considers the degree of inequality across wealth quintiles over mean rates of: (1) infant mortality; (2) child mortality; (3) stunting; and (4) underweight; relying on data from the World Health Organization (WHO) Health Equity monitor. Since all these variables are bounded between 0 and 1, Silber (2015) uses six indices, all of which are consistent (in terms of the choice between attainments and shortfalls). The first index used is *CE* in equation (18.21). The second index, also proposed by Erreygers but in a different paper (Erreygers, 2009a), is a form of normalized standard deviation:

$$VE = \frac{2}{(h^{max} - h^{min})}\sqrt{\frac{1}{n}\sum_{i=1}^{n}(h_i - \bar{h})^2},$$

where: $\bar{h} \equiv \frac{1}{n}\sum_{i=1}^{n}h_i$. Again, if only group data are available for the computation of *VE* then the operations need to be performed in terms of *G* groups, as opposed to *n* individuals. The third index used by Silber (2015) is the following member of the family proposed by Lasso de la Vega and Aristondo (2012):

$$LA(0.5) = \left[\frac{\sqrt{I(H)} + \sqrt{I(H_{max} - H)}}{2}\right]^2,$$

where $I()$ is an inequality index, H is the distribution of bounded health attainments, and $H_{max} - H$ is the corresponding distribution of health shortfalls. Silber (2015) uses the Gini for $I()$. The fourth, fifth and sixth indices used by Silber (2015) are choices from three families of consistent inequality indices derived by Chakravarty et al. (2015). From the family of Atkinson consistent inequality indices, Silber (2015) chooses the Euclidean-mean version as the fourth index:

$$AC = \sqrt{\frac{1}{n^2}\sum_{i=1}^{n}\sum_{j=1}^{n}|h_i - h_j|^2}$$

From the family of Kolm consistent indices, Silber (2015) chooses the following member as the fifth index:

$$KC = \frac{1}{2}\ln\left(\frac{1}{n^2}\sum_{i=1}^{n}\sum_{j=1}^{n}\exp 2|h_i - h_j|\right)$$

Finally, Silber (2015) chooses the Theil consistent index as the fifth index for the empirical analysis:

$$TC = \left[\exp\frac{1}{n^2}\sum_{i=1}^{n}\sum_{j=1}^{n}\ln(1 + |h_i - h_j|)\right] - 1$$

In all the previous cases, again, if only group data are available, then the operations need to be performed in terms of *G* groups, as opposed to *n* individuals. For the case of infant mortality rates, Silber (2015) finds reductions in socioeconomic inequality according to most indices and in all surveyed countries. However, as mentioned, the results are not always robust across indices. For example, in the case of Cambodia (2000–2010), *VE*, *AC*, and *KC* all point to reduction. By contrast, the other three indices suggest either an increase or no movement (in the case of *CE*). On the other hand, for the Philippines (1998–2008) all indices concur in stating that socioeconomic inequality decreased. The lack of robustness in some country experiences should not come as a surprise. Consistent indices only ensure that the rankings will not be altered by the choice of attainment versus shortfall. Yet they do not guarantee that different indices will rank consistently between them. For the latter to occur a dominance condition needs to be met. In this case, the absolute Lorenz curves must not cross in order for a comparison (for example, one year against another one for the same country) to be robust to different index choices. Precisely because sometimes the dominance condition is not met, the exercise of Silber (2015) exemplifies the importance of assessing inequality trends with several inequality indices (in addition to performing dominance tests).

Similar situations arise for the case of stunting. In Nepal (2001–2011), for example, socioeconomic inequality increased robustly across the six indices. By contrast, in Bangladesh (1996–2007) some indices show an increase in inequality (*CE, LA, TC*) while the others present the opposite result (*VE, AC, KC*). Again, for child mortality some results are robust, as for Bangladesh (1993–2007) and Nepal (2001–2011), where all indices indicate inequality reduction; whereas others are not, such as for Vietnam (1997–2002) and Cambodia (2000–2010). The same situation arises for underweight, featuring some robust results such as an increase in inequality in Cambodia (2000–2010) and Nepal (2001–2011), whereas Bangladesh shows outcomes which depend on the choice of inequality index. Finally, Silber (2015) also provides us with a reminder that even within the same well-being dimension, for example health, the trends in socioeconomic or total inequality may vary by indicator (for example, child mortality, stunting, and so on).

18.5 CONCLUSION

The goal of this chapter was to familiarise the reader with some of the standard empirical methods used to measure social inequality, based on the different interpretations of this concept. We divided the discussions into two main sections based on the kind of data we face. Section 18.3 deals with social inequality when the variable of interest is ordinal. We started by briefly discussing attempts at cardinalising the ordinal variable. Then we moved onto more preferred methods that handle the discrete distributions directly. We provided both own and literature-based examples of empirical applications of the inequality measurement methods for ordinal variables discussed by our companion chapter (Lasso de la Vega, Chapter 17 in this *Handbook*). The section discusses methods, and provides empirical illustrations, for the measurement of between-group, or socio-economic, inequality when the variable of interest (for example, self-assessed health) is ordinal, and the group-defining variable (for example, education level) is discrete. We considered methods more appropriate for unordered and ordered socioeconomic variables, respectively.

Section 18.4 of the chapter is dedicated to the measurement of between-group, or socioeconomic, inequality for cardinal data. We started with a brief explanation of methods for the measurement of socioeconomic inequality when the variable of interest is cardinal (for example, income) and the socioeconomic group is unordered (for example, ethnic group), followed by own and literature's empirical illustrations. Then we moved onto the measurement of between-group inequality when the socioeconomic variable is continuous. Here we delved into concentration curves, the main method devised for this data setting.

We provided a few own and literature examples, while acknowledging that the empirical literature on concentration curves is vast and better covered in other collections (see, e.g., Fleurbaey and Schokkaert, 2011). We finished this section with a brief overview of the most recent empirical applications of the relatively new methods developed to measure between-group inequality with bounded cardinal data (which are more thoroughly discussed in the companion chapter in this *Handbook*, Chapter 17 by Lasso de la Vega).

One of the main lessons stemming from the empirical literature is that our narrative and understanding of trends in social inequality relies heavily on our methodological choices: the choice of indicator for the variable or dimension of interest; the choice of variable(s) used to define the socioeconomic groups; the choice of inequality index. Whether the results are robust to alternative choices is an empirical question. At least in the case of index choices, there is often the possibility of performing stochastic dominance analysis for inequality measurement. We discussed some of these methods, for example, S-dominance (Allison and Foster, 2004) and the matrix approach by Zheng (2011). When the dominance condition is fulfilled, then an inequality comparison (for example, year 1 versus year 2, or country A versus B) is robust to the choice of a broad family of measures. However, sometimes the condition is not fulfilled, in which case a pairwise comparison will depend on the choice of measure. For that same reason, dominance analysis can rarely rank a whole set of distributions fully. Moreover, even when dominance conditions hold across the board, they only provide an ordinal ranking. They do not tell us much as to the inequality gap between two distributions. Hence the need to use inequality indices as well.

In this chapter our focus has primarily been on the most basic methods of social inequality measurement; therefore, we have bypassed some important measurement and behavioural aspects. Firstly, we have not really delved into the determinants of social inequality. While measurement of social inequality is important, it is equally important to understand the determinants behind it. Secondly, we have not discussed the decomposition methods used, especially in the health literature, in order to quantify descriptively the (associative rather than causal) contribution of socioeconomic and contextual covariates to social inequality trends. Several of the papers cited above also illustrate these more sophisticated methods of analysis.

We have also not covered the notions of social polarization and bipolarization; both different concepts from social inequality, despite apparent similarities on the surface. Albeit briefly discussed, regression-based analysis needs to be more fully explored. Still, we hope that this chapter will encourage more rigorous applications on measuring and understanding social inequality.

ACKNOWLEDGEMENTS

We are grateful to Conchita D'Ambrosio for her support, encouragement and patience. The usual disclaimer applies.

NOTES

1. The reader is invited to track the popularity of the word 'inequality' in English-speaking countries using Google Trends.
2. This is, for instance, the definition of the related Wikipedia article titled 'Social inequality'.
3. For standard inequality measures see Foster and Sen (1997) and Cowell (2011).
4. $\tau = 0.73$ ensures that $AP = 0.5$ when $m = 5$ and the distribution across categories is uniform, as explained by the authors, citing Apouey (2007. p. 885). Note that the intuition of this measure is based on the notion of polarisation.
5. A value of τ that would render the index equal to 0.5 when the variable is uniformly distributed across four categories.
6. For a comprehensive treatment of dissimilarity measurement see Andreoli and Zoli (2014).
7. Further indices in this spirit can be found in Reardon (2009).
8. We continue the discussion on concentration curves below.
9. The authors also compute other statistics based on measurement concepts not covered in this review.
10. If the groups are defined by an ordered variable, then other measurement methods such as concentration curves can be more relevant and/or insightful. We discuss these below.
11. As explained by Lasso de la Vega (Chapter 17 in this *Handbook*), Ebert (2010) has identified a third different family of inequality indices which are decomposable into different definitions of between- and within-group components.
12. We gratefully acknowledge the permission granted by Professor Galbraith to reproduce Figure 18.1.
13. Should the concentration curve be above the 45-degree line then the opposite would ensue: poorer people would have more QUALY.
14. We are not considering papers from the inequality of opportunity literature, which, as mentioned previously, is not being covered in this chapter.
15. Note that h can be normalized so that $h^{max} = 1$ and $h^{min} = 0$, leading to $CE = \frac{8}{n^2}\sum_{i=1}^{n} z_i h_i$, as shown by Baeten et al. (2013).

REFERENCES

Abul Naga, R., C. Stepenhurst, and G. Yalonetzky (2016). Statistical inference for ordinal inequality preorderings. mimeo.

Abul Naga, R. and T. Yalcin (2008). Inequality measurement for ordered response health data. *Journal of Health Economics* 27, 1614–1625.

Abul Naga, R. and T. Yalcin (2010). Median independent inequality orderings. Mimeo.

Acemoglu, D. and J. Robinson (2012). *Why Nations Fail: The Origins of Power, Prosperity and Poverty*. Crown, New York.

Alesina, A., R. Di Tella, and R. MacCulloch (2004). Inequality and happiness: are Europeans and Americans different?. *Journal of Public Economics* 88(9–10), 2009–2042.

Allison, A. and J. Foster (2004). Measuring health inequality using qualitative data. *Journal of Health Economics* 23, 505–524.

Andreoli, F. and C. Zoli (2014). Measuring dissimilarity. University of Verona Department of Economics WP-23.

Apouey, B. (2007). Measuring health polarisation with self-assessed health data. *Health Economics* 16, 875–894.

Apouey, B. and J. Silber (2013). Inequality and bi-polarization in socioeconomic status and health: ordinal approaches. In P.R. Dias and O. O'Donnell (eds), *Health and Inequality* (Research on Economic Inequality), Vol. 21, pp. 77–109. Emerald, Bingley.

Aristondo, O. and C. Lasso de la Vega (2013). Measuring the inequality of bounded distributions: a joint analysis of attainments and shortfalls, In P.R. Dias and O. O'Donnell (eds), *Health and Inequality* (Research on Economic Inequality, Vol. 21). pp. 33–52. Emerald, Bingley.

Badgett, M.V.L. and H.L. Hartmann (1995). *Economic Perspectives on Affirmative Action*, The effectiveness of equal employment opportunity policies. University Press of America, Lanham, MD.

Baeten, S., T. van Ourti and E. van Doorslaer (2013). Rising inequalities in income and health in China: who is left behind?. *Journal of Health Economics* 32(6), 1214–1229.

Balestra, C. and N. Ruiz (2015). Scale-invariant measurement of inequality and welfare in ordinal achievements: an application to subjective well-being and education in OECD countries. *Social Indicators Research* 123, 479–500.

Chakravarty, S., N. Chattopadhyay and C. D'Ambrosio (2015). On a family of achievement and shortfall inequality indices. *Health Economics* 25(12), 1503–1513.

Chen, S. and B. Zheng (2014). Socioeconomic inequality in happiness in the United States. In *Economic Well-Being and Inequality: Papers from the Fifth ECINEQ Meeting* (Research on Economic Inequality, Vol. 22), pp. 217–236. Emerald, Bingley.

Costa Font, J. and F. Cowell (2013). Measuring health inequality with categorical data: some regional patterns. In P.R. Dias and O. O'Donnell (eds), *Health and Inequality* (Research on Economic Inequality), Vol. 21, pp. 535–576. Emerald, Bingley.

Cowell, F. (2011). *Measuring Inequality* (3 edn). Oxford University Press, Oxford.

Cowell, F. and E. Flachaire (2012). Inequality with ordinal data. Public Economics Programme Discussion Paper No. 16, London School of Economics and Political Sciences, London.

D'Ambrosio, C. and I. Permanyer (2015). Measuring social polarpolarization with ordinal and categorical data. *Journal of Public Economic Theory* 17(3), 311–327.

Di Tella, R., R. MacCulloch and A. Oswald (2006). The macroeconomics of happiness. *Review of Economics and Statistics* 85(4), 809–827.

Dorling, D. (2011). *Injustice: Why Social Inequality Persists*. Policy Press, Bristol.

Dutta, I. and J. Foster (2013). Inequality of happiness in the US: 1972–2010. *Review of Income and Wealth* 59(3), 393–415.

Dutta, I., P. Madden, and A. Mishra (2014). Group inequality and conflict. *Manchester School* 82(3), 257–283.

Ebert, U. (2010). The decomposition of inequality reconsidered: weakly decomposable measures. *Mathematical Social Sciences* 60, 94–103.

Erreygers, G. (2009a). Can a single indicator measure both attainment and shortfall inequality?. *Journal of Health Economics* 28(4), 885–893.

Erreygers, G. (2009b). Correcting the concentration index. *Journal of Health Economics* 28, 504–515.

Esteban, J.-M. and D. Ray (1994). On the measurement of polarization. *Econometrica* 62(4), 819–851.

Esteban, J.-M. and D. Ray (2008). On the salience of ethnic conflict. *American Economic Review* 98, 2185–2202.

Ferreira, F. and J. Gignoux (2011). The measurement of inequality of opportunity: theory and an application to Latin America. *Review of Income and Wealth* 57(4), 622–657.

Fleurbaey, M. and E. Schokkaert (2011). Equity in health and health care. In M. Pauly, T. McGuire and P. Barros (eds), *Handbook of Health Economics*, Vol. 2, pp. 1003–1092. North–Holland, Amsterdam.

Foster, J. and A. Sen (1997). Annexe. *On Economic Inequality*, pp. 107–220. Oxford University Press.

Foster, J. and A. Shneyerov (2000). Path independent inequality measures. *Journal of Economic Theory* 91, 199–222.

Frick, J. and N. Ziebarth (2013). Welfare-related health inequality: does the choice of measure matter?. *European Journal of Health Economics* 14, 431–442.

Fryer Jr, R. (2011). Racial inequality in the 21st century: the declining significance of discrimination. In O. Ashenfelter and D. Carel (eds), *Handbook of Labor Economics*, Vol. 4, pp. 855–971. North–Holland, Amsterdam.

Fusco, A. and J. Silber (2014). On social polarization and ordinal variables the case of self-assessed health. *European Journal of Health Economics* 15, 841–851.

Galbraith, J. and T. Hale (2009). The evolution of economic inequality in the United States, 1969–2007: evidence from data on inter-industrial earnings and inter-regional incomes. University of Texas Inequality Project, 57.

Holzer, H. and D. Neumark (2000). Assessing affirmative action. *Journal of Economic Literature* 38(3), 483–568.

Jones, A., N. Rice, S. Robone and P. Rosa Dias (2011). Inequality and polarisation in health systems' responsiveness: a cross-country analysis. *Journal of Health Economics* 30, 616–625.

Kakwani, N., A. Wagstaff and E. van Doorslaer (1997). Socioeconomic inequalities in health: measurement, computation, and statistical inference. *Journal of Econometrics* 77, 87–103.

Kjellsson, G. and U. Gerdtham (2013). Lost in translation: rethinking the inequality equivalence for bounded health variables. In P.R. Dias and O. O'Donnell (eds), *Health and inequality* (Research on Economic Inequality, Vol. 21, pp. 3–32. Emerald, Bingley.

Kjellsson, G., U. Gerdtham and D. Petrie (2015). Lies, damned lies, and health inequality measurements. understanding the value judgments. *Epidemiology* 26(5), 673–680.

Lambert, P. and B. Zheng (2011). On the consistent measurement of attainment and shortfall inequality. *Journal of Health Economics* 30(1), 214–219.

Lasso de la Vega, C. and O. Aristondo (2012). Proposing indicators to measure achievement and shortfall inequality consistently. *Journal of Health Economics* 31(4), 578–583.

Lazar, A. and J. Silber (2013). On the cardinal measurement of health inequality when only ordinal information is available on individual health status. *Health Economics* 22(1), 106–113.

Lv, G., Y. Wang and Y. Xu (2015). On a new class of measures for health inequality based on ordinal data. *Journal of Economic Inequality* 13, 465–477.

Madden, D. (2010). Ordinal and cardinal measures of health inequality: an empirical comparison. *Health Economics* 19, 243–250.

Madden, D. (2011). The impact of an economic boom on the level and distribution of subjective well-being: Ireland 1994–2001. *Journal of Happiness Studies* 12, 667–679.

Majumdar, M. and S. Subramanian (2011). Capability failure and group disparities: some evidence from India for the 1980s. *Journal of Development Studies* 37(5), 104–140.

Marmot, M. (2005). Social determinants of health inequalities. *Lancet* 365, 1099–1104.

Marmot, M., G. Smith, S. Stansfeld, et al. (1991). Health inequalities among British civil servants: the Whitehall II study. *Lancet* 337(8754), 1387–1393.

Murage, P., J. Hamm and M. Brannan (2012). The Slope Index of Inequality (SII) in life expectancy: interpreting it and comparisons across London. London Health Inequalities Network.

O'Donnell, O., E. van Doorslaer, A. Wagstaff and M. Lindelow (2008). Analyzing health equity using household survey data. World Bank.

Reardon, S. (2009). Measures of ordinal segregation. In Y. Flückiger, S.F. Reardon and Jaques Silber (eds), *Occupational and Residential Segregation*, (Research on Economic Inequality, Vol. 17), pp. 129–155. Emerald, Bingley.

Roemer, J. (2014). Economic development as opportunity equalization. *World Bank Economic Review* 28(2), 189–209.

Roemer, J. and A. Trannoy (2015). Equality of opportunity. In A. Atkinson and F. Bourguignon (eds), *Handbook of Income Distribution*, Vol. 2, pp. 217–300. North–Holland, Amsterdam.

Shorrocks, A. (1980). The class of additively decomposable inequality measures. *Econometrica* 48, 613–625.

Silber, J. (2015). On inequality in health and pro-poor development: the case of Southeast Asia. *Journal of Economic Studies* 42(1), 34–53.

Silber, J. and G. Yalonetzky (2011). Measuring inequality in life chances with ordinal variables. In J.G. Rodríguez (ed.), *Inequality of Opportunity: Theory and Measurement*, (Research on Economic Inequality, Vol. 19), pp. 77–98. Emerald, Bingley.

Stevenson, B. and J. Wolfers (2008). Economic growth and subjective well-being: reassessing the Easterlin paradox. *Brookings Papers on Economic Activity* 39(1), 1–102.

Stewart, F. (2009). Horizontal inequalities as a cause of conflict. Bradford Development Lecture.

Stewart, F., G. Brown and L. Mancini (2005). Why horizontal inequalities matter: some implications for measurement. CRISE Working Paper No. 19.

van Doorslaer, E. and A. Jones (2003). Inequalities in self-reported health: validation of a new approach to measurement. *Journal of Health Economics* 22(1), 61–87.

van Kippersluis, H., T. van Ourti, O. O'Donnell and E. van Doorslaer (2009). Health and income across the life cycle and generations in Europe. *Journal of Health Economics* 28(4), 818–830.

Veenhoven, R. (1990). Inequality in happiness: inequality in countries compared across countries. MPRA Paper 11275.

Wagstaff, A. and E. van Doorslaer (2000). Income inequality and health: what does the literature tell us?. *Annual Review of Public Health* 21, 543–567.

Wang, H. and Y. Yu (2015). Increasing health inequality in China: an empirical study with ordinal data. *Journal of Economic Inequality*. DOI 10.1007/s10888-015-9315-1.

Weitzman, M. (1970). Measures of overlap of income distributions of white and Negro families in the United States. US Bureau of the Census.

Zheng, B. (2011). A new approach to measure socioeconomic inequality in health. *Journal of Economic Inequality* 9(4), 555–577.

19. Income and social polarization: theoretical approaches
Iñaki Permanyer

19.1 INTRODUCTION

Over the last two decades, we have witnessed a growing interest in the conceptualization and measurement of polarization. This interest can be partly attributable to the existing relationship between polarization, socioeconomic stability and economic growth. Loosely speaking, polarization has to do with the clustering of individuals forming groups in different parts of a given distribution, particularly in its extremes. In politics, a society can be said to become more polarized if its members fly away from a moderate 'centre position' and become more radicalized towards opposing and irreconcilable poles. In the case of income distributions, societies become more polarized when the middle class is hollowed-out and greater proportions of individuals fall in the 'poor' and 'rich' categories. It has been persuasively argued elsewhere that the disappearance of the middle class hinders economic mobility and economic growth. Moreover, highly polarized societies are more prone to experience episodes of social unrest, tension, revolt and even armed conflict.

For many years, it has been common to relate the origins of social conflictivity with high levels of inequality. In this respect, the empirical literature offers, at best, mixed and inconclusive evidence. As will be shown in a companion chapter of this volume, polarization measures have typically performed better than their inequality counterparts when explaining episodes of social tension or conflict. This chapter, however, is of a more theoretical and technical nature. Because of space limitations, the measures presented in this chapter are not discussed in great depth (the interested reader can check the corresponding references for greater detail). Rather, its main goal is to provide a wide overview of the different approaches that have been proposed so far in the conceptualization and measurement of polarization.

As with many other terms related to socioeconomic phenomena (for example, 'inequality', 'poverty' and 'well-being'), the term 'polarization' means different things to different people. The many and diverse ways in which researchers have tried to formalize the intuitions underlying the notion of polarization has generated a myriad of measures – each of which attempts to approach the same object from a different angle – that are explored in this chapter. During the last 20 years or so, when this literature has been blossoming, it has not been uncommon to see some confusion regarding the notions of polarization and inequality because of the close relationship existing between them. This is why many contributions to the polarization literature – particularly the original ones in the mid-1990s – have made strong efforts to establish a clear distinction and avoid misunderstandings. As will be seen in this chapter, even if the notion of inequality is intimately embedded in the conceptualization of polarization, and it has been particularly influential in the developments of the latter, the two ideas are fundamentally different and very often lead to opposing views and results when evaluating states of affairs.

Roughly speaking, most of the contributions to the measurement of polarization can be classified under the headings of 'income polarization' and 'social polarization' measures. Income polarization indices measure the extent to which individuals are clustered around local and antagonistic poles in the income distribution; they will be reviewed in section 19.2. That section examines the so-called 'bipolarization' indices and the 'multipolar' ones. Clearly, when a particular income polarization index is chosen, alternative income distributions will be ranked completely; that is, given any couple of distributions the index will be able to establish which one of them is more polarized than the other. However, if we use different indices, there may be different rankings of the distributions. In this context, it is common to seek classes of indices that produce the same orderings of alternative sets of income distributions. The incipient literature on polarization orderings – which is very much related to the literature on inequality and poverty orderings – is also explored in section 19.2.

It has been argued that social tension or conflict may be articulated along certain factors other than income distributions, such as culture or biology. These factors typically include ethnicity, race or religion. The measures attempting to capture the notion of polarization when the salient characteristic that divides a given society is of that nature can be classified under the label of 'social polarization'. They are analysed in section 19.3. Given the fact that social tension can take place along economic and non-economic lines, it is also desirable to have polarization measures able to capture both factors simultaneously. These are the so-called 'hybrid polarization' measures, which are described in section 19.4. Lastly, section 19.5 is devoted to future research lines that need to be further investigated.

Throughout this chapter, the following general notation is used. A polarization index is denoted by P and the corresponding sub-index and super-index. The super-index is typically an acronym with the first letter of the author's last name, and the sub-index indicates the kind of index referred to. More specifically, P_I denotes an income polarization index, P_S a social polarization index, P_H a hybrid polarization index, and P_M a multidimensional polarization index.

19.2   INCOME POLARIZATION MEASURES

As many other subfields in welfare analysis, the first polarization measures introduced in the literature were primarily interested in the distribution of income across the population. This section is devoted to exploring the different income polarization measures that have been proposed so far. For that purpose we need to introduce some notation. For a population of size N, an income distribution will be given by a pair (n, y), where $y = (y_1, \ldots, y_k)$ is the vector of different income levels and $n = (n_1, \ldots, n_k)$ is the vector of corresponding population sizes (that is, n_i is the number of individuals with income exactly equal to y_i). Clearly, $\sum_i n_i = N$. Defining $\pi_i := n_i/N$, $\pi = (\pi_1, \ldots, \pi_k)$ is the vector of corresponding population shares. It is assumed that each y_i belongs to a right-open interval of the real line R^1: $[a, +\infty)$ with $a \geq 0$. The set of income distributions for such population will be denoted by D. For any $(n, y) \in D$, the mean and the median will be denoted by $\mu(n, y)$ and $m(n, y)$ respectively (or μ, m for short). We will denote by 1^k the k-coordinated vector of ones. Assuming that the y_i's are ordered non-decreasingly, we denote by y^U (resp. y^L) the vector of such y_i's above (resp. below) the median m. The expressions μ^U and μ^L will be used to denote the mean values of the numbers in y^U and y^L respectively.

An income polarization index is defined as a real-valued function $P_I:D \to R^1$. For all $(n, y) \in D$, the value $P_I(n, y)$ indicates the level of polarization corresponding to the distribution (n, y).

Income polarization indices can be classified in two subgroups: the so-called 'bipolarization' indices (that basically measure the extent to which an income distribution is clustered around the 'poor' and 'rich' poles) and 'multipolar' indices (that measure the extent to which an income distribution has an arbitrary number of antagonistic poles). Before exploring the corresponding indices that have been proposed in the literature (see below) we will briefly examine their normative foundations, that is: the axiomatic properties upon which they are based. Some of these axioms apply for both bipolarization indices and multipolar ones, but some of them are group-specific. The most basic axioms are the following:

Normalization: If $(n, y) \in D$ is such that there exists $j \in \{1,\ldots,k\}$ with $n_j = N$, then $P_I(n, y) = 0$.

Scale invariance: For all $(n, y) \in D$ and all scalars $\lambda > 0$, $P_I(n, y) = P_I(n, \lambda y)$.

Translation invariance: For all $(n, y) \in D$ and all scalars $\lambda > 0$, $P_I(n, y) = P_I(n, y+\lambda 1^k)$.

Symmetry: For all $(n, y) \in D$, $P_I(n, y) = P_I(n\Pi, y\Pi)$, where Π is any $k \times k$ permutation matrix.

Population principle: For all $(n, y) \in D$, $P_I(n, y) = P_I(\lambda n, y)$, where $\lambda > 0$.

Continuity: P_I is a continuous function in its arguments.

These axioms are so mild that they are not able to pin down a specific polarization index. As a matter of fact they are so general that they have also been applied with minor modifications when characterizing inequality or poverty indices, so they will not be discussed here. The following two axioms are the cornerstones upon which income bipolarization measures are based:

Increased spread: Consider any $(n, y) \in D$ and $(n, x) \in D$ such that $m(n, y) = m(n, x) = m$. Consider the following scenarios: (1) There exists $j \in \{1,\ldots,k\}$ such that $x_j < y_j < m$ and $x_i = y_i$ for all $i \neq j$; (2) There exists $l \in \{1,\ldots,k\}$ such that $m < y_l < x_l$ and $x_i = y_i$ for all $i \neq l$. If either (1), (2) or both (1) and (2) are true, then $P_I(n, x) > P_I(n, y)$.

This axiom basically states that greater distancing between the groups below and above the median should make the distribution more polarized (see Figure 19.1).

Increased bipolarity: Consider any $(n, y) \in D$ and $(n, x) \in D$ such that $m(n, y) = m(n, x) = m$. Consider the following scenarios: (1) x has been obtained from y by a progressive transfer of income from richer person 'b' to poorer person 'a' with $y_b < m$; (2) x has been obtained from y by a progressive transfer of income from richer person 'd' to poorer person 'c' with $y_c > m$. If either (1), (2) or both (1) and (2) are true, then $P_I(n, x) > P_I(n, y)$.

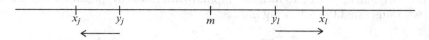

Figure 19.1   Illustration of 'increasing spread'

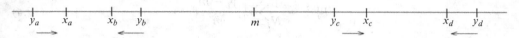

Figure 19.2   Illustration of 'increased bipolarity'

Increased bipolarity is a clustering or bunching principle. It basically states that when egalitarian transfers between individuals on the same side of the median take place, polarization should increase (see Figure 19.2). This axiom is what essentially distinguishes polarization from inequality. While all inequality measures satisfying the Pigou–Dalton transfers principle would decrease after the transfer, increased bipolarity states that polarization should increase.

With these and other similar axioms, different authors have characterized some of the income bipolarization measures reviewed next.

19.2.1   Income Bipolarization Measures

The first bipolarization measures were proposed in Foster and Wolfson (1992 [2010]) and later used in Wolfson (1994, 1997). While originally derived from a polarization ordering approach (see section 19.3), the authors proposed the following bipolarization index:

$$P_I^{FW} = (T - G)\frac{\mu}{m} \tag{19.1}$$

where $T = (\mu^U - \mu^L)/\mu$ and G is the relative Gini index. The value of T is known as the relative median deviation. When the distribution is symmetric, $\mu = m$, so bipolarization simply equals the difference between T and G, which is always non-negative. Foster and Wolfson (1992 [2010]) also showed that P_I^{FW} can be written as:

$$P_I^{FW} = (G_B - G_W)\frac{\mu}{m} \tag{19.2}$$

where G_B and G_W are the between- and within-group inequality values (as measured with the Gini index) in a partitioning of the population in two groups: those above the median and those below it.[1] Equation (19.2) clearly shows that in some cases, inequality and polarization can go in opposite directions: *ceteris paribus*, a greater level of within group inequality raises overall inequality but lowers polarization. The bipolarization index P_I^{FW} is simple, intuitive and – as will be shown below – it has been generalized in different directions. To be sure, it should be pointed out that different authors speak about the Wolfson index when referring to P_I^{FW}. The indices shown in equations (19.1) and (19.2) are written in relative terms (that is, the expressions between parentheses are divided by the mean μ). It is straightforward to obtain their absolute counterparts substituting G and T with the absolute Gini and the absolute median deviation respectively.

Another original approach to measure bipolarization was proposed by Wang and Tsui (2000), who suggested the following indices:

$$P_I^{WTa} = \frac{1}{N}\sum_{i=1}^{k} n_i |y_i - m|^r \tag{19.3}$$

$$P_I^{WTr} = \frac{1}{N}\sum_{i=1}^{k} n_i \left|\frac{y_i - m}{m}\right|^r \tag{19.4}$$

where $r \in (0,1)$. The Wang and Tsui indices simply aggregate the deviations of the individual incomes from the median when those are measured in absolute or relative terms (equations 19.3 and 19.4, respectively). Larger values of parameter r give more importance to very large deviations from the median.

Extensions

The indices presented in the previous section gave way to a number of extensions and generalizations aiming to improve some of the former deficiencies. As noted in Chakravarty and Majumder (2001) and Chakravarty et al. (2007), the indices shown in equations (19.1)–(19.4) are purely descriptive regarding the distribution of incomes around the median, but they were derived without making any use of welfare concepts. For this reason, these authors suggested using relative and absolute indices of bipolarization using explicit forms of social welfare functions. The relative index proposed by Chakravarty and Majumder (2001) can be written as follows:

$$P_I^{CM} = \frac{\mu^U(1 - I(y^U)) + 2\mu^U + \mu^L(1 - I(y^L)) - B(m)\mu^L}{2m} + H(m) \tag{19.5}$$

where $B(m)$ and $H(m)$ are chosen so that the bipolarization axioms are satisfied and $I(y^U)$ (resp. $I(y^L)$) is the value of an inequality index for the numbers in the vector y^U (resp. y^L). Equation (19.5) generalizes the Foster–Wolfson index by using other indices of inequality rather than the original Gini; in fact, whenever I is the Gini index, equation (19.5) essentially reduces to the Foster–Wolfson bipolarization index shown in equations (19.1) and (19.2). When alternative inequality formulations like the Atkinson or the Theil indices are chosen, the corresponding polarization index satisfies other ethical principles the decision-maker might be interested in. In a very similar fashion, Chakravarty et al. (2007) proposed the following index:

$$P_I^{CMR} = \frac{\mu^U(1 - I(y^U)) + 2\mu^U + \mu^L(1 - I(y^L)) - \tilde{B}(m)\mu^L}{2} + \tilde{H}(m) \tag{19.6}$$

where $\tilde{B}(m)$ and $\tilde{H}(m)$ serve the same purpose as the $B(m)$ and $H(m)$ in equation (19.5). Clearly, (19.6) is the absolute version of (19.5); it can also be interpreted as a generalization of the absolute version of the Foster–Wolfson index.

Also similar to the Foster–Wolfson index, Rodriguez and Salas (2003) proposed the so-called extended Wolfson bipolarization measure as:

$$P_I^{RS} = G_B(v) - G_W(v) \tag{19.7}$$

where $G_B(v)$ (resp. $G_W(v)$) is the between-group (resp. within-group) component associated with the Donaldson and Weymark (1980) extended Gini inequality index[2] assuming that the population is bi-partitioned across the median. In order to satisfy the increased bipolarity axiom, Rodriguez and Salas (2003) show that parameter v must lie somewhere in the interval [2, 3]. The idea of defining bipolarization as the difference of between-group and within-group inequality when the population is split in two across the median income was also present in the index proposed by Silber et al. (2007):

$$P_I^{SDH} = (G_B - G_W)/G \tag{19.8}$$

Following the same basic idea, bipolarization has also been defined as:

$$P_I^{ZK_G} = G_B/G_W \tag{19.9}$$

Clearly, equation (19.9) can be seen as a 'multiplicative' version of equations (19.7) and (19.8); that is, rather than using the difference in between-group and within-group inequalities, one uses their ratio. Equation (19.9) is very similar to the hybrid polarization measure proposed by Zhang and Kanbur (2001) and presented in equation (19.41) below. The similarity between equations (19.2), (19.7), (19.8) and (19.9) is clear. As is clear from equation (19.9), such a polarization index can be problematic when there is no within-group inequality. In this respect, it is easy to show that $P_I^{SDH} = (P_I^{ZK_G} - 1)/(P_I^{ZK_G} + 1)$, so this measure avoids the eventual problem of zero denominators. An axiomatic characterization of a broad class of bipolarization indices can be found in Bossert and Schworm (2008).

Chakravarty (2009, p. 117) proposed the following bipolarization indices:

$$P_I^{C_\varepsilon} = \frac{\left(\dfrac{1}{N}\sum_{i=1}^{k} n_i |m - y_i|^\varepsilon\right)^{1/\varepsilon}}{m}, \quad 0 < \varepsilon < 1 \tag{19.10}$$

$P_I^{C_\varepsilon}$ is the ratio between the generalized mean of order ε of deviations of individual incomes from the median and the median. The absolute version of equation (19.10) is given by:

$$P_I^{C_a\varepsilon} = \left(\frac{1}{N}\sum_{i=1}^{k} n_i |m - y_i|^\varepsilon\right)^{1/\varepsilon} = m P_I^{C_\varepsilon}, \quad 0 < \varepsilon < 1 \tag{19.11}$$

While not being exactly the same, the indices $P_I^{C_\varepsilon}$ and $P_I^{C_a\varepsilon}$ are reminiscent of the bipolarization indices proposed by Wang and Tsui (2000) in equations (19.3) and (19.4).

19.2.2 Polarization Orderings

As is well known, different bipolarization indices might rank alternative distributions in different directions. In some cases, one might be interested in having a more robust procedure to rank distributions that remains unchanged when choosing all possible indices belonging to a particular class. This partial ordering approach is reviewed in this section, in which we assume that the population weights $n_i = 1$ for all i to simplify notation and define $\overline{N} = (N + 1)/2$. Similarly to the Lorenz curve in the inequality framework, different authors have defined polarization curves to rank distributions in terms of polarization in a robust manner.

The first authors to speak about polarization curves were Foster and Wolfson (1992 [2010]), who defined the so-called relative polarization curve. That curve shows the extent to which a given distribution is different from the hypothetical situation in which everybody has an income equal to the median. The ordinate corresponding to the population proportion q/N equals:

$$FWC_R(y,q) = \begin{cases} \dfrac{1}{N}\displaystyle\sum_{q \leq i \leq \overline{N}} \dfrac{(m(y) - y_i)}{m(y)} & if\ 1 \leq q \leq \overline{N} \\ \dfrac{1}{N}\displaystyle\sum_{\overline{N} \leq i \leq q} \dfrac{(y_i - m(y))}{m(y)} & if\ \overline{N} \leq q \leq N \end{cases} \quad (19.12)$$

Note that the ordinate at $\overline{N}/N$ involves the income level $m(y)$. Whenever q is not an integer, the corresponding ordinate is obtained via linear interpolation (see Chakravarty, 2009 for details). For a typical income distribution, FWC_R is decreasing up to $\overline{N}/N$, at $\overline{N}/N$ the curve coincides with the horizontal axis and then it increases monotonically (see Figure 19.3). In case of an equal distribution ($y_i = m$ for all i), the FWC_R curve corresponds to a horizontal line passing through the origin. Interestingly, the area under FWC_R corresponds to the Foster and Wolfson (1992 [2010]) bipolarization index shown in equations (19.1) and (19.2).[3]

The FWC_R curve allows introducing the definition of dominance criteria. For any two income distributions x, y, we say that 'x relative FW dominates y' (written as $x \geq_{FW_R} y$) if and only if $FWC_R(x, q) \geq FWC_R(y, q)$ for all $q \in \{1, \ldots, N\}$ and the strict inequality

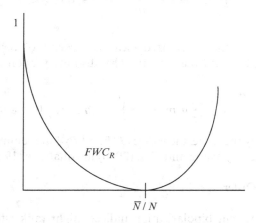

Figure 19.3   An illustration of a relative polarization curve

holds at least once. The next one is the kind of result a polarization ordering approach aims to establish:

Theorem 1 (Chakravarty, 2009): Let x, y be a couple of arbitrary income distributions. Then, the following conditions are equivalent: (1) $x \geq_{FW_R} y$; (2) $P_I(x) > P_I(y)$ for all relative bipolarization indices that satisfy increased spread, increased bipolarity and symmetry.

Extensions

The notion of relative polarization curve (FWC_R) can be extended in several directions. The easiest one is to consider an absolute polarization curve, which is simply obtained from FWC_R scaling up by the median. This is the approach followed by Chakravarty et al. (2007). According to that paper, one has that: (1) the area under the absolute polarization curve corresponds to the absolute version of the Foster and Wolfson index P_I^{FW}; and (2) Theorem 1 can be restated simply using absolute bipolarization indices.

As is known, relative polarization curves (and the corresponding indices) remain unchanged with proportional changes in all incomes, and absolute polarization curves (and the corresponding indices) remain unchanged if the same amount is added to all individual incomes. However, there are intermediate concepts of invariance which have been explored in the field of income inequality (see, e.g., Pfingsten, 1986). In an interesting contribution, Chakravarty and D'Ambrosio (2010) define an 'intermediate polarization curve' as:

$$IPC_1(y,q,\lambda) = \begin{cases} \dfrac{1}{N}\displaystyle\sum_{q \leq i \leq \overline{N}} \dfrac{(m(y) - y_i)}{\lambda m(y) + 1 - \lambda} & \text{if } 1 \leq q \leq \overline{N} \\ \dfrac{1}{N}\displaystyle\sum_{\overline{N} \leq i \leq q} \dfrac{(y_i - m(y))}{\lambda m(y) + 1 - \lambda} & \text{if } \overline{N} \leq q \leq N \end{cases} \qquad (19.13)$$

where λ is a real parameter between 0 and 1. Clearly, when $\lambda = 1$, IPC_1 corresponds to the relative polarization curve (FWC_R) and when $\lambda = 0$, IPC_1 corresponds to the absolute polarization curve. Chakravarty and D'Ambrosio (2010) show that: (1) the area under IPC_1 is another bipolarization index (called the intermediate polarization index); (2) Theorem 1 can be generalized for the case of intermediate polarization indices.

In this line, Lasso de la Vega et al. (2010) propose other notions of intermediateness. In particular, they propose the following generalization of the intermediate polarization curve shown in equation (19.13):

$$IPC_2(y,q,\lambda,\varepsilon) = \begin{cases} \dfrac{1}{N}\displaystyle\sum_{q \leq i \leq \overline{N}} \dfrac{(m(y) - y_i)}{(\lambda m(y) + 1 - \lambda)^\varepsilon} & \text{if } 1 \leq q \leq \overline{N} \\ \dfrac{1}{N}\displaystyle\sum_{\overline{N} \leq i \leq q} \dfrac{(y_i - m(y))}{(\lambda m(y) + 1 - \lambda)^\varepsilon} & \text{if } \overline{N} \leq q \leq N \end{cases} \qquad (19.14)$$

Clearly, when $\varepsilon = 1$, IPC_2 corresponds to IPC_1. This family of curves comes from the adoption of the Krtscha-type notion of intermediateness (Krtscha, 1994). In turn, Lasso de la Vega et al. (2010) also show that the area under IPC_2 corresponds to a Krtscha-type intermediate polarization index and elaborate the corresponding version of Theorem 1 for Krtscha-type intermediate bipolarization indices. Interestingly, Lasso de la Vega et al. (2010) also show the conditions under which their intermediate bipolarization indices satisfy the 'polarization version' of the unit consistency[4] axiom proposed by Zheng in the context of inequality and poverty measurement. That axiom is not satisfied by the intermediate polarization indices proposed by Chakravarty and D'Ambrosio (2010).

Lastly, Duclos and Echevin (2005) introduce simple dominance tests for income distributions. Defining $d_y(i) = |1 - y_i/m|$ and $Q_y(\lambda) = N^{-1}\sum_{i=1}^{N} I(d_y(i) \geq \lambda)$ – where $I(.)$ is an indicator function that takes the value of 1 if its argument is true and 0 otherwise – the authors suggest that a reasonable way to test bipolarization dominance between any two income distributions x, y is to compare the relative position of the curves $Q_x(\lambda)$ and $Q_y(\lambda)$ for all $\lambda > 0$ (see Duclos and Echevin, 2005, for details). Recall that $Q_y(\lambda)$ gives the proportion of the population whose proportional distance from the median exceeds λ.

19.2.3   Income Multipolar Indices

The different bipolarization measures presented in the previous sections were constructed under the assumption that a society is split into two equal-sized groups: the 'poor' and the 'rich' (that is, those below and above the median income). However, this is just one possible partition, and one might wonder what happens when alternative groupings of the population are proposed. This intuition has led to the creation of other polarization indices that will be investigated in this section.

In a fundamental contribution, Esteban and Ray (1994) proposed a polarization measure (henceforth ER) that attempted to measure the extent to which an income distribution is clustered around an arbitrary number of poles. For that purpose, the authors presented the so-called 'identification–alienation' approach (IA). According to IA, polarization can be assumed to be equal to the sum of all possible effective antagonisms existing in a given society, which in turn depend on individuals' sense of identification and alienation. On the one hand, individuals are assumed to feel identified with other individuals who are 'similar' to themselves. On the other hand, individuals are assumed to feel alienated vis-à-vis other individuals who are 'very different'. More specifically, Esteban and Ray (1994) posit that the interpersonal antagonism $T(i,a)$ of a person with an income level x with respect to one with an income level y is the result of their own sense of identity i, which depends on the group size n_i, and of the interpersonal alienation a, which is assumed to depend on the income distance $|y - x|$. Moreover, it is assumed that T is some function increasing in its second argument with $T(0,a) = T(i,0) = 0$. Therefore, the IA approach is summarized in the following hypothesis:

Hypothesis: Polarization in a given society is postulated to be the sum of all effective antagonisms:

$$P_I(n,y) = \sum_i \sum_j n_i n_j T(n_i,|y_i - y_j|) \tag{19.15}$$

This assumption is a bit of a black box and some extra work is necessary to derive it from other – much weaker – axioms. Be that as it may, Esteban and Ray (1994) proposed the following three axioms to pin down an explicit functional form for equation (19.15) so that it could be implemented empirically.[5] All three axioms are based on an income distribution constituted by three different values $y_1 = 0 < y_2 < y_3$ and the corresponding population masses n_1, n_2 and n_3:

Axiom ER1: Let $n_1 > n_2 = n_3 > 0$. Fix $n_1 > 0$ and $y_2 > 0$. There exists $c_1 > 0$ and $c_2 > 0$ (possibly depending on n_1 and y_2) such that if $|y_2 - y_3| < c_1$ and $n_2 < c_2 n_1$, then joining of the masses n_2 and n_3 at their mid-point $(y_2 + y_3)/2$ increases polarization.

Axiom ER2: Let n_1, n_2, $n_3 > 0$, $n_1 > n_3$ and $|y_2 - y_3| < y_2$. There exists $c_3 > 0$ such that if n_2 is moved to the right towards n_3 by an amount not exceeding c_3, polarization increases.

Axiom ER3: Let n_1, n_2, $n_3 > 0$, $n_1 = n_3$ and $y_2 = y_3 - y_2 = c_4$. Any new distribution formed by shifting population mass from the central mass n_2 equally to the two lateral masses n_1 and n_3, each c_4 units of distance away, must increase polarization.

Imposing axioms ER1, ER2 and ER3 to the functional form of equation (19.15), Esteban and Ray (1994) derived the following polarization index:

$$P_I^{ER}(n,y) = c \sum_i \sum_j n_i^{1+\alpha} n_j |y_i - y_j| \qquad (19.16)$$

where $c > 0$ is a proportionality constant and $\alpha \in (0, 1.6]$. Recall that when $\alpha = 0$, P_I^{ER} corresponds to the (absolute) Gini index. Therefore, α is usually interpreted as a polarization sensitivity parameter: the greater the value of α, the greater the difference between inequality and polarization. Interestingly, the maximum possible value of P_I^{ER} is attained when the population is split in two equal-sized income groups, and is minimal when all population is concentrated on a single income group. In another contribution, Esteban and Ray (1999) show that polarization indices like the one shown in equation (19.16) arise naturally in behavioural models that link the level and pattern of social conflict to the society-wide distribution of individual characteristics.

Variants and extensions
The polarization index suggested by Esteban and Ray (1994) has been generalized in a number of directions that attempt to overcome some of its shortcomings. One of the problems with the *ER* framework is that in most real-world cases, income distributions are modelled using continuous distributions rather than with a discrete list of income values $\{y_1, \ldots, y_k\}$. In this vein, Duclos et al. (2004) proposed an axiomatically characterized continuous version of the ER index, which will be referred to as *DER*. In order to characterize the new index, Duclos et al. (2004) introduced the notion of basic densities, that is, un-normalized, symmetric, unimodal densities with compact support. Those basic densities are used to model income distributions. The axioms used in that paper are listed below:

Axiom DER1: If a distribution is composed of a single basic density, then a squeeze[6] of that density cannot increase polarization.

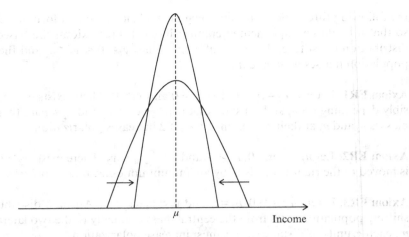

Figure 19.4   An illustration of a single squeeze

After squeezing a basic density, this one is more concentrated towards the mean and the distribution is more homogeneous (see Figure 19.4), so it seems natural to expect that polarization should reduce in such case.

Axiom DER2: If a symmetric distribution is composed of three basic densities with mutually disjoint supports, then a symmetric squeeze of the side densities cannot reduce polarization.

This is the basic axiom that makes polarization essentially different from inequality measurement. Since the squeezes of the side densities are accomplished via Pigou–Dalton progressive transfers, virtually all inequality measures would reduce, while polarization goes in the opposite direction because more cohesive antagonistic groups are formed after the transfers (see Figure 19.5).

Axiom DER3: Consider a symmetric distribution composed of four basic densities with mutually disjoint supports, as in Figure 19.6. Slide the two middle densities to the side as shown (keeping all supports disjoint). Then polarization must increase.

After the slides of the two middle densities to the corresponding sides, it looks as if two more cohesive and antagonistic groups emerged from the distribution: the first corresponding to the two densities to the right and the second to the two densities to the left. Since these changes depart from a uniform-like distribution and approach the bipolar case, it is expected that polarization should increase.

In a well-known result, Duclos et al. (2004, p. 1744) prove that a polarization index defined in the IA framework satisfies axioms DER1, DER2, DER3 and a continuous version of the population principle if and only if it is proportional to:

$$P_I^{DER} \equiv \int\int f^{1+\alpha}(x)f(y)|x - y|dxdy \qquad (19.17)$$

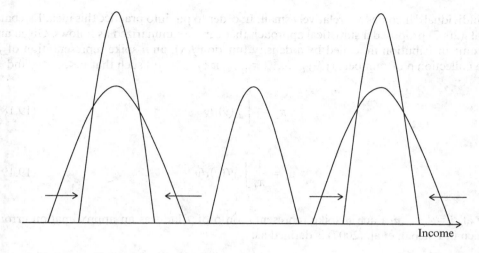

Figure 19.5 An illustration of a double squeeze

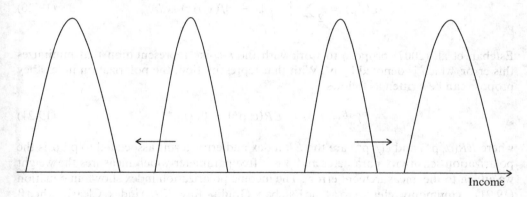

Figure 19.6 An illustration of a symmetric outward slide

In this formula, $f(x)$ is the density function corresponding to the original income distribution and $\alpha \in [0.25, 1]$. As before, when $\alpha = 0$, P_I^{DER} corresponds to the continuous version of the Gini index, so α can be treated as a polarization sensitivity parameter: the larger its values, the greater the difference between polarization and inequality. In order to facilitate the empirical implementation of P_I^{DER}, Abdelkrim and Duclos (2007) have introduced a polarization module in their distributive analysis software DASP (Distributive Analysis Stata Package) which can be freely downloaded from http://dasp.ecn.ulaval.ca. In an interesting contribution, Esteban and Ray (2012) discuss the axiomatic characterization of *DER* and compare it with other characterizations presented in the literature for other well-known measures like the Foster and Wolfson (1992 [2010]) and the Wang and Tsui (2000) indices shown in equations (19.1)–(19.4).

Another criticism directed against the *ER* and *DER* indices is that individuals are assumed to feel identified only with other individuals with exactly the same income level. However, it has been argued that such identification might also exist when the differences in individuals' incomes are relatively small. In order to put into practice this idea, Esteban et al. (2007) proposed a statistical approach that can be summarized as follows. Given an income distribution modelled by a density function $f(x)$, an n-spike representation of f is a collection ρ of numbers $(y_0, y_1, \ldots, y_n; \pi_1, \ldots, \pi_n; \mu_1, \ldots, \mu_n)$ such that $y_0 < \ldots < y_n$ and:

$$\pi_i = \int_{y_{i-1}}^{y_i} f(y)\,dy \tag{19.18}$$

$$\mu_i = \frac{1}{\pi_i} \int_{y_{i-1}}^{y_i} yf(y)\,dy \tag{19.19}$$

for all $i = 1, \ldots, n$. Each n-spike representation ρ of f induces an approximation error, which in Esteban et al. (2007) is defined as:

$$\varepsilon(f,\rho) = \frac{1}{2}\sum_i \int_{y_{i-1}}^{y_i} \int_{y_{i-1}}^{y_i} |x - z| f(x) f(z)\,dx\,dz \tag{19.20}$$

Esteban et al. (2007) propose to work with the n-spike representation that minimizes this error, which is denoted by ρ^*. With that representation, the polarization index they propose can be written as follows:

$$P_I^{EGR}(f,\alpha,\beta) = ER(\alpha,\rho^*) - \beta\varepsilon(f,\rho^*) \tag{19.21}$$

where $ER(\alpha, \rho^*)$ and $\varepsilon(f, \rho^*)$ are the ER index and error terms associated to ρ^*; α is the polarization sensitivity parameter and β is a free parameter which measures the weight we attach to the 'measurement error'. The income polarization index shown in equation (19.21) is commonly referred to as the Esteban–Gradín–Ray (*EGR*) index. Clearly, when $\beta = 0$ *EGR* reduces to *ER*. Interestingly, for the special case where there are only two groups ($n = 2$) and $\alpha = \beta = 1$, one has that:

$$P_I^{EGR}(f,1,1) = \frac{m}{2} P_I^{FW} \tag{19.22}$$

That is: the Foster and Wolfson (1992 [2010]) index of bipolarization can be seen as a particular case of the *EGR* index. This approach has the virtue of casting both measures – each of which derived from a completely different perspective – in the context of a statistically unified framework. Again, the *EGR* index can be implemented empirically using the software package DASP implemented by Abdelkrim and Duclos (2007).

Assuming that the income distribution is partitioned into different groups, Lasso de la Vega and Urrutia (2006) have proposed a variant of the *EGR* index that can be written as follows:

$$P_I^{LU} = \sum_i \sum_j \pi_i^{1+\alpha} \pi_j (1 - G_i)^\theta |y_i - y_j| \tag{19.23}$$

In this equation, G_i stands out as the Gini index for group i and $\theta \geq 0$ is a constant representing the sensitivity towards group cohesion. Introducing the term $(1 - G_i)^\theta$, the P_f^{LU} index is also sensitive to within group dispersion.

19.3 SOCIAL POLARIZATION

It has been argued that social tension might arise not only because of particular characteristics of the income distribution, but by other salient characteristics like ethnicity or religiosity. In this respect, several researchers have attempted to measure polarization on the basis of alternative groupings of the population (typically based on ethnic or religious lines) that do not depend exclusively on the distribution of income or wealth. These constructs will be referred to as 'social polarization measures'. One of the most well-known examples of a social polarization index was introduced by Reynal-Querol (2002) and is defined as:

$$RQ = 1 - \sum_{i=1}^{k}\left(\frac{1/2 - \pi_i}{1/2}\right)^2 \pi_i = 4\sum_{i=1}^{k}\pi_i^2(1 - \pi_i) \qquad (19.24)$$

where we assume there are k exogenously given groups with population shares π_i. According to Montalvo and Reynal-Querol (2002), the RQ index satisfies the following basic properties:

Property 1: If there are three groups with shares π_1, π_2 and π_3, and $\pi_1 > \pi_2 \geq \pi_3$, then if we merge the two smallest groups into a new group, the new distribution is more polarized than the original one.

Property 2: Suppose there are two groups with shares π_1, π_2. Take one of the groups and split it into $g \geq 2$ groups in such a way that $\pi_1 = \tilde{\pi}_1 \geq \tilde{\pi}_i \ \forall i = 2. \ldots ,g + 1$, with strict inequality for at least one i, where $\tilde{\pi}$ is the new vector of population shares. Then polarization under $\tilde{\pi}$ is smaller than under π.

Property 3: Assume there are three groups with shares π_1, π_2 and $\pi_3 = \pi_1$. Then, if we shift mass from the second group equally to the other two groups, polarization increases.

These properties are reminiscent of the different axioms used to characterize the income polarization index P_f^{ER}. It should be noted that RQ takes its maximal value of 1 when a population is split in two equal-sized groups (the bipolar case) and it takes its minimal value of 0 when there is only a single group. As a matter of fact, the original purpose of the index was to capture how far the distribution of the different groups is from the $(1/2,0,\ldots,0,1/2)$ bipolar distribution, so RQ can be interpreted as an index measuring 'how bipolar' a given population distribution is. In this respect, RQ differs substantially from other well-known heterogeneity measures that have been widely used in the literature, like the fractionalization index shown below:

$$FRAC = 1 - \sum_{i=1}^{k} \pi_i^2 = \sum_{i=1}^{k} \pi_i(1 - \pi_i) \tag{19.25}$$

As is known, $FRAC$ should be interpreted as the probability that two randomly selected individuals do not belong to the same group. Keeping all else constant, when we increase arbitrarily the number of groups (k), RQ will decrease but $FRAC$ will increase, so the two measures are fundamentally different. (See also Ciommi et al., Chapter 23 in this *Handbook*.)

19.3.1   Axiomatic Characterization of RQ

In its original formulation, the RQ index was not axiomatically characterized (observe that RQ satisfies properties 1, 2 and 3, but these do not characterize the index univocally). In an attempt to fill this gap, Chakravarty and Maharaj (2011) axiomatically character-ized RQ, a useful exercise that is important to fully understand the normative foundations upon which an index is based. In that paper, the authors posit that a social polarization index has to be of the following form:

$$P_S^{CM}(\pi_1,\ldots,\pi_k) = \sum_{i=1}^{k} \psi(\pi_i) \tag{19.26}$$

where $\psi:[0,1]\to R$ is a continuous function called 'influence function' and $\psi(\pi_i)$ is assumed to represent the impact of group i on overall polarization. In this context, Chakravarty and Maharaj (2011) propose the following axioms:

Axiom S1: For all k and all $\pi = (\pi_1,\ldots,\pi_k)$, $0 \le P_S^{CM} \le 1$.

Axiom S2: For all k, $P_S^{CM}(\pi) = 0$ if π is some permutation of $(1,0,\ldots,0)$.

Axiom S3: For all k, $P_S^{CM}(\pi) = 1$ if π is some permutation of $(1/2,1/2,0,\ldots,0)$.

Axiom S4: Consider the distribution $\pi = (\pi_1,\ldots,\pi_k)$ and the distribution $\pi'=((\pi_1 + \pi_2)/2, (\pi_1 + \pi_2)/2, \pi_3,\ldots, \pi_k)$. Then the polarization difference $P_S^{CM}(\pi) - P_S^{CM}(\pi')$ can be expressed as:

$$P_S^{CM}(\pi) - P_S^{CM}(\pi') = (\pi_1 - \pi_2)^2 f(\pi_1 + \pi_2) \tag{19.27}$$

where $f:[0,1]\to R$ is a continuous function.

Axiom S5: $P_S^{CM}(1/k,\ldots,1/k)$ becomes arbitrarily small for sufficiently large k.

All these axioms – which are identified by the letter 'S' standing for 'social' – are quite clear and simple (except perhaps for axiom S4, which might not look as intuitive as the others). With them, the following result can be presented:

Theorem 2 (Chakravarty and Maharaj, 2011): Let P_S^{CM} be a function as in (19.26) for which the influence function ψ is twice continuously differentiable. Then the following statements are equivalent:

1. P_S^{CM} satisfies axioms S1, S2, S3, S4 and Property 1.
2. P_S^{CM} satisfies axioms S1, S2, S3, S4 and Property 2.
3. P_S^{CM} satisfies axioms S2, S3, S4 and Property 3.
4. P_S^{CM} satisfies axioms S2, S3, S4 and S5.
5. P_S^{CM} is precisely the index RQ.

Moreover, Chakravarty and Maharaj (2011) also show that the different sets of axioms are independent (see their Theorem 7).

19.3.2   Variants and Extensions

One of the greatest advantages of the RQ index is its simplicity: its values can be easily calculated simply knowing the population shares of the subgroups $\pi_1, \ldots, \pi_k$. In turn, this leaves room for a significant number of extensions in alternative directions. For instance, Chakravarty and Maharaj (2012) have proposed the so-called 'generalized RQ-index of order θ', which is defined as:

$$RQ_\theta = 4 \sum_{i=1}^{k} \pi_i^2 (1 - \pi_i) + \theta \sum_{1 \leq i_1 < i_2 < i_3 \leq k} \pi_{i_1} \pi_{i_2} \pi_{i_3} \qquad (19.28)$$

where $\theta \in [0,3]$ and $k \geq 3$. The first term appearing in equation (19.28) gives a multiple of the probability that out of three randomly selected individuals, two will belong to a single group and the third to another one. The second term gives a multiple of the probability that all three individuals belong to three different groups. Since RQ_θ is a linear combination of both probabilities, its values can be interpreted as an extent of heterogeneity of a population partitioned in k groups. Clearly, when $\theta = 0$, RQ_θ reduces to RQ.

In Montalvo and Reynal-Querol (2002), the RQ index is presented as a particular case of the so-called discrete polarization index:

$$P_S^{DP}(\alpha,\theta) = \theta \sum_{i=1}^{k} \sum_{j \neq i} \pi_i^{1+\alpha} \pi_j \qquad (19.29)$$

It is trivial to show that $P_S^{DP}(1,4) = RQ$. This equation bears a lot of resemblance to the *ER* income polarization index shown in equation (19.16). Rather than using the term $|y_i - y_j|$ for measuring distance between groups, equation (19.29) uses a discrete metric that takes a value of 1 when two individuals belong to different groups and 0 otherwise.

It can be argued that the discrete distance measure might be too crude to capture appropriately the existing distances between alternative social groups. In this respect, Permanyer (2012) proposes to greatly enrich this distance measure in the following way. Firstly, it is postulated that social polarization is greatly influenced by the extent to which different individuals feel identified with the group to which they belong. The intensity with which individuals feel belonging to their particular group is called the 'radicalism degree', and it is measured with a real number x ($x \in R^+$). For each population group i there is an un-normalized density function $f_i(x)$ that measures the way in which radicalism degrees are distributed therein. We denote by $f = (f_1(x), \ldots, f_k(x))$ the collection of the k density functions. In order to operationalize the IA approach, it is postulated that an individual belonging to group i with radicalism degree x has a feeling of identification proportional to $f_i(x)$. Regarding alienation, two different assumptions are made: one of them posits that alienation can only be felt between members of different groups[7] (assumption A1) and the second one states that alienation can also be felt between members of the same group[8] (assumption A2). Under assumption A1, Permanyer (2012) axiomatically characterizes the following social polarization index:

$$P_S^{P1}(f) = \sum_{i=1}^{k} \sum_{j \neq i} \pi_i^{1+\alpha} \pi_j (\mu_i + \mu_j) \tag{19.30}$$

where μ_i is the mean of radicalism degrees' density function $f_i(x)$ and $\alpha \in (0,1]$. As usual, α is interpreted as a polarization sensitivity parameter. Recall that this measure can be seen as a generalization of the discrete social polarization measure $P_S^{DP}(\alpha, \theta)$ shown in equation (19.29): the absence of an alienation component has been substituted by a much richer structure that is sensitive to individuals' radicalism distributions in equation (19.30). Clearly, if $\mu_i = \mu_j \forall i \neq j$, $P_S^{P1} \equiv P_S^{DP}(\alpha, \theta)$. Interestingly, (19.30) also bears some resemblance with equation (19.42) (see below), the difference being that in equation (19.30) one deals with radicalism degrees distributions while in equation (19.42) one deals with income distributions.

Since one could argue that alienation might operate not only between individuals of different groups but also between individuals of the same group (assumption A2), Permanyer (2012) also characterizes axiomatically the following index:

$$P_S^{P2}(f) = \sum_{i=1}^{k} \iint f_i^{1+\alpha}(x) f_i(y) |x - y| dx dy + \sum_{i=1}^{k} \sum_{j \neq i} \iint f_i^{1+\alpha}(x) f_j(y) (x + y) dx dy \tag{19.31}$$

where the polarization sensitivity parameter α is bounded between 1/2 and 1. This formulation bears some resemblance with the income polarization index *DER* shown in equation (19.17). As before, however, equation (19.31) is based on radicalism degrees distributions, but equation (19.17) is based on income distributions.

The main challenge when attempting to implement empirically the polarization indices shown in equations (19.30) and (19.31) is to measure radicalism degrees and their distribution $f_i(x)$. In the empirical application shown in Permanyer (2012), religious radicalism degree is proxied applying principal components analysis to a set of attitudinal questions regarding religiosity. In order to facilitate the computation of equations (19.30) and (19.31), Abdelkrim and Duclos (2007) have implemented a specific module in the software package DASP.

19.3.3 Polarization Measures on the Basis of Ordinal Information

So far, the polarization indices shown in this chapter have been computed on the basis of cardinal or categorical data. In the former category we can find the income polarization indices of section 19.2 plus the social polarization indices shown in equations (19.30)–(19.31). In the latter category we can find the other social polarization indices. However, in many circumstances important dimensions might be coded with ordinal variables (a typical example is that of health, which in many circumstances is measured via respondents' self-assessments on an ordinal scale). Interestingly, other socioeconomic indices have made room for ordinal variables as well, for instance in the field of inequality and multidimensional poverty measurement (e.g., Allison and Foster, 2004; Alkire and Foster, 2011, among many others).

In this subsection we will show a couple of polarization measures that are meant to be used with ordinal information. Before that, we introduce some basic notation. The number of categories will be denoted by k, and the number of individuals in category i by n_i. As before, let $\pi_i = n_i / \sum_{i=1}^{k} n_i$. For each category $c \in \{1, \ldots, k\}$ we define $N_c = \sum_{i=1}^{c} n_i$ and $\Pi_c = \sum_{i=1}^{c} \pi_i$. In an original contribution, Apouey (2007) presented the following polarization indices on the basis of ordinal data:

$$P_S^{A1} = \theta \left[\left(\frac{N_k}{2} \right)^\beta - \frac{1}{k-1} \sum_{c=1}^{k-1} \left| N_k \left(\frac{N_c}{N_k} - \frac{1}{2} \right) \right|^\beta \right] \tag{19.32}$$

$$P_S^{A2} = 1 - \frac{2^\beta}{k-1} \sum_{c=1}^{k-1} \left| \Pi_c - \frac{1}{2} \right|^\beta \tag{19.33}$$

where θ is a strictly positive constant and $\beta \in (0,1)$. In equation (19.32), θ is a proportionality constant that can be used to normalize the values of the index into the desired range. In equations (19.32) and (19.33), parameter β reflects the importance that is given to the median category. When $\beta \to 0$ (resp. $\beta \to 1$), the relative contribution of the median category increases (resp. decreases) whereas the relative contribution of the other categories decrease (resp. increase).

The ordinal polarization indices shown in equations (19.32) and (19.33) are similar to Wang and Tsui's (2000) cardinal bipolarization measures (see equations 19.3 and 19.4). That is, it is assumed that the population is divided in two subgroups: those below the median and those above it. In this respect, the polarization indices P_S^{A1}, P_S^{A2} are meant to satisfy the ordinal version of the axioms of increased spread and increased bipolarity (see Apouey, 2007 for details). Essentially, both P_S^{A1} and P_S^{A2} measure how far a given distribution is from the extreme bipolar case where half the population is concentrated in the lower end of the distribution and the other half in the upper extreme. Therefore, both measures are maximized in the bipolar case and minimized in the case where all population is concentrated in a single category. This property is shared with all income bipolarization measures shown in section 19.2.1 and with the RQ index.

D'Ambrosio and Permanyer (2015) presented a new class of social polarization indices meant for those cases where an attribute of interest (for example, health, happiness or degree of satisfaction) is measured in an ordinal scale and the population is assumed to be partitioned in exogenously given groups $g_1, \ldots, g_k$ (for example, along ethnic, religious or other lines). In that paper, the authors use the IA approach, so polarization is assumed to be proportional to the sum of all effective antagonisms in the population. As is usual, individuals' identification is assumed to be proportional to the size of the group to which they belong. Regarding alienation, the authors propose two different alternatives: symmetric and asymmetric alienation. For symmetric alienation between groups g_i, g_j, the 'discrete overlap coefficient' has been proposed:

$$\theta_{ij} = \sum_{c=1}^{k} \min \{p_{g_i, c}, p_{g_j, c}\} \tag{19.34}$$

where $p_{g_i, c}$ is the share of group g_i in category c. This coefficient lies between 0 (disjoint groups) and 1 (perfectly overlapping groups). Alienation is then defined as $1 - \theta_{ij}$, taking the value 0 when the groups overlap completely and 1 when the groups are completely disjoint. The greater the degree of overlap, the more similar the groups are, and hence the less the degree of alienation between them. Alternatively, it has been argued that feelings of alienation between groups should not necessarily be reciprocal. Consider, say, a comparison between a poor and a rich individual: while the poor person might have reason to feel animosity towards the rich person, the opposite might not hold necessarily. In this context, alienation between groups 'i' and 'j' can be defined as a function of:

$$A_{ij} = \frac{\sum_{s=1}^{N_i} \sum_{t=1}^{N_j} \delta_{st}}{N_i N_j} \tag{19.35}$$

where δ_{st} equals 1 if individual 'i' from group i is ranked below individual 't' from group j and 0 otherwise. This procedure yields an asymmetric function $(A_{ij} \neq A_{ji})$, consistent with the alienation felt by the underprivileged towards more privileged groups not necessarily being reciprocated (this contrasts with traditional income-polarization measures, where alienation is always symmetric). The value of A_{ij} measures the extent to which group g_i is underprivileged with respect to group g_j. When $A_{ij} = 1$, all of the members of group g_i are ranked below any member of group g_j with respect to the ordinal attribute we take into consideration: this is the case of maximal alienation. At the other extreme, $A_{ij} = 0$ when no member of group g_i is ranked below any member of group g_j, which refers to minimal alienation.

With these symmetric and asymmetric alienation functions, D'Ambrosio and Permanyer (2015) axiomatically characterized the following social polarization measures:

$$P_S^{AP1} \equiv \sum_{s=1}^{k} \sum_{t=1}^{k} \pi_s^{1+\alpha} \pi_t (1 - \theta_{st}) \tag{19.36}$$

$$P_S^{A2P} \equiv \sum_{s=1}^{k} \sum_{t=1}^{k} \pi_s^{1+\alpha} \pi_t A_s \tag{19.37}$$

where $\alpha \in [\alpha^*, 1]$, with $\alpha^* = \frac{2 - \log_2 3}{\log_2 3 - 1} \approx 0.71$ is the polarization sensitivity parameter. Once again, these polarization indices can be seen as generalizations of the polarization index $P_S^{DP}(\alpha, \theta)$ shown in equation (19.29) where the discrete distance function has been substituted by a richer structure that is sensitive to the way in which a given attribute of interest is distributed across individuals and groups.

19.4   HYBRID POLARIZATION MEASURES

The income polarization measures shown in section 19.2 describe the extent to which the distribution of income is clustered around certain poles. Following a different approach, the social polarization indices shown in section 19.3 basically measure the extent to which a population is clustered around certain poles defined on the basis of non-income characteristics such as race, ethnicity or religion. This section describes other polarization indices that lie somewhere in between the aforementioned intuitions; that is, the distribution of a given attribute – typically income – as well as other qualitative characteristics play a non-trivial role when defining the groups among which polarization is going to be measured. For this reason, indices of this kind are referred to as 'hybrid'. In this respect, the polarization indices P_S^{AP1} and P_S^{AP2} shown in equations (19.36) and (19.37) could also be considered as hybrid because the distribution of an (ordinal) attribute and the existence of exogenously given groups are relevant when defining the alienation component.

Zhang and Kanbur (2001) defined a simple and intuitive hybrid index of polarization on the basis of the *Generalized Entropy* (*GE*) index of inequality (Shorrocks, 1980). If we assume that the population has n members, the index is written as:

$$I(y) = \begin{cases} \sum_{i=1}^{n} f(y_i)\left[\left(\frac{y_i}{\mu}\right)^c - 1\right] & \text{if } c \neq 0,1 \\ \sum_{i=1}^{n} f(y_i)\left(\frac{y_i}{\mu}\right)\log\left(\frac{y_i}{\mu}\right) & \text{if } c = 1 \\ \sum_{i=1}^{n} f(y_i)\log\left(\frac{y_i}{\mu}\right) & \text{if } c = 0 \end{cases} \tag{19.38}$$

Recall that *GE* is additively decomposable; that is, if we assume that the population is split in k groups, total inequality can be written as the sum of within-group and between-group inequalities. This is generally written as:

$$I(y) = \sum_{g=1}^{k} w_g I_g + I(\mu_1 e_1, \ldots, \mu_k e_k) \tag{19.39}$$

where e_g is a vector of ones of length n_g, μ_g is the mean of group g, I_g is the internal inequality within group g and:

$$
w_g = \begin{cases} \dfrac{n_g}{N}\left(\dfrac{\mu_g}{\mu}\right)^c & \text{if } c \neq 0,1 \\[2ex] \dfrac{n_g}{N}\left(\dfrac{\mu_g}{\mu}\right) & \text{if } c = 1 \\[2ex] \dfrac{n_g}{N} & \text{if } c = 0 \end{cases} \tag{19.40}
$$

Taking advantage of this well-known inequality index, Zhang and Kanbur (2001) proposed the following hybrid polarization measure:

$$
P_H^{ZK} = \frac{I(\mu_1 e_1, \ldots, \mu_k e_k)}{\displaystyle\sum_{g=1}^{k} w_g I_g} \tag{19.41}
$$

This simple index satisfies the most basic intuitions regarding a polarization index; namely, it increases with larger between group inequality and it decreases with larger within group inequality. It must be emphasized that the income polarization index shown in equation (19.9) is very similar to the index shown in (19.41): in the former, it is assumed that the population is split into two non-overlapping groups – those above the median income and those below it – and the inequality measure used is the Gini index rather than GE.[9]

In an interesting contribution, D'Ambrosio (2001) proposed other hybrid polarization measures inspired in the IA approach. Essentially, it is assumed that the population is split in k relevant groups, each of which with the corresponding income distribution $f_i(x)$. With this notation, the D'Ambrosio (2001) hybrid polarization measure can be written as:

$$
P_H^A = \sum_i \sum_j \pi_i^{1+\alpha} \pi_j \, Kov_{ij} \tag{19.42}
$$

where $Kov_{ij} = \frac{1}{2}\int |f_i(y) - f_j(y)| dy$ is the Kolmogorov measure of variation distance. This is a measure of the lack of overlap between income distributions $f_i(x)$ and $f_j(x)$. $Kov_{ij} = 0$ if $f_i(x) = f_j(x)$ for all x and Kov_{ij} reaches its maximum of 1 when $f_i(x)$ and $f_j(x)$ do not overlap. There is a clear relationship between the Kolmogorov measure of variation distance and the overlap coefficient shown in equation (19.34), which can be rewritten in its continuous version as:

$$
\theta_{ij} = \int_{-\infty}^{\infty} \min\{f_i(x), f_j(x)\} \, dx \tag{19.43}
$$

The statistical properties of the overlap coefficient θ_{ij} and some of its multivariate generalizations have been explored in detail by Anderson et al. (2009). Other interesting hybrid polarization measures have been proposed – albeit not axiomatically characterized – in Duclos et al. (2004). Following the IA approach, the authors consider the case in which notions of identification are mediated not just by group membership but also by income similarities as well, while the antagonism equation remains untouched. Then they get what one might call social polarization with income-mediated identification, which can be written as:

$$P_H^{DER1} = \sum_{j=1}^{k} (1 - n_j) \int_x f_j(x)^\alpha dF_j(x) \tag{19.44}$$

Duclos et al. (2004) also make the assumption that alienation can also be income-mediated (for alienation, two individuals must belong to different groups and have different incomes). According to the authors, 'groups have only a demarcating role – they are necessary (but not sufficient) for identity, and they are necessary (but not sufficient) for alienation' (Duclos et al., 2004, p. 1760). The corresponding index would look as follows:

$$P_H^{DER2} = \sum_{j=1}^{k} \sum_{k \neq j} \int_x \int_y f_j(x)^\alpha |x - y| dF_j(x) dF_k(y) \tag{19.45}$$

19.5 FUTURE RESEARCH LINES

As has been shown in this literature review, the measurement of polarization has expanded considerably in the last two decades since the seminal contributions of Foster and Wolfson (1992 [2010]) and Esteban and Ray (1994). However, much work remains to be done and this chapter ends by indicating some research lines in polarization measurement that deserve to be further explored.

Among the most promising lines of research in the field of polarization measurement is that of multidimensional polarization. As has been the case with inequality or poverty measurement, it is possible to conceive the notion of polarization in a multidimensional setting where attributes other than income are taken into account when trying to identify clusters and distances between them. In this respect, it is worth highlighting that there have already been some initial attempts to produce such measures. In an innovative contribution, Gigliarano and Mosler (2009) introduce a polarization index defined on the basis of many attributes at the same time. If we denote by X an $n \times k$ matrix with non-negative entries (n being the number of individuals in the society and k the number of attributes that are being taken into account), the authors posit that multidimensional polarization should be written as follows:

$$P_M^{GM}(X) = \varsigma(B(X), W(X), S(X)) \tag{19.46}$$

where $B(X)$ and $W(X)$ are indices that measure between- and within-group inequality, respectively; $S(X)$ is an index of relative group size; and ς is a function that increases on B and S and decreases on W. In other words, the authors construct multivariate polarization indices using the between and within decomposition by subgroups of certain indices of multivariate inequality. Clearly, this formulation is an attempt to generalize the functional forms of the polarization indices shown in equations (19.2), (19.7), (19.8), (19.9) and

(19.41). In order to be able to obtain meaningful between- and within-group inequality decompositions, Gigliarano and Mosler (2009) use different inequality decompositions via generalized entropy indices, multivariate extensions of Atkinson's inequality index and Gini decompositions where the supports of the different groups have no geometric overlap. To simplify matters, the authors further assume that equation (19.46) must take one of the following forms:

$$P_M^{GM1}(X) = \phi\left(\frac{B(X)}{W(X) + c}\right)S(X) \tag{19.47}$$

$$P_M^{GM2}(X) = \psi(B(X) - W(X))S(X) \tag{19.48}$$

$$P_M^{GM3}(X) = \tau\left(\frac{B(X)}{B(X) + W(X) + c}\right)S(X) \tag{19.49}$$

Recall that these are quite general functional forms that include relatively similar versions of the polarization indices of Foster and Wolfson (1992 [2010]), Zhang and Kanbur (2001) and Silber et al. (2007), as particular cases. Interestingly, Gigliarano and Mosler (2009) also propose a list of desirable axioms a multidimensional polarization index should satisfy. Among these, a couple that are specifically multidimensional are the 'between groups correlation increasing majorization property' and the 'within groups correlation increasing majorization property'. Both describe the way in which a polarization index should respond under correlation increasing switches among attributes.[10] Despite the interest that these measures have generated, it is fair to say that multidimensional polarization measurement is still in its infancy and much work remains to be done. Among other things, the polarization indices shown in (19.46)–(19.49) are not axiomatically characterized and their structure is somewhat arbitrary. It would be interesting to derive other – more general – functional forms from weaker assumptions than those imposed in the aforementioned equations.

In this vein, another topic that to the author's knowledge has never been explored before, and which might be interesting to investigate in the future, is the possibility of defining multidimensional polarization orderings. The literature of inequality and poverty measurement has already introduced the notions of multidimensional inequality and multidimensional poverty orderings (e.g., Duclos et al., 2011; Bourguignon and Chakravarty, 2008). One might just wonder whether it might be possible to generalize the existing ideas on polarization orderings to a multivariate setting.

After reading the existing list of polarization indices, it seems clear that there is room for much further improvement in the measurement of polarization on the basis of ordinal information. In many cases the variables of interest are not cardinal, particularly when they refer to non-income dimensions (for example, health or educational attainment). This issue has also been highlighted by Alkire and Foster (2011), who argue that in multidimensional poverty measurement it is very useful to define indices admitting ordinal structures. To date, there are only a couple of measures defined on an ordinal basis (see above), and these measures can be expanded in many different directions. In particular, it might also be of interest to follow Alkire and Foster's approach and to define multidimensional polarization indices that can be constructed with non-cardinal variables.

An important issue that definitely needs to be further explored is the definition of appropriate socioeconomic distance functions between groups when these are defined along a variety of economic or social lines (for example, wealth, income, class, race, ethnicity or religion). As has been shown in this chapter, the literature has already proposed different ways of approaching this issue, but none of them has gained widespread adherence. In this respect, it may be anticipated that the methodology used to measure distances in trees (for instance, linguistic trees; see Greenberg, 1956; Fearon and Laitin, 2000; Laitin, 2000; Desmet et al., 2009; Desmet et al., 2012) could be useful to generate distance or alienation functions between groups. Similarly, it may be speculated that the ideas behind the construction of diversity theories (e.g., Weitzman 1992, 1998; Nehring and Puppe, 2002, 2004) could be fruitful when attempting to define compelling intergroup distance functions.

NOTES

1. Since these two subgroups are non-overlapping, one has that overall inequality as measured with the Gini index (G) can be written as $G = G_B + G_W$.
2. In its continuous version, the extended Gini inequality index is defined as $G(v) = 1 - v(v - 1)\int_0^1 (1 - q)^{v-2} L(q) dq$, where v is an inequality aversion parameter such that $v>1$ and L is the Lorenz curve.
3. In that paper, the polarization curve was introduced first and the Foster–Wolfson polarization index was defined after it.
4. A bipolarization measure P_I is unit consistent if for any distributions x, y such that $P_I(x) < P_I(y)$, then $P_I(\theta x) < P_I(\theta y)$ for any $\theta > 0$.
5. The formulation of these axioms is taken from Chakravarty (2009), who in turn adapted them from Esteban and Ray (1994).
6. Technically speaking, a λ-squeeze of a basic density f is the following mean-preserving reduction in the spread of f: $f^\lambda(x) \equiv (1/\lambda)f(x - (1 - \lambda)\mu/\lambda)$, where μ is the mean of f.
7. In case radicalism degrees of different individuals from different groups equal x and y, their alienation is assumed to be $x+y$.
8. In case radicalism degrees of different individuals from the same group equal x and y, their alienation is assumed to be $|x-y|$.
9. The Gini index is not additively decomposable (that is, it does not satisfy equation 19.39) in general. However, in the particular case where the different groups are non-overlapping, it is possible to write the Gini as the sum of between group and within group inequalities.
10. In the multi-attribute welfare literature, a 'correlation increasing switch' is defined as follows. Assume we are comparing two individuals i and j in a two-dimensional achievement space associated with attributes a and b. Assume also that i has more of a but less of b than j does. If we interchange the achievements in attribute b between the two persons, now individual i has more of a and more of b, so there has been an increase in the correlation of the attributes. Such change is called a correlation increasing switch.

REFERENCES

Abdelkrim, A. and J.-Y. Duclos (2007), *DASP: Distributive Analysis Stata Package*, PEP, World Bank, UNDP and Université Laval.

Alkire, S. and J. Foster (2011), 'Counting and multidimensional poverty measurement', *Journal of Public Economics*, 95 (7/8), 476–487.

Allison, R. and J. Foster (2004), 'Measuring health inequality using qualitative data', *Journal of Health Economics*, 23, 505–524.

Anderson, G., Y. Ge and L. Wah (2009), 'Distributional overlap: simple, multivariate, parametric and non-parametric tests for alienation, convergence and general distributional difference issues', *Econometric Reviews*, 29 (3), 247–275.

Apouey, B. (2007), 'Measuring health polarization with self-assessed health data', *Health Economics*, 16, 875–894.

Bossert, W. and W. Schworm (2008), 'A class of two-group polarization measures', *Journal of Public Economic Theory*, 10, 1169–1187.

Bourguignon, François and Satya Chakravarty (2008), 'Multi-dimensional poverty orderings: theory and applications', in K. Basu and R. Kanbur (eds), *Essays for a Better World: Essays in Honor of Amartya Sen*, Volume I, Oxford University Press, Oxford.

Chakravarty, Satya (2009), *Inequality, Polarization and Poverty: Advances in Distributional Analysis*, Springer, Berlin.

Chakravarty, S. and C. D'Ambrosio (2010), 'Polarization orderings of income distributions', *Review of Income and Wealth*, 56 (1), 47–64.

Chakravarty, S. and B. Maharaj (2011), 'Measuring ethnic polarization', *Social Choice and Welfare*, 37, 431–452.

Chakravarty, S. and B. Maharaj (2012), 'Ethnic polarization orderings and indices', *Journal of Economic Interaction and Coordination*, 7, 99–123.

Chakravarty, S. and A. Majumder (2001), 'Inequality, polarization and welfare: theory and applications', *Australian Economic Papers*, 40 (1), 1–13.

Chakravarty S., A. Majumder and R. Roy (2007), 'A treatment of absolute indices of polarization', *Japanese Economic Review*, 58, 273–293.

D'Ambrosio, C. (2001), 'Household characteristics and the distribution of income in Italy: an application of social distance measures', *Review of Income and Wealth*, 47 (1), 43–64.

D'Ambrosio, C. and I. Permanyer (2015), 'Measuring social polarization with ordinal and categorical data', *Journal of Public Economic Theory*, 17 (3), 311–327.

Desmet, K., I. Ortuño-Ortín and R. Wacziarg (2012), 'The political economy of ethnolinguistic cleavages', *Journal of Development Economics*, 97 (1), 322–332.

Desmet, K., I. Ortuño-Ortín, and S. Weber (2009), 'Linguistic diversity and redistribution', *Journal of the European Economic Association*, 7 (6), 1291–1318.

Donaldson, D. and J. Weymark (1980), 'A single-parameter generalization of the Gini indices of inequality', *Journal of Economic Theory*, 22, 67–86.

Duclos, J.Y. and D. Echevin (2005), 'Bipolarization comparisons', *Economics Letters*, 87, 249–258.

Duclos, J.-Y., J. Esteban and D. Ray (2004), 'Polarization: concepts, measurement, estimation', *Econometrica*, 72, 1737–1772.

Duclos, J.-Y., D. Sahn and S. Younger (2011), 'Partial multidimensional inequality orderings', *Journal of Public Economics*, 95 (3/4), 225–238.

Esteban, J., C. Gradín and D. Ray (2007), 'An extension of a measure of polarization, with an application to the income distribution of five OECD countries', *Journal of Economic Inequality*, 5, 1–19.

Esteban, J. and D. Ray (1994), 'On the measurement of polarization', *Econometrica*, 62, 819–852.

Esteban, J. and D. Ray (1999), 'Conflict and distribution', *Journal of Economic Theory*, 87, 379–415.

Esteban, Joan and Debraj Ray (2012), 'Comparing polarization measures', in M. Garfinkel and S. Skaperdas, *Oxford Handbook of the Economics of Peace and Conflict*, Oxford University Press, Oxford.

Fearon, J. and D. Laitin (2000), 'Violence and the social construction of ethnic identity: review essay', *International Organization*, 54 (4), 845–77.

Foster, J. and M. Wolfson (1992 [2010]), 'Polarization and the decline of the middle class: Canada and the US', Mimeo, Vanderbilt University; published in the *Journal of Economic Inequality* (2010), 8, 247–273.

Gigliarano, C. and K. Mosler (2009), 'Constructing indices of multivariate polarization', *Journal of Economic Inequality*, 7, 435–460.

Greenberg, J. (1956), 'The measurement of linguistic diversity', *Language*, 32 (1), 109–115.

Krtscha, M. (1994), 'A new compromise measure of inequality', in W. Eichhorn (ed.), *Models and Measurement of Welfare and Inequality*, Springer, Heidelberg.

Laitin, D. (2000), 'What is a language community?', *American Journal of Political Science*, 44 (1), 142–155.

Lasso de la Vega, C. and A. Urrutia (2006), 'An alternative formulation of the Esteban–Gradin–Ray extended measure of bipolarization', *Journal of Income Distribution*, 15, 42–54.

Lasso de la Vega, C., A. Urrutia and H. Diez (2010), 'Unit consistency and bipolarization of income distributions', *Review of Income and Wealth*, 56 (1), 65–83.

Montalvo, J. and M. Reynal-Querol (2002), 'Why ethnic fractionalization? Polarization, ethnic conflict and growth', Universitat Pompeu Fabra, Economics Working Paper No. 660.

Nehring, K. and C. Puppe (2002), 'A theory of diversity', *Econometrica*, 70 (3), 1155–1198.

Nehring, K. and C. Puppe (2004), 'Modelling phylogenetic diversity', *Resource and Energy Economics*, 26, 205–235.

Permanyer, I. (2012), 'The conceptualization and measurement of social polarization', *Journal of Economic Inequality*, 10 (1), 45–74.

Pfingsten, A. (1986), 'Distributionally-neutral tax changes for different inequality concepts', *Journal of Public Economics*, 30, 385–393.

Reynal-Querol, M. (2002), 'Ethnicity, political systems and civil wars', *Journal of Conflict Resolution*, 46 (1), 29–54.

Rodriguez, J. and R. Salas (2003), 'Extended bipolarization and inequality measures', *Research on Economic Inequality*, 9, 69–83.

Shorrocks, A. (1980), 'The class of additively decomposable inequality measures', *Econometrica*, 48, 613–625.

Silber, J., J. Deutsch and M. Hanoka (2007), 'On the link between the concepts of kurtosis and bipolarization', *Economics Bulletin*, 4, 1–6.

Wang, Y. and K. Tsui (2000), 'Polarization orderings and new classes of polarization indices', *Journal of Public Economic Theory*, 2, 349–363.

Weitzman, M. (1992), 'On diversity', *Quarterly Journal of Economics*, 107 (2), 363–405.

Weitzman, M. (1998), 'The Noah's Ark problem', *Econometrica*, 66 (6), 1279–1298.

Wolfson, M. (1994), 'When inequalities diverge', *American Economic Review P&P*, 94, 353–358.

Wolfson, M. (1997), 'Divergent inequalities: theory and empirical results', *Review of Income and Wealth*, 43, 401–421.

Zhang, X. and R. Kanbur (2001), 'What differences do polarization measures make? An application to China', *Journal of Development Studies*, 37, 85–98.

20. Income and social polarization: empirical findings
Chiara Gigliarano

20.1 INTRODUCTION

Polarization is a recent but rapidly expanding concept in economics. It concerns the presence in a given society of two or more groups, or poles, of individuals who share similar characteristics with the other members of the same group, but are different, in terms of the same features, from the individuals of other groups. In general, we say that the distribution of one variable over a given population is polarized if the relative frequency of observations is low in correspondence to the central value(s) (properly defined) of the distribution, and it is high at the tails, in such a way that the society is split into groups that are homogeneous inside and different from each other. Therefore, polarization can be measured in two ways: either by looking at the dispersion of the society from central value(s) of the distribution towards the extreme points, or considering the population as made up by well distinct groups.

Polarization immediately recalls inequality: both concepts deal with the disparity existing in a society, but in distinct ways. Inequality focuses on the interpersonal differences over the entire distribution, while polarization monitors two contrasting forces: (1) the inequality between the population groups; and (2) the equality within them.

The notion of polarization is not so widespread and well-known as that of inequality. Amiel et al. (2010) investigate people's perceptions of the meaning of income polarization. The responses suggest that the important features that differentiate polarization from inequality (in particular, the idea that polarization increases if the inequality within the groups reduces) are not widely accepted and understood.

Many different variables can be used to evaluate polarization in a society. These include: (1) monetary variables, such as income, wealth and expenditure; as well as (2) non-monetary indicators such as religion, ethnicity, language, race and political opinion. The former case is referred to as 'income polarization', while the latter case is defined as 'social polarization'.

The first systematic works on income polarization measurement date back to Foster and Wolfson (1992, 2010) and Esteban and Ray (1994), who propose the first rigorous treatments of such phenomenon. In their works, these authors underline different aspects of the phenomenon of polarization, distinguishing two main strands in the literature on income polarization. The first, originating from Esteban and Ray (1994), focuses on the rise of separated income groups: polarization increases if the groups become more homogeneous internally, more separated from each other, and more equal in size. This approach is followed, among others, by Gradín (2000), Milanovic (2000), D'Ambrosio (2001), Zhang and Kanbur (2001), Duclos et al. (2004), Esteban et al. (2007), Yitzhaki (2010) and Lasso de la Vega and Urrutia (2006).

The second strand, going back to Foster and Wolfson (1992, 2010), describes the decline of the middle class, measuring how the centre of the income distribution is emptied. Authors such as Wolfson (1994, 1997), Wang and Tsui (2000), Chakravarty and Majumder (2001), Rodrıguez and Salas (2003), Chakravarty et al. (2007), Chakravarty et al. (2007), Deutsch et al. (2007), Chakravarty and D'Ambrosio (2010) and Lasso de la Vega et al. (2010) develop and extend this alternative approach.

Most researchers have focused on measuring polarization of income distributions, while a few of them have studied social polarization (see, among others, D'Ambrosio, 2001; Zhang and Kanbur, 2001; Duclos et al., 2004; Montalvo and Reynal-Querol, 2005; Permanyer, 2012; Chakravarty and Maharaj, 2012; D'Ambrosio and Permanyer, 2015). These authors assume that the factors that determine individuals' identity do not depend solely on their income levels but, rather, are culturally, ideologically, historically, biologically or socially driven.

The reason that motivates the increasing interest in the analysis of income and social polarization is the idea that high levels of polarization, in terms of the presence of contrasting groups (according to the Esteban and Ray's approach), or in terms of a weak and hollowed-out middle class (in the case of Wolfson's method) can lead to an instable society, causing possible social conflicts and revolts. Pressman, in particular, stresses the importance of the middle class for avoiding social conflicts and tensions:

> a large and vibrant middle class is important to every nation. For many reasons, a thriving middle class contributes to economic growth as well as to social and political stability . . . A middle class serves as buffer between the poor and the wealthy . . . Those with low incomes may never be able to become rich, but they will have reasonable dreams of achieving middle class status. Thus, they will be less likely to revolt against the system and more likely to work hard. (Pressman, 2007, p. 1)

Therefore, a flourishing middle class prevents polarization inside a country; social unrest, in fact, usually starts when income becomes polarized.

Esteban and Ray (1999) also show that the level of conflict increases with the level of polarization. In particular, they develop a behavioural model that is aimed at detecting the type of distributions that are most likely to be highly correlated with conflict, and they prove that conflict is maximized at some symmetric bimodal distribution of the population. This property is closely related to the notion of polarization.

For a long time the literature on social conflict has focused on indices of inequality and indices of fractionalization, and these measures have been used in several empirical studies of conflict. In particular, income inequality has been viewed as closely related to conflict. However, Lichbach (1989) shows in his survey article that the empirical studies on the relationship between inequality and conflict have only come up with inconclusive results. Recently, there seems to be agreement that groups rather than individuals are the decisive actors in large-scale violent conflicts.

The notion of fractionalization – or of 'power concentration' – is the complement of the well-known Hirschman–Herfindahl measure of concentration. The measure of fractionalization can be understood as the probability that two randomly chosen individuals happen to be of different groups. Polarization and fractionalization try to capture different aspects of the distribution of the population over a set of characteristics. The measures of fractionalization and of polarization differ in two major aspects. Firstly, a larger number of groups increases fractionalization, while it decreases polarization.[1] Secondly, most measures of polarization consider inter-group distances to be crucial, while fractionalization measures do not include this information.

Esteban and Ray (2008) provide a theoretical framework that clarifies the role of polarization and fractionalization on conflict. They show that the relationship between polarization or fractionalization and conflict is non-monotonic, and the intensity of conflict depends positively on the degree of polarization. In highly polarized societies, the occurrence of open conflict should be rare but its intensity is very severe, whenever it happens. On the other hand, highly fractionalized societies are prone to the occurrence of conflict, but its intensity will be moderate.[2]

Most of the literature fails to find any significant evidence of ethnic fractionalization as a determinant of conflict. This negative finding is underlined by Montalvo and Reynal-Querol (2005), who show, on the contrary, a significant relationship between ethnic polarization and conflict incidence. Some empirical works (e.g., Montalvo and Reynal-Querol, 2003) provide evidence suggesting that polarization outperforms fractionalization as a predictor of civil conflict and, hence, measures of polarization have become more and more popular in empirical studies of conflict.

The aim of this chapter is to provide a review of the main empirical findings and evidence obtained from applications of the income and social polarization indices described in Chapter 19 of this *Handbook*. The remainder of this chapter is organized as follows. Section 20.2 focuses on income polarization and distinguishes between Wolfson's approach (subsection 20.2.1) and Esteban and Ray's approach (subsection 20.2.2). Subsection 20.2.3 illustrates alternative methods for monitoring income polarization based on nonparametric density estimation techniques. Section 20.3 discusses the main empirical applications of social polarization indices. In section 20.4 we discuss other applications, such as health polarization, effects of taxation on income polarization and the link between wage polarization and labour market mobility. Section 20.5 illustrates briefly the available software for computing polarization indices, while section 20.6 concludes the chapter.

20.2 INCOME POLARIZATION MEASURES: EMPIRICAL FINDINGS

As already mentioned in the introduction, there are two main approaches to measuring income polarization: on the one hand, measures following Foster and Wolfson's approach consider only two poles in the population (the poor and the rich) and, therefore, are referred to as income bipolarization measures (subsection 20.2.1); on the other hand, indices inspired by Esteban and Ray's perspective allow for a generic number of groups and are referred to here as income multipolar indices (subsection 20.2.2). Beside these two approaches, an alternative way to analyse income polarization has been recently developed in the economic literature, based on nonparametric density estimation techniques (subsection 20.2.3).

20.2.1 Income Bipolarization Measures

This strand of the literature on income polarization measurement focuses on the case of a society splitting into only two groups; the phenomenon of polarization is defined as the hollowing-out of the centre of the distribution, rather than as the rise of two opposed peaks. Therefore, the focus is on the size of the middle part of the income distribution, often nominated as the middle class. Other phrases associated with discussions of the concept of polarization include a distribution that is more 'spread out from the middle', 'a hollowed out middle', or 'a tendency toward bimodality' (Wolfson, 1997).

The first attempts to study the decline of the middle class (or bipolarization) in the income distribution trace back to the 1980s, when a considerable number of papers and press articles appeared about the phenomenon of hollowing-out in the United States middle class (e.g., Blackburn and Bloom, 1985; Thurow, 1987; Horrigan and Haugen, 1988; Beach et al., 1997; Pressman, 2007). This issue involved not only the United States of the late 1970s and 1980s, but also other countries, such as Australia, the United Kingdom, the Netherlands, Sweden and Taiwan; see, in particular, the empirical analysis in Pressman (2007).

A more rigorous analysis of the phenomenon was then proposed by Wolfson (1994, 1997), who explained that bipolarization refers to a particular type of change in the distribution: a movement of observations from the middle of the distribution towards both tails. The following first discusses the relevant issue of how to define the middle class, and then reviews the most important empirical applications of Foster and Wolfson's index.

Bipolarization as decline of the middle class: how to define the middle class?
In the analysis of bipolarization the middle class constitutes a crucial element. This class refers to a group of people who are close enough in their socioeconomic status to be able to cooperate and form a common political will. According to Pressman (2007) the economic interpretation of the middle class consists of a group of individuals whose income level is more or less in the middle of the income distribution. A strong middle class has a beneficial influence on the society, as it provides a buffer between the extreme tendencies of the lower and upper social classes. Easterly (2001), for example, shows that a higher share of income for the middle class is associated with higher growth, more education, better health status and less political instability in the society. In this context, the decline of the middle class in a developed country implies a threat to economic growth and socio-political stability.

There are two main steps for measuring the disappearing middle class: (1) the definition of 'middle class'; and (2) the measure of its shrinkage. In the economic literature, there still exists an open debate on how to define the middle class: the notion of 'middle class' still appears to be vague and arbitrary, as no consensus exists among researchers on how to cut income distribution in order to separate the middle from the remaining population. Several authors have already pointed out this issue, including Atkinson and Brandolini (2013), Eisenhauer (2008), Pressman (2007) and Jenkins (1995).

On one side, Foster and Wolfson (1992, 2010) and the authors who have followed their approach (in particular, Wolfson, 1994, 1997; Wang and Tsui, 2000; Chakravarty and Majumder, 2001; Rodrıguez and Salas, 2003; Chakravarty et al., 2007; Chakravarty and D'Ambrosio, 2010) use the median income as a reference point, considering the middle class as the group of individuals whose income is equal to the median income. The closer incomes are to the median, the less polarized is the distribution; while the presence of two well-separated poles at the right and left of the median income identifies a highly polarized income distribution.

On the other side, there exist some contributions in the economic literature that define the middle class starting from an interval of income values. A group of authors interested in monitoring the declining middle class in the United States (including Blackburn and Bloom, 1985; Thurow, 1987; Horrigan and Haugen, 1988; Beach et al., 1997; Pressman, 2007) identifies the middle class either: (1) as the *h* per cent of the population closest to the centre of the distribution (with *h* equal, for example, to 20, 30 or 60); or (2) as the group of individuals whose income belongs to the interval between the *p* per cent and the *q* per cent of the median income, with *p* and *q* given (for example, *p* = 60 and *q* = 225 in Blackburn and Bloom, 1985). These authors then measure the decline of the middle class by looking only inside this central class, and monitoring either its size or its income range or share.

The first approach (called the 'people space approach') identifies the middle class by an income interval delimited by some quantiles of population, and it measures its disappearance in terms of income share related to this class. Beach et al. (1997), for example, consider as the population portion the middle 20 per cent, 30 per cent and 60 per cent, while Beach (1989) considers only the middle 60 per cent of the population.

The second approach (called the 'income space approach') is opposite to the first one, as instead of defining the middle class in terms of a percentage of the population and monitoring the income share of this group, it inverts the order: the middle class is defined in terms of income interval delimited by two fractions of the median income, and then the number of people within this interval are counted up; for example, Blackburn and Bloom (1985). Beach et al. (1997) and Horrigan and Haugen (1988) consider several values for the lower (*p*) and upper (*q*) bound of the middle class: percentages (*p, q*) equal to (75, 125), (50, 150), (25, 175), (25, 200).

For example, Atkinson and Brandolini (2013) provide an application of the people space approach, based on the Luxembourg Income Study (LIS) data. The middle class is defined as the central 60 per cent part of the population. Results show that in the more egalitarian countries of Northern and Central Europe the richest person in the middle class has an income that is around 1.4 times the median; twice the income of the lowest middle class person. This ratio increases in countries with more unequal distributions: in Mexico, for example, the top middle class income is four times the bottom middle class income. This means that in the years considered by the authors, the middle class's income share is larger in the Nordic and continental European countries; and smaller in Italy, the United States, the United Kingdom and, especially, Mexico.

Atkinson and Brandolini (2013) also illustrate the income space approach, according to which people are in the middle class if their income lies between some proportion of the median income. Here several alternative boundaries are considered (75–125 per cent, 75–167 per cent, 75–200 per cent, 75–300 per cent). According to their empirical analysis, changing the definition of the middle class may lead to different results. Moreover, the size of the middle class has declined over time in most countries, but not in Mexico, Norway, Denmark, Italy and France.

The definition of the middle class considered so far is applied mainly to developed countries. Alternative definitions are typically considered when dealing with the middle class in developing countries or, more generally, for the entire world. Just as middle-income classes within countries are deemed necessary for a 'healthy political democracy' (Thurow, 1987), middle-income countries may be important in promoting global peace and stability.

In particular, Milanovic and Yitzhaki (2002) focus on the world income distribution and propose a definition of the middle class for the world's countries. They divide the world into three groups: (1) the rich G7 countries and those with similar income levels; (2) the middle-income countries (defined as those countries with per capita income between Brazil's and Italy's); and (3) the less developed countries (whose per capita income is less than or equal to Brazil's). The authors find little overlap among these three groups, meaning that very few people living in developing countries have incomes in the range of those in rich countries.

Ravallion (2010) raises some criticism, affirming that the definition of the middle class usually proposed for rich countries may not have any relevance to poor countries. The author criticizes the degree of arbitrariness in this definition: 'Why 75% and 125% of the median? Why Brazil and Italy? Why $2 and $10? Why should the upper bound be 10 times the lower one?' (ibid., p. 446). Ravallion suggests defining the developing world's middle class as the group of those individuals who are not considered poor by the standards of developing countries, but are still poor by the standards of rich countries. As an upper bound, the author uses the United States poverty line, while for the lower bound he considers the median amongst 70 national poverty lines for developing countries, drawn from World Bank data. Ravallion (2010) shows that, in 1990, about one person in three in the developing world belonged to the middle class by this definition; while in 2005 the proportion had risen to to one in two.

Empirical applications of Wolfson's measure and its extensions
Several empirical applications are available in the economic literature of Foster and Wolfson's index and their extensions and generalizations. Here the focus is on the ones that allow for cross-country comparisons. An interesting application of the Foster and Wolfson's index is proposed in Atkinson and Brandolini (2013), who report the change in the Foster and Wolfson index, between the mid-1980s and the mid-2000s, for a selection of 15 LIS countries in comparison with the change in the overall income inequality measured by the Gini index. The results reveal that inequality and polarization are interconnected but distinct phenomena, as their variations differ in size and even move in opposite directions in some countries. Income distribution becomes more polarized in most countries, but not in Mexico, Norway, Denmark, Italy and France.

Seshanna and Decornez (2003) propose an empirical application of Foster and Wolfson's polarization index involving all the world's countries and using data from the Penn World Tables and the World Bank. The aim of their analysis is to assess whether the rich countries have become richer and the poor have become poorer over the period between 1960 and 2000. The paper also examines whether greater economic integration across countries (globalization) has been accompanied by increases in inter-country polarization and inequality. The study is done on the basis of inter-country comparisons for the world as a whole, as well as subgroups of the world (based on association to a supranational institution, income level, geographic location and openness to trade). The variable of interest is the country's average gross domestic product (GDP) per capita, corrected for inflation, population size and exchange rates. The authors conclude that the richer a group of countries is, the less intra-group polarization there is; with the exception of high-income non-Organisation for Economic Co-operation and Development (OECD) countries. East Asia, Latin America and sub-Saharan Africa show increases in polarization. In general, the richer a group of countries is (whether classified by income group or region), the less polarized it tends to be, and the more its Wolfson index decreases.

Seshanna and Decornez (2003) also show that world income polarization has grown continuously during the period 1960–2000, and this evidence contributes to diminishing the importance of the supposedly beneficial effects of world economic growth. Their findings are partly contradicted by Duro (2005), who provides further evidence on the international income polarization trend by using updated and revised income data from the latest version of the Penn World Tables (PWT 6.0) and by using polarization indexes (both Wolfson's and Esteban et al.'s, 2007 extended measures). The empirical evidence suggests that polarization follows a curvilinear pattern, with initial growth followed by decline, in contrast to the pattern of monotonous growth found by Seshanna and Decornez (2003). The main reason for the discrepancy between the two analyses could be the different data source, since criticism has been expressed concerning the lack of the veracity of the data for countries such as China and India in previous versions of Penn World Tables. The results seem to reinforce the non-pessimistic views about the effects of globalization on international income distribution.

20.2.2   Income Multipolar Indices

This section focuses on the most relevant applications and empirical findings related to the second strand of the income polarization literature, that traces back to Esteban and Ray (1994). As already discussed in Chapter 10 of this *Handbook*, the first formulation of the Esteban and Ray (1994) polarization index reveals some empirical limitations; therefore, Esteban et al. (2007) propose an extended version of the original polarization index in order to overcome the drawbacks. This section first summarizes the Esteban and Ray (1994) measure's drawbacks and illustrates the main applications of the extended Esteban et al. (2007) measure. Then, it presents some other interesting applications related to further extensions of the Esteban and Ray (1994) measure, and in particular to the Esteban et al. (2007) index.

The first main limitation of the Esteban and Ray (1994) measure is that it should be used only after having grouped the population in a way that captures the group identification structure of the society. However, the classes into which the population could be grouped (for example, deciles) may be very far from the conceptual grouping based on the alienation/identification framework. The following briefly reviews the main solutions proposed in the literature to overcome this issue.

The approach proposed in Esteban et al. (2007) to overcome this first limitation of the Esteban and Ray (1994) index is the following: if the number of groups is fixed and given, one should first choose the cut-off points by minimizing the dispersions within the clusters, and then apply the Esteban and Ray measure to these groups, including a correction for the intra-group dispersion. This corresponds to the extended polarization measure P^{EGR} (f, α, β), defined in Chapter 19 of this *Handbook*.

Esteban et al. (2007) also propose an empirical application on household income polarization in five OECD countries (United States, United Kingdom, Canada, Germany and Sweden) for the period 1974–2000. The authors compute the extended polarization index P^{EGR} (f, α, β) choosing three groups, the sensitivity parameter β equal to 1.16 and β equal to 1 (in the paper, different values of α and different numbers of groups are also considered). The results reveal that, at the beginning of the period under consideration, Sweden appears as the country with lowest polarization, Germany is as polarized as the United Kingdom (UK), and both are nearly as polarized as Canada and the United States (US). By the end of the period two types of countries emerge with clearly different levels of polarization: the US and the UK are highly polarized countries, while Sweden, Germany and Canada exhibit low polarization, with a significant gap in between.

The extended measure of polarization has also been applied by Esteban (2000) to the measurement of polarization in the inter-regional distribution of per capita income in Spain; by Gradin (2000) to the study of income bipolarization in the different Spanish regions; and by many others. In particular, Gradin (2000) applies the Esteban et al. (2007) extended measure in order to analyse the role of different household characteristics (for example, educational level, position in the labour market, and region) in the formation of groups in the Spanish expenditure distribution. Two approaches are considered. On the one hand, he assumes that groups are determined by characteristics that their members share, and he studies which gives rise to a higher level of polarization. The idea is that, despite polarization occurring in the income space, groups in the distribution are the result of similarities with respect to a relevant attribute other than income, such as, for instance, race or education. This approach is referred to as 'group polarization'. On the other hand, Gradin (2000) also investigates which characteristics better explain an observed level of polarization, assuming that income proximity determines the group to which one belongs. This second approach is referred to as 'explained polarization'.

Empirical results show that in Spain the educational level attained by the householders is the main determinant of the observed levels in bipolarization, when the groups are built according to proximity in spending levels (explained polarization approach). The geographical variables appear as the main factor explaining depolarization during the 1970s, while the socioeconomic condition plays that role during the 1980s.

When each characteristic is the criterion in forming groups (group polarization approach), then the author finds that educational level displays the highest levels of polarization, despite its decrease during the 1980s. The socioeconomic condition exhibits stable distribution for the 1973–1980 period but is strongly less polarized after the 1980s. Despite polarization declines in Spain for most characteristics, there are several for which it has increased, as in the case of the autonomous regions and provinces during the 1980s, these becoming more polarized among them and internally more identified.

Ezcurra and Pascual (2007) follow the approach of Esteban et al. (2007) and examine spatial polarization in the regional distribution of per capita income in a set of European Union countries over the period 1980–2001. The data used are drawn from the Cambridge Econometrics regional database and include information on GDP and population of 191 NUTS-2 regions belonging to 12 countries (Belgium, Germany, Greece, Spain, France, Italy, the Netherlands, Austria, Portugal, Finland, Sweden and the UK). The results obtained using the extended polarization measure proposed by Esteban et al. (2007), assuming two groups, show considerable cross-country variation in regional polarization levels in the sample considered. In particular, Portugal, Belgium and Italy are the nations where the partition of income distribution into two well-differentiated groups is more evident. The lowest average regional polarization levels over the 22-year period examined are found in Greece, Finland and the Netherlands. In addition, the empirical evidence proposed by the authors emphasizes the role played by national development processes in this context. The estimations show that, beyond a certain level of per capita income, regional polarization decreases as the process of economic development advances. The authors also emphasize that there are signs to suggest that regional polarization increases once a relatively high level of per capita income is attained, although this rise is less marked than the decrease experienced previously.

The second drawback related to the Esteban and Ray (1994) polarization measure regards the choice of its key parameter α, which is known as 'polarization sensitivity'. A larger α indicates a greater departure of Esteban and Ray (1994) from inequality measurement, while as α equals zero, Esteban and Ray (1994) simply becomes proportional to the Gini index. In Esteban and Ray (1994), α has permissible values falling within the interval [1, 1.6]. The indeterminacy of α actually makes the Esteban and Ray (1994) measure produce a partial order for polarization. Moreover, although an interval of α leaves the researcher freedom of choosing their most ideal polarization sensitivity, there are no criteria for making this choice given one's certain beliefs about how far the polarization measure should diverge from inequality measurement. More importantly, empirical evidence from Anderson (2004b) indicates that Esteban and Ray (1994) with $\alpha = 1.5$ may not concur with the polarization test developed from the stochastic dominance conditions.

Geng (2012) focuses on this second limitation of the Esteban and Ray (1994) measure and aims at finding an exact value for α. The results of the paper help to avoid potential debates over the choice of α, hence providing a unified way of specifying Esteban and Ray polarization index in applications. Another important novelty of the cited paper is to build the polarization index on the absolute income (or other attributes of interest), as contrasted with the logarithm of income considered in Esteban and Ray (1994). Geng (2012) notes that when the income in levels is considered, axioms in Esteban and Ray (1994) are no longer proper as some of them are not mean preserving. The paper proposes a set of mean-preserving axioms so that comparisons of polarization can be made directly between distributions. Overall, these axioms pin down a unique polarization index out of the class of Esteban and Ray (1994) measures, which corresponds to the value of α equal to 1.

Lasso de la Vega and Urrutia (2006) point out some problems with the extended version of the polarization measure proposed by Esteban et al. (2007). More precisely, the measure proposed by Esteban et al. (2007) fails to verify one of the basic features of polarization: namely that higher heterogeneity across groups should lead to an increase in polarization. The authors provide a counter-example that shows this problem, and provide an alternative formulation for the extension of the Esteban and Ray (1994) measure that is able to solve the problem (see measure P^{LU} in Chapter 19 of this *Handbook*). The alternative measure P^{LU} is applied to data from 22 Latin American countries from 1970 to 1998, showing that in Latin America the use of information on group cohesion plays a critical role in modifying the qualitative behaviour of the Esteban and Ray polarization.

Hussain (2009) proposes an interesting decomposition of the Duclos et al. (2004) polarization into three specific components:

$$P^{DER} = A * I * (1 + \rho),$$

where A is average alienation (= two times the Gini coefficient), I is average identification, and ρ is the normalized covariance between alienation and identification.

The application is built on data from administrative registers in Statistics Denmark. It is a longitudinal representative dataset of the Danish population for the years 1984–2002. Empirical results show that polarization increased by about 5 per cent from 1984 to 2002 when applying either Duclos et al.'s measure, or the Foster and Wolfson bipolarization measure. This increase has been caused by more alienation (inequality), and faster income growth among high incomes relative to the middle. In particular, identification is almost unchanged in the period, whereas alienation (the Gini coefficient) increased by almost 10 per cent. Alienation (inequality) is indeed the driving force behind the observed change in polarization.

20.2.3 Bipolarization Analysis Based on Nonparametric Density Estimation

Beyond the two main approaches to the measurement of polarization reviewed so far (Esteban and Ray, 1994, on the one hand; and Foster and Wolfson, 1992 and 2010, on the other hand), an alternative method for monitoring the phenomenon of polarization, based on nonparametric density estimation, has been proposed.

Kernel estimation methods have been often employed for investigating the shape of the cross-country distribution of per capita income. Quah (1997) proposes an analogous method for studying the convergence hypothesis, and revealing, where appropriate, polarization and clumping within subgroups. The data show little cross-country convergence; instead, the important features are persistence, immobility and polarization, exemplified by convergence club or twin peaks dynamics. The world seems to be converging to a distribution where many remain wealthy and many remain poor, and the middle-income class is vanishing.

Jenkins (1995) proposes to investigate the shrinking middle class hypothesis using kernel density estimation methods. The approach reveals new evidence of changes in the concentration of middle incomes in the United Kingdom during the 1980s. Breakdowns by family economic status demonstrate that a major cause of the aggregate changes was a moving apart of the income distributions for working and non-working households.

Pittau and Zelli (2010) argue that kernel estimation methods for the detection of multiple modes are likely to be less informative, when investigating the convergence hypothesis, than approaches that model the distribution as a mixture of component densities. The mixture approach is able to detect the presence of multiple components in a distribution even if that multiplicity does not manifest itself as multimodality. The authors implement the mixture approach using cross-country per capita income Penn World Data for the period 1960 to 2000. In contrast to the commonly held view that the cross-country distribution of per capita income exhibits two modes, the statistical tests that the authors use indicate the presence of three-component densities in each of the nine years examined. For each year they estimate a three-component mixture model and label the components as 'poor', 'middle' and 'rich'. They find that the evident 'hollowing-out' of the middle of the distribution is largely attributable to the increased concentration of the rich and poor countries around their respective component means. The among-components mobility during the period considered is low; this leads the authors to interpret the multiple mixture components detected as representing convergence clubs. Finally, they use the estimated mixture densities to compute the Duclos et al. (2004) measure of polarization and find that polarization increased over the sample period, mainly due to the decreased variances of the poor and rich components.

A similar approach has been proposed by Anderson (2004a, 2004b). The idea consists of thinking of the income distribution as a mixture of sub-populations (typically, the poor and the rich) and studying polarization in the context of changes of such sub-distributions. In particular, stochastic dominance conditions are proposed as means of defining the degree and the nature of separateness of the sub-distributions. The paper presents tests for polarization both between and within population distributions.

Anderson (2010) extends the results in the multivariate context, providing measures that rely upon nonparametric kernel density estimation techniques. He tries to characterize the sense of polarization that the poor experience in a multivariate context, which in turn may be used to reflect a sense of their relative impoverishment. Measures of 'overlap' and 'trapezoidal' polarization have been proposed which, in the context of comparisons of poor and rich groups, encompass the difficulties associated with defining poverty thresholds in relative poverty measures. Application of the techniques to world income and life expectancy distributions reveals an overall improvement in the conditions of the poor (largely due to the advances made by China and India over those years). However, when applied specifically to a comparison of Africa and the Rest of the World it revealed that Africa's relative position is deteriorating. This deterioration is largely due to increases in the degree of alienation, measured by the Euclidean distance, between the Africa's distributional mode and that of the Rest of the World, as a consequence of an increased African within-group variation.

A nonparametric density estimation approach has also been followed by other authors in order to analyse regional polarization and interregional territorial imbalances. Maza and Villaverde (2004), for example, analyse the regional inequalities in the per capita GDP of 12 European Union (EU) countries (France, Spain, Portugal, Ireland, the UK, Italy, Belgium, Denmark, Germany, Greece, Luxembourg, the Netherlands) and their evolution over the years 1980–1996. Their analysis is based on nonparametric density estimation of the per capita GDP distribution, and suggests the existence of clusters of rich and poor regions in the EU, which means that the regional per capita GDP distribution is characterized by polarization. In particular, the authors assess that the regional income distribution in the EU is characterized by spatial dependence, as EU regions have outcomes similar to their neighbouring regions, regardless of which country they belong. Regions with high income have neighbours with similarly high income, while regions with low income have neighbours with similarly low income. The presence of polarization in the EU regions concentrates the richer regions in the north of Europe (mainly Germany, Denmark, the north of Italy and some regions in France) and the poor regions in the south (mainly Spanish, Portuguese, Greek and southern Italian regions). Also, their empirical findings stress that regional distribution of per capita GDP in the EU regions is very persistent, and therefore regional mobility is quite low.

Ezcurra et al. (2005), similar to the previous cited work, analyse the distribution of regional per capita income in the EU. The authors combine a nonparametric approach together with the information provided by measures of inequality and polarization. Also in their work, empirical findings reveal the importance of the role played by the spatial dimension. An additional result concerns the dynamics of regional inequality and polarization: the authors show that these two phenomena decreased in Europe over the period 1977–1999. In particular, the results reveal an overall reduction in regional inequality over the period 1977–1999; the greater part of this reduction took place at the end of the 1970s, while in the next 20 years no big changes occurred. According to the Esteban–Gradin–Ray measure, regional polarization also diminished over the period, mainly in the 1970s and 1980s, while in the 1990s polarization tended to remain stable.

20.3 SOCIAL POLARIZATION

The economic literature usually refers to social polarization when the factors that determine tensions or conflicts in a given population are socially driven (depending, in particular, on ethnic, religious or nationalistic feelings) and do not depend on the distribution of income. The following subsections review some empirical results on religious and ethnolinguistic polarization.

20.3.1 Religious Polarization

Reynal-Querol (2002) emphasizes the importance of religious differences as a cause of ethnic civil wars and conflicts. Religious divisions are more likely to cause conflict between societies than resources, interest groups or language divisions, since religion is not negotiable. The author shows empirically that religious polarization is one of the most important factors to explain social ethnic conflicts. An index of religious polarization is proposed (see the RQ index defined in Chapter 19 in this *Handbook*), which can be considered the corresponding polarization index by Esteban and Ray (1994) for a discrete metric.

The author then performs several logistic regression models, revealing a positive and significant effect of religious polarization in explaining the incidence of ethnic civil war. Also, there is a positive and significant effect of linguistic fragmentation on ethnic civil wars, due to the fact that communication problems increase diversity. However, the author shows that the effect of language fragmentation disappears when religious polarization is included in the regression analysis. This suggests that religious differences are more important than linguistic diversity.

Montalvo and Reynal-Querol (2003), moreover, show empirically that the religious polarization index is more appropriate to measure the effect of potential conflicts on economic development than the traditional fragmentation index. Instead of considering religion simply in terms of the proportion of each religious group (as in the religious fragmentation index), the authors also take into account the potential conflictive relationship among them. The index of religious fragmentation increases when the number of groups increases, while the index of religious polarization proposed by Reynal-Querol (RQ) index is instead maximum when there are two religious groups of equal size. For a given number of groups, the threat is higher, the larger the size of another group relative to the size of the reference group.

Empirical evidence shows that for low values of polarization the relationship between fractionalization and polarization is positive and linear (for countries showing high level of religious homogeneity). However, for higher values of polarization (greater than 0.6) the relationship is close to zero; it means that there is no correlation in countries that are highly religiously heterogeneous (such as the African countries). Interestingly, the authors re-estimate an augmented Solow model that includes indices of religious diversity. Empirical findings show that religious fragmentation has no significant effect on long-term growth, while religious polarization has a significant and negative effect on economic development. Thus, empirically the religious polarization index is superior to the religious fragmentation index in explaining economic development.

Esteban and Ray (2008) clarify the roles of polarization and fractionalization and their relationship with conflict. When society is highly polarized, the potential cost of rebellion is extremely high, and this cost may serve as the guarantor of peace. So, in highly polarized societies, the occurrence of open conflict should be rare but its intensity will be very severe, when it happens. On the other hand, highly fractionalized societies are prone to the occurrence of conflict, but its intensity will be moderate. Specifically, within a theoretical framework the authors show that the relationship between polarization or fractionalization and conflict is non-monotonic, and that the intensity of conflict depends positively on the degree of polarization.[3]

20.3.2 Ethno-Linguistic Polarization

The number of papers dealing with the effects of ethnic diversity on issues of economic interest is growing at a fast rate. Most of these papers use the index of ethno-linguistic fractionalization as the indicator of ethnic diversity. However, many authors have found that, even though ethnic fractionalization seems to be a powerful explanatory variable for economic growth, it is not significant in the explanation of civil wars and other kinds of conflicts. Fearon and Laitin (2003) and Collier and Hoeffler (2004) find that neither ethnic fractionalization nor religious fractionalization has any statistically significant effect on the probability of civil wars.

The index of polarization by Esteban and Ray (1994) was initially thought of as a measure of income or wealth polarization. However, in terms of income or wealth it is not clear which levels distinguish different groups with a common identity. Where does the middle class start? How rich is rich? In the case of ethnic diversity the identity of the groups is less controversial, but the distance between different ethnic groups is much more difficult to measure than income or wealth. Montalvo and Reynal-Querol (2005) assume that the distance across groups is generated by a discrete metric (0-1).

Montalvo and Reynal-Querol (2005) compare three main data sources that can be used for analysis on ethno-linguistic diversity across countries: the *World Christian Encyclopedia* (WCE), the *Encyclopedia Britannica* (EB) and the *Atlas Narodov Mira* (ANM). Montalvo and Reynal-Querol (2005) consider that the most accurate description of ethnic diversity is the one in the WCE, which contains details for each country on the most diverse classification level, which may coincide with an ethno-linguistic family or subfamilies.

Ethnic polarization has been shown to be an important determinant not only of the incidence of civil wars (Montalvo and Reynal-Querol, 2005) but also of its duration. This is shown in Montalvo and Reynal-Querol (2010). They apply the Reynal-Querol (RQ) index for analysing the relationship between ethnic polarization and the duration of civil wars. The authors argue that the duration of civil wars increases, the more ethnically polarized a society is. Empirical results show that ethnically polarized countries have to endure longer civil wars than ethnically less polarized societies. The authors use the Uppsala/PRIO25 dataset, which includes wars that cause at least 25 yearly deaths.

The database contains 117 civil wars corresponding to 74 countries during the period 1960–1999.

As a preliminary indication the authors look at the survivor functions of civil wars in highly polarized countries versus countries with lower level of ethnic polarization. To separate these two groups they use the median value of ethnic polarization. Results show that the Kaplan–Meier estimated survivor function of the countries with a higher degree of ethnic polarization almost everywhere dominates the survivor function of the countries with lower ethnic polarization. Since the failure time in this case is the end of a civil war, and the time at risk is the period of civil war, the dominance of the survivor function of highly polarized countries implies that the duration of wars is longer in those countries. The authors then move to an analysis of duration in a parametric setting, resorting to the Weibull model and looking at the hazard functions for highly polarized countries versus countries with low polarization. They show that the hazard function for the end of a civil war is much lower for highly polarized countries.

Montalvo and Reynal-Querol (2008) apply the index of discrete ethnic polarization for explaining genocides. Most of the recent papers on the determinants of civil wars and genocides fail to find any significant effect for ethnic heterogeneity, measured as fractionalization. Their empirical results show that ethnic fractionalization has no effect on genocides; while substituting the index of ethnic fractionalization by the index of ethnic polarization, the authors find a positive and statistically significant effect on the incidence of genocide. Moreover, when including both measures together, ethnic fractionalization has no effect, while ethnic polarization has a positive and significant effect on the incidence of genocides and politicides. Therefore, ethnic heterogeneity, measured as ethnic polarization, is also important for the explanation of genocides.

The RQ index, which is one of the most-used measures of religious or ethnic polarization in the literature, does not take into account alienation between individuals, a fundamental component in a polarization index. In his paper, Permanyer (2012) presents two axiomatically characterized social polarization indices incorporating this alienation component: the first one focuses on between-group alienation only and the second one takes also into account alienation within groups (see Chapter 19 in this *Handbook* for more details). Data used are from the World Value Surveys (WVS), a set of internationally comparable household surveys that have been collected in both developed and developing countries. Their questionnaire contains many questions regarding the religiosity of individuals. Empirical results suggest that the new indices might be good predictors of the occurrence of conflict.

Recently, Esteban et al. (2012) provide further evidence on the importance of considering polarization measures for explaining civil conflicts. In particular, they are motivated by the fact that more than half of the civil conflicts recorded since the end of the Second World War have been classified as ethnic or religious. The authors illustrate that ethnic divisions do influence social conflict. In particular, they show that the two different measures of ethnic division – polarization and fractionalization – jointly influence conflict.

Their study is based on 138 countries over the period 1960–2008, with the time period divided into five-year intervals. Using data from the jointly maintained database under the Uppsala Conflict Data Program and the Peace Research Institute of Oslo (see Gleditsch et al., 2002), the authors construct a discrete measure of conflict, which is equal to 0 if the country is at peace in those five years; to 1 if it has experienced low-intensity conflict (more than 25 battle-related deaths but less than 1000) in any of these years; or to 2 if the country has been in high-level conflict (more than 1000 casualties) in any of the five years. A second measure of conflict intensity is computed from the Cross-National Time-Series Data Archive (see Banks and Wilson, 2013), which provides a continuous measure of several manifestations of social unrest, with no threshold dividing peace from war.

To compute the index of ethnic polarization, the authors consider as a proxy for intergroup distances the linguistic distance between two groups. The idea behind this choice is that linguistic distance is associated with cultural distance. The authors run a cross-sectional regression of conflict on both fractionalization and polarization measures, also controlling for other variables that are considered relevant in explaining civil conflict: population size; gross domestic product per capita, which raises the opportunity cost of supplying conflict resources; natural resources, measured by the presence of oil or diamonds; the percentage of mountainous terrain, which facilitates guerrilla warfare; non-contiguity, referring to countries with territory separated from the land area containing the capital city either by another territory or by 100 km of water; measures of the extent of democracy; the degree of power afforded to those who run the country, which is a proxy for the size of the public prize; time dummies to capture possible global trends; and regional dummies to capture patterns affecting entire world regions. Also, because current conflict is deeply affected by past conflict, the authors use lagged conflict as an additional control.

Their empirical findings reveal that polarization affects ethnic conflicts more when the winners enjoy a 'public' prize (such as political power or religious hegemony), while fractionalization has more influence when the prize is 'private' (such as government subsidies, or infrastructures).

20.4   OTHER APPLICATIONS

Recently, the analysis of polarization has been extended in new directions, such as the impact of taxation on income polarization (subsection 20.4.1), the measurement of health polarization (subsection 20.4.2), and the relationship between wage polarization and mobility (subsection 20.4.3).

20.4.1   Income Polarization and Taxation

Oliver et al. (2010) proposes one of the first attempts to analyse the effects on polarization of some tax benefits reforms. In particular, the authors perform an evaluation of the impact on efficiency, income inequality and polarization of the replacement of the Spanish system with the systems of France, Denmark and the UK, using a micro-simulation model. The main findings show that each of the new systems would reduce income inequality; while the effects of the reforms are ambiguous when considering the Esteban and Ray polarization index. For some values of the parameter, polarization would increase, while for other choices it would reduce.

20.4.2 Polarization and Health

Up to now dispersion in health distribution has been measured using inequality indices only. However, some aspects of dispersion are not captured by inequality measures. One of the first attempts to link the notion of polarization with that of health economics traces back to Apouey (2007), who proposes an axiomatic foundation for new measures of polarization that can be applied to ordinal distributions such as self-assessed health (SAH) data. This is an improvement over the existing measures of polarization that can only be used for cardinal variables. The new measures of health polarization avoid one difficulty that the related measures for evaluating health inequalities face: inequality measures are mean-based, and since only cardinal variables have a mean, SAH has to be cardinalized to compute a mean, which can then be used to calculate an inequality measure. In contrast, the new polarization measures are median-based and hence do not require the imposition of cardinal scaling on the categories. An empirical illustration using data from the British Household Panel Survey demonstrates that SAH polarization is also a relevant question on empirical grounds. Interestingly, the family of polarization measures proposed in Apouey (2007) can be applied to characterize many other self-assessed measures, for example, happiness, well-being and political opinions.

Apouey (2010) provides an extension of the Wolfson's index of social polarization for health. The main novelty is that individuals are ordered according to income and not to health, and split into two groups divided by the median income. Then, quantification of income-related health polarization is made possible using Wolfson's index and a modified Wolfson's index. The two income-related health polarization indices are minimum when the health status of the richer individuals is poor while the poorer individuals have excellent health. On the contrary, polarization is maximum when the poorer have poor health and the richer are also healthier. These measures can also be rewritten, analogously to the Rodriguez and Salas (2003) measure, as a function of the difference between social inequality between groups and social inequality within groups. They can also be decomposed into their causes. Their application provides empirical findings on the self-assessed health status of French women grouped by age.

The analysis proposed by Pérez and Ramos (2010) also examines the effect of income polarization on individual self-assessed health. The authors argue that income polarization captures much better the social tensions and conflicts that are behind the link between income disparities and individual health, and which have traditionally been proxied by inequality. Two factors are particularly relevant: the psychosocial stress resulting from strategies of dominance and conflict; and the lower provision of public goods such as health, education and police. Their empirical findings show that there is a negative relationship between income polarization among socioeconomic subgroups and health in Spain over the years 1994–2001. The interpretation of polarization is in accordance with Esteban and Ray (1994), based on the feelings of alienation and identification, while the measure applied is Zhang and Kanbur's (2001) based on the Theil inequality indices.

Using jointly the ordinal SAH and the categorical ethnicity variable, D'Ambrosio and Permanyer (2015) compute new polarization indices for the different Chilean regions and compare their values with ones obtained from existing indices. This method allows comparison of the rankings of the regions according to the values of the different polarization indices. An empirical application is provided using Chilean data: results suggest that the rankings provided by new polarization indices when compared to other polarization and inequality measures can be substantially different.

20.4.3   Wage Polarization and Mobility in Labour Market

Poggi and Silber (2010) combine the analysis of wage polarization with that of wage mobility. Using the polarization index recently proposed by Deutsch et al. (2007), the authors show that a distinction can be made between a change over time in polarization that is the consequence of 'structural mobility' (change over time in the overall, between- and within-groups inequality) and a change in polarization that is the sole consequence of 'exchange mobility' (changes over time in the ranks of the individuals). This approach is applied to the 1985–2003 Work Histories Italian Panel (WHIP), an employer–employee linked panel database. The authors would like to check whether there is eventually a relationship between labour market segmentation and potential seniority. The empirical investigation is aimed at analysing changes in the level of polarization over time in order to understand the possible origins of tensions and conflicts among individuals with the same potential seniority. It appears that the distribution of wages at the time of entry into the labour market has the highest degree of polarization when the two groups selected are highly paid versus the other workers. Polarization between male and female workers is quite low but increases with seniority, and structural mobility increases polarization, while exchange mobility decreases polarization. When making a distinction between individuals with low and high levels of education, it can be observed that polarization decreases with seniority: structural mobility turns out to decrease polarization, and it overcomes the opposite effect of exchange mobility.

20.5   SOFTWARE AVAILABLE FOR IMPLEMENTING POLARIZATION INDICES

DASP is a comprehensive package of Stata modules that helps to analyse the distribution of living standards. DASP is freely distributed and freely available. A manual for users is Araar and Duclos (2013).

The income polarization indices available in DASP are the following: the Duclos et al. (2004) (together with standard errors and confidence intervals for comparing two distributions), the Foster and Wolfson (1992, 2010) (together with standard errors and confidence intervals for comparing two distributions) and the extended Esteban et al. (2007) measure. As a measure of social polarization DASP provides the Permanyer (2012) measures, together with their decomposition into group components. Also, decomposition of the Duclos et al. (2004) index is implemented, as proposed by Araar (2008), by population subgroups and by income sources.

20.6   DISCUSSION AND CONCLUDING REMARKS

This chapter has provided a review of the main empirical findings and evidence drawn from applications of the most common indices of income and social polarization. Within the literature on income polarization measurement it has distinguished between Wolfson's approach, Esteban and Ray's approach, and alternative methods based on nonparametric density estimation techniques. It then discussed the main empirical applications of social polarization indices and reviewed other applications, such as health polarization, effects of taxation on income polarization, and the link between wage polarization and labour market mobility.

The literature on the measurement of polarization has focused mainly on one sole variable, such as income, religion or ethno-linguistic variables. However, the socioeconomic status of a person and the distance between individuals (and groups) are not determined by income alone but also by other monetary and nonmonetary characteristics of well-being, such as wealth, education and health; persons differ from each other according to several attributes, so that the same level of income can provide two individuals with different degrees of satisfaction of their needs. This discussion illustrates the necessity to move from income polarization or social polarization to a multivariate concept of polarization.

NOTES

1. According to the Duclos et al. (2004) index, the maximum level of polarization is reached for two equally sized groups.
2. For further discussion on the link between polarization and social conflicts, see also Esteban and Schneider (2008) and Esteban and Ray (2011), and the review of theoretical works therein.
3. See also Ginsburgh and Weber (2010) for an extensive discussion about the difference between ethnic fractionalization and ethnic polarization indices.

REFERENCES

Amiel, Y., Cowell, F. and Ramos, X. (2010) Poles apart? An analysis of the meaning of polarization. *Review of Income and Wealth* 56, 23–56.

Anderson, G. (2004a) Making inferences about the polarization, welfare and poverty of nations: a study of 101 countries 1970–1995. *Journal of Applied Econometrics* 19, 537–550.

Anderson, G. (2004b) Toward an empirical analysis of polarization. *Journal of Econometrics* 122, 1–26.

Anderson, G. (2010) Polarization of the poor: multivariate relative poverty measurement sans frontiers. *Review of Income and Wealth* 56, 84–101.

Apouey, B.H. (2007) Measuring health polarization with self-assessed health data. *Health Economics* 16, 875–894.

Apouey, B.H. (2010) On measuring and explaining socioeconomic polarization in health with an application to French data. *Review of Income and Wealth* 56, 141–170.

Araar, A. (2008) On the decomposition of polarization indices: illustrations with Chinese and Nigerian household surveys. Cahiers de recherche 08-06 CIRPEE.

Araar, A. and Duclos, J. (2013) User Manual for Stata Package *DASP: Version 2.3*, PEP, World Bank, UNDP and Université Laval.

Atkinson, A.B. and Brandolini, A. (2013) On the identification of the 'middle class'. In J.C. Gornick and M. Jäntti (eds), *Income Inequality: Economic Disparities and the Middle Class in Affluent Countries*, pp. 77–100. Stanford, CA: Stanford University Press.

Banks, A.S. and Wilson, K.A. (2013) Cross-National Time-Series Data Archive. Jerusalem: Databanks International. http://www.databanksinternational.com.

Beach, C.M. (1989) Dollars and dreams: a reduced middle class? Alternative explanations. *Journal of Human Resources* 24, 162–193.

Beach, C., Chaykowski, R. and Slotsve, G. (1997) Inequality and polarization of male earnings in the United States, 1968–1990. *North American Journal of Economics and Finance* 8, 135–152.

Blackburn, M.L. and Bloom, D.E. (1985) What is happening to the middle class?. *American Demographics* 7, 18–25.

Chakravarty, S.R. and D'Ambrosio, C. (2010) Polarization orderings of income distributions. *Review of Income and Wealth* 56, 47–64.

Chakravarty, S.R. and Maharaj, B. (2012) Ethnic polarization orderings and indices. *Journal of Economic Interaction and Coordination* 7, 99–123.

Chakravarty, S.R. and Majumder, A. (2001) Inequality, polarization and welfare: theory and applications. *Australian Economic Papers* 40, 1–13.

Chakravarty, S.R., Majumder, A. and Roy, S. (2007) A treatment of absolute indices of polarization. *Japanese Economic Review* 58, 273–293.

Collier, P. and Hoeffler, A. (2004) Greed and grievance in civil war. *Oxford Economic Papers* 56, 663–595.

D'Ambrosio, C. (2001) Household characteristics and the distribution of income in Italy: an application of social distance measures. *Review of Income and Wealth* 47, 43–64.

D'Ambrosio, C. and Permanyer, I. (2015) Measuring social polarization with ordinal and categorical data. *Journal of Public Economic Theory* 17, 311–327.

Deutsch, J., Hanoka, M. and Silber, J. (2007) On the link between the concepts of kurtosis and bipolarization. *Economics Bulletin* 4, 1–6.

Duclos, J.-Y., Esteban, J. and Ray, D. (2004) Polarization: concepts, measurement, estimation. *Econometrica* 72, 1737–1772.

Duro, J.A. (2005) Another look to income polarization across countries. *Journal of Policy Modeling* 27, 1001–1007.

Easterly, W. (2001) The middle class consensus and economic development. *Journal of Economic Growth* 6, 317–335.

Eisenhauer, J.G. (2008) The economic definition of the middle class. *Forum for Social Economics* 37, 103–113.

Esteban, J. (2000) An analysis of the polarization of the distribution of provincial income in Spain, 1955–1993 (in Spanish). *Moneda y Crédito* 211, 11–50.

Esteban, J., Gradin, C. and Ray, D. (2007) An extension of a measure of polarization, with an application to the income distribution of five OECD countries. *Journal of Economic Inequality* 5, 1–19.

Esteban, J., Mayoral, L. and Ray, D. (2012) Ethnicity and conflict: theory and facts. *Science* 336, 858–865.

Esteban, J. and Ray, D. (1994) On the measurement of polarization. *Econometrica* 62, 819–851.

Esteban, J. and Ray, D. (1999) Conflict and distribution. *Journal of Economic Theory* 87, 379–415.

Esteban, J. and Ray, D. (2008) Polarization, fractionalization and conflict. *Journal of Peace Research* 45, 163–182.

Esteban, J. and Ray, D. (2011) Linking conflict to inequality and polarization. *American Economic Review* 101, 1345–1374.

Esteban, J. and Schneider, G. (2008) Polarization and conflict: theoretical and empirical issues. *Journal of Peace Research* 45, 131–141.

Ezcurra, R., Gil, C., Pascual, P. and Rapun, M. (2005) Inequality, polarization and regional mobility in the European Union. *Urban Studies* 42, 1057–1076.

Ezcurra, R. and Pascual, P. (2007) Regional polarization and national development in the European Union. *Urban Studies* 44, 99–122.

Fearon, J. and Laitin, D. (2003) Ethnicity, insurgency, and civil war. *American Political Science Review* 97, 75–90.

Foster, J.A. and Wolfson, M.C. (1992) Polarization and the decline of the middle class: Canada and the US. mimeo, Vanderbilt University.

Foster, J. and Wolfson, M. (2010) Polarization and the decline of the middle class: Canada and the US. *Journal of Economic Inequality* 8, 247–273.

Geng, D. (2012) Identifying the unique polarization index: a mean-preserving axiomatic approach. *Journal of Public Economic Theory* 14, 791–812.

Ginsburgh, V. and S. Weber (2010) *The Economics of Linguistic Diversity: How Many Languages Make Sense?*, Princeton, NJ: Princeton University Press.

Gleditsch, N.P., Wallensteen, P., Eriksson, M., Sollenberg, M. and Strand, H. (2002) Armed conflict 1946–2001: a new dataset. *Journal of Peace Research* 39, 615–637.

Gradin, C. (2000) Polarization by sub-populations in Spain, 1973–1991. *Review of Income and Wealth* 46, 457–474.

Horrigan, M.W. and Haugen, S.E. (1988) The declining middle-class thesis: a sensitivity analysis. *Monthly Labor Review* 111, 3–13.

Hussain, M.A. (2009) The sensitivity of income polarization: time, length of accounting periods, equivalence scales, and income definitions. *Journal of Economic Inequality* 7, 207–223.

Jenkins, S. (1995) Did the middle class shrink during the 1980s? UK evidence from kernel density estimates. *Economics Letters* 49, 407–413.

Lasso de la Vega, C. and Urrutia, A. (2006) An alternative formulation of the Esteban–Gradin–Ray extended measure of polarization. *Journal of Income Distribution* 15, 42–54.

Lasso de la Vega, C., Urrutia, A. and Diez, H. (2010) Unit consistency and bipolarization of income distributions. *Review of Income and Wealth* 56, 65–83.

Lichbach, M.I. (1989) An evaluation of 'Does economic inequality breed political conflict?' studies. *World Politics* 41, 431–470.

Maza, A. and Villaverde, J. (2004) Regional disparities in the EU: mobility and polarization. *Applied Economics Letters* 11, 517–522.

Milanovic, B. (2000) A new polarization measure and some applications. Washington, DC: World Bank.

Milanovic, B. and Yitzhaki, S. (2002) Decomposing world income distribution: does the world have a middle class?. *Review of Income and Wealth* 48, 155–178.

Montalvo, J.G. and Reynal-Querol, M. (2003) Religious polarization and economic development. *Economics Letters* 80, 201–210.

Montalvo, J.G. and Reynal-Querol, M. (2005) Ethnic polarization, potential conflict and civil war. *American Economic Review* 95, 796–816.

Montalvo, J.G. and Reynal-Querol, M. (2008) Discrete polarization with an application to the determinants of genocides. *Economic Journal* 118, 1835–1865.

Montalvo, J.G. and Reynal-Querol, M. (2010) Ethnic polarization and the duration of civil wars. *Economics of Governance* 11, 123–143.

Oliver, X., Piccoli, L. and Spadaro, A. (2010) A microsimulation evaluation of efficiency, inequality, and polarization effects of implementing the Danish, the French, and the UK redistribution system in Spain. *Review of Income and Wealth* 56, 186–214.

Pérez, C.B. and Ramos, X. (2010) Polarization and health. *Review of Income and Wealth* 56, 171–185.

Permanyer, I. (2012) The conceptualization and measurement of social polarization. *Journal of Economic Inequality* 10, 45–74.

Pittau, M.G. and Zelli, R. (2010) Mixture models, convergence clubs and polarization. *Review of Income and Wealth* 56, 102–121.

Poggi, A. and Silber, J. (2010) On polarization and mobility: a look at polarization in the wage-career profile in Italy. *Review of Income and Wealth* 56, 123–140.

Pressman, S. (2007) The decline of the middle class: an international perspective. *Journal of Economic Issues* 41, 181–200.

Quah, D.T. (1997) Empirics for growth and distribution: stratification, polarization, and convergence clubs. *Journal of Economic Growth* 2, 27–59.

Ravallion, M. (2010) The developing world's bulging (but vulnerable) middle class. *World Development* 38, 445–454.

Reynal-Querol, M. (2002) Ethnicity, political systems, and civil wars. *Journal of Conflict Resolution* 46, 29–54.

Rodrıguez, J. and Salas, R. (2003) Extended bi-polarization and inequality measures. *Research on Economic Inequality* 9, 69–83.

Seshanna, S. and Decornez, S. (2003) Income polarization and inequality across countries: an empirical study. *Journal of Policy Modeling* 25, 335–358.

Thurow, L. (1987) A surge in inequality. *Scientific American* 256, 30–37.

Wang, Y. and Tsui, K. (2000) Polarization orderings and new classes of polarization indices. *Journal of Public Economic Theory* 2, 349–363.

Wolfson, M.C. (1994) When inequalities diverge. *American Economic Review* 48, 353–358.

Wolfson, M.C. (1997) Divergent inequalities: theory and empirical results. *Review of Income and Wealth* 43, 401–421.

Yitzhaki, S. (2010) Is there room for polarization?. *Review of Income and Wealth* 56, 7–22.

Zhang, X. and Kanbur, R. (2001) What difference do polarisation measures make? An application to China. *Journal of Development Studies* 37, 85–98.

21. Segregation: theoretical approaches
Oscar Volij

21.1 INTRODUCTION

Segregation and its measurement has been an object of interest for sociologists since at least the late 1940s. More recently, economists as well have become interested in segregation and its effects on the wage gender gap, the educational attainment of minorities and on other socio-economic variables. The concept of segregation, nevertheless, has proved to be quite elusive. Indeed, since the seminal paper of Duncan and Duncan (1955), the literature on segregation has generated a plethora of indices. To make some order, Massey and Denton (1988) identified five different aspects that could be captured by the concept of segregation, namely, evenness, exposure, concentration, centralization and clustering. Evenness refers to the extent to which the members of the different groups are similarly distributed across units; exposure, to the extent to which members of the minority groups are exposed to members of other groups; concentration, to the proportion of space occupied by the members of the minority in the city; centralization, to the degree to which the members of the minority group are located near the center of the city; and finally, clustering refers to the closeness of the units occupied by the members of the minority. They have also classified 20 indices into five categories corresponding to the above aspects. One of the differences among the various indices is that they require qualitatively different data. Thus, while indices of evenness and exposure typically take as an input the raw number of members of each group in each unit, indices of concentration and clustering additionally require geographical data such as the areas of different units and their distances from the center. Similarly, indices of clustering require data on the proximity between the different units. More formally, the domains on which the various indices are defined are not the same which makes any comparison between them absurd.

This chapter surveys the segregation literature with a focus on axiomatic models. It particularly mentions James and Taeuber (1985), who propose a short list of properties for the evaluation of evenness and exposure indices for the case of two groups, and Reardon and Firebaugh (2002), who evaluate several such indices, for the multigroup case. Full characterizations of indices or of families of indices, however, did not appear until Philipson (1993). The chapter concentrates on indices defined within the traditional model of segregation in which members of different groups, for example men and women, or blacks, whites and Hispanics, are located in different locations. These locations could be neighborhoods, schools or occupations. A number of recent papers, however, have opted for a different model in which members of different groups are located on a network. Two notable exponents of this novel approach are Echenique and Fryer (2007), and Ballester and Vorsatz (2013). In Echenique and Fryer (2007) the model is given by a weighted directed graph where the nodes represent individuals, the arcs represent the existence of an interaction between the corresponding individuals, and the weight measures the intensity of the interaction. In addition, each individual belongs to a particular ethnic group. The segregation index they propose, called the spectral segregation index, can be thought of as a measure of isolation because it tries to capture the degree to which individuals tend to interact with members of their own group.[1] Ballester and Vorsatz (2013) also model a city as a graph, but in their case the nodes represent locations which can contain several individuals belonging to various groups. They complement the graph with a Markov matrix with an absorbing state that describes the probabilities of transitions from one location to another. The segregation index they propose captures the probabilities that in the long run members of the same group end up in the same location.

This chapter is organized as follows. After the basic notation is introduced in section 21.2, section 21.3 defines the Lorenz segregation ordering on two-group cities and enumerates several properties that it satisfies. Section 21.4 introduces some well known examples of segregation indices. Section 21.5 enumerates additional axioms that a segregation index may satisfy, and section 21.6 states three characterization results. Finally, section 21.7 focuses on the case in which the number of groups is variable and formulates another characterization theorem.

21.2 NOTATION

Throughout the chapter the language of urban ethnic segregation is used. The definitions and results, however, apply in other contexts as well, including occupational gender segregation, religious segregation in schools, and so on.

The initial, and perhaps the most important modeling choice concerns the domain on which the segregation measures are to be defined. Some axioms may characterize a particular ordering over a particular domain, but not over some alternative one. In this part of the chapter attention is restricted to a domain with a fixed number of racial groups. Furthermore, for ease of exposition attention is further restricted to two groups only, referred to as blacks and whites. This entails little loss of generality since most of the results generalize (some in a straightforward way) to the many groups case. Section 21.7 focuses on a domain with a variable number of groups.

A neighborhood n is characterized by a pair (B_n, W_n) of non-negative real numbers, at least one of which is positive. The pair (B_n, W_n) is the neighborhood's ethnic composition. Namely, the first and second components are the numbers of blacks and whites, respectively, in n. A city is a finite collection of neighborhoods, at least one of which has a positive number of blacks and at least one of which has a positive number of whites. Formally, a city is a system $\langle N, (B_n, W_n)_{n \in N} \rangle$ such that $\sum_{n \in N} B_n > 0$ and $\sum_{n \in N} W_n > 0$, where N is the set of neighborhoods and for each $n \in N$, (B_n, W_n) is n's racial composition.

Given a city $\langle N, (B_n, W_n)_{n \in N} \rangle$, we denote by B and W the total numbers of blacks and whites, respectively: $B = \sum_{n \in N} B_n$ and $W = \sum_{n \in N} W_n$. Also, the following notation will be useful:

$P = \dfrac{B}{B + W}$: the proportion of blacks in the city

$p_n = \dfrac{B_n}{B_n + W_n}$: the proportion of blacks in neighborhood n

$T = B + W$: the total population of the city

$T_n = B_n + W_n$: the total population of neighborhood n

$b_n = \dfrac{B_n}{B}$: the proportion of the city's blacks that live in neighborhood n

$w_n = \dfrac{W_n}{W}$: the proportion of the city's whites that live in neighborhood n.

For any city $X = \langle N, (B_n, W_n)_{n \in N} \rangle$ and any positive constant α, αX denotes the city that results from multiplying the number of blacks and whites in each neighborhood of X by α, namely, $\alpha X = \langle N, (\alpha B_n, \alpha W_n)_{n \in N} \rangle$. For any two cities $X = \langle N_X, (B_n, W_n)_{n \in N_X} \rangle$ and $Y = \langle N_Y, (B_n, W_n)_{n \in N_Y} \rangle$, with disjoint sets of neighborhoods, $X \circ Y$ denotes the concatenation of the two. Formally, $X \circ Y = \langle N_X \cup N_Y, (B_n, W_n)_{n \in N_X \cup N_Y} \rangle$. For convenience, we will sometimes denote a city $X = \langle N, (B_n, W_n)_{n \in N} \rangle$ simply by $(B_n, W_n)_{n \in N}$.

The city's ethnic distribution is given by $(P, 1 - P)$ and neighborhood n's ethnic distribution is given by $(p_n, 1 - p_n)$. Neighborhood n is representative of the city if the proportions of the city's blacks and of the city's whites who live in the neighborhood are equal; that is, if $b_n = w_n$.

21.3   LORENZ ORDERING

We are interested in ordering cities according to their level of segregation. This task is not an easy one, as is evident from the large number of existing segregation indices. However, there are some instances in which the comparison of cities according to their segregation seems to be straightforward. These instances are identified by axioms. Before presenting some of the axioms, let us motivate them by means of a particular partial order defined on the class of two-group cities, namely the Lorenz order.

Let $X = \langle N, (B_n, W_n)_{n \in N} \rangle$ be a city, and let $\phi : \{1, 2, \ldots, |N|\} \to N$ be an ordering of the neighborhoods such that $i \leq j \Rightarrow p_{\phi(i)} \geq p_{\phi(j)}$. Namely, ϕ orders neighborhoods in a non-increasing manner according to their proportion of blacks. Also let $\beta_0 = \omega_0 = 0$, and for $i = 1, 2, \ldots, |N|$, let $\beta_i = \beta_{i-1} + b_{\phi(i)}$ and $\omega_i = \omega_{i-1} + w_{\phi(i)}$. That is, β_i is the proportion of blacks that reside in the i neighborhoods with the highest proportions of blacks. Similarly, ω_i is the proportion of whites that reside in these same neighborhoods. The Lorenz curve *of* X is the graph that is obtained by plotting the points (β_i, ω_i) and connecting the dots.[2] Note that the line segment that connects the points $(\beta_{i-1}, \omega_{i-1})$ and (β_i, ω_i) has a slope of $w_{\phi(i)}/b_{\phi(i)}$. It can be checked that $b_i/(b_i + w_i) \geq b_j/(b_j + w_j) \Leftrightarrow p_i \geq p_j$. Therefore, the Lorenz curve is invariant to the choice of ordering ϕ as long as it satisfies $i \leq j \Rightarrow p_{\phi(i)} \geq p_{\phi(j)}$. Figure 21.1 illustrates the Lorenz curve of a city with three neighborhoods.

Based on the Lorenz curves described above we can now define the Lorenz partial order:

Definition 1 Let X and Y be two cities. We say that Y is at least as segregated as X according to the Lorenz criterion, denoted by $Y \succeq_L X$, if the Lorenz curve of Y is nowhere above the Lorenz curve of X.

Figure 21.2 depicts the Lorenz curves of two cities, X and Y, the latter being more segregated than the former according to the Lorenz criterion. The relation 'being at least

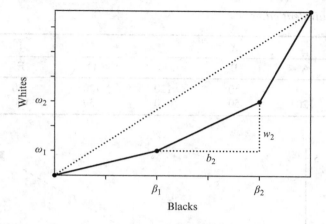

Figure 21.1   The Lorenz curve of a three-neighborhood city

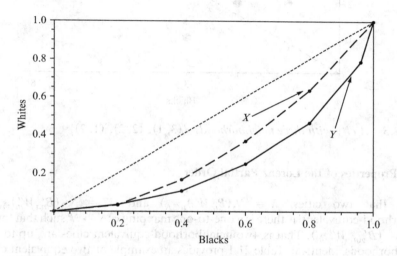

Figure 21.2   Y is more segregated than X according to the Lorenz criterion

as segregated as, according to the Lorenz criterion' is an example of a segregation order. A segregation order is a binary relation that is used to compare cities according to their respective levels of segregation. More formally, if we denote the set of all cities with two ethnic groups by C_2, a segregation order, $\geqslant$, is a reflexive and transitive binary relation on C_2. We interpret $X \geqslant Y$ to mean that 'city X is at least as segregated as city Y according to $\geqslant$'. The relations $\sim$ and $>$ are derived from $\geqslant$ in the usual way.[3] Much of the segregation literature is interested in identifying segregation orders that satisfy desirable properties. In order to motivate them, we next analyze some of the properties that the Lorenz order satisfies.

Table 21.1   Equivalent cities

	X			Y		
	A	B	C	D	E	F
Blacks	30	50	120	120	30	50
Whites	120	50	30	30	120	50

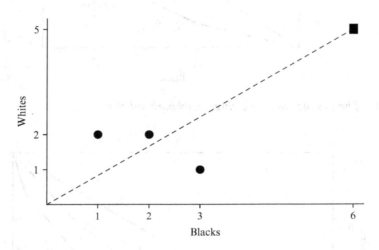

Figure 21.3   A city with three neighborhoods: $\langle(3, 1), (2, 2), (1, 2)\rangle$

21.3.1   Properties of the Lorenz Partial Order

We say that two cities, $X = \langle N,(B_n, W_n)_{n \in N}\rangle$ and $X' = \langle N',(B'_m, W'_m)_{m \in N'}\rangle$, are 'neighborhood-equivalent' if there is a one-to-one mapping $\varphi:N \to N'$ such that for all $n \in N$, $(B_n, W_n) = (B'_{\varphi(n)}, W'_{\varphi(n)})$. That is, two neighborhood-equivalent cities are, up to renaming of neighborhoods, identical. Table 21.1 provides an example of two equivalent cities.

It is clear that two neighborhood-equivalent cities have the same Lorenz curves. Therefore, the Lorenz order satisfies the following axiom:

Neighborhood-Anonymity (N-ANON) An order $\geqslant$ on $\mathcal{C}_2$ satisfies neighborhood-anonymity if for any two neighborhood-equivalent cities X and Y we have that $X \sim Y$.

Neighborhood-anonymity allows us to represent any city $\langle N,(B_n, W_n)_{n \in N}\rangle$ graphically by drawing the collection of points $(B_n, W_n)_{n \in N}$. Figure 21.3 depicts a city with three neighborhoods. The rectangle represents the city's total population of blacks and whites, (B, W). The slope of the dotted line is the city's ratio of whites over blacks. It can be seen that blacks are over-represented in one of the neighborhoods and under-represented in the other two.

Consider now the cities $X = \langle N,(B_n, W_n)_{n \in N}\rangle$ and $Y = \langle N,(\alpha B_n, \beta W_n)_{n \in N}\rangle$, the latter

Table 21.2 Doubly scaled cities

	X			Y		
	A	B	C	D	E	F
Blacks	3	5	12	30	50	120
Whites	120	50	30	60	25	15

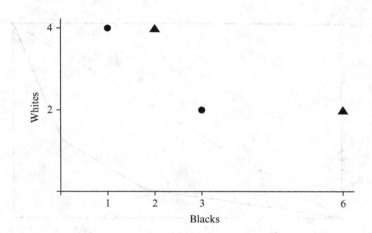

Figure 21.4   Two cities: one is obtained from the other by scaling down the number of blacks

being obtained from X by multiplying the number of X's blacks by $\alpha > 0$ and the number of X's whites by $\beta > 0$. Table 21.2 depicts an example of two such cities.

Since for all n, neighborhood n in both cities contain the same proportions b_n and w_n of the total number of blacks and whites, respectively, X and Y have the same Lorenz curve. Therefore, the Lorenz order satisfies the following axiom:

Composition Invariance (CI) Let $X = \langle N, (B_n, W_n)_{n \in N} \rangle$ be a city and let $Y = \langle N, (\alpha B_n, \beta W_n)_{n \in N} \rangle$ be the city that is obtained from X by multiplying the number of agents of a given group by the same nonzero factor in all neighborhoods. An order $\geqslant$ on $\mathcal{C}_2$ satisfies composition invariance if for any such cities we have $X \sim Y$.

Figure 21.4 depicts two cities, one of which has, for each of its neighborhoods, the same number of whites and half the number of blacks as the other one. According to Composition Invariance, these two cities are equally segregated.

Now let $X = \langle N, (B_n, W_n)_{n \in N} \rangle$ be a city and consider the city Y that is obtained from X by splitting a particular neighborhood n into two neighborhoods n_1 and n_2 with the same ethnic distribution. Namely, $(B_{n_1}, W_{n_1}) = (\alpha B_n, \alpha W_n)$ and $(B_{n_2}, W_{n_2}) = ((1 - \alpha) B_n, (1 - \alpha) W_n)$ for some $\alpha \in (0, 1)$. Table 21.3 illustrates two such cities.

Then, we have $b_n = b_{n_1} + b_{n_2}$, $w_n = w_{n_1} + w_{n_2}$, and $p_{n_1} = p_{n_2} = p_n$. Therefore, both X

Table 21.3   Splitting a neighborhood and keeping its ethnic distribution

	X			Y			
	A	B	C	A_1	A_2	B	C
Blacks	30	50	120	20	10	50	120
Whites	120	50	30	80	40	50	30

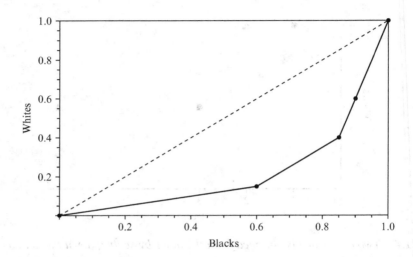

Figure 21.5   The two Lorenz curves

and *Y* have the same Lorenz curve, as depicted in Figure 21.5. Indeed, the segment that represents neighborhood *n* in *X* is split into two segments representing neighborhoods n_1 and n_2 in *Y*.

As a result, the Lorenz order satisfies the following axiom:

Organizational Equivalence (OE) Let $X \in C_2$ be a city and let (B_n, W_n) be a neighborhood of *X*. Also let *Y* be the city that results from *X* by dividing (B_n, W_n) into two neighborhoods, (B_{n_1}, W_{n_1}) and (B_{n_2}, W_{n_2}), with the same ethnic distribution. Namely, $p_{n_1} = p_{n_2}$. An order $\geqslant$ on C_2 satisfies organizational equivalence if for any such cities we have $X \sim Y$.

In order to motivate the next axiom, consider a city $X = \langle N, (B_n, W_n)_{n \in N} \rangle$. Let $i, j \in N$ be two neighborhoods such that $0 < p_i < 1$ and $p_j \leq p_i$. That is, neighborhood *i* contains both blacks and whites, but has proportionally less whites than neighborhood *j*.

Let $\varepsilon \in (0, W_i]$, and let *Y* be the city that is obtained from *X* by moving ε whites from neighborhood *i* to neighborhood *j*. That is, $Y = \langle N, (B'_n, W'_n)_{n \in N} \rangle$ in which $(B'_i, W'_i) = (B_i, W_i - \varepsilon)$, $(B'_j, W'_j) = (B_j, W_j + \varepsilon)$, and $(B'_n, W'_n) = (B_n, W_n)$ for all $n \neq i, j$. Then we have that

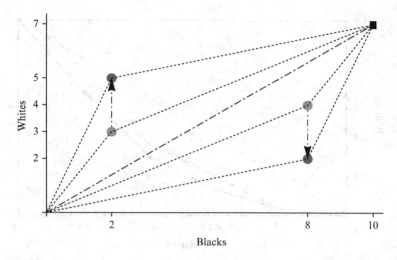

Figure 21.6   Transferring whites from a neighborhood with a relatively low percentage of whites to one with a relatively high percentage of whites

$$w_n/b_n = w'_n/b'_n \text{ for all } n \neq i,j$$

$$w'_i/b'_i < w_i/b_i \leq w_j/b_j < w'_j/b'_j.$$

Figure 21.6 depicts the outcome of transferring white individuals from a neighborhood with relatively few whites to another one with relatively more whites.

It can be checked that the Lorenz curve of X lies nowhere below the Lorenz curve of Y, while it is not true that the Lorenz curve of Y lies nowhere below the Lorenz curve of X. (See Figure 21.7 for an example of the effect of a transfer of white residents on the Lorenz curve.) Therefore, the Lorenz order satisfies the following axiom.

The W Transfer Principle (WT) For any city $X = \langle N,(B_n,W_n)_{n\in N}\rangle$, let $i, j \in N$ be two neighborhoods such that $B_i W_i > 0$ and

$$\frac{W_i}{B_i + W_i} \leq \frac{W_j}{B_j + W_j}.$$

Also let $\varepsilon \in (0, W_i]$, and Y be the city that is obtained from X by moving ε whites from neighborhood i to neighborhood j. A segregation order $\geqslant$ on $\mathcal{C}_2$ satisfies the W Transfer Principle if for any such cities we have that $Y > X$.

Analogously, the Lorenz order satisfies the following axiom.[4]

The B Transfer Principle (BT) For any city $X = \langle N,(B_n,W_n)_{n\in N}\rangle$, let $i, j \in N$ be two neighborhoods such that $B_i W_i > 0$ and

$$\frac{B_i}{B_i + W_i} \leq \frac{B_j}{B_j + W_j}.$$

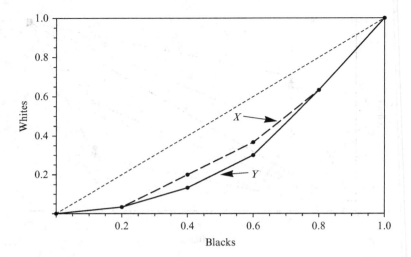

Figure 21.7   Lorenz curves before (X = {(30, 5), (30, 25), (30, 25), (30, 40), (30,
55)}) and after the transfer (Y = {(30, 5), (30, 15), (30, 25), (30, 50),
(30, 55)})

Also let $\varepsilon \in (0, B_i]$, and Y be the city that is obtained from X by moving ε blacks from neighborhood i to neighborhood j. A segregation order $\geqslant$ on $\mathcal{C}_2$ satisfies the B Transfer Principle if for any such cities we have $Y > X$.

We can summarize the two axioms in the following.

The Transfer Principle (T) A segregation order $\geqslant$ on $\mathcal{C}_2$ satisfies the transfer principle if it satisfies both WT and BT.

The Lorenz order satisfies the above four axioms, but it may not be the only ordering of cities that does this. It turns out that any order that satisfies the above four axioms must be consistent with the Lorenz order, and conversely, any order that is consistent with the Lorenz ordering must satisfy the four axioms. This result, which is stated in the following Proposition, was demonstrated by Hutchens (1991) for the case in which all neighborhoods have an identical number of blacks or an identical number of whites. It was also mentioned, without proof, in James and Taeuber (1985, p. 19), and in Hutchens (2001). For a proof, see Lasso de la Vega and Volij (2014).

Proposition 1 *Let $\geqslant$ be an order on $\mathcal{C}_2$. It satisfies Neighborhood-Anonymity, Composition Invariance, Organizational Equivalence and the Transfer Principle if and only if for all two cities $X, Y \in \mathcal{C}_2$ the following implications hold:*

$$Y >_L X \Rightarrow Y > X \tag{21.1}$$

$$Y \sim_L X \Rightarrow Y \sim X. \tag{21.2}$$

Hutchens (2015) studies the implications of adding the following symmetry axiom to the ones listed in the above Proposition. For any city $X = \langle N, (B_n, W_n)_{n \in N} \rangle$ its dual is the city $X^D = \langle N, (W_n, B_n)_{n \in N} \rangle$ that is obtained from X by, for each neighborhood n, interchanging the numbers of blacks and whites.

Symmetry (S) Let $X = \langle N, (B_n, W_n)_{n \in N} \rangle$, be a city and let $X^D = \langle N, (W_n, B_n)_{n \in N} \rangle$ be its dual. A segregation order $\geqslant$ on $\mathcal{C}_2$ satisfies symmetry if for any two such cities we have $X \sim X^D$.

The Lorenz partial order does not satisfy Symmetry because in general, the Lorenz curves of a city and its dual cross each other, which renders them incomparable by the Lorenz criterion. Hutchens (2015) proposes the following modification of the Lorenz partial order:

Definition 2 Let X and Y be two cities. We say that Y is at least as segregated as X according to the weak Lorenz criterion, denoted by $Y \geqslant_{WL} X$, if either $Y \geqslant_L X$ or $Y^D \geqslant_L X$.

In other words, Y is at least as segregated as X according to the weak Lorenz criterion, if either it is at least as segregated as X according to the Lorenz criterion or would be so should Y's blacks become white and Y's whites become black.

Hutchens (2015) obtains the following characterization of the segregation orders that are weak-Lorenz consistent:

Proposition 2 *Let $\geqslant$ be an order on $\mathcal{C}_2$. It satisfies Neighborhood-Anonymity, Composition Invariance, Organizational Equivalence, the Transfer Principle and Symmetry if and only if for all two cities $X, Y \in \mathcal{C}_2$ the following implications hold:*

$$Y >_{WL} X \Rightarrow Y > X \qquad (21.3)$$

$$Y \sim_{WL} X \Rightarrow Y \sim X. \qquad (21.4)$$

21.4 SEGREGATION ORDERINGS AND THEIR MEASURES

As we have seen, the above four axioms let us identify a partial order among cities. But the literature on segregation is interested in identifying reasonable complete orderings, so that *any* two cities could be compared according to their respective segregation levels. Complete segregation orders are usually represented by segregation indices, which are functions that assign to each city a nonnegative number that is meant to capture its level of segregation. Given a segregation index S, the associated segregation order is defined by $X \geq Y \Leftrightarrow S(X) \geq S(Y)$. Clearly, a segregation order may be represented by more than one index.

Additional axioms to the ones presented above have been proposed in order to identify reasonable segregation orderings. Before introducing them, a number of segregation indices that have been widely used to measure segregation are listed.

21.4.1   Examples of Segregation Indices

The following is one of the most widely-used indices of segregation:

The Index of Dissimilarity. It is defined as:

$$D(X) = \sum_{n \in N: b_n > w_n} (b_n - w_n). \tag{21.5}$$

This index was introduced to the literature by Jahn et al. (1947). It assigns to each city the proportion of either blacks or whites that would need to be relocated in order to obtain perfect integration. For example, if $b_n > w_n$, one needs to remove a proportion $b_n - w_n$ of the city's blacks from neighborhood n for the neighborhood to be representative, and if $b_n < w_n$, one needs to add a proportion $w_n - b_n$ of the city's blacks to neighborhood n for the neighborhood to be representative. The index of dissimilarity can be represented graphically as the maximum distance between the Lorenz curve and the 45 degree line. Since two Lorenz curves may have the same maximum distance to the 45 degree line with one being below the other, the index of dissimilarity is not consistent with the Lorenz ordering. Indeed, as we shall see below, it does not satisfy the transfer principle. Karmel and MacClachlan (1988) proposed a slight modification to the dissimilarity index that takes into account the city's ethnic distribution. It is given by:

$$2P(1 - P)D(X).$$

This index calculates the number of people that would need to be relocated in order to obtain perfect integration, keeping each of the neighborhoods' population unchanged, and normalizes it so that the index ranges between 0 and 1. Like the Dissimilarity index, the Karmel and MaClachlan index is not consistent with the Lorenz ordering. Since the value of the index depends on the city's ethnic distribution it does not satisfy composition invariance.

The Gini Index. It is defined as:

$$G(X) = \frac{1}{2} \sum_{n \in N} \sum_{m \in N} |b_n w_m - b_m w_n|. \tag{21.6}$$

This index is adapted from the income inequality index of the same name. As in the case of the Index of Dissimilarity, this index is also related to the Lorenz curve. Indeed, it can be shown that $G(X)$ equals twice the area between the Lorenz curve and the 45 degree line.

The next two indices are related to the concept of entropy. The entropy of a random variable is the expected number of bytes needed to transmit the value of its realization. In the case of a two-value random variable with distribution $(q, 1 - q)$, its entropy is given by:

$$h(q, 1 - q) = q \log_2\left(\frac{1}{q}\right) + (1 - q)\log_2\left(\frac{1}{1 - q}\right).$$

The entropy of a random variable is a measure of the uncertainty contained in it.

One can interpret a city's ethnic distribution as the distribution of a random variable, that is, the ethnicity of a city's resident. Therefore, the entropy of a city's ethnic distribution $(P, 1 - P)$ represents the uncertainty concerning the ethnicity of a randomly chosen city resident. Similarly, the entropy of a neighborhood's ethnic distribution, $(p_n, 1 - p_n)$, represents the uncertainty concerning the ethnicity of a randomly chosen individual, conditional on knowing that he belongs to that neighborhood. Although the entropy of a given neighborhood may be higher or lower than the entropy of the whole city, the entropy of the latter is at least as high as the average entropy of its neighborhoods.[5] The next two indices compare the entropy of a city's ethnic distribution with the average entropy of its neighborhoods.

The Mutual Information Index. It is defined as:

$$MI(X) = h(P, 1 - P) - \sum_{n \in N} \frac{T_n}{T} h(p_n, 1 - p_n) \tag{21.7}$$

where h is the entropy function.

The Mutual Information is the average reduction in entropy that results from learning the neighborhood in which a randomly chosen individual lives. This index was first proposed by Theil (1971) and has been applied by Fuchs (1975) and Mora and Ruiz-Castillo (2003, 2004). In the case of two ethnic groups, many of its properties, have been pointed out by Mora and Ruiz-Castillo (2005).

The Entropy Index. It is defined as:

$$H(X) = \sum_{n \in N} \frac{T_n}{T} \frac{h(P, 1 - P) - h(p_n, 1 - p_n)}{h(P, 1 - P)}. \tag{21.8}$$

Note that $H(X) = MI(X)/h(P, 1 - P)$.

The Entropy Index is the average decrease in entropy that results from learning the neighborhood, relative to the whole city's entropy. It was proposed by Theil (1972) and Theil and Finizza (1971).

The next index has been used in several applications:

Index of Isolation. It is given by:

$$J(X) = \frac{\left(\sum_{n \in N} b_n p_n \right) - P}{1 - P}. \tag{21.9}$$

This index calculates the gap between the average of the neighborhoods' proportions of blacks (weighted by the neighborhood's fraction of the city's blacks) and the city's overall proportion of blacks, and normalizes it so that it ranges between 0 and 1. It turns out that this index is symmetric with respect to ethnic groups. Therefore, it also equals the normalized gap between the average of the neighborhoods' proportions of whites (weighted by the neighborhood's fraction of the city's whites) and the city's overall proportion of whites. This index was originally proposed by Bell (1954). James and Taeuber (1985) refer to J as the variance ratio index. Massey and Denton (1988) call it the correlation ratio. Reardon and Firebaugh (2002) call it the index of Normalized Exposure. A variant of this index was used by Cutler et al. (1999) to measure the evolution of segregation in American cities.

The following family of indices, called generalized entropy measures, was introduced and characterized by Hutchens (2004). It is defined for $\beta \in (0, 1)$ as follows:

$$O_\beta = 1 - \left[\sum_{n \in N} w_n^{1-\beta} b_n^\beta \right].$$

When $\beta = 1/2$, the corresponding generalized entropy measure, sometimes called the square root index, is:

$$O_{1/2} = 1 - \sum_{n \in N} \sqrt{w_n b_n}.$$

A closely related family of segregation measures is the Atkinson's family which was introduced by James and Taeuber (1985). For $\beta \in (0, 1)$ it is defined as follows:

$$A_\beta = 1 - \frac{P}{1-P} \left[\frac{1}{PT} \sum_{n \in N} T_n (1 - p_n)^{1-\beta} p_n^\beta \right]^{\frac{1}{1-\beta}}.$$

By routine substitutions this expression can be rewritten as:

$$A_\beta = 1 - \left[\sum_{n \in N} w_n^{1-\beta} b_n^\beta \right]^{\frac{1}{1-\beta}}.$$

It is readily seen that measure A_β is obtained from O_β by means of a monotonic transformation. Indeed:

$$O_\beta = 1 - (1 - A_\beta)^{1-\beta}.$$

Consequently, for any $\beta \in (0, 1)$, the indices A_β and O_β represent the same segregation ordering. In particular, the symmetric Atkinson measure $A_{1/2}$ represents the same segregation order as the Square Root index $O_{1/2}$.

21.5 MORE AXIOMS

Since there is such a great variety of indices that are available for researchers to measure segregation it is worth asking if any are more desirable than others? This section discusses a number of properties to help answer this question.[6]

The next axiom is similar to the Transfer Principle in that it states circumstances under which the overall city's segregation increases. Specifically, it states that if a neighborhood is split into two neighborhoods with different ethnic distributions, then segregation must increase. Formally:

Neighborhood Division Property (NDP) Let $X \in C_2$ be a city and let n be a neighborhood of X. Also let Y be the city that results from dividing n into two neighborhoods, n_1 and n_2. If n_1 and n_2 have different ethnic distributions (that is, $p_{n1} \neq p_{n2}$), then $Y > X$.

Frankel and Volij (2011) show that Organizational Equivalence and the Transfer Principle imply the Neighborhood Division Property. The next claim, the proof of which can be found in the Appendix, shows that, assuming Organizational Equivalence, the Transfer Principle and the Neighborhood Division Property are in fact equivalent. One advantage of the Neighborhood Division Property over the Transfer Principle, however, is that while the former is naturally extended to cities with more than two groups, the latter is not.

Claim 1 *Let $\geqslant$ be an order on C_2 that satisfies Organizational Equivalence. Then, it satisfies the Transfer Principle if and only if it satisfies the Neighborhood Division Property.*

The next axiom states that segregation does not depend on which ethnic group is called black and which one is called white:

Group Symmetry (GS) Segregation in a city is unaffected by relabeling the ethnic groups: $\langle N, (B_n, W_n)_{n \in N} \rangle \sim \langle N, (W_n, B_n)_{n \in N} \rangle$.

This axiom is satisfied by all the indices presented in section 21.4.1 except for the Atkinson indices with parameter $\beta \neq 1/2$. These latter indices view segregation not as a feature of the city as a whole, but as the relation between the city and its minority group which is given a different weight than the one received by the other group.

The next axiom states that adjoining the same set of neighborhoods to two cities with the same population and ethnic distribution preserves their order:

Independence (IND) Let X and Y be two cities with the same number of blacks and whites. Then $X \geqslant Y$ if and only if $X \circ Z \geqslant Y \circ Z$, for all cities Z.

Figure 21.8 illustrates the independence axiom. Two cities are depicted, one consisting of the two neighborhoods that are denoted by small dots, and the other of the two neighborhoods that are denoted by large dots. Note that these two cities have the same number of blacks and whites. Independence requires that no matter how these two cities are ranked by the segregation order, the annexation of the neighborhood denoted by a triangle to both of them does not affect their ranking. The Mutual Information index as well as the whole family of Atkinson indices satisfy independence. The Gini and the Dissimilarity indices do not.

Independence is a strong axiom in the sense that it requires order preservation whenever any set of of neighborhoods is adjoined to the existing ones. The next axiom weakens

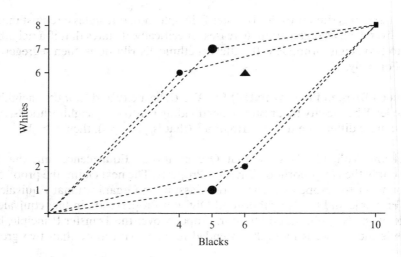

*Figure 21.8   IND: Adding the triangular neighborhood to the small-dot and large-dot
cities does not affect their segregation ranking*

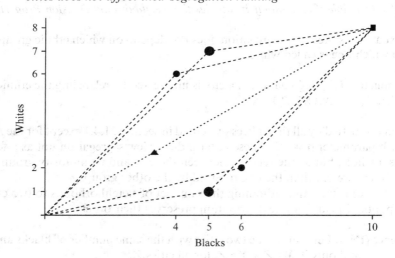

*Figure 21.9   WIND: adding the triangular neighborhood to the small-dot and large-dot
cities does not affect their segregation ranking*

Independence in that order preservation is required only if the set of neighborhoods that
is added, Z, has the same ethnic distribution as the two existing cities:

Weak Independence (WIND) Let X Y and Z be three cities. Suppose all three of them have
the same proportion of blacks, and that X and Y have the same total populations. Then
$X \succcurlyeq Y$ if and only if $X \circ Z \succcurlyeq Y \circ Z$.

Figure 21.9 illustrates Weak Independence. Two cities are depicted, one consisting of the two small-dot neighborhoods and the other of the two large-dot neighborhoods. A hypothetical isolated neighborhood is also depicted there by a triangle. This neighborhood has the same proportion of blacks and whites as the other two cities. Weak Independence requires that however these two cities are ranked, the annexation of the black neighborhood to both of them does not affect the ranking. If the annexed neighborhood did not have the same ethnic distribution as the other two cities, then Weak Independence (as opposed to Independence) would not have required anything.

Although the Dissimilarity index does not satisfy Independence, it does satisfy Weak Independence. The Gini index, however, does not satisfy this weaker axiom.

For the same reason that not all preference relations can be represented by a utility function, not all segregation orders can be represented by a segregation index. Furthermore, the segregation literature is usually interested not just in segregation indices but in continuous ones.[7] In order to guarantee that a continuous representation exists, a continuity axiom is often needed. The following one, which is satisfied by all the indices introduced so far, requires that certain similar cities must have similar segregation levels:

Continuity (C) For any cities X Y and Z, where X and Y have the same proportion of blacks and the same total population, the sets:

$$\{c \in [0,1]: cX \circ (1 - c)Y \geqslant Z\} \text{ and } \{c \in [0,1]: Z \geqslant cX \circ (1 - c)Y\}$$

are closed.

All the axioms presented thus far impose conditions on the segregation order. The literature also offers axioms which impose conditions directly on segregation indices. One example is the next one, which turns out to be closely related to IND:

Aggregation (AGG) An index S is Aggregative if there is a function F such that $S(X \circ Y) = F(S(X), S(Y), B(X), W(X), B(Y), W(Y))$, where F is a continuous function, strictly increasing in its first and second arguments.

The next claim, which is proved in the appendix, shows that Independence and Aggregation are to some extent equivalent axioms:

Claim 2 *If an index S satisfies Aggregation then it also satisfies Independence. Furthermore, a continuous index that satisfies Independence satisfies Aggregation as well.*

21.6   IMPLICATIONS OF THE AXIOMS

This section presents two results that show the implications of the axioms presented in section 21.5.[8] As stated before, Neighborhood-Anonymity, the Transfer Principle and Organizational Equivalence are minimal requirements that any segregation ordering should satisfy. Furthermore, Composition Invariance is a requirement that cannot be violated if the dimension of evenness is to be captured by the ordering. Group Symmetry is an uncontroversial axiom if we want to be color blind, namely, if segregation is to be independent of the name of the ethnic groups. Continuity is a technical requirement which is also uncontroversial; similar cities should have similar segregation levels. The following result, which can be found in Frankel and Volij (2007), shows that adding Weak Independence to the above axioms yields a very convenient additive representation:

Theorem 1 *The segregation ordering* $\geqslant$ *satisfies Neighborhood-Anonymity, Group Symmetry, Composition Invariance, the Transfer Principle, Weak Independence, Organizational Equivalence, and Continuity, if and only if there is a function* $f:[0, 1] \times [0, 1] \to \mathbb{R}$ *with the following properties:*

1. *For all cities X and Y:*

$$X \geq Y \text{ if and only if } \sum_{i \in N(X)} f(b_i, w_i) \geq \sum_{j \in N(Y)} f(b_j, w_j).$$

2. *f is symmetric, homogeneous of degree 1, and strictly convex on the simplex* $\Delta = \{(b, w) \in [0, 1]: b + w = 1\}.$

In addition, the function $f(c, 1 - c)$ *is unique up to a positive affine transformation. That is, f and g both satisfy properties 1 and 2 if and only if there are constants* $\alpha \in (0, \infty)$ *and* $\beta \in \mathbb{R}$, *such that:*

$$f(c, 1 - c) = \alpha g(c, 1 - c) + \beta \quad \forall c \in [0, 1].$$

Hutchens (2001) proved a similar result by replacing Weak Independence and Continuity with the requirement of Additivity. This axiom requires the ordering to be represented by an index of the form $\sum_{i \in N} f(b_i, w_i)$ for some continuous function f.

As Theorem 1 shows, there are many indices that satisfy Weak Independence, Composition Invariance and Continuity, along with the basic axioms of Group Symmetry, Anonymity, Organizational Equivalence, and the Transfer Principle. The next theorem, proved by Hutchens (2004), shows that by strengthening the weak independence axiom one obtains a full characterization of a single ordering:

Theorem 2 *Let* $S:\mathcal{C}_2 \to \mathbb{R}$ *be a continuous aggregative segregation index that satisfies Neighborhood-Anonymity, Group Symmetry, Composition Invariance, the Transfer Principle, Organizational Equivalence. Then, S is a strictly increasing transformation of the square root index,* $O_{1/2}$.

In fact, Frankel and Volij (2008b, Theorem 2) show that Continuity is not needed:

Theorem 3 *The ordering represented by the Symmetric Atkinson index,* $A_{1/2}$, *is the only one that satisfies Neighborhood-Anonymity, Organizational Equivalence, Neighborhood Division Property, Composition Invariance, Group Symmetry, and Independence on* $\mathcal{C}_2$.

Table 21.4 provides a summary of the satisfied properties, or those that fail to be satisfied by the indices presented in section 21.4.1. For proofs, see Frankel and Volij (2008a).

Table 21.4 Which indices violate which axioms?

		N-Anon	OE	CI	T	WIND	GS	IND	NDP	CONT
1	Symmetric Atkinson: $A_{1/2}(X)$	✓	✓	✓	✓	✓	✓	✓	✓	✓
2	Asymmetric Atkinson: $A_w(X)$	✓	✓	✓	✓	✓	✗	✓	✓	✓
6	Mutual Information: $M(X)$	✓	✓	✗	✓	✓	✓	✓	✓	✓
11	Dis-similarity: $D(X)$	✓	✓	✓	✗	✓	✓	✗	✗	✓
13	Gini Index: $G(X)$	✓	✓	✓	✓	✗	✓	✗	✓	✓
14	Entropy Index: $H(X)$	✓	✓	✗	✓	✓	✓	✗	✓	✓
15	Isolation: $J(X)$	✓	✓	✗	✓	✓	✓	✓	✓	✓

Note: A '✓' means that the axiom is satisfied, while '✗' indicates that it is not.

21.7 VARIABLE NUMBER OF GROUPS

As mentioned before, most of the axioms can be extended to segregation orderings defined on any class with a fixed number of groups. Moreover, both Theorem 1 and Theorem 3 can be extended to these classes. However, if one is interested to characterize a segregation order on the whole class of cities, an axiom that restricts the order when it compares cities with different numbers of groups is required. This section presents one such axiom, and states a characterization of the Mutual Information index that is based on it.

Before introducing the new axiom, it is necessary to define an extended class of cities that allows for a variable number of ethnic groups:

Definition 3 A *city* is a system, $\langle N, G, ((T_n^g)_{g \in G})_{n \in N} \rangle$, where N is a finite nonempty set of neighborhoods, G is a finite nonempty set of ethnic groups, and for each ethnic group $g \in G$ and neighborhood $n \in N$, T_n^g is a nonnegative real number that represents the number of members of ethnic group g that reside in neighborhood n.

We denote by C the class of all cities.

As before, $T_n = \sum_{g \in G} T_n^g$ denotes the total number of people located in neighborhood n, and $T = \sum_{n \in N} T_n$ denotes the city's total population. The total number of members of ethnic group g is denoted by T^g, and the proportion of group g members in the city is denoted by P^g. The city's ethnic distribution is given by the list $(P^g)_{g \in G}$. Similarly, the proportion of neighborhood n's population that belongs to ethnic group g is denoted by p_n^g, and neighborhood n's ethnic distribution by $(p_n^g)_{g \in G}$. The entropy of a distribution $(q^g)_{g \in G}$ is now given by:

$$h((q^g)_{g \in G}) = \sum_{g \in G} q^g \log_2 \left(\frac{1}{q^g} \right).$$

The extension of the Mutual Information index to the class of all cities is given by the function $M: C \to \mathbb{R}$ defined by:

$$M(X) = h((P^g)_{g \in G}) - \sum_{n \in N} \frac{T^n}{T} h((p_n^g)_{g \in G}).$$

In words, the Mutual Information of a city is the difference between the entropy of the city's ethnic distribution and the average entropy of its neighborhoods' ethnic distributions. Alternatively, it is the average reduction of entropy that results from the knowledge of the neighborhood where a randomly chosen individual is located.

As in the case of two ethnic groups, we would like segregation orderings defined on the class of all cities to be invariant to the renaming of both neighborhoods and ethnic groups. For this purpose, it is convenient to identify cities that are equivalent, up to the renaming of groups and neighborhoods. We say that two cities, $X = \langle N, G, ((T_n^g)_{g \in G})_{n \in N} \rangle$ and $X' = \langle N', G', ((T_n'^g)_{g \in G'})_{n \in N'} \rangle$, are equivalent if there are one-to-one mappings $\phi: N \to N'$ and $\psi: G \to G'$ such that for all $n \in N$ and $g \in G$, $(T_n^g) = (T_{\phi(n)}^{\psi(g)})$. The following axiom states that only the racial composition of neighborhoods and not their names matter.

Anonymity (ANON) A segregation ordering satisfies anonymity if any two equivalent cities are equally segregated.

Anonymity is the conjunction of the Neighborhood-Anonymity and Group Symmetry axioms defined in sections 21.3 and 21.5.

We are now ready to state the above-mentioned axiom. It states that splitting a group, say blacks, into two subgroups, say black females and black males, while keeping their distribution across neighborhoods constant, should not affect segregation. Formally:

Group Division Property (GDP) Let $X \in \mathcal{C}$ be a city in which the set of ethnic groups is G. Let X' be the result of partitioning some group $g \in G$ into two subgroups, g_1 and g_2, such that the two subgroups have the same distribution across neighborhoods; namely, $T_n^{g_1}/T_n^g$ is independent of n, and thus equals T^{g_1}/T^g. Then $X' \sim X$.

One of the main axioms used in previous results is CI, which is an essential axiom of any index that wants to capture the dimension of evenness. However, there are some segregation orders, in particular those that intend to capture the dimension of isolation, that fail to satisfy CI. To measure isolation, a weaker requirement is enough.

Scale Invariance (SI) Let X be a city and let $Y = \alpha X$ be the city that is obtained from X by multiplying the number of residents by a positive factor α. An order $\geqslant$ on $\mathcal{C}$ satisfies scale invariance if for any such cities we have $X \sim Y$.

Scale invariance states that for the purpose of measuring segregation one does not need to know whether people of the various ethnic groups are measured in units, tens, or thousands, as long as they are measured in the same units.

The axioms of Independence, Organizational Equivalence and Continuity are generalized for the case of a variable number of ethnic groups in a straightforward way.

The next result, proved in Frankel and Volij (2011), provides a characterization of the Mutual Information order on the class of all cities:

Theorem 4 *An ordering on C satisfies Scale Invariance, Independence, Organizational Equivalence, the Neighborhood Division Property, the Group Division Property, Anonymity,and Continuity if and only if it is represented by the Mutual Information index.*

Not all the indices we have discussed in section 21.4.1 can be generalized to the many-group case in a straightforward way. However, the symmetric Atkinson index, the Gini index and the Entropy index can.[9] The information that appears in Table 21.4 is still valid for the multigroup version of these indices, except of course for the transfer principle. Note, however, that none of the above-mentioned indices satisfy the Group Division property. See Frankel and Volij (2011) for details.

Finally, a relationship can be pointed out between the Mutual Information index and the informativeness of information structures. A city can be interpreted as an information structure where neighborhoods are signals that provide information about the ethnicity of a randomly chosen city resident. Consequently, we can adopt Blackwell's (1953) partial order, which ranks information structures according to their informativeness, and use it to partially order cities. It turns out that since the Mutual Information index does not satisfy Composition Invariance, it is not consistent with Blackwell's order. However, as argued in Frankel and Volij (2011), if one restricts comparisons to pairs of cities with the same ethnic distribution, the Mutual Information index is consistent with Blackwell's ordering.

21.8   CONCLUDING COMMENTS

The axiomatic approach, by emphasizing the essential properties that the various measures share and those on which they differ, can help researchers select the segregation indices that best fit their purposes. This chapter has surveyed some of what we believe are the most interesting theoretical results that employ this approach.

We first noted that the Lorenz order satisfies the four basic properties of neighborhood-anonymity, composition invariance, organizational equivalence and the transfer principle. We further saw that every segregation order that satisfies these properties must agree with the Lorenz order. Therefore, the Lorenz order is the common denominator of all segregation orders that satisfy them.

It was later shown that adding independence to the above list of axioms results in a full characterization of the segregation order that is represented by the symmetric Atkinson index, also known as the Square Root index. We also saw that by weakening the independence axiom and by adding a continuity requirement one obtains a family of segregation measures that have a convenient additive representation.

Finally, it was demonstrated that for the class of a variable number of ethnic groups, weakening composition invariance and adding the group division property results in the characterization of the Mutual Information index.

ACKNOWLEDGEMENTS

We thank Casilda Lasso de la Vega for her useful comments. Our discussions much improved this survey. I also thank the Spanish Ministerio de Educacin y Ciencia (under project ECO2015-67519-P) and the Gobierno Vasco (under the project IT568-13) for research support.

NOTES

1.   Isolation is to be understood as the opposite of exposure.
2.   The cities' Lorenz curves are usually referred to as segregation curves. Note that the segregation curve of X is the standard Lorenz curve of an income distribution in which blacks play the role of individuals and whites play the role of income.
3.   That is, $X \sim Y$ if both $X \geqslant Y$ and $Y \geqslant X$; $X > Y$ if $X \geqslant Y$ but not $Y \geqslant X$.
4.   The two transfer principles are not equivalent. When one of the neighborhoods has no blacks, blacks cannot be transferred from it. Therefore, in this case only the W Transfer Principle is not vacuous.
5.   This is just a restatement of the fact that the entropy function h is concave.
6.   With some abuse of language, let us say that a segregation index satisfies a property if its induced segregation order does.
7.   Any city with $|N|$ neighborhoods can be seen as a point in a $\mathbb{R}^{2|N|}$ Euclidean space.
8.   Henceforth, attention is restricted to complete segregation orders.
9.   For generalizations of the Dissimilarity index and the Isolation index, see Reardon and Firebaugh (2002).

REFERENCES

Ballester, C. and M. Vorsatz (2013), Random-Walk-Based Segregation Measures. *Review of Economics and Statistics* 96, 383–401.
Bell, W. (1954), A Probability Model for the Measurement of Ecological Segregation. *Social Forces* 32, 357–364.
Blackwell, D. (1953), Equivalent Comparisons of Experiments. *Annals of Mathematical Statistics* 24, 265–272.
Cutler, D., E. Glaeser and J. Vigdor (1999), The Rise and Decline of the American Ghetto. *Journal of Political Economy* 107, 455–506.
Duncan, O.D. and B. Duncan (1955), A Methodological Analysis of Segregation Indices. *American Sociological Review* 20, 210–217.
Echenique, F. and R.G. Fryer, Jr (2007), A Measure of Segregation Based on Social Interactions. *Quarterly Journal of Economics* 122, 441–485.
Frankel, D. and O. Volij (2007), Measuring Segregation. Mimeo, http://volij.co.il/publications/papers/segin dex17.pdf.
Frankel, D. and O. Volij (2008a), Unpublished Appendix to Measuring School Segregation. Mimeo, http://volij. co.il/publications/papers/appendix25.pdf.
Frankel, D. and O. Volij (2008b), Scale-Invariant Measures of Segregation. Mimeo, http://volij.co.il/publica tions/papers/atkinsonFull.pdf.
Frankel, D. and O. Volij (2011), Measuring School Segregation. *Journal of Economic Theory* 146, 1–38.
Fuchs, V. (1975), A Note on Sex Segregation in Professional Occupations. *Explorations in Economic Research* 2, 105–111.
Hutchens, R. (1991), Segregation Curves, Lorenz Curves, and Inequality in the Distribution of People across Occupations. *Mathematical Social Sciences* 21, 31–51.
Hutchens, R. (2001), Numerical Measures of Segregation: Desirable Properties and Their Implications. *Mathematical Social Sciences* 42, 13–29.
Hutchens, R. (2004), One Measure of Segregation. *International Economic Review* 45, 555–578.
Hutchens, R. (2015), Symmetric Measures of Segregation, Segregation Curves, and Blackwell's Criterion. *Mathematical Social Sciences* 73, 63–68.
Jahn, J., C.F. Schmidt and C. Schrag (1947), The Measurement of Ecological Segregation. *American Sociological Review* 12, 293–303.
James, D.R. and K.E. Taueber (1985), Measures of Segregation. *Sociological Methodology* 15, 1–32.

Karmel, T. and M. MacLachlan (1988), Occupational Sex Segregation – Increasing or Decreasing?. *Economic Record* 64, 187–195.
Lasso de la Vega, C. and O. Volij (2014), Segregation, Informativeness and Lorenz Dominance. *Social Choice and Welfare* 43, 547–564.
Massey, D.S. and N.A. Denton (1988), The Dimensions of Racial Segregation. *Social Forces* 67, 281–315.
Mora, R. and J. Ruiz-Castillo (2003), Additively Decomposable Segregation Indices: The Case of Gender Segregation by Occupations and Human Capital Levels in Spain. *Journal of Economic Inequality* 1, 147–179.
Mora, R. and J. Ruiz-Castillo (2004), Gender Segregation by Occupations in the Public and the Private Sector: The Case of Spain. *Investigaciones Economicas* 28, 399–428.
Mora, R. and J. Ruiz-Castillo (2005), The Axiomatic Properties of an Entropy Based Index of Segregation. Universidad Carlos III de Madrid working paper no. 05-62.
Philipson, T. (1993), Social Welfare and Measurement of Segregation. *Journal of Economic Theory* 60, 322–334.
Reardon, S.F. and G. Firebaugh (2002), Measures of Multigroup Segregation. *Sociological Methodology* 32, 33–67.
Theil, H. (1971), *Principles of Econometrics*, Wiley & Sons, New York.
Theil, H. (1972), *Statistical Decomposition Analysis*, North-Holland, Amsterdam.
Theil, H. and A.J. Finizza (1971), A Note on the Measurement of Racial Integration in Schools. *Journal of Mathematical Sociology* 1, 187–193.

APPENDIX

Proof of Claim 1. Let $\geq$ be a segregation order that satisfies OE and T. We will show that it satisfies NDP as well. Let X be a city and let n be a neighborhood of X. Let Y be the city that results from dividing n into two neighborhoods, n_1 and n_2. Assume that n_1 and n_2 don't have the same ethnic distributions. Further assume, without loss of generality, that the proportion of blacks is higher in n_1 than in n_2; namely, $B_{n_1} W_{n_2} > B_{n_2} W_{n_1}$. Neighborhood n in city X can be written $(B_n, W_n) = (B_{n_1} + B_{n_2}, W_{n_1} + W_{n_2})$. Let $\alpha = \frac{B_{n_1} + W_{n_1}}{B_n + W_n}$ and let X' be the city that results from X by splitting neighborhood n into the following two neighborhoods: $n_1' = \alpha(B_n, W_n)$ and $n_2' = (1 - \alpha)(B_n, W_n)$. By organizational equivalence, $X \sim X'$. Since $B_{n_1} W_{n_2} > B_{n_2} W_{n_1}$ we have:

$$B_{n_1} > \alpha B_n.$$

Transfer $B_{n_1} - \alpha B_n > 0$ blacks from from n_2' to n_1', (since $B_{n_1} - \alpha B_n < (1 - \alpha) B_n$, this can be done). Further transfer the same amount of whites from n_1' to n_2'. The city that results is Y. By the transfer principle, this operation strictly raises segregation; namely, $Y > X' \sim X$, so by transitivity, $Y > X$.

We will now show that NDP implies WT. The proof that it also implies BT is analogous and is left to the reader. Let $X = \langle N, (B_n, W_n)_{n \in N} \rangle$, and let $i, j \in N$ be two neighborhoods such that $B_i W_i > 0$ and:

$$B_i W_j \geq B_j W_i$$

Let $\varepsilon \in (0, W_i)$, and let Y be the city that is obtained from X by moving ε whites from neighborhood i to neighborhood j. That is, $Y = \langle N, (B_n', W_n')_{n \in N} \rangle$ in which $(B_i', W_i') = (B_i, W_i - \varepsilon)$, $(B_j', W_j') = (B_j, W_j + \varepsilon)$, and $(B_n', W_n') = (B_n, W_n)$ for all $n \neq i, j$. We need to show that $Y > X$. If $B_j = 0$, then Y is the result of splitting neighborhood (B_i, W_i) into $(B_i, W_i - \varepsilon)$ and $(0, \varepsilon)$ and then merging $(0, \varepsilon)$ with $(0, W_j)$. By NDP, the splitting operation increases segregation, and by OE, the merging of two neighborhoods with the same proportion of whites leaves segregation unchanged. Therefore, $Y > X$.

If $B_j > 0$, define the following values:

$$\alpha = \frac{W_j + \varepsilon}{B_j}$$

$$\beta = \frac{W_i - \varepsilon}{B_i}$$

$$\gamma = \frac{\varepsilon}{\alpha - \beta} = \frac{\varepsilon B_i B_j}{B_i(W_j + \varepsilon) - B_j(W_i - \varepsilon)}$$

Since $W_j B_i \geq W_i B_j$, we have that γ, β, $\alpha > 0$. Split (B_i, W_i) into $(B_i - \gamma, W_i - \alpha\gamma)$ and $(\gamma, \alpha\gamma)$. Similarly, split (B_j, W_j) into $(B_j - \gamma, W_j - \beta\gamma)$ and $(\gamma, \beta\gamma)$. (This can be done because $\gamma < \min\{B_i, B_i\}$. Indeed:

$$\gamma = \frac{\varepsilon B_i B_j}{B_i(W_j + \varepsilon) - B_j(W_i - \varepsilon)} < \frac{B_i B_j}{B_i + B_j}$$

Therefore, $\gamma(B_i + B_j) < B_i B_j$ or equivalently, which implies that $\gamma < B_i$ and $\gamma < B_j$.) By NDP the resulting city is more segregated. Now merge $(B_i - \gamma, W_i - \alpha\gamma)$ with $(\gamma, \beta\gamma)$ and also merge $(B_j - \gamma, W_j - \beta\gamma)$ with $(\gamma, \alpha\gamma)$. Since:

$$\frac{W_i - \alpha\gamma}{B_i - \gamma} = \beta$$

$$\frac{W_j - \beta\gamma}{B_j - \gamma} = \alpha$$

by OE this merger does not affect segregation. The resulting pair of neighborhoods is:

$$(B_i, W_i - \alpha\gamma + \beta\gamma) \text{ and } (B_j, W_j - \beta\gamma + \alpha\gamma)$$

which happen to be $(B_i, W_i - \varepsilon)$ and $(B_j, W_j + \varepsilon)$, respectively.

Proof of Claim 2. (Based on Frankel and Volij, 2011) Let X and Y be two cities with the same number of blacks and the same number of whites and let Z be any city:

$X \circ Z \succcurlyeq Y \circ Z$
   $\Leftrightarrow S(X \circ Z) \geq S(Y \circ Z)$
   $\Leftrightarrow F(S(X), S(Z), B, W, B(Z), W(Z)) \geq F(S(Y), S(Z), B, W, B(Z), W(Z))$
   $\Leftrightarrow S(X) \geq S(Y)$
   $\Leftrightarrow X \succcurlyeq Y.$

Conversely, assume that $\geqslant$ satisfies IND and that it is represented by a continuous index S. Define $F: \mathbb{R}^6 \to \mathbb{R}$ by:

$$F(s_x, s_y, b_x, w_x, b_y, w_y) = S(X \circ Y)$$

where X is a city with $S(X) = s_x$, $B(X) = b_x$, $W(X) = w_x$ and Y is a city with $S(Y) = s_y$, $B(Y) = b_y$, $W(Y) = w_y$. First note that F is well-defined. Indeed, if X' and Y' are cities such that $X \sim X'$, $Y \sim Y'$, $B(X) = B(X')$, $W(X) = W(X')$, $B(Y) = B(Y')$, $W(Y) = W(Y')$, then by IND applied twice:

$$S(X \circ Y) = S(X' \circ Y) = S(X' \circ Y').$$

Second, note that by IND, F is increasing in its first two arguments. Third, since S is continuous, so is F.

22. Segregation: empirical findings
Ricardo Mora and Jacques Silber

22.1 INTRODUCTION

Social scientists have long been interested in the empirical analysis of segregation. Among the most intensively researched issues, we can find the tendency of men and women to work in different occupations (referred to as gender occupational segregation), the tendency of students of different races or ethnic groups to attend separated schools (referred to as racial or ethnic school segregation), and the tendency of individuals of different races or ethnic groups to live in different areas within the same city (referred to as racial or ethnic residential segregation). We can think of these topics as the three major areas in which empirical segregation studies are usually classified. However, these three major areas are by no means exhaustive. Psychologists, economists and sociologists have also found systematic associations between human groups defined in terms of other types of status such as age, religion, nationality, and organizational units such as occupations, neighborhoods, schools, firms, industries, and the like. Moreover, different forces which lead to segregation manifest themselves simultaneously, so that the empirical literature is enriched by studies on the interactions of, say, racial and gender segregation.

Hence, the empirical literature on segregation is vast and complex, and in this chapter we cannot aim to provide a complete review of this topic. Consequently, and given the space limitations, we assign to ourselves two more realistic aims. In the first place, we focus on more recent contributions in major areas of segregation which we consider as promising lines of research. In the second place, we present an in-depth review of the development in the last decades of one major area: the case of racial school segregation in the United States. We think that the case of racial school segregation is worth reviewing in detail for two reasons. Firstly, it is arguably the topic most widely covered in the literature.[1] More fundamentally, we believe that this larger interest in academia reflects the fact that racial school segregation in the context of desegregation policies in the United States is a nice illustration of an area of research with clear empirical content and policy implications. Its evolution over time has been strongly influenced by the actual implementation of desegregation policies that were: (1) themselves motivated, at least partly, by academic research; and (2) difficult to imagine in any other context of segregation due to their wide scope and intensity.

We start the chapter by covering the topic of racial or ethnic residential segregation. In comparison with the other notions of segregation, residential segregation requires measures that take into account the spatial patterning of the geographical units on the basis of which it is measured. Consequently, empirical research on residential segregation has been greatly influenced by the development of new measures or indexes that aim to overcome some of the shortcomings of the measures traditionally used in the analysis of segregation in the workplace or in the schools. Then, after devoting some comments to some developments in the literature on economic segregation, we end this section with a review of some more recent empirical studies of residential segregation both in the United States and in some other countries.

In the next section we emphasize differences between the economic and sociological approaches to the study of gender segregation in the labor market. We also briefly review the more recent contributions to studies of the trends and differences between the European Union (EU) and the United States (US) in gender segregation. We then turn to racial segregation in the labor market. First we compare different approaches to the topic. Then we review recent studies of racial and ethnic workplace segregation in the United States and other countries.

The chapter ends with a rather detailed survey of empirical studies of racial school segregation, our focus being on the US case. We first briefly describe the development of the school desegregation policies that took place in the second half of the twentieth century. Then we look at trends in racial school segregation and review the studies on the effects of desegregation. We end this section with a brief discussion of the empirical literature on the effects of racial isolation on students' outcomes.

22.2 THE CASE OF RACIAL OR ETHNIC RESIDENTIAL SEGREGATION

22.2.1 The Specificity of Residential Segregation Measurement

The most popular index of segregation, whether one refers to occupational, school or residential segregation, remains the dissimilarity index originally proposed by Duncan and Duncan (1955). Additional segregation indices have appeared in the literature (see, for example, Reardon and Firebaugh, 2002, for a review of indices of multi-group segregation; Silber, 2012, for a survey of the measurement of segregation, with a focus on occupational segregation; and Volij, Chapter 21 in this *Handbook*, for a more recent survey on segregation measurement) but these indices are usually 'aspatial' because they tend to ignore the spatial patterning of the geographical units (for example, census tracts) on the basis of which segregation is measured. Massey and Denton (1988, p. 282) have defined residential segregation as 'the degree to which two or more groups live separately from one another, in different parts of the urban environment'. They argue, however, that groups may be segregated in different ways, and make a distinction between five ways in which these groups may live apart from one another:

- Evenness: this refers to the fact that minority members may be overrepresented in some areas and underrepresented in others.
- Exposure: the idea here is that minority members may not often be in contact with majority members because they rarely share a neighborhood with them.
- Concentration: the emphasis here is on the fact that minority members may be concentrated within a small area when compared to majority members.
- Centralization: here the accent is put on whether minority members live mainly in, say, the center of cities.
- Cluster: the feature which is stressed here is whether minority members live in one large 'contiguous enclave' rather than being scattered across various neighborhoods.

Massey and Denton (1988) then review various measures of segregation which reflect one of the five aspects of residential segregation which have just been mentioned.

Reardon and O'Sullivan (2004) criticized the use of 'aspatial' measures of segregation when attempting to measure residential segregation. They stressed two flaws of such an aspatial approach. The first one is the 'checkerboard problem', which amounts to saying that aspatial measures of segregation ignore the spatial proximity of neighborhoods and focus only on, say, their racial composition. Assume each square in a checkerboard represents either an exclusively black or an exclusively white neighborhood. If you now move all the black squares to one side of the board and all the white squares to the other side, there certainly should be an increase in segregation because, first, in each neighborhood there are either only black or only white individuals; but, second, there is now a situation where most neighborhoods are located near neighborhoods that are similar from a racial point of view. Unfortunately, aspatial measures of segregation will not display an increase in segregation in such a case.

The second issue emphasized by Reardon and O'Sullivan (2004) is the 'modifiable areal unit problem' (MAUP). The idea is that residential units reported by a database may be quite arbitrary, so that two individuals living very close to each other, but in different residential units, will be considered as being more distant from each other than two individuals living in the same residential area but at each end of the area.

Reardon and O'Sullivan (2004) were also quite critical of the distinction made by Massey and Denton (1988) between evenness and clustering, because both concepts depend on the scale of aggregation. More precisely, Reardon and O'Sullivan (2004) argue that, 'in principle, if we derived a segregation measure from information about the exact locations and spatial environments of individuals and their proximities to one another in residential space, there would be no conceptual difference at all between evenness and clustering'. These authors therefore prefer to emphasize the following two basic aspects of spatial residential segregation:

- Spatial exposure: this refers to the probability that members of one group meet members of another group in their 'local spatial environments'.
- Spatial evenness or clustering: the accent here is put on the 'extent to which groups are similarly distributed in the residential space'.

Reardon and O'Sullivan (2004) then proposed several indices of spatial segregation which they classified respectively as spatial exposure segregation indices, information theory and spatial segregation indices, diversity and spatial segregation indices, and spatial dissimilarity indices.

22.2.2   The Case of Income Segregation

Reardon (2011), in a short review of the literature on the measurement of economic segregation, makes a distinction between three approaches: measures based on categories, on 'variation-ratios' and on spatial autocorrelation.

'Category-based' measures of income segregation

Some studies of income segregation divide the population into only two categories separated by some threshold, so that traditional measures of segregation, such as the dissimilarity or Gini index, can be used. Jenkins et al. (2008), for example, divided the population of children at school into two categories: those with a high and a low social position. They then computed school segregation on the basis of the dissimilarity index and the square root index (see Hutchens, 2001). High and low social position in each country analyzed were defined in terms of the national distribution of social position index values: 'high' referring to having a value above, and 'low' to a value equal to or below the median social position. Such an approach has clear shortcomings: the loss of information resulting from a grouping of income into only two categories, and the choice of threshold. Some researchers (e.g., Massey and Eggers, 1993) have applied the same approach to more than two categories, applying, for example, the dissimilarity index to every pair of categories and computing afterwards an average value of the dissimilarity index. Others have used segregation indices, such as Theil's entropy-related index, which can be applied to more than two categories. Thus Fong and Shibuya (2000) analyzed the spatial separation of the poor in Canadian cities, while Telles (1995) studied socioeconomic segregation in Brazil.

Measures of income segregation based on 'variation-ratios'

This approach defines income segregation as the ratio of between neighborhoods dispersion in mean income (or wealth) over total population variation in income (wealth). Various measures of dispersion have been used in empirical works. Wheeler (2006) and Wheeler and La Jeunesse (2006) used the variance of incomes; Jargowsky (1996) the standard deviation; Kim and Jargowsky (2009) the Gini index; Ioannides (2004) the variance of the logarithms of income; and Ioannides and Seslen (2002) the Bourguignon–Theil entropy-related index. Such approaches evidently have drawbacks as they often rely on a parametric estimation of income distributions, but they are certainly preferable to a simple category-based approach to the measurement of income segregation. A somehow different approach was adopted by Watson (2009), who defined what she called the Centile Gap Index, a measure of income segregation which has the advantage of not being sensitive to rank preserving variations in incomes.

Spatial autocorrelation measures of income segregation

Dawkins (2004, 2006) takes a different approach. He proposed an extension of the traditional Gini index of segregation, the distinction between both concepts being similar to that which exists between the so-called concentration ratio and the Gini index (on this distinction, see Kakwani, 1980).

Jargowsky and Kim (2005b) took still another approach when they defined what they called the Generalized Neighborhood Sorting Index (GNSI). Jargowsky started from the idea that segregation measures are usually defined for discrete groups such as gender, race or ethnic groups. As a consequence they cannot be easily applied to the case of a continuous variable such as income. This is why researchers have often decided to divide the income distribution into discrete income categories, a transformation which allowed them to then use segregation indices such as the dissimilarity index. The problem with such an approach is that fixing the boundaries of the income categories is quite arbitrary so that a change in the boundaries may well lead to important changes in the value of the segregation index that was selected. This is why Jargowsky (1996) recommended using what he called the Neighborhood Sorting Index (NSI), which is the ratio of the standard deviation of neighborhood mean household income to the standard deviation of individual household incomes. In other words, the NSI is equal to the ratio of the standard deviation of the between (census) tracts (average) incomes over the overall (all tracts combined) standard deviation of the individual incomes.

Therefore, if the mean incomes in the various neighborhoods are quite different from the overall (whole population) mean income, we will observe neighborhoods with either high or low incomes, and this would imply a relatively high degree of segregation. If, on the contrary, the mean incomes in the various neighborhoods are relatively close to the overall mean income, we would have a low numerator and hence a low level of segregation. The various neighborhoods could be heterogeneous but there would not be much difference between them. Note that the NSI is only a limited measure of spatial segregation. On the one hand it indicates how much information about variation in household income is lost by aggregating data at the (census) tract level, but on the other hand it does not take into account the spatial arrangement of the different neighborhoods. The NSI could, for example, have the same value if all high-income neighborhoods are clustered in one part of, say, a metropolitan area or if they are scattered throughout the metropolitan area. Moreover the NSI measure is sensitive to the way the tracts are defined, that is, to the previously mentioned MAUP.

To solve this issue Jargowsky and Kim (2005a) introduced a new measure which they called the Generalized Neighborhood Sorting Index (GNSI) which has the advantage of being a geographically sensitive measure of spatial segregation. The main difference between the GNSI and NSI measures is that the numerator of the GNSI includes a 'moving window' which allows estimation of the economic level of a neighborhood without taking into account only those individuals living in the neighborhood itself. The idea is to eventually also take into account contiguous neighborhoods, or all those neighborhoods which are within a certain distance of the neighborhood.

The approach of Reardon (2011): combining the 'category-based' and the 'variation-ratios' approaches to income segregation measurement
In a paper on ordinal segregation, Reardon (2009) defined an ordinal segregation measure. To define the ordinal variation of a variable, Reardon (2009), following previous work on the topic, assumes that the degree of variation of an ordinal variable is maximal when half of the individuals are located in the lowest category and half of them in the highest category. Ordinal variation evidently takes its minimal value when all the individuals are in the same category. Combining the concept of ordinal variation with ideas he applied to the measurement of spatial segregation (see Reardon and Firebaugh, 2002), Reardon (2011) then defined three spatial rank-order measures of income.

22.2.3 Some Empirical Studies of Residential Segregation

Platt Boustan (2011) examines racial segregation in American cities. Following Cutler et al. (1999) she stresses the fact that residential segregation could be generated by three possible factors. First, there might be black self-segregation if blacks prefer to live near other blacks, either because they enjoy the company of black neighbors or because they have common preferences for local amenities such as neighborhood restaurants. Second, whites may use collective action to exclude blacks from white neighborhoods. Third, residential segregation may simply be the result of individual moves by white households away from integrated neighborhoods.

Reardon et al. (2009) examined what happened to racial residential segregation during the last decade of the twentieth century. They investigated in particular how the geographic scale of racial residential segregation patterns in US metropolitan areas varied between 1990 and 2000. They concluded that both Hispanic–white and Asian–white segregation increased modestly, while black–white segregation declined during the same period. The latter segregation, however, did not decline at a 4000 macro-scale, so that the decline in segregation observed in tract-level studies implies that nearby neighborhoods had become more racially similar, but there was no large-scale redistribution of black and white populations. These authors then regressed 1990–2000 changes in segregation on covariates such as the percentage change in the metropolitan area's population size; changes in group-specific population shares and in the foreign-born population share; changes in the suburbanization ratio and the group-specific suburbanization ratios; and in the group-specific per capita income ratios. It then appears that these covariates explain quite well the observed trends in the macro-type of segregation (4000 m radius). This model, however, was less successful in explaining the observed trends in micro-segregation (500 m radius).

Other studies looked at income segregation. It was, for example, found (see Pew Research Center, 2012) that residential income segregation had increased during the past three decades across the United States as well as in 27 of the 30 largest metropolitan areas. This study also stressed the fact that 28 percent of lower-income households in 2010 were located in a majority lower-income census tract (against 23 percent in 1980), whereas 18 percent of upper-income households were located in a majority upper-income census tract (versus only 9 percent in 1980). These changes are likely to be related to the long-term increase in income inequality in the United States, as well as to the shrinkage of the middle class from 85 percent in 1980 to 76 percent in 2010. This Pew analysis also suggested adding together the share of lower-income households living in a majority lower-income tract and the share of upper-income households living in a majority upper-income tract. They called this sum the Residential Income Segregation index (RISI), the maximal value of which is evidently 200. Looking at the ten largest metropolitan areas, the authors of this report concluded that Houston (61) and Dallas (60) have the highest RISI scores, while Atlanta (41), Chicago (41) and Boston (36) have the lowest scores.

There have also been studies of residential segregation in other countries. Monkkonen (2010), for example, looked at residential segregation in urban Mexico. His study confirmed the clustering of high-income groups in a central zone and the greater income heterogeneity of high-income areas as compared to those of low-income areas. Monkkonen (2010) also concluded that levels of segregation of low-income households and ethnic minorities were not high in Mexico when compared with those in the United States and Europe.

Vincent et al. (2012) analyzed income segregation in France. Their study was implemented at two different geographical scales called, respectively, IRIS (Ilots Regroupés pour l'Information Statistique), which is an area comprising 1800–5000 inhabitants, and 'Grand Quartier', being a grouping of several adjoining IRIS inside a city. The authors then concluded that, whatever the geographical scale, there was an increase in income-based segregation between 2001 and 2004, but a decrease afterwards. At the IRIS scale the cities of Bayonne, Nice and Bordeaux seem to be the least segregated, while Le Havre and Lille are the most income-segregated cities. An analysis at the 'Grand Quartier' level did not modify this picture.

22.3   ON GENDER SEGREGATION IN THE LABOR MARKET

22.3.1   Contrasting the Economic and Sociological Approaches

Economists as well as sociologists have been trying for several decades to measure segregation by gender in the labor market, to determine its causes and assess its implications. Since the measurement of segregation is a topic that was covered in Chapter 21 of this *Handbook*, we will focus our attention in this section firstly on the ways sociologists and economists look at segregation by gender in the labor force; and secondly on some of the more recent empirical studies of occupational segregation by gender, special emphasis being given to the situation in the United States and in the European Union.

Among economists the most popular approach to occupational segregation by gender remains the neo-classical human capital model which stresses the role of three sets of determinants related, respectively, to labor supply, labor demand, and institutional and labor segmentation theories (see Anker, 1997). As far as labor supply is concerned, the idea is that women have lower levels of human capital because (at least until recently) they have lower levels of education and in less relevant fields of study, but also less labor market experience since they often tend to stop working when they have children. As stressed by Anker (1997, p. 317), this approach implies that women 'would rationally choose occupations with relatively high starting pay, relatively low returns on experience, and relatively low penalties for temporary withdrawal from the labor force'. Such an approach, however, cannot be the only one explaining segregation by gender in the labor force, since in recent decades the educational level of women has considerably increased, often being higher than that of men. Also observed are an increase in the commitment of women to the labor force, and a rise in the share of female-headed households and, as a consequence, in the proportion of women working full-time.

Human capital theory also has implications as far as labor demand is concerned. Employers are thus likely to prefer hiring men when the job offered is supposed to require a higher level of education, and/or when job experience and on-the-job training are important. Such attitudes on the part of employers are also driven by the supposedly higher rates of absenteeism and labor turnover among women.

Economists also mention the role of institutions, in particular that of unions, which often play a crucial role when hiring, firing or promotion decisions have to be made. The theory of labor market segmentation (see Doeringer and Piore, 1971) can thus be considered as an approach emphasizing the institutional side; the idea being that there is a primary sector with good jobs in terms of pay and security and working conditions, and a secondary market with little protection and poor conditions as far as pay and promotion perspectives are concerned. Economists such as Bergmann (1974) have argued that women tend to be overcrowded in this secondary market. Another theory related to labor market segmentation stresses the role of statistical discrimination (see Phelps, 1972; Arrow, 1973). This approach starts by arguing that there are productivity differences between groups of workers such as men and women. Since recruiting or promoting someone involves high search and information costs, it becomes rational for an employer to discriminate against the group of workers who are supposed on average to have lower productivity.

While economists tend generally to attribute the association between the gender of a worker and their career achievement to the characteristics and preferences of individual workers or employers, the sociological approach emphasizes *'societal-level* systems of differentiation and stratification' (Reskin and Bielby, 2005, p. 71), underlining in particular the role of socialization. 'Men and women develop different preferences and skills that are considered to be appropriate for their sex by cultural standards' (Okamoto and England, 1999, p. 561). Thus women who value traditional roles will be more likely to choose female jobs (see Corcoran and Courant, 1985). More generally, 'social differentiation refers to social processes that mark certain personal characteristics as important' (Reskin and Bielby, 2005, p. 72). People are thus often differentiated by traits such as their birth cohort, marital status or gender. Although such differentiation does not imply that members of different categories are not treated equally, it is somehow a prerequisite for social stratification, which refers to a 'systematic inequality in the distribution of socially valued resources on the basis of people's personal characteristics' (Reskin and Bielby, 2005, p. 72). While some characteristics (for example, religion) result in unequal rewards in only some domains, it seems that gender and age lead to stratification across almost all domains, so that most societies give an advantage to men over women in almost all aspects of well-being. The sexual division of labor is probably the most blatant expression of sex differentiation in activities, since for a long time men would specialize in market and women in domestic work. Although such a simple allocation of work is less clear-cut nowadays there still exists an important sexual division of labor within market work, since genders are very often assigned to different tasks within a given occupation. The sociological approach to segregation by gender emphasizes the fact that the sexual division of labor is not only a function of individual preferences, whether of workers or employees. It is also reflected in the way employment structure and practices are implemented. A good illustration is that of part-time work, which is much more prevalent for female jobs. The sex composition of jobs evidently has an impact on who applies for a job and who gets it. It should therefore be clear that the sociological approach to gender inequality in career outcomes puts a great weight on 'the personnel practices through which workers are matched to jobs' (Reskin and Bielby, 2005, p. 80).

22.3.2   Gender Segregation in the Labor Market: The Case of the European Union

Despite important changes that have occurred during the past decades and which seem to have led to a less clear-cut classification of the labor force into male- and female-dominated occupations, gender differences in occupations remain important in the European Union. It thus appears (see Eurostat, 2008) that concentration in some occupations is much higher among women than men. The Eurostat study stresses the fact that almost 36 percent of the women working in the European Union were employed in just six of the 130 standard occupational categories, the corresponding proportion for working men being

25 percent. The six most concentrated occupations for women were: (1) shop salespersons and demonstrators; (2) domestic and related helpers, cleaners and launderers; (3) personal care and related workers; (4) other office clerks; (5) administrative associate professionals; and (6) housekeeping and restaurant service workers. The corresponding occupations for men were: (1) motor vehicle drivers; (2) building frame and related trade workers; (3) managers of small enterprises; (4) building finishers and related trades workers; (5) physical and engineering science technicians; and (6) machinery mechanics and fitters.

Turning now to the extent of segregation and the changes observed during the 15 years to 2009, it appears (European Commission, 2009) that the picture is more complex. For the EU-12 group, for which the longest time series is available, segregation does not seem to have changed much since 1992, whether one measures it via the Duncan and Duncan (1955) or the Karmel and MacLachlan (1988) indices. If one looks at the EU-27 data, then there seems to have been a slight upward movement in occupational segregation over time. Relatively low segregation levels are observed for Greece, Romania, Malta, Italy and the Netherlands. The countries with high levels of segregation are Estonia, Slovakia, Latvia, Finland, Bulgaria, Lithuania, Cyprus and Hungary.

When attempting to decompose changes in the segregation indices, the authors of this report (European Commission, 2009) found that in the short run the structure of employment (where and to what extent total employment grows) is the most important determinant, while in the long run it is clearly 'desegregation' within occupations.

22.3.3   Comparing Occupational Segregation by Gender in the EU and the US

Using a single cross-section corresponding to the year 1999, Dolado et al. (2002) attempted to uncover converging trends in occupational segregation by gender between the US and the EU, by checking whether the differential between the two continents was declining across age cohorts. They reached the following conclusions:

1.   The population weights of highly educated women in the EU were slowly converging to those of the US, while the employment rates of less-educated women were much lower in the EU.
2.   The occupational structures on the two continents were quite different, with European women having a larger share of employment in social services and North American women in private services. Occupational segregation has been declining across age cohorts among more educated women (still being higher in the EU), but has remained quite constant among individuals with lower educational levels.
3.   Occupational segregation seems to be positively correlated with the share of part-time jobs (which are typically female) in the economy.

22.4   ON RACIAL SEGREGATION IN THE LABOR MARKET

22.4.1   Orthodox versus Less Orthodox Economic Approaches

The *Cambridge Dictionaries Online* defines discrimination as the practice of treating particular people, companies or products differently from others, especially in an unfair way.

This same dictionary defines segregation as the separation of one group of people from another, especially one sex or race from another. The two concepts are, however, linked. Becker (1957), for example, argues that an increase in discrimination decreases trade, while a decrease in trade implies an increase in economic segregation. As a consequence he concludes that an increase in discrimination goes together with an increase in segregation. The relationship between discrimination and segregation, however, is not straightforward.

Let us start with what could be called the orthodox approach to racial segregation. In his famous book, Becker (1957) thus argues (see Darity and Mason, 1998, p. 82) that:

> if two groups share similar productivity profiles under competitive conditions where at least some employers prefer profits to prejudice, eventually all workers must be paid the same wages. The eventual result may involve segregated workforces – say, with some businesses hiring only white men and others only black women – but as long as both groups have the same average productivity, they will receive the same pay.

This approach may be refined, and models have indeed been proposed where discrimination may lead to a rise in profits, or where not discriminating may reduce profits. Discrimination by customers, a concept which was already introduced by Becker (1957), allows wage discrimination even when employers do not discriminate. This would be particularly true when a product must be delivered via face-to-face contact. Madden (1975) thus suggests that consumer discrimination may lead to occupational segregation rather than to wage discrimination. Her argument is as follows. Assume that the wage of minority workers (for example, blacks or women) decreases when the consumer contact in a given job increases. These minority workers would then prefer to find employment in jobs requiring less contact, and wages would be higher. It is only in cases where there are not enough such jobs with minimal contact that consumer discrimination might lead to wage differentials. Most jobs, however, do not require consumer contact, so that consumer discrimination will segregate minority workers into these jobs but not cause wage differentials.

Statistical discrimination theory, which was mentioned previously, is another extension of the orthodox approach but, as stressed by Darity and Williams (1985), if average group differences are perceived rather than real, at some stage employers will start learning that their prejudices are not justified. There would then be a need to explain why such beliefs should persist.

A more realistic view of what really happens in the labor market may involve self-fulfilling prophecies. For example, low expectations of employment opportunities can decrease the propensity of minority members to acquire additional human capital, and such a phenomenon may be transmitted from one generation to the next with clear implications concerning occupational segregation and wage discrimination.

22.4.2 Empirical Studies of Racial and Ethnic Workplace Segregation

We focus here on some recent studies of this issue. Hellerstein and Neumark (2008) use the 1990 Decennial Employer–Employee Database (DEED) to examine workplace segregation by education, language, race and ethnicity in the United States. They first provide measures of workplace segregation based on education, language, race and ethnicity. Then they check the relationship which may exist between skill (mainly education) segregation on one hand, and racial or ethnic segregation on the other hand. The idea, for example, is that since race (for example, whites versus blacks) may be correlated with skill, racial segregation may in fact be the consequence of segregation by skills. Similarly, ethnic segregation (for example, Hispanics versus whites) may be simply the by-product of differences in English proficiency. The authors conclude, first, that education does not play an important role in generating workplace segregation by race. There is hence a need to look for other sources of segregation such as discrimination, residential segregation or labor market networks. Second, segregation by language proficiency seems to explain one-third of the overall Hispanic–white segregation. Finally, it appears that among poor English speakers there is segregation of Hispanics from others, so that there is likely to be some complementarity between workers who speak the same language. Another interesting finding is that segregation across workplaces tends to decrease with establishment size.

While Hellerstein and Neumark (2008) computed segregation indices for some partitions of the population by relevant characteristics (education, language proficiency, and so on), Gradin (2010) tried to control for many attributes at the same time by adapting to segregation analysis a technique originally proposed by DiNardo et al. (1996) to decompose wage differentials between two distributions across the entire distribution. The idea is to compute, first, an unconditional segregation by comparing, for example, the distribution of white and black workers among the various occupations. Then, using a propensity score approach one would compare the occupational distribution of whites and blacks, assuming for example that blacks have the same distribution of relevant characteristics (educational level, language proficiency, immigrant status, geographical location and age) as the whites. This would give the unexplained amount of segregation. The difference between the unexplained and explained segregation will then give the amount of segregation that is a consequence of the characteristics mentioned previously. Gradin (2010) concluded that the lack of English proficiency, educational attainment and recent immigration to the US explain a large part of the relatively high level of unconditional segregation for Hispanics and for Asians (50–60 percent for Hispanics, and 30–35 percent for Asians). For blacks, who were mostly born in the US, the unconditional segregation is relatively low and a smaller share of this segregation is due to the attributes mentioned previously, so that they have a higher level of conditional segregation. Gradin (2010) also notes that if minorities had the same geographical distribution across the countries as whites, their segregation would be even greater, so that their uneven geographical distribution reduces the level of segregation that would otherwise be observed.

Salardi (2012) took another approach to measuring occupational segregation. She attempted to assess changes in Brazilian occupational structure and the magnitude of occupational segregation, over time; her analysis encompassing both gender and racial segregation. She also made a distinction between the formal, informal and self-employed labor markets and tried to identify specific demographic, educational sectorial and spatial patterns. Finally, using the so-called Shapley decomposition procedure (see Sastre and Trannoy, 2002; Chantreuil and Trannoy, 2013; Shorrocks, 2013) to decompose changes in occupational segregation, as originally suggested by Deutsch et al. (2009), she broke down changes over time in segregation into changes in gender and racial composition within occupations, changes in the overall occupational structure, and variations in the shares of the different population subgroups distinguished. She concluded that there was a large increase in female labor force participation and in the share of non-white workers. She also found that the share of the non-formal labor markets remained relatively constant between 1987 and 2006 and that the tertiary sector had rapidly grown during that period, absorbing almost all the additional female and non-white workers who entered the labor force. She also noted an increase in the share of women, especially non-white women, in the labor force. As far as segregation is concerned, Salardi (2012) found that gender segregation was much greater than racial segregation. Although racial segregation declined in the formal sector, it increased in recent years in the informal sector. She also noted that non-whites are heavily concentrated in low-skill occupations, and that racial segregation is quite high among better-educated and young workers, in urban areas and in the South and South-East regions. The implementation of the Deutsch et al. (2009) approach allowed the author to conclude also that the decline in both gender and racial segregation is mainly the consequence of a more homogeneous gender and racial composition within occupations. But these improvements seem to have been offset in the non-formal labor markets by changes in the occupational structure, and the entry of new groups into the labor force, changes that per se would have led to an increase in segregation.

22.5 ON RACIAL SCHOOL SEGREGATION

In the previous sections of the chapter we have chosen to focus on more recent contributions in major areas of segregation which we consider as promising lines of research. In this section, in contrast, we present an in-depth review of the development in the last decades of one major area: the case of racial school segregation and desegregation policies in the United States. This choice is an explicit recognition of the very special roles that both research and policy implementation in this area have had on the evolution of each other.

Social scientists have long recognized the social and political relevance and research complexity of the interactions between race and equal opportunity in education. Coleman, only three years after the publication in 1966 of the landmark Coleman Report on *Equality of Education Opportunity* (Coleman et al., 1966), would offer a simple mental experiment to highlight these complexities:

> For suppose we carry out a mental experiment in which Negroes and whites were subject to precisely the same school resources, for example, in a single school in a single town, with a single school class at each grade. One might be prepared to say . . . that this situation would provide such equality. But suppose, in this mental experiment, that the school met for only one hour each week. Would we still be prepared to assert that it provided equality of educational opportunity? (Coleman, 1967, p. 5)

As argued by Clotfelter et al. (2009), racial gaps in education are arguably one of the most concerning issues about race and equity in education in the US. Moreover, racial isolation in the schools appears to most observers as a potentially destabilizing factor in the racial relations in American society. With these concerns in mind, the policies of school desegregation that started by the end of the 1960s were a bold attempt to solve this issue once and for all. This shift in school policy has recently been referred to as 'one of the most dramatic social experiments of the twentieth century' (Baum-Snow and Lutz, 2011, p. 3019). Not surprisingly, the trends and consequences of racial school segregation in the US have been at the origin of numerous studies. Here we aim at reviewing only the most salient contributions. First, we describe the development of the school desegregation policies that took place in the second half of the twentieth century. Then we look at trends in racial school segregation and review the studies on the effects – both intended and unintended – of desegregation. We end this section with a brief discussion of the empirical literature on the effects of racial isolation on students' outcomes.[2]

22.5.1 School Desegregation in the US

In 1954, the US Supreme Court decision in *Brown v. Board of Education* declared separate public schools for black and white students unconstitutional. The decision was of crucial importance as it put an end to a decades-long policy based on the legal doctrine that a public system that separated individuals by race would not be unconstitutional if the individuals were given equal access to services and facilities. Among the arguments held by the Supreme Court, two had clear empirical content. The first one was that the 'separate but equal' system had failed in the case of education and had instead perpetuated systematic differences in the resources devoted to black and white students. The second argument was partly motivated by research conducted among children in the segregated South in the late 1930s. Psychologists Kenneth B. Clark and Mamie Phipps Clark had found that, confronted with identical dolls except in their skin and hair color, all white and black children showed a clear preference to play with the white doll (Clark and Clark, 1939). This finding seemed to suggest that low self-esteem among black children could be related to segregation, and that an integrated school system would improve the academic performance of minority children.

The *Brown* decision led to the first establishment of a desegregation policy in several districts. Desegregation in this first stage simply meant the elimination of a racial system by the introduction of Freedom of Choice plans. Parents were given the freedom to choose the school for their children. However, this freedom seems to have led to very little reassignment of black students and practically no movement from 'white' to 'black' schools for white students. In fact, regional estimates of school segregation do not reveal any significant change around 1954 (Boozer et al., 1992).

In 1968 the Supreme Court held that the Freedom of Choice plan in New Kent county district was not appropriate to achieve the goal of a non-racial system in the district (*Green v. County School Board of New Kent County*, 391 US 430, 1968). The decision was the first one of several during the early 1970s which effectively marked the end of Freedom of Choice plans and the beginning of other methods, such as 'busing', to achieve racial integration in the public schools. As Coleman et al. (1975) put it, by 1973 desegregation had moved from meaning the dismantling of a system by which children were sent away to segregate them by race, to a system by which children were sent to distant schools to integrate them.

This trend towards more intensive use of involuntary integrating policies ended abruptly in 1974. In that year, the *Milikan v. Bradley* ruling substantially limited the conditions for inter-district integration policies. In the following decades, desegregation policies were influenced by additional court decisions that put further limits on involuntary measures such as busing and admissions policies based on race. By the 1990s, an increasing number of court cases granted districts 'unitary' status so that they were freed from court supervision of their desegregation efforts. After *Parents Involved*,[3] affirmative action programs have been limited to situations where race-neutral approaches are unworkable, and they do not involve decisions based on the student's race.[4]

22.5.2 School Segregation Trends

The first round of studies on the effects of desegregation focused on its impact on racial trends in school districts. Because of lack of data availability, there are few studies that provide aggregate estimates of the extent of segregation prior to 1968. An interesting example is Boozer et al. (1992). Using retrospective self-reported data from the 1980 National Survey of Black Americans, the authors constructed a time series of data on school segregation over the 1924 to 1971 period for individuals who grew up in the South and Border states.[5] Their estimates show that segregation levels measured as percentage of black schools did not decline immediately after *Brown*, but may have started to decline around four years before *Green*.[6]

Coleman et al. (1975) use biennial school enrollment data from the Office of Civil Rights (OCR) for the period 1968 to 1973.[7] The authors use the proportion of white children in the school with the average black child as a measure of interracial school contact, and its relative deviation with respect to the district average of white students as a measure of within-district segregation. Using basic statistical and regression techniques they find that although there had been a large reduction in segregation after 1968, it was clear that desegregation was also contributing to increasing segregation between central city districts and the suburbs.

By the end of the 1980s, there was already a large number of studies that corroborated these findings. Using the OCR data for a sample of 125 school districts that represents half of minority enrollment in the US, Welch and Light (1987) find that during the 1967 to 1985 period segregation – measured via the dissimilarity index – declined in 93 percent of them, while in 74 districts exposure increased, measured by the average proportion of white classmates in schools minorities attend (see also Orfield, 1983; Orfield and Monfort, 1992; Boozer et al., 1992). These positive trends, however, were concurrent with a pronounced decline in white enrollment, a fact upon which a consensus had developed during the decade (see Wilson, 1985, and the references therein).

Rivkin (1994) also studies the evolution of racial school segregation with OCR enrollment data. He looks at the beginning and end of the period available at the time, 1968 and 1988, and also reports results for 1980: a relevant intermediate year because many more districts carried out desegregation policies in the 1970s than in the 1980s. His findings on general trends are in line with previous results in the literature. He also confirms two major demographic shifts: the increasing demographic importance of Hispanics and Asians, and the existence of regional trend differentials. In all regions but the North-East segregation, measured by the Gini index, had declined and black students' exposure to white students had increased (especially in the South). Motivated by the constraints imposed to involuntary desegregation policies by *Milikan*, Rivkin (1994) argues that, as of 1994, there is little scope for improvements in school integration by policies directly carried out by local educational authorities. He notes that the geographic racial concentration in school districts sets an upper bound to the potential integrative effects of school district policies. Gini measurements at district level provide estimates of the level of school segregation arising from location choices by parents and, therefore, mark a lower bound for the contribution of residential segregation to the overall school segregation of students. Rivkin (1994) identifies the within-district school segregation – referred to as school district segregation – as the difference between the Gini segregation index for student enrollments at school level and the Gini segregation index at school district level, referred to as residential segregation.[8] The main results are summarized in his Table 2. On average, the Gini indices of school segregation are 0.93, 0.84 and 0.77 in 1968, 1980 and 1988, respectively. The values for the school district level measures are 0.76, 0.78 and 0.77, respectively. Thus, while within-district segregation declined from 0.17 to 0.05, residential segregation remained stable at around 0.77, or 94 percent of total segregation. He concludes that even if all school districts became fully integrated – that is, if the proportions of white and minority students in the schools mirrored those of the school district – school segregation by race would decrease by less than five percentage points (see Rivkin and Welch, 2006, for an update of the analysis).

The quantitative accuracy of these dramatic findings was put into question because of three methodological issues. The first one comes from the limitation of using, like in most previous studies, data that sample districts and preclude the analysis of metropolitan segregation. The second was that, in spite of its policy relevance, the focus on the interracial contact between black and white students could underestimate the importance of desegregation policies for other minorities. The last methodological criticism stems from the well-known fact that the Gini index is not decomposable, in the sense that a reduction in the measure of within-district segregation may also simultaneously lead to an increase in the measure of school district segregation (Allison, 1978; Reardon and Firebaugh, 2002).

By the end of the 1990s a number of papers using the Common Core of Data (CCD) attempted to address these problems. Using data from the academic year 1994/1995, Clotfelter (1999) provides the first systematic evaluation of the importance of racial school segregation patterns in metropolitan areas. Using a normalized exposure – which is decomposable in the two-group case – and the Gini index, Clotfelter (1999) finds that, by 1995, metropolitan areas exhibit levels of segregation close to those estimated for the US with the OCR enrollment data. Moreover, most of the segregation found in metropolitan areas comes from racial disparities between districts. Thus, his results seem to confirm Rivkin's (1994) major policy result with accurate metropolitan information from the CCD. In arguably the first large-scale multiracial study of school segregation, Reardon et al. (2000) use the CCD from 1989 to 1995 to track the evolution of patterns of school segregation, capturing the extent of segregation among minority groups. The authors exploit a weak decomposability property satisfied by Theil's entropy index of segregation to conclude that while metropolitan segregation between whites and minority students increased, segregation within minorities decreased, resulting in a rather stable overall level of multi-group segregation. The entropy index of segregation also allows for a decomposition of metropolitan segregation into between- and a within-districts terms (Reardon and Firebaugh, 2002). Using this property, the authors find that the observed increase in segregation between whites and minority students was largely due to an increase in enrollment disparities between city and suburban districts. In their Table 3, Reardon et al. (2000) present a two-way decomposition of multiracial metropolitan school segregation for 1995. The results again confirmed the importance of between-districts segregation, although the levels are somewhat lower than those obtained with the Gini index, 67.8

percent of segregation can be accounted for by between-districts segregation. Around two-thirds of this segregation stems from racial enrollment differences between central cities and suburban districts (see also Reardon and Yun, 2001).

Frankel and Volij (2011) study the evolution of multi-group segregation from the academic year 1987/1988 to the academic year 2007/2008. As they compare how different segregation indexes perform, they note that indexes which are invariant to the overall distribution of students by race report small decreases. For example, the Atkinson index with symmetric weights shows a decline from 0.64 to 0.52, or 18.8 percent in 21 years. In contrast, the composition-sensitive indexes (that is, indexes that are not invariant) tend to show large increases: for instance, the non-normalized version of the entropy index – the so-called mutual information index – shows an increase of 17.9 percent during the same period. Normalized composition-sensitive indexes, like the Gini and the entropy index, report little change in overall segregation: the Gini index shows a decline from 0.82 to 0.79, while the entropy index registers a 6.7 percent decrease. Hence, as Frankel and Volij argue, normalization seems to ameliorate the influence on the composition-sensitive measures of the growing ethnic diversity observed during the period.[9] Using the mutual information index, the authors then compute segregation at four geographic levels: states, metropolitan areas (core-based statistical area: CBSA), districts and schools. For the academic year 2007/2008, within-district segregation can account for only 19.8 percent of the total segregation. The most important source of school segregation is the ethnic differentiation of districts within metropolitan areas, which accounts for 32.3 percent of the total, and is mainly due to the separation of blacks from whites and Asians. Segregation between the states is also important, accounting for 31.9 percent of total segregation. This is mainly due to the residential patterns of Hispanics. Thus, the results corroborate previous findings according to which desegregation policies at school district level have little scope for sizable improvements in integration.

22.5.3 Consequences of Segregation

Intentional versus natural studies and intended versus unintended outcomes
It is useful to distinguish two types of studies on segregation outcomes: studies on the effects of racial isolation in the schools and studies of desegregation programs. While the former are concerned with the channel through which any successful school desegregation policy will affect individual performances, the latter is focused on the efficacy and practical justification of actually implemented desegregation policies. Crain and Mahard (1978) refer to this second type of studies as 'intentional' since they focus on the effects of intentional desegregation operations; while they refer to the first type of studies as 'natural' because they mostly relate individual outcomes to the racial mixing 'naturally' observed in the schools.

Based on the variable of interest, intentional studies can be further classified into those that focus on intended outcomes and those that focus on unintended outcomes. In the former group of intentional studies we can include those that focus on the consequences – both for the minority group and for the white students – for which desegregation policies were initially justified, at least partly. Among these intended outcomes we find academic achievement, self-esteem and racial attitudes. In contrast, unintended outcomes focus on effects that were not planned or desired when the first round of involuntary desegregation programs were implemented. Arguably, two of the most significant alleged unintended consequences of desegregation were the 'white flight' of whites from public to private schools, and from urban areas to more racially homogeneous suburban regions.

The methodological problems faced in these studies are well known. Experimental data hardly provide evidence which is easy to extrapolate to other contexts; while for observational data in which there is no randomized-out control group, causal effects are frequently difficult to identify. Although several strategies can be used to approximate the experimental data ideal, no solution is perfect. In some cases, strategies frequently found in other research fields seem very inappropriate. For example, the strategy of using siblings of the transferred students as controls is likely to exacerbate self-selection bias, as parents will probably take into account children factors associated with test scores but unobserved by the researcher. In voluntary plans, self-selection may also bias results. Parents in desegregated schools may have motivations that affect their involvement both in desegregation operations and in the performance of their children. In districts in which all students are reassigned, improvements must be identified by comparing the outcomes of reassigned black students with those of another cohort, with those of white students, or with national norms. In general, the use of covariates to make the comparison more credible is likely to be incomplete. Estimates obtained using blacks' improvements in test scores over improvements from initially similar white students may capture confounding effects arising from race-specific trends in test scores unrelated to desegregation plans. Results from cross-sectional studies that use black students attending a segregated school as a control are difficult to interpret if local unobserved factors triggering the desegregation policy in the treated group – or its absence in the control group – are associated with students' performances. Cohort studies where reassigned black students are compared with similar black students before desegregation rely on the absence of trends in academic performance. Even in longitudinal studies with detailed personal background information, the additional use of pre-test scores as a control will not eliminate these problems entirely, as children experience individual-specific time-heterogeneous cognitive improvements.

Desegregation intended outcomes
Early analyses focused on short-run effects on academic achievement. Crain and Mahard (1978, p. 18) report a growing consensus in relation to the effects on white students, noting that 'virtually every writer on the subject has agreed that the test performance of white students is unaffected by school desegregation'. Their verdict on black achievement is somewhat less clear, as they find that out of 77 research studies, 40 show that desegregation has a positive effect on black achievement, and 12 show a negative result. Focusing on the 39 studies involving mandatory assignments, they find a four-to-one ratio favoring positive outcomes. The only two studies reviewed by Crain and Mahard (1978) using experimental data, that of Zdep (1971) and of Mahan and Mahan (1971), did find positive outcomes for reassigned students. However, a study using observational data with a credible identification strategy, that of Schellenberg and Halteman (1976), did not find positive results. Schellenberg and Halteman (1976) studied the desegregation program in Grand Rapids, Michigan. Black students were reassigned from inner-city overcrowded schools to white suburban schools. As the reassigned students were those who lived in areas which were the furthest away from their local schools, Schellenberg and Halteman

(1976) argue that students who lived a few blocks nearer their local school would be compelling controls. Somewhat surprisingly, results covering a period of two years fail to give any evidence of a positive effect.

There are no simple reasons for this lack of consensus in the early literature. Studies differ not only in the desegregation policies actually implemented, but also in the data available and the identification strategy pursued. Moreover, as Crain and Mahard (1978) convincingly argue, under certain conditions, desegregation effects may well not be positive:

> Student performance can be affected by community conflict, by school desegregation that is not reinforced by neighborhood integration, and by the racial attitudes of black and white students and staff. For example, desegregation may have a short-term negative effect if teachers do not adapt their teaching methods to their new students, or if black students do not make the transition to a white school easily and are upset by racial issues or simply by the change in schools. (Crain and Mahard, 1978, p.22)

In the early 1980s, the National Institute of Education established a representative panel of experts to review the evidence on black achievement, and selected 19 studies for review. All the selected studies fulfilled a quasi-experimental design with a segregated control group. The results reported by the members of the panel using meta-analysis techniques do provide some patterns. First, average negative effects seem to be ruled out. Second, no positive effects for math achievement are found. Finally, there is some evidence of short-term positive effects in reading levels. However, these positive effects seem to be concentrated in a number of school districts, making the average effect difficult to interpret (Cook, 1984; Armor, 1984). By the mid-1990s two different lines of study had enlarged the scope of analysis. First, understanding the reasons why some desegregation plans were effective while others seemed to produce no improvements among black students soon became the main focus of many research strategies. While a growing number of researchers questioned the effectiveness of mandatory reassignments and some researchers argued that voluntary strategies actually result in more integration (see Rossell, 1995, and the references therein), national estimates of desegregation outcomes using pooled cross-sections and panel data started to provide a clear overall picture. Among the latter studies, one work deserves special attention. Using 125 school districts identified in Welch and Light (1987), Guryan (2004) examined the impact of school desegregation on the probability of dropping out of high school using county census data from 1970 and 1980. The key identification strategy is based on the role of precedent in the US legal process. Guryan (2004) argues that the private civil rights groups that initiated court proceedings to trigger desegregation court mandates chose to bring suit in school districts when and where they expected a higher probability of victory, rather than a larger benefit for students. Hence, a plausible identification strategy is to use a sample of school districts that did implement a desegregation plan and exploit district heterogeneity at the time the plan was started. He then compares high-school-aged blacks in counties in which a school district desegregated between 1970 and 1979 with those in counties in which a school district desegregated both before and after. Difference-in-differences estimates controlling for county fixed-effects suggest that desegregation plans caused drop-out rates to decline by two to three percentage points.

Several recent papers show positive effects not only on test scores, but also on a wide variety of outcomes such as dropout rates, earnings, crime and adult health status (Lutz, 2005; Weiner et al., 2009; Johnson, 2011). There are several channels through which these effects materialize. First, black students may benefit from positive peer effects and also develop a greater amount of self-confidence. Perhaps transferred black students benefit from better schools in terms of their facilities and staff. Perhaps desegregation also improves educational services through a large increase in resources. Usually it is difficult to disentangle each source of improvements, but in a recent study, Reber (2010) develops an ingenious strategy to give an estimation of the relative importance of the last two channels. Using aggregated district-level data in the 1960–1975 period, she examines the effects on continuation rates at different grades of large desegregation interventions in Louisiana school districts. In 1964, only about 1 percent of black students were in school with any whites. By 1970, after the implementation of large-scale mandatory desegregation plans, the average black student was in a school that was more than 30 percent white. As it turned out, Reber (2010) shows that blacks in 1960 high black enrollment share districts saw smaller increases in exposure to whites, but larger increases in resources in their schools. This asymmetry opens the way for a novel identification strategy, because blacks' initial educational attainment in 1960 was not significantly related to initial black enrollment share: in its simplest specification, a positive estimate for the coefficient of the 1960 black enrollment share on changes in continuation rates attainment suggests a larger role for resources and a smaller role for exposure to whites in accounting for black students reductions in dropout rates. For example, a significant positive coefficient of 0.185 for 12th graders suggests that the additional funding that came with desegregation was more important than increased exposure to whites in increasing black educational continuation rates after grade 12.

The white flight and other unintended outcomes from desegregation

Research on desegregation effects has been concerned not only with the alleged positive effects it would bring to black students, but also with unintended responses by white families and state and local authorities. In Coleman et al. (1975), the final conclusion left an open question concerning the extent to which desegregation actually caused white flight from central cities:

> The emerging problem of school segregation in large cities is a problem of metropolitan area residential segregation, black central cities and white suburbs, brought about by a loss of whites from the center of cities. This loss is intensified by extensive school desegregation in those central cities, but in cities with high proportions of blacks and predominantly white suburbs, it proceeds at a relatively rapid rate with or without desegregation. (Coleman et al., 1975, p. 80)

As pointed out by Rivkin and Welch (2006), most early studies report a short-run relation between desegregation and white flight, although the magnitude of the effect varies. To analyze long-term effects, Wilson (1985) looks at OCR data for a subsample of districts, mainly from the South, for the 1968–1982 period. Using an autoregressive model, he relates white enrollment changes to changes in white exposure to non-whites. He interprets his results as suggesting that white losses are independent of the nature of the desegregation program and limited to the year the program is implemented. However, the simultaneity between the control and the dependent variable complicates the causal interpretation of the regression results.

Welch and Light (1987) extend the period of analysis to 1982 and match the OCR data with district-level data. They also restrict the set of districts to every district with 50 000 or more students in 1968, and 20 percent to 90 percent minority representation (a total of 125 large districts). They relate changes in white enrollment to changes in the index of dissimilarity by timing and desegregation plan and find that white losses were largest one year before implementation of desegregation and that they remained above pre-plan level one year after implementation. They further find larger negative effects for some mandatory segregation plans, a result later confirmed using alternative datasets by several authors (Rossell, 1995; Rossell and Armor, 1996).

Reber (2005) uses school-level data for a sample of 108 large districts from the Welch and Light (1987) data with at least one court-ordered desegregation plan at some time between 1961 and 1986 and – similar to Guryan (2004) – exploits variation in the timing of court-ordered desegregation plans to study how desegregation plans affected white public school enrollment. Difference-in-differences estimates suggest annual losses to be large – over 10 percent – and persistent in the long term, especially in districts with many nearby school districts and with desegregation plans that increased whites' exposure to non-whites. As the author points out, these findings provide evidence that desegregation may have failed to reduce segregation in the long run by the decision to exclude suburban districts.

More recently, Baum-Snow and Lutz (2011) employ an identification strategy similar to that of Reber (2005) to evaluate the importance of white flight to the private school system. First, using aggregates of tract-level data from the decennial census assigned to school districts for 92 metropolitan areas with central districts that experienced major court-ordered school desegregation between 1960 and 1990, they obtain similar or marginally smaller results than Reber (2005) for white enrollment decline. Then they find large positive estimates on white private enrollment in central city districts, especially outside of the South. However, the size estimates imply that these effects were not determinants of the decline of the white population in central cities. As the authors report: 'Even without court-ordered desegregation . . . aggregate central district white population would have fallen by 10 percent between 1960 and 1990 rather than the decline of 13 percent actually observed' (Baum-Snow and Lutz, 2011, p. 3044). Using a similar identification strategy and the same data as in Reber (2010), Reber (2011) also studies white flight to private schools in Louisiana school districts. Her results suggest that increases in private school enrollment accounted for about 60 percent of the differential decline in public school enrollment in blacker districts. Finally, using information on per pupil revenue she also finds that white flight did not adversely affect the finances of school districts.

Natural studies on racial peer effects
In this section we review the empirical literature on the effects of racial isolation on the academic achievement of blacks. Since Coleman et al. (1966), there had not been a clear consensus on this issue. Although the Coleman Report and others provided early empirical evidence that racial isolation harms achievement (see also Crain, 1970; Boozer et al., 1992) several papers provided contradictory results (see, e.g., Armor 1984; Bridge et al., 1979).

A well-known reason behind the difficulty in reaching an early consensus is the fact that racial composition in the schools is an outcome of decisions by families and authorities. Hence, a causal interpretation of a significant coefficient for the proportion of black students must assume that the sorting of students into schools and classes is unrelated to academic achievement; an assumption likely to be false in many empirical situations.

More recent attempts to identify peer racial effects by identification strategies that minimize school selection bias include Hoxby (2000), Grogger (1996) and Rivkin (2000). Hoxby's (2000) identification strategy for peer effects is based on the intuition that student cohorts close in age in the same school are more comparable than other students. Hence, she proposes to use changes in the racial (and gender) composition of a grade in a school in adjacent years as control. As stressed by Hanushek et al. (2009), a problem with this approach is that differences across cohorts may still be related to both racial composition and achievement.

Using longitudinal data, Grogger (1996) attempts to identify the effect of school quality on the black–white wage gap. As an additional control, he includes in all specifications the proportion black in the school, but finds no significant effects (point estimates are negative). As Rivkin (2000) argues, even with longitudinal data and family background information, it is likely that school choices will still be conditioned by a myriad of unobservable factors, including educational preferences and children's abilities. He investigates the impact of school racial composition on 12th-grade score, years of school attained and the log of monthly earnings for a sample of black men and women who attended high school in large urban districts in 1982. To minimize the endogeneity of school choice, he controls for parental education, family income and a measure of achievement at the beginning of the period. Results suggest no effect of the exposure to whites on academic attainment or earnings. However, the fact that he uses high school seniors questions the validity of the results for the black school population as a whole.

A similar type of criticism is faced by Card and Rothstein (2007). They use college entry test scores of black students for the 1998–2001 cohorts. After controlling for family background, school-level and city-level controls, they find a significant neighborhood effect, but their estimate of the school racial composition effect is not significant (they cannot reject that both effects are equal). Clearly, focusing on workers who previously self-selected into taking college entry tests raises similar questions for the interpretation of the results as those from Rivkin (2000).

Hanushek et al. (2009) exploit a unique rich panel of three successive cohorts of Texas public elementary students as they progress through school over 3000 public schools. The most recent cohort in the dataset attended 5th grade in 1996. Using a variety of fixed effects specifications, they attempt to identify racial isolation effects from other dimensions of school quality and family and individual specific effects. The findings suggest that black isolation – measured by the proportion of blacks at the school – lowers mathematics achievement, while the corresponding estimates on whites are not significant.

More recently, Billings et al. (2014) study the impact of the proportion of minority students at school level on educational and criminal outputs. They exploit redrawing of school boundaries by the end of race-based busing in Charlotte-Mecklenburg schools in 2001. They compare outputs from students who lived on opposite sides of newly drawn boundaries and find that students assigned to schools with more minority students obtained lower educational outcomes (such as exam grades and completion rates). Moreover, for minority male students a 10 percentage point increase in minority share is found to be associated to a 7 percent increase in the probability of ever being arrested and incarcerated. As they further find that increased resources did not mitigate the effects on crime incidence, they conclude that the end of busing widened racial inequality.

22.6 CONCLUDING COMMENTS

A huge literature has attempted in the past few decades to measure segregation, whether it be occupational, school or residential segregation. The focus of part of this literature was on measurement issues, and indeed there is by now quite a long list of segregation indices. Most of the papers in this field were, however, empirical studies of segregation, and the present chapter aimed at reviewing this type of literature. Given the space constraints which we had to face, we were not able to present an exhaustive survey of all the empirical studies that looked at occupational, school and residential segregation. We decided therefore to give the priority to school segregation and devote relatively more space to this topic. As a consequence the review of occupational segregation by gender or race as well as of residential segregation is much more succinct, although we tried to show what the main research directions in these domains were.

As far as the literature on residential segregation is concerned, our review confirms the specificity of this type of segregation which requires, when one wants to evaluate its extent, the use of spatial measures of segregation which do not ignore the spatial proximity of neighborhoods and are flexible enough so that they are not sensitive to the arbitrariness in which residential units are defined. More recent studies seem to indicate that towards the end of the twentieth century, both Hispanic–white and Asian–white residential segregation in the United States increased modestly, while black–white segregation declined. The latter decline, however, was limited in the sense that although nearby neighborhoods had become more racially similar, there was no large-scale redistribution of black and white populations. Concerning income segregation, it seems that residential income segregation increased during the past three decades across the United States as well as in 27 of the thirty 30 largest metropolitan areas.

When analyzing occupational segregation by gender, economists tend to look at three main determinants – labor demand, labor supply and institutional factors – while the sociological approach stresses the role of socialization. As far as trends are concerned, occupational segregation by gender does not seem to have changed much since 1992 for the EU-12 group, while for the EU-27 there seems to have been a slightly upward movement. In the United States occupational segregation has been declining across age cohorts among more educated women, but has remained quite constant among individuals with lower educational levels. In both the EU and the USA occupational segregation seems to be positively correlated with the share of part-time jobs (which are typically female) in the economy.

Recent studies of occupational segregation by race suggest that in the United States segregation by language proficiency is important, as it can explain up to one-third of the overall Hispanic–white segregation. These studies also find that segregation across workplaces tends to decrease with establishment size. If a distinction is made between conditional and unconditional segregation, it then appears that the lack of English proficiency, educational attainment and recent immigration to the US explain a large part of the relatively high level of unconditional segregation for Hispanics and for Asians, whereas for blacks a much smaller share of occupational segregation is due to the attributes mentioned previously.

For school segregation in the United States there seems to be quite a large consensus according to which, although there has been a large reduction in segregation after 1968, it is also clear that desegregation policies contributed to increasing segregation between central city districts and suburbs. If school segregation is computed at different geographic levels such as states, metropolitan areas, districts and schools, it then appears that the most important source of school segregation is the ethnic differentiation of districts within metropolitan areas, which is mainly due to the separation of blacks from whites and Asians. Segregation between the states is also important but it is mainly due to the residential patterns of Hispanics.

ACKNOWLEDGEMENTS

Ricardo Mora gratefully acknowledges the financial support by the Ministerio Economía y Competitividad (Spain), through grant ECO2015-65204-P and also the financial support from grants MDM 2014-0431 and MadEco-CM (S2015/HUM-3444).

NOTES

1. A search in Google Scholar for 'racial school segregation "United States"' gives approximately 242 000 results. A search for 'occupational segregation' or 'residential segregation' gives 146 000 and 181 000 results, respectively.
2. There is also an increasing number of international studies on school racial segregation, particularly in the UK, that we cannot address due to space limitations. See, among others, Burgess et al. (2005), Jenkins et al. (2008) and Wilson (1985).
3. *Parents Involved in Community Schools v. Seattle School District No. 1*, 551 US 701, 2007.
4. For reviews of landmark school desegregation court cases, see Weiler (1998) and Rivkin and Welch (2006). See also US Office for Civil Rights (2017) for current Federal Government guidance to school districts on how to implement desegregation policies.
5. The National Survey of Black Americans (NSBA) asked respondents whether they attended an 'all black' or 'mostly black' grammar school, junior high, or high school.
6. This change in 1964 is possibly explained by prohibition by the Civil Rights Act of federal aid to segregated schools. Guryan (2004) presents corroborative evidence for Louisiana counties.
7. This survey does not provide student assignments to class level, and for the years of the study it was a sample drawn from districts with enrollments larger than 300 students. Since weights are provided to compute national aggregates, and data for the districts included are quite detailed, despite its limitations it has become one of the two main sources of information to evaluate racial school segregation in the US. The other nationwide source that is frequently used in segregation studies, the Common Core of Data (CCD), from the US Department of Education's National Center for Education Statistics, started in academic year 1987/1988.
8. He also presents evidence using Lorenz curves.
9. See also Mora and Ruiz-Castillo (2010). When expressed in percentage points, the entropy and the mutual information indexes give the same decomposition, so that their distinction is only relevant in the evaluation of trends in overall levels of segregation.

REFERENCES

Allison, P.D. (1978) 'Measures of inequality', *American Sociological Review*, 43(6): 865–880.
Anker, R. (1997) 'Theories of occupational segregation by sex: an overview', *International Labour Review*, 136(3): 315–339.
Armor, D.J. (1984) 'The evidence on desegregation and black achievement', in T. Cook, D. Armor, R. Crain, N. Miller, W. Stephan, H. Walberg and P. Wortman (eds), *School Desegregation and Black Achievement*, Washington, DC: National Institute of Education, pp. 43–67.
Arrow, K.J. (1973) 'The theory of discrimination', in O. Ashenfelter and A. Rees (eds), *Discrimination in Labor Markets*, Princeton, NJ: Princeton University Press, pp. 3–33.
Baum-Snow, N. and B.F. Lutz (2011) 'School desegregation, school choice, and changes in residential location patterns by race', *American Economic Review*, 101(7): 3019–3046.
Becker, G.S. (1957) *The Economics of Discrimination*, Chicago, IL: University of Chicago Press.
Bergmann, B. (1974) 'Occupational segregation, wages and profits when employers discriminate by wage or sex', *Eastern Economic Journal*, 1(2): 103–1101.
Billings, S.B., D.J. Deming and J. Rockoff (2014) 'School segregation, educational attainment, and crime: evidence from the end of busing in Charlotte-Mecklenburg', *Quarterly Journal of Economics*, 129(1): 435–476.
Boozer, M., A. Krueger and S. Wolkon (1992) 'Race and school quality since Brown v. Board of Education', Brookings Papers on Economic Activity, Microeconomics.
Bridge, R.G., Judd, C.M. and P.R Moock (1979) *The Determinants of Educational Outcomes: The Impact of Families, Peers, Teachers, and Schools*, Cambridge, MA: Ballinger.
Burgess, R.G., D. Wilson and R. Lupton (2005) 'Parallel lives? Ethnic segregation in schools and neighbourhoods', *Urban Studies*, 42(7): 1027–1056.
Card, D. and J. Rothstein (2007) 'Racial segregation and the black–white test score gap', *Journal of Public Economics*, 91(11/12): 2158–2184.
Chantreuil, F. and A. Trannoy (2013) 'Inequality decomposition values: the trade-off between marginality and efficiency', *Journal of Economic Inequality*, 11: 83–98.
Clark, K.B. and M.K. Clark (1939) 'The development of consciousness of self and the emergence of racial identification in Negro preschool children', *Journal of Social Psychology*, 10(4): 591–599.
Clotfelter, C. (1999) 'Public school segregation in metropolitan areas', *Land Economics*, 75(4): 487–504.
Clotfelter, C., H. Ladd and J. Vigdor (2009) 'The academic achievement gap in grades 3 to 8', *Review of Economics and Statistics*, 91(2): 398–419.
Coleman, J.S. (1967) 'Equality of educational opportunity, reconsidered', Discussion paper, Center for the Study of Social Organization of Schools, Johns Hopkins University, Baltimore, MD.
Coleman, J.S., E.Q. Campbell, C.J. Hobson, F. McPartland, A.M. Mood, F.D. Weinfeld and R.L. York (1966) *Equality of Education Opportunity*, Washington, DC: US Government Printing Office.
Coleman, J.S., S.D. Kelly and J.A. Moore (1975) 'Trends in school segregation, 1968–73', Discussion paper, Urban Institute Paper 722-03-01, Washington, DC.
Cook, T.D. (1984) 'What have black children gained academically from school desegregation: examination of the metaanalytic evidence', in T. Cook, D. Armor, R. Crain, N. Miller, W. Stephan, H. Walberg and P. Wortman (eds), *School Desegregation and Black Achievement*, Washington, DC: National Institute of Education, pp. 6–42.
Corcoran, M.E. and P.N. Courant (1985) 'Sex role socialization and labor market outcomes', *American Economic Review*, 75: 275–278.
Crain, R.L. (1970) 'School integration and occupational achievement of Negroes', *American Journal of Sociology*, 75(4): 593–606.
Crain, R.L. and R.E. Mahard (1978) 'Desegregation and black achievement: a review of the research', *Law and Contemporary Problems*, 42(3): 17–43.
Cutler, D.M., E.L. Glaeser and J.L. Vigdor (1999) 'The rise and decline of the American ghetto', *Journal of Political Economy*, 107: 455–506.
Darity, W.A., Jr and P.L. Mason (1998) 'Evidence on discrimination in employment: codes of color, codes of gender', *Journal of Economic Perspectives*, 12(2): 63–90.
Darity, W., Jr and R. Williams (1985) 'Peddlers forever? Culture, competition and discrimination', *American Economic Review*, 75(2): 256–261.
Dawkins, C.J. (2004) 'Measuring the spatial pattern of residential segregation', *Urban Studies*, 41(4): 833–851.
Dawkins, C.J. (2006) 'The spatial pattern of black–white segregation in US metropolitan areas: an exploratory analysis', *Urban Studies*, 43(11): 1943–1969.
Deutsch, J., Y. Flückiger and J. Silber (2009) 'Analyzing changes in occupational segregation: the case of Switzerland 1970–2000', *Occupational and Residential Segregation, Research on Economic Inequality*, 17: 173–204.

DiNardo, J., N.M. Fortin and T. Lemieux (1996) 'Labor market institutions and the distribution of wages, 1973–1992: a semiparametric approach', *Econometrica*, 64: 1001–1044.

Doeringer, P. and M. Piore (1971) *Internal Labor Markets and Manpower Analysis*, Lexington, MA: Heath & Co.

Dolado, J.J., F. Felgueroso and J.F. Jimeno (2002) 'Recent trends in occupational segregation by gender: a look across the Atlantic', IZA (Institute for the Study of Labor), Discussion Paper No. 524.

Duncan, O.D. and B. Duncan (1955) 'A methodological analysis of segregation indexes', *American Sociological Review*, 20(2): 210–217.

European Commission (2009) *Gender Segregation in the Labour Market: Causes, Implications and Policy Responses in the EU*. Directorate-General for Employment, Social Affairs and Equal Opportunities, Unit G1.

Eurostat (2008) *The Life of Women and Men in Europe: A Statistical Portrait*.

Fong, E. and K. Shibuya (2000) 'The spatial separation of the poor in Canadian cities', *Demography*, 37(4): 449–459.

Frankel, D.M. and O. Volij (2011) 'Measuring school segregation', *Journal of Economic Theory*, 146(1): 1–38.

Gradin, C. (2010) 'Conditional occupational segregation of minorities in the US', ECINEQ Working Paper No. 185.

Grogger, J. (1996) 'Does school quality explain the recent black/white wage trend?', *Journal of Labor Economics*, 14(2): 231–253.

Guryan, J. (2004) 'Desegregation and black dropout rates', *American Economic Review*, 94(4): 919–943.

Hanushek, E.A., J.F. Kain and S.G. Rivkin (2009) 'New evidence about Brown v. Board of Education: the complex effects of school racial composition on achievement', *Journal of Labor Economics*, 27(3): 349–383.

Hellerstein, J.K. and D. Neumark (2008) 'Workplace segregation in the United States: race, ethnicity and skill', *Review of Economics and Statistics*, 90(3): 459–477.

Hoxby, C. (2000) 'Peer effects in the classroom: learning from gender and race variation', Working Paper 7867, National Bureau of Economic Research.

Hutchens, R.M. (2001) 'Numerical measures of segregation: desirable properties and their implications', *Mathematical Social Sciences*, 42: 13–29.

Ioannides, Y.M. (2004) 'Neighborhood income distributions', *Journal of Urban Economics*, 56(3): 435–457.

Ioannides, Y.M. and T.N. Seslen (2002) 'Neighborhood wealth distributions', *Economics Letters*, 76: 357–367.

Jargowsky, P.A. (1996) 'Take the money and run: economic segregation in US metropolitan areas', *American Sociological Review*, 61(6): 984–998.

Jargowsky, P.A. and J. Kim (2005a) 'A measure of spatial segregation: the Generalized Neighborhood Sorting Index', Political Economy Working Paper 10/04, School of Social Sciences, University of Texas at Dallas.

Jargowsky, P.A. and J. Kim (2005b) 'A measure of spatial segregation: the Generalized Neighborhood Sorting Index', National Poverty Center Working Paper Series #05-3, University of Michigan, Ann Arbor, MI.

Jenkins, S.P., J. Micklewright and S.V. Schnepf (2008) 'Social segregation in secondary schools: how does England compare with other countries?', *Oxford Review of Education*, 34(1): 21–37.

Johnson, R.C. (2011) 'Long-run impacts of school desegregation and school quality on adult attainments', Working Paper 16664, National Bureau of Economic Research.

Kakwani, N.C. (1980) *Income Inequality and Poverty: Methods of Estimation and Policy Applications*, Oxford: World Bank and Oxford University Press.

Karmel, T. and M. MacLachlan (1988) 'Occupational sex segregation – Increasing or decreasing?', *Economic Record*, 64: 187–195.

Kim, J. and P.A. Jargowsky (2009) 'The Gini coefficient and segregation on a continuous variable', in Y. Flückiger, S.F. Reardon and J. Silber (eds), *Occupational and Residential Segregation*, Vol. 17 of Research on Economic Inequality, Bingley: Emerald Group Publishing, pp. 57–70.

Lutz, B.F. (2005) 'Post Brown vs. the Board of Education: the effects of the end of court-ordered desegregation', Finance and Economics Discussion Series, Divisions of Research and Statistics and Monetary Affairs Federal Reserve Board, Washington, DC.

Madden, J.F. (1975) 'Discrimination – a manifestation of male market power?', in C. Lloyd (ed.), *Sex, Discrimination and the Division of Labor*, New York: Columbia University Press, pp. 146–174.

Mahan, T.W. and A.M. Mahan (1971) 'The impact of schools on learning: inner-city children in suburban schools', *Journal of School Psychology*, 9(1): 1–11.

Massey, D.S. and N.A. Denton (1988) 'The dimensions of residential segregation', *Social Forces* 67(2): 281–315.

Massey, D.S. and M.L. Eggers (1993) 'The ecology of inequality: minorities and the concentration of poverty', *American Journal of Sociology* 95(5): 1153–1188.

Monkkonen, P. (2010) 'Measuring residential segregation in urban Mexico: levels and patterns', Institute of Urban and Regional Development, Working Paper 2010-05, Berkeley, CA.

Mora, R. and J. Ruiz-Castillo (2010) 'Entropy-based segregation indices', *Sociological Methodology*, 41: 159–194.

Okamoto, D. and P. England (1999) 'Is there a supply side to occupational sex segregation', *Sociological Perspectives*, 42(4): 557–582.

Orfield, G. (1983) 'Public school desegregation in the United States, 1968–1980', Joint Center for Political Studies, Washington, DC.

Orfield, G. and F. Montfort (1992) 'Status of school desegregation: the next generation', Discussion Paper, Council of Urban Boards of Education, National School Boards Association, Alexandria, VA.

Pew Research Center (2012) 'The rise of residential segregation by income', Pew Social and Demographic Trends, Washington, DC.

Phelps, E. (1972) 'The statistical theory of racism and sexism', *American Economic Review*, 62(4): 659–661.

Platt Boustan, L. (2011) 'Racial residential segregation in American cities', in N. Brooks, K. Donaghy and G. Knaap (eds), *Handbook of Urban Economics and Planning*, Oxford: Oxford University Press, pp. 318–339.

Reardon, S.F. (2009) 'Measures of ordinal segregation', in Y. Flückiger, S.F. Reardon and J. Silber (eds), *Occupational and Residential Segregation*, Vol. 17 of Research on Economic Inequality, Bingley: Emerald, pp. 129–155.

Reardon, S.F. (2011) 'Measures of income segregation', mimeo, Center for Education Policy Analysis, Stanford University.

Reardon, S.F., C.R. Farrell, S.A. Matthews, D. O'Sullivan, K. Bischoff and G. Firebaugh (2009) 'Race and space in the 1990s: changes in the geographical scale of residential segregation, 1990–2000', *Social Science Research*, 38: 55–70.

Reardon, S.F. and G. Firebaugh (2002) 'Measures of multi-group segregation', *Sociological Methodology*, 32, 33–67.

Reardon, S.F. and D. O'Sullivan (2004) 'Measures of spatial segregation', *Sociological Methodology*, 34(1), 121–162.

Reardon, S.F. and J.T. Yun (2001) 'Suburban racial change and suburban school segregation, 1987–95', *Sociology of Education*, 74(2): 79–101.

Reardon, S.F., J. Yun and T. Eitle (2000) 'The changing structure of school segregation: measurement and evidence of multiracial metropolitan-area school segregation, 1989–1995', *Demography*, 37(3): 351–364.

Reber, S.J. (2005) 'Court-ordered desegregation successes and failures integrating american schools since Brown versus Board of Education', *Journal of Human Resources*, 40(3): 559–590.

Reber, S.J. (2010) 'School desegregation and educational attainment for blacks', *Journal of Human Resources*, 45(4): 893–914.

Reber, S.J. (2011) 'From separate and unequal to integrated and equal? school desegregation and school finance in Louisiana', *Review of Economics and Statistics*, 93(2): 404–415.

Reskin, B.F. and D.D. Bielby (2005) 'A sociological perspective on gender and career outcomes', *Journal of Economic Perspectives*, 19(1): 71–86.

Rivkin, S.G. (1994) 'Residential segregation and school integration', *Sociology of Education*, 67(4): 279–292.

Rivkin, S.G. (2000) 'School desegregation, academic attainment, and earnings', *Journal of Human Resources*, 35(2): 333–346.

Rivkin, S.G. and F. Welch (2006) 'Has school desegregation improved academic and economic outcomes for blacks?', *Handbook of the Economics of Education*, 2: 1019–1049.

Rossell, C.H. (1995) 'Controlled-choice desegregation plans not enough choice, too much control?', *Urban Affairs Review*, 31(1): 43–76.

Rossell, C.H. and D.J. Armor (1996)): 'The effectiveness of school desegregation plans, 1968–1991', *American Politics Research*, 24(3): 267–302.

Salardi, P. (2012) 'The evolution of gender and racial occupational segregation across formal and non-formal labour markets in Brazil – 1987 to 2006', ECINEQ Working Paper 243.

Sastre, M. and A. Trannoy (2002) 'Shapley inequality decomposition by factor components: some methodological issues', in P. Moyes, C. Seidl and A.F. Shorrocks (eds), *Inequality: Theory, Measurement and Applications, Journal of Economics*, Supplement 9: 51–82.

Schellenberg, J. and J. Halteman (1976) 'Bussing and academic achievement: a two-year follow up', *Urban Education*, 10(4): 357–365.

Shorrocks, A.F. (2013) 'Decomposition procedures for distributional analysis: a unified framework based on the Shapley value', *Journal of Economic Inequality*, 11: 99–126.

Silber, J. (2012) 'Measuring segregation: basic concepts and extensions to other domains', in J. Bishop and R. Salas (eds), *Inequality, Mobility, and Segregation: Essays in Honor of Jacques Silber*, Vol. 20 of Research on Economic Inequality, Bingley: Emerald, pp. 1–35.

Telles, E.E. (1995) 'Structural sources of socioeconomic segregation in Brazilian metropolitan areas', *American Journal of Sociology*, 100(5): 1199–1223.

US Office for Civil Rights (2017) 'Guidance on the voluntary use of race to achieve diversity and avoid racial isolation in elementary and secondary schools', https://www2.ed.gov/about/offices/list/ocr/docs/guidance-ese-201111.pdf (accessed 11 January 2017).

Vincent, P., F. Chantreuil and B. Tarroux (2012) 'Appraising the breakdown of unequal individuals in large French cities', Université de Rennes 1 Working Paper 2012-20.

Watson, T. (2009) 'Inequality and the measurement of residential segregation by income in American neighborhoods', *Review of Income and Wealth*, 55(3): 820–844.

Weiler, J. (1998) 'Recent changes in school desegregation. ERIC/CUE Digest Number 133', Discussion paper, ERIC Clearinghouse on Urban Education, New York.

Weiner, D.A., B.F. Lutz and J. Ludwig (2009) 'The effects of school desegregation on crime', National Bureau of Economic Research Working Paper 15380.

Welch, F. and A. Light (1987) 'New evidence on school desegregation', Discussion Paper, US Commission of Civil Rights, Washington, DC.

Wheeler, C.H. (2006) 'Urban decentralization and income inequality: is sprawl associated with rising income segregation across neighborhoods?', Federal Reserve Bank of St-Louis, Research Division, Working Paper 2006-037B.

Wheeler, C.H. and E.A. La Jeunesse (2006) 'Neighborhood income inequality', Federal Reserve Bank of St-Louis, Research Division, Working Paper 2006-039B.

Wilson, F.D. (1985) 'The impact of school desegregation programs on white public-school enrollment, 1968–1976', *Sociology of Education*, 58(3): 137–153.

Zdep, S.M. (1971) 'Educating disadvantaged urban children in suburban schools: an evaluation', *Journal of Applied Social Psychology*, 1(2): 173–186.

23. Diversity and social fractionalization: theoretical approaches

*Mariateresa Ciommi, Ernesto Savaglio and
Stefano Vannucci*

23.1 INTRODUCTION

The use of indices of diversity or variation has a long-standing tradition in ecology and biology, and is arguably a hallmark of modern statistics. In the last decade, however, a more general assessment and measurement of diversity has attracted a growing interest from other disciplines including economics and other social sciences. The motivations of such a remarkably increased focus on diversity measurement come from a wide variety of concerns, including those for biodiversity and the effectiveness of conservation policies, and for several instances of socioeconomic diversity both agreeable (for example, diversity in juries and other representative bodies or 'undominated diversity' in the allocation of resources; Van Parijs, 1995) and detrimental (for example, severe inequalities of access to resources and opportunities).

Accordingly, the extant literature on diversity measurement also displays a considerable variety of aims and emphases.[1] Thus, while biodiversity is invariably treated, in all the discussions on environmental issues, as a valuable characteristic to be preserved or optimized, on the contrary socioeconomic diversities enjoy a much more mixed status. Biodiversity-oriented measures typically take into account the population size in order to address sustainability-related issues. Some measures of socioeconomic diversity are allowed to disregard the population size issue (see, e.g., Baumgärtner, 2007, which aptly emphasizes this point). Furthermore, and partly as a consequence of the large variety of contexts where diversity measurement issues arise, the formats of the relevant data structures are themselves considerably diverse.

This chapter consists of two main sections. Section 23.2 is devoted to the concept of diversity and its measurement. In particular, we elucidate some alternative classifications proposed in the extant literature, and we discuss the axiomatic approach to the analysis of diversity. Section 23.3 of the chapter is devoted to the analysis of diversity when the population is partitioned according to social attributes, namely the measurement of fractionalization. In particular, we review the most relevant indices used to account for fractionalization, highlighting the links with other disciplines. In fact, as stressed above, diversity attracts a variety of scholars: sociologists, biologists, ecologists, political scientists and economists, to name just a few. In addition, the extant literature accounts for several different approaches to the analysis of diversity. Consequently, alternative taxonomies have been proposed: Stirling (2007) suggests (see below) summarizing the concept of diversity with the concept of variety, balance and disparity, independently of the specific context in which the notion of diversity is applied; and Page (2011) defines diversity as diversity within a type or diversity of types, distinguishing among variation, entropy, distance, attributes and population measures (see section 23.2.1). Both these taxonomies meet the aims of biodiversity analysis. In fact, an ecosystem can be identified as the vector of species abundances. Hence, the classification species implies their partition into types: two species considered similar belong to the same type. Consequently, such a classification does not allow for possible differences of the levels of diversity. Gravel (2008) (see section 23.2.1) provides a classification of diversity measures in terms of cardinal (Weitzman, 1992; Bossert et al., 2003) or ordinal notions of dissimilarity (Pattanaik and Xu, 2000; Bervoets and Gravel, 2007), where the main difference between a cardinal and an ordinal (or qualitative) measure of dissimilarity is that the latter only enables the formulation of statements such as 'the object a is more dissimilar from b than the object c is from d', without any further quantification of such a dissimilarity. Basili and Vannucci (2013) (section 23.2.2) discuss the literature on diversity focusing on the structure of the type-space, including several alternative metric-like spaces. We further distinguish between theory-based and frequency-based measures of diversity (section 23.2.3).

Finally, if the analysis of diversity moves from the comparison of sets of objects/species to the comparison of populations which can be partitioned according to one or more social characteristics, such as language, religion or nationality, a new class of measures focusing on social fractionalization can be introduced (section 23.3).

23.2   MEASURING DIVERSITY

In the last decade, several scholars have classified diversity measures according to the specific context where they have been defined. The next paragraphs will be devoted to the analysis of these different classifications.

23.2.1   Classifications of Diversity Measures: Stirling (2007), Gravel (2008) and Page (2011)

A first interesting attempt to provide a unified classification of diversity measures is due to Stirling (2007), who claims that the notion of diversity in different contexts could be described by taking into account a combination of three basic properties – variety, balance and disparity – each of which tries to answer three distinct questions concerning a given (for example, biological) system: 'How many types of objects do we have in the system?', 'How much of each type of objects do we have in the system?' and 'How different from each other are the types of objects that we have in the system?'. Thus, variety refers to the number of types or classes into which the elements of a system could be partitioned. That definition was developed in a biological context, but could be applied and adapted to other fields: in ecology, for instance, scholars are interested in computing the number of species in a system (species-number indices; McIntosh, 1967) while in economics, they may be interested in enumerating the firms in a region or the products of a firm. The diversity computed by indices based on the variety increases as long as the variety increases (notwithstanding the rest). Balance is the analogous of what statisticians call variance (see Pielou, 1977), also called evenness by ecologists and concentration by economists. Stirling (2007, p. 709) refers to it as a 'function of the pattern of apportionment of elements across categories'. Formally, it can be represented by a set of (positive) fractions summing up to 1. Indices capturing such information are Gini (1912), Simpson (1949) and Shannon and Weaver (1962). The more even the balance, the greater is diversity, *ceteris paribus*. Finally, disparity concerns the level of possible distinction among objects. Formally, it can be set up using distance measures, and diversity increases if the elements of the system become more disperse, *ceteris paribus*.

Beside Stirling's (2007) classification, Gravel (2008) proposed an alternative classification that distinguishes three different approaches to the study of diversity. The first, developed by biologists, is based on the generalized entropy. The second, called aggregate dissimilarity approach, distinguishes between the aggregate cardinal dissimilarity suggested by Weitzman (1992), Bossert et al. (2003) and Van Hees (2004), and the aggregate ordinal dissimilarity (see Pattanaik and Xu, 2000; Bervoets and Gravel, 2007). Finally, the third approach is based on the valuation of realized attributes (Nehring and Puppe, 2002, 2003). That is, when a categorization of objects according to their attributes is provided, the diversity of a set of objects is computed as the sum of the attributes possessed by its elements.

However, the current literature accounts for additional attempts to classify the different notions and measures of diversity. Indeed, more recently, Page (2011) distinguished among diversity within types, diversity across types and diversity across populations of types. Diversity within type is what biologists call variation; whereas diversity across types is what commonly people call diversity. In particular, diversity across type refers to differences in kinds; for instance, the different available types of dishes on a menu. Conversely, diversity within type refers to the differences in the amount of some attributes; for instance, the prices of dishes on the menu. Page regards variance and coefficient of variation of a random variable as the typical measure of diversity within types. Furthermore, he distinguishes three main classes of diversity across types: (generalized) entropy measures, attribute diversity measure and distance-based measures. In particular, entropy measures take into account both the number of types and the evenness of the distributions across those types.[2] Formally, entropy measures model several indices simply changing a single parameter, which is the power to which the probabilities of different types are raised. This means that such a coefficient may be interpreted as a propensity to have a more spread-out distribution. The major weakness of the entropy measures is their difficulty in capturing the inner type differences.[3] Although Page's (2011) classification is sensible and helpful, it relies on a very informal notion of what a type is.

23.2.2 An Alternative Type-Metric Classification

An alternative classification of diversity measures is obtained by focusing on the structure of the type space of the relevant population. Indeed, the type spaces encountered in the extant literature on diversity assessment include premetric,[4] semimetric[5] and metric[6] spaces (see, e.g., Weitzman, 1992; Pattanaik and Xu, 2008; Bossert et al., 2001; Pattanaik and Xu, 2000; Van Hees, 2004), relational systems consisting of preference profiles as supplemented with a binary similarity relation (Peragine and Romero-Medina, 2006) or with a quaternary dissimilarity relation representing a total preorder of binary dissimilarities (Bervoets and Gravel, 2007), (subspaces of) suitably preordered mixture spaces (Nehring and Puppe, 2002, 2003), partially ordered sets or posets (Basili and Vannucci, 2013).

Weitzman (1992) introduces a pure diversity function that relies on a dissimilarity metric, and is uniquely defined up to an additive constant of integration: the larger the pairwise dissimilarities between elements of a subpopulation, the larger the diversity of the subpopulation. If the dissimilarity metric is in fact an ultrametric[7] then the diversity value of a subset is the length of the associated tree. If not, the diversity value provides a numerical assessment of 'the tightest or most parsimonious feasible reconstruction, in the sense of being the minimal number of character-state changes required to account for diversity of a set' (Weitzman, 1992, p. 378).

A characterization of the ranking induced by Weitzman's diversity function is provided by Bossert et al. (2001) within a dissimilarity semimetric space (X, d): they first characterize the class of rankings consistent with a certain lexicographic distance induced by d, and then show that the Weitzman's diversity ranking is precisely the only ranking of that class which satisfies two restricted monotonicity and independence conditions, plus a related indifference for link elements property requiring that certain elements do not contribute to the diversity rank of certain subsets. Thus, the Weitzman ranking is essentially the lexicographic distance-based total preorder, which is singled out by the requirement that the aggregation of the distances involved be additive (see Bossert et al., 2001).

The instrumental role of diversity assessments in the evaluation of subsets in terms of freedom of choice is another major source of the growing concern for diversity rankings (see Barberà et al., 2004, for an extensive survey of the literature on rankings of opportunity sets, including freedom-of-choice rankings). Pattanaik and Xu (2000) is an early contribution to the literature on diversity that is mainly motivated by the concern for such freedom-rankings of opportunity sets. That work relies on a simple – that is, two-valued – dissimilarity semimetric, which induces in an obvious way a binary similarity relation on the set of options. Then, Pattanaik and Xu provide a characterization of the total preorder that ranks opportunity sets according to the sizes of their smallest – that is, coarsest – similarity-based partitions. In a subsequent work of theirs, the same authors consider a weaker (finite) dissimilarity space (namely a symmetric premetric space, where the identity of indiscernibles principle may not hold), and offer a characterization of the partial preorder of subsets dictated by a dominance ranking induced by the underlying premetric (see Pattanaik and Xu, 2008).

Working in the same vein, but within a much richer environment which combines a binary similarity relation with a variable profile of preferences chosen from a given reference set of total preorders on the basic set, Peragine and Romero-Medina (2006) characterize two distinct total preorders which rank subsets according to the number of dissimilar unilateral optima (of unilateral dissimilar optima, respectively) they include. Van Hees (2004) also starts from a dissimilarity metric space of options, and considers several extended point-to-set distances relying on that dissimilarity metric. He shows that several combinations of distance-respecting independence properties for diversity rankings are inconsistent with the requirement of equi-diversity for singletons when the underlying dissimilarity space of options includes linear sequences of three or four options such that: (1) adjacent options are at equal distances; and (2) the distance between the extremal options is given by the sum of intermediate distances (see Van Hees, 2004).

Bossert et al. (2003) discuss the axiomatic foundations of several (pre)metric-oriented diversity rankings proposed in the extant literature from a quite general perspective, distinguishing between ordinal and ratio-scale (pre)metrics. By definition, the former – as opposed to the latter – do not attach any significant role to comparisons concerning differences between distances. For instance, the Pattanaik–Xu similarity-based ranking and the premetric-based dominance ranking mentioned above all rely on ordinal (pre)metrics, while Weitzman's diversity ranking and some of the diversity rankings considered by Van Hees (2004) rely on a ratio-scale metric.

Bervoets and Gravel (2007) model diversity by means of a quaternary dissimilarity relation on the given population, or equivalently a total preorder of dissimilarities between pairs of population units, and provide a characterization of the maxi-max diversity ranking of subpopulations, namely the ranking induced by maximizing maximum dissimilarity.

Some papers by Nehring and Puppe (2002, 2003) contribute a quite different (pre) metric-free approach to diversity measurement. Indeed, Nehring and Puppe (2002) introduce a binary multi-attribute representation of subsets. Next, starting from a submodular non-negative diversity function they show via conjugate Möbius inversion[8] that choosing that function amounts to selecting the set of relevant binary attributes and their (positive) weights. Moreover, they show that if: (1) the option set is suitably embedded in a mixture space of lotteries over opportunity sets; and (2) such a mixture space is endowed with a total preorder (to be interpreted as preference for diversity) obeying the standard set of von Neumann–Morgenstern axioms as supplemented with a mild positivity requirement, then the foregoing diversity function may be regarded as an expected diversity function representing those preferences (see Nehring and Puppe, 2002). Finally, Nehring and Puppe focus on the problem of establishing some conditions on the structure of relevant binary attributes, ensuring that such a diversity function only depends on binary dissimilarity information, with special emphasis on the case of monotonic dependence (see Nehring and Puppe, 2002, 2003).

Most of the data structures considered above include an implicit or explicit order-theoretic (sub)structure, namely a partially ordered set or poset. And, in fact, posets display a somewhat unique combination of extreme informational parsimony and ubiquity (see Basili and Vannucci, 2013 for a few characteristic examples including the general case of dominance ordered multi-attribute spaces with ordinal criteria and evolutionary trees). Indeed, Basili and Vannucci (2013) focus on the assessment of (a prominent sort of) diversity when the relevant type space of population units is just a finite poset. They follow the widely held notion that diversity should somehow depend on the assessment of dissimilarity between each pair of units. However, they take incomparability to be the 'intrinsic' dissimilarity relation of the given type-poset. Next, they compare the diversity of subpopulations via maximum dissimilarity, choosing to assess the latter by the size of the largest totally dissimilar subset(s) – or largest antichain – included in any given subpopulation. As a result, Basili and Vannucci (2013) suggest width-based rankings for the assessment of diversity among populations when the type space is a finite poset.

An earlier use of the undominated width-ranking in the specialized case of multi-preferential setting (but with no explicit reference to diversity assessment) was first introduced and characterized in Pattanaik and Xu (1998). Moreover, the criterion of 'undominated diversity' for allocations (see Van Parijs, 1995) amounts to selecting allocations of endowments whose individual components form an anti-chain with respect to the unanimity partial (pre)order and are therefore of maximum width for the relevant population of agents.

23.2.3 Theory-Based and Frequency-Based Measures of Diversity

In the economic literature, the use of theory-based and frequency-based measures of diversity is particularly relevant in order to distinguish two different but not mutually inconsistent approaches. At the most abstract level, all the problems of diversity appraisal could be represented by a simple formal structure. A set of objects (such as, for example, options to freely choose, living species, media opinions, and so on) is given and its subsets are to be compared in terms of diversity. The evaluation process, which depends on the information available on those objects, may or may not rely on some explicit theory about what is diversity. If a classification of objects by types is available, then frequency-based measures can be introduced. Indeed, most diversity indicators use information on the relative frequency of those objects. However, if objects are types, one has to rely on a diversity relation, possibly induced by a metric-like structure. This is the typical concern of what we denote as theory-based measures of diversity. They are well represented by the two seminal contributions of Weitzman (1992) and Nehring and Puppe (2003).

Weitzman (1992) suggests that diversity measurement should rely on a cardinal-based dissimilarity metric $d:X \times X \rightarrow R_+$ where X is a non-empty universal set of objects (for example, biological species, types or options of a menu): d evaluates the dissimilarity between two objects $x,y \in X$. The dissimilarity function has value zero if $x = y$ and the distance between an alternative and a set A is assumed to be the $min[d(x,y)]$ for any $y \in A\backslash\{x\}$ if $\{x\} \neq A$. Weitzman (1992) defines a recursive function $V:P \rightarrow R_+$, based upon d, where P is the set of all possible subsets of X, as follows: $V(A) = max_{a_i \in A}\{(V(A - \{a_i\}) - d(a_i,A)\}$ for all $A \in X$ with $V(A) = 0$ if A is a singleton. $V(\cdot)$ assigns a value to each set and induces an ordering on the sets of P such that we interpret the statement $A \geqslant B$ as the diversity offered by the set A is at least as great as the diversity offered by the set B if and only if $V(A) \geq V(B)$.

Bossert et al. (2001) provide an axiomatic characterization of Weitzman's diversity ordering that relies on the following properties:

Simple Monotonicity. For all $x,y,z,w \in X$:

$$\{x,y\} \geqslant \{z,w\} \text{ if and only if } d(x,y) \geq d(z,w)$$

that links together the dissimilarity between pairs of options and their relative ranking.

Independence. For all $A,B \in P$, *for all* $x \in X\backslash A$, *for all* $y \in X\backslash B$ if the dissimilarity between x (resp. y) and each element of A (resp. B) is less than the dissimilarity among the elements of A (resp. B), then:

$$A \geqslant B \text{ if and only if } A \cup \{x\} \geqslant B \cup \{y\}.$$

That requires that addition of options to a set, which are less dissimilar than the elements of the set itself, be irrelevant for their relative ranking.

If the dissimilarity between a species c and other two $\{a,b\}$ is no greater than the dissimilarity between a and b, and if the dissimilarity between x and y is the sum of the dissimilarity between a and b and the dissimilarity between c and $\{a,b\}$, then c is the so-called link-species, namely:

Link Indifference. For all $x,y,a,b \in X$ with $x \neq y$ and a,b,c being pairwise distinct, if $\{x,y\} > \{a,b\}$ and c is a link element of $\{a,b\}$ relative to $\{x,y\}$, then:

$$\{x,y\} \sim \{a,b,c\}.$$

Thus, working within a dissimilarity semimetric space (X,d), Bossert et al. (2001): first characterize the class of rankings consistent with a certain lexicographic distance induced by d, and then show that Weitzman's diversity ranking is precisely the only ranking of that class which satisfies two d-restricted monotonicity and independence conditions, plus Link Indifference. Thus, the Weitzman ranking is essentially the lexicographic-distance-based total preorder, which is singled out by the requirement that the aggregation of the distances involved, be additive (see Bossert et al., 2001).

Additivity is also the basis of the multi-attribute approach developed by Nehring and Puppe (2002, 2003). They denote by $\geqslant \subseteq X \times C$ a relation describing the characteristics of each species, that is, $(x,c) \in \geqslant$ if the species $x \in X$ has characteristic $c \in C$, with C the set of all characteristics that could eventually be considered relevant in a biological environment. If we define with $\omega_c \geq 0$ the weight of the c characteristic, then the diversity value of a set S of species is:

$$v(S) = \sum_{c \in C:(x,c) \in \geqslant \text{ for some } x \in S} \omega_c$$

In words, the total weight of all different characteristics of some species in S determines the diversity value of a set of species. Further, the value of the contribution of each species to diversity is due to all those characteristics that are typical of such species and which are not held by another one. It is worth noticing that the diversity function $v(S)$ satisfies the mildest and more suitable condition in the theory of ranking sets of objects (see Barberà et al., 2003), that is, (anti-)monotonicity with respect to set-inclusion. It says that the diversity added by a species to any biological environment cannot increase as we consider more comprehensive environment: for all X, Y and x, if $X \subseteq Y$ then $v(X \cup \{x\} - v(X)) \geq v(Y \cup \{x\} - v(Y))$.

23.2.4   Frequency-Based Measures of Diversity: An Axiomatic Approach

Let $X = (x_1, \ldots, x_N)$ be the distribution vector of a population of size $N \in \mathbb{N}$. We denote by $i \in (1,2,\ldots,k)$ the types in the population. Here, type means the different realizations of a single attribute that characterizes a given society. Roughly speaking, an individual characteristic is a variable that we want to analyse such as, for example, language, nationality or ethnicity. Hence, if we consider language, the types consist of the languages taken into consideration.

In what follows, we focus on the unidimensional measurement of diversity, that is, we fix an attribute and we partition the society accordingly. As a consequence, let $n = (n_1, \ldots, n_N)$ be the vector of the corresponding population, that is, n_i be the number of elements (individuals, plants or objects) that share the same i-th type, such that

$\sum_{i=1}^{k} n_i = N$ and $P = (p_1, \ldots, p_k)$ be the vector of corresponding population share, where $p_i = \frac{n_i}{N}$ represents the proportion of the i-th type in the population, with $\sum_{i=1}^{k} p_i = 1$. Thus, a diversity index D is a real valued function $D: \cup_{N \geq 2} \mathbb{R}_N^+ \to \mathbb{R}$ where $\cup_{N \geq 2} \mathbb{R}_N^+$ denotes the set of all finite N dimensional distributions. $D(X)$ and $D(P)$ represent the value of the diversity index computed taking into account the original distribution or the proportions respectively.

As for the poverty measurement (Foster, 2006) or the inequality measurement (Cowell, 2000), a diversity measure $D(\cdot)$ should satisfy:

Positivity [POS]: $D(P) \geq 0$.

Maximal diversity [MAXD]: *Let* p_i $i \in \{1, \ldots, k\}$ *denote the proportion of individuals having the i-th attribute. Then $D(P)$ assumes the maximum value if for all i, $p_i = \frac{1}{n}$.*

The Positivity axiom requires that at least the value of the diversity index should not be negative. Maximal diversity occurs when each type is represented equally, that is, a diversity index takes its maximum value when types are in equal proportions. A second set of axioms requires that a diversity index ignores certain aspects of the distribution, namely:

Normalization of proportions [NORP]: $D(P) = 0$ *if* $p_i = 1$ and $p_j = 0$ for all $j \in \{1, \ldots, k\}$ $\setminus \{i\}$.

Normalization of the distributions [NORD]: $D(P) = 0$ *if* $x_i = x$ for all $i \in \{1, \ldots, n\}$ and $x_j = 0$ for all $j \in \{1, \ldots, k\} \setminus \{i\}$.

Normalization of proportions and Normalization of the distribution axioms assert that if in a population all the individuals belong to the same group, then there is no diversity. Both axioms state that a diversity index takes the value zero if aggregate disparity is 0, namely when all the elements are effectively identical. In these situations, the population is said to be perfectly homogeneous.

Symmetry (Anonymity) [SYM]: *Let* $X = (x_1, \ldots, x_n)$ *and* $Y = (x_{\sigma(1)}, \ldots, x_{\sigma(n)})$ *be two populations, where* $\sigma: \mathbb{R} \to \mathbb{R}$ *is a permutation function, then* $D(X) = D(Y)$.

Replication invariance [REIN]: *If* $X = (X, \ldots, X)$ *is obtained from* $X = (x_1, \ldots, x_n)$ *by a m-replication of X, then* $D(X) = D(Y)$.

Scale invariance (0-Homogeneity) [SLIN]: *Let* $X = (x_1, \ldots, x_n)$ *and* $Y = (tx_1, \ldots, tx_n)$ *be two populations, where* $t \in \mathbb{R}$ *is a factor scale, then* $D(X) = D(Y)$.

Symmetry means that a reordering of individuals leaves the diversity value unchanged. This axiom is called 'symmetry between species' by Gravel (2008) and it ensures that the only thing that is relevant in the evaluation of diversity is the abundance of each species in the population. Bossert et al. (2011) refer to it as Anonymity, since it requires that individuals be treated impartially.

Replication invariance allows comparability across populations of different sizes.

It asserts that when one distribution is an m-fold replication of another, then the two distributions are distributionally equivalent. Roughly speaking, the population size does not matter, and all that matters is the proportion of individuals in the population who are sharing different attributes. This is a standard requirement when populations of different size are compared. Homogeneity of degree zero refers to the fact that population size is not important to compute diversity. Scale invariance axioms have been investigated in-depth by Gravel (2008). He suggests that those axioms are controversial in the diversity appraisal since they imply equal diversity of $S_1 = (10,10)$ and $S_2 = (10^6, 10^6)$.

On the contrary, an index can be sensitive to the population size by imposing the scaling up of a society by some factor, namely:

1-Homogeneity [1HOM]: *Let $X = (x_1, \ldots, x_n)$ and $Y = (tx_1, \ldots, tx_n)$ be two populations, where $t \in \mathbb{R}$ is a factor scale, then $D(Y) = tD(X)$.*

The following axiom could be interpreted as the counterpart of the Transfer Principle defined in the poverty measurement theory. It suggests how diversity changes in the case of redistribution:

Redistribution on proportions [REP]: *For all distributions $P = (p_1, p_2, \ldots, p_k)$ and for a fixed $k > 1$, $D(P)$ must decrease (or, at least, not increase) when some larger proportions are redistributed in order to approach the equalizing vector $(\underbrace{\frac{1}{k}, \frac{1}{k}, \ldots, \frac{1}{k}}_{k-\text{times}})$*

Thus, it states that if we redistribute some large proportion such that, after the distribution process, groups showing smaller proportions now are more equal distributed, then the diversity index should at least not increase.

Monotonicity (on the number of types) [MONC]: *Given two distributions $P = (p_1, p_2, \ldots, p_k)$ and $P' = (p_1, p_2, \ldots, p_{k'})$ such that each type is represented equally, then $D(P) \geq D(P')$ if $k \geq k'$.*

Monotonicity ensures that when types are equally distributed, then the number of types matters. In particular, diversity depends monotonically on the number of species: when this number varies among populations or over time, the larger the number of types or species, the higher the diversity of the population, other things being equal. Solow and Polasky (1994) propose a similar version of this axiom, calling it Monotonicity of variety. They assert that, if the elements are evenly balanced and equally disperse, then the diversity value should increase monotonically. Weitzman (1992, p. 376) considers this axiom as 'a basic axiom that is reasonable to impose on any diversity function' and he refers to it as monotonicity in species. Following Weitzman, it is also possible to interpret this axiom as follows: the extinction of any species in a system produces a reduction in the value of diversity. Monotonicity on the number of types is a very general requirement. It is the counterpart of the monotonicity axiom proposed by Sen (1976) in poverty measurement theory. A further quite natural requirement is the following:

Continuity axiom [CON]: *$D(X)$ is continuous on its domain.*

Clearly, continuity ensures that there are no jumps in the value of the diversity index, that is, that the diversity index varies continuously with the distribution.

There are properties establishing a connection between the overall diversity measure and the diversity in population subgroups, that is a quite helpful requirement if one takes for granted that total diversity should be equal to the sum of the within and between components of a system, formally:

Additive decomposable axiom [ADDE]: Let $X = (x_1,...,x_N)$ be a population partitioned into K subgroups each containing B types, such that $N=KB$. Denoting by q_j the probability of the j attributes and p_{jl} the probability of each type, where l the type within the j attribute. Then the following identity for $D(P) = D(p_{11}, p_{12},..., p_{1B},..., p_{KB})$ holds:

$$D(P) = D_K(q_1,...,q_K) + \sum_{j=1}^{K} q_j D_B \left(\frac{p_{j1}}{q_j}, \frac{p_{j2}}{q_j},..., \frac{p_{jB}}{q_j} \right)$$

where D_K and D_B are respectively the within and between component.

Alternatively, it is possible to aggregate individuals in a recursive way. The following axiom, prosed by Ciommi and Lasso de la Vega (2014), suggests that a diversity index for a society in which a new individual is added should be composed of two components, namely the diversity of the original population and the diversity of all the individuals with respect to the new one. Formally:

Aggregativity axiom [AGG]: For every $N \geq 2$ there exist strictly positive weighting functions $\alpha(N,1)$ and $\beta(N,1)$ such that, for a given individual $l \notin \{1,...,N\}$ $D(X \cup l) = \alpha(N,1)D(X) + \beta(N,1) \sum_{1 \leq i \leq N} d(x_i, 1)$ where $d(x_i, 1)$ is the distance between individuals i and l.

This axiom is the counterpart of the Ebert (2010) axiom in inequality measurement.

Finally, there are properties that force the index to have a particular functional form:

Link axiom [LIN]: Given a distribution X with $k \geq 2$ species, there exists at least one species j, the so-called link species, that satisfies $D(X)=d(j, X\backslash\{j\})+D(X\backslash\{i\})$ where, in general, $d(l,Z)$ denotes the minimum distance from individual j and a member of population Z.

As pointed out by Weitzman, this axiom provides a natural connection between the value of the diversity index for any society and the primary notion of distance. In addition, it forces an additive functional form of the diversity index and, using recursive techniques, it enables diversity computation when new individuals are added.[9]

An additional requirement for a diversity index, concerning the way to add irrelevant attributes, has also been considered in the extant literature. Let us introduce the following example to clarify the idea. Suppose that we are measuring diversity of language and there exist individuals speaking some language that are not already present in the population under analysis. Let us suppose that these individuals are of the same type as other individuals belonging to the population. Then, if these individuals are added in the population, the diversity should not change. Formally, following Weitzman (1992) we have:

Twin property [TW]: *Suppose that for a given distribution X there exists some types $l \notin \{1,...,k\}$ identical to some types $j \in \{1,..., k\}$, such that $d(j,l) = 0$ and $d(j,i) = d(k,i)$ for all $j \in \{1,...,k\}$ then $D(X) = D(X \cup \{i\})$.*

That property is quite important since it suggests how to add or subtract types. It is a sort of continuity of diversity in species, since if we add a species that is very closely related to an existing one, then the index should be affected only by 'a very small amount that goes to zero in the limit as the added species becomes an identical twin with an existing species' (Weitzman, 1992, p. 391).

Examples of diversity indices
In what follows, we list some of the most widely used frequency-based diversity measures. Let K be the total number of types in a society and p_i the proportion of individuals belonging to the i-th type, we have the following.

Berger-Parker index (1970): $D(P) = \max_i p_i$. It is defined as the proportional abundance of the most abundant species. The major limitation of this index is that, by definition, it uses only partial information about the relative abundance of the various species. The lower the value of $D(P)$, the more diverse the sample (or, similarly, the less dominant[10] any one of the types represented in the population). For this reason, the reciprocal of the index $1/D(P)$. is often used so that an increase in the value of the index stands for an increase in the diversity (and a reduction in dominance). If we need an index whose range is in the interval $[0,1)$, the complement to one of the Berger–Parker index is computed. In addition, one of the main advantage of the last formulation is that it satisfies *POS, MAXD, NORP, NORD, SYM, REIN* and *SLIN*.

Simpson diversity index (1949): $D(P) = 1 - \Sigma_{i=1}^{k} p_i^2$. The Simpson index, proposed by Simpson (1949), considers the number of species of a given habitat and their relative abundance. It represents the probability that two randomly selected individuals (in a habit) belong to the same species. Formally $S_S = \Sigma_{i=1}^{k} p_i^2$ with range in $[0,1]$ with value (close to) 0 if the system is more diverse and (close to) 1 when the system is homogeneous (only one species). The Simpson index is a suitable diversity measure and is used in several different contexts. Indeed, it is applied for instance to the analysis of the effect of religious diversity on economic development (see Montalvo and Reynal-Querol, 2002, below) or as a measure of the relative size of the firms with respect to the industry, namely the Herfindahl–Hirschmann index (HHI).[11] Finally, ecologists use the complement of the Simpson index as a measure of diversity (Simpson, 1949), while biologists use its inverse (Lande, 1996).

The Simpson diversity index satisfies *POS, MAXD, NORP, SYM, REIN, SLIN, REP, MONC, CON* and *ADDE*.

Gini index of diversity: $D(P) = \sum_{i=1}^{k} p_i^2$ This index is defined as the complement to one of the Simpson diversity index; consequently, it represents the probability that two randomly selected individuals in the habitat belong to the same species.

Shannon (1948) diversity index (first-order diversity): $D(P) = -c\sum_{i=1}^{k} p_i \ln p_i$ It was first formulated as a measure accounting for entropy. The Shannon diversity index is also based on relative abundance like the Simpson diversity index. It gives a measure of both type-size numbers and their evenness. It means that if we transform into binary code words each types in our ecosystem, such that short code words represent the most abundant types, and suppose we walk around our ecosystem and name all the types we see, then if we have used an efficient code to denote the population units we will be able to save energy in naming the most abundant types. If so, the average code word length we call out as we wander around will be close to the Shannon diversity index. The Shannon diversity index satisfies *POS, MAXD, SYM, REIN, SLIN, MONC, CON* and *ADDE*.

All in all, we can distinguish between frequency-based measures of diversity that have an additive structure and those constructed by choosing different values of a parameter that defines the so-called generalized alpha-order means.[12] Some of the most applied diversity indices can be derived using both methods as shown in Table 23.1.[13]

Table 23.1   Diversity indices

Name of the index	$D(P)$	$\left(\sum_{i=1}^{k} p_i^{\alpha}\right)^{\frac{1}{1-\alpha}}$ where $\alpha \in \mathbb{R}$	$\sum_{i=1}^{k} \phi(p_i)$ where $\phi:[0,1] \to \widetilde{\mathbb{R}}$ is a concave function
Number of types	k	$\alpha = 0$	$\phi(p_i) = 1$
Diversity index	$\left(\sum_{i=1}^{k} p_i^2\right)^{-1}$	$\alpha = 2$	
Simpson index	$\sum_{i=1}^{k} p_i^2 = G = 1 - S$ where G is the Gini index and S the Simpson diversity index		$\phi(p_i) = p_i^2$
Inverted Berger–Parker Dominance index	$\dfrac{1}{p^*}$ $p^* = \max_i p_k$	$\alpha \to \infty$	
Shannon entropy index	$-c\sum_{i=1}^{k} p_i \ln p_i$ with $0 \ln 0 = 0$	$\alpha \to 1$	$\phi(p_i) = -p_i \ln p_i$

23.3 MEASURING SOCIAL FRACTIONALIZATION

As stressed by Luce et al. (1990, p. 323), 'when measurement is more problematic . . . we are strongly tempted to imitate the methods of the sciences allied to physics by finding new applications of these same physical measures'. That approach was followed in social fractionalization measurement, which started as an index-focused endeavour. In particular, the well-known Simpson (1949) diversity index used by biologists and ecologists to quantify the biodiversity of a habitat, has been widely adopted as the leading measure.

Indeed, the ethnic fragmentation or ethno-linguistic fractionalization index (ELF) for a country is defined as the probability that two individuals, randomly selected from the overall population belong to different ethnic groups. It is computed through three steps. First, the overall population is partitioned into k ethnic groups. Then, for every group, the population share (p_i) is computed. Finally, all the shares are raised to the second power, added and the obtained value subtracted to 1, namely:

$$ELF = 1 - \sum_{i=1}^{k} p_i^2 \qquad (23.1)$$

ELF is computed for social as well as physical attributes such as language, religion, ethnicity, and so on; that is the reason why scholars are used to refer to it as the linguistic fractionalization index, religious fractionalization index or ethnic fractionalization index. Easterly and Levine (1997) interpreted equation (23.1) as the probability that two randomly selected individuals belong to the same ethnic group. Moreover, as pointed out by Bossert et al. (2011), ELF is a decreasing transformation of the Herfindahl–Hirschman index (Herfindahl, 1945; Hirschman, 1950) as applied to population shares instead of market shares.

Fearon (2003) gives a very intuitive idea of how ELF works, computing ELF for eight theoretical countries. For a perfectly homogeneous society, $ELF = 0$, (minimum value of the index). A society with n equally distributed groups shows the highest level of fractionalization, that is, $ELF = 1-(1/n)$.

However, according to Posner (2004), the ELF index has three types of drawbacks, namely specific problems, general problems and problems of applications. The specific problems concern the ambiguity of ethnographic data used in order to compute the index.[14] The general problems refer to the unreliability of the use of single statistics to summarize the complex scenario of a country. The problems of application arise from the use of the measure. Posner (2004) observes that in most of the studies aiming at linking ethnic diversity with low rates of growth, there exists a mismatch between the causal mechanism and the measure of diversity that is used to test that mechanism.

As observed by Montalvo and Reynal-Querol (2005), despite such weaknesses, there are at least two main reasons that support the use of a fractionalization index. Firstly, in the industrial organization literature, economists usually exploit the Herfindahl–Hirschman index that summarizes the relationship between market structure and profitability. In this context, it is possible to derive the index using a non-cooperative game in which oligopolistic firms decide to play Cournot strategies. The second theoretical foundation arises from inequality measurement theory. In fact, it is easy to show that one of the most important inequality indices, namely the Gini index, reduces to the ELF when using a discrete dichotomic metric instead of the Euclidean distance:

$$Gini = \sum_{i=1}^{k} \sum_{j \neq i} p_i p_j = \sum_{i=1}^{k} p_i \sum_{j \neq i} P_j = \sum_{i=1}^{k} p_i(1 - p_i) = ELF$$

In order to overcome the criticisms of ELF summarized by Posner (2004), other indices have been proposed in the economics and other disciplines. Berger and Parker (1970) consider only one charac$(0,1]$teristic at a time (for instance, language, religion, culture, ethnicity) and observe the higher fraction of people it belongs to. Therefore, their index, called the Berger–Parker index of dominance (hereafter, BP), is simply the proportion of the most abundant types in the population. Formally, $BP = \frac{s}{N}$, where s and N. denote the size of the largest group in the population and the total number of living beings in the population units, respectively. In words, s expresses the proportional importance of the most abundant types and BP ranges in, assuming the maximum value for the case of a unique species. The BP index, which is very intuitive and easy to calculate, could have a bias for those countries with a large variety of different outcomes for the same attributes (for example, some African countries).

23.3.1   The Greenberg Indices of Diversity

Analysing the map of the linguistic distributions, Greenberg (1956, p. 109) has proposed a measure that distinguishes regions of the world with a great linguistic diversity from those with relative uniformity, 'in order to render such impressions more objective, allow the comparing of disparate geographical areas, and eventually to correlate varying degrees of linguistic diversity with . . . non-linguistic factors'.

He called this measure the 'monolingual non-weighted method' (hereafter, A) and this index is what economists refer to as Herfindahl index or fractionalization index, since formally it coincides with the ELF formulation. In fact, for a given area and two individuals randomly selected in a population, A represents the probability that the two individuals do not speak the same language, and p_i denotes the share of individuals speaking a given language: $A = 1 - \sum_{i=1}^{k} p_i^2 = ELF$.

Primarily based on the consideration that the degree of resemblance among languages have to play a role in measuring linguistic diversity, Greenberg proposed to modify A, by defining the monolingual weighted method (hereafter, B). The word 'monolingual' stresses the idea that in both formulations each individual is counted as speaking a single language. The idea behind B is the following: assuming the same proportional distribution among the languages, a given area registers more diversity than a second one, if the former exhibits a greater number of less-related languages or languages that are not closely related descendants of the same original language than the second one.

Formally, we denote (following Greenberg's notation) with M and N a pair of languages and m and n the proportions of population units speaking M and N, respectively. According to Greenberg, for each pair of languages, the product mn represents the probability of randomly selecting successively a person speaking language M and a second one speaking N. Then, let r_{mn} be a real number (in the range $(0,1)$), called resemblance factor, obtained using an arbitrary but fixed basic vocabulary and representing the proportion of resemblances between each pair of languages.[15] Finally, as for the usual fractionalization index, let us to compute the sum of the weighted products and subtract it from 1, that is: $B = 1 - \sum_{mn} (mn) r_{mn}$

Therefore, A can be viewed as a particular case of B, supposing that r_{mn} assumes only dichotomous values, that is $r_{mn} = 1$ if $m = m$ and $r_{mn} = 0$ if $m \neq m$. In addition, B is always smaller than or equal to A, and the two indices coincide if the resemblance among all pairs of languages is zero.

Beside A and B, Greenberg (1956) proposed six additional linguistic diversity indices in the case of polylingualism. The idea is to allow multiple counting, roughly speaking: an individual speaking l distinct languages is counted as l distinct people. Among these indices, the so-called Index of Communication (hereafter, H) has received some attention. H defines the probability that two randomly selected members of the population have at least one language in common. The index is obtained by first partitioning the population into proportions of people speaking any one language only, or any particular combination of languages. Then, the products of each pair of such proportions is computed, and each of these products is then divided into as many parts as the product of the number of languages in each group. Finally, each of these values is multiplied by 1 if the pairs are identical and by 0 if diverse.

The literature counts only few attempts at the use of the Greenberg's indices. For instance, Lieberson (1964) elaborates a modification of Greenberg's H index, trying to compute the probability that an individual in a country will be able to communicate with an individual living in another country. More recently, Laitin (2000) discussed the potential utility of the B index, analysing six post-Soviet countries. Similarly, Fearon (2003) proposed to measure diversity in a population taking into account language instead of ethnicity, following Greenberg's A index. Finally, Bossert et al. (2011) show that B can be derived as a special case of the generalized fractionalization index they proposed.[16]

23.3.2   The Montalvo and Reynal–Querol Index

Let us suppose to compute the ELF for two societies, the first one composed by ten equally sized groups and the second one containing only two equally sized groups. The value of the index results to be greater in the former; consequently the first population is more fractionalized. However, it seems quite intuitive that the second society may be more unstable than the first one.[17] Based on this observation, Montalvo and Reynal-Querol (2002) introduced a polarization index (hereafter, MR), where p_i denotes the share of group i in the population and k is the total number of groups in which a population is partitioned: $MR = 1 - \sum_{i=1}^{k} (\frac{0.5 - p_i}{0.5})^2 p_i$.

The index here captures the distance of any distribution from the situation that leads to the maximum conflict. In other words, as shown in Montalvo and Reynal-Querol (2005), the original purpose of the polarization index is to capture how far the distribution of the ethnic group is from the $(0.5, 0, \ldots, 0, 0.5)$ distribution, which represents the maximum level of polarization.

MR is maximal for two equally sized groups and decreases as the society diverges from an equally split one. The authors show that the correlation between MR and ELF is negative for high levels of ELF, highly positive for low levels. On the other hand, MR and ELF

are uncorrelated for intermediate levels. In addition, their cross-country regression analysis shows that ethnic polarization has a positive impact on the likelihood of the occurrence of a civil war and a negative effect on the growth rate of a country.

More on the relationship between fractionalization and polarization

In the special case of two population groups, the *ELF* and *MR* indices coincide up to a scale factor. In fact, using the so-called 'rule of completing the square' and the fact that $p_1 + p_2 = 1$, *ELF* can be written as:

$$ELF = 1 - (p_1^2 + p_2^2) = 1 - [(p_1 + p_2)^2 - 2p_1p_2] = 2p_1p_2.$$

On the other hand, *MR* takes the following form:

$$MR = 4\{p_1^2(1 - p_1) + p_2^2(1 - p_2)\} = 4p_1p_2.$$

Coinsequently, $MR = 2 \times ELF$. Of course, that relationship fails if we move from a population with two groups to a population with three or more groups.

The basic difference between the *ELF* and *MR* indices lies in the weights associated to the probability p_i. In *MR*, p_i has weight equal to the relative size of group i. By contrast, in the *ELF* index, the size of each group has zero effect on the weight of the probability that two individuals belong to different groups. This is a crucial point that gives information about the contribution of each group to the final value of the index. In particular, following Mtalvo and Reynal-Querol (2005), we define with w_i^{ELF} and w_i^{MR} the proportional contribution of group i respectively to the *ELF* and *MR* indices. Therefore, we have:

$$w_i^{ELF} = \frac{p_i(1 - p_i)}{\sum_i p_i(1 - p_i)} \text{ and } w_i^{MR} = \frac{p_i^2(1 - p_i)}{\sum_i p_i^2(1 - p_i)}$$

the two weights coincide if all the groups have equal size: $w_i^{ELF} = w_i^{MR} = p_i$.

Let us suppose to increase the size of one group.[18] Concerning the *ELF* index, we have that the new proportional contribution of the largest group is smaller than its relative size, that is, $\widetilde{w}_i^{ELF} < p_i$, but we obtain the opposite result for the *MR* index, that is, $\widetilde{w}_i^{ELF} > p_i$. Summing up, large groups contribute to the *MR* (*ELF*) index proportionally more (less) than their relative size and the reverse happens for small groups..

23.3.3   The Posner Index

Posner (2004) affirms that the crucial problem of the *ELF* index lies in its definition. He claims that, for each country, the data from which the *ELF* has been computed[19] refers to several groups that are ethnically distinct but, for the most part, do not participate in politics as such. For this reason, he introduces the so-called politically relevant ethnic groups index (hereafter, *PREG*), 'a new index of ethnic fractionalization' (as the author himself reports in the abstract of his paper; ibid., p. 849), based on the subclass of the politically relevant ethnic groups. While several fractionalization indices are available for most of the countries of the world, *PREG* is available only for 42 African countries. However, Posner calculates his index every ten years, from the 1960s to the 1990s (replicating Easterly and Levine's 1997 influential article on Africa's 'growth tragedy'). His results confirm that, for the tested countries, *PREG* captures the policy-mediated effect of ethnic diversity on growth much better than *ELF* The main novelty of the *PREG* index is that, at the same time, it includes ethnic groups such as single political coalitions and excludes all the groups that do not contribute directly to the process of macroeconomic policy-making. Since it is essentially constructed using the Herfindahl concentration equation, as for the usual fractionalization index, *PREG* has the same drawbacks as the latter. In particular, it is insensitive to variation in the size of groups and it does not take into account the depth of the divisions among ethnic groups in the country and their concentration. Anyway, it has some advantages since it integrates the list provided by the *Atlas Noradov Mira*, including, as explained before, groups that try to influence macroeconomic policy. In fact, as Posner stressed, 'the quality of the new index depends fundamentally on the quality of the (necessarily subjective) decisions that were made to consolidate or drop groups from the original Atlas counts' (Posner, 2004, p. 855).

23.3.4 Bossert, D'Ambrosio and La Ferrara's Generalized Fractionalization Index

As stressed in the previous sections, a limitation of the *ELF* index is that it accounts only for one attribute and individuals are pre-assigned to given groups according to this attribute. Indeed, a measure of fractionalization, that only considers the population share, presents several drawbacks. Bossert et al. (2011) maintain that a measure of fractionalization must take into account the degree of similarity among individuals in a country. In fact, individuals may differ in several aspects: in age, gender, race, educational background, physical ability, geographic location, marital status, political affiliation or work experience, in addition to ethnicity, language and religious beliefs. Authors introduce and characterize what they call the generalized fractionalization index (hereafter, *GELF*) that takes as primitive the individuals, and partitions them into groups according to the similarity they present. The *GELF* index is defined as the complement to one of the sum of the elements of a similarity matrix (that is, a matrix whose entries are the pairwise distances among all individuals belonging to the same region) normalized by the square of the number of individuals. In the limit case where the information is purely binary, *GELF* reduces to the ethno-linguistic fractionalization index. The authors provide an empirical application, comparing their *GELF* with *ELF* and computing diversity for the US, using census data[20] at individual level regarding four variables: race, income, education and employment. In their illustration, in order to generate the partition, they use five racial groups and measure similarity among these groups along the remaining dimensions. As pointed out by the authors, the choice of race as a variable for partitioning society is purely instrumental and necessary to compare their results with the *ELF* index based on racial share. They show that for all of the US in 1990, *GELF* and *ELF* are positively correlated but, as stressed by the authors, the relationship among them is far from being linear (the value of the correlation coefficient is 0.59).

In particular, with respect to only racial share, several states – for instance Hawaii, California and Nevada – are much more heterogeneous. What emerges from the US data is that accounting for the value of similarity among individuals according to several attributes (instead of only one: race) may indeed alter the picture of ethnic diversity.

To the best of our knowledge, this is the only paper that provides a characterization of a fractionalization index.[21] The strength of the Bossert et al. (2011) paper is the use of an axiomatic approach to define fractionalization indices. The authors require that their index satisfy some very intuitive axioms that are widely accepted in several fields, including poverty, inequality and social exclusion studies. The first axiom they impose is Normalization, requiring that the index takes value zero in a society with no diversity and, consequently, it assumes positive value if there is diversity among individuals. The second axiom, Anonymity, is an invariance axiom since it requires that the diversity index be invariant with respect to permutations of individuals. The third axiom they consider is Additivity. It ensures that the value of the fractionalization index computed combining two distinct societies (in their case, two similarity matrices) is obtained summing up the single corresponding fractionalization indices of both the societies. Finally, the last axiom is the Replication invariance axiom, allowing comparisons among society containing a different number of individuals, and requiring the index to be invariant with respect to multiple replies of the original population. The authors prove that a diversity measure satisfies these four axioms if and only if it is their *GELF*. In addition, they prove that it is a natural extension of *ELF*. Bossert et al.'s paper represents a link between economic literature on ethnic diversity (e.g., Laitin, 2000; Alesina et al., 2003; Fearon, 2003) and the theoretical economic literature on the measurement of diversity (Weitzman, 1992, 1998; Pattanaik and Xu, 2000; Nehring and Puppe, 2002; Bossert et al., 2003, to name but a few).

NOTES

1. For instance, in biology, diversity typically denotes the number of variety and species in a region and their spatial distribution. Sociologists define the diversity of a society as the probability that two randomly selected group members belong to the same group. Whereas, in a context of organization theory, Harrison and Klein identify three different aspects of diversity: separation, variety and variation (see Harrison and Klein, 2007, Table 1 p.1203 for more details).
2. This class of measures corresponds to a mixture of what Stirling (2007) calls variety and balance.
3. Distance measures overcoming this limitation as shown by Greenberg (1956), who first proposed using a distance function to define several measures of linguistic diversity. Later, Weitzman (1992) assumed an a priori notion of distance among pairs of objects.
4. A premetric defined on set X is a function $d:X \times X \to \mathbb{R}$ such that for any $x,y \in X$, $d(x,y) \geq 0$ (non-negativity) and $d(x,y) = 0$ implies $x = y$ (indiscernibility of identicals) hold. A premetric is symmetric if for any $x,y \in X$, $d(x,y) = d(y, x)$ (symmetry) holds.
5. A semimetric is a symmetric premetric such that for any $x,y \in X$, $d(x,y) = 0$ entails $x = y$ (the identity of indiscernibles principle).
6. A metric is semimetric that also satisfies triangular inequality, or equivalently a subadditive semimetric.
7. A metric $d:X \times X \to \mathbb{R}$ is an ultrametric if $d(x,z) \leq \max\{d(x,y), d(y,z)\}$. for all $x,y,z \in X$.
8. Given an attribute valuation function λ that assigns a non-negative value $\lambda(S)$ to any subset S of X a diversity indicator $I_d:P(x) \to \mathbb{R}$ has a conjugate Möbius inverse $\lambda:P(x) \to \mathbb{R}$ defined for every set B as: $\lambda(B) = \Sigma_{S \subseteq B}(-1)^{|B \setminus S|+1}I_d(X \setminus S)$ and satisfying for every set A the equality: $I_d(A) = \Sigma_{S:S \cap A \neq 0}\lambda(S)$. As reported by Gravel (2008), the non-negative conjugate Möbius inverse can be interpreted as a method for valuing the attributes, that is any set receiving a positive value is considered as an attribute. (See Nehring, 1999; Nehring and Puppe, 2002; Gravel, 2008, for more details).
9. It is easy to show that LIN implies MONC.
10. Here 'dominance' refers to the extent to which a species is abundant in the ecosystem.
11. The economists Orris C. Herfindahl (1945) and Albert O. Hirschman (1950) proposed the HHI or concentration index independently. For more detail on the background of the index, see Hirschman (1964).

Formally, it is defined as the sum of the squares of the market shares of the 50 largest firms (or summed over all the firms if there are fewer than 50) within an industry.

12. From a mathematical point of view, generalized means are a family of functions for aggregating sets of numbers. Such a family is also known as power means or Hölder means.

13. For instance, assuming $\phi(p_i) = 1$ or, similarly $\alpha = 0$ we get $D(P) = k$ that is the number of types in the society. On the other hand, if $\phi(p_i) = p_i^2$ we obtain the complement to one of the Simpson index that is the Gini Index. Then again, positing $\phi(p_i) = -p_i \ln p_i$ with $0 \ln 0 = 0$, that is approaching α to 1, the well-known Shannon diversity index (Shannon, 1948) is achieved: $D(P) = -c\sum_{i=1}^{k} p_i \ln p_i$ where c is a constant depending on the unit of measurement of entropy.

14. ELF computation is mainly based on ethno-linguistic classification provided by sources from the Atlas Narodov Mira compiled in 1964. See section 24.2 of Chapter 24 in this *Handbook*.

15. To compute such a coefficient, Greenberg (1956) proposed to use the glottochronology list that is a fixed basic vocabulary. Laitin (2000) observes that what Greenberg calls glottochronology is probably the so-called 'lexico-statistics' that allows for cross-sectional comparisons (see Laitin, 2000, p. 147, footnote 5).

16. The Bossert et al. (2011) index will be discussed in-depth later.

17. Here the word 'unstable' is used to denote countries where there are several changes in the elite running the country (see Mauro, 1995).

18. In consequence, the size of another group must decrease by the same amount.

19. The author observes that oldest dataset (that is, the *Atlas Noradov Mira* dataset) as well as the newer ones (that is, Roeder, 2001; Alesina et al., 2003; Fearon, 2003) suffer from the same inconvenience.

20. The dataset they use is the 5 per cent IPUMS from the 1990 Census.

21. Vigdor (2002) presents and discuss a simple method linking individual behaviour to the composition of community, showing how fractionalization indices are 'most clearly motived when using geographically aggregated data' (ibid., p. 272)

REFERENCES

Alesina, A., Devleeschauwer, A., Easterly, W., Kurlat, S., Wacziarg, R. (2003) 'Fractionalization', *Journal of Economic Growth*, 8, 155–194.

Barberà, S., Bossert, W., Pattanaik, P.K. (2004) 'Ranking sets of objects', in Barberà, S., Hammond, P.C., Seidl, C. (eds), *Handbook of Utility Theory, Vol. II, Extensions* (pp. 893–977), Kluwer Academic Publishers, Dordrecht.

Basili, M., Vannucci, S. (2013) 'Diversity as width', *Social Choice and Welfare*, 40, 913–936.

Baumgärtner, S. (2007) 'Why the measurement of species diversity requires prior value judgments', in Kontoleon, A., Pascual, U., Swanson, T. (eds), *Biodiversity Economics: Principles, Methods and Applications* (pp. 293–310), Cambridge University Press, Cambridge, UK and Heidelberg, Germany.

Berger, W.H., Parker, F.L. (1970) 'Diversity of planktonic Foramenifera in deep sea sediments', *Science*, 168, 1345–1347.

Bervoets, S., Gravel, N. (2007) 'Appraising diversity with an ordinal notion of similarity: an axiomatic approach', *Mathematical Social Sciences*, 53, 259–273.

Bossert, W., D'Ambrosio, C., La Ferrara, E. (2011) 'A generalized index of fractionalization', *Economica*, 78, 723–750.

Bossert, W., Pattanaik, P.K., Xu, Y. (2001) 'The measurement of diversity', Working Paper CRDE 17-2001, Montreal.

Bossert, W., Pattanaik, P.K., Xu, Y. (2003) 'Similarity of options and the measurement of diversity', *Journal of Theoretical Politics*, 15, 405–421.

Ciommi, M., Lasso de la Vega, C. (2014) 'Measuring diversity in a counting approach', Mimeo.

Cowell, F.A. (2000) 'Measurement of inequality', in Atkinson, A.B., Bourguignon, F. (eds), *Handbook of Income Distribution* (pp. 87–166), North Holland, Amsterdam.

Easterly, W., Levine, R. (1997) 'Africa's growth tragedy: policies and ethnic divisions', *Quarterly Journal of Economics*, 112, 1203–1250.

Ebert, U. (2010) 'The decomposition of inequality reconsidered: weakly decomposable measures', *Mathematical Social Sciences*, 60, 94–103.

Fearon, J.D. (2003) 'Ethnic and cultural diversity by country', *Journal of Economic Growth*, 8, 195–222.

Foster, J.E. (2006) 'Poverty indices', in de Janvry, A., Kanbur, R. (eds), *Poverty, Inequality and Development: Essays in Honor of Erik Thorbeck* (pp. 41–65), Springer US, New York.

Gini, C. (1912) 'Variabilità e mutabilità' (Variability and mutability), reprinted in Pizetti, E., Salvemini, T. (eds), *Memorie di metodologica statistica* (p. 1), Libreria Eredi Virgilio Veschi, Rome.

Gravel, N. (2008) 'What is diversity?', in Boylan, T., Gekker, R. (eds), *Economics, Rational Choice and Normative Philosophy* (pp. 15–55), Routledge, London.

Greenberg, J.H. (1956) 'The measurement of linguistic diversity', *Language*, 32, 109–115.

Harrison, D.A., Klein, K.J. (2007) 'What's the difference? Diversity construct as separation, variety, or disparity in organizations', *Academy of Management Review*, 32, 1199–1228.

Herfindahl, O.C. (1945) *National Power and the Structure of Foreign Trade*, University of California Press, Berkeley, CA.

Hirschman, A.C. (1950) 'Concentration in the US steel industry', Doctoral Thesis, Columbia University.

Hirschman, A.O. (1964) 'The paternity of an index', *American Economic Review*, 54, 761–762.

Laitin, D.D. (2000) 'What is a language community?', *American Journal of Political Science*, 44, 142–155.

Lande, R. (1996) 'Statistics and partitioning of species diversity, and similarity among multiple communities', *Oikos*, 76, 5–13.

Lieberson, S. (1964) 'An extension of Greenberg's linguistic diversity measures'. *Language*, 40, 526–531.

Luce, R.D., Krantz, D.H., Suppes, P., Tvwesky, A. (1990) *Foundations of Measurement, Vol 3: Representation, Axiomatization and Invariance*, Academic Press, San Diego, CA.

Mauro, P. (1995) 'Corruption and growth', *Quarterly Journal of Economics*, 110, 681–712.

McIntosh, R.P. (1967) 'An index of diversity and the relation of certain concepts to diversity', *Ecology*, 48, 392–404.

Montalvo, J.G., Reynal-Querol, M. (2002) 'Why ethnic fractionalization? Polarization, ethnic conflict and growth', UPF Working Paper, No. 660.

Montalvo, J.G., Reynal-Querol, M. (2005) 'Ethnic polarization, potential conflict, and civil wars', *American Economic Review*, 95, 796–816.

Nehring, K. (1999) 'Preference for flexibility in a Savagian framework', *Econometrica*, 67, 101–119.

Nehring, K., Puppe C. (2002) 'A theory of diversity', *Econometrica*, 70, 1155–1198.

Nehring K., Puppe C. (2003) 'Diversity and dissimilarity in lines and hierarchies', *Mathematical Social Sciences*, 45, 167–183.

Page, S.E. (2011) *Diversity and Complexity*, Princeton University Press, Princeton, NJ.

Pattanaik, P.K., Xu, Y. (1998) 'On preference and freedom', *Theory and Decision*, 48, 173–198.

Pattanaik, P.K., Xu, Y. (2000) 'On diversity and freedom of choice', *Mathematical Social Sciences*, 40, 123–130.

Pattanaik, P.K., Xu, Y. (2008) 'Ordinal distance, dominance, and the measurement of diversity', in Pattanaik, P., Tadenuma, K., Xu, Y., Yoshihara, N. (eds), *Rational Choice and Social Welfare: Theory and Applications* (pp. 259–269), Springer, Heidelberg.

Peragine, V., Romero-Medina, A. (2006) 'On preference, freedom and diversity', *Social Choice and Welfare*, 27, 29–40.

Pielou, E.C. (1977) *Mathematical Ecology*, John Wiley & Sons, New York.

Posner, D.N. (2004) 'Measuring ethnic fractionalization in Africa', *American Journal of Political Science*, 48, 849–863.

Roeder, P.G. (2001) 'Ethnolinguistic fractionalization (ELF) indices, 1961 and 1985', 16 February, http//:weber.ucsd.edu/~proeder/elf.htm (accessed 17 September 2013).

Sen, A. (1976) 'Poverty: an ordinal approach to measurement', *Econometrica*, 44(2), 219–231.

Shannon, C.E. (1948) 'A mathematical theory of communication', *Bell System Technical Journal*, 27, 379–423.

Shannon, C.E., Weaver, W. (1962) 'The mathematical theory of communication', University of Illinois Press, Urbana, IL.

Simpson, E.H. (1949) 'Measurement of diversity', *Nature*, 163, 688.

Solow, A., Polasky, S. (1994) 'Measuring biological diversity', *Environmental Ecological Statistics*, 1, 95–107.

Stirling, A. (2007) 'A general framework for analysing diversity in science, technology and society', *Journal of the Royal Society Interface*, 4, 707–719.

Van Hees, M. (2004) 'Freedom of choice and diversity of options: some difficulties', *Social Choice and Welfare*, 22, 253–266.

Van Parjis, P. (1995) *Real Freedom for All*, Oxford University Press, Oxford.

Vigdor, J.L. (2002) 'Interpreting ethnic fragmentation effects', *Economics Letters*, 75, 271–276.

Weitzman, M.L. (1992) 'On diversity', *Quarterly Journal of Economics*, 107, 363–405.

Weitzman, M.L. (1998) 'The Noah's Ark problem', *Econometrica*, 66, 1279–1298.

24. Diversity and social fractionalization: empirical findings

Mariateresa Ciommi

24.1 INTRODUCTION

When people think about the meaning of the word 'diversity', it usually pertains to difference in type. However, this is only one way to speak of diversity. Another interesting point of view is to consider diversity as the composition of society. Scott E. Page (2011, p. 23) affirms that 'diversity can refer to difference in community or population composition'. I embrace this definition. Hence, with the word 'diversity', I refer to differences among individuals and groups in a society. Such differences include economic, cultural as well as physical aspects, such as difference of race, language, ethnicity, nationality, gender, sexual orientation, political and religious affiliation, or socioeconomic status.

In the empirical literature on cross-country studies, the diversity of a population or a society is defined and measured through fractionalization or polarization indices,[1] looking at the resulting partitions that are specified by taking into account some of the above-mentioned traits. In particular, diversity is measured with respect to language or ethnic groups.[2] Usually, 'fractionalization' and 'diversity' are used synonymously, but the idea behind these two terms is completely different. In fact, while a 'diverse society' or a 'diverse country' is a non-homogenous place, a 'fractionalized society' or 'fractionalized country' refers to a place in which individuals are partitioned – that is, fractionalized – according to or with respect to some specific characteristics, such as ethnicity, nationality, language, religion, and so on. This situation can be well captured by a specific measure that involves both the number and the size of groups, in which it is possible to separate individuals belonging to the society under analysis. That is, recurring to the fractionalization index, also called the ethnolinguistic fractionalization index (henceforth, ELF), defined as the probability that two individuals, randomly selected from the overall population of a country will belong to different ethnic groups. Formally:

$$ELF = 1 - \sum_{i=1}^{n} p_i^2 \qquad (24.1)$$

where n represents the number of ethnic groups and p_i is the population share in each group. Depending on the attribute used to partition the society scholars use to refer to it simply as the linguistic fractionalization index, religious fractionalization index or ethnic fractionalization index.

Figure 24.1 is a useful instrument to get an intuitive idea of what the most fractionalized countries are, according to ethnicity in 2012. Most of the European countries, North Africa and Australia belong to the less ethnically fractionalized countries, while the most fractionalized countries are located in the centre of Africa.

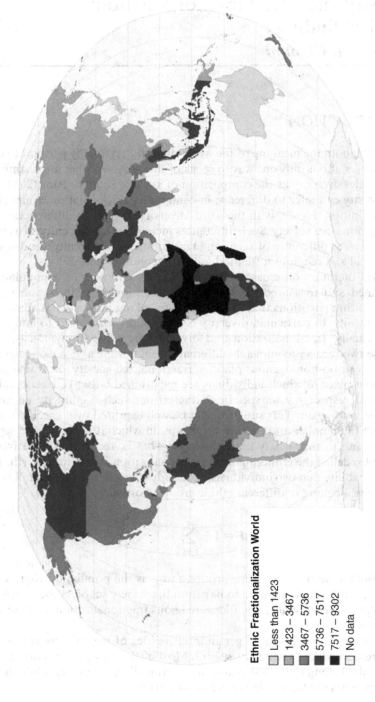

Figure 24.1 World ethnic fractionalization (2012)

This chapter surveys the empirical literature on social fractionalization and diversity, focusing on two crucial aspects of the field, which correspond to the main sections: the choice of the variable to identify groups (and, as a consequence, the dataset) and the implications that social fractionalization and diversity have for the economy of a country. One of the first problems in providing a measure of social fractionalization and diversity is the choice of the dataset to use in order to calculate the fractionalization of a country. The first main section of this chapter (section 14.2) reviews about 15 datasets used in literature which are in my opinion the most important, moving from the oldest, the *Statesman's Yearbook* first published in 1864 (Martin, 1865), to the Desmet et al. (2012), and going through the *Atlas Narodow Mira* (1964) dataset, the *L'Etat des Religions Dans le Mond* (Clévenot, 1987), the Alesina et al. (2003) dataset, and the Fearon (2003) dataset. That section also examines the relationship among the corresponding fractionalization indices obtained using the above-mentioned datasets, showing that most of them present a very high correlation. It has been argued that social fractionalization and diversity deals with several strands of economic as well as social literature. As a matter of fact, there are numerous empirical studies analysing the impact of ethnic, religious, linguistic or cultural diversity on growth (Mauro, 1995; Easterly and Levine, 1997; Collier, 2001; Posner, 2004), on the level of development (Florida and Gates, 2001; Florida, 2002), on the quality of institutions (La Porta et al., 1999; Alesina et al., 2003), on the rise of conflict (Annett, 2001) and on hourly wages (Ottaviano and Perri, 2005). In addition, these relationships have been investigated in depth at several administrative levels, obtaining results for continents and countries as well as for cities, both developed and developing. They are analysed in section 24.3. Lastly, section 24.4 is devoted to future research lines that need to be further investigated.

24.2 DATA SOURCES FOR ETHNOLINGUISTIC FRACTIONALIZATION

In order to distinguish among groups, there are manifold objective attributes usually used, such as language, race, religion, tribe, descent, nationality, or some combination. The standard way to compute the fractionalization index is to create one ethnic fractionalization measure that differentiates ethnic groups by the languages spoken, under the assumption that language ties are the most salient features that describe the ethnicity of an individual. There exist several distinct datasets compiled by researchers and teams as well as official institutions. The next paragraphs are devoted to an in-depth description of them.

24.2.1   The Statesman's Yearbook

The *Statesman's Yearbook* (henceforth, ST) is the oldest published database and it is essentially based on national sources (Martin, 1865). The first release dates from 1864 and since 2006, the ST has been launched online.[3] In 2009, the website was uploaded with a complete archive from 1864 to 2009. The ST collects yearly information on every country in the world. For each country, there is geographic, historic, economic, political, social and cultural information. In particular, it gives information on social statistics, government, religion, culture, social institutions, as well as several economic character-istics such as gross domestic product (GDP), energy, natural resources, industry and international trade.

As for other datasets (such as the *World Christian Encyclopedia* and *L'Etat des Religions Dans le Monde*), it collects data from the following religious groups: Animist religion, Bahaism, Buddhism, Chinese Religion, Christians, Confucianism, Hinduism, Jews, Muslims, Syncretic cults, Taoism, and other religions. As stressed by Montalvo and Reynal-Querol (2005a), one of the biggest advantages of this dataset is its extremely detailed account of Animist religion.

24.2.2   Ethnologue

The *Ethnologue*, also called *Languages of the World*, is a comprehensive reference volume that catalogues all the known living languages. The 2013 release contains statistics for 7105 languages belonging to 145 language families.[4] It provides information on the number of speakers, location, dialects, linguistic affiliations, availability of the Bible in the language, and an estimate of language viability. The first edition was published in 1951 by Pittman as a mimeograph of ten pages, whereas the first edition as a book was published in 1958 (Pittman and Canonge, 1958). New editions of the *Ethnologue* are published approxi-mately every four years. Despite the great amount of information provided by the dataset, no political scientists use it as a measure of ethnic fractionalization. The main reason is that even if in some places, such as Africa, language seems to be the best way to categorize individuals, in countries such as those in South America, most of the people speak the same language (Spanish), but at the same time they belong to different cultural, racial and religious groups. Consequently it is better to refer to ethnicity by taking into account not only language but also race, cultural identity and, often, religion.

24.2.3   Atlas Narodov Mira

The most widely used dataset of worldwide ethnolinguistic fractionalization was con-structed in 1960 by a group of 70 Soviet ethnographic researchers from the Moscow Miklukho-Maklai Ethnological Institute[5] and printed in 1964 as the *Atlas Narodov Mira* (usually referred to also as the *Atlas of Peoples of the World*, Atlas or ANM). This dataset is mainly based on the linguistic and historical origins of various groups and it is widely used in contemporary research, especially for the calculation of the ethnolinguistic frac-tionalization index following the work of Taylor and Hudson (1972), which refers to this simply as the ELF index. The Soviet variable ethnic measures the probability that, select-ing at random two individuals in a country, they will belong to two different ethnolinguis-tic groups. By definition, this variable increases with the number of ethnolinguistic groups and increases the more equal the size of the groups. Easterly and Levine (1997) report the 15 most and least fractionalized countries according to the ethnic variable, calculated by Taylor and Hudson (1972) using the ANM dataset. The computed index ranges from 1 to 93. Among the 66 analysed countries, Tanzania (93), Uganda and Zaire (90) are the most fractionalized countries, whereas Haiti, Japan and Portugal (1) are very homogeneous in terms of ethnicity. More in general, the great majority of the most ethnically heterogene-ous countries in the world belong to the African continent.

The ANM has several strengths: it is complete, since it covers about 1600 languages and almost all the countries in the world, and presents high-quality maps. In addition, as affirmed by Taylor and Hudson (1972), the construction of the database was not influenced by ideological bias, even if some countries such as North and South Korea, North and South Vietnam, Taiwan and Southern Yemen are not listed in the dataset, probably because they were not recognized as countries by the Soviet government.

However, ANM presents some weaknesses, and many outstanding scholars have questioned the validity of the data (see, e.g., Fearon, 2003; Alesina et al., 2003; Posner, 2004; Bridgman, 2008; Weidmann et al., 2010). In fact, as observed by Weidmann et al. (2010), the source of the information in the ANM is rather ambiguous. Soviet researchers cite three different types of sources[6] with no documentation about either its methodology or its definition of ethnicity. Bridgman (2008) investigates whether the ANM data correspond to the likelihood of marrying within the group, defining an ethnic group as 'a set of people that are endogamous and for which no endogamous subgroup exists' (Bridgman, 2008, p. 2). The main result obtained by the author is that the ANM has a tendency to underestimate the level of ethnic division, and as a natural consequence, empirical research based on ANM data will likely underestimate the effect of ethnic division.[7]

A second weakness is that the construction of the ANM is based on the situation in the 1960s, which is outdated compared to the current situation. More recently, the University of Harvard provides a digital map of the *Atlas Narodov Mira*,[8] within the Georeferencing of Ethnic Groups (GREG) project. This world map project employs geographic information systems (GIS) to represent group territories as polygons. The GREG dataset consists of 8969 polygons.

Regarding the third weakness stressed above, the ANM seems to misspecify certain ethnic groups. The most famous case is the non-distinction between Hutu and Tutsi in Rwanda. This problem has been overcome by several newer datasets, such as that provided in 2001 by Annett; in 2003 in two distinctive works by Alesina et al. and Fearon; and in 2004 by Posner.

Finally, the last critique of the wide use of this dataset is its inability to properly distinguish between ethnic and linguistic differences. Even if this does not represent a major problem for most of the countries in Africa or Europe (since people identify themselves by both ethnic group and language), for Latin America this is crucial: people are quite homogeneous in terms of language, but are distinct in terms of ethnic membership.

24.2.4 Roberts

The Roberts dataset (Roberts, 1962) presents a strong correlation with the ANM. It covers 66 Asian and African countries and summary statistics from Latin America, but it includes some countries missing from the ANM such as South and North Korea, South and North Vietnam and Taiwan. The dataset focuses on the challenges of linguistic communication due to industrial development in these countries. Easterly and Levine (1997) investigate this dataset, concluding that it presents several weakness. It not only covers fewer countries but also omits many language groups. For instance, in Chad, the dataset dismisses several groups that cover 42 percent of the population; and in Ivory Coast about 26 percent of the population is not included according to the ANM measure.

24.2.5   Muller

The Muller (1964) dataset is essentially linguistic. It covers 144 languages with at least one million speakers each, and 56 additional languages selected considering supplementary aspects, such as political, cultural or anthropological importance. The construction of this database involves primary data, since Muller uses census reports. However, he limits the analysis to the 200 most important word languages, whereas the ANM takes into account 1300 languages. Easterly and Levine (1997) observe that the main consequence of this restriction is the omission of several African ethnic groups in the analysis. For instance, like Roberts (1962), he only mentions the largest Kenyan group; and in Liberia he omits to consider the Kru language, thereby leaving out about 30 percent of the population.

24.2.6   Taylor and Hudson

Using data from the Soviet Union for the *Atlas Narodiv Mira*, in 1972 Charles L. Taylor and Michael C. Hudson published the first edition of the *Handbook of Political and Social Indicators*.[9] This huge dataset was widely used to build standard measures of ethnic diversity for a long time.

24.2.7   World Christian Encyclopedia

One of the most used and cited sources on data for religious diversity across countries is the Barrett (1982) dataset also referred to as the *World Christian Encyclopedia* (henceforth, WCE). One of the most important advantages of this dataset is that it contains a cross-section of time series, providing, in the first edition, information for three distinct years: 1970, 1975 and 1980.

After the first edition, Barrett et al. published a second one in 2001. More recently, data incorporated into the *World Christian Encyclopedia* are available online.[10] As reported on the website of the new project that supports and integrates the book, extensive religious and secular statistics are available on 9000 Christian denominations, 238 countries and 13 000 ethnolinguistic groups. Data are also available at local level, for 5000 cities and 3000 provinces.

The WCD dataset also includes statistical information on population and religious adherents for 1900, 1970, 2000, 2005 and 2010, as well as predictions for 2025 and 2050. Specifically, it incorporates information on demography (birth rate, adult percentage, and life expectancy), health (HIV rates, access to water, mortality), education (literacy percentage, schools, universities) and communication (scripture access, religious freedom). It also takes into account a good deal of religious information, such as Christian personnel, Evangelism rates, the status of mission work, lists of Christian denominations in every country, regional and global estimates of Pentecostals and Charismatics, and the status of Bible translation. However, this data source exhibits several shortcomings, as observed by Montalvo and Reynal-Querol (2002a). The most important is that the data do not admit the possibility of double practice, which is a very common customary action in several countries, such as some sub-Saharan African and Latin American countries. Finally, comparing this dataset with others, the authors realize that Zaire shows a religion distribution very similar to that of Spain or Italy, and so conclude that the data are biased towards the Christian religion.

24.2.8 L'état des Religions Dans le Monde

L'Etat des Religions Dans le Monde (henceforth, ET) provides information on the proportions of followers of Animist and Syncretic cults. The ET dataset includes, as the name suggests, very exhaustive data on religious affiliation for a wide range of countries, published in 1987 (Clévenot, 1987). It contains information from the *World Christian Encyclopedia*, but this is corrected using national sources. A strength of this dataset is that it takes into account the proportions of both Animists (in sub-Saharan African countries) and Syncretics (in Latin American countries) – cult followers. Data are collected for 183 countries around the world.

24.2.9 Black Africa: A Comparative Handbook

The first edition of *Black Africa: A Comparative Handbook*, published in 1972, contains data on the political, social, economic, religious, as well as ecological and demographic characteristics of 32 Black African nations in the late 1950s and 1960s. In 1989, Morrison et al. published an updated version, covering 41 Black African nations as well as providing a modern comparative analysis of African states (Morrison et al., 1989). In particular, the data focus on political regime characteristics such as the existence and nature of political parties, elections, the nature of the judicial system and civil wars, among others; economic aspects including government expenditures, public investment, defence budgets, energy, industrial production, international trade, educational expenditure, economic welfare, communication, transportation, and so on; as well as information on the military and security systems, cultural pluralism, language and religion, and primary and secondary school enrolment. The main strength of this dataset is the comparability of data on a wide range of topics among African countries. As the authors stress in their introduction, the *Comparative Handbook* intends to provide reliable information to make an easier comparison of political, economic and social analysis.

24.2.10 The World Factbook

Each year, since 1980, the United States Central Intelligence Agency (CIA) publishes an accurate dataset, called the *World Factbook* (hereafter, WF). The WF provides information on the history, people, government, economy, geography, communications, transportation, military and transnational issues of 267 world entities. On the related webpage of the project,[11] it is possible to find accurate and free-of-charge data on religions practiced[12] as well as on languages spoken.[13] Fearon and Laitin (2003) use the WF to construct two measures of Fearon and ethnic fractionalization; whereas Montalvo and Reynal-Querol (2005a) assert that it is more detailed than the ST, but less than the ET or the WCE.

24.2.11 Encyclopedia Britannica

Encyclopedia Britannica Inc. (henceforth, EB) annually provides statistical information on about 220 countries. The EB uses an estimation of statistics based on its own collections, census data (government publications), public and private reports concerning social and economic indicators, as well as membership figures of the churches concerned. However, it also uses the WCE as a basic source and, as a consequence, it is subject to most of the same biases.

Data include information on population, social indicators, agriculture, labour, manufacturing, trade, finance, transportation, and so on. In particular, as social indicators, it takes into account religion and languages. For each country, it provides data concerning religious affiliations, and also presents the distribution of religious groups for a given year. For this reason, it is one of the most-used databases for constructing fractionalization indices, and in particular for religion fractionalization indices.

There are several examples in the economic literature where the EB is used as the main source for the construction of religious variables. For instance, for their religious fractionalization index, Alesina et al. (2003) use the EB combined with WF variables, while the language variable as well as the religious one are totally based on the 2001 edition of the EB.

Comparing EB with the *Ethnologue*, the second dataset is much more disaggregated than the first one. For instance, the *Ethnologue* lists 291 living languages in Mexico, while the Britannica lists only 21. However, in contrast with the WF estimate for Algeria (99 per cent 'Arab-Berber') the EB gives more detailed information, taking into account several distinct groups (Algerian Arab, 59.1%; Berber, 26.2%, of which Arabized Berber, 3.0 per cent; Bedouin Arab, 14.5 per cent; other, 0.2 per cent).

24.2.12 Roeder

Based on the ANM dataset, in 2001, Roeder makes available on his webpage[14] several ethnolinguistic fractionalization (ELF) measures for two distinct years: 1961 and 1986. For both years, he calculates ELF as defined by Taylor and Hudson (1972) in three different ways. The first way uses none of the groupings reported in the sources when data on subgroups is available. The second way consists of imposing that racial distinctions within linguistic groups do not constitute separate ethnic groups. Finally, the last way in which the author calculates the index is by considering ethnic groups defined by language, putting together racial groups and cultural subgroups within linguistic groups.

24.2.13 Alesina, Devleeschauwer, Easterly, Kurlat and Wacziard

Constructed in 2003 by Alesina et al., the Fractionalization dataset[15] covers two general areas: the quality of institutions and economic growth. The measure is calculated for 215 countries and it accounts for 1055 major linguistic as well as 650 ethnic groups. The dataset contains data for one year for each country. To assemble the dataset, authors collected data by merging several sources, such as the Encyclopaedia Britannica Inc. Britannica World Data (2001 edition), the CIA's *World Factbook* (2000 edition), Levinson's (1998)

Ethnic Groups Worldwide, Minority Rights Group International's (1997) *World Directory of Minorities* and, for selected African countries, Mozaffar and Scarrit (1999). In most cases, the primary source is the national censuses. In particular, the language and religion indices are based on data from 2001, whereas most of the data involved in calculating the ethnic fractionalization indices are from the 1990s or older. In 2008, using census data, Alesina and Zhuravskaya extend this dataset by adding about 100 countries on a regional level.

24.2.14 Fearon

This dataset is mainly used to construct fractionalization indices based on ethnic variables. Fearon (2003) builds this dataset[16] by identifying 822 ethnic and ethno-religious groups in 160 countries that made up at least 1 percent of the country's population in the early 1990s. The construction of this dataset comes from the comparisons of the WF and EB datasets. Since, according to Fearon's (2003) analysis, the two datasets lead to discrepant results, he integrates them, involving country-specific sources; for instance, using Morrison et al. (1989) for African countries.

24.2.15 Desmet, Ortuño-Ortin and Weber

The last dataset described here was formulated by Desmet et al. in 2012 as a variant of Fearon's formalization. It is essentially based on linguistic variables. As its main novelty, the authors focus on language families, rather than on the single language spoken. For the construction of their dataset, the authors use the 15 levels of aggregation available in the linguistic classification provided by the *Ethnologue* dataset.[17] The sample obtained contains 226 observations.

As stressed by the authors, the key strength of this dataset is that it allows a more in-depth understanding of the concept of diversity. For example, the measures of diversity commonly used make Chad and Zambia look very similar, belonging to the top deciles. Moreover, the introduction of language families rather than single languages, gives a completely different picture. Chad continues to be one of the most diverse countries (it is ranked 7 out of 225), whereas now Zambia looks very homogeneous (176 out of 225). Finally, the idea behind the measure obtained using this dataset is closer to the Greenberg (1956) measure of diversity rather than to the traditional fractionalization index. This section concludes by reporting the correlation among the datasets mentioned above.

24.2.16 A Comparison among Datasets

As the long list of presented datasets shows, the diversity – measured as ethnicity, religion, language, and so on – of a country is, in a certain sense, a subjective concept and, depending on the main source used it will lead to different outcomes and, in particular, to different rankings of countries. In the next paragraphs, I illustrate the correlation among pairs of most of the above-quoted datasets, showing the similarity and dissimilarity among them.

Alesina, Devleeschauwer, Easterly, Kurlat and Wacziarg; and Annett
In their paper, Alesina et al. (2003) calculate three different indices of fractionalization. The first is an ethnic fractionalization index, considering 650 groups belonging to 190 countries. The second index they compute is a linguistic fractionalization measure, using 1055 groups in 201 countries, where groups are identified according to the language spoken. The third is the religion fractionalization index, estimated for 215 countries with respect to 294 different religions.

Similarly, Annett (2001) computes what he defines as a new index of fractionalization, with data from the WCE dataset. The author chooses this dataset since it provides an extremely detailed breakdown of ethnolinguistic groups, within each country. With respect to the Barrett (1982) ranking, this one has several advantages: it includes more countries (150) and the data are more recent.

The correlation between Alesina et al.'s (2003) dataset and Annett's (2001) is very high. As Alesina et al. (2003) affirm, restricting only on the overlap between the samples of two datasets, the value between the Annett ethnolinguistic fractionalization variable and the Alesina ethnicity variable is 0.89, and the correlation between the religious fractionalization variable is 0.84.

Alesina, Devleeschauwer, Easterly, Kurlat and Wacziarg; and the ANM
Alesina et al. (2003) compute the correlation between their dataset and the ANM. Although there exists a relatively high correlation between the ethnic and linguistic index calculated by Alesina et al. and the fractionalization index computed using ANM (0.76 and 0.88, respectively), the same result does not occur for religious fractionalization for which the correlation is quite low.

Authors show that there is a low correlation between ethnic and religious fractionalization (0.14) and language and religion (0.27). These values imply that a country that is highly fractionalized in ethnicity does not necessary present the same degree of fractionalization in religion, whereas high fractionalization in languages is often associated with high fractionalization in ethnicity (the correlation coefficient is 0.70).

Alesina, Devleeschauwer, Easterly, Kurlat and Wacziarg; Fearon; and Posner
Posner (2004) observes that, restricting the sample of world countries to only sub-Saharan African countries, Alesina et al. (2003) and Fearon (2003) show quite high correlation (0.73). In addition, both of them correlate with his calculation at under 0.54.

Montalvo and Reynal-Querol; the ANM; and Alesina, Devleeschauwer, Easterly, Kurlat and Wacziarg
Montalvo and Reynal-Querol (2005a) compute the correlation between their fractionalization index (basically the WCE), the fractionalization index obtained using ANM data, and the fractionalization index calculated by Alesina et al. (2003). They discover a very high correlation (0.86) between their index and the ANM. The authors also show that, focusing only on linguistic diversity, the correlation between their measure and the ELF increases, stepping up to 0.92.

Annett; ANM; Muller; and Roberts
Annett (2001) computes all the correlations between his new index of fractionalization and the same index calculated using the ANM, Muller and Roberts datasets, respectively. The highest correlation is with Roberts (0.85). The ANM is also very highly correlated (0.84); whereas the relatively lower level of correlation is with the Muller dataset (0.66). For the sake of comparison, Annett (2001) also calculates the correlation among the three datasets, showing that here also the correlation is very high. In particular, the correlation between the ANM and Muller is 0.83; and the correlation between Muller and Roberts is 0.93.

Fearon; and the ANM
The bivariate correlation for the common countries (135) between the aggregate measure of ethnic fractionalization provided by the ANM and the Fearon one is quite high (0.76). As Fearon (2003) reports, this result holds except in the Middle East and North Africa, and Latin America and the Caribbean.[18]

Montalvo and Reynal-Querol; EB; and WCE
As observed by Montalvo and Reynal-Querol (2005a), considering only religious fractionalization, the correlation between their index, obtained using the ET and ST, and the indices obtained using the EB and WCE, is very high: 0.76 and 0.84, respectively.

PREG; the ANM; Alesina, Devleeschauwer, Easterly, Kurlat and Wacziarg; Roeder; and Fearon
Finally, I compare the alternative formulation of the fractionalization index introduced by Posner (2004), the PREG index[19] and some of the most important measures mentioned above. The author provides these correlations only for a subsample of African countries that are common to all five measures. The correlation ranges from 0.44 (with Fearon) to 0.67 (ELF; that is, ANM), suggesting that the PREG index is quite different from the other measures. As stressed by Posner, these low correlation values do not imply that PREG is a sort of 'noisy proxy for the other measure' (Posner, 2004, p. 857), since the ranking of the most and least fractionalized countries differs from the ANM ranking.[20]

Additional consideration among datasets
Montalvo and Reynal-Querol (2005a) show that it is necessary to be careful with the datasets one uses, since they have several missing values. In fact, they illustrate that it is possible to obtain different results depending on the source of data. In fact, while all the datasets – namely the WCE, ST, WF and ET – report information on large religions, this is not the case of Animist and Syncretic cults. Thus, they focus on the treatment of these last two, showing that neither the WCE nor the WF account for Syncretic cults, whereas the ST is not very detailed. On the other hand, the Animist cult is reported in detail in the ST; whereas the WCE reports only some countries. Thus, according to Montalvo and Reynal-Querol (2005a), the most complete dataset is the ET, since it accounts for all three: the large religions, Animist cults and Syncretic cults.

The consequences of these results are that if we are interested in calculating religious diversity focusing only on large religions, the results obtained using the WCE and ET are almost identical. On the contrary, if in our analysis we also need to take into account

Animists and Syncretic cults, the best option is to use the ET. Similarly, if we are interested only in Animists cults, the best dataset is the ST. In other words, the datasets should be chosen depending on the object of the analysis.[21]

24.3   RELATIONSHIP WITH ECONOMIC AND SOCIAL OUTCOMES

Many scholars have investigated the relationship between diversity – intended as diversity in ethnicity, religion, language or culture – and its effects on social and economic aspects of a country. Some authors have argued that an ethnically diverse society can have a higher probability of ethnic conflicts and, consequently, ethnic conflicts negatively affect growth. Diversity also causes high level of corruption and holds back the diffusion of technological innovations. Ethnic diversity reduces business affecting the levels of economic activities and influences trade. In addition, some government expenditure may favour some ethnic groups. The negative relationship between ethnic diversity and growth can be interpreted as a consequence of a high probability of conflict associated with a more fractionalized society. For this reason most of the papers use a fractionalization index as the main indicator of ethnic heterogeneity. In fact, an index of fractionalization aims at capturing the degree to which a society is split into distinct groups.

As a matter of fact, there are a lot of economic studies affirming that a high level of diversity, measured as more fractionalized society (with respect to ethnicity, religion, language, culture, and so on) correlates positively with a high level of economic development (Florida, 2002; Florida and Gates, 2001), with higher hourly wages (Ottaviano and Peri, 2005). However, the same variables cause inefficiency and corruption and prevent economic growth (Mauro, 1995; Easterly and Levine, 1997; Collier, 2001); they are related to the quality of institutions (La Porta et al., 1999; Alesina et al., 2003), they impact upon political instability (Easterly and Levine, 1997; Annett, 2001), and they influence education (Easterly and Levine, 1997). Finally, fractionalization indices may also be unable to give a unambiguous answer, for instance in the case of civil conflicts (Annett, 2001) or growth (Posner, 2004).

In terms of empirical findings,[22] the implication of diversity in economics has been investigated in depth. In particular, scholars have analysed the consequences at several administrative levels (for continents and countries as well as for cities) and several degree of development (for developed and developing countries). The following paragraphs are devoted to analysing the results in these directions in greater depth.

24.3.1   Fractionalization and Polarization

As highlighted by Alesina et al. (2003), the fractionalization indices are not the only available measures of ethnic, religious and linguistic heterogeneity, even if they are the most used in the literature. Following Montalvo and Reynal-Querol (2002b), a measure of polarization rather than fractionalization has been introduced in empirical applications. In doing so, fractionalization and polarization indices are usually employed to describe and measure the ethnic composition of the society. Even if for a statistical perspective, fractionalization and polarization indices are, in a certain sense, two sides of the same coin since both aim at measuring ethnic division, for a given society; the computation of a polarization index points out at capturing the divergence from a bipolar distribution.[23] In addition, as pointed out by Esteban et al. (2012), these two indices generate very different results for societies with three or more ethnic group. Authors also claim that in the study of social conflict fractionalization is not an appropriate measure.[24] In the same context, Esteban and Ray (2008) prove that when a society is highly polarized, conflicts are rare since the costs of rebellion are extremely high, but if they occur, their intensity is very severe. Differently, conflicts mainly occur in highly fractionalized societies but with a moderate intensity. Esteban and Ray (2008) also show that measures of fractionalization and polarization tend to run in opposite directions, and the relationship between polarization and conflict, or fractionalization and conflict, is non-monotonic.

This divergence is portrayed by Montalvo and Reynal-Querol (2005a).[25] They plot the fractionalization index and the polarization index as a function of the number of groups, under the hypothesis that all of them have the same size. They show that, for a fixed and constant distance between groups, the polarization index achieves the maximum value for two equal-sized groups, whereas the fractionalization index (called by authors 'fragmentation') does so for a huge number of small groups, increasing as the number of the groups grows. In this way, one can argue that the index of polarization largely captures the potential conflicting relationships between groups, compared to the fractionalization measure, since the latter is essentially based on their number.

Montalvo and Reynal-Querol (2005b) also prove that their polarization index (hereafter, RQ) coincides with the ethnolinguistic index (barring for a factor scale) in the case of two groups. Hence, for two groups, polarization and fractionalization should have an extremely high correlation; whereas if the number of groups is greater than two, they are truly different. Analysing 138 countries, they find that for low levels of fractionalization, the relationship between them is positive (and close to linear). For the medium range, it is almost zero, and for a high level of diversity the correlation between fractionalization and polarization is negative.[26]

24.3.2 Fractionalization and Growth

There is an increasing body of literature that recognizes that ethnic fractionalization is correlated with growth. In fact, fractionalization has direct effects as well as indirect effects (through civil wars, crime, revolutions, instability, low school rate, and so on) on the path of growth of a country.

There are many factors that influence the level of economic development of a country. Alesina and Rodrik (1994) show that the more unequal the distribution of resources (such as income and land) is in a given society, the lower is the rate of economic growth. Moreover, not only economic variables have an impact on growth: in fact, as discussed in Barro (1996), political and social factors can also influence growth.[27]

Mauro (1995) proves that economic growth decreases with ethnolinguistic fractionalization. Similarly, Easterly and Levine (1997) find empirical evidence in support of ethnic heterogeneity as the explanatory variable for growth, showing how, in several African polarized countries, a very high level of ethnic diversity is one of the prominent factors in their poor economic performance. They conclude that this negative relationship is a major determinant of Africa's poor economic performance.

However, this relationship is not unambiguous. Collier (2000) tracks down a negative effect of fractionalization on growth only in non-democratic regimes, while democratic ones manage better to deal with ethnic diversity. A similar result has been provided by Easterly (2001); the author argues that 'ethnic diversity has a zero-marginal effect on economic growth at maximum institutional development' (ibid., p. 691). As Easterly stresses, this result is 'related to the findings that democracy eliminates the adverse effect of ethnolinguistic fractionalization on growth' (ibid.).

For Annett (2001) the effects of ethnic diversity on growth can be found in the instability that it generates, so fractionalization has only an indirect effect on growth. Alesina et al. (2003) affirm that the null hypothesis of no direct effect of the index of religious fractionalization cannot be rejected, which means that the impact of the index on growth is negative and robust. However, since an ethnolinguistic index is also correlated with GDP and quality of government, it is difficult to reach conclusions about the causality. On the other hand, Posner (2004) claims that an ethnolinguistic index is an inappropriate tool for testing the effect of ethnic diversity on growth, through its effect on macroeconomic policies, proposing the use of the Politically Relevant Ethnic Groups (PREG) index.

Patsiurko et al. (2012) calculate fractionalization indices (ethnic, religion and language) for two years, 1985 and 2000, analysing the variation of these indices over time and their impact on the growth rates of Organisation for Economic Co-operation and Development (OECD) countries. The authors find that ethnic fractionalization scores change for nine out of 30 countries analysed, and the rank also changes significantly.[28] The main cause of these shifts is attributed to immigration. Calculating the correlations between their fractionalization indices for 1985 and the growth rates for 1989–1999, they find -0.33 for ethnic, -0.17 for linguistic and -0.23 for religious; these values confirm the leading literature results. However, using fractionalization indices for 2000 a positive correlation between their religious fractionalization index and the growth rates appears. As the authors conclude, since none of these relationships is significant statistically, this suggests that if fractionalization affects growth, the effect may be indirect (that is, through public policies, public goods, quality of government, and so on).

24.3.3   Fractionalization and Public Policies

There are several studies devoted to analysing the relationship between fractionalization and public policies (Easterly and Levine, 1997; La Porta et al., 1999; Alesina et al., 2003). The authors find a negative correlation between a fractionalization index and the quality of infrastructure, school rating and literacy; and a positive correlation with political instability, bureaucratic delay and infant mortality. This section surveys and assesses most of the literature concerning the impact of ethnic, linguistic, religious and cultural fractionalization on economic policies and outcomes.[29]

Fractionalization and public goods

Easterly and Levine (1997) show that ethnically fractionalized societies may be affected by rent-seeking behaviour, since ethnic groups may raise difficulties in agreeing on the choice of certain public goods. Alesina et al. (1999) prove that there is a negative correlation between racial fractionalization of a city and the provision of public goods such as hospitals, roads and schools. In particular, they find that the more a city is fragmented, the less the government takes care of these infrastructures, since spending on public goods is lower in fragmented countries.

Ethnic fractionalization and quality of government

The empirical investigation of the determinants of the quality of government by La Porta et al. (1999) covers up to 152 countries. They show that ELF is negatively correlated with the quality of the government. Higher fractionalization is associated with lower government efficiency, such as more corruption, longer delays, worse property rights and regulation, lower consumption and less political freedom, especially for countries that are poor and closer to the equator. These results have been confirmed by Alesina et al.'s (2003) analysis. The authors show that while high ethnic fractionalization is associated with low quality of government, the reverse is true only with respect to religious fractionalization.

Ethnic fractionalization and politic instability

Annett (2001) reports a positive correlation between fractionalization and instability, even if ethnolinguistic fractionalization and religious fractionalization are treated independently. He presents a theoretical model establishing that an ethnically or religiously fractionalized society is potentially unstable. His results suggest that greater fractionalization influences political instability, which in turn leads to higher government consumption.

Easterly and Levine (1997) demonstrate that the cross-country differences in ethnic diversity explain the cross-country differences in political instability. Their paper quantifies this empirical relationship for some African countries in the 1960s, 1970s, and 1980s; the results stress that Africa's high level of ethnic diversity may explain what the authors call its tragic growth performance.

Ethnic fractionalization, civil wars and social conflicts

In support of the importance of the relationship between fractionalization and civil wars and social conflicts, Esteban et al. (2012) observe that half of the civil conflicts recorded after the Second World War have been classified as ethnic or religious. Analysing 98 countries, of which 27 had civil wars of varying duration during the period, Collier and Hoeffler (1998) report a positive (even if not monotonic) relationship between ELF and risk of conflict. However, they conclude by saying that it is not the ethnolinguistic fractionalization that penalizes the society, but rather the degree of fractionalization which most facilitates insurgent coordination. They explain that the many African civil wars are due to poverty instead of ethnolinguistic fractionalization.

Montalvo and Reynal-Querol (2005a) highlight that, although ethnic fractionalization is a powerful explanatory variable for economic growth, it is not significant in the explanation of civil war or of other types of conflict. Fearon and Laitin (2003) achieve the same results, showing that both ethnic and religious fractionalization do not have statistically significant effects on the probability that civil wars occur.

In analysing the occurrence and intensity of social conflicts, Esteban and Ray (2008) show that for a highly fractionalized society, conflicts may occur but with a moderate intensity. Finally, Esteban et al. (2012) obtained the same results, concluding that fractionalization indices are not appropriate measures for at least two reasons. Firstly, the size of the group plays a role. In other words, groups require a minimum size to fight one another. Secondly, this measure assumes that all groups are symmetrically positioned with respect to other groups, but in general this is not true. In fact, fractionalization indices consider every pair group as 'equally different' (Esteban et al., 2012, p. 859).

Fractionalization and corruption

Mauro (1995) provides one of the most important attempts to calculate the relationship between fractionalization and corruption. He observes that ethnic fractionalization measured using data from the ANM decreases institutional efficiency, political stability and bureaucratic efficiency, and increases corruption. He resorts to a fractionalization index in order to avoid and correct any potential source of endogenous bias. Assuming that the ethnolinguistic fractionalization for a country is exogenous and unrelated to economic variables apart from its effects on institutional efficiency, he finds a negative and significant correlation between the ethnolinguistic fractionalization index and institutional efficiency (-0.38), political stability (-0.41), bureaucratic efficiency (-0.28) and corruption (-0.31).[30]

Racial fractionalization and redistribution

Alesina and La Ferrara (2002) show that racial politics affect redistributive policies. These authors assert that in a more fractionalized society according to racial origins, inhabitants are less willing to redistribute income because the racial majority feels that redistributive flows would favour a racial minority. Lind (2007) also underlines the impact of fractionalization on politics and in particular on the support of redistribution. In his paper, he provides a theoretical basis showing that fractionalization reduces the amount of redistribution in democratic politics. In addition, in his opinion for a fractionalized society inequality between and within groups have opposite effects.[31]

Social fractionalization and fiscal deficit

Analyzing 57 developed and developing countries over the period 1970–1990, with respect to more than 40 economic, socio-political and institutional variables, Woo (2003) shows that social fractionalization implies a negative effect on fiscal deficits in countries with weak institutions.

Fractionalization and human capital

Easterly and Levine (1997) observe that in a highly ethnically fractionalized society, public goods such as education bring less satisfaction because of disagreements between ethnic groups on issues such as the language of instruction or the learning content. As a consequence, this may cause a low level of investment in human capital.

Analysing US cities, Florida (2002) stresses that high diversity attracts human capital. In particular, constructing a heterogeneity index (which is not directly related to canonical definition of ethnicity, but involves some characteristics that differentiate individuals), he shows that a high value of this heterogeneity corresponds to higher human capital.

Fractionalization and school performance

There are several works underlining the negative relationship between racial fractionalization and school performance. Easterly and Levine (1997) find a negative relationship between the degree of ethnolinguistic fractionalization and the number of years of schooling in a country. Using US data for county, metropolitan and city areas collected by the Bureau of the Census for 1994 (County and City Data Book), Alesina et al. (1999) show that racial diversity lowers spending on education.

Hall and Leeson (2010) analyse the relationship between racial fractionalization and the performance of Ohio students. Using a sample of 607 school districts in the state of Ohio obtained by merging two different data sources (the US 'Census 2000 School District Tabulation' and the 'Cupp Report') for 1999/2000 school terms, they report that the relationship between the district passage rates on the 9th grade maths test and racial fractionalization is negative. In particular, the authors empirically prove that school district passage rates are lower in more racially fractionalized communities. In addition they conclude that the passage rate on the state maths exam falls (about 7–17.5 percentage points) if one moves from a homogenous school district to another with two racial groups having equal population shares.

Linguistic fractionalization and productivity
There is increasing attention given to the investigation of the relationship between fractionalization and productivity. In a pioneer work, using country data from Taylor and Hudson (1972) on linguistic fractionalization and gross national product (GNP) per capita, Pool (1990, p. 250) shows that 'development-oriented elites in multilingual countries typically perceive a conflict between linguistic pluralism and modernization, and no wonder that they typically propose to solve this conflict by promoting linguistic assimilation'.

Considering only US cities and using Census data (160 cities for 1970, 1980 and 1990), Ottaviano and Perri (2005) investigate the effects of linguistic diversity on the wage of US-born white males, between 40 and 50 years old. After controlling for various other determinants, they find a positive effect of linguistic diversity on labour productivity, since richer diversity is associated with higher hourly wages.[32]

Fractionalization and trade and immigration
Easterly and Levine (1997) and Ortega and Peri (2012) investigate the relationship between fractionalization and trade and immigration. Easterly and Levine (1997) affirm that fractionalization causes conflicts, and this may affect trade since people could engage in trade only among individuals belonging to the same groups. On the other hand, Ortega and Peri (2012) show that even if immigration does not have a direct effect on the Gini coefficient, it increases linguistic fractionalization, which in turn has a negative effect on income. Finally, they find that a higher migration share is associated with increases in ethnic fractionalization as well as in linguistic fractionalization. In contrast, trade shares are not associated with higher fractionalization.

Cultural diversity and rents
Considering US-born citizens and using a fractionalization index as a proxy for the diversity of the cities,[33] Ottaviano and Perri (2006) analyse the effect of a culturally diverse population on productivity, through two different effects: wages and rental prices. They find a positive relationship, which means that US-born individuals living in cities that are more diverse pay higher rents compared to those living in more homogenous ones.[34]

Cultural fractionalization and ethnic fractionalization

Similarly, to the construction of the ELF index, in particular in the modified version of Greenberg (1956), Fearon (2003) constructs a measure of cultural fractionalization based on the proximity of language. Even if the cultural fractionalization index is highly correlated with ELF (about 0.82), considering this cultural–linguistic similarity, Latin America is more homogeneous with respect to the usual fractionalization index.[35] In addition, analysing metropolitan regions, Florida and Gates (2001) and Florida (2002) show that a higher degree of cultural diversity corresponds to higher levels of economic development.

Religious fractionalization and the size of the non-profit sector

It seems reasonable that fractionalization, and in particular religious fractionalization, is also correlated with the size of the non-profit sector. In fact, where considerable heterogeneity exists in a population and, as a consequence, there is not unanimous consensus about which public goods to generate through the public sector, people look for non-profit organizations to supply the public goods they cannot obtain through either the market or the state. This circumstance has been broadly investigated by Salamon et al. (2000). In order to test whether correlation exists between the size of the non-profit sector in a country and the degree of heterogeneity in the population, they collect data about the type of non-profit entities for 22 countries, using religious variables as a proxy of a more general diversity. They find that countries with similar levels of fractionalization vary largely in the size of their non-profit sectors.[36] In fact, Colombia and Ireland have a low level of diversity but a different size of non-profit sector; while Argentina and Japan present a similar size but a completely different level of diversity. The regression coefficient between the sector's size and heterogeneity is not statistically significant, suggesting that this relationship does not exist.

24.4   CONCLUDING REMARKS

In the last decades, there has been an increasing interest in the study of social fractionalization and diversity, focused mainly on analysing their economic implications. The starting point of this chapter's survey was the description of fractionalization datasets, showing the correlation among the rankings provided, using most of them to calculate fractionalization indices. Finally, the chapter investigated the direct and indirect relationships between fractionalization and several economic and social outcomes such as political instability, income redistribution, growth, civil war, school performance and immigration.

However, some problems persist with the use of fractionalization measures, since people differ in several respects, such as language, religion, and race or other physical attributes. In some countries, language is the borderline that better splits individuals into groups; in others it is religion. So, what dimension should one use? This is an important decision, since using one key factor instead of another may lead to different results. Therefore, I believe that the choice of the variables should be carried with maximum care in the empirical analysis. In my opinion, it is also necessary to improve the measurement of social fractionalization and diversity.

A further important direction for research consists of providing diversity measures over time besides cross-countries. I believe that the time dimension in the calculation of fractionalization may play a role, especially to evaluate the effects of changes of the value of the index on economic performance.

Finally, I believe that in analysing the possible effects of ethnic, linguistic and religious diversity on economic outcomes, great care should be employed, since depending on the context they could lead to different results. In particular, new effort is necessary to investigate the possible correlation between social fractionalization and the dimensions of economic well-being.

ACKNOWLEDGEMENTS

The author thanks Conchita D'Ambrosio, Casilda Lasso de la Vega, Ernesto Savaglio and Stefano Vannucci for their helpful comments and suggestions.

NOTES

1. See the chapters on income and social polarization in this *Handbook*. See also Esteban and Ray (1994), Easterly and Levine (1997), Reynal-Querol (2002), Alesina et al. (2003) and Fearon (2003), among others.
2. Anthropologists Comaroff and Comaroff (2009) define an ethnic group as a cluster of people whose elements (members) are characterized through a common trait or attribute. People belonging to the same ethnic group may share the same language or have a common heritage and/or a common culture, or they may also possess a common ancestry or may profess the same religion. Other anthropologists, James Peoples and Garrick Bailey (2010, p. 389), suggest a more subjective definition of 'ethnic group', based on the perception of diversity suffered by individuals, saying: 'an ethnic group is a named social category of people based on perceptions of shared social experience or ancestry. Members of the ethnic group see themselves as sharing cultural traditions and history that distinguish them from other groups . . . In contrast to social stratification, which divides and unifies people along a series of horizontal axes on the basis of socioeconomic factors, ethnic identities divide and unify people along a series of vertical axes.' Moreover, usually, sociologists denote by 'ethnic group' a group whose members belong to the same race.
3. http://www.statesmansyearbook.com/.
4. For more detail, see http://www.ethnologue.com.
5. This Institute was a part of the Department of Geodesy and Cartography of the USSR State Geological Committee.
6. The ethnographic and geographic maps assembled by the Institute of Ethnography at the USSR Academy of Sciences, population census data and ethnographic publications of government agencies.
7. See Bridgman (2008, p. 3) for details.
8. See http://worldmap.harvard.edu/data/geonode:Naradov_Mira_GREG for details on the Harvard Project.
9. The second edition was published in 1983 by Taylor Jodice.
10. http://worldchristiandatabase.org/.
11. See https://www.cia.gov/library/publications/the-world-factbook.
12. See https://www.cia.gov/library/publications/the-world-factbook/fields/2122.html.
13. See https://www.cia.gov/library/publications/the-world-factbook/fields/2098.html.
14. See http://weber.ucsd.edu/~proeder/elf.htm.
15. That overall dataset is downloadable from: http://www.anderson.ucla.edu/faculty_pages/romain.wacziarg/papersum.html.
16. Replication Data are available at http://www.stanford.edu/group/ethnic/publicdata/publicdata.html.
17. They use the 15th edition of this source.
18. See Fearon (2003, p. 210, figure 3) for a graphical representation of such correlations.
19. The Politically Relevant Ethnic Groups (PREG) was introduced by Posner (2004). It is based on an accounting for politically relevant ethnic groups and it is available for 42 African countries.
20. See Posner (2004, p. 857, Table 2) for all pairs correlations among the PREG, ELF, Alesina et al. (2003) and Fearon (2003) measures of fractionalization.
21. See Montalvo and Reynal-Querol (2005a, p. 297, Table 1).

22. See Alesina and La Ferrara (2005) for a survey.
23. See Chapters 19 and 20 on income and social polarization in this *Handbook*.
24. See paragraph 24.3.3 for more details.
25. See Montalvo and Reynal-Querol (2005a, p. 305, figure 1).
26. See Montalvo and Reynal-Querol (2005a, p. 307, figure 2), for a comparison between ethnic polarization and ethnic fractionalization through WCE data. Montalvo and Reynal-Querol (2005a, p. 307, figure 3) also provide a scatterplot for the relationship between religious polarization versus religious fractionalization using data from the ET. Finally, the same authors (Montalvo and Reynal-Querol, 2005b) give a scatterplot for the relationship between ethnic polarization versus ethnic fractionalization using the ANM (ibid., p. 803, figure 3), and ethnic polarization versus ethnic fractionalization using data collected by Alesina et al. (2003), (Montalvo and Reynal-Querol, 2005b, p. 804, figure 4).
27. Barro (1996) shows that, for a given starting-level GDP, the growth rate is reinforced by social factors such as higher initial schooling and life expectancy and lower fertility, as well as political factors such as lower government consumption, better maintenance of the rule of law, lower inflation and improvements in the terms of trade.
28. See Patsiurko et al. (2012, pp. 205, 206, figures 1 and 2).
29. See Alesina and La Ferrara (2005) for a detailed survey focused on communities of different size and organizational structure.
30. The corruption index is calculated using data drawn from The Economist Intelligent Unit, see Mauro (1995, Section II) for more details.
31. In particular, the within-group inequality increases the support for redistribution whereas the between-group inequality reduces the support for it (Lind, 2007, p. 64, Proposition 3).
32. They explain the logarithm of average hourly wage by linguistic diversity and additional variables such as average schooling of the population, share of whites, racial fractionalization, unemployment and so on. All other things being equal, they find that an increase of 0.20 of the linguistic diversity increases the average hourly wage by 12–20 per cent.
33. They consider a city as diverse if it has a high share of foreign-born people.
34. See Ottaviano and Peri (2006, p. 19, figure 2) for a graphical representation of the relationship between rents of US-born and diversity.
35. See Fearon (2003, p. 213, figure 4) for more details.
36. See Salamon et al. (2000, p. 9, figure 4).

REFERENCES

Alesina, A., R. Baqir and W. Easterly (1999) 'Public Goods and Ethnic Divisions', *Quarterly Journal of Economics*, 114, 1243–1284.
Alesina, A., A. Devleeschauwer, E. William, S. Kurlat and R. Wacziarg (2003) 'Fractionalization', *Journal of Economic Growth*, 8, 155–194.
Alesina A. and E. La Ferrara (2002) 'Who Trusts Others?', *Journal of Public Economics*, 85, 207–234.
Alesina A. and E. La Ferrara (2005) 'Ethnic Diversity Economic Performance', *Journal of Economic Literature*, 43, 762–800.
Alesina, A. and D. Rodrik (1994) 'Distributive Politics and Economic Growth', *Quarterly Journal of Economics*, 109, 465–490.
Alesina, A. and E. Zhuravskaya (2008) 'Segregation and the Quality of Government in a Cross-Section of Countries', Center for Economic and Financial Research, Working Papers w0120.
Annett, A. (2001) 'Social Fractionalization, Political Instability, and the Size of the Government', *IMF Staff Papers*, 46, 561–592.
Atlas Narodov Mira (1964) Moscow: Miklukho-Maklai Ethnological Institute at the Department of Geodesy and Cartography of the State Geological Committee of the Soviet Union.
Barrett, D.B. (ed.) (1982) *World Christian Encyclopedia*, Oxford: Oxford University Press.
Barrett, D.B., G.T. Kurian and T.M. Johnson (2001) *World Christian Encyclopedia: A Comparative Survey of Churches and Religions in the Modern World*, 2 vols, Oxford: Oxford University Press.
Barro, R.J. (1996) 'Determinants of Economic Growth: A Cross-Country Empirical Study', National Bureau of Economic Research, No. w5698.
Bridgman, B. (2008) 'What Does the *Atlas Narodov Mira* Measure?', *Economics Bulletin*, 10, 1–8.
CIA (various years) *CIA World Fact Book*, https://www.cia.gov/library/publications/the-world-factbook/index.html.
Clévenot, M. (1987) *L'Etat des Religions dans le Monde*, Paris: La Découverte.

Collier, P. (2000) 'Ethnicity, Politics and Economic Performance', *Economics and Politics*, 12, 225–245.
Collier, P. (2001) 'Implications of Ethnic Diversity', *Economic Policy*, 32, 127–166.
Collier, P. and A. Hoeffler (1998) 'On Economic Causes of Civil War', *Oxford Economic Papers*, 50, 563–573.
Comaroff, J.L. and J. Comaroff (2009) *Ethnicity, Inc.*, Chicago, IL: University of Chicago Press.
Desmet, K., I. Ortuño-Ortín and R. Wasziarg (2012) 'The Political Economy of Linguistic Cleavages', *Journal of Development Economics*, 97, 322–338.
Easterly, W. (2001) 'Can Institutions Resolve Ethnic Conflicts?', *Economic Development and Cultural Change*, 49, 687–706.
Easterly, W. and R. Levine (1997) 'Africa's Growth Tragedy: Policies and Ethnic Divisions', *Quarterly Journal of Economics*, 111, 1203–1250.
Encyclopedia Britannica Inc. (annual) 'Britannica World Data', Chicago, IL: Encyclopedia Britannica Inc.
Esteban, J., L. Mayoral and D. Ray (2012) 'Ethnicity and Conflict: Theory and Fact', *Science*, 336, 858–865.
Esteban, J. and D. Ray (1994) 'On the Measurement of Polarization', *Econometrica*, 62, 819–851.
Esteban, J. and D. Ray (2008), 'Polarization, Fractionalization and Conflict', *Journal of Peace Research*, 45, 163–182.
Fearon, J.D. (2003) 'Ethnic and Cultural Diversity by Country', *Journal of Economic Growth*, 8, 195–222.
Fearon, J.D. and D.D. Laitin (2003) 'Ethnicity, Insurgency, and Civil War', *American Political Science Review*, 97, 75–90.
Florida, R. (2002) 'The Economic Geography of Talent', *Annals of the Association of American Geographers*, 92, 743–755.
Florida, R. and G. Gates (2001) 'Technology and Tolerance: The Importance of Diversity to High-Tech Growth', Brookings Institute Discussion Paper, Washington, DC.
Greenberg, J.H. (1956) 'The Measurement of Linguistic Diversity', *Language*, 32, 109–115.
Hall, J.C. and P.T. Leeson (2010) 'Racial Fractionalization and School Performance', *American Journal of Economics and Sociology*, 69, 736–758.
La Porta, R., F. Lopez-de-Silanes, A. Shleifer and R. Vishny (1999) 'The Quality of Government', *Journal of Law, Economics and Organization*, 15, 222–279.
Levinson, D. (1998) *Ethnic Groups Worldwide*, A Ready Reference Handbook, Phoenix, AZ: Oryx Press.
Lind, J.T. (2007) 'Fractionalization and the Size of Government', *Journal of Public Economics*, 91, 51–76.
Martin, F. (ed.) (1865) *The Statesman's Year-Book: A Statistical, Genealogical, and Historical Account of the States and Sovereigns of the Civilised World for the Year 1865.* London and Cambridge: Macmillan & Co.
Mauro, P. (1995) 'Corruption and Growth', *Quarterly Journal of Economics*, 110, 681–712.
Minority Rights Group International (1997) *World Directory of Minorities*, London: Minority Rights Group International.
Montalvo, J.G. and M. Reynal-Querol (2002a) 'The Effect of Ethnic and Religious Conflict on Growth', PRPES Working Paper No. 15.
Montalvo, J.G. and M. Reynal-Querol (2002b) 'Why Ethnic Fractionalization? Polarization, Ethnic Conflict and Growth', UPF Working Paper No. 660.
Montalvo, J.G. and M. Reynal-Querol (2005a) 'Ethnic Diversity and Economic Development', *Journal of Development Economics*, 76, 293–323.
Montalvo, J.G. and M. Reynal-Querol (2005b) 'Ethnic Polarization, Potential Conflict, and Civil Wars', *American Economic Review*, 95, 796–816.
Morrison, D., R. Mitchell and J. Paden (1989) *Black Africa: A Comparative Handbook*, 2nd edn, New York: Paragon House.
Mozaffar, S. and J. Scarrit (1999) 'The Specification of Ethnic Cleavages and Ethnopolitical Groups for the Analysis of Democratic Competition in Contemporary Africa', *Nationalism and Ethnic Politics*, 5, 82–117.
Muller, S. (1964) *The World's Living Languages*, New York: Frederick Ungar.
Ortega, F. and G. Peri (2012) 'The effect of trade and migration on income', National Bureau of Economic Research, No. w18193.
Ottaviano, G. and G. Peri (2005) 'Cities and Cultures', *Journal of Urban Economics*, 58, 304–337.
Ottaviano, G. and G. Peri (2006) 'The Economic Value of Cultural Diversity: Evidence from US Cities', *Journal of Economic Geography*, 6, 9–44.
Page, S.E. (2011) *Diversity and Complexity*, Princeton, NJ: Princeton University Press.
Patsiurko, N., J.L. Campbell and J.A. Hall (2012) 'Measuring Cultural Diversity: Ethnic, Linguistic and Religious Fractionalization in the OECD', *Ethnic and Racial Studies*, 35, 195–217.
Peoples, J. and G. Bailey (2010) *Humanity: An Introduction to Cultural Anthropology*, 9th edn, Belmont, CA: Wadsworth Cengage Learning.
Pittman, R. and E. Canonge (1958) *The Ethnologue of Bibleless Tribes for Prayer Intercessors, Bible Translators, Missionaries, Prospective Missionaries, Mission Councils*, 5th edn, Glendale, CA: Whycliffe Bible Translators.
Pool, J. (1990) 'Language Regimes and Political Regimes', in Brian Weinstein (ed.), *Language Policy and Political Development* (pp. 241–261), Norwood, NJ: Ablex.

Posner, D.N. (2004) 'Measuring Ethnic Fractionalization in Africa', *American Journal of Political Science*, 48, 849–863.

Reynal-Querol, M. (2002) 'Ethnicity, Political Systems and Civil War', *Journal of Conflict Resolution*, 46, 29–55.

Roberts, J. (1962) 'Sociocultural Change and Communication Problems', in F. Rice (ed.), *Study of the Role of Second Languages in Asia, Africa, and Latin America* (pp. 105–123), Washington, DC: Center for Applied Linguistics, Modern Language Association of America.

Roeder, P.G. (2001) 'Ethnolinguistic Fractionalization (ELF) Indices, 1961 and 1985', 16 February, http//:weber.ucsd.edu/~proeder/elf.htm (accessed 17 September 2013).

Salamon, L.M., S.W. Sokolowski and H.K. Anheier (2000) 'Social Origins of Civil Society: An Overview', Working Papers of the Johns Hopkins Comparative Nonprofit Sector Project, no. 38.

Taylor, C.L. and M.C. Hudson (1972) *World Handbook of Political and Social Indicators II*, 2nd edn, New Haven, CT: Yale University Press.

Weidmann, N.B., J.K. Rød and L. Cederman (2010) 'Representing Ethnic Groups in Space: A New Dataset', *Journal of Peace Research*, 47, 491–499.

Woo, J. (2003) 'Economic, Political, and Institutional Determinants of Public Deficits', *Journal of Public Economics*, 87, 387–426.

Index